Security Analysis, Portfolio Management, and Financial Derivatives

Security Analysis, Portfolio Management, and Financial Derivatives

Cheng Few Lee
Rutgers University, USA

Joseph Finnerty
University of Illinois, Urbana-Champaign, USA

John Lee
Center for PBBEF Research, USA

Alice C Lee
State Street Corp., USA

Donald Wort
California State University East Bay, USA

World Scientific

NEW JERSEY • LONDON • SINGAPORE • BEIJING • SHANGHAI • HONG KONG • TAIPEI • CHENNAI

Published by

World Scientific Publishing Co. Pte. Ltd.

5 Toh Tuck Link, Singapore 596224

USA office: 27 Warren Street, Suite 401-402, Hackensack, NJ 07601

UK office: 57 Shelton Street, Covent Garden, London WC2H 9HE

British Library Cataloguing-in-Publication Data
A catalogue record for this book is available from the British Library.

SECURITY ANALYSIS, PORTFOLIO MANAGEMENT, AND FINANCIAL DERIVATIVES

ISBN 978-981-4343-56-5

In-house Editor: Agnes Ng

Typeset by Stallion Press
Email: enquiries@stallionpress.com

Printed in Singapore by B & Jo Enterprise Pte Ltd

Preface

In this edition, we have extensively updated and expanded the topics of futures and option. Therefore, we use a new title *Security Analysis, Portfolio Management, and Financial Derivatives.* The major changes of this edition are described as follows:

(A) Update and expansion of the material of original chapters.
(B) Update of empirical examples in original chapters.
(C) There are 27 chapters in this edition. The new chapters included in this new edition are as follows:

Chapter 18	Decision Tree and Microsoft Excel Approach for OPM
Chapter 19	Normal, Log-normal Distribution, and Option Pricing Model
Chapter 20	Comparative Static Analysis of the Option Pricing Models
Chapter 25	Capturing Equity Risk Premia
Chapter 26	Simultaneous Equation Models for Security Valuation

(D) The chapters in this book fall into five parts: (i) Information and Security Valuation, (ii) Portfolio Theory and Asset Pricing, (iii) Futures and Option, (iv) Applied Portfolio Management, and (v) Special Topics.

Based upon our personal teaching experience at various universities, we find that this book can be used in an investment analysis course, portfolio management course, or option and futures course. For an investment analysis course, we suggest instructors cover Chapters 2, 3, 4, 5, 6, 7, 8, 9, 12, 13, 21, 22, 25, and 26. For a portfolio management course, we suggest instructors cover Chapters 3, 4, 5, 7, 8, 9, 10, 11, 12, 13, 14, 15, 16, 17, 21, 22, 23, 24, and 25. For option and future course, we suggest instructors cover Chapters 14, 15, 16, 17, 18, 19, 20, 22, 23, 24, and 27.

We suggest project assignments for Parts I, II, III, and IV. Chapter 25 can be used as a reference for both Project II and Project IV. Chapter 26 can be used as a reference for Project I. Chapter 27 can be used as a reference for Project III.

For this edition, we appreciate the comments from our MBA and undergraduate students at Rutgers University, University of Illinois — Champaign and Urbana, and California State University, Hayward. In addition, we appreciate the help from our research assistant Hong-Yi Chen, Tzu Tai, and Miranda Lu. In particular, the extensive help from Hong-Yi Chen at National Central University, Taiwan, is most appreciated. Finally, we would like to express our thanks for the financial support from the Wintek Corporation and the Polaris Financial Group that allowed us to write this second edition.

There are undoubtedly some errors in the finished product, both typographical and conceptual. We would like to invite readers to send suggestions, comments, criticisms, and corrections to the first author Professor Cheng F. Lee at the Department of Finance and Economics, Rutgers University, Janice H. Levin Building Room 141, Rockafeller Road, Piscataway, NJ 08854-8054, USA (lee@business.rutgers.edu).

Cheng Few Lee
Joseph Finnerty
John Lee
*Alice C. Lee**
Donald Wort

*Any views or opinions presented in this publication are solely those of the authors and do not necessarily represent those of State Street Corporation. State Street Corporation is not associated in any way with this publication and accepts no liability for the contents of this publication.

Preface for *Security Analysis and Portfolio Management*

Security Analysis and Portfolio Management integrates the many topics of modern investment analysis. It provides a balanced presentation of theories, institutions, markets, academic research, and practical applications, and presents both basic concepts and advanced principles. Topic coverage is especially broad: in analyzing securities, we look at stocks and bonds, options and futures, foreign exchange, and international securities. The discussion of options and futures includes a detailed analysis of hedging strategies. A unique chapter on market indices teaches students the basics of index information, calculation, and usage and illustrates the important roles that these indices play in model formation, performance evaluation, investment strategy, and hedging techniques. In addition, complete sections on program trading, portfolio insurance, duration and bond immunization, performance measurements, and the timing of stock selection provide real-world applications of investment theory.

Security Analysis and Portfolio Management first discusses how finance theory and statistical and mathematical tools can be used effectively to analyze and determine the market value of bonds, stocks, options, futures, and options on futures. Second, based on this information, the text investigates issues related to equity portfolios, bond portfolios, and international portfolios. For equity-portfolio selection, the text discusses Markowitz's full-information methods, Sharpe's index methods, and the performance measure method. Finally, the efficient-market hypothesis, mutual-fund timing and selectivity, and portfolio insurance are also explored in detail.

The chapters in this book fall into five groups. The material in Chapters 2–7 review and extend the concepts and methods that students have learned from basic corporate finance and investment courses.

Chapters 8–11 present both the theoretical and empirical issues concerning the use of the market model, the CAPM, the APT, and risk diversification in security analysis and portfolio management. Chapters 12–15 use the theories and methods presented in the first 11 chapters to investigate futures and options. Chapters 16–21 cover applications of portfolio theories and models developed in the preceding chapters. Finally, Chapter 22 is meant only for advanced students who require an in-depth derivation of the Black–Scholes option pricing model in terms of stochastic differential equations. It can be skipped over without loss of continuity.

Accounting information is essential for business decision making because it describes both the financial assets and the real assets of a firm. Historical accounting information has been used extensively by security analysis and portfolio managers, while proponents of the semi-strong form of the efficient-market hypothesis regard such information as valueless. In Chapter 2, ratio analysis, regression analysis, and earnings-per-share estimation are considered. The use of financial information in security analysis is emphasized. The role of the investment advisor in evaluating and rating the financial instruments of various companies is employed as an example of the ways that accounting information can be used to make valuation recommendations.

Chapter 3 deals with the measurement and the growth determination of rates of return on security investments. In addition to defining the holding-period return and the holding-period yield, three alternative methods for calculating average rates of return are discussed. These estimates can be used either to determine historical investment performance or to forecast future performance. It is known that a weighted unbiased estimator can be used to reduce or eliminate the bias in forecasting rates of return.

Alternative methods of estimating growth rates are also discussed in Chapter 3. The relative advantages of these alternative methods are explored both theoretically and empirically. Possible applications of growth-rates estimation in security analysis and portfolio management are discussed.

Chapter 4 reviews both pre-Modigliani and Miller and M&M valuation theories in detail. The basic concepts of the capital asset pricing model (CAPM) and the option pricing model are also explored in order to construct a rectangular theoretical framework of valuation. This chapter reviews basic theories that students have learned from a first course on either financial management or investment. Topics in this chapter can be used as a review or as major theoretical background for understanding later chapters of this text.

Chapter 5 extends the valuation analysis to the specific case of the debt instruments of corporations. Issues related to the yield curve, the term structure of interest rates, and bonds ratings are carefully analyzed. Chapter 6 discusses the computation of alternative market indices and examines the possible biases associated with using these indexes in investment analysis. The historical behavior of market indices and index forecasting are also explored. The Wilshire 5000 index is discussed in detail.

In Chapter 7, sources of risk and basic portfolio analysis are investigated and used as a framework for further analysis of the CAPM and the market model. Chapter 8 discusses utility theory and Markowitz's full-information model of portfolio selection in detail. In Chapter 9, the market model and the CAPM are evaluated both theoretically and empirically. The applications of the market model to risk decomposition are analyzed using both fixed-coefficient regression models. Methods of forecasting beta coefficients are explored, using both accounting and market information.

Chapter 10 addresses how Markowitz's full-information portfolio-selection process can be simplified through the use of index models. In Chapter 11, multi-index models and the arbitrage pricing theory (APT) are discussed from both a theoretical and an empirical basis.

Chapter 12 discusses the basic issues of futures markets and futures contracts. In addition, two alternative hedging methods are investigated in detail. Chapter 13 explores the use of commodity futures, financial futures, and stock-index futures. The valuation of these futures and their use in hedging is investigated. Chapters 14 and 15 outline the basic concepts of put and call options, and the option pricing model is derived using a binomial-model approach. Alternative applications of the option pricing theory (OPT) in the making of investment decisions are explored in detail.

Chapter 16 deals with the concept of an efficient market and the empirical evidence that supports or refutes this hypothesis. The implications of market efficiency for security analysts and portfolio managers are also stressed. Chapter 17 discusses timing and selectivity of stocks and mutual funds from both a fundamental-analysis and technical-analysis perspective. Some forecasting models are examined, and Fama's breakdown of overall investment performance into several specific components is also covered.

Chapter 18 illustrates how the Sharpe and Treynor performance measures can be used to simplify the portfolio-selection procedure. In Chapter 19, issues relating to international diversification, exchange-rate risk, the international CAPM, and international portfolio-selection methods are investigated in detail. Chapter 20 presents a discussion of the issues involved in the management of a fixed-income portfolio. Both duration and bond immunization are carefully analyzed in this chapter. Chapter 21 examines the use of hedging and portfolio-insurance strategies for equity and bond portfolio.

This book is suitable for a second investment course at both the undergraduate and the graduate level. However, because *Security Analysis and Portfolio Management* addresses both the theoretical and the empirical sides of issues, and because it discusses both basic concepts and more advanced topics, it is suitable for a more quantitatively oriented first course in investment.

In the development of this book, we have benefited from the reviews and comments of many individuals, including colleagues and students from the University of Illinois at Urbana-Champaign and other universities. We especially want to acknowledge the insightful comments and corrections of Louis Scott, University of Georgia; Steve Sears, Texas Tech; Cheryl Frohlich-Plumber, University of North Florida; Kent Zumwalt, Colorado State University; Henry R. Oppenheimer, Rhode Island University; A. G. Malliaris, Loyala University; Charles Corrado, Loyala University; Ron Moy, Rutgers University; John C. Lee, Laventhol and Horwath; C. C. Yang, National Taiwan University; and Raymond Altimix, First of America Bank.

Cheng Few Lee
Joseph Finnerty
Donald Wort

Contents in Brief

Contents

Project I Financial Statement Analysis and Security Valuation

Chapter 1

Introduction

The growth in the number of financial instruments, and in the volume of trade in these instruments, today offers both a challenge and an opportunity to the student of finance. What is the challenge? It is to master the descriptive characteristics and uses of financial instruments. The opportunity? A highly rewarding investment career.

Such a challenge is timely, crucial, and apropos to current market activities. Figure 1.1 and Table 1.1 show that the volume in U.S. capital markets of new issues of traditional financial instruments (bonds and stocks) has more than tripled between 1980 and 1988. Most growth has occurred in debt securities, probably in response to the large decline in interest rates between 1980 and 1988; and common stock has likewise experienced an increase during this period. However, the new issues during 2006 to 2010 experienced a dramatic decrease due to the financial crisis in 2007.

Increases in new issues of primary-market securities reflect an increase in demand for capital by business units. The primary market for corporate offerings involves the sale of securities by the issuing firm. The proceeds of the sale of these securities are received by the firm in the form of new capital to be used either for new investments or for refinancing maturing debt obligations.

Secondary markets involve already existing issues that are traded among investors. In this case, the instruments are traded between the current investors and the potential investors in a corporation. The proceeds of the sale do not go to the firm but to the current owners of the security. Secondary markets serve two major roles. First, they provide liquidity

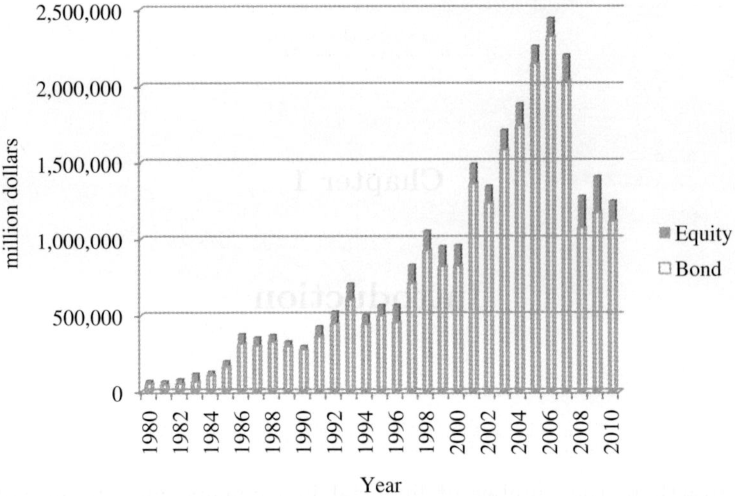

Fig. 1.1. Volume of New Issues Sold in the U.S., 1980–2010.

to investors who acquire securities in the primary market. The amount of trading in the secondary market has experienced growth, as shown in Table 1.2 and Figure 1.2. Second, these markets provide a continuous mechanism for price determination from which firms have an idea about the amount of capital they could raise and the terms they need to offer to in order to induce potential investors to purchase new issue of securities.

Another dimension of the growth of financial markets is the increase in the types of financial instrument being issued in both the primary and secondary markets. Table 1.3 is a partial list of the exchanges and the types of futures contracts and options currently traded around the world.

The 1980s have been marked by far-reaching changes in international capital markets. In particular, the financial markets have been characterized by increasing liberalization of regulation and innovation as well as intense competition. Barriers to diversification through portfolio investment in transnational security markets are being lowered, and financial risks are being repackaged and redistributed into different portfolios. The emergence of swaps, which permit borrowers (and investors) to separate the choice of markets (and credits) from the choice of currency and/or interest-rate risk, has been an important development in the international portfolio-management scene. The daily trading volume of interest rate swaps exceeded $4 billion in the first four months of 2010.

Table 1.1. Volume of New Issues Sold in the U.S. (million dollars).

Year	Stock	Bonds
1980	20,489	53,206
1981	25,349	44,642
1982	30,562	53,226
1983	51,579	68,370
1984	22,628	109,903
1985	35,515	165,754
1986	61,830	313,502
1987	53,349	301,349
1988	42,455	327,864
1989	32,203	297,114
1990	23,441	275,760
1991	65,268	361,971
1992	78,457	443,911
1993	101,554	603,119
1994	60,398	441,287
1995	68,473	496,296
1996	112,546	453,963
1997	117,880	708,188
1998	126,755	923,771
1999	131,568	818,683
2000	134,917	822,012
2001	128,554	1,356,879
2002	110,435	1,232,618
2003	127,141	1,579,311
2004	144,603	1,737,342
2005	115,256	2,141,496
2006	119,165	2,318,379
2007	168,654	2,030,248
2008	206,598	1,069,815
2009	233,967	1,171,218
2010	131,135	1,113,799

Source: Federal Reserve Bulletin.

The opportunity in investment careers can either be in security analysis or portfolio management for both domestic and international firms. A more rapid increase in the size international capital markets also enhances the opportunity for investment careers.

With this innovative and growing environment serving as a backdrop, this study of security analysis and portfolio management begins with an explanation of the objectives of each of these areas.

Table 1.2. Average Daily Trading Volume in NYSE Listed Issues (millions of shares).

Year	Volume
1980	44.87
1981	46.85
1982	65.05
1983	85.33
1984	90.96
1985	109.17
1986	141.03
1987	188.54
1988	161.46
1989	165.47
1990	156.78
1991	178.92
1992	202.27
1993	264.52
1994	291.35
1995	346.10
1996	412.30
1997	525.68
1998	673.59
1999	809.18
2000	1041.58
2001	1239.96
2002	1441.02
2003	1398.40
2004	1466.79
2005	1647.13
2006	1826.67
2007	2119.63
2008	2609.83

Source: NYSE Statistics Archive in NYSE Euronext website (http://www.nyse.com/financials/1022221393023.html).

1.1. Objective of Security Analysis

The ultimate objective of security analysis is to develop theoretical models that can be used to determine the value of financial instruments such as stocks, preferred stocks, bonds, options, futures, and options on futures, so that a comparison can be made of these values with the prices at which these instruments are currently trading in securities markets. Such a comparison aids investors and security analysts wishing to make investment decisions.

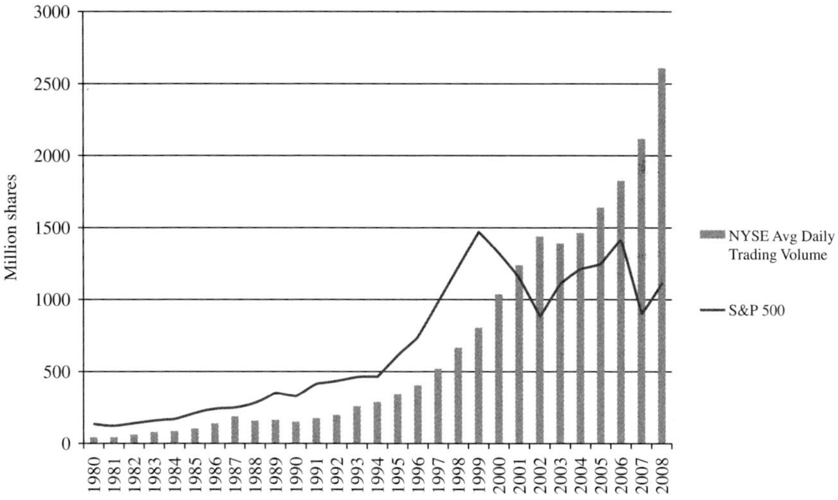

Fig. 1.2. Average Daily Trading Volume of NYSE and S&P 500 (Million shares). *Source*: NYSE Statistics Archive in NYSE Euronext website (http://www.nyse.com/financials/1022221393023.html).

Security analysts are continually looking for undervalued or overvalued situations. Undervalued situations, where the theoretical value is higher than the present market value, offer the opportunity to invest in instruments that are expected to have above-average returns; overvalued situations, where the theoretical value is below the current market value, offer the opportunity to sell instruments whose prices are expected to fall. An even more aggressive investor can short sell the overvalued instruments for above-average returns.

There are many factors to be considered in security analysis and many general approaches that can be taken. A selection of those considered most useful to security analysts are covered in detail in the first and final sections of this book.

1.2. Objective of Portfolio Management

Portfolio management seeks to combine securities so that the overall return of the portfolio is enhanced and the risk to the portfolio is reduced. Thus, determination of superior performance is made for the entire portfolio or combination of securities, rather than separately for each individual security.

Table 1.3. Options and Futures Exchanges.

American Stock Exchange	*COMEX*	*New York Mercantile Exchange*
Major Market Index Option	Gold	No. 2 Heating Oil
	Silver	Crude Oil
Chicago Board of Trade	Gold Option	Leaded Gasoline
T-Bond	Silver Option	Unleaded Gasoline
T-Bond Option		
10-Year T-Note	*FINEX*	*Pacific Stock Exchange*
10-Year T-Note Option	U.S. Dollar Index	Technology Index Option
Major Market Index	European Currency Unit	
Maxi Stock Index		*MATIF PARIS*
Municipal Bond Index	*Hong Kong Futures Exchange*	French 7–10 Year Government Note
NASDAQ 100 Index	Hong Kong Stock Index	French 90–Days T-Bill
Chicago Mercantile Exchange	*International Petroleum Exchange*	*Philadelphia Stock Exchange*
British Pound	Gas Oil	British Pound Option
Canadian Dollar		Canadian Dollar Option
Deutsch Mark	*Kansas City Board of Trade*	Deutschemark Option
Japanese Yen		Japanese Yen Option
Swiss Franc	Value Line Average Index	Swiss Franc Option
European Currency Unit		European Currency Unit Option
British Pound Option		
Canadian Dollar Option	*LIFFE*	Value Line Average Index Option
Deutschemark Option	Eurodollar	
Japanese Yen Option	Pound Sterling	
Swiss Franc Option	Sterling Currency	*SIMEX*
S&P 500 Index	Long Gilt	Deutsch Mark
S&P 250 OTC Index	FTSE 100 Index	Japanese Yen
S&P 500 Option	U.S. Treasury Bond	Eurodollar
Eurodollar	Pound/Dollar Option	
T-Bill		
Eurodollar Option	*Montreal Stock Exchange*	*Sydney Futures Exchange*
T-Bill Option	T-Bill Option	All Ordinaries Stock Index
		90-Day Bank Bill
	Canadian Bond Option	U.S. Dollar
Chicago Board Options Exchange		Australian 10-Year T-Bond
S&P 100 Option	*New York Futures Exchange*	
S&P 500 Option		
	NYSE Composite Index	*Tokyo Stock Exchange*
British Pound Option	NYSE Composite Index Option	Yen Bond
Canadian Dollar Option	CRS Index	

(*Continued*)

Table 1.3. (*Continued*)

Deutschemark Option		*Toronto Futures Exchange*
French Franc	*New York Stock Exchange*	TSE 300 Index
Japanese Yen Option	Composite Index Option	
Swiss Franc Option	Double Index Option	*Toronto Stock Exchange*
T-Bond Option	Beta Index Option	TSE 300 Index Option
5-Year T-Note Option		

Source: Adapted from Future's Magazine's 1989 Reference Guide to Futures-Options Markets, pp. 112–127.

1.3. Basic Approaches to Security Analysis and Portfolio Management

There are many approaches to security analysis. The most traditional categorization has been to divide security analysis into **fundamental analysis** and **technical analysis**. Fundamental analysis rests on the belief that at any point in time, there is a basic intrinsic value for the stock market, for industries and for individual securities. These values depend on the relationship between information and the theoretical determinants of value. The fundamental analysis approach requires both a correct theoretical model of valuation and access to relevant information.

Technical analysis is based on the idea that prices of financial instruments move in trends that persist through time and also recur over time. It is based on the belief that as random information comes to the financial markets, it is not immediately reflected in security prices. Rather, as knowledge of the information spreads among the market participants, they react to it by buying and selling financial instruments. This spreading of the information indicates that the changes in market prices move in trend over a period of time. Technical analysis stems from the premise that investors can identify the movements or trends in the movement of prices and use this information to generate above-average returns.

The last two decades have seen the development of the **efficient-market hypothesis (EMH)**. This explanation for the behavior of prices in financial markets is based on the concept of a "fair game" model. This model requires that the price-determination process uses all of the relevant information that is available at any point in time to determine the value or price of a financial instrument. For ease of empirical testing of the EMH, three forms of the hypothesis have evolved: (i) the weak form, (ii) the semi-strong form, and (iii) the strong form. The weak form states that current stock prices fully reflect all historical information including the historical sequence of price, price changes, trading volume, and so on. Hence knowledge of past events or the use of a trading rule based on past events will not consistently generate above-average investment performance. The semi-strong form states that stock prices (in addition to historic information of the weak form) fully reflect all public information such as corporate earnings, dividends, economic or political news, and so forth. This implies that investors who purchase securities based on information that is public will pay a price for a security that has already been adjusted for the value of the information. The strong form states that security prices fully reflect all information, both public and private. Hence it implies that no group of investors or market participants can outperform the market even though they have monopolistic access to information. In Chapter 16, extensive discussions of the empirical and the implications of the EMH for portfolio management and security analysis are presented.

In terms of basic philosophy about portfolio management and security analysis, it is our belief that an investor with superior training, intellect and judgment can turn in a superior performance. One of the roles of security analysis is to keep the market relatively efficient. There are currently two extreme views about the stock market:

1. Institutional investors dominate the market and it is impossible for the individual investor to outperform the professional portfolio manager.
2. The professional portfolio manager cannot consistently outperform the market; therefore, even the most naïve individual investor has a chance to turn in a superior performance as a result of blind luck.

The philosophy of this text falls somewhere between the two opposing views. Professional investment management should be able to provide superior performance vis-a-vis private individuals; but some knowledgeable individuals will be able to outperform the professionals in certain special circumstances. The question of how to evaluate the various aspects of the performance of security analysts and portfolio managers is discussed in Chapters 17 and 18.

A final dimension of the performance issue that needs special emphasis is time. Studies by Summers (1986) and Fama and French (1988) indicate that given a longer time horizon, the financial markets may not be as efficient as was once generally believed. Either because of the econometric problems with previous research methodology (as pointed out by Summers) or because of the long-run negative serial correlation of security returns (found by Fama and French) there is some doubt about the evidence that supports the EMH.

1.4. Source of Information

Four levels of information are necessary for the security analyst and portfolio manager:

1. Economy-wide information;
2. Financial market information;
3. Industry information; and
4. Individual company information.

The Economy

The condition of the U.S. and world economies has important impact on the activities and performance of financial market participants. Table 1.4 lists some of the sources of information about the U.S. and world economies.

Financial Markets

Data on the prices and trading volume of various financial instruments provide input to various valuation models used by the security analyst and portfolio manager to determine investment value. Table 1.5 lists some of the various sources of information about the financial markets.

Industry Information

The majority of information about individual industries is provided by the various trade associations of each specific industry. In Table 1.6, the sources of industry information are shown.

Corporate Information

The most obvious source of information about a specific company is the company itself. Either because of disclosure regulations or voluntary disclosure, a large amount of information about each publicly traded company becomes available each day. Table 1.7 lists the major sources of information about individual companies.

Given the large amount of information that is available, it is the job of security analysts and portfolio managers to analyze this information in order to make knowledgeable investment decisions.

Table 1.4. Sources of Information about the U.S. and World Economies.

GOVERNMENT SOURCES	
Statistical Abstracts of the U.S.	Prepared by the Bureau of the Census, this contains extensive social, political, and economic statistics.
Survey of Current Business	A monthly publication of the Department of Commerce. Twice a year the Business Statistics Supplement is published; this contains more than 2,500 time series of monthly, quarterly, and yearly data about the U.S. economy. A detailed description of each series is provided.
Federal Reserve Bulletin	A monthly publication of the Board and Governors of the Federal Reserve System, its major emphasis is on the monetary statistics and other financial statistics of the U.S. economy.
Business Conditions Digest	The Department of Commerce publishes a monthly series of data and charts of leading economic indicators, coincident indicators, and lagging indicators of the U.S. economy.
Economic Report of the President	The President sends a report of the state of the U.S. economy to Congress at the beginning of each year. Each report contains a summary of the past year's economic events and the major problems the economy will be facing the next year. Additionally there are statistical series of economic variables for the U.S. economy.
International Finance Statistics and U.N. Statistical Notebook	Good sources of data on worldwide economics and finance.
GENERAL FINANCIAL PRESS	
The Wall Street Journal	A daily newspaper covering the economy and the financial markets. It offers extensive price data for securities.
Business Week	A weekly focusing on topics about business and the economy.
Fortune	A biweekly featuring articles about business and the economy.
Economist	A weekly filled with articles and reports relating to the world economy.

1.5. Structure of the Book

There are 27 chapters in this book and they are divided into five parts. Part I discusses information and security valuation. Part II discusses portfolio theory and asset pricing. Part III discusses futures and options. Part IV presents applied portfolio management. Part V discusses special topics. The material in Chapters 2–6 review and extend the concepts and methods that

Table 1.5. Sources of Information about the Financial Markets.

GENERAL FINANCIAL PRESS	
The New York Times	Either local or national editions are available daily throughout the country, featuring articles and price information on the major financial markets.
Commercial and Financial Chronicle	A weekly offering price information on equity securities.
Barron's	A weekly magazine featuring articles and price information on most financial markets, domestic as well as international.
Finance	A monthly magazine providing articles about financial markets.
Euromoney	A monthly magazine with articles and data on international capital and money markets.
Institutional Investor	A monthly featuring articles aimed at the managers of large institutional portfolios.
Financial Analysts Journal	A bimonthly featuring articles of interest to financial analysts.
Journal of Portfolio Management	A quarterly publishing articles of interest to portfolio managers.
GOVERNMENT SOURCES	
Statistical Bulletin	A monthly publication of the Securities and Exchange Commission (SEC) emphasizing equity securities.
Annual Report of the SEC	A yearly report of the SEC highlighting major events in the financial markets.
PRIVATE SOURCES	
New York Stock Exchange (NYSE) Fact Book	An annual published by the NYSE; it contains extensive data on the trading on the NYSE.
AMEX Statistical Review	An annual of the AMEX; it contains data on the trading on the AMEX.
Dow Jones Investor's Handbook	A yearly publication of the earnings, dividends and prices of the Dow Jones Averages; published since 1939.
Standard & Poor's Trading and Security Statistics	Published yearly, featuring historical data on all of the S&P indexes.

students have learned from basic corporate finance and investment courses. Chapters 7–13 present both the theoretical and empirical issues concerning the use of the market model, the CAPM, the APT and risk diversification in security analysis and portfolio management. Chapters 14–20 use the theories and methods presented in the first thirteen chapters to investigate futures and options. Chapters 21–24 cover applications of portfolio theories and models developed in the preceding chapters. Finally, Chapters 25–27

Table 1.6. Sources of Information about Industries.

TRADE ASSOCIATIONS AND INDUSTRY PUBLICATIONS	
Iron and Steel Ages	*Computers*
Institute of Life Insurance	*Chemical Week*
American Bankers Association	*Aviation Week*
Machine Tool Association	*Automotive News*
PRIVATE SOURCES	
Dun and Bradstreet Key Business Ratios	Lists financial ratios for 125 industries.
Robert Morris Associates	Lists financial ratios for medium- and small-sized firms in various industries.
Standard & Poor's Investment Advisory Service, Industry Surveys, and Outlook	Provides information and data on major events in various industries.
Moody's Manuals	Provides information and financial data on various industries.
GOVERNMENT	
U.S. Industrial Outlook	An annual analysis of 200 industries.
Reports on specific industries	*Census of Mineral Industries*
	Census of Selected Service Industries
	Census of Construction Industry
	Census of Transportation
	Census of Retail Trade
	Census of Wholesale Trade
	Annual Survey of Manufactures
	Financial Census for Manufacturing Corporations

discuss special topics related to risk premia, security valuation, and Ito's calculus for advanced students. Special topics can be skipped over without loss of continuity.

Accounting information is essential for business decision making because it describes both the financial assets and the real assets of a firm. Historical accounting information has been used extensively by security analysis and portfolio managers, while proponents of the semi-strong form of the efficient-market hypothesis regard such information as valueless. In Chapter 2, ratio analysis, regression analysis, and earnings-per-share estimation are considered. The use of financial information in security analysis is emphasized. The role of the investment advisor in evaluating and rating the financial instruments of various companies is employed as an example of the ways that accounting information can be used to make valuation recommendations.

Table 1.7. Sources of Information about Individual Companies.

CORPORATE	
Annual and Quarterly Reports	All firms whose securities are publicly held and traded are required to disseminate to their security holders an annual report of operations and financial position. Basic financial statements such as income statement, balance sheet, sources and uses of funds, as well as changes in retained earnings are included in all annual reports.
Security Prospectus	If a firm is issuing new securities, financial information about the firm must be released to the public before the new securities can be issued.
GOVERNMENT	
Required Report	Form 10K: Form 10K is a very detailed annual report that publicly traded firms must submit to the SEC. These reports will be furnished to the public upon request to the firm. Information is also submitted every quarter in the form of a 10Q report.
PRIVATE	
Standard & Poor's Corporation Record	Provides annual financial data on individual companies.
Moody's Manuals	Provides annual historical and financial data on individual firms.
Value Line Investment Service	Offers historical and financial information on 1,700 companies, as well as quality recommendations as to the investment value of specific firms.
Brokerage Firms' Reports	Usually offer specific recommendations about the investment worth of individual firms' securities — for example, buy, sell, hold.
PRIVATE COMPUTERIZED DATABASES	
Compustat	S&P computerized database has approximately 3,500 companies covering 20 years of financial and market-price data.
University of Chicago Stock Price Tapes	The Center for Research on Security Price (CRSP) offers monthly and daily price data from various exchanges.
I/B/E/S	Provides detailed and consensus estimates featuring up to 26 forecast measures including GAAP and pro-forma EPS, revenue/sales, net income, pre-tax profit and operating profit, and price targets and recommendations for more than 60,000 companies in 67 countries worldwide.
Wharton Research Data Service	Provides data compiled from independent sources that specialize in specific historical data. Some sources include Capital IQ, NYSE Euronext, CRSP, and Thomson Reuters.

Chapter 3 deals with the measurement and the growth determination of rates of return on security investments. In addition to defining the holding-period return and the holding-period yield, three alternative methods for calculating average rates of return are discussed. These estimates can be used either to determine historical investment performance or to forecast future performance. It is known that a weighted unbiased estimator can be used to reduce or eliminate the bias in forecasting rates of return. Alternative methods of estimating growth rates are also discussed in Chapter 3. The relative advantages of these alternative methods are explored both theoretically and empirically. Possible applications of growth-rate estimation in security analysis and portfolio management are discussed.

Chapter 4 reviews both pre-Modigliani and Miller and M and M valuation theories in detail. The basic concepts of the CAPM and the option-pricing model are also explored in order to construct a rectangular theoretical framework of valuation. This chapter reviews basic theories that students have learned from a first course on either financial management or investment. Topics in this chapter can be used as a review or as major theoretical background for understanding later chapters of this text.

Chapter 5 extends the valuation analysis to the specific case of the debt instruments of corporations. Issues related to the yield curve, the term structure of interest rates, and bonds ratings are carefully analyzed. Chapter 6 discusses the computation of alternative market indexes and examines the possible biases associated with using these indexes in investment analysis. The historical behavior of market indexes and index forecasting are also explored.

In Chapter 7, sources of risk and basic portfolio analysis are investigated and used as a framework for further analysis of the CAPM and the market model. Chapter 8 discusses utility theory and Markowitz's full-information model of portfolio selection in detail. In Chapter 9, the market model and the CAPM are evaluated both theoretically and empirically. The applications of the market model to risk decomposition are analyzed using both fixed-coefficient regression models. Methods of forecasting beta coefficients are explored, using both accounting and market information.

Chapter 10 addresses how Markowitz's full-information portfolio-selection process can be simplified through the use of index models. Chapter 11 illustrates how the Sharpe and Treynor performance measures can be used to simplify the portfolio-selection procedure. Chapter 12 deals with the concept of an efficient market and the empirical evidence that supports or refutes this hypothesis. The implications of market efficiency for security analysts and portfolio managers are also stressed. In Chapter 13, multi-index models and the APT are discussed from both a theoretical and an empirical basis. The intertemporal CAPM is also discussed in some detail.

Chapter 14 discusses the basic issues of futures markets and futures contracts. In addition, two alternative hedging methods are investigated in detail. Chapter 15 explores the use of commodity futures, financial futures, and stock-index futures. The valuation of these futures and their use in hedging is investigated. Chapter 16 and 17 outline the basic concepts of put and call options, and the option-pricing model is derived using a binomial-model approach. Payoff and profits of different option strategies are also discussed in Chapter 16. Binomial option-pricing model and its applications in the making of investment decisions are explored in Chapter 17. Chapter 18 uses a Microsoft Excel workbook to create the decision trees for the binomial option-pricing model. Chapter 19 uses bivariate normal density function to evaluate American option price. An Excel program for the evaluation of stock option model is also provided in Chapter 19. Chapter 20 shows the comparative static analysis of the option-pricing models with respect to their determinants. Derivations and applications are discussed in detail.

Chapter 21 discusses timing and selectivity of stocks and mutual funds from both a fundamental analysis and technical analysis perspective. Some forecasting models are examined, and Fama's breakdown of overall investment performance into several specific components is also covered. In Chapter 22, issues relating to international diversification, exchange-rate risk, the international CAPM, and international portfolio-selection methods are investigated in detail. The valuations of currency option and index option are also discussed in Chapter 22. Chapter 23 presents a discussion of the issues involved in the management of a fixed-income portfolio. Both duration and bond immunization are carefully analyzed in this chapter. Chapter 24 examines the use of hedging and portfolio-insurance strategies for equity and bond portfolio.

Chapter 25 presents three long/short strategies and empirically examines whether these strategies can capture equity risk premia. Chapter 26 shows how simultaneous-equation models can be used in financial planning and forecasting. The case of Johnson and Johnson is used in an empirical example of this technique. In addition, two alternative models for security valuation provided by Feltham and Ohlson are discussed in detail. Finally, Chapter 27 provides an in-depth derivation of the

Black–Scholes option-pricing model in terms of the stochastic differential equation.

1.6. Summary

In this chapter, we have used the new issues data of both equity and bond and trading volume of equity to show the expansion taking place in the financial markets around the world. Therefore, it requires a firm foundation in the relevant theories and methods of valuation to make a right decision in investing financial instruments.

This chapter has identified the objectives of portfolio management and security analysis. In addition, we also discuss the sources of economy-wide information, financial market information, industry information, and individual company information, which are necessary for the security analyst and portfolio manager. Finally, the structure of this book has discussed in some detail.

Questions and Problems

1. Please discuss the differences between the primary market and the secondary market.
2. Please discuss the issuing value of bonds and stocks during the period from 1980 to 2010. In addition, please calculate the growth rate of the new issue of these two instruments.
3. Please discuss the average daily trading volume of equity during the period from 1980 to 2009. In addition, please calculate the growth rate of the average daily trading volume of equity during this period.
4. What are security analysis and portfolio management? Is there any relationship between these two topics?

Bibliography

Bodie, Z., A. Kane and A. Marcus. *Investments*, 9th ed. New York: McGraw-Hill Book Company, 2010.

Brealey, R. A. *An Introduction to Risk and Return from Common Stock*, 2nd ed. Cambridge, MA: MIT Press, 1981.

Darst, D. M. *The Handbook of the Bond and Money Markets.* New York: McGraw-Hill, 1981.

Fama, E. F. and K. R. French. "Permanent and Temporary Components of Stock Prices." *Journal of Political Economy*, v. 96 (April 1988), pp. 246–273.

Fama, E. F. and M. H. Miller. *The Theory of Finance.* New York: Holt, Rinehart and Winston, 1972.

Graham, B., D. Dodd and S. Cottle. *Security Analysis: Principles and Techniques,* 4th ed. New York: McGraw-Hill, 1962.

Kohler, H. *Statistics for Business and Economics,* 3rd ed. New York: Harper-Collins Publisher, 1994.

Lee, A. C, J. C. Lee and C. F. Lee. *Financial Analysis, Planning and Forecasting: Theory and Application,* 2nd ed. Singapore: World Scientific Publishing Company, 2009.

Malkiel, B. A. *A Random Walk Down Wall Street,* 4th ed. New York: W. W. Norton & Company, Inc., 2011.

Ross S., R. Westerfield and J. Jaffe. *Corporate Finance,* 9th ed. New York: McGraw-Hill Book Company, 2010.

Summers, L. H. "Do We Really Know that Financial Markets are Efficient?" Discussion Paper No. 1237, Harvard Institute of Economic Research, 1986.

West, R. R. "The Teaching of Investment: Is Witchcraft Still Appropriate?" *Journal of Financial and Quantitative Analysis,* v. 9 (November 1974), pp. 789–793.

Part I

Information and Security Valuation

Chapter 2

Accounting Information and Regression Analysis

2.1. Introduction

Accounting information, market information, and basic aggregated economic data are the basic inputs needed for financial analysis and planning; statistical methods, regression analysis, operation research programming techniques, and computer programming knowledge are important tools for achieving financial planning and forecasting. In performing financial analysis and planning, it is important to know how to use the appropriate tools in analyzing the relevant data.

The main purposes of this chapter are (i) to show how algebraic and statistical methods are used in cost–volume–profit (CVP) analysis and (ii) to demonstrate how modern econometric methods can be used to analyze the dynamic adjustment process of financial ratios and obtain new insights into the use of financial ratios in the financial analysis, planning, and forecasting. Recall that for financial management, the three major policies of the firm are investment, financing, and dividend policy. The basic concept of CVP analysis can be used in the areas of investment and financing, specifically for capital budget decision making and leverage analysis. Similarly, ratio analysis can be used to determine a firm's liquidity position, leverage position, the effectiveness of asset utilization, and profitability performance.

This chapter is organized as follows. Section 2.2 reviews four important financial statements: the balance sheet, the statement of earnings, the statement of equity, and the statement of cash flow. Section 2.3 discusses possible weaknesses of accounting information, and proposes possible methods to minimize these weaknesses. In Section 2.4, static ratio analysis is reviewed and dynamic financial ration analysis is presented. Both single-equation and simultaneous-equation approaches to dynamic financial analysis are explored. In Section 2.5, CVP analysis is extended from deterministic analysis to stochastic analysis. The concepts of statistical distributions are used to improve the robustness of CVP analysis. The relationship between accounting income and economic income is explored in Section 2.6. Finally, Section 2.7 summarizes the key concepts the chapter. In addition, there are two appendixes to this chapter reviewing basic econometric methods. Appendix A reviews basic concepts and methods of simple regression and multiple regressions, and Appendix B discusses basic concepts and methods of instrumental variables and two-stage least-squares regression.

2.2. Financial Statements: A Brief Review

Corporate annual and quarterly reports generally contain four basic financial statements: balance sheet, statement of earnings, statement of retained earnings, and statement of changes in financial position. Using Johnson & Johnson (JNJ) annual consolidated financial statements as examples, we discuss in turn the usefulness of, and problems associated with the use of, each of these statements in financial analysis and planning. Finally, the use of annual versus quarterly financial data is addressed.

2.2.1. *Balance Sheet*

The balance sheet describes a firm's financial position at one specific point in time. It is a static representation, as if a snapshot had been taken, of the firm's financial composition of assets and liabilities at one point in time. The balance sheet of JNJ, shown in Table 2.1, is broken down into two basic areas of classification — total assets (debit) and total liabilities and shareholders' equity (credit).

On the debit side, accounts are divided into six groups: current assets, marketable securities — non-current, property, plant and equipment, intangible assets, deferred taxes on income, and other assets. Current assets represents those accounts that are of a short-term nature such as cash and cash equivalent, marketable securities and accounts receivable, inventories, deferred tax on income, and prepaid expense. It should be noted that

Table 2.1. Consolidated Balance Sheets of Johnson & Johnson Corporation and Consolidated Subsidiaries (2004–2009) (Dollars in Millions).

Assets	2004	2005	2006	2007	2008	2009
Current Assets						
Cash and Cash Equivalent ($)	9,203	16,055	4,083	7,770	10,768	15,810
Marketable Securities	3,681	83	1	1,545	2,041	3,615
Account Receivable	6,831	7,010	8,712	9,444	9,719	9,646
Inventory	3,744	3,959	4,889	5,110	5,052	5,180
Deferred Taxes on Income	1,737	1,845	2,094	2,609	3,430	2,793
Prepaid Expenses and Other Receivable	2,124	2,442	3,196	3,467	3,367	2,497
Total Current Assets	**27,320**	**31,394**	**22,975**	**29,945**	**34,377**	**39,541**
Marketable Securities — Non-current	46	20	16	2	—	—
Property, Plant and Equipment, Net	10,436	10,830	13,044	14,185	14,365	14,759
Intangible Assets, Net	11,842	12,175	28,688	28,763	27,695	31,185
Deferred Taxes on Income	551	385	3,210	4,889	5,841	5,507
Other Assets	3,122	3,221	2,623	3,170	2,634	3,690
Total Assets	**53,317**	**58,025**	**70,556**	**80,954**	**84,912**	**94,682**
Liabilities and Shareholder's Equity						
Current Liabilities						
Loans and Notes Payable	280	668	4,579	2,463	3,732	6,318
Account Payable	5,227	4,315	5,691	6,909	7,503	5,541
Accrued Liabilities	3,523	3,529	4,587	6,412	5,531	5,796
Accrued Rebates, Returns, and Promotion	2,297	2,017	2,189	2,318	2,237	2,028
Accrued Salaries, Wages, and Commissions	1,094	1,166	1,391	1,512	1,432	1,606
Taxes on Income	1,506	940	724	223	417	442
Total Current Liabilities	**13,927**	**12,635**	**19,161**	**19,837**	**20,852**	**21,731**
Long-term Debt	2,565	2,017	2,014	7,074	8,120	8,223
Deferred Tax liability	403	211	1,319	1,493	1,432	1,424
Employee-related Obligations	2,631	3,065	5,584	5,402	7,791	6,769
Other Liabilities	1,978	2,226	3,160	3,829	4,206	5,947

(*Continued*)

Table 2.1. (*Continued*)

Assets	2004	2005	2006	2007	2008	2009
Shareowners' Equity						
Preferred Stock-without Par Value	—	—	—	—	—	—
Common Stock-Par Value $1.00	3,120	3,120	3,120	3,120	3,120	3,120
Net Receivable from Employee Stock Plan	−11	—	—	—	—	—
Accumulated Other Comprehensive Income	−515	−755	−2,118	−693	−4,955	−3,058
Retained Earnings	35,223	41,471	49,290	55,280	63,379	70,306
Less: Common Stock Held in Treasury	6,004	5,965	10,974	14,388	19,033	19,780
Total Shareowners' Equity	**31,813**	**37,871**	**39,318**	**43,319**	**42,511**	**50,588**
Total Liabilities and Shareholders' Equity	**53,317**	**58,025**	**70,556**	**80,954**	**84,912**	**94,682**

deferred tax on income in this group is a current deferred tax and will be converted into income tax within one year. Property encompasses all fixed or capital assets such as real estate, plant and equipment, and special tools and the allowance for depreciation and amortization. Intangible assets refer to the assets of research and development (R&D).

The credit side of the balance sheet in Table 2.1 is divided into current liabilities, long-term liabilities, and shareowner's equity. Under current liabilities the following accounts are included: accounts, loans, and notes payable; accrued liabilities; accrued salaries; and taxes on income. Long-term liabilities include various forms of long-term debt, deferred tax liability, employee-related obligations, and other liabilities. The stockholder's equity section of the balance sheet represents the net worth of the firm to its investors. For example, as of December 31, 2004, JNJ had $0 million preferred stock outstanding, $3,120 million in common stock outstanding, and $35,223 million retained earnings. Sometimes there are preferred stock and hybrid securities (e.g., convertible bonds and convertible preferred stock) on the credit side of the balance sheet.

The balance sheet is useful because it depicts the firm's financing and investment policies. The use of comparative balance sheets, those that present several years' data, can be used to detect trends and possible future problems. JNJ has presented on its balance sheet information from six periods, December 31, 2004; December 31, 2005; December 31, 2006; December 31, 2007; December 31, 2008; and December 31, 2009. The balance sheet, however, is static and therefore should be analyzed with caution in financial analysis and planning.

2.2.2. *Statement of Earnings*

JNJ's statement of earnings is presented in Table 2.2 and describes the results of operations for a 12-month period ending December 31. The usual income-statement periods are annual, quarterly, and monthly. JNJ has chosen the annual approach. Both the annual and quarterly reports are used for external as well as internal reporting. The monthly statement is

Table 2.2. Consolidated Statements of Earnings of JNJ Corporation and Subsidiaries (2004–2009) (Dollars in Millions).

(Dollars in Millions Except Per Share Figures)	2004	2005	2006	2007	2008	2009
Sales to Customers ($)	47,348	50,514	53,324	61,095	63,747	61,897
Cost of Products Sold	13,422	13,954	15,057	17,751	18,511	18,447
Gross Profit	33,926	36,560	38,267	43,344	45,236	43,450
Selling, Marketing, and Administrative Expenses	15,860	16,877	17,433	20,451	21,490	19,801
Research Expense	5,203	6,312	7,125	7,680	7,577	6,986
Purchased In-process Research and Development	18	362	559	807	181	—
Interest Income	−195	−487	−829	−452	−361	−90
Interest Expense, Net of Portion Capitalized	187	54	63	296	435	451
Other (income) expense, Net	15	−214	−671	1,279	−1,015	547
	21,088	22,904	23,680	30,061	26,307	27,695
Earnings Before Provision for Taxes on Income	12,838	13,656	14,587	13,283	16,929	15,755
Provision for Taxes on Income	4,329	3,245	3,534	2,707	3,980	3,489
Net Earnings	8,509	10,411	11,053	10,576	12,949	12,266
Basic Net Earnings per Share ($)	2.87	3.50	3.76	3.67	4.62	4.45
Diluted Net Earnings per Share ($)	2.84	3.46	3.73	3.63	4.57	4.40

used primarily for internal purposes such as the estimation of sales and profit targets, judgment of controls on expenses, and monitoring progress toward longer-term targets. The statement of earnings is more dynamic than the balance sheet because it reflects changes for the period. It provides an analyst with an overview of a firm's operations and profitability of the firm on a gross, and operating, and a net income basis. JNJ's income includes sales, interest income, and other net income/expenses. Costs and expenses for JNJ's include the cost of goods sold; selling, marketing, and administrative expenses; and depreciation, depletion, and amortization. The difference between the income and cost and expenses results in the company's Net Earnings. A comparative statement of earnings is very useful in financial analysis and planning because it allows insight into the firm's operations, profitability, and financing decisions over time. For this reason JNJ presents the statement of earnings of six consecutive years, 2004, 2005, 2006, 2007, 2008, and 2009. Armed with this information, evaluating the firm's future is easier.

2.2.3. *Statement of Equity*

JNJ's statements of equity are shown in Table 2.3. These are the earnings that a firm retains for reinvestment rather than paying them out to shareholders in the form of dividends. The statement of equity is easily understood if it is viewed as a bridge between the balance sheet and the statement of earnings. The statement of equity presents a summary of those categories that have an impact on the level of retained earnings: the net earnings and the dividends declared for preferred and common stock. It also represents a summary of the firm's dividend policy and shows how net income is allocated to dividends and reinvestment. JNJ's equity is one source of funds for investment, and this internal source of funds is very important to the firm. With these three statements, one can analyze important firm decisions on the capital structure, cost of that capital, capital budgeting, and dividend policy.

2.2.4. *Statement of Cash Flows*

Another extremely important part of the annual and quarterly report is the statement of cash flows. This statement is very helpful in evaluating a firm's use of its funds and in determining how these funds were raised. Statements of cash flow for JNJ are shown in Table 2.4. These statements

Table 2.3. Consolidated Statements of Equity of JNJ Corporation and Subsidiaries (2004–2009) (Dollars in Millions).

(Dollars in millions)	Total	Comprehensive Income	Retained Earnings	Note Receivable From Employee Stock Ownership Plan (ESOP)	Accumulated Other Comprehensive Income	Common Stock Issued Amount	Treasury Stock Amount
Balance, December 28, 2003	**$27,464**		**31,098**	**(18)**	**(590)**	**3120**	**(6,146)**
Net earnings	8,180	8,180	8,180				
Cash dividends paid	(3,251)		(3,251)				
Employee stock compensation and stock option plans	1,339		(64)				1,403
Conversion of subordinated debentures	105		(18)				123
Repurchase of common stock	(1,384)						(1,384)
Business combinations							
Other comprehensive income, net of tax:							
Currency translation adjustment	268	268			268		
Unrealized gains/(losses) on securities	59	59			59		
Pension liability adjustment	(282)	(282)			(282)		

(Continued)

Table 2.3. (*Continued*)

(Dollars in millions)	Total	Comprehensive Income	Retained Earnings	Note Receivable From Employee Stock Ownership Plan (ESOP)	Accumulated Other Comprehensive Income	Common Stock Issued Amount	Treasury Stock Amount
Reclassification adjustment		(10)					
Total comprehensive income		8,215					
Note receivable from ESOP	7			7			
Balance, January 2, 2005	**$32,505**		**35,945**	**(11)**	**(545)**	**3,120**	**6,004**
Net earnings	10,060	10,060	10,060				
Cash dividends paid	(3,793)		(3,793)				
Employee stock compensation and stock option plans	1,485		27				1,458
Conversion of subordinated debentures	369		(132)				501
Repurchase of common stock	(1,717)		203				
Business combinations	1,366		1,302				(1,920)
Other comprehensive income, net of tax:							
Currency translation adjustment	(415)	(415)			(415)		

(*Continued*)

Table 2.3. (*Continued*)

(Dollars in millions)	Total	Comprehensive Income	Retained Earnings	Note Receivable From Employee Stock Ownership Plan (ESOP)	Accumulated Other Comprehensive Income	Common Stock Issued Amount	Treasury Stock Amount
Unrealized gains/(losses) on securities	(16)	(16)			(16)		
Gains/(losses) on derivatives & hedges	165	165			165		
Reclassification adjustment		(15)					
Total comprehensive income		9,779					
Note receivable from ESOP	11			11			
Balance, January 1, 2006	**38,654**		**42,310**		**(811)**	**3,120**	**(5,965)**
Net earnings	11,053	11,053	11,053				
Cash dividends paid	(4,267)		(4,267)				
Employee stock compensation and stock option plans	1,858		181				1,677
Conversion of subordinated debentures	26		(10)				36
Repurchase of common stock	(6,722)						(6,722)

(*Continued*)

Table 2.3. *(Continued)*

(Dollars in millions)	Total	Comprehensive Income	Retained Earnings	Note Receivable From Employee Stock Ownership Plan (ESOP)	Accumulated Other Comprehensive Income	Common Stock Issued Amount	Treasury Stock Amount
Other comprehensive income, net of tax:							
Currency-translation adjustment	362	362			362		
Unrealized gains/(losses) on securities	(9)	(9)			(9)		
Pension liability adjustment	(1,710)	(34)			(1,710)		
Gains/(losses) on derivates & hedges	(6)	(6)			(6)		
Reclassification adjustment		(9)					
Total comprehensive income		11,357					
Note receivable from ESOP							
Balance, December 31, 2006	**$39,239**		**49,267**		**(2,174)**	**3,120**	**(10,974)**
Net earnings	10,576	10,576	10,576				
Cash dividends paid	(4,670)		(4,670)				
Employee stock compensation and stock option plans	2,311		131				2,180

(Continued)

Table 2.3. *(Continued)*

(Dollars in millions)	Total	Comprehensive Income	Retained Earnings	Note Receivable From Employee Stock Ownership Plan (ESOP)	Accumulated Other Comprehensive Income	Common Stock Issued Amount	Treasury Stock Amount
Conversion of subordinated debentures	9		(4)				13
Repurchase of common stock	(5,607)						(5,607)
Adoption of FIN 48	(19)		(19)				
Other comprehensive income, net of tax:							
Currency translation adjustment	786	786			786		
Unrealized gains on securities	23	23			23		
Pension liability adjustment	670	670			670		
Losses on derivatives & hedges	(54)	(54)			(54)		
Reclassification adjustment		(5)					
Total comprehensive income		11,996					
Note receivable from ESOP							
Balance, December 30, 2007	**$43,264**		**55,281**		**(749)**	**3,120**	**(14,388)**
Net earnings	12,949	12,949	12,949				
Cash dividends paid	(5,024)		(5,024)				
Employee stock compensation and stock option plans	2,180		175				2,005

(Continued)

Table 2.3. (*Continued*)

(Dollars in millions)	Total	Comprehensive Income	Retained Earnings	Note Receivable From Employee Stock Ownership Plan (ESOP)	Accumulated Other Comprehensive Income	Common Stock Issued Amount	Treasury Stock Amount
Conversion of subordinated debentures			(1)				1
Repurchase of common stock	(6,651)						(6,651)
Other comprehensive income, net of tax:							
Currency translation adjustment	(2,499)	(2,499)			(2,499)		
Unrealized gains on securities	(59)	(59)			(59)		
Pension liability adjustment	(1,870)	(1,870)			(1,870)		
Gains on derivatives & hedges	166	166			166		
Reclassification adjustment		(27)					
Total comprehensive income		8,660					
Note receivable from ESOP							
Balance, December 28, 2008	**$42,456**		**63,380**		**(5,011)**	**3,120**	**(19,033)**
Net earnings	12,266	12,266	12,266				
Cash dividends paid	(5,327)		(5,327)				

(*Continued*)

Table 2.3. (*Continued*)

(Dollars in millions)	Total	Comprehensive Income	Retained Earnings	Note Receivable From Employee Stock Ownership Plan (ESOP)	Accumulated Other Comprehensive Income	Common Stock Issued Amount	Treasury Stock Amount
Employee stock compensation and stock option plans	1,402		25				1,377
Conversion of subordinated debentures	2		(4)				6
Repurchase of common stock	(2,130)						(2,130)
Other comprehensive income, net of tax:							
Currency-translation adjustment	1,363	1,363			1,363		
Unrealized gains on securities	(55)	(55)			(55)		
Pension liability adjustment	565	565			565		
Gains on derivatives & hedges	24	24			24		
Reclassification adjustment							
Total comprehensive income		14,163					
Note receivable from ESOP							
Balance, January 1, 2006	**50,533**		**70,307**	—	**(3,114)**	**3,120**	**(19,780)**

Table 2.4. Consolidated Statements of Cash Flow of JNJ Corporation and Subsidiaries (Dollars in millions).

(Dollars in Millions)	2004	2005	2006	2007	2008	2009
Cash flows from operating activities						
Net earnings	$8,180	10,060	11,053	10,576	12,949	12,266
Adjustments to reconcile net earnings to cash flows:						
Depreciation and amortization of property and intangibles	2,124	2,093	2,177	2,777	2,832	2,774
Purchased in-process research and development	18	362	559	807	181	—
Deferred tax provision	−676	−235	−1,168	−1,762	22	−436
Accounts receivable allowances	3	−31	−14	22	86	58
Changes in assets and liabilities, net of effects from acquisitions:						
Increase in accounts receivable	−111	−568	−699	−416	−736	453
(Increase)/decrease in inventories	11	−396	−210	14	−101	95
(Decrease)/increase in accounts payable and accrued liabilities	607	−911	1,750	2,642	−272	−507
Decrease/(increase) in other current and noncurrent assets	−437	542	−269	−1,578	−1,600	1,209
Increase in other current and non-current liabilities	863	343	410	564	984	31
Net cash flows from operating activities	10,582	11,259	13,589	13,646	14,345	15,943
Cash flows from investing activities						
Additions to property, plant and equipment	−2,175	−2,632	−2,666	−2,942	−3,066	−2,365
Proceeds from the disposal of assets	237	154	511	457	785	154
Acquisitions, net of cash acquired	−580	−987	−18,023	−1,388	−1,214	−2,470
Purchases of investments	−11,617	−5,660	−467	−9,659	−3,668	−10,040
Sales of investments	12,061	9,187	426	7,988	3,059	7,232
Other (primarily intangibles)	−273	−341	−72	−368	−83	−109

(*Continued*)

Table 2.4. (*Continued*)

(Dollars in millions)	2004	2005	2006	2007	2008	2009
Net cash used by investing activities	−2,347	−279	−20,291	−5,912	−4,187	−7,598
Cash flows from financing activities						
Dividends to shareholders	−3,251	−3,793	−4,267	−4,670	−5,024	−53,273
Repurchase of common stock	−1,384	−1,717	−6,722	−5,607	−6,651	−2,130
Proceeds from short-term debt	514	1,215	6,385	19,626	8,430	9,484
Retirement of short-term debt	−1,291	−732	−2,633	−21,691	−7,319	−6,791
Proceeds from long-term debt	17	6	6	5,100	1,638	9
Retirement of long-term debt	−395	−196	−13	−18	−24	−219
Proceeds from the exercise of stock options	684	774	1,135	1,562	1,486	882
Net cash used by financing activities	−5,106	−4,443	−6,109	−5,698	−7,464	−4,092
Effect of exchange rate changes on cash and cash equivalents	190	−225	180	275	−323	161
Increase/ (Decrease) in cash and cash equivalents	3,826	6,852	−11,972	3,687	2,998	5,042
Cash and cash equivalents, beginning of year	5,377	9,203	16,055	4,083	7,770	10,768
Cash and cash equivalents, end of year	9,203	16,055	4,083	7,770	10,768	15,810
Supplemental cash flow data						
Cash paid during the year for:						
Interest	222	151	143	314	525	533
Income taxes	3,880	3,429	4,250	4,099	4,068	2,368
Supplemental schedule of noncash investing and financing activities						
Treasury stock issued for employee compensation and stock option plans, net of cash proceeds	802	818	622	738	593	541
Conversion of debt	105	369	26	9	—	2
Acquisitions						
Fair value of assets acquired	595	1,128	19,306	1,620	1,328	3,345
Fair value of liabilities assumed	−15	−141	−1,283	−232	−114	−8,751
Net cash paid for acquisitions	580	987	18,023	1,388	1,214	2,470

of cash flow are composed of three sections: cash flows from operating activities, cash flows from investing activities, and cash flows from financing activities. The statement of cash flows, whether developed on a cash or working capital basis, summarizes long-term transactions that affect the firm's cash position. For JNJ, the sources of cash are essentially provided by operations. Application of these funds includes dividends paid to stockholders and expenditures for property, plant and equipment, etc. Therefore, this statement reveals some important aspects of the firm's investment, financing, and dividend policies, making it an important tool for financial planning and analysis.

The cash flow statement shows how the net increase or decrease in cash has been reflected in the changing composition of current assets and current liabilities. It highlights changes in short-term financial policies. It helps answer question such as: Has the firm been building up its liquidity assets or is it becoming less liquid?

The statement of cash flow can be used to help resolve differences between finance and accounting theory. There is value for the analyst in viewing the statement of cash flow over time, especially in detecting trends that could lead to technical or legal bankruptcy in the future. Collectively, these four statements present a fairly clear picture of the firm's historical and current position.

2.2.5. *Interrelationship among Four Financial Statements*

It should be note that balance sheet, statement of earnings, statement of equity, and statement of cash flow are interrelated. These relationships are briefly described as follows:

(1) Retained earnings calculated from statement of equity for current period should be used to replace the retained earnings item in the balance sheet of previous period. Therefore, the statement of equity can be regard as a bridge for balance sheet and statement of earnings.
(2) We need the information of balance sheet, statement of earnings, and statement of equity to compile the statement of cash flow.
(3) Cash and cash equivalent item can be found in the statement of cash flow. In other words, the statement of cash flow has described how the cash and cash equivalent has been changed during the period. It is known that the first item of the balance sheet is cash and cash equivalent.

2.2.6. *Annual Versus Quarterly Financial Data*

Both annual and quarterly financial data are important to financial analysts; which one is the most important depends on the time horizon of the analysis. Depending upon the patterns of fluctuation in the historical data, either annual or quarterly data could prove more useful. As Gentry and Lee (1983) discuss, understanding the implications of using quarterly data versus annual data is important for proper financial analysis and planning.

Quarterly data has three components: trend-cycle, seasonal, and irregular or random components. It contains important information about seasonal fluctuations that "reflects and intra-year pattern of variation which is repeated constantly or in evolving fashion from year to year."[1] Quarterly data have the disadvantage of having a large irregular, or random, component that introduces noise into analysis.

Annual data is composed of two components, rather than the three of quarterly data, the trend-cycle and the irregular component, but no seasonal component. The irregular component is much smaller in annual data than in quarterly data. While it may seem that annual data would be most useful for long-term financial planning and analysis, seasonal data reveal important permanent patterns that underlie the short-term series in financial analysis and planning. In other words, quarterly data can be used for intermediate-term financial planning to improve financial management.

Use of either quarterly or annual data has a consistent impact on the mean-square error of regression forecasting (see Appendix A), which is composed of variance and bias. Changing from annual to quarterly data will generally reduce variance while increasing bias. Any difference in regression results, because of the use of different data, must be analyzed in light of the historical patterns of fluctuation in the original time-series data.

2.3. Critique of Accounting Information

2.3.1. *Criticism*

At first glance, accounting information seems to be heavily audited and regulated, automatically determining what numbers are presented. However, careful analysis makes it apparent that accountants work with a fairly broad framework of rules that increase the distance between accounting and financial valuation. This leeway in accounting rules also

[1]See Gentry and Lee (1983).

tends to make accounting information more random. In addition, Hong (1977) shows that the selection of "last in, first out" (LIFO) or "first in, first out" (FIFO) methods for tax and depreciation based upon historic cost generally introduce a bias in a firm's market-value determination. This combination of discrepancy, bias, and randomness means that accounting information does not represent the "true" information. As a result, both time-series and cross-sectional comparisons of accounting information are difficult to analyze.

A major problem with use of accounting information rises from errors made in classifying transactions into individual accounts. There are several types of classification errors.

One classification error occurs when a bookkeeper enters an item in the wrong account. This is dealt with by modern auditing through the use of sampling techniques where the auditor certifies that the probability of a material error, that is, an error that would alter a manager's or investor's decision, is within an acceptable limit.

The difference between accountancy and finance theory is another case of classification error. An accountant defines income as the change is shareholder's wealth due to operations of the firm. This includes the use of accruals in wealth determination. The finance discipline defines a firm's income as cash income, or the difference between cash revenues and cash expenses (those payments made to generate current revenue).[2] Due to the accruals used in accounting, accounting income is numerically different from cash income because of a difference in timing.

Another problem with accounting information relates to depreciation costs. There are various accepted ways to spread the cost of an asset over its useful life.[3] The choice of a depreciation method can cause a wide variation in net income.[4] A straight-line method will reduce income less than an

[2]See Haley and Schall (1979).

[3]Depreciation is a procedure that allocates the acquisition costs of the asset to subsequent periods of time on a systematic and rational basis. There are several widely used methods of allocating the acquisition costs: straight-line, declining balance, and sum-of-the-years digits.

[4]There is a limit on the ability of the firm to manipulate its financial statements by repeatedly changing accounting methods, for depreciation, inventory valuation, or any other of the numerous decisions permitted by generally accepted accounting principles (GAAP). The limitation on constant changes in accounting methods is provided by several sources. Accounting Principle Board 20 requires that any changes must be justified on the basis of fair presentation and that the change and the justification be disclosed.

accelerated method in the first years of depreciation. In the later years, accelerated depreciation will reduce income less than a straight-line method.

The use of historical costs for pricing an asset acquisition also causes problems in using accounting information. Such reliance on historical cost is particularly troublesome in times of high inflation because historical cost values are no longer representative of the underlying values of the assets and liabilities of the firm. The accounting profession is attempting to deal with this problem through the use of supplementary disclosure of selected financial statement items, as required by Financial Accounting Standard Board 33, for large, publicly traded firms.[5] Accountants are also developing replacement cost and other inflation-adjusted accounting procedures.

2.3.2. *Methods for Improvement*

Three possible methods for improving the representativeness or accuracy of accounting information in financial analysis and planning are the use of alternative information, statistical tools, and finance and economic theories.

2.3.2.1. *Use of Alternative Information*

Of the many types of alternative information that could be used to improve the accounting data, the most practical and consistent type is market information. Stock prices and replacement costs can be used to adjust reported accounting earnings. According to the theory of efficient capital markets, the market price of a security represents the market's estimate of the value of that security. Furthermore, the market value (or the "intrinsic" value) of a common stock represents the firm's "true" earning potential perceived by investors. An example of the use of market information to complement accounting information is the use of the option-pricing model in capital budgeting under uncertainty in Chapter 10.

2.3.2.2. *Statistical Adjustments*

Another method of improving accounting information is the use of statistical tools. By using a time-series decomposition technique suggested

The American Institute of Certified Public Accountants, through the Auditing Standards Board, requires that the auditor certify that accounting principles have been consistently observed in the current period in relation to the preceding periods [AU 150.02].

[5]Financial Accounting Standards Board Statement #33, Stamford CT, June 1974.

by Gentry and Lee (1983), quarterly earnings can be divided into three components: trend-cyclical, seasonal, and irregular. This decomposition procedure can be used to remove some undesirable noise associated with accounting numbers. Therefore, this statistically adjusted accounting earnings data can be used to improve its usefulness in determining a firm's intrinsic value.

For long-term financial planning and analysis, the trend-cyclical component is the major source of information. The seasonal and irregular components introduce noise that clouds the analysis, and this noise can be removed. For short-term (or intermediate-term) planning and analysis, the seasonal component also produces valuable information. Thus, both trend-cycle and seasonal components should be used in working capital management. Note that the source(s) of noise can also be eliminated by moving average or other statistical methods.

2.3.2.3. *Application of Finance and Economic Theories*

The third method of improving accounting information is the use of finance and economic theories. For example, there are the Modigliani and Miller valuation theory, the capital-asset pricing theory, and option pricing theory, which will be discussed in Chapters 4, 9, and 17. By applying these theories, one can adjust accounting income to obtain a better picture of income measurement, i.e., finance income (cash flow). Also, the use of finance theory combined with market and other information gives an analyst another estimate of income measurement. In addition, the various earnings estimates can shed additional light on the firm's value determination. To do these kinds of empirical tests, Lee and Zumwalt (1981) use a multiple regression model to investigate the association between six alternative accounting profitability measures and security rate-of-return determination. Their empirical results suggest that accounting profitability information is an important extra-market component information of asset pricing. In other words, it is shown that different accounting profitability measures should be used by security analysts and investors to determine the equity rates of return for different industries.

2.4. Static Ratio Analysis and Its Extension

In order to make use of financial statements, an analyst needs some form of measure for analysis. Frequently, ratios are used to relate one piece of financial data to another. The ratio puts the two pieces of data on an equivalent base, which increases the usefulness of the data. For example, net income as an absolute number is meaningless to compare across firms of different sizes. If one creates a net profitability ratio (NI/Sales), however, comparisons are made easier. Analysis of a series of ratios will give us a clear picture of a firm's financial condition and performance.

Analysis of ratios can take one of two forms. First, the analyst can compare the ratios of one firm with those of similar firms or with industry averages at a specific point in time. This is one type of cross-sectional analysis technique that may indicate the relative financial condition and performance of a firm. One must be careful, however, to analyze the ratios while keeping in mind the inherent differences between firms' production functions and operations. Also, the analyst should avoid using "rules of thumb" across industries because the composition of industries and individual firms varies considerably. Furthermore, inconsistency in a firm's accounting procedures can cause accounting data to show substantial differences between firms, which can hinder comparability through the use of ratios. This variation in accounting procedures can also lead to problems in determining the "target ratio" (to be discussed later).

The second method of ratio comparison involves the comparison of a present ratio with that same firm's past and expected ratios. This form of time-series analysis will indicate whether the firm's financial condition has improved or deteriorated. Both types of ratio analysis can take one of the two following forms: static determination and analysis, or dynamic adjustment and its analysis.

2.4.1. *Static Determination of Financial Ratios*

The static determination of financial ratios involves the calculation and analysis of ratios over a number of periods for one company, or the analysis of differences in ratios among individual firms in one industry. An analyst must be careful of extreme values in either direction because of the interrelationships between ratios. For instance, a very high liquidity ratio is costly to maintain, causing profitability rations to be lower than they need be. Furthermore, ratios must be interpreted in relation to the raw data from which they are calculated, particularly for ratios that sum accounts in order to arrive at the necessary data for the calculation. Even though this analysis must be performed with extreme caution, it can yield important conclusions in the analysis for a particular company. Table 2.5 presents ratio data for the domestic pharmaceutical industry.

Table 2.5. Company Ratios Period 2008–2009.

Ratio Classification	Formula	JNJ 2008	JNJ 2009	Industry 2008	Industry 2009
Liquidity Ratio					
(1) Current Ratio	$\frac{\textit{Current asset}}{\textit{Current liabilities}}$	1.65	1.82	2.18	2.06
(2) Quick Ratio	$\frac{CA - \textit{inventory} - \textit{other } CA}{\textit{Current liabilities}}$	0.61	0.89	1.61	1.51
Leverage Ratio					
(3) Debt-to-Asset	$\frac{\textit{Total debt}}{\textit{Total asset}}$	0.48	0.45	0.48	0.49
(4) Debt-to-Equity	$\frac{\textit{Total debt}}{\textit{Total equity}}$	0.96	0.84	1.02	1.04
(5) Equity Multiplier	$\frac{\textit{Total asset}}{\textit{Total equity}}$	2.00	1.87	2.10	2.12
(6) Times Interest Paid	$\frac{EBIT}{\textit{Interest expenses}}$	27.78	30.39	26.49	27.16
Activity Ratios					
(7) Average collection period	$\frac{\textit{Account Receivable}}{\textit{Sales}/365}$	54.11	56.32	72.73	73.14
(8) Accounts receivable Turnover	$\frac{\textit{Sales}}{\textit{Accounts Receivable}}$	6.65	6.39	5.81	5.88
(9) Inventory Turnover	$\frac{\textit{Cost of Good Sold}}{\textit{Inventory}}$	3.09	3.04	2.40	2.38
(10) Fixed Asset Turnover	$\frac{\textit{Sales}}{\textit{Fixed assets}}$	1.26	1.12	3.82	3.82
(11) Total Asset Turnover	$\frac{\textit{Sales}}{\textit{Total assets}}$	0.75	0.65	0.67	0.71
Profitability Ratios					
(12) Profit margin	$\frac{\textit{Net income}}{\textit{Sales}}$	20.30%	19.80%	19.47%	19.43%
(13) Return on assets	$\frac{\textit{Net income}}{\textit{Total assets}}$	15.25%	12.95%	12.41%	12.38%
(14) Return on equity	$\frac{\textit{Net Income}}{\textit{Total equity}}$	30.20%	26.40%	25.07%	24.51%
Market value					
(15) Price/earnings	$\frac{\textit{Market price per share}}{\textit{Earning per share}}$	12.95	14.47	17.32	20.99
(16) Price-to-book-value	$\frac{\textit{Market price per share}}{\textit{Book value per share}}$	3.90	3.51	3.63	4.27

2.4.1.1. *Liquidity Ratios*

Liquidity ratios are calculated from information on the balance sheet; they measure the relative strength of a firm's financial position. Crudely interpreted, these are coverage ratios that indicate the firm's ability to meet short-term obligations. The current ratio (ratio 1 in Table 2.5) is the most popular of the liquidity ratios because it is easy to calculate and has intuitive appeal. It is also the most broadly defined liquidity ratio, as it does not take into account the differences in relative liquidity among the individual components of current assets. A more specifically defined liquidity ratio is the quick or acid-test ratio (ratio 2), which excludes the least liquid portion of current assets, inventories.

2.4.1.2. *Leverage Ratios*

If an analyst wishes to measure the extent of a firm's debt financing, a leverage ratio is the appropriate tool to use. This group of ratios reflects the financial risk posture of the firm. The two sources of data from which these ratios can be calculated are the balance sheet and the statement of earnings.

The balance-sheet leverage ratio measures the proportion of debt incorporated into the capital structure. The debt–equity ratio measures the proportion of debt that is matched by equity; thus this ratio reflects the composition of the capital structure. The debt–asset ratio (ratio 3), on the other hand, measures the proportion of debt-financed assets currently being used by the firm. Other commonly used leverage ratios include equity multiplier, ratio (4) and time interest paid, ratio (6).

The income-statement leverage ratio measures the firm's ability to meet fixed obligations of one form or another. The time interest paid, which is earnings before interest and taxes over interest expense, measures the firm's ability to service the interest expense on its outstanding debt. A more broadly defined ratio of this type is the fixed-charge coverage ratio, which includes not only the interest expense but also all other expenses that the firm is obligated by contract to pay. (This ratio is not included in Table 2.5 because there is not enough information on fixed charges for these firms to calculate this ratio.)

2.4.1.3. *Activity Ratios*

This group of ratios measures how efficiently the firm is utilizing its assets. With activity ratios one must be particularly careful about the interpretation of extreme results in either direction; very high values may indicate possible problems in the long term, and very low values may indicate a current problem of not generating enough sales or of not taking a loss for assets that are obsolete. The reason that high activity may not be good in the long term is that the firm may not be able to adjust to an even higher level of activity and therefore may miss out on a market opportunity. Better analysis and planning can help a firm get around this problem.

The days-in-accounts-receivable or average collection-period ratio (7) indicates the firm's effectiveness in collecting its credit sales. The other activity ratios measure the firm's efficiency in generating sales with its current level of assets, appropriately termed turnover ratios. While there are many turnover ratios that can be calculated, there are three basic ones: inventory turnover (9), fixed assets turnover (10), and total assets turnover (11). Each of these ratios measures a quite different aspect of the firm's efficiency in managing its assets.

2.4.1.4. *Profitability Ratios*

This group of ratios indicates the profitability of the firm's operations. It is important to note here that these measures are based on past performance. Profitability ratios generally are the most volatile, because many of the variables affecting them are beyond the firm's control. There are three groups of profitability ratios: those measuring margins, those measuring returns, and those measuring the relationship of market values to book or accounting values.

Profit-margin ratios show the percentage of sales dollars that the firm was able to convert into profits. There are many such ratios that can be calculated to yield insightful results, namely profit margin (12), return on asset (13), and return on equity (14).

Return ratios are generally calculated as a return on assets or equity. The return on assets ratio (13) measures the profitability of the firm's asset utilization. The return on equity (14) indicates the rate of return earned on the book value of owner's equity. Market-value analyses include (i) market-value/book-value ratio and (ii) price per share/earnings per share (P/E) ratio. These ratios and their applications will be discussed in Chapter 6.

Overall, all four different types of ratios (as indicated in Table 2.5) have different characteristics stemming from the firm itself and the industry as a whole. For example, the collection-period ratio (which is Accounts Receivable times 365 over Net Sales) is clearly the function of the billings, payment, and collection policies of the pharmaceutical industry. In addition, the fixed-asset turnover ratios for those firms are different. This might imply that different firms have different capacity utilization.

2.4.1.5. *Estimation of the Target of a Ratio*

An issue that must be addressed at this point is the determination of an appropriate proxy for the target of a ratio. For an analyst, this can be an insurmountable problem if the firm is extremely diversified, and if it does not have one or two major product lines in industries where industry averages are available. One possible solution is to determine the relative industry share of each division or major product line, then apply these percentages to the related industry averages, and then derive one target ratio for the firm as a whole with which its ratio can be compared. One must be very careful in any such analysis because the proxy may be extremely over- or underestimated. The analyst can also use Standard Industrial Classification (SIC) codes to properly define the industry of diversified firms. He/she can then use 3- or 4-digit codes and compute his/her own weighted industry average.

Often an industry average is used as a proxy for the target ratio. This can lead to another problem, the appropriate calculation of an industry average, even though the industry and companies are fairly well defined. The issue here is the appropriate weighting scheme for combining the individual company ratios in order to arrive at one industry average. Individual ratios can be weighted according to equal weights, asset weights, or sales weights. The analyst must determine the extent to which firm size, as measured by asset base or market share, affects the relative level of a firm's ratios and the tendency for other firms in the industry to adjust toward the target level of this ratio. One way this can be done is to calculate the coefficients of variation for a number of ratios under each of the weighting the schemes and to compare them to see which scheme most consistently has the lowest coefficient variation. This would appear to be the most appropriate weighting scheme. Of course, one could also use a different weighting scheme for each ratio, but this would be very tedious if many ratios were to be analyzed. Note that the median rather than the average or mean can be used, to avoid needless complications with respect to extreme values that might distort the computation of averages.

In the dynamic analysis that follows, the equal-weighted average is used throughout.

2.4.2. *Dynamic Analysis of Financial Ratios*

In basic finance and accounting courses, industry norms are generally used to determine whether the magnitude of a firm's financial ratios is acceptable. Taken separately, ratios are mere numbers. This can lead to some problems in making comparisons among and drawing conclusions from them. In addition, by making only static, one-ratio-to-another comparisons, we are not taking advantage of all the information they can provide. A more dynamic analysis can improve our ability to compare companies with one another and to forecast future ratios. Regressing current ratios against past ratios helps one analyze the dynamic nature and the adjustment process of a firm's financial ratio.

2.4.2.1. *Single-Equation Dynamic Adjustment Process*

1. Basic Model. Lev (1969) uses the concept of the partial-adjustment model to define a dynamic financial-ratio adjustment process as

$$Y_{j,t} = Y_{j,t-1} + \delta_j (Y^*_{j,t} - Y_{j,t-1}), \tag{2.1}$$

where $0 \leq \delta_j \leq 1$, and

δ_j = A partial adjustment coefficient;
$Y_{j,t}$ = Firm's jth financial ratio period t;
$Y_{j,t-1}$ = Firm's jth financial ratio period $t-1$; and
$Y^*_{j,i}$ = Firm's jth financial ratio target in period t.

This model is used in a wide variety of empirical applications of the dynamic properties of financial analysis and forecasting, such as the investment, financing, dividend decisions, and forecasting. The relationship postulates that at any time, t, only a fixed fraction of the desired adjustment is achieved in that period. Thus, the coefficient of adjustment, δ_j, reflects the fact that there are limitations to the periodic adjustment of ratios.

Lev (1969) suggests that differences across ratios in their speed of adjustment coefficient, δ_j, are a function of two conflicting types of costs: (1) the cost of adjustment, and (2) the cost of being out of equilibrium. These two costs must be balanced for each ratio. Equation (2.1) implies that a firm's current financial ratio is equal to the last period's financial ratio plus and adjustment term. The adjustment factor depends upon two elements: the partial adjustment coefficient, δ_i, and the difference between $Y^*_{j,t}$ and $Y_{j,t-1}$. However, $Y^*_{j,t}$ is not an observable variable, so we must find some alternative proxy.

To resolve the problem associated with determining the target ratio ($Y^*_{j,t}$), Lev assumes that: (1) $Y^*_{j,t}$ is exactly equal to the industry average of the jth financial ratio in the previous period, denoted as $X_{j,t-1}$ and (2) $Y^*_{j,t}$ is proportional to $X_{j,t-1}$, that is $CX_{j,t-1}$ where C is the related proportional constant. A generalized proxy of $Y^*_{j,t}$ can be defined as

$$Y^*_{j,t} = CX_{j,t-1} + \tau_{j,t}, \tag{2.2}$$

where $0 \leq C \leq 1$ and $\tau_{j,t}$ represents the proxy error. Proxy error is the error arising from the fact that the substitute, or proxy, ratio only partially approximates the desired target ratio. If $C = 1$ and $\tau_{j,t} = 0$, then $X_{j,t-1}$ is the perfect proxy for $Y^*_{j,t}$. Then we can substitute $X_{j,t-1}$ for $Y^*_{j,t}$ in Equation (2.1) and obtain:

$$Y_{j,t} - Y_{j,t-1} = \delta_j[X_{j,t-1} - Y_{j,t-1}]. \tag{2.3}$$

In order to estimate the partial adjustment coefficient, δ_j, a simple time-series regression can be run and used in the empirical study. The linear form of this regression is defined as

$$Z_{j,t} = A_j + B_j W_{j,t-1} + \varepsilon_{j,t} \tag{2.4}$$

where

$$\begin{aligned} Z_{j,t} &= Y_{j,t} - Y_{j,t-1}, \\ W_{j,t-1} &= X_{j,t-1} - Y_{j,t-1}, \\ A_j \text{ and } B_j &= \text{regression parameters,} \end{aligned}$$

and

$$\varepsilon_{j,t} = \text{the error term.}$$

2. Extensions of this model. Lev also suggests a log-linear form of this model in order to study the dynamic ratio-adjustment process:

$$Z'_{j,t} = A'_j + B'_j W'_{j,t-1} + \varepsilon'_{j,t}, \tag{2.5}$$

where

$$\begin{aligned} Z'_{j,t} &= \log(Y_{j,t}) - \log(Y_{j,t-1}), \\ W'_{j,t-1} &= \log(X_{j,t-1}) - \log(Y_{j,i-1}), \end{aligned}$$

and

$$\varepsilon'_{j,t} = \text{the error term.}$$

One of the possible advantages of the log-linear form of this model over the linear form is that the estimated B'_j represents the elasticity of change, while the estimated B_j does not. The argument is based upon the fact that

$$B'_j = \frac{\partial \log(Y_{j,t}/Y_{j,t-1})}{\partial \log(X_{j,t-1}/Y_{j,t-1})} = \frac{\%\text{ change in }[Y_{j,t}/Y_{j,t-1}]}{\%\text{ change in }[X_{j,t-1}/Y_{j,t-1}]}. \quad (2.6)$$

This model can be generalized by assuming that the optimal ratio level attained by the firm is last period's industry ratio average times an adjustment factor, as follows:

$$Y^*_{j,t} = CX_{j,t-1}. \quad (2.7)$$

The adjustment coefficient, C, indicates that firms tend to maintain a fixed deviation from the industry mean in their adjustment process. Furthermore, the analysis of the coefficient and the partial adjustment coefficient (δ_j) should be very helpful in demonstrating the dynamic nature of a firm's financial structure, its financial ratios, and their adjustment toward the industry mean.

As for predicting future ratios, Lev finds that the model's predictive powers can be enhanced substantially through the following extension to multiple regression:

$$Y_{j,t} = \hat{A} + \hat{B}_1 X_{j,t-1} + \hat{B}_2 Y_{j,t-1} + \varepsilon_{j,t}. \quad (2.8)$$

This model is found to be substantially more accurate in prediction of future ratios, while the model detailed in Equation (2.4) is better at estimating the partial adjustment coefficient, B_j. With this model, analysts can forecast future possibilities. Furthermore, once the future ratios are estimated, one can work backward and determine the estimated levels of individual accounts; this procedure facilitates planning ahead to meet unpleasant future economic situations.

3. Empirical Data. Annual financial ratio data for JNJ and the industry as a whole will be used to show how Equations (2.4) and (2.5) perform in empirical financial ratio analysis. The sample period is from 1992 to 2004 for JNJ in terms of Equation (2.5) has been empirically estimated. The estimated B'_j and A'_j and the information needed to estimate these two regression parameters are listed in Table 2.6. Based upon the procedure

Table 2.6. Dynamic Adjustment Ratio Regression Results.

Variable	CR	LR
Mean Z	0.0075	−0.03083
Mean W	−0.14583	0.361666667
Var(Z)	0.013039	0.006099
Cov(Z, W)	0.074	0.009
B'_j	0.810*	0.259
t-statistics	[3.53]	[1.06]
A'_j	0.032	−0.042

*Partial adjustment coefficient significant at 95% level

discussed in Appendix A, the estimated mean Z, mean W, Var (W), and COV (Z, W) used to estimate B'_j and A'_j estimates of Table 2.6 indicate that the partial adjustment coefficients associated with both current ratio and leverage ratio for JNJ.

The accounting general ledger items used in calculating ratios are interrelated. A ratio is merely calculated by using at least two such items. Hence, important financial ratios of a firm may be interrelated. The correlation coefficient matrix among current ratio (CR), asset turnover (AT), gross profit margin (GPM), and leverage ratio (LR) for JNJ is presented in Table 2.7 to show the interrelationship. Fisher's z-statistics imply that the sample correlation coefficients between CR and GPM, CR and LR, AT and LR, and GPM and LR are statistically significant at the 95% level. Based upon approximations of Fisher's z-statistics the sample correlation coefficients (as indicated in Table 2.7) can be statistically tested.[6]

As shown in Table 2.7, the LR is fairly negatively correlated with CR (−0.51175) and GPM (−0.05028) but positively correlated the activity ratio

Table 2.7. Ratio Correlation Coefficient Matrix.

	CR	AT	GPM	LR
CR	1.0			
AT	−0.443841	1.0		
GPM	0.363273	0.381393	1.0	
LR	−0.51175	0.21961	−0.05028	1.0

[6] z-statistics $==1/2\log[(1+\rho)/(1-\rho)]$, where ρ is the simple correlation coefficient.

(AT, 0.21961). Also, GPM is somewhat positively correlated with the CR (0.363273). It can thus show that these ratios are interrelated. This tells us that we must use a system of ratios in simple analysis, or use simultaneous equations in a statistical analysis.

2.4.2.2. *Simultaneous Determination of Financial Ratios*

The high correlation between some ratios implies that the financial ratio adjustment process may well be determined by a combination of financial circumstances. To test this hypothesis, a two-equation for CR and LR can be specified as

$$Z_{1,t} = A_0 + A_1 Z_{2,t} + A_2 W_1 + \varepsilon_{1,t}, \tag{2.9a}$$

$$Z_{2,t} = B_0 + B_1 Z_{1,t} + B_2 W_2 + \varepsilon_{2,t}, \tag{2.9b}$$

where A_i, B_i $(i = 0, 1, 2)$ are coefficients, ε_1 and ε_2 are error terms, and

$Z_{1,t}$ = Individual firm's CR in period t – individual firm's CR in period $t - 1$;
$Z_{2,t}$ = Individual firm's leverage ratio in period t – individual firm's leverage ratio period $t - 1$;
$W_{1,t}$ = Industry average CR in period $t - 1$ – individual firm's CR period $t - 1$;
$W_{2,t}$ = Industry average leverage ratio in period $t - 1$ – individual firm's leverage ratio in period $t - 1$.

The equation system above includes two endogenous (Z_1, Z_2) and two exogenous variables (W_1, W_2). The exogenous variable in Equation (2.9a) is different from the one in Equation (2.9b). Therefore, this equation system is just-identified equation system [see Appendix B for the exact definition of endogenous and exogenous variables and the procedure for identifying an equation system].

There are random errors (sampling errors) in both Z_1 and Z_2, the independent variables in Equations (2.9a) and (2.9b), respectively, which bias the estimated coefficients, A_1 and B_1. [See Appendix B for a discussion on bias.] In order to obtain unbiased estimates for both coefficients, A_1 and B_1, we use the instrumental-variable technique [discussed in Appendix B] to estimate the parameters Equations (2.9a) and (2.9b). The empirical results for this simultaneous equation system for the current and leverage

Table 2.8. JNJ Empirical Results for the Simultaneous Equation System.

	$A_0(B_0)$	$A_1(B_1)$	$A_2(B_2)$
(2.9a)	−0.071 [−1.80]	−0.378 [−5.52]	0.080 [1.20]
(2.9b)	−0.0577 [−1.59]	−0.842 [−6.07]	0.074 [0.91]

ratios of JNJ are shown in Table 2.8. The results indicate that the estimated coefficients associated with endogenous variables, A_1 and B_1, are statistically different from 0 at the 95% significance level, implying that the current and leverage ratio adjustment processes are jointly determined for. Hence, single-equation ratio analysis and forecasting might be subject to simultaneous-equation bias (see Appendix B.). This is why we use the system of ratios (e.g., the DuPont System) in elementary financial management. In addition, results of Table 2.8 indicate that exogenous variables, W_1 and W_2, are not statistically important in explaining the fluctuations of JNJ's CR and leverage ratio over time.

2.4.3. *Statistical Distribution of Financial Ratios*

Normal and log-normal distributions are two of the most popular statistical distributions used in accounting and financial analysis. The density function of a normal distribution is

$$F[X] = \frac{1}{\sigma\sqrt{2\pi}} e^{-(X-\mu)^2/2\sigma^2} \quad (-\infty < \mathrm{X} < +\infty), \tag{2.10}$$

where μ and σ^2 are the population mean and variance, respectively, and e and π are given constants; that is, $\pi = 3.14159$ and $e = 2.71828$.

Normal distributions with different means and variances are graphed in Figs. 2.1 and 2.2. In these two figures, $F(X)$ represents the frequency of the variable X. The variance of Fig. 2.1 is larger than the variance of Fig. 2.2.

If a variable is normally distributed, the information that fully describes the distribution is the mean and the variance. The relative skewness of normal distribution is 0, and the kurtosis of a normal distribution is equal to 3.

There is a direct relationship between the normal distribution and the log-normal distribution. If Y is log-normally distributed, then $X = \log Y$ is normally distributed. Following this definition, the mean and the variance

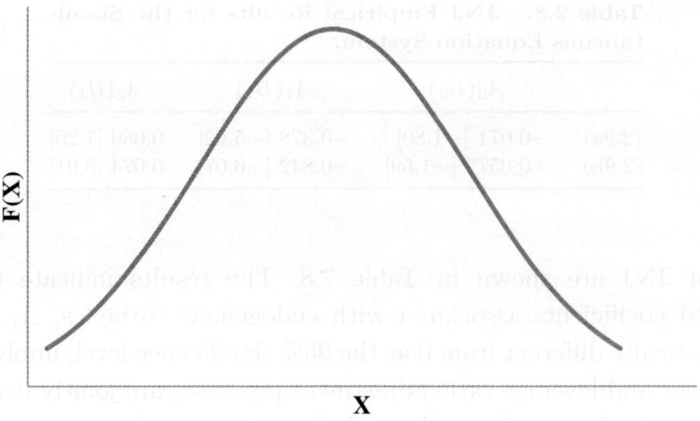

Fig. 2.1. Normal Distribution with Large Variance.

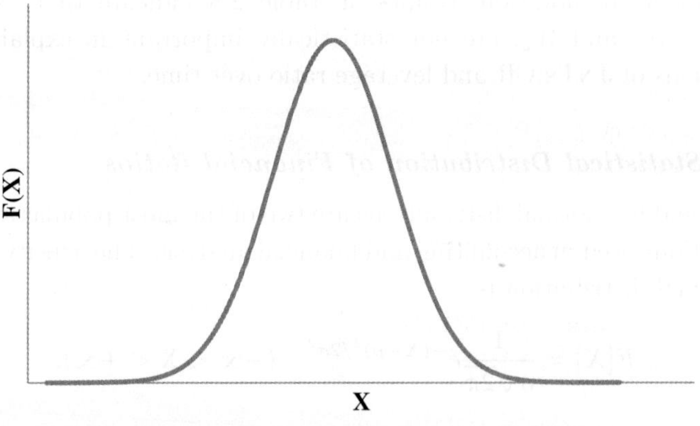

Fig. 2.2. Normal Distribution with Small Variance.

of Y can be defined as

$$\mu_Y = \exp\left(\mu_x + \frac{1}{2}\sigma_x^2\right), \tag{2.11a}$$

$$\sigma_Y^2 = \exp(2\mu_x + \sigma_x^2)(\exp(\sigma_x^2) - 1), \tag{2.11b}$$

where exp represents an exponential with base e.

Deakin (1976) finds that the cross-sectional distribution of financial ratios is log-normally instead of normally distributed. Upon analyzing the raw data, he finds that, within the pharmaceutical industry, only the debt-asset ratio is normally distributed; this occurs in 15 of the 19 years of his dataset. All other ratios are log-normally distributed. However, after taking the log transformation, the CR becomes normally distributed in 12 of the 19 years, while the normality of the debt-asset ratio drops from 15 to only 6 of the 19 years.

Generally, it seems that financial ratios are not normally distributed and that log transformation does help normalize the data in some, but not in all cases. The reason we need a normal distribution for analyzing ratios is in testing the significance of a difference, for example, between the behavior of firm and industry figures for the same ratio. Therefore, it is necessary for the analyst to look at data with and without transformations, in order to determine which set of data fits the normal distribution more closely.

2.5. Cost–Volume–Profit Analysis and its Applications

Cost–volume–profit (CVP) analysis is a synthesized analysis of the statement of earnings. Volume, price per unit, variable cost per unit, and the total fixed cost are the key variables for doing this kind of analysis. The basic type of CVP analysis is the break-even analysis, which can be extended to operating and financial leverage analysis. All of these analyses are important tools of financial analysis and control. Technically, ratio-variable inputs are required for performing these analyses. Conceptually, CVP and its derived relationships are designed to analyze the statement of earnings in terms of an aggregated ratio indicator. Hence, CVP analysis can be regarded as one kind of financial ratio analysis.

2.5.1. *Deterministic Analysis*

Deterministic break-even analysis is an important concept in basic microeconomics, accounting, finance, and marketing courses. Mathematically, the operating [earnings before interest and tax (EBIT)] can be defined as

$$\text{Operating Profit} = \text{EBIT} = Q(P - V) - F, \tag{2.12}$$

where

Q = Quantity of goods sold;
P = Price per unit sold;
V = Variable cost per unit sold;
F = Total amount of fixed costs; and
$P - V$ = Contribution margin.

If operating profit is equal to zero, Equation (2.12) implies that $Q(P-V)-F=0$ or that $Q(P-V)=F$, that is

$$Q^* = \frac{F}{(P-V)}. \tag{2.13}$$

Equation (2.13) represents the break-even quantity, or that quantity of sales at which fixed costs are just covered. There are two kinds of break-even analysis, linear and nonlinear. The two forms are shown graphically in Figs. 2.3 and 2.4.

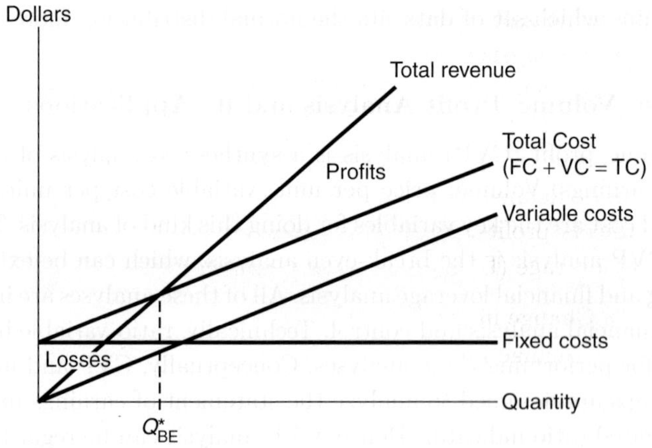

Fig. 2.3. Linear Break-even Analysis.

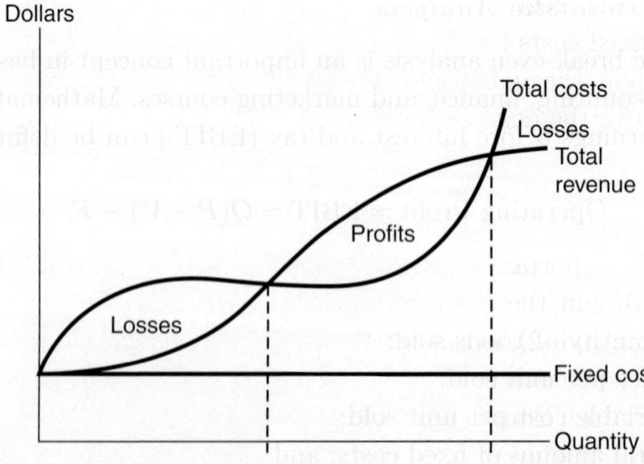

Fig. 2.4. Nonlinear Break-even Analysis.

There are very important economic interpretations of these alternative break-even analyses. Linear representation of the total revenue curve implies that the firm operates within a perfect output or product market; the linear total cost curve implies that the input market is linear or perfect and the return (economies) to scale is constant. If these conditions do not hold, linear break-even analysis becomes either unrealistic or only an approximation of the real situation facing the firm.

In the real world, returns (economies) to scale can either be constant, increasing, or decreasing. A nonlinear representation of the variable cost and total revenue curves is a more accurate representation of the real one break-even level of sales using this form of analysis.

Break-even analysis can be used in three separate but related ways in financial management. That is: (i) to analyze a program of modernization and automation, (ii) to study the effects of a general expansion in the level of operations, and (iii) in new-product decision. These operating leverage decisions can be defined more precisely in terms of the way a given change in volume affects profits. For this purpose we use the definition of degree of operating leverage (DOL) defined in Equation (2.14):

$$\text{DOL} = \frac{\%\text{ Change in profits}}{\%\text{ Change in sales}} = \frac{Q(P-V)}{Q(P-V)-F} = 1 + \frac{\text{Fixed Costs}}{\text{Profits}}. \tag{2.14}$$

The first equality in Eq. (2.14) is the basic definition of DOL; the second equality is obtained by substituting the definition of profits and sales from Equation (2.12) (see Appendix 6B for derivation). The third equality implies that the degree of operating leverage increases with a firm's exposure to fixed costs (see Appendix 6B for derivation).

Based upon the definition of linear break-even quantity defined in Equation (2.13), the degree of operating leverage can be rewritten as

$$DOL = \frac{1}{[1-(Q^*/Q)]}. \tag{2.15}$$

There are two important implications of this formulation: (1) if $Q > Q^*$, then DOL > 0, and the change in profits is in the same direction as the change in sales; and (2) if $Q < Q^*$, then DOL < 0 and the change in losses is in the opposite direction from the change in sales (i.e., if sales increase, losses will decrease). Both Equations (2.14) and (2.15) can be used to calculate the degree of operating leverage at any level of output, Q. If company XYZ's break-even quantity Q^* is 50,000 units, then DOL at 100,000 production units is 2. This implies that 1% change of XYZ's sales will generate 2% change of its profit.

2.5.2. *Stochastic Analysis*

In reality, net profit is a random variable because the quantity used in the analysis should be the quantity sold, which is unknown and random, rather than the quantity produced, which is internally determined. This is the simplest form of stochastic CVP analysis; for there is only one stochastic variable and one need not be concerned about independence among the variables. The distribution of sales is shown graphically in Fig. 2.5.

A slightly more complicated form of stochastic CVP analysis is obtained when it is assumed that both the quantity of good sold (Q) and the contribution margin ($P - V$) are stochastic variables and are independently distributed. The independence assumption is reasonable because the second stochastic variable is defined as the contribution margin, rather than the three separate random variables Q, P, and V. In this situation, quantity and price are probably not independent, because both distributions are determined by imperfections in the product market. Furthermore, these three variables are generally highly negatively correlated, while the normality of their distributions is questionable (and needs further empirical testing). Under the contribution margin approach, one variable that is subtracted from prices, variable costs, has a distribution that is determined by imperfections in the input market. This drastically reduces the degree of correlation with the quantity sold.

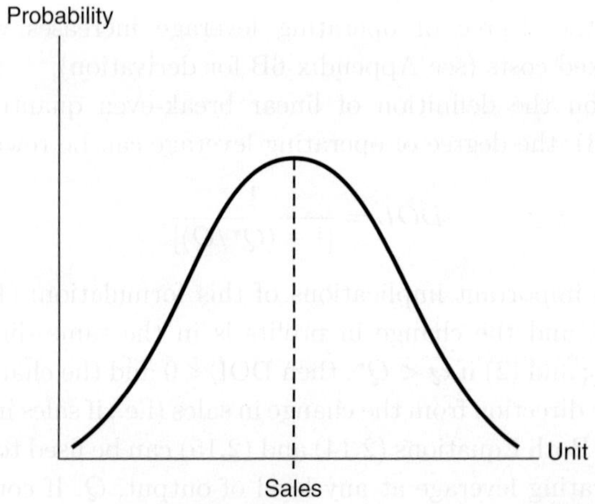

Fig. 2.5. Distribution of Sales.

While the assumption of independence seems to be fairly accurate in some cases, there is need for more research in this area. Hilliard and Leitch (1975) addressed this problem through the use of a log-normal approach to CVP analysis under uncertainty. They have developed an easily implemented model that can handle dependence among input variables, and that should prove to be helpful to the practitioner.

Equation (2.12) can be generalized to allow Q, P, and V to be stochastic variables. Profits also become a stochastic variable, as represented in Equation (2.16):

$$\text{Operating profit} = \text{EBIT} = Q^{\pi}(P^{\pi} - V^{\pi}) - F. \tag{2.16}$$

This formulation for CVP analysis under uncertainty is very important for the decision-maker. Because it is becoming increasingly important to move from point (certainty) to interval (uncertainty) estimates, particularly in today's dynamic business environment, the stochastic nature of this CVP formulation allows one to calculate the point estimate and also the related interval estimate based on the combined probability distributions. This application of probabilistic models greatly enhances the degree of realism. Uncertainty break-even analysis has been generalized by Wei (1979) and Yunker and Yunker (1982) to take into account the crucial elements of random demand and the level of production in the determination of actual sales and resulting profits.

Besides the applications discussed in this section, both CVP and break-even analysis can be integrated with the net present value method of capital budgeting decisions to do financial analysis. Reinhardt (1973) uses this approach to do break-even analysis for Lockheed's Tri Star Program. The major difference between the net present value (NPV) type of break-even analysis and the "naive" break-even analysis does not take account of the cost of capital. This will be explored in the capital budgeting under certainty chapter in detail.

2.6. Accounting Income Versus Economic Income[7]

There are three ways of describing income: accounting earnings, finance income, and economic income. Accounting earnings are based upon recording transactions according to GAAP using accruals and deferrals, rather than cash flows. Accountants measure the change in stockholders'

[7]This section is based, in part, on Haley and Schall (1979), pp. 8–10.

wealth due to the operations of the firm. Economic earnings are more abstract than accounting earnings. The historic definition of economic income, as given by Hicks (1965), is the maximum value at which an individual can consume during a period and still be as only the change in wealth due to realized gains and obvious losses (those that are realized as well as those that are inevitable). Economic income measures the change in wealth based upon both realized and unrealized gains and losses.

Finance income is based on cash flow changes in wealth. Cash income is cash revenues less cash expenses. Finance income defines change in wealth as net cash flow, or net cash income less cash investment outlays. Technically economic income rather than accounting earnings should be used to determine the value of a firm, but theoretical economic income is not directly observable, so accounting earnings are generally used as proxy for them. Conceptually, the relationship between accounting earnings and economic income can be defined as

$$E_t = A_t + P_t, \tag{2.17}$$

where

E_t = Economic income,
A_t = Accounting earnings, and
P_t = Proxy errors.

In estimating the cost of capital for the utility industry, Miller and Modigliani (1966) take accounting earnings as a proxy for economic income, using instrumental-variable technique, to remove the proxy errors (as discussed in Appendix B). Finance income (cash flows instead of accounting income) will be used to evaluate alternative capital budgeting decisions, which will be used to evaluate alternative capital budgeting decisions and are discussed in Chapters 9 and 10. The main difference between accounting income and cash flows (finance income) is that the former does not focus on cash flows when they occur, while the latter does. The cash flows, for example, correctly deduct the entire expenditure for investment in plant and equipment at the time the cash outflows occur.

2.7. Summary

In this chapter, the usefulness of accounting information in financial analysis is conceptually and analytically evaluated. Both statistical methods and regression analysis techniques are used to show how accounting information can be used to perform active financial analysis for the pharmaceutical industry.

In these analyses, static ratio analysis is generalized to dynamic ratio analysis. The necessity of using simultaneous-equation technique in conducting dynamic financial ratio analysis is also demonstrated in detail. In addition, both deterministic and stochastic CVP analyses are examined. The potential applications of CVP analysis in financial analysis and planning are discussed in some detail. Overall, this chapter gives readers a good understanding of basic accounting information and econometric methods, which are needed for financial analysis and planning.

Questions and Problems

1. What is the value of accounting information in the process of financial analysis and planning? What are the components to annual and quarterly accounting information and their respective advantages and disadvantages for financial analysis and planning?
2. Define the following terms:

   (a) Real versus financial market
   (b) M_1 and M_2
   (c) Leading economic indicators
   (d) NYSE, AMEX, and OTC
   (e) Primary versus secondary stock market
   (f) Bond market
   (g) Options and futures markets.

3. What are limits related to the use of accounting information? What are differences between accounting information and that of economics and finance that can result? How can these limits be overcome and differences reconciled?
4. Discuss the major difference between the linear and nonlinear break-even analysis?
5. What can ratio analysis contribute to financial planning and analysis? What are the determinants of the dynamic adjustment process? How are target ratios derived?
6. What is the relationship between CVP and ratio analysis? How can it be used in financial analysis and planning?

7. Briefly discuss the issue related to net income (EAIT) in financial analysis and planning.
8. A market model is defined as

$$R_{jt} = A_j + B_j R_{mt} + \in_j,$$

where R_{jt}, R_{mt} are rate of return for jth security and market rates of return, respectively; A_j is the intercept and B_j is the slope. Use the Ordinary Least Squares (OLS) theory and method discussed in Appendix A of this chapter to show how A_j and B_j can be estimated.
9. Parts of financial records for Company XYZ are:

Anticipated sales = \$400,000
Degree of financial leverage = 4/3
Variable cost = \$200,000
Combined leverage effect = 2
Quantity sold = \$100,000 units
Profit margin = 5%
Total debt = \$200,000
Leverage ratio = 1/2
Common stock outstanding = 10,000 shares
Current price per share = \$40
Retention rate = 1/2
IRR = 8%

Calculate the following:

(a) The total interest expense.
(b) The total fixed cost.
(c) The degree of operating leverage.
(d) The break-even quantity.
(e) The EAIT.
(f) Total corporation income tax expense.
(g) The return on net worth.
(h) The return on total asset.
(i) The EPS.
(j) The P/E ratio for common stock.
(k) The pay-out ratio for dividend.
(l) The growth rate for the common stock.
(m) The required rate of return.
(n) Total asset turnover.

(o) Analyze the financial situation of Company XYZ.
(p) If the probabilistic concepts are applied to break-even analysis, how should the analyses in (o) be revised?

10. Use the ratio information listed in Table 2.6 of the text to estimate the partial ratio adjustment model for GM and interpret the related results.
11. ABC Company's financial records are as follows:

Quantity of goods sold = 10,000
Price per unit sold = \$20
Variable cost per unit sold = \$10
Total amount of fixed cost = \$50,000
Corporate tax rate = 50%

(a) Calculate EAIT.
(b) What is the break-even quantity?
(c) What is the DOL?
(d) Should the ABC Company produce more for greater profits?

12. ABC Company's predictions for next year are as follows:

	Probability	Quantity	Price (\$)	Variable Cost/Unit (\$)	Corporate Tax Rate
State 1	0.3	1,000	10	5	0.5
State 2	0.4	2,000	20	10	0.5
State 3	0.3	3,000	30	15	0.5

In addition, we also know that the fixed cost is \$15,000. What is the next year's expected EAIT?
13. Use an example to discuss four alternative depreciation methods.
14. XYX, Inc. currently produces one product that sells for \$330 per unit. The company's fixed costs are \$80,000 per year; variable costs are \$210 per unit. A salesman has offered to sell the company a new price of equipment which will increase fixed costs to \$100,000. The salesman claims that the company's break-even number of units sold will not be altered if the company purchases the equipment and raises its price (assuming variable costs remain the same).

(a) Find the company's current break-even level of units sold.
(b) Find the company's new price if the equipment is purchased and prove that the break-even level has not changed.

15. Consider the following financial data of a corporation:

Sales = $500,000
Quantity = 25,000
Variable cost = $300,000
Fixed cost = $50,000

(a) Calculate the DOL at the above quantity of output.
(b) Find the break-even quantity and sales levels.

16. On the basis of the following firm and industry norm ratios, identify the problem that exists for the firm:

Ratio	Firm	Industry
Total Asset Utilization	2.0	3.5
Average Collection Period (days)	45	46
Inventory Turnover (times)	6	6
Fixed Asset Utilization	4.5	7.0

17. The financial ratios for Wallace, Inc., a manufacturer of consumer household products, are given below along with the industry norm:

Ratio	Firm			Industry
	1986	1987	1988	
Current Ratio	1.44	1.31	1.47	1.2
Quick Ratio	0.66	0.62	0.65	0.63
Average Collection Period (days)	33	37	32	34
Inventory Turnover	7.86	7.62	7.72	7.6
Fixed Asset Turnover	2.60	2.44	2.56	2.8
Total Asset Turnover	1.24	1.18	2.8	1.20
Debt to Total Equity	1.24	1.14	0.84	1.00
Debt to Total Assets	0.56	0.54	0.46	0.50
Times Interest Earned	2.75	5.57	7.08	5.00
Return on Total Assets	0.02	0.06	0.07	0.06
Return on Equity	0.06	0.12	0.12	0.13
Net Profits Margin	0.02	0.05	0.05	0.05

Analyze Wallace's ratios over the three-year period for each of the following categories:

(a) Liquidity
(b) Asset utilization

(c) Financial leverage
(d) Profitability

18. Below are the Balance Sheet and the Statement of Earnings for Nelson Manufacturing:

Balance Sheet for Nelson on 12/31/88

Assets	
Cash and Marketable Securities	\$125,000
Accounts Receivable	\$239,000
Inventories	\$225,000
Prepaid Expenses	\$11,000
Total Current Assets	\$600,000
Fixed Assets (Net)	\$400,000
Total Assets	\$1,000,000
Liabilities and Stockholder's Equity	
Account Payable	\$62,000
Accruals	\$188,000
Long-Term Debt Maturing in 1 year	\$8,000
	\$258,000
Long-Term Debt	\$221,000
Total Liabilities	\$479,000
Stockholder's Equity	
Preferred Stock	\$5,000
Common Stock (at par)	\$175,000
Retained Earnings	\$341,000
Total Stockholder's Equity	\$521,000
Total Liabilities and Stockholder's Equity	\$1,000,000

Statement of Earnings for Nelson for Year Ending 12/31/88

Net sales	$800,000
Less: Cost of Goods Sold	$381,600
Selling, General, and Administrative Expense	$216,800
Interest Expense	$20,000
Earnings before Taxes	$181,200
Less: Tax Expense (40%)	$72,480
Net Income	$108,720

(a) Calculate the following ratios for Nelson.

	Nelson	*Industry*
(1) Current Ratio		3.40
(2) Quick Ratio		2.43
(3) Average Collection Period		88.65
(4) Inventory Turnover		6.46
(5) Fixed Asset Turnover		4.41
(6) Total Asset Utilization		1.12
(7) Debt to Total Equity		0.34
(8) Debt to Total Assets		5.25
(9) Times Interest Earned		12.00
(10) Return on Total Assets		0.12
(11) Return on Equity		0.18
(12) Net Profit Margin		0.12

(b) Identify Nelson's strengths and weaknesses relative to the industry norm.

Appendix 2A: Simple Regression and Multiple Regression

2A.1. *Introduction*

Algebra, basic calculus, and linear regression topics are usually required for both undergraduate and graduate business students. This appendix reviews simple regression and multiple regression. (Appendix B will (i) review basic algebraic simultaneity, and (ii) integrate the algebraic simultaneous equation concept with multiple regression, in order to introduce the concepts of instrumental variable and econometric simultaneous equation.) This appendix enables the reader to use the standard multiple regression and simultaneous equation statistic packages that are available (i.e., North Carolina State University's SAS and University of Illinois SOUPAC) to estimate and interpret the empirical results of financial analysis and planning.

2A.2. *Simple Regression*

If we want to explain the variation of the CR for JNJ Company in period t $[Y_t]$, given the auto industry's CR in period $t-1$ $[X_{t-1}]$, we can choose either a linear or log linear model, as defined below.

$$Y_t = a + bX_{t-1} + \varepsilon_t, \tag{2A.1a}$$

$$\log Y_t = a' + b' \log X_{t-1} + \varepsilon'_t, \tag{2A.1b}$$

where ε_t and ε'_t are error terms representing the difference between actual CRs and the predicted CRs. The choice between Equation (2A.1a) and Equation (2A.1b) depends on whether the related variables, Y_t and X_{t-1}, are normally or log-normally distributed.

In order to obtain the best linear model to predict Y_t, given X_{t-1}, we want to find the equation that minimizes the squared error terms. The error terms $(\hat{\varepsilon}_t)$ represent the difference between the actual and current ratio (Y_t) and the current ratio predicted by the estimated linear model $(\hat{Y_t})$. The estimated current ratio can be defined as $Y = \hat{a} + \hat{b}X_{t-1}$. The theory and method of estimating a and b are one of the main issues of this appendix.

In Equation (2A.1a), if the unconditional probability distribution of Y_t is normally distributed with mean $\overline{Y}$ and variance σ^2_Y, the conditional probability distribution of $Y_t, \tilde{Y_t} \mid X_{t-1}$ will be a normal distribution with mean $(a + b\bar{X}_{t-1})$ and variance σ^2_ε.

Applying the variance operator to both sides of Equation (2A.1a) we have

$$\begin{aligned} Var[Y_t] &= Var[a + bX_{t-1} + \varepsilon_t] \\ &= Var[a] + Var[bX_{t-1}] + Var[\varepsilon_t] + 2\text{cov}[a, bX_{t-1}] \\ &\quad + 2\text{cov}[a, \varepsilon_t] + 2\text{cov}[bX_{t-1}, \varepsilon_t], \end{aligned} \tag{2A.2a}$$

$$Var[Y_t] = b^2\, Var[X_{t-1}] + Var[\varepsilon_t]. \tag{2A.2b}$$

The conditions for obtaining Equation (2A.2b) are

(i) Both a and b must be constants. Equation (2A.1) is a fixed coefficient model instead of a random coefficient model.
(ii) X_{t-1} must be uncorrelated with ε_t. This implies that there is no errors-in-variables problem inherent in the raw data associated with the independent variable. (The errors-in-variables problem is discussed in the instrumental variables and two-stage least-squares analysis in Appendix B.)

Equation (2A.2b) implies that the total variance Y_t, $Var[Y_t]$,can be decomposed into two components: (1) explained variance, $b^2 Var[X_{t-1}]$ and (2) unexplained variance, $Var[\varepsilon_t]]$. If X_{t-1} has any explanatory power, then $Var[Y_t]$ will be larger than $Var[\varepsilon_t]$. The degree of explanatory power X_{t-1} can be defined as

$$R^2 = \frac{\text{Variation explained by the explanatory variable}}{\text{Total variation in the dependent variable}}$$

$$= \frac{b^2 Var[X_{t-1}]}{Var[Y_t]}. \tag{2A.3}$$

To obtain the best estimates of a and b, we want to find the equation that minimizes the error sum of squares (ESS) as defined below:

$$ESS = \sum_{t=1}^{n}[Y_t - \hat{Y}_t]^2 = \sum_{t=1}^{n}[Y_t - \hat{a} - \hat{b}X_{t-1}]^2. \tag{2A.4}$$

ESS evaluates the predicted relationship by summing the squares of the differences between actual and predicted values of the dependent variable, Y_t. In order to minimize the value of ESS, we must take the derivative of ESS with respect to $\hat{a}$ and $\hat{b}$, and set the results equal to zero, as shown in Eq. (2A.5a) and (2A.5b):

$$\frac{\partial(ESS)}{\partial a} = -2\sum_{t=1}^{n}(Y_t - \hat{a} - \hat{b}X_{t-1}) = 0, \tag{2A.5a}$$

$$\frac{\partial(ESS)}{\partial b} = -2\sum_{t=1}^{n}X_{t-1}(Y_t - \hat{a} - \hat{b}X_{t-1}) = 0. \tag{2A.5b}$$

In order to jointly solve for estimates of the parameters a and b, Equations (2A.5a) and (2A.5b) are used to formulate a two-equation simultaneous system as follows:

$$\hat{a}n + \hat{b}\sum_{t=1}^{n} X_{t-1} = \sum_{t=1}^{n} Y_t, \tag{2A.6a}$$

$$\hat{a}\sum_{t=1}^{n} X_{t-1} + \hat{b}\sum_{t=1}^{n} X_{t-1}^2 = \sum_{t=1}^{n} X_{t-1}Y_t. \tag{2A.6b}$$

In these normal equations, two parameters are to be solved for from the give information: $\sum_{t=1}^{n} X_{t-1}$; $\sum_{t=1}^{n} Y_t$; $\sum_{t=1}^{n} X_{t-1}^2$ and $\sum_{t=1}^{n} X_{t-1}Y_t$. By Cramer's rule (see also Chapter 3), we have

$$\hat{b} = \frac{\begin{vmatrix} n & \sum_{t=1}^{n} Y_t \\ \sum_{t=1}^{n} X_{t-1} & \sum_{t=1}^{n} X_{t-1}Y_t \end{vmatrix}}{\begin{vmatrix} n & \sum_{t=1}^{n} X_{t-1} \\ \sum_{t=1}^{n} X_{t-1} & \sum_{t=1}^{n} X_{t-1}^2 \end{vmatrix}}$$

$$= \frac{n\left(\sum_{t=1}^{n} X_{t-1}Y_t\right) - \left(\sum_{t=1}^{n} X_{t-1}\sum_{t=1}^{n} Y_t\right)}{n\sum_{t=1}^{n} X_{t-1}^2 - \left(\sum_{t=1}^{n} X_{t-1}\right)^2}, \tag{2A.7a}$$

$$\hat{b} = \frac{Cov[X_{t-1}, Y_t]}{Var[X_{t-1}]}, \tag{2A.7b}$$

$$\hat{a} = \frac{\begin{vmatrix} \sum Y & \sum X_{t-1} \\ \sum X_{t-1}Y_t & \sum X_{t-1}^2 \end{vmatrix}}{\begin{vmatrix} n & \sum X_{t-1} \\ \sum X_{t-1} & \sum X_{t-1}^2 \end{vmatrix}}$$

$$= \frac{\left(\sum_{t=1}^{n} Y_t\right)\left(\sum_{t=1}^{n} X_{t-1}^2\right) - \left(\sum_{t=1}^{n} X_{t-1}\right)\left(\sum_{t=1}^{n} X_{t-1}Y_t\right)}{n\sum_{t=1}^{n} X_{t-1}^2 - \left(\sum_{t=1}^{n} X_{t-1}\right)^2}$$

$$= \frac{\begin{array}{l}\left(\sum_{t=1}^{n} Y_t/n\right)\left[n\left(\sum_{t=1}^{n} X_{t-1}^2\right) - \left(\sum_{t=1}^{n} X_{t-1}\right)^2\right] \\ \quad - \left(\sum_{t=1}^{n} X_{t-1}/n\right)\left[n\left(\sum_{t=1}^{n} X_{t-1}Y_t\right) - \left(\sum_{t=1}^{n} X_{t-1}\right)\left(\sum_{t=1}^{n} X_{t-1}\right)\right]\end{array}}{n\sum_{t=1}^{n} X_{t-1}^2 - \left(\sum_{t=1}^{n} X_{t-1}\right)^2}. \tag{2A.8a}$$

$$\hat{a} = \bar{Y} - \bar{X}\hat{b}. \tag{2A.8b}$$

Equations (2A.7b) and (2A.8b) can be used to estimate the parameters of Equation (2A.1a). For JNJ's CR and the related industry average data, we have:

$$\bar{X} = 1.730 \qquad Var[X_{t-1}] = 0.0481$$
$$\bar{Y} = 1.587 \qquad Var[Y_{t-1}] = 0.0967$$
$$Cov[Y_t, X_{t-1}] = 0.0402$$
$$\hat{b} = 08358 \qquad \hat{a} = 0.1411.$$

Before the estimated $\hat{a}$ and $\hat{b}$ are used, they should be tested to determine whether they are statistically different from zero or not. To perform the null hypothesis test, the variance of $\hat{b}$ and $\hat{a}$ should be derived.

Variance of $\hat{b}$

Equation (2A.7b) implies that

$$\hat{b} = \sum_{t=1}^{n} \frac{(x_{t-1}y_t)}{\sum_{t=1}^{n} x_{t-1}^2} = \sum_{t=1}^{n} W_{t-1}y_t, \tag{2A.7c}$$

where

$$x_{t-1} = X_{t-1} - \bar{X},$$
$$y_t = Y_t - \bar{Y},$$
$$W_{t-1} = \frac{x_{t-1}}{\sum_{t=1}^{n} x_{t-1}^2}.$$

Substituting $y_t = bx_{t-1} + \varepsilon_t$ into Eq. (2A.7b), we have

$$\hat{b} = \sum_{t=1}^{n} W_{t-1}bx_{t-1} + \sum_{t=1}^{n} W_{t-1}\varepsilon_t \tag{2A.7d}$$

Through the application of the variance operator on Equation (2A.7d), we have

$$Var(\hat{b}) = E(\hat{b} - b)^2$$
$$= E\left(\sum_{t=1}^{n} W_{t-1}bX_{t-1} + \sum_{t=1}^{n} W_{t-1}\varepsilon_t - b\right)^2$$

$$= E\left[\left(\sum_{t=1}^{n} W_{t-1}x_{t-1} - 1\right)b + \sum_{t=1}^{n} W_{t-1}\varepsilon_t\right]^2$$

$$= E\left(\sum_{t=1}^{n} W_{t-1}\varepsilon_t\right)^2 \quad \text{since } \sum_{t=1}^{n} W_{t-1}x_{t-1} = 1.$$

Therefore,

$$Var(\hat{b}) = E[(W_0\varepsilon_1)^2 + 2(W_0W_1\varepsilon_1\varepsilon_2) + (W_1\varepsilon_2)^2 + \cdots]. \tag{2A.9}$$

If ε_t if serially uncorrelated, that is, $E[\varepsilon_t, \varepsilon_{t-1}] = 0$, then Equation (2A.9) implies that

$$Var(\hat{b}) = E(W_0\varepsilon_1)^2 + E(W_1\varepsilon_2)^2 + \cdots$$
$$= W_0^2 E(\varepsilon_1^2) + W_1^2 E(\varepsilon_2^2) + \cdots.$$

In generalized form,

$$Var(\hat{b}) = \sum_{t=1}^{n} W_{t-1}^2 E(\varepsilon_t^2)$$
$$= \sigma_\varepsilon^2 \sum_{t=1}^{n} W_{t-1}^2$$

But

$$\sum_{t=1}^{n} W_{t-1}^2 = \frac{\sum_{t=1}^{n} x_{t-1}^2}{(\sum_{t=1}^{n} x_{t-1}^2)^2} = \frac{1}{\sum_{t=1}^{n} x_{t-1}^2}.$$

Therefore,

$$Var(\hat{b}) = \frac{\sigma_\varepsilon^2}{\sum_{t=1}^{n} x_{t-1}^2}. \tag{2A.10}$$

Using a similar derivation, we can derive $Var(\hat{a})$ and $Cov(\hat{a}, \hat{b})$:

$$Var(\hat{a}) = \sigma_\varepsilon^2 \frac{\sum_{t=1}^{n} x_{t-1}^2}{n\sum_{t=1}^{n} x_{t-1}^2}. \tag{2A.11}$$

$$Cov(\hat{a}, \hat{b}) = -\sigma_\varepsilon^2 \frac{\bar{X}}{\sum_{t=1}^{n} x_{t-1}^2}. \tag{2A.12}$$

Multiple Regression

If the current ratio for JNJ in period t $[Y_t]$ is a function of the pharmaceutical industry's current ratio in period $t-1$ $[X_{1,t-1}]$ and the pharmaceutical industry's leverage ratio in period $t-1$ $[X_{2,t-1}]$, the linear relationship can be defined as

$$Y_t = a + bX_{1,t-1} + cX_{2,t-1} + \varepsilon_t. \tag{2A.13a}$$

The ESS can be defined as

$$ESS = \sum \hat{\varepsilon}_t^2 = \sum (Y_t - \hat{Y}_t)^2,$$

where

$$\hat{Y}_t = \hat{a}_t + \hat{b}X_{1,t-1} + \hat{c}X_{2,t-1}.$$

To obtain the least-squares estimates of the parameters a, b, and c, we can minimize ESS by calculating its partial derivatives with respect to these three unknown parameters, equating each to zero, and solving:

$$\frac{\partial ESS}{\partial a} = 0 \text{ or } \sum Y_t = na + b\sum X_{1,t-1} + c\sum X_{2,t-1}, \tag{2A.14a}$$

$$\frac{\partial ESS}{\partial b} = 0 \text{ or } \sum X_{1,t-1}Y_t$$
$$= a\sum X_{1,t-1} + b\sum X_{1,t-1}^2 + c\sum X_{1,t-1}X_{2,t-1}, \tag{2A.14b}$$

$$\frac{\partial ESS}{\partial c} = 0 \text{ or } \sum X_{2,t-1}Y_t$$
$$= a\sum X_{2,t-1} + b\sum X_{1,t-1}X_{2,t-1} + c\sum X_{2,t-1}^2. \tag{2A.14c}$$

Substituting $y_t = Y_t - \hat{Y}$, $x_{1,t-1} = X_{1,t-1} - \hat{X}$ and $x_{2,t-1} = X_{2,t-1} - \hat{X}$ for Y_t, $X_{1,t-1}$ and $X_{2,t-1}$, Equations (2A.14a), (2A.14b), and (2A.14c), respectively, can be rewritten as

$$0 = na + b(0) + c(0), \tag{2A.15a}$$

$$\sum x_{1,t-1}y_t = a(0) + b\sum x_{1,t-1}^2 + c\sum x_{1,t-1}x_{2,t-1} \tag{2A.15b}$$

$$\sum x_{2,t-1}x_t = a(0) + b\sum x_{1,t-1}x_{2,t-1} + c\sum x_{2,t-1}^2. \tag{2A.15c}$$

The important conditions used to obtain Equation (2A.15) are

(i) $\sum y_t = 0$,
(ii) $\sum x_{1,t-1} = 0$,
(iii) $\sum x_{2,t-1} = 0$.

Equation (2A.15a) implies that $a = 0$. Therefore, we can use Equations (2A.15b) and (2A.15c) to solve $\hat{b}$ and $\hat{c}$. Based upon Cramer's rule, we have

$$\hat{b} = \frac{\sum x_{1,t-1}y_t(\sum x_{2,t-1}^2) - \sum x_{2,t-1}y_t \sum x_{1,t-1}x_{2,t-1}}{(\sum x_{1,t-1}^2)(\sum x_{2,t-1}^2) - (\sum x_{1,t-1}x_{2,t-1})^2}, \tag{2A.16a}$$

$$\hat{c} = \frac{\sum x_{2,t-1}y_t(\sum x_{1,t-1}^2) - \sum x_{1,t-1}y_t \sum x_{1,t-1}x_{2,t-1}}{(\sum x_{1,t-1}^2)(\sum x_{2,t-1}^2) - (\sum x_{1,t-1}x_{2,t-1})^2}. \tag{2A.16b}$$

Substituting Equations (2.A.16a) and (2.A.16b) into Eq. (2.A.14a), and dividing both sides of Eqs. (2.A.14a) by n, we have

$$\hat{a} = \hat{Y} - \hat{b}\bar{X}_1 - \hat{c}\bar{X}_2. \tag{2A.17}$$

Using the concept of estimating standard errors of regression parameters as discussed earlier, standard errors of $\hat{a}$, $\hat{b}$ and $\hat{c}$ (S_a, S_b, and S_c, respectively) can be estimated. The empirical results for JNJ's ratio are listed in Equation (2A.13b).

The multiple regression result associated with JNJ's dynamic CR adjustment process is

$$\begin{aligned} Y_t = {} & -0.2837 \quad +0.7564X_{1,t-1} \quad +0.2990X_{2,t-1}. \\ & (0.4323) \qquad (0.3288) \qquad\qquad (0.2240) \end{aligned} \tag{2A.13b}$$

Figures below the regression coefficients are standard errors of estimated regression coefficients.
Substituting related estimates into (2A.17), we obtain

$$\begin{aligned} \hat{a} &= 1.7071\,(0.7564)(1.8448)(0.2990)(1.6904) \\ &= 0.2837. \end{aligned}$$

There exists a similar coefficient of determination (R^2) for the multiple regression.

The difference between $Y1/2t$ and its mean, $Y^{\mathrm{TM}}\sim$, can be broken down as

$$(Y_t - \bar{Y}_t) = (Y_t - \hat{Y}_t) + (\hat{Y}_t - \bar{Y}_t), \tag{2A.18}$$

where

$$\hat{Y}_t = \hat{a} + \hat{b}X_{1,t-1} + \hat{c}X_{2,t-1}. \tag{2A.19}$$

Note that $\hat{Y}$ is the estimated dependent variable and Y_t is the actual dependent variable; $Y_t - \hat{Y}$ is the residual term for the tth period, and $(\hat{Y}_t - \bar{Y})$ represents the difference between the overall mean and the estimated dependent variable in period t (conditional mean). Squaring both sides of Eq. (2.A.18) and summing over all observations (1 to n), we obtain

$$\underset{\text{TSS}}{\sum(Y_t - \bar{Y}_t)^2} = \underset{\text{ESS}}{\sum(Y_t - \hat{Y}_t)^2} + \underset{\text{RSS}}{\sum(\hat{Y}_t - \bar{Y}_t)^2}, \tag{2A.20}$$

where

TSS = Total sum of squares;
ESS = Explained sum of squares; and
RSS = Residual sum of squares.

The R^2 can now be defined as

$$R^2 = \frac{\text{RSS}}{\text{TSS}} = \frac{\sum(\hat{Y}_t - \bar{Y}_t)^2}{\sum(Y_t - \bar{Y}_t)^2} = 1 - \frac{\sum \hat{\varepsilon}_t^2}{\sum(Y_t - \bar{Y}_t)^2}. \tag{2A.21}$$

Here R^2 measures the portion of variation in Y that is explained by the multiple regression. The term R^2 is often informally interpreted as a measure of "goodness of fit" and used as a statistic for comparison of the validity of the regression results under alternative specifications of the independent variables of the model.

The difficulty with R^2 as a measure of "goodness of fit" is that R^2 pertains to the explained and unexplained variation in Y and therefore does not account for the number of degrees of freedom in the problem. Originally there are n degrees of freedom in a sample of n observations, but one degree of freedom is used up in calculating $\bar{Y}$ leaving only $n - 1$ degrees of freedom for residuals $(Y - \bar{Y})$ to calculate $Var(Y_t)$. Similarly k degrees of freedom are used up in calculating k regressors, leaving only

$n-k$ degrees of freedom for calculating $Var(\hat{\varepsilon}_t)$. To correct for this problem, the corrected R^2 ($\bar{R}^2$) is defined as

$$R^2 = 1 - \frac{\sum \hat{\varepsilon}_t^2}{Var(Y_t)}, \tag{2A.22}$$

where

$$Var(\hat{\varepsilon}_t) = \sigma_\varepsilon^2 = \frac{\sum \hat{\varepsilon}_t^2}{n-k},$$

$$Var(Y_t) = \frac{\sum (Y_t - \bar{Y})^2}{n-1}.$$

and k = the number of independent variables.

Even though the ESS will decrease (or remain the same) as new explanatory variables are added, the residual variance need not decrease. From Equations (2A.21) and (2A.22), the relationship between R^2 and $\overline{R}^2$ can be defined as

$$\bar{R}^2 = 1 - (1 - R^2)\frac{n-1}{n-k}. \tag{2A.23}$$

Some implications of Equation (2A.23) are

(a) If $k = 1$, then $R^2 > \bar{R}^2$;
(b) If $k > 1$, then $R^2 > \bar{R}^2$;
(c) $\bar{R}^2$ can be negative.

The R^2 and $\bar{R}^2$ associated with Equation (2A.13b) are 0.4901 and 0.4350, respectively. If the error, $\hat{\varepsilon}_t$, is normally distributed, t-tests can be applied to test the regression coefficient because $(\hat{a}-a)/S_a$, $(\hat{b}-b)/S_b$ and $(\hat{c}-c)/S_c$ are all t-distributions with $n-k$ degrees of freedom. The t-statistics associated with $\hat{a}$, $\hat{b}$, and $\hat{c}$ are -0.6565, 2.3005, and 1.3345, respectively. The estimated regression coefficients, the standard errors and t-statistics, $\bar{R}^2$are printed out by most regression programs.

In addition to the t-statistics, the regression program also prints F-statistics, R^2 and $\bar{R}^2$. The relationship between the F-statistic and R^2 can be defined as

$$F(k-1, n-k) = \frac{R^2}{1-R^2}\frac{n-k}{k-1},$$

where $F(k-1, n-k)$ represents F-statistic with $k-1$ and $n-k$ degrees of freedom.

Strictly speaking, the $F(k-1,\ n-k)$-statistic allows us to test the hypothesis that none of the explanatory variables helps to explain the variation of Y about its mean. In other words, the F-statistics used to test the joint hypothesis, H (0): $a = b = c = 0$. The F-statistic for JNJ's current ratio is $F(2, 24) = 11.7689$. This statistic is significantly different from zero at the 95% confidence level. The multiple regression explored here will be used in the chapters on cost of capital and dividend policy.

Appendix 2B: Instrumental Variables and Two-Stages Least Squares

In Appendix A, we assumed that each of the independent variables in the linear regression model was uncorrelated with the true error term. If this assumption does not hold, then the estimated slope will not necessarily be unbiased. If the sample slope estimator is equal to the population slope estimator, then this sample slope estimate is an unbiased estimator. There are three instances when independent variables may be correlated with the associated error term:

(1) One or more of the independent variables is measured with error.
(2) One or more of the independent variables is determined in part (through one or more separate equations) by the dependent variable.
(3) One or more of the independent variables is a lagged dependent in a model which the error term is serially correlated.

All three of these cases appear in empirical finance research.

There exist error-in-variable problems in the estimation of systematic risk and in the estimation of the relative effect of dividends and retained earnings on the price of common stocks. There are simultaneous equation problems in estimating the joint determination of financial ratios (as discussed in Chapter 2) and in estimating the cost of capital. There exist serial correlation problems in estimating the dynamic ratio-adjustment process, as indicated in Chapter 2, and in estimating partial adjustment coefficients in the dividend decision model. All these problems can be resolved by the instrumental variable, two-stage least squares, or modified instrumental variable technique of estimation.

2B.1. *Errors-in-Variable Problem*

In Chapter 7, we will use the market model to estimate systematic risk. The market model is defined as

$$R_{j,t} = A_j + B_j R_{m,t} + \varepsilon_t, \tag{2B.1}$$

where $R_{j,t}$ and $R_{m,t}$ are the rates of return for the jth security in period t and the market rate of return in period t, respectively. As true market rate of return, $R_{m,t}$ is not directly observable, the equity market rate of return, $R^*_{m,t}$ is used as a proxy. Hence, there are proxies errors that result from the use of $R^*_{m,t}$ to replace $R_{m,t}$. The relationship between $R_{m,t}$ and $R_{m,t}$ can be defined as

$$R^*_{m,t} = R_{m,t} + V_t, \tag{2B.2}$$

where V_t is the proxy error (or measurement error), and

$$Var(R^*_{m,t}) = Var(R_{m,t} + V_t) = \sigma^2_m + \sigma^2_V. \tag{2B.3}$$

Substituting Equation (2B.2) into Equation (2B.1) yields the actual empirical regression model shown in Equation (2B.4):

$$R_{j,t} = A_j + B_j R^*_{m,t} + \varepsilon^*_t, \tag{2B.4}$$

where $\varepsilon^* = \varepsilon - B_j V_j$.

In Equation (2B.4), $\mathrm{Cov}[R^*_{m,t}, \varepsilon^*_t] = -B_j \sigma^2_V$; that is, the independent variable $R^*_{m,t}$ is correlated with the error terms. Therefore, the least-squares estimates of regression parameters will be biased. In addition, this implies that the standard least-squares slope estimates are not reliable systematic risk measures for investment analysis and financial management.

Based upon the OLS estimate for $B1/2j$ derived in Appendix A, we have

$$\begin{aligned}\hat{B}_j &= \frac{Cov(R^*_{m,t}, R_{jt})}{Var(R^*_{m,t})} = \frac{Cov(R_{m,t} + V_t, \alpha_j + B_j R_{m,t} + \varepsilon_t)}{Var(R_{m,t}) + Var(V_t)} \\ &= \frac{B_j Cov(R_{m,t}, R_{m,t}) + Cov(V_t, \varepsilon_t)}{Var(R_{m,t}) + Var(V_t)} = \frac{B_j}{1 + \sigma^2_V/\sigma^2_M}\end{aligned} \tag{2B.5}$$

if $Cov(V_{t1}, \varepsilon_t) = 0$.

Equation (2B.5) shows that even if measurement errors are assumed to be independent of $R_{m,t}$ and ε_t, the estimated slope, b, will be biased downward; σ^2_V/σ^2_M is generally used to measure the quality of the data.

There are two generally accepted techniques for overcoming the problems of errors in variables: (1) grouping, and (2) instrumental variables. Black *et al.* (1972) and Lee (1976) use the grouping method to estimate beta coefficients. The grouping method can reduce measurement errors because the errors of individual observations tend to be cancelled out by their mutual independence. Hence, there is less measurement error in a group average than there would be if sample data were not grouped. In addition,

Lee also suggests an instrumental variable method to estimate the beta coefficients.

2B.2. *Instrumental Variables*

Instrumental variables can be defined from both the error-in-variable and the two-stage, least-squares (2SLS) estimation viewpoints. In classical error-in-variable problems, an instrumental variable is one that is highly correlated with the independent variable, but independent of the measurement error associated with independent variable, V_t, and the true regression error, ε_t. If Z_t is the instrumental variable to be used to reduce the measurement error associated with $R^*_{m,t}$ in estimated beta, as discussed in Section 2B.1, then $Z_t$should be independent of both $Z_t$and ε_t. Lee (1976) uses the rank order (i.e., with values $1, 2, 3, \ldots, N$) as the variable Z for estimating Beta coefficients. Taking the covariance of Z with respect to all variables in Equation (2B.1) yields:

$$Cov(R_j, Z) = B_j Cov(R_m, Z) + Cov(Z, \varepsilon) \tag{2B.6}$$

If $Cov[Z, V] = Cov[Z, \varepsilon]$, then:

$$\hat{B}_j = \frac{Cov(R_j, Z)}{Cov(R^*_m, Z)} = \frac{Cov(R_j, Z)}{Cov(R_m, Z)}. \tag{2B.7}$$

Here $\hat{B}_j$ is a consistent estimator of B_j. Note that this method is sometimes called the "covariance" method of estimating beta.

In estimating the parameters of simultaneous equation system, a 2SLS estimator is generally an instrumental variable estimably more than a single equation regression can capture. Specifically, seldom is a variable determined by a single relationship (equation). Normally a variable determined simultaneously with many other variables in a whole system of simultaneous equations. For example, the current ratio is determined simultaneously with the leverage ratio, the activity ratio, and the profitability ratio, as discussed earlier.

Using a two-equation system to serve as an example to discuss identification problems, we have

$$Y_1 = A_0 + A_1 Y_2 + E_1, \tag{2B.8a}$$

$$Y_2 = B_0 + B_1 Y_1 + B_2 Z_1 + E_2; \tag{2B.8b}$$

$$Y_1 = A_0 + A_1 Y_2 + A_2 Z_2 + E_1, \tag{2B.9a}$$

$$Y_2 = B_0 + B_1Y_1 + B_2Z_1 + E_2; \tag{2B.9b}$$

$$Y_1 = A_0 + A_1Y_2 + A_2Z_2 + A_3Z_3 + E_1Y, \tag{2B.10a}$$

$$Y_2 = B_0 + B_1Y_1 + B_2Z_1 + E_2. \tag{2B.10b}$$

Equations (2B.8), (2B.9), and (2B.10) are three different simultaneous equation systems. Y_1 and Y_2 are endogenous variables determined within the system of equations, while Z_1, Z_2, and Z_3 are exogenous variables and E_1 and E_2 are residual terms. There are two methods to distinguish between the endogenous and exogenous variables. Conceptually, the exogenous variables, Z_1Z_2, and Z_3, are determined outside this system of equations. They can also be referred to as predetermined variables. The essential point is that their values are determined elsewhere and are not influenced by Y_1, Y_2, E_1 or E_2. On the other hand, Y_1 and Y_2 are jointly dependent, or endogenous, variables: their values are determined within the model, and thus they are influenced Z_1Z_2, Z_3, E_1 and E_2 Statistically, Y_2 and E_1 and Y_1 and E_2 are dependent. Therefore, they face the error-in-variable problem (or simultaneous equation bias) when the OLS method is used to estimate the parameters of the model. The exogenous variables, Z_1Z_2, and Z_3, and the error terms, E_1 and E_2, are statistically independent.

A requirement for identifying an equation is that the number of exogenous variables that are excluded from the equation (K) must be at least equal to the number of endogenous variables that are included on the right-hand side of that equation (H). The equations above are defined as follows:

(1) In Equations (2B.8a), (2B.9a), (2B.9b), and (2B.10a), $K = H$. These are "exactly identified" equations.
(2) In Equation (2B.8b), $K < H$. Equation (2B.8b) is an "under identified" equation.
(3) In Equation (2.B.10b), $K > H$. Equation (2B.10b) is an "over identified" equation.

In an under identified equation, the related regression parameters cannot be statistically estimated. If an equation is either exactly identified or over identified, the instrumental variable and the (2SLS) technique can be used to statistically estimate the related regression parameters. Johnston and Dinardo (1996) has shown that 2SLS and instrumental-variable techniques are equivalent procedures, on the condition that the first stage system and on the condition that the instrument used in the instrumental-variable procedure is the fitted value of the first-stage regression.

2B.3. *Two-Stage, Least-Square*

Equations (2B.10a) and (2B.10b) will serve as an example in the discussion of the 2SLS estimation procedure.

Stage 1: Use OLS to estimate the following two reduced-form equations:

$$Y_1 = C_0 + C_1 Z_1 + C_2 Z_2 + C_3 Z_3 + E_1, \tag{2B.11a}$$

$$Y_2 = D_0 + D_1 Z_1 + D_2 Z_2 + D_3 Z_3 + E_2. \tag{2B.11b}$$

Stage 2: Use OLS to estimate the following structural equations:

$$Y_1 = A_0 + A_1 \hat{Y}_2 + A_2 Z_2 + A_3 Z_3 + E_1, \tag{2B.10$'$a}$$

$$Y_2 = B_0 + B_1 \hat{Y}_1 + B_2 Z_1 + E_2, \tag{2B.10$'$b}$$

where $\hat{Y}_1$ and $\hat{Y}_2$ are the estimates of Y_1 and Y_2.

The stochastic components associated with the error terms E_1 and E_2 have been purged in Stage 1. The estimated parameters, $\hat{C}_0, \hat{C}_1, \hat{C}_2, \hat{C}_3, \hat{D}_0, \hat{D}_1, \hat{D}_2$, and $\hat{D}_3$, are reduced-form parameters, while the estimated parameters, $\hat{A}_0, \hat{A}_1, \hat{A}_2, \hat{A}_3, \hat{B}_0, \hat{B}_1$ and $\hat{B}_2$ are structural parameters. Johnston and Dinardo (1996) has used the relationship between the structural parameters and reduced-form parameters to discuss the identification problem. An equation is unidentified if there is no way of estimating all the structural parameters from the reduced-form parameters. Furthermore, an equation is exactly identified if a unique value is obtainable for some parameters.

The 2SLS estimating method is used by Modigliani and Miller (1966) to reduce the measurement errors of accounting earnings, in estimating the cost of capital for the electric utility industry. The simultaneous current ratio and leverage ratio determination process was defined in Equation (2.9) of this chapter, and was estimated by using JNJ's ratio data. The first-stage regression results associated with Equations (2B.11a) and (2B.11b), in terms of JNJ's current ratio and leverage ratio, are

$$\begin{aligned} Y_1 = {} & -0.2399 + 0.8198 Z_1 - 1.9004 Z_1, \quad R^2 = 0.3449, \\ & \ (0.1012) \quad (0.2802) \qquad (1.245) \end{aligned} \tag{2B.12a}$$

$$\begin{aligned} Y_2 = {} & \ 0.0746 \ - 0.1133 Z_1 + 0.7849 Z_2, \quad R^2 = 0.4240, \\ & (0.0195) \quad (0.0541) \qquad (0.2405) \end{aligned} \tag{2B.12b}$$

where the digits below the regression coefficients are standard errors of estimates, and Z_1 and Z_2 represent the firm's current-ratio and leverage-ratio deviations from the related industry average in previous period.

Based upon Equations (2B.12a) and (2B.12b), the estimated current ratio and leverage ratio for JNJ Corporation can be estimated. These estimated endogenous variables are then used in the structural equations, as indicated in Equations (2B.10′a) and (2B.10′b) to obtain the results of second-stage regressions.

Bibliography for Appendix 2

Black, F., M. C. Jensen and M. Scholes. "The Capital Asset Pricing Model: Some Empirical Tests," in M. C. Jensen, ed., *Studies in the Theory of Capital Markets*, pp. 79–121. New York: Praeger, 1972.

Greene, W. H. *Econometric Analysis*, 7th ed. Englewood Cliffs, NJ: Prentice Hall Inc., 2011.

Hamilton, J. D. *Time Series Analysis*, Princeton, NJ: Princeton University Press, 1994.

Johnston, J. and J. Dinardo. *Econometrics Methods*, 4th ed. New York: McGraw-Hill, 1996.

Lee, C. F. "Performance Measure, Systematic Risk, and Errors-in-Variable Estimation Method." *Journal of Economics and Business* (Spring 1976), 122–127.

Miller, M. H., and F. Modigliani. "Some Estimates of the Cost of Capital for the Electric Utility Industry, 1954–57." *American Economic Review* (June 1966), 333–391.

Bibliography

Bodie, Z., A. Kane and A. Marcus. *Investments*, 7th ed. New York: McGraw-Hill Book Company, 2006.

Brealey, R. and S. Myers. *Principles of Corporate Finance*, 9th ed. New York: McGraw-Hill Book Company, 2007.

Brigham, E. F. and M. C. Ehrhardt. *Financial Management-Theory and Practice*, 12th ed. Hinsdale, OH: South-Western College Pub, 2007.

Copeland, T. E. and J. F. Weston. *Financial Theory and Corporate Policy*, 4th ed. Reading, MA: Addison-Wesley Publishing Company, 2004.

Deakin, E. B. "Distribution of Financial Accounting Ratios." *The Accounting Review*, v. 51 (1976), 90–96.

Gentry, J. A. and C. F. Lee. "Measuring and Interpreting Time, Firm and Ledger Affect." in C. F. Lee ed.: *Financial Analysis and Planning: Theory and Application — A Book of Readings*, Boston: Addison-Wesley Publishing Company, 1983.

Haley, C. W. and L. D. Schall. *The Theory of Financial Decisions*. New York: McGraw Hill, 1979.

Hicks, J. R., *Capital and Growth.* London: Oxford University Press, 1965.

Hicks, J. R., *Value and Capital*, 2nd ed. London: Oxford University Press, 1975.

Hilliard, J. E. and R. A. Leitch. "Cost–Volume-Profit Analysis under Uncertainty: A Log-Normal Approach." *The Accounting Review*, v. 51 (1975), 69–80.

Hong, H. "Inflation and Market Value of the Firm: Theory and Test." *Journal of Finance*, v. 32 (1977), 1031–1048.

Lee, C. F. and A. C. Lee, *Encyclopedia of Finance*, New York, NY: Springer, 2006.

Lee, C. F. and J. K. Zumwalt. "Associations between Alternative Accounting Profitability Measures and Security Returns." *Journal of Financial and Quantitative Analysis*, v. 16 (1981), 71–93.

Lev, B. "Industry Averages as Targets for Financial Ratios." *Journal of Accounting Research* (Autumn 1969), 290–299.

Manes, R. "A New Dimension of Break-Even Analysis." *Journal of Accounting Research*, v. 4 (Spring 1966), 87–100.

Penman, S. H. *Financial Statement Analysis and Security Valuation*, 4th ed. New York: McGraw-Hill/Irwin, 2009.

Reinhardt, U. E. "Break-Even Analysis for Lockheed's Tri-Star: An Application." *Journal of Finance*, v. 28 (1973), 821–838.

Ross, S. A., R. W. Westerfield and J. Jaffe. *Corporate Finance*, 9th ed. New York: McGraw-Hill/Irwin, 2009.

Snedecor, G. W. *Statistical Methods*, 8th ed. Ames, Iowa: Iowa State College Press, 1989.

van Horne, J. C. *Financial Management and Policy*, 13th ed. Englewood Cliffs, NJ: Prentice Hall Inc., 2008.

Wei, S. "*A General Discussion Model for Cost-Volume-Profit Analysis Under Uncertainty*," The Accounting Review **54** (October 1979): 687–706.

Yunker, J. A. and P. J. Yunker. "Cost–Volume-Profit Analysis under Uncertainty: An Integration of Economic and Accounting Concepts." *Journal of Economics and Business*, v. 34 (1982), 21–37.

Chapter 3

Common Stock: Return, Growth, and Risk

Investors in financial assets are compensated for the assumption of risk by earning an appropriate rate of return. This rate of return is composed of a percentage change in the market value of the assets and the yield of interest or dividends. The concept of return is crucial to the study of security analysis and portfolio management; therefore, accurate measurement of the rate of return is of vital concern. In the first part of this chapter, the concepts of holding-period return (HPR), holding-period yield (HPY), arithmetic mean, and geometric mean are defined and examined. This is followed by a discussion of a mixture of the arithmetic mean and geometric mean, as well as various ways of determining growth. The final section of the chapter presents different kinds of risks and the analytical measures commonly used to quantify risk. Appendix 3A presents logarithms and their properties.

In security analysis and portfolio management, growth-rate estimates of earnings, dividends, and price per share are important factors in determining the value of an investment. A regression method was demonstrated in Chapter 2, and in the latter part of this chapter both the compound-sum and the regression methods are developed in detail. Data from Johnson & Johnson (J&J) for 1999–2009 are used to show how alternative growth-rate estimation methods can be useful in security analysis.

3.1. Holding-Period Return

To measure the relative ending wealth, **HPR** is proposed by the financial profession to do the analysis. The HPR is the ratio of the terminal value of the investment (plus all cash distributions — that is, interest or dividend payments — received during the holding period) to the initial value of the investment. Mathematically, this can be expressed as

$$\text{HPR}_t = (1 + r_t) = \frac{P_t + C_t}{P_{t-1}}, \quad (3.1)$$

where

P_t and P_{t-1} = the market value of the investment in period t and period $t-1$, respectively; and

C_t = the cash distributions paid during the holding period.

Sample Problem 3.1 illustrates the calculation of the HPR.

Sample Problem 3.1

Table 3.1 lists J&J stock price and dividend data for 11 years. In order to calculate the HPR for 2009, the terminal value of the stock ($64.41) is added to the dividend received during 2009 ($1.91) and the sum is divided by the initial value of the stock for 2008 ($59.83).

Solution

$$\text{HPR}(2009) = \frac{\$64.41 + \$1.91}{\$59.83} = \frac{\$66.32}{\$59.83} = 1.108.$$

Table 3.1. Johnson & Johnson Company HPR and HPY.

Year	Closing Price ($)	Annual Dividend ($)	Annual HPR	Annual HPY (%)
1999	93.25	1.04	—	—
2000	105.10	1.22	1.14	14
2001	59.10	0.66	0.569	−43.1
2002	53.71	0.78	0.922	−7.8
2003	51.66	0.91	0.979	−2.1
2004	63.42	1.08	1.249	24.9
2005	60.10	1.26	0.968	−3.2
2006	66.02	1.44	1.222	22.2
2007	66.70	1.60	1.035	3.5
2008	59.83	1.77	0.924	−7.6
2009	64.41	1.91	1.108	10.8

Source: Moody's *Industrial Manual*, 2010.

3.2. Holding-Period Yield

Holding-period yield (HPY) is a measure of investment performance related to HPR. The HPY is the ratio of the change in the market value of the investment plus cash distributions received during the period divided by the original value of the investment. This is represented by

$$\mathrm{HPY}_t = (r_t) = \frac{(P_t - P_{t-1}) + C_t}{P_{t-1}} = \frac{P_t + C_t}{P_{t-1}} - 1. \tag{3.2}$$

From this expression it is easy to see that HPY equals -1. Thus, the 2009 HPY for J&J, as indicated in the fifth column of Table 3.1, is expressed as

$$\mathrm{HPY}(2009) = \frac{(\$64.41 - \$59.83) + \$1.91}{\$59.83} = 0.108, \text{ or } 10.8\%.$$

The HPY defined in Equation (3.2) is a discrete type of HPY. It assumes that the cash flows and investments occur at specific points in time. In this case, \$59.83 is invested at the beginning of the year, and \$1.91 is assumed to be received at year end, when the price is \$64.41. The HPR and HPY of J&J during 1999–2009, as indicated in Table 3.1, reflect the investment performance during this period.

The time-series distribution of the HPR is important in the analysis of security investments and the management of security portfolios. As shall be seen at the end of this chapter, when the riskiness of an investment is considered, the variability of the HPR or HPY is one of its measures. The two most important types of probability distributions used in investment analysis are the normal and the log-normal distributions. If the HPR is normally distributed, the mean and the standard deviation are sufficient to describe the shape of the HPR distribution adequately. If some skewness to the distribution exists, the log-normal distribution will be more appropriate in describing the distribution of returns.

In this study of portfolio theory, we assume that investors make their portfolio decisions on the basis of mean and standard deviation of rate of return. Since the normal distribution is fully represented by the mean and standard deviation, it is important to know whether the distribution being used in portfolio analysis is indeed normal. The distribution of stock returns has been shown by Fama (1965) to be abnormal. Additionally, Elton and Gruber (1974), using the concept of limited liability for investors, argue that normality and limited liability are inconsistent. The most an investor can lose is 100%, whereas the potential gain from an investment is limitless in

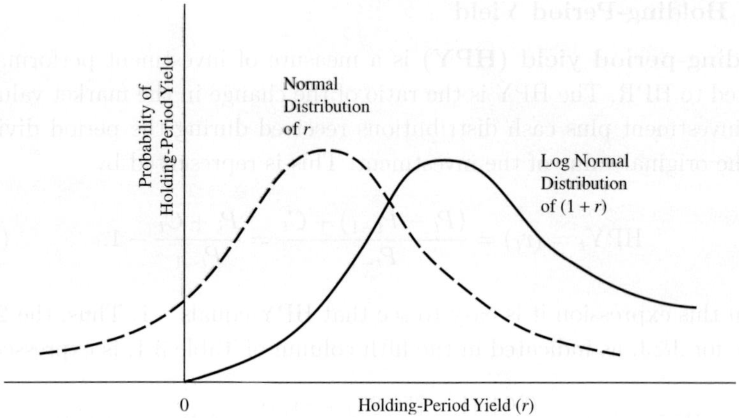

Fig. 3.1. Normal and Log Normal Distributions.

theory; hence, the distribution of returns cannot be normal where infinitely large gains have a nonzero probability.

Figure 3.1 shows the log-normal and normal probability distributions for the HPR $(1+r)$ and HPY (r).

Assuming that returns are log-normally distributed (which more correctly reflects the state of the world) does not negate the use of the mean and standard deviation in portfolio analysis. Further issues related to log-normal distributions are covered in the portfolio theory section of the text.

Table 3.1 uses a one-period or discrete model for calculating the HPR and HPY, assuming that the cash flow occurs at the end of the period. It is usually more realistic to deal with many periods and compounded returns when evaluating real-world investments.

The frequency of compounding influences the HPR and HPY calculations in the following way:

$$\text{HPY}_t^c = \ln\left(\frac{P_t + C_t}{P_{t-1}}\right), \tag{3.3}$$

where HPY_t^c is the holding-period rate of return with continuous compounding, and ln is the natural logarithm.

If $P_t = \$64.41$, $P_{t-1} = \$59.83$, and $C_t = \$1.91$, then

$$\text{HPY}_t^c = \ln\left(\frac{\$64.41 + \$1.91}{\$59.83}\right) = 0.103.$$

More generally, the rate of return with continuous compounding for a given period is expressed by

$$\text{HPR}_t^d = 1 + \text{HPY}^d = \exp(\text{HPY}^c), \quad (3.4)$$

where HPY_t^d is the discrete holding-period rate of return and $\exp(e)$ is 2.718, the base of natural logarithms. By taking the natural log of both sides of Equation (3.4):

$$\ln(1 + \text{HPY}^d) = \text{HPY}^c. \quad (3.5)$$

For example, if \$1,000 invested for one year produces an ending cash flow of \$1,271, the HPR^d is 1.271 for a HPY^d of 27.1%. The continuously compounded rate implicit in this investment is calculated by using Equation (3.5):

$$\ln(1 + 0.271) = 0.24,$$

for a HPY^c of 24%. In every case except $\text{HPY}^d = 0$, the continuously compounded return is always less than the discrete return.

On the other hand, given a continuous return, the discrete return can be calculated using Equation (3.6):

$$\text{HPY}^d = \exp(\text{HPY}^c) - 1. \quad (3.6)$$

For example, if the HPY^c is 18.5%, the HPY^d is $e^{0.185} - 1$, or 20.3%.

3.2.1. *Arithmetic Mean*

The **arithmetic mean** of HPY is one of the measures used to evaluate the performance of an investment. The arithmetic mean is the sum of the values of the data points divided by the number of such data points. In computational form, this can be expressed as

$$\bar{X} = \frac{\sum_{t=1}^{n} X_t}{n}, \quad (3.7)$$

where

$\bar{X}$ = the arithmetic mean of HPY; and
$\bar{X}$ = the HPY in tth year.

From Table 3.1, the arithmetic mean of J&J stock HPYs over a 10-year period, 1999–2009, can be calculated as

$$\bar{X} = \frac{0.015}{10} = 0.0015.$$

This implies that, on average, the investment has increased in value by 0.15% per year. Is this really a meaningful number? Probably not.

There are some complications to be aware of when employing the arithmetic mean. First, the arithmetic mean is quite sensitive to extreme values. For example, suppose that over a five-year period, a stock returned 5% in four years and 50% in one year. The arithmetic mean would be $0.70/5 = 0.14$, or 14%. With only the arithmetic mean as a guide, the returns might be expected to be scattered about 14%. Upon inspection, however, it is found that the stock was returned only 5% most of the time. The implication is that arithmetic mean has an upward bias that increases directly with the variability of the data. Another disadvantage of using the arithmetic mean relating to variability is of particular concern to security analysts. This problem can best be described by the following. Consider a stock whose price rises from \$10 to \$15 one year and drops back to \$10 the next. The annual HPY would be 50% in the first year and −33% in the second year. While the annual arithmetic mean return would be 8.5%, it is clear that the return equals zero, as the value of the investment is still \$0. Another measure of the mean return is necessary.

3.2.2. *Geometric Mean*

An alternative average measure for evaluating the investment performance is the **geometric mean**. The geometric mean is the nth root of the product of the n values of the data points:

$$\bar{g} = \sqrt[n]{X_1 \cdot X_2 \cdot \cdots \cdot X_n}. \tag{3.8}$$

HPRs rather than HPYs are used in calculating the geometric mean of rates of return because negative or zero yields will result in meaningless answers, a consequence of necessarily taking the nth root of negative numbers. The nth roots of negative numbers are imaginary numbers. There is no economic interpretation of an imaginary number.

To see how the geometric mean deals with the problems encountered with the arithmetic mean, it is useful to return to the examples of the previous section. The geometric average annual rate of return ($\bar{g}$) for a stock yielding 5% for four years and 50% for one year would be calculated as

$$\begin{aligned}\bar{g} &= \sqrt[5]{1.50 \times 1.05 \times 1.05 \times 1.05 \times 1.05}\\ &= \sqrt[5]{1.823}\\ &= 1.128.\end{aligned}$$

Subtracting 1.0 from the HPR, the HPY is 0.128, or 12.8%. This is less than the 14% arithmetic mean. In dealing with the other arithmetic-mean problems — that is, computing an average return when the actual return is zero — the geometric mean provides a suitable solution.

$$\begin{aligned}\bar{g} &= \sqrt{1.50 \times 0.667}\\ &= \sqrt{1.0} = 1.0.\end{aligned}$$

Subtracting 1.0 from the HPR, the HPY is 0.0, or 0%.

The geometric mean HPR of J&J stock as indicated in Table 3.1 for the 10-year period noted above is expressed as

$$\bar{g} = \sqrt[10]{0.8401} = 0.9827.$$

The geometric-mean return (HPY) is −1.73%, considerably different from the arithmetic-mean estimate of 0.15%. Comparison of the terminal wealth that would be accumulated using the geometric- and arithmetic-mean return estimates with the actual terminal wealth will help determine which is more accurate.

The original price of J&J stock was \$93.25. Cash dividends amounting to \$12.63 were distributed over the 10-year period, and the terminal price of the stock was \$64.41. Thus, the actual terminal wealth, assuming no reinvestment of the intermediate cash flow, was \$77.04. Since application of 1.05% growth rate to the initial price of \$93.25 over 10 years yields a terminal wealth position of \$103.51, use of the arithmetic mean overstates the terminal wealth by \$26.47. This is an underestimated value. Use of the geometric mean of −1.73%, on the other hand, yields the result of \$78.32, where the difference between the actual terminal wealth and estimated terminal wealth is \$1.28.

The best estimate of a future value for a given distribution is still the arithmetic average because it represents the expected value of the distribution. The arithmetic mean is most useful for determining the central tendency of a distribution *at a point in time* (i.e., for cross-sectional analysis). However, the geometric average mean is best suited for measuring a stock's compound rate of return over time (i.e., time-series analysis). Hence, the geometric average or compound return should always be used when dealing with the returns of securities over time.

The rationale for this particular observation revolves around the biases involved in the calculations of the arithmetic and geometric means. The arithmetic mean tends to be biased toward extreme observations, whereas the geometric mean penalizes extreme observations. That is, the geometric mean provides more of a smoothing process.

In analyzing past time-series data the geometric mean is usually more representative of actual data (as in the J&J example).

In order to simplify the computations involved in calculating the geometric mean, logarithms can be used to calculate the nth root.[1]

$$\bar{g} = \sqrt[n]{X_1 \cdot X_2 \cdot \cdots \cdot X_n}, \tag{3.9}$$

$$\ln(\bar{g}) = \frac{1}{n}(\ln X_1 + \ln X_2 + \cdots + \ln X_n),$$

$$\text{antilog}\,[\log(\bar{g})] = \text{antilog}\left(\frac{1}{n}\sum_{t=1}^{n} \log X_t\right),$$

$$\bar{g} = \text{antilog}\left(\frac{1}{n}\sum_{t=1}^{n} \log X_t\right). \tag{3.10}$$

For a three-year period example, in which the holding periods were $X_t = 1.0$, $X_2 = 1.15$, and $X_3 = X_n = 0.98$, the use of Equation (3.3) would give the following results:

$$\begin{aligned}\bar{g} &= \sqrt[3]{1.10 \times 1.15 \times 0.98}\\ &= \sqrt[3]{1.2397}\\ &= 1.074.\end{aligned}$$

Using Equation (3.10) as follows, the same result can be obtained:

$$\begin{aligned}\bar{g} &= \text{antilog}\left[\frac{1}{3}(\log 1.10 + \log 1.15 + \log 0.98)\right]\\ &= \text{antilog}\left[\frac{1}{3}(0.0414 + 0.0607 - 0.0088)\right]\end{aligned}$$

[1] In this application, the use of base 10 or ordinary logarithms will yield the same results.

$$= \text{antilog}\left[\frac{1}{3}(0.0933)\right]$$

$$= \text{antilog } 0.0311$$

$$= 1.074.$$

3.2.3. *Weighted Unbiased Mean*

When consideration is given to the types of applications for average rates of return to (1) determine the historical profit rate of an investment and (2) to assess the long-run expected rate of return of some investment instruments, the importance of accuracy and a lack of bias are apparent. For example, an executive who is enrolled in a company's pension plan would certainly try to assess the magnitude of his or her retirement fund when determining a current schedule of personal savings. As another example, an actuary calculating premiums for a life-insurance policy would need to make some assumption about long-run expected rates of return and would typically base assessments of future rates of return upon past experience. Blume (1974) has investigated the possible bias in using either arithmetic average ($\bar{x}$) or geometric average ($\bar{g}$) to forecast such expected rates of return and has proposed four alternative unbiased estimators: (1) simple unbiased, (2) overlapped unbiased, (3) weighted unbiased, and (4) adjusted unbiased. Since Blume has also mathematically and empirically shown that the weighted unbiased estimator is the most efficient estimator and is the most robust for non-normal and nonstationary data, only this estimator is discussed here. The definition of the weighted unbiased estimator, $M(W)$, is

$$M(W) = \left(\frac{n-T}{n-1}\right)\bar{X} + \left(\frac{T-1}{n-1}\right)\bar{g}, \tag{3.11}$$

where

$n =$ the number of HPRs used to estimate the historical average returns; and

$T =$ the number of investment-horizon periods for which a particular investment is to be held.

For example, to estimate the average HPR for a five-year horizon using the J&J Company data, it can be seen that $n = 10$, $T = 5$, and

$$M(W) = \frac{10-5}{10-1}(1.0105) + \frac{5-1}{10-1}(-1.0079)$$

$$= \frac{5}{9}(1.0105) + \frac{4}{9}(0.9827)$$
$$= 0.5614 + 0.4368$$
$$= 0.9982.$$

Therefore, application of the weighted unbiased estimator approach would lead to an estimated average HPR of −0.18%, if the holding period is expected to be five years. A shorter holding-period assumption would result in a higher estimated HPR (i.e., closer to $\bar{X}$), and a longer holding-period assumption would result in a lower estimated HPR (i.e., closer to $\bar{g}$). These results are consistent with investors' intuitive inclination to be more conservative with longer-term estimates of return.

3.3. Common-Stock Valuation Approaches

Arithmetic, geometric, and weighted unbiased means are three alternative averages useful in evaluating the historical performance of an investment. Nevertheless, while it is important to be aware of an investment's past performance, it is crucial to understand the ingredients for determining the market value of common stock in future investment performance evaluation. There are four logically equivalent approaches for estimating the market value of common stock.

(1) The stream of dividends approach
(2) The current earnings plus future investment opportunities approach
(3) The discounted cash-flow approach
(4) The stream of earnings approach

These four methods are explored in more detail in Chapter 4. For now, the derivation and implications of the stream of dividends approach is presented. In general, there are three ways to express this approach, as indicated in Equations (3.12), (3.13), and (3.14):

$$P_0 = \sum_{t=1}^{n} \frac{d_t}{(1+k)^t}, \tag{3.12}$$

$$P_0 = \frac{d_1}{k - g}, \tag{3.13}$$

$$P_0 = \frac{d_1}{k}, \tag{3.14}$$

where

P_0 = current price per share;
d_t = expected dividends per share in period t;
k = capitalization rate;
n = terminal time period; and
g = the growth rate of dividends per share.

Both Equations (3.13) and (3.14) can be derived from Equation (3.12). If n approaches infinity, k is larger than g, and dividends grow at a constant rate so that $d_t = d_0(1+g)^t$, it can be shown that Equation (3.12) reduces to Equation (3.13), commonly called the Gordon dividend model.[2] If the growth rate of dividends is zero, Equation (3.13) reduces to Equation (3.14). These three valuation expressions are important for security analysis and portfolio management because they can be used to calculate the theorctical value of common stock, and variations on them can be used to calculate the value of bonds and other investment instruments. To use these models, estimates of the appropriate capitalization rate (k) and the growth rate (g) for dividends are required. In the following section, alternative methods for estimating the growth rate are explored in accordance with the concepts of the compounding process and linear regression.

3.4. Growth-Rate Estimation and its Application

The purpose of this section is to show how growth rates can be mathematically estimated. The application of these estimated growth rates is briefly discussed.

3.4.1. *Compound-Sum Method*

One method of estimating the growth rate uses the compounding process. Both discrete and continuous compounding are basic concepts in financial

---

[2]Substituting $d_i = d_0(1+g)^t$ into Equation (3.12) and letting $k > g$ and n approach infinity:

$$P_0 = d_0\left[\left(\frac{1+g}{1+k}\right) + \left(\frac{1+g}{1+k}\right)^2 + \cdots + \left(\frac{1+g}{1+k}\right)^n\right]$$

$$= d_0\left(\frac{1+g}{1+k}\right)\left[\frac{1}{1-\left(\frac{1+g}{1+k}\right)}\right] = \frac{d_0(1+g)}{k-g} = \frac{d_1}{k-g}.$$

management and investment analysis. These concepts are expressed mathematically in Equations (3.15) and (3.16):

$$d_n = d_0(1+i)^n, \tag{3.15}$$

$$d_n = d_0e^{in}, \tag{3.16}$$

where

d_0 = the dividend per share at time zero;
d_n = the dividend per share at time n;
i = the compound interest rate; and
e = a constant equal to 2.718.

Equation (3.15) describes a discrete compounding process and Equation (3.16) describes a continuous compounding process.

The relationship between Equations (3.15) and (3.16) can be illustrated by using an intermediate expression such as

$$d_n = d_0\left(1+\frac{i}{m}\right)^{mn}, \tag{3.17}$$

where m is the frequency of compounding in each year. If $m = 4$, Equation (3.17) is a quarterly compounding process; if $m = 365$, it describes a daily process; and if m approaches infinity, it describes a continuous compounding process. Thus Equation (3.16) can be derived from Equation (3.17) in the following manner. Based upon the definition

$$\lim_{m\to\infty}\left(1+\frac{1}{m}\right)^{m} = e = 2.718. \tag{3.18}$$

Equation (3.17) can be rewritten as

$$\lim_{m\to\infty} d_n = \lim d_0\left(1+\frac{1}{m/i}\right)^{m/i(in)} = d_0e^{in}. \tag{3.19}$$

The growth rate of earnings or dividends can be estimated either mathematically or statistically. Mathematically, the growth rate can be estimated by using either Equation (3.15) or (3.16). Rewriting Equation (3.15) using the symbol for growth rate, g, in place of i gives:

$$d_n = d_0(1+g)^n. \tag{3.20}$$

From Equation (3.20), it is clear that

$$(1+g)^n = \frac{d_n}{d_0}. \tag{3.21}$$

Table 3.2. Dividend Behavior of Firms ABC and XYZ in Dividends per Share (DPS, dollars).

Year	ABC	XYZ
2005	1.00	1.00
2006	1.00	1.10
2007	1.00	1.21
2008	1.00	1.33
2009	1.00	1.46
2010	1.00	1.61
2011	1.77	1.77

Given values for d_0, d_n, and n, and using a compound sum table, the value of g can easily be obtained. This approach is called the **compound-sum method** for estimating growth rates. While the advantage of this method is its simplicity, it ignores other information points between the first and last period.

Suppose there are two firms whose dividend payments patterns are as shown in Table 3.2, using the compound-sum method the growth rate of firm ABC can be calculated as

$$(1+g)^m = \frac{d_m}{d_0} = \frac{1.77}{1.00}.$$

Using a compound-sum table where $n = 6$ and interest factor $= 1.77$, $g = 10\%$. The compound-sum method also yields a growth rate of 10% for firm XYZ. Yet it becomes clear that the dividend behavior of these firms is distinctly different when looking at the dividends per share in Table 3.2.

3.4.2. *Regression Method*

To use all the information available to the security analysts, two regression equations can be employed. These equations can be derived from Equations (3.15) and (3.16) by letting $i = g$ and taking the logarithm (ln):

$$\ln d_n = \ln d_0 + n \ln(1+g), \tag{3.22}$$

$$\ln d_n = \ln d_0 + gn. \tag{3.23}$$

Both Equations (3.22) and (3.23) indicate that d_n is linearly related to n. Using the data in Table 3.2 for companies ABC and XYZ, we can estimate the growth rates for their respective dividend streams. Graphs of the regression equations for ABC and XYZ are shown in Fig. 3.2. The slope

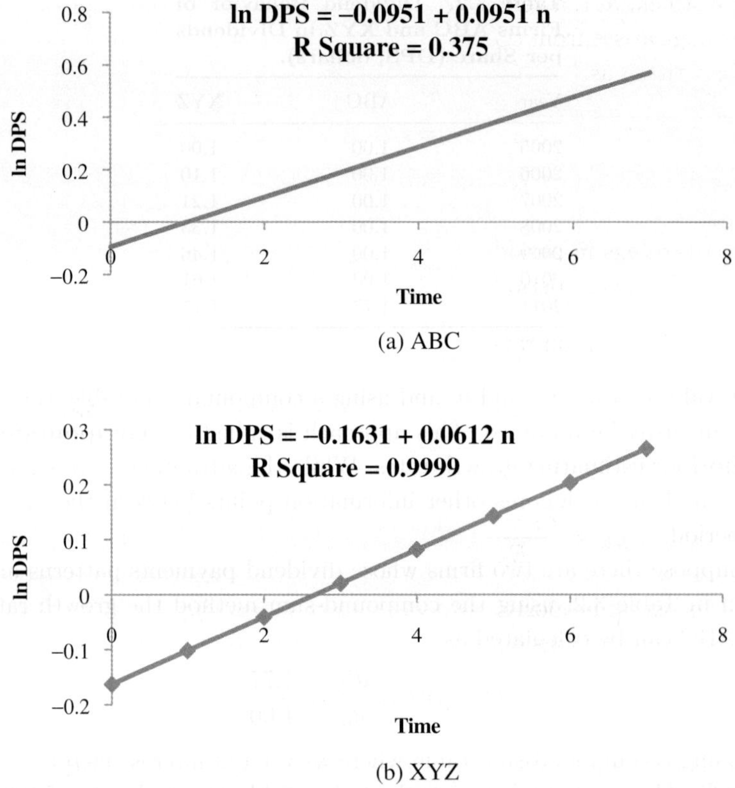

Fig. 3.2. Regression Models for ABC and XYZ.

of the regression using Equation (3.23) for ABC shows an estimated value for growth of about 6%. The estimate for XYZ is 9.5%. If Equation (3.22) had been used to estimate the growth, then the antilog of the regression slope estimate would equal the growth rate.

3.4.3. *One-Period Growth Model*

Another method of estimating the growth rate involves the use of percentage change in some variable such as earnings per share, dividend per share, or price per share in a **one-period growth model**. The one-period growth model is the model in which the same growth will continue forever. If b stands for the fraction of earnings retained within the firm, r stands for the rate of return the firm will earn on all new investments, and I_t stands for investment at t, a very simple expression for growth is obtained. Growth in earnings arises from the return on new investments. Therefore, earnings can be written as

$$E_t = E_{t-1} + rI_{t-1}, \tag{3.24}$$

where

E_t = earnings in period t; and
E_{t-1} = earnings in period $t-1$.

If the firm's retention rate (b) is constant, then:

$$E_t = E_{t-1} + rbE_{t-1} = E_{t-1}(1+rb). \tag{3.25}$$

Growth in earnings is the percentage change in earnings, or

$$g_E = \frac{E_t - E_{t-1}}{E_{t-1}} = \frac{E_{t-1}(1+rb) - E_{t-1}}{E_{t-1}} = rb. \tag{3.26}$$

Since a constant proportion of earnings is assumed to be paid out each year, the growth in earnings equals the growth in dividends, or

$$g_E = g_D = rb.$$

If firm M has a retention rate of 50% and an average return on investment of 20%, then the expected growth in dividends on earnings can be expressed as

$$g_E = g_D = rb = (0.20)(0.50) = 0.1, \text{ or } 10\%.$$

Using this expression for growth, Equation (3.13) can be rewritten as

$$P = \frac{D_1}{k - rb}. \tag{3.27}$$

Alternatively, this model can be stated in terms of the capitalization rate:

$$k = \frac{D_1}{P_0} + rb. \tag{3.28}$$

It is worthwhile to examine the implication of this model for the growth in stock prices over time. The growth in stock price is

$$g_P = \frac{P_{t+1} - P_t}{P_t}. \tag{3.29}$$

Recognizing that P_t and P_{t+1} can be defined by Equation (3.27), with the exception that D_{t+1} must be replaced by $D(1 + br)$:

$$g_P = br.$$

Thus, under the assumption of a constant retention rate, for a one-period model, dividends, earnings, and prices are all expected to grow at the same rate.

Investors may use a one-period model in selecting stocks, but future profitability of investment opportunities plays an important role in determining the value of the firm and its earnings per share (EPS) and dividend per share (DPS). The rate of return on new investments can be expressed as a fraction, c (perhaps larger than one), of the rate of return security holders require, or

$$r = ck.$$

Substituting this into Equation (3.28) and rearranging:

$$k = \frac{(1 - b)E}{(1 - cb)P_0}. \tag{3.30}$$

If a firm has no extraordinary investment opportunities ($r = k$), then $c = 1$ and the rate of return that security holders require is simply the inverse of the stock's price/earnings ratio. On the other hand, if the firm has investment opportunities that are expected to offer a return above that required by the firm's stockholders ($c > 1$), the earnings/price ratio at which the firm sells will be below the rate of return required by investors.

An investor could predict next year's dividends, the firm's long-term growth rate, and the rate of return stockholders require for holding the stock. Equation (3.13) could then be solved for the theoretical price of the stock that could be compared with its present price. Stocks that have theoretical prices above actual price are candidates for purchase; those with theoretical prices below their actual price are candidates for sale or for short sale. Sample Problem 3.2 provides further illustration of the one-period growth model.

Sample Problem 3.2

The use of the one-period model can be illustrated with a simple using the J&J data from Table 3.3.

Table 3.3. Selected Financial Data for J&J.

Year	Time X_1	EPS X_2 (\$)	DPS Price X_3	Price per Share X_4 (\$)
1997	1	2.41	0.93	65.88
1998	2	2.23	0.95	83.88
1999	3	2.94	1.04	93.25
2000	4	3.39	1.22	105.06
2001	5	1.83	0.66	59.10
2002	6	2.16	0.78	53.71
2003	7	2.39	0.91	51.66
2004	8	2.83	1.08	63.42
2005	9	3.46	1.26	60.10
2006	10	3.73	1.44	66.02
2007	11	3.63	1.60	66.70
2008	12	4.57	1.77	59.83
2009	13	4.40	1.91	64.41
Mean (\$)		3.0744	1.1894	68.6933
Standard Deviation		0.8684	0.3918	15.7600
Coefficient of Variation		0.2825	0.3294	0.2294

Source: Moody's *Industrial Manual*, 1987.

Solution

At the end of 2009, J&J's stock was selling for \$64.41 a share. The capitalization rate can be calculated using Equation (3.28):

$$k = \frac{d_1}{P_0} + rb, \quad \text{or} \quad k = \frac{d_1}{P_0} + g.$$

The current dividend yield is expressed:

$$\frac{d_1}{P_0} = \frac{\$1.91}{\$64.41} = 0.0297, \text{ or } 2.97\%.$$

If J&J's dividend is expected to grow at 10% per year:

$$k = 2.97 + 10.00$$

$$k = 12.97.$$

Thus, the required rate of return as estimated is 12.97%.

Alternatively, Equation (3.27) could be used to estimate the theoretical value of J&J stock. If the dividend is expected to stay at \$1.91, and $k = 12.97$, then estimates for the retention rate and the expected return for investment are required. For the sake of example, it is assumed that a retention rate of 50% and an expected return from investment of 18% yields a value of 9% for b times r. This gives an estimated value for the stock of

$$P = \frac{d_1}{k - br} = \frac{1.91}{0.1297 - (0.5)(0.18)} = \$48.11.$$

While J&J's stock would seem to be overvalued selling at $64.41 a share, notice the sensitivity of this valuation equation to both the estimate of the appropriate discount rate (required rate of return) and the estimate of the long-term growth rate. For example, if J&J's required rate of return had been 11.965% rather than 12.97%, its theoretical price would have been $64.41.

It seems logical to assume that firms that have grown at a very high rate will not continue to do so in the infinite future. Likewise, firms with very poor growth might improve in the future. Although a single growth rate could be found, it is difficult to estimate this single number. In order to give greater flexibility to this technique many analysts have turned to multiple period (two or three periods) growth-rate models. Each period has a specific growth rate associated with the firm's prospects in the short run and also the long run.

3.4.4. *Two-Period Growth Model*

The simplest extension of the one-period model is to assume that a period of extraordinary growth will continue for a certain number of years, after which growth will change to a level at which it is expected to continue indefinitely. This kind of model is called the **two-period growth model**.

If it is assumed that the length of the first period is n year, that the growth rate in the first period is g_1, and that P_n is the price at the end of period n, the value of the stock can be written as

$$P = \frac{d_1}{1+k} + \frac{d_1(1+g_1)}{(1+k)^2} + \frac{d_1(1+g_1)^2}{(1+k)^3} + \cdots + \frac{d_1(1+g_1)^{n-1}}{(1+k)^n} + \frac{P_n}{(1+k)^n},$$

where

d_1 = the current dividend per share; and
g_i = the growth rate during period i.

Using the formula for the sum of geometric progression as defined as (the first term of the series) [1 − (common ratio)^n]/(1 − common ratio), where n is the number of terms summed over, the value of the stock can be written as

$$P_0 = d_1\left(\frac{1-\left(\frac{1+g_1}{1+k}\right)^n}{k-g_1}\right) + \frac{P_n}{(1+k)^n}. \tag{3.31}$$

After n periods, it is assumed that the firm exhibits a constant growth forever. If g_2 is the growth in the second period and d_{n+1} is the dividend in the $n+1$ period, then:

$$P_n = \frac{d_{n+1}}{k-g_2}.$$

The dividend in the $n+1$ period can be expressed in terms of the dividend in first period:

$$d_{n+1} = d_1(1+g_1)^n(1+g_2).$$

Making substitutions for P_n and d_{n+1} the two-period model becomes:

$$P_0 = d_1\left(\frac{1-\left(\frac{(1+g_1)^n}{(1+k)^n}\right)}{k-g_1}\right) + \frac{d_1}{(k-g_2)}\left(\frac{1+g_1}{1+k}\right)^n(1+g_2). \tag{3.32}$$

This formula can easily be solved for the theoretical price of any stock. For example, Firm OPQ pays a dividend of \$1.00 per share which is expected to grow at 10% for five years and 5% thereafter. The investors in OPQ require a rate of return of 15%. The current price of OPQ stocks using Equation (3.32) should be

$$\begin{aligned} P &= 1.00\left(\frac{1-\frac{(1+0.10)^5}{(1.15)^5}}{0.15-0.10}\right) + \frac{1.00}{0.15-0.05}\left(\frac{1+0.10}{1+0.15}\right)^5(1+0.05) \\ &= 3.985 + 8.405 \\ &= \$12.39. \end{aligned}$$

3.4.5. *Three-Period Growth Model*

A logical extension of the two-period model is the **three-period growth model**. The three-period growth model implies that there exist three different growth rates for the whole growth valuation process. The resultant model would assume that in the first period growth is expected to be constant at some level. A forecast must be of both the level of growth and the duration of period one. During period two, the growth changes from its value in period one to a different level. Both the duration and the pattern of change of growth in period two must be forecast. The third and final period is the period of steady-state growth.

Look at Firm OPQ again. If instead of forecasting a growth rate of 5% during the second period, the three-period model is used to forecast at a 7% growth rate during the sixth through tenth years and at a 5% growth rate from the eleventh year thereafter, the price of OPQ stock can be calculated using Equation (3.32).

$$P = d_1\left(\frac{1-\frac{(1+g_1)^n}{(1+k)^n}}{k-g_1}\right) + d_1(1+g_1)^n(1+g_2)\left(\frac{1-\frac{(1+g_2)^{M-n}}{(1+k)^{M-n}}}{k-g_2}\right) + \frac{D(1+g_1)^n(1+g_2)^{M-n}(1+g_3)}{(1+k)^M(k-g_3)}, \quad (3.32A)$$

where M is the end of the second period and other terms are defined as before.

$$\begin{aligned} P &= 1.00\left(\frac{1-\frac{(1.10)^5}{(1.15)^5}}{0.15-0.10}\right) + 1.00(1.10)^5(1.07)\left(\frac{1-\frac{(1.07)^5}{(1.15)^5}}{0.15-0.07}\right) \\ &\quad + \frac{1.00(1.1)^5(1.07)^5(1.05)}{(1.15)^{10}(0.15-0.05)} \\ &= 3.985 + 6.520 + 5.862 \\ &= \$16.367. \end{aligned}$$

The additional information about the three periods of OPQ's growth yields a different answer for the theoretical market price of the shares. Since the firm experiences five years of growth at 7% during the second period, which is larger than the 5% growth assumed in the two-period model, the market price per share is $3.66 per share higher when we use the three-period model.

In Sample Problem 3.3, a set of actual data is employed to show how these concepts can be used to help security analysts and portfolio managers analyze the expected value of a firm.

Sample Problem 3.3

To demonstrate how the concepts of growth rate and stock-valuation model discussed in the previous sections can be analyze securities, the per-share values for price, earnings, and dividends of J&J during 1997–2009 are used. (See Table 3.3.) The mean and the standard deviations of the EPS are higher than the mean and standard deviation of the DPS. As expected, on average J&J earns more per share in earnings than they pay out in dividends; nevertheless, the variability of the earning stream is greater than the variability of the dividend stream. In comparing the dispersion of two different series there generally is a problem with simply comparing the magnitude of the respective standard deviations. The standard deviation is an absolute measure of dispersion and as such is influenced by the numbers in the series. To compare the dispersion of two series, the **coefficient of variation (CV)**, is usually employed. The CV is defined as the standard deviation (SD) divided by the expected return (ER). The larger the CV, the greater the dispersion relative to the mean. In this case, the EPS still has a greater dispersion than the dividend series.

The expected value per share for J&J is determined using the Gordon model as expressed in Equation (3.13). To use this valuation approach, it is necessary to estimate the dividends per share in the next period, the capitalization rate, and the growth rate of dividends per share. The capitalization rate can be estimated by the earnings yield method, the weighted cost of capital method, or the capital asset pricing model (CAPM) method (discussed in Chapter 9). The following numerical example uses a required return of 16% for J&J and the compound-sum method of computing dividends per share growth rate. (Use of Equation (3.21) yields a growth rate of 13%.) Substituting these values into Equation (3.13) yields:

$$P_0 = \frac{1.91}{0.16 - 0.13} = \$63.67.$$

This theoretical value is a higher than the average price for the period ($68.69) and the current price ($64.41). The primary problems associated with this stock-valuation approach involve the adequacy of using averages of past data to estimate the future and using the compound-sum method to estimate the growth rate.

The data from Table 3.3 can be used to show how the growth rates of dividends and earnings per share can be estimates by the regression method. To estimate the related regression parameters and to provide a base for discussion of other implications, covariances and correlation coefficients

Table 3.4A. Covariance Matrix.

Variable		Time 1	EPS 2	DPS 3	PPS 4	ln EPS 5	ln DPS 6	ln PPS 7
Time	1	14.00	2.4115	1.1540	−26.2025	0.7596	0.9200	−0.3353
EPS	2		0.6961	0.3048	0.8114	0.2276	0.2547	0.0147
DPS	3			0.1417	0.0710	0.0989	0.1169	0.0034
PPS	4				229.2706	0.4840	0.3867	3.0251
ln EPS	5					0.0756	0.0841	0.0077
ln DPS	6						0.0986	0.0071
ln PPS	7							0.0403

Table 3.4B. Correlation Matrix.

Variable		Time 1	EPS 2	DPS 3	PPS 4	ln EPS 5	ln DPS 6	ln PPS 7
Time	1	1	0.7725	0.8193	−0.4625	0.7382	0.7831	−0.4463
EPS	2		1	0.9704	0.0642	0.9920	0.9723	0.0878
DPS	3			0.1752	4.722	−0.0127	0.1069	0.1535
PPS	4				292.4578	1.5915	2.9146	8.7230
ln EPS	5					0.0888	−0.0050	0.0403
ln DPS	6						0.0658	0.0949
ln PPS	7							0.2667

for time, EPS, DPS, PPS, ln PPS are presented in Tables 3.4A and 3.4B. The covariance matrix in Table 3.4A presents variances (elements on the diagonal) and covariances (elements off the diagonal). The correlation matrix in Table 3.4B presents correlation coefficients.

Conceptually, both the covariance and the correlation coefficient can be used to measure the extent to which two variables move together. The correlation coefficient is most commonly used because it is a standardized unit-free measure. Correlation coefficients range from −1.0 (perfect negative correlation) to +1.0 (perfect positive correlation). The concepts introduced here will be useful in understanding the diversification process discussed later in this book.

Some implications can be drawn from the sign and the magnitude of the correlation coefficients in Table 3.4B. The correlation coefficient between time and price per share (row 1, column 4) is −0.4625, indicating that the price has decreased over time. The coefficient between time and dividends per share (row 1, column 3) is 0.8193, implying that dividends were generally increasing over time. The coefficient of correlation between time and earnings per share (row 1, column 2) is 0.7725, which is positive, and this implies increased in earnings over time.

Following the format of Equations (3.22) and (3.23), the models for regressing X_5 and X_6 on X_1 can be defined:

$$X_5 = a_0 + a_1 X_1 + e_5, \tag{3.33}$$

$$X_6 = b_0 + b_1 X_1 + e_6, \tag{3.34}$$

where

a_0, a_1 and b_0, b_1 = regression parameters; and
e_5 and e_6 = error terms.

The formulas necessary to estimate the slopes a_1 and b_1 are represented by

$$a_1 = \text{Cov}(X_1, X_5)/\text{Var}(X_1), \tag{3.35}$$

$$b_1 = \text{Cov}(X_1, X_6)/\text{Var}(X_1). \tag{3.36}$$

Based on the information listed in Table 3.4A, the estimates slopes are

$$a_1 = \frac{0.7596}{14.00} = 0.0543 \quad (t = 3.6292),$$

$$b_1 = \frac{0.9200}{14.00} = 0.0657 \quad (t = 4.1760).$$

The estimated student's t-statistic, shown in parentheses, is used to show whether the regression estimate is significantly different from zero. Given values of the regression estimate and the degrees of freedom, we see that a_1 is not significantly different from zero and that b_1 is statistically significant. This verifies the aforementioned implications, which were drawn from the correlation matrix — that is, the growth rate of earnings per share as estimated by a_1 is essentially zero (5.43%) and the growth rate of dividends per share as estimated by b_1 is positive at 6.57%.

Use of the regression-generated growth rate for dividends per share of 6.17% in the valuation equation yields:

$$P_0 = \frac{\$1.91}{0.16 - 0.0657} = \$20.25,$$

which is closer to the average price for the period (\$68.69) than the 2009 price of \$64.41 per share. Thus, use of the regression method in this case is not as useful as the compound-sum method in valuing the shares of J&J.

3.5. Risk

Up to this point the discussion has centered only on various measures of return. Whenever return is considered, risk must be considered as well. In this section, various types of risk are defined and the various quantitative measures of risk are presented.

3.5.1. *Definitions of Risk*

In general, **risk** can be defined as the probability of success or failure. More specifically, any investment that has more than one possible return for a given holding period is defined as risky. As long as expectation of return cannot be guaranteed, the investor is facing risk. By this definition, every asset possesses some degree of risk; even Treasury bills (T-bills) involve some risk with respect to the real rate of return. Unless the nominal rate of discount on T-bill is exactly equal to the normal expected return of investors, investors in T-bills are facing risk. This is so because realized inflation may be different from expected inflation.

All investments involve some degree of risk, and there are large differences between the risks of various financial instruments. For example, T-bills have a different degree of risk than stocks or options. In order to discuss the relative as well as the absolute degree of the risk of various financial instruments, quantitative measures of risk are needed. Consistent with the definition of risk, such measures should provide a summary of the degree to which realized return is different from expected return. That is to say, such measures give an indication of the dispersion of the possible returns.

If the distribution of returns is symmetrical, two meaningful measures of dispersion are available: the **variance** and the standard **deviation**. The variance is equal to the average of the squared deviations from the mean of the distribution. It is generally by the symbol σ^2 and is defined:

$$\sigma^2 = \sum_{i}^{n} (\bar{X} - X_i)^2 P_r(x_i), \quad \text{or} \qquad (3.37)$$
$$= E(X^2) - [E(X)]^2,$$

where

$\bar{X}$ = the mean of the distribution and $\bar{X} = E(X)$;
X_i = the ith observation of return;
$P_r(x_i)$ = the probability that x_i will be realized;

$E(X^2)$ = the expectation of the return squared; and
$[E(X)]^2$ = the square of the mean return.

To obtain the standard deviation, σ, merely take the square root of the variance. So long as the distribution of return is symmetrical with a finite variance and an investor's risk aversion can be approximated by an appropriate utility function, the variance or the standard deviation is a useful measure of risk.

The calculations of variance and standard deviation of returns for Company A and Company B are illustrated in Table 3.5. As shown in Table 3.5, security B is riskier than security A because the dispersion of possible outcomes for B is larger than for A. When the variance or standard deviations are employed to measure risk for individual securities, it is assumed that the securities are not being held in a portfolio.

3.5.2. *Sources of Risk*

Sources of risk are important for understanding the degree of fluctuation for an investment over time. Sources of risk can be from firm-specific factors or market and economic factors.

Table 3.5. Calculation of Variance and Standard Deviation of Returns.

Returns x_i	Probability of x_i	$(x_i - \bar{x})^2$	$(x_i - \bar{x})^2 P_r x_i$
Company A			
0.10	0.10	0.0004	0.00004
0.11	0.20	0.0001	0.00002
0.12	0.40	0.0	0.0
0.13	0.20	0.0001	0.00002
0.14	0.10	0.0004	0.00004
			$\sigma^2 = 0.00012$
$\bar{X}_A = 12\%$			$\sigma = 0.0109$
Company B			
−0.10	0.20	0.0264	0.052812
0.05	0.30	0.00016	0.000048
0.10	0.30	0.0014	0.000421
0.20	0.20	0.0189	0.003781
			$\sigma^2 = 0.057062$
$\bar{X}_B = 6.5\%$			$\sigma = 0.2388$

3.5.2.1. *Firm-Specific Factors*

The total risk of a firm's security can be divided into two categories: (1) those that relate to the issuer of the security and (2) those that relate to all securities. The types of risk that are issuer specific are called **business risk** and **financial risk**. Business risk relates to the fluctuations in the growth of the operating cash flows of the issuers. Financial risk is related to the mix of debt and equity in the capital structure of the issuer.

For a corporate issuer of securities, business risk is determined by the fluctuations of prices of its products, demand for its products, the costs of production, and technological change and managerial efficiency. Securities of firms in different industries have different dispersions of returns because of these factors; for example, a utility has quite constant returns, whereas an automobile firm has more variable returns.

The second factor that affects the variability of return from investment in corporate securities is the financial structure of the issuer. The assets of a firm can be financed by either debt or equity. The use of debt promises the investor a fixed return, and equity holder's return is leveraged or the fluctuation of return magnified. For investors in both debt and equity, the greater the amount of debt in the firm's capital structure, the greater is the variance of returns.

3.5.2.2. *Market and Economic Factors*

As has been noted, the return on investment is made up of the cash flow from interest or dividends and the future price of the security. The price that is realized when the security matures or is sold may be fixed or variable. Additionally, if the security is sold before it matures, the future price is uncertain. Hence the variance of return (risk) is significantly related to the degree of price volatility over time. Prices of financial instruments vary as the general rates of interest change. There is an inverse relationship between interest rates and the price of securities — that is, when interest rates go up the price of a security falls. Decrease in interest rates, on the other hand, causes the price to rise.

The impact of the change in interest rates on the rate of return of government bonds is a good example of how interest rates can affect the return of investors. Government bonds are not subject to business or financial risk, but the rate of return realized by investors depends upon the movements in interests in interest rates. As will be shown in Chapter 5, the relationship between movements in the interest rate and the prices of securities depends upon such factors as the maturity of the security, the timing and size of the cash flows, and the rate of reinvestment available to the investor.

Actual rates of inflation are rarely equal to the rates of inflation expected by investors. The difference adds another element of uncertainty to the variability of returns. Investors in a bond expect to receive a stream of promised nominal cash flows in the future. If the level of prices changes differently from what investors expect, then their realized real rate of return will differ from what they expected at the time of investment. If the price level increases to a greater degree than what investors expect, their realized return will bc smallcr, and if prices do not increase as rapidly as investors expect, their realized return will be greater than they anticipated. For investors in equities, as the level of inflation increases the amount of uncertainty with respect to how inflation will help or harm the economy, industries, companies, and financial markets increases; and this increase in uncertainty has an adverse effect on the rates of return realized by investors. Hence, not only does inflation affect risk but the level of inflation also is an important variable as well. High levels of inflation present an opportunity for greater variability and uncertainty, thereby adversely affecting security returns, while low levels of inflation reduce uncertainty about future price level changes, thus favorably affecting security prices.

3.6. Covariance and Correlation

The **covariance** is a measure of how returns on assets move together. If the time series of returns are moving in the same direction, the covariance is positive. If one series is increasing and the other is decreasing, the covariance is negative. If series move in an unrelated fashion relative to one another, the covariance is a small number or zero.

If we divide the covariance between the return series of two assets by the product of the standard deviations of the two series, we have the correlation coefficient between the two series. Basically it is similar to a covariance that has been standardized by the variability of each series. Its range of values falls between +1 (perfectly positively correlated) −1 (perfectly negatively correlated).

The formulas for the covariance and the correlation coefficient are shown in Equations (3.38) and (3.39).

$$\mathrm{Cov}(XY) = \sigma_X \sigma_Y \rho_{XY} = \frac{\sum_{i=1}^{n} (X_i - \bar{X}_i)(y_i - \bar{y}_i)}{n}, \tag{3.38}$$

Table 3.6. Covariance and Correlation of Security Returns.

Company X		Company Y						
Time Period	Return	Time Period	Return	$(X-\bar{X})$	$(Y-\bar{Y})$	$(X-\bar{X})(Y-\bar{Y})$	$(X-\bar{X})^2$	$(Y-\bar{Y})^2$
1	0.10	1	−0.10	0.05	−0.09	−0.0045	0.0025	0.0081
2	−0.05	2	0.05	−0.1	0.06	−0.006	0.01	0.0036
3	0.15	3	0.0	0.1	0.01	0.001	0.01	0.0001
4	0.05	4	−0.10	0.00	−0.09	0.0	0.0	0.0081
5	0.0	5	0.10	−0.05	−0.04	0.002	0.0025	0.0016
Mean = 0.05		Mean = −0.01				−0.0075	0.0250	0.0215

$N = 5$

$\sigma_x^2 = 0.025/5 = 0.005$

$\sigma_x = 0.0707$

$\sigma_y^2 = 0.0215/5 = 0.0043$

$\sigma_y = 0.0656$

$\text{Cov}(XY) = \frac{-0.0075}{5} = -0.0015$ Correlation coefficient $\rho_{XY} = \frac{-0.0015}{(0.0707)(0.0656)} = -0.3234$

where

ρ_{XY} = the correlation coefficient between series X and Y; and
$\bar{X}_i$ and $\bar{Y}_i$ = the means of the X and Y series, respectively.

Based upon the definition of covariance, ρ_{XY} can be defined:

$$\rho_{XY} = \frac{\text{Cov}(XY)}{\rho_X \rho_Y}. \tag{3.39}$$

In Table 3.6 the covariance and the correlation of security returns are calculated. From Table 3.6, we can see that the returns of securities A and B are slightly negatively correlated, and the covariance of X and Y is a small negative number. As will be seen in Chapter 7, these may be good securities to hold together in a portfolio because of the lack of correlation between their returns.

3.7. Systematic Risk, Unsystematic Risk, and the Market Model

In the discussion of the sources of risk, we identified sources of risk that originated from the issue of the security and sources of risk that affected securities in general. In these sections, this distinction is developed further in the context of the market model. The issuer-specific risk is called **unsystematic risk**, because it is unique to each issuer of securities and does not affect all financial securities. The market-related risk affecting all securities is called the **systematic risk**.

In order to analyze or measure the degree of systematic and unsystematic risk that a security contains, a model of the return-generating process must be identified. A widely accepted model to achieve this is called the **market model** and is shown by Equation (3.40):

$$R_{it} = \alpha_i + \beta_i R_{mt} + e_{it}, \tag{3.40}$$

where

R_{it} = return on the ith security during time t;
α_i = the intercept of the regression model;
β_i = a measure of systematic risk of the ith security;
R_m = the random return on the market index in period t; and
e_{it} = the measure of unsystematic risk of security i.

In general, Equation (3.40) identifies a linear relationship between the return on the market (R_m) and the return on an individual security (R_i). (A more complete discussion of the market model is presented later in this text.)

In addition to the return on a security, investors are also interested in its risk or variability. Using Equation (3.40), the market model, it is possible to identify the components of risk for an individual stock in terms of the variance of return for the stock i. This is shown in Equation (3.41):

$$\sigma^2(R_i) = \beta_i \sigma^2(R_m) + \sigma^2(e_i), \tag{3.41}$$

where

$\sigma^2(R_m)$ = the degree of systematic risk; and
$\sigma^2(e_i)$ = the degree of unsystematic risk contained in the total risk of security $i, \sigma^2(R_i)$.

The size of β_i, in general, depends on how closely the movements of the individual security returns are correlated with the movements of the market index. Using the definitions of the slope coefficient of a regression equation as discussed in Chapter 1:

$$\beta_i = \frac{\mathrm{Cov}(R_i, R_m)}{\sigma^2(R_m)} = \frac{E(R_i, R_m) - E(R_i)E(R_m)}{\sigma^2(R_m)}. \tag{3.42}$$

As has been seen before, the covariance between two variables is equal to the respective standard deviations times the correlation coefficient. The

β_i in Equation (3.42) can therefore be in terms of the correlation coefficient, as shown in Equation (3.43):

$$\beta_i = \frac{\sigma(R_i)\sigma(R_m)\rho_{im}}{\sigma^2(R_m)} = \sigma(R_i)\frac{\rho_{im}}{\sigma(R_m)}. \tag{3.43}$$

In general, the measure of systematic risk of security is a function of the variability of return of both the security and the market, $\sigma(R_i)$ and $\sigma(R_m)$, and the correlation between the movement of returns of the security and the market ρ_{im}.

The systematic risks of various securities differ due to their relationships with the market. Hence, ranking securities by their correlation coefficient is equivalent to ranking them by their systematic risks. Securities with large βs are high-risk securities. Securities with $\beta = 1$ imply that the risk characteristics of these securities are identical with that market. Securities with low βs are defensive securities, and their returns are less volatile than the market.

A firm's β can be estimated by regression analysis. This approach assumes that the past relationship between a stock's return and market return will continue into the future. Ordinary least-squares regression is used to identify the historical relationship.

The use of regression analysis to determine the firm's β requires the selection of an appropriate index of market returns. In Chapter 6, a discussion of the various indexes will be presented; as will be seen, the theory of portfolio construction and capital asset pricing requires that the appropriate market index be a value weighted portfolio of all the risky assets. It is difficult to find such an index, so various proxies are often used, such as the Dow Jones Industrial Average (DJIA), Standard and Poor's 500(S&P 500), the New York stock Exchange composite, the Fisher Index, and so on. Once a suitable index has been selected, the next decision involves the time period over which the returns data should be collected.

The basic problem centers around the tradeoff of using a large volume of data for long periods versus using only current relevant data. For statistical reasons, the greater the number of observations, the better the forecasting properties. However, the more current the data, the more relevant it is to the future because conditions may have changed in the market, making data from distant past relatively useless. As a general rule, five years of monthly data seems to be used quite frequently as a balance between relevance and having a large enough number of observations.

The next step is to calculate the rate of return for the individual security and the market index. In general, it is best to use the continuous compounding HPY as calculated by Equation (3.3).

$$\mathrm{HPY}_t^c = \ln\left(\frac{P_t + C_t}{P_{t-1}}\right), \tag{3.3}$$

After the index, time-period, and HPYs have been calculated, the next step is to run the ordinary least-squares regression of

$$\ln\left(\frac{P_t + C_t}{P_{t-1}}\right) = \alpha + \beta \ln\left(\frac{I_t + C_t}{I_{t-1}}\right), \tag{3.44}$$

in which I_t is the index value and the other variables are as previously defined.

A final variable of interest is the R^2 or coefficient of determination. This variable measures the fraction of variability of the dependent variable that is explained by the influence of the independent variable. The closer the R^2 is to 1.0, the higher the percentage of the variability in the security's return than is explained by movements on the return on the market portfolio. The R^2 provides a measure of a stock's unsystematic risk. Stocks with a large R^2 have low unsystematic risk, whereas if the R^2 is closed to zero, the unsystematic risk of the security is large. Sample Problem 3.4 provides further illustration.

Sample Problem 3.4

Using a Excel program the market model is run on return for J&J, International Business Machines (IBM), and S&P 500 index (^GSPC) during May 1, 2005 to April 30, 2010. The data and results of this analysis are shown in Table 3.7.

Table 3.7 shows the estimates of systematic risk (β) and R^2 (adjusted coefficient of determination) for J&J and IBM.

Table 3.7. Estimates of Systematic Risk (β) and R^2 (Adjusted Coefficient of Determination) for J&J and IBM.

J&J	IBM
$\beta = 0.5667$	$\beta = 0.77623$
$R^2 = 0.4434$	$R^2 = 0.3774$

The security return of J&J moves very closely with the market while IBM is somewhat less. About 55% and 62% of the total risk of J&J and IBM, respectively, are embodied in unsystematic risk. This can be seen by looking at the R^2 statistic. Since the regressions have R^2 of approximately 0.44 and 0.38, systematic risk makes up about 44% and 38% of the total risk for J&J and IBM, respectively. The remaining risk, $1 - R^2$, is the unsystematic risk.

There are differences in the methods of calculating returns — using different indexes; using different holding periods (daily, weekly, monthly); and using different time periods. This causes estimates of systematic and unsystematic risk to vary from one analyst to another for a given security; hence, care should be taken in using the beta estimate for forecasting security returns. A good knowledge of the various variable used is necessary in order to ensure a reasonable forecast.

The Market Model for Sample Problem 3.4: $\ln(1 + R_i) = \alpha + \beta \ln(1 + R_m) + e_i$.

Date	S&P 500	J&J	IBM	Date	S&P 500	J&J	IBM
May-05	0.03	−0.0176	−0.0082	Nov-07	−0.044	0.0458	−0.091
Jun-05	−0.0001	−0.0312	−0.0179	Dec-07	−0.0086	−0.0153	0.0278
Jul-05	0.036	−0.0161	0.1248	Jan-08	−0.0612	−0.0533	−0.0092
Aug-05	−0.0112	−0.0037	−0.0318	Feb-08	−0.0348	−0.0122	0.0671
Sep-05	0.0069	−0.0018	−0.005	Mar-08	−0.006	0.0469	0.0113
Oct-05	−0.0177	−0.0104	0.0207	Apr-08	0.0475	0.0343	0.0482
Nov-05	0.0352	−0.0088	0.0883	May-08	0.0107	0.0017	0.0767
Dec-05	−0.001	−0.0266	−0.0753	Jun-08	−0.086	−0.036	−0.0842
Jan-06	0.0255	−0.0427	−0.011	Jul-08	−0.0099	0.0642	0.0797
Feb-06	0.0005	0.0076	−0.0106	Aug-08	0.0122	0.0354	−0.0452
Mar-06	0.0111	0.0272	0.0278	Sep-08	−0.0908	−0.0164	−0.0391
Apr-06	0.0122	−0.0102	−0.0016	Oct-08	−0.1694	−0.1146	−0.2051
May-06	−0.0309	0.0338	−0.0261	Nov-08	−0.0748	−0.037	−0.1174
Jun-06	0.0001	−0.005	−0.0386	Dec-08	0.0078	0.0213	0.0314
Jul-06	0.0051	0.044	0.0077	Jan-09	−0.0857	−0.0359	0.089
Aug-06	0.0213	0.0396	0.0502	Feb-09	−0.1099	−0.126	0.0097
Sep-06	0.0246	0.0044	0.012	Mar-09	0.0854	0.0518	0.0527
Oct-06	0.0315	0.0378	0.1267	Apr-09	0.0939	−0.0045	0.0652

(Continued)

(*Continued*)

Date	S&P 500	J&J	IBM	Date	S&P 500	J&J	IBM
Nov-06	0.0165	−0.0166	−0.0012	May-09	0.0531	0.0627	0.0351
Dec-06	0.0126	0.0017	0.0569	Jun-09	0.0002	0.0299	−0.0175
Jan-07	0.0141	0.0118	0.0206	Jul-09	0.0741	0.0719	0.1294
Feb-07	−0.0218	−0.0525	−0.0598	Aug-09	0.0336	0.0007	0.0057
Mar-07	0.01	−0.0424	0.0142	Sep-09	0.0357	0.0074	0.0132
Apr-07	0.0433	0.0656	0.0843	Oct-09	−0.0198	−0.0302	0.0084
May-07	0.0325	−0.0083	0.0471	Nov-09	0.0574	0.0726	0.0523
Jun-07	−0.0178	−0.0261	−0.0127	Dec-09	0.0178	0.025	0.036
Jul-07	−0.032	−0.0181	0.0513	Jan-10	−0.037	−0.0241	−0.065
Aug-07	0.0129	0.0282	0.0583	Feb-10	0.0285	0.0099	0.0436
Sep-07	0.0358	0.0633	0.0096	Mar-10	0.0588	0.0349	0.0086
Oct-07	0.0148	−0.008	−0.0143	Apr-10	0.0148	−0.0138	0.0058

JNJ Regression Output		IBM Regression Output	
Constant	0.00088	Constant	0.00967
Standard error of Y estimate	0.03042	Standard error of Y estimate	0.04761
R^2	0.4434	R^2	0.3774
Number of Observations	60	Number of Observations	60
Degrees of Freedom	58	Degrees of Freedom	58
X coefficient(s)	0.5667	X coefficient(s)	0.77623
Standard Error of Coefficient	0.0818	Standard Error of Coefficient	0.12802

3.8. Summary

This chapter has examined return, growth, and risk for common-stock variation. First discussed were the three alternative means — arithmetic, geometric, and weighted unbiased means — used to calculate the HPR and HPY. An analysis was then presented of two alternative methods — compound-sum and regression methods — used to calculate the growth rate of EPS and DPS. Finally, sources of risk were qualitatively identified and quantitatively analyzed. An understanding of these concepts is crucial, for this information and these techniques are essential to accurate security analysis and successful portfolio management.

Questions and Problems

1. What is the relationship between HPR and HPY?
2. Suppose you purchased XYZ Corporation's stock last year at a price of $100, and you sold it this year for $107 after receiving a $5 dividend. Calculate your HPR and your HPY.
3. Use the data given in Sample Problem 3.1 to calculate the HPR and HPY if you purchased Pennzoil stock in 1980 and sold it in 1986.
4. How does the normal distribution differ from the log-normal distribution? Is there any reason why one distribution is preferred?
5. What is the relationship between discrete HPY and the continuous HPY?
6. What is the arithmetic mean? What is the geometric mean? What are the advantages and disadvantages of each?
7. What is the weighted unbiased mean? When does it approach the arithmetic mean? When does it approach the geometric mean?
8. Use the data given in Sample Problem 3.1 to calculate the weighted unbiased mean for Pennzoil HPR. Assume the number of investment horizon period is six and that you will be using the HPR for 1980–1986 in your estimate.
9. What is risk? How is it measured? What are the components of risk?
10. What is systematic risk? What is unsystematic risk? What is the significance of these two types of risk?
11. You are given the security-return information about two companies as shown in the table at the top of page 68.
    (a) Find the covariance and correlation between the returns for companies A and B.
    (b) Explain why correlation and covariance are important in portfolio management.

Time Period	Return A	Return B
1	0.10	0.09
2	0.08	0.10
3	0.07	0.09
4	0.05	0.12

12. Evaluate the following statement: "Because investors dislike risk (as measure by the standard deviation) they require a higher rate of

return for holding stock that have a higher standard deviation of their returns."

13. What is the market model? What is beta? Why is beta important to portfolio management? How can we estimate beta?
14. What is regression analysis? Why is it an important tool for portfolio managers?
15. Use the data given in Problem 9 of Chapter 2 to forecast sales using regression analysis. Use a nonlinear trend model and a sales growth model.
16. You are given the following information about XYZ Company's stock.

Return on XYZ's Stock (%)	
1980	8.0
1981	10.0
1982	–4.0
1983	5.3
1984	12.2
1985	14.3
1986	–10.2
1987	19.3
1988	16.4

(a) Calculate the arithmetic mean for the company's returns.
(b) Calculate the geometric mean for the company's returns.
(c) Why do the answers in (a) and (b) differ?

Appendix 3A: Logarithms and their Properties

Logarithms were originally developed to simplify computations. Today calculators and computers make this use of logarithms obsolete; nevertheless, they still have useful properties for application in rate of return estimation.

If M and N are positive numbers and b is a positive number that is a base, then:

$$M = b^x, \quad N = b^y, \quad \text{and} \quad MN = b^{x+y}.$$

From these relations we have

$$\log_b M = x, \quad \log_b N = y, \quad \text{and} \quad \log_b MN = x + y.$$

Using these relations, some useful properties can be discussed.

(1) The logarithm of a product is the sum of the logarithms of the components:

$$\log_b(MN) = \log_b M + \log_b N.$$

(2) Since

$$\begin{aligned} \frac{M}{N} &= \frac{b^x}{b^y} = b^{x-y} \\ \log_b(M/N) &= x - y \\ &= \log_b M - \log_b n. \end{aligned}$$

The logarithm of a quotient is the logarithm of the numerator minus the logarithm of the denominator.

(3) Since

$$\begin{aligned} M^r &= b^{xr} \\ \log_b M^r &= xr \\ &= r \log_b M. \end{aligned}$$

The logarithm of a number raised to a power equals the power times the logarithm of the number.

The natural logarithm is in terms of the base e, where e is a number equal to 2.71828. As it turns out, the limit of $\left(1 + \frac{1}{n}\right)^n = e$ as n approaches infinity. This is important in finance because the compounding term used is of the form in the parentheses. The symbol ln is used to represent natural logarithms instead of $\log_e$.

Bibliography

Blume, M. E. "Unbiased Estimators of Long-Run Expected Rates of Return." *Journal of the American Statistical Association*, v. 69 (September 1974), 634–638.

Blume, M. E. and I. Friend. "Risk, Investment Strategy and the Long-Run Rates of Return." *The Review of Economics and Statistics*, v. 56 (August 1974), 259–269.

Bodie, Z., A. Kane and A. Marcus. *Investments*, 9th ed. New York: McGraw-Hill Book Company, 2010.

Cheng, P. L. and M. K. Deets. "Statistical Biases and Security Rates of Return." *Journal of financial and Quantitative Analysis*, v. 6 (June 1971), 977–994.

Elton, E. J. and M. J. Gruber. "Portfolio Theory When Investment Relatives are Lognormally Distributed." *Journal of Finance*, v. 29 (September 1974), 1265–1273.

Fama, E. F. "The Behavior of Stock Market Prices. "*Journal of Business*, v. 38 (January 1965), 34–105.

Latane, H. A., D. L. Tuttle and C. P. Jones. *Security Analysis and Portfolio Management*, 2nd ed. New York: Ronald Press, 1975.

Lee, C. F. *Financial Analysis and Planning: Theory and Application.* Reading, MA: Addison-Wesley Publishing Company, 1985.

Lee, A. C, J. C. Lee and C. F. Lee. *Financial Analysis, Planning and Forecasting: Theory and Application*, 2nd ed. Singapore: World Scientific Publishing Company, 2009.

Levy, R. "Measurement of Investment Performance." *Journal of Financial and Quantitative Analysis*, v. 3 (March 1968), 35–37.

Long, S. W. "Risk-Premium Curve vs. Capital Market Line: Differences Explained." *Financial Management* (Spring 1978), 60–64.

Pratt, S. R. "Relationship between Variability of Past Return and Levels of Future Returns for Common Stocks, 1920–60," in E. B. Frederickson, *Frontier of Investment Analysis*, 2nd ed., pp. 338–353. London: International Textbook Co., 1971.

Reilly, F. K. Investment Analysis and Portfolio Management, 2nd ed. Hinsdale, IL: The Dryden Press, 1985.

Rogalski, R. J. and S. M. Tinic. "Risk-Premium Curve vs. Capital Market Line: A Re-Examination." *Financial Management* (Spring 1978), 73–84.

Rothstein, M. "On Geometric and Arithmetic Portfolio Performance Indexes." *Journal of Financial and Quantitative Analysis*, v. 7 (September 1972), 1983–1992.

Soldofsky, R. M. and R. L. Miller. "Risk-Premium Curve vs. Capital Market Line: A Further Word." *Financial Management*, v. 7 (Spring 1978), 65–72.

Young, W. E. and R. H. Trent. "Geometric Mean Approximations of Individual Security and Portfolio Performance." *Journal of Financial and Quantitative Analysis*, v. 4 (June 1969), 179–199.

Chapter 4

Introduction to Valuation Theories

Value determination of financial instruments is important in security analysis and portfolio management. Valuation theories are the basic tools for determining the intrinsic value of alternative financial instruments. This chapter provides a general review of the financial theory that most students of finance would have already received in basic corporate finance and investment classes. Synthesis and integration of the valuation theories are necessary for the student of investments in order to have a proper perspective of security analysis and portfolio management.

The basic policy areas involved in the management of a company are investment policy, (2) financial policy, (3) dividend policy, and (4) production policy. Since the determination of the market value of a firm is affected by the way management sets and implements these policies, they are of critical importance to the security analyst. The security analyst must evaluate management decisions in each of these areas and convert information about company policy into price estimates of the firm's securities. This chapter examines these policies within a financial theory framework, dealing with valuation models.

There are four alternative but interrelated valuation models of financial theory that might be useful for the analysis of securities and the management of portfolios:

(1) Discounted cash-flow valuation theory (classical financial theory)
(2) M&M valuation theory (neoclassical financial theory)
(3) Capital asset pricing model (CAPM)
(4) Option pricing theory (OPT)

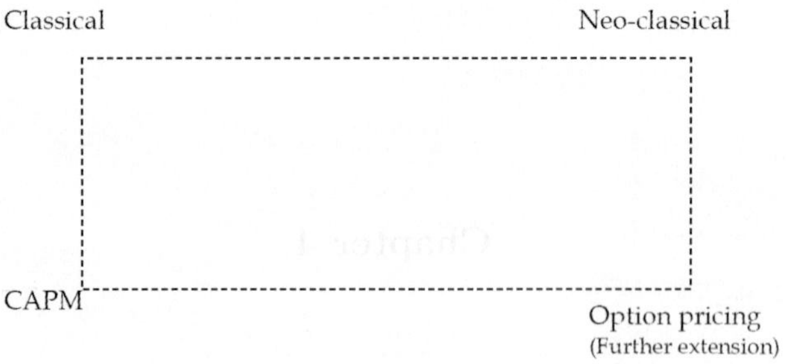

Fig. 4.1. Relationship of the Four Different Theories.

The relationship among these four different theories can be described by Fig. 4.1.

The discounted cash-flow valuation and M&M theories are discussed in the typical required corporate-finance survey course for both bachelor's and master's programs in business. The main purpose of this chapter is to review these theories and discuss their interrelationships. The discounted cash-flow model is first reviewed by extending some of the basic valuation concepts that were introduced in Chapter 3. In the second section, the four alternative evaluation methods developed by M&M in their 1961 article are discussed. Their three propositions and their revision with taxes are explored, including possible applications of their theories in security analysis. Miller's inclusion of personal taxes is discussed. The third section includes a brief overview of CAPM concepts, which is covered in more detail in Chapter 9; and the fourth section introduces option pricing theory, which is discussed in Chapters 16 and 17.

4.1. Discounted Cash-Flow Valuation Theory

Discounted cash-flow valuation theory is the basic tool for determining the theoretical price of a corporate security. The price of a corporate security is equal to the present value of future benefits of ownership. For example, for common stock, these benefits include dividends received while the stock is owned plus capital gains earned during the ownership period. If we assume a one-period investment and a world of certain cash flows, the price paid for a share of stock, P_0, will equal the sum of the present value of a certain dividend per share, d_1 (assumed to be paid as a single flow at year end), and the selling price per share P_1:

$$P_0 = \frac{d_1 + P_1}{1 + k}, \tag{4.1}$$

in which k is the rate of discount assuming certainty; P_1 can be similarly expressed in terms of d_2 and P_2:

$$P_1 = \frac{d_2 + P_2}{1 + k}. \tag{4.2}$$

If P_1 in Equation (4.1) is substituted into Equation (4.2), a two-period expression is derived:

$$P_0 = \frac{d_1}{(1+k)} + \frac{d_2}{(1+k)^2} + \frac{P_2}{(1+k)^2}. \tag{4.3}$$

It can be seen, then, that an infinite time-horizon model can be expressed as the

$$P_0 = \sum_{t=1}^{\infty} \frac{d_t}{(1+k)^t}. \tag{4.4}$$

Equation (4.4) is identical to Equation (3.12) of previous chapter.

Since the total market value of the firms' equity is equal to the market price per share multiplied by the number of shares outstanding, Equation (4.4) may be re-expressed in terms of total market value MV_0:

$$MV_0 = \sum_{t=1}^{\infty} \frac{D_t}{(1+k)^t}, \tag{4.5}$$

in which $D_t =$ total dollars of dividends paid during year t.

Using this basic valuation approach as a means of expressing the appropriate objective of the firm's management, the valuation of a firm's securities can be analyzed in a world of certainty.

Sample Problem 4.1

XYZ Company will pay dividends of \$3 and \$4 in years one and two, respectively. In addition, the market price per share is predicted to be \$30 at the end of second year, and the discount rate is 12%. Substituting this information into Equation (4.3) the current theoretical price per share can be calculated.

Solution

$$\begin{aligned} P_0 &= \frac{\$3}{(1+0.12)} + \frac{\$4 + \$30}{(1+0.12)^2} \\ &= \$29.78. \end{aligned}$$

4.2. Bond Valuation

Bond valuation is a relatively easy process, as the income stream the bondholder will receive is known with a high degree of certainty. Barring a firm's default, the income stream consists of the periodic coupon payments and the repayments of the principal at maturity. These cash flows must be discounted to the present using the required rate of return for the bond.

The basic principles of bond valuation are represented in the equation:

$$\mathrm{PV} = \sum_{t=1}^{n} \frac{\mathrm{CF}_t}{(1+k_b)^t}, \tag{4.6}$$

where

$\mathrm{PV} =$ present value of the bond;
$n =$ the number of periods to maturity;
$\mathrm{CF}_t =$ the cash flow (interest and principal) received in period t;
$k_b =$ the required rate of return of the bondholders (equal to risk-free rate i plus a risk premium).

4.2.1. *Perpetuity*

The first (and most extreme) case of bond valuation involves a **perpetuity**, a bond with no maturity date and perpetual interest payments. Such bonds do exist. In 1814, the English government floated a large bond issue to consolidate the various small issues they had used to pay for the Napoleonic Wars. Such bonds are called *consols*, and the owners are entitled to a fixed amount of interest income annually in perpetuity. In this case, Equation (4.6) collapses into:

$$\mathrm{PV} = \frac{\mathrm{CF}}{k_b}. \tag{4.7}$$

Thus, the valuation depends directly on the periodic interest payment and the required rate of return for the bond. It can be seen that required rates of return, necessitated by a higher rate of inflation or an increase in the perceived risk of the bond, lower the present value, decreasing the bond's market value. For example, if the stated annual interest payment on the perpetuity bond is \$50 and the required rate of return in the market is 10%, the price of the security is stated:

$$\mathrm{PV} = \$50/0.10 = \$500.$$

If its issuing price had been \$1,000, it can be seen that the required rate of return would have been only 5% (k_b = CF/PV = \$50/\$1,000 = 0.05, or 5%).

4.2.2. *Term Bonds*

Most bonds are **term bonds**, which mature at some definite point in time. Thus, Equation (4.6) should be respecified to take this fact into account:

$$PV = \sum_{t=1}^{n} \frac{I_t}{(1+k_b)^t} + \frac{P_n}{(1+k_b)^n}, \tag{4.8}$$

where:

I_t = the annual coupon interest payment;
P_n = the principal amount (face value) of the bond; and
n = the number of periods to maturity.

Sample Problem 4.2

If a corporate bond issued by XYZ Company has the following characteristics:

Annual coupon payment = \$90
Face value = \$1,000
Number of years till bond matures = 5
Return required by bondholders = 12%

Then Equation (4.8) can be used to calculate the theoretical value of this bond.

$$\begin{aligned} PV &= \frac{\$90}{(1+0.12)} + \frac{\$90}{(1+0.12)^2} + \frac{\$90}{(1+0.12)^3} \\ &\quad + \frac{\$90}{(1+0.12)^4} + \frac{\$90}{(1+0.12)^5} + \frac{\$1{,}000}{(1+0.12)^5} \\ &= \$891.83. \end{aligned}$$

Again, it should be noted that the market price, PV, of a bond is affected by changes in the rate of inflation. If inflation increases, the discount rate must also increase to compensate the investor for the resultant decrease in the value of the debt repayment. The present value of each period's interest payment thus decreases, and the price of the bond falls.

The bondholder is always exposed to interest-rate risk, the variance of bond prices resulting from fluctuations in the level of interest rates. Interest-rate risk, or price volatility of a bond caused by changes in interest-rate levels, is directly related to the term to maturity. There are two types of risk premiums associated with interest-rate risk as it applies to corporate bonds. The **bond maturity premium** refers to the net return from investing in long-term government bonds rather than the short-term bills. Since corporate bonds generally possess default risk, another of the components of corporate bond rates of return is **default premium**. The bond default premium is the net increase in return from investing in long-term corporate bonds rather than in long-term government bonds.

Additional features of a bond can affect its valuation. **Convertible bonds**, those with a provision for conversion into shares of common stock, are generally more valuable than firm's straight bonds for several reasons. First, the investor receives the potential of positive gains from conversion when the market price of a firm's common stock rise above the conversion price. If the stock price is greater than conversion price, the convertible bond generally sells at or above its conversion value. Second, the bondholder also receives the protection of fixed income payment, regardless of the current price of the stock — assuring the investor that the price of the bond will be at least equal to that of a straight bond, should stock prices fail to increase sufficiently. Third, for any given firm the coupon rate of return from its bonds is generally greater than the dividend rate of return (dividend yield) from their common stock — thus causing a measure of superiority for a convertible bond over its conversion into common sock until stock dividends rise above the bond's coupon rate. Even then, the convertible bond may be preferred by investors because of the higher degree of certainty of interest payments as compared to dividends that would decline when earnings fall.

A sinking-fund provision may also increase the value of a bond, at least at its time of issue. A sinking-fund agreement specifies a schedule by which the sinking fund will retire the bond issue gradually over its life. By providing cash to the sinking fund for use in redeeming the bonds, this provision ensures the investor some potential demand for the bond, thus slightly increasing the liquidity of the investment.

Finally, the possibility that the bond may be called will generally lower the value relative to a noncallable bond. A call provision stipulates that the bond may be retired by the issuer at a certain price, usually above par or face value. Therefore, in periods of large downward interest movements, a company may be able to retire a high coupon bond and issue new bonds with a lower interest payment requirement. A call feature increases the risk to an investor in that his expected high interest payments may be called away from him, if overall interest rate levels decline.

4.3. Common-Stock Valuation

Common-stock valuation is complicated by an uncertainty of cash flows to the investor, necessarily greater than that for bond valuation.[1]

Not only might the dividends voted to shareholders each period change in response to management's assessment concerning the current level of earnings stability, future earnings prospects, of other factors, but the price of the stock may also either rise or fall, resulting in either capital gains or losses if the shares are sold. Thus the valuation process requires the forecasting of both capital gains and the stream of expected dividends. Both must also be discounted at the required rate of return of the common stockholders.

$$P_0 = \frac{d_1}{1+k} + \frac{d_2}{(1+k)^2} + \cdots + \frac{P_n}{(1+k)^n}, \tag{4.9}$$

where

P_0 = the present value, or price, of the common stock per share;
d = the dividend payment per share;
k = the required rate of return of the common stockholders; and
P_n = the price of the stock in period n when sold.

However, P_n can also be expressed as the sum of all discounted dividends to be received from period n forward into the future. Thus, the value at the present time can be expressed as an infinite series of discounted dividend payments:

$$P_0 = \sum_{t=1}^{\infty} \frac{d_t}{(1+k)^t}, \tag{4.4}$$

in which d_t is the dividend payment in period t. Several possibilities exist regarding the growth of dividend payments over time. First, dividends may be assumed to be a constant amount, and the formula for the stock's

[1]This is true because foregoing interest puts the firm into default, while missing dividend payments does not.

valuation is simple Equation (4.7), where CF is the constant dividend and k is the required rate of return of the common stockholder.

Second, dividends may be expected to grow at some constant rate, g. In such a case, a dividend at time t is simply the compound value of the present dividend (i.e., $P_t = (1+g)^t d_0$). Under this assumption, as in Chapter 3, if $g < k$, the valuation equation can be simplified to

$$P_0 = \frac{d_1}{(k-g)}. \tag{4.10}$$

This equation represents the **Gordon growth model**, which is identical to Equation (3.13) of the last chapter. Note that a critical condition for this model is that the constant growth of dividends must be less than the constant required rate of return. The zero-growth situation is a special case of this model, in which

$$P_0 = \frac{d_1}{k}. \tag{4.11}$$

This is Equation (3.14) of the previous chapter.

Finally, dividends can exhibit a period of supernormal growth (i.e., $g > k$) before declining to the normal growth situation assumed in the Gordon model ($g < k$). Supernormal growth often occurs during the "takeoff" phase in a firm's life cycle. That is, a firm may experience a life cycle analogous to that of a product: first, a low-profit introductory phase, then a takeoff phase of high growth and high profits, leveling off at a plateau during its mature stage, perhaps followed by a period of declining earnings. Computer and electronics manufacturers experienced a period of supernormal growth during the 1960s, as did semiconductor firms during the 1970s. Bioengineering firms appear to be the super growth firms of the 1980s. Internet firms experienced a high growth during the 1990s. Recently, solar energy firms appear to be the super growth firms.

Sample Problem 4.3

LBO, Inc., has just paid a dividend of \$6 per share. In addition, dividends are expected to grow at a constant rate of 3% per year. If shareholders require a 7% annual rate of return, what should be the current theoretical price of LOB's stock?

Equation (4.10) can be used to calculate the current theoretical price. However, Equation (4.10) uses the dividend expected to be received next year, while the current information relates to the dividend received this year. Because dividends are expected to grow at a constant rate, next year's dividend should just be the future value of this year's dividend compounded at the growth rate of dividends.

Solution

$$\begin{aligned} d_1 &= d_0(1+g) \\ &= \$6(1+0.03) \\ &= \$6.18. \end{aligned}$$

Substituting into Equation (4.10) gives the current theoretical price of LBO's stock.

$$\begin{aligned} P_0 &= \frac{\$6.18}{0.07-0.03} \\ &= \$154.50. \end{aligned}$$

The valuation of a supernormal growth stock requires some estimate of the length of the supernormal growth period. The current price of the stock will then consist of two components: (1) the present value of the stock during the supernormal growth period, and (2) the present value of the stock price at the end of the supernormal growth period:

$$P_0 = \sum_{t=1}^{n} \frac{d_0(1+g_s)^t}{(1+k)^t} + \frac{\frac{d_{n+1}}{k-g_n}}{(1+k)^n}, \tag{4.12}$$

where:

g_s = supernormal growth rate;
n = the number of periods before the growth drops from supernormal to normal;
k = the required rate of return of the stockholders; and
g_n = the normal growth rate of dividends (assumed to be constant thereafter).

Equation (4.12) is similar to Equation (3.3) of the last chapter.

As we can see from our development of the discounted cash-flow financial theory, the primary determinant of value for securities is the cash flow received by the investors. Anything that affects the cash flow, such as the dividend policy, investment policy, financing policy, and production policy of the firm, needs to be evaluated in order to determine a market price.

Some shortcomings of this approach include the overemphasis on the evaluation of the individual firm to the exclusion of portfolio concepts and the interrelationship with the overall market indexes. Most of the classical models are also static in nature, overlooking the concept of dynamic growth. Nevertheless, a fundamental approach to security valuation — the stream of dividends approach — has evolved from this theory.

4.4. M&M Valuation Theory

Miller and Modigliani (M&M, 1961) have proposed four alternative valuation methods to determine the theoretical value of common stocks. This section discusses these valuation approaches in some detail. M&M's four more or less distinct approaches to the valuation of common stock are:

(1) The discounted cash-flow approach;
(2) The current earnings plus future investment opportunities approach;
(3) The stream of dividends approach;
(4) The stream of earnings approach.

Working from a valuation expression referred to by M&M as the "fundamental principle of valuation":

$$P_0 = \frac{1}{1+k}(d_1 + P_1). \tag{4.13}$$

M&M further developed a valuation formula to serve as a point of reference and comparison among the four valuation approaches:

$$V_0 = \sum_{t=0}^{\infty} \frac{1}{(1+k)^{t+1}}(X_t - I_t), \tag{4.14}$$

where:

V_0 = the current market value of the firm;
X_t = net operating earnings in period t; and
I_t = new investment during period t.

In this context, the discounted cash-flow approach can be expressed as

$$V_0 = \sum_{t=0}^{\infty} \frac{1}{(1+k)^{t+1}}(R_t - O_t), \tag{4.15}$$

in which R_t is the stream of cash receipts by the firm and O_t is the stream of cash outlays of the firm. This fundamental principle is based on the assumption of "perfect markets," "rational behavior," and "perfect certainty" as defined by M&M. Since X_t differs from R_t and I_t differs from O_t only by the cost of goods sold and depreciation expense, if $(R_t - O_t)$ equals $(X_t - I_t)$, then (4.15) is equivalent to (4.14) and the discounted cash-flow approach is an extension of Equation (4.13), the fundamental valuation principle. Hence, the security analyst must be well versed in generally accepted accounting principles in order to evaluate the worth of accounting earnings of $(X_t - I_t)$.

The **investment-opportunities approach** seems in some ways the most natural approach from the standpoint of an investor. This approach takes into account the ability of the firm's management to issue securities at "normal" market rates of return and invest in the opportunities, providing a rate higher than the normal rate of return. M&M develop from this framework the following expression, which they show can also be derived from Equation (4.14):

$$V_0 = \frac{X_0}{k} + \sum_{t=0}^{\infty} \frac{I_t(k_t^* - k)}{(1+k)^{t+1}}, \tag{4.16}$$

in which X_0 is the perpetual net operation earning and k_t^* is the "higher than normal" rate of return on new investment I_t.

From the expression it can be seen that if a firm cannot generate a rate of return of its new investments higher than the normal rate, k, the price/earnings ratio applied to the firm's earnings will be equal to $1/k$, thus implying simple expansion rather than growth over time. An important variable for security analysis is a firm's price/earning (P/E) ratio (or earnings multiple), defined as

$$\text{P/E ratio} = \frac{\text{Market price}}{\text{Earnings per share}}.$$

Conceptually the P/E ratio is determined by three factors: (1) the investor's required rate of return (K), (2) the retention ratio of the firm's earning, b, where b is equal to 1 minus the dividend payout ratio, and (3) the firm's expected return on investment (r). Using the constant-growth model (Equation 4.10):

$$\begin{aligned} P_0 &= \frac{d_1}{k-g}, \\ P_0 &= \frac{E_1(1-b)}{k-(br)}, \\ \frac{P_0}{E_1} &= \frac{1-b}{k-(br)}, \end{aligned} \tag{4.17}$$

in which b is the retention rate and E_1 is the next period's expected profit.

The P_0/E ratio is theoretically equal to the payout ratio of a firm, divided by the difference between the investor's required return and the firm's growth rates. In the above relationship a direct relationship has been identified between P/E ratio and discount cash-flow valuation model.

The **stream-of-dividends approach** has been by far the most popular in the literature of valuation; it was developed in the pre-M&M period. Assuming an infinite time horizon, this approach defines the current market price of a share of common stock as equal to the discounted present value of all future dividends:

$$P_0 = \sum_{t=0}^{\infty} \frac{1}{(1+k)^{t+1}}(d_t). \tag{4.18}$$

Restating in terms of total market value:

$$V_0 = \sum_{t=0}^{\infty} \frac{1}{(1+k)^{t+1}}(D_t). \tag{4.19}$$

With no outside financing, it can be seen that $D_t = X_t - I_t$ and

$$V_0 = \sum_{t=0}^{\infty} \frac{1}{(1+k)^{t+1}}(X_t - I_t),$$

which is Equation (4.14). With outside financing through the issuance of shares of new common stock, it can be shown that

$$V_0 = \sum_{t=0}^{\infty} \frac{1}{(1+k)^{t+1}}(D_t + V_{t+1} - m_{t+1}{}^* P_{t+1}), \tag{4.20}$$

in which m_{t+1} is the number of new shares issued at price P_{t+1}. For the infinite horizon, the value of the firm is equal to the investments it makes and the new capital it raises, or

$$V_{t+1} - (m_{t+1})(P_{t+1}) = I_t - (X_t - D_t).$$

Thus, Equation (4.20) can also be written as

$$V_0 = \sum_{t=0}^{\infty} \frac{1}{(1+k)^{t+1}}(X_t - I_t),$$

which is same as Equation (4.14).

Given the M&M ideal assumptions, the above result implies irrelevance of dividends because the market value of the dividends provided to the new stockholders must always be precisely the same as the increase in current dividends. This is in direct disagreement with the findings of the discounted cash-flow model, where dividends are a major determinant of value. In this case, dividends have no impact on value, and the firm's investment policy is the most important determinant of value. Security analysis should concern itself with the future investment opportunities of the firm and forget about dividends.

M&M also developed the **stream-earnings approach**, which takes account of the fact that additional capital must be acquired at some cost in order to maintain the stream of future earnings at its current level. The capital to be raised is I_t and its cost is $K\%$ per period thereafter; thus, the current value of the firm under this approach can be stated as

$$V_0 = \sum_{t=0}^{\infty} \frac{1}{(1+k)^{t+1}}(X_t - I_t),$$

which, again, is Equation (4.14).

Because under none of these four theoretical approaches does the term D_t remain in the final valuation expression and because X_t, I_t, and k are assumed to be independent of D_t, M&M conclude that the current value of a firm is independent of its current and future dividend decisions. The amount gained by stockholders is offset exactly by the decline in the market value of their stock. In the short run, this effect is observed when a stock goes ex-dividend — that is, if the market price of the stock falls by the amount of the dividend on the last day, the old shareholders are entitled to receive a dividend payment. The stock's value is then dependent only upon the expected future earnings stream of the firm. Security analysts spend much time and effort forecasting a firm's expected earnings.

While the above analysis ignores the case in which external financing is obtained through the issuance of debt, in such a situation M&M's *position* then rests upon their indifference proposition with respect to leverage (M&M, 1958), discussed elsewhere in this chapter. Since that analysis shows that under a set of assumptions consistent with their "fundamental principal of valuation," the real cost of debt in a world of no taxation is equal to the real cost of equity financing, M&M conclude that the means of external financing used to offset the payment of dividends does not affect their hypothesis that dividends are irrelevant.

Prior to M&M's 1961 article, the classical view held that dividend policy was a major determinant of the value of the corporation and that firms should seek their "optimal payout ratios" to maximize their value. M&M's conclusions about the irrelevance of dividend policy given investment policy, collided head-on with the existing classical view. The view that the value of the firm is independent of dividend policy also extends into a world with corporate taxes but without personal taxes.

4.4.1. *Review and Extension of M&M Proposition I*

The existence of optimal capital structure has become one of the important issues for academicians and practitioners in finance. While classical finance theorists argue that there is an optimal capital structure for a firm, the new classical financial theory developed by M&M (1958, 1963) has cast doubt upon the existence of such an optimal structure. The specific assumptions that they made, consistent with the dividend irrelevance analysis previously outlined, include:

(1) Capital markets are perfect (frictionless).
(2) Both individuals and firms can borrow and lend at the risk-free rate.
(3) Firms use risk-free debt and risky equity.
(4) There are only corporate taxes (i.e., there are no wealth taxes or personal income taxes).
(5) All cash flow streams are perpetuities (i.e., no growth).

Developing the additional concepts of risk class and homemade leverage, M&M derived their well-known **Proposition I**, both with and without corporate taxes.[2]

If all firms are in the same risk class, then their expected risky future net operating cash flow ($\dot{X}$) varies only by a scale factor. Under this circumstance, the correlation between two firms' net operating income (NOI) within a risk class should be equal to 1.0. This implies that the rates of return will be equal for all firms in the same risk class, that is

$$R_{it} = \frac{\dot{X}_{it} - \dot{X}_{it-1}}{\dot{X}_{it-1}}, \tag{4.21}$$

[2]In 1985, Franco Modigliani won the Nobel Prize for his work on the life cycle of savings and his contribution to what has become known as the M&M theory, discussed in this section.

and because $\dot{X}_{it} = C\dot{X}_{jt}$, where C is the scale factor:

$$R_{jt} = \frac{C\dot{X}_{jt} - C\dot{X}_{jt}}{C\dot{X}_{jt-1}} = R_{it}, \tag{4.22}$$

in which R_{it} and R_{jt} are rates of return for the ith and jth firms, respectively. Therefore, if two streams of cash flow differ by only a scale factor, they will have the same distributions of returns and the same risk, and they will require the same expected return.

The concept of **homemade leverage** is used to refer to the leverage created by individual investors who sell their own debt while **corporate leverage** is used to refer to the debt floated by the corporation. Using the assumption that the cost of homemade leverage is equal to the cost of corporate leverage, M&M (1958) derived their Proposition I both with and without taxes. However, the Proposition I with taxes was not correct, and they subsequently corrected this result in their 1963 paper. Mathematically, M&M's Proposition I can be defined as

$$V_j = (S_j + B_j) = X_j/\rho_k, \tag{4.23}$$

and Proposition I with taxes can be defined as

$$V_j^L = \frac{(1-\tau_j)X_j}{\rho_k^\tau} + \frac{\tau I_j}{r} = V_j^U + \tau B_j. \tag{4.24}$$

In Equation (4.23), B_j, S_j, and V_j are the market value of debt, common shares, and the firm, respectively; X_j is the expected profit before deduction of interest, ρ_k the required rate of return or the cost of capital in risk class k. In Equation (4.24), ρ_k^τ is the required rate of return used to capitalize the expected returns net of tax for the unlevered firm with long-run average earnings before tax and interest of (X_j) in risk class k; τ_j is the corporate tax rate for the jth firm, I_j is the total interest expense for the jth firm, and r is the market interest rate used to capitalize the certain cash inflows generated by risk-free debt; B_j is total risk-free debt floated by the jth firm, and V^L and V^U are the market values of the leveraged and unleveraged firms, respectively.

By comparing these two equations, we find that the advantages of a firm with leverage will increase that firm's value by $\tau_j B_j$ — that is, the corporate tax rate times the total debt floated by that firm. One of the important implications of this proposition is that there is no optimal capital structure for the firm unless there are bankruptcy costs associated with its debt flotation. If there are bankruptcy costs, then a firm will issue debt until its tax benefit is equal to the bankruptcy cost, thus providing, in such a case, an optimal capital structure for the firm. In addition to the bankruptcy costs, information signaling (see Leland and Pyle (1977) and Ross (1977)) and differential expectations between shareholders and bondholders can be used to justify the possible existence of an optimal structure of a firm. The existence of optimal capital structure is an important issue for security analysts to investigate because it affects the value of the firm and the value of the firm's securities. Is a firm with a high level of debt more valuable than a similar firm with very little debt? M&M say either it does not matter or that the highly leveraged firm is more valuable.

The important assumptions used to prove the M&M Proposition I with taxes are that (1) there are no transaction costs; (2) homemade leverage is equal to corporate leverage; (3) corporate debt is riskless; and (4) there is no bankruptcy cost. Overall, M&M's Proposition I implies that there is no optimal capital structure. If there is a tax structure that systematically provides a lower after-tax real cost of debt relative to the after-tax real cost of equity, the corporation will maximize the proportion of debt in their capital structure and will issue as much debt as possible to maximize the tax shield associated with the deductibility of interest.

Stiglitz (1969) extends M&M's proposition using a general equilibrium state preference framework. He is able to show that M&M's results do not depend on risk classes, competitive capital markets, or agreement by investors. The only two fundamental assumptions are that there is no bankruptcy and individuals can borrow at the same rate as firms. Stiglitz (1974) develops the argument that there may exist a determinate debt-equity ratio for the economy as a whole, but not for the individual firm.

4.4.2. *Miller's Proposition on Debt and Taxes*

Miller (1977) argues that although there is no optimal capital structure for an individual firm, in the aggregate case there may be an optimal structure. In balancing bankruptcy cost against tax shelter, an optimal capital structure is derived, just as the classical view has always maintained.

The Tax Reform Act of 1986 taxes dividends and long-term capital gains at the same top rate of 28%. This is a major change from the old 50% rate on dividends and 20% rate on long-term capital gains. The new tax bill has also shifted the major tax burden to corporations and away from individuals. Even though the maximum corporate tax rate will decrease to

34% from the current top rate of 46%, corporations will be paying more taxes because of the loss of the Investment Tax Credits and the Accelerated Cost Recovery System depreciation allowances.

These changes in the tax code will shift the emphasis of corporate management from retaining earnings in order to generate price appreciation and capital gains to the payout of corporate funds in the form of dividends.

In his presidential address at the Annual Meeting of the American Finance Association, Merton Miller (1977) incorporates personal taxes into the M&M (1958, 1963) argument for the relationship between the firm's leverage and cost of capital.

M&M's Proposition I shows that the value of the leveraged firm equals the value of the unleveraged firm plus the tax shield associated with interest payments, as shown by Equation (4.24):

$$V^L = V^U + t_C B, \tag{4.24}$$

where

V^L = the value of the leveraged firm;
V^U = the value of the unleveraged firm;
t_c = the corporate tax rate; and
B = the value of the firm's debt.

Miller generalizes the M&M relationship shown in Equation (4.24) to include personal taxes on dividends and capital gains as well as taxes on interest income, to yield:

$$V^L = V^U + \left[1 - \frac{(1 - t_C)(1 - t_{ps})}{(1 - t_{pB})}\right] B, \tag{4.25}$$

in which t_{ps} is the personal tax rate on income from stock and t_{pB} is the personal tax rate on income from bonds.

Using Equation (4.25) and the assumption of market equilibrium, and the fact that individual investors can defer income on stocks indefinitely (or that there exists a group of investors who are tax exempt, namely $t_{ps} = 0$). Miller argues that for the economy as a whole there is an optimal amount of debt, but for individual firms there is no optimal capital structure. Using Equation (4.25) the impact on firm value caused by the tax code changes embodied in the Tax Reform Act of 1986 was examined.

In general, by using the 1963 M&M relationship and the 1977 Miller relationship for tax shields, we can identify an upper and lower bound for

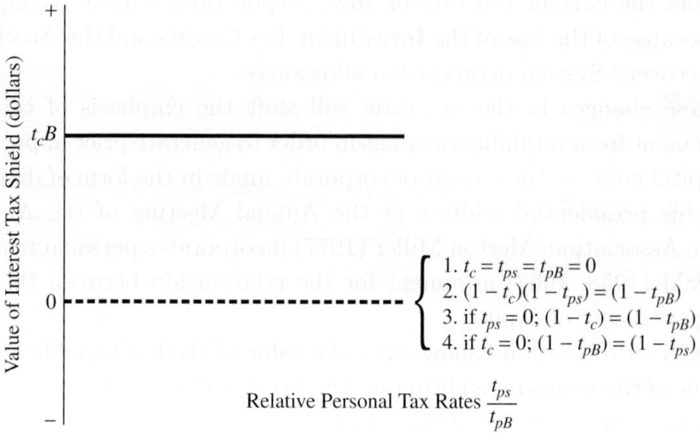

Fig. 4.2. Upper and Lower Bounds on the Value of Interest Tax Shelter.

the change in value associated with interest tax shields. These upper and lower bounds are shown in Fig. 4.2.

The upper bound is defined by the M&M arguments as t_cB — or, as discussed by Miller, the case where equity and debt income are taxed at the same rate. The lower bound is zero, which can occur under four circumstances, labeled 1 through 4 in Fig. 4.2. If there is no corporate or personal tax then there is no tax shield from interest deductibility. Case 2 shows that if the product of the after-tax factors for corporate and personal tax on equals the after-tax factor for debt, then the term

$$\frac{(1 - t_c)(1 - t_{ps})}{1 - t_{pB}}$$

equals one and the tax shield has zero value. This means that the after-tax cost of equity is equal to the after-tax cost of debt; it is highly unlikely that this could occur and so it is only shown as a feasible reason for a zero value of the tax shield. Cases 3 and 4 are of more practical interest: although not addressed directly in Miller's article, they serve as the limiting case to discuss the relationship between personal tax on equity and bond income and the size of the interest tax shield. Case 3 can be generalized to $t_{ps} < t_{pB}$ (the tax on equity income is less than the tax on equity income), and case 4 to $t_{pB} < t_{ps}$ (the tax on bond income is less than the tax on equity income).

In Fig. 4.2 the x- (horizontal) axis is defined as the relative personal tax rate, that is, the ratio of t_{ps} to t_{pB}. Three situations for the value of t_{ps}/t_{pB} are considered: it may be (1) less than one, (2) equal to one, or

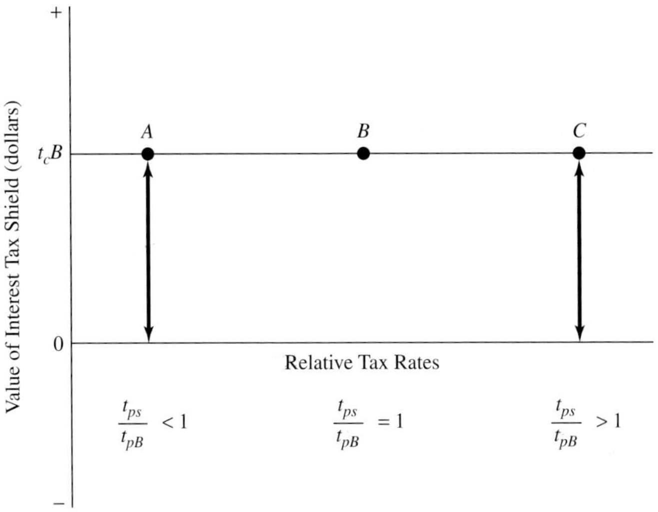

Fig. 4.3. The Relationship between t_{ps} and t_{pB} and the Value of the Tax Shield on Interest.

(3) greater than one. These three cases are shown in Fig. 4.3 by the letters A, B, and C.

Case A. In this situation, if $t_{pB} > t_{ps}$, the tax rate on debt income will be higher than the tax rate on stock income, which was quite feasible under the old tax system where capital gains received preferential tax treatment. The value of the tax shield could be almost as high as the upper bound. To the other extreme, the tax shield could be zero or even negative if t_{ps} was very large and t_{pB} was close to zero. Clearly, if the tax shield became negative, corporations would cease issuing debt securities — so zero is actually the lower bound of this case.

Case B. If the taxation on bond income is the same as the taxation of stock income, the value of the tax shield under Miller's approach will equal the original M&M value of t_cB, as shown by case B in Fig. 4.3.

Case C. Finally, if the personal tax on stock income is higher than the personal tax on bond income, a range of values for the tax shield on interest is possible, as shown by C in Fig. 4.3. The lower end of the range approaches zero for small values of t_{pB} and large values of t_{ps}. If the tax rate on equity is very high and the tax rate on bonds is very low, the value of the tax shield will approach zero. At the upper end of the range, if the tax rate on equity income is only slightly larger than the tax rate on debt income, the value of the interest tax shield will approach $t_c B$.

4.5. The Tax Reform Act of 1986 and Its Impact on Firm Value

Before the Tax Reform Act of 1986, the situation was generally similar to Case A. The tax rate on equity income was less than the tax rate on debt income. This can be shown to be true for two reasons: (1) the capital-gains portion of equity income was taxed at relatively low rates (i.e., 20% maximum), and (2) the equity investors could defer the realization of capital gains indefinitely (i.e., they were taxed at a zero rate). In either case, the tax rate on equity income was lower than the tax rate on debt income. One of the provisions of the Tax Reform Act was to abolish the preferential treatment for capital-gains income. By itself this would cause t_{ps} to move toward equality with t_{pB}, and the situation would be approaching that of Case B.

Another aspect of the Tax Reform Act was to lower the marginal corporate tax rate. By itself this would tend to lower the upper bound or reduce the value of the tax shield on interest. However, this reduction in the corporate tax rate was offset by a reduction in many of the tax credits that were formerly available to corporations. Therefore, it would appear that even though the benefit derived from the tax shield on interest is being reduced, the number and value of other tax shields are also being reduced or eliminated; this would in general cause the interest tax shield to be more highly valued because of the scarcity of other tax shields. The increase in the interest tax-shield value can be accomplished by the corporation issuing more bonds, thereby increasing the value of B in the relationship $t_c B$. Even though t_c is going down, the decrease can be offset by an increase in B. The actual change in the value of the tax shield of interest is an empirical question, but it appears that because of risk considerations, the decrease in t_c will have a greater impact than the possible offsetting increase in B. Therefore, the upper bound on the value of the interest tax shield will undoubtedly shift downward.

Considering these changes in the tax code — reduction of personal rates, equaling of personal tax rate on bond and equity income, and the reduction in the corporate tax rate — we envision the following scenario. Figure 4.4 illustrates the general position of the value of the interest tax shield up to the end of 1986. The upper bound is the value of the tax shield

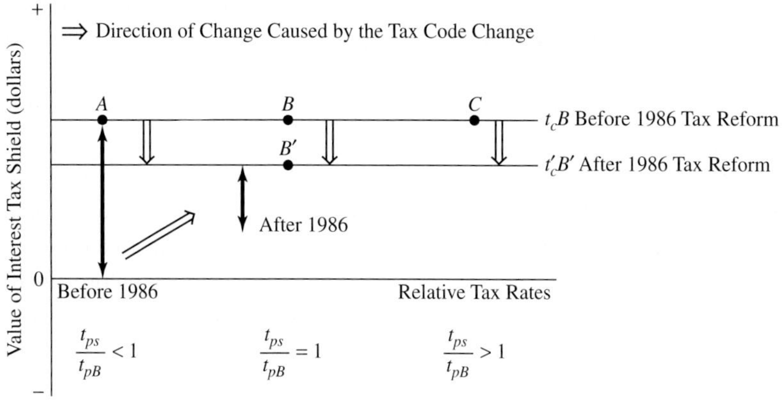

Fig. 4.4. The Impact of the Tax Reform Act of 1986 on the Value of the Interest Tax Shield.

of t_cB, and the situation is as in Case A. The reduction in the tax rate on corporations will reduce the upper bound of the tax shield to t'_cB'. The elimination of the preferential treatment of capital gains will lead from a Case A situation to a Case B situation. However, the fact that investors can still defer capital gains will prevent t_{ps} from equaling t_{pB} exactly, so a Case B situation will not be totally achieved.

4.6. Corporate Response to the Tax Reform Act of 1986

The Tax Reform Act of 1986 raises the after-tax cost to borrow and invest for both individuals and businesses. Hence the new tax law will cause investors to place more importance on dividends, at the same time reducing the amount of investment of firms, thereby allowing them to increase dividends.

But dividends will still remain inferior to capital gains from the perspective of certain taxpayers because of the double taxation problem. Dividends are paid out of corporate profits on an after-tax basis, and then the dividend income is taxed a second time for certain recipients. In contrast, if a firm reinvests the cash flows and causes the firm to gain in price, the investor will receive a capital gain because of price appreciation. The tax on the capital gain can be deferred by the investor until some future time, which is an advantage.

Firms faced with substantial capital investments in the near future will be placed in a precarious position. As the tax benefits of income tax credit (ITC) and accelerated cost recovery system (ACRS) are eliminated or reduced, the remaining tax shields will become more valuable, even though the reduction in tax rates will reduce the marginal value of the tax shield. Thus a greater reliance on financing corporate needs through the issuance of debt is the predicted trend.

Both of these changes, the dividend effect and the debt increase, will noticeably impact the economy and the financial markets. Additionally, the level of uncertainty for the decision maker concerning tax policy has increased. For example, the ITC has been eliminated twice before since its introduction in 1962, and in both cases it was restored within 1.5 years.

Taggart (1980) introduces uncertainty into the bond's cost (recall that previous work assumed bonds to be risk free). Since costs might stem from several sources, undergoing or attempting to avoid the bankruptcy process may consume real resources; conflicts of interest between shareholders and bondholders could lead to suboptimal decisions from the firm's standpoint, and negotiation and enforcement of debt contracts might be costly. Taggart extends Miller's analysis of the relationship between tax considerations and corporate capital structures to conditions of incomplete capital markets and special costs associated with corporate debt. Unlike Miller's model, however, the capital structure of any one firm is not found to be a matter of indifference to all shareholders at a market equilibrium. This is attributable in part to the costs of debt, which dictate a tendency for more debt to be issued by those firms with lower costs. With the introduction of uncertainty, corporate shares and tax-exempt bonds are no longer perfect substitutes. Therefore, two distinct clienteles emerge, one demanding that firms have as much debt as possible, and one demanding firms have as little debt as possible. Firms in a given risk class would move to one or the other extreme in proportion to the relative demands from the two clienteles. In the presence of debt costs, the high-leverage firms will be those with the lowest debt costs.

DeAngelo and Masulis (1980) extend Miller's (1977) analysis to include other tax shields, such as depreciation and investment tax credit. They find that a constant marginal personal tax on debt versus declining marginal corporate tax savings from leverage leads to an optimum degree of leverage, which equates the marginal personal tax cost and the marginal corporate tax benefit. The marginal corporate tax benefit declines as more debt is added to the capital structure, because of the probability of at least partial loss of the debt tax shield in the presence of corporate tax shield substitutes for debt and existing debt tax shield, since there is a ceiling on the total use of tax shields. This optimum degree of leverage is a unique interior solution in market equilibrium.

Shelton (1981) contests the M&M assumption that homemade leverage is equal to corporate leverage. He calls this "equal access" and points out that, in reality, corporations have better access to the debt markets than individuals. Individuals must pay a premium in the market as a result of the information asymmetry about their capacity and willingness to repay. This unequal access, in combination with the fact that individuals in differing tax brackets benefit in varying ways from the corporate leverage, complicates M&M's analysis. The implication is that individuals cannot recreate the same position by buying the unleveraged firm and issuing their own debt as they could obtain by buying the stock of a leveraged firm. Since M&M's assumptions generally do not hold, it can be shown that there is an optimum debt for a corporation. Barnea *et al.* (1981) use market imperfections and agency costs to show that an optimal structure consistent with the classical financial theory does exist. Hence, the choice of an optimal amount of debt is an important issue in security analysis and portfolio management.

For the no-tax version, it appears that M&M are ignoring the fact that within prudent ranges of usage, debt is a low-cost source of funds. Nevertheless, M&M's argument here is that the increase in perceived financial risk with an increase of debt in the capital structure will cause an increase in required rate of return for the equity holders of the firm that will just offset the use of more low-cost debt capital. When corporate taxes are assumed, however, the tax deductibility of interest payments leads to the implication within their model that the firm should use as much debt as possible (see Equation (4.24)). The reason for this apparently extreme result is their original assumption of no bankruptcy costs. Since in reality bankruptcy costs are quite large, use of imprudent levels of debt would be so costly that an optimal capital structure is still implied.

The important implications of this section for security analysts are that dividend policy and leverage policy may not be as significant in the determination of the market value of the firm as originally assumed, and that primary emphasis should be put on the investment policy of the firm. The impact of dividend policy seems to be closely involved with the information content included in the dividend decisions of management, as the same valuation can be determined using approaches that do not specifically include dividends. The impact of debt leverage is heavily dependent upon the tax laws concerning the deductibility of interest payments. The degree of financial leverage observed empirically varies substantially from industry to industry and even between firms in the same industry, depending largely upon the coexistent degree of operating leverage and the level of sales volatility. Firms with relatively low business risk are able to support a high percentage of debt in their capital structure, and firms with relatively high business risk cannot.

4.7. Capital Asset Pricing Model

At about the same time as M&M were developing their work, developments in portfolio theory were leading to a model describing the formation of capital asset prices in world of uncertainty: the **CAPM**.

The CAPM is a generalized version of M&M theory in which M&M theory is provided with a link to the market:

$$E(R_j) = R_f + \beta_j[E(R_m) - R_f], \tag{4.26}$$

where

R_j = the rate of return for security j;
β_j = a volatility measure relating the rate of return on security j with that of the market over time;
R_m = the rate of return for the overall market (typically measured by the rate of return reflected by a market index, such as the S&P 500); and
R_f = the risk-free rate available in the market (usually the rate of return on U.S. Treasury bills is used as a proxy).

In the CAPM framework, the valuation of a company's securities is dependent not only upon their cash flows but also upon those of other securities available for investment. It is assumed that much of the total risk, as measured by standard deviation of return, can be diversified away by combining the stock of a firm being analyzed with those of other companies. Unless the cash flows from these securities are perfectly positively correlated, smoothing or diversification will take place. Thus, the security return can be divided into two components: a systematic component that is perfectly correlated with the overall market return and an unsystematic component that is independent of the market return:

$$\text{Security return} = \text{Systematic return} + \text{Unsystematic return}. \tag{4.27}$$

Since the security return is perfectly correlated with the market return, it can be expressed as a constant, **beta**, multiplied by the market return

(R_m). The beta is a volatility index, measuring the sensitivity of the security return to changes in the market return. The unsystematic return is residual of the relationship of R_j with R_m.

As has been previously noted, the standard deviation of the probability distribution of a security's rate of return is considered to be an appropriate measure of the total risk of that security. This total risk can be broken down into systematic and unsystematic components, just as noted above for security return:

$$\text{Total security risk} = \text{Systematic risk} + \text{Unsystematic risk.} \tag{4.28}$$

Diversification is achieved only when securities that are not perfectly correlated with one other are combined. The unsystematic risk components tend to cancel each other since they are all residuals from the relationship of security returns with the overall market return. In the process; the portfolio risk measure declines without any corresponding lowering of portfolio return (see Fig. 4.5). It is assumed in this illustration that the selection of additional securities as the portfolio size is increased is performed in some random manner, although any selection process other than intentionally choosing perfectly correlated securities will suffice. Unsystematic risk is shown to be gradually eliminated until the portfolio risk is completely market related. While for an actual portfolio the systematic risk will not remain constant as securities are added, the

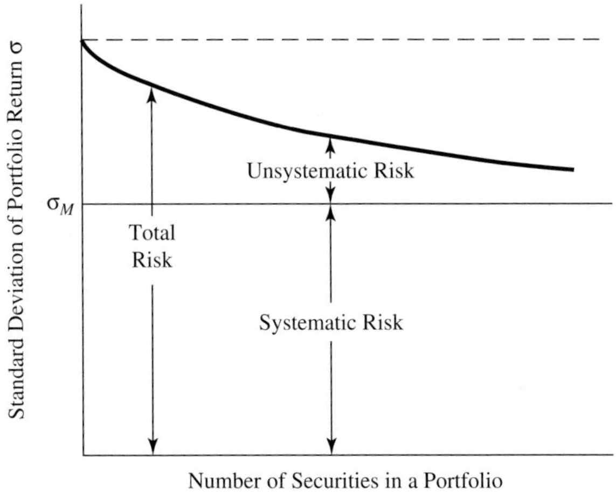

Fig. 4.5. Diversification Process.

intent is to show that the unsystematic-risk portion can be diversified away, leaving the market-related systematic portion as the only relevant measure of risk. Empirical studies have shown that a portfolio of about 20 securities not highly correlated with one another will provide a high degree of diversification. Although capital-market theory assumes that all investors will hold the market portfolio, it is neither necessary nor realistic to assume that all investors will be satisfied with the market level of risk. There are basically two ways that investors can adjust their risk level within the CAPM theoretical framework. First, funds for investment can be divided between the market portfolio and risk-free securities. The capital-market line (CML) is derived assuming such a trade-off function.

This is illustrated in Fig. 4.6, in which point M is the market portfolio and points on the CML below and above M imply lending and borrowing at the risk-free rate, respectively. The second way of adjusting the portfolio risk level is by investing in a fully diversified portfolio of securities (i.e., the correlation coefficient of the portfolio with the market, r_{pm} is equal to 1.0) that has a weighted average beta equal to the systematic-risk level desired:

$$\beta_p = \sum_{j=1}^{n} W_j B_j, \tag{4.29}$$

in which W_j is the proportion of total funds invested in security j. Since in the CAPM systematic risk as measured by beta is the only risk that need be undertaken, it follows that no risk premium should be expected for the bearing of unsystematic risk. With that in mind, the relationship between expected return and risk can be better defined through the illustration

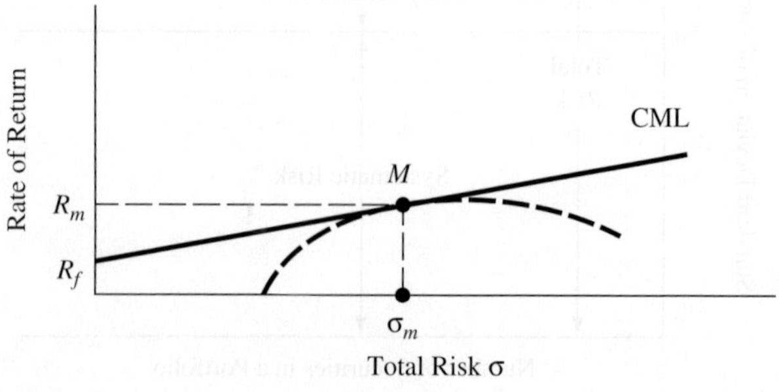

Fig. 4.6. Capital-Market Line.

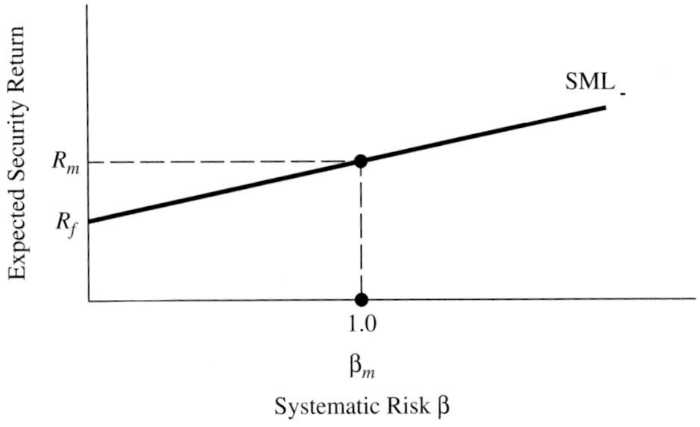

Fig. 4.7. Security-Market Line.

of the security-market line (SML) in Fig. 4.7 in which R_m and β_m are the expected return and risk level of the market portfolio, respectively. In equilibrium, all securities and combinations of securities are expected to lie along this line. In contrast, only fully diversified portfolios would be expected to fall along the CML, because only with full diversification is total risk equal to systematic risk alone. Sample Problem 4.4 provides further illustration, and a much more detailed description of the use of CAPM in making investment decisions is included in later chapters of this book.

Sample Problem 4.4

The following is known about the market and LBO, Inc.:

$$\text{Three-month } T\text{-bill rate} = 8\%$$

$$\text{Expected return on the S\&P 500} = 11\%$$

$$\text{Estimated beat for LBO's stock} = 1.5$$

Substituting into Equation (4.26) solves for the expected return on LBO's stock.

Solution

$$\begin{aligned} E(R_{\text{LBO}}) &= 8\% + 1.5(11\% - 8\%) \\ &= 12.5\% \end{aligned}$$

4.8. Option Valuation

Option contracts give their holders the right to buy and sell a specific asset at some specified price on or before a specified date. Since these contracts can be valued in relation to common stock, the basic concepts involved have a number of applications to financial theory and to the valuation of other financial instruments. (A more theoretical discussion of option pricing theory is included in Chapters 14 and 15.)

While there are a variety of option contracts — for example, call options, put options, combinations of calls and puts, convertible securities, and warrants — this chapter's discussion is limited to **call options**. A call option gives the holder the right to buy a share of stock at a specified price, known as the exercise price, and the basic American option can be exercised at any time through the expiration date. The value of the option at expiration is the difference between the market price of the underlying stock and its exercise price (with a minimum value of zero, of course).

While several factors affect the value of an option, the most important factor is the price volatility of the stock — the greater the volatility, the greater the value of the option, other things remaining the same. We will also note that the longer the time left before expiration and the higher the level of interest rates in the market, the greater the option value, all other things held the same.

The theoretical value of a call option at expiration is the difference between the market price of the underlying common stock, p_s, and the exercise price of the option, E, or zero, whichever is greater:

$$C = \text{Max}(P_s - E, 0). \tag{4.30}$$

When the price of the stock is greater than the exercise price, the option has a positive theoretical value which will increase dollar for dollar with the price of the stock. When the market price of the stock is equal to or less than the exercise price, the option has a theoretical value of zero, as shown in Fig. 4.8. Nevertheless, as long as some time remains before expiration, the actual market price of the option (referred to as the option premium at the time of issue) is likely to be greater than its theoretical value. This increment above the theoretical value is called the *time value* or *speculative value* of the option, and its size will depend primarily on the perceived likelihood of a profitable move on the price of the stock before expiration of the option. Sample Problem 4.5 provides further illustration.

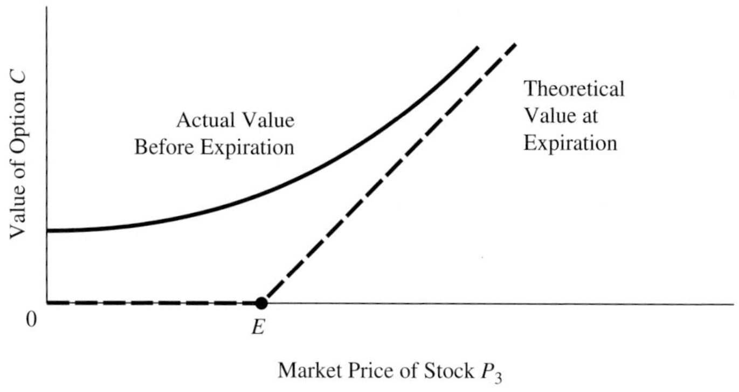

Fig. 4.8. Theoretical and Actual Values of a Call Option.

Sample Problem 4.5

A call option written on LBO, Inc.'s stock has an exercise price of \$95. Calculate the value of the call option when the option expires if the price of the stock at expiration is (a) \$106, (b) \$92.

Solution

According to Equation (4.30), the call option can take on only two values. If the call option expires "in the money," its value will be the difference between the stock price and the exercise price. If the call option expires "out of the money," its value will be equal to zero because the option holder does not have to exercise this option.

(a) Call expires "in the money":

$$\begin{aligned} C &= \$106 - \$95 \\ &= \$11 \end{aligned}$$

(b) Call expires "out of the money," so option will not be exercised:

$$C = \$0$$

The full range of possible values for the market price of the option is from the theoretical value on the low side to the market price of the stock itself on the high side. For the option price to be equal to the stock price, an infinite time to expiration would be implied. For the option price to be equal to the theoretical value only, imminent expiration would be implied. For virtually all options for which the value would be determined, however, the option price would fall somewhere between these two extremes. Because an option costs less than its underlying stock, the percentage change in option price is greater than the percentage change in stock price, given some increase in the market price of the stock. Thus, a leveraged rate of return can be earned by investment in the option rather than the stock. As stock price continues to increase, the difference between the percentage change in option price and the percentage change in stock price will tend to converge.

Thus far it has been shown that the value of an option will be a function of the underlying stock price, the exercise price of the option, and the time to maturity. Yet there is still another factor that is probably the single most important variable affecting the speculative value of the option. That is the **price volatility** of the underlying stock. The greater the probability of significant change in the price of the stock, the more likely it is that the option can be exercised at a profit before expiration. Sample Problem 4.6 provides further illustration.

Sample Problem 4.6

At the beginning of some time period, investment may be considered in options on stock A and stock B, both of which have an exercise price of \$48. If the probabilities of stock price at the end of the period are as indicated in Table 4.1, the theoretical values of option A and option B can also be determined using Equation (4.29). While the expected value of the stock prices for A and B is the same, \$50, the expected theoretical values are \$3.40 for option A and \$5.40 for option B.

$$\begin{aligned}\text{Option A} &= (0)(0.1) + (0)(0.2) + (2)(0.4) + (7)(0.2) + (12)(0.1)\\ &= \$3.40.\\ \text{Option B} &= (0)(0.1) + (0)(0.2) + (2)(0.4) + (12)(0.2) + (22)(0.1)\\ &= \$5.40.\end{aligned}$$

Table 4.1. Stock Price and Option Price.

Probability	0.1	0.2	0.4	0.2	0.1
Price of stock A (\$)	40	45	50	55	60
Theoretical value of option A (\$)	0	0	2	7	12
Price of stock B (\$)	30	40	50	60	70
Theoretical value of option B (\$)	0	0	2	2	22

Exercise price of option A = Exercise price of option B = \$48

The greater expected value of the option with greater stock-price volatility that is shown, therefore, results from the fact that the value of an option cannot be less than zero. Consequently, the value of an option is not a function of the expected value of the stock price at a point in time but a function of the volatility of stock price.

There is another factor affecting the speculative premium for options. This is the level of interest rates in the market — specifically for option analysis, the *call money* rate charged by brokers for the use of margin in common-stock accounts. As this concept is discussed later, it is sufficient here to point out that the leverage achieved through option investment is similar to that achieved through direct margin purchase of the underlying common stock, but without the explicit interest cost involved in the latter. Thus, the higher the call money rate, the greater the savings from the use of options and the greater the speculative value of the option.

To summarize, there are five variables necessary to determine the value of an American call option (ignoring dividends on the common stock, the effect of which is discussed in Chapter 14):

1. Stock price and 2. *Exercise price*: The relationship between these two prices determines whether the option has a positive theoretical value.
3. *Time to maturity*: The longer the time to maturity, the greater the speculative value of the option because the chances for a profitable movement in the price of the stock are increased.
4. *Volatility of stock price*: There is a positive relationship between the volatility of the underlying stock price and the speculative value of the option because with greater volatility, there is greater potential for gain on the upside and greater benefit from the downside protection involved with the option.
5. *Interest rate*: The higher the call money rate for direct margin purchase of common stock, the greater the relative value of being able to achieve equal amounts of leverage through the alternative of option purchase.

The factors that affect the value of an option can be written in a functional form:

$$C = f(S, X, \sigma^2, T, r_f), \tag{4.31}$$

where

C = value of the option;
S = stock price;

X = exercise price;
σ^2 = variance of the stock;
T = time to expiration; and
r_f = risk-free rate.

The value of the option increases as a function of the value of the stock for a given exercise price and maturity date — the lower the exercise price, the greater the value of the option; and the longer the time to maturity, the higher the value of the option. The holder of an option will prefer more variance in the price of the stock. The greater the variance (price volatility) the greater the probability that the stock price will exceed the exercise price and thus benefit the holder.

Considering two related financial securities — common stock and the option on the common stock — it is possible to illustrate how a risk-free hedged position can be developed. In this way, unprofitable price movements in one of the securities will be offset by profitable price movements in the other. The hedge ratio determines the portion of stock held long in relation to the options in the short position (or vice-versa). With a complete hedge, the value of the hedged position can be shown to be the same regardless of the stock-price outcome. In efficient financial markets, the rate of return earned on perfectly hedged positions will be the risk-free rate. Consequently, it is then possible to determine the appropriate option price at the beginning of the period. If the actual market price is above or below this value, arbitrage would then drive the option price toward its correct level. In Chapter 14, this process and the development of the Black and Scholes (1973) continuous type of option-pricing model and Cox *et al.*'s (1979) discrete type of binomial option-pricing model will be analyzed in some detail. Option pricing models and their applications are discussed (in great detail) in Chapters 14, 15, and 21.

4.9. Summary

This chapter has reviewed and summarized four alternative valuation theories — discounted cash flow, M&M, CAPM, and OPT — which are basic to introductory course in financial management or investments. These theories can directly and indirectly become guidelines for further study of security analysis and portfolio management. Derivations and applications of CAPM and OPT to security analysis and portfolio management are studied in detail in later chapters.

Question and Problems

1. What is arbitrage? Why is it such an important concept in security analysis and portfolio management?
2. Calculate the value of a security that will pay \$10/year in perpetuity, if investors require an 8% return.
3. Calculate the value of a bond that has an annual coupon rate of 9% and a maturity value of \$1,000. Assume the bond matures in five years and that bondholders require an 11% return.
4. What is a callable bond? Other things being equal, which bond will have greater value, a callable bond or a noncallable bond?
5. Evaluate the following statement: "Because investors purchase a security for its expected cash flow, the dividend policy of a firm will affect the value of the firm's stock."
6. You are given the following information:

$$\text{Return on three-month T-bills} = 6\%$$
$$\text{Expected return on S\&P 500} = 9\%$$

   (a) Draw the security-market line.
   (b) Calculate the expected rate of return on a stock with a beta equal to 1.5.

7. Define the following terms:

   (a) call option
   (b) put option
   (c) exercise price.

8. What are the advantages of purchasing a call option on IBM stock rather than purchasing the stock itself? Are there any disadvantages?
9. Evaluate the following statement: "Because most individuals dislike risk, the higher the variance of IBM's stock price, the lower the value of put and call options written on IBM's stock."
10. What is the call money rate? Carefully explain the relationship between the call money rate and the value of an option.
11. What is a perpetuity? What would a bond that pays \$110 per year in perpetuity be worth if bondholders required a 12% return?
12. Briefly explain M&M's Proposition I and its importance to modern financial theory.

Bibliography

Black, F. and M. Scholes. "The Pricing of Options and Corporate Liabilities." *Journal of Political Economy*, v. 81 (May–June 1973), pp. 637–654.

Barnea, A., R. A. Haugen and L. W. Senbet. "Market Imperfections, Agency Problems, and Capital Structure: A Review." *Financial Management*, v. 10 (Summer 1981), pp. 7–22.

Beranek, W. "Research Directions in Finance." *Quarterly Journal of Economics and Business*, v. 21 (Spring 1981), pp. 6–24.

Bodie, Z., A. Kane and A. Marcus. *Investments*, 9th ed. New York, NY: McGraw-Hill/Irwin, 2010.

Brealey, R. and S. Myers. *Principles of Corporate Finance.* New York, NY: McGraw-Hill Book Company, 1988.

Brigham, E. F. *Financial Management: Theory and Practice*, 4th ed. Orlando, FL: Dryden Press, 1988.

Copeland, T. E. and J. F. Weston. *Financial Theory and Corporate Policy*, 4th ed. Reading, MA: Addison-Wesley Publishing Company, 2004.

Cox, J. C., S. A. Ross and M. Rubinstein. "Option Pricing: A Simplified Approach." *Journal of Financial Economics*, v. 7 (September 1979), pp. 229–263.

DeAngelo, H. and L. DeAngelo. "The Irrelevance of the MM Dividend Irrelevance Theorem." *Journal of Financial Economics*, v. 79 (2006), pp. 293–315.

DeAngelo, H. and R. W. Masulis. "Optimal Capital Structure Under Corporate and Personal Taxation." *Journal of Financial Economics*, v. 8 (March 1980), pp. 3–29.

Fama, E. F. and M. H. Miller. *Theory of Finance.* New York, NY: Holt, Rinehart and Winston, 1972.

Galai, D. and R. W. Masulis. "The Option Pricing Model and the Risk Factor of Stock." *Journal of Financial Economics*, v. 3 (March 1976), pp. 53–81.

Haley, C. W. and L. D. Schall. *Theory of Financial Decision*, 2nd ed. New York, NY: McGraw-Hill Book Company, 1979.

Hsia, C. C. "Coherence of the Modern Theories of Finance." *The Financial Review*, v. 16 (Winter 1981), pp. 27–42.

Jensen, M. C. and W. H. Meckling. "Can the Corporation Survive?" *Financial Analysts Journal*, v. 34 (January/February 1978), pp. 31–37.

Lee, A. C., J. C. Lee and C. F. Lee, *Financial Analysis, Planning and Forecasting: Theory and Application*, 2nd ed. Hackensack, NJ and Singapore: World Scientific, 2009.

Lee, C. F. *Financial Analysis and Planning: Theory and Application. A Book of Readings.* Reading, MA: Addison-Wesley Publishing Company, 1983.

Lee, C. F. *Financial Analysis and Planning: Theory and Applications.* Reading, MA: Addison-Wesley Publishing Company, 1985.

Lee, C. F. and J. E. Finnerty. *Corporate Finance: Theory, Method, and Applications.* Harcourt Brace Jovanovich, SUA, 1990.

Lee, C. F. and J. C. Junkus. "Financial Analysis and Planning: An Overview." *Journal of Economics and Business*, v. 34 (August 1983), pp. 257–283.

Lee, C. F. and A. C. Lee. *Encyclopedia of Finance.* Berlin, Germany: Springer, 2006.

Lee, C. F., A. C. Lee and J. Lee. *Handbook of Quantitative Finance and Risk Management.* Berlin, Germany: Springer, 2010.

Leland, H. and D. H. Pyle. "Informational Asymmetries, Financial Structure and Financial Intermediation." *Journal of Finance*, v. 32 (September 1977), pp. 371–387.

Mao, J. C. T. *Quantitative Analysis of Financial Decisions.* New York: The Macmillan Company, 1969.

Miller, M. H. "The Modigliani–Miller Proposition after 30 Years." *Journal of Economic Perspectives*, v. 2 (Fall 1988), pp. 99–120.

Miller, M. H. "Debt and Taxes." *Journal of Finance*, v. 32 (May 1977), pp. 101–175.

Miller, M. H. and F. Modigliani. "Dividend Policy Growth and the Valuation of Share." *Journal of Business*, v. 34 (1961), pp. 411–433.

Modigliani, F. and M. Miller. "The Cost of Capital, Corporation Finance and the Theory of Investment." *American Economic Review*, v. 48 (June 1958), pp. 261–297.

Modigliani, F. and M. Miller. "Corporate Income Taxes and the Cost of Capital: A Correction." *American Economic Review*, v. 53 (June 1963), pp. 433–443.

Pogue, G. A. and K. Lull. "Corporate Finance: An Overview." *Sloan Management Review*, v. 15 (Spring 1974), pp. 19–38.

Reilly, F. K. *Investment Analysis and Portfolio Management*, 2nd ed. Orlando, FL: Dryden Press, 1985.

Ross, S. A. "The Determination of Financial Structure: The Incentive Signalling Approach." *Bell Journal of Economics* (Spring 1977), pp. 23–40.

Ross, S., A. R. W. Westerfield and J. Jaffe. *Corporate Finance*, 9th ed. New York, NY: McGraw-Hill/Irwin, 2009.

Ross, S. A., R. W. Westerfield and B. Jordan. *Fundamentals of Corporate Finance*, 9th ed. New York, NY: McGraw-Hill/Irwin, 2009.

Shelton, J. "Equal Access and Miller's Equilibrium." Journal of Financial and Quantitative Analysis, v. 16 (November 1981), pp. 603–623.

Stiglitz, J. E. "A Re-Examination of the Modigliani-miller Theorem." *The American Economic Review*, v. 54 (December 1969), pp. 784–793.

Stiglitz, J. E. "On the Irrelevance of Corporate Financial Policy." *The American Economic Review*, v. 54 (December 1974), pp. 851–866.

Taggart, R. A., Jr. "Taxes and Corporate Capital Structure in an Incomplete Market." *NBER Working Paper* (1980).

van Horne, J. C. *Financial Management and Policy*, 6th ed. New Jersey, NJ: Prentice-Hall, 1985.

Weston, J. F. "Developments in Finance Theory." *Financial Management*, v. 10 (Tenth Anniversary Issue, 1981), pp. 5–22.

Weston, J. F. and T. E. Copeland. *Managerial Finance*, 8th ed. Orlando, FL: Dryden Press, 1986.

Chapter 5

Bond Valuation and Analysis

Of the many investment vehicles available to individuals and portfolio managers, the **bond** is one of the best known and most widely used. While, in general, a bond can be defined as a long-term fixed obligation of an issuer, there are many types of bonds that can be purchased. For example, bonds can vary by the type issuer: U.S. Treasury, federal agencies, municipalities, and corporations. Bonds available in the market also vary according to their maturity, coupon rate, callability, and sinking-fund provisions. These bond fundamentals are discussed in the first section.

The second section focuses on the basic model, which states that an investor's required rate of return on any bond is equal to the risk-free rate plus a risk premium. This risk premium can be quantified using the capital asset pricing model (CAPM) approach. Through the use of market return and beta of the CAPM, we explore the computation and use of bond betas.

In the third section, bond-rating procedures are examined and related to the systematic risk of bonds — that is, the bond beta. Theory and estimation for the term structure of interest rates are the topics of the next section; emphasis is placed on the use of this analysis in making better investment decisions. The fundamentals of convertible-bond investment are included in the final section.

5.1. Bond Fundamentals

Types of issuer and bond provisions are two fundamental factors to consider in analyzing bond valuation.

5.1.1. *Type of Issuer*

Bonds issued by different agencies represent different return and risk. Therefore, it is important to understand the classification of a bond issuer.

5.1.1.1. *U.S. Treasury*

As almost everyone is aware, the U.S. government is a large issuer of debt securities. While much of this debt is in the form of short maturity **Treasury bills (T-bills)**, which are short-term debt obligations of the U.S. government, there are also many T-note or T-bond issues available for purchase. Both **T-notes** and **T-bonds** are long-term, government debt instruments. T-notes have initial maturities of 10 years or less and T-bonds have maturities longer than 10 years. The primary distinguishing factor of federal debt is its virtually nonexistent default risk. At the time of issue, their maturity is 10 years or more, and they carry a coupon rate, which means that a specified amount of interest is paid semiannually over the life of the issue in addition to the face-value repayment at maturity. The Treasury usually has included a five-year-before-maturity call provision, in which the Treasury can call back the bonds from the investors by repaying the principal and any accumulated interest, but the most recent issues have eliminated this provision. By convention, the callable bonds are priced in the market using the first call date as the effective maturity and by using fractions of a 365-day year to compute accumulated interest.

T-bonds are sold on an auction basis through the Federal Reserve banks and their branch offices. They can be on either a registered or bearer basis. While in the case of registered T-bonds the owners' names are recorded in the Treasury's books, thus lowering the risk from theft, bearer bonds are simpler to transfer and have attached coupons, which can be "clipped" and submitted to any bank for collection of the semiannual interest payments as they become due.

In addition to T-bonds, the Treasury also issues short- and intermediate-term marketable securities via T-bills and T-notes. The notes differ from the bonds in terms of initial maturity only. They are limited by law to an original maturity of 1 to 10 years, while T-bonds can have any maturity longer than 10 years. Both tend to be issued for a minimum denomination of $1,000 and pay interest semiannually.

T-bills are highly liquid and free of default risk. They are sold weekly through a competitive-bidding process conducted by the Federal Reserve System. Currently there are three maturity categories: (1) 13 weeks,

Table 5.1. Yield, Time to Maturity, and Coupon Rates for Treasury Bonds and Notes as of February 16, 2011.

(1) R_t	(2) t	(3) x	(1) R_t	(2) t	(3) x	(1) R_t	(2) t	(3) x
0.0618	0.117808	0.875	0.409	1.161644	1.375	0.7933	2	3.875
0.043	0.117808	4.75	0.4309	1.20274	1	0.8481	2.063014	2.75
0.1088	0.2	0.875	0.4157	1.20274	4.5	0.8981	2.10411	1.375
0.1194	0.2	4.875	0.4516	1.243836	1.375	0.8785	2.147945	2.5
0.1154	0.284932	0.875	0.4717	1.287671	0.75	0.9392	2.189041	1.75
0.1096	0.284932	4.875	0.469	1.287671	4.75	0.9126	2.230137	3.125
0.1355	0.367123	1.125	0.4969	1.328767	1.875	0.9895	2.271233	1.375
0.1353	0.367123	5.125	0.5159	1.369863	0.625	0.9264	2.271233	3.625

(2) 26 weeks, and (3) 52 weeks. Bills are sold in minimum denominations of \$10,000 and in multiples of \$5,000, thereafter. Furthermore, they are issued only in book-entry form. Purchases are evidenced by printed receipts.

The **Treasury yield curve** is a widely used tool for investors and traders. Table 5.1 presents the data necessary to determine the yield curve. The yield to maturity (YTM) is defined as the interest rate that equates the current price of a bond or a bill with the present value of the future cash flows that will occur over the life of the bond or bill.

Table 5.1 lists parts of the important information from Table 5A.1 for each government bond issue: the coupon rate (x), the maturity (t), and the YTM (R_t). The information of Table 5.1 can be found from the website of *Wall Street Journal* (http://online.wsj.com/). In the following sections, we will discuss how this kind of data can be used to draw the yield curve and how to forecast the YTM.

The **bid and ask prices** represent the prices at which dealers in government bonds are willing to buy and sell the various T-bonds and T-notes. For T-bills, the bid and ask prices are quoted in terms of discount from par. Suppose, for instance, a bill has 30 days to maturity and it is currently quoted at a discount of 5.8%, its price can be determined by using Equation (5.1):

$$d = \frac{360}{n}\frac{100 - P}{100}, \tag{5.1}$$

where

$d =$ the discount rate;
$n =$ the number of days until maturity; and

P = the price per \$100 of face value of the bill.

$$0.058 = \frac{360}{30}\frac{100 - P}{100}$$

$$P = \$99.517 \text{ per } \$100 \quad \text{of face value}$$

In general, a **bid and ask spread** (the difference at which the market maker or dealer is willing to buy or sell a security) is the price of liquidity service provided by the dealer who bridges the gap between buying and selling in the marketplace. The size of the bid and ask spread is a function of the frequency of trading of the security. More actively traded securities have narrow bid and ask spreads, whereas less actively traded securities have much wider spreads.

Using the data listed in Table 5.1, the yield curve can be constructed; moreover, both the freehand and regression methods can be used to construct the yield curve. These results are discussed in Section 5.4. Figure 5.1 presents the yield curve in terms of the freehand method on March 1, 2011. In Fig. 5.1, the vertical axis represents YTM and the horizontal axis represents the time to maturity.

Usually the yield curve is positive, as shown in Fig. 5.1, with long-term issues yielding more than short-term issues. The higher yield for a 23-year

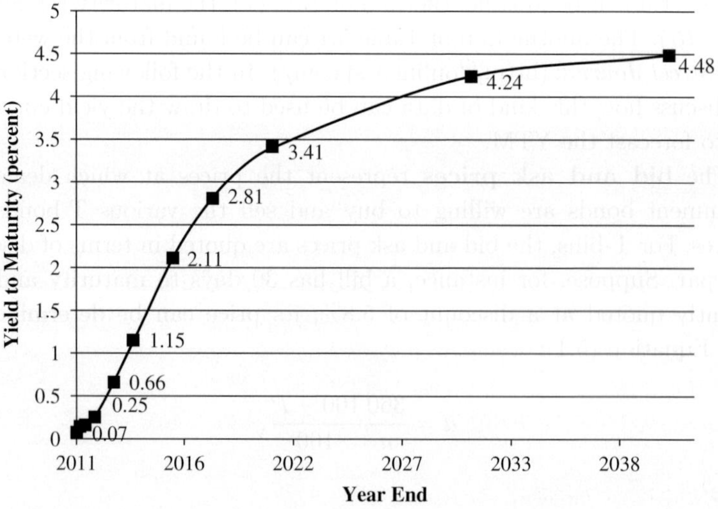

Fig. 5.1. U.S. Government Bond Yield Curve as of March 01, 2011.
Source: U.S. Department of The Treasury, 2011.

bond compared with a three-month bill, for example, would compensate a bond investor for the greater risk of price declines and the uncertainty about the long-term economic outlook.

Investors can use yield curves in several ways. First, although yield curves may not be highly reliable and accurate indicators of future interest rates, they form a consensus of how the market participants think interest rates will move in the future. An upward-sloping yield curve indicates that rates are expected to rise, and a downward-sloping yield curve indicates that rates are expected to fall. Second, the investor can use the yield curve to help select the maturity of his investments. For example, if an investor plans to invest a sum of money for five years, there are many alternative ways to reach this objective — buy a five-year bond and hold it until it matures; buy a one-year bond and, when it matures, buy another one-year bond, and so forth until the desired maturity date is reached; buy a longer-term bond, say 10 years, and sell it after five years have passed. These are three of the many alternative ways that the investor can obtain his or her objective. Analysis of the yield curve can aid the investor in evaluating the profit potential of various strategies.

A third and final use of the yield curve is in identifying individual issues that are either greatly overpriced or underpriced relative to the current yield curve. (For example, if you found a 20-year U.S. government bond yielding 6%, when the yield curve shown in Fig. 5.1 shows similar maturity bonds yielding 3½% to 4%, you undoubtedly would be interested in finding out why this individual bond was priced differently.)

5.1.1.2. *Federal Agencies*

Federal agencies such as the Government National Mortgage Association (GNMA or "Ginny Mae") and government-sponsored enterprises such as the Small Business Administration (SBA) also issue bonds.

Neither type of **agency bond** is a direct obligation of the Treasury even though some agencies are government sponsored or guaranteed. The net effect is that agency bonds are considered almost default-risk free (if not legally so in all cases) and, therefore, are typically priced to provide only a slightly higher yield than their corresponding T-bond counterparts.

5.1.1.3. *Municipalities*

"Municipality" is a general term commonly used to include all nonfederal government entities. Therefore, **municipal bonds** include those issued by states, counties, cities, and state and local government–established authorities (nonfederal agencies).

There are basically only two types of municipal bonds — general-obligation bonds (GOBs) and revenue bonds. **GOBs** are backed by the "full faith and credit" of the issuing governmental unit, which basically means that the unit may tax its constituents to the legal limit, if necessary, to pay the principal and interest on the bonds.

On the other hand, **revenue bonds** are backed only by the revenues generated by the project being financed. The issuing governmental unit is not directly responsible for any debt service on such bonds beyond which it is self-generated. Obviously, since it is a market reality that municipalities with outstanding revenue issues in default will be severely handicapped in securing any future revenue bond financing, investors tend to expect the sponsoring units to cover project revenue shortages. The degree of this expectation varies between municipalities, but the extent to which it exists the yields on revenue bonds will be only slightly higher than those on GOBs.

In recent years, large variability in interest rates has hampered commercial and economic development in the U.S. particularly at the local level. As a result, creative financing plans for such projects as new shopping centers, downtown business redevelopment, and even hotels have include the cooperation of local municipalities, most often city governments. This cooperation has taken the form of city issues of tax-free industrial revenue and economic development bonds. Buyers of these issues tend not to look to the cities for ultimate payment, because the municipalities are not likely to accept the same level of responsibility that they would for city-originated projects. Therefore, the marketability and yields of these bonds are more directly related to the financial strength of the business entity involved. Congress has tightened regulations, and in some cases eliminated certain types of issues, in order to limit the volume of industrial revenue and economic development bonds because of perceived abuses in which many municipalities have been considered too lax.

The primary distinguishing feature of municipal bonds is the federal income-tax exemption. This exemption is in effect a federal subsidy to state and local governments to assist them in financing their needs.

For many investors the exemption provides an attractive vehicle for investment. Since tax-free municipal bonds are priced in the market according to the average marginal tax rate of their buyers, those investors at the high end of the tax-rate spectrum stand to benefit the most. The equation most commonly used for determining the equivalent taxable yield (ETY) of a tax-exempt issue is

$$\text{ETY} = \frac{\text{Tax-exempt coupe rate}}{(1-\tau)}, \tag{5.2}$$

where τ = the marginal tax rate of the investor. So an investor in the 30% tax bracket would consider a 9% municipal bond to be equivalent to a 13% taxable bond $[9/(1-0.3)=13]$.

However, this equation is only applicable to bonds that are selling at par value because capital gains and their different rate of taxation are ignored. For issues not selling at par, the yield portions from interest and capital gains must be estimated and evaluated at their appropriately different rates of taxation in order to get a true after-tax comparison.[1] In general for municipal bonds, the interest payments are tax exempt and any capital gains are taxed as normal income.

5.1.1.4. *Corporations*

Corporations issue a variety of long-term debt securities. They differ mainly in the type of collateral supporting the bonds. These range from mortgage bonds secured by real assets to debentures secured simply by the general credit of the issuing firm.

While public utilities dominate the corporate bond sector, corporate bonds are also issued by industrial, transportation, financial, and other types of firms. Corporate bonds are attractive to many investors because of their high yields relative to government debt and their low risk compared to corporate equity issues.

5.1.2. *Bond Provisions*

Bond provisions such as maturity classes, debentures, coupons, maturity, callability, and sinking funds are discussed in this section.

5.1.2.1. *Maturity Classes*

Bonds are usually grouped by their maturity classes. **Short-term bonds** are any bonds maturing within five years. **Medium-term bonds** mature

[1] For more precise measures, see Leibowitz (1974).

in 5–10 years. **Long-term bonds** may run 20 years or more. Short-term bonds may be secured or unsecured and are common in industrial financing. Real-estate of equipment mortgages or other securities usually attempt to secure medium-term bonds, as do railroads and utilities. Capital-intensive industries such as airlines and utilities with long expectations of equipment life and associated costs are heavy users of long-term bonds.

5.1.2.2. *Mortgage Bond*

A **mortgage bond** is an issue secured with a lien on real property or buildings. A *blanket mortgage* is an issue secured with a lien on all assets of a firm. The mortgage bond may be open-end, limited open-end, or closed-end, or it may contain an after-acquired property clause. An open-end mortgage allows more bonds to be issued on the same mortgage contract. There are usually limitations on the amount of additional borrowing. Normally, the open-end mortgage contains an after-acquired property clause, which provides that all property acquired after the first mortgage was issued be added to the property already pledged as security by the contract. A limited open-end mortgage allows the firm to use additional borrowings up to a specified maximum amount; a closed-end mortgage prohibits additional borrowing on that property. The type of mortgage and the provisions that are behind the mortgage bond determine its risk and return.

5.1.2.3. *Debentures*

Debentures are unsecured bonds. They are issued with no liens against specific property, although a claim against earnings exists. All assets not specifically pledged, or any balance remaining after payment of secured debts from previously pledged assets, are available to pay the legal claims of general creditors. *Subordinate debentures* are debentures that are specifically made subordinate to all other general creditors holding claims on assets.

5.1.2.4. *Coupons*

A **bonds coupon** is the stated amount of interest that the firm (or government) promises to pay each year of the bond's life. In practice it is most often paid semiannually and is frequently expressed as a percentage of the par value of the bond. The par value is the stated amount of principal that will be paid at the termination of the bond. (For corporate bonds, the par value is almost always $1,000 and will be assumed to be so in our examples, unless otherwise stated.) While the coupon rate is one of the determinants of a bond's investment yield, coupon rates are only equal among bonds selling at the par value.

5.1.2.5. *Maturity*

Another important factor affecting the investment return of bonds is their maturity, or time remaining for repayment of principal. In fact, the most popular yield measure for bonds is **YTM**, or promised yield. The YTM is defined as the discount rate that will equate the present value of all remaining cash flows to the bond investor (periodic interest payment and par value at maturity) to the current price in the market. (It is identical to the market rate of discount used in Chapter 4 in discussing bond valuation.)

5.1.2.6. *Callability*

The **call provision** allows the issuing firm to terminate the bond issue before maturity. This provision may include a deferral clause that prevents the firm from exercising this right for a number of years. Such a clause is more valued by investors during periods in which coupons are historically high. In any case, this provision, as well as any other provision perceived to be an advantage to either the issuer or the buyer, has an impact on the pricing of the issue.

Since the call provision is clearly an advantage to the issuer, the effective yield that must be provided to new-issue buyers is higher for callable bonds. Callability is also used with increasing frequency in issues of preferred stock and is probably most important to the issuer of convertible bonds. This latter point is discussed in more detail later in the chapter.

The call provision has an impact on bond investment yields in another important way. To the extent that a bond issue is expected to be called, the call provision shortens the bond's expected maturity. Investors allow for this by relying on computed estimates of **yield to call (YTC)** rather than YTM. The computational procedure is similar to that for YTM, in that the YTC is the discount rate that equates the present value of all the cash flows expected through the point of call — that is, the interest payments and the call price. The only differences are fewer interest payments and the substitution of the call price at the call date for the face-value payment at the stated maturity date. Thus, the key distinguishing feature is the effective maturity.

The **call price** is the sum of the face value and the call premium, both of which are set in the bond indenture at the time of original issue. It should also be noted that the YTC is more uncertain rate than the YTM. This is so because the call date is often difficult to estimate, while the maturity date is fixed. As a result, there may be more variability in bond prices for bonds that can be called.

The linkage of bonds and put options has occurred in recent years. A putable debenture is a bond that carries a put option providing that the investor can sell the bond back to the issuer at a specified exercise price prior to the maturity date of the bond. A putable bond can be viewed as a regular debt instrument that has a bundle of put options written by the issuer of the bond to the investors who own the bond. These options grant valuable sale rights to investors and impose purchase obligations on the issuer. Investors pay for these valuable rights by accepting a coupon rate on the bond that is lower than that normally associated with a similar bond without the put provision. A very common example of a putable bond is a U.S. Savings Bond. Each bond specifies a redemption schedule of increasing prices at which the investor can sell the bond back to the Treasury at a specific date in the future. An investor can choose to sell the bond back to the Treasury or hold the bond until it matures.

5.1.2.7. *Sinking Funds*

The effective maturity of a bond is also impacted by the sinking-fund provision. The typical **sinking fund** involves a partial liquidation of the total issue each year as specified in the indenture. Therefore, the average maturity of the individual bonds making up the issue is reduced. While this process will impact the investment yield in a less drastic way than an expected call, the relatively small number of bonds being retired each year has not led to the calculation of a special yield similar to the YTC.

Theoretically, sinking-fund bonds are priced on the basis of a weighted-average maturity. The **yield to weighted-average maturity (YTWAM)** could be computed as the discount rate that would equate all the cash inflows, including the sinking-fund early retirements, to the current price of the bond. The payoff inflows would have to be selling at prices that are higher than the call price, or at an estimated market price, if they are expected to be selling at less than the call price. Again it is clear that uncertainty is injected into the pricing process.

5.2. Bond Valuation, Bond Index, and Bond Beta

Bond valuation, bond index, bond beta, and other related issues are the subjects of this section.

5.2.1. *Bond Valuation*

The valuation or price determination of bonds was stated in Chapter 4 to be accomplished by computing the present value of all future cash flows to be received by the security holder. That is

$$P_0 = \sum_{t=1}^{n} = \frac{C_t}{(1+k_b)^t} + \frac{P_n}{(1+k_b)^n}, \tag{5.3}$$

where

P_0 = the price of the bond at the time zero;
C_t = coupon interest payment in period t;
P_n = face value of bond to be paid at period n;
k_b = required rate of return of bondholders; and
n = number of periods to maturity.

Sample Problem 5.1 provides further illustration.

Sample Problem 5.1

In 1988, the IBM 9% bonds maturing in 2003, when the required rate of return of bondholders is 10%, should be selling for \$922.785.

$$\begin{aligned} P_0 &= \sum_{t=1}^{30} \frac{\$45}{(1+0.05)^t} + \frac{\$1,000}{(1.05)^{30}} \\ &= \$45(15.373) + \$1,000(0.231) \\ &= \$691.785 + \$231 \\ &= \$922.785. \end{aligned}$$

It should be noted that since corporate bonds pay interest semiannually, Equation (5.3) must be adjusted to reflect these semiannual payments. This can be done by dividing the annual interest payment of \$90 per year by two, thereby increasing the number of periods till maturity from 15 years to 30 six-month intervals, and dividing the required rate of return by two.

In this chapter, the same process indicated in Equation (5.3) is used to determine the investors' yield, given the existence of the current bond price. The bond yields most used by investors and analysts are: (1) current yield (CY), (2) YTM (also called promised yield), (3) YTC, and (4) realized yield (RY).

Current yield is computed by dividing the coupon interest payment by the current market price of the bond.

$$\mathrm{CY} = \frac{C}{P_0}. \tag{5.4}$$

Sample Problem 5.2 provides further illustration.

Sample Problem 5.2

For the IBM bond of Sample Problem 5.1, the current yield is 9.75%. This can be calculated in terms of Equation (5.4) as

$$\mathrm{CY} = \frac{\$90}{\$922.785} = 0.0975.$$

This is a measure that reflects the rate of return on actual investment, but it is not a complete measure of a bond investor's rate of return. It is used by some analysts to compare with dividend yields on alternative investments in common stocks.

A more complete measure of bond return is the YTM, because it takes into account all of the cash flows to be received over the entire life of the bonds. It is commonly considered the appropriate discount Rate [k_b in Equation (5.3)] and can be computed on a trial-and-error basis (most investor use special-function calculators or bond-yield tables) given the values of P_0, C_t, P_n, and n. There is also an approximation method based on a return on investment approach:

$$\mathrm{AYTM} = \frac{C + \dfrac{P_n - P_0}{n}}{\dfrac{P_n + P_0}{2}}, \tag{5.5}$$

where

C = annual coupon interest payment;
$P_n - P_0$ = amount of discount at which bond is selling; and
$\frac{P_n + P_0}{2}$ = the average investment over the period to maturity.

Sample Problem 5.3 provides further illustration.

Sample Problem 5.3

If an AT&T 2001 bond with a coupon of 7% was selling for \$790 in 1988, its actual yield to maturity (AYTM) could be calculated by using Equation (5.5).

$$\begin{aligned}\text{AYTM} &= \frac{70 + \dfrac{1000 - 790}{13}}{\dfrac{1000 + 790}{2}} \\ &= 9.6\%.\end{aligned}$$

In fact, the AYTM for this bond, given this information, is 9.78%.

When it seems likely that a bond will be called before maturity, the time to the expected call date is a more appropriate measure of the maturity of the issue. In this case, analysts will try to estimate the most likely call date and compute the YTC. Both Equations (5.3) and (5.5) can be adjusted to allow for this. For clarity of exposition, the approximation Equation (5.5) is adjusted as

$$\text{AYTC} = \frac{C + \dfrac{P_c - P_0}{n_c}}{\dfrac{P_c + P_0}{2}}, \tag{5.6}$$

where

P_c = estimated market price at the call date; and
n_c = time to estimated call date.

Often, the first possible call date is used by analysts as the estimated call date, particularly when the coupon rate is high and the bond seems likely to be called. Sample Problem 5.4 illustrates this concept.

Sample Problem 5.4

If the AT&T 2001 bond of Sample Problem 5.3 is called in 1995 at \$1,010, the approximate YTC can be calculated by using Equation (5.6).

$$\begin{aligned}\text{AYTC} &= \frac{70 + \dfrac{1010 - 790}{7}}{\dfrac{1010 + 790}{2}} \\ &= 11.26\%.\end{aligned}$$

Table 5.2. Semiannual Adjustments.

AT&T	Annual Rate (%)	Adjustment for Semiannual Interest (%)
AYTM	9.6	4.81 semiannual = 9.62 annualized
AYTC	11.26	5.63 semiannual = 11.26 annualized

This is higher than the YTM for two reasons: (1) $1,010 is earned at call instead of $1,000 at maturity, and (2) the capital gain is earned over a shorter period of time — 7 instead of 13 years.

ARY can be computed as the *ex-post* rate of return earned over a past period, or it can be more usefully referred to as an expected yield to be realized over a holding period shorter than the time to maturity. Using the approximation format:

$$\text{ARY} = \frac{C + \dfrac{P_{hp} - P_0}{n_{hp}}}{\dfrac{P_{hp} + P_0}{2}}, \tag{5.7}$$

where

P_{hp} = estimated market price at the end of the holding period; and
n_{hp} = time to the end of the estimated holding period.

As shown in the example for calculating the price of a bond using Equation (5.3), an adjustment for semiannual compounding must be made. The general rule for this adjustment is to multiply n by 2 and to divide C and K by 2. The results of these adjustments for the examples of this section are shown in Table 5.2.

5.2.2. *Bond Indices*

The Salomon Brothers High-Grade, Long-Term Bond Index and the Lehman Brothers, Kuhn, Loeb (LBKL) Bond Index are the best known and most widely quoted bond indices available today. Before specifying their content and makeup, it is useful to consider some of the general problems involved in trying to accurately index the overall bond market. Published yield data cover only a relatively few of the total number of issues. Most bonds are not listed on the major exchanges but trade in the over-the-counter market (OTC). There is no central location or source of transaction prices for bonds. Another problem is that many issues, even those listed on major exchanges, are not actively traded, thus leading to inefficient pricing. As interest rates change over time, "old" price quotes become totally inaccurate. In addition, even for listed bonds, the larger institutional sales and purchases will often take place off the exchanges at prices that can be significantly different from the odd-lot type transactions taking place on the exchanges.

To avoid the problems mentioned above, bond traders at Salomon Brothers individually priced all publicly offered issues rated AA or better and make up a package of indices over various spans of time — for example, the latest month, the last three months, the calendar year to date, the past twelve months, and the past four quarters. Their monthly report includes several useful subcategories of the overall market data, but the basic measure is the total rate of return index, using a market value weighted approach.

LBKL take a completely different approach to resolving the pricing problems of corporate bonds. They compute theoretical prices by programming in factors such as bond ratings, maturities, coupon rates, sinking-fund provisions, call and call-protection provisions, and dollar amounts outstanding. Yield-curve and yield-spread factors are programmed in on a monthly basis in order to stay as up-to-date as possible with market conditions. Verification with market quotations is made for those issues that have current active data available, and actual quotations are used for U.S. Treasury and agency bonds. The LBKL group also produces a package of bond indices, including the bond Index, the Long-Term Corporate Bond Indices, and the U.S. Government/Agency Bond Index. Several thousand corporate bonds of BBB grade or better, and several hundred government and agency issues, are included in the indices at any given time. The LBKL group also subcategorizes its index information in ways useful to bond analysts and investors.

5.2.3. *Bond Beta*

The **bond beta** is computed similar to its counterpart, the **stock beta**. The bond beta is a ratio of the covariance of bond return with the market to the variance in the market. As a useful risk measure, the bond beta should be related to the risk of default and the price-level risk associated with interest-rate changes. Since bond ratings have been used for many years to relate a firm's operating and financial characteristics to the likelihood of default, it was logical to expect these ratings to be inversely related to bond betas.

Prior studies by Beaver *et al.* (1970) and others have shown that there is a significant relationship between stock betas and internal corporate variables. In addition, Pinches and Mingo (1973) and others have found that internal corporate variables have a significant relationship with bond ratings. Following from such leads, Reilly and Joehnk (1976) and Weinstein (1981 and 1983) have studied the relationship of bond betas with bond ratings and interest-rate risk.

Before looking further into the results of these interesting empirical studies, it is essential to define the bond beta in the following linear regression model:

$$\tilde{R}_{bt} = \alpha + \beta\tilde{R}_{mt} + \tilde{\epsilon}_{bt}, \tag{5.8}$$

where

$\tilde{R}_{bt}$ = the estimated holding-period return on bond b at time t;
$\tilde{R}_{mt}$ = the estimated holding-period return on some market index at time t;
$\tilde{\epsilon}_{bt}$ = the residual random-error term (assumed to have a mean of zero);
α = the regression intercept; and
β = the bond beta.

An important question involving this regression is what to use as the market index. Is an index like the S&P 500, commonly used to compute stock betas, appropriate for bond betas? Would an index totally consisting of bonds provide superior results? Reilly and Joehnk (1976) use five different market indexes.

1. Moddy's Average Corporate Bond Yield Index;
2. Moddy's Lagged Corporate Bond Yield Index;
3. Moddy's Segregated Group-Rating Bond Yield Index;
4. S&P 500 Composite Stock Price Index; and
5. Moddy's Average Corporate Bond Index converted to a price basis.

Weinstein (1981) estimates bond beta using the following different market indices:

1. The CRSP value-weighed NYSE index (including dividends).[2]

[2]CRSP is the Center for Research on Security Prices; the CRSP index contains every stock listed on the New York Stock Exchange. Each security is weighted in the index by its market value as a percentage of the total value of the New York Stock Exchange. Hence large, high-value firms such as IBM would have a greater weight than smaller-value firms.

2. A bond index developed by Ibbotson and Singuefield (1979), and
3. A combined index with a 0.7 weight on the CRSP index and 0.3 on the Ibbotson index.

This third index is used again by Weinstein (1983) because the earlier study seems to show that this is the best market-portfolio measure of the three used in that study.

Weinstein computes correlation coefficients between βs calculated from each market index for each year of his study (1962–1975). The results indicate a very high degree of correlation between the stock index and the combined index (mostly 0.89 or higher), a moderately high correlation between the bond index and the combined index (0.3 to 0.8); but mixed results for the correlation between the stock index and the bond index (negative in the early years and positive in the later years). In general, his estimations of bond betas using the three different market indices show that the choice of index is quite important. He concludes that the combined index provides the most reliable results.

As will be shown, the market model illustrated by Equation (5.8) requires a market index that, in theory, is representative of all risky assets. Hence Weinstein's results are supportive of the theory. When measuring a security's systematic risk (β), the more representative the index, the better the measure.

Reilly and Joehnk (1976) find that among the three bond-yield series used to measure market return, the Average Corporate Bond Yield Index (measure number 1 in the list above) and the Segregate Group-Rating Bond Yield Index (measure number 3) are both clearly superior to the Lagged Corporate Bond Yield Index (measure number 2). This "superiority" as measured by Reilly and Joehnk is in terms of lower unsystematic risk or standard error of the estimate (SEE). A perfect market-portfolio measure would have no unsystematic risk.

Reilly and Joehnk (1976) also compare market measures 4 and 5, the S&P 500 Composite Stock Price Index and the Average Corporate Bond Index converted to a price basis. While the former is better in terms of lower autocorrelation results, the bond-price index is clearly superior in terms of lower unsystematic risk (SEE).

To summarize, both the Weinstein and Reilly and Joehnk studies show:

1. The choice of a market index has a significant effect on the bond betas determined therefrom.

2. Indices made up of only common stocks are inferior to those including at least some bonds determining bond beta.
3. Bonds have a low level of systematic risk as measured by bond beta.

The next topic we examine is the relationship between this risk measure and the rating assigned to bonds by agencies such as Moody's and Standard & Poor's.

It would be expected, if beta is a useful measure of the risk inherent in bond investment, that this measure is inversely related to the bond ratings assigned to the issuing firms. However, the results from the Reilly and Joehnk study (1976) do not consistently support this hypothesis. The authors conjecture that this may be true because bond ratings are assigned by the agencies on the likelihood of default, while the market risk measure (beta) depends upon the relationship between the changes in market yields (prices). The major short-run determinants of bond yields are overall macroeconomic factors, which will tend to have a similar effect on all risk classes of bonds. Therefore, the risk measured by beta would not necessarily be closely related to bond ratings that concentrate on the probability of default. The change of default generally involves not only macroeconomic but also individual firm factors.

Weinstein (1981) finds similar results over the first four classes, AAA to BAA, that is, there is no consistent relationship between bond betas and bond ratings. Nevertheless, he does find a significant relationship in the inverse direction, as would be predicted, when the lower-class bonds (BA, B, and below) are considered. This likely because the probability of default is so low for high-rated bonds and only becomes a factor in beta measurements for the low-rated bonds. In any case, Weinstein (1981) and Reilly and Joehnk (1976) find that the systematic risk (beta) of corporate bonds is an important factor to be considered by security analysts and portfolio managers.

5.3. Bond-Rating Procedures

Bond ratings obviously are of interest to the academic community as evidenced by the number of bond-rating studies published in recent years. Ratings are even more important to the issuers and purchasers of the securities. From the investor's viewpoint, the ratings are an indication of the quality or safely of the issue; while from the issuers' viewpoint, the ratings have a direct impact on cost of their funds.

Bonds are classified according to credit risk by three bond-rating companies: (1) Moody's Investor Services, (2) Standard & Poor's, and (3) Fitch Investor Services. The purpose of their ratings is to provide investors a measure of default risk that would be difficult and costly to obtain on their own.

The rating categories for the two best-known services, Moody's and Standard & Poor's, are described in Table 5.3. The services tend to emphasize that their ratings are based upon a mixture of qualitative and quantitative factors that cannot be simulated by models that rely entirely on performance ratios or other quantitative measurements. A number of

Table 5.3. Moody's and Standard & Poor's Rating Categories for Bonds.

Moody's Rating	Description	Standard & Poor's Rating	Description
Aaa	Bonds of highest quality	AAA	Bonds of highest quality
Aa	Bonds of high quality	AA	High-quality debt obligations
A	Bonds whose security of principal and interest is considered adequate but may be impaired in the future	A	Bonds that have a strong capacity to pay interest and principal but may be susceptible to adverse effects
Baa	Bonds of medium grade that are neither highly protected nor poorly secured	BBB	Bonds that have an adequate capacity to pay interest and principal, but are more vulnerable to adverse economic conditions or changing circumstances
Ba	Bonds of speculative quality whose future cannot be considered well assured	BB	Bonds of lower medium grade with few desirable investment characteristics
B	Bonds that lack characteristics of a desirable investment		
Caa	Bonds in poor standing that may be defaulted	B & CCC	Primarily speculative bonds with great uncertainties and major risk if exposed to adverse conditions
Ca	Speculative bonds that are often in default	C	Income bonds on which no interest is being paid
C	Bonds with little probability of any investment value (lowest rating)	D	Bonds in default

researchers have attempted in various ways to develop models that will predict either the ratings themselves or the occurrence of rating changes. Probably the best known of these studies is one conducted by Pinches and Mingo (1973) in which they develop and test a factor analysis/multiple discriminant analysis (MDA) model for predicting bond ratings. Using the factor analysis as a screen, 35 firm- or issue-related variable believed to influence the rating of a bond issue are reduced to seven factors or dimensions that explain 63% of the variation in the data.[3] These seven factors include:

1. Size
2. Financial leverage
3. Long-term capital intensiveness
4. Return on investment
5. Short-term capital intensiveness
6. Earnings stability
7. Debt and debt-coverage stability

One variable from each factor is entered into a MDA procedure in order to determine which variables best describe the differences between the ratings groups. The MDA model performing best includes the following variables.

(1) Subordination
(2) Years of consecutive dividends
(3) Issue size
(4) The five-year mean of (net income + interest)/interest
(5) The five-year mean of long-term debt/total assets
(6) Net income/total assets

Linear classification procedures are then used to determine that 70% of the original sample, 65% of a holdout sample, and 56% of a new sample are correctly classified, respectively.[4] The Baa group, which includes both subordinated and nonsubordinated bonds, is the most difficult to classify. Only 4 of 25 Baa-rated bonds are correctly classified in the holdout and new samples. Pinches and Mingo's conclusion about this result is that the Baa class is difficult to predict because of the subordination feature. All

[3]Some variables were standardized and a log transformation was applied to others to improve normality and reduce heteroskedasticity.

[4]The holdout sample consisted of bonds in the same year as the original sample, while the new sample consisted of bonds issued in the first six months of the following year.

sample bonds rated below Baa are subordinated, while all but two sample bonds rated above Baa are nonsubordinated.[5] Thirteen of the bonds rated Baa are subordinated and 12 are nonsubordinated.

In their 1975 follow-up study, Pinches and Mingo conclude that quadratic rather than linear classification rules are superior. Two alternative models are presented. The first approach uses the quadratic procedure and determines that 65% of the bonds are correctly classified. Pinches and Mingo's second approach is completed in two steps. The bonds are first divided into two groups, subordinated and nonsubordinated, and one discriminate model is then developed for each group. When the classification results are combined, more than 75% of the bonds are correctly classified.

In a study using the 132-bond data base of the Pinches and Mingo studies, Zumwalt and Wort (1980) develop MDA models for all adjacent groups of three classifications (Aa-A, A-Baa, Ba-B), as well as for the Pinches and Mingo (1973) five-group model. First looking at the Zumwalt and Wort (1980) results for the five-group model, 84 of the 132 bonds (63.6%) are correctly classified, and, as in the case of the Pinches and Mingo (1973) study, those bonds rated as Baa are the most difficult to classify. Only 6 of 25, or 24% of the Baa, are correctly classified. In order to examine the problem more closely, group overlap statistics are computed. While group means for the variables may be significantly different, classification can still be quite difficult, if the groups exhibit a substantial amount of overlap among the individual variables for each bond. In fact, the results do show a substantial amount of overlap of the A, Baa- and Ba-rated bonds with less overlap between Aa and A and Ba and B. These results help explain the difficulty encountered in classifying the Baa-rated bonds.

The adjacent group classifications are quite good overall, with 87.5% of the Aa-A groups, 68.6% of the A-Baa groups, 71.0% of the Baa-Ba groups, and 88.1% of the Ba-B groups, correctly classified. Even the percentage of correct Baa classifications is an improvement, 52% when paired with A-rated bonds and 44% when paired with Ba-rated bonds — an average of 48%.

Zumwalt and Wort also find some interesting results when comparing the percentage of total discriminating power among the five variables. While the five-group model identifies years of consecutive dividends and issue

[5]In Pinches and Mingo's follow-up study (1975), they eliminate the two A-rated subordinated bonds in order to more directly compare the results of several models and to focus on the subordination feature.

size, which are the two most important variables in the overall model, the two-group analysis allows more specific insights. For example, years of consecutive dividends is the most important variable for the two lowest ratings comparisons (Baa-Ba and Ba-B) and the second most important for the highest rating comparison (Aa-A). Issue size is the most important variable for the two highest rating comparisons (Aa-A and A-Baa) and is third and fifth, respectively, in importance for the Baa-Ba and Ba-B comparisons. In examining the rationale for these results, it must be understood that these variables are really proxies for more basic investment attributes, such as creditworthiness and probability of default. For example, issue size is likely to be directly correlated with creditworthiness. While it is common for firms issuing Aa- and A-rated bonds to have paid dividends for many years consecutively (thus rendering this variable comparatively useless as a distinguishing factor), relative creditworthiness can be judged on the basis of issue size as indicated in the linkage described above. For firms issuing the lower-rated bonds, the size range of bond issues may be limited somewhat by the lack of creditworthiness as indicated more directly by continuing ability to make dividend payments to the firm's common stockholders.

The use of quantitative models to predict bond ratings or the changes in bond ratings may be just an academic exercise. Several empirical studies have shown that the investment marker adjusts bond prices in response to new information items much more efficiently than the bond-ratings services. That is, by the time a bond rating has been changed upward or downward by the services, the information that caused the rating to change has already been reflected in the bond price. Hence what investors need is a better understanding of what types of information affect the pricing of bonds.

Hettenhouse and Sartoris (1976) and Weinstein (1977) show that the ratings changes have very little informational value to analysts and investors. While the bond market has generally been found to be less efficient than the stock market, it is apparently efficient enough to be able to price bonds independently of the information supplied by rating agencies. While this is true, the continuing of rating services indicates that some segments of the market consider bond ratings useful information in the assessment of relative risk. Hence, it is important to understand the procedures and information used to evaluate the bonds by the bond-rating agencies, as discussed in this section. The next section focuses on an important concept — term structure of interest for bond valuation.

5.4. Term Structure of Interest

The theory of term structure and its estimators is investigated in this section. In addition, applications of term structure are discussed.

5.4.1. *Theory*

Market interest rates influence the rate of return on bond investments as well as the variability of that rate of return. It is important, therefore, to examine the development and impact of term or maturity structure on the market interest rates.

The **term structure of interest rates** is typically described by the yield curve, a static representation of the relationship between term to maturity and YTM that exists at a given point time, within a given risk class of bonds. All other bond features, such as coupon, callability, and market sector, should also remain constant in this cross-sectional comparison. Khoury (1983) points out that term structure and yield curves are only equivalent for pure discount bonds, that is, for bonds that have no interim coupon payments, only a simple payment at the maturity of the issue.[6] This is so because the YTM of coupon issues is more properly a function of a weighted average term to maturity. This problem is again addressed in Chapter 20 in connection with the concept of bond duration.

Yield curves, measured at a point in time, show the market yield/maturity expectations at the time of measurement only. These expectations can and do change over time, sometimes abruptly. In general, the yield curve approximates four patterns or shapes, as shown in Fig. 5.2.

Historically, the increasing yield curve has been most common. It has an added intuitive appeal to investors because of the implication that farther distant cash flows should require a higher risk premium, while other things remain the same. The decreasing curve for the most part has not been common in the past, although it occurred frequently in the 1970s and early 1980s as interest rates reached historically high levels. The humped curve tends to occur during transition periods from high to low levels and reflects

[6]Pure discount bonds are also called zero-coupon bonds. Some investment dealers in the bond market have recently begun to manufacture zero-coupon bonds from regular U.S. Treasury issues by "stripping" the coupon payments away from the overall bond-payment structure and marketing them separately as single-payment investments. Early in 1985, the U.S. Treasury began making this process easier by separating the registration of coupon payments and maturity payments upon issuance.

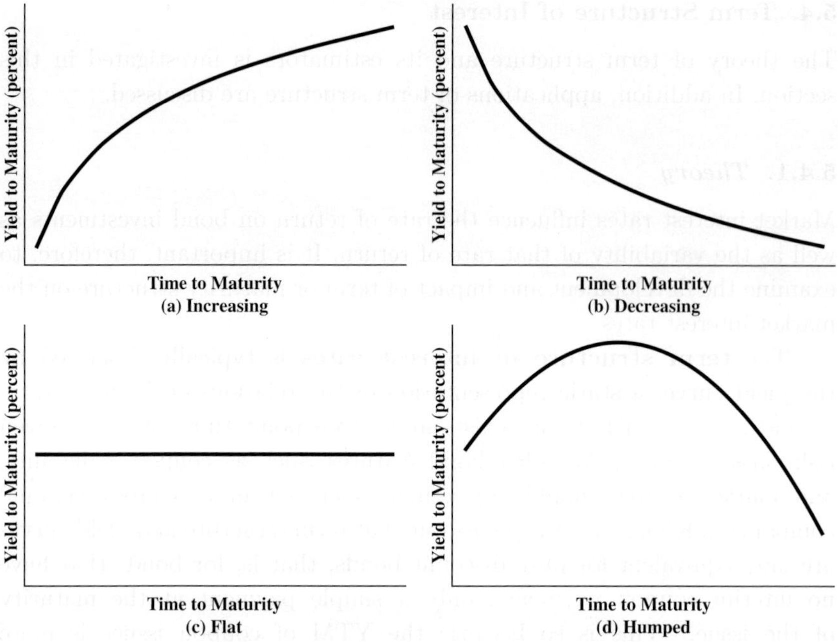

Fig. 5.2. Yield-Curve Patterns.

this transition through higher intermediate-term rates. Flat curves occur rarely for any significant period of time. There are theories that have been developed to explain the yield-curve patterns. The most common of these are: (1) the expectations hypothesis, (2) the liquidity-preference hypothesis, (3) the market-segmentation hypothesis, and (4) preferred habitat.

Most economists agree that the expectations hypothesis is the best single description of this theoretical foundation of term structure. According to this demand-based theory, the expectations of market participants concerning the likely course of future interest-rate movements determine the market demand for each bond maturity class. Given a set of appropriate assumptions, it can be shown through this approach that the interest rate for any long-term issue can be measured as the geometric mean of the series of expected single-period interest rates leading up to the maturity period of the issue being examined; or more simply, that long-term rates are the geometric mean of expected short-term rates. The expectations hypothesis implies that investors, as are indifferent to the specific maturities held and that on average, bonds of all maturities are perfect substitutes for one another:

$$(1 + R_n) = \left[\prod_{t=1}^{n} (1 + r_t) \right]^{1/n}, \tag{5.9}$$

where

R_n = YTM for a bond with n years to maturity; and
r_t = one-year forward rate that is expected to occur in year t.

Sample Problem 5.5 provides further illustration.

Sample Problem 5.5

As indicated in Fig. 5.3, the forward rate r_t takes on the values 5%, 6%, and 4% for $t = 1, 2$, and 3, respectively. Each of these is a forward rate occurring at some future time. Equation (5.9) can be used to calculate the yield-to-maturity rate R_n, where $n = 2$.

$$\begin{aligned} 1 + R_2 &= \sqrt{(1 + r_1)(1 + r_2)} \\ &= \sqrt{(1 + 0.05)(1 + 0.06)} \\ R_2 &= 1.055 - 1 \\ &= 0.055. \end{aligned}$$

In using the expectations hypothesis to evaluate long-term bonds, investors are unlikely to try to estimate each period's expected forward rate to the point of maturity. However, they can use rates available on

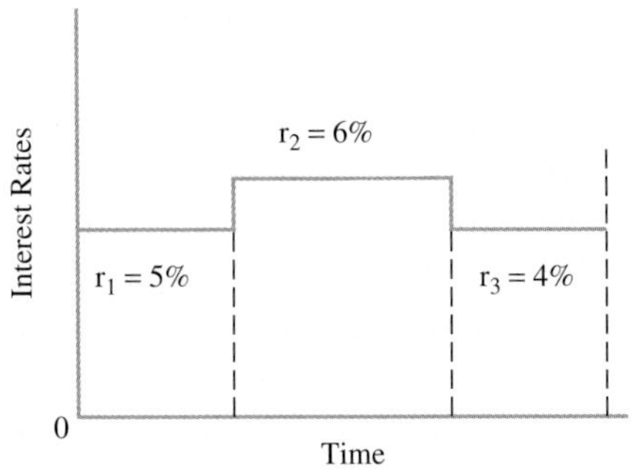

Fig. 5.3. Pattern of Forward Rate.

existing issue of varying maturities to estimate implied one-year yields. To do so, Equation (5.9) can be rewritten as

$$(1 + r_n) = \frac{(1 + R_n)^n}{(1 + R_{n-1})^{n-1}}. \tag{5.10}$$

Sample Problem 5.6 provides further illustration.

Sample Problem 5.6

If six-year Treasury bonds have a current YTM of 9% and five-year Treasury bonds have a current YTM of 8%, the implied one-year forward rate expected in year six would be

$$\begin{aligned}(1 + r_6) &= \frac{(1.09)^6}{(1.08)^5} = \frac{1.68}{1.47} \\ &= 1.14,\end{aligned}$$

and r_6 is expected to be 14%. Note that the implied one-year forward rate beginning in the sixth year is greater than either the current five- or six-year YTMs. This is the result of an upward-sloping yield curve and the time value of money.

While the pure version of the expectations theory assumes investors' risk neutrality at the margin, the liquidity-preference theory can be considered to be another version of the expectations theory with investors' risk aversion assumed at margin. That is, investors are assumed to view long-term maturities as inherently riskier than short-term maturities.

$$(1 + R_n) = \left[\prod_{t=1}^{n} (1 + r_t + L_t)\right]^{1/n}, \tag{5.11}$$

in which L_t is the liquidity premium demanded by investors and increases as t increases from 1 to n.

With liquidity premiums built into the yield curve, the implied forward rates that can be extracted from the interest-rate term structures are higher than the future rates otherwise expected by investors — that is, they are upward-biased estimates. This upward bias means that the yield curves will always have relatively higher slopes than under the pure expectations hypothesis, which produces unbiased estimates. An implication is that investors will no longer view bonds of different maturity as perfect substitutes for one another. With liquidity premiums included YTMs on coupon bonds will not be fully realized, even if all the expected future rates are realized, because the investor is paying a higher price the longer the maturity of the bond. This higher price will reduce the yield that the investor actually receives.

In terms of substitutability, the third theory, the market-segmentation hypothesis, assumes that bonds of different maturities are not adequate substitutes for one another. Under this hypothesis, the maturity requirements of investors are so strong that they will tend to restrict their investments to specific segments of the term structure. For example, insurance companies will invest in intermediate-term maturities, while commercial banks will invest in shorter maturities. While many institutional investors will try to match asset and liability maturities, it is not clear that such preferences will cause the term structure to primarily reflect supply and demand within maturity subcategories rather than the investor's expectations and liquidity premiums.

The consensus of empirical evidence concerning term-structure hypotheses seems to favor a combination of the expectations theory and the liquidity-preference theory (see Kessel, 1971). There has been little support for the market-segmentation hypothesis. While it has adherents among practitioners, it has been generally ignored by academicians as a viable supporting hypothesis. Modigliani and Swatch (1967) do attempt to blend all three hypotheses into what they call the preferred-habitat theory, which states that investors who ordinarily invest only in a given maturity range could be induced into other maturities by a sufficient risk premium. Their theory is characterized by a multiple-horizon market and a willingness on the part of investors to acquire instruments within a range called a habitat. Risk for the investors will increase as the maturity of an investment exceeds the investor's horizon, and with risk increasing return will be required. However, the market will not be willing to pay these ever increasing returns. Borrowers will eventually find investors with risk profiles dictated by the longer horizon needed by the borrower, within an acceptable interest-rate range for both parties.

Any yield-curve shape can be explained by the expectations theory. A descending curve stems from the belief that future short-term rates will be less than current short-term rates. An ascending curve results from investor forecasts of higher short-term rates. The humped yield curve can be explained by saying rates are expected to rise in the near term before they decline in the distant future.

Any yield-curve shape explained by the expectations theory can be explained by the liquidity-preference theory. However, the observed market yield curve is higher than that predicted by the expectations theory by the amount of the liquidity premium. The liquidity-preference theory helps explain why upward-sloping curves are considered the norm.

Both the segmentation theory and the preferred-habitat theory explain the yield-curve shape through supply and demand forces within the various maturity horizons of the curve. Modigliani and Swatch were not able to conclusively verify their hybrid theory empirically, but many economists do believe that term structure can be best understood only with proper attention being allotted to expectations, liquidity premiums, and supply/demand factors.

5.4.2. *Estimation*

There are two methods that can be used to estimate yield curves: (1) the **freehand method** and (2) the **regression method.**

To construct a yield curve using the freehand method, a graph is plotted of the YTM and time to maturity for government bonds. Table 5.1 illustrates this. Table 5.1 presents the yields for Treasury bonds, notes, and bills from *The Wall Street Journal* for Wednesday, February 16, 2011. To plot a yield curve, the first step is to convert the date the bond matures into years. This is done by first looking at bonds that mature on April 30, 1989. To convert this maturity date into years, the number of days until the bond matures is divided by 365. In this case, the bond matures in 39 days, or 0.1068 years (39/365). This process is continued until all maturity dates have been converted into years. Table 5A.1 in the appendix at the end of this chapter presents the yield maturity and time to maturity for the Treasury bonds and notes. Column 1 lists the YTM and column 2 lists the time to maturity. To plot the yield curve using the freehand method, simply plot the time to maturity on the x-axis and the YTM on the y-axis. Figure 5.4 gives a scatter plot of time to maturity and YTM for Treasury bonds and notes on February 16, 2011.

The freehand method for estimating the yield curve simply involves drawing a curve through the scatter plot of Fig. 5.4. It is clear that the location of the curve is somewhat arbitrary. In Fig. 5.4 notice that the yield curve is increasing — that is, as time to maturity increases, the yield on Treasury securities rise.

One criticism of the freehand method is that it cannot be relied upon by investors to be reproducible — where the curve will be drawn is arbitrary. In addition, the yield curve uses securities that are not fully homogeneous.

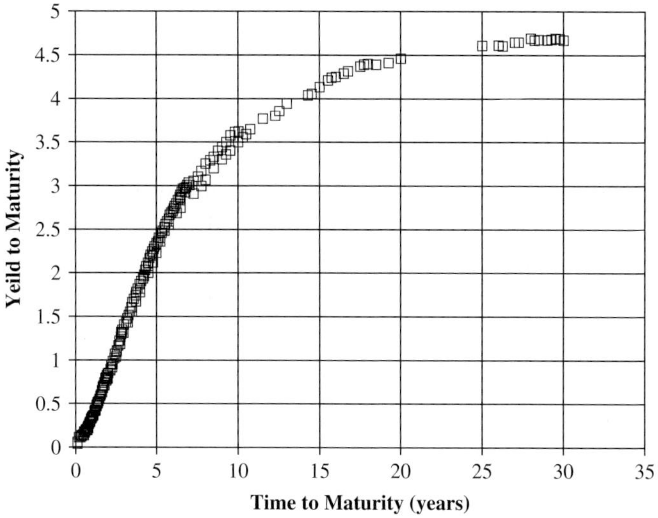

Fig. 5.4. Yield Curve for U.S. Treasury Bonds and Notes as of February 16, 2011.

For example, the bonds, notes, and bills used to plot the Treasury yield curve have differences in coupons and callability.

Echols and Elliott (1976) develop a revised construction approach in order "... to present a reproducible analytical structure for extracting yield curves from market data." Basically, they use regression techniques to fit the curve, rather than the Treasury's freehand approach, and they specifically include the impact of coupon on the shape of the yield curve. Starting from Equation (5.9), they derive a regression equation which can be used to estimate the yield curve.

$$(1 + R_n) = \left[\prod_{t=1}^{n} (1 + r_t)\right]^{1/n}. \tag{5.9}$$

This can be rewritten as

$$(1 + R_n) = (1 + R_1)^{1/n} \left[\prod_{t=2}^{n} (1 + r_t)\right]^{1/n}. \tag{5.12}$$

Taking the logs of both sides yields:

$$\ln(1 + R_n) = \frac{1}{n} \ln(1 + R_1) + \frac{1}{n} \sum_{t=2}^{n} \ln(1 + r_t). \tag{5.13}$$

If the forward rate structures are an exponential progression, it can be shown that

$$\frac{1}{n}\sum_{t=2}^{n-1}\ln(1+r_t)=\ln k_1-\frac{k_2}{2}-\frac{\ln k_1}{n}+\frac{k_2}{2}n, \tag{5.14}$$

where k_1 and k_2 are constants and t is the maturity of a given bond. Substituting this expression into Equation (5.13):

$$\ln(1+R_t)=\frac{1}{t}[\ln(1+R_1)-\ln k_1]+t(k_2/2)+\ln k_1-\frac{k_2}{2}, \tag{5.15}$$

or, in regression form:

$$\ln(1+R_t)=a(1/t)+b(t)+c+e_t, \tag{5.16}$$

where a, b, and c are estimated regression coefficients.

This regression model provides a framework that can be used to measure yield curves that are rising, humped, decreasing, or flat by using the estimated values of the regression coefficients a and b.

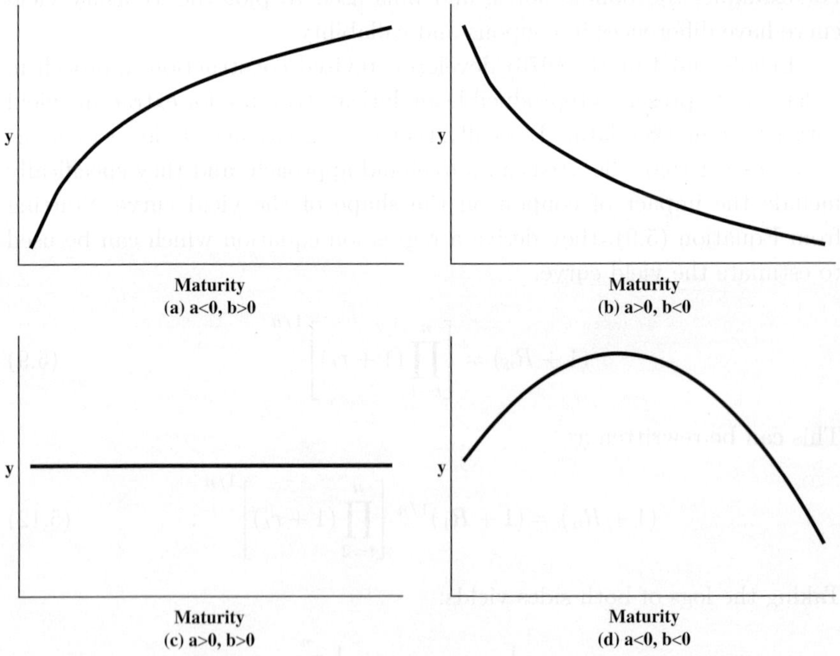

Fig. 5.5. Regression Coefficients and Yield-Curve Shape.

The model shown by Equation (5.16) can be modified to incorporate the effect of coupon values on the term structure by assigning an additional variable for the coupon values of the bonds being used to estimate the yield curve:

$$\ln(1 + R_t) = a(1/t) + b(t) + c + d(x) + e_t, \tag{5.17}$$

where x is the coupon rate of the bond. Sample Problem 5.7 provides further illustration.

Sample Problem 5.7

Using the data on Treasury bonds, notes, and bills shown in Table 5A.1, the regression shown in Equation (5.17) was run yielding estimates of a, b, c, and d. The regression results are presented in Table 5.4. In addition, Table 5.5 presents the results that incorporate coupons into the regression.

The correct calculations of forward market rates of interest involve only yields on fully discounted notes. In the regression model used for estimating the yield curve, a correction for the coupon effect has been incorporated. The use of the model to estimate an implied forward rate insures that

Table 5.4. Regression Results for Sample Problem 5.7.

Regression Output: $\ln(1 + R_t) = a(1/t) + b(t) + c + e_t$		
Constant (c)		0.783093
Standard error of constant		0.028184
R^2		0.742913
Number of observations		223
Degrees of freedom		220
	a	b
X coefficient(s)	−0.18219	0.047286
Standard error of coefficients	0.017992	0.002624

Table 5.5. Regression Results for Sample Problem 5.7 Incorporating Coupons.

Regression output: $\ln(1 + R_t) = a(1/t) + b(t) + d(x) + c + e_t$			
Constant (c)			0.673866
Standard error of constant			0.034919
R^2			0.76818
Number of observations			223
Degrees of freedom			219
	a	b	d
X coefficient(s)	−0.17833	0.042615	0.03791
Standard error of coefficients	0.017143	0.002674	0.007759

a correction for variations in the coupon effect over time is taken into consideration.

In capital-market theory, the risk-free rate is a concept with considerable theoretical significance. The YTM on a coupon-bearing risk-free government bond depends upon the rate at which the future interest cash inflows can be reinvested. Because this future reinvestment is uncertain, a coupon-bearing risk-free government bond is not truly risk free even though it has no default risk. The only strictly risk-free yield is the rate on a zero-coupon government bond.

A two-year Treasury note with a 1.375% coupon could be expected to yield 5.87% based on the February 16, 2011, term structure as indicated in Table 5.6 below.

Table 5.6. Estimated Yield of a Two-Year, 1.375% Coupon Note.

$$\begin{aligned}\ln(1+R_t) &= -0.17833(1/2) - 0.042615(2) - 0.03791(1.375) + 0.673866\\ &= 0.722056\end{aligned}$$

To transform $\ln(1+R_t)$ into the YTMy, take the exponential of both sides of the equation:

$$\begin{aligned}1+R_t &= \exp[0.722056]\\ &= 1.058661\\ R_t &= 1.058661 - 1\\ &= 0.058661 \quad \text{or} \quad 5.87\%\end{aligned}$$

As with any extrapolation, there may be a problem with extrapolating outside of the sample range. Hence, caution should be exercised in using the risk-free yield estimate obtained from this technique.

5.5. Convertible Bonds and their Valuation

Convertible bonds are long-term debt securities that can be converted into a specified number of shares of common stock at the option of the bond-holder. The ratio of exchange can be expressed either in terms of a conversion ratio (CR), which is simply the number of shares into which one bond is convertible — for example, 20 shares per bond — or in terms of a conversion price (CP), which is equal to the bond's face value (FV) divided by the conversion ratio.

$$\text{CP} = \frac{\text{FV}}{\text{CR}}. \tag{5.18}$$

With a face value of \$1,000 and a conversion ratio of 20, the conversion price is \$1,000/20 or \$50.

Often these basic conversion terms change over the life of the convertible-bond issue. For example, the conversion price may increase in discrete stages — that is, \$50 for the first five years, \$55 for the next five years, and so on. The reason the issuer might employ such a strategy is to shorten the time before conversion if the common-stock price increased enough to make conversion otherwise likely.

The conversion price should not be confused with the bond's conversion value (CV), the total market value of the bond in terms of the stock into which it is convertible. The conversion value can be computed by multiplying the conversion ratio by the price of the firm's common stock, P_s:

$$\text{CV} = (\text{CR})(P_S). \tag{5.19}$$

For the current example, if the price of the stock is \$40 per share, the conversion value would be (20)(\$40) = \$800. Because it would otherwise cause arbitrage opportunities, the convertible bond will not sell in the market for less than its conversion value.

The convertible bond also provides the investor with a fixed return in the form of its coupon payments. The present value of these periodic coupons (usually paid semiannually, as for regular nonconvertible bonds) plus the present value of the face value to be paid at maturity will equal what is called the investment value (IV) of the convertible bond:

$$\text{IV} = \sum_{t=1}^{n} \frac{I}{(1+k)^t} + \frac{FV}{(1+k)^n}, \tag{5.20}$$

where

FV = the face value of the bond;
I = the periodic coupon payment;
k = the investor's required rate of return; and
n = the number of periods until the maturity of the issue.

Because a convertible bond is effectively a hybrid security with some of the features of bonds and some of common stock, its value both as a bond and as common stock must be considered in order to value it. When the conversion value exceeds the investment value, the convertible-bond price (P_{CV}) is related primarily to the conversion value; and when the conversion value is less than the investment value, P_{CV} is related primarily to the investment value. Figure 5.6 provides further illustration.

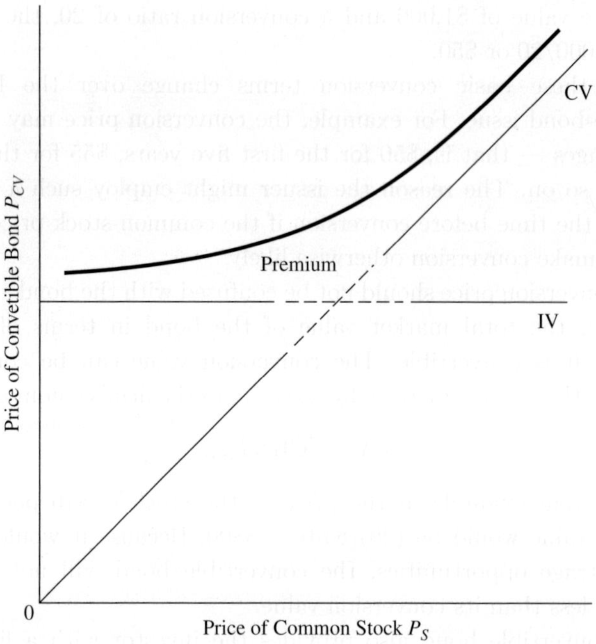

Fig. 5.6. Investment Value, Conversion Value, and the Price of a Convertible Bond.

A convertible bond will ordinarily sell at a premium over the investment value, primarily because of the conversion option, and will sell at a premium above the conversion value because of the floor established by its investment value. This investment-value floor is not constant over time, but will actually vary with interest-rate movements and perceived changes in the financial risk of the issuing company. For example, if interest rates increase or the firm's financial risk increases (possibly accompanied by a lower bond rating) the floor can decrease, thus providing less protection to the convertible bondholder. If the face value of the convertible is higher than the investment value (as it ordinarily would be at the time of issue because of the bond's conversion potential), the investment value will increase over time, while other things are held constant. This is true because the ultimate price is always the face value at maturity. The size of the premiums reflected in the convertible bond's price would be larger the more volatile the underlying stock price is if the bond had a significant conversion potential.

As indicated above, the convertible bond actually has two types of premiums, the premium over investment value (IV) and the premium over conversion value (CV). At relatively common-stock prices, the value of the investment floor becomes negligible and the IV becomes insignificant: the bond is selling at price very close to its conversion value. Another factor causing P_{CV} to closely approximate CV at high stock prices is that if the conversion value exceeded the call price of the bond, the firm could exercise its call option and effectively force conversion. Upon conversion, the convertible bond would be worth only its conversion value. If, on the other hand, the convertible-bond price were close to the investment value, it would be an indication that the conversion potential of the bond is negligible.

The main reason for convertible-bond premium is the hybrid nature of the security. It offers downside protection against stock-price declines at the same time that it provides upside price-appreciation potential similar to straight common-stock investment. However, other factors also influence the size of the premiums to some extent. For example, transaction costs charged for convertible-bond purchases are ordinarily lower than for common-stock purchases. This should increase the convertible-bond premiums, other things held constant. Another factor that might have an upward influence is the fact that certain regulated financial institutions are more restricted in their common-stock investment than in their purchase of convertible bonds (see Brigham, 1966). An additional factor taken into account by convertible-bond investors is the comparison of the common-stock dividend yield (d/P_s) and the current yield (I/P_{CV}) of the convertible bond. The greater the common stock's dividend yield is relative to the convertible bond's interest yield, the less attractive the convertible and the lower the premiums on it.

With the definitions of investment value, conversion value, and the premiums associated with them in hand, it is possible to take a more rigorous approach to the convertible bonds. Using the simplifying assumptions of a single-period investment horizon and a constant term structure of interest rates over that horizon, convertible bonds can be separated into two categories: (1) those for which IV > CV and (2) those for which CV > IV.

For convertible bonds in which IV > CV, investors set prices for these securities primarily for their bond value and only secondarily because of their conversion potential. The single-period cash flows could be expressed as the sum of the face value (FV), the coupon payment (I), and the expected gain upon conversion. This last flow is a function of the stock price per share in state i at period $1(P_{si1})$. For all values of P_{si1} greater than the corresponding values of IV/CR:

$$\text{Expected conversion profit} = \sum_{i=1}^{m} [(P_{si1})(\text{CR}) - \text{IV}_{i1}] \left[\prod{}_{i1}\right], \qquad (5.21)$$

where

$$(P_{si1})(\mathrm{CR}) = \mathrm{CV}_1$$

$\prod_{i1}$ = the probability of occurrence for P_s values at time i.

Therefore:

$$\text{Expected CV} = \mathrm{FV}_1 + I_1 + \sum_{i=1}^{m} [(P_{si1})(\mathrm{CR}) - \mathrm{IV}_{i1}] \left[\prod{}_{i1}\right]. \qquad (5.22)$$

Using the k_d, the required rate of return for straight debt investments, and k_s, the required rate of return for straight common-stock investments, the value of the debt-dominated convertible bond (IV > CV) can be expressed:

$$P_{CVD} = \frac{\mathrm{FV}_1 + I_1}{(1+k_d)} + \frac{\sum_{i=1}^{m} [(P_{si1})(\mathrm{CR}) - \mathrm{IV}_{i1}] [\prod_{i1}]}{(1+k_s)}. \qquad (5.23)$$

Since $\mathrm{FV}_1 + I_1/(1+k_d)$ is equal to IV_0 Equation (5.24) can be written:

$$P_{CVD} = \mathrm{IV}_0 + \frac{\sum_{i=1}^{m} [(P_{si1})(\mathrm{CR}) - \mathrm{IV}_1] [\prod_{i1}]}{(1+k_s)}. \qquad (5.24)$$

The price of a convertible bond with IV > CV is equal to its current investment value and the present value of the expected conversion profit. Since $P_{\mathrm{CVD}} - \mathrm{IV}$ is equal to the current premium over investment value, IP,

$$\mathrm{IP} = \frac{\sum_{i=1}^{m} [(P_{si1})(\mathrm{CR}) - \mathrm{IV}_{i1}] [\prod_{i,1}]}{(1+k_s)}. \qquad (5.25)$$

That is, IP is equal to the present value of the expected conversion profit.

For convertible bonds in which CV > IV, investors set prices for these securities primarily for their conversion potential and secondarily for their investment-value floor protection. This floor protection is also a function of the common-stock price probability distribution. For all values of P_{si1} less than or equal to the corresponding value of $\mathrm{IV}_1/\mathrm{CR}$:

$$\text{Expected floor protection} = \sum_{i=1}^{m} [\mathrm{IV}_{i1} - (P_{si1})(\mathrm{CR})] \left[\prod{}_{i1}\right]. \qquad (5.26)$$

Therefore:

$$\text{Expected } CV_1 = (\mathrm{CR})\,[E(P_{si1})] + I_1 + \sum_{i-1}^{m} [\mathrm{IV}_{i1} - (P_{si1})(CR)] \left[\prod{}_{i1}\right]. \qquad (5.27)$$

Discounting at the appropriate rates, the value of the stock-dominated convertible bond (CV > IV) can be expressed:

$$P_{CVS} = \frac{(\text{CR})\,[E(P_{si1})] + \sum_{i=1}^{m} [\text{IV}_{i1} - (P_{si1})(\text{CR})]\,[\prod i1]}{(1+k_s)} + \frac{I}{(1+k_d)}. \tag{5.28}$$

Since the current price of common stock, P_{s0}, can be written in terms of the present value of the sum of the expected period-1 price P_1 and the expected period-1 dividends d:

$$P_0 = \frac{E(P_1) + E(d_1)}{(1+k_s)}, \tag{5.29}$$

it can also be shown that

$$\frac{(\text{CR})\,[E(P_{si1})]}{(1+k_s)} = (\text{CR})(P_0) - \frac{(\text{CR})\,[E(d_1)]}{(1+k_s)}. \tag{5.30}$$

Substituting into Equation (5.28):

$$P_{\text{CVS}} = (\text{CR})(P_0) + \frac{I}{(1+k_d)} - \frac{E(d_1)(\text{CR})}{(1+k_s)} + \frac{\sum_{i=1}^{m} \text{IV}_1 - [(\text{CR})(P_{si1})][\prod i1]}{(1+k_s)}. \tag{5.31}$$

Thus, with (CR) $(P_0) = \text{CV}_0$:

$$P_{\text{CVS}} = \text{CV}_0 + \left\{\frac{I_1}{(1+k_d)} - \frac{E(d_1)(\text{CR})}{(1+k_s)}\right\} + \frac{\sum_{i=1}^{m} \text{IV}_{\text{i}1} - (\text{CR})(P_{si1})[\prod i1]}{(1+k_s)}. \tag{5.32}$$

The price of a convertible bond with CV > IV is then equal to the sum of its current conversion value, the present value of the difference between the coupon interest payments on the bond and the expected dividend that would be paid upon conversion, and the present value of the expected floor protection.

Since $P_{CVS}-\text{CV}$ is equal to the current premium over investment value CP:

$$\text{CP} = \left\{\frac{I_1}{(1+k_d)} - \frac{E(d_1)(\text{R})}{(1+k_s)}\right\}^t + \frac{\sum_{i=1}^{m} \text{IV}_{\text{i}1} - [(\text{CR})(P_{si1})]\,[\prod i1]}{(1+k_s)}. \tag{5.33}$$

That is, CP is equal to the present value of the income-stream differential between the bond and an equivalent amount of common stock, and the present value of the floor protection.

Even though the preceding analysis of convertible-bond valuation was made under simplifying assumptions, the removal of each of them could be shown to uphold the basic logic and results that were found. Empirical testing by Walter and Que (1973) and West and Largay (1972) essentially shows that the relationships developed here seems to hold up in the markets for convertible bonds. For example, Walter and Que notes that for bonds with CV > IV, premiums decline at a decreasing rate as the difference between CV and IV increases. They also note that the premiums are positively correlated with the difference between bond coupon and stock dividends. For bonds with IV > CV, Walter and Que find that the premium declines at a decreasing rate as the CV/IV ratio declines, that is, as the probability of profitable conversion decreases. West and Largay study's results basically agree with those of Walter and Que. However, neither study finds conclusive results concerning the impact of systematic risk on bond premiums. An alternative way of viewing convertible bonds is presented by Brennan and Schwartz (1977, 1980). In their view, a convertible bond is a combination of a regular bond and a call option.

5.6. Summary

This chapter has considered how security analysts and portfolio managers deal with some of the complex problems associated with the analysis and valuation of bonds. A study was made of the types of bonds available and the basic fundamentals relating to their valuation. The impact of systematic risk on the valuation models was analyzed and some of the available empirical evidence was reviewed. From the evidence, it seems clear that the choice of a market index is quite important and that the inclusion of bonds in the market index is helpful in explaining the relationship between return and risk.

Bond ratings were examined and prediction models were developed to help identify the factors that need to be considered by investors. The ratings seem to be impounded efficiently into bond prices, so that their informational content to investors is suspect. Considerable emphasis was placed on the theories of the term structure of interest rates and the resulting yield curves. It appears that properly constructed yield curves can be useful to investors in the forecasting of interest rates, to help identify mispriced bonds to help investors manage their bond portfolios, and to provide an analytical base for investment strategies, such as riding the yield curve.

In the final section, convertible bonds were separated for further analysis because their hybrid nature (an investment mixture of debt and stock) causes special problems for analysts trying to value them in the market. It was demonstrated that the valuation process is more manageable with some simplifying assumptions and the categorization of convertible bonds according to the relative sizes of their investment value and their conversion value. It was shown that the premium over the investment value is equal to the sum of the present value of the difference between bond coupons and expected stock dividends and the present value of the bond's floor protection.

Bond valuation and analysis can be used in security analysis and portfolio management to determine fair value of bond prices and the potential risk-related interest-rate fluctuations of liquidity conditions. Consequently, both security analysts and portfolio managers need command of the concepts, theory, and techniques discussed in this chapter.

Questions and Problems

1. Define the following terms.

   (a) par value
   (b) YTM
   (c) zero-coupon bond
   (d) yield curve
   (e) coupon interest rate

2. You notice that the yield curve for Treasury securities has the shape shown in the figure.

   (a) Discuss in detail some of the theories that might explain the shape of the yield curve.

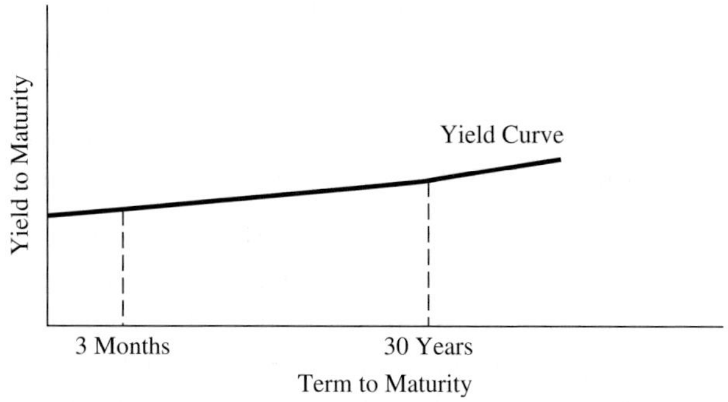

   (b) If you were buying these bonds, would you buy long-term or short-term bonds?

3. You are given the following information about ABC Corporation's bonds.

Years until bond matures	3 years
Coupon rate	12%
Maturity value	$1,000
Current market price	$1,050

If you assume that interest payments are made annually and that you require a 10% rate of return, would you purchase this bond?

4. Calculate the YTM for a bond that matures in five years and has a coupon rate of 9%, a par value of $1,000, and a current market price of $953. Assume that interest payments are made semiannually.
5. You are considering two bonds for investment purposes:

   Bond A: A$10,000 par-value zero-coupon bond with a term to maturity of five years and a market yield of 9%.
   Bond B: A$10,000 par-value coupon bond with a 9% coupon rate, a term to maturity of five years, and a market yield of 9%.

   (a) Calculate the initial price of both bonds at a market yield of 9%, assuming semiannual compounding.
   (b) Calculate the percentage change in the price of the bonds if the market yields rise by three percentage points (300 basis points).

6. What is call risk? What effect does call risk have on the promised yield to maturities?
7. Compare the following two bonds:

   Bond A: A tax-free municipal bond selling at par with a coupon rate of 6%, a maturity value of $10,000, and a term to maturity of four years.
   Bond B: A corporate bond selling at par with a coupon rate of 9%, a maturity value of $10,000, and a term to maturity of four years.

   If you assume that both bonds have the same default risk and that your marginal tax rate is 28%, which bond would you purchase?

8. What are revenue bonds? What are general-obligation bonds (GOBs)? If New York City would be both expected to have the greater risk? Which type of bond would have the greater YTM?
9. Briefly explain the relationship between bond prices and market rate of interest.

10. A bond that matures in 20 years has a call date five years from today. If the coupon rate is 9%, the maturity value is \$10,000, and the current market price is \$11,000, calculate the appropriate yield.

Appendix 5A: Worksheets for Yield Curves

Table 5A.1. Yield, Time to Maturity and Coupon Rates for Treasury Bonds and Notes as of February 16, 2011.

(1) R_t	(2) t	(3) x	(1) R_t	(2) t	(3) x	(1) R_t	(2) t	(3) x
0.0618	0.117808	0.875	0.409	1.161644	1.375	0.7933	2	3.875
0.043	0.117808	4.75	0.4309	1.20274	1	0.8481	2.063014	2.75
0.1088	0.2	0.875	0.4157	1.20274	4.5	0.8981	2.10411	1.375
0.1194	0.2	4.875	0.4516	1.243836	1.375	0.8785	2.147945	2.5
0.1154	0.284932	0.875	0.4717	1.287671	0.75	0.9392	2.189041	1.75
0.1096	0.284932	4.875	0.469	1.287671	4.75	0.9126	2.230137	3.125
0.1355	0.367123	1.125	0.4969	1.328767	1.875	0.9895	2.271233	1.375
0.1353	0.367123	5.125	0.5159	1.369863	0.625	0.9264	2.271233	3.625
0.1458	0.452055	1	0.5034	1.369863	4.875	0.9576	2.315068	3.5
0.1381	0.452055	4.875	0.5273	1.410959	1.5	1.0293	2.356164	1.125
0.1461	0.493151	5	0.5574	1.454795	0.625	1.011	2.39726	3.375
0.167	0.536986	1	0.5595	1.454795	4.625	1.0691	2.438356	1
0.1725	0.536986	4.625	0.5931	1.49589	1.75	1.0369	2.482192	3.375
0.1866	0.619178	1	0.5662	1.49589	4.375	1.113	2.523288	0.75
0.1914	0.619178	4.5	0.6087	1.539726	0.375	1.083	2.523288	4.25
0.2108	0.70411	1	0.5916	1.539726	4.125	1.088	2.567123	3.125
0.2038	0.70411	4.625	0.6444	1.580822	1.375	1.1674	2.608219	0.75
0.2229	0.745205	1.75	0.6574	1.621918	0.375	1.157	2.649315	3.125
0.2453	0.786301	0.75	0.6369	1.621918	4.25	1.2163	2.690411	0.5
0.2423	0.786301	4.5	0.7001	1.663014	1.375	1.2179	2.734247	2.75
0.2656	0.827397	1.125	0.711	1.706849	0.375	1.2563	2.731507	0.5
0.287	0.871233	1	0.6779	1.706849	3.875	1.1699	2.731507	4.25
0.2927	0.871233	4.625	0.7456	1.747945	1.375	1.2661	2.772603	2
0.3065	0.912329	1.125	0.7099	1.747945	4	1.2953	2.813699	0.75
0.3162	0.956164	0.875	0.7496	1.789041	0.5	1.3104	2.857534	1.5
0.3211	0.956164	4.75	0.7088	1.789041	3.375	1.3434	2.89863	1
0.3354	0.99726	1.375	0.7942	1.830137	1.125	1.3384	2.942466	1.75
0.3423	0.99726	4.875	0.8023	1.873973	0.625	1.3997	2.983562	1.25
0.3504	1.035616	0.875	0.7645	1.873973	3.625	1.3096	2.983562	4
0.3486	1.035616	4.625	0.8251	1.915068	1.375	1.3889	3.019178	1.875
0.3626	1.076712	1.375	0.8392	1.958904	0.625	1.4282	3.10411	1.75
0.3956	1.120548	1	0.7789	1.958904	2.875	1.4757	3.186301	1.875
1.5079	3.271233	2.25	2.3681	5.063014	2.625	3.0019	6.90137	2.75
1.5515	3.353425	2.625	2.409	5.147945	2.375	3.0288	6.986301	2.625

(Continued)

Table 5A.1. (*Continued*)

(1) R_t	(2) t	(3) x	(1) R_t	(2) t	(3) x	(1) R_t	(2) t	(3) x
1.5977	3.438356	2.625	2.4363	5.230137	2.625	3.0062	7.027397	3.5
1.5634	3.479452	4.25	2.3992	5.271233	5.125	3.0511	7.271233	3.875
1.6612	3.523288	2.375	2.3637	5.271233	7.25	2.9049	7.271233	9.125
1.6947	3.605479	2.375	2.4581	5.315068	3.25	3.1047	7.523288	4
1.7417	3.690411	2.375	2.4865	5.39726	3.25	3.1662	7.775342	3.75
1.6727	3.731507	4.25	2.5263	5.482192	3.25	2.9979	7.775342	9
1.7794	3.772603	2.125	2.488	5.523288	4.875	3.2507	8.027397	2.75
1.8158	3.857534	2.625	2.5655	5.567123	3	3.0691	8.027397	8.875
1.8648	3.942466	2.25	2.5921	5.649315	3	3.2892	8.273973	3.125
1.8246	3.983562	4	2.6241	5.734247	3.125	3.3314	8.526027	3.625
1.778	3.983562	11.25	2.5895	5.775342	4.625	3.1969	8.526027	8.125
1.9036	4.060274	2.375	2.5587	5.775342	7.5	3.3943	8.778082	3.375
1.9303	4.145205	2.5	2.666	5.816438	2.75	3.4429	9.030137	3.625
1.9814	4.227397	2.5	2.6863	5.90137	3.25	3.3005	9.030137	8.5
1.9563	4.268493	4.125	2.7073	5.986301	3.125	3.4965	9.276712	3.5
2.0309	4.312329	2.125	2.6763	6.027397	4.625	3.3523	9.276712	8.75
2.0703	4.394521	1.875	2.734	6.063014	3	3.5763	9.528767	2.625
2.112	4.479452	1.75	2.7579	6.147945	3.25	3.4047	9.528767	8.75
2.0764	4.520548	4.25	2.793	6.230137	3.125	3.616	9.780822	2.625
1.9998	4.520548	10.625	2.7655	6.271233	4.5	3.6193	10.03288	3.625
2.1709	4.564384	1.25	2.6806	6.271233	8.75	3.4958	10.03288	7.875
2.2055	4.646575	1.25	2.8329	6.315068	2.75	3.5484	10.27671	8.125
2.2467	4.731507	1.25	2.8672	6.39726	2.5	3.5904	10.52603	8.125
3.6425	10.77808	8	4.2513	16.02192	6.625	4.6023	26.27397	5
3.7672	11.52603	7.25	4.2889	16.51781	6.375	4.6436	27.02466	4.375
3.7995	12.27397	7.625	4.3119	16.76986	6.125	4.644	27.26849	4.5
3.856	12.52603	7.125	4.3724	17.52055	5.5	4.6873	28.00548	3.5
3.9425	13.02192	6.25	4.3924	17.7726	5.25	4.6714	28.24932	4.25
4.035	14.27671	7.5	4.3993	18.02466	5.25	4.6665	28.24932	4.5
4.0571	14.52877	7.625	4.3882	18.52055	6.125	4.6747	28.50137	4.375
4.1296	15.02466	6.875	4.4112	19.26575	6.25	4.6685	29.00822	4.625
4.2027	15.52877	6	4.4605	20.02192	5.375	4.6793	29.26027	4.375
4.2129	15.52055	6.75	4.6037	25.02466	4.5	4.687	29.51233	3.875
4.2404	15.76986	6.5	4.6089	26.0274	4.75	4.6832	29.76438	4.25
						4.6702	30.01644	4.75

Bibliography

Beaver, W., H. P. Kettler and M. Scholes. "The Association Between Market Determined and Accounting Determined Risk Measures." *Accounting Review*, v. 45 (1970), pp. 654–682.

Bodie, Z., A. Kane and A. Marcus. Investments, 9th ed. New York: McGraw-Hill Book Company, 2010.

Brennan, M. J. and E. Schwartz. "Analyzing Convertible Bonds." *Journal of Financial and Quantitative Analysis*, v. 15 (November 1980), pp. 907–929.

Brennan, M. J. and E. Schwartz. "Convertible Bonds: Valuation and Optimal Strategies for Call and Conversion." *Journal of Finance*, v. 32 (December 1977), pp. 1699–1715.

Brigham, E. F. "An Analysis of Convertible Debentures: Theory and Some Empirical Evidence." *Journal of Finance*, v. 21 (1966), pp. 35–54.

Echols, M. E. and J. W. Elliott. "A Quantitative Yield Curve Model of Estimating the Term Structure of Interest Rates." *Journal of Financial and Quantitative Analysis*, v. 11 (March 1976), pp. 87–114.

Fisher, L. and R. L. Weil. "Coping with the Risk of Interest Rate Fluctuations: Returns to Bond Holders from Naïve and Optimal Strategies." *Journal of Business*, v. 44 (October 1971), pp. 408–431.

Folger, H. R. "Managing Bond Portfolios." In *Investment Managers Handbook*, Summer Levine, ed., Chapter 9, pp. 316–317. Homewood, IL: Dow Jones-Irwin, 1980.

Gushee, C. H. "How to Hedge a Bond Investment." *Financial Analysts Journal*, v. 37 (March/April 1981), pp. 44–51.

Hettenhouse, G. W. and W. L. Sartoris. "An Analysis of the Informational Value of Bond-Rating Changes." *Quarterly Review of Economics and Business*, v. 16 (Summer 1976), pp. 68–78.

Homer, S. and M. L. Leibowitz. *Inside the Yield Book*. New York, NY: Prentice-Hall, Inc., and New York Institute of Finance, 1972.

Hopewell, M. H. and G. G. Kaufman. "Bond Price Volatility and Term to Maturity: A Generalized Respecification." *American Economic Review*, v. 63 (September 1973), pp. 749–753.

Ibbotson, R. G. and R. A. Singuefield. *Stock, Bonds, Bills, and Inflation: Historical Returns (1926–1981)*. Charlottesville, VA: Financial Analysts Researchers Foundation, 1982.

Ibbotson, R. G. and R. A. Singuefield. "Stocks, Bonds, Bills and Inflation: Updates." *Financial Analysts Journal*, v. 35 (July–August 1979), pp. 40–44.

Kessel, R. A. "Inflation-Caused Wealth Redistribution: A Test of a Hypothesis." *American Economic Review*, v. 46 (1956), pp. 128–141.

Kessel, R. A. "The Cyclical Behavior of the Term Structure of Interest Rates." J. M. Guttentag, ed.: *Essays on Interest Rates*, v. 2 (1971), pp. 337–390.

Khoury, S. J. *Investments*. New York, NY: Macmillan Publishing Company, 1983.

Lee, C. F. and A. C. Lee. *Encyclopedia of Finance*. New York: Springer, 2006.

Lee, A. C., J. C. Lee and C. F. Lee. *Financial Analysis and Planning and Forecasting: Theory and Application*. Singapore: World Scientific, 2009.

Leibowitz, M. L. *Total After-Tax Bond Performances and Yield Measures*. New York: Salomon Brothers, 1974.

McCulloch, H. J. "An Estimation of the Liquidity Premium." *Journal of Political Economy*, v. 83 (January/February 1975), pp. 95–119.

Modigliani, F. and R. Swatch. "Debt Management and the Term Structure of Interest Rates: An Empirical Analysis of Recent Experience." *Journal of Political Economy*, v. 75 (Supplement, August 1967), pp. 569–589.

Pinches, G. E. and K. A. Mingo. "A Multivariate Analysis of Industrial Bond Ratings." *Journal of Finance*, v. 28 (March 1973), pp. 1–18.
Pinches, G. E. and K. A. Mingo. "The Role of Subordination and Industrial Bond Ratings." *Journal of Finance*, v. 30 (March 1975), pp. 201–206.
Reilly, F. K. and M. D. Joehnk. "The Association between Market-Determined Risk Measures for Bonds and Bond Ratings." *Journal of Finance*, v. 31 (December 1976), pp. 1387–1403.
Walter, J. E. and A. V. Que. "The Valuation of Convertible Bonds." *Journal of Finance*, v. 28 (July 1973), pp. 713–732.
Weinstein, M. I. "The Systematic Risk of Corporate Bonds." *Journal of Finance and Quantitative Analysis*, v. 16 (September 1981), pp. 257–287.
Weinstein, M. I. "Bond Systematic Risk and the Option Pricing Model." *Journal of Finance*, v. 38 (December 1983), pp. 1415–1430.
Weinstein, M. I. "The Effect of Rating Change Announcement on Bond Price." *Journal of Financial Economics*, v. 5 (December 1977), pp. 329–350.
West, R. R. "Bond Ratings, Bond Yields and Financial Regulations." *Journal of Law and Economics*, v. 1 (April 1973), pp. 159–168.
West, R. R. and J. A. Largay III. "Premium on Convertible Bonds: Comments." *Journal of Finance*, v. 27 (December 1972), pp. 1156–1162.
Zumwalt, J. K. and D. Wort. "An Examination of Factors Influencing Bond Rating." *Akron Business and Economics Review* (Fall 1980), pp. 31–35.

Chapter 6

The Uses and Calculation of Market Indexes

The topic of market indexes has always been of great importance in the world of security analysis and portfolio management because the indexes are commonly used by investors to reflect the level and performance of the market. These market measures can be used as a standard of investment performances as well as a critical factor in the determination of required rates of return for individual security for a security investment through the use of the capital asset pricing model (CAPM), which necessitates an estimate of the current level of return on the market portfolio — usually proxied by a broadly based market index. Market-index values have also been commonly used to provide insights into such economic variables as the growth of economic output and corporate returns. Recent years, however, have seen an explosion in the potential value of market-index information because of new options and futures contracts, in addition to the development of market-index mutual funds that have made these indexes directly tradable investment opportunities. The full set of implications for security analysts and portfolio managers, as well as for the individual investor, has not yet been fully developed in the literature of finance. Some of these implications are explored in later sections of this chapter.

This chapter discusses five main topics. Section 6.1 discusses alternative methods for compiling stock and price indexes, while Section 6.2 describes alternative market indexes. Section 6.3 provides a discussion of the uses of market indexes. Section 6.4 investigates both the historical behavior of market indexes and the implications of their use for forecasting, and Section 6.5 focuses on market-index proxy errors and their impact on beta estimates and efficient-market hypothesis (EMH) tests.

6.1. Alternative Methods for Compilation of Stock and Price Indexes

Many different indexes are computed and compiled for the use of investors. While some indexes have been developed using an equal weighting approach (equal dollar amounts assumed to be invested in each component), the primary types utilized are either price weighted or value weighted. Both these methods are employed in the compilation of stock consumer-price (cost) indexes. Stock indexes are directly used in security analysis and portfolio management, and consumer-price (cost) indexes are used in measuring the change of purchasing power. It should be noted that consumer-price (cost) information is also useful in security analysis and portfolio management.

6.1.1. *Price-Weighted and Quantity-Weighted Indexes*

In a **price-weighted index** the basic approach is to sum the prices of the component securities used in the index and divide this sum by the number of components, in other words, to compute a simple arithmetic average. The Dow–Jones Industrial Average (DJIA) is the most familiar index of this type. To allow for the impact of stock splits and stock dividends, which could destroy the consistency and comparability of price-weighted index data over time, an adjustment of either the reported price data or the divisor is required. As will be seen below, the DJIA has used a divisor adjustment for some time now.

A price-weighted index such as the DJIA is not strictly speaking as index at all — it is an average. The concept of indexing involves the comparison of currently computed averages with some base value. For example, the current levels of the Standard & Poor's 500 index (S&P 500) are compared with the average level for the base period of 1941–1943. The S&P 500 is also the most widely used example of a **value-weighted stock index**. In such an index, the weight of each component stock is equal to its market value in relation to that of all the stocks included. The use of market value (price per share multiplied by the number of shares outstanding) obviates the necessity of adjusting for stock splits or stock dividends.

Two classical forms of indexes are the Paasche index and the Laspeyres index. They measure price inflation because quantity is held constant.

$$\text{Paasche price index} = \frac{\sum P_{jt}Q_{jt}}{\sum P_{j0}Q_{jt}}, \tag{6.1}$$

$$\text{Laspeyres price index} = \frac{\sum P_{jt}Q_{j0}}{\sum P_{j0}Q_{j0}}, \tag{6.2}$$

where

P_{jt} = price per unit for jth commodity in period t;
P_{j0} = price per unit for jth commodity in period 0;
Q_{jt} = the quantity of jth commodity in period t; and
Q_{j0} = the quantity of jth commodity in period 0.

Equations (6.1) and (6.2) can be used to construct Fisher's ideal price index:

$$\begin{array}{l}\text{Fishers ideal}\\ \text{Price index}\end{array} = \sqrt{\left(\frac{\sum P_{jt}Q_{jt}}{\sum P_{j0}Q_{jt}}\right)\left(\frac{\sum P_{jt}Q_{j0}}{\sum P_{j0}Q_{j0}}\right)}. \tag{6.3}$$

Similarly, **quantity-weighted indexes** can be defined:

$$\text{Laspeyres price index} = \frac{\sum Q_{jt}P_{j0}}{\sum Q_{j0}P_{j0}}, \tag{6.4}$$

$$\text{Paasche price index} = \frac{\sum Q_{jt}P_{jt}}{\sum Q_{j0}P_{jt}}, \tag{6.5}$$

$$\begin{array}{l}\text{Fishers ideal}\\ \text{Price index}\end{array} = \sqrt{\left(\frac{\sum Q_{jt}P_{j0}}{\sum Q_{j0}P_{j0}}\right)\left(\frac{\sum Q_{jt}P_{jt}}{\sum Q_{j0}P_{jt}}\right)}. \tag{6.6}$$

Sample Problem 6.1 provides further illustration.

Sample Problem 6.1

To show how the indexes mentioned above can be used to analyze real-world issues, we demonstrate how the price index is compiled; the Laspeyres price index for the second week is calculated as follows. The data of the first two tables indicate that the total cost of purchasing the quantities shown (in hundreds of thousands of shares) in the first week, which will be used as base period, was (in million):

$$(121.4)(64.56)+(177.6)(39.47)+(514.3)(19.49)+(22.2)(46.81) = \$25{,}910.345.$$

At the prices prevailing in the second week the total cost of purchasing the same shares would have been

$$(121.4)(63.20)+(177.6)(38.87)+(514.3)(18.96)+(22.2)(44.53)=\$33{,}135.429.$$

Substituting these numbers into Equation (6.2), the Laspeyres price index for the second week is obtained:

$$100\left(\frac{33{,}135.429}{25{,}910.345}\right)=127.88.$$

The Paasche price index for the second week is calculated as follows. The data of the first two tables indicate that the total cost of purchasing the quantities shown (in hundreds of thousands of shares) in the first week, which will be used as base period, was (in million):

$$(121.4)(64.56)+(177.6)(39.47)+(514.3)(19.49)+(22.2)(46.81)=\$25{,}910.345.$$

At the prices prevailing in the second week the total cost of purchasing the same shares would have been

$$(121.4)(63.20)+(177.6)(38.87)+(514.3)(18.96)+(22.2)(44.53)=\$33{,}135.429.$$

Substituting these numbers into Equation (6.2), the Laspeyres price index for the second week is obtained:

$$100\left(\frac{33{,}135.429}{25{,}910.345}\right)=127.88.$$

Prices of Stock in Four Pharmaceutical Corporations for the First 12 Weeks or 2010, with the Unweighted Aggregate Index of Prices.

Week	Date	JNJ	MRK	PFE	MJN	Average	Index of Average
1	2010/1/11	64.56	39.47	19.49	46.81	42.58	100.00
2	2010/1/19	63.20	38.87	18.96	44.53	41.39	97.20
3	2010/1/25	62.86	38.18	18.66	45.23	41.23	96.83
4	2010/2/1	62.64	36.73	17.96	46.29	40.91	96.06
5	2010/2/8	62.72	36.92	17.80	45.05	40.62	95.40
6	2010/2/16	63.81	37.49	17.99	46.78	41.52	97.50
7	2010/2/22	63.00	36.88	17.55	47.30	41.18	96.71
8	2010/3/1	64.04	37.49	17.48	49.91	42.23	99.17
9	2010/3/8	64.18	37.16	17.08	51.99	42.60	100.05
10	2010/3/15	65.11	38.06	16.91	51.39	42.87	100.67
11	2010/3/22	64.38	37.43	17.14	51.83	42.70	100.26
12	2010/3/29	65.77	37.71	17.08	52.90	43.37	101.84

Average Volume of Transactions in Shares of Four Pharmaceutical Corporations for the First 12 Weeks of 2010 (hundreds of thousands).

Week	Date	JNJ	MRK	PFE	MJN
1	2010/1/11	121.4	177.6	514.3	22.2
2	2010/1/19	141.8	209.6	741.1	27.0
3	2010/1/25	151.1	164.4	508.9	33.2
4	2010/2/1	136.4	180.3	811.4	26.2
5	2010/2/8	104.5	153.0	583.2	21.0
6	2010/2/16	105.5	143.7	573.3	23.6
7	2010/2/22	101.5	161.6	572.6	18.5
8	2010/3/1	92.6	116.7	682.0	18.6
9	2010/3/8	137.7	155.7	587.7	24.2
10	2010/3/15	118.5	182.8	635.8	18.4
11	2010/3/22	95.0	133.6	642.6	18.1
12	2010/3/29	96.7	110.5	546.8	10.7

Weighted Aggregate Price Indexes for First Twelve Weeks of 2010.

Week	Laspeyres Price Index	Paasche Price Index	Fisher's Price Index
1	100.00	100.00	100.00
2	127.88	97.67	111.76
3	106.97	96.59	101.65
4	127.22	93.90	109.30
5	97.01	93.61	95.30
6	95.57	95.06	95.31
7	96.32	93.27	94.79
8	95.51	93.57	94.53
9	106.61	93.83	100.02
10	108.52	93.78	100.88
11	95.63	93.10	94.36
12	83.99	93.89	88.80

Source: http://finance.yahoo.com/.

6.1.2. *Value-Weighted Indexes*

So far, indexes of quantity as well as price have been defined. It would seem appropriate to measure total cost of the consumer's purchases in terms of cost index as

$$\text{Cost index} = \frac{\sum P_{jt}Q_{jt}}{\sum P_{j0}Q_{j0}}. \tag{6.7}$$

The cost index is the basic form used for compiling the **value-weighted stock index**.

The Paasche index tends to underestimate the inflation rate, while the Laspeyres index are intended to be a measure of value growth. The standard form of value-weighted stock indexes is expressed as

$$\text{Stock index} = \frac{\sum P_{jt} \sum Q_{jt}}{\sum P_{j0} \sum Q_{j0}}. \tag{6.8}$$

Therefore, changes in the index level could be the result of either price changes or volume changes. The price effect can be separated out by using one of the constant-quantity approaches s defined in Equations (6.1), (6.2), or (6.8). From a security analyst's point of view, it might even be useful to divide indexes such as the S&P 500 into subgroups that are either inflation favorable or inflation unfavorable. The quantity effect is also not really an exogenous factor. It can be separated out by using one of the constant-price approaches as defined in Equations (6.4), (6.5), or (6.6). There are at least three ways in which the concept of quantity is important in index construction. First, there is the number of shares outstanding, which is used to determine a firm's market value. Experienced analysts know that this quantity is an understatement of the true number of shares implied in price determination in the market. Even the accounting profession has taken steps to force companies to include "share equivalents" when computing earnings-per-share figures that will be reported to their stockholders. To the extent that share equivalents change over time, the rate of change in value-weighed stock indexes will be misstated, as will the level of the indexes. A second quantity-effect concept deals with market-volume figures — the number of shares traded in the market per unit of time. The implications of this technical concept are not well understood and are not taken account of in the stock indexes. A stock-velocity measure might be useful to financial analysts, similar to the money-velocity measurements used by economists. A third quantity-effect concept is related to supply-and-demand relationships, in which the amount of securities issued depends positively on the securities' selling price. Thus, stock quantity will increase relatively (because of new issues) during periods in which prices are perceived to be high and will decline relatively (because of repurchases) during periods in which prices are perceived to be low. More will be said about this quantity effect in later chapters dealing with market efficiency and the capital asset pricing model.

6.2. Alternative Market Indexes

In this section, the seven important stock indexes mentioned earlier are discussed. Following each discussion an illustration is provided.

6.2.1. *Dow Jones Industrial Average*

The DJIA is probably the best known and most widely quoted of all the market indexes. Its latest value is broadcast many times a day, even on the least news-oriented top-40 radio stations. The financial News Cable Network reports it every 90 seconds during a trading day. It is also probably the most criticized representation of the overall market among the available major stock indexes. The DJIA is a price-weighted arithmetic average of 30 large, well-known industrial stocks, all of which are listed on the New York Stock Exchange (NYSE). The computation involves summing the current prices of the 30 stocks and then dividing by a divisor that is adjusted to allow for any stock splits or large stock dividends.

$$\text{DJIA} = \sum_{i=t}^{30} \frac{P_{it}}{DV_t}, \tag{6.9}$$

where

P_{it} = the closing price of stock i on day t; and
DV_t = the adjusted divisor on day t.

As can be seen in Table 6.1, the adjustment process is designed to keep the index value the same as it would have been if the slit had not occurred. Similar adjustments have been made when it has been found necessary to replace one of the component stocks with the stock of another company. The consistency and comparability of index values at different points in time are thus protected. Nevertheless, the adjustment process used for the DJIA has not been accepted without criticism. Since price weighting itself causes high-priced stocks to dominate the series, this same effect can cause a shift in this balance when fast-growing firms split their stock. For example, a 20% increase in the price of Stock A from Table 6.1 would in itself have caused a 10% increase in the value of the sample index before the split, while a 20% increase in Stock B would have cause only a 5% increase in the index value. After the two-for-one split of Stock A, a 20% increase in either Stock A or Stock B would produce the same effect on the index value (a 6.7% increase), illustrating a downward shift in the importance of Stock

Table 6.1. Adjustment of DJIA Divisor to Allow for a Stock Split.

Stock	Price before Split	Price after 2-for-1 Stock Split by Stock A
A	60	30
B	30	30
C	20	20
D	10	10
	120	90
	Average $= \frac{120}{4} = 30$	Adjustment of Divisor $= \frac{90}{30} = 3$
		Average $= \frac{90}{3} = 30$
	Divisor before Split = 4	Divisor after Split = 3

A relative to the other stocks in the sample. This type of an effect could lead to the fastest-growing stocks having the least importance in determining the index values.

Other criticisms of the DJIA center around its emphasis on using only large, mature, "blue-chip" firms (and a small number of them at that) that do not seem to be similar to most companies in the market. The attitude of the multitudes that watch its daily movement seems to be "as the DJIA goes, so goes the economy." Since studies measuring the correlation of daily price changes of the DJIA with other broader indexes of NYSE stocks have found correlation coefficients ranging from 0.89 to 0.92, this attitude may be justified in the short run.[1]

6.2.2. *Standard & Poor's Composite 500 Index*

The second most popular market index, **Standard & Poor's Composite 500 Index (S&P 500)**. is a value-weighted index of 400 industrial stocks, 40 utility stocks, 20 transportation stocks, and 40 financial stocks. It is computed as follows:

$$\text{S \& P}_t = \frac{\sum P_{it}Q_{it}}{\sum P_{i0}Q_{i0}} \times 10, \tag{6.10}$$

where

P_{it} = price of stock i in period t;
Q_{it} = number of shares outstanding for stock i in period t;

[1]See Reilly, F. K. *Investments Analysis and Portfolio Management*. Chicago: Dryden Press, 1985.

P_{i0} = price of stock i in the base period 0; and
Q_{i0} = number of shares outstanding for stock i in base period 0;

and the base period is 1941–1943.

Since 1976, when the makeup of the S&P 500 was changed to include financial stocks, the index had for the first time included stocks from the over-the-counter (OTC) market. ("Over the counter" recalls the trading practices of the 1800s, when buyers and sellers of unlisted stocks traded their stocks over the bank counter.) This was necessary because many of the stocks of major financial institutions are traded on the OTC market.

While the S&P 500 is much more comprehensive in makeup — thus more representative of the overall market — than the DJIA, its total number of components is still small compared to the theoretically available market portfolio of all investment opportunities. The value-weighting computational approach is also subject to the criticism that firms with the largest market values have the most influence on the computed level. While this is certainly true, it is also true of the market portfolio itself, and should not be a problem except to the extent that the S&P 500 sample does not sufficiently reflect the makeup of the market portfolio. This cannot be properly evaluated empirically because of the impossibility of specifying the market portfolio accurately. In any case, the S&P 500 has gained added significance recently because of the development of options, futures contracts, and options on futures contracts for this index.[2] This has created a new opportunity for portfolio managers by providing a new means to adjust the risk and return of a portfolio to desired levels. By adjusting the proportion of the futures position to the valuation of the portfolio, the portfolio manager can theoretically attain any risk-return combination desired. These opportunities are discussed in further detail in later chapters.

6.2.3. *New York Stock Exchange Composite Index*

Following Fisher (1966), another commonly used value-weighted index is the **New York Stock Exchange Composite Index**, inaugurated in 1966 and consisting of the market values of all of the common stocks listed on the NYSE. While it includes many more stocks than the S&P 500 (about 1,700), this index can still be criticized as a proxy for the market portfolio

[2]Other indexes for which options and futures contracts have been developed include the NYSE Composite Index, the Value Line Stock Index, and a subset of the S&P 500, the S&P 100.

because it contains none of the companies that cannot be listed, or choose not to be listed, on the NYSE.

6.2.4. *Wilshire 5000 Equity Index*

The **Wilshire 5000 Equity Index**, prepared by Wilshire Associates of Santa Monica, California, is a value-weighted and equal-weighted index that is increasing in usage because it contains most equity securities available for investment, including all NYSE and AMEX issues plus the most active stocks on the OTC market.

The following formula is used to compute the index:

$$I_t = I_{t-1}\left(\frac{\sum_{j=1}^{n}(S_{jt})P_{jt}}{\sum_{j=1}^{n}(S_{jt-1})P_{jt-1}}\right), \tag{6.11}$$

where

I_t = index value for the tth period;
n = number of stocks in index;
P_{jt} = price of the jth security for the tth period; and
S_{jt} = shares outstanding of the jth security for the tth period.

In the event that P_{jt} is not available for a given security, that security is dropped from the summations. If P_{jt-1} is not available but P_{jt} is — that is, a security has just resumed trading — the last available price is substituted for P_{jt-1}.

6.2.5. *Standard & Poor's Composite 100 Index*

Very recently a subset of the S&P 500 called the **S&P 100** was developed for use in the futures and options markets. Although it may seem strange in the context of the increasing development of broader indexes that this more narrowly based index would be formed, it will become clear that the basis for its popularity is related to margin requirement in the options market. Sample Problem 6.2 provides further illustration.

Sample Problem 6.2

To illustrate the seven indexes just discussed, daily quotations from *The Wall Street Journal* for January 10 to January 25, 2010, are presented in Table 6.2.

Table 6.2. Major Stock Indexes for January 11, 2010–January 25, 2010.

Indexes	DJIA	Nasdaq	S&P 500	Wilshire 5000	S&P 100
11-Jan	10663.99	2312.41	1146.98	11838.1	528.61
12-Jan	10627.26	2282.31	1136.22	11697.8	524.29
13-Jan	10680.77	2307.90	1145.68	11819.2	527.93
14-Jan	10710.55	2316.74	1148.46	11846.8	529.60
15-Jan	10609.65	2287.99	1136.03	11715	524.11
19-Jan	10725.43	2320.40	1150.23	11865.5	530.21
20-Jan	10603.15	2291.25	1138.04	11744.9	524.73
21-Jan	10389.88	2265.70	1116.48	11539.8	514.13
22-Jan	10172.98	2205.29	1091.76	11289.1	502.35
25-Jan	10196.86	2210.80	1096.78	11331.5	504.54

6.3. The User and Uses of Market Indexes

People from many walks of life use and are affected by market indexes. Economists and statisticians use stock-market indexes to study long-term growth patterns in the economy, to analyze and forecast business of economic activity. Investors, both individual and institutional, use the market index as a benchmark against which to evaluate the performance of their own or institutional portfolios. The answer to the question, "Did you beat the market?" has important ramifications for all types of investors. Market technicians in many cases base their decisions to buy and sell on the patterns that appear in the time series of the market indexes. The final use of the market index is in portfolio analysis. In discussions of the market model and systematic risk earlier in this chapter, it became evident that the relevant riskiness of a security is determined by the relationship between that security's return and the return on the market.

Among economists and statisticians, one of the major uses of stock-market indexes is as a leading economic indicator. Judging by how long they have been employed, leading indicators of economic activity must be considered a forecasting success. Unlike econometric modeling, the leading economic indicator approach to forecasting does not require assumptions about what causes economic behavior. Instead, it relies on statistically detecting patterns among economic variables that can be used to forecast turning points in economic activity. Table 6.3 presents a list of the time series currently being used by the U.S. Department of Commerce as leading economic indicators.

A recent development in the financial market is the growth of futures and options on stock-market indexes. Index options have been by far the

Table 6.3. The Index of Leading Indicators (Includes 12 Data Series).

BEA Series Number	Description of Series	Weight
1	Average workweek of production workers, manufacturing	0.984
3	Layoff rate, manufacturing (inverted)	1.025
8	New order, consumer goods and materials, 1972 dollars	1.065
12	Index of net business formation	0.984
19	Index of stock prices (Standard and Poor)	1.079
20	Contracts and orders, plant and equipment, 1972 dollars	0.971
29	Building permits, private housing	1.025
32	Vendor performance	0.930
36	Change in inventories on hand and on order, 1972 dollars	0.957
92	Percentage change in sensitive prices (smoothed)	0.971
104	Percentage change in total liquid assets (smoothed)	1.011
105	Money supply (M1), 1972 dollars	1.065

Source: Department of Commerce. *Handbook of Cyclical Indicators* (May 1977).

most important of the numerous new financial instruments introduced during the 1980s. The development of the index options has made it possible for institutional investors to deal with the entire market rather than individual stocks, and thus to open up new kinds of investment strategies. As will be shown, the potential for options and futures strategies to reduce risk and change return patterns is almost limitless.

Besides the seven indexes discussed in the last section, Merrill Lynch and Wilshire Associates have compiled an index called the **Merrill Lynch and Wilshire Capital Markets Index (CMI).** The CMI is a market-value weighted index created to measure the total return performance of the combined domestic taxable fixed-income and equity market. This unique new investment tool currently tracks more than 10,000 bonds and stocks. The CMI has been used in (1) asset-allocation decisions, (2) performance measurement, (3) sector-investment analysis, and (4) portfolio structuring.

6.4. Historical Behavior of Market Indexes and the Implications of their Use for Forecasting

It is useful at this point to observe how some of the market indexes have behaved historically and to study the implications of their use in forecasting.

6.4.1. *Historical Behavior*

Table 6.4 compare annualized rates of return computed over one-year through ten-year holding periods for pairs of the most widely used market

Table 6.4. Annualized Rates of Return: DJIA versus S&P 500 (Dividends Included).

Holding Period (years)	DJIA	S&P 500
2001	3.7	−11.6
2002	−9.0	−15.0
2003	−10.8	−9.7
2004	15.1	16.3
2005	2.7	6.3
2006	6.7	6.6
2007	22.0	20.5
2008	−7.3	−8.5
2009	−35.0	−34.4
2010	23.4	18.5

indexes. These rates of return are computed using May 1, 2000, as the closing date of each holding period.

As can be seen in Table 6.4, there are some differences, notably in rates of return for any given year, but the relative year-to-year movement is very similar. The correlation coefficient between rates of return computed from these two indexes over this time period is 0.952989. This means that 95.30% of the movement in the returns on the DJIA can be considered to be related to the concurrent movement in returns on the S&P 500. So even though there are substantial differences in the way these indexes are computed, there is a high correlation in the way they behave. Figure 6.1 presents the historical graph of the S&P 500 during the period 1991–2009.

6.4.2. *Implications*

What are the implications for security analysts and portfolio managers who might be using such indexes as proxies for the return on the market portfolio? The results seem to imply that differences among the available indexes, although occasionally significant over short time periods, are not very great over longer time periods. In his study using daily price changes, Reilly (1985) finds that even on a short-run basis the DJIA is highly correlated with other indexes that are based primarily on stocks listed on the NYSE. In fact, the consensus of stock-index research seems to indicate that the main cause of lower correlated return is the use of relatively higher-risk samples, such as samples made up primarily of American Stock Exchange or over-the-counter stocks (see Reilly (1985)). It would therefore

Fig. 6.1. The S&P 500, 1991–2009.

seem appropriate for forecasters of market return to use market-index proxies that are broadly based in nature and that basically reflect the average risk across all investment opportunities. Roll's (1978) research, in which use of different indexes was shown to give conflicting portfolio-performance decisions in marginal situations, has clearly demonstrated that this can be important and has probably led to the increased use in recent years of indexes such as the Wilshire 5000. (The Wilshire 5000 Equity Index is graphed in Fig. 6.2. Monthly returns for the Wilshire 5000 Equity Indexes are listed in Appendix 6A.)

6.5. Market-Index Proxy Errors and their Impact on Beta Estimates and Efficient-Market-Hypothesis Tests

This section concerns how the stock index can be used to calculate the market rates of return. The issue related to proxy error in estimating the market model (see Chapter 4) is also studied.

Market indexes are used as proxy variables to calculate the return on the market portfolio R_m in the "market model."

$$R_{jt} = \alpha_j + \beta_j R_{mt} + e_{jt}, \qquad (6.12)$$

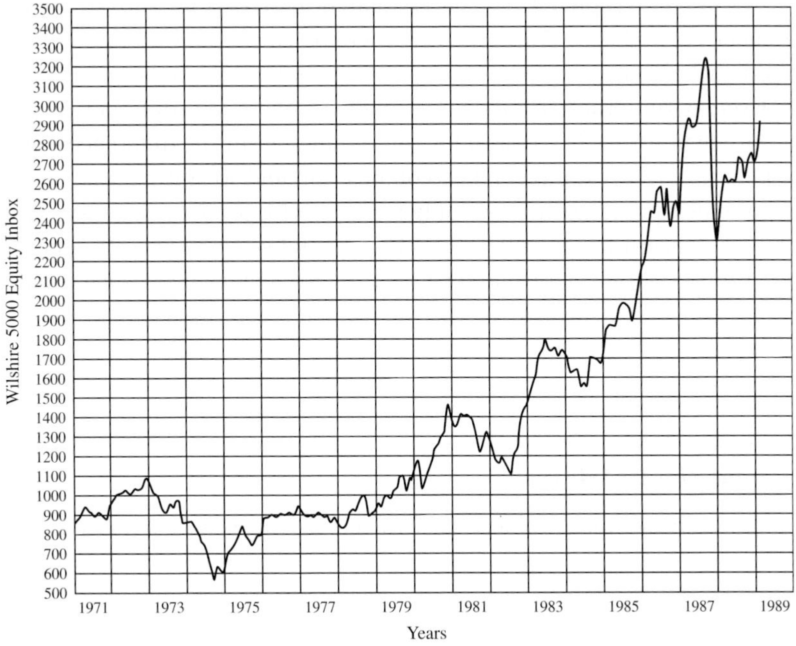

Fig. 6.2. The Wilshire 5000 Equity Index.
Source: Wilshire Associates.

where

R_{jt} = the return in the jth security in period t;
α_j = the intercept of a market model for the jth security;
β_j = the systematic risk measure of security j;
R_{mt} = the return on the market index in period t; and
e_{jt} = a random error term.

Estimations of β_j(beta) can be made empirically by regressing R_{it} on R_{mt}, where R_m is proxied by using a rate of return based on a market index, such as the S&P 500. For example:

$$R_{mt} = \frac{I_t - I_{t-1} + d_t}{I_{t-1}}, \tag{6.13}$$

where I_{t-1} and I_t are the S&P 500 index levels at the beginning and end of period t, respectively, and d_t is the dividends paid on the index stocks during period t.

It should be noted that the estimated R_{mt} can be subject to measurement error (Lee, 1976; Roll, 1978). Globally, the market rate of return should include not only the equity return but also bonds, gold, and so on. Even within the various equity indexes there are different levels of measurement error. The reason for this is inherent in the differences among the indexes — for example, index composition and weighting scheme. This kind of index-proxy error is not only a concern for academicians but should also be a concern for industry practitioners and security as well, especially since the development of market-index investment vehicles such as index options and index futures. (These instruments are discussed in detail in Chapters 12 through 16.)

6.6. Index-Proxy Error, Performance Measure, and the EMH Test

A potentially serious problem is involved in the use of a market index to represent the market portfolio. Strictly speaking, the market portfolio consists of all available investment opportunities, weighted according to their proportion of the total market value. While an index such as the S&P 500 is also value weighted and includes many more component firms than a narrowly based index such as the DJIA, it includes only common-stock investments, and only a small proportion of the total available. Because of this, many financial analysts are beginning to use broader indexes, such as the Wilshire 5000. Nevertheless, while this index is value weighted and includes all stocks for which daily prices are available, it still does not include "all available investment opportunities." Richard Roll (1977) questions the adequacy of using a market index as a market-portfolio proxy. He points out that the linear relationship between beta and the required rate of return for a security follows from the efficiency of the market portfolio, and that this linearity is not independently testable. A proxy, such as the S&P 500, may be mean-variance efficient, while the market portfolio is not, and it might be mean-variance inefficient when the market portfolio is efficient. Roll thinks that the CAPM and the market portfolio are therefore untestable without accurate specification of the "true" market portfolio. Since the latter is impossible, therefore, so is the former. Roll (1978) strengthens his argument by showing that different indexes used as proxies for the market portfolio can cause different portfolio-performance rankings.

This is quite a serious matter, indeed, because many financial analysts and portfolio managers are evaluated using CAPM-based performance-measurement models — for example, the Jensen model, in which "alpha" values are measured to determine whether a portfolio is performing well. The alpha is the intercept value of an *ex-post* regression of the risk premiums achieved over time by as individual portfolio analyzed on the market-risk premium over the same time period. Since

$$R_{pt} - R_{ft} = \alpha_p + \beta_p(R_{mt} - R_{ft}) + e_{pt}, \tag{6.14}$$

where

R_{pt} = rate of return for a portfolio in period t;
R_{ft} = riskless rate in period t;
R_{mt} = market rate of return in period t;
β_p = systematic risk for a portfolio; and
e_{pt} = an error term.

It follows that Jensen's performance measurement can be computed:

$$\alpha_p = [\bar{R}_p - R_f] - \beta_p[\bar{R}_m - R_f], \tag{6.15}$$

where $\bar{R}_p$ and $\bar{R}_m$ represent rates of return for a portfolio and market rates of return, respectively.

A plot of risk-premium characteristic lines for three portfolios is shown in Fig. 6.3. It can be said that Portfolio X has shown superior performance over the time period analyzed because its alpha is significantly positive. This is true because the CAPM model leads to the conclusion that, under equilibrium conditions, the alpha intercept should be equal to zero. Figure 6.3 also suggests that Portfolio Z has shown inferior performance because of the significantly negative alpha, and Portfolio Y has performed as would be predicted by the CAPM. (Other model, such those developed by Sharpe and Treynor, are studied in more detail in later chapters of this book.) The point being made here is that beta-estimation problems can have important and far-reaching implications. These empirical problems, as well as problems dealing with the fundamental assumptions of the theory, have led other researchers suck as Stephen Ross (1976) to seek alternative models, among them the arbitrage pricing theory (APT) discussed in Chapter 11. As will be seen in later chapters, these alternative models have empirical and theoretical problems of their own.

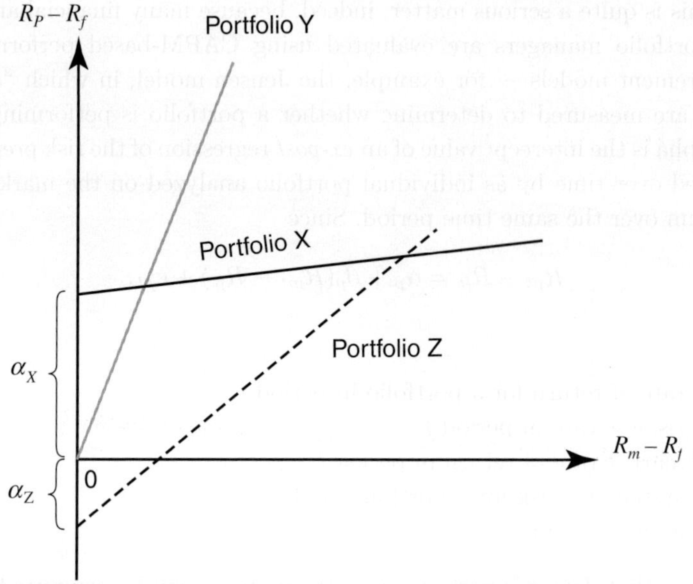

Fig. 6.3. Risk-Premium Characteristic Lines.

Market-index proxy errors, through their impact on beta estimation, also impact heavily upon tests of the EMH. This is true because a test of market efficiency (security prices fully reflect all available information) must be based on a model of market equilibrium (e.g., the CPAM), and any test therefore simultaneously a test of efficiency and a test of the assumed equilibrium model. (EMH is discussed in Chapter 16.)

6.7. Summary

This chapter has described basic market-index information needed to do security analysis and portfolio management, as well as methods of compiling stock-market and price indexes and historical behavior of stock indexes. Moreover, the impact of proxy errors associated with market rates of return on beta estimation discussed in this chapter underscore the importance of alternative stock indexes for both individual and institutional investors.

Questions and Problems

1. What is a market index? What are some of the uses of market indexes for security analysis?

2. Give two different methods used to weight indexes.
3. Compare the Paasche and Laspeyres price indexes. What are the benefits and disadvantages of each index?
4. What is the DJIA? How many stocks are included in the index? What method is used to weight the stocks?
5. What stocks makeup the S&P 500? What method is used to weight the stocks? Why do some people consider this index to be a better measure of market performance than the DJIA?
6. Carefully explain the differences between calculating an index using a geometric average versus an arithmetic average.
7. Briefly explain Roll's criticism of market indexes as proxies of the market portfolio.
8. Briefly compare the advantages and disadvantages of using a narrowly focused index such as the DJIA with that of a broad-based index like the Wilshire 5000.
9. Using section C of *The Wall Street Journal*, define the major indexes and discuss their usefulness.

Appendix 6A: Monthly Returns for the Wilshire 5000 Equity Indexes

Table 6A.1. Monthly Returns for the Wilshire 5000 Equity Indexes, January 29, 1971–December 31, 1984.

	Value-Weight Index			Equal-Weighted Index		
Month Ending	Price Appreciation* (%)	Dividends Yield (%)	Total Return (%)	Price Appreciation (%)	Dividends Yield (%)	Total Return (%)
1/29/71	5.184	0.127	5.311	14.528	0.114	14.642
2/26/71	1.381	0.418	1.799	4.982	0.216	5.198
3/31/71	4.266	0.209	4.475	5.702	0.199	5.901
4/30/71	3.479	0.104	3.583	3.857	0.100	3.957
5/28/71	−3.707	0.401	−3.306	−4.692	0.217	−4.475
6/30/71	0.226	0.166	0.392	−1.534	0.182	−1.352
7/30/71	−3.688	0.103	−3.585	−4.822	0.100	−4.722
8/31/71	3.524	0.450	3.974	3.870	0.241	4.111
9/30/71	−0.540	0.163	−0.377	−0.346	0.180	−0.166
10/29/71	−4.035	0.179	−3.856	−5.471	0.123	−5.348
11/30/71	−0.704	0.416	−0.288	−3.481	0.253	−3.228
12/31/71	8.966	0.177	9.143	11.667	0.200	11.867

(*Continued*)

Table 6A.1. (*Continued*)

	Value-Weight Index			Equal-Weighted Index		
Month Ending	Price Appreciation* (%)	Dividends Yield (%)	Total Return (%)	Price Appreciation (%)	Dividends Yield (%)	Total Return (%)
1/31/72	2.895	0.120	3.015	10.110	0.109	10.219
2/29/72	2.976	0.395	3.371	4.606	0.209	4.815
3/30/72	0.726	0.202	0.928	0.524	0.168	0.692
4/28/72	0.629	0.106	0.735	0.896	0.102	0.998
5/31/72	1.363	0.416	1.779	−1.782	0.221	−1.561
6/30/72	−2.228	0.149	−2.079	−3.400	0.178	−3.222
7/31/72	3.120	0.386	3.506	1.070	0.221	1.291
8/31/72	3.120	0.386	3.506	1.070	0.221	1.291
9/29/72	−0.938	0.164	−0.774	−2.794	0.166	−2.628
10/31/72	0.762	0.138	0.900	−1.241	0.135	−1.106
11/30/72	4.273	0.418	4.691	4.017	0.257	4.274
12/29/72	0.928	0.136	1.064	−1.513	0.188	−1.325
1/31/73	−2.801	0.115	−2.686	−2.973	0.090	−2.883
2/28/73	−4.688	0.357	−4.331	−7.707	0.190	−7.517
3/30/73	−0.842	0.154	−0.688	−2.921	0.194	−2.727
4/30/73	−5.066	0.127	−4.939	−7.340	0.135	−7.205
5/31/73	−2.830	0.453	−2.377	−8.621	0.262	−8.359
6/29/73	−0.986	0.170	−0.816	−4.213	0.201	−4.012
7/31/73	5.483	0.140	5.623	11.303	0.135	11.438
8/31/73	−3.472	0.431	−3.041	−4.686	0.261	−4.425
9/28/73	5.101	0.156	5.257	7.770	0.174	7.944
10/31/73	−0.029	0.173	0.144	0.125	0.149	0.274
11/30/73	−12.684	0.474	−12.210	−18.335	0.274	−18.061
12/31/73	0.833	0.200	1.033	−4.521	0.285	−4.236
1/31/74	0.214	0.158	0.372	13.350	0.165	13.515
2/28/74	−0.175	0.467	0.292	0.513	0.279	0.792
3/29/74	−2.682	0.199	−2.483	0.682	0.246	0.928
4/30/74	−4.691	0.180	−4.511	−5.788	0.173	−5.615
5/31/74	−4.944	0.556	−4.388	−7.562	0.322	−7.240
6/28/74	−2.702	0.238	−2.464	−3.620	0.287	−3.333
7/31/74	−7.192	0.180	−7.012	−5.687	0.192	−5.495
8/30/74	−9.659	0.670	−8.989	−9.071	0.369	−8.702
9/30/74	−11.289	0.296	−10.993	−8.507	0.319	−8.188
10/31/74	16.250	0.313	16.563	9.238	0.252	9.490
11/29/74	−4.934	0.714	−4.220	−5.554	0.408	−5.146
12/31/74	−2.883	0.297	−2.586	−8.634	0.417	−8.217
1/31/75	14.431	0.194	14.625	31.170	0.241	31.411
2/28/75	5.525	0.672	60197	5.510	0.351	5.861
3/31/75	2.444	0.281	2.725	8.283	0.346	8.629

(*Continued*)

Table 6A.1. *(Continued)*

	Value-Weight Index			Equal-Weighted Index		
Month Ending	Price Appreciation* (%)	Dividends Yield (%)	Total Return (%)	Price Appreciation (%)	Dividends Yield (%)	Total Return (%)
4/30/75	4.615	0.212	4.827	3.092	0.190	3.282
5/30/75	5.015	0.614	5.629	7.483	0.352	7.835
6/30/75	4.720	0.240	4.960	7.321	0.298	7.619
7/31/75	−6.321	0.188	−6.133	−1.078	0.187	−0.891
8/29/75	−2.644	0.532	−2.112	−5.116	0.316	−4.800
9/30/75	−4.129	0.286	−3.843	−4.324	0.356	−3.968
10/31/75	5.332	0.252	5.584	1.418	0.217	1.635
11/28/75	2.618	0.544	3.162	1.688	0.326	2.014
12/31/75	−1.247	0.255	−0.992	−0.396	0.381	−0.015
1/30/76	12.283	0.204	12.487	19.963	0.180	20.143
2/27/76	0.161	0.511	0.672	10.993	0.279	11.272
3/31/76	2.448	0.249	2.697	2.346	0.289	2.635
4/30/76	−1.088	0.132	−0.956	−0.453	0.237	−0.216
5/28/76	−1.580	0.624	−0.956	−2.003	0.306	−1.697
6/30/76	4.011	0.224	4.235	2.938	0.172	3.110
7/30/76	−0.762	0.142	−0.620	0.446	0.162	0.608
8/31/76	−0.761	0.589	−0.172	−1.725	0.348	−1.377
9/30/76	2.199	0.227	2.426	1.490	0.287	1.777
10/29/76	−2.262	0.184	−2.078	−2.539	0.185	−2.354
11/30/76	−0.072	0.693	0.621	2.530	0.388	2.918
12/31/76	6.108	0.213	6.321	10.683	0.341	11.024
1/31/77	−3.702	0.161	−0.3541	3.324	0.175	3.499
2/28/77	−2.056	0.589	−1.467	0.143	0.306	0.449
3/31/77	−1.240	0.246	−0.994	1.150	0.289	1.439
4/29/77	0.520	0.143	0.663	1.576	0.092	1.668
5/31/77	−1.260	0.129	−1.131	2.302	0.249	2.551
6/30/77	4.196	0.912	5.108	5.182	0.298	5.480
7/29/77	−1.471	0.131	−1.340	4.165	0.172	4.357
8/31/77	−1.991	0.697	−1.294	−0.605	0.340	−0.265
9/30/77	−0.021	0.283	0.262	1.036	0.268	1.304
10/31/77	−4.040	0.212	−3.828	−2.208	0.215	−1.993
11/30/77	3.616	0.835	4.451	7.258	0.372	7.630
12/30/77	0.589	0.258	0.847	1.602	0.348	1.950
1/31/78	−5.724	0.191	−5.533	−1.132	0.176	−0.956
2/28/78	−1.734	0.730	−1.004	2.291	0.374	2.66
3/31/78	3.106	0.341	3.447	6.506	0.332	6.892
4/28/78	8.092	0.179	8.271	8.538	0.171	8.709
5/31/78	1.553	0.822	2.375	6.640	0.367	7.007
6/30/78	−1.362	0.273	−1.089	0.525	0.299	0.824

(Continued)

Table 6A.1. (*Continued*)

	Value-Weight Index			Equal-Weighted Index		
Month Ending	Price Appreciation* (%)	Dividends Yield (%)	Total Return (%)	Price Appreciation (%)	Dividends Yield (%)	Total Return (%)
7/31/78	5.579	0.183	5.762	5.241	0.169	5.410
8/31/78	3.608	0.671	4.279	9.303	0.331	9.634
9/29/78	−0.802	0.286	−0.516	0.085	0.258	0.343
10/31/78	−10.961	0.251	−10.710	−18.607	0.201	−18.406
11/30/78	2.415	0.812	3.227	3.949	0.412	4.361
12/29/78	1.589	0.288	1.877	1.050	0.371	1.421
1/31/79	4.564	0.235	4.799	9.601	0.222	9.823
2/28/79	−3.009	0.688	−2.321	−2.253	0.349	−1.904
3/30/79	6.601	0.285	6.886	8.463	0.326	8.789
4/30/79	0.710	0.238	0.948	2.573	0.216	2.789
5/31/79	−2.344	0.845	−1.499	−0.916	0.359	−0.557
6/29/79	4.798	0.272	5.070	5.153	0.321	5.474
7/31/79	0.966	0.224	1.190	1.886	0.211	2.097
8/31/79	5.746	0.797	6.543	7.507	0.386	7.893
9/28/79	0.365	0.267	0.632	−0.528	0.240	−0.288
10/31/79	−7.422	0.294	−7.128	10.276	0.229	−10.047
11/30/79	5.427	0.774	6.201	6.253	0.405	6.658
12/30/79	2.354	0.295	2.649	4.735	0.357	5.092
1/31/80	6.930	0.242	7.172	9.144	0.231	9.375
2/29/80	−0.454	0.679	0.225	−2.590	0.338	−2.252
3/31/80	−12.429	0.284	−12.145	−16.146	0.319	−15.827
4/30/80	4.516	0.226	4.742	5.061	0.222	5.283
5/30/80	5.108	0.781	5.889	6.819	0.412	7.231
6/30/80	3.371	0.333	3.704	3.892	0.385	4.277
7/31/80	6.646	0.245	6.891	9.722	0.207	9.929
8/29/80	2.006	0.559	2.565	5.548	0.327	5.875
9/30/80	2.635	0.283	2.918	3.068	0.281	3.349
10/31/80	2.257	0.274	2.531	2.958	0.224	3.182
11/28/80	10.252	0.595	10.847	5.230	0.274	5.504
12/31/80	−4.230	0.265	−3.965	−3.813	0.288	−3.525
1/30/81	−4.445	0.171	−4.274	−0.195	0.166	−0.029
2/27/81	0.691	0.595	1.286	−0.205	0.288	0.083
3/31/81	4.706	0.306	5.012	7.561	0.293	7.854
4/30/81	−0.986	0.227	−0.759	2.820	0.227	30.47
5/29/81	0.705	0.634	1.339	4.220	0.276	4.496
6/30/81	−1.387	0.636	−0.751	−1.274	0.267	−1.007
7/31/81	−0.655	0.177	−0.478	−2.009	0.149	−1.860
8/31/81	−6.155	0.638	−5.517	−7.317	0.240	−7.077
9/30/81	−6.843	0.286	−60557	−9.007	0.222	−8.785
10/30/81	5.711	0.327	6.038	8.065	0.215	8.280

(*Continued*)

Table 6A.1. (*Continued*)

	Value-Weight Index			Equal-Weighted Index		
Month Ending	Price Appreciation* (%)	Dividends Yield (%)	Total Return (%)	Price Appreciation (%)	Dividends Yield (%)	Total Return (%)
11/30/81	3.818	0.684	4.502	2.573	0.267	2.840
12/31/81	−3.015	0.286	−2.729	−1.155	0.246	−0.909
1/29/82	−3.023	0.144	−2.879	−1.679	0.118	−1.561
2/26/82	−6.172	0.645	−5.527	−4.759	0.233	−4.526
3/31/82	−1.424	0.398	−1.026	−0.409	0.274	−0.135
4/30/82	4.139	0.183	4.322	5.772	0.214	5.986
5/28/82	−3.629	0.815	−2.814	−2.402	0.269	−2.133
6/30/82	−2.825	0.345	−2.480	−3.410	0.255	−3.155
7/30/82	−2.261	0.166	−2.095	−0.546	0.121	−0.425
8/31/82	10.934	0.997	11.931	7.799	0.318	8.117
9/30/82	1.300	0.290	1.590	3.905	0.219	4.124
10/29/82	11.453	0.246	11.699	13.863	0.174	14.037
11/30/82	4.214	0.676	4.890	9.551	0.243	9.794
12/31/82	1.130	0.233	1.363	3.254	0.214	3.468
1/31/83	3.953	0.206	4.159	12.194	0.141	12.335
2/28/83	2.594	0.613	3.207	5.266	0.241	5.507
3/31/83	3.365	0.298	3.653	6.182	0.215	6.397
4/29/83	7.302	0.130	7.432	8.207	0.110	8.317
5/31/83	0.758	0.533	1.291	10.085	0.214	10.299
6/30/83	3.572	0.300	3.872	4.785	0.186	4.971
7/29/83	−3.251	0.126	−3.125	−1.396	0.103	−1.293
8/31/83	0.040	0.545	0.585	−2.505	0.200	−2.305
9/30/83	1.368	0.293	1.661	0.448	0.161	0.609
10/31/83	−2.867	0.175	−2.692	−5.417	0.121	−5.296
11/30/83	2.331	0.503	2.834	4.127	0.190	4.317
12/30/83	−1.352	0.244	−1.108	−1.563	0.185	−1.378
1/31/84	−1.797	0.191	−1.606	0.738	0.162	0.900
2/29/84	−4.472	0.494	−3.978	−5.108	0.179	−4.929
3/30/84	1.054	0.343	1.397	1.188	0.198	1.386
4/30/84	0.089	0.174	0.263	−1.674	0.118	−1.556
5/31/84	−5.831	0.519	−5.312	−4.530	0.180	−4.350
6/29/84	2.029	0.390	2.419	1.873	0.207	2.080
7/31/84	−2.191	0.203	−1.988	−4.293	0.125	−4.168
8/31/84	10.749	0.591	11.340	10.609	0.207	10.816
9/28/84	−0.238	0.297	0.059	0.518	0.154	0.672
10/31/84	−0.306	0.293	−0.013	−1.563	0.148	−1.415
11/30/84	−1.533	0.454	−1.079	−2.358	0.170	−2.188
12/31/84	2.105	0.329	2.434	1.388	0.191	1.579

*Represents monthly percentage change in Wilshire 5000 Equity Index.
Source: Wilshire Associates.

Table 6A.2. Monthly Return for Wilshire 5000 Equity Indexes: January 31, 1985–January 31, 1989.

	Value-Weight Index			Equal-Weighted Index		
Month Ending	Price Appreciation* (%)	Dividends Yield (%)	Total Return (%)	Price Appreciation (%)	Dividends Yield (%)	Total Return (%)
1/31/85	8.415	0.237	8.652	13.453	0.163	13.616
2/28/85	1.249	0.448	1.697	5.711	0.174	5.885
3/29/85	−0.456	0.322	−0.134	−0.087	0.185	0.098
4/30/85	−0.377	0.178	−0.199	0.028	0.121	0.149
5/31/85	5.154	0.583	5.737	3.346	0.187	3.533
6/28/85	1.519	0.326	1.845	0.913	0.153	1.066
7/31/85	−0.0246	0.226	−0.020	−3.231	0.098	3.329
8/30/85	−1.007	0.652	−0.355	0.514	0.251	0.765
9/30/85	−4.192	0.282	−3.910	−5.128	0.152	−4.976
10/31/85	4.208	0.243	4.451	3.324	0.118	3.442
11/29/85	6.501	0.432	6.933	6.505	0.158	6.663
12/31/85	4.236	0.305	4.541	4.359	0.152	4.511
1/31/86	0.897	0.177	1.074	5.399	0.103	5.502
2/28/86	6.952	0.450	7.402	6.647	0.144	6.791
3/31/86	5.107	0.257	5.364	5.642	0.154	5.796
4/30/86	−0.858	0.174	−0.684	2.602	0.100	2.702
5/30/86	4.713	0.378	5.091	4.540	0.125	4.665
6/30/86	1.128	0.241	1.369	1.744	0.138	1.882
7/31/86	−6.142	0.172	−5.970	−6.760	0.119	−6.641
8/29/86	6.263	0.358	6.621	3.434	0.141	3.575
9/30/86	−8.183	0.220	−7.963	−4.870	0.179	−4.691
10/31/86	4.869	0.172	5.041	3.818	0.090	3.908
11/28/86	1.139	0.360	1.499	0.357	0.115	0.472
12/31/86	−2.742	0.262	−2.480	−2.195	0.153	−2.042
1/30/87	12.651	0.153	12.804	13.557	0.098	13.655
2/27/87	4.550	0.348	4.898	8.979	0.126	9.105
3/31/87	2.157	0.242	2.399	5.461	0.139	5.600
4/30/87	−1.902	0.235	−1.667	−0.546	0.097	−0.449
5/29/87	0.319	0.210	0.529	1.187	0.111	1.298
6/30/87	4.225	0.251	4.476	3.550	0.130	3.680
7/31/87	4.314	0.135	4.449	4.800	0.092	4.892
8/31/87	3.550	0.334	3.884	2.348	0.116	2.464
9/30/87	−2.306	0.195	−2.111	−1.476	0.143	−1.333
10/30/87	−22.948	0.169	−22.779	−25.555	0.068	−25.487
11/30/87	−7.525	0.395	−7.130	−5.429	0.180	−5.249
12/31/87	6.979	0.315	7.294	6.612	0.210	6.822
1/29/88	4.166	0.174	4.340	10.303	0.118	10.421
2/29/88	4.684	0.597	5.281	8.278	0.206	8.484
3/31/88	−1.965	0.290	−1.675	5.960	0.168	6.128

(Continued)

Table 6A.2. (*Continued*)

Month Ending	Value-Weight Index: Price Appreciation* (%)	Value-Weight Index: Dividends Yield (%)	Value-Weight Index: Total Return (%)	Equal-Weighted Index: Price Appreciation (%)	Equal-Weighted Index: Dividends Yield (%)	Equal-Weighted Index: Total Return (%)
4/29/88	0.951	0.172	1.123	1.482	0.096	1.578
5/31/88	−0.227	0.431	0.204	−0.547	0.168	−0.379
6/30/88	4.881	0.271	5.152	5.555	0.204	5.759
7/29/88	−1.004	0.285	−0.719	−0.054	0.157	0.103
8/31/88	−3.285	0.465	−2.820	−2.324	0.160	−2.164
9/30/88	3.567	0.250	3.817	2.011	0.204	2.215
10/31/88	1.631	0.303	1.934	−1.043	0.120	−0.923
11/30/88	−2.210	0.466	−1.744	−3.820	0.194	−3.626
12/30/88	1.799	0.356	2.155	2.312	0.235	2.547
1/31/89	6.531	0.281	6.812	6.173	0.151	6.324

*Represents monthly percentage change in Wilshire 5000 Equity Index.
Source: Wilshire Associates.

Bibliography

Bodie, Z., A. Kane and A. J. Marcus. *Investments*, 9th ed. New York: McGraw-Hill/Irwin, 2010.

Cootner, P. "Stock Market Indexes — Fallacies and Illusions." *Commercial and Financial Chronicle*, September 29, 1966, p. 18.

Eubank, A. A. "Risk-Return Contrasts: NYSE, AMEX and OTC." *Journal of Portfolio Management*, v. 3 (Summer 1977), pp. 25–30.

Fisher, L. "Some New Stock Market Indexes." *Journal of Business*, v. 39 (January 1966), pp. 191–225.

Fisher, L. and J. Lorie. "Some Studies of Variability of Returns on Investments in Common Stock." *Journal of Business*, v. 43 (April 1970), pp. 99–134.

Latane, H. A., D. L. Tuttle and W. E. Young. "Market Indexes and Their Implications for Portfolio Management." *Financial Analysts Journal*, v. 27 (September/October 1971), pp. 75–85.

Lee, C. F. "Investment Horizon and the Functional Form of the CAPM." *Review of Economics and Statistics*, v. 58 (August 1976), pp. 356–363.

Lee, C. F. and A. C. Lee. *Encyclopedia of Finance*. New York: Springer, 2006.Lee, A. C., J. C. Lee and C. F. Lee. *Statistics for Business and Financial Economics*. Singapore: World Scientific Publishing Company, 1999.

Lee, C. F., A. C. Lee and J. C. Lee . *Handbook of Quantitative Finance and Risk Management*. New York: Springer, 2010.

Newbold, P. *Statistics for Business and Economics*, 1st ed. New Jersey, NJ: Prentice-Hall, Inc., 1984.

Reilly, F. K. *Investments Analysis and Portfolio Management*. Chicago: Dryden Press, 1985.

Reilly, F. K. *Investment Analysis and Portfolio Management*, 9th ed. Boston, MA: South-Western College Publishing, 2008.

Roll, R. "A Critique of the Asset Pricing Theory's Tests." *Journal of Financial Economics*, v. 4 (March 1977), pp. 129–176.

Roll, R. "Ambiguity When Performance is Measured by the Securities Market Line." *Journal of Finance*, v. 33 (September 1978), pp. 1051–1069.

Roll, R. "Performance Evaluations and Benchmark Error I and II." *Journal of Portfolio Management*, v. 6 and 7 (Summer 1980 and Winter 1981), pp. 5–12, 17–22.

Ross, S. A. "The Arbitrage Theory of Capital Asset Pricing." *Journal of Economic Theory*, v. 13 (December 1976), pp. 341–360.

Rudd, A. T. "The Revised Dow-Jones Industrial Average: New Wine in Old Bottles?" *Financial Analysts Journal*, v. 35 (October/November 1979), pp. 57–61, 63.

Part II

Portfolio Theory and Asset Pricing

Chapter 7

Sources of Risks and Their Determination

This chapter focuses on the various types of risk. An understanding of the sources of risk and their determination is very useful for doing meaningful security analysis and portfolio management; thus, discussing risk prior to an exploration of portfolio-selection models is essential. In this chapter, methods of measuring risk are defined by using basic statistical methods, and both the concepts and applications of the dominance principle and portfolio theory are discussed in some detail.

A discussion of the different types of risk and their classification is followed by a review of the concepts and applications of portfolio analysis. The dominance as well as the necessity of using performance measures as a means to compare performance among different portfolios are discussed. The determination of the commercial lending rate in accordance with risk and return concepts is then analyzed, and the final section of this chapter concerns calculations of the market rate of return and the market risk premium.

7.1. Risk Classification and Measurement

Chapter 3 discussed the rates of returns on financial assets and the total, systematic, and unsystematic risks associated with these returns. **Risk** is defined as the probability of success or failure. To be able to measure risk, it is necessary to define the range of outcomes and the probability that these outcomes will occur. A probability distribution may be determined either subjectively or objectively; a subjective determination is made by the individual about the likelihood of various future outcomes, while an objective determination involves measuring past data that are associated with the frequency of certain types of outcomes.

In either case, a subjective or objective determination requires a quantitative measure of risk. The measure most commonly used is the standard deviation or the variance of the possible returns. In considering two securities, A and B, it is possible to use a subjective approach, an objective approach, or a combination of the two approaches to indicate the expected range of outcomes and the probability that each outcome will occur. Figure 7.1 illustrates the distribution of return possibilities for these two securities.

While the standard deviation is stated in rates of return, the variance is stated in terms of the rate of return squared. Since it is more natural to discuss rates of return rather than rates of return squared, risk is usually measured with the standard deviation of returns. Nevertheless, for statistical purposes, it is usually more convenient to use the variance rather than the standard deviation. Either risk measure is appropriate because the standard deviation is merely a simple mathematical transformation of the variance.

It is the job of the security analyst to provide estimates of a financial asset's risk. Supplying estimates of a security variance or standard deviation is one method of estimating the total risk of a security.

Why do securities have differing levels of total risk? What factors cause the returns of securities to vary? Table 7.1 defines various types of risk and in so doing offers answers to these questions, and in analyzing the risks defined in Table 7.1 the following paragraphs provide further illustration.

At any point, a security or a portfolio could be subject to a number of these risks. In general, the various risks are neither mutually exclusive nor additive. By mutually exclusive, it is meant that the fact that a portfolio contains a certain kind of risk does not mean that it also contains other types of risk. By additive, it is meant that if a portfolio contains a number of different types of risk, the total risk of the portfolio is simply the sum of the individual risks. Additionally, some of the risks defined in Table 7.1 are easily quantified or measured — for example, using beta to measure systematic risk — while other types of risk may not have well-defined quantitative risk measures, such as management risk or political risk. Finally, it should be noted that the types of risk listed on Table 7.1 are mutually exclusive.

Security A

i	r	P_{ri}
1	−0.30	0.04
2	−0.20	0.06
3	−0.10	0.10
4	0.00	0.30
5	0.10	0.30
6	0.20	0.10
7	0.30	0.06
8	0.40	0.04

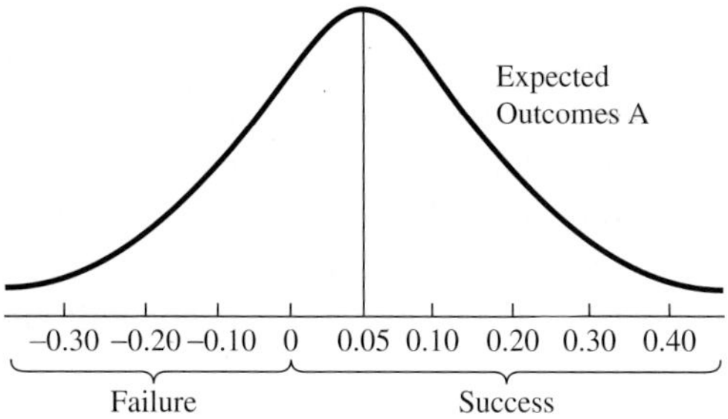

Expected return A

$$\begin{aligned} E(R) &= -0.3(0.04) - 0.2(0.06) - 0.1(0.1) \\ &\quad + 0(0.3) + 0.1(0.3) + 0.2(0.1) \\ &\quad + 0.3(0.06) + 0.4(0.04) \\ &= 0.05 \end{aligned}$$

Variance A

$$\begin{aligned} \sigma_A^2 &= (-0.3 - 0.05)^2(0.04) \\ &+ (-0.2 - 0.05)^2(0.06) \\ &+ (-0.01 - 0.05)^2(0.1) \\ &+ (0 - 0.05)^2(0.3) \\ &+ (0.1 - 0.05)^2(0.3) \\ &+ (0.2 - 0.05)^2(0.1) \\ &+ (0.3 - 0.05)^2(0.06) \\ &+ (0.4 - 0.05)^2(0.04) \\ &= 0.001812 \end{aligned}$$

Security B

i	r	P_{ri}
1	−0.10	0.10
2	0.00	0.40
3	0.10	0.40
4	0.20	0.10

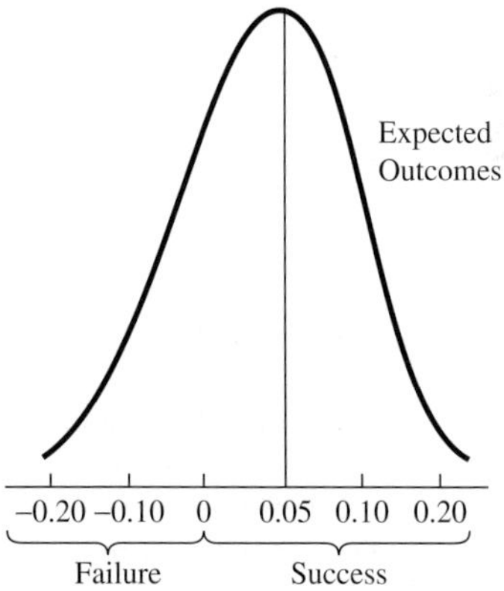

Expected return B

$$\begin{aligned} E(R) &= -0.1(0.1) + 0(0.4) + 0.1(0.4) \\ &\quad + 0.2(0.1) \\ &= 0.05 \end{aligned}$$

Variance B

$$\begin{aligned} \sigma_B^2 &= (-0.1 - 0.05)^2(0.1) \\ &+ (0 - 0.05)^2(0.4) \\ &+ (0.1 - 0.05)^2(0.4) \\ &+ (0.2 - 0.05)^2(0.4) \\ &= 0.00149 \end{aligned}$$

Fig. 7.1. Probability Distributions Between Securities A and B.

7.1.1. *Call Risk*

An investor who purchases a security, whether it is a debt instrument or equity, usually has a pretty good idea of his or her investment horizon — that is, how long he or she intends to hold the security. If the issuer calls the bond or repurchases the stock at a point in time prior to the end of the investor's investment horizon, the return earned by the investor may be less than expected. The investor is facing **call risk** (see Table 7.1 for a detailed definition).

Generally all corporate bonds and preferred stocks are callable at some point during the life of the security. Investors do not like this call feature because bonds are most often called after interest rates have fallen, so that the issue can replace them with a new issue of bonds at a lower interest rate. When a bond is called, instead of receiving the expected interest flows for the remainder of his or her investment horizon, the

Table 7.1. Types of Risk.

Risk Type	Description
Call risk	The variability of return caused by the repurchase of the security before its stated maturity.
Convertible risk	The variability of return caused when one type of security is converted into another type of security.
Default risk	The probability of a return of zero when the issuer of the security is unable to make interest and principal payments — or for equities, the probability that the market price of the stock will go to zero when the firm goes bankrupt.
Interest-rate risk	The variability of return caused by the movement of interest rates.
Management risk	The variability of return caused by bad management decisions; this is usually a part of the unsystematic risk of a stock, although it can affect the amount of systematic risk.
Marketability risk	The variability of return caused by the commissions and price concessions associated with selling an illiquid asset.
Political risk	The variability of return caused by changes in laws, taxes, or other government actions.
Purchasing-power risk	The variability of return caused by inflation, which erodes the real value of the return.
Systematic risk	The variability of a single security's return caused by the general rise or fall of the entire market.
Unsystematic risk	The variability of return caused by factors unique to the individual security.

investor must reinvest the proceeds received from the issuer at a lower rate of interest. It is this reinvestment at a new lower rate of interest that causes the yield or return of the bond to be different than what the investor expected.

For this reason, in periods of high interest rates, when interest rates are expected to drop to lower levels in the future, bonds that are call-protected for a certain number of years usually sell at a higher price than callable bonds. Thus a deferred call feature can cause an interest spread or differential to develop vis-à-vis a similar issue with no call feature or an issue that is immediately callable. The size of the interest differential varies with the investor's expectations about the future movement of interest rates.

Whether a bond is callable immediately after it is issued or after a deferred period, the actual call of the bond involves the payment of a premium over the par value of the bond by the issuer.

7.1.2. *Convertible Risk*

If a bond or a preferred stock is convertible into a stated number of shares of common stock of the corporation issuing the original security, the rate of return of the investment may vary because the value of the underlying common stock has increased or decreased. This kind of investment is facing **convertible risk**, as described in Table 7.1. A convertible security normally has a lower coupon rate, or stated dividend (in the case of preferred stocks), because investors are willing to accept a lower contractual return from the company in order to be able to share in any raise in the price of the firm's common stock. The size of the yield spread between straight and convertible securities is dependent on the future prospects of the individual firm and the general level of interest rates.

The difference between the value paid for the conversion right and the actual returns experienced over the life of the security increases the variability of returns associated with the investment.

7.1.3. *Default Risk*

The quality of the issue or the chances of bankruptcy for the issuer have a significant impact on the rate of return of a security. A lower-quality issue will sell at a lower price and thus offers a higher yield than a similar security issued by a higher-quality issuer. This is true in all segments of the securities markets. Hence, most investors hold diversified portfolios in order to reduce their exposure to any one security going into default or the issuer going bankrupt. The risk relating to default or bankruptcy is called **default risk**, as described in Table 7.1.

7.1.4. *Interest-Rate Risk*

As the general level of interest rates changes, the value of an individual security also changes. As interest rates rise, the value of existing securities falls, and *vice versa*. Additionally, longer-term securities are more affected by a given change in the general level of interest rates than are shorter-term securities. The fluctuation of security returns caused by the movement of interest rates is called **interest-rate risk**, as described in Table 7.1.

For example, Bond A has a coupon of 7% and a maturity of five years. If interest rates increases from 7% to 8%, the price of A will fall $6.75 for each $100 of par value, whereas the price of B will fall only $4.00 for each $100 of par value.

Another factor that affects the amount of price change for a given interest rate changes is the size of the coupon. The lower the coupon rate of an issue, the more widely its price will change for a given change in interest rates. For example, Bond C is a 20-year bond with a percentage coupon and a market value of $68 when the general level of interest rates is 7%. Bond D is a 20-year bond with 7% coupon, so its market value is par $100. If interest rates increases from 7% to 8%, the value of Bond C will fall to $60.38, a decrease in value of 11.3% based on its market price [(60.38−68)/68], whereas Bond D's value will fall by 9.8% [(90.2−100)/100].

In general, a shorter-maturity, higher-coupon security is subjected to less interest-rate risk than a long-term, low-coupon security.

7.1.5. *Management Risk*

Management Risk, as indicated in Table 7.1, is caused by errors of a firm's managers when they make business and financing decisions. **Business risk** refers to the degree of fluctuation of net income associated with different types of business operations. This kind of risk is related to different types of business and operating strategies. **Financial risk** refers to the variability of returns associated with leverage decisions. The question then arises as to how much of the firm should be financed with equity and how much should be financed with debt.

It should be noted that both business risk and financial risk are not necessarily constant over time. Both risks can be affected by the fluctuations of the business cycle or by changes in government policy.

Jensen and Meckling (1976) have presented a theory, called **agency theory** that deals with the problem of management errors and their impact on security owners. An agent–principal relationship exists when decision-making authority is delegated. The modern corporation is a good example of this phenomenon. The owners or shareholders of the firm delegate the decision-making authority to the firm's managers, who are in reality employees or agents of the owners. Other things being equal, the managers make decisions that satisfy the needs of the managers rather than the desires of the owners unless the firm's owners can protect themselves from management decisions. Some have argued that it is the function of financial arrangements using bond covenants, options, and so on, to narrow the divergence of goals between a firm's owners and its managers. In any case, it is the possibility of management error or divergent goals that is one of the causes of variability of return for securities.

7.1.6. *Marketability (Liquidity) Risk*

The marketability risk (or liquidity risk) of a security (see the description in Table 7.1) affects the rate of return received by its owner. Marketability is made up of two components: (1) the volume of securities that can be bought or sold in a short period of time without adversely affecting the price, and (2) the amount of time necessary to complete the sale of a given number of securities. Other things being equal, the less marketable a security, the lower its price or the higher its yield. A highly liquid security — for example, IBM shares traded on the New York Stock Exchange (NYSE) — can be purchased or sold in large quantities in a very short time. Millions of shares of IBM are traded every day on the NYSE. The stock of a small firm traded over the counter (OTC) may trade only a few hundred shares a week and is said to be illiquid.

One good measure of the marketability of a security is the spread between the bid price and ask price. The **bid price** is the current price at which the security can be sold and the **ask price** is the current price at which the security can be bought. The bid price is always lower than the ask price. The bid-ask spread is the cost of selling the asset quickly. That is to say, it is the amount of margin required by the market maker to stand ready to buy or sell reasonable amounts of the security quickly. The more illiquid the security, the wider the bid-ask spread.

7.1.7. *Political Risk*

International **Political Risk** (as described in Table 7.1) stems from the political climate and conditions of a foreign country. For instance, if a government is unstable, as is the case in some South American countries, there may be wild fluctuations in interest rates due to a lack of confidence by the population and the business community. There may even be some chance of sabotage of plant and equipment or other acts of terrorism. Contracts may not be upheld or enforceable. These are all factors that may cause the rate of return on certain securities to vary.

Domestic political risk takes the form of laws, taxes, and government regulations. As the government changes the tax law, the returns of securities can be greatly affected. For example, the Tax Reform Act of 1986 probably had a very important role in the bull market of January to August 1987, when the Dow-Jones Industrial Average went from below 1900 to above 2700.

7.1.8. *Purchasing-Power Risk*

Purchasing-Power Risk, as described in Table 7.1, is related to the possible shrinkage in the real value of a security even though its nominal value is increasing. For example, if the nominal value of a security goes from \$100 to \$200, the owner of this security is pleased because the investment has doubled in value. But suppose that, concurrent with the value increase of 100%, the rate of inflation is 200% — that is, a basket of goods costing \$100 when the security was purchased now costs \$300. The investor has a "money illusion" of being better off in nominal terms. The investment did increase from \$100 to \$200: nevertheless, in real terms, whereas the \$100 at time zero could purchase a complete basket of goods, after the inflation only two-third of a basket can now be purchased. Hence, the investor has suffered a loss of value.

7.1.9. *Systematic and Unsystematic Risk*

In Chapter 3, **total risk** was defined as the sum of **systematic and unsystematic risk** (see Table 7.1). Total risk is also equal to the sum of all the risk components just discussed. However, the importance and the contribution to total risk depend on the type of security under consideration. The total risk of bonds contains a much larger fraction of interest-rate risk than the total risk of a stock. Each of the types of risk discussed may contain a systematic component that cannot be diversified away and an unsystematic component that can be reduced or eliminated, if the securities are held in a portfolio.

It is assumed throughout this text that rational investors are average to risk, whatever its source; hence the knowledge of various risk-management techniques is essential. Toward that end, this chapter now focuses on the management of risk through diversification.

7.2. Portfolio Analysis and Application

Essential to adequate diversification is the knowledge of the primary concepts of portfolio analysis and their application. This section focuses on basic analysis and applications; more advanced portfolio theory and methods will be discussed in Chapters 8, 10, and 18.

A portfolio can be defined as any combination of assets or investments. **Portfolio analysis** is used to determine the return and risk for these combinations of assets. Portfolio concepts and methods are employed here to formally develop the idea of the dominance principle and some other measures of portfolio performance.

7.2.1. *Expected Return on a Portfolio*

The **rate of return on a portfolio** is simply the weighted average of the returns of individual securities in the portfolio. For example, 40% of the portfolio is invested in a security with a 10% expected return (security A); 30% is invested in security B with a 5% expected return; and 30% is invested in security C with a 12% expected return. The expected rate of return on this portfolio can be expected as

$$\begin{aligned}\bar{R}_p &= W_a\bar{R}_a + W_b\bar{R}_b + W_c\bar{R}_c\\ &= (0.4)(0.1) + (0.3)(0.5) + (0.3)(0.12)\\ &= 0.091,\end{aligned}$$

in which W_a, W_b, and W_c are the percentages of the portfolio invested in securities A, B, and C, respectively. The summation of these weights is equal to one. Here, R_p represents the expected rate of return for the portfolio and is the weighted average of the securities' expected rate of return. In general, the expected return on an n-asset portfolio is defined by Equation (7.1):

$$\bar{R}_p = \sum_{i=1}^{n} \bar{R}_i W_i, \tag{7.1}$$

where

$\sum_{i=1}^{n} W_i = 1$
W_i = the proportion of the individual's investment allocated to security i; and
R_i = the expected rate of return for security i.

7.2.2. *Variance and Standard Deviation of a Portfolio*

The riskiness of a portfolio is measured by the **standard deviation** (or **variance**) of the portfolio. To calculate the standard deviation of a portfolio, we should first identify the covariance among the securities within the portfolio. The covariance between two securities used to formulate a portfolio can be defined as

$$\begin{aligned} \mathrm{Cov}(W_1R_1, W_2R_2) &= \sum_{t=1}^{N} \frac{(W_1R_{1t} - W_1\bar{R}_1)(W_2R_{2t} - W_2\bar{R}_2)}{N-1} \\ &= W_1W_2 \sum_{t=1}^{N} \frac{(R_{1t} - \bar{R}_1)(R_{2t} - \bar{R}_2)}{N-1} \\ &= W_1W_2\mathrm{Cov}(R_1, R_2), \end{aligned} \tag{7.2}$$

where

R_{1t} = the rate of return for the first security in period t;
R_{2t} = the rate of return for the second security in period t;
$\bar{R}_1$ and $\bar{R}_2$ = average rates of return for the dirst security and the second security, respectively; and
$\mathrm{Cov}(R_1, R_2)$ = the covariance between R_1 and R_2.

The covariance as indicated in Equation (7.2) can be used to measure the covariability between two securities (or assets) when they are used to formulate a portfolio. With this measure, the variance for a portfolio with two securities can be derived:

$$\mathrm{Var}(W_1R_{1t} + W_2R_{2t}) = \sum_{t=1}^{N} \frac{[(W_1R_{1t} + W_2R_{2t}) - (W_1\bar{R}_1 + W_2\bar{R}_2)]^2}{N-1}. \tag{7.3}$$

For a three-security portfolio, the variance of portfolio can be defined:

$$\begin{aligned}\text{Var}(R_p) &= \sum_{i=A}^{C}\sum_{j=A}^{C} W_i W_j r_{ij}\sigma_i\sigma_j \\ &= W_A W_A r_{AA}\sigma_A\sigma_A + W_A W_B r_{AB}\sigma_A\sigma_B + W_A W_C r_{AC}\sigma_A\sigma_C \\ &\quad + W_B W_A r_{AB}\sigma_B\sigma_A + W_B W_B r_{BB}\sigma_B\sigma_B + W_B W_C r_{BC}\sigma_B\sigma_C \\ &\quad + W_C W_A r_{CA}\sigma_C\sigma_A + W_C W_B r_{CB}\sigma_C\sigma_B + W_C W_C r_{CC}\sigma_C\sigma_C. \end{aligned} \tag{7.4}$$

Again simplifying and rearranging yields:

$$\begin{aligned}\text{Var}(R_p) &= W_A^2\sigma_A^2 + W_B^2\sigma_B^2 + W_C^2\sigma_C^2 + 2(W_A W_B r_{AB}\sigma_A\sigma_B \\ &\quad + W_A W_C r_{AC}\sigma_A\sigma_C + W_B W_C r_{BC}\sigma_B\sigma_C). \end{aligned} \tag{7.5}$$

Thus, as the number of securities increases from two to three, there is one more variance term, and two more covariance terms. The general formula for determining the number of terms that must be computed (NTC) to determine the variance of a portfolio with N securities is

$$\text{NTC} = N \text{ variances} + \frac{N^2 - N}{2} \text{ covariances.}$$

Table 7.2 clearly illustrates the tremendous estimation and computational load that exists using the Markowitz diversification approach. Later chapters will illustrate how this problem can be alleviated.

Table 7.2. Portfolio Size and Variance Computations.

Number of Securities	Number of Variance and Covariance Terms
2	3
3	6
4	10
5	15
10	55
15	120
20	210
25	325
50	1,275
75	2,850
100	5,050
250	31,375
500	125,250

Sample Problem 7.1

If you have two securities, you can use Equation (7.2) to calculate the portfolio variance as follows:

Security 1		*Security 2*	
$W_1 = 40\%$		$W_2 = 60\%$	
$t = 1$	$\bar{R}_{1t} = 10\%$	$t = 1$	$\bar{R}_{2t} = 5\%$
$= 2$	15%	$= 2$	10%
$= 3$	20%	$= 3$	15%
$\bar{R}_1 = 15\%$		$\bar{R}_1 = 10\%$	

$$\begin{aligned}
&\mathrm{Var}(W_1 R_{1t} + W_2 R_{2t})\\
&\quad = \sum_{t=1}^{N} \frac{[(W_1 R_{1t} + W_2 R_{2t}) - (W_1 \bar{R}_1 + W_2 \bar{R}_2)]^2}{N-1}\\
&\quad = [(0.4)(0.1) + (0.6)(0.05) - (0.4)(0.15) + (0.6)(0.1)]^2/2\\
&\qquad + [(0.4)(0.15) + (0.6)(0.1) - (0.4)(0.15) + (0.6)(0.1)]^2/2\\
&\qquad + [(0.4)(0.2) + (0.6)(0.15) - (0.4)(0.15) + (0.6)(0.1)]^2/2\\
&\quad = \frac{(0.07 - 0.12)^2}{2} + \frac{(0.12 - 0.12)^2}{2} + \frac{(0.17 - 0.12)^2}{2}
\end{aligned}$$

Var portfolio $= 0.0025$.

The riskiness of a portfolio can be measured by the standard deviation of returns, as indicated in Equation (7.2.2):

$$\sigma_p = \sqrt{\frac{\sum_{t=1}^{N} (\bar{R}_{pt} - \bar{R}_p)^2}{N-1}}, \tag{7.6}$$

where σ_p is the standard deviation of the portfolio's return and $\bar{R}_p$ is the expected return of the n possible returns. Figure 7.2 illustrates possible distributions for two portfolios, assuming the same expected return but different levels of risk. Since portfolio B's variability is greater than that of portfolio A, investors regard portfolio B as riskier than portfolio A.

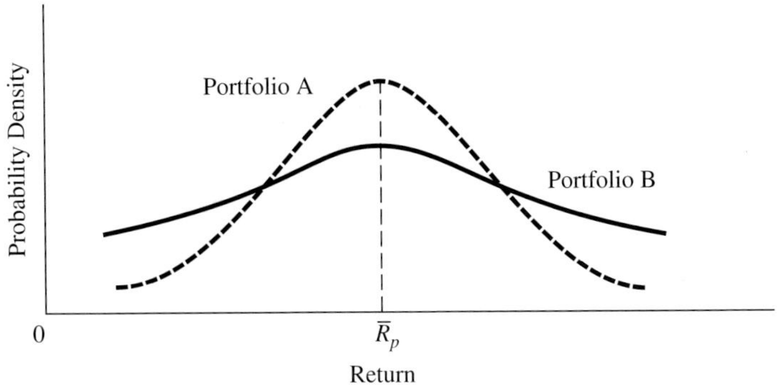

Fig. 7.2. Probability Distributions of Returns for Two Portfolios.

7.2.3. *The Two-Asset Case*

To explain the fundamental aspect of the risk-diversification process in a portfolio, consider the **two-asset case**. Following Equation (7.7):

$$\begin{aligned}\sigma_p &= \sqrt{\frac{\sum_{t=1}^{N}(R_{pt}-\bar{R}_p)^2}{N-1}}\\ &= \sqrt{\frac{\sum_{t=1}^{N}[W_1^2(R_{1t}-\bar{R}_1)^2+W_2^2(R_{2t}-\bar{R}_2)^2+2W_1W_2(R_{1t}-\bar{R}_1)(R_{2t}-\bar{R}_2)]}{N-1}}\\ &= \sqrt{W_1^2\text{Var}(R_{1t})+W_2^2\text{Var}(R_{2t})+2W_1W_2\text{Cov}(R_1,R_2)},\end{aligned} \tag{7.7}$$

where $W_1 + W_2 = 1$. By the definitions of correlation coefficients between R_1 and $R_2(\rho_{12})$, the CovR_1, R_2 can be rewritten:

$$\text{Cov}(R_1, R_2) = \rho_{12}\sigma_1\sigma_2, \tag{7.8}$$

where σ_1 and σ_2 are the standard deviations of the first and second security, respectively. From Equations (7.7) and (7.8), the standard deviation of a two-security portfolio can be defined as

$$\begin{aligned}\sigma_p &= \sqrt{\text{Var}(W_1R_{1t}+W_2R_{2t})}\\ &= \sqrt{W_1^2\sigma_1^2+(1-W_1)^2\sigma_2^2+2W_1(1-W_1)\rho_{12}\sigma_1\sigma_2}.\end{aligned} \tag{7.9}$$

Sample Problem 7.2 provides further illustration.

Sample Problem 7.2

For securities 1 and 2 used in the previous example, applying Equation (7.9) should give the same results for portfolio variance.

Security 1	*Security 2*
$\sigma_1^2 = 0.0025$	$\sigma_2^2 = 0.0025$
$W_1 = 0.4$	$W_2 = 0.6$
$\rho_{12} = +1$	

$$\begin{aligned}\sigma_p &= \sqrt{(0.4)^2(0.0025) + (0.6)^2(0.0025) + 2(0.4)(0.6)(1)(0.05)(0.05)}\\ &= \sqrt{0.0025}\end{aligned}$$

$\sigma_p = 0.05$ or Var portfolio $= 0.0025$, the same answer as for Sample Problem 7.1.

If $\rho_{12} = 1.0$, Equation (7.9) can be simplified to the linear expression:

$$\sigma_p = W_1\sigma_1 + W_2\sigma_2,$$

where $W_2 = (1 - W_1)$. Since Equation (7.9) is a quadratic equation, some value of W_1 minimizes σ_p. To obtain this value, differentiate Equation (7.9) with respect to W_1 and set this derivative equal to zero. Solving for W_1:

$$W_1 = \frac{\sigma_2(\sigma_2 - \rho_{12}\sigma_1)}{\sigma_1^2 + \sigma_2^2 - 2\rho_{12}\sigma_1\sigma_2}. \tag{7.10a}$$

A condition needed for Equation (7.10a) is that $W_1 \leq 1$ that is, no more than 100% of the portfolio can be in any single security, and negative positions (short positions) can be maintained on any security.

If $\rho_{12} = 1$, Equation (7.10a) reduces from

$$\begin{aligned}\frac{\partial\sigma_p}{\partial W_1} &= [W_1^2\sigma_1^2 + (1 - W_1)^2\sigma_2^2 + 2W_1(1 - W_1)\rho_{12}\sigma_1\sigma_2]^{-1/2}\\ &\quad\times[2W_1\sigma_1^2 - 2(1 - W_1)\sigma_2^2 + 2(1 - 2W_1)\rho_{12}\sigma_1\sigma_2]\\ &= \frac{W_1[\sigma_1^2\sigma_2^2 - 2\int_{12}\sigma_1\sigma_2] - [\sigma_1^2 - \rho_{12}\sigma_1\sigma_2]}{[W_1^2\sigma_1^2 + (1 - W_1)^2\sigma_2^2 + 2W_1(1 - W_1)\rho_{12}\sigma_1\sigma_2]}\end{aligned}$$

to

$$\begin{aligned}W_1 &= \frac{\sigma_2(\sigma_2 - \sigma_1)}{(\sigma_2 - \sigma_1)(\sigma_2 - \sigma_1)}\\ &= \frac{\sigma_2}{\sigma_2 - \sigma_1}.\end{aligned} \tag{7.10b}$$

Returning to the sample problems for securities 1 and 2, since the standard deviations are equal and the securities are perfectly positively correlated, Equation (7.10b) indicates that there is no value for W_1 that will minimize the portfolio variance. The weight from W_1 that gives the minimum-variance portfolio is 0.05/(0.05 – 0.05) or 0.05/0, which is undefined.

If $\rho_{12} = -1$, Equation (7.10a) reduces to

$$W_1 = \frac{\sigma_2(\sigma_2 + \sigma_1)}{(\sigma_1 + \sigma_2)(\sigma_1 + \sigma_2)} \\ \frac{\sigma_2}{(\sigma_2 + \sigma_1)}. \tag{7.10c}$$

However, if the correlation coefficient between 1 and 2 is −1, then the minimum-variance portfolio must be divided equally between security 1 and security 2 — that is

$$W_1 = \frac{0.05}{0.05 + 0.05} \\ = 0.5.$$

As an expanded form of Equation (7.9), a portfolio can be written:

$$\sigma_p = \left[\sum_{i=1}^{n} W_1^2 \sigma_1^2 + 2 \sum_{i=1}^{n-1} \sum_{j=i+1}^{n} W_i W_j \rho_{ij} \sigma_i \sigma_j \right]^{1/2} , \\ = \left[\sum_{j=1}^{n} \sum_{i=1}^{n} W_i W_j \mathrm{Cov}(R_{it}, R_{jt}) | \right]^{1/2} \tag{7.11}$$

where

W_i and W_j = the investor's investment allocated to security i and security j, respectively;

ρ_{ij} = the correlation coefficient between security i and security j; and

n = the number of securities included in the portfolio.

Since Equation (7.11) has n securities, there are n variance terms (i.e., $W_1^2 \sigma_1^2$) and $(n^2 - n)$ covariance terms (i.e., $W_i W_j \rho_{12} \sigma_i \sigma_j$). If $n = 200$, Equation (7.8) will have 200 variance terms and 39,800 covariance terms, and any practical will require a great amount of information as well as many computations. Sample Problem 7.3 provides further illustration.

Sample Problem 7.3

Consider two stocks, A and B: $\bar{R}_A = 10, \bar{R}_B = 15, \sigma_A = 4$, and $\sigma_{\mathrm{B}} = 6$. (1) If a riskless portfolio could be formed from A and B, what would be the expected return of R_p? (2) What would the expected return be if $\rho_{AB} = 0$?

Solution

1. $\sigma_p = (W_A^2\sigma_A^2 + (1 - W_A)^2\sigma_B^2 + 2W_A(1 - W_A)\rho_{AB}\sigma_A\sigma_B)^{1/2}$

   If we let $\rho_{AB} = -1$

$$\begin{aligned}\sigma_p &= [W_A\sigma_A - (1 - W_A)\sigma_B]\\ \sigma_p &= 0 = 4W_A - 6(1 - W_A)R_B\\ W_A &= 3/5.\end{aligned}$$

   So

$$\begin{aligned}\bar{R}_p &= W_A\bar{R}_A + (1 - W_A)R_B\\ &= \left(\frac{3}{5}\right)(10) + \left(\frac{2}{5}\right)(15)\\ &= 12\%.\end{aligned}$$

2. If we let $\rho_{AB} = 0$

$$\begin{aligned}\sigma_p &= [W_A^2\sigma_A^2 + (1 - W_A)^2\sigma_B^2]^{1/2}\\ \frac{\partial\sigma_p}{\partial W_A} &= \frac{1}{2}[2W_A\sigma_A^2 + 2(1 - W_A)\sigma_B^2(-1)][W_A^2\sigma_A^2 + (1 - W_A)^2\sigma_B^2]^{-1/2}\\ &= 0\end{aligned}$$

$$W_A\sigma_A^2 - (1 - W_A)\sigma_B^2 = 0$$

$$\begin{aligned}W_A &= \sigma_B^2/(\sigma_A^2 + \sigma_B^2)\\ &= \sigma_B^2/(4^2 + 6^2)\\ &= 9/13\\ \bar{R}_P &= \frac{9}{13}(10) + \frac{4}{13}(15)\\ &= 11.54\%.\end{aligned}$$

7.2.4. *Asset Allocation among Risk-Free Asset, Corporate Bond, and Equity*

From the previous discussion, we know that the riskier investments offer higher average returns, while less risky investments offers lower average returns. Therefore, a rational investor makes optimal portfolio choice between risky and risk-free securities instead of making all-or-nothing choices from these investment classes. They can and do construct their portfolios using securities from all asset classes. For example, some of the portfolio may be in risk-free Treasury bills, some in high-risk stocks.

The most straightforward way to control the risk of the portfolio is through the fraction of the portfolio invested in Treasury bills and other safe money market securities versus risky assets. The capital allocation decision is an example of an asset allocation choice — a choice among broad investment classes, rather than among the specific securities within each asset class. Most investment professionals consider asset allocation as the most important part of portfolio construction.

Sample Problem 7.4

Assume that the total market value of a private fund is \$500,000, of which \$100,000 is invested in a risk-free asset for practical purposes. The remaining \$400,000 is invested in risky securities, where \$240,000 in equities (E) and \$160,000 in long-term bonds (B). Under such assumption, the risky portfolio consists 60% of E and 40% of B, and the weight of the risky portfolio in the mutual fund is 80%.

Suppose that the fund manager wishes to decrease risk by reducing the allocation to the risky portfolio from 80% to 70% and not change the proportion of each asset in the risky portfolio. The risky portfolio would then total only $0.7 \times \$500{,}000 = \$350{,}000$, requiring the sale of \$50,000 of the original \$400,000 of risky holdings, with the proceeds used to purchase more shares in risk-free asset. Total holdings in the risk-free asset will increase $\$500{,}000 \times (1 - 0.7) = \$150{,}000$, the original holdings (\$100,000) plus the new contribution (\$50,000).

Because the weights of E and B in the risky portfolio are 60% and 40%, respectively, to leave the proportions of each asset in the risky portfolio unchanged, the fund manager should sell $0.6 \times \$50{,}000 = \$30{,}000$ of E and $0.4 \times \$50{,}000 = \$20{,}000$ of B. After the sale, the proportions of each asset in the risky portfolio are in fact unchanged:

$$\text{E: } W_E = \frac{240{,}000 - 30{,}000}{400{,}000 - 50{,}000} = 0.6$$

$$\text{B: } W_B = \frac{160{,}000 - 20{,}000}{400{,}000 - 50{,}000} = 0.4.$$

7.3. The Efficient Portfolio and Risk Diversification

Utilizing the definitions of standard deviation of expected return of a portfolio discussed previously, this section discusses the concepts of the **efficient portfolio** and **risk diversification.**

7.3.1. *The Efficient Portfolio*

By definition, a portfolio is efficient, if there exists no other portfolio having the same expected return at a lower variance of returns. Moreover, a portfolio is efficient if no other portfolio has a higher expected return as the same risk of returns.

This suggests that given two investments, A and B, investment A will be preferred to B if

$$E(\mathrm{A}) > E(\mathrm{B}) \quad \text{and} \quad \mathrm{Var(A)} = \mathrm{Var(B)}$$

or

$$E(\mathrm{A}) = E(\mathrm{B}) \quad \text{and} \quad \mathrm{Var(A)} < \mathrm{Var(B)},$$

where

$E(\mathrm{A})$ and $E(\mathrm{B})$ = the expected returns of A and B; and
Var(A) and Var(B) = their respective variances or risk.

The mean returns and variance of every investment opportunity can be calculated and plotted as a single point on a mean-standard deviation diagram, as shown in Fig. 7.3.

All points below curve EF represent portfolio combinations that are possible. Point D represents a portfolio of investments with a return R_D and risk σ_D. All points above EF are combinations of risk and returns that do not exist. Point B would therefore represent risk and return that cannot be obtained with any combination of investments.

The EF curve is also called the **efficient frontier** because all points below the curve are dominated by a point found on the curve. For instance, suppose a firm is willing to assume a maximum risk level σ_D. It can obtain a return of R_D with portfolio D or move to point C on the frontier and receive a higher return R_C with that portfolio. Therefore, C dominates D because it would be preferred to D. For the same level of risk, it has a higher return.

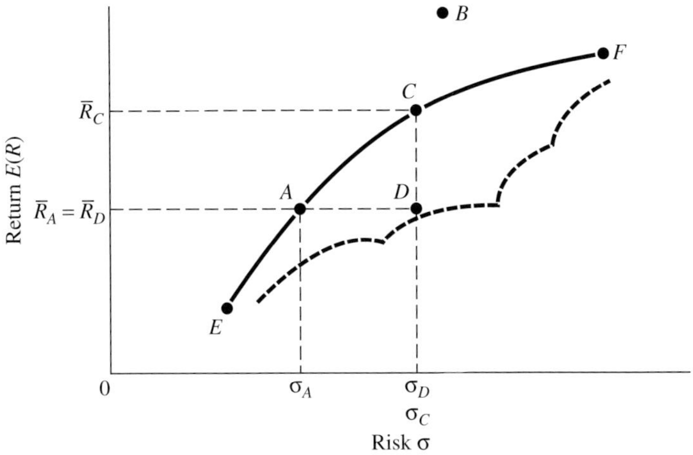

Fig. 7.3. The Efficient Frontier in Portfolio Analysis.

A similar argument could be made in terms of risk. If the firm wants to achieve a return of R_A, it will select portfolio A over D, because A represents the same return at a smaller level of risk or standard deviation: $\sigma_A < \sigma_B$. Therefore, point D is not efficient but points A and C are. A decision maker could, therefore, select any point on the frontier and feel secure in knowing that a better portfolio is not available. Sample Problem 7.5 further illustrates this concept.

Sample Problem 7.5

To show how the portfolio concepts and methods discussed in this section can be used to do practical analysis, monthly rates of return from April 2001 to April 2010 for Johnson & Johnson (JNJ) and IBM are used as examples. The basic statistical estimates for these two firms are average monthly rates of return and the variance–covariance matrix. The average monthly rates of return for JNJ and IBM are 0.0080 and 0.0050, respectively. The variances and covariances are listed in the following Table 7.3.

Table 7.3. Variance–Covariance Matrix.

	JNJ	IBM
J&J	0.0025	0.0007
IBM	0.0007	0.0071

From Equation (7.10), we have

$$W_1 = \frac{0.0071 - .0007}{0.0025 + 0.0071 + 2(0.0007)}$$
$$= \frac{0.0064}{0.011}$$
$$= 0.5818$$
$$W_2 = 1.0 - 0.5818 = 0.4182.$$

Using the weight estimates and Equations (7.2) and (7.3):

$$E(\bar{R}_P) = (0.5818)(0.0080) + (0.4182)(0.0050)$$
$$= 0.0067454$$
$$\sigma_P^2 = (0.5818)^2(0.0025) + (0.4182)^2(0.0071)$$
$$+ 2(0.5818)(0.4182)(0.0007)$$
$$= 0.0024$$
$$\sigma_P = 0.0493.$$

When ρ_{12} is less than 1.00, it indicates that the combination of the two securities will result in a total risk less than their added respective risks. This is the diversification effect. If ρ_{12} is equal to 1.00, this would mean that the combination of the two securities has no diversification effect at all.

The correlation coefficient of $\rho_{12} = 0.1660735469$ indicates that a portfolio combining JNJ and IBM would show a diversification effect and a reduction in risk.

7.3.2. *Corporate Application of Diversification*

The effect of diversification is not necessarily limited to securities but may have wider applications at the corporate level. Frequently, managers will justify undertaking many product lines because of the effects of diversification. Instead of "putting all the eggs in one basket," the investment risks are spread out among many lines of services or products in hope of reducing the overall risks involved and maximizing returns. To what degree this diversification takes place in other types of corporate decisions depends on the decision maker's preference for risk and return. The overall goal is to reduce business risk fluctuations of net income. However, it should be noted that investors can do their own homemade diversification, which generally reduces the need of corporate diversification.

This type of corporate diversification can be taken to the multinational level. For example, General Motors has overseas divisions throughout the world. Although these divisions all produce the same product, autos and auto parts, GM's status as a multinational corporation allows it to take advantage of the diversifying effects of different exchange rates and political and economic climates. This issue will be explored in detail in Chapter 19.

7.3.3. *The Dominance Principle*

The **dominance principle** has been developed as a means of conceptually understanding the risk/return tradeoff. As with the efficient-frontier analysis, we must assume an investor prefers returns and dislikes risks. For example, as depicted in Fig. 7.4, if an individual is prepared to experience risk associated with σ_A, he or she can obtain a higher expected return with portfolio $A(R_A)$ than with portfolio $B(R_B)$. Thus A dominates B and would be preferred. Similarly, if an individual were satisfied with a return of $\bar{R}_B$, he or she would select portfolio B over C because the risks associated with B are less ($\sigma_B < \sigma_C$). Therefore using the dominance principle reinforces the choice of an efficient portfolio and is also a method in determining it.

Figure 7.4 makes clear that points A and B are directly comparable because they have a common standard deviation, σ_A. Points B and C are directly comparable because of a common return, $\bar{R}_B$. Now consider portfolio D. How does its risk versus return compare with the other portfolios shown in Fig. 7.4? It is difficult to say because the risk and

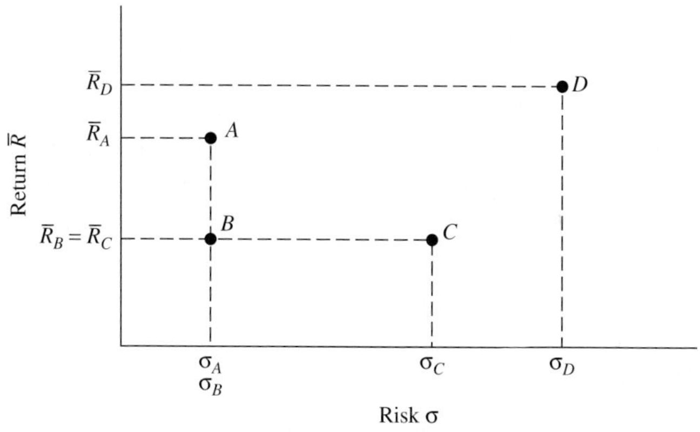

Fig. 7.4. The Dominance Principle in Portfolio Analysis.

return are not directly comparable using the dominance principle. This is the basic limitation of the dominance principle — that portfolios without a common risk or return factor are not directly comparable.

7.3.4. *Three Performance Measures*

For such a situation it becomes necessary to use some other performance measure. There are basically three important portfolio performance measures taught in investment courses: (1) the Sharpe, (2) the Treynor, and (3) the Jensen measures.

The **Sharpe measure (SP)** (Sharpe, 1966) is of immediate concern. Given two of the portfolios depicted in Fig. 7.4, portfolios B and D, their relative risk–return performance can be compared using the equations:

$$\mathrm{SP}_D = \frac{\bar{R}_D - R_f}{\sigma_D} \quad \text{and} \quad \mathrm{SP}_B = \frac{\bar{R}_B - R_f}{\sigma_B},$$

where

SP_D, SP_B = Sharpe performance measures;
$\bar{R}_D$, $\bar{R}_B$ = the average return of each portfolio;
R_f = risk-free rate; and
σ_D, σ_B = the respective standard deviation on risk of each portfolio.

Because the numerator is the average return reduced by the risk-free rate, it represents the average risk premium of each portfolio. Dividing the risk premium by the total risk per portfolio results in a measure of the return (premium) per unit of risk for each portfolio. The Sharpe performance measure equation will therefore allow a direct comparison of any portfolio, given its risk and returns.

Consider Fig. 7.5 where portfolio A is being compared to portfolio B. If a riskless rate exists, then all investors would prefer A to B because combinations of A and the riskless asset give higher returns for the same level of risk than combinations of the riskless asset and B. The preferred portfolio lies on the ray passing through R_f that is furthest in the counterclockwise direction (the ray that has the greatest slope). Sample Problem 7.6 further illustrates this concept.

Sample Problem 7.6

An insurance firm is trying to decide between two investment funds. From past performance indicated in Table 7.4, they were able to calculate the

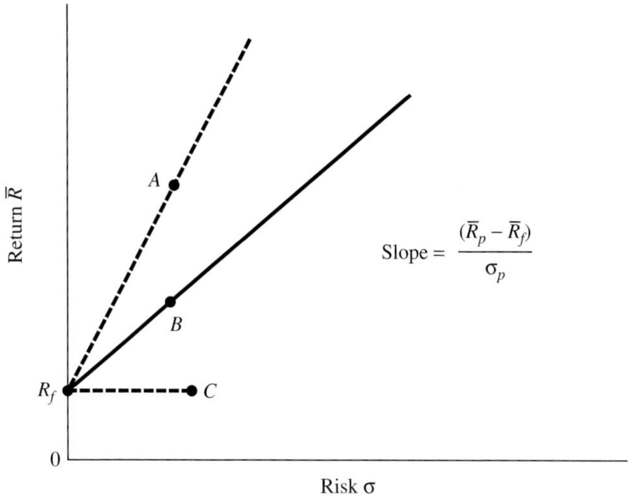

Fig. 7.5. Combinations of Portfolio and the Risk-Free Investment.

Table 7.4. Past Performance of the Insurance Firm.

	Smyth Fund	Jones Fund
Average return R (%)	18	16
Standard deviation σ (%)	20	15
Risk-free rate $= R_f(\%) = 9.5$		

average returns and standard deviations for these funds. The current T-bill rate is 9.5% and the firm will this will use this as a measure of the risk-free rate.

Using the Sharpe performance measure, the risk–return measurements for these two firms are

$$SP_{\text{Smyth}} = \frac{0.18 - 0.095}{0.20} = 0.425$$

$$SP_{\text{Jones}} = \frac{0.16 - 0.095}{0.15} = 0.433.$$

It is clear that the Jones fund has a slightly better performance and would be the better alternative of the two.

The SP looks at the risk-return decision from the point of view of an investor choosing a portfolio to represent the majority of his or her investment. An investor choosing a portfolio to represent a large part of his or her wealth would likely be concerned with the full risk of the portfolio, and the standard deviation is a measure of that risk.

On the other hand, if the risk level of the portfolio is already determined by the investor and what is important is to evaluate the performance of the portfolio over and above the total market performance, perhaps the proper risk measure would be the relationship between the return on the portfolio and the return on the market, or beta. All combinations of a riskless asset and a risky portfolio lie on a straight line connecting them. The slope of the line connecting the risky asset A and the risk-free rate is $(\bar{R}_A - R_f)/\sigma_A$. Here, as in the SP, an investor would prefer the portfolio on the most counterclockwise ray emanating from the riskless asset. This measure, called the **Treynor measure (TP)**, developed by Treynor in 1965, examines differential return when beta is the risk measure. Sample Problem 7.7 provides further illustration.

Sample Problem 7.7

Rank the portfolios shown in Table 7.5 based on the SP. Assume $R_f = 8\%$. If $R_f = 5\%$, how does the order change?

Solution

SP

$$\mathrm{SP}_M = \frac{\bar{R}_M - R_f}{\sigma}$$

$$\mathrm{SP}_A = 0.84$$

$$\mathrm{SP}_B = 0.73$$

$$\mathrm{SP}_C = 0.78$$

$$\mathrm{SP}_D = 0.20$$

$$\mathrm{SP}_E = 0.50.$$

Table 7.5. Past Performances of Portfolios A to E.

Portfolio	Return (%)	Risk (%)
A	50	50
B	19	15
C	12	9
D	9	5
E	8.5	1

Ranked by the SP, A > B > E > C > D. The SP indicates that portfolio A is the most desirable: it has the highest return per unit of risk.

For $R_f = 5\%$

$$\text{SP}_A = 0.90$$
$$\text{SP}_B = 0.933$$
$$\text{SP}_C = 0.78$$
$$\text{SP}_D = 0.80$$
$$\text{SP}_E = 3.5.$$

The order changes to E > B > A > D > C. Now E is the best portfolio as it has the highest return per unit of risk.

The TP can be expressed by the following:

$$\text{TP} = \frac{\bar{R}_j - R_f}{\beta_j}, \tag{7.13}$$

where

$\bar{R}_j$ = average return of jth portfolio;
R_f = risk-free rate; and
β_j = beta coefficient for jth portfolio.

The Treynor performance measure uses the beta coefficient (systematic risk) instead of total risk for the jth portfolio (σ_j) as a risk measure. Applications of the TP are similar to the SP as discussed previously.[1]

Jensen (1968, 1969) has proposed a measure referred to as the *Jensen differential performance index* **(Jensen's measure or JM)**. The differential return can be viewed as the difference in return earned by the portfolio compared to the return that the capital asset pricing line implies should be earned.

Consider the line connecting the riskless rate and the market portfolio. A manager could obtain any point along this line by investing in the market portfolio and mixing this with the riskless asset to obtain the desired risk level. If the constructed portfolio is actively managed, then one measure of performance is the difference in return earned by actively managing the portfolio, compared with what would have been earned if the portfolio had

[1]Discussion of the Treynor measure adapted from Treynor J. "How to Rate Management of Investment Funds." *Harvard Business Review*, v. 43 (January/February 1965), pp. 63–75. Adapted by permission.

been passively constructed of the market portfolio and the riskless asset to achieve the same risk level. The slope of the line connecting the riskless asset and the market portfolio is $(\bar{R}_M - R_f)/\beta_M$, and the intercept must be the riskless rate. The beta on the market portfolio is one; therefore, the CAPM equation results in

$$\bar{R}_P = R_f + (\bar{R}_M - R_f)\beta_P. \tag{7.14}$$

JM is the differential return of the managed portfolio's actual return less the return on the portfolio of identical beta that lies on the line connecting the riskless asset and the market portfolio. Algebraically, JM is expressed as

$$\text{JM} = \bar{R}_P - [R_f + (\bar{R}_M - R_f)\beta_p]. \tag{7.15}$$

Figure 7.6 depicts portfolio rankings for the JM, and Sample Problem 7.8 provides further illustration.

Sample Problem 7.8

Rank the portfolio in Table 7.6 according to JM:

(1) Assuming $R_M = 10\%$ and $R_f = 8\%$
(2) Assuming $R_M = 12\%$ and $R_f = 8\%$

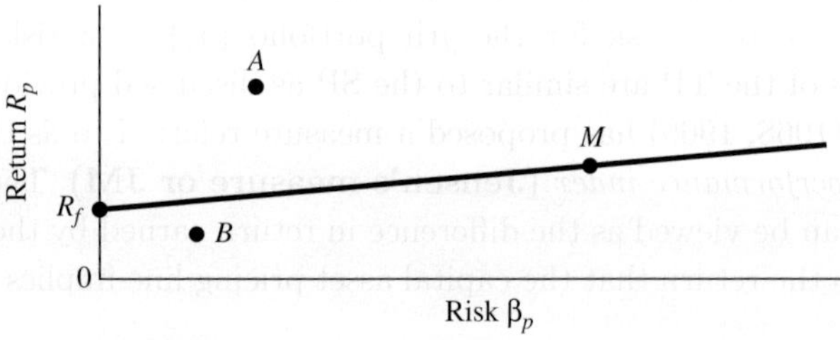

Fig. 7.6. Jensen's Measure for Portfolio Rankings.

Table 7.6. Past Performances and Betas of Portfolios A to E.

Portfolio	$R_i(\%)$	$\sigma(\%)$	β_i
A	50	50	2.5
B	19	15	2.0
C	12	9	1.5
D	9	5	1.0
E	8.5	1	0.25

(3) Assuming $R_M = R_f = 8\%$
(4) Assuming $R_M = 12\%$ and $R_f = 4\%$

Solution

$$R_i = R_f + \beta_i(R_M - R_f) \qquad \text{JM} = (R_i - R_f) - \beta_i(R_M - R_f)$$

(1)
$$\begin{aligned} \text{JM}_A &= 37\% \\ \text{JM}_B &= 7\% \\ \text{JM}_C &= 1\% \\ \text{JM}_D &= -2\% \\ \text{JM}_E &= 0\% \end{aligned}$$

Ranked by the JM A > B > C > E > D.

(2)
$$\begin{aligned} \text{JM}_A &= 32\% \\ \text{JM}_B &= 3\% \\ \text{JM}_C &= -2\% \\ \text{JM}_D &= -3\% \\ \text{JM}_E &= -0.5\% \end{aligned}$$

The rank changes to A > B > E > C > D.

(3)
$$\begin{aligned} \text{JM}_A &= 42\% \\ \text{JM}_B &= 11\% \\ \text{JM}_C &= 4\% \\ \text{JM}_D &= 1\% \\ \text{JM}_E &= 0.5\% \end{aligned}$$

The rank is A > B > C > D > E.

(4)
$$\begin{aligned} \text{JM}_A &= 26\% \\ \text{JM}_B &= -1\% \\ \text{JM}_C &= -4\% \\ \text{JM}_D &= -3\% \\ \text{JM}_E &= 2.5\% \end{aligned}$$

The rank now is A > E > B > D > C.

7.3.5. *Interrelationship among Three Performance Measures*

It should be noted that all three performance measures are interrelated. For instance, if $\rho_{pm} = \sigma_{pm}/\sigma_p\sigma_m = 1$, then the JM divided by σ_p becomes equivalent to the SM. Since

$$\beta_p = \sigma_{pm}/\sigma_m^2 \quad \text{and} \quad \rho_{\text{pm}} = \sigma_{pm}/\sigma_p\sigma_m, \tag{7.16}$$

the JM must be multiplied by $1/\sigma_p$ in order to derive the equivalent SM:

$$\begin{aligned}\frac{\text{JM}}{\sigma_P} &= \frac{[\bar{R}_P - R_F]}{\sigma_P} - \frac{[\bar{R}_M - R_F]}{\sigma_m}\frac{(\sigma_{pm})}{\sigma_m\sigma_p} \\ &= \frac{[\bar{R}_P - R_F]}{\sigma_P} - \frac{[\bar{R}_M - R_F]}{\sigma_m} \\ &= \text{SP}_P - \text{SP}_m \quad \text{(common constant)}\end{aligned} \tag{7.17}$$

If the JM is divided by β_P, it is equivalent to the TM plus some constant common to all portfolios:

$$\begin{aligned}\frac{\text{JM}}{\beta_P} &= \frac{[\bar{R}_P - R_F]}{\beta_P} - \frac{[\bar{R}_M - R_F]\beta_P}{\beta_P} \\ &= \text{TM}_P - [\bar{R}_M - R_F] \\ &= \text{TM}_P - \text{common constant.}\end{aligned} \tag{7.18}$$

Sample Problem 7.9 provides further illustration.

Sample Problem 7.9

Continuing with the example used for the Sharpe performance measure in Sample Problem 7.6, assume that in addition to the information already provided the market return is 10%, the beta of the Smyth Fund is 0.8, and the Jones Fund beta is 1.1. Then, according to the capital asset pricing line, the implied return earned should be

$$\begin{aligned}\bar{R}_{\text{Smyth}} &= 0.095 + (0.10 - 0.095)(0.8) = 0.099 \\ \bar{R}_{\text{Jones}} &= 0.095 + (0.10 - 0.095)(1.1) = 0.1005.\end{aligned}$$

Using the JM, the risk-return measurements for these two firms are

$$\begin{aligned}\text{JM}_{\text{Smyth}} &= 0.18 - 0.099 = 0.081 \\ \text{JM}_{\text{Jones}} &= 0.16 - 0.1005 = 0.0595.\end{aligned}$$

From these calculations, it is clear that the Smyth Fund has a better performance and would be the better alternative of the two. Note that this is the opposite of the results determined from the Sharpe performance measure in Sample Problem 7.6. Computing the TP would reinforce the Jensen results. More analysis of these performance measures will be undertaken in detail in Chapter 18.

7.4. Determination of Commercial Lending Rate

This section concerns a process for estimating the lending rate a financial institution would extend to a firm or the borrowing rate a firm would feel is reasonable based on economic, industry, and firm-specific factors.

As shown previously, part of the rate of return is based on the risk-free rate. The risk-free rate R_f must first be forecasted for three types of economic conditions — boom, normal, and poor.

The second component of the lending rate is the risk premium (R_P). This can be calculated individually for each firm by examining the change in earnings before interest and taxes (EBIT) under the three types of economic conditions. The EBIT is used by the lender as an indicator of the ability of the potential borrower to repay borrowed funds.

Table 7.7 has been constructed based on the methods discussed previously. In total there are nine possible lending rates under the three different economic conditions. The construction of these lending rates is shown in Table 7.8. This table shows that during a boom the risk-free rate is set at 12%, but the risk premium can taken on different values. These is a 40% chance that it will be 3%, a 30% chance it will be 5%, and a 30% chance it will be 8%. The products of the R_P probabilities and the R_f probability are the joint probabilities of occurrence for the lending rates computed from these parameters. Therefore, there is a 10% chance that a firm will be faced with a 15% lending rate during a boom, a 7.5% chance

Table 7.7. Possible Lending Rates.

Economic Conditions	R_f (%)	Probability	EBIT ($ millions)	Probability	R_p (%)
Boom	12.0	0.25	2.5	0.40	3
			1.5	0.30	5
			0.5	0.30	8
Normal	10.0	0.50	2.5	0.40	3
			1.5	0.30	5
			0.5	0.30	8
Poor	8.0	0.25	2.5	0.40	3
			1.5	0.30	5
			0.5	0.30	8

Table 7.8. Construction of Actual Lending Rates.

Economic Conditions	(*A*) R_f (%)	(*B*) Probability	(*C*) R_p (%)	(*D*) Probability	($B \times D$) Joint Probability of Occurrence	($A + C$) Lending Rate (%)
Boom	12	0.25	3.0	0.40	0.100	15
			5.0	0.30	0.075	17
			8.0	0.30	0.075	20
Normal	10	0.50	3.0	0.40	0.200	13
			5.0	0.30	0.150	15
			8.0	0.30	0.150	18
Poor	8	0.25	3.0	0.40	0.100	11
			5.0	0.30	0.075	13
			8.0	0.30	0.075	16

of a 17% rate, and a 7.5% chance of an 18% rate. This process applies for the other conditions, normal and poor, as well.

Based upon the mean and variance Equations (7.1) and (7.2) it is possible to calculate the expected lending rate and its variance. Using the information provided in Table 7.8, the weighted average can be calculated:

$$\begin{aligned} R = {} & (0.100)(15\%) + (0.075)(17\%) + (0.075)(20\%) + (0.200)(13\%) \\ & + (0.150)(15\%) + (0.150)(18\%) + (0.100)(11\%) + (0.075)(13\%) \\ & + (0.075)(16\%) \\ = {} & 15.1\%. \end{aligned}$$

With a standard deviation of

$$\begin{aligned} \sigma = {} & [(0.100)(15 - 15.1)^2 + (0.075)(17 - 15.1)^2 + (0.075)(20 - 15.1)^2 \\ & + (0.200)(13 - 15.1)^2 + (0.150)(15 - 15.1)^2 + (0.150)(18 - 15.1)^2 \\ & + (0.100)(11 - 15.1)^2 + (0.075)(13 - 15.1)^2 + (0.075)(16 - 15.1)^2]^{1/2} \\ = {} & (0.001 + 0.271 + 1.801 + 0.882 + 0.0015 + 1.2615 + 1.681 \\ & + 0.331 + 0.061) \\ = {} & 2.51\%. \end{aligned}$$

If this distribution is indeed approximately normal, the mean and standard deviation can be employed to make some statistical inferences. Figure 7.7 makes it clear that 68.3% of the observations of a standard normal distribution are within one standard deviation of the mean, 95.4% are within three.

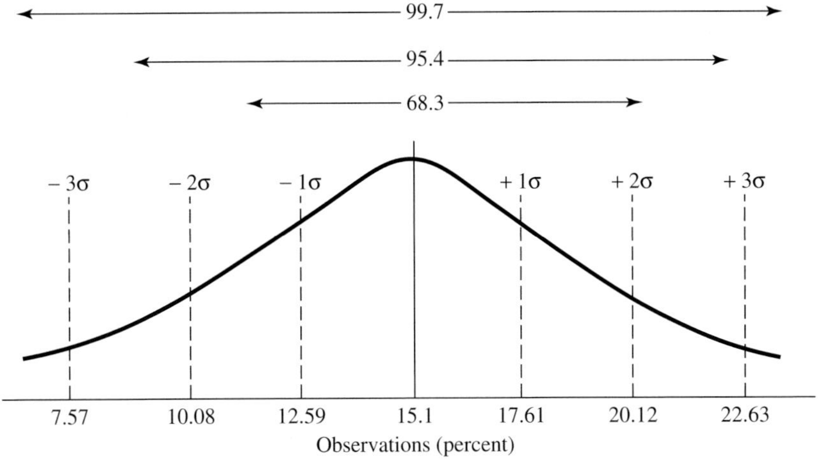

Fig. 7.7. Probability of X_i in the Intervals $\pm 1\sigma, \pm 2\sigma, \pm 3\sigma$.

Since the average lending rate is assumed to be normally distributed with a mean of 15.1% and a standard deviation of 2.51%, it is clear that almost all (99.7%) of the lending rates will lie in the range from 7.57% to 22.63%, because 7.57% is three standard deviations below 15.1% and 22.63% is three standard deviations above the mean. It is also clear that 68.3% of the rates will lie in the range of 12.59%–17.61%.

7.5. The Market Rate of Return and Market Risk Premium

The **market rate of return** is the return that can be expected from the market portfolio. This portfolio contains all risky assets — that is, stocks, bonds, real estate, coins, and so on. Because *all* risky assets are included, the market portfolio is a completely diversified portfolio. All unsystematic risks related to each individual asset would, therefore, be diversified away. The remaining risk is systematic risk that which influences all risky assets.

The market rate of return can be calculated using one of several types of market indicator series, such as the Dow-Jones Industrial Average, the Standard and Poor (S&P) 500, or the NYSE Index, using the following equation:

$$\frac{I_t - I_{t-1}}{I_{t-1}} = R_{mt}, \tag{7.19}$$

where

R_{mt} = market rate of return at time t;
I_t = market index at t; and
I_{t-1} = market index at $t - 1$.

This equation calculates the percent change in the market index during period t and the previous period $t - 1$. This change is the rate of return an investor would expect to receive in t had he or she invested in $t - 1$.

A **risk-free investment** is one in which the investor is sure about the timing and amount of income streams arising from that investment. However, for most types of investments, investors are uncertain about the timing and amount of income of their investments. The types of risks involved in investments can be quite broad, from the relatively riskless T-bills to highly risky speculative stocks.

The reasonable investor dislikes risks and uncertainty and would, therefore, require an additional return on his investment to compensate for this uncertainty. This return, called the **risk premium**, is added to the nominal risk-free rate. The risk premium is derived from several major sources of uncertainty or risk, as was discussed at the beginning of this chapter.

Table 7.9 illustrates this concept. In this table, the market rate of return using the S&P 500 was calculated using Equation (7.9) to devise average quarterly returns. Quarterly T-bill rates are listed in the fourth column. The T-bill rate was deducted from the market return rate ($R_m - R_f$) to devise the risk premium. In most of 1981 and the first two quarters of 1982, the market was in decline, with low returns resulting in each quarter. This allowed the T-bill investors to obtain a higher than the market return and resulted in negative risk premiums.

The second half of 1982 demonstrated an increasing market level and higher market returns. The fourth quarter of 1982 was a 16.79% return, the highest in the past eight quarters. This allowed market rates to leap beyond the riskless T-bill rate, and the result was a positive risk premium. The first half of 1983 also revealed a positive risk premium. However, the market-risk premiums from the third quarter of 1983 to the first quarter of 1985 were all negative. Negative risk premiums also occurred through 1986 and 1987 during the period of fluctuation in the level of stock market prices. The fourth quarter of 1987 reflects the October 1987 stock-market crash, which resulted in a loss of almost 25% in the S&P average.

Table 7.9. Market Returns and T-Bill by Quarters.

Quarter	S&P 500	(*A*) Market Return (%)	(*B*) T-Bill Rate (%)	(*A*)–(*B*) Risk Premium (%)
1980				
IV	135.76			
1981				
I	136.00	+0.18	13.36	−13.18
II	131.21	−3.52	14.73	−18.25
III	116.18	−12.94	14.70	−27.64
IV	122.55	+5.48	10.85	−5.37
1982				
I	111.96	−8.64	12.68	−21.32
II	110.61	−1.21	12.47	−13.68
III	120.42	+8.87	7.92	+0.95
IV	140.64	+16.79	7.94	+8.85
1983				
I	152.96	+8.76	8.35	0.41
II	168.11	+9.90	8.79	1.11
III	166.07	−1.22	9.00	−10.22
IV	164.93	−0.69	9.00	−9.69
1984				
I	159.18	−3.49	9.52	−13.01
II	153.18	−3.77	9.87	−13.64
III	166.10	+8.43	10.37	−1.94
IV	167.24	+0.68	8.06	−7.37
1985				
I	180.66	+8.02	8.52	−0.50
II	188.89	+4.55	6.95	−2.4
III	184.06	−2.62	7.10	−9.72
IV	207.26	+12.60	7.07	+5.53
1986				
I	232.33	+12.09	6.56	+5.53
II	245.30	+5.58	6.21	−0.63
III	238.27	−2.86	5.21	−8.07
IV	248.61	+4.33	5.43	−1.10
1987				
I	292.47	+17.64	5.59	+12.05
II	301.36	+3.03	5.69	−2.66
III	318.66	+5.74	6.40	+0.05
IV	240.96	−24.38	5.77	−30.10

Theoretically it is not possible for a risk premium required by investors to be negative. Taking on risk involves some positive cost. Nevertheless, using short-run estimators as in Table 7.9 may result in negative figures because they reflect the fluctuations of the market. The basic problem with using actual market data to assess risk premiums has to do with the difference between expected returns (which are always positive) and realized returns (which may be positive or negative). It becomes evident that investors' expectations will not always be realized.

7.6. Summary

This chapter has defined the basic concepts of risk and risk measurement. The efficient-portfolio concept and its implementation were demonstrated using the relationships of risk and return. The dominance principle and performance measures were also discussed and illustrated. Finally, the interest rate and market rate of return were used as measurements to show how the commercial lending rate and the market risk premium can be calculated.

Overall, this chapter has introduced uncertainty analysis assuming previous exposure to certainty concepts. Further application of the concepts discussed in this chapter as related to security analysis and portfolio management are explored in later chapters.

Questions and Problems

1. What is risk? What are some of the ways to measure risk?
2. Define the following terms:

   (a) call risk (b) convertible risk
   (c) default risk (d) interest-rate risk
   (e) management risk (f) marketability risk
   (g) purchasing risk (h) systematic risk
   (i) unsystematic risk (j) efficient portfolio

3. Calculate the expected return and variance for a portfolio consisting of two stocks. A and B.

$$E(R_A) = 12\% \qquad E(R_B) = 16\%$$
$$W_A = 0.3 \qquad \text{Var}(R_B) = 3\%$$
$$\text{Var}(R_A) = 2\% \qquad \text{Cov}(R_A, R_B) = 1\%$$

4. If a portfolio consists of 25 stocks, how many variance terms will there be? How many different covariance terms will there be?
5. You are given the information in the table about three stocks under different economic conditions.

Economic Conditions	R_A (%)	R_B (%)	R_C (%)	P_i (%)
Recession	10	9	20	20
Normal Growth	11	8	10	30
Inflation	12	6	20	50

(a) Calculate the expected return and variance for each security.
(b) Calculate the covariance and correlation coefficient for each pair of assets.
(c) Find the expected return for a portfolio consisting of equal amounts of stocks A, B, and C.

6. Carefully explain the dominance explain the dominance principle and its importance to portfolio theory.
7. Compare the SP of portfolio performance with the TP. Under what conditions will they be equivalent?
8. Rank the portfolios A through F in the table using both the SP and TP. Assume that the risk-free rate is 5%.

Portfolios	$E(R)$ (%)	σ (%)	β (%)
A	10	4	2
B	8	12	3
C	11	9	2.4
D	13	20	1.5
E	9	6	1.7
F	7	2	0.3

9. Compare the JM of portfolio performance to the TP.

Bibliography

Ben-Horin, M. and H. Levy. "Total Risk, Diversifiable Risk and Non-Diversifiable Risk: A Pedagogic Note." *Journal of Financial and Quantitative Analysis*, v. 15(June 1980), pp. 289–295.

Bowman, R. G. "The Theoretical Relationship between Systematic Risk and Financial (Accounting) Variables." *Journal of Finance*, v. 34 (June 1979), pp. 617–630.

Elton, E. J., M. J. Gruber, S. J. Brown and W. N. Goetzmann. *Modern Portfolio Theory and Investment Analysis*, 7th ed. New York: John Wiley & Sons, 2006.

Evans, J. L. and S. H. Archer. "Diversification and the Reduction of Dispersion: An Empirical Analysis." *Journal of Finance*, v. 23 (December 1968), pp. 761–767.

Francis, J. C. and S. H. Archer. *Portfolio Analysis*. Englewood Cliffs, NJ: Prentice-Hall, Inc., 1979.

Ibbotson, R. G. and R. A. Sinquefield. "Stocks, Bonds, Bills, and Inflation: Simulations of the Future (1976–2000)." *Journal of Business*, v. 49 (July 1976), pp. 313–338.

Jensen, M. C. "The Performance of Mutual Funds in the Period 1945–1964." *Journal of Finance*, v. 23 (May 1968), pp. 389–416.

Jensen, M. C. "Risk, the Pricing of Capital Assets, and the Evaluation of Investment Portfolios." *Journal of Business*, v. 42 (April 1969), pp. 167–185.

Jensen, M. and W. Meckling, "Theory of the Firm: Managerial Behavior, Agency Costs, and Ownership Structure," *Journal of Financial Economics*, v. 3 (October 1976), pp. 305–360.

Lee, C. F. and A. C. Lee, *Encyclopedia of Finance*, New York, NY: Springer, 2006.

Lee, C. F., J. C. Lee and A. C. Lee. *Statistics for Business and Financial Economics*. Singapore: World Scientific Publishing Co., 2000.

Lee, C. F. and S. N. Chen. "The Sampling Relationship Between Sharpe's Performance Measure and Its Risk Proxy: Sample Size, Investment Horizon and Market Conditions," *Management Science*, v. 27 (June 1981), pp. 607–618.

Lee, C. F. and S. N. Chen. "The Effects of the Sample Size, the Investment Horizon and Market Conditions on the Validity of Composite Performance Measures: A Generalization," *Management Science*, v. 32 (November 1986), pp. 1410-1421.

Lee, C. F. and S. N. Chen. "On the Measurement Errors and Ranking of Composite Performance Measures," *Quarterly Review of Economics and Business*, v. 24 (Autumn, 1984), pp. 6–17.

Markowitz, H. M. *Portfolio Selection: Efficient Diversification of Investments*. New York: John Wiley and Sons, Inc., 1959.

Modigliani, F. and G. A. Pogue. "An Introduction to Risk and Return." *Financial Analysis Journal*, v. 30 (May–June 1974), pp. 69–86.

Robichek, A. A. and R. A. Cohn. "The Economic Determinants of Systematic Risk." *Journal of Finance*, v. 29 (May 1974), pp. 439–447.

Schall, L. D. "Asset Valuation, Firm Investment, and Firm Diversification." *Journal of Business*, v. 45 (January 1972), pp. 11–28.

Sharpe, W. F. "Mutual Fund Performance." *Journal of Business*, v. 39 (January 1966), pp. 119–138.

Thompson, D. J. "Sources of Systematic Risk in Common Stocks." *Journal of Business*, v. 49 (April 1976), pp. 173–188.

Tobin, J. "Liquidity Preference as Behavior toward Risk." *Review of Economic Studies*, v. 25 (February 1958), pp. 65–86.

Treynor, J. "How to Rate Management of Investment Funds." *Harvard Business Review*, v. 43 (January/February 1965), pp. 63–75.

Chapter 8

Risk-Aversion, Capital Asset Allocation, and Markowitz Portfolio-Selection Model

In this chapter, basic portfolio analysis concepts and techniques are discussed in the Markowitz portfolio-selection model and other related issues in portfolio analysis. Before Harry Markowitz (1952, 1959) developed his portfolio-selection technique into what came to be called modern portfolio theory (MPT), security-selection models focused primarily on the returns generated by investment opportunities. The Markowitz theory retained the emphasis on return, but it elevated risk to a coequal level of importance, and the concept of portfolio risk was born. Although risk has been considered an important factor and variance an accepted way of measuring risk, Markowitz was the first to clearly and rigorously show how the variance of a portfolio can be reduced through the impact of diversification. He demonstrated that by combining securities that are not perfectly positively correlated into a portfolio, the portfolio variance can be reduced.

The **Markowitz model** is based on several assumptions concerning the behavior of investors:

A probability distribution of possible returns over some holding period can be estimated by investors.

Investors have single-period utility functions in which they maximize utility within the framework of diminishing marginal utility of wealth.

Variability about the possible values of return is used by investors to measure risk.

Investors use only expected return and risk to make investment decisions.

Expected return and risk as used by investors are measured by the first two moments of the probability distribution of returns-expected value and variance.

Return is desirable; risk is to be avoided.

It follows, then, that a security or portfolio is considered efficient if there exists no other investment opportunity with a higher level of return at a given level of risk and no other opportunity with a lower level of risk at a given level of return.

8.1. Utility Theory, Utility Functions, and Indifference Curves

In this section, utility theory and functions, which are needed for portfolio analysis and capital asset models will be discussed in detail.

8.1.1. *Utility Theory*

Utility theory is the foundation for the theory of choice under uncertainty. Following Henderson and Quandt (1980), cardinal and ordinal theories are the two major alternatives used by economists to determine how people and societies choose to allocate scarce resources and to distribute wealth among one another over time.[1]

8.1.2. *Utility Functions*

Economists define the relationships between psychological satisfaction and wealth as "utility." An upward-sloping relationship, as shown in Fig. 8.1, identifies the phenomena of increasing wealth and increasing satisfaction as being directly related. These relationships can be classified into linear, concave, and convex utility functions.

In Fig. 8.1(a), for each unit change in wealth, there is a linear utility function, and equal increase in satisfaction or utility. A doubling of wealth will double satisfaction, and so on. If an investor's utility function is a linear

[1] A *cardinal utility* implies that a consumer is capable of assigning to every commodity or combination of commodities a number representing the amount or degree of utility associated with it. An *ordinary utility* implies that a consumer will not be able to assign numbers that represent (in arbitrary unit) the degree or amount of utility associated with commodity or combination of commodity. The consumer can only rank and order the amount or degree of utility associated with commodity.

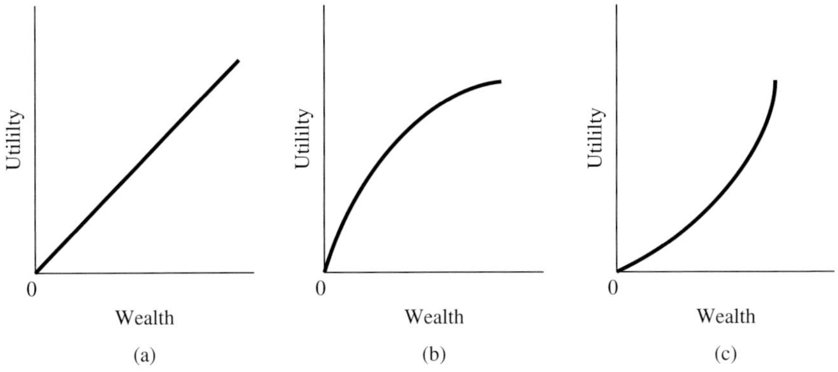

Fig. 8.1. Utility Functions, (a) Linear, (b) Concave Function, (c) Convex Function.

utility function, we call this kind of investor as risk-neutral investor. This is probably not very realistic: \$1 increase in wealth from \$1 to \$2 is probably more important than an increase from \$1 million to \$2 million, because the marginal utility diminishes with increased wealth.

In Fig. 8.1(b), the concave utility function shows the relationship of an increase in wealth and a less than proportional increase in utility. In other words, the marginal utility of wealth decreases as wealth increases. As mentioned above, the \$1 increase from \$1 to \$2 of wealth is more important to the individual than the increase from \$1,000,000 to \$1,000,001. Each successive increase in wealth adds less satisfaction as the level of wealth rises. We call an investor with a concave utility function as risk-averse investor.

Finally, Fig. 8.1(c) is a convex utility function, which denotes a more than proportional increase in satisfaction for each increase in wealth. Behaviorally, the richer you are the more satisfaction you receive in getting an additional dollar of wealth. Investors with convex utility functions are called risk-seeking investors.

The utility theory, primarily used in finance, is developed by Von Neumann and Morgenstern (VNM, 1947). VNM define investor utility as a function of rates of return or wealth. Mao (1969) points out that the VNM utility theory is really somewhere between the cardinal and ordinal utility theories. The function associated with the VNM's utility theory in terms of wealth can be defined as

$$U = f(\mu_w, \sigma_w),$$

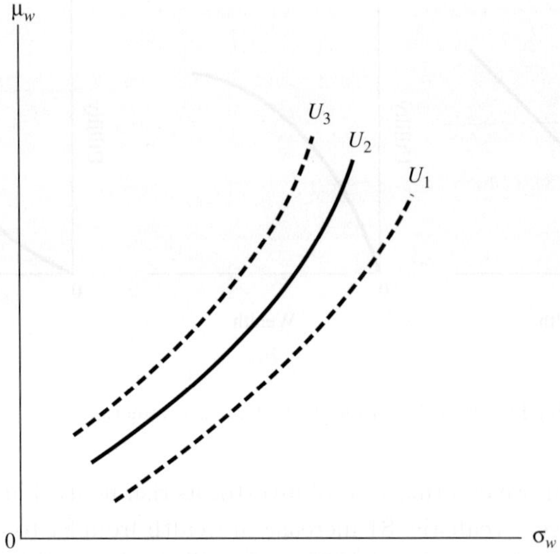

Fig. 8.2. Indifference Curves of Utility Functions.

where μ_w indicates expected future wealth and σ_w represents the predicted standard deviation of the possible divergence of actual future wealth from μ_w.

Investors are expected to prefer a higher expected future wealth to a lower value. Moreover, they are generally risk averse as well. That is, they prefer a lower value of σ_w to a higher value, given the level of μ_w.[2] These assumptions imply that the **indifference curves** relating to μ_w and σ_w will be upward sloping, as indicated in Fig. 8.2. In Fig. 8.2, each indifference curve is an expected utility isoquant showing all the various combinations of risk and return that provide an equal amount of expected utility for the investor.

In explaining how investment decisions or portfolio choices are made, utility theory is used here not to imply that individuals actually make decisions using a utility curve, but rather as an expository vehicle that helps explain how investors presumably act. In general, humans behave as if more is better than less (the utility curve is upward sloping) and marginal utility is decreasing (the utility curve is concave).

[2]Technically, these conditions can be represented mathematically by $\partial U/\partial \mu_w > 0$ and $\partial U/\partial \sigma_w < 0$.

In an uncertain environment it becomes necessary to ascertain how different individuals will react to risky situations. The risk is defined as the probability of success or failure. Alternatively, risk could be described as variability of outcomes, payoffs, or returns. This implies that there is a distribution of outcomes associated with each investment decisions. What is needed is a linkage between utility or expected utility and risk. Expected utility has been defined as the numerical value assigned to the probability distribution associated with a particular portfolio's return. This numerical value is calculated by taking a weighted average of the utilities of the various possible returns. The weights are the probabilities of occurrence associated with each of the possible returns. It is calculated by the following formula:

$$E(U) = \sum_{i}^{n} U(w_i)P_i, \tag{8.1}$$

where

$E(U)$ = expected utility;
$U(w_i)$ = the utility of the ith outcome w_i; and
P_i = the probability of the ith outcome.

Sample Problem 8.1 provides further illustration.

Sample Problem 8.1

Given investments A and B as shown in Table 8.1, determine the utilities of A and B for the given utility functions.

$$U(w) = w_i$$
$$U(w) = w_i^2$$
$$U(w) = w_i^2 - w_i$$

Table 8.1. Possible Outcomes of Investments A and B.

A		B	
Outcome w_i	Probability	Outcome w_i	Probability
10	2/5	9	2/3
5	2/5	3	1/3
1	1/5		

Solution

For $U(w) = w_i$

$$\text{Expected Utility of A} = \frac{2}{5}(10) + \frac{2}{5}(5) + \frac{1}{5}(1) = 6\frac{1}{5}$$

$$\text{Expected Utility of B} = \frac{2}{3}(9) + \frac{1}{3}(3) = 7$$

For $U(w) = w_i^2$

$$\text{Expected Utility of A} = \frac{2}{5}(100) + \frac{2}{5}(25) + \frac{1}{5}(1) = 50\frac{1}{5}$$

$$\text{Expected Utility of B} = \frac{2}{3}(81) + \frac{1}{3}(9) = 57$$

$U(w) = w_i^2 - w_i$ (use results from 1 and 2)

$$\text{Expected Utility of A} = 50\frac{1}{5} - 6\frac{1}{5} = 44$$

$$\text{Expected Utility of B} = 57 - 7 = 50$$

In all three cases, B has the higher degree of utility because it has a higher expected value as well as a smaller dispersion than A.

8.1.2.1. Linear Utility Function and Risk

It is useful to consider how the shape of an individual's utility function affects his or her reaction to risk. Assume that an individual who has \$5,000, and whose behavior is a linear utility function (Fig. 8.1(a)), is offered a chance to gain \$10,000 with a probability of 1/2 or to lose \$10,000 with a probability of 1/2. What should he or she pay for such an opportunity? The answer is nothing, for as can be seen in Fig. 8.3, this individual would be no better or worse off accepting or rejecting this opportunity. If he rejected the offer, his wealth would be \$5,000 with utility U_1; if he paid nothing for the opportunity, his wealth would remain as \$5,000 with utility U_1. Any payment for this chance would reduce his wealth and therefore be undesirable. This is so because the expected value of the fair game is zero:

$$\frac{1}{2}(10,000) + \frac{1}{2}(-10,000) = 0.$$

Figure 8.3 illustrates this linear utility function concept. In the following section, we will analyze the implication of concave utility function.

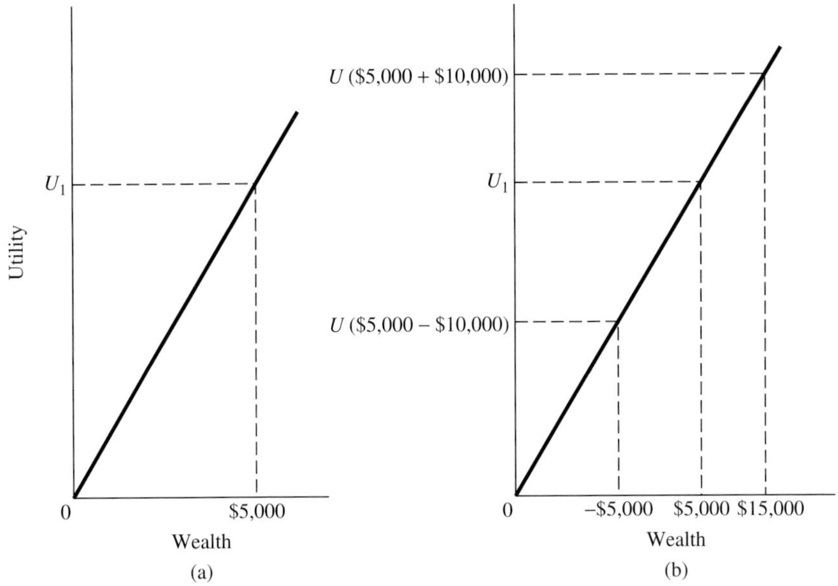

Fig. 8.3. Risk-Neutral Investors and Fair Games, (a) Initial Position, (b) Expected Utility if Offer is Accepted.

8.1.2.2. Concave Utility Function and Risk

Now consider an individual whose behavior is a concave utility function. If this individual participates and wins, his or her utility is shown by point U_W in Fig. 8.4. But if the individual loses, his or her position is shown by U_L. The expected value of this fair game, having a 50% chance of winning and a 50% chance of losing, is shown by point A.[3] The utility of the fair game is U_F. A comparison of U_F with the initial position, U_i, shows that the investor should not accept this fair game.

As shown in Fig. 8.4, the utility of winning $(U_W - U_i)$ is less than the utility of losing $(U_i - U_L)$. Therefore, the utility of doing nothing is greater than the expected utility of accepting the fair game. In fact, the individual should be willing to pay up to the difference between the utility of winning and the utility of losing $(U_i - U_L)$–$(U_W - U_i)$ to avoid being involved in this situation. Alexander and Francis (1986) theoretically analyze this issue in

[3]Following Fama (1970) and Alexander and Francis (1986, p. 177) a fair game means that the expected returns, given information set θ, equal the expected returns without the information set. Note that this does not mean the expected returns are zero or positive — they could be negative.

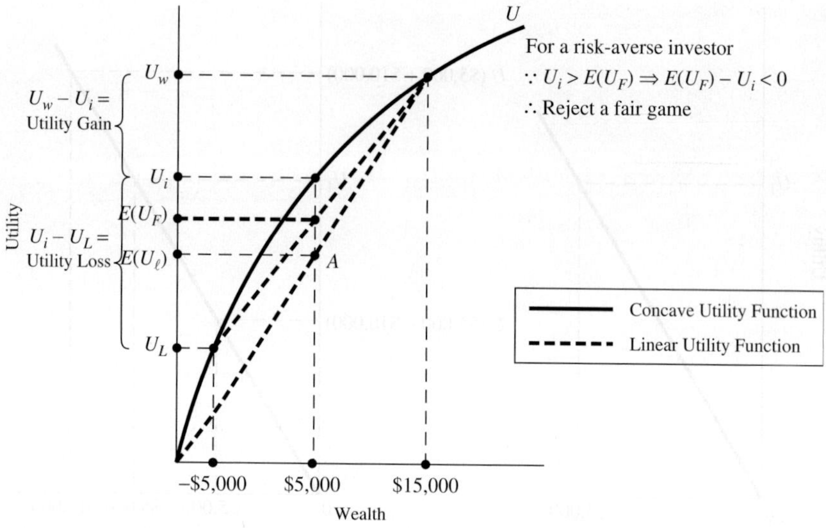

Fig. 8.4. Utility Function for Risk-Averse Investor.

more detail. Hence investors with concave utility functions are said to be risk averse. That is, they would reject a fair game because the utility derived from winning is less than the utility lost should they lose the game. In other words, the expected utility of participating in a fair game is negative. Sample Problem 8.2 will provide illustration of linear, concave, and convex utility function cases for different investment decisions.

$E(U_F) = \frac{1}{2}(U_w + U_L)$ is the expected utility of the fair game under a concave utility function.

$E(U_\ell)$ is the expected utility of the fair game under a linear utility function.

Sample Problem 8.2

Given the following utility functions for four investors, what can you conclude about their reaction toward a fair game?

(1) $u(w) = w + 4$
(2) $u(w) = w - \frac{1}{2}w^2$ (quadratic utility function)
(3) $u(w) = -e^{-2w}$ (negative exponential utility function), and
(4) $u(w) = w^2 - 4w$.

Evaluate the second derivative of the utility functions according to the following rules.

$u''(w) < 0$ implies risk averse
$u''(w) = 0$ implies risk neutral
$u''(w) > 0$ implies risk seeker

Solution

$$u(w) = w + 4$$
$$u'(w) = 1$$
$$u''(w) = 0$$

This implies risk neutrality; it is indifference for the investor to accept or reject a fair gamble.

$$u(w) = w - \frac{1}{2}w^2$$
$$u'(w) = -w^2$$
$$u''(w) = -2w < 0$$

(We assume wealth is non-negative.)

This implies the investor is risk averse and would reject a fair gamble.

$$u(w) = -e^{-2w}$$
$$u'(w) = 2e^{-2w}$$
$$u''(w) = -4e^{-2w} < 0$$

This implies risk adversity; the investor would reject a fair gamble.

$$u(w) = w^2 - 4w$$
$$u'(w) = 2w - 4$$
$$u''(w) = 2 > 0$$

This implies risk preference; the investor would seek a fair gamble.

The convex utility function is not realistic in real-world decisions; therefore, it is not further explored at this point. The following section discusses the implications of alternative utility functions in terms of indifference curves.

8.1.3. *Risk Aversion and Asset Allocation*

When risk increases along with return, the most attractive portfolio is not obvious. How can investors quantify the rate at which they are willing to trade off return against risk? By assuming that each investor can assign a welfare, or utility, score to competing investment portfolios based on the expected return and risk of those portfolios. Higher utility values are assigned to portfolios with more attractive risk-return profiles. Portfolios receive higher utility scores for higher expected returns and lower scores for higher volatility.

Assigning a portfolio with expected return and variance of returns, the following utility score:

$$U = E(r) - \frac{1}{2} \times A \times s^2, \tag{8.2}$$

where

U = utility;
$E(r)$ = expected return on the asset or portfolio;
A = coefficient of risk aversion; and
s^2 = variance of returns.

Sample Problem 8.3

Consider three investors with different degrees of risk aversion: A1 = 2.0, A2 = 3.0, and A3 = 4.0, all of whom are evaluating the three portfolios in Table 8.2. Because the risk-free rate is assumed to be 5%, utility score implies that all three investors would assign a utility score of 0.05 to the

Table 8.2. Utility Scores Assigned by Each Investor to Each Portfolio.

Investor: Risk Aversion (A)	Utility Score Portfolio (L) $E(r) = .07$; $\sigma = .05$	Utility Score Portfolio (M) $E(r) = .09$; $\sigma = .1$	Utility Score Portfolio (H) $E(r) = .13$; $\sigma = .2$
2.0	$0.07 - \frac{1}{2} \times 2 \times 0.05^2 = 0.0675$	$0.09 - \frac{1}{2} \times 2 \times 0.1^2 = 0.0800$	$0.13 - \frac{1}{2} \times 2 \times 0.2^2 = 0.0900$
3.0	$0.07 - \frac{1}{2} \times 3 \times 0.05^2 = 0.0663$	$0.09 - \frac{1}{2} \times 3 \times 0.1^2 = 0.0750$	$0.13 - \frac{1}{2} \times 3 \times 0.2^2 = 0.0700$
4.0	$0.07 - \frac{1}{2} \times 4 \times 0.05^2 = 0.0650$	$0.09 - \frac{1}{2} \times 4 \times 0.1^2 = 0.0700$	$0.13 - \frac{1}{2} \times 4 \times 0.2^2 = 0.0500$

risk-free alternative. Table 8.2 presents the utility scores that would be assigned by each investor to each portfolio. The portfolio with the highest utility score for each investor appears in bold. Notice that the high-risk portfolio, H, would be chosen only by the investor with the lowest degree of risk aversion, A1 = 2.0, while the low-risk portfolio, L would be passed over even by the most risk-averse of our three investors. All three portfolios beat the risk-free alternative for the investors with levels of risk aversion given in Table 8.2.

Sample Problem 8.4

Assuming an investor who faces a risk-free rate and a risky portfolio with expected return and standard deviation will find that for any choice of W, the expected return of the complete portfolio is given by

$$E(r_C) = r_f + W[E(r_p) - r_f]. \tag{8.3}$$

The variance of the complete portfolio is

$$\sigma_C^2 = W^2\sigma_p^2. \tag{8.4}$$

The investor attempts to maximize utility by choosing the best allocation to the risk asset, W. To solve the utility maximization problem, we write the problem as follows:

$$Max\ U = E(r_C) - \frac{1}{2}A\sigma_C^2 = r_f + W[E(r_p) - r_f] - \frac{1}{2}AW^2\sigma_p^2. \tag{8.5}$$

Taking derivative of U with respective to W and set the derivative of this expression to zero, W yields the optimal position for risk-averse investors in the risk asset, W*, as follows:

$$W^* = \frac{E(r_p) - r_f}{A\sigma_p^2}. \tag{8.6}$$

In the numerical example, we assume that the expected rate of return on risky asset is $E(r_p) = 16\%$ and $\sigma_P = 20\%$, and the risk-free rate is $r_p = 6\%$. The optimal solution for an investor with a coefficient of risk aversion $A = 3$ is

$$W^* = \frac{0.16 - 0.06}{3 \times (0.20)^2} = 0.83. \tag{8.7}$$

Therefore, the investor will invest 83% of his investment budget in the risky asset and 17% of his investment budget in the risk-free asset.

8.1.4. *Indifference Curves*

Indifference (utility-function) curves are abstract theoretical concepts. They cannot, as a practical matter, be used to actually measure how individuals make investment decisions — or any other decisions. They are, however, useful tools for building models that illustrate the relationship between risk and return. An investor's utility function can be utilized conceptually to derive an indifference curve, which shows individual preference for risk and return.[4] An indifference curve can be plotted in the risk–return space such that the investor's utility is equal all along its length. The investor is indifferent to various combinations of risk and return; hence, the name indifference curve. Various types of investor's indifference curves are shown in Fig. 8.5.

In the same level of satisfaction, the risk-averse investor requires more return for an extra unit of risk than the return the investor asks for previous one unit increase of risk. Therefore, the indifference curve is convex. Figure 8.5(a) presents two indifference curves which are risk-averse, and $U_1 > U_2$ (higher return and lower risk). For a risk-neutral investor, the indifference curve is a straight line. In the same level of satisfaction, the investor requires the same return for an extra unit of risk as the return he or she asks for previous one unit increase of risk. Figure 8.5(b) presents two indifference curves which are risk-neutral, and $U_1 > U_2$. For a risk-seeking investor, the indifference curve is a concave function. In the same level of satisfaction, the investor requires less return for an extra unit of risk than the return he asks for previous one unit increase of risk. Figure 8.5(c) presents two indifference curves which are risk-seeking, and $U_1 > U_2$.

The more risk-averse individuals will claim more premiums when they face uncertainty (risk). In Fig. 8.5(d), when facing σ_0, investor 1 and investor 2 have the same expected return, $E(R_0)$. However, when the risk adds to σ_1, the expected return $E(R_1)$ investor 1 asks is higher than the expected return $E(R_2)$ investor 2 asks. Thus, investor 1 is more risk-averse than investor 2. Therefore, in return-risk plane, the larger slope of indifference curve which the investor has, the higher risk-averse level the investor is.

Later in this chapter different levels of risk and return are evaluated for securities and portfolios when a decision must be made concerning which

[4]By definition, an indifference curve shows all combinations of products (investments) A and B that will yield same level of satisfaction or utility to consume. This kind of analysis is based upon ordinal rather than cardinal utility theory.

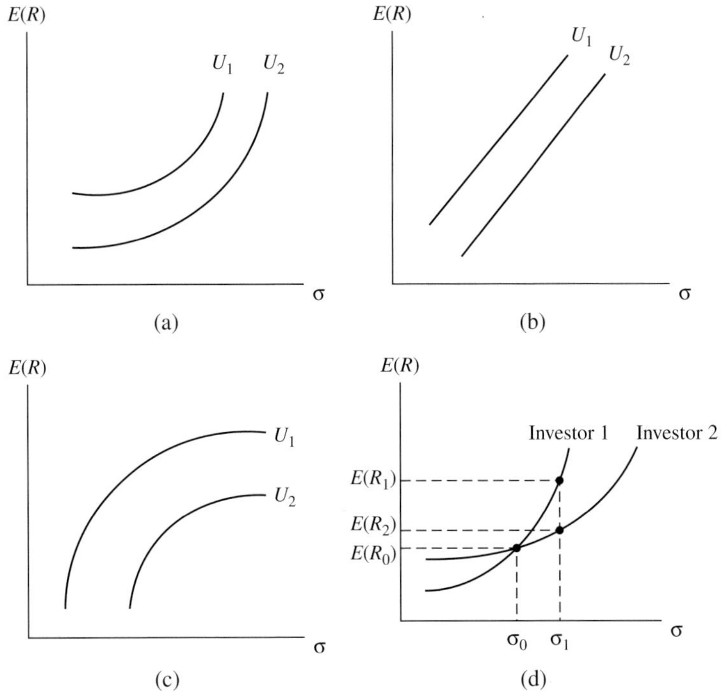

Fig. 8.5. Indifference Curves for Various Types of Individuals, (a) Risk-Averse investor, (b) Risk-Neutral Investor, (c) Risk-Seeking Investor, (d) Level of Risk-Aversion.

security or portfolio is better than another. It is at that point in the analysis that indifference curves of hypothetical individuals are employed to help determine which securities or portfolios are desirable and which ones are not. Basically, values for return and risk will be plotted for a number of portfolios as well as indifference curves for different types of investors. The investor's optimal portfolio will then be the one identified with the highest level of utility for the various indifference curves.

Investors generally hold more than one type of investment asset in their portfolio. Besides securities, an investor may hold real estate, gold, art, and so on. Thus, as the measures of risk and return for individual securities developed, the measures of risk and return may be used for portfolios of risky assets. Risk-averse investors hold portfolios rather than individual securities as a means of eliminating unsystematic risk; hence the examination of risk and return will continue in terms of portfolios rather than individual securities. Indifference curves can be used to indicate investors' *willingness* to trade risk for return; now investors' ability to trade risk for return needs to be represented in terms of indifference curves and efficient portfolios, as discussed in the next section.

8.2. Efficient Portfolios

As discussed in Chapter 7, **efficient portfolios** may contain any number of asset combinations. The asset combinations can be illustrated in Fig. 8.6, where the area within curve $XVYZ$ is the feasible opportunity set representing all possible portfolio combinations. The curve YV represents all possible efficient portfolios and is the efficient frontier. The line segment VX is on the feasible opportunity set, but not on the efficient frontier; all points on VX represent inefficient portfolios.

The portfolios and securities that lie on the frontier VX in Fig. 8.6 would not be likely candidates for investors to hold. This is so because they do not meet the criteria of maximizing expected return for a given level of frisk or minimizing risk for a given level of return. This is easily seen by comparing the portfolio represented by points X and X'. Since investors always prefer more expected return than less for a given level of risk, X' is always better than X. Using similar reasoning, investors would always prefer V to X because it has both a higher return and a lower level of risk. In fact, the portfolio at point V is identified as the **minimum-variance portfolio**, since no other portfolio exists that has a lower variance.

8.2.1. *Portfolio Combinations*

For each of the combinations of individual securities and inefficient portfolios in Fig. 8.6, there is a corresponding portfolio along the efficient frontier that either has a higher return given the same risk or a lower risk given the same return. However, points on the efficient frontier do not dominate one another. While point Y has considerably higher return than point V, it also has considerably higher risk. The optimal portfolio along the efficient frontier is not unique with this model and depends upon the risk/return tradeoff utility function of each investor. Portfolio selection, then, is determined by plotting investors' utility functions together with the efficient-frontier set of available investment opportunities. No two investors will select the same portfolio except by chance or if their utility curves are identical. In Fig. 8.6, two sets of indifference curves labeled U and U' are shown together with the efficient frontier. The U curves have a higher slope, indicating a greater level of risk aversion. The investor is indifferent to any

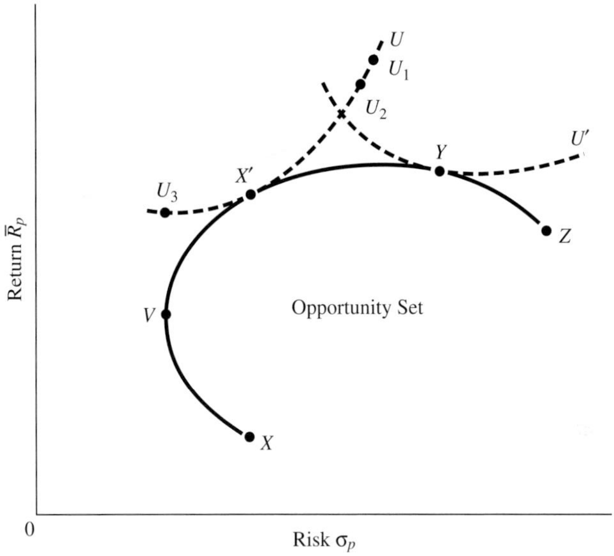

Fig. 8.6. Indifference Curves and the Minimum-Variance Set.

combination of R_p and σ_p along a given curve, for example, U_1, U_2, or U_3. The U' curve would be appropriate for a less risk-averse investor — that is, one who would be willing to accept relatively higher risk to obtain higher levels of return. The optimal portfolio would be the one that provides the highest utility — a point in the northwest direction (higher return and lower risk). This point will be at the tangent of a utility curve and the efficient frontier. The tangency point investor in Fig. 8.6 is point X'; for the risk-averse it is point Y. Each investor is logically selecting the optimal portfolio given his or her risk–return preference, and neither is more correct than the other.

Individual investors sometimes find it necessary to restrict their portfolios to include a relatively small number of securities. Mutual-fund portfolios, on the other hand, often contain securities from more than 500 different companies. To give some idea of the number of securities that is necessary to achieve a high level of diversification, Levy and Sarnat (1971) considered a naïve strategy of equally weighted portfolios — that is, of dividing the total investment into equal proportions among component securities. Plotting the variance of the portfolios developed in this manner against the number of securities making up the portfolios will result in a function similar to that illustrated in Fig. 8.7. As can be seen, the additional

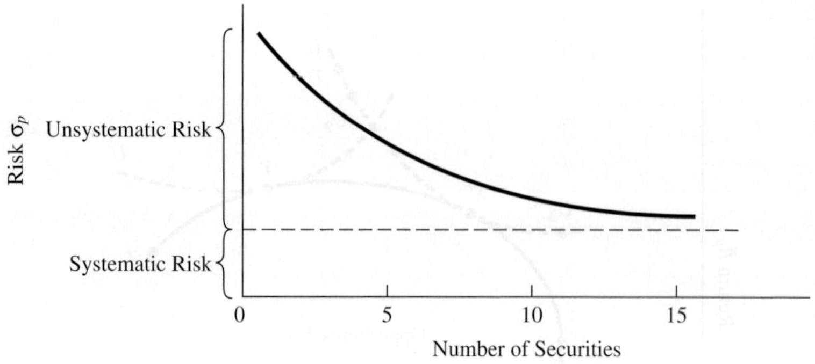

Fig. 8.7. Naive Diversification Reduces Risk to the Systematic Level in a Randomly Selected Portfolio.
Source: Levy and Sarnat (1971).

reduction in portfolio variance rapidly levels off as the number of securities is increased beyond five. An earlier study by Evans and Archer (1968) shows that the percentage of diversification that can be achieved with randomly selected, equally weighted portfolios levels off rapidly beyond a portfolio size of about 15.

8.2.2. *Short Selling*

Short selling (or "going short") is a much regulated type of market transaction. It involves selling shares of a stock that are borrowed in expectation of a fall in the security's price. When and if the price declines, the investor buys an equivalent number of shares of the same stock at the new lower price and returns to the lender the stock that was borrowed. The Federal Reserve Board requires short-selling customers to deposit 50% of the net proceeds of such short sales with the brokerage firm carrying out the transaction. Another key requirement of a short sale, set by the Securities and Exchange Act of 1934, is that the short sale must occur at a price higher than the preceding sale — or at the same price as the preceding sale, if that took place at a higher price than a preceding price. This is the so-called uptick or zero-tick rule. It prevents the price of a security from successively falling because of continued short selling.

Relaxing the assumption of no short selling in this development of the efficient frontier involves a modification of the analysis of the previous section. The efficient frontier analyzed in the previous sections was bounded on both ends by Y and the minimum variance portfolio V, respectively, as shown in Fig. 8.6. Point Y is called the **maximum-return portfolio**, since there is no other portfolio with a higher return. This point is normally an efficient security or portfolio with the greatest level of risk and return. It could also be a portfolio of securities, all having the same highest levels of risk and return. Point Z is normally a single security with the lowest level of return, although it could be a portfolio of securities, all having the same low level of return.

The Black (1972) model is identical to the Markowitz model except that it allows for short selling.[5] That is, the non-negativity constraint on the amount that can be invested in each security is relaxed, $W_A \gtrless 0$. A negative value for the weight invested in a security is allowed, tantamount to allowing a short sale of the security. The new efficient frontier that can be derived with short selling is shown in Fig. 8.8(a).

The major difference between the frontier in Fig. 8.8(a) (short selling) and Fig. 8.8(b) (no short selling) is the disappearance of the end points Y and Z. An investor could sell the lowest-return security (Y). If the number of short sales is unrestricted, then by a continuous short selling of X and reinvesting in Y, the investor could generate an infinite expected return. Hence the upper bound of the highest-return portfolio would no longer be Y but infinity (shown by the arrow on the top of the efficient frontier). Likewise, the investor could short sell the highest-return security U and reinvest the proceeds into the lowest-yield security X, thereby generating a return less than the return on the lowest-return security. Given no restriction on the amount of short selling, an infinitely negative return can be achieved, thereby removing the lower bound of X on the efficient frontier. But rational investors will not short sell a high-return stock and buy a low-return stock.

The portfolios on $VZ\prime$ always dominate those of VX, as shown in Fig. 8.8(a).

Whether an investor engages in any of this short-selling activity depends on the investor's own unique set of indifference curves. Hence, short selling generally will increase the range of alternative investments from the minimum-variance portfolio to plus or minus infinity. However, in the Black model with short selling, no provision was made for the Securities and Exchange Commission (SEC) margin requirement. Dyl (1975) imposed the margin requirement on short selling and added it to the Markowitz development of the efficient frontier.

[5]Most texts do not identify the Markowitz model with restrictions on short sale. Markowitz (1952) in fact, excluded short sales.

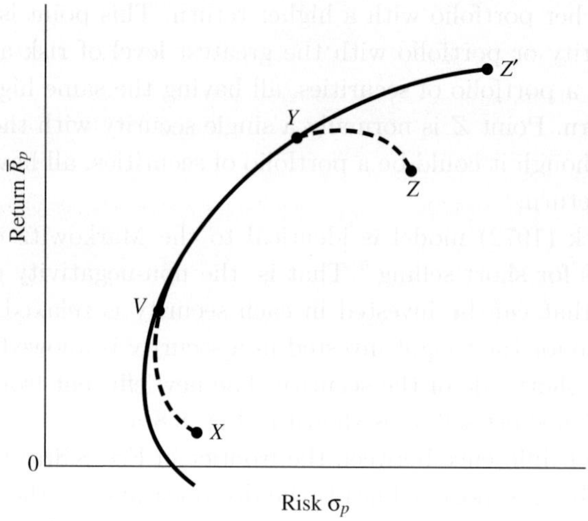

Fig. 8.8(a). The Efficient Frontier with Short Selling.

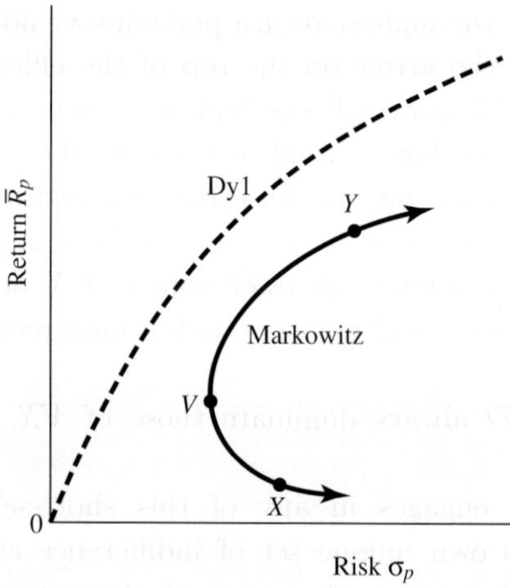

Fig. 8.8(b). Efficient Frontiers with and without Short Selling and Margin Requirements.
Source: Dyl (1975).

The Dyl Model. Dyl introduced short selling with margin requirements by creating a new set of risky securities, the ones sold short, which are negatively correlated with the existing set of risky securities. These new securities greatly enhance the diversification effect when they are placed in portfolios. The **Dyl model** affects the efficient frontier in two ways: (1) If the investor were to combine in equal weight any long position in a security or portfolio with a short position in a security or a portfolio, the resulting portfolio would yield zero return and zero variance and (2) any combination of unequal weighted long or short positions would yield portfolios with higher returns and lower risk levels. Overall, these two effects will yield an efficient frontier that dominates the Markowitz efficient frontier. Figure 8.8(b) compares the Dyl and Markowitz efficient frontiers.

Even though the inclusion of short selling changes the location and boundaries of the efficient frontier, the concavity of the curve is still intact. This is important in that it preserves the efficient frontier as the locus of optimal portfolios for risk-average investors. As long as the efficient frontier remains concave, by using indifference curves it will be possible to locate the optimal portfolio for each investor.

8.3. Techniques for Calculating the Efficient Frontier with Short Selling

Since there are thousands of securities from which the investor can choose for portfolio formation, it can be very costly and time consuming to calculate the efficient frontier set. One way of determining the optimal investment proportions in a portfolio is to hold the return constant and solve for the weighting factors ($W_1 \ldots, W_n$for n securities) that minimize the variance, given the constraint that all weights sum to one and that the constant return equals the expected return developed from the portfolio. The optimal weights can then be obtained by minimizing the Lagrange function C for portfolio variance.

$$C = \sum_{i=1}^{n}\sum_{j=1}^{n} W_i W_j r_{ij}\sigma_i\sigma_j + \lambda_1\left(1 - \sum_{i=1}^{n} W_i\right) + \lambda_2\left[E^* - \sum_{i=1}^{n} W_i E(R_i)\right], \tag{8.8}$$

in which λ_1 and λ_2 are the Lagrange multipliers; E^* and $E(R_i)$ are targeted rate of return and expected rate of return for security i, respectively; ρ_{ij} is the correlation coefficient between R_i and R_j; and other variables are as previously defined.

Function C has $n+2$ unknowns: $W_1, \ldots, W_n, \lambda_1$, and λ_2. By differentiating C with respect to W_i, λ_1, and λ_2 and equating the first derivatives to zero, $n+2$ equations can be derived to solve for $n+2$ unknowns. As shown in the empirical example later in this chapter, matrix algebra is best suited to this solution process. By using this approach, the minimum variance can be computed for any given level of expected portfolio return (subject to the other constraint that the weights sum to one). In practice it is best to use a computer because of the explosive increase in the number of calculations as the number of securities considered grows. The efficient set that is generated by the aforementioned approach (Equation (8.1)) is sometimes called the **minimum-variance set** because of the minimizing nature of the Lagrangian solution.

Thus far no specific distribution for measuring returns has been assumed. In most cases, specific distribution of returns will be needed when applying the portfolio model. The normal and log normal are two of the most commonly used distribution.

8.3.1. *The Normal Distribution*

As you undoubtedly are aware, the **normal (probability) distribution** is a bell-shaped curve centered on the mean of a given population or sample distribution. The area under the curve is an accumulation of probabilities that sum to one. With half of the area lying to the left and half to the right of the mean, probability statements may be made about underlying sample that makes up the distribution.

Within the scope of the Markowitz model, the normal distribution may be applied because of the use of the mean-variance assumptions. The formation of probability statements from the underlying sample is a result of the standard deviation (square root of the variance) quantifying the spread of the distribution. If the sample is normally distributed, approximately 68% of the observations will lie within one standard deviation on either side of the mean, approximately 95% will lie within two standard deviations, and approximately 99% will lie within three standard deviations. This ability to ascertain intervals of confidence for the observations allows the utilization of the normal distribution to predict ranges within which the portfolio returns will lie.

Utilizing the standard normal distribution (mean of zero, standard deviation of one), any set of mean-variance data can be standardized to develop probability statements about returns on a given portfolio. Standardization is an algebraic operation in which the mean is subtracted from a given return and this difference is divided by the standard deviation. The resultant metric is then standard normal and can be compared with tabulated values to calculate probabilistic quantities of occurrence. Within this framework, any hypothesized level of return can be assigned a probability of occurrence given a probabilistic value of occurrence that is based upon the nature of the sample.

For expository purposes, suppose the mean return on a particular investment is 10% for a given period, and that historically these returns have a variance of 0.16%, it is of interest to know what the probabilities are of obtaining a 15% or greater return, or a return less than or equal to 8%. These probabilities may be evaluated by using the normal distribution, as stated in notation below:

$$P(X \geq 0.15|\bar{R}_p = 0.1, \sigma_p^2 = 0.0016),$$
$$P(X \leq 0.18|\bar{R}_p = 0.1, \sigma_p^2 = 0.0016),$$

by standardizing the probability statements to z values:

$$\begin{aligned} &P\left(z \geq \frac{0.15 - 0.1}{0.04} = 1.25\right), \\ &P\left(z \leq \frac{0.08 - 0.1}{0.04} = -0.5\right). \end{aligned} \tag{8.9}$$

These standardized values can then be compared with the tabulated z values found in tables of the standardized normal distribution. For $z \geq 1.25$ the probability is 10.56% (50%–39.44%), and for $z = -0.05$ the probability is 0.3085. Therefore this investment has an 11.51% chance of obtaining a 15% or more return, and a 30.85% chance of obtaining 8% or less.

It is extremely difficult to make probabilistic statements when using the normal distribution. Given that the return data utilized are *ex post*, the predictive ability of the normal distribution based on historical data is limited. The past does not always predict the future; hence, this problem is somewhat alleviated by an assumption that the security under consideration is in a static state. Nevertheless, as shown by research and common sense, this assumption is rather bold, and the use of the normal distribution should be limited to comparisons of various past portfolio returns.

Another difficulty with the normal distribution is that if the distribution of the sample is skewed in any way, the standard deviation will not properly reflect the equivalent areas under the curve on either side of the mean. This problem will be discussed and solved in the next section through the application of the **log-normal distribution.** A variable is log-normally distributed if a logarithm of this variable is normally distributed. In addition, Simkowitz and Beedles (1978) have discussed implications of skewness on the diversification of the portfolio.

8.3.2. *The Log-Normal Distribution*

The log-normal distribution discussed in Chapter 19 will be explored further in this section. The approach outlined in the last section for delineating the efficient frontier assumes that the security-return data are normally distributed. In reality, most financial researchers would agree that security-return data tend to be positively skewed. This skewness can be a serious problem in accurately developing an efficient frontier with the Markowitz model because of the assumption that only the first two moments of the return distribution, mean and variance, are important.

One reason for returns being positively skewed is the inability of the investor to lose more than 100% of his or her investment, effectively creating a lower bound to portfolio returns. This is called the limited-liability constraint. But since capital gains and dividends could conceivably be infinite, the upper tail of the distribution of returns has no upper bounds. The range of probable returns is spread toward the positive side and therefore contains a potential bias when it is utilized in developing statistical estimates.

If the return distributions are significantly skewed, the efficient frontier can be more accurately determined with the use of logarithmically transformed holding-period returns. That is, each holding-period return for security i with holding period $T(1 + R_{iT})$ is transformed by computing its natural logarithm, $\ln(1 + R_{iT})$. The logarithmic transformation converts a data set of discretely compounded returns into continuously compounded returns. The larger the differencing interval used to measure the returns, the more positively skewed the distribution of discrete time returns; that is, if skewness exists in the return distribution, annual data will be more positively skewed than monthly data, which will be more skewed than weekly data.

The continuous compounding implied in the logarithmically transformed data will virtually eliminate any positive skewness existing in the raw return data when rates of return are log-normally distributed. It is practically possible to directly derive the efficient frontier using means and variances of logarithmically transformed data. Under this circumstance, assume that utility functions use continuous returns and variances, and then use the $\ln(1 + R_p)$ transformation on discrete data. To deal with the untransformed log-normally distributed data, Elton and Padberg (1976) use the mean and variance of log-normal distributed as discussed in Chapter 2 to derive the efficient frontier. In other words, they first delineate the efficient frontier by using the means and variances of the untransformed data and then determine the subset of the $[E(1+R_p), \sigma(1+R_p)]$ efficient frontier in terms of log-transformed data, $\ln(1+R_p)$.

Use of the logarithmic transformation can also be shown to eliminate less desirable portfolios in the lowest-return segment of the efficient frontier computer using the raw data.[6] Before moving on to an example, however, it will be useful to briefly summarize the portfolio-selection process.

8.3.3. *Mathematical Method to Calculate Efficient Frontier*[7]

The Markowitz model of portfolio selection is a mathematical approach for deriving optimal portfolios, that is, portfolios that satisfy the following conditions.

The least risk for a given level of expected return (minimum-variance portfolios)

The greatest expected return for a given level of risk (efficient portfolios).

How does a portfolio manager apply these techniques in the real world?

The process would normally begin with a universe of securities available to the fund manager. These securities would be determined by the goals and objectives of the mutual fund. For example, a portfolio manager who runs a mutual fund specializing in health-care stocks would be required to select securities from the universe of health-care stocks. This would greatly reduce the analysis of the fund manager by limiting the number of securities available.

The next step in the process would be to determine the proportions of each security to be included in the portfolio. To do this, the fund manager would begin by setting a target rate of return for the portfolio. After determining the target rate of return, the fund manager can determine the different proportions of each security that will allow the portfolio to reach this target rate of return.

The final step in the process would be for the fund manager to find the portfolio with the lowest variance given the target rate of return.

The optimal portfolio can be obtained mathematically through the use of the Lagrangian multipliers. The Lagrangian method allows the

[6]See Baumol (1963).

[7]We also provide graphical method to calculate efficient frontier. Please see Appendix 8A for detailed graphical method to calculate efficient frontier.

minimization or maximization of an objective function when the objective function is subject to some constraints. To do mathematical analysis, we need to calculate the expected return and variance of the portfolio which have been discussed in Chapter 7.

One of the goals of portfolio analysis is minimizing the risk or variance of the portfolio, subject to the portfolio attaining some target expected rate of return, and also subject to the portfolio weights summing to one. The problem can be stated mathematically:

$$\text{Min } \sigma_p^2 = \sum_{i=1}^{n}\sum_{j=1}^{n} W_i W_j \sigma_{ij} \tag{8.10}$$

Subject to

(i) $$\sum_{i=1}^{n} W_i E(R_i) = E^*$$

where E^* is the target expected return and

(ii) $$\sum_{i=1}^{n} W_i = 1.0.$$

The first constraint simply says that the expected return on the portfolio should equal the target return determined by the portfolio manager. The second constraint says that the weights of the securities invested in the portfolio must sum to one.

The Lagrangian objective function can be written:

$$\begin{aligned} C = {} & \sum_{i=1}^{n}\sum_{j=1}^{n} W_i W_j \text{Cov}(R_i R_j) + \lambda_1\left(1 - \sum_{i=1}^{n} W_i\right) \\ & + \lambda_2\left[E^* - \sum_{i=1}^{n} W_i E(R_i)\right]. \end{aligned} \tag{8.11}$$

For three securities case, the Lagrangian objective function is as follow:

$$\begin{aligned} C = {} & W_1^2\sigma_1^2 + W_2^2\sigma_2^2 + W_3^2\sigma_3^2 + 2W_1W_2\sigma_{12} + 2W_1W_3\sigma_{13} \\ & + 2W_2W_3\sigma_{23} + \lambda_1(1 - W_1 - W_2 - W_3) + \lambda_2 E^* \\ & - W_1E(R_1) - W_2E(R_2) - W_3E(R_3). \end{aligned}$$

Taking the partial derivatives of (8.12) with respect to each of the variables, $W_1, W_2, W_3, \lambda_1, \lambda_2$ and setting the resulting five equations equal to zero yields the minimization of risk subject to the Lagrangian constraints. We can obtain the following equations.

$$\frac{\partial C}{\partial W_1} = 2W_1\sigma_1^2 + 2W_2\sigma_{12} + 2W_3\sigma_{13} - \lambda_1 - \lambda_2 E(R_1) = 0,$$
$$\frac{\partial C}{\partial W_2} = 2W_2\sigma_2^2 + 2W_1\sigma_{12} + 2W_3\sigma_{23} - \lambda_1 - \lambda_2 E(R_2) = 0,$$
$$\frac{\partial C}{\partial W_3} = 2W_3\sigma_3^2 + 2W_1\sigma_{13} + 2W_2\sigma_{23} - \lambda_1 - \lambda_2 E(R_3) = 0, \quad (8.12)$$
$$\frac{\partial C}{\partial \lambda_1} = 1 - W_1 - W_2 - W_3 = 0,$$
$$\frac{\partial C}{\partial \lambda_2} = E^* - W_1 E(R_1) - W_2 E(R_2) - W_3 E(R_3) = 0.$$

This system of five equations and five unknowns can be solved by the use of matrix algebra. Briefly, the Jacobian matrix of these equations is

$$\begin{bmatrix} 2\sigma_{11} & 2\sigma_{12} & 2\sigma_{13} & -1 & -E(R_1) \\ 2\sigma_{21} & 2\sigma_{22} & 2\sigma_{23} & -1 & -E(R_2) \\ 2\sigma_{31} & 2\sigma_{32} & 2\sigma_{33} & -1 & -E(R_3) \\ 1 & 1 & 1 & 0 & 0 \\ E(R_1) & E(R_2) & E(R_3) & 0 & 0 \end{bmatrix} \times \begin{bmatrix} W_1 \\ W_2 \\ W_3 \\ \lambda_1 \\ \lambda_2 \end{bmatrix} = \begin{bmatrix} 0 \\ 0 \\ 0 \\ 1 \\ E^* \end{bmatrix}. \quad (8.13)$$

Therefore, it is possible to premultiply both sides of the matrix equation of (8.13), AW = K, by the inverse of A (denoted A^{-1}) and solve for the W column. This is possible because all values in the A and K matrices are known or arbitrarily set.

The first problem is the inversion of the matrix of coefficients. First, derive the determinant of matrix A. Next, after developing the signed, inverted matrix of cofactors for A, divide the cofactors by the determinant, resulting in the inversion of the original matrix. Finally, premultiply the column vector for the investment weights.

Sample Problem 8.4

This example focuses on the returns and risk of the first three industrial companies, Johnson & Johnson (JNJ), International Business Machines Corp. (IBM), and Boeing Co. (BA), for the period April 2001 to April 2010. The data used are tabulated in Table 8.3.

Table 8.3. Data for Three Securities.

Company	$E(r_i)$	σ_i^2	$\text{Cov}(R_i, R_j)$
JNJ	0.0080	0.0025	$\sigma_{12} = 0.0007$
IBM	0.0050	0.0071	$\sigma_{23} = 0.0006$
BA	0.0113	0.0083	$\sigma_{13} = 0.0007$

Plugging the data listed in Table 8.3 and $E^* = 0.00106$ into the matrix above yields:

$$\begin{bmatrix} 0.0910 & 0.0018 & 0.0008 & -1 & -0.0053 \\ 0.0036 & 0.1228 & 0.0020 & -1 & -0.0055 \\ 0.0008 & 0.0020 & 0.1050 & -1 & -0.0126 \\ 1 & 1 & 1 & 0 & 0 \\ 0.0053 & 0.0055 & 0.0126 & 0 & 0 \end{bmatrix} \times \begin{bmatrix} W_1 \\ W_2 \\ W_3 \\ \lambda_1 \\ \lambda_2 \end{bmatrix} = \begin{bmatrix} 0 \\ 0 \\ 0 \\ 1 \\ 0.00106 \end{bmatrix}. \tag{8.14}$$

When matrix A is properly inverted and postmultiplied by K, the solution vector A^{-1}K is derived:

$$\begin{matrix} W & & \text{A}^{-1}\text{K} \\ \begin{bmatrix} W_1 \\ W_2 \\ W_3 \\ \lambda_1 \\ \lambda_2 \end{bmatrix} & = & \begin{bmatrix} 0.9442 \\ 0.6546 \\ -0.5988 \\ 0.1937 \\ -20.1953 \end{bmatrix} \end{matrix}. \tag{8.15}$$

With the knowledge of the efficient-portfolio weights given that $E(R_p)$ is equal to 0.00106, 0.00212, and 0.00318, the variances of the efficient portfolios may be derived from plugging the numbers into Equation (8.2). Taking the square root of the variances to derive the standard deviation, the various risk–return combinations can be plotted and the efficient frontier graphed, as shown in Fig. 8.8 in the previous section. As can be seen from comparing this figure to the graphical derivation of the efficient frontier derived graphically, the results are almost the same.

8.3.4. *Portfolio Determination with Specific Adjustment for Short Selling*

By using a definition of short sales developed by Lintner (1965), the computation procedure for the efficient frontier can be modified. Lintner defines short selling as putting up an amount of money equal to the value of the security sold short. Thus the short sale is a use rather than a source of funds to the short seller. The total funds the investor invests short, plus the funds invested long, must add up to the original investment. The proportion of funds invested short is $|X_i|$, since $X_i < 0$. The constraint in the minimization problem concerning the weights of the individual securities needs to be modified to incorporate this fact. Additionally, the final portfolio weight (output of the matrix inversion) must be rescaled so the sum of the absolute value of the weights equals one. By defining short sales in this manner, the efficient frontier does not extend to infinity (as shown in Fig. 8.8(a)) but resembles the efficient frontier in Fig. 8.8(b).

Monthly rates of return for JNJ, IBM, and BA are used to perform the analysis in this section. The sample period is from January 2001 to September 2007. The Markowitz model determines optimal asset allocation by minimizing portfolio variance using a constrained optimization procedure:

$$\text{Min } \operatorname{Var}(R_p) = \sum_{i=1}^{3}\sum_{j=1}^{3} W_i W_j \sigma_{ij}. \tag{8.16}$$

Subject to

(i) $$\sum_{i=1}^{3} W_i E(R_i) = E^*,$$

(ii) $$\sum_{i=1}^{3} |W_i| = 1.0,$$

where the E^* is the investors' desired rate of return, and where the absolute value of the weights $|W_i|$ allows for a given W to be negative (sold short) but maintains the requirement that all funds are invested or their sum equals one.

The Lagrangian function is

$$\text{Min } L = \sum_{i=1}^{n}\sum_{j=1}^{n} W_i W_j + \lambda_1 \sum_{i=1}^{n} [W_i E(R_i) - E^*] + \lambda_2 \left(\sum_{i=1}^{n} W_i - 1 \right). \tag{8.17}$$

By using JNJ, IBM, and BA a three-security portfolio will be formed and optimal weights will be solved for.

Security	Monthly $E(R_i)$	σ_i^2	σ_{12}	σ_{13}	σ_{23}
JNJ	0.0080	0.0025	0.0007	0.0006	0.0007
IBM	0.0050	0.0071			
BA	0.0113	0.0083			

Substituting these values into the matrix:

$$\begin{bmatrix} 0.1008 & 0.0014 & 0.0012 & 0.0080 & 1 \\ 0.0014 & 0.1756 & 0.0014 & 0.0050 & 1 \\ 0.0012 & 0.0014 & 0.1820 & 0.0113 & 1 \\ 0.0080 & 0.0050 & 0.0113 & 0 & 0 \\ 1 & 1 & 1 & 0 & 0 \end{bmatrix} \times \begin{bmatrix} W_1 \\ W_2 \\ W_3 \\ \lambda_1 \\ \lambda_2 \end{bmatrix} = \begin{bmatrix} 0 \\ 0 \\ 0 \\ E* \\ 1 \end{bmatrix}, \tag{8.18}$$

$$E^* = 0.013.$$

By solving using the identity-matrix technique, the weights for the three securities can be obtained:

$$\text{Johnson \& Johnson} = -0.0406$$
$$\text{American Express} = -0.0146$$
$$\text{Exxon Mobile} = 1.0552.$$

By using the following relationship to rescale these weights so that the second constraint for the sum of the absolute values of the weights to equal one is satisfied:

$$W_{|A|} = \frac{|A|}{|A| + |B| + |C|}. \tag{8.19}$$

The resealed absolute weights are

$$W_{JNJ} = \frac{0.0406}{0.0406 + 0.0146 + 1.0552} = 0.0366,$$

$$W_{AXP} = \frac{0.0146}{0.0406 + 0.0146 + 1.0552} = 0.0131,$$

$$W_{XOM} = \frac{1.0552}{0.0406 + 0.0146 + 1.0552} = 0.9503.$$

The return on this portfolio is

$$\overline{R}_p = (0.0366)(0.0053) + (0.0131)(0.0055) + (0.9503)(0.0126)$$
$$= 1.22\%.$$

The variance:

$$\sigma_p^2 = (0.0366)^2(0.0455) + (0.0131)^2(0.0614) + (0.9503)^2(0.0525)$$
$$+ 2(0.0366)(0.0131)(0.0009) + 2(0.0366)(0.9503)(0.0004)$$
$$+ 2(0.0131)(0.9503)(0.0010)$$
$$= 0.0475.$$

8.3.5. *Portfolio Determination without Short Selling*

The minimization problem under study can be modified to include the restriction of no short selling by adding a third constraint:

$$W_i \geq 0, \quad i = 1, \ldots, N. \tag{8.20}$$

The addition of this non-negativity constraint precludes negative values for the weights (i.e., no short selling). The problem now is a quadratic programming problem similar to the ones solved so far, except that the optimal portfolio may fall in an unfeasible region. In this circumstance, the next best optimal portfolio is elected that meets all of the constraints. An example of this situation is shown in Fig. 8.9.[8]

In Fig. 8.9(a) the optimal portfolio is located in the region of positive values for weights W_i^*, and thereby satisfies the constraint $W_i^* \geq 0$. In Fig. 8.9(b), the optimal portfolio shown by W_i^* falls in a region where W_1 is negative, and so the constraint is not satisfied. The next best optimal portfolio is shown by B, and this is the solution of the problem that satisfies the non-negativity constraint. Additional discussion of the problems is presented in later chapters. Most recently, Lewis (1988) has developed a simple algorithm for the portfolio-selection problem. His method is based on an interactive use of the Markowitz critical-line method for solving quadratic programs. In Figs. 8.9(a) and 8.9(b) the vertical axis is defined as $(\bar{R}_p - R_f)\ \sigma_p$ which is a Sharpe performance mean, as defined in Chapter 7,

[8]In Figs. 8.9(a) and 8.9(b), the vertical axis is defined as $(\bar{R}_p - R_f)/\sigma_p$, which is the Sharpe performance measure.

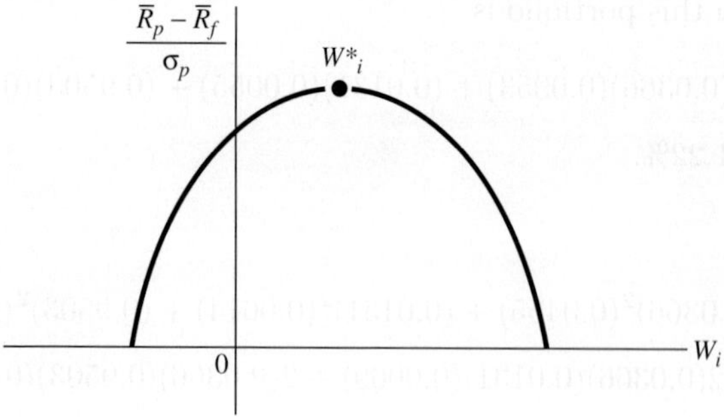

(a)

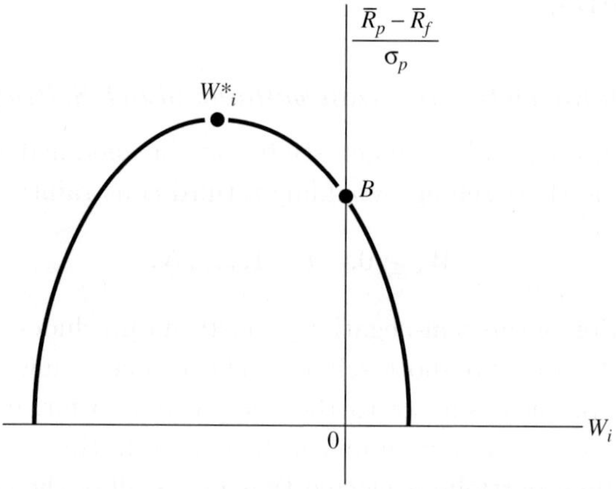

(b)

Fig. 8.9. Optimal Portfolio in Feasible and Unfeasible Regions, (a) Optimal Portfolio in Feasible Region ($W_i^* > 0$), (b) Optimal Portfolio in Unfeasible Region ($W_i^* < 0$).

and can be regarded as the objective function for a portfolio selection. Chapter 11 will discuss topics in detail.

8.4. Summary

This chapter has focused on the foundations of Markowitz's model and on derivation of efficient frontier through the creation of efficient portfolios of varying risk and return. It has been shown that an investor can increase expected utility through portfolio diversification as long as there is no perfect positive correlation among the component securities. The extent of the benefit increases as the correlation is lower, and also increases with the number of securities included.

The Markowitz model can be applied to develop the efficient frontier that delineates the optimal portfolios that match the greatest return with a given amount of risk. Also, this frontier shows the dominant portfolios as having the lowest risk given a stated return. This chapter has included methods of solving for the efficient frontier both graphically and through a combination of calculus and matrix algebra, with and without explicitly incorporating short selling.

Next chapters will illustrate how the crushing computational load involved in implementing the Markowitz model can be alleviated through the use of the index portfolio, and how the tenets of the Markowitz efficient frontier are still met.

Questions and Problems

1. Calculate the expected return of a portfolio 25% of which consists of stock A, with an expected return of 8%, and 75% of which is stock B, with an expected return of 12%.
2. Carefully explain why the variance of a portfolio is not represented by a weighted average of the variances of the individual securities which make up the portfolio.
3. Determine the risk preferences of investors with the following utility functions when $w = 0$.

   (a) $U(w) = Ae^{Bw} A, B > 0$
   (b) $U(w) = 5w + 2w^{-3}$
   (c) $U(w) = W^{-2/3}$
   (d) $U(w) = 3w - e^{-2w}$

4. What is a fair game? Will risk-averse investors, risk-neutral investors, and risk-preferring investors, enter into a fair game?
5. You are given the following information about two stocks

State of Economy	Return A (%)	Return B (%)	Probability P_i
Recession	10	9	30
Normal Growth	11	7	20
Inflation	12	4	50

(a) Calculate the risk and return for stock A and stock B.
(b) Calculate the risk and return of a portfolio consisting 60% of stock A and 40% of stock B.

6. Define what is meant by an efficient portfolio and an inefficient portfolio. How can the dominance principle be used to define the concept of the efficient portfolio?
7. What is short selling? What is the efficient frontier? How does the efficient frontier change when short selling is not allowed?
8. Carefully explain how margin requirements on short sales affect the efficient frontier.
9. Draw the relationship between risk and return for a portfolio consisting of two stocks, A and B, when:

   (a) correlation between A and B is 0;
   (b) correlation between A and B is +1; and
   (c) correlation between A and B is −1.

10. You are given the following information about stocks A and B.

$$E(R_A) = 16\%$$
$$E(R_B) = 10\%$$
$$\sigma_A = 3\%$$
$$\sigma_B = 2\%$$
$$\rho_{AB} = 0.8$$

You have $20,000 to invest.

   (a) Find the expected rate of return and variance on a portfolio consisting of the optimal weights for A and B.
   (b) Suppose you would like to invest an additional $5,000 in the portfolio consisting of A and B. If there is a risk-free asset that has a rate of return of 5%, explain how you would do this. What is the rate of return and variance on this investment?

11. You are the investment advisor for John Doe, a young hot-shot lawyer, and also for Jane Roe, an elderly widow. John can be considered a very aggressive investor, while Jane is a very conservative investor. Carefully explain how the portfolios you select for them would differ.
12. Discuss the procedure of using Markowitz's optimal portfolio-selection model to determine the optimal weights for a portfolio.

13. Based on the dataset in Appendix 8.A, please use the Markowitz model to calculate the optimal weights of JNJ, IBM, and BA when the required rate of return of the portfolio is 10%.
14. Based on the dataset in Appendix 8.A, please use the Markowitz model to calculate the optimal weights of JNJ, IBM, BA, and CAT when the required rate of return of the portfolio is 12%.
15. Based upon the data of JNJ, IBM, and BA from Appendix 8.A, please use Markowitz optimal portfolio-selection model to determine the optimal weights of three securities for a portfolio with a 0.5% monthly required rate of return when the short-selling is allowed.
16. Based upon the data of JNJ, IBM, BA, and CAT from Appendix 8.A, please use Markowitz optimal portfolio-selection model to determine the optimal weights of four securities for a portfolio with a 1% monthly required rate of return when the short-selling is allowed.

Appendix 8A: Graphical Analysis in Markowitz Portfolio-Selection Model: Three-Security Empirical Solution

The process of finding the efficient frontier graphically described in this appendix is originally developed by Markowitz (1952). Francis and Archer (1979) have discussed this subject in detail. To facilitate a realistic example, actual data have been taken from a set of monthly returns generated by the Dow-Jones 30 Industrials. This example focuses on the returns and risk of the first three industrial companies — JNJ, IBM, and BA — for the period April 2000–April 2010. The data used are tabulated in Table 8A.1. Using historical data, we can obtain the expected monthly returns, variances, and covariances of JNJ, IBM, and BA as indicated in Table 8.3. Both graphical and mathematical analyses are employed to obtain an empirical solution.

Graphical Analysis. To begin to develop the efficient frontier graphically, it is necessary to move from the three dimensions necessitated by the three-security portfolio to a two-dimensional problem by transforming the third security into an implicit solution from the other two. To do this it must be noted that since the summation of the weights of the three securities is equal to unity, then implicitly:

$$W_3 = 1 - W_1 - W_2 \tag{8A.1}$$

Table 8A.1. Adjusted Prices for JNJ, IBM, and BA (April 2000–April 2010).

Date	JNJ	IBM	BA	CAT	Date	JNJ	IBM	BA	CAT
2000/3	27.19	103.26	30.12	14.72	2003/3	46.67	69.64	20.9	20.21
2000/4	31.93	97.26	31.62	14.84	2003/4	45.46	75.39	22.75	21.75
2000/5	34.76	93.72	31.23	14.39	2003/5	44.03	78.32	25.72	21.56
2000/6	39.56	95.69	33.43	12.75	2003/6	41.88	73.39	28.79	23.02
2000/7	36.14	98.04	39.02	12.94	2003/7	41.95	72.28	27.78	28.07
2000/8	35.83	115.43	43.01	13.97	2003/8	40.35	73.1	31.52	29.88
2000/9	36.61	98.47	51.72	11.78	2003/9	40.3	78.73	28.94	28.64
2000/10	35.9	86.12	54.37	13.47	2003/10	40.96	79.76	32.45	30.63
2000/11	39.1	81.86	55.49	15.1	2003/11	40.32	80.85	32.51	31.79
2000/12	41.08	74.41	53.03	18.18	2003/12	42.25	82.76	35.69	34.7
2001/1	36.41	98.05	47.01	17.12	2004/1	43.69	88.61	35.36	32.8
2001/2	38.18	87.56	50.13	16.1	2004/2	44.28	86.31	36.87	31.8
2001/3	34.32	84.3	44.9	17.18	2004/3	41.66	82.14	34.92	33.19
2001/4	37.85	100.92	49.81	19.57	2004/4	44.38	78.86	36.29	32.78
2001/5	38.17	98.11	50.82	21.11	2004/5	46	79.4	39.12	31.78
2001/6	39.34	99.6	44.93	19.51	2004/6	45.99	79	43.64	33.5
2001/7	42.6	92.32	47.3	21.62	2004/7	45.63	78.04	43.35	31.15
2001/8	41.64	87.82	41.5	19.62	2004/8	48.21	76.06	44.78	30.82
2001/9	43.77	80.59	27.15	17.58	2004/9	46.75	77.01	44.27	34.1
2001/10	45.75	94.96	26.42	17.68	2004/10	48.45	80.61	42.8	34.32
2001/11	46.16	101.69	28.6	18.75	2004/11	50.29	84.8	46.12	39.01
2001/12	46.83	106.42	31.59	20.66	2004/12	52.88	88.71	44.57	41.55
2002/1	45.57	94.92	33.36	20.02	2005/1	53.95	84.07	43.56	38.13
2002/2	48.41	86.44	37.6	22.11	2005/2	54.93	83.47	47.55	40.68
2002/3	51.63	91.62	39.47	22.64	2005/3	56.24	82.39	50.57	39.13
2002/4	50.76	73.79	36.49	21.89	2005/4	57.47	68.86	51.48	37.86
2002/5	48.93	71.01	35.02	20.95	2005/5	56.46	68.3	55.5	40.46
2002/6	41.68	63.55	36.95	19.62	2005/6	54.7	67.08	57.32	40.98
2002/7	41.95	62.14	34.09	18.06	2005/7	53.82	75.45	57.33	46.58
2002/8	43.48	66.68	30.58	17.63	2005/8	53.62	73.06	58.43	47.94
2002/9	43.29	51.58	28.15	15.04	2005/9	53.52	72.69	59.24	50.76
2002/10	47.03	69.83	24.54	16.66	2005/10	52.97	74.2	56.35	45.64
2002/11	45.8	77.03	28.24	20.35	2005/11	52.5	80.75	59.67	50.15
2002/12	43.14	68.68	27.36	18.64	2005/12	51.1	74.67	61.47	50.14
2003/1	43.06	69.3	26.2	18.07	2006/1	48.92	73.85	59.78	59.16
2003/2	42.3	69.22	22.98	19.31	2006/2	49.3	73.07	63.88	63.68
2006/3	50.64	75.1	68.48	62.57	2008/4	60.28	113.1	76.87	74.28
2006/4	50.12	74.98	73.33	66.21	2008/5	60.38	121.78	75.32	74.97
2006/5	51.81	73.02	73.41	63.77	2008/6	58.21	111.52	59.81	66.97
2006/6	51.55	70.21	72.23	65.1	2008/7	61.95	120.41	55.61	63.44
2006/7	53.82	70.75	68.27	62.22	2008/8	64.14	114.98	60.03	64.55
2006/8	55.96	74.29	66.3	58.25	2008/9	63.09	110.47	52.51	54.39
2006/9	56.2	75.18	69.8	57.77	2008/10	55.86	87.81	48	35.21
2006/10	58.33	84.72	70.69	53.53	2008/11	53.79	77.51	39.33	37.78

(Continued)

Table 8A.1. (*Continued*)

Date	JNJ	IBM	BA	CAT	Date	JNJ	IBM	BA	CAT
2006/11	57.36	84.62	78.64	54.69	2008/12	54.94	79.94	39.36	41.18
2006/12	57.46	89.43	78.92	54.08	2009/1	52.97	87.05	39.03	28.74
2007/1	58.13	91.27	79.56	56.78	2009/2	46.29	87.89	29.3	22.93
2007/2	55.09	85.81	77.82	57.1	2009/3	48.7	92.53	33.15	26.05
2007/3	52.75	87.03	79.29	59.4	2009/4	48.48	98.56	37.32	33.58
2007/4	56.21	94.37	82.93	64.63	2009/5	51.52	102.03	42.2	33.46
2007/5	55.75	98.81	90.04	69.94	2009/6	53.05	100.24	39.99	31.18
2007/6	54.29	97.56	86.07	69.69	2009/7	56.87	113.21	40.38	42.1
2007/7	53.3	102.56	92.58	70.43	2009/8	56.91	113.85	47.19	43.3
2007/8	54.81	108.54	86.85	67.72	2009/9	57.33	115.36	51.44	49.05
2007/9	58.28	109.58	94.3	70.1	2009/10	55.6	116.32	45.41	53
2007/10	57.81	108.01	88.55	67	2009/11	59.64	122.41	50.23	56.2
2007/11	60.46	98.18	83.41	64.56	2009/12	61.13	126.81	51.88	54.85
2007/12	59.53	100.91	78.83	65.16	2010/1	59.66	118.57	58.08	50.62
2008/1	56.35	99.99	74.98	64.1	2010/2	60.25	123.74	60.94	55.29
2008/2	55.67	106.69	74.99	65.31	2010/3	62.35	124.8	70.06	60.91
2008/3	58.28	107.89	67.36	70.7	2010/4	62.9	124.8	70.43	62.01

Additionally, the above relation may be substituted into Equation (8A.1):

$$\begin{aligned} E(R_p) &= W_1E(R_1) + W_2E(R_2) + W_3E(R_3) \\ &= W_1E(R_1) + W_2E(R_2) + (1 - W_1 - W_2)E(R_3) \\ &= W_1E(R_1) + W_2E(R_2) + E(R_3) - W_1E(R_3) - W_2E(R_3) \\ &= [E(R_1) - E(R_3)]W_1 + [E(R_2) - E(R_3)]W_2 + E(R_3). \end{aligned} \tag{8A.2}$$

Finally, inserting the values for the first and second securities yields:

$$\begin{aligned} E(R_p) &= (0.0080 - 0.0113)W_1 + (0.0050 - 0.0113)W_2 + 0.0113 \\ &= -0.0033W_1 - 0.0063W_2 + 0.0113. \end{aligned} \tag{8A.3}$$

As can be seen, Equation (8A.3) is a linear function in two variables and as such is readily graphable. Since given a certain level of portfolio return the function will solve jointly for the weights of securities 1 and 2, it solves indirectly for the weight of security 3.

The variance formula shown in Equation (8.2) is converted in a similar manner by substituting in Equation (8A.1) as follows:

$$\begin{aligned}
\sigma_p^2 &= \sum_{i=1}^{3}\sum_{j=1}^{3} W_i W_j \mathrm{Cov}(R_i, R_j) = \mathrm{Var}(R_p) \\
&= W_1^2\sigma_{11} + W_2^2\sigma_{22} + W_3^2\sigma_{33} + 2W_1W_2\sigma_{12} + 2W_1W_3\sigma_{13} + 2W_2W_3\sigma_{23} \\
&= W_1^2\sigma_{11} + W_2^2\sigma_{22} + (1 - W_1 - W_2)^2\sigma_{33} + 2W_1W_2\sigma_{12} \\
&\quad + 2W_1(1 - W_1 - W_2)\sigma_{13} + 2W_2(1 - W_1 - W_2)\sigma_{23} \\
&= (\sigma_{11} + \sigma_{33} - 2\sigma_{13})W_1^2 + (2\sigma_{33} + 2\sigma_{12} - 2\sigma_{13} - 2\sigma_{23})W_1W_2 \\
&\quad + (\sigma_{22} + \sigma_{33} - 2\sigma_{23})W_2^2 + (-2\sigma_{33} + 2\sigma_{13})W_1 \\
&\quad + (-2\sigma_{33} + 2\sigma_{13})W_2 + \sigma_{33}. \qquad (8A.4)
\end{aligned}$$

Inserting the covariances and variances of the three securities from Table 8.3:

$$\begin{aligned}
\sigma_p^2 &= [0.0025 + 0.0083 - 2(0.0007)]W_1^2 + [2(0.0083) + 2(0.0007) \\
&\quad - 2(0.0007) - 2(0.0006)]W_1W_2 + [0.0071 + 0.0083 \\
&\quad - 2(0.0006)]W_2^2 + [-2(0.0083) + 2(0.0007)]W_1 \\
&\quad + [-2(0.0083) + 2(0.0007)]W_2 + 0.0083 \\
&= 0.0094W_1^2 + 0.0154W_1W_2 + 0.0142W_2^2 - 0.0152W_1 \\
&\quad - 0.0152W_2 + 0.0083. \qquad (8A.5)
\end{aligned}$$

Minimum-Risk Portfolio. Part of the graphical solution is the determination of the minimum-risk portfolio. Standard partial derivatives are taken of Equation (8A.4) with respect to the directly solved weight factors as follows:

$$\begin{aligned}
\frac{\partial\sigma_p^2}{\partial W_1} &= 2(\sigma_{11} + \sigma_{33} - 2\sigma_{13})W_1 \\
&\quad + (2\sigma_{33} + 2\sigma_{12} - 2\sigma_{13} - 2\sigma_{23})W_2 + (-2\sigma_{33} + 2\sigma_{13}) = 0 \\
\frac{\partial\sigma_p^2}{\partial W_2} &= (2\sigma_{33} + 2\sigma_{12} - 2\sigma_{13} - 2\sigma_{23})W_1 \\
&\quad + 2(\sigma_{22} + \sigma_{33} - 2\sigma_{23})W_2 + (2\sigma_{23} - 2\sigma_{33}) = 0.
\end{aligned} \qquad (8A.6)$$

When these two partial derivatives are set equal to zero and the unknown weight factors are solved for, the minimum risk portfolio is derived. Using the numeric values from Table 8.3:

$$\begin{aligned}\frac{\partial\sigma_p^2}{\partial W_1} &= 2[0.0025 + 0.0083 - 2(0.0007)]W_1 + [2(0.0083) + 2(0.0007) \\ &\quad - 2(0.0007) - 2(0.0006)]W_2 + [-2(0.0083) + 2(0.0007)] \\ &= 0.0188W_1 + 0.0154W_2 - 0.0152 = 0. \\ \frac{\partial\sigma_p^2}{\partial W_2} &= [2(0.0083) + 2(0.0007) - 2(0.0007) - 2(0.0006)]W_1 \\ &\quad + 2[0.0071 + 0.0083 - 2(0.0006)]W_2 + [-2(0.0083) + 2(0.0007)] \\ &= 0.0154W_1 + 0.0284W_2 - 0.0152 = 0.\end{aligned} \tag{8A.7}$$

By solving these two equations simultaneously the weights of the minimum-risk portfolio are derived. This variance represents the lowest possible portfolio-variance level achievable, given variance and covariance data for these stocks. This can be represented by the point V of Fig. 8.6. This solution is an algebraic exercise that yields $W_1 = 0.6659$ and $W_2 = 0.1741$ and therefore, through Equation (8A.1), $W_3 = 0.16$.

The Iso-Expected Return Line. The variance and return equations have been derived and it is now time to complete the graphing procedure. To begin the graphing, the iso-expected return function lines must be delineated given various levels of expected return. The **iso-expected return line** is a line that has the same expected return on every point of the line. Utilizing Equation (8A.3), three arbitrary returns are specified: 0.0082, 0.01008, 0.01134. These three monthly returns are then set equal to Equation (8A.3), and graphing is now possible by setting W_1 equal to zero or other values to solve for W_2. For example, if $W_2 = 0$ and $E(R_p) = 0.0080$, then W_1 can be solved as follows (see Table 8A.2 for final results).

$$\begin{aligned}0.008 &= -0.0033W_1 - 0.0063(0) + 0.0113, \\ 0.0033W_1 &= 0.0113 - 0.008 = 0.0033, \\ W_1 &= 1.0000.\end{aligned}$$

In a similar fashion, other points are calculated and are listed in Table 8A.2. A line may be drawn between the points to develop the various iso-expected return function lines. There are a multitude of possible return functions, but only these three lines (IR_1, IR_2, and IR_3) in terms of the data listed in Table 8A.2 are shown in Fig. 8A.1. In Fig. 8A.1, vertical axis and horizontal axis represent W_1 and W_2, respectively.

Table 8A.2. Iso-Return Lines.

	Target Return		
W_2	0.008 W_1	0.010 W_1	0.012 W_1
−1.0	2.9091	2.3030	1.6970
−0.5	1.9545	1.3485	0.7424
0.0	1.0000	0.3939	−0.2121
0.5	0.0455	−0.5606	−1.1667
1.0	−0.9091	−1.5152	−2.1212

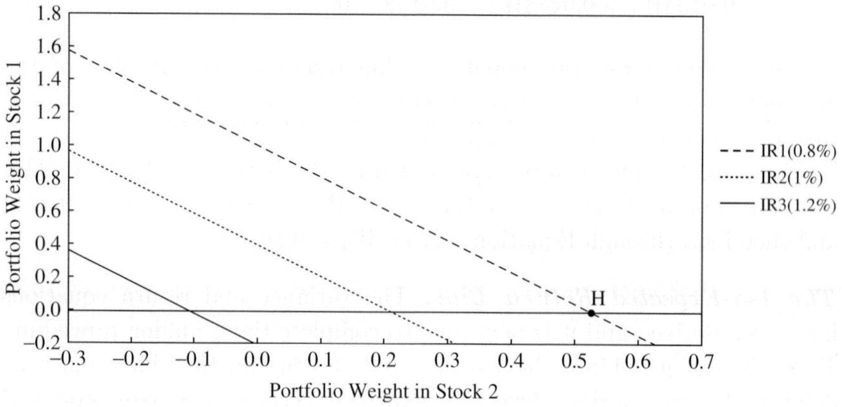

Fig. 8A.1. Iso-Return Lines.

Each point on the iso-expected return line of Fig. 8A.1 represents a different combination of weights placed in the three securities. The issue now is to determine the portfolio that lies on the iso-expected return line with the lowest variance. Table 8A.3 shows the portfolio variances as we move along the iso-expected return line. For example, moving along the iso-expected return line associated with an expected return of 0.80%, note that the minimum variance portfolio is associated with weights of 0.1803 in security 2 and 0.6558 in security 1.

Iso-Variance Ellipses. As is seen from Table 8A.3, the minimum-variance portfolio can be found by moving along the iso-expected return line until the minimum-variance portfolio is reached. To better visualize this, examine the variance of a portfolio as the proportions in security 1 and security 2 are changed. A plot of these points will allow the family of iso-variance ellipses to be traced. The **iso-variance ellipses** are the ellipses that have the same variance on every point of this ellipse curve. It should

Table 8A.3. Portfolio Variance along the Iso-Return Line.

	0.0082		0.0100		0.0120	
W_2	W_1	Var	W_1	Var	W_1	Var
−1.0000	2.9091	0.0284	2.3030	0.0173	1.6970	0.0130
−0.7500	2.4318	0.0184	1.8258	0.0103	1.2197	0.0092
−0.5000	1.9545	0.0107	1.3485	0.0058	0.7424	0.0077
−0.4713	1.8998	0.0100	1.2937	0.0054	0.6876	0.0077*
−0.2500	1.4773	0.0054	0.8712	0.0036	0.2652	0.0086
−0.1455	1.2778	0.0039	0.6717	0.0034*	0.0657	0.0097
0.0000	1.0000	0.0025	0.3939	0.0038	−0.2121	0.0119
0.1803	0.6558	0.0019*	0.0497	0.0054	−0.5563	0.0158
0.2500	0.5227	0.0020	−0.0833	0.0063	−0.6894	0.0176
0.5000	0.0455	0.0038	−0.5606	0.0113	−1.1667	0.0257
0.7500	−0.4318	0.0081	−1.0379	0.0187	−1.6439	0.0361
1.0000	−0.9091	0.0147	−1.5152	0.0284	−2.1212	0.0490

*Minimum variance portfolios.

be noted that an ellipse is an egg-shaped circle of points with a common center and orientation. The minimum-risk portfolio variance is the center of all possible ellipses as it has the least risk. It will be desirable, then, to find this minimum risk value, as no other weighting scheme of these three securities will develop a lesser risk. The solutions of Equation (8A.7) have determined that the weights associated with the minimum-risk portfolio are $W_1 = 0.3857, W_2 = 0.2810$, and $W_3 = 0.3333$. Substituting this information listed in Table 8A.1 into Equation (8.2), the variance of the minimum-risk portfolio is: W_1

$$\begin{aligned}\text{Var}(R_p) &= \sum_{i=1}^{n}\sum_{j=1}^{n} W_i W_j \text{Cov}(R_i R_j)\\ &= W_1^2\sigma_{11} + W_2^2\sigma_{22} + W_3^2\sigma_{33} + 2W_1W_2\sigma_{12} + 2W_2W_3\sigma_{23}\\ &\quad + 2W_1W_3\sigma_{13} = (0.6558)^2(0.0025) + (0.1803)^2(0.0071)\\ &\quad + (0.1639)^2(0.0083) + 2(0.6558)(0.1803)(0.0007)\\ &\quad + 2(0.1803)(0.1639)(0.0006) + 2(0.6558)(0.1639)(0.0007)\\ &= 0.0019.\end{aligned}$$

Note that the variance of the minimum-risk portfolio can be used as a base for graphing the iso-variance ellipses. It can be completed by taking Equation (8A.3) and holding one of the weights, say W_2 portfolio variance $\text{Var}(R_p)$, constant. Bring the $\text{Var}(R_p)$ to the right-hand side of the equation, and notice that the equation is of a quadratic form and can be solved using the quadratic formula:

$$W_1 = \frac{-b \pm \sqrt{b^2 - 4ac}}{2a}, \quad (8A.8)$$

where

$a =$ all coefficients of W_1^2;
$b =$ all coefficients of W_1; and
$c =$ all coefficients that are not multiplied by W_1, or W_1^2: or
$a = \sigma_{11} + \sigma_{33} - 2\sigma_{13}$;
$b = (2\sigma_{33} + 2\sigma_{12} - 2\sigma_{13} - 2\sigma_{23})W_2 - 2\sigma_{33} + 2\sigma_{13}$; and
$c = (\sigma_{22} + \sigma_{33} - 2\sigma_{23})W_2^2 + (-2\sigma_{33} + 2\sigma_{23})W_2 + \sigma_{33} - \text{Var}(R_p)$.

Substituting the numbers from the data of Table 8A.1 into Equation (8A.4) yields:

$$\begin{aligned}\text{Var}(R_p) &= 0.0094W_1^2 + 0.0154W_1W_2 + 0.0142W_2^2 - 0.0152W_1 \\ &\quad - 0.0152W_2 + 0.0083 \\ 0 &= 0.0094W_1^2 + 0.0154W_1W_2 + 0.0142W_2^2 - 0.0152W_1 \\ &\quad - 0.0152W_2 + 0.0083 - \text{Var}(R_p),\end{aligned}$$

where:

$$a = 0.0094;$$

$$b = 0.0154W_2 - 0.0152; \quad \text{and}$$

$$c = 0.0142W_2^2 - 0.0152W_2 + 0.0083 - \text{Var}(R_p).$$

When these expressions are plugged into the quadratic formula:

$$W_1 = \frac{-(0.0154W_2 - 0.0152) \pm \sqrt{b^2 - 4ac}}{2(0.0094)}, \quad (8A.9)$$

where

$$\begin{aligned}b^2 &= (0.0154W_2 - 0.0152)^2; \\ 4ac &= 4\{(0.0094)[0.0142W_2^2 - 0.0152W_2 + 0.0083 - \text{Var}(R_p)]\}.\end{aligned}$$

This is a solution for the two points of W_1(W_{11} and W_{12}) for a given portfolio variance and weight of the second security (W_2). When selecting the level of $\text{Var}(R_p)$ *it is best to choose a value that is slightly larger than the minimum-risk value. This assures the calculation of a possible portfolio, since no portfolio of these three securities may have less risk. Additionally, an initial selection of a value for* W_2 close to the minimum-risk portfolio W_2 will be desirable.

In sum, Equation (8A.9) can be used to construct the iso-variance ellipse for given $\text{Var}(R_p)$ in terms of arbitrary W_2. By jointly considering iso-expected return lines and iso-variance ellipses, efficient portfolios can be identified that are defined as the portfolios with the minimum variance given the expected rate of return. This task can be done by computer, as mentioned in the last section. To obtain the weights of an efficient portfolio, the following set of instructions must be entered into the computer.

Find the portfolio weights that minimize portfolio variance, subject to the target expected rate-of-return constraint. For this case, target rates of return are 0.82%, 1.008%, or 1.1134%. The sum of the portfolio weights for all stocks in the portfolio must be equal to one. Mathematically, this instruction is defined in Equation (8A.2).

The expected return and variance for a three-security portfolio is defined in Equations (8A.3) and (8A.5), respectively.

The estimated expected return, variance, and covariance as defined in Table 8.3 should be entered into the computer for estimation.

Using $E(R_p) = 0.80\%$ as an example, $\text{W}_1 = 0$ and $W_2 = 0.5238$. From the relationship, $W_3 = 1 - W_1 - W_2 = 1 - 0 - 0.5238 = 0.4762$. In other words, the point H represents three portfolio weights for the three stocks. The computer substitutes weights, variances, and covariances (listed in Table 8A.1) into Equation (8A.5) to obtain portfolio variance. The portfolio variance consistent with the weights of point H is computed. The computer now moves by some predetermined distance either northeast or southwest along the 0.80% iso-expected return line. From this kind of search, the minimum variance associated with this 0.82% iso-expected return line is identified to be 0.0019, as indicated in Table 8A.3. By a similar procedure, the minimum variances associated with 1% and 1.20% iso-expected return lines are identified to be 0.0034 and 0.0077, respectively. When minimum variances associated with predefined iso-expected return are identified, the optimal weights associated with expected returns equal to 1% and 1.20% in terms of data indicated in Table 8A.1 are also calculated. These results are indicated in Table 8A.3.

Using the minimum variances associated with iso-expected returns (0.80%, 1%, and 1.20%), three iso-variance ellipses can be drawn as IV_1, IV_2, and IV_3.

When $\text{Var}(R_p) = 0.0182$ and $W_2 = 0.3$, the quadratic formula from Equation (8A.9) above yields two roots.

$$W_{11} = \frac{-(0.0730) + \sqrt{(0.0730)^2 - (-0.0052)}}{2(0.0972)}$$
$$= 0.4247.$$
$$W_{12} = \frac{-(0.0730) - \sqrt{(0.0730)^2 - (-0.0052)}}{2(0.0972)}$$
$$= 0.3263.$$

To solve for W_{11} and W_{12}, we need $b^2 > 4ac$. Solving for the variance:

$$(0.104W_2 - 0.1042)^2$$
$$-4\{(0.0972) > [0.1119W_2^2 - 0.103W_2 + 0.0525 - \text{Var}(R_p)]\}.$$

If W_2 and $\text{Var}(R_p)$ are not selected so that $b^2 > 4ac$, Equation (8A.9) will require taking the square root of a negative number, and mathematically the solution will be an imaginary number. Solving W_2 in terms of an imaginary number is not meaningful; therefore, we only consider the case when $b^2 > 4ac$.

The variance chosen was the minimum variance of the portfolio associated with $E(R_p) = 0.0082$. Actually, any variance might have realistically been chosen as long as it exceeded the minimum-risk portfolio variance. Table 8A.4 lists various W_{11} and W_{12} values for given levels of W_2 and

Table 8A.4. Various W_1 given W_2 and $\text{Var}(R_p)$.

W_2	Var (R_p)	b	b^2	C	4ac	W_{11}	W_{12}
0.14	0.0019	−0.013044	0.000170	0.004522	0.000170	0.711205	0.676454
0.16	0.0019	−0.012736	0.000162	0.004300	0.000162	0.716669	0.638223
0.18	0.0019	−0.012428	0.000154	0.004088	0.000154	0.706925	0.615203
0.20	0.0019	−0.012120	0.000147	0.003888	0.000146	0.689362	0.600000
0.22	0.0019	−0.011812	0.000140	0.003699	0.000139	0.663195	0.593401
−0.20	0.0034	−0.018280	0.000334	0.008548	0.000321	1.162299	0.782382
0.00	0.0034	−0.015200	0.000231	0.004900	0.000184	1.172396	0.444625
0.20	0.0034	−0.012120	0.000147	0.002388	0.000090	1.046640	0.242722
0.40	0.0034	−0.009040	0.000082	0.001012	0.000038	0.832359	0.129343
0.60	0.0034	−0.005960	0.000036	0.000772	0.000029	0.452575	0.181467
−0.60	0.0077	−0.024440	0.000597	0.014952	0.000562	1.615217	0.984783
−0.20	0.0077	−0.018280	0.000334	0.004248	0.000160	1.674858	0.269823
0.20	0.0077	−0.012120	0.000147	−0.001912	−0.000072	1.431458	−0.142096
0.60	0.0077	−0.005960	0.000036	−0.003528	−0.000133	1.006820	−0.372777
1.00	0.0077	0.000200	0.000000	−0.000600	−0.000023	0.242231	−0.263508

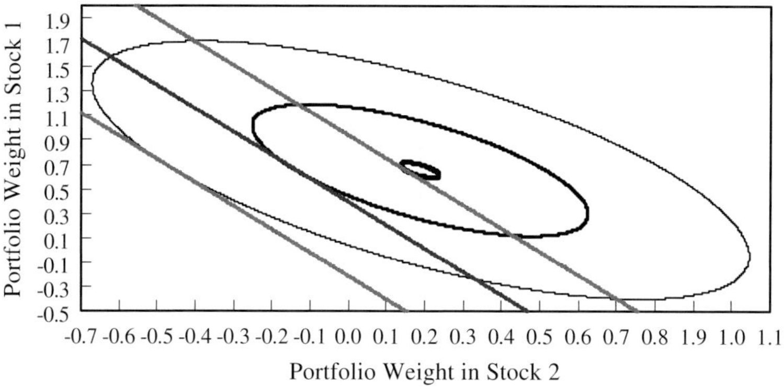

Fig. 8A.2. Iso-Variance Ellipses.

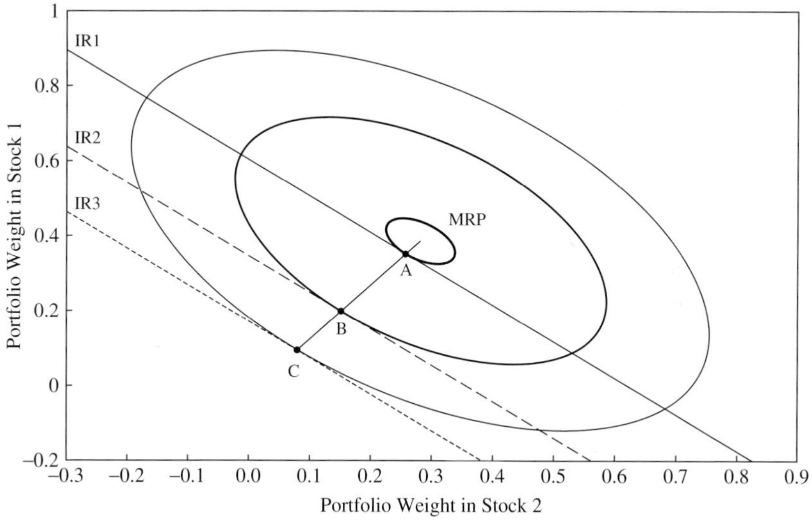

Fig. 8A.3. Iso-Variance Ellipses and Iso-Return Lines.

$\text{Var}(R_p)$. In addition, Table 8A.4 presents the value of b^2 and $4ac$ to check whether or not the root is a real number. It should be noticed that all possible variances are higher than the minimum-risk portfolio variance. Data from Table 8A.4 are used to draw three iso-variance ellipses, as indicated in Figs. 8A.2 and 8A.3.

The Critical Line and Efficient Frontier. After the iso-expected return functions and iso-variance ellipses have been plotted, it is an easy

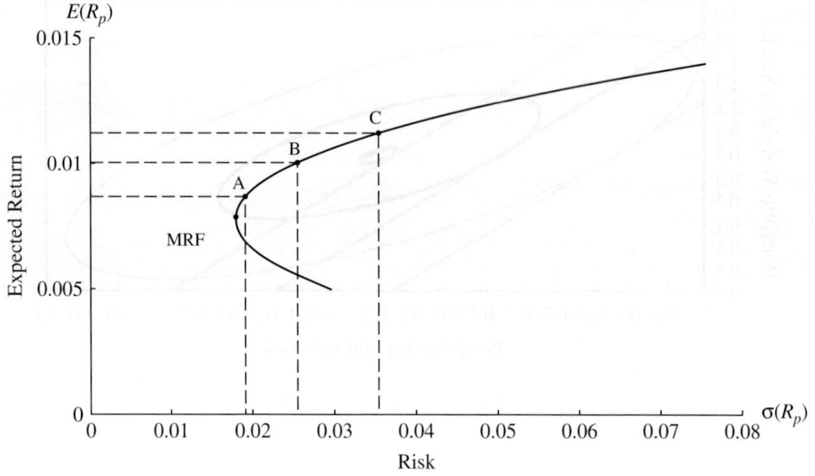

Fig. 8A.4. The Efficient Frontier for the Data of Table 8A.5.

task to delineate the efficient frontier. By definition, the efficient portfolio is the portfolio with the highest return for any given risk. In Fig. 8A.3, the efficient portfolios are those where a given iso-expected return line is just tangent to the variance ellipse. *MRPABC* is denoted as the **critical line**; all portfolios that lie between points *MRP* and *C* are said to be efficient, and the weights of these portfolios may be read directly from the graph. From the graph, portfolio weights for the portfolios that minimize variances, given a 0.80%, 1%, or 1.20% expected rate of return are listed in Table 8A.3. It is possible, given these various weights, to calculate the $E(R_p)$ and the variances of these portfolios, as indicated in Table 8A.5. The efficient frontier is then developed by plotting each risk–return combination, as shown in Fig. 8A.4.

In this section a step-wise graphical approach has been employed to obtain optimal weights for a three-security portfolio. In the next section a

Table 8A.5. Weights, $\bar{R}_p$, and σ_p for Efficient Points.

Portfolio*	W_1	W_2	W_3	$E(R_p)$	$Var(R_p)$	$\sigma(R_p)$
A	0.3521	0.2577	0.3902	0.0082	0.0182	0.1349
B	0.1983	0.1510	0.0795	0.01008	0.0258	0.1606
C	0.3902	0.6507	0.8252	0.01134	0.0368	0.1918

*Portfolios A, B, and C represent expected returns of 0.82%, 1.008%, and 1.134%, respectively.

mathematical optimization approach is used to calculate the optimal weight for a three-security portfolio.

Bibliography

Alexander, G. J. and J. C. Francis. *Portfolio Analysis.* New York: Prentice-Hall, Inc., 1986.

Baumol, W. J. "An Expected Gain-Confidence Limit Criterion for Portfolio Selection." *Management Science*, v. 10 (October 1963), 171–182.

Bertsekas, D. "Necessary and Sufficient Conditions for Existence of an Optimal Portfolio." *Journal of Economic Theory*, v. 8 (June 1974), 235–247.

Black, F. "Capital Market Equilibrium with Restricted Borrowing." *Journal of Business*, v. 45 (July 1972), 444–455.

Blume, M. "Portfolio Theory: A Step toward Its Practical Application." *Journal of Business*, v. 43 (April 1970), 152–173.

Bodie, Z., A. Kane and A. Marcus. *Investments*, 9th ed. New York: McGraw-Hill Book Company, 2010.

Brealey, R. A. and S. D. Hodges. "Playing with Portfolios." *Journal of Finance*, v. 30 (March 1975), 125–134.

Breen, W. and R. Jackson. "An Efficient Algorithm for Solving Large-Scale Portfolio Problems." *Journal of Financial and Quantitative Analysis*, v. 6 (January 1971), 627–637.

Brennan, M. J. "The Optimal Number of Securities in a Risky Asset Portfolio Where There are Fixed Costs of Transaction: Theory and Some Empirical Results." *Journal of Financial and Quantitative Analysis*, v. 10 (September 1975), 483–496.

Cohen, K. and J. Pogue. "An Empirical Evaluation of Alter native Portfolio-Selection Models." *Journal off Business*, v. 46 (April 1967), 166–193.

Dyl, E. A. "Negative Betas: The Attractions of Selling Short." *Journal of Portfolio Management*, v. I (Spring 1975), 74–76.

Elton, E. J. and Martin Gruber. "Portfolio Theory When Investment Relatives are Log Normally Distributed." *Journal of Finance*, v. 29 (September 1974), 1265–1273.

Elton, E. J. and M. E. Padberg. "Simple Criteria for Optimal Portfolio Selection." *Journal of Finance*, v. 11 (December 1976), 1341–1357.

Elton, E. J. and M. E. Padberg. "Simple Criteria for Optimal Portfolio Selection: Tracing Out the Efficient Frontier." *Journal of Finance*, v. 13 (March 1978), 296–302.

Elton, E. J., M. J. Gruber, S. J. Brown and W. N. Goetzmann. *Modern Portfolio Theory and Investment Analysis*, 7th ed. New York: John Wiley & Sons, 2006.

Evans, J. and S. Archer. "Diversification and the Reduction of Dispersion: An Empirical Analysis." *Journal of Finance*, v. 3 (December 1968), 761–767.

Fama, E. F. "Efficient Capital Markets: A Review of Theory and Empirical Work." *Journal of Finance*, v. 25 (May 1970), 383–417.

Feller, W. *An Introduction to Probability Theory and Its Application*, Vol. 1. New York: John Wiley and Sons, Inc., 1968.

Francis, J. C. and S. H. Archer. *Portfolio Analysis*. New York: Prentice-Hall, Inc., 1979.

Gressis, N., G. Philiippatos and J. Hayya. "Multiperiod Portfolio Analysis and the Inefficiencies of the Market Portfolio." *Journal of Finance*, v. 31 (September 1976), 1115–1126.

Henderson, J. and R. Quandt. *Microeconomic Theory: A Mathematical Approach*, 3rd ed. New York: McGraw-Hill, 1980.

Lee, C. F. and A. C. Lee. *Encyclopedia of Finance*. New York: Springer, 2006.

Lee, C. F., J. C. Lee and A. C. Lee. *Statistics for Business and Financial Economics*. Singapore: World Scientific Publishing Co., 2000.

Lee, C. F., A. C. Lee and J. C. Lee. *Handbook of Quantitative Finance and Risk Management*. New York: Springer, 2010.

Levy, H. and M. Sarnat. "A Note on Portfolio Selection and Investors' Wealth." *Journal of Financial and Quantitative Analysis*, v. 6 (January 1971), 639–642.

Lewis, A. L. "A Simple Algorithm for the Portfolio Selection Problem." *Journal of Finance*, v. 43 (March 1988), 71–82.

Lintner, J. "The Valuation of Risk Assets and the Selection of Risky Investments in Stock Portfolio and Capital Budgets." *Review of Economics and Statistics*, v. 47 (February 1965), 13–27.

Maginn, J. L., D. L. Tuttle, J. E. Pinto and D. W. McLeavey. *Managing Investment Portfolios: A Dynamic Process*, CFA Institute Investment Series, 3rd ed. New York: John Wiley & Sons, 2007.

Mao, J. C. T. *Quantitative Analysis of Financial Decisions*. New York: The Macmillan Company, 1969.

Markowitz, H. M. "Markowitz Revisited." *Financial Analysts Journal*, v. 32 (September/October 1976), 47–52.

Markowitz, H. M. Mean-Variance Analysis in Portfolio Choice and Capital Markets. New York: Blackwell, 1987.

Markowitz, H. M. *Portfolio Selection*. Cowles Foundation Monograph 16. New York: John Wiley and Sons, Inc., 1959.

Markowitz, H. M. "Portfolio Selection." *Journal of Finance*, v. 1 (December 1952), 77–91.

Martin, A. D., Jr. "Mathematical Programming of Portfolio Selections." Management Science, v. 1 (1955), 152–166.

Merton, R. "An Analytical Derivation of Efficient Portfolio Frontier." *Journal of Financial and Quantitative Analysis*, v. 7 (September 1972), 1851–1872.

Mossin, J. "Optimal Multiperiod Portfolio Policies." *Journal of Business*, v. 41 (April 1968), 215–229.

Ross, S. A. "On the General Validity of the Mean-Variance Approach in Large Markets," in W. F. Sharpe and C. M. Cootner, *Financial Economics: Essays in Honor of Paul Cootner*, 52–84. New York: PrenticeHall, Inc., 1982.

Sharpe, W. F. *Portfolio Theory and Capital Markets*. New York: McGraw-Hill, 1970.

Simkowitz, M. A. and W. L. Beedles. "Diversitifcation in a Three-Moment World." *Journal of Finance and Quantitative Analysis*, v. 13 (1978), 927–941.

Von Neumann, J. and O. Morgenstern. *Theory of Games and Economic Behavior*, 2nd ed. Princeton, NJ: Princeton University Press, 1947.

Wackerly, D., W. Mendenhall and R. L. Scheaffer. *Mathematical Statistics with Applications*, 7th ed. California: Duxbury Press, 2007.

Chapter 9

Capital Asset Pricing Model and Beta Forecasting

One of the important financial theories is the **capital asset pricing model**, commonly referred to as CAPM. Briefly touched upon in Chapter 4, it constitutes the major topic of this chapter; in addition, alternative methods for forecasting beta (systematic risk) are discussed.

Using the concepts of basic portfolio analysis and the dominance principle discussed in the last two chapters, two alternative methods are employed to derive the CAPM. The discussion concerns how the market model can be used to decompose (i.e., divide) risk into two components, systematic and unsystematic risk, as well as applications of the beta coefficient and procedures for forecasting a beta coefficient.

A graphical approach is first utilized to derive the CAPM, after which a mathematical approach to the derivation is developed that illustrates how the market model can be used to decompose total risk into two components. This is followed by a discussion of the importance of beta in security analysis and further exploration of the determination and forecasting of beta. The discussion closes with the applications and implications of the CAPM, and the appendix offers empirical evidence of the risk–return relationship.

9.1. A Graphical Approach to the Derivation of the CAPM

Following the risk–return tradeoff principle and the portfolio diversification process, Sharpe (1964), Lintner (1965), and Mossin (1966) have developed an asset pricing model that can determine both the market price of a portfolio and the price of an individual security. They focus upon the pricing determination of those parts of security risk that can be eliminated through diversification as well as those that cannot.

Systematic risk is that part of total risk that results from the common variability of stock prices and the subsequent tendency of stock prices to move together with the general market. The other portion of total risk is **unsystematic risk**, the result of variables peculiar to the firm or industry — for example, a labor strike or resource shortage.

Systematic risk, also referred to as *market risk*, reflects the swings of the general market. Some stocks and portfolios can be very sensitive to movements in the market, while others show more independence and stability. The universally accepted notion for the measure of a stock's or a portfolio's relative sensitivity to the market based upon its past record is the Greek letter **beta (β)**. The estimation, application, and forecasting of beta are discussed in the following sections.

9.1.1. *The Lending, Borrowing, and Market Portfolios*

Chapter 7 assumed that the efficient frontier was constructed with risky assets only. If there existed both risk-free and risky assets, investors would then have the choice of investing in one or the other, or in some combination of the two.

The concept of the risk-free asset is generally proxied by a government security, such as the Treasury bill (T-bill). T-bills are backed by the Federal government and are default free, hence considered riskless. An investor's portfolio can be composed of different combinations of riskless and risky assets. Figure 9.1 is a graph of different sets of portfolio opportunities; it includes the risk-free asset with a return of R_f. Since the riskless asset has zero risk, it is represented by a point on the vertical axis.

With the additional alternative to invest in risk-free assets that yield a return of R_f, the investor is able to create new combinations of portfolios that combine the risk-free assets with the risky assets. The investor is thus able to achieve any combination of risk and return that lies along the line connecting R_f and a tangent point M_p, the market portfolio. All portfolios along the line R_fM_pC are preferred to the risky portfolio opportunities on the curve AM_pB. Therefore, the points on the line R_fM_pC represent the best attainable combinations of risk and return.

At point R_f, the investor has all available funds invested in the riskless asset and expects to receive the return of R_f. The portfolios along the line R_fM_p are lending portfolios and contain combinations of investments in

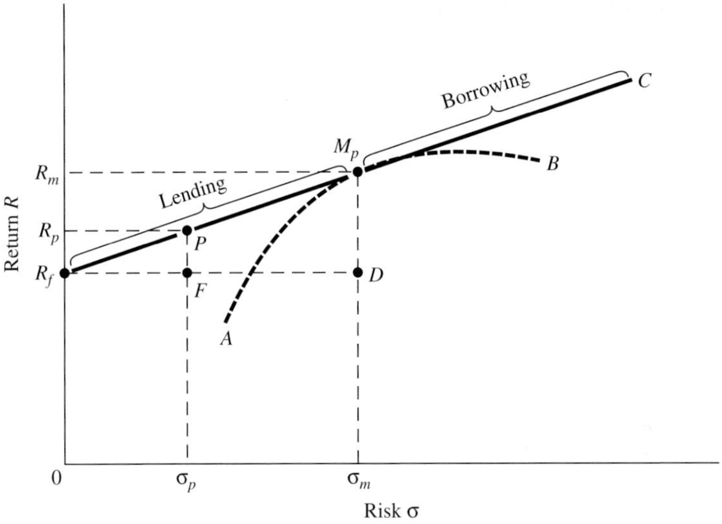

Fig. 9.1. The Capital Market Line.

the risk-free asset and investments in a portfolio of risky assets M_p. These are called *lending portfolios* because investors are, in effect, lending money to the government at the risk-free rate, when they invest in the risk-free asset.

At point M_p the investor wants only risky assets and has put his wealth into the risky-asset portfolio, which is called the **market portfolio**. The investor at this point is neither lending nor borrowing. An alternative view is that at this point the investor may be lending and borrowing equal amounts that just offset each other. At M_p investors receive a rate of return R_m and undertake risk σ_m.

If it is assumed that the investor can borrow money at the risk-free rate R_f and invest this money in the risky portfolio M_p, he or she will be able to derive portfolios with higher rates of return but with higher risks along the line extending beyond M_pC. The portfolios along line M_pC are **borrowing portfolios**. They are so called because they contain a negative amount of the risk-free asset. The negative amount invested in the risk-free asset can be viewed as borrowing funds at the risk-free rate and investing in risky assets. The borrowing for investment is called *margin* and is controlled by the government. Therefore, the new efficient frontier becomes R_fM_pC and is referred to as the **capital market line (CML)**. The CML describes the relationship between expected return and total risk.

9.1.2. *The Capital Market Line*

An illustration and explanation of the CML have already been provided; the equation for the CML is

$$E(R_p) = R_f + [E(R_m) - R_f]\frac{\sigma_p}{\sigma_m}, \tag{9.1}$$

where

R_f = the risk-free rate;
R_m = return on market portfolio M_p;
R_p = return on the portfolio consisting of the risk-free asset and portfolio M_p; and
$\sigma_p\sigma_m$ = the standard deviations of the portfolio and the market, respectively.

The implementation of Equation (9.1) can be explained graphically. An investor has three choices in terms of investments. He or she may invest in the riskless asset R_f in the market portfolio M_p or in any other efficient portfolio along the CML, such as portfolio P of Fig. 9.1.

If the investor puts his or her money into the riskless asset, he or she can receive a certain return of R_f; if his or her investments are put into the market portfolio he or she can expect an average return of R_m and risk of σ_m; if he or she invests in portfolio P, he or she can expect an average return of R_p with risk of σ_p. The difference between R_m and $R_f(R_m - R_f)$ is called the **market risk premium**.

The investor of portfolio P only needs to take on risk of σ_p so his or her risk premium is $(R_p - R_f)$. This is less than the market risk premium because the investor is taking on a smaller amount of risk, $\sigma_p < \sigma_m$.

By geometric theory, triangles R_fPF and R_fM_pD are similar. Consequently, they are directly proportional. Thus:

$$E(R_p) - R_f = [E(R_m) - R_f]\frac{\sigma_p}{\sigma_m}.$$

At equilibrium, all investors will want to hold a combination of the risk-free asset and the tangency portfolio (M_p). Since the market is cleared at equilibrium — that is, prices are such that the demand for all marketable assets equals their supply — the tangency portfolio M_p must represent the market portfolio. An individual security's proportional makeup (X_i) in the market portfolio will be the ratio of its market value (its equilibrium price times the total number of shares outstanding) to the total market value of all securities in the market, or:

$$X_i = \frac{\text{Market value of individual asset}}{\text{Market value of all assets}}. \quad (9.2)$$

Thus, at equilibrium, prices are such that supply is equated to demand, and all securities in the market will be represented in the market portfolio according to their market value.

Given the CML, assuming that investors are interested only in mean and variance of return, the CML will dominate all other attainable portfolios and securities because of the dominance principle, as discussed in Chapter 7. This implies that they will attempt to put some portion of their wealth into the market portfolio of risky assets, depending on their individual risk preference.

Since it has been established that the market portfolio is the only relevant portfolio of risky assets, the relevant risk measure of any individual security is its contribution to the risk of the market portfolio. The beta coefficient relates the covariance between security and market to the market's total variance, and it is the relevant market-risk measure. This will be explored in the next two sections. Notationally, beta is

$$\beta_i = \frac{\sigma_{im}}{\sigma_m^2} = \frac{\text{Cov}(R_i, R_m)}{\text{Var}(R_m)}.$$

Sample Problem 9.1 provides further illustration about risk/return tradeoffs.

Sample Problem 9.1

Describe the kinds of assets that could characterize the risk/return tradeoffs depicted by A, B, and C in Fig. 9.2.

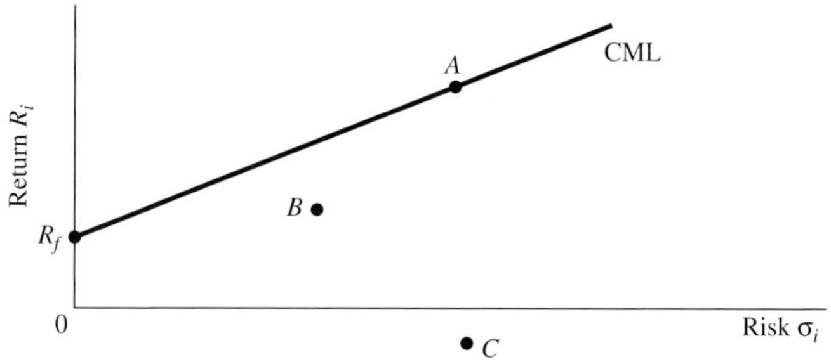

Fig. 9.2. The Capital Market Line.

Solution

A is a correctly priced asset, perhaps a stock or a portfolio. B is an overpriced asset, perhaps a bond selling at too large a premium. C is an asset with expected negative return — for example, a lottery ticket. The price of the lottery ticket is too high to be justified by the expected value of winning the jackpot. Even though the jackpot may be large, the probability of winning it is very small, hence its expected value is small. Therefore, the cost of the ticket is greater than the expected value of winning, which yields a negative return.

9.1.3. *The Security Market Line — The Capital Asset Pricing Model*

An asset's systematic risk with the market, β, is the only relevant risk measure of capital asset pricing for the individual asset and the portfolio. Consequently, a derivation of the relationship between systematic risk and return can be made where the expected linear relationship between these two variables is referred to as the **security market line (SML)**, illustrated by Fig. 9.3.

To derive the graphical picture of the SML, it is necessary to list a few assumptions concerning the investors and the securities market.

(1) Investors are risk averse.
(2) The CAPM is a one-period model because it is assumed that investors maximize the utility of their end-of-period wealth.

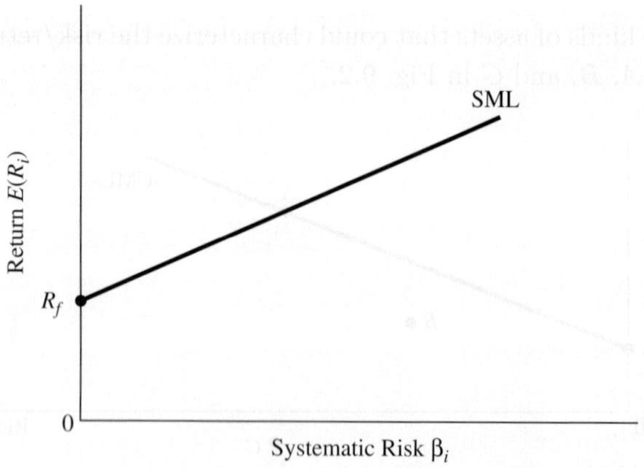

Fig. 9.3. The CAPM Showing the SML.

(3) All investors have the same efficient frontier — that is, they have homogeneous expectations concerning asset returns and risk.
(4) Portfolios can be characterized by their means and variances.
(5) There exists a risk-free asset with a return R_f, the rate at which all investors borrow or lend. The borrowing rate is equal to the lending rate.
(6) All assets are marketable and perfectly divisible, and their supplies are fixed.
(7) There are no transaction costs.
(8) Investors have all information available to them at no cost.
(9) There are no taxes or regulations associated with trading.

All individual assets or portfolios will fall along the SML. The position of an asset will depend on its systematic risk or beta. The required risk premium for the market is $R_m - R_f$, and β_m is equal to one. Given the SML, the return on a risky asset is equal to

$$E(R_i) = R_f + \beta_i[E(R_m) - R_f], \tag{9.3}$$

where

$E(R_i)$ = the expected rate of return for asset i;
R_f = the expected risk-free rate;
β_i = the measure of normalized systematic risk (beta) of asset i, and
$E(R_m)$ = the expected return on the market portfolio.

(*Note*: This SML is also generally called the CAPM. The mathematical derivation of this model will be shown in the next section.)

The relationship between the CML and the SML can be seen by rearranging the definition of the beta coefficient:

$$\beta_i = \frac{\text{Cov}(R_i, R_m)}{\text{Var}(R_m)} = \frac{\sigma_{im}}{\sigma_m^2} = \frac{\rho_{i,m}\sigma_i\sigma_m}{\sigma_m^2} = \frac{\sigma_{i,m}\sigma_i}{\sigma_m}, \tag{9.4}$$

where

σ_i = standard deviation of a security's rate of return;
σ_m = standard deviation of the market rate of return;
$\sigma_{i,m}$ = the correlation coefficient of R_i and R_m; and
$\sigma_{im} = \frac{\sigma_{im}}{\sigma_i\sigma_m}$.

If $\sigma_{im} = 1$, then Equation (9.3) reduces to

$$E(R_i) = R_f + \frac{\sigma_i}{\sigma_m}[E(R_m) - R_f]. \tag{9.3$'$}$$

If $\sigma_{i,m} = 1$, this implies that this portfolio is an efficient portfolio. If i is an individual security, it implies that the returns and risks associated with the asset are perfectly correlated with the market as a whole. There are several implications:

(1) Equation (9.3) is a generalized case of Equation (9.3′).
(2) The SML instead of the CML should be used to price an individual security or an inefficient portfolio.
(3) The CML prices the risk premium in terms of total risk, and the SML prices the risk premium in terms of systematic risk.

Sample Problem 9.2 provides further illustration.

Sample Problem 9.2

Suppose the expected return on the market portfolio is 10% and that $R_f = 6\%$. Further, suppose that you were confronted with an investment opportunity to buy a security with return expected to be 12% and with $\beta = 1.2$. Should you undertake this investment?

Solution

$$R_i = a + b\beta_i$$

for the market portfolio with $\beta = 1$ we have

$$0.10 = a + (b \times 1) = a + b,$$

and for the risk-free rate with $\beta = 0$, we have

$$0.06 = a + (b \times 0) = a.$$

Solving these equations for a and b yields:

$$a = 0.06$$

$$b = 0.04.$$

For the security with $\beta = 1.2$ the expected return given the SML is

$$R_i = 0.06 + 0.04(1.2) = 0.108.$$

Since 12% > 10.8%, the security is undervalued — that is, the security should be purchased since its return is above the equilibrium return of 10.8% for that level of the risk.

9.2. Mathematical Approach to the Derivation of the CAPM

Using the assumptions about efficient and perfect markets stated earlier in the chapter, we can show how Sharpe derived the CAPM.

Sharpe (1964) used a general risky asset that did not lie along the CML and dubbed it i. Risk and return for the possible combinations of security i with the market portfolio M are shown by Fig. 9.4. The average return and standard deviation for any I–M combination can be approached in the Markowitz fashion for a two-asset case:

$$\begin{aligned} &\text{(i)} \qquad E(R_p) = w_i E(R_i) + (1 - w_i)E(R_m), \\ &\text{(ii)} \qquad \sigma(R_p) = \left(w_i^2\sigma_i^2 + (1 - w_i)^2\sigma_m^2 + 2(1 - w_i)w_i\sigma_{im}\right)^{1/2}, \end{aligned} \tag{9.5}$$

in which w_i represents excess demand for i or demand greater than its equilibrium weight in portfolio M.

The changes in mean and standard deviation as the proportion w_i changes are represented by

$$\frac{\partial E(R_p)}{\partial w_i} = E(R_i) - E(R_m),$$

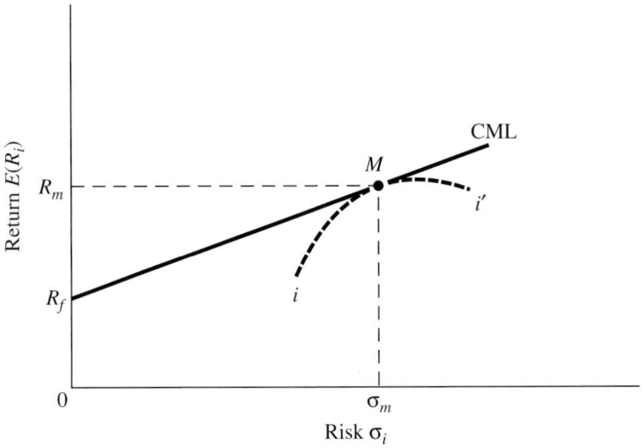

Fig. 9.4. The Opportunity Set Provided by Combinations of Risky Asset i and the Market Portfolio M.

$$\frac{\partial\sigma(R_p)}{\partial w_i} = 1/2[w_i^2\sigma_i^2 + (1-w_i)^2\sigma_m^2 + 2w_i(1-w_i)\sigma_{im}]^{-1/2} \times[(2w_i\sigma_i^2 - 2\sigma_m^2 + 2w_i\sigma_m^2 + 2\sigma_{im} - 4w_i\sigma_{im})]. \tag{9.6}$$

When $w_i = 0$, the ith security is held in proportion to its total market value, and there is no excess demand for security i. This is the key insight to Sharpe's argument, for when $w_i = 0$, it is possible to equate the slope of the curve iMi' with the CML, thus obtaining an expression for the return on any risky security i. At equilibrium when $w_i = 0$, the slope along the iMi' curve will be equal to

$$\frac{\partial E(R_p)}{\partial\sigma(R_p)} = \frac{\dfrac{\partial E(R_p)}{\partial w_i}}{\dfrac{\partial\sigma(R_p)}{\partial w_i}} = \frac{E(R_i) - E(R_m)}{\dfrac{\sigma_{im} - \sigma_m^2}{\sigma_m}}. \tag{9.7}$$

The slope of the CML at point M is

$$\frac{E(R_m) - R_f}{\sigma_m}. \tag{9.8}$$

Setting Equation (9.7) equal to Equation (9.8) and rearranging the terms to solve for $E(R_i)$ gives the equation for the SML or CAPM:

$$E(R_i) = R_f + [E(R_m) - R_f]\frac{\sigma_{im}}{\sigma_m^2}. \tag{9.9}$$

This represents the return on any risky asset i. At equilibrium, every risky asset will be priced so that it lies along the SML. It should be noted that the term σ_{im}/σ_m^2 represents the beta coefficient for the regression of R_i versus R_m so that Equation (9.9) can be rewritten as

$$E(R_i) = R_f + [E(R_m) - R_f]\beta_i, \tag{9.10}$$

which is the formula for the CAPM.

9.3. The Market Model and Risk Decomposition

To use the CAPM, the market model must be employed to estimate the beta (systematic risk). In addition, the market model can be used to do risk decomposition. Both the market model and risk decomposition are discussed in this section.

9.3.1. *The Market Model*

As noted previously, the total risk of a portfolio or security can be conceived as the sum of its systematic and unsystematic risks. The equation that expresses these concepts states that the return on any asset at time t can be expressed as a linear function of the market return at time t plus a random error component. Thus, the market model is expressed as

$$R_{i,t} = \alpha_i + \beta_i R_{m,t} + e_{i,t}, \tag{9.11}$$

where

$R_{i,t}$ = the return of the ith security in time t;
α_i = the intercept of the regression;
β_i = the slope;
$R_{m,t}$ = the market return at time t; and
$e_{i,t}$ = random error term.

9.3.2. *Risk Decomposition*

The regression model of Equation (9.11), which describes the risky asset's characteristics relative to the market portfolio, is also called the *characteristic line*. Since beta is the slope coefficient for this regression (market model), it demonstrates how responsive returns for the individual earning assets are to the market portfolio. By using the market model, the total variance for security $i(\sigma_i^2)$ can be represented by and decomposed into

$$\sigma_i^2 = \beta_i^2 \sigma_m^2 + \sigma_{ei}^2, \tag{9.12}$$

in which $\beta_i^2 \sigma_m^2$ is the systematic-risk component of total risk and σ_{ei}^2 is the unsystematic component.

The CAPM as developed here is expressed in terms of expected values. Since expected values are not directly measured, we must transform the CAPM into an expression that uses observable variables. Assuming that on average expected returns $E(R_{i,t})$ for a security equal realized returns, returns can be expressed as

$$R_{i,t} = E\left(R_{i,t}\right) + \beta_i \left[R_{m,t} - E\left(R_{m,t}\right)\right] + e_{i,t}, \tag{9.13}$$

in which $e_{i,t}$ is a random error term.

Assuming that the expected value of the error term is 0, that it is uncorrelated with the term $[R_{m,t} - E(R_{m,t})]$ and that $\mathrm{Cov}(e_{i,t}, e_{i,t-1}) = 0$, the expression for $E(R_{i,t})$ can be substituted from the CAPM equation (9.10) into (9.13):

$$R_{i,t} = R_{f,t} + [E(R_{m,t}) - R_{f,t}]\beta_i + [R_{m,t} - E(R_{m,t})]\beta_i + e_{i,t}.$$

Simplifying this equation:

$$R_{i,t} - R_{f,t} = \alpha_i + \beta_i(R_{m,t} - R_{f,t}) + e_{i,t}, \tag{9.14}$$

where α_i is the intercept. All variables of Equation (9.14) can be estimated from observed data. Equation (9.14) is called the **risk-premium version** of the market model. It is similar to the market model indicated in Equation (9.11), except that instead of using the total returns R_i and R_m, it uses the risk-premium portion of the returns, or $R_i - R_f$ and $R_m - R_f$. Sample Problem 9.3 provides further illustration.

Sample Problem 9.3

To show how Equations (9.11) and (9.12) can be used, we will use monthly return data from Johnson & Johnson (J&J) and IBM. The time period covers from March 2000 to April 2010. Their average return, beta coefficient, total variance, and residual variance are as indicated in Table 9.1. We can see that IBM with $\beta = 1.1964$ is more sensitive to the fluctuations of the market than J&J with $\beta = 0.3726$.

Both the magnitude of total variance and beta of IBM were larger than for J&J, although the average rates of return for J&J were higher for IBM. Hence J&J was a more desirable security, if that was the only choice the investor had.

9.3.3. *Why Beta is Important for Security Analysis*

Implications and applications of beta coefficients in security analysis will be discussed in this section. Beta is used as a measurement of risk: it gauges the sensitivity of a stock or portfolio relative to the market, as indicated

Table 9.1. Average Return, Beta Coefficient, Total Variance, and Residual Variance of J&J and IBM.

	Avg. Return	Beta	Residual Variance	Total Variance
Johnson & Johnson	0.008	0.3726	0.0022	0.0025
IBM	0.005	1.1964	0.0041	0.007

in Equation (9.11). A beta of 1.0 is characteristic of a broad market index such as the NYSE index or the S&P 500. A beta of 2.0 indicates that the stock will swing twice as far in either direction than a fall or rise in the market average. If the market gains 15%, a security of $\beta = 2$ is expected to gain 30%. Conversely, should the market fall 15%, the stock is expected to fall 30%.

A beta of 0.50 indicates that the stock is more stable than the market and will move only half as much as the market. For example, if the market loses 20%, a stock with $\beta = 0.50$ will lose only 10% of the market, and if the market should gain 20%, the stock will gain only 10%. High-beta stocks have been classified as aggressive while low-beta stocks are referred to as defensive. From Table 9.1 it is clear that IBM is an offensive stock while J&J is a defensive stock.

The CAPM has illustrated the concept that risks are associated with portfolios where the relevant (systematic) risk of an individual security is dependent upon the security's effect on portfolio risk. Therefore, the CAPM equation $E(R_i) = R_f + \beta_i[E(R_m) - R_f]$ represents a description of how rates of return are established in the marketplace assuming investors behave according to the assumptions of the model. Thus a stock's beta measures its contributions to the risk of the portfolio and is therefore a measure of the stock's riskiness relative to the market.

In the previous section it was found that the rates of return of stock i are presumed to bear a linear relationship with the market rate of return as defined in Equation (9.11). Equation (9.11) is a fixed-coefficient market model. Following Fabozzi and Francis (1978), Sunder (1980), and Lee and Chen (1980), a random-coefficient market model can be defined as Equation (9.15a) or Equation (9.15b):

$$R_{it} = \alpha_i + \beta_{it} R_{mt} + e_{it}, \tag{9.15a}$$

$$R_{it} - R_{ft} = \alpha_i^{'} + \beta_{it}^{'}(R_{mt} - R_{ft}) + e_{it}, \tag{9.15b}$$

in which $\beta_{it} = \beta_i + \eta_{it} \cdot \eta_{it}$ represents the random fluctuation associated with the beta coefficient. Using the random-coefficient market model, the total risk can be decomposed into three components, as defined in Equation (9.16):

$$\sigma_i^2 = \beta_j^2 \sigma_m^2 + \sigma_{\varepsilon i}^2 + \sigma_\eta^2 \sigma_m^2, \tag{9.16}$$

in which $\sigma_\eta^2 \sigma_m^2$ represents an interaction risk between the market and the random fluctuation of the beta. Equation (9.16) is a generalized case of Equation (9.12). It contains systematic risk, unsystematic risk, and a risk term that reflects any interaction between the systematic and unsystematic risk.

Both fixed-coefficient and random-coefficient market models can be used to do security analysis and portfolio selection, discussed later in this text.

The relationship between total risk, market risk, and firm-specific risk can be shown as

$$\text{Total risk} = \text{Market risk} + \text{Firm-specific risk.}$$

Since firm-specific risk can be eliminated by diversification:

$$\text{Relevant risk} = \text{Market risk.}$$

Beta is important for the investment manager because it can be used (1) to select individual stocks for investment; (2) to construct portfolios of financial assets with desired levels of risk and return; and (3) to evaluate the performance of portfolio managers. Details of the various uses of beta and the CAPM are provided later in this text. Sample Problem 9.4 provides further illustration.

Sample Problem 9.4

Given the SML $\overline{R}_i = 0.06 + 0.08\beta_i$ what should the expected return of a security be if it has a beta twice as great as a similar security returning 18%?

Solution

$$\overline{R}_i = 0.06 + 0.08\beta = 0.18.$$

Solving for β yields

$$\beta = 1.5.$$

Therefore, the security's β is $2 \times 1.5 = 3.0$ and the required return is

$$\begin{aligned}\overline{R}_i &= 0.06 + 0.08(3.0)\\ &= 0.30.\end{aligned}$$

A 30% return is required.

9.3.4. *Determination of Systematic Risk*

As mentioned above, systematic risk is nondiversifiable because it runs across industries and companies and affects all securities. Chapter 7 discussed many factors that determine risk. At this point we are interested only in those management decisions that can be related to the degree of systematic risk a firm exhibits — namely, the operating decisions and the financing decisions of management.

There are two dimensions of risk that affect a firm's systematic risk. The first is **financial risk**, the additional risk placed on the firm and its stock holders due to the firm's decision to be leveraged — that is, to take on additional debt. The second, **business risk**, is the riskiness involved with a firm's operations, if it takes on no debt.

A particular firm's capital structure affects the riskiness inherent in the company's common stock and thus affects its required rate of return and the price of the stock. A company's capital-structure policy requires choosing between risk and return. Taking on increasing levels of debt increases the riskiness of the firm's earning stream, but it usually also results in a higher expected rate of return. High levels of risk tend to lower a stock's price, but a high level of expected rates of return tends to raise it. Therefore, striking a balance with the optimal capital structure maximizes the price of the stock.

Business risk is the risk inherent in a firm's operations. It can also be defined as the uncertainty inherent in projection of future operating income or **earnings before interest and taxes (EBIT)**. Fluctuations in EBIT can result from a number of factors. On the national level these can be economic factors such as inflationary or recessionary times. At the industry level some factors may be the level of competition between similar industries, natural or man-made catastrophes, labor strikes, price controls, and so on. There are a host of possibilities that affect EBIT by raising or lowering its level.

Uncertainty regarding future income flows is a function of the company's business risk. It may fluctuate among industries, among firms, and across time. The extent of business risk is dependent upon the firm and the Industry. Cyclical industries such as steel production or automobile manufacture have especially high business risks because they are dependent upon the strength of the economy. The retail food industry is considered to be quite stable because food is a necessary good that will be purchased regardless of the state of the economy.

Business risk is dependent upon several factors, the most important of which are listed here:

(1) *Demand variability*: Stability in the levels of demand for the firm's product results in a reduction *of* business risk.

(2) *Sales price variability*: Highly volatile prices result in high-risk, volatile markets; therefore, stability of prices results in reduction *of* business risk.
(3) *Suppliers' price variability*: Firms whose input prices are highly variable are exposed to higher levels of risk.
(4) *Output price flexibility relative to input prices*: As a result of inflation, a firm that is able to raise its output prices with increasing input costs minimizes its business risk.

When a firm uses debt or financial leverage, business risk and financial risk are concentrated on the stockholders. For example, if a firm is capitalized only with common equity, then the investors all share the business risk in proportion to their ownership of stock. If, however, a firm is 50% levered (50% of the corporation is financed by debt, the other half by common equity), the investors who put up the equity will then have to bear all business risk and some financial risk.

The effect of leverage upon return on assets (ROA) and return on equity (ROE) and its effect upon the stockholders can be generalized as follows:

(1) The use of leverage or debt generally increases ROE.
(2) The standard deviation of ROA (σ_{ROA}) is a measure of business risk, whereas the standard deviation of ROE (σ_{ROE}) is a measure of the risk borne by stockholders; $\sigma_{\text{ROA}} = \sigma_{\text{ROE}}$ if the firm is not levered; otherwise with the use of debt $\sigma_{\text{ROE}} > \sigma_{\text{ROA}}$ an indication that business risk is being borne by stockholders.
(3) The difference between σ_{ROE} and σ_{ROA} is the actual risk stockholders face and a measure of the increased risk resulting from financial leverage. Thus

$$\text{Risk of financial leverage} = \sigma^2_{\text{ROE}} - \sigma^2_{\text{ROA}}.$$

9.4. Growth Rates, Accounting Betas, and Variance in EBIT

Besides leverage, other financial variables associated with the firm can affect the beta coefficient. These are the growth rate, accounting beta, and variance in EBIT.

9.4.1. *Sustainable Growth Rates*

In Chapter 3, we have discussed two methods for estimating growth rate. Alternatively, the **growth rate** can be measured in terms of the growth in total assets or the growth in sales. It is determined by the percentage change between two periods.

$$\frac{\text{sales}_t - \text{sales}_{t-1}}{\text{sales}_{t-1}} \times 100\% \quad \text{or} \quad \frac{\text{total assets}_t - \text{total assets}_{t-1}}{\text{total assets}_{t-1}} \times 100\%.$$

Based upon this definition, Higgins (1977, 1981, and 2008) has developed a sustainable growth rate. Growth and its management present special problems in financial planning. From a financial perspective, growth is not always a blessing. Rapid growth can put considerable strain on a company's resources, and unless management is aware of this effect and takes active steps to control it, rapid growth can lead to bankruptcy. It becomes necessary, therefore, to define a company's sustainable growth rate:

$$\frac{\Delta S}{S} = g^* = \frac{P(1-D)(1+L)}{T - P(1-D)(1+L)} = \frac{(1-D)ROE}{1-(1-D)ROE}, \tag{9.17}$$

where

P = the profit margin on all sales;
D = the target dividend payout ratio;
L = the target debt to equity ratio;
T = the ratio of total assets to sales;
S = annual sales; and
ΔS = the increase in sales during the year.

How is Equation (9.17) derived? Assuming a company is not raising new equity, the cash to finance growth must come from retained profits and new borrowings:

$$\begin{aligned}\text{Retained profits} &= \text{Profits} - \text{Dividends}\\ &= \text{Profit margin} \times \text{Total sales} - \text{Dividends}\\ &= \text{P}(S + \Delta S)(1 - D).\end{aligned}$$

Further, because the company wants to maintain a target debt-to-equity ratio equal to L, each dollar added to the owners' equity enables it to increase its indebtedness by \$$L$. Since the owners' equity will rise by an amount equal to retained profits:

$$\begin{aligned}\text{New borrowings} &= \text{Retained profit} \times \text{Target debt-to-equity ratio}\\ &= P(S + \Delta S)(1 - D)L.\end{aligned}$$

The use of cash represented by the increase in assets must equal the two sources of cash (retained profits and new borrowings):

$$
\begin{aligned}
\text{Uses of cash} &= \text{Sources of cash} \\
\text{Increases in assets} &= \text{Retained profits} + \text{New borrowings} \\
\Delta ST &= P(S+\Delta S)(1-D) + P(S+\Delta S)(1-D)L, \\
\Delta ST &= P(1-D)(1+L)S + P(1-D)(1+L)\Delta S, \\
\Delta S[T - P(1-D)(1+L)] &= P(1-D)(1+L)S, \\
\frac{\Delta S}{S} &= \frac{P(1-D)(1+L)}{T-P(1-D)(1+L)}.
\end{aligned}
$$

In Equation (9.17), the $\Delta S/S$ or g^* is the firm's sustainable growth rate assuming no infusion of new equity. Therefore, a company's growth rate in sales must equal the indicated combination of four ratios, P, D, L, and T. In addition, if the company's growth rate differs from g^*, one or more of the ratios must change. For example, suppose a company grows at a rate in excess of g^*, then it must either use its assets more efficiently or it must alter its financial policies. Efficiency is represented by the profit margin and asset-to-sales ratio. It therefore would need to increase its profit margin (P) or decrease its asset-to-sales ratio (T) in order to increase efficiency. Financial policies are represented by payout or leverage ratios. In this case, a decrease in its payout ratio (D) or an increase in its leverage (L) would be necessary to alter its financial policies to accommodate a different growth rate. It should be noted that increasing efficiency is not always possible and altering financial policies not always wise. (For other available methods to alter growth the reader is referred to Chapter 11 of Lee *et al.* (2009).)

If we divide both numerator and denominator of Equation (9.17) by T and make some arrangement, then we can show that the sustainable growth rate can be shown as

$$\frac{\Delta S}{S} = \frac{P(1-D)(1+L)}{T-P(1-D)(1+L)} = \frac{(1-D)ROE}{1-(1-D)ROE}, \tag{9.17a}$$

where ROE = the rate of return on equity.

Since sustainable growth rate does not allow company to use external equity, by allowing company to use both external debt and equity, Lee *et al.* (2011) have derived a generalized sustainable growth rate as

$$g(t) = \frac{(1-D)ROE}{1-(1-D)ROE} + \frac{\lambda \cdot \Delta n \cdot p/E}{1-(1-D)ROE}, \tag{9.17b}$$

where

$\lambda =$ degree of market imperfection;
$\Delta n =$ number of shares of new equity issued;
$p =$ price per share of new equity; and
$E =$ total equity.

9.4.2. *Accounting Beta*

The **accounting beta** can be calculated from earnings-per-share (EPS) data. Using EPS as an example, beta can be computed as follows:

$$\text{EPS}_{i,t} = \alpha_i + \beta_i \text{EPS}_{m,t} + e_{i,t},$$

where

$\text{EPS}_{i,t} =$ earnings-per-share of firm i at time t;
$\text{EPS}_{m,t} =$ earnings-per-share of market average at time t; and
$e_{i,t} =$ error term.

The estimate of β_i is the EPS type of accounting beta.

9.4.3. *Variance in EBIT*

The variance in EBIT (X) can be defined as

$$\frac{\sum_{t=1}^{n} \left(X_t - \overline{X}\right)^2}{n-1},$$

in which $X_t =$ earnings before interest and taxes in period t, and $\overline{X} =$ average EBIT.

The total variance of EBIT can be used to measure the overall fluctuation of accounting earnings for a firm.

9.4.4. *Capital–Labor Ratio*

The **capital–labor ratio** has an impact upon the magnitude of the beta coefficient. In order to examine this impact, it is necessary to examine the capital–labor ratio.

A production function is a function that can be seen as a function of labor and capital:

$$Q = f(K, L), \tag{9.18}$$

where K = capital and L = labor. K/L (the capital–labor ratio) is generally used to measure a firm's degree of capital intensity. Corporations often choose between increasing their capital intensity through installation of computers, use of robotics in place of labor, and increase in labor inputs. Small industries that specialize in hand-crafted or -tooled goods will have to increase their capital ratio in order to increase production. However, it has been the trend in recent years for many growth-oriented firms, whether manufacturers or other members of the business sector, to increase their efficiencies through increased investments in capital. Auto manufacturers are finding that robots can assemble cars of high and consistent quality at only a fraction of the cost of workers.

Capital intensity results in increased total risks and generally results in an increase in beta. Large investments are often needed to fully automate a plant or to computerize a bank completely. Taking on debt or issuing securities is normally how these capitalization increases are financed. If the capital–labor ratio is greater than one — that is, if K is greater than L — a firm is capital intensive. If the capital–labor ratio is less than one — that is, if K is less than L — then there is a reduction in capital intensity and a shift toward human-resource investment.

9.4.5. *Fixed Costs and Variable Costs*

Business risk is dependent upon the extent a firm builds **fixed costs** into its operations. If a large percentage of a firm's costs are fixed, costs cannot decline proportionally when demand falls off. If fixed costs are high, then a slight drop in sales can lead to large declines in EBIT. Therefore, the higher a firm's fixed costs are, the greater its business risk and, generally, the higher its beta.

A firm with a large amount of fixed costs is said to have a *large degree of operating leverage*. An example of these costs may be the highly skilled workers of an engineering firm. The firm cannot hire and fire experienced and highly skilled workers easily; therefore, the workers must be retained and paid during a period of slack demand. Similarly, a firm that is highly leveraged will be characterized by the scenario that small changes in sales will result in large changes in operating income.

Variable costs have the opposite effect, because they are adjustable to the firm's needs. Should a drop in sales occur, variable costs can be lowered to meet the lowered output.

The extent to which firms can control their operating leverage is dependent upon their technological needs. Companies that require large investments in fixed assets — such as steel mills, auto manufacturers, and airlines — will have large fixed costs and operating leverages. Therefore, how much a company is willing to undertake operating leverages must come into play during capital-budgeting decisions. If the company is risk averse, it may opt for alternatives with smaller investments and fixed costs.

A company having a larger percentage of fixed costs generally implies that they use more capital-intensive types of technology in production. For example, an auto manufacturer such as General Motors (GM) has a higher percentage of fixed costs than a food manufacturer such as General Foods. Therefore, GM's capital–labor ratio can be expected to be higher than that of General Foods. An implication of this phenomenon is that General Foods has a lower beta than GM.

9.4.6. *Beta Forecasting*

Analysts and investment managers who use the CAPM and beta are interested in whether the beta coefficient and the standard-deviation statistics for different securities and portfolios are stable through time or whether they change in a predictable fashion. If the beta coefficient and standard deviation are stable, then using a beta derived from current and historical price data is fine, because the beta today is the same as the beta in the future. However, if the beta coefficient and standard deviation are unstable or vary through time, the analyst or manager must forecast a beta's future value before employing it.

The available evidence on the stability of beta indicates that the beta on an individual security is generally not stable, whereas portfolios have stable betas. Hence we are faced with the problem of forecasting future betas in order to use the CAPM for individual securities. **Beta forecasting** refers to using the historical beta estimates or other historical financial information to forecast future betas.

Beaver *et al.* (1970) argue that if it is possible to find the underlying determinants of beta, such knowledge can be used to help forecast future betas. They used accounting information from the financial statements of firms to help in the estimation of beta and concluded that using both price and accounting information shows promise for better beta estimates.

Rosenberg and Marathe (1975) used 54 factors in 6 categories to estimate betas. Their factors included historical price information, price/earnings (P/E) ratios, financial ratios, and statistical measures associated with the market model. They support the notion that betas are determined by fundamental factors related to firms in addition to market pricing data.

Given that the most useful beta is one that can be forecasted correctly, and that the beta is related to the financial and business risk of the firm as well as the degree to which a firm's businesses co-vary with the total economy, it becomes necessary to determine the best way to forecast beta. The next section addresses this issue.

9.4.7. *Market-Based Versus Accounting-Based Beta Forecasting*

Market-based beta forecasts are based upon market information alone. Historical betas of firms are used as a proxy for their future betas. This implies that the unadjusted sample beta, $\hat{\beta}_t$, is equal to the population value of future beta:

$$\beta_{t+1} = \hat{\beta}_t. \tag{9.19a}$$

Alternatively, there may be a systematic relationship between the estimated betas for the first period and those of the second period, as shown by Blume (1971):

$$\hat{\beta}_{i,t+1} = a_0 + a_1\hat{\beta}_{i,t}, \tag{9.19b}$$

in which $\hat{\beta}_{i,t+1}$ and $\hat{\beta}_{i,t}$ estimated beta for the ith firm in period $t+1$ and t, respectively. Sample Problem 9.5 provides further illustration.

Sample Problem 9.5

If $\hat{a}_0 = 0.35, \hat{a}_1 = 0.80$, and $\hat{\beta}_{i,t} = 0.12$, then the future beta can be either

$$\beta_{t+1} = 1.2 \quad \text{or}$$

$$\hat{\beta}_{t+1} = 0.35 + (0.80)(1.2) = 1.31.$$

It is worthwhile to note that Value Line uses Equation (9.19b) to estimate the future beta.

Accounting-based beta forecasts rely upon the relationships of accounting information such as the growth rate of the firm, EBIT, leverage, and the accounting beta as a basis for forecasting beta. To use accounting information in beta forecasts, the historical beta estimates are first cross-sectionally related to accounting information such as growth rate, variance of EBIT, leverage, accounting beta, and so on:

$$\beta_i = a_0 + a_1 X_{1i} + a_2 X_{2i} + a_j X_{ji} + \cdots + a_m X_{mi}, \tag{9.20}$$

where X_{ji} is the jth accounting variables for ith firm, and a_j is the regression coefficient.

Some researchers have found that the historically based beta is the best forecast, whereas others have found that the accounting-based beta is best. Lee *et al.* (1986) used composite concepts to show that both accounting and market information are useful for beta forecasting. They found that neither beta forecasts based upon market information nor those based on accounting information are conditionally more efficient with respect to each other. It can be inferred, then, that each set of forecasts contains useful information for the prediction of systematic risk.

The statistical procedure used by Lee *et al.* (1986) is the ordinary least-squares method. Ordinary least squares is a statistical procedure for finding the best fitting straight line for a set of points; it seems in many respects a formalization of the procedure employed when fitting a line by eye. For instance, when visually fitting a line to a set of data, the ruler is moved until it appears that the deviations of the points from the prospective line have been minimized. If the predicted value of y_i (dependent variable) obtained from the fitted line is denoted as $\hat{y}_i$ the prediction equation becomes:

$$\hat{y}_i = \hat{\beta}_0 + \hat{\beta}_1 x_i,$$

where $\hat{\beta}_0$ and $\hat{\beta}_1$ represent estimates of the true β_0 and β_1; x_i is an independent variable.

Graphically, the vertical lines drawn from the prediction line to each point represent the deviations of the points from the predicted value of y. Thus the deviation of the ith point is $y_i - \hat{y}_i$.

In order to find the best fit, it is necessary to minimize the deviations of the points. A criterion of best fit that is often employed is known as the *principle of least squares*. It may be stated as follows: Choose the best fitting line as the one that minimizes the sum of squares of the errors (SSE) of the observed values of Y from those predicted. Expressed mathematically,

$$\text{SSE} = \sum_{i=1}^{n} (y_i - \hat{y}_i)^2.$$

Further, the mean sum of squares of the error (MSSE) of the observed values of Y could be minimized from the predicted mean. Expressed mathematically as

$$\text{MSSE} = \frac{\sum_{i=1}^{n}(y_i - \hat{y}_i)^2}{n}.$$

Mincer and Zarnowitz (1969) suggest a decomposition of the mean squared error term into three components representing bias, inefficiency, and random error. Mathematically, this is represented as

$$\frac{\sum_{i=1}^{n}(y_i - \hat{y}_i)^2}{n} = (y_i - \hat{y}_i)^2 + (S_y - \rho S_y)^2 + (1 - \rho^2)S_y^2,$$

where $\bar{y}$, and S_y represent the mean, standard deviation, and correlation coefficient of y, respectively.

Using the ordinary least-squares method, Lee *et al.* (1986) showed that it is possible to achieve better forecasts by combining two types of betas. Using an ordinary least-squares estimate of β_{OLS} and a Bayesian adjustment procedure of Vasicek (1973) as defined in Equation (9.21):

$$\beta_V = \frac{\dfrac{\bar{\beta}}{V(\hat{\beta})} + \dfrac{\hat{\beta}_{\text{OLS}}}{V(\hat{\beta}_{\text{OLS}})}}{\dfrac{1}{V(\hat{\beta})} + \dfrac{1}{V(\hat{\beta}_{\text{OLS}})}}, \tag{9.21}$$

where

β_{OLS} = the least-squares estimate of a first-period individual beta;
$V(\hat{\beta}_{\text{OLS}})$ = variance estimate of β_{OLS};
$\bar{\beta}$ = the cross-sectional mean value of estimated β_{OLS};
$V(\hat{\beta})$ = the cross-sectional variance of estimated β_{OLS}; and
β_V = the Bayesian adjusted beta.

Equation (9.21) indicates that the Vasicek type of Bayesian adjustment beta is a weighted average of $\bar{\beta}$ and β_{OLS}. The weights are

$$w_1 = \frac{\dfrac{1}{V(\hat{\beta})}}{\dfrac{1}{V(\hat{\beta})} + \dfrac{1}{V(\hat{\beta}_{\text{OLS}})}} \quad \text{and} \quad w_2 = \frac{\dfrac{1}{V(\hat{\beta}_{\text{OLS}})}}{\dfrac{1}{V(\hat{\beta})} + \dfrac{1}{V(\hat{\beta}_{\text{OLS}})}}.$$

The authors first use first-period regressions projected forward to obtain forecasts of the second-period betas. The summary of the stepwise regression for the first-period data is given in Table 9.2. Table 9.3 summarizes

Table 9.2. Summary of Stepwise Regression Results for First-Period Data.

Dependent Variable Adjusted R^2	$\hat{\beta}_{\text{OLS}}$	$\hat{\beta}_v$
	0.245	0.236
Independent Variables	*Coefficients (t-values)*	
Intercept	0.911	1.037
	(11.92)	(12.71)
Financial leverage	0.704	0.599
	(5.31)	(5.81)
Dividend payout	−0.175	−0.108
	(−3.50)	(−2.85)
Sales	0.030	0.018
	(3.02)	(2.28)
Operating income	0.011	0.026
	(2.18)	(2.28)
Assets	—	−0.026
	—	(−2.41)

Source: Lee *et al.* (1986, p. 59).

Table 9.3. Mean Squared Error Decompositions for Forecasts of Second-Period Betas.

	Market-Based Forecasts		*Accounting-Based Forecasts*	
	Without Bayesian Adjustment	*With Bayesian Adjustment*	*Without Bayesian Adjustment*	*With Bayesian Adjustment*
Bias	0.0003	0.0000	0.0003	0.0000
Inefficiency	0.0309	0.0090	0.0015	0.0001
Random error	0.0581	0.0577	0.0659	0.0638
Total mean squared errors	0.0893	0.0667	0.0677	0.0640

Source: Lee *et al.* (1986, p. 600).

the overall mean squared errors together with the mean squared error decomposition.

Lee *et al.* (1986) note that for forecasts developed without the Bayesian adjustment, the accounting-based forecast is better, in terms of overall mean squared error. This advantage results entirely from inefficiency in the Mincer–Zarnowitz sense of the market-based forecast. By contrast, the Bayesian-adjusted market-based forecasts suffer far less from this problem and, as a result, the mean squared prediction error for Bayesian-adjusted

Table 9.4. Results for the Estimation of Market- and Accounting-Based Composite With and Without Bayesian Adjustment.

	Without Bayesian Adjustment $\hat{\beta}_{OLS}(2) = a + b_1\hat{\beta}^A_{OLS} + b_2\hat{\beta}_{OLS} + w$		
	Intercept	$\hat{\beta}^A_{OLS}$	$\hat{\beta}_{OLS}$
Coefficients	0.251	0.399	0.370
Standard errors	0.104	0.102	0.052
		MSE = 0.0545	
	With Bayesian Adjustment $\hat{\beta}_{OLS}(2) = a + b_1\hat{\beta}^A_V + b_2\hat{\beta}_V + w$		
	Intercept	$\hat{\beta}^A_V$	$\hat{\beta}_V$
Coefficients	−0.096	0.606	0.475
Standard errors	0.134	0.133	0.067
		MSE = 0.0530	

Source: Lee *et al.* (1986, p. 61).

market-based forecasts are only marginally larger than the accounting-based forecasts — 0.0667 compared to 0.0640.

Lee *et al.* (1986) tested a composite predictor for beta consisting of both a market beta and an accounting beta. Table 9.4 shows the results of using this composite method to forecast beta for both the Bayesian-adjusted and nonadjusted model. In Table 9.4, β_{OLS} (2) represents the OLS-estimated beta in the second period; β^A_{OLS} and $\hat{\beta}^A_V$ represent accounting-based beta without and with Bayesian adjustment, respectively. By comparing both MSE (market) of 0.893 and 0.0667 and MSE (accounting) of 0.0677 and 0.0640 with MSE (composite) of 0.0545 and 0.0530, respectively, it can be concluded that on the basis of mean squared error, the composite predictor outperforms either the market- or accounting-information predictor. Of the models used for the composite predictor, it appears that the Bayesian adjustment case is superior.

From research it appears, then, that accounting-based and market-based forecasts can be combined to produce a superior composite forecast of beta.

9.5. Some Applications and Implications of the CAPM

Since its development, the uses of the CAPM have extended into all areas of corporate finance and investments. The CAPM can be applied to two aspects of the capital-budgeting problem: (1) determining the cost of capital and (2) assessing the riskiness of a project under consideration. The CAPM can also be useful in a real-estate problem, deciding to lease or buy.

The use of the CAPM can be extended into valuation of the entire firm. Because of its impact upon firm valuation, the CAPM has been of great use in the merger-analysis area of financial analysis. The CAPM has also been used to test various financial theories. By including a dividend term and considering its effects, the CAPM can be used to test the effects of the firm's dividend policy. An area that has received a great deal of attention is the use of the CAPM in testing the efficient-market hypothesis.

An application of the CAPM to the capital-budgeting process concerns the valuation of risky projects. If accurate estimates can be made about the systematic risk of a project, then the CAPM can be used to determine the return necessary to compensate the firm for the project's risk. If the sum of the estimated cash flows discounted by the CAPM-calculated required rate of return is positive, then the firm should undertake the project.

Rubinstein (1973) demonstrates how the CAPM can be used to value securities and to calculate their risk-adjusted equilibrium price. First, the CAPM must be converted to using price variables instead of expected return. It may be rewritten:

$$E(R_i) = \frac{P_1 - P_0}{P_0},$$

where

R_i = the expected returns for the ith firms;
P_1 = the price of stock in time 1; and
P_0 = the price of stock in the previous period.

Thus, the CAPM is redefined:

$$\frac{E(P_1) - P_0}{P_0} = R_{f \cdot t} + [E(R_m) - R_f]\frac{\sigma_{im}}{\sigma_m^2}, \tag{9.22}$$

or, rearranging Equation (9.22):

$$P_0 = \frac{E(P_1)}{1 + R_f + [E(R_m) - R_f]\frac{\sigma_{im}}{\sigma_m^2}}.$$

Thus the rate of return used to discount the expected end-of-period price contains a risk premium dependent upon the security's systematic risk.

CAPM has also been applied in the analysis of mergers. It has been shown that the risks of a portfolio can be substantially reduced with the inclusion of securities that are not perfectly correlated in terms of returns. This principle also applies with respect to the mergers between firms. The merging of two firms with different product lines, called a *conglomerate merger*, creates diversification, considered of great benefit. Suppose that one firm sells a product that is recession resistant, then a decrease in earnings of one division of the conglomerate will be offset by the steady earnings of another division. The overall result will be a relatively stable income stream despite shifting trends in the economy.

9.6. Summary

This chapter has discussed the basic concepts of risk and diversification and how they pertain to the CAPM. The procedures for deriving the CAPM itself were presented, and the CAPM was shown to be an extension of the CML theory. The possible uses of the CAPM in financial management were also indicated.

The concept of beta and its importance to the financial manager was introduced. Beta represents the systematic risk of a firm and is a comparison measure between a particular firm's security or portfolio risk and the market average. Systematic risk was further discussed through an investigation of the beta coefficient and the impact of other important financial variables on the magnitude of the beta coefficient.

The statistical method of least squares and its application were introduced, and beta forecasts based on the least-squares method were compared with those based on market information, accounting information, and a composite-predictor beta forecast composed of both accounting and market information. The composite predictor appears to yield a better forecast than either the market-information or accounting-information forecasts separately.

Questions and Problems

1. What is the CML? What is the SML? What are the differences between the two? What is their relationship?
2. You are the insurance commissioner in the state of California. BBB Insurance Company's stock has a rate of return of 9%. BBB's executives argue that this is too low and that they should be granted a rate

increase. If the risk-free rate is 5%, the expected return on the NYSE is 9% and BBB's stock has a $\beta = 2$, would you grant the rate increase?

3. You are trying to decide whether to purchase the stock of ABC Company. To make this decision, you have the following information available to you:

$$\begin{aligned} \text{Current price} &= \$100 \\ \text{Expected price next year} &= \$105 \\ \text{Dividend paid next year} &= \$10 \\ R_f &= 5\% \\ E(R_m) &= 8\% \\ \beta_{\text{ABC}} &= 1.5 \end{aligned}$$

   Should you purchase ABC's stock?

4. You are given the following information about two correctly priced securities.

$$\begin{aligned} E(R_A) &= 7\% \quad \beta_A = 0.7 \\ E(R_B) &= 9\% \quad \beta_B = 1.3 \end{aligned}$$

   (a) Derive the equation for the SML.
   (b) Plot the SML.
   (c) If stock C has an expected return of 15% and a beta value of 2, is it correctly priced?

5. Define the market model. How can the parameters of a market model be estimated?
6. Explain how to derive the CAPM with the existence of borrowing and lending rates.
7. You are given the following equation for the standard CAPM.

$$E(R_j) = 0.07 + 0.12\beta_j$$

   (a) What is the risk-free rate?
   (b) What is the return on the market?
   (c) What is the market risk premium?

8. What is beta? Why is beta a better measure of risk than the standard deviation?
9. Briefly discuss some of Roll's (1977) criticisms regarding empirical tests of the CAPM. (See Appendix 9A.)

10. You are given the following information about Widget Company and the market.

$$\text{Cov}(R_w, R_m) = 0.003$$
$$\sigma_m = 2\%$$
$$E(R_m) = 9\%$$
$$R_f = 5\%$$

Calculate the expected return on Widget Company's stock.

11. Economists have tested the empirical CAPM.

$$R_i = R_f + \beta_i(R_m - R_f) + e_i$$

by estimating the equation

$$\bar{R}_i = a_0 + a_1 b_i + e_i$$

in which $\bar{R}_i = R_i - R_f$ and b_i = the estimate of β from the market model regression.

(a) What parameter estimates a_0 and a_1 would be consistent with the CAPM?
(b) Discuss briefly the results of some of these empirical tests.
(c) What are some of the econometric problems associated with these tests?

12. You are given the following information about stock A and the market.

$$E(R_m) = 10\% \qquad \sigma_m = 6\%$$
$$\sigma_A = 3\% \qquad \text{Cov}(R_A R_m) = 0.0048$$

Assume you can borrow or lend as much as you like at the risk-free rate of 5%. What is the systematic risk of stock A? Using the assumptions of the CAPM, find the expected return on A.

13. Discuss how the beta coefficient can be forecasted. How can accounting-based and composite-based models be used to forecast the beta coefficient?

Appendix 9A: Empirical Evidence for the Risk–Return Relationship

The validity of the CAPM can be borne out partly through observations of actual portfolios held in the marketplace. As discussed in Chapters 7 and 8, there exist two primary relationships between risk and return. First, the rates of return of efficient portfolios are linear functions of their riskiness as measured by their standard deviation. This is illustrated by the CML. Second, the rate of return of an individual asset is determined by its contribution of risk to the portfolio, and this is measured by beta, where beta has a linear relationship with the security's expected rate of return. This is illustrated by the SML.

The performance of mutual funds can be employed to test the explanatory powers of the linear relationship between risk and return of the CML. Mutual funds are professionally managed and therefore the most visible type of portfolio, easily used for comparison testing. One study was performed by Sharpe (1966) to test the performance of a fund and the relationship between its rate of return and risk over time. Sharpe computed average annual returns and the standard deviations of these returns for 34 mutual funds from 1954 to 1963. His model implies that portfolios with higher risks will receive higher returns. This Sharpe found to be true for all 34 funds. He calculated the correlation between average returns and their standard deviations to be 0.836, indicating that more than 80% of the difference in returns was due to differences in risk.

Sharpe also found that there was a linear relationship between returns and risks, except in the region of very high risks. Sharpe's study provides basic support to the contention that the CML explains the relationship between risk and return, both in portfolio theory and in the marketplace.

Another study was performed by Jensen (1969). He studied the correlation of beta coefficients (market sensitivity) and the expected return of mutual funds. On the basis of analysis of 115 mutual funds over a nine-year period he was able to conclude that high returns were associated with high volatility or high systematic risks. He also found evidence that beta coefficients are a valid and accurate measure of risk.

Both the Sharpe and Jensen studies on the risk and return of mutual funds show that an empirical risk-return relationship does exist among mutual funds. (However, Sharpe used the capital market line to perform his empirical tests, while Jensen used the SML, derived by Sharpe (1964).)

The second implication of the risk-return relationship is that the risk premium on individual assets depends on the contribution each makes to the riskiness of the entire portfolio.

The CAPM is a simple linear model expressed in terms of expected returns and expected risk. In its *ex-ante* form:

$$E(R_i) = R_f + [E(R_m) - R_f]\beta_i. \tag{9A.1}$$

Although many of the aforementioned extensions of the model support this simple linear form, others suggest that it may not be linear, that factors other than beta are needed to explain $E(R_i)$, or that the R_f is not the appropriate riskless rate.

The first step necessary to empirically test the theoretical CAPM is to transform it from expectations (*ex-ante*) form into a form that uses observed data. On average, the expected rate of return on an asset is equal to the realized rate of return. This can be written as

$$R_{it} = E(R_{it}) + \beta_i \delta_{mt} + e_{it},$$

where

$$\begin{aligned} \delta_{mt} &= R_{mt} - E(R_{mt}); \\ E(\delta_{mt}) &= 0; \\ e_{it} &= \text{a random error term}; \\ \text{Cov}(e_{it}, \delta_{mt}) &= 0; \\ \text{Cov}(e_{it}, e_{it-1}) &= 0; \quad \text{and} \\ \beta_{it} &= \text{Cov}(R_{it} R_{mt}) \text{Var}(R_{mt}). \end{aligned}$$

When CAPM is empirically tested it is usually written in the following form:

$$R'_{pt} = \gamma_0 + \gamma_1 \beta_p + e_{pt}, \tag{9A.2}$$

where

$$\begin{aligned} \gamma_1 &= \bar{R}_{mt} - \bar{R}_{ft} \\ R'_{pt} &= R_{pt} - R_{ft}. \end{aligned}$$

These relationships can be stated as follows.

(1) The intercept term γ_0 should not be significantly different from zero.
(2) Beta should be the only factor that explains the rate of return on a risky asset. If other terms, such as residual variance, dividend yields, P/E ratios, firm size, or beta squared are included in an attempt to explain return, they should have no explanatory power.
(3) The relationship should be linear in beta.
(4) The coefficient of beta, "II" should be equal to $\bar{R}_{mt} - \bar{R}_{ft}$.
(5) When the equation is estimated over very long periods of time, the rate of return on the market portfolio should be greater than the risk-free rate.

The work of Jensen (1972) provides a comprehensive and unifying review of the theoretical developments and the empirical work done in the field until that year. In his paper he points out that

> the main result of the original papers in this area is the demonstration that one can derive the individual's demand function for assets, aggregate these demands to obtain equilibrium prices (or expected returns) solely as a function of potentially measurable market parameters. Thus the model becomes testable.

Let us now summarize the empirical work of Douglas (1969), Black *et al.* (1972), and Fama and MacBeth (1973). The first published test of the CAPM was by Douglas (1969), who regressed the returns of a large cross-sectional sample of common stocks on their own variances and on their beta coefficients β_i obtained by market models. His results are in variance with the Sharpe–Lintner–Mossin (S–L–M) model, for he found that the return was positively related to the variance of the security but not the covariance with the index of returns.

Douglas also summarizes some of the work of Lintner (1965), who estimates beta from a typical market model. Douglas then adds a term for the standard deviation of error (proxy for unsystematic risk). He finds that the coefficient for the unsystematic risk is both positive and significant, the intercept term is higher than the appropriate risk-free rate, and the coefficient for the market risk premium is too low.

Black *et al.* observed that cross-sectional tests may not provide direct validation of the CAPM, and they proceeded to construct a time-series test, which they considered more powerful. Their results lead them to assert that the usual form of the CAPM does not provide an accurate description of the structure of security returns. Their results indicate that β s are nonzero and are directly related to the risk level. Low-beta securities earn significantly more on average than predicted by the model, and high-risk securities earn significantly less on average than predicted by the model. They go on to argue for a two-factor model:

$$R_{it} = (1 - \beta_i)R_{zt} + \beta_i(R_{mt}) + e_{it}. \tag{9A.3}$$

If $E(R_z) = 0$ then the S–L–M CAPM would be consistent with this model. However, the cross-sectional term for the intercept is a constant and not equal to zero. They then proceed to look for a rationale of this finding in Black's zero-beta model.

Fama and MacBeth (1973) tested (1) a linear relationship between return on the portfolio and the portfolio's beta and (2) whether unsystematic risk has an effect between portfolio return and a risk measure in addition to beta. Their basic estimation equation is:

$$\tilde{R}_{it} = \tilde{\gamma}_{0t} + \tilde{\gamma}_{1t}\bar{\beta}_i + \tilde{\gamma}_{2t}\bar{\beta}_i^2 + \tilde{\gamma}_{3t}\bar{\sigma}_i^2(\mu) + \tilde{e}_{it}, \tag{9A.4}$$

in which $\tilde{\gamma}_{0t}$ is the intercept term, $\bar{\beta}_i$ is the average of the β_i for all individual securities in portfolio i, and $\bar{\sigma}_i(\mu)$ is the average of the residual standard deviations from all securities in portfolio j.

Although they found that there are variables in addition to the portfolio beta that systematically affect period-by-period returns (which are apparently related to the average squared beta of the portfolio and the risk factor other than beta), they dismissed the latter as "almost surely proxies," since "there is no rationale for their presence in our stochastic risk–return model." Their results seem to suggest that the S–L–M model does not hold. The intercept factor, $\tilde{\gamma}_{0t}$ is generally greater than R_F, and $\tilde{\gamma}_{1t}$ is substantially less than $\bar{R}_m - \bar{R}_f$. This seems to indicate that the zero-beta model is more consistent with the data.

Blume and Husick (1973) found empirical evidence to indicate that historical rates of return may sometimes foreshadow changes in future betas, and that stocks with higher transaction costs should yield somewhat higher gross expected returns. Their data indicate that beta is not stationary over time, that it does change over time as a function of price. Transaction-cost effects appear less important than the informational effects of price in explaining future returns or future betas. Therefore, the return-generating process may be more complex than what has been assumed.

Blume and Friend (1973) examine both theoretically and empirically the reasons why the CAPM does not adequately explain differential returns on financial assets. Empirically the risk–return tradeoffs implied by stocks on the New York Stock Exchange for three different periods after World War II casted doubt on the validity of the CAPM either in its S–L–M form or zero-beta form. However, they do confirm the linearity of the relationship for NYSE stocks.

Rosenberg and McKibben (1973) observed that predictions of the riskiness of returns on common stocks can be based on fundamental accounting data for the firm and also on the previous history of stock prices. This paper tries to combine both sources of information to provide efficient predictions. A stochastic model of the parameters is built and the mean squared error is used as a criterion for the evaluation of the forecasting performance of estimators. They concluded that the results "strongly confirm the usefulness of the specific risk predictions based on the accounting descriptors."

Merton (1980) is concerned with the estimation of the expected return on the market. He notes that the current practice for estimating the expected market return adds the historical average realized excess market returns to the current observed interest rate. However, while this model explicitly reflects the dependence of the market return on the interest rate, it fails to account for the effects of changes in the level of market risk. Three models of equilibrium-expected market returns are elaborated, and estimation procedures that incorporate the prior restriction that equilibrium-expected excess returns on the market must be positive are derived and applied to return data for the period 1926–1978. The following are the principal conclusions of the study.

(1) The non-negativity restriction above should be explicitly included as part of the specifications.
(2) Estimators that use realized returns should be adjusted for heteroskedasticity.

Roll (1977) directs an attack on the empirical tests of the CAPM. Although recognizing that the theory is testable in principle, he asserts that "no correct and unambiguous test to the theory [has] appeared in the literature and there is practically no possibility that such a test can be accomplished in the future." This conclusion is derived from the mathematical equivalence between the individual return beta linearity and the market portfolio's mean variance efficiency. Therefore, any valid test presupposes complete knowledge of the market portfolio's composition. The major results reported by Roll from his theoretical inquiry include:

(1) The only testable hypothesis is that the market portfolio is mean-variance efficient.
(2) All other so-called implications of the CAPM are not independently testable.
(3) In any sample, there will always be an infinite number of *ex post* mean-variance efficient portfolios; betas calculated will satisfy the linearity relation exactly, whether or not the true market portfolio is mean-variance efficient.
(4) The theory is not testable unless the exact composition of the true market portfolio is known and used in the tests.

(5) Using a proxy for the market portfolio does not solve the problem, for the proxy itself might be mean-variance efficient even when the true market portfolio is not, and conversely.
(6) Empirical tests that reject the S–L–M model have results fully compatible with the S–L–M model and a specification error in the measured market portfolio.
(7) If the selected index is mean-variance efficient, then the betas of all assets are related to their mean returns by the same linear function (all assets and portfolios fall exactly on the SML).
(8) For every ranking of performances obtained with a mean-variance inefficient index, there exists another nonefficient index that reverses the ranking.

Roll's critique is a broad indictment of most of the accepted empirical evidence concerning the CAPM theory.

9A.1. Anomalies in the Semi-Strong Efficient-Market Hypothesis

Three anomalies in the semi-strong efficient-market hypothesis are noteworthy. Four authors — Basu, Banz, Reinganum, and Keirn — deal with these three anomalies: (1) P/E ratios; (2) size effects; and (3) the January effect.

Basu (1977) empirically notes that a firm with a low P/E ratio, when adjusted for risk, has an excess return over firms that have a high P/E ratio. If this is true, then there are implications for the market's efficiency, the validity of the CAPM, or both. However, Basu found that the excess returns, when adjusted for transaction costs, taxes, and so forth, were so much smaller as to be insignificant. Therefore, CAPM and market efficiency were supported. In conjecturing why a difference in P/E ratios could affect the returns of the firm, we believe that the relationship may involve the firm's ability to raise debt. A low P/E ratio may indicate more difficulty in raising capital than a high P/E ratio. This difficulty in raising capital could result in different lending and borrowing rates for different firms. Therefore, a Brennan version of the standard CAPM pricing model may be more applicable. Or the APT model (see Chapter 11) may be more appropriate in pricing the assets where one of the factors involved captures the P/E effect.

Reinganum (1981) also empirically tests the P/E effect and finds the same results as Basu. In addition, Reinganum was concerned with the efficiency of the market. In order to see if the market was informationally efficient, Reinganum also looked at returns of firms with neither high nor low P/E ratios. He found these firms to be correctly priced. From these results he conjectures that the market was informationally efficient, but CAPM did not allow for the P/E effect on returns. Therefore an APT model with the P/E effect as one of its factors would be preferable to the CAPM model.

Banz (1981) empirically tests the effect of firm size, finding that small-company stock returns were higher than large-company stock returns. Banz argues that the P/E ratio serves as a proxy for the size of a firm and not vice versa. His conjecture about why this anomaly exists centers around informational distribution. A small firm's information distribution is somewhat limited, which causes investors to be wary of buying the stock and depresses the price. Banz suggests that the APT valuation model may be more robust than the CAPM in that the APT would be able to capture the size effect by using a P/E ratio as a proxy for the size effect as a factor in the model. Since the distribution of information affects a firm's ability to raise capital (less information on a firm may cause a firm to pay a premium for capital), the premium would indicate that the lending and borrowing rates of different firms are not the same. A valuation model capturing different lending and borrowing rates was provided by Brennan (1971). The utilization of this model could be implemented where rates differed for large and small firms. If small firms do not borrow in the capital market, then Black's no-borrowing CAPM would be more suitable than the standard CAPM.

Keim (1983) empirically tests one of the most baffling anomalies, the January effect. He found that for stocks with excess returns, over 50% of these excess returns were realized in January. In addition, 50% of the January excess return occurs in the first week of January. This phenomenon of excess returns occurring in the month following the tax-year end has been found empirically in Great Britain also. Although Keim offers no rationale for this phenomenon, others have tried to find tax reasons for this anomaly. The selling of assets in January rather than December to postpone capital gains taxes to the next taxable year has been one suggested rationale. Unlike the P/E and size effects, this anomaly does not have a clear proxy that could be utilized as a factor in an APT model. CAPM does not capture the effect well, and without any theoretical or economical rationale for this effect, any valuation model would be hard pressed to account for it.

Many of the authors seem to conclude that the standard CAPM is not working well, and that alternative valuation models should be considered to capture these anomalies. This might imply that security analysis and portfolio management techniques can be used to beat the market.

Bibliography

Banz, R. W. "The Relationship between Return and Market Value of Common Stocks." *Journal of Financial Economics*, v. 9 (March 1981), pp. 3–18.

Basu, S. "Investment Performance of Common Stocks in Relation to Their Price-Earnings Ratios: A Test of the Efficient Markets Hypothesis." *Journal of Finance*, v. 32 (June 1977), pp. 663–682.

Beaver, W., P. Kettler and M. Scholes. "The Association between Market Determined and Accounting Determined Risk Measures." *Accounting Review*, v. 45 (October 1970), pp. 654–682.

Black, F., M. C. Jensen and M. Scholes. "The Capital Asset Pricing Model: Some Empirical Tests," in M. C. Jensen (ed.), *Studies in the Theory of Capital Markets*, pp. 20–46. New York: Praeger, 1972.

Blume, M. E. "On the Assessment of Risk." *Journal of Finance*, v. 26 (March 1971), pp. 1–10.

Blume, M. E. and I. Friend. "A New Look at the Capital Asset Pricing Model." *Journal of Finance*, v. 28 (March 1973), pp. 19–34.

Blume, M. E. and F. Husick. "Price, Beta, and Exchange Listing." *Journal of Finance*, v. 28 (March 1973), pp. 283–299.

Brennan, M. J. "Capital Market Equilibrium with Divergent Borrowing and Lending Rate." *Journal of Financial and Quantitative Analysis*, v. 7 (December 1971), pp. 1197–1205.

Douglas, G. W. "Risk in the Equity Markets: An Empirical Appraisal of Market Efficiency." *Yale Economic Essays*, v. 9 (Spring 1969), pp. 3–45.

Elton, E. J., M. J. Gruber, S. J. Brown and W. N. Goetzmann. *Modern Portfolio Theory and Investment Analysis*, 7th ed. New York: John Wiley & Sons, 2006.

Fabozzi, F. J. and J. C. Francis. "Beta as a Random Coefficient." *Journal of Financial and Quantitative Analysis*, v. 13 (March 1978), pp. 101–116.

Fama, E. F. "Risk, Return and Equilibrium: Some Clarifying Comments." *Journal of Finance*, v. 23 (March 1968), pp. 29–40.

Fama, E. F. and J. MacBeth. "Risk, Return and Equilibrium: Empirical Tests." *Journal of Political Economy*, v. 31 (May–June 1973), pp. 607–636.

Francis, J. C. *Investments: Analysis and Management*, 4th ed. New York, NY: McGraw-Hill Book Company, 1986.

Higgins, R. C. *Analysis for Financial Management*, 9th ed. New York, NY: McGraw-Hill, Inc, 2008.

Higgins, R. C. "How Much Growth Can a Firm Afford?" *Financial Management*, v. 6 (1977), pp. 7–16.

Higgins, R. C. "Sustainable Growth under Inflation." *Financial Management*, v. 10 (1981), pp. 36–40.

Jensen, M. C. "Capital Markets: Theory and Evidence." *The Bell Journal of Economic and Management Science*, v. 3 (Autumn 1972), pp. 357–398.

Jensen, M. C. "Risk, the Pricing of Capital Assets, and the Evaluation of Investment Portfolio." *Journal of Business*, v. 42 (April 1969), pp. 607–636.

Keim, D. B. "Size-Related Anomalies and Stock Return Seasonality: Further Empirical Evidence." *Journal of Financial Economics*, v. 11 (June 1983), pp. 13–32.

Lee, A. C., J. C. Lee and C. F. Lee. *Financial Analysis and Planning and Forecasting: Theory and Application.* Singapore: World Scientific, 2009.

Lee, C. F., A. C. Lee andJ. C. Lee . *Handbook of Quantitative Finance and Risk Management.* New York: Springer, 2010.

Lee, C. F. and S. N. Chen. "A Random Coefficient Model for Reexamining Risk Decomposition Method and Risk-Return Relationship Test." *Quarterly Review of Economics and Business*, v. 20 (March 1980), pp. 58–69.

Lee, C. F., M. C. Gupta, H. Y. Chen and A. C. Lee. "Optimal Payout Ratio under Uncertainty and the Flexibility Hypothesis: Theory and Empirical Evidence" *Journal of Corporate Finance* v. 17 (June 2011), pp. 483–501.

Lee, C. F., P. Newbold, J. E. Finnerty and C. C. Chu. "On Accounting-Based, Market-Based and Composite-Based Beta Predictions: Methods and Implications." *The Financial Review*, v. 21 (February 1986), pp. 51–68.

Lintner, J. "The Valuation of Risk Assets and the Selection of Risky Investments in Stock Portfolios and Capital Budgets." *Review of Economics and Statistics*, v. 47 (February 1965), pp. 13–37.

Merton, R. C. "On Estimating the Expected Return on the Market, an Exploratory Investigation." *Journal of Financial Economics*, v. 8 (December 1980), pp. 323–361.

Miller, M. and M. Scholes. "Rates of Return in Relation to Risk: A Reexamination of Some Recent Findings," in in M. C. Jensen (ed.), *Studies in the Theory of Capital Markets*, pp. 47–78. New York, NY: Praeger, 1972.

Mincer, J. and V. Zarnowitz. "The Evaluation of Economic Forecasts," in J. Mincer (ed.), *Economic Forecasts and Expectations.* New York, NY: National Bureau of Economic Research, 1969, pp. 1–46.

Mossin, J. "Equilibrium in a Capital Asset Market." *Econometria*, v. 34 (October 1966), pp. 768–873.

Reinganum, M. R. "Misspecification of Capital Asset Pricing: Empirical Anomalies Based on Earnings Yields and Market Values." *Journal of Financial Economics*, v. 8 (March 1981), pp. 19–46.

Roll, R. "Ambiguity When Performance is Measured by the Securities Market Line." *Journal of Finance*, v. 33 (September 1978), pp. 1051–1069.

Roll, R. "A Critique of the Asset Pricing Theory's Tests-Part I: On Past and Potential Testability of the Theory." *Journal of Financial Economics*, v. 4 (March l977), pp. 129–176.

Rosenberg, B. and V. Marathe. "Tests of the Capital Asset Pricing Hypothesis." Working Paper No. 32 of the Research Program in France. Graduate School of Business and Public Administration, University of California, Berkeley, May 1975.

Rosenberg, B. and W. McKibben. "The Prediction of Systematic and Specific Risk in Common Stocks." *Journal of Finance and Quantitative Analysis*, v. 8 (March 1973), pp. 317–333.

Rubinstein, M. E. "A Mean-Variance Synthesis of Corporate Financial Theory." *Journal of Finance*, v. 28 (March 1973), pp. 167–168.

Sharpe, W. "Capital Asset Prices: A Theory of Market Equilibrium under Conditions of Risk." *Journal of Finance*, v. 19 (September 1964), pp. 425–442.

Sharpe, W. "Mutual Fund Performance." *Journal of Business*, v. 39 (January 1966), pp. 119–138.

Sunder, S. "Stationarity of Market Risk: Random Coefficients Tests for Individual Stocks." *Journal of Finance*, v. 35 (September 1980), pp. 883–896.

Vasicek, O. A. "A Note on Using Cross-Sectional Information in Bayesian Estimation of Security Betas." *Journal of Finance*, v. 28 (December 1973), pp. 1233–1239.

Chapter 10

Index Models for Portfolio Selection

Chapter 8 presented and discussed the Markowitz model for delineating the efficient frontier. Numerous examples were shown that indicated the potentially crushing number of computations resulting from the calculations for even a three-security portfolio. This chapter offers some simplifying assumptions that reduce the overall number of calculations through the use of the Sharpe single-index and multiple-index models.

The essential difference between the single- and multiple-index models is the assumption that the single-index model explains the return of a security or a portfolio with only the market. The multiple-index model (MIM) describes portfolio returns through the use of more than one index. The investor may quantify the return on a portfolio by seeking an index that is representative of the market together with indexes that are representative of the industries of which the component securities are members or exhibit some other common factor. More is said about the MIM later in the chapter; for now the single-index model is the focus of discussion.

10.1. The Single-Index Model

The major simplifying assumption that yields the index model from Markowitz's portfolio theory is that covariances between individual securities contained in the portfolio are zero. This assumption greatly reduces the number of calculations needed to find the set of efficient portfolios. The use of the index model necessitates additional statistical estimates for the parameters of the index; nevertheless, these additions are minor in comparison to the reduction in the calculation load as a result of ignoring the covariance terms between securities.

Suggested by Markowitz (1959), the **single-index model** was fully developed by Sharpe (1970), who assumed that the covariances could be overlooked. The return of an individual security was tied to two factors — a random effect and the performance of some underlying market index. Notationally:

$$R_{it} = a_i + b_i R_{It} + e_{it}, \tag{10.1}$$

where

a_i and b_i = regression parameters for the ith firm;
R_{It} = the tth return of some underlying market index;
R_{it} = the tth return on security i; and
e_{it} = the tth random effect for the ith security.

Equation (10.1) is the market model as discussed in the last chapter. This regression makes several assumptions about the random effect term.

(1) The expected value of the tth random effect for security i is zero. More explicitly, $E(e_{it}) = 0$.
(2) The variance of the error terms is constant. This amounts to the assumption that the errors are homoscedastic.
(3) There is no relationship between the errors and the return on the market: $\mathrm{Cov}(e_{if}, R_{It}) = 0$.
(4) The random effects are not serially correlated: $E(e_{it}, e_{it+n}) = 0$.
(5) The ith security's random effect is unrelated to any other random effects of any other security: $E(e_{it}, e_{jt}) = 0$.

The fifth assumption guarantees that the regression coefficients a_i and b_i are the best unbiased linear estimators of the true parameters.

An investigation of some of the results of the previous assumptions is in order. The expected value of the return on security i is equal to the sum of the intercept, the adjusted return on the index, and some random effect. This can be expressed as

$$\begin{aligned} E(R_i) &= E(a_i + b_i R_{It} + e_{it}) \\ &= E(a_i) + E(b_i R_{It}) + E(e_{it}). \end{aligned} \tag{10.2}$$

Because a_i and b_i are constants, and $E(e_{it})$ is equal to zero:

$$r_i = E(R_i) = a_i + b_i r_I, \tag{10.3}$$

where r_I is equal to the mean of the returns on the market index.

If the mean of the returns on security i equals r_i then the variance of security i is equal to the expected value of squared deviations from r_{it}. This translates to

$$\begin{aligned}\sigma_i^2 &= E(R_{it} - r_i)^2 \\ &= E[(a_i + b_i R_{It} + e_{it}) - (a_i + b_i r_I)]^2 \\ &= E[b_i(R_{It} - r_I) + e_{it}]^2 \\ &= b_i^2 E(R_{It} - r_I)^2 + 2b_i E[e_{it}(R_{It} - r_I)] + E(e_{it})^2.\end{aligned} \tag{10.4}$$

By the third assumption, the covariance of the random effect and the deviation of the index return from its mean are zero; also, the expected value of the squared errors is equal to the variance of the random effect. Thus:

$$\begin{aligned}\sigma_i^2 &= b_i^2 E(R_{It} - r_I)^2 + E(e_{it})^2 \\ &= b_i^2 \sigma_I^2 + \sigma_{ei}^2.\end{aligned} \tag{10.5}$$

This is equivalent to saying that the variance of the returns on a security is made of some adjusted quantity of the variance of the market (usually referred to as systematic risk) plus the variance of the random effects exclusive to that particular security (unsystematic risk).

The last result to be investigated from these assumptions involves a minor step into abstraction in which the possibility of interaction between two securities and the market index is considered. It is suggested that because variations in the returns of two different securities are not interrelated but only connected to the market index, the covariance between the two securities can be derived from the twice-adjusted variance of the market index (once by the b coefficient of the first security with the market and again by the b coefficient of the second security with the market). The investigation starts with a statement about the covariance of the two securities:

$$\begin{aligned}\sigma_{ij} &= E[(R_{it} - r_i)(R_{jt} - r_j)] \\ &= E[((a_i + b_i R_{It} + e_{it})(a_i + b_i r_I)) \\ &\quad \times ((a_j + b_j R_{It} + e_{jt})(a_j + b_j r_I)] \\ &= E[(b_i(R_{It} - r_I) + e_{it}) \times (b_j(R_{It} - r_I) + e_{jt})] \\ &= b_i b_j E(R_{It} - r_I)^2 + b_i E(e_{jt}(R_{It} - r_I)) \\ &\quad + b_j E(e_{it}(R_{It} - r_I)) + E(e_{it}e_{jt}).\end{aligned} \tag{10.6}$$

Since according to the third and fourth assumptions the last three terms of the last summation are equal to zero:

$$\sigma_{ij} = b_i b_j \sigma_I^2. \tag{10.7}$$

The number of calculations necessary to utilize the Markowitz model is $N + (N^2 - N)/2$, as shown in Chapter 8. For a portfolio with a hundred securities, this translates to 5,050 calculations. With the Sharpe single-index model, only 100 estimates are needed for the various security-regression coefficients and only one variance calculation, the variance of the returns on the market. In addition, 100 estimates of the unsystematic risk σ_{ei}^2 are also needed for the single-index model. Hence, the single-index model has dramatically reduced the input information needed.[1]

10.1.1. *Deriving the Single-Index Model*

So far only the Sharpe single-index model has been utilized to study the returns of a single security i as determined by its relation to the returns on a market index.

10.1.1.1. Expected Return of a Portfolio

Now consider the return of a portfolio of n securities. The return of a portfolio of n securities is the weighted summation of the individual returns of the component securities. Notationally:

$$E(R_{pt}) = \sum_{i=1}^{n} x_i E(R_i),$$

where Rpt is the rate of return for a portfolio in period t and X_i is the weight associated with the ith security.

$$R_{it} = a_i + b_i R_{It} + e_{it}$$

$$\begin{aligned} R_{pt} &= \sum_{i=1}^{n} x_i(a_i + b_i R_{It} + e_{it}) \\ &= \sum_{i=1}^{n} x_i(a_i + e_{it}) + \sum_{i=1}^{n} x_i(b_i R_{It}) \qquad (10.8a) \\ &= \sum_{i=1}^{n} x_i a_i + \sum_{i=1}^{n} (x_i b_i)(R_{It}) + \sum_{i=1}^{n} x_i e_{it}. \end{aligned}$$

[1]Discussion of the single-index model adapted in part from Sharpe (1970). Adapted with permission.

Thus,

$$E(R_{pt}) = \sum_{i=1}^{n} x_i a_i + \sum_{i=1}^{n} (x_i b_i) E(R_{It}). \tag{10.8b}$$

This equation indicates that the return of a portfolio may be decomposed into the summation of the weighted returns peculiar to the individual securities and the summation of the weighted adjusted return on the market index. Thus the portfolio may be viewed as a combination of n basic securities and a weighted adjusted return from an investment in the market index.

10.1.1.2. Variance of a Portfolio

To derive the variance of the portfolio σ_p^2, consider first that the mean return of the portfolio is equal to the expected value of the return on the portfolio. Then, following the definition of σ_p^2 in Chapter 7 and Equations (10.5) and (10.7), we obtain:

$$\begin{aligned}\sigma_p^2 &= E[(R_{pt} - E(R_{pt}))^2] \\ &= \sum_{i=1}^{n} x_i^2 \sigma_{ei}^2 + \sum_{i=1}^{n}\sum_{j=1}^{n} x_i x_j b_i b_j \sigma_I^2 \\ &= \left[\sum_{i=1}^{n} x_i b_i\right]\left[\sum_{j=1}^{n} x_j b_j\right]\sigma_i^2 + \sum_{i=1}^{n} x_i^2 \sigma_{ei}^2.\end{aligned} \tag{10.9}$$

Because the weighted sum of the b_i coefficients is equal to the coefficient of the portfolio $\sum_{i=1}^{n} x_i b_i = b_p$, similarly $\sum_{j=1}^{n} x_j b_j = b_p$. Hence, the last equation reduces to

$$\sigma_p^2 = b_p^2 \sigma_I^2 + \sum_{i=1}^{n} x_i^2 \sigma_{ei}^2. \tag{10.10}$$

It was shown in Chapter 8 that when the number of component securities in a portfolio approaches 15, the unique risk of the component securities is reduced through diversification. In Equation (10.10), the last term, the weighted sum of the random effect variances, approaches zero as n increases. So again, as the number of securities increases, the unsystematic risk is reduced and the remaining risk of the portfolio is the adjusted variance of the market index. Sample Problem 10.1 further illustrates this concept.

Sample Problem 10.1

Given the following information, what should the β of the portfolio (b_p) be?

$$\sigma_p^2 = 0.082 \quad \sigma_I^2 = 0.021 \quad \sum_{i=1}^{n} x_i^2 \sigma_{ei}^2 = 0.04$$

Solution

Substituting related information into Equation (10.10):

$$\begin{aligned} b_p^2 &= \frac{\sigma_p^2 - \sum_{i=1}^{n} x_i^2 \sigma_{ei}^2}{\sigma_p^2} \\ &= \frac{0.082 - 0.04}{0.021} \\ &= 2.0. \end{aligned}$$

Therefore, $b_p = 1.414$.

Equation (10.8b) implies that the portfolio can be viewed as an investment in n basic securities and a weighted adjusted return in the market, or

$$\sum_{i=1}^{n} (x_i b_i) E(R_{It}).$$

The return on the market can be decomposed as a combination of the expected return plus some random effect. When this random effect is positive, the atmosphere is bullish and when it is negative, the atmosphere is bearish. Notationally:

$$\begin{aligned} R_{It} &= E(R_{It}) + e_{n+1,t} \\ &= a_{n+1} + e_{n+1,t}. \end{aligned} \tag{10.11}$$

This bit of algebraic maneuvering enables the weighted adjusted investment in the market to be viewed as an investment in an artificial security, the $(n+1)$th of an n-security portfolio. The weight for this $(n+l)$th security is the sum of the n weights multiplied by their respective related coefficients to the market index. Thus:

$$x_{n+1} = \sum_{i=1}^{n} x_i b_i. \tag{10.12}$$

The reason for this divergence in notation resulting in the definition of the $(n + l)$th security's return and weight is that Equation (10.8) can be simplified to yield a working model for portfolio analysis. Substituting the last results for X_{n+1} and R_{It} into Equation (10.8B) yields:

$$\begin{aligned} R_{pt} &= \sum_{i=1}^{n} x_i(a_i + e_{it}) + x_{n+1}(a_{n+1} + e_{n+1,t}) \\ &= \sum_{i=1}^{n+1} x_i(a_i + e_{it}). \end{aligned} \tag{10.13}$$

Because the expected value of the random-effect terms is zero, the summation that results after the application of the expectations operator can be expressed as

$$\begin{aligned} E(R_{pt}) &= \sum_{i=1}^{n} x_i a_i + x_{n+1} E(R_{It}) \\ &= \sum_{i=1}^{n+1} x_i a_i. \end{aligned} \tag{10.14}$$

This yields a formula for the return of a portfolio that is easily applied to portfolio analysis. Before proceeding, however, it is necessary to simplify the variance formula so that it may be used as well.

Remembering that the variance of the portfolio is the expected value of the squared deviations from the expected market return, the last results concerning R_{pt} and $E(R_{pt})$ may be applied:

$$\begin{aligned} \mathrm{Var}(R_{pt}) &= E\left\{\left[\sum_{i=1}^{n+1} x_i(a_i + e_{it})\right] - E\left[\sum_{i=1}^{n+1} x_i(a_i + e_{it})\right]\right\}^2 \\ &= E\left\{\left[\sum_{i=1}^{n+1} x_i(a_i + e_{it})\right] - \sum_{i=1}^{n+1} x_i[E(a_i) + E(e_{it})]\right\}^2 \\ &= E\left\{\left[\sum_{i=1}^{n+1} x_i\,(a_i + e_{it})\right] - \sum_{i=1}^{n+1} x_i E(a_i)\right\}^2 \\ &= E\left(\sum_{i=1}^{n+1} x_i e_{it}\right)^2 \\ &= \mathrm{Var}\left(\sum_{i=1}^{n+1} x_i e_{it}\right). \end{aligned} \tag{10.15}$$

Table 10.1. Single Index Model.

R_{It}	R_{it}	α_i	$\beta_i R_{It}$	e_i
4	12	2	8	$12 - 2 - 8 = 2$
6	14	2	12	$14 - 2 - 12 = 0$
10	20	2	20	$20 - 2 - 20 = -2$
8	18	2	16	$18 - 2 - 16 = 0$
28	64	8	56	0

This result follows from the assumption that the covariances are equal to zero. Additionally, each variance term is only a weighted sum of the errors around the market return. The direct usefulness of the last two conclusions will become apparent when solving for the security weights. Sample Problem 10.2 provides further illustration.

Sample Problem 10.2

Given R_{It}, R_{it}, and α_i as indicated in Table 10.1 and the fact that $\sum_{t=1}^{n} \beta_i R_{It} = 56$, using the relationship

$$\sum_{t=1}^{n} R_{It} = n\alpha_i + \sum_{t=1}^{n} \beta_i R_{It} + \sum_{t=1}^{n} e_{it},$$

find the values for α_i, β_i, and e_i.

Solution

$$\sum_{t=1}^{n} R_{It} = 28, \quad \text{so } \beta_i = \frac{\sum_{t=1}^{n} \beta_i R_{It}}{\sum_{t=1}^{n} R_{It}}$$
$$= \frac{56}{28}$$
$$= 2.$$

Substitute the values $\sum_{t=1}^{n} R_{It} = 64$, $\sum_{t=1}^{n} \beta_i R_{It} = 56$, $n = 4$ into the regression line

$$\sum_{t=1}^{n} R_{It} = n\alpha_i + \sum_{t=1}^{n} \beta_i R_{It} + \sum_{t=1}^{n} e_{it}$$

and solve for α_i.

The $\beta_i R_{It}$ column in Table 10.1 is filled by simply multiplying $\beta(=2)$ by the R_{It} column. The e_i's are the amounts such that $R_{it} = \alpha + \beta_i R_{mt} + e_{it}$ is an equality, so $R_{it} = \alpha_i + \beta_i R_{It} + e_{it}$ is satisfied. From the last column of the table we know that $\sum_{i=1}^{n} e_{it} = 0$. Therefore

$$\alpha_i = \frac{64 - 56 + 0}{4} = 2.$$

In this section, the expected return $E(R_{pt})$ and the variance of a portfolio $\mathrm{Var}(R_{pt})$ in terms of the single-index model has been derived. In the following section, the optimal portfolio selection procedures discussed in Chapter 8 are used to explore the single-index optimum-portfolio selection model.

10.1.2. *Portfolio Analysis and the Single-Index Model*

Before beginning the portfolio analysis using the single-index model, it is necessary to explain a derivation of security weights through the use of the Lagrangian calculus maximization discussed in Chapter 8. The maximization procedure maximizes a linear combination of the following two equations[2]:

$$\begin{aligned} \text{Max } E(R_p) &= \sum_{i=1}^{n+1} E(R_i) \quad \text{or} \\ -\mathrm{Var}(R_p) &= -\mathrm{Var}\left(\sum_{i=1}^{n+1} x_i e_{it}\right) \end{aligned} \tag{10.16a}$$

$$\text{subject to } \sum_{i=1}^{n+1} x_i = 1 \quad \text{and} \quad x_{n+1} = \sum_{i=1}^{n} x_i b_i. \tag{10.16b}$$

The first constraint is equivalent to requiring that the sum of the weights of the component securities is equal to one. The second constraint requires that the weight of the market index within the portfolio returns is equal to the summation of the weighted adjustment factors of the component securities. This requirement is as described in Equation (10.16b).

[2]The maximization of the negative of the variance is equivalent to the minimization of the variance itself. This can be viewed as originating from the negative spectrum of the number line and maximizing toward zero.

Combining the above two objective functions with the two constraints yields a Lagrangian function:

$$P = \Phi E(R_p) - \text{Var}(R_p) + \lambda_1 \left(\sum_{i=1}^{n} x_i - 1 \right) + \lambda_2 \left(\sum_{i=1}^{n} x_i b_i - x_{n+1} \right)$$

$$= \Phi \sum_{i=1}^{n+1} x_i a_i - \sum_{i=1}^{n+1} \text{Var}(e_{it}) + \lambda_1 \left(\sum_{i=1}^{n} x_i - 1 \right) + \lambda_2 \left(\sum_{i=1}^{n} x_i b_i - x_{n+1} \right). \tag{10.16c}$$

The only difference between this maximization function and the minimization shown in Chapter 8, beyond intent, is that instead of fixing some arbitrary value of return needed (E^*), an attempt can be made to quantify the level of risk aversion that the investors of the portfolio require, thereby placing the portfolio on the efficient frontier not by desired return but by level of utility, as discussed in Chapter 8. This coefficient of risk aversion is denoted by the Greek letter Φ (*Phi*). When low values are exhibited, risk aversion is pronounced; when high values are in evidence, substantial risk taking is allowed. This notion of the level of risk aversion is best pictured in Fig. 10.1. In Fig. 10.1, A represents an investor's objective function to minimize the risk only — therefore, the aggressiveness to return is zero; C represents an investor's objective function to maximize returns only — therefore, the aggressiveness to return is infinite. At B an investor's attitude toward return and risk is between A and C.

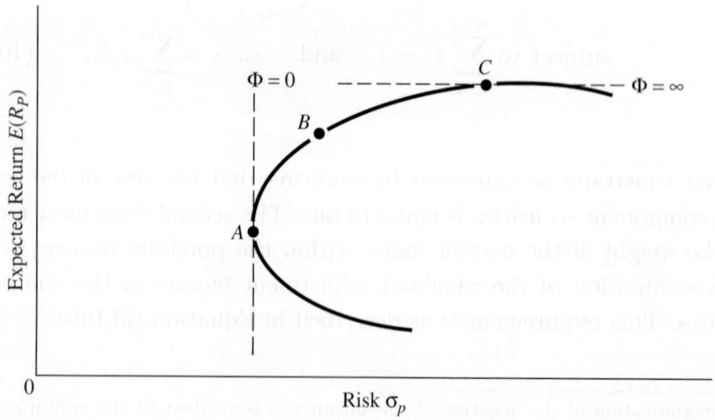

Fig. 10.1. Level of Risk Aversion and Investors' Investment Attitude.

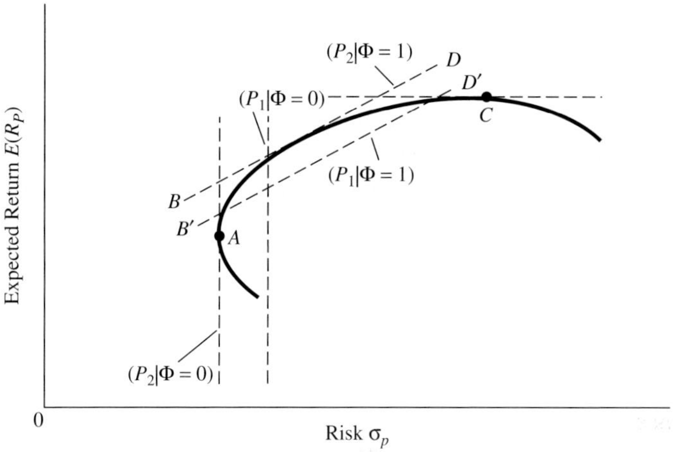

Fig. 10.2. Level of Risk Aversion and Objective Function.

Figure 10.2 provides further illustration of the approach being utilized. What is depicted is the variation of the objective function P as the parameter denoting risk is varied. Again, notice that the risk–return relation for a low Φ is lower than that for the more risk-taking, high value of Φ. Points A and C are as discussed for Fig. 10.1. Lines BD and $B'D'$ represent the objective function when the risk-aversion parameter is equal to one. Note that BD instead of $B'D'$ represents the maximization of the objective function. In sum, different values of Φ generate different optimal objective functions.

Consider now the three-security portfolio. In this framework, the preceding objective function expands to

$$\begin{aligned} P = {} & \Phi x_1 a_1 + \Phi x_2 a_2 + \Phi x_3 a_3 + \Phi x_4 a_4 - x_1^2 \mathrm{Var}(e_{1t}) \\ & - x_2^2 \mathrm{Var}(e_{2t}) - x_3^2 \mathrm{Var}(e_{3t}) - x_4^2 \mathrm{Var}(e_{4t}) + \lambda_1 x_1 + \lambda_1 x_2 \\ & + \lambda_1 x_3 - \lambda_1 + \lambda_2 x_1 b_1 + \lambda_2 x_2 b_2 + \lambda_2 x_3 b_3 - \lambda_2 x_4. \end{aligned} \tag{10.17}$$

Take note of all terms in the preceding equation that contain a_4 and x_4. By utilizing the relations of the individual securities to the market, it has been possible to delete most of the calculations necessitated by the full Markowitz variance–covariance model. The return that will be generated from an optimal portfolio derived through this maximization rests on the estimation of the future expected return and variance of the index. This will lead to the availability of ranging analysis for these estimations, which will produce robust estimates for the security weights highlighted at the end of this section.

To proceed with the Lagrangian maximization it is necessary to notice that the above equation has six unknowns — the four weights and the two Lagrangian coefficients. All other values are expected to be known or estimated. To maximize, the partial derivative of the objective function is taken with respect to each of the six variables:

$$\begin{aligned}
\frac{\partial P}{\partial x_1} &= \Phi a_1 - 2x_1\sigma_1^2 + \lambda_1 + \lambda_2 b_1 = 0\\
\frac{\partial P}{\partial x_2} &= \Phi a_2 - 2x_2\sigma_2^2 + \lambda_1 + \lambda_2 b_2 = 0\\
\frac{\partial P}{\partial x_3} &= \Phi a_3 - 2x_3\sigma_3^2 + \lambda_1 + \lambda_2 b_3 = 0\\
\frac{\partial P}{\partial x_4} &= \Phi a_4 - 2x_4\sigma_4^2 - \lambda_2 = 0\\
\frac{\partial P}{\partial \lambda_1} &= x_1 + x_2 + x_3 - 1 = 0\\
\frac{\partial P}{\partial \lambda_2} &= x_1 b_1 + x_2 b_2 + x_3 b_3 - x_4 = 0,
\end{aligned} \tag{10.18}$$

where

$\sigma_1^2 = \text{Var}(e_{1t})$;
$\sigma_2^2 = \text{Var}(e_{2t})$;
$\sigma_3^2 = \text{Var}(e_{3t})$; and
$\sigma_4^2 = \text{Var}(e_{4t})$.

Equation (10.18) is a set of six equations in six unknowns when set equal to zero. These six equations can be rewritten in matrix format:

$$\overset{A}{\begin{bmatrix} -2\sigma_1^2 & 0 & 0 & 0 & 1 & b_1\\ 0 & -2\sigma_2^2 & 0 & 0 & 1 & b_2\\ 0 & 0 & -2\sigma_3^2 & 0 & 1 & b_3\\ 0 & 0 & 0 & -2\sigma_4^2 & 0 & -1\\ 1 & 1 & 1 & 0 & 0 & 0\\ b_1 & b_2 & b_3 & -1 & 0 & 0 \end{bmatrix}} \overset{x}{\begin{bmatrix} x_1\\ x_2\\ x_3\\ x_4\\ \lambda_1\\ \lambda_2 \end{bmatrix}} = \overset{k}{\begin{bmatrix} -\Phi a_1\\ -\Phi a_2\\ -\Phi a_3\\ -\Phi a_4\\ 1\\ 0 \end{bmatrix}}. \tag{10.19a}$$

Equation (10.19a) has related the individual securities to the index and has discarded the use of numerous covariance terms. The majority of the elements of the matrix indicated in the first matrix of Equation (10.19a) are zero. For three securities case, the inputs needed for Equation (10.19a) are three alphas, three betas, and three residual variances for individual securities. In addition, we also need the information of mean and variance of market rate of return. Similarly, for n securities case, we need $3n + 2$ inputs. From Chapter 8, we know that we need $2n + \frac{n^2 - n}{2}$ inputs if we use Markowitz model to obtain the optimal weight of the portfolio.

As in Chapter 8, to solve for the x column vector of variables, the P matrix is inverted and each side of the equation is premultiplied by A^{-1}. This yields the x column vector of variables on the left-hand side and A^{-1} multiplied by k, the solution column vector, on the right-hand side.

$$\begin{aligned} \mathrm{A}x &= k \\ \mathrm{A}^{-1}\mathrm{A}x &= \mathrm{A}^{-1}k \\ \mathrm{I}x &= \mathrm{A}^{-1}k, \end{aligned} \tag{10.19b}$$

where I is the identity matrix.

The procedure for solving Equations (10.19a) and (10.19b) was discussed in Chapter 8. A linear-programming (LP) approach to solve this kind of model is discussed in Appendix 10A.

In order to estimate a single-index type of optimal portfolio, the estimates of a market model are needed; a discussion of the market model and beta estimates is therefore needed as well.

Sample Problem 10.3

During the discussion of the single-index model, a method was presented for determining optimal portfolio weights given different levels of risk aversion. In this section, a three-security portfolio is examined in which the returns of the securities are related to a market index.

The same securities are used as in Chapter 8 (Table 8.3); the S&P 500 are included as the market index. The securities and the index have the following observed parameter estimates taken from actual monthly returns during the period from April 2000 to April 2010 (see Table 10.2). The table includes the calculation of the beta estimate for each security. Check these figures, remembering that beta is equal to the covariance of security i with the market divided by the variance of the market returns.

Table 10.2. Single Index Model: Three Securities Case.

	$\bar{R}_i$	$Var(\bar{R}_i)$	$\text{Cov}(R_i, R_j)$	b_i
JNJ	0.0080	0.0025	0.0007	0.37
IBM	0.0050	0.0071	0.0006	1.20
BA	0.0113	0.0083	0.0007	1.04
S&P 500	−0.0009	0.0021	0.0021	1.00

As shown in Equation (10.19a), a matrix can be developed by utilizing the set of data in the first table of this problem and a Φ of 1.0 (denoting moderate risk aversion):

$$\begin{array}{ccc} A & x = & k \end{array}$$

$$\begin{bmatrix} -0.0050 & 0 & 0 & 0 & 1 & 0.37 \\ 0 & -0.0142 & 0 & 0 & 1 & 1.2 \\ 0 & 0 & -0.0166 & 0 & 1 & 1.04 \\ 0 & 0 & 0 & -0.0042 & 0 & 0 \\ 1.0 & 1.0 & 1.0 & 0 & 0 & 0 \\ 0.37 & 1.2 & 1.04 & -1.0 & 0 & 0 \end{bmatrix} \begin{bmatrix} x_1 \\ x_2 \\ x_3 \\ x_4 \\ \lambda_1 \\ \lambda_2 \end{bmatrix} = \begin{bmatrix} -0.0080 \\ -0.0050 \\ -0.0113 \\ 0.0009 \\ 1.0 \\ 0 \end{bmatrix}$$

When the P matrix is invented and premultiplies each side of the equation:

$$x = A^{-1}k$$

$$\begin{bmatrix} x_1 \\ x_2 \\ x_3 \\ x_4 \\ \lambda_1 \\ \lambda_2 \end{bmatrix} = \begin{bmatrix} 1.7092 \\ -0.6821 \\ -0.0271 \\ -0.2143 \\ 0.0073 \\ -0.0184 \end{bmatrix}.$$

This solution vector shows that investment should be divided 170.92% in JNJ, −68.21% in IBM, and −2.71% in BA. Additionally, the weight of x_4 is the sum of the weighted adjustments as indicated in Equation (10.16b). The return on this portfolio is the weighted sum of the individual returns:

$$\begin{aligned} E(R_p) &= \sum_{i=1}^{n} x_i E(R_i) \\ &= [(1.7092 \times 0.0080) + (-0.6821 \times 0.0050) + (-0.0271 \times 0.0113)] \\ &= 0.0100. \end{aligned}$$

The variance of the portfolio is the sum of the weighted variance and covariance terms:

$$\mathrm{Var}(R_p) = \sum_{i=1}^{n}\sum_{j=1}^{n} x_i x_j \sigma_{ij}.$$

Taking the covariance expressions:

$$\begin{aligned}\mathrm{Var}(R_p) &= [(1.7092^2 \times 0.0025) + (-0.6821^2 \times 0.0071) \\ &\quad + (-0.0271^2 \times 0.0083) + 2 \times (1.7092 \times -0.6821 \times 0.0007) \\ &\quad + 2 \times (1.7092 \times -0.0271 \times 0.0007) \\ &\quad + 2 \times (-0.6821 \times -0.0271 \times 0.0006) \\ &= 0.0089.\end{aligned}$$

A portfolio has been developed that is efficient within the realm of this model. By varying the utility factor Φ from risk averse to more aggressive risk posture we can develop an efficient frontier under the Sharpe single-index model. For a fuller graph, the analyst would continue the calculations with ever higher values of Φ stretching the efficient frontier.

10.1.3. *The Market Model and Beta*

Equation (10.2) defines the market model:

$$R_{it} = a_i + b_i R_{It} + e_{it}.$$

From this market model, a_i, b_i, $\mathrm{Var}(e_{it})$, and $\mathrm{Var}(R_{It})$ can be estimated: all are required for the single-index type of optimal portfolio.

So far the regression coefficient has been referred to as b_i when, in fact, it is a risk relationship of a security with the market. Quantified as the covariance of security i with the market index divided by the variance of the return of the market, beta is a relational coefficient of the returns of security i as they vary with the returns of the market. Notationally:

$$b_i = \frac{\sigma_{i,I}}{\sigma_I^2} = \sum_{t=1}^{n} \frac{[(R_{it} - r_{it})(R_{It} - r_{It})]}{(R_{It} - r_{It})^2}. \tag{10.20}$$

Of course, due to the continuous nature of security returns, the result of the above calculation is an estimate and therefore subject to error. This error can be quantified by the use of standard error estimates, which provide the ability to make interval estimations for future predictions. The following discussion is related to the **beta estimate** and its forecasting as discussed in Chapter 9.

Because of the linkage between security returns and the firm's underlying fundamental nature, beta estimates will vary over time. It is the job of the security analyst to decide how to modify not only the beta estimate but also the period of time from which the sample of returns is to be drawn. Some popular security-evaluation techniques use a tiered growth model to correspond to the product life-cycle theory. Within the scope of this theory, beta estimates for the relation of that security to the market will vary with respect to the time period chosen for the sample of returns. It is obvious that the returns generated by a firm in its infancy have very little correlation with returns during the growth or maturity phase. It is up to the analyst to judge which phase a company may be in and to adjust the beta estimates accordingly.

Assume for expository purposes that all stocks move in perfect alignment with the market, and therefore the security returns all produce beta estimates of 1. It could then be said that any estimation of betas above 1 would indicate positive sampling error, and all estimates below 1 indicate negative sampling error. Future periods would show returns that caused movement from either side of the estimate deviation back toward 1. Blume (1975) shows that the adjustment of a beta in one period could accurately predict the adjustment in subsequent periods. Utilizing regression analysis, Blume demonstrates that a historical beta could be adjusted successfully to predict future levels. Large brokerage houses have taken this theory a little further by applying weighted averages of historic and average betas in adjusting beta estimates. This has the advantage of being simple to calculate, but it has the ability nevertheless to adjust beta back toward an average level. (This kind of beta-adjustment process was discussed in the last chapter; the Value Line beta estimate is essentially based upon this process, as explored in Chapter 9.)

Historic beta estimates give the analyst a feeling of how the firm is generating returns to an investor but provide very little guidance about the firm's underlying fundamental nature. It is held that a firm's balance-sheet ratios over time can indicate how risky the firm is relative to the market. Using seven financial quantities of a firm, Beaver *et al.* (BKS, 1970) show that betas can be estimated by multiple regression relating the financial levels to the riskiness of the firm by using

(1) Dividend payout;
(2) Asset growth;

(3) Leverage;
(4) Liquidity;
(5) Asset size;
(6) Earnings volatility; and
(7) Accounting beta (relation of earnings of the firm with the earnings of the economy as a whole).

BKS show not only that each of the variables carries a logical relation to the market but also that the multiple regression is significant. Other studies, most notably that of Rosenberg and Guy (1976), use many more fundamental factors in the regression for estimating betas.

Historic betas are of consequence because of their relation with market returns; nevertheless, the sampling period tends to crowd out the information contained in returns due to recent developments of the firm. Fundamental betas tend to recognize significant changes in the makeup of a firm — for example, a change in debt structure, or liquidity. The disadvantage related to fundamental betas is that they treat intercompany responsiveness as constant. It is patently obvious that a small firm taking on a large debt will be at much more risk than a Ford or GM doing the same.

Because of the advantages and disadvantages apparent in both types of beta estimates, it has been shown that a combination of the estimates is more suitable to risk classification. Rosenberg and McKibben (1973) found that intercompany responsiveness is substantial, so an analysis was undertaken to introduce these variations into the regression. Utilizing a set of dummy variables to capture the advantages of both types of betas, Rosenberg and Marathe (1974) have described a multiple regression for the beta estimate of a firm that include information such as variability, level of success, relative size, and growth potential. By using a very large and complex model, they found that the forecasting ability of the regression analysis is substantial, but they were inconclusive as to whether the benefit of the analysis outweighs the computational cost.

Forecasting future beta levels holds its roots in the difficulty of forecasting the fundamental nature of the firm itself. This section has briefly looked over some of the available adjustment processes for beta estimation. While reasonable in its scope, this coverage of the adjustment process is by no means complete. Additional research material is cited at the end of this chapter for use in further study. It should be kept in mind during future readings that the more sophisticated an adjustment process is, the more likely it is that the computational costs will outweigh the improvement of the beta forecast.

10.2. Multiple Indexes and the MIM

The previous section reviewed the possibilities of adjusting the beta estimate in the single-index model to capture some of the information concerning a firm not contained in the historic returns. The **MIM** pursues the same problem as beta adjustment, but approaches the problem from a different angle. The MIM tackles the problem of relation of a security not only to the market by including a market index but also to other indexes that quantify other movements. For example, U.S. Steel has returns on its securities that are related to the market, but due to the declining nature of the American steel industry there is also some relation to the steel industry itself. If an index could be developed that represented the movement of the U.S. steel industry, it could be utilized in the return analysis, and a more accurate estimate of possible security returns for U.S. Steel could be derived.

The assumption underlying the single-index model is that the returns of a security vary only with the market index. The expansion provided by the MIM includes factors that affect a security's return beyond the effects of the market as a whole. Realistically any index might be used, but well-known, published indexes are usually incorporated. These may include general business indicators, industry-specific indicators, or even self-constructed indexes concerning the structure of the firm itself. The model to be addressed contains L indexes; nevertheless, a few examples of possible indexes of interest are offered. The MIM is related to the arbitrage pricing model developed by Ross (1976, 1977), which will be explored in detail in the next chapter.

The covariance of a security's return with other market influences can be added directly to the index model by quantifying the effects through the use of additional indexes. If the single-index model were expanded to take into account interest rates, factory orders, and several industry-related indexes, the model would change to

$$R_i = a_i^* + b_{i1}^* I_1^* + b_{i2}^* I_2^* + \cdots + b_{iM}^* I_M^* + c_i. \qquad (10.21)$$

In this depiction of the MIM, I_j^* is the actual level of index j, while b_{ij}^* is the actual responsiveness of security i to index j. If the component of the security return is not related to any of the indexes then this index model can be divided into two parts: (1) a_i, the expected value of the unique return, and (2) c_i which represents the distribution of the random effect; c_i has a mean effect of zero and a variance of $\sigma^2_{c_i}$.

This model can be utilized with multiple regression techniques, but if the indexes are unrelated to each other, the calculations would be made much simpler. This assumption reduces the number of calculations, as compared with the Markowitz full variance-covariance model, but is obviously more complex than the single-index model. To assure that the indexes are unrelated, the index variables can be orthogonalized (made uncorrelated) by completing inter-regressions on the indexes themselves.

Assume there is a hypothetical model that deals with two indexes:

$$R_i = a_i^* + b_{i1}^* I_1^* + b_{i2}^* I_2^* + c_i. \tag{10.22}$$

Suppose the indexes are the market index and an index of wholesale prices. If these two indexes are correlated, the correlation may be removed from either index.

To remove the relation between I_1^* and I_2^*, the coefficients of the following equation can be derived by regression analysis:

$$I_2^* = e_0 + e_1 I_1^* + d_i,$$

where

e_0 and e_1 = the regression coefficients; and
d_i = the random error term.

By the assumptions of regression analysis, d_i is uncorrelated with I_1. Therefore:

$$\hat{d}_i = I_2^* - (\hat{e}_0 + \hat{e}_1 I_1^*),$$

which is an index of the performance of the sector index without the effect of I_1 (the market removed). Defining:

$$I_2 = \hat{d}_i = I_2^* - \hat{e}_0 - \hat{e}_1 I_1^*,$$

an index is obtained that is uncorrelated with the market. By solving for I_2^* and substituting into Equation (10.5):

$$R_i = a_i^* + b_{i1}^* I_1^* + b_{i2}^* I_2 - b_{i2}^* \hat{e}_0 - b_{i2}^* \hat{e}_1 I_1^* + c_i.$$

Rearranging:

$$R_i = (a_i^* - b_{i2}^* \hat{e}_0) + (b_{i1}^* - b_{i2}^* \hat{e}_1) I_1^* + b_{i2}^* I_2 + c_i.$$

If the first set of terms in the brackets is defined as a_i and the second set of terms is defined as $b_{i1}, b^*_{i2} = b_{i2}$, $I^*_1 = I_1$, and $c_i = e_i$, the equation can be expressed:

$$R_i = a_i + b_{i1}I_1 + b_{i2}I_2 + e_i, \tag{10.23}$$

in which I_1 and I_2 are totally uncorrelated: the goal has been achieved. As will be seen later, these simplifying calculations will make the job of determining variance and covariance much simpler.

The expected return can be expressed:

$$\begin{aligned} E(R_{it}) &= E(a_i + b_{i1}I_{1t} + b_{i2}I_{2t} + e_{it}) \\ &= E(a_i) + E(b_{i1}I_{1t}) + E(b_{i2}I_{2t}) + E(e_{it}) \\ &= a_i + b_{i1}\bar{I}_1 + b_{i2}\bar{I}_2. \end{aligned} \tag{10.24}$$

Since a_i, b_{i1}, and b_{i2} are constants, $E(e_i) = 0$ by assumption, where $\bar{I}_1 = E(I_{1t})$ and $\bar{I}_2 = E(I_{2t})$.

Variance can be expressed:

$$\begin{aligned} \sigma^2 &= E(R_{it} - R_i)^2 \quad \text{where } R_i = E(R_{it}) \\ &= E[(a_i + b_{i1}I_1 + b_{i2}I_2 + e_{it}) - (a_i + b_{i1}\bar{I}_1 + b_{i2}\bar{I}_2)]^2 \\ &= E[(a_1 + a_i) + b_{i1}(I_{1t} + \bar{I}_1) + b_{i2}(I_{2t} + \bar{I}_2) + e_{it}]^2 \\ &= E[b^2_{i1}(I_{1t} + \bar{I}_1)^2 + 2b_{i1}b_{i2}(I_{1t} + \bar{I}_1)(I_{2t} + \bar{I}_2) \\ &\quad + b^2_{i2}(I_{2t} + \bar{I}_2)^2 + 2b_{i1}(I_{1t} + \bar{I}_1)e_{it} \\ &\quad + 2b_{i2}(I_{2t} + \bar{I}_2)e_{it} + e^2_{it} \\ &= b^2_{i1}E(I_{1t} + \bar{I}_1)^2 + b_{i1}b_{i2}E[(I_{1t} + \bar{I}_1)(I_{2t} + \bar{I}_2)] \\ &\quad + b^2_{i2}E(I_{2t} + \bar{I}_2) + b_{i1}E[(I_{1t} + \bar{I}_1)e_i] \\ &\quad + b_{i2}E[(I_{2t} + \bar{I}_2)e_i] + E(e^2_i). \end{aligned}$$

But by assumption:

$$\begin{aligned} E[(I_{1t} + \bar{I}_1)(I_{2t} + \bar{I}_2)] &= 0, \\ E[(I_{1t} + \bar{I}_1)e_i] &= 0, \\ E[(I_{2t} + \bar{I}_2)e_i] &= 0, \end{aligned}$$

and

$$E(I_{1t} + \bar{I}_1)^2 = \sigma_1^2,$$
$$E(I_{2t} + \bar{I}_2)^2 = \sigma_2^2,$$
$$E(e_i^2) = \sigma_{ei}^2;$$

therefore,

$$\sigma_i^2 = b_{i1}^2\sigma_1^2 + b_{i2}^2\sigma_2^2 + \sigma_{ei}^2. \tag{10.25}$$

Covariance between security i and security j can be expressed as

$$\begin{aligned}
\sigma_{ij} &= E[(R_{it} - R_i)(R_{jt} - R_j)][\text{where } R_i = E(R_{it}) \quad \text{and} \quad R_j = E(R_{jt}) \\
&= E\{[(a_i + b_{i1}I_1 + b_{i2}I_{2t} + e_{1t}) - (a_i + b_{i1}\bar{I}_1 + b_{i2}\bar{I}_2)] \\
&\quad \times [(a_j + b_{j1}I_{1t} + b_{j2}I_{2t} + e_{jt}) - (a_j + b_{j1}\bar{I}_1 + b_{j2}\bar{I}_2)]\} \\
&= E\{[b_{i1}(I_{1t} - \bar{I}_1) + b_{i2}(I_{2t} - \bar{I}_2) + e_i] \times [b_{j1}(I_{1t} - \bar{I}_1) \qquad (10.26) \\
&\quad + (b_{j2}(I_{2t} - \bar{I}_2) + e_{jt}]\} \\
&= E[b_{i1}b_{j1}(I_{1t} - \bar{I}_1)^2 + b_{i2}b_{j2}(I_{2t} - \bar{I}_2)^2] \\
&= b_{i1}b_{j1}\sigma_1^2 + b_{i2}b_{j2}\sigma_2^2.
\end{aligned}$$

since all remaining expected values of the cross-product terms equal zero.

The extended results of expected return variance and covariance for a multi-index and more than two indexes can be found in Appendix 10B of this chapter.

One simplifying way of applying the MIM is to start with the basic market model and add indexes to reflect industry-related effects. If the firm has 100% of its operations in one industry, Equation (10.23) can be used to represent a two-index model with market index and industry index. In general this approach reduces the number of data inputs to $4N + 2I + 2$. These data inputs are: (1) the expected return and variance for each stock and market index; (2) the covariance between the individual security and the market index and the industry index; and (3) the mean and variance of each industry index. Although this is a larger number of data inputs than for the simple market model, the accuracy of the estimation of security return increases. So the tradeoff is one of more information (higher cost to use) versus greater accuracy of the forecasted security return.

Care must be taken in applying the MIM. It is often the case that the additional information resulting from the application of a higher-complexity model is outweighed by the computational cost increase. In an attempt at making the model as parsimonious as possible, it is necessary to judge the increased information gained by utilizing the more complex model. This can be accomplished by examining the mean square error for the forecast of the actual historic values. Although not within the scope of this text, the ability to judge the accuracy of a forecast is essential and can be acquired from any good statistical forecasting text. Sample Problem 10.3 provides further illustration of the single-index model.

10.3. Summary

This chapter has discussed the essentials of single- and multiple-index models. The theoretical underpinnings of the theories have been explored and numerical examples have been provided. An efficient boundary has been derived under the guidelines of the model and the quantitative analysis of the related parameters has been studied. It has been shown that both single-index and multi-index models can be used to simplify the Markowitz model for portfolio section; remember, however, that the MIM is much more complicated than the single-index model.

Questions and Problems

1. You are given monthly return data for two stocks and the NYSE as shown in the table.

Month	D (percent)	E (percent)	NYSE (percent)
1	5.30	7.3	4.5
2	6.25	8.2	5.2
3	−2.12	−10.2	1.1
4	12.75	15.4	10.3
5	−3.4	−2.0	−1.3
6	8.6	9.5	10.5
7	9.2	8.2	7.6
8	−2.1	−1.0	0
9	−8.3	−10.2	−7.4
10	10.2	11.5	9.3
11	5.4	5.9	4.2
12	6.2	7.2	8.5

(a) Calculate the α (alpha) and β (beta) for each stock.
(b) Compute the variance of the residuals of each regression.
(c) Calculate the correlation between each stock and the market.
(d) Compute the mean return and variance of an optimal portfolio consisting of these two stocks in terms of the single-index model.

2. Assume that you have determined that a two-index model best describes the return process. The first index is a market index, while the second is an industry index. Is it possible to remove the impact of the market from the industry?
3. Derive the formulas for the expected return, variance, and covariance of any stock given a two-index model in which the indexes are orthogonal.
4. Assume that returns are generated by an L-index model:

$$R_i = a_i + b_{i1}I_1 + b_{i2}I_2 + \cdots + b_{iL}I_L + e_i$$

(a) Interpret the coefficients $a_i, b_i, \ldots, b_{iL}$.
(b) Derive the variance of this model.

5. Carefully explain the relationship between the single-index model and the Markowitz model of portfolio theory. How many different terms must be calculated in a portfolio consisting of n securities using the Markowitz model? How many different terms must be calculated in a portfolio consisting of n securities using the single-index model?
6. Using three alternative methods (substitution, Cramer's rule, and matrix inversion) solve the following simultaneous equation system.

$$\begin{aligned} -x_1 + 2x_2 + 4x_3 &= 15 \\ 2x_1 - 8x_2 + 2x_3 &= -8 \\ 4x_1 + 2x_2 - 5x_3 &= -7 \end{aligned}$$

Appendix 10A: A Linear-Programming Approach to Portfolio-Analysis Models

Sharpe (1967) developed a simplified portfolio-analysis model designed to be formulated as an LP problem. Jacob (1974) developed an LP model for small investors that delineates efficient portfolios composed of only a few securities. Both of these approaches have as their objectives: (1) a reduction in the amount of data required and (2) a reduction in the amount of computer capability required to solve the portfolio-selection problem.

Sharpe approaches the problem of capturing the essence of mean-variance portfolio selection in an LP formulation by

(1) Making a diagonal transformation of the variables that will convert the problem into a diagonal form, and
(2) Using a piecewise linear approximation for each of the terms for variance.

The LP that results from the use of market responsiveness as the risk measure and the imposition of an upper limit on investment in each security is

$$\text{Max } P = \lambda \left[\sum_{i=1}^{n} x_i E(R_i) \right] - (1 - \lambda) \left[\sum_{i=1}^{n} x_i \beta_i \right], \tag{10A.1}$$

subject to

$$\sum_{i=1}^{n} x_i = 1,$$

$$0 \leq x_i \leq U,$$

where

$x_i =$ the fraction of the portfolio invested in security i;
$E(R_i) =$ the expected returns of security i;
$\beta_i =$ the beta coefficient of security i;
$U =$ the maximum fraction of the portfolio that may be held in any one security; and
$\lambda =$ a parameter reflecting the degree of risk aversion.

The λ is used in generating the efficient frontier. The value of λ corresponds to the rate of substitution of return for risk measured by the individual security β, while the U maximum percentage to be invested in any one security greatly reduces the number of securities that will be needed for diversification.

Building on this framework, Jacob derives an LP model that allows the small investor explicit control over the number of securities held. Jacob's LP model incorporates the effects of unsystematic risk as well as systematic risk, the beta in the Sharpe LP. Jacob's model is to minimize

$$\sigma^2(R_p) = \underbrace{\frac{1}{K}\left(\sum_{i=1}^{n} x_i\beta_i\right)^2 \sigma^2(R_m)}_{\text{Systematic risk}} + \underbrace{\left(\frac{1}{K}\right)^2 \sum_{i=1}^{n} x_i^2\sigma^2(e_i)}_{\text{Unsystematic risk}}, \tag{10A.2}$$

subject to

$$\frac{1}{K}\sum_{i=1}^{n} x_i E(R_i) \le E^*(R_p),$$

$$\frac{1}{K}\sum_{i=1}^{n} x_i = K, \quad x_i = 0 \text{ or } 1,$$

where

x_i = the investment in security i — all, or nothing;
$E(R_i)$ = the expected return on security i equal to $\alpha_i + \beta_i R_m$;
K = the desired upper bound on the number of securities the investor is willing to consider, usually in the range of 15 to 20;
β_i = the measure of systematic risk;
$\sigma^2(e_i)$ = the measure of unsystematic risk; and
$E^*(R_p)$ = the lowest acceptable rate of return the investor is willing to earn on his or her portfolio.

An additional simplification is to turn the objective function of Equation (10A.2) into a linear relationship. Since the decision variables (x_i) are binary valued, the unsystematic-risk term of the objective function is already linear. Given that the portfolio beta $\left(\sum_{i=1}^{n} x_i\beta_i\right)/K$ is very close to unity, a reasonable linear approximation to the first term in the objective function is provided by

$$\frac{1}{K}\left[\sum_{i=1}^{n} x_i\beta_i\sigma^2(R_m)\right] = \sigma^2(R_m)\left(\frac{1}{K}\sum_{i=1}^{n} x_i\beta_i\right)^2.$$

After division by K and rearrangement of terms, the objective function can be restated as

$$Z = \sum_{i=1}^{n} x_i\left[\beta_i\sigma^2(R_m) + \frac{1}{K}\sigma^2(e_i)\right].$$

Letting $Z_i = \beta_i\sigma^2(R_m) + (1/K)\sigma^2(e_i)$, the problem can be cast as

$$\text{Minimize } Z = \lambda\sum_{i=1}^{n} X_i Z_i - (1-\lambda)\sum_{i=1}^{n} X_i E(R_i),$$

subject to

$$\sum_{i=1}^{n} X_i = 1.0, \quad 0 \le X_i \le 1/K, \quad i = 1, 2, \ldots, N,$$

in which λ is varied from zero to one. This problem can be solved by the LP approach suggested by Sharpe (1967). An example of solving this problem can be found in Jacob (1974).

Appendix 10B: Expected Return, Variance, and Covariance for an MIM

Using the orthogonalization technique discussed in the text, the MIM is transformed into

$$R_i = a_i + b_{i1}I_1 + b_{i2}I_2 + \cdots + b_{iL}I_L + c_i, \tag{10B.1}$$

in which all I_j are uncorrelated with each other. To interpret the transformed indexes, notice that I_2 is now the difference between the actual level of the index and the level it would be, given the level of the other indexes. Also, b_{i2} is now the sensitivity of security i's return to a change in I_2, given that all other indexes are held constant.

It is also convenient, beyond making the indexes uncorrelated, to assume that the covariance of the residuals with the indexes is equal to zero. With this final assumption, the MIM can be recapped as follows. Generalized equation:

$$R_i = a_i + b_{i1}I_1 + b_{i2}I_2 + \cdots + b_{iL}I_L + c_i$$

for all securities $i = 1$ to N, and

(1) $E(c_i) = 0$
(2) Var $(c_i) = \sigma^2_{ci}$
(3) Var $(I_j) = \sigma^2_{Ij}$
(4) Cov $(I_j, I_k) = E[(I_j - \bar{I}_j)(I_k - \bar{I}_k)] = 0,\ \bar{I}_j = E(I_j), \bar{I}_{ci} = E(I_{ci})$
(5) $\text{Cov}(c_i, I_j) = E[c_i(I_j - \bar{I}_j)] = 0$
(6) $\text{Cov}(c_i, c_j) = E(c_i, c_j) = 0$ for all $i, j,$ and k.

The last statement is equivalent to the residuals being unrelated, which is to say that the only reason for common co-movement of returns is due to the movement of the indexes. Although this is like ignoring some of a model's shortcomings, it facilitates a usable model to obtain a quantified idea of future return patterns.

The expected value of the model with the multiple indexes is

$$\begin{aligned} E(R_i) &= E(a_i + b_{i1}I_1 + b_{i2}I_2 + \cdots + b_{iL}I_L + c_i) \\ &= E(a_i) + E(b_{i1}I_1) + E(b_{i2}I_2) + \cdots + E(b_{iL}I_L) + E(c_i), \end{aligned}$$

because a and the b are constants, and the expected value of the residuals is equal to zero

$$r_i = a_i + b_{i1}\bar{I}_1 + b_{i2}\bar{I}_2 + \cdots + b_{iL}\bar{I}_L, \tag{10B.2}$$

where $\bar{I}_j$ is the expected value of index j.

The variance of the returns using multiple indexes is

$$\sigma_i^2 = E(R_i - r_i)^2,$$

where r_i is the expected value of the returns of security i. Substituting R_i and r_i from above:

$$\begin{aligned} \sigma_i^2 = E[&(a_i + b_{i1}I_1 + b_{i2}I_2 + \cdots + b_{iL}I_L + c_i) \\ &- (a_i + b_{i1}\bar{I}_1 + b_{i2}\bar{I}_2 + \cdots + b_{iL}\bar{I}_L)]^2. \end{aligned}$$

Rearranging, and noticing that the a_i cancel, yields:

$$\sigma_i^2 = E[b_{i1}(I_1 - \bar{I}_1) + b_{i2}(I_2 - \bar{I}_2) + \cdots + b_{iL}(I_L - \bar{I}_L) + c_i]^2.$$

Next, the terms in the brackets are squared. To proceed with this concentrate on the first index, arid the rest of the terms involving the other indexes follow directly. The first index times itself and all other terms yields

$$\begin{aligned} E[&b_{i1}^2(I_1 - \bar{I}_1)^2 + b_{i1}b_{i2}(I_1 - \bar{I}_1)(I_2 - \bar{I}_2) + \cdots \\ &+ b_{i1}b_{iL}(I_1 - \bar{I}_1)(I_L - \bar{I}_L) + b_{i1}(I_1 - \bar{I}_1)(c_i)]. \end{aligned}$$

Remembering that

$$E[(I_i - \bar{I}_i)(I_j - \bar{I}_j)] = 0 \quad \text{and} \quad E[(I_i - \bar{I}_i)c_i] = 0,$$

the only nonzero term involving index one is expressed as

$$b_{i1}^2 E(I_1 - \bar{I}_1)^2 = b_{i1}^2 \sigma_{I1}^2.$$

Because all terms involving c_i are zero and $E(c_i)^2 = \sigma_{ci}^2$:

$$\sigma_i^2 = b_{i1}^2 \sigma_{I1}^2 + b_{i2}^2 \sigma_{I2}^2 + \cdots + b_{iL}^2 \sigma_{IL}^2 + \sigma_{ci}^2. \qquad (10B.3)$$

The covariance of the returns between security i and j utilizing the MIM can be expressed as

$$\sigma_{ij} = E[(R_i - r_i)(R_j - r_j)].$$

Again, substituting for R_i, r_i, R_j, and r_j:

$$\begin{aligned}\sigma_{ij} = E[[&(a_i + b_{i1}I_1 + b_{i2}I_2 + \cdots + b_{iL}I_L + c_i)\\ &- (a_i + b_{i1}\bar{I}_1 + b_{i2}\bar{I}_2 + \cdots + b_{iL}\bar{I}_L)]^*\\ &\times [(a_j + b_{j1}I_1 + b_{j2}I_2 + \cdots + b_{jL}I_L + c_j)\\ &- (a_j + b_{j1}\bar{I}_1 + b_{j2}\bar{I}_2 + \cdots + b_{jL}\bar{I}_L)]].\end{aligned}$$

Again, noting that a_i cancels and combining the terms involving the same b's:

$$\begin{aligned}\sigma_{ij} = E\{&[b_{i1}(I_1 - \bar{I}_1) + b_{i2}(I_2 - \bar{I}_2) + \cdots + b_{iL}(I_L - \bar{I}_L) + c_i]\\ &\times [b_{j1}(I_1 - \bar{I}_1) + b_{j2}(I_2 - \bar{I}_2) + \cdots + b_{jL}(I_L - \bar{I}_L) + c_j]\}.\end{aligned}$$

Next multiply out terms, again concentrating on the terms involving b_{i1}:

$$\begin{aligned}E[&b_{i1}b_{j1}(I_1 - \bar{I}_1)^2 + b_{i1}b_{i2}(I_1 - \bar{I}_1)(I_2 - \bar{I}_2) + \cdots\\ &+ b_{i1}b_{jL}(I_1 - \bar{I}_1)(I_L - \bar{I}_L) + b_{i1}(I_1 - \bar{I}_1)c_j].\end{aligned}$$

Because the covariance between two indexes is zero, and the covariance between any residual and an index is zero:

$$b_{i1}b_{j1}E(I_1 - \bar{I}_1)^2 = b_{i1}b_{j1}\sigma_{I1}^2.$$

To conclude, remember that the covariance of the residuals is equal to zero and therefore:

$$\sigma_{ij} = b_{i1}b_{j1}\sigma_{I1}^2 + b_{i2}b_{j2}\sigma_{I2}^2 + \cdots + b_{iL}b_{jL}\sigma_{IL}^2. \tag{10B.4}$$

Appendix 10C: Using Microsoft Excel to Calculate Optimal Weights of a Portfolio

This appendix will contain three portions. Part I will discuss matrix inversion method to solve a simultaneous equation system. Part II will use the method of Part I to obtain the optimal weights of Markowitz model. Part III will present how to use Microsoft Excel to obtain the optimal weights of Index model.

Part I

This part illustrates how to solve a simultaneous equation system by matrix inversion method. Given simultaneous equations as follows:

$$\begin{aligned} 3x_1 + 2x_2 + 4x_3 &= 32, \\ 2x_1 + 3x_3 &= 19, \\ 4x_1 + 2x_2 + 3x_3 &= 29. \end{aligned}$$

The simultaneous equations can be written as the matrix forms

$$\underbrace{\begin{bmatrix} 3 & 2 & 4 \\ 2 & 0 & 3 \\ 4 & 2 & 3 \end{bmatrix}}_{A} \underbrace{\begin{bmatrix} x_1 \\ x_2 \\ x_3 \end{bmatrix}}_{X} = \underbrace{\begin{bmatrix} 32 \\ 19 \\ 29 \end{bmatrix}}_{K}.$$

Then we can obtain the elements of matrix X by multiplying the inverse matrix A^{-1} and the matrix K. In the following part, we will illustrate the calculation of the inverse matrix in Excel.

Part II

Here we use the monthly prices of Johnson & Johnson (JNJ), International Business Machines (IBM), Boeing Company (BA), and S&P 500 index

(GSPC) during March 1, 2000, to April 30, 2010, as the example. The process includes data collection, the statistic analysis of samples, the results of the market model, and the calculation of the optimal weights of Markowitz model.

Data Collection

The collection of the monthly returns starts from the Yahoo Finance website: http://finance.yahoo.com/ and inputs the stock ticker "**JNJ**" to get quotes.

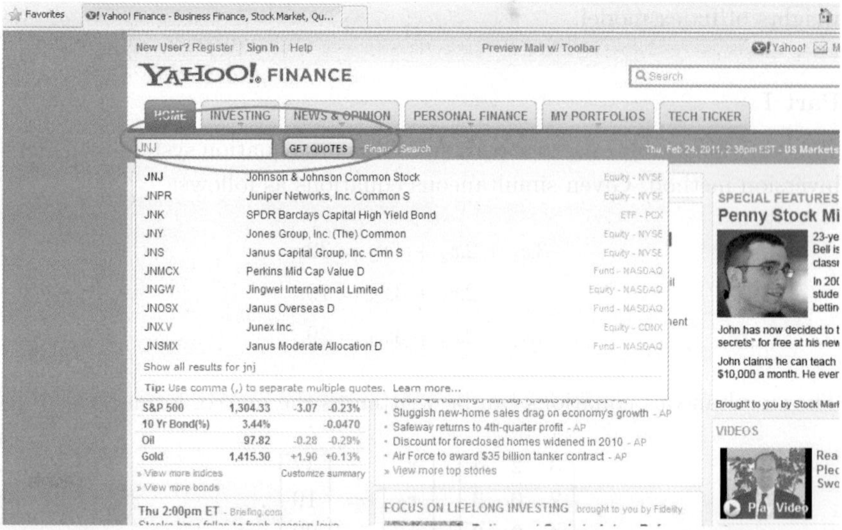

The second step is to get the stock prices: select "**Historical Prices**" on the left panel of the website, input the range of data from March 1, 2000, to April 30, 2010, select "**Monthly**" data and press "**Get Prices**." After the webpage shows the historical prices, scroll down to the bottom of the webpage and select "**Download to Spreadsheet**," and then we can get the monthly prices of JNJ. Here we only need the data of the adjusted prices and use "**Sort**" function on Excel to make price in ascending order.

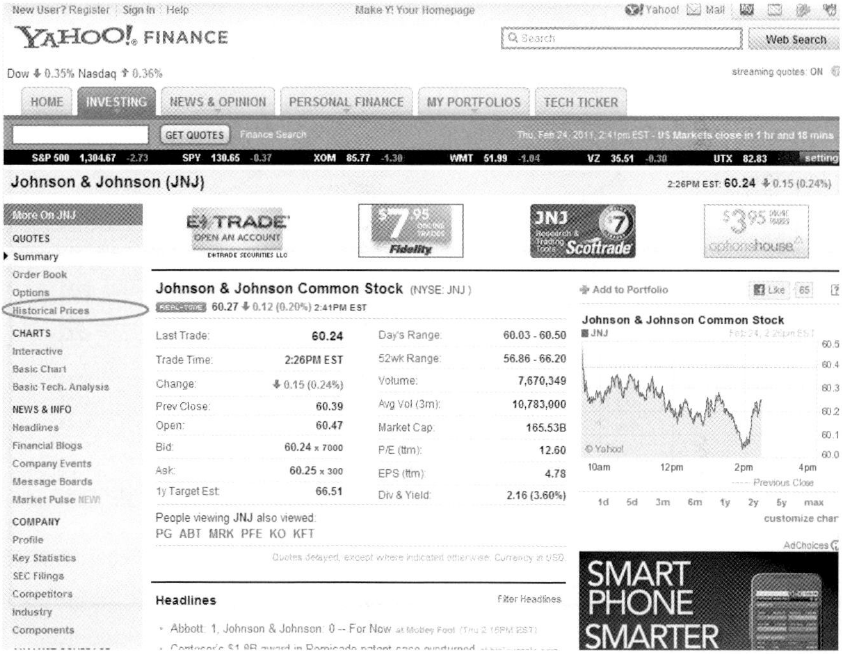

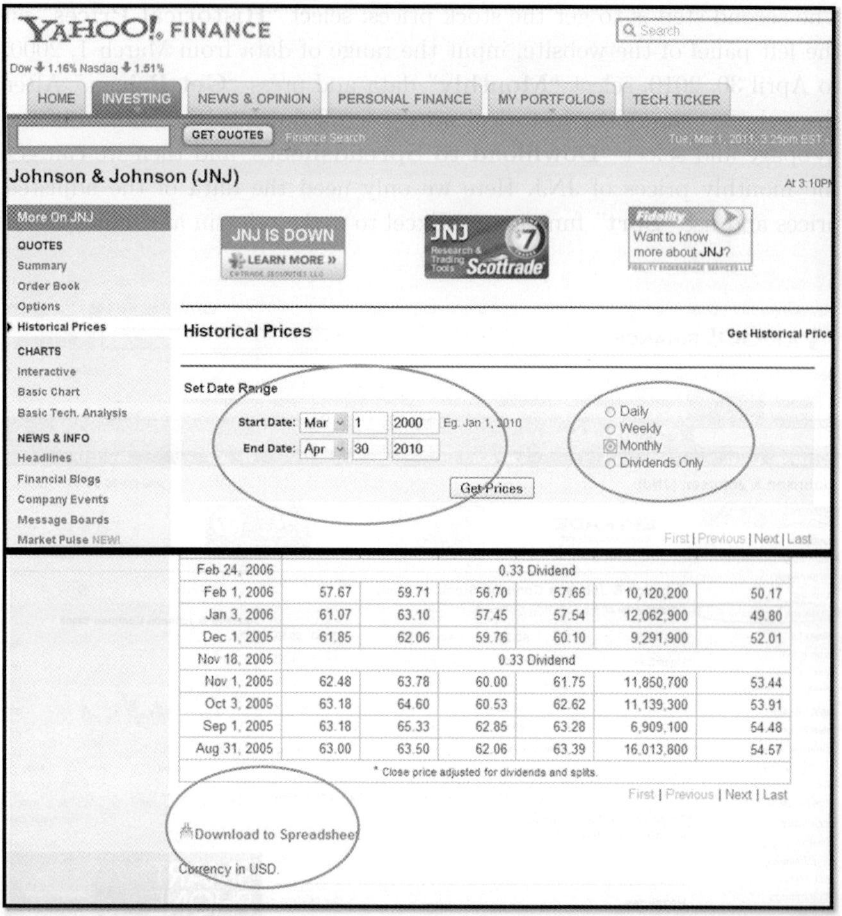
YAHOO! FINANCE
Search
Dow 1.16% Nasdaq 1.51%
HOME
INVESTING
NEWS & OPINION
PERSONAL FINANCE
MY PORTFOLIOS
TECH TICKER
GET QUOTES
Finance Search
Tue, Mar 1, 2011, 3:25pm EST
Johnson & Johnson (JNJ)
At 3:10PM
More On JNJ
QUOTES
Summary
Order Book
Options
Historical Prices
CHARTS
Interactive
Basic Chart
Basic Tech. Analysis
NEWS & INFO
Headlines
Financial Blogs
Company Events
Message Boards
Market Pulse NEW!
JNJ IS DOWN
LEARN MORE »
JNJ
Research & Trading Tools
Scottrade
Fidelity
Want to know more about JNJ?
Historical Prices
Get Historical Prices
Set Date Range
Start Date: Mar 1 2000
End Date: Apr 30 2010
Eg. Jan 1, 2010
Daily
Weekly
Monthly
Dividends Only
Get Prices
First | Previous | Next | Last
Feb 24, 2006 0.33 Dividend
Feb 1, 2006 57.67 59.71 56.70 57.65 10,120,200 50.17
Jan 3, 2006 61.07 63.10 57.45 57.54 12,062,900 49.80
Dec 1, 2005 61.85 62.06 59.76 60.10 9,291,900 52.01
Nov 18, 2005 0.33 Dividend
Nov 1, 2005 62.48 63.78 60.00 61.75 11,850,700 53.44
Oct 3, 2005 63.18 64.60 60.53 62.62 11,139,300 53.91
Sep 1, 2005 63.18 65.33 62.85 63.28 6,909,100 54.48
Aug 31, 2005 63.00 63.50 62.06 63.39 16,013,800 54.57
* Close price adjusted for dividends and splits.
First | Previous | Next | Last
Download to Spreadsheet
Currency in USD.

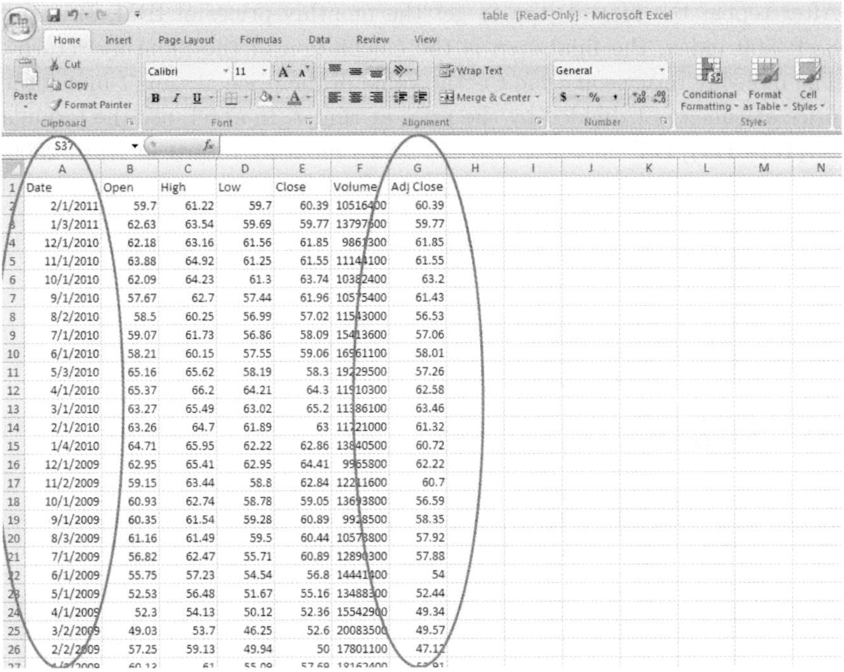

	Date	Open	High	Low	Close	Volume	Adj Close
2	2/1/2011	59.7	61.22	59.7	60.39	10516400	60.39
3	1/3/2011	62.63	63.54	59.69	59.77	13797600	59.77
4	12/1/2010	62.18	63.16	61.56	61.85	9861300	61.85
5	11/1/2010	63.88	64.92	61.25	61.55	11144100	61.55
6	10/1/2010	62.09	64.23	61.3	63.74	10382400	63.2
7	9/1/2010	57.67	62.7	57.44	61.96	10575400	61.43
8	8/2/2010	58.5	60.25	56.99	57.02	11543000	56.53
9	7/1/2010	59.07	61.73	56.86	58.09	15413600	57.06
10	6/1/2010	58.21	60.15	57.55	59.06	16961100	58.01
11	5/3/2010	65.16	65.62	58.19	58.3	19229500	57.26
12	4/1/2010	65.37	66.2	64.21	64.3	11910300	62.58
13	3/1/2010	63.27	65.49	63.02	65.2	11386100	63.46
14	2/1/2010	63.26	64.7	61.89	63	11721000	61.32
15	1/4/2010	64.71	65.95	62.22	62.86	13840500	60.72
16	12/1/2009	62.95	65.41	62.95	64.41	9965800	62.22
17	11/2/2009	59.15	63.44	58.8	62.84	12211600	60.7
18	10/1/2009	60.93	62.74	58.78	59.05	13693800	56.59
19	9/1/2009	60.35	61.54	59.28	60.89	9928500	58.35
20	8/3/2009	61.16	61.49	59.5	60.44	10578800	57.92
21	7/1/2009	56.82	62.47	55.71	60.89	12890300	57.88
22	6/1/2009	55.75	57.23	54.54	56.8	14441400	54
23	5/1/2009	52.53	56.48	51.67	55.16	13488300	52.44
24	4/1/2009	52.3	54.13	50.12	52.36	15542900	49.34
25	3/2/2009	49.03	53.7	46.25	52.6	20083500	49.57
26	2/2/2009	57.25	59.13	49.94	50	17801100	47.12

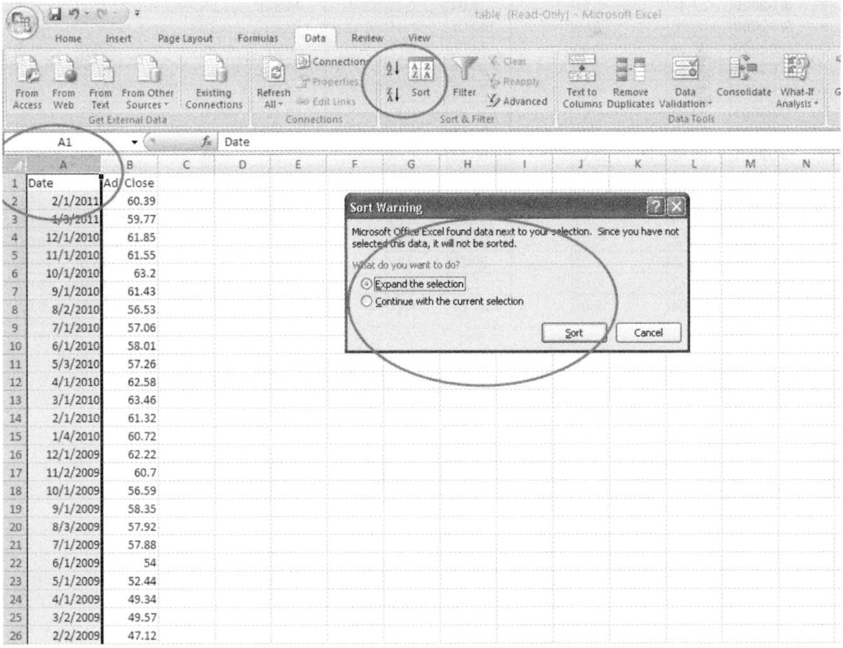

	Date	Adj Close
2	2/1/2011	60.39
3	1/3/2011	59.77
4	12/1/2010	61.85
5	11/1/2010	61.55
6	10/1/2010	63.2
7	9/1/2010	61.43
8	8/2/2010	56.53
9	7/1/2010	57.06
10	6/1/2010	58.01
11	5/3/2010	57.26
12	4/1/2010	62.58
13	3/1/2010	63.46
14	2/1/2010	61.32
15	1/4/2010	60.72
16	12/1/2009	62.22
17	11/2/2009	60.7
18	10/1/2009	56.59
19	9/1/2009	58.35
20	8/3/2009	57.92
21	7/1/2009	57.88
22	6/1/2009	54
23	5/1/2009	52.44
24	4/1/2009	49.34
25	3/2/2009	49.57
26	2/2/2009	47.12

After repeat the second step to get the monthly prices of IBM, BA, and S&P 500 index, the final step is the calculation of the monthly returns. The monthly returns at time t is the value of the price at time t minus the price at time $t-1$ divided by the price at time t. In excel, use the formula "**=(B4−B3)/B3**" in cell C4 to get JNJ's monthly return in April 2000, and then by the same way we can get the monthly returns of the individual securities and S&P 500 index.

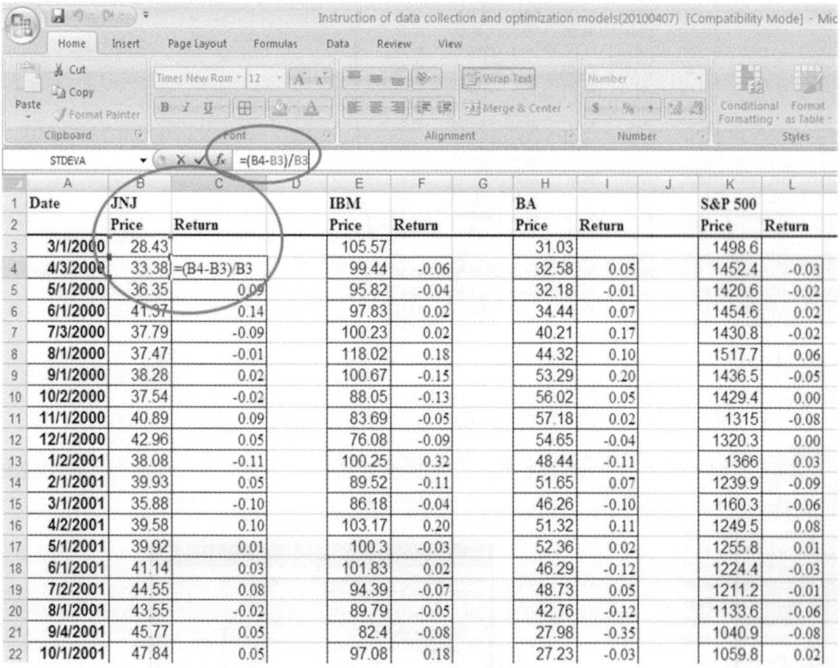

Date	JNJ Price	JNJ Return	IBM Price	IBM Return	BA Price	BA Return	S&P 500 Price	S&P 500 Return
3/1/2000	28.43		105.57		31.03		1498.6	
4/3/2000	33.38	=(B4-B3)/B3	99.44	-0.06	32.58	0.05	1452.4	-0.03
5/1/2000	36.35	0.09	95.82	-0.04	32.18	-0.01	1420.6	-0.02
6/1/2000	41.37	0.14	97.83	0.02	34.44	0.07	1454.6	0.02
7/3/2000	37.79	-0.09	100.23	0.02	40.21	0.17	1430.8	-0.02
8/1/2000	37.47	-0.01	118.02	0.18	44.32	0.10	1517.7	0.06
9/1/2000	38.28	0.02	100.67	-0.15	53.29	0.20	1436.5	-0.05
10/2/2000	37.54	-0.02	88.05	-0.13	56.02	0.05	1429.4	0.00
11/1/2000	40.89	0.09	83.69	-0.05	57.18	0.02	1315	-0.08
12/1/2000	42.96	0.05	76.08	-0.09	54.65	-0.04	1320.3	0.00
1/2/2001	38.08	-0.11	100.25	0.32	48.44	-0.11	1366	0.03
2/1/2001	39.93	0.05	89.52	-0.11	51.65	0.07	1239.9	-0.09
3/1/2001	35.88	-0.10	86.18	-0.04	46.26	-0.10	1160.3	-0.06
4/2/2001	39.58	0.10	103.17	0.20	51.32	0.11	1249.5	0.08
5/1/2001	39.92	0.01	100.3	-0.03	52.36	0.02	1255.8	0.01
6/1/2001	41.14	0.03	101.83	0.02	46.29	-0.12	1224.4	-0.03
7/2/2001	44.55	0.08	94.39	-0.07	48.73	0.05	1211.2	-0.01
8/1/2001	43.55	-0.02	89.79	-0.05	42.76	-0.12	1133.6	-0.06
9/4/2001	45.77	0.05	82.4	-0.08	27.98	-0.35	1040.9	-0.08
10/1/2001	47.84	0.05	97.08	0.18	27.23	-0.03	1059.8	0.02

The Way to Collect the Monthly Risk-Free Rates

We use Three-Month Treasury Constant Maturity Rate from Federal Reserve Bank of St. Louis (http://research.stlouisfed.org/fred2/series/GS3M). Press "**Download Data**" on the website, select the date range from April 1, 2000, to April 30, 2010, and press "**Download Data**" again.

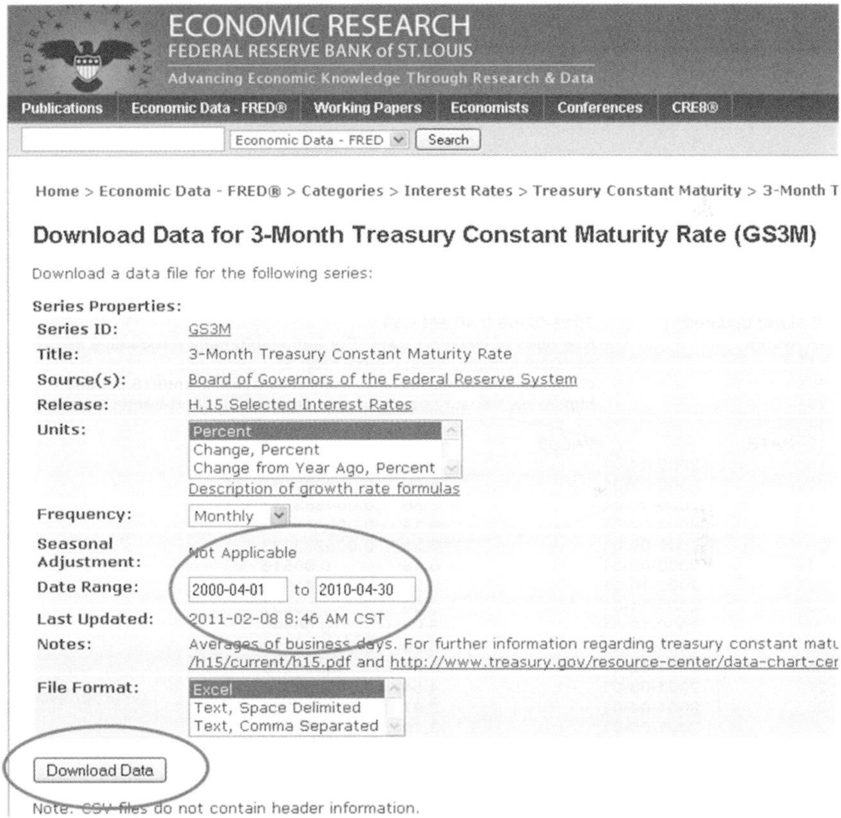

Here, the risk-free rate is in the form of percentage of annual rate, but the monthly returns of individual securities and S&P 500 index are in the form of decimal of monthly rate. To adjust the risk-free rate to monthly risk-free rate, we should divide the risk-free rate by 12. Further, to adjust the monthly risk-free rate to decimal, we should divide it by 100.

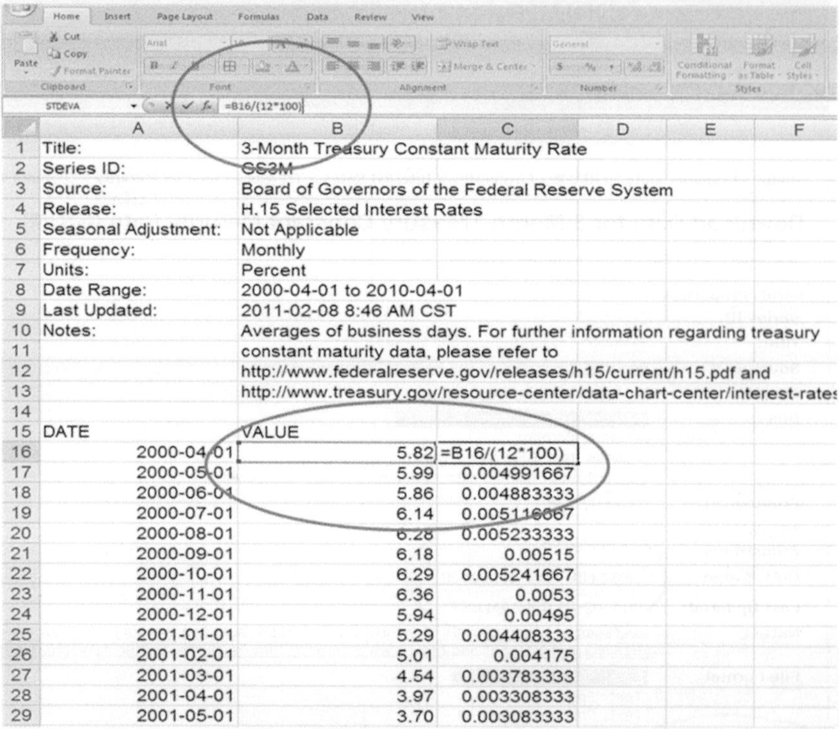

STDEVA =B16/(12*100)

	A	B	C	D	E	F
1	Title:	3-Month Treasury Constant Maturity Rate				
2	Series ID:	GS3M				
3	Source:	Board of Governors of the Federal Reserve System				
4	Release:	H.15 Selected Interest Rates				
5	Seasonal Adjustment:	Not Applicable				
6	Frequency:	Monthly				
7	Units:	Percent				
8	Date Range:	2000-04-01 to 2010-04-01				
9	Last Updated:	2011-02-08 8:46 AM CST				
10	Notes:	Averages of business days. For further information regarding treasury				
11		constant maturity data, please refer to				
12		http://www.federalreserve.gov/releases/h15/current/h15.pdf and				
13		http://www.treasury.gov/resource-center/data-chart-center/interest-rate				
14						
15	DATE	VALUE				
16	2000-04-01	5.82	=B16/(12*100)			
17	2000-05-01	5.99	0.004991667			
18	2000-06-01	5.86	0.004883333			
19	2000-07-01	6.14	0.005116667			
20	2000-08-01	6.28	0.005233333			
21	2000-09-01	6.18	0.00515			
22	2000-10-01	6.29	0.005241667			
23	2000-11-01	6.36	0.0053			
24	2000-12-01	5.94	0.00495			
25	2001-01-01	5.29	0.004408333			
26	2001-02-01	5.01	0.004175			
27	2001-03-01	4.54	0.003783333			
28	2001-04-01	3.97	0.003308333			
29	2001-05-01	3.70	0.003083333			

The Statistic Analysis of Samples

Copy the monthly returns of JNJ, IBM, BA, S&P 500 index, and the monthly risk-free rates into new sheet. The values of average and variance are calculated by "**AVERAGE**" and "**VARP**" functions and the covariance matrix is calculated by "**Covariance**" in "**Data Analysis**."

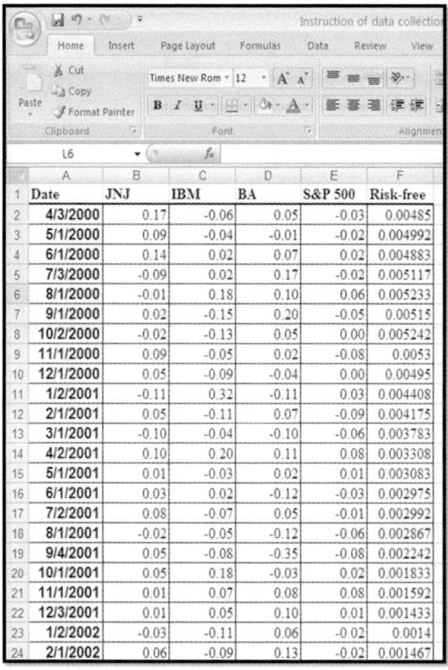

L6

	A	B	C	D	E	F
1	Date	JNJ	IBM	BA	S&P 500	Risk-free
2	4/3/2000	0.17	-0.06	0.05	-0.03	0.00485
3	5/1/2000	0.09	-0.04	-0.01	-0.02	0.004992
4	6/1/2000	0.14	0.02	0.07	0.02	0.004883
5	7/3/2000	-0.09	0.02	0.17	-0.02	0.005117
6	8/1/2000	-0.01	0.18	0.10	0.06	0.005233
7	9/1/2000	0.02	-0.15	0.20	-0.05	0.00515
8	10/2/2000	-0.02	-0.13	0.05	0.00	0.005242
9	11/1/2000	0.09	-0.05	0.02	-0.08	0.0053
10	12/1/2000	0.05	-0.09	-0.04	0.00	0.00495
11	1/2/2001	-0.11	0.32	-0.11	0.03	0.004408
12	2/1/2001	0.05	-0.11	0.07	-0.09	0.004175
13	3/1/2001	-0.10	-0.04	-0.10	-0.06	0.003783
14	4/2/2001	0.10	0.20	0.11	0.08	0.003308
15	5/1/2001	0.01	-0.03	0.02	0.01	0.003083
16	6/1/2001	0.03	0.02	-0.12	-0.03	0.002975
17	7/2/2001	0.08	-0.07	0.05	-0.01	0.002992
18	8/1/2001	-0.02	-0.05	-0.12	-0.06	0.002867
19	9/4/2001	0.05	-0.08	-0.35	-0.08	0.002242
20	10/1/2001	0.05	0.18	-0.03	0.02	0.001833
21	11/1/2001	0.01	0.07	0.08	0.08	0.001592
22	12/3/2001	0.01	0.05	0.10	0.01	0.001433
23	1/2/2002	-0.03	-0.11	0.06	-0.02	0.0014
24	2/1/2002	0.06	-0.09	0.13	-0.02	0.001467

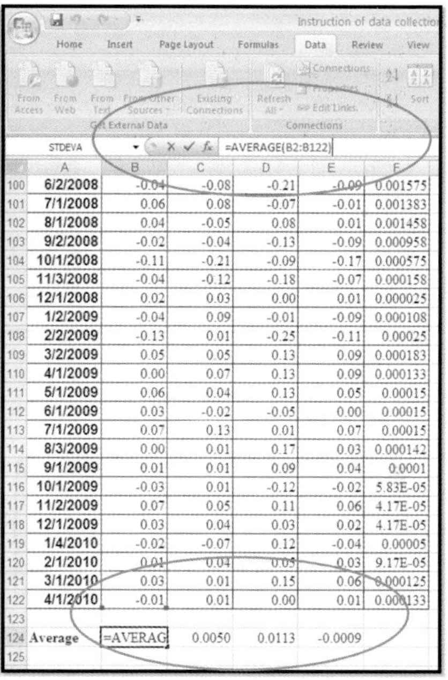

STDEVA =AVERAGE(B2:B122)

	A	B	C	D	E	F
100	6/2/2008	-0.04	-0.08	-0.21	-0.09	0.001575
101	7/1/2008	0.06	0.08	-0.07	-0.01	0.001383
102	8/1/2008	0.04	-0.05	0.08	0.01	0.001458
103	9/2/2008	-0.02	-0.04	-0.13	-0.09	0.000958
104	10/1/2008	-0.11	-0.21	-0.09	-0.17	0.000575
105	11/3/2008	-0.04	-0.12	-0.18	-0.07	0.000158
106	12/1/2008	0.02	0.03	0.00	0.01	0.000025
107	1/2/2009	-0.04	0.09	-0.01	-0.09	0.000108
108	2/2/2009	-0.13	0.01	-0.25	-0.11	0.00025
109	3/2/2009	0.05	0.05	0.13	0.09	0.000183
110	4/1/2009	0.00	0.07	0.13	0.09	0.000133
111	5/1/2009	0.06	0.04	0.13	0.05	0.00015
112	6/1/2009	0.03	-0.02	-0.05	0.00	0.00015
113	7/1/2009	0.07	0.13	0.01	0.07	0.00015
114	8/3/2009	0.00	0.01	0.17	0.03	0.000142
115	9/1/2009	0.01	0.01	0.09	0.04	0.0001
116	10/1/2009	-0.03	0.01	-0.12	-0.02	5.83E-05
117	11/2/2009	0.07	0.05	0.11	0.06	4.17E-05
118	12/1/2009	0.03	0.04	0.03	0.02	4.17E-05
119	1/4/2010	-0.02	-0.07	0.12	-0.04	0.00005
120	2/1/2010	0.01	0.04	0.05	0.03	9.17E-05
121	3/1/2010	0.03	0.01	0.15	0.06	0.000125
122	4/1/2010	-0.01	0.01	0.00	0.01	0.000133
123						
124	Average	=AVERAG	0.0050	0.0113	-0.0009	
125						

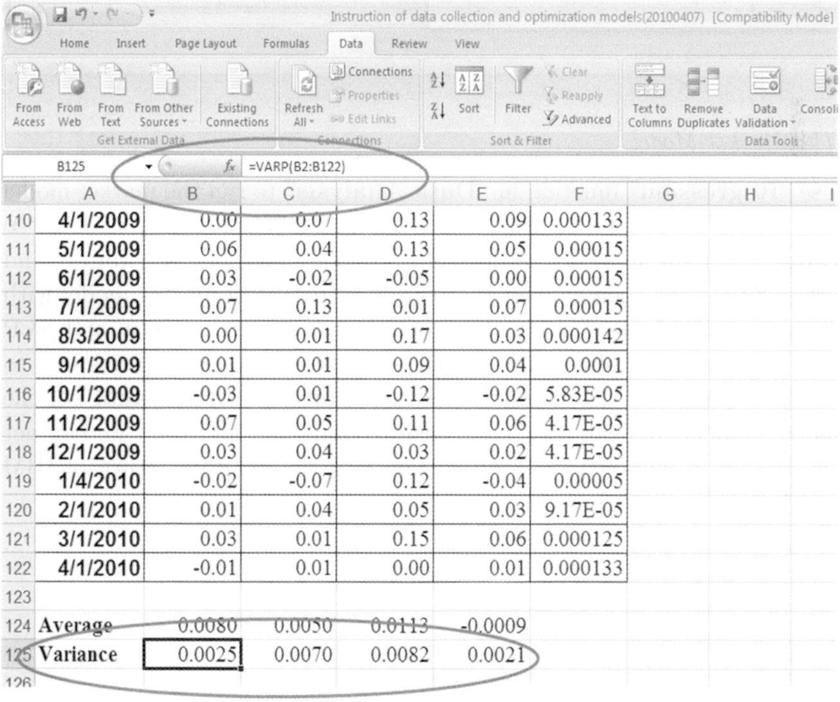

Instruction of data collection and optimization models(20100407) [Compatibility Mode]

B125 =VARP(B2:B122)

	A	B	C	D	E	F
110	4/1/2009	0.00	0.07	0.13	0.09	0.000133
111	5/1/2009	0.06	0.04	0.13	0.05	0.00015
112	6/1/2009	0.03	-0.02	-0.05	0.00	0.00015
113	7/1/2009	0.07	0.13	0.01	0.07	0.00015
114	8/3/2009	0.00	0.01	0.17	0.03	0.000142
115	9/1/2009	0.01	0.01	0.09	0.04	0.0001
116	10/1/2009	-0.03	0.01	-0.12	-0.02	5.83E-05
117	11/2/2009	0.07	0.05	0.11	0.06	4.17E-05
118	12/1/2009	0.03	0.04	0.03	0.02	4.17E-05
119	1/4/2010	-0.02	-0.07	0.12	-0.04	0.00005
120	2/1/2010	0.01	0.04	0.05	0.03	9.17E-05
121	3/1/2010	0.03	0.01	0.15	0.06	0.000125
122	4/1/2010	-0.01	0.01	0.00	0.01	0.000133
123						
124	Average	0.0080	0.0050	0.0113	-0.0009	
125	Variance	0.0025	0.0070	0.0082	0.0021	

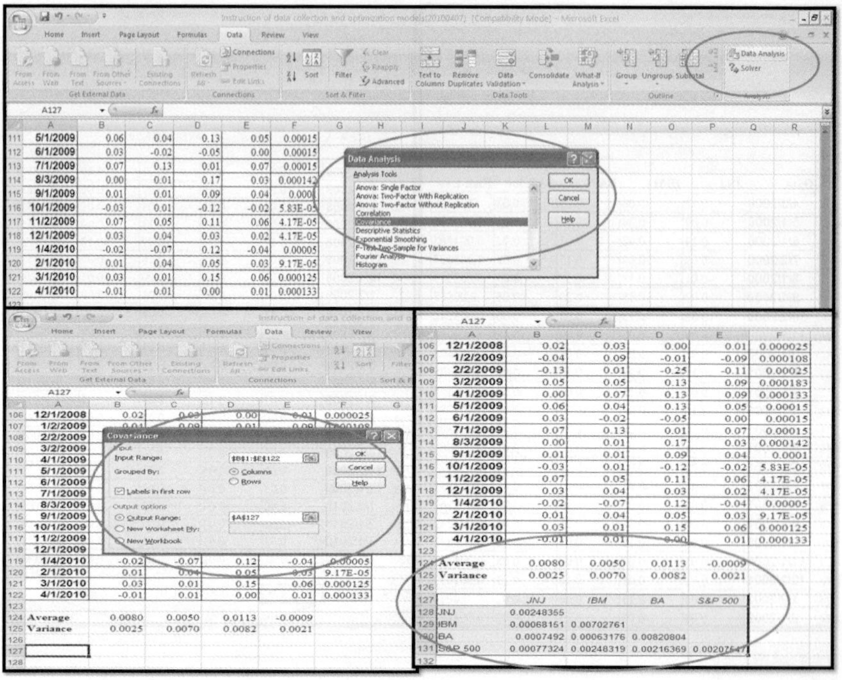

The Market Model

Use "**Regression**" function in "**Data Analysis**" to run the market model with respect to JNJ's returns, select the monthly returns of JNJ in "**Y range**" and the monthly returns of S&P 500 index in "**X range**," and press "**OK**." We then can get the regression results of market model with respect to JNJ in new sheet. The coefficients of intercept term and S&P 500 index are "**Alpha**" and "**Beta**" of market model with respect to JNJ's return. The MS of residual is the "**Variance of residual**" of the market model. Repeat the "**Regression**" function, and then we can get the results of market model with respect to the monthly return of IBM and BA.

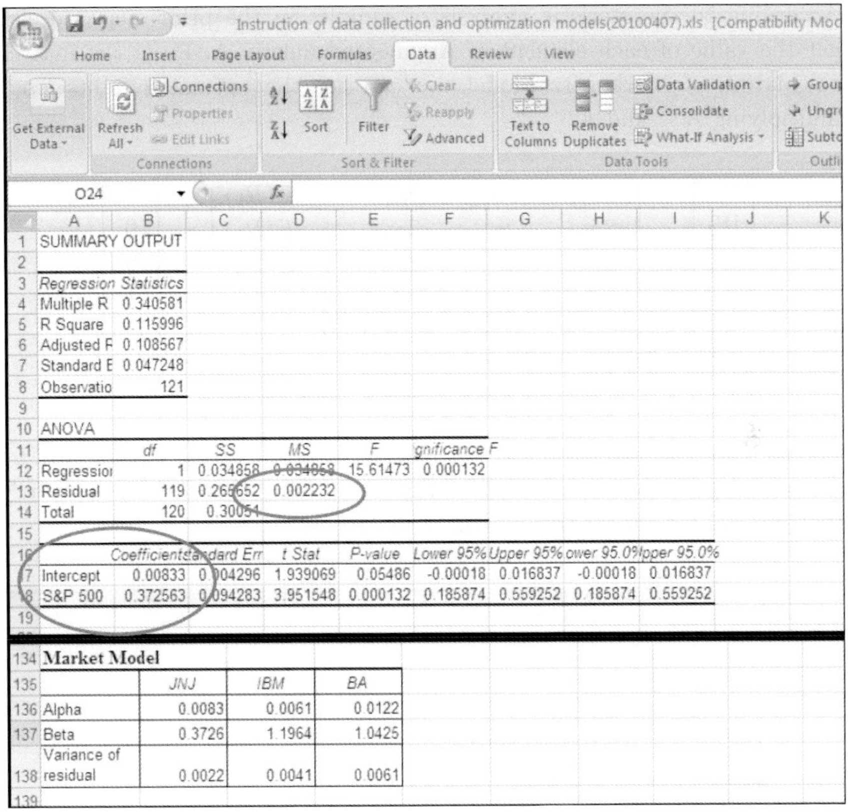

	A	B	C	D	E	F	G	H	I
1	SUMMARY OUTPUT								
2									
3	*Regression Statistics*								
4	Multiple R	0.340581							
5	R Square	0.115996							
6	Adjusted F	0.108567							
7	Standard E	0.047248							
8	Observatio	121							
9									
10	ANOVA								
11		*df*	*SS*	*MS*	*F*	*gnificance F*			
12	Regressio	1	0.034858	0.034858	15.61473	0.000132			
13	Residual	119	0.265652	0.002232					
14	Total	120	0.30051						
15									
16		*Coefficients*	*tandard Err*	*t Stat*	*P-value*	*Lower 95%*	*Upper 95%*	*ower 95.0%*	*pper 95.0%*
17	Intercept	0.00833	0.004296	1.939069	0.05486	-0.00018	0.016837	-0.00018	0.016837
18	S&P 500	0.372563	0.094283	3.951548	0.000132	0.185874	0.559252	0.185874	0.559252

134	**Market Model**			
135		*JNJ*	*IBM*	*BA*
136	Alpha	0.0083	0.0061	0.0122
137	Beta	0.3726	1.1964	1.0425
138	Variance of residual	0.0022	0.0041	0.0061

Markowitz Model

In Markowitz Model, we know

$$\underbrace{\begin{bmatrix} 2\sigma_{11} & 2\sigma_{12} & 2\sigma_{13} & 1 & E(R_1) \\ 2\sigma_{21} & 2\sigma_{22} & 2\sigma_{23} & 1 & E(R_2) \\ 2\sigma_{31} & 2\sigma_{32} & 2\sigma_{33} & 1 & E(R_3) \\ 1 & 1 & 1 & 0 & 0 \\ E(R_1) & E(R_2) & E(R_3) & 0 & 0 \end{bmatrix}}_{A} \underbrace{\begin{bmatrix} W_1 \\ W_2 \\ W_3 \\ \lambda_1 \\ \lambda_2 \end{bmatrix}}_{W} = \underbrace{\begin{bmatrix} 0 \\ 0 \\ 0 \\ 1 \\ E^* \end{bmatrix}}_{K}.$$

According to the statistic analysis of samples in the prior step, we can get the value of each element of Augmented matrix A. From the matrix calculation of Markowitz Model, we can get the optimal weights from multiplying A^{-1} and K.

$$\underbrace{\begin{bmatrix} W_1 \\ W_2 \\ W_3 \\ \lambda_1 \\ \lambda_2 \end{bmatrix}}_{W} = \underbrace{\begin{bmatrix} 2\sigma_{11} & 2\sigma_{12} & 2\sigma_{13} & 1 & E(R_1) \\ 2\sigma_{21} & 2\sigma_{22} & 2\sigma_{23} & 1 & E(R_2) \\ 2\sigma_{31} & 2\sigma_{32} & 2\sigma_{33} & 1 & E(R_3) \\ 1 & 1 & 1 & 0 & 0 \\ E(R_1) & E(R_2) & E(R_3) & 0 & 0 \end{bmatrix}^{-1}}_{A^{-1}} \underbrace{\begin{bmatrix} 0 \\ 0 \\ 0 \\ 1 \\ E^* \end{bmatrix}}_{K}.$$

To calculate the inverse matrix of matrix A, select a range from A37 to E41 and type "**=Minverse(A37:E41)**" and press "**Ctrl+Shift+Enter,**" then we can get the inverse matrix of matrix A.

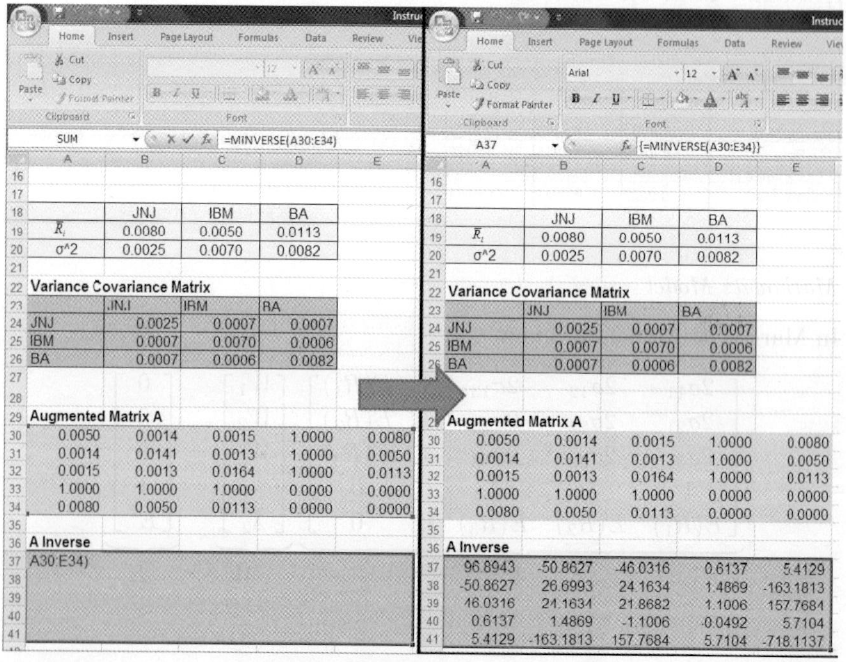

Input the value of each element of matrix K where E^* is the required return of investor. To multiply the matrixes A^{-1} and K, select a range from

A114 to A118 and type **"=MMULT(A98:E102,A106:A110)."** Press **"Ctrl+Shift+Enter,"** then we can get the optimal weight matrix W with short selling.

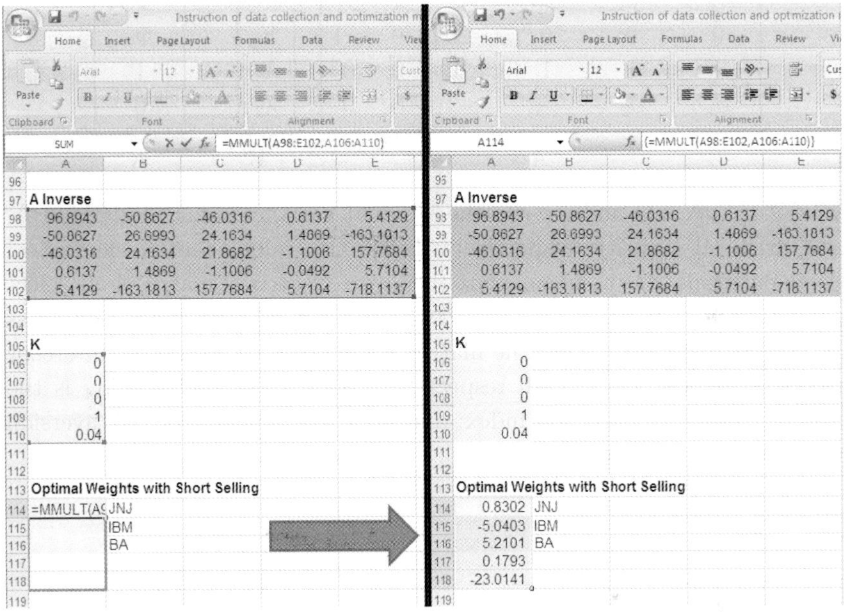

When short selling is constrained, the optimal weights can be rescaled by

$$W_{|A|} = \frac{|A|}{|A| + |B| + |C|}.$$

The rescaled absolute weights are shown in the matrix below.

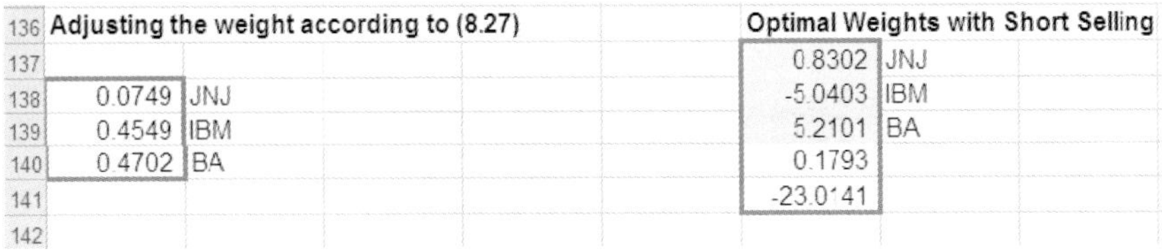
Adjusting the weight according to (8.27)
0.0749 JNJ
0.4549 IBM
0.4702 BA
Optimal Weights with Short Selling
0.8302 JNJ
-5.0403 IBM
5.2101 BA
0.1793
-23.0141

Part III

The data used in Index Model comes from the statistic analysis of samples and market model discussed in Part II. Here we use the variance of S&P 500 index as the residual variance of the artificial security. In Index Model, we know

$$\underbrace{\begin{bmatrix} -2\sigma_1^2 & 0 & 0 & 0 & 1 & \beta_1 \\ 0 & -2\sigma_2^2 & 0 & 0 & 1 & \beta_2 \\ 0 & 0 & -2\sigma_3^2 & 0 & 1 & \beta_3 \\ 0 & 0 & 0 & -2\sigma_4^2 & 0 & -1 \\ 1 & 1 & 1 & 0 & 0 & 0 \\ \beta_1 & \beta_2 & \beta_3 & -1 & 0 & 0 \end{bmatrix}}_{A} \underbrace{\begin{bmatrix} X_1 \\ X_2 \\ X_3 \\ X_4 \\ \lambda_1 \\ \lambda_2 \end{bmatrix}}_{W} = \underbrace{\begin{bmatrix} -\Phi\alpha_1 \\ -\Phi\alpha_2 \\ -\Phi\alpha_3 \\ -\Phi\alpha_4 \\ 1 \\ 0 \end{bmatrix}}_{K},$$

where σ_1^2, σ_2^2, σ_3^2, and σ_4^2 are the residual variances of JNJ, IBM, BA, and artificial security, respectively. Input the value of each element of Augmented matrix A and calculate the inverse matrix of matrix A via select a range from A167 to F172, type "**=Minverse(A159:F164)**" and press "**Ctrl+Shift+Enter**." For the matrix K, the α_1, α_2, α_3 are the intercept terms of market model with respect with JNJ, IBM, and BA; α_4 is the average return of S&P 500 index; and Φ is the indicator of risk aversion (here we assume equal to one).

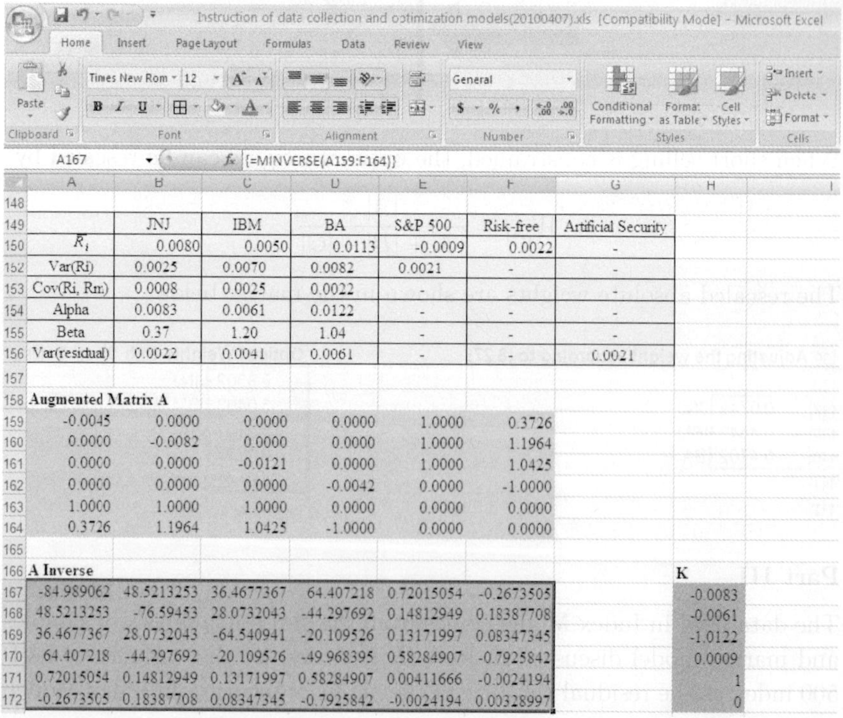

	A	B	C	D	E	F	G	H
149		JNJ	IBM	BA	S&P 500	Risk-free	Artificial Security	
150	$\bar{R}_i$	0.0080	0.0050	0.0113	-0.0009	0.0022	-	
152	Var(Ri)	0.0025	0.0070	0.0082	0.0021	-	-	
153	Cov(Ri, Rm)	0.0008	0.0025	0.0022	-	-	-	
154	Alpha	0.0083	0.0061	0.0122	-	-	-	
155	Beta	0.37	1.20	1.04	-	-	-	
156	Var(residual)	0.0022	0.0041	0.0061	-	-	0.0021	
158	**Augmented Matrix A**							
159	-0.0045	0.0000	0.0000	0.0000	1.0000	0.3726		
160	0.0000	-0.0082	0.0000	0.0000	1.0000	1.1964		
161	0.0000	0.0000	-0.0121	0.0000	1.0000	1.0425		
162	0.0000	0.0000	0.0000	-0.0042	0.0000	-1.0000		
163	1.0000	1.0000	1.0000	0.0000	0.0000	0.0000		
164	0.3726	1.1964	1.0425	-1.0000	0.0000	0.0000		
166	**A Inverse**							**K**
167	-84.989062	48.5213253	36.4677367	64.407218	0.72015054	-0.2673505		-0.0083
168	48.5213253	-76.59453	28.0732043	-44.297692	0.14812949	0.18387708		-0.0061
169	36.4677367	28.0732043	-64.540941	-20.109526	0.13171997	0.08347345		-1.0122
170	64.407218	-44.297692	-20.109526	-49.968395	0.58284907	-0.7925842		0.0009
171	0.72015054	0.14812949	0.13171997	0.58284907	0.00411666	-0.0024194		1
172	-0.2673505	0.18387708	0.08347345	-0.7925842	-0.0024194	0.00328997		0

From the matrix calculation of Index Model, we can get the optimal weights from multiplying A^{-1} and K.

$$\underbrace{\begin{bmatrix} X_1 \\ X_2 \\ X_3 \\ X_4 \\ \lambda_1 \\ \lambda_2 \end{bmatrix}}_{W} = \underbrace{\begin{bmatrix} -2\sigma_1^2 & 0 & 0 & 0 & 1 & \beta_1 \\ 0 & -2\sigma_2^2 & 0 & 0 & 1 & \beta_2 \\ 0 & 0 & -2\sigma_3^2 & 0 & 1 & \beta_3 \\ 0 & 0 & 0 & -2\sigma_4^2 & 0 & -1 \\ 1 & 1 & 1 & 0 & 0 & 0 \\ \beta_1 & \beta_2 & \beta_3 & -1 & 0 & 0 \end{bmatrix}^{-1}}_{A^{-1}} \underbrace{\begin{bmatrix} -\Phi\alpha_1 \\ -\Phi\alpha_2 \\ -\Phi\alpha_3 \\ -\Phi\alpha_4 \\ 1 \\ 0 \end{bmatrix}}_{K}.$$

Select a range from A175 to A180, type " =**MMULT(A167:F172,H167:H172)**" and press "**Ctrl+Shift+Enter**," then we can get the optimal weight matrix W. The average return on optimal portfolio and the variance of optimal portfolio are calculated by the functions $\sum_{i=1}^{3} X_i \bar{R}_i$ and $\sum_{i=1}^{3}\sum_{j=1}^{3} X_i X_j Cov(R_i, R_j)$.

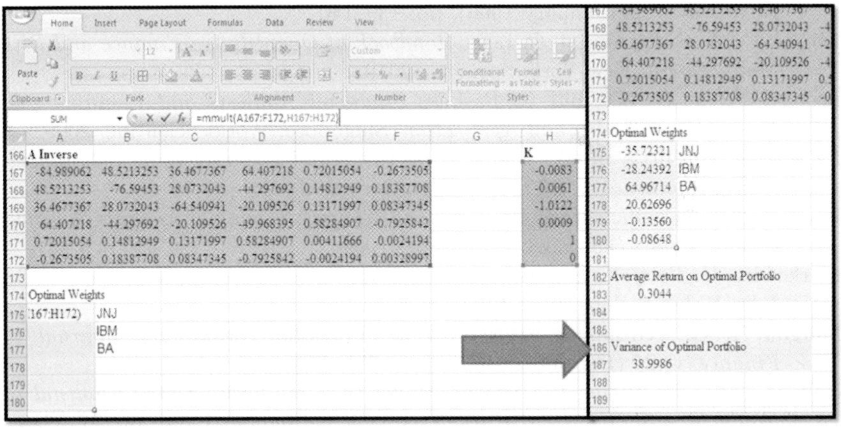

Bibliography

Beaver, W., P. Kettler and M. Scholes. "The Association between Market Determined and Accounting Determined Risk Measures." *The Accounting Review*, v. 45 (October 1970), pp. 654–682.

Blume, M. "Betas and Their Regression Tendencies." *Journal of Finance*, v. 20 (June 1975), pp. 785–795.

Brenner, M. "On the Stability of the Distribution of the Market Component in Stock Price Changes." *Journal of Financial and Quantitative Analysis*, v. 9 (December 1974), pp. 945–961.

Elton, E. J., M. J. Gruber and T. Urich. "Are Betas Best?" *Journal of Finance*, v. 23 (December 1978), pp. 1375–1384.

Elton, E. J., M. J. Gruber, S. J. Brown and W. N. Goetzmann. *Modern Portfolio Theory and Investment Analysis*, 7th ed. New York: John Wiley & Sons, 2006.

Fouse, W., W. Jahnke and B. Rosenberg. "Is Beta Phlogiston?" *Financial Analysts Journal*, v. 30 (January/February 1974), pp. 70–80.

Frankfurter, G. and H. Phillips. "Alpha-Beta Theory: A Word of Caution. "*Journal of Financial Management*, v. 3 (Summer 1977), pp. 35–40.

Frankfurter, G. and J. Seagle. "Performance of the Sharpe Portfolio Selection Model: A Comparison." *Journal of Financial and Quantitative Analysis*, v. 11 (June 1976), pp. 195–204.

Gibbons, M. R. "Multivariate Tests of Financial Models, a New Approach." *Journal of Financial Economics*, v. 10 (March 1982), pp. 3–27.

Haugen, R. and D. Wichern. "The Intricate Relationship between Financial Leverage and the Stability of Stock Prices. " *Journal of Finance*, v. 20 (December 1975), pp. pp. 1283–1292.

Jacob, N. "A Limited-Diversification Portfolio Selection Model for the Small Investor." *Journal of Finance*, v. 19 (June 1974), pp. 847–856.

King, B. "Market and Industry Factors in Stock Price Behavior." *Journal of Business*, v. 39 (January 1966), pp. 139–140.

Lee, C. F., A. C. Lee and J. C. Lee . *Handbook of Quantitative Finance and Risk Management.* New York: Springer, 2010.

Lee, A. C., J. C. Lee and C. F. Lee. *Financial Analysis and Planning and Forecasting: Theory and Application.* Singapore: World Scientific, 2009.

Latane, H., D. Tuttle and A. Young. "How to Choose a Market Index." *Financial Analysts Journal*, v. 27 (September/October 1971), pp. 75–85.

Levy, R. "Beta Coefficients as Predictors of Return." *Financial Analysts Journal*, v. 30 (January/February 1974), pp. 61–69.

Markowitz, H. *Portfolio Selection.* Cowles Foundation Monograph 16. New York: John Wiley & Sons, Inc., 1959.

Morgan, I. G. "Grouping Procedures for Portfolio Formation." *Journal of Finance*, v. 21 (December 1977), pp. 1759–1765.

Roll, R. "Bias in Fitting the Sharpe Model to Time Series Data." *Journal of Financial and Quantitative Analysis*, v. 4 (September 1969), pp. 271–289.

Rosenberg, B. and J. Guy. "Prediction of Beta from Investment Fundamentals." *Financial Analysts Journal*, v. 32 (May/June 1976), pp. 60–72.

Rosenberg, B. and J. Guy. "Prediction of Beta from Investment Fundamentals, Part II." *Financial Analysts Journal*, v. 32 (July/August 1976), pp. 62–70.

Rosenberg, B. and W. McKibben. "The Prediction of Systematic and Specific Risk in Common Stocks." *Journal of Financial and Quantitative Analysis*, v. 8 (March 1973), pp. 317–333.

Rosenberg, B. and V. Marathe. "The Prediction of Investment Risk: Systematic and Residual Risk." Berkeley Working Paper Series, 1974.

Ross, S. A. "Arbitrage Theory of Capital-Asset Pricing." *Journal of Economic Theory*, v. 8 (December 1976), pp. 341–360.

Ross, S. A. "Return, Risk and Arbitrage," in Friend and J. L. Bicksler (eds.), *Risk and Return in Finance*, vol. 1, pp. 187–208. Cambridge, MA: Ballinger, 1977.

Sharpe, W. F. "A Linear Programming Algorithm for Mutual Fund Portfolio Selection." *Management Science*, v. 13 (1967), pp. 499–510.

Sharpe, W. F. *Portfolio Theory and Capital Markets.* New York: McGraw-Hill Book Co., 1970.

Smith, K. V. "Stock Price and Economic Indexes for Generating Efficient Portfolios." *Journal of Business*, v. 42 (July 1969), pp. 326–335.

Stone, B. "A Linear Programming Formulation of the General Portfolio Selection Problem." *Journal of Financial and Quantitative Analysis*, v. 8 (September 1973), pp. 621–636.

Chapter 11

Performance-Measure Approaches for Selecting Optimum Portfolios

Previously, we have discussed Markowitz's (1952, 1959) full variance–covariance approach to determine optimal weights of a portfolio. Moreover, we also utilized Sharpe's index-model approach to simplify Markowitz's optimal portfolio-selection process. This chapter assumes the existence of a risk-free borrowing and lending rate and advances one step further to simplify the calculation of the optimal weights of a portfolio and the efficient frontier. First discussed are Lintner's (1965) and Elton *et al.*'s (1976) Sharpe performance-measure approaches for determining the efficient frontier with short sales allowed. This is followed by a discussion of the Treynor performance-measure approach for determining the efficient frontier with **short sales allowed**. The Treynor-measure approach is then analyzed for determining the efficient frontier with **short sales not allowed**. And finally, Dow-Jones 30 data from January 2003 through December 2007 are employed to demonstrate how the Treynor method can be applied in the real world. Overall, this chapter relates the performance-measure concepts and methods to the portfolio-selection models and makes more accessible the insights of optimal portfolio selection.

11.1. Sharpe Performance-Measure Approach With Short Sales Allowed

In deriving the capital asset pricing model (CAPM), Lintner (1965) suggests a performance-measure approach for determining the efficient frontier discussed in previous chapters. Lintner arrived at this approach through a sequence of logical steps.

Following previous chapters, the objective function for portfolio selection can be expressed:

$$\text{Max}\, L = \sum_{i=1}^{n} W_i\bar{R}_i + \lambda_1 \left\{ \left[\sum_{j=1}^{n}\sum_{i=1}^{n} \text{Cov}(R_i, R_j) \right]^{1/2} - \sigma_p \right\} + \lambda_2 \left(\sum_{i=1}^{n} W_i - 1 \right), \tag{11.1}$$

where

$\bar{R}_i$ = average rates of return for security i;
W_i (or W_j) = the optimal weight for ith (or jth) security;
$\text{Cov}(R_i, R_j)$ = the covariance between R_i and R_j;
σ_p = the standard deviation of a portfolio; and
λ_1, λ_2 = Lagrangian multipliers.

Markowitz portfolio selection model minimizes the variance given the targeted expected rate of return. Equation (11.1) maximizes the expected rates of return given targeted standard deviation.

If a constant risk-free borrowing and lending rate R_f is subtracted from Equation (11.1):

$$\text{Max}\, L' = \sum_{i=1}^{n}(W_i\bar{R}_i) - R_f + \lambda_1 \left\{ \left[\sum_{i=1}^{n}\sum_{j=1}^{n} W_iW_j\text{Cov}(R_i, R_j) \right]^{1/2} - \sigma_p \right\} + \lambda_2 \left(\sum_{i=1}^{n} W_i - 1 \right). \tag{11.2a}$$

Equations (11.1) and (11.2a), both formulated as a constrained maximization problem, can be used to obtain optimum portfolio weights $W_i(i = 1, 2, \ldots, n)$. Since R_f is a constant, the optimum weights obtained from Equation (11.1) will be equal to those obtained for Equation (11.2a). Previous chapters used the methodology of **Lagrangian multipliers**; it can be shown that Equation (11.2a) can be replaced by a nonconstrained maximization method as follows. Incorporating the constant $\sum_{i=1}^{n} W_i = 1$

into the objective function by substituting

$$R_f = (1)R_f = \left(\sum_{i=1}^{n} W_i\right) R_f = \sum_{i=1}^{n} W_i R_f$$

into Equation (11.2a):

$$\operatorname{Max} L' = \sum_{i=1}^{n} W_i(\bar{R}_i - R_f) + \lambda_1 \left[\left(\sum_{i=1}^{n}\sum_{j=1}^{n} W_i W_j \operatorname{Cov}(R_i, R_j)\right)^{1/2} - \sigma_p\right]. \tag{11.2b}$$

A two-Lagrangian multiplier problem has been reduced to a one-Lagrangian problem as indicated in Equation (11.2b). By using a special property of the relationship between $\sum_{i=1}^{n}(\bar{R}_i - R_f)$ and $(\sum_{i=1}^{n}\sum_{j=1}^{n} W_i W_j \operatorname{Cov}(R_i, R_j))^{1/2}$ the constrained optimization of Equation (11.2b) can be reduced to an unconstrained optimization problem, as indicated in Equation (11.3)[1]

$$\operatorname{Max} L = \frac{\sum_{i=1}^{n} W_i(\bar{R}_i - R_f)}{\left(\sum_{i=1}^{n} W_i^2\sigma_i^2 + \sum_{i=1}^{n}\sum_{j=1}^{n} W_i W_j \sigma_{ij}\right)^{1/2}} \quad (i \neq j), \tag{11.3}$$

where $\sigma_{ij} = \operatorname{Cov}(R_i, R_j)$. Alternatively, the objective function of Equation (11.3) can be developed as follows. This ratio L is equal to excess average rates of return for the ith portfolio divided by the standard deviation of the ith portfolio. This is a **Sharpe performance measure**.

Following Sharpe (1964) and Lintner (1965), if there is a risk-free lending and borrowing rate (R_f) and short sales are allowed, then the efficient frontier (efficient set) will be linear, as discussed in previous chapters. In terms of return (R_p) standard-deviation σ_p space, this linear efficient frontier is indicated as line R_fE in Fig. 11.1. AEC represents a feasible investment opportunity in terms of existing securities to be included in the portfolio when there is no risk-free lending and borrowing rate. If there is a risk-free lending and borrowing rate, then the efficient frontier becomes R_fE. An infinite number of linear lines represent the combination of a riskless asset and risky portfolio, such as R_fA, R_fB, and R_fE. It is

[1]Since the ratio of Equation (11.3) is homogeneous of degree zero with respect to W_i. In other words, the ratio L is unchanged by any proportionate change in the weight of W_i.

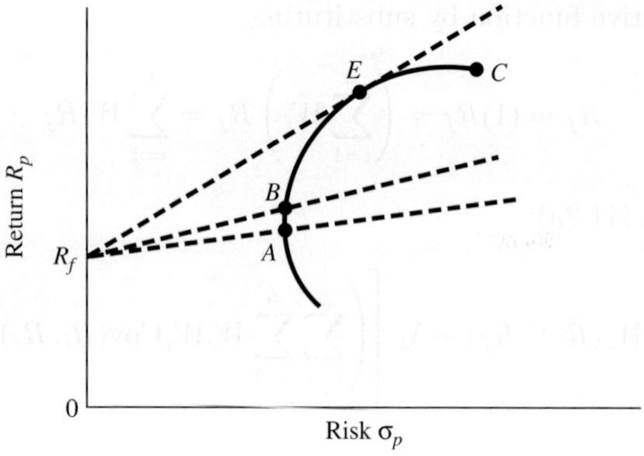

Fig. 11.1. Linear Efficient Frontier.

obvious that line R_fE has the highest slope, as represented by

$$\Theta = \frac{\bar{R}_p - R_f}{\sigma_p}, \tag{11.4}$$

in which $\bar{R}_p = \sum_{i=1}^{n} W_i\bar{R}_i$, R_f, and σ_p are defined as in Equation (11.2a). Thus the efficient set is obtained by maximizing Θ. By imposing the constraint $\sum_{i=1}^{n} W_i = 1$, Equation (11.4) is expressed:

$$\Theta' = \frac{\bar{R}_p - R_f}{\sigma_p} + \lambda\left(\sum_{i=1}^{n} W_i - 1\right). \tag{11.5a}$$

By using the procedure of deriving Equation (11.2b), Equation (11.5a) becomes

$$\Theta' = \frac{\sum_{i=1}^{n} W_i(\bar{R}_i - R_f)}{\sum_{i=1}^{n} W_i^2\sigma_i^2 + \sum_{i=1}^{n}\sum_{i=1}^{n}\sigma_{ij}}, \tag{11.5b}$$

$i \neq j$; where j.

This equation is equivalent to Equation (11.3). This approach is used by Elton and Gruber (1987) to derive their objective function for optimal portfolio selection.[2]

Following the maximization procedure discussed earlier in previous chapters, it is clear that there are n unknowns to be solved in either Equation (11.3) or Equation (11.5b). Therefore, calculus must be employed to compute n **first-order conditions** to formulate a system

[2]See Elton *et al.* (2006).

of n simultaneous equations:

$$\begin{aligned} &1 \quad \frac{dL}{dW_1} = 0 \\ &2 \quad \frac{dL}{dW_2} = 0 \\ &\vdots \qquad\quad \vdots \\ &n \quad \frac{dL}{dW_n} = 0. \end{aligned}$$

From Appendix 11A, the n simultaneous equations used to solve H_i are

$$\begin{aligned} \bar{R}_1 - R_f &= H_1\sigma_1^2 + H_2\sigma_{12} + H_3\sigma_{13} + \cdots + H_n\sigma_{1n}, \\ \bar{R}_2 - R_f &= H_1\sigma_{12} + H_2\sigma_2^2 + H_3\sigma_{23} + \cdots + H_n\sigma_{2n}, \\ &\vdots \\ \bar{R}_m - R_f &= H_1\sigma_{1n} + H_2\sigma_{2n} + H_3\sigma_{3n} + \cdots + H_n\sigma_n^2, \end{aligned} \tag{11.6a}$$

where $H_i = kW_i (i = 1, 2, \ldots, n)$; and

$$k = -\frac{\bar{R}_p - R_f}{\sigma_p^2}.$$

The H_S is proportional to the optimum portfolio weight $W_i (i = 1, 2, \ldots, n)$ by a constant factor K. To determine the optimum weight W_i, H_i is first solved from the set of equations indicated in Equation (11.6). Having done so, H_i must be called to calculate W_i, as indicated in Equation (11.7).

$$W_i = \frac{H_i}{\sum_{i=1}^{n} H_i}. \tag{11.7}$$

If there are only three securities, then Equation (11.6a) reduces to:

$$\begin{aligned} \bar{R}_1 - R_f &= H_1\sigma_1^2 + H_2\sigma_{12} + H_3\sigma_{13} \\ \bar{R}_2 - R_f &= H_1\sigma_{12} + H_2\sigma_2^2 + H_3\sigma_{23} \\ \bar{R}_3 - R_f &= H_1\sigma_{13} + H_2\sigma_{23} + H_3\sigma_3^2. \end{aligned} \tag{11.6b}$$

Sample Problem 11.1 provides further illustration.

Sample Problem 11.1

Let

$$\bar{R}_1 = 15\% \quad \bar{R}_2 = 12\% \quad \bar{R}_3 = 20\%$$
$$\sigma_1 = 8\% \quad \sigma_2 = 7\% \quad \sigma_3 = 9\%$$

$$r_{12} = 0.5 \quad r_{13} = 0.4 \quad r_{23} = 0.2$$
$$R_f = 8\%.$$

Substituting this information into Equation (11.6b):

$$15 - 8 = 64H_1 + (0.5)(8)(7)H_2 + (0.4)(8)(9)H_3$$
$$12 - 8 = (0.5)(8)(7)H_1 + 49H_2 + (0.2)(7)(9)H_3$$
$$20 - 8 = (0.4)(8)(9)H_1 + (0.2)(7)(9)H_2 + 81H_3.$$

Simplifying:

$$\begin{aligned} 7 &= 64H_1 + 28H_2 + 28.8H_3 \\ 4 &= 28H_1 + 49H_2 + 12.6H_3 \\ 12 &= 28.8H_1 + 12.6H_2 + 81H_3. \end{aligned} \tag{11.6c}$$

Using Cramer's rule, H_1, H_2, and H_3 can be solved as follows:

$$H_1 = \frac{\begin{vmatrix} 7 & 28 & 28.8 \\ 4 & 49 & 12.6 \\ 12 & 12.6 & 81 \end{vmatrix}}{\begin{vmatrix} 64 & 28 & 28.8 \\ 28 & 49 & 12.6 \\ 28.8 & 12.6 & 81 \end{vmatrix}}$$

$$= \frac{(4{,}233.6 + 1{,}451.5 + 27{,}783) - (1{,}111.3 + 9{,}072 + 16{,}934.4)}{(10{,}160.6 + 10{,}160.6 + 254{,}016) - (10{,}160.6 + 63{,}504 + 40{,}642.6)}$$

$$= \frac{33{,}648.1 - 27.1177}{160{,}030} = \frac{6{,}350.4}{160{,}030} = 3.97\%.$$

$$H_2 = \frac{\begin{vmatrix} 64 & 7 & 28.8 \\ 28 & 4 & 12.6 \\ 28.8 & 12 & 81 \end{vmatrix}}{\begin{vmatrix} 64 & 28 & 28.8 \\ 28 & 49 & 12.6 \\ 28.8 & 12.6 & 81 \end{vmatrix}}$$

$$= \frac{(2{,}540.2 + 9{,}676.6 + 20{,}736) - (9{,}676.8 + 15{,}876 + 3{,}317.8)}{160{,}030}$$

$$= \frac{32{,}952.8 - 28{,}870.6}{160{,}030} = 2.55\%.$$

$$H_3 = \frac{\begin{vmatrix} 64 & 28 & 28.8 \\ 28 & 49 & 12.6 \\ 28.8 & 12.6 & 81 \end{vmatrix}}{\begin{vmatrix} 64 & 28 & 28.8 \\ 28 & 49 & 12.6 \\ 28.8 & 12.6 & 81 \end{vmatrix}}$$

$$= \frac{(3,225.6 + 2,469.6 + 37,632) - (3{,}225.6 + 9{,}480 + 9{,}878.4)}{160{,}030}$$

$$= \frac{20{,}815.2}{160{,}030} = 13.01\%.$$

Using Equation (11.7), W_1, W_2, and W_3 are obtained:

$$\begin{aligned} W_1 &= \frac{H_1}{\sum_{i=1}^3 H_i} = \frac{3.97}{3.97 + 2.55 + 13.01} = \frac{3.97}{18.53} \\ &= 20.33\% \\ W_2 &= \frac{H_2}{\sum_{i=1}^3 H_i} = \frac{2.55}{19.53} \\ &= 13.06\% \\ W_3 &= \frac{H_3}{\sum_{i=1}^3 H_i} = \frac{13.01}{19.53} \\ &= 66.61\%. \end{aligned}$$

Here $\bar{R}_p$ and σ_p^2 can be calculated by employing these weights:

$$\begin{aligned} \bar{R}_p &= (15)(0.2033) + (12)(0.1306) + (20)(0.0061) \\ &= 3.049 + 1.5672 + 13.322 \\ &= 17.9382\% \\ \sigma_p^2 &= \sum_{i=1}^{3} W_i^2 \sigma_i^2 + \sum_{i=1}^{3} \sum_{j=1}^{3} W_i W_j r_{ij} \sigma_i \sigma_j \quad i \neq j \\ &= (0.2033)^2(64) + (0.1306)^2(49) + (0.6661)^2(81) \\ &\quad + 2(0.2033)(0.1306)(0.5)(8)(7) \\ &\quad + 2(0.2033)(0.6661)(0.4)(8)(9) \\ &\quad + 2(0.2)(0.1306)(0.6661)(7)(9) \\ &= 2.645 + 0.836 + 35.939 + 1.487 + 7.8 + 2.192 \\ &= 50.899\%. \end{aligned}$$

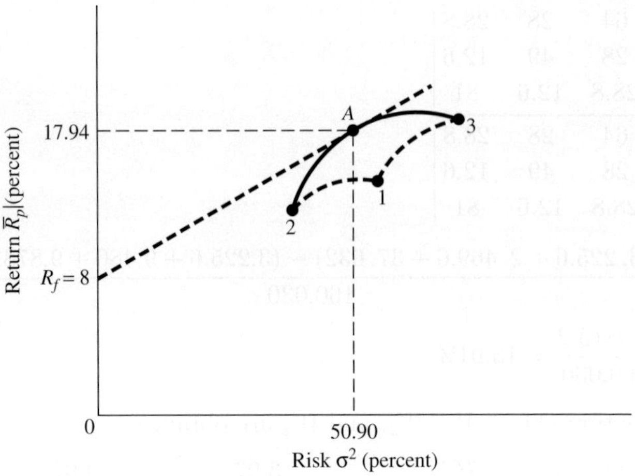

Fig. 11.2. Efficient Frontier for Example 11.1.

The efficient frontier for this example is shown in Fig. 11.2. Here A represents an efficient portfolio with $\bar{R}_p = 17.94\%$ and $\sigma_p^2 = 50.90\%$.

In addition to Cramer's rule used in this example, we can also use the matrix inversion method to solve this question. Equation (11.6b) can be written in the matrix form as following:

$$\begin{bmatrix} \bar{R}_1 - R_f \\ \bar{R}_2 - R_f \\ \bar{R}_3 - R_f \end{bmatrix} = \begin{bmatrix} \sigma_1^2 & \sigma_{12} & \sigma_{13} \\ \sigma_{21} & \sigma_2^2 & \sigma_{23} \\ \sigma_{31} & \sigma_{32} & \sigma_3^2 \end{bmatrix} \begin{bmatrix} H_1 \\ H_2 \\ H_3 \end{bmatrix}.$$

Then Equation (11.6c) can be written as following:

$$\begin{bmatrix} 7 \\ 4 \\ 12 \end{bmatrix} = \begin{bmatrix} 64 & 28 & 28.8 \\ 28 & 49 & 12.6 \\ 28.8 & 12.6 & 81 \end{bmatrix} \begin{bmatrix} H_1 \\ H_2 \\ H_3 \end{bmatrix}.$$

By using inverse matrix method in Appendix 10C of Chapter 10, we can obtain H_1, H_2, and H_3.

$$\begin{bmatrix} H_1 \\ H_2 \\ H_3 \end{bmatrix} = \begin{bmatrix} 64 & 28 & 28.8 \\ 28 & 49 & 12.6 \\ 28.8 & 12.6 & 81 \end{bmatrix}^{-1} \begin{bmatrix} 7 \\ 4 \\ 12 \end{bmatrix}$$

$$= \begin{bmatrix} 0.024 & -0.012 & -0.007 \\ -0.012 & 0.027 & 0 \\ -0.007 & 0 & 0.015 \end{bmatrix} \begin{bmatrix} 7 \\ 4 \\ 12 \end{bmatrix} = \begin{bmatrix} 0.0397 \\ 0.0255 \\ 0.1301 \end{bmatrix}.$$

The Sharpe performance-measure method discussed in this section is the most popular method used in empirical studies of portfolio management. For example, Chiou *et al.* (2010) have used this method to study stock returns, risk, and legal environment around the world. The empirical results of this paper can be found in Chapter 22 of this book.

11.2. Treynor-Measure Approach With Short Sales Allowed

Using the single-index market model discussed in previous chapter, Elton *et al.* (1976) define:

$$\sigma_p = \left(\sum_{i=1}^{n} W_i^2 \beta_i^2 \sigma_m^2 + \sum_{i=1}^{n} \sum_{\substack{j=1 \\ j \neq i}}^{n} W_i W_j \beta_i \beta_j \sigma_m^2 + \sum_{i=1}^{n} W_i^2 \sigma_{\in i}^2 \right)^{1/2}.$$

Substituting of this value of σ_p into Equation (11.3):

$$L = \frac{\sum_{i=1}^{n} W_i(\bar{R}_i - R_f)}{\sigma_p = \left(\sum_{i=1}^{n} W_i^2 \beta_i^2 \sigma_m^2 + \sum_{i=1}^{n} \sum_{\substack{j=1 \\ j \neq i}}^{n} W_i W_j \beta_i \beta_j \sigma_m^2 + \sum_{i=1}^{n} W_i^2 \sigma_{\in i}^2 \right)^{1/2}}. \tag{11.8}$$

In order to find the set of $W_i s$ that maximizes L, take the partial derivative of the above equation with respect to each W_i and some manipulation. Then we can obtain

$$W_i = \frac{H_i}{\sum_{i=1}^{n} H_i}, \tag{11.9}$$

where

$$H_i = \frac{(\bar{R}_i - R_f)}{\sigma_{\in i}^2} - \left(\frac{\sigma_m^2 \sum_{j=1}^{n} \frac{(\bar{R}_j - R_f)}{\sigma_{\in i}^2}}{1 + \sigma_m^2 \sum_{j=1}^{i} \frac{\beta_j^2}{\sigma_{ej}^2}} \right) \left(\frac{\beta_i^2}{\sigma_{\in i}^2} \right). \tag{11.10}$$

The procedure of deriving Equations (11.9) and (11.10) can be found in Appendix 11B. The $H_i s$ must be calculated for all the stocks in the portfolio. If H_i is a positive value, this indicates the stock will be held long, whereas a negative value indicates that the stock should be sold short.

This method is called the Treynor measure approach. The argument will be clearer when the case of portfolio selection with short sales not allowed is discussed.

To determine the optimum portfolio from the H_is (such that 100% of funds are invested), the weights must be scaled. One method follows the standard definition of short sales, which presumes that a short sale of stock is a source of funds to the investor; it is called the **standard method of short sales**. This standard scaling method is indicated in Equation (11.10). In Equation (11.10), H_i can be positive or negative. This scaling factor includes a definition of short sales and the constraint:

$$\sum_{i=1}^{n} W_i = 1.$$

A second method (**Lintner's** (1965) **method of short sales**) assumes that the proceeds of short sales are not available to the investor and that the investor must put up an amount of funds equal to the proceeds of the short sale. The additional amount of funds serves as collateral to protect against adverse price movements. Under these assumptions, the constraints on the W_is can be expressed as

$$\sum_{i=1}^{n} |W_i| = 1.$$

And the scaling factor is expressed as

$$W_i = \frac{H_i}{\sum_{i=1}^{n} |H_i|}. \tag{11.11}$$

Sample Problem 11.2 provides further illustration.

Sample Problem 11.2

The following example shows the differences in security weights in the optimal portfolio due to the differing short-sale assumptions. Data associated with regressions of the single-index model are presented in Table 11.1. The mean return, $\bar{R}$, the excess return $\bar{R}_i - R_f$, the beta coefficient β_i, and the variance of the error term $\sigma^2_{\in i}$ are presented from columns 2 through 5.

Table 11.1. Data Associated with Regressions of the Single-Index Model.

(1) Security Number	(2) $\overline{R}_i$	(3) $\overline{R}_i - R_f$	(4) β_i	(5) $\sigma^2_{\in i}$
1	15	10	1	30
2	13	8	2	50
3	10	5	1.43	20
4	9	4	1.33	10
5	7	2	1	30

From the information in Table 11.1, using Equations (11.9) and (11.10). $H_i(i = 1, 2, \ldots, 5)$ can be calculated as

$$H_1 = \left(\frac{1}{30}\right)\left(\frac{15-5}{1}\right) - 3.067 = 0.2311$$

$$H_2 = \left(\frac{2}{50}\right)\left(\frac{13-5}{2}\right) - 3.067 = 0.0373$$

$$H_3 = \left(\frac{1.43}{20}\right)\left(\frac{10-5}{1.43}\right) - 3.067 = 0.0307$$

$$H_4 = \left(\frac{1.33}{10}\right)\left(\frac{9-5}{1.33}\right) - 3.067 = -0.0079$$

$$H_5 = \left(\frac{1}{30}\right)\left(\frac{7-5}{1}\right) - 3.067 = -0.0356.$$

If this same example is scaled using the standard definition of short sales $(\sum_{i=1}^{5} H_i)$, which provides funds to the investor:

$$\sum_{i=1}^{5} H_i = 0.2556$$

$$W_1 = \frac{0.2311}{0.2556} = 0.9041$$

$$W_2 = \frac{0.0373}{0.2556} = 0.1459$$

$$W_3 = \frac{0.0307}{0.2556} = 0.1201$$

$$W_4 = \frac{-0.0079}{0.2556} = -0.0309$$

$$W_5 = \frac{-0.0356}{0.2556} = -0.1393.$$

Using this definition of short sales provides that the investor should invest 90.41% of his or her money in security 1, and so on. If all $W_i s$ are added together, they equal 100%. This is true because the definition says that the funds received from selling short a security should be used to purchase more of the other securities.

According to Lintner's method:

$$\sum_{i=1}^{5} |H_i| = 0.3426.$$

Now to scale the H_i values into an optimum portfolio, apply Equation (11.11):

$$W_1 = \frac{0.2311}{0.3426} = 0.6745$$

$$W_2 = \frac{0.0373}{0.3426} = 0.1089$$

$$W_3 = \frac{0.0307}{0.3426} = 0.0896$$

$$W_4 = \frac{-0.0079}{0.3426} = -0.0231$$

$$W_5 = \frac{-0.0356}{0.3426} = -0.1039.$$

Thus the Lintner model states that an investor should invest 67.45% in security 1, 10.89% in security 2, and 8.96% in security 3. The investor should then sell short 2.31% and 10.39% of securities 4 and 5, respectively.

The difference between Lintner's method and the standard method is due to the different definitions of short selling discussed earlier. The standard method assumes that the investor has the proceeds of the short sale, while Lintner's method assumes that the short seller does not receive the proceeds and must provide funds as collateral.

The method discussed in this section does not require the inputs of covariance among individual securities. Hence, it is a simpler method than that of the Sharpe performance-measure method discussed in the previous section. The relative advantage of the Sharpe performance method over the Treynor performance method is exactly identical to the relative advantage of the Markowitz model over the Sharpe single-index model. In sum, the Treynor performance method for portfolio selection requires the information of both the risk-free rate and the market rates of return.

11.3. Treynor-Measure Approach With Short Sales Not Allowed

Equation (11.10) can be modified to

$$H_i = \frac{\beta_i}{\sigma_{\in i}^2}\left(\frac{\bar{R}_i - R_f}{\beta_i} - C^*\right), \tag{11.12}$$

in which $\frac{(\bar{R}_i - R_f)}{\beta_i}$ is the **Treynor performance measure** and C^* can be defined as

$$C^* = \frac{\sigma_m^2 \sum_{j=1}^{i} \frac{(\bar{R}_i - R_f)\beta_i}{\sigma_{\in j}^2}}{1 + \sigma_m^2 \sum_{j=1}^{i} \frac{\beta_j^2}{\sigma_{\in j}^2}}. \tag{11.13}$$

Elton *et al.* (1976) also derive a Treynor-measure approach with short sales not allowed. From Appendix 11C, Equation (11.13) should be modified to

$$H_i = \frac{\beta_i}{\sigma_{\in i}^2}\left(\frac{\bar{R}_i - R_f}{\beta_i} - C^*\right) + \mu_i, \tag{11.14}$$

where

$$H_i \geq 0, \quad \mu_i \geq 0, \quad \text{and} \quad H_i \mu_i = 0,$$

then

$$C^* = \frac{\sigma_m^2 \sum_{j=1}^{d} \frac{\bar{R}_j - R_f}{\sigma_{\in j}^2}\beta_j}{1 + \sigma_m^2 \sum_{j=1}^{d} \frac{\beta_j^2}{\sigma_{\in j}^2}}, \tag{11.15}$$

where d is a set which contains all stocks with positive H_i.

If all securities have positive β_is, the following three-step procedure from Elton *et al.* can be used to choose securities to be included in the optimum portfolio[3]:

(1) Use the Treynor performance measure $(\bar{R}_i - R_f)/\beta_i$ to rank the securities in descending order.
(2) Use Equation (11.16) to calculate C_i^* for first ith securities.
(3) Include i securities for which $(\bar{R}_i - R_f)/\beta_i$ are larger than C_i^*. Then C^* is equal to C_i^*.
(4) Use Equation (11.5) to calculate optimum weights for i securities.

Sample Problem 11.3 provides further illustration.

Sample Problem 11.3

The Center for Research in Security Prices tape was the source of five years of monthly return data, from January 2006 through December 2010, for the 30 stocks in the Dow-Jones Industrial Averages (DJIAs). The value-weighted average of the S&P 500 index was used as the market while three-month Treasury-bill rates were used as the risk-free rate.

The single-index model was used with an ordinary least-squares regression procedure to determine each stock's beta. The following data were compiled for each stock.

(1) The mean monthly return $\bar{R}_i$;
(2) The mean excess return $\bar{R}_i - R_f$;
(3) The beta coefficient;
(4) The variance of the residual errors; and
(5) The Treynor performance measure $(\bar{R}_i - R_f)/\beta_i$.

All data are listed in the following worksheet, which lists the companies in descending order of Treynor performance measure.

To calculate the C_i^* as defined in Equation (11.16), $(\bar{R}_j - R_f)\beta_j/\sigma_{\epsilon j}^2$, $\sum_{j=1}^{i}[(\bar{R}_j - R_f)\beta_j/\sigma_{\epsilon j}^2]$ and $\beta_j^2/\sigma_{\epsilon j}^2$. $\sum_{j=1}^{i}(\beta_j^2/\sigma_{\epsilon j}^2)$ are calculated and presented in the worksheet. Substituting $\sigma_m^2 = 0.00207$, $\sum_{j=1}^{i}[(\bar{R}_j - R_f)\beta_j/\sigma_{\epsilon j}^2]$, and $\sum_{j=1}^{i}(\beta\sigma_j^2/\sigma_{\epsilon j}^2)$ into Equation (11.16) produces C_i^* for every firm as listed in the last column in the worksheet.

[3]If the beta coefficient β_i for ith security is positive, then the size of H_i depends on the sign of the term in parentheses. Therefore, if a security with a particular $(\bar{R}_i - R_f)/\beta_i$ is included in the optimum portfolio, all securities with a positive beta that have higher values of $(\bar{R}_i - R_f)/\beta_i$ must be included in the optimum portfolio.

Worksheet for DJIAs

TICKER	Mean $\overline{R}_1$	Standard Deviation σ_1	(1) $\overline{R} - R_f$	(2) β_1	(3) $\sigma^2_{\in i}$	(4) $\frac{(\overline{R}_i - R_f)}{\beta_i}$	(5) $\frac{(\overline{R}_i - R_f)\beta_i}{\sigma^2_{\in i}}$	(6) Cumulative Sum of Column (5)	(7) $\frac{\beta_i^2}{\sigma^2_{\in i}}$	(8) Cumulative Sum of Column (7)	(9) C_i^*
MCD	0.0173	0.0461	0.0155	0.4868	0.0015	0.0318	5.1718	5.17	162.78	162.78	0.0103
VZ	0.0095	0.0571	0.0077	0.6171	0.0022	0.0125	2.1822	7.35	174.64	337.42	0.0109
KO	0.0093	0.0510	0.0075	0.6107	0.0015	0.0122	2.9839	10.34	244.09	581.52	0.0112
WMT	0.0051	0.0473	0.0032	0.2939	0.0020	0.0110	0.4715	10.81	42.89	624.41	0.0112
IBM	0.0093	0.0603	0.0074	0.7494	0.0020	0.0099	2.7704	13.58	278.72	903.13	0.0109
MRK	0.0086	0.0778	0.0068	0.6950	0.0047	0.0097	0.9974	14.58	102.44	1005.57	0.0108
TRV	0.0072	0.0537	0.0054	0.5595	0.0020	0.0096	1.5043	16.08	156.46	1162.03	0.0107
CVX	0.0087	0.0624	0.0069	0.7161	0.0024	0.0096	2.0276	18.11	211.22	1373.25	0.0106
DIS	0.0109	0.0700	0.0091	1.0495	0.0017	0.0086	5.6156	23.72	650.72	2023.97	0.0100
UTX	0.0094	0.0616	0.0076	0.9454	0.0012	0.0080	6.0253	29.75	754.36	2778.32	0.0095
PG	0.0051	0.0489	0.0032	0.5031	0.0017	0.0064	0.9697	30.72	151.09	2929.41	0.0094
XOM	0.0048	0.0520	0.0030	0.4699	0.0021	0.0063	0.6699	31.39	105.85	3035.27	0.0093
T	0.0055	0.0616	0.0037	0.6707	0.0025	0.0055	0.9805	32.37	179.27	3214.53	0.0091
MSFT	0.0058	0.0802	0.0039	1.0130	0.0035	0.0039	1.1424	33.51	294.94	3509.47	0.0087
HPQ	0.0044	0.0752	0.0026	1.0496	0.0025	0.0024	1.0913	34.60	448.21	3957.68	0.0081
KFT	0.0030	0.0623	0.0012	0.6072	0.0028	0.0020	0.2581	34.86	129.35	4087.04	0.0079
CAT	0.0029	0.1279	0.0011	1.8954	0.0059	0.0006	0.3565	35.22	610.24	4697.27	0.0070
DD	0.0024	0.0872	0.0006	1.3410	0.0023	0.0004	0.3358	35.55	766.25	5463.52	0.0061
JNJ	0.0019	0.0443	0.0001	0.5758	0.0010	0.0002	0.0639	35.62	331.58	5795.10	0.0058

(Continued)

(*Continued*)

TICKER	Mean $\overline{R}_1$	Standard Deviation σ_1	(1) $\overline{R} - R_f$	(2) β_1	(3) $\sigma^2_{\in i}$	(4) $\frac{(\overline{R}_i - R_f)}{\beta_i}$	(5) $\frac{(\overline{R}_i - R_f)\beta_i}{\sigma^2_{\in i}}$	(6) Cumulative Sum of Column (5)	(7) $\frac{\beta_i^2}{\sigma^2_{\in i}}$	(8) Cumulative Sum of Column (7)	(9) C_i^*
MMM	0.0019	0.0665	0.0000	0.7421	0.0029	0.0000	0.0071	35.63	192.91	5988.01	0.0056
PFE	0.0012	0.0638	−0.0006	0.6569	0.0028	−0.0009	−0.1368	35.49	151.62	6139.63	0.0055
CSCO	−0.0010	0.0892	−0.0029	1.2445	0.0035	−0.0023	−1.0299	34.46	447.41	6587.04	0.0050
JPM	−0.0016	0.0991	−0.0034	1.1347	0.0061	−0.0030	−0.6362	33.82	209.63	6796.67	0.0047
BA	−0.0036	0.0965	−0.0055	1.2556	0.0048	−0.0044	−1.4447	32.38	331.72	7128.39	0.0043
INTC	−0.0041	0.0855	−0.0059	1.0853	0.0039	−0.0055	−1.6467	30.73	300.84	7429.23	0.0040
HD	−0.0028	0.0768	−0.0046	0.7130	0.0045	−0.0065	−0.7319	30.00	113.42	7542.65	0.0038
AXP	−0.0094	0.1230	−0.0113	1.7421	0.0063	−0.0065	−3.1098	26.89	480.54	8023.19	0.0032
AA	−0.0211	0.1765	−0.0229	2.6867	0.0101	−0.0085	−6.1104	20.78	716.57	8739.77	0.0023
GE	−0.0135	0.1126	−0.0154	1.6787	0.0045	−0.0092	−5.7667	15.01	629.83	9369.59	0.0015
BAC	−0.0370	0.2225	−0.0388	2.6688	0.0290	−0.0145	−3.5646	11.45	245.28	9614.87	0.0011
R_m	−0.0013									Max C_i^*	0.0112
$Var(R_m)$	0.00294										
R_f	0.00183										

Table 11.2. Positive Optimum Weight for Three Securities.

TICKER	H_i	$\frac{\beta_i}{\sigma^2_{\in i}}$	$\frac{(\overline{R_i}-R_f)}{\beta_i}$	(A) Optimum Percentage	(B) Mean $\overline{R_i}$	(A) × (B)
MCD	6.8729	334.4223	0.0318	0.9001	0.0173	0.0156
VZ	0.3609	282.9821	0.0125	0.0473	0.0095	0.0005
KO	0.4016	399.6946	0.0122	0.0526	0.0093	0.0005
Total	7.635466			1	$\overline{R_p}$	0.0165
C*	0.0112					

Using company VZ as an example:

$$C^*_{VZ} = \frac{(0.00294)(7.35)}{1 + (0.00294)(337.42)} = 0.0109.$$

From C_i^* of the worksheet, it is clear that there are three securities that should be included in the portfolio. The estimated $\beta_i/\sigma^2_{\in i}$, $(\bar{R}_i - R_f)/\beta_i$ and C_i^* of these three securities are listed in Table 11.2. Substituting this information into Equation (11.15) produces H_i for all three securities. Using security MCD as an example:

$$H_{MCD} = (334.4223)(0.0318 - 0.0112) = 6.8729.$$

Using Equation (11.12), the optimum weights can be estimated for all three securities, as indicated in Table 11.2. In other words, 90.01% of our fund should be invested in security MCD, 4.73% in security VZ, 5.26% in security KO. Based upon the optimal weights, the average rate for the portfolio $\bar{R}_p$ is calculated as 1.65%, as presented in the last column of Table 11.2.

11.4. Impact of Short Sales on Optimal-Weight Determination

The Markowitz model of portfolio analysis requires a large number of inputs as it is necessary to estimate the covariance between each pair of securities. Previously, the analysis was simplified by the assumption that security returns were related through a common response to some market index. This model, known as Sharpe's single-index model greatly reduces the number of inputs necessary to analyze the risk and return characteristics of portfolios. In both the Markowitz and Sharpe models, the analysis is facilitated by the presence of short selling.

This chapter discusses a method proposed by Elton and Gruber for the selection of optimal portfolios. Their method involves ranking securities based on their excess return to beta ratio, and choosing all securities with a ratio greater than some particular cutoff level C^*. It is interesting to note that while the presence of short selling facilitated the selection of the optimum portfolio in both the Markowitz and Sharpe models, it complicates the analysis when we use the Elton and Gruber approach. From Example 11.3, using the DJIA, absence of short selling allowed formation of the optimal portfolio using only eight stocks.

11.5. Economic Rationale of the Treynor Performance-Measure Method

Cheung and Kwan (1988) have derived an alternative simple rate of optimal portfolio selection in terms of the single-index model. First, Cheung and Kwan relate C^* as defined in Equation (11.13) to the correlation coefficient between the portfolio rates of return with i securities R_i and market rates of return $R_m(\rho_i)$:

$$\rho_i = \frac{C^*}{\sigma_m \Theta_i}, \tag{11.16}$$

where

$\rho_i = \sigma_{im}/\sigma_i\sigma_m$;
σ_{im} = covariance between R_i and R_m;
$\Theta_i = (\bar{R}_i - R_f)/\sigma_i$, the Sharpe performance measure associated with the ith portfolio; and
σ_i and σ_m = standard deviation for ith portfolio and market portfolio, respectively.

Cheung and Kwan show that ρ_i and C_i^* display the same functional behavior for optimal portfolio selection. In other words, if portfolios are formed by adding securities successively from the highest rank to the lowest rank, the optimal portfolio is reached when the correlation of the portfolio returns and the index is at its maximum. Since the expected return on the index must be positive if the investor is to invest in stocks, an objective of the investor's using the single-index model to establish the risk-return tradeoff is to pick securities that benefit the most from a market upswing. Hence, the role of index in the selection of securities for an optimum portfolio is demonstrated explicitly.

Based upon the single-index model and the risk decomposition discussed in previous chapters, the following relationships can be defined:

$$\begin{aligned} &1. \quad \rho_i = \frac{\sigma_{im}}{\sigma_i \sigma_m} \\ &2. \quad \sigma_{im} = \beta_i \sigma_m^2 \\ &3. \quad \sigma_i^2 = \beta_i^2 \sigma_m^2 + \sigma_{\in i}^2 \end{aligned} \tag{11.17}$$

From Equation (11.17), Cheung and Kwan define ρ_i in terms of β_i^2, σ_m^2, and σ_i.

$$\rho_i = \sqrt{\beta_i^2 \sigma_m^2 / \sigma_i^2 + \sigma_{\in i}^2} = \sqrt{1 - \frac{\sigma_{\in i}^2}{\sigma_i^2}},$$

in which $\sigma_{\in i}^2$ is the nonsystematic risk for the ith portfolio. They use both ρ_i and Θ_i to select securities for an optimum portfolio, and they conclude that ρ_i can be used to replace Θ_i in selecting securities for an optimum portfolio. Nevertheless, Θ_i information is still needed to calculate the weights for each security. Hence, Cheung and Kwan's ρ_i criteria is good only for understanding Elton and Gruber's performance-measure method for portfolio selection.

11.6. Summary

Following Elton *et al.* (1976) and Elton and Gruber (1987), we have discussed the performance-measure approaches to selecting optimal portfolios. We have shown that the performance-measure approaches for optimal portfolio selection are complementary to the Markowitz full variance–covariance method and the Sharpe index-model method. These performance-measure approaches are thus worthwhile for students of finance to study following an investigation of the Markowitz variance–covariance method and Sharpe's index approach.

Questions and Problems

1. Define or explain the following terms:
   (a) short selling (b) single-index model
   (c) Treynor measure (d) Sharpe measure
2. A portfolio earns an annual rate of return of 15% with a standard deviation of 10%. The risk-free rate is 7% and the return to the market is 12%. The portfolio beta is 0.8.

(a) Calculate Sharpe's performance index.
(b) Calculate Treynor's performance index.
(c) Which measure is most useful in assessing performance?

3. Given the information in the following table, calculate each security's weight in the optimal portfolio using (a) Lintner's method and (b) the standard method. Why are the weights different?

Security	$\overline{R}_i$	$\overline{R}_i - R_f$	β_i	σ_i^2
A	10	6	1.3	30
B	9	5	1.2	20
C	8	4	1.7	50
D	7	3	0.6	10

4. Given the following information, use the Sharpe performance-measure approach with short sales allowed to calculate the return and risk of the optimum portfolio. Draw a graph of the efficient frontier.

Security	$\overline{R}_i$	σ_i	r_{AB}	r_{AC}	r_{BC}	R_f
A	10%	10%	0.5			6%
B	8%	6%		0.3		
C	7%	5%			0.8	

5. Review and compare the alternative portfolio-selection methods discussed in Chapters 8, 10, and 11. Which method do you like most? Why?

Appendix 11A: Derivation of Equation (11.6a)

The objective function L as defined in Equation (11.3) can be rewritten as

$$\text{Max}\, L = \left[\sum_{i=1}^{n} W_i(\bar{R}_i - R_f)\right]\left[\sum_{i=1}^{n} W_i^2\sigma_i^2 + \sum_{i=1}^{n}\sum_{j=1}^{n} W_iW_j\sigma_{ij}\right]^{-1/2} \quad (i \neq j).$$

Then, following the product and chain rule, we have

$$\frac{dL}{dW_i} = \frac{d}{dW_i}\left[\sum_{i=1}^{n} W_i(\bar{R}_i - R_f)\right]\left[\sum_{i=1}^{n} W_i\sigma_i^2 + \sum_{i=1}^{n}\sum_{j=1}^{n} W_j\sigma_{ij}\right]^{-1/2} \quad (i \neq j)$$

$$= \left[\sum_{i=1}^{n} W_i^2\sigma_i^2 + \sum_{i=1}^{n}\sum_{j=1}^{n} W_iW_j\sigma_{ij}\right]^{-1/2} \times \frac{d}{dW_i}\left[\sum_{i=1}^{n} W_i(\bar{R}_i - R_f)\right]$$

$$+ \left[\sum_{i=1}^{n} W_i(\bar{R}_i - R_f)\right]\frac{d}{dW_i}\left[\sum_{i=1}^{n} W_i\sigma_i^2 + \sum_{i=1}^{n}\sum_{j=1}^{n} W_j\sigma_{ij}\right]^{-1/2}$$

$$= \left[\sum_{i=1}^{n} W_i^2\sigma_i^2 + \sum_{i=1}^{n}\sum_{j=1}^{n} W_iW_j\sigma_{ij}\right]^{-1/2} [\bar{R}_i - R_f]$$

$$-\frac{1}{2}\left[\sum_{i=1}^{n} W_i(\bar{R}_i - R_f)\right]\left[\sum_{i=1}^{n} W_i^2\sigma_i^2 + \sum_{i=1}^{n}\sum_{j=1}^{n} W_iW_j\sigma_{ij}\right]^{-3/2}$$

$$\times \left[2W_i\sigma_i^2 + 2\sum_{j=1}^{n} W_j\sigma_{ij}\right]$$

$$= 0 \quad (i = 1, 2, \ldots, n) \tag{11A.1}$$

Multiplying Equation (11A.1) by $[\sum_{i=1}^{n} W_i^2\sigma_i^2 + \sum_{i=1}^{n}\sum_{j=1}^{n} W_iW_j\sigma_{ij}]^{1/2}$, $i \neq j$, and rearranging yields:

$$\bar{R}_i - R_f = \left(\frac{\sum_{i=1}^{n} W_i(\bar{R}_i - R_f)}{\sum_{i=1}^{n} W_i^2\sigma_i^2 + \sum_{j=1}^{n}\sum_{j=1}^{n} W_iW_j\sigma_{ij}} \atop i \neq j\right)\left(W_i\sigma_i^2 + \sum_{j=1}^{n} W_j\sigma_{ij}\right). \tag{11A.2}$$

Defining

$$k = \frac{\sum_{i=1}^{n} W_i(\bar{R}_i - R_f)}{\sum_{i=1}^{n} W_i^2\sigma_i^2 + \sum_{i=1}^{n}\sum_{j=1}^{n} W_iW_j\sigma_{ij}}, \quad i \neq j$$

yields

$$-k\left(W_i\sigma_i^2 + \sum_{i=1}^{n} W_i\sigma_{ij}\right) + (\bar{R}_i - R_f) = 0, \quad j \neq i.$$

Therefore,

$$\frac{dL}{dW_i} = -(kW_1\sigma_{1i} + kW_2\sigma_{2i} + \cdots + kW_i\sigma_i^2 + \cdots + kW_n\sigma_{ni}) + (\bar{R}_i - R_f)$$
$$= 0$$

Define $H_i = kW_i$, where W_i are the fractions to invest in each security and H_i are proportional to this fraction. Substituting H_i for kW_i:

$$\bar{R}_i - R_f = H_i\sigma_{1i} + H_2\sigma_{2i} + \cdots + H_i\sigma_i^2 + \cdots + H_n\sigma_{ni}$$

There is one equation like this for each value of i.

$$\begin{aligned}\bar{R}_1 - R_f &= H_1\sigma_1^2 + H_2\sigma_{12} + \cdots + H_n\sigma_{1n}\\ \bar{R}_2 - R_f &= H_1\sigma_{21} + H_2\sigma_2^2 + \cdots + H_n\sigma_{2n}\\ &\vdots\\ \bar{R}_n - R_f &= H_1\sigma_{n1} + H_2\sigma_{n2} + \cdots + H_n\sigma_n^2\end{aligned}$$

This is Equation (11.6a) in the text.

Appendix 11B: Derivation of Equation (11.10)

Following the optimization procedure for deriving Equation (11A.2) in Appendix 11A:

$$\frac{dL}{dW_i} = (\bar{R}_i - R_f) - \frac{\sum_{i=1}^n W_i(\bar{R}_i - R_f)}{\sigma_p^2} \times \left(W_i\beta_i^2\sigma_m^2 + \beta_i\sum_{j=1}^n W_j\beta_j\sigma_m^2 + W_i\sigma_{\in i}^2\right) = 0, \quad j \neq i.$$

Let $H_i = [(\bar{R}_p - R_f)/\sigma_p^2]W_i$ and, solving for any H_i,

$$H_i = \frac{\bar{R}_i - R_f}{\sigma_{\in i}^2} - \frac{\beta_i\sigma_m^2\sum_{j=1}^n H_j\beta_j}{\sigma_{\in i}^2}. \tag{11B.1}$$

Multiplying both sides of the equation by β_i:

$$H_i\beta_i = \frac{(\bar{R}_i - R_f)\beta_i}{\sigma_{\in i}^2} - \frac{\beta_i\sigma_m^2\sum_{j=1}^n H_j\beta_j^2}{\sigma_{\in i}^2}. \tag{11B.2}$$

Adding together the n equation of this form yields:

$$\sum_{j=1}^{n} H_j\beta_j = \frac{\sum_{j=1}^{n} \frac{(\bar{R}_j - R_f)\beta_j}{\sigma^2_{\in i}}}{1 + \sigma^2_{\in i} \sum_{j=1}^{n} \frac{\beta_j^2}{\sigma^2_{\in i}}}. \tag{11B.3}$$

By substituting Equation (11B.3) into Equation (11B.1), we can obtain (11.10)

$$H_i = \frac{(\bar{R}_i - R_f)}{\sigma^2_{\in i}} - \left(\frac{\sigma^2_m \sum_{j=1}^{n} \frac{(\bar{R}_j - R_f)}{\sigma^2_{\in i}}}{1 + \sigma^2_m \sum_{j=1}^{i} \frac{\beta_j^2}{\sigma^2_{ej}}} \right) \left(\frac{\beta_i^2}{\sigma^2_{\in i}} \right).$$

Appendix 11C: Derivation of Equation (11.15)

This appendix discusses the use of performance measure to examine the optimal portfolio with short sales not allowed. Therefore, Equation (11B.1) from Appendix 11.B must be modified:

$$H_i = \frac{\bar{R}_i - R_f}{\sigma^2_{\in i}} - \frac{\beta_i \sigma^2_m}{\sigma^2_{\in i}} \sum_{j=1}^{n} \beta_j H_j + \mu_i, \tag{11C.1}$$

where $H_i \geq 0$, $\mu_i \geq 0$, and $\mu_i H_i = 0$ for all i.

The justification of this equation can be found in Elton *et al.* (1976). Assuming all stocks that would be in an optimal portfolio (called d) can be found, and then arranging these stocks as $i = 1, 2, \ldots, d$, for the subpopulation of stocks that make up the optimal portfolio:

$$H_i = \frac{\bar{R}_i - R_f}{\sigma^2_{\in i}} - \frac{\beta_i \sigma^2_m}{\sigma^2_{\in i}} \sum_{j=1}^{d} H_j\beta_j \quad \text{and} \quad \mu_i = 0. \tag{11C.2}$$

Multiplying both sides by β_j, summing over all stocks in d, and rearranging yields:

$$\sum_{j=1}^{d} H_j\beta_j = \frac{\sum_{j=1}^{d} \left(\frac{\bar{R}_j - R_f}{\sigma^2_{\in j}} \right) \beta_j}{1 + \sigma^2_m \sum_{j=1}^{d} \frac{\beta_j}{\sigma^2_{\in j}}}. \tag{11C.3}$$

Notice since the set d contains all stocks with positive H_i:

$$\sum_{j=1}^{n} H_j\beta_j = \sum_{j=1}^{d} H_j\beta_j,$$

and let:

$$C^* = \sigma_m^2 \frac{\sum_{j=1}^{d} \frac{\bar{R}_j - R_f}{\sigma_{\in j}^2} \beta_j}{1 + \sigma_m^2 \sum_{j=1}^{n} \frac{\beta_j^2}{\sigma_{\in j}^2}}. \tag{11C.4}$$

Using (11C.4), the following equation for H_i is obtained after substitution and rearranging from Equation (11C.1):

$$H_i = \frac{\beta_i}{\sigma_{\in i}^2}\left(\frac{\bar{R}_i - R_f}{\beta_i} - C^*\right) + \mu_i. \tag{11C.5}$$

Since $\mu_i \geq 0$, the inclusion of μ_i can only increase the value of H_i. Therefore, if H_i is positive, $\mu_i = 0$ can never make it zero and the security should be included. If $H_i < 0$ when $\mu_i = 0$, positive values of μ_i can increase H_i. However, because the product of μ_i and H_i must equal zero, as indicated in Equation (11C.1), positive values of μ_i imply $H_i = 0$. Therefore, any security $H_i < 0$ when $\mu_i = 0$ must be rejected. Therefore, Equation (11.15) in the text can be used to estimate the optimal weight of a portfolio.

Appendix 11D: Quardratic Programming and Kuhn–Tucker Conditions

The quadratic programming algorithm is based on a technique from advanced calculus called Kuhn–Tucker conditions. This technique can solve the optimal portfolio with short sales not allowed. The problem can be stated as

$$\text{Max}_{\{W_i, i=1,2,\ldots n\}} F(W) = \frac{\overline{R_p} - R_f}{\sigma_p}.$$

Subject to

$$\sum_{i=1}^{n} W_i = 1, \quad W_i \geq 0, \quad i = 1, 2, \ldots n$$

where

$$\overline{R_p} = \sum_{i=1}^{n} W_i \bar{R}_i,$$

$$\sigma_p = \left[\sum_{i=1}^{n} W_i^2 \sigma_i^2 + \sum_{i=1}^{n} \sum_{j=1}^{n} W_i W_j \sigma_{ij}\right]^{1/2}.$$

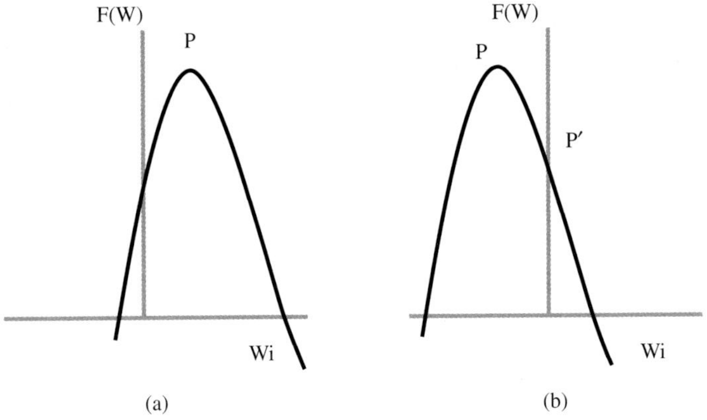

Fig. 11D.1. Value of the Function $F(W)$ as W_i Changes.

To find the maximum value of $F(W)$, there are two cases of the optimal weights $W = (W_1, W_2, \ldots W_n)$ in Fig. 11D.1

If $F(W)$ is a function of W_i in Fig. 11D.1(a), then the maximum value of $F(W)$ occurs at P, where $\frac{dF(W)}{dW_i} = 0$ at positive optimal weight ($W_i > 0$). However, in Fig. 11D.1(b), the maximum feasible value of $F(W)$ occurs at P' instead of P because of short sell not allowed, then $\frac{dF(W)}{dW_i} < 0$ at optimal weight ($W_i = 0$). Therefore, in general, we can obtain the optimal weights under conditions:

$$\frac{dF(W)}{dW_i} \leq 0,$$

$$\frac{dF(W)}{dW_i} W_i = 0.$$

We can rewrite the conditions as five Kuhn–Tucker conditions:

$$\frac{dF(W)}{dW_i} + A_i = 0,$$

$$W_i A_i = 0,$$

$$W_i \geq 0,$$

$$A_i \geq 0,$$

$$\sum_{i=1}^{n} W_i = 1.$$

When maximum feasible value occurs on $\frac{dF(W)}{dW_i} < 0$, A_i is positive and W_i is equal to zero. If maximum feasible value occurs on $\frac{dF(W)}{dW_i} = 0$, then A_i is equal to zero and W_i is positive. In the following part, we will solve the optimal weights under Kuhn–Tucker conditions by Excel.

Given an example in Fig. 11D.2: initial weights $W = (0.1, 0.2, 0.7)$, $\frac{dF(W)}{dW_i}$ can be calculated by the Equation (11A.2) in Appendix 11A and the value of the excess return and covariance matrix as below.

Then we use "***Solver***" function in Excel to find the optimal weights W. Set target cell B5 equal to the value of 1 (the fifth Kuhn–Tucker condition), select the range from B2 to C4 as change cells, and select the first and second Kuhn–Tucker conditions as the constraints.

For the third and fourth Kuhn–Tucker conditions, press "***Options***" into **Solver Options**, select "***Assume Non-Negative***" and press "***OK***." Then go back to **Solver Parameters** and press "***Solve***".

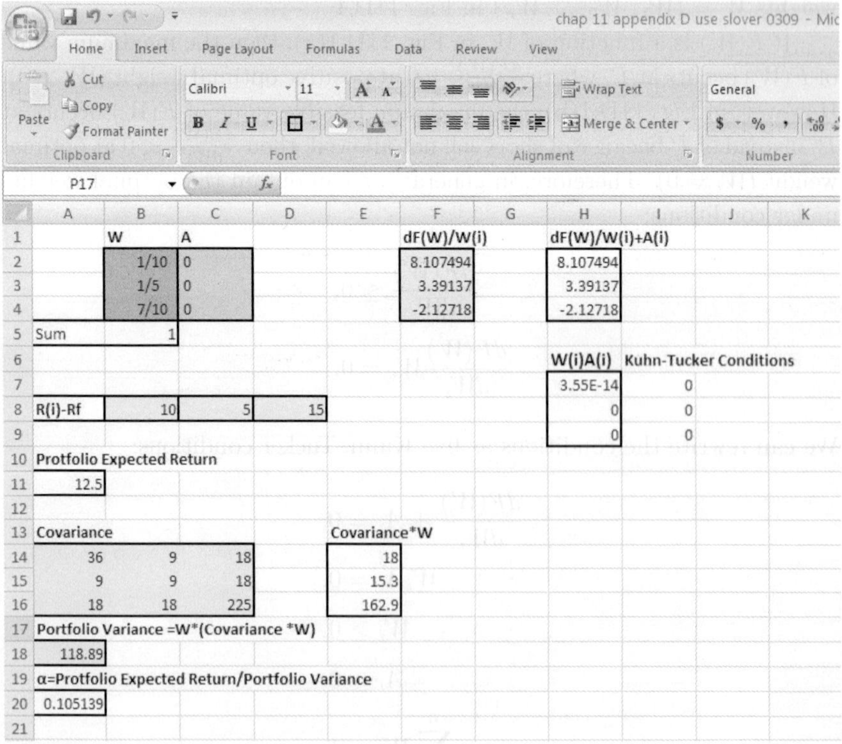

Fig. 11D.2. Solver Function in Excel.

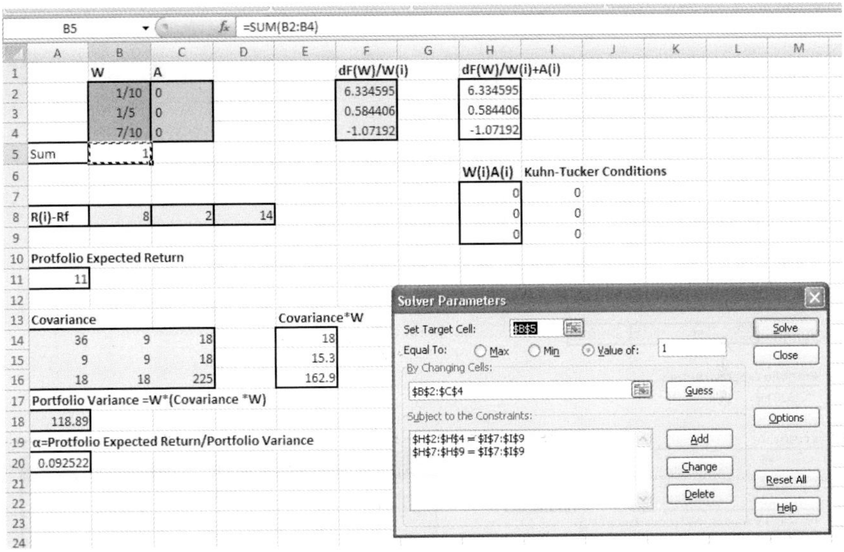

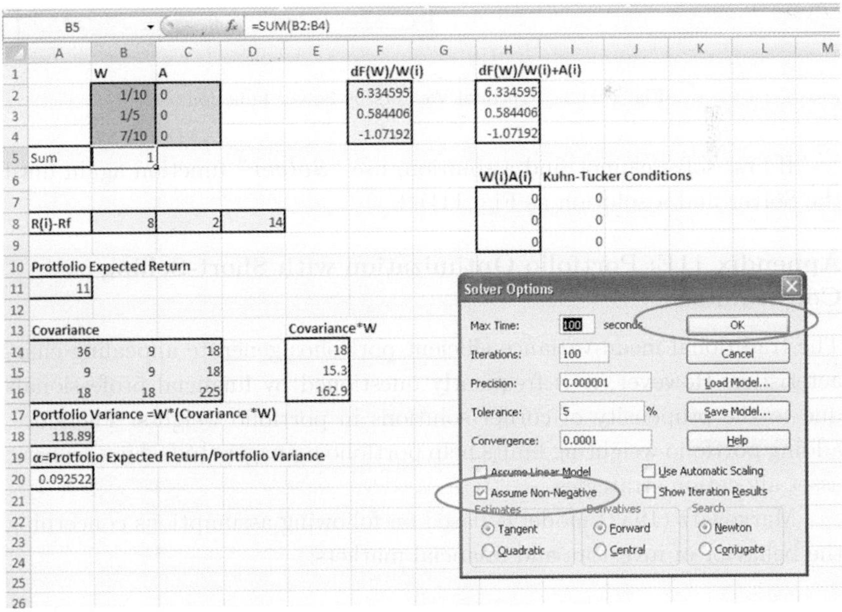

Fig. 11D.2. (*Continued*)

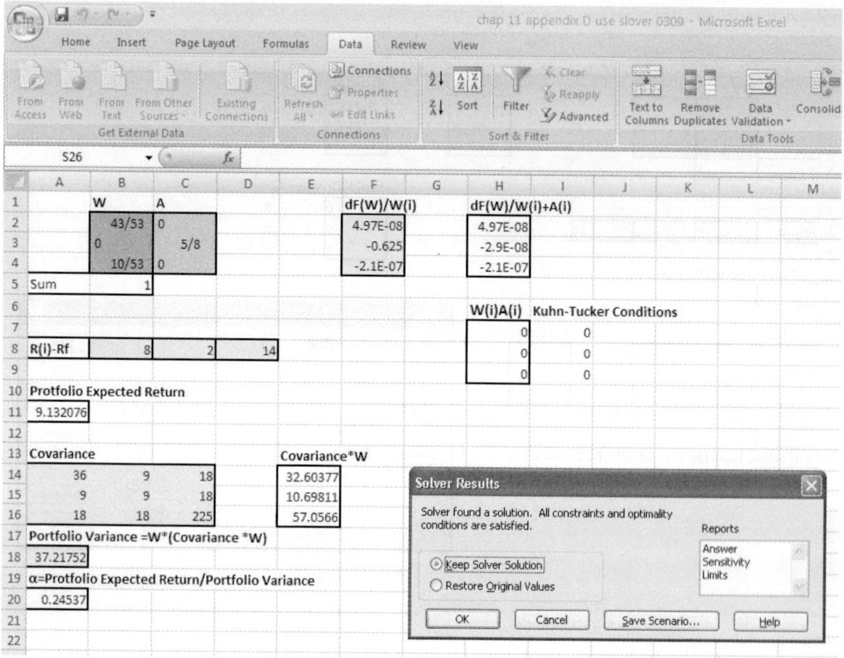

Fig. 11D.3. Optimal Weights by Solver Function.

If first solve cannot find a solution, use "***Solver***" function again until the Solver find a solution as Fig. 11D.3.

Appendix 11E: Portfolio Optimization with Short-Selling Constraints[4]

The traditional mean-variance efficient portfolios generate appealing characteristics. However, it is frequently questioned by financial professionals due to the propensity of corner solutions in portfolio weights. Therefore, adding portfolio weighting limits help portfolio managers to fashion realistic asset allocation strategies.

Markowitz (1952) model is based on following assumptions concerning the behavior of investors and financial markets:

(1) Investors have single-period utility functions in which they maximize utility within the framework of diminishing marginal utility of wealth. Return is desired but risk is to be avoided.

[4]This appendix is contributed by Paul Chiou at Central Michigan University.

(2) Investors care only about the first two moments of the returns of their portfolios over the investment period.
(3) Investors can long- and short-sell assets without limits.
(4) Financial markets are frictionless, that is, there are no taxes and costs.

Suppose risky asset investments can be characterized as a vector of multivariate returns of N securities, $\mathbf{R}^{\mathrm{T}}$. The expected risk premiums and variance-covariance of asset returns can be expressed as a vector $\boldsymbol{\mu}$ and a positive definite matrix $\mathbf{V}$, respectively. Let Ω be the set of all real vectors $\mathbf{w}$ that define the weights of assets such that $\mathbf{w}^{\mathrm{T}}\mathbf{1} = 1$, where $\mathbf{1}$ is an N-vector of ones. The expected return of the portfolio is $\mu_p = \mathbf{w}^{\mathbf{T}}\boldsymbol{\mu}$ and the variance of the portfolio is $\sigma_p = \mathbf{w}^{\mathrm{T}}\mathbf{V}\mathbf{w}$. Considering all constraints given the objective to minimize the portfolio's risk, the efficient frontier can be then expressed as a Lagrangian function:

$$\min_{\{\mathbf{w},\varphi,\eta\}} \Xi = \frac{1}{2}\mathbf{w}^{\mathrm{T}}\mathbf{V}\mathbf{w} + \phi(\mu_p - \mathbf{w}^{\mathrm{T}}\boldsymbol{\mu}) + \eta(1 - \mathbf{w}^{\mathrm{T}}\mathbf{1}). \tag{11E.1}$$

As described in the previous section, the optimal portfolio weights are a function of means, variances, and covariances of asset returns. Consider a generalized case with N assets, let

$$\mathbf{A} = \mathbf{1}^{\mathrm{T}}\mathbf{V}^{-1}\mathbf{R}, \quad \mathbf{B} = \mathbf{R}^{\mathrm{T}}\mathbf{V}^{-1}\mathbf{R}, \quad \mathbf{X} = \mathbf{1}^{\mathrm{T}}\mathbf{V}^{-1}\mathbf{1}, \quad \text{and} \quad \Delta = \mathbf{BX} - \mathbf{A}^2,$$

the solution of the above quadratic function is (see Pennacchi (2008))

$$\mathbf{w}_{\mathrm{p}} = \frac{1}{\Delta}[(\mathrm{X}\mu_{\mathrm{p}} - \mathrm{A})(\mathbf{V}^{-1}\mathbf{R}) + (\mathrm{B} - \mathrm{A}\mu_{\mathrm{p}})(\mathbf{V}^{-1}\mathbf{1})]. \tag{11E.2}$$

The short-selling constraints are further considered in Markowitz model. The inequalities that represent non-negative portfolio weights are

$$\mathbf{w}_1 \geq 0, \quad \mathbf{w}_2 \geq 0, \ldots, \mathbf{w}_{\mathrm{N}} \geq 0, \text{ where } \mathbf{w} = [\mathbf{w}_1, \mathbf{w}_2, \ldots, \mathbf{w}_{\mathrm{N}}]. \tag{11E.3}$$

The solution of this constrained diversification is to incorporate Equation (11E.3) in Equation (11E.1). Although the constraints on portfolio weights ($\mathbf{w}^{\mathrm{T}}\mathbf{1} = 1$ and Equation (11E.1)) are linear, the objective function, which is to minimize σ_{p}, is nonlinear as it contains the squares and cross-products of portfolio weights. There is no standard package to solve this quadratic programming issue because of the inequality restriction on each of elements in $\mathbf{w}$.[5]

Kuhn–Tucker conditions are frequently applied to solve the above problem. Consider the quadratic property in the objective function; the

[5]For detailed discussion, see Chapters 6 and 9 in Elton *et al.* (2007).

traditional Lagrangian techniques encounter difficulty to solve the global optimum. When inequalities are active, they will be treated as equalities and are included in the Lagrangian. Once the equalities are inactive, they should be left out. The advantage is that Kuhn–Tucker conditions require the objective function gradient to be expressible as a multiplier-weighted combination of constrained gradient. The quadratic programming problem becomes complicated once there are more constraints included and can be solved by computer program.[6] However, the results of such constrained optimization in asset allocation generate more feasible portfolios than the unconstrained optimization.[7]

A Numerical Example

Considering a three-asset case exemplified in the previous section, we have the following objective and constraint functions:

$$\min \sigma_p^2 = \sum_{j=1}^{3}\sum_{i=1}^{3} W_j W_i Cov(R_j, R_i), \tag{11E.4}$$

$$\text{s.t.} \quad E(R_p) = \sum_{i=1}^{3} W_i E(R_i),$$

$$\sum_{i=1}^{3} W_i = 1,$$

$$W_1 \geq 0, \quad W_2 \geq 0, \quad W_3 \geq 0.$$

Replacing the variables in Equation (11E.4), we can rewrite Equation (11E.1) as

$$\min \Xi = \left[W_1^2\sigma_{11} + W_2^2\sigma_{22} + W_3^2\sigma_{33}) \right. \\ \left. + 2(W_1W_2\sigma_{12} + W_1W_3\sigma_{13} + W_2W_3\sigma_{23}) \right.$$

[6]See Chapter 6 in Elton *et al.* (2007) and Chapter 14 in Rardin (1998).

[7]See Jagannathan and Ma (2003) and Chiou *et al.* (2009). Empirically investigate the impact of weighting constraints on international diversification and suggest that including upper and lower bounds in portfolio weights enhance feasibility of asset allocation.

$$- \phi\left(E(R_p) - \sum_{i=1}^{3} W_i E(R_i)\right) - \eta\left(\sum_{i=1}^{3} W_i - 1\right)$$

$$\left. - \lambda_1 W_1 - \lambda_2 W_2 - \lambda_3 W_3 \right], \tag{11E.5}$$

where ϕ, η, and λ_i $i = 1, 2, 3$, are Lagrange multipliers (LMs). They represent the shadow prices, or the penalty, of the constraints. The corresponding complementary slackness conditions are

$$\begin{aligned}
\phi\left(E(R_p) - \sum_{i=1}^{3} W_i E(R_i)\right) &= 0, \\
\eta\left(\sum_{i=1}^{3} W_i - 1\right) &= 0, \\
-\lambda_1 W_1 &= 0, \\
-\lambda_2 W_2 &= 0, \\
-\lambda_3 W_3 &= 0.
\end{aligned} \tag{11E.6}$$

The above complementary slackness conditions indicate that either inequality constraints should be active at a local optimum or the corresponding Lagarange variable should equal zero. For differentiable nonlinear program, solutions W_i, ϕ, η, λ_i, $i = 1, 2, 3$, satisfy the Kuhn–Tucker conditions if they fulfill complementary slackness conditions, primal constraints, and gradient equation

$$\nabla \frac{\partial \sigma_p^2}{\partial W_i} = \sum \nabla \text{ Constraint}(W_1, W_2, W_3) \cdot \text{LM}. \tag{11E.7}$$

Any combination of W_i, $i = 1, 2, 3$, for which there exist a corresponding LMs satisfying these conditions is called a Kuhn–Tucker point.

Our portfolio model has the following objective function gradient

$$\nabla \frac{\partial \sigma_p^2}{\partial W_i} = \begin{pmatrix} 0.91W_1 + 0.0018W_2 + 0.0008W_3 \\ 0.0018W_1 + 0.1228W_2 + 0.002W_3 \\ 0.0008W_1 + 0.002W_2 + 0.105W_3 \end{pmatrix} \tag{11E.8}$$

and those of the five linear constraints are

$$\begin{aligned}
\nabla\text{Constraint}_1(W_1, W_2, W_3) &= (0.0053, 0.0055, 0.0126) \\
\nabla\text{Constraint}_2(W_1, W_2, W_3) &= (1, 1, 1) \\
\nabla\text{Constraint}_3(W_1, W_2, W_3) &= (1, 0, 0) \\
\nabla\text{Constraint}_4(W_1, W_2, W_3) &= (0, 1, 0) \\
\nabla\text{Constraint}_5(W_1, W_2, W_3) &= (0, 0, 1).
\end{aligned} \tag{11E.9}$$

Therefore the gradient equation part of Kuhn–Tucker conditions is

$$\begin{aligned}
0.0053\phi + 1\eta + 1\lambda_1 &= 0.91W_1 + 0.0018W_2 + 0.0008W_3 \\
0.0055\phi + 1\eta + 1\lambda_2 &= 0.0018W_1 + 0.1228W_2 + 0.002W_3 \\
0.0126\phi + 1\eta + 1\lambda_3 &= 0.0008W_1 + 0.002W_2 + 0.105W_3
\end{aligned} \tag{11E.10}$$

plus the primal constraints as part of the conditions

$$\begin{aligned}
E(R_p) &= \sum_{i=1}^{3} W_i E(R_i), \\
\sum_{i=1}^{3} W_i &= 1, \\
W_1 &\geq 0, \\
W_2 &\geq 0, \\
W_3 &\geq 0.
\end{aligned} \tag{11E.11}$$

and complementary slackness conditions in Equation (11E.6).

Notice that the weights are functions of five LMs and bounded by inequality constraints. Since the functions of solutions of W_i are multidimensional, we cannot show their relation on a graph. One may start from any feasible point and then search an improving feasible direction $\Delta(W_1, W_2, W_3)$ chased by implementations of feasible and small steps of LMs. The stop of an improving feasible search not necessarily represents the current Kuhn–Tucker point is the global optimum but suggests it is a local optimum. Since there is no close-form solution function for each weight, one may need to continue the search until no improvement can be found. In our case, if

$$\nabla \frac{\partial \sigma_p^2}{\partial W_i} \cdot \Delta(W_1, W_2, W_3) < 0, \tag{11E.12}$$

there is an improvement in objective function. The time-consuming calculation of the constrained portfolio selection can be speeded by applying computer software such as Microsoft Excel and Matlab.[8]

We use the same data set to construct the nonconstrained (NC) efficient frontier and short-selling constrained (SS) efficient frontier, which is shown in Fig. 11E.1. When the portfolio weights have no limits, theoretically, the investor can expand the upper bound of efficient frontier unlimitedly by allocating assets in extreme long and short positions in different securities. The maximum return of NC efficient frontier can be infinite if the investor is willing to take infinite risk. In Fig. 11E.1, the SS optimal diversification is a subset of the NC portfolio.

The global minimum variance (MV) for the two kinds of portfolio is identical in this case. The information is listed in Table 11E.1. The conclusion of the same MV under different constraints does not always

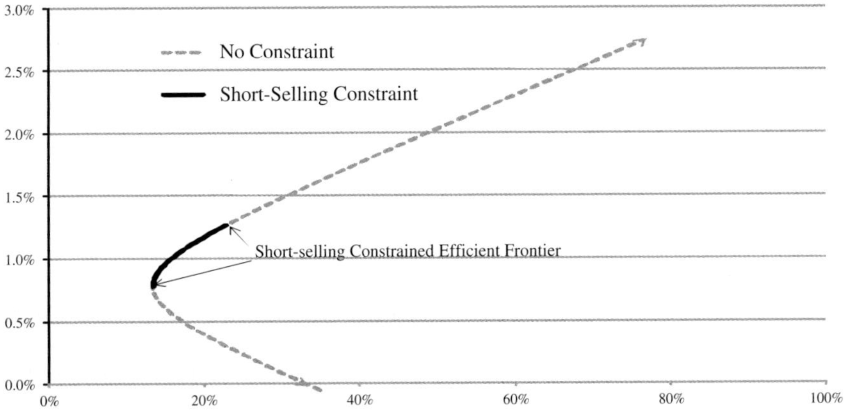

Fig. 11.E.1. Efficient Frontiers.

Table 11E.1. Minimum-Variance Portfolio.

E(R)(%)	σ(%)	Portfolio Weight	w_1(%)	w_2(%)	w_3(%)
0.78	13.39		38.57	28.10	33.33

[8]For example, the Matlab syntax `frontcon` allows users to enter a matrix which defines constraints related to minimum and maximum for assets. For more in-detail discussion, readers may refer the text of Matlab's finance function.

Table 11E.2. Portfolios on Efficient Frontier.

E(R)(%)	σ(%)	Sharpe Ratio	Portfolio Weight	w_1(%)	w_2(%)	w_3(%)
0.78	13.39	0.0333		38.57	28.10	33.33
1.04	16.87	0.0422		16.86	13.04	70.10
1.24	22.38	0.0406		−25.82	−16.90	142.72
2.63	72.96	0.0315		−100.53	−199.47	400.00
3.38	101.30	0.0300		−366.73	66.73	400.00

happen when the coefficients of correlation among securities and the relative magnitudes of return among assets change. Note that the optimal diversification strategies are sensitive to the variation in the first two moments of asset returns in the portfolio.

Notice that, theoretically, the maximum return of NC efficient frontier can be infinite if the investor is willing to take infinite risk by allocating assets in extremely huge long and short positions. However, the effectiveness of such extreme-weight diversification strategies is questionable due to their low mean-variance efficiency. As the portfolios on efficient frontiers shown in Table 11E.2, assuming the long-term annual risk-free interest rate is 4%, the portfolios of corner solutions are less mean-variance efficient than the ones without negative and extremely positive weights.

Bibliography

Alexander, G. J. and B. J. Resnick. "More on Estimation Risk and Single Rule for Optimal Portfolio Selection." *Journal of Finance*, v. 40 (March 1985), pp. 125–134.

Bodie, Z., A. Kane and A. Marcus. *Investments*, 7th ed. New York: McGraw-Hill Book Company, 2006.

Chen, S. N. and S. J. Brown. "Estimation Risk and Simple Rules for Optimal Portfolio Selection." *Journal of Finance*, v. 38 (September 1983), pp. 1087–1093.

Cheung, C. S. and C. C. Y. Kwan. "A Note on Simple Criteria for Optimal Portfolio Selection." *Journal of Finance*, v. 43 (March 1988), pp. 241–245.

Chiou, W. P., A. C. Lee and C. A. Chang. "Do Investors Still Benefit From International Diversification with Investment Constraints?" *Quarterly Review of Economics and Finance*, v. 49 (2009), pp. 449–483.

Chiou, W. P., A. C. Lee and C. F. Lee. "Stock Return, Risk and Legal Environment around the World." *International Review of Economics and Finance*, v. 19 (2010), pp. 95–105.

Elton, E. J and M. J. Gruber. "Profesionally Managed Publicly Traded Commodity Funds." Journalf of Business, v. 60 (April 1987), pp. 175–199.

Elton, E. J., M. J. Gruber, S. J. Brown and W. N. Goetzmann. *Modern Portfolio Theory and Investment Analysis*, 7th ed. New York: John Wiley & Sons, 2006.

Elton, E. J., M. J. Gruber and M. W. Padberg. "Simple Criteria for Optimal Portfolio Selection." *Journal of Finance*, v. 31 (December 1976), pp. 1341–1357.

Jagannathan, R. and T. Ma. "Risk Reduction in Large Portfolios: Why Imposing the Wrong Constraints Helps." *Journal of Finance*, v. 58 (2003), pp. 1651–1683.

Kwan, C. C. Y. "Portfolio Analysis Using Single Index, Multi-Index, and Constant Correlation Models: A Unified Treatment." *Journal of Finance*, v. 39 (December 1984), pp. 1469–1483.

Lee, C. F. and A. C. Lee. *Encyclopedia of Finance.* New York: Springer, 2006.

Lee, C. F., A. C. Lee and J. C. Lee . *Handbook of Quantitative Finance and Risk Management.* New York: Springer, 2010.

Lee, C. F., J. C. Lee and A. C. Lee. *Statistics for Business and Financial Economics.* Singapore: World Scientific Publishing Co., 2000.

Lintner, J. "The Valuation of Risk Asset on the Selection of Risky Investments in Stock Portfolio and Capital Budgets." *The Review of Economics and Statistics*, v. 57 (February 1965), pp. 13–37.

Maginn, J. L., D. L. Tuttle, J. E. Pinto and D. W. McLeavey. *Managing Investment Portfolios: A Dynamic Process*, CFA Institute Investment Series, 3rd ed. New York: John Wiley & Sons, 2007.

Markowitz, H. "Portfolio Selection." *Journal of Finance*, v. 7 (March 1952), pp. 77–91.

Markowitz, H. *Portfolio Selection: Efficient Diversification of Investments.* New York: John Wiley and Sons, 1959.

Pennacchi, G. *Theory of Asset Pricing.* Boston: Addison-Wesley, 2008.

Rardin, R. *Optimization in Operations Research.* New Jersey: Prentice Hall, 1998.

Sharpe, W. F. "A Simplified Model for Portfolio Analysis." *Management Science*, v. 9 (January 1963), pp. 277–293.

Sharpe, W. F. "Capital Asset Prices: A Theory of Market Equilibrium under Conditions of Risk." *Journal of Finance*, v. 19 (September 1964), pp. 425–442.

Wackerly, D., W. Mendenhall and R. L. Scheaffer. *Mathematical Statistics with Applications*, 7th ed. California: Duxbury Press, 2007.

Chapter 12

The Efficient-Market Hypothesis and Security Valuation

Previous chapters have discussed alternative theories and methods for evaluating stocks, bonds, futures, options on futures, and other securities. One of the assumptions used to discuss valuation theory and methods is that the capital market is efficient. In an *efficient capital market*, security prices fully reflect all available information. Therefore, empirical investigation of whether the capital market is efficient is important for security analysis and portfolio management. In finance research, a statistical hypothesis used to test whether the capital market is efficient is called the **efficient-market hypothesis (EMH)**.

This chapter focuses on the EMH and its relationship to security valuation. Valuation concepts and financial theories and models discussed in previous chapters are utilized to show the degree of efficiency with which both market-based and accounting information is reflected in current stock prices. Four major areas are discussed. The first is the relationship between market value and book value. Following this is an analysis of the market model and the capital asset pricing model (CAPM) used for testing the EMH. The EMH is then divided into three forms according to strength of efficiency, and the empirical evidence of market efficiency is presented. Last to be discussed are other recent issues related to the EMH.

12.1. Market Value Versus Book Value

One source of data used in security analysis is economic and market information. Another source — the primary source of information available to the security analyst — is accounting information from the financial statements of the firm, discussed earlier in Chapter 2. One of the key accounting items — assets — is the focus of the following section.

12.1.1. *Assets*

In general, the financial statements of the firm value the physical assets at historical cost less accumulated depreciation. This is known as **book value.** Unfortunately, the expired service of assets recorded as depreciation rarely reflects the change in the actual market value of the assets. For this reason, the book value of assets is often not relevant to the valuation of the firm.

The Securities and Exchange Commission (SEC) now requires the nation's largest companies to disclose replacement-cost information for the firm's assets. This information allows investors to analyze the difference between the book value and the cost of replacing the firm's current productive capacity. The SEC also requires disclosure of replacement cost and depreciation charges estimated on the basis of replacement cost of productive capacity.

Conventional accounting procedures do not allow assets to be written up in value except when purchased. If one firm acquires another firm at a purchase price in excess of book value, some of the assets of the acquired firm may be written up if they are deemed undervalued.

Land is not depreciated in the financial statements of the firm; neither is any increase in the **market value** (value in terms of market price) of property recognized in the balance sheet, unless some "arm's length" transaction has taken place to objectively verify the value.

The firm's portfolio of marketable equity securities is usually recorded at the lower of initial cost or market value. Marketable debt securities are generally recorded at historical cost, although the lower of cost or market value may be used for debt investments as well. A decline in the market value of an equity-security portfolio below its cost is recorded in the valuation-allowance account. This loss on the valuation of marketable equity securities flows through the income statement. Any subsequent increase in the market value of the portfolio is recognized as a recovery of loss on the valuation of marketable equity securities. However, the recovery of loss can never exceed the amount previously recorded in the valuation-allowance account. This means that securities are always valued at the lower of cost or market value.

Long-term bond investments are recorded at initial cost. Any difference between initial cost and the face value of the bond is amortized over the remaining life of the bond. The investment account is adjusted periodically to reflect the amortization of the discount or premium. Generally, the market value of the bond investment and its net carrying value differ substantially. Note that bonds in default must be marked to market.

Stock held as an investment in another corporation can be accounted for under one of two methods: (1) the equity method or (2) the lower-of-cost or market-value method. The equity method is used if the investing firm exercises significant control over the other corporation (investee). Under this method, the investment is recorded at cost. Any net earnings of the investee are recorded in proportion to the investor's share of ownership as an increase in the investment account of the investor. Dividends or net losses of the invested result in a decrease in the investing firm's investment account. The lower of the cost or market value is used if no evidence of significant control exists. These securities are handled in the same way as marketable equity securities.

12.1.2. *Liabilities and Owner's Equity*

Most current liabilities reflect their current values because they mature in less than one year. However, long-term debt in the form of bonds presents a more difficult problem.

Bond liabilities are recorded at the price at which they were sold when issued. If the bonds were not sold at par value, the discount or premium is amortized over the life of the issue. At the date of each interest payment, the amortization of a bond premium is deducted from the bonds-payable account, while amortization of a discount is added to the bonds-payable account. Obviously, the market value of the bond issue will change radically with interest-rate fluctuations over time. However, the balance-sheet account will steadily change (due to the amortization) toward the par value on the maturity date of the issue.

The stockholders' equity account of the firm consists of contributed and earned capital. Contributed capital includes capital stock and additional paid-in capital. Earned capital is better known as retained earnings. When a firm issues common stock, the capital-stock account is increased by the par value of the issue. The par value is a nominal value per share. If stock is issued at a value greater than par value, a premium results. This increases the additional paid-in capital of the firm. Stock issued at less than par value results in a discount and decreases the additional paid-in-capital account. Again, the book value of the stockholders' equity can differ greatly from the actual market value of common stock.

The true market value of any firm is the sum of the market prices of all the firm's outstanding debt and equity issues. This value is often substantially different than the accounting value or book value of the firm.

12.1.3. *Ratios and Market Information*

Many ratios computed using accounting data can also be computed using market information (as discussed in Chapter 3). For example, the long-term debt-to-assets ratio might be computed using the market value of all outstanding debt. The return-on-equity ratio could be computed using accounting information for earnings and market information for the value of equity.

Ratios should be calculated using both kinds of information to determine whether there is a difference (relative to each other or to other firms in the industry) between the two methods. Large differences indicate a need for further analysis. The following section examines some market information-related ratios.

12.1.4. *Market-to-Book Ratio*

The ratio of market-to-book value for common equity is defined as

$$\frac{\text{Price per share of common stock}}{\text{Book value per share}} = \text{Market-to-book ratio}, \qquad (12.1)$$

in which the book value per share is computed by dividing the total of stockholders' equity from the balance sheet by the number of common shares outstanding. The **market-to-book ratio** is a measure of the management's ability to operate the company and to manage its financial affairs profitable. It also is an indication of the premium the market is willing to pay for the stock, given expectations about the future profitability of the firm. If this ratio is less than one, the market has taken a dim view of the future prospects for the company. Conversely, if it is greater than one, the market is favorably impressed with the firm. Sample Problem 12.1 provides further illustration.

Table 12.1. XYZ Company Year-End Balance Sheet (Dollars in million).

XYZ Company Year-End Balance Sheet ($ million)			
Current assets	$10	Current liabilities	$10
Fixed assets	$20	Long-term debt	$25
Intangibles	$10	Equity (in shares outstanding*)	$5
Total assets	$40	Total liabilities and equity	$40

Note: 1 million shares are outstanding.

Sample Problem 12.1

The XYZ Company's financial statements and certain market information are given in the Table 12.1 below. Calculate the market-to-book ratio and indicate what it implies about XYZ. The stock sells for $20 per share.

Solution

$$\frac{\text{Price per share}}{\text{Book value per share}} = \text{Market-to-book ratio}$$

$$\frac{\$20}{\frac{\$5{,}000{,}000}{1{,}000{,}000 \text{ shares}}} = 4/1.$$

A market-to-book ratio greater than one indicates that the market likes the future prospects of XYZ. This may be due to the understatement of the value of XYZ's assets on the balance sheet (they are recorded at historic cost instead of future profitability potential), or because the market is placing value on something that does not appear on the balance sheet — for example, a new breakthrough or discovery, market leadership, expected increases in future earnings, and so on.

When attempting to estimate the weighted average cost of capital for a firm, only market values should be used in calculating the relative debt and equity weights as well as current interest costs and required returns. Book values reflect conditions at the date of issuance of the securities, whereas market values reflect the current situation facing the firm.

In addition to the market-to-book ratio given in Equation (12.1), the relationship between price per share and earnings per share (**P/E ratio**) as in Equation (12.2) is an important market-value-related ratio.

$$\text{P/E ratio} = \frac{\text{Price per share}}{\text{Earnings per share}}. \tag{12.2}$$

This ratio has been widely used by security analysts to determine whether the market price per share is reasonable. Sample Problem 12.2 provides further illustration.

Sample Problem 12.2

Given the data about XYZ Company from Sample Problem 12.1, and the income statement for the current period in the Table 12.2 below, calculate the P/E ratio for XYZ and indicate what it implies about the company. The market P/E ratio for the New York Stock Exchange (NYSE) average is 15.

Solution

$$\text{Earnings per share} = \frac{\$1{,}330{,}000}{1{,}000{,}000} = \$1.33$$

$$\frac{\text{Price per share}}{\text{Earnings per share}} = \text{P/E ratio}$$

$$\frac{\$20}{\$1.33} = 15 \text{ times.}$$

XYZ is selling at 15 times current earnings — that is, it has a P/E ratio of 15. The current market P/E ratio for a broad-based average (NYSE) is 15. This implies that the market views XYZ's earnings as similar to the average firm listed on the NYSE.

A ratio called **Tobin's *q* ratio** [developed by Tobin (1969)] as defined in Equation (12.3) has recently been used by financial managers

Table 12.2. XYZ Company Year-End Income Statement (Dollars in million).

XYZ Company Year-End Income Statement ($ million)	
Revenues	$90
Expenses	−86
Operating income	4
Interest	− 2
Taxable income	2
Tax	− 0.67
Profit	1.33/1,000,000 shares = $1.33/share

to determine a firm's investment behavior.

$$q = \frac{\text{Firm's market value}}{\text{Firm's replacement cost}}, \tag{12.3}$$

where the firm's market value is taken to be the sum of the market value of common stock, the market value of preferred stock, and the market value of the firm's debt. A firm's replacement cost can be found in its financial-accounting reports either as a supplementary statement or in the notes to the financial statement. Lindenberg and Ross (1981) have developed some theoretical and empirical implications associated with the Tobin q for economic and financial analysis. The q ratio might be useful to security analysts in determining the future market value of a firm (especially in light of the recent wave of takeovers). Sample Problem 12.3 provides further illustration.

Sample Problem 12.3

Again, this problem concerns XYZ Company. Information about its replacement value and the market value of its debt is given below. Calculate Tobin's q ratio for XYZ and indicate what information it conveys about the firm.

Replacement cost of total assets	\$50 million
Market value of XYZ's debt	\$30 million

Solution

$$\frac{\text{Firm's market value}}{\text{Firm's replacement cost}} = q$$

$$\frac{\$30\text{ million} + \$20\text{ million}}{\$50\text{ million}} = 1.$$

A q ratio of 1 indicates that the firm is fairly priced in terms of the current or replacement cost of its assets. A look at the q and P/E ratios for XYZ shows that they are fairly priced by the market. The high market-to-book ratio is caused by the understatement of the value of the firm's assets resulting from the use of historical costs for accounting purposes.

Overall, market/book ratio, P/E ratio, and Tobin's q ratio are calculated by dividing market information by some form of accounting information. These ratios are important for both security analysts and portfolio managers.

12.2. Market Efficiency in a Market-Model and CAPM Context

The quality of market valuation methods depends heavily on the concept of **market efficiency.** An efficient capital market is an important part of the economy. This is an ideal capitalistic economy in which prices are accurate signals for capital allocation. If the capital market is to function properly in the allocation of economic and financial resources, prices of securities must be accurate indicators of intrinsic value.

A useful way to begin a discussion of efficient markets is to note the difference between *perfect* capital markets and *efficient* capital markets. A **perfect market** means an economy in continuous equilibrium — that is, a market which instantly and correctly responds to new information, providing signals for real economic decisions. The following are necessary conditions for perfect capital markets.

(1) Markets are frictionless.
(2) Production and securities markets are perfectly competitive.
(3) Markets are informationally efficient.
(4) All individuals are rational expected-utility maximizers.

Given these conditions, it follows that both product and securities markets will be both allocationally and operationally efficient. Markets are allocationally efficient when resources are directed to the best available opportunities, signaled correctly by relative prices; markets are operationally efficient when transaction costs are reduced to the minimum level possible.

The overall concept of **allocational efficiency** is one in which security prices are set in such a way that investment capital is directed to its optimal use. Because of the position of the U.S. in the world economy, the allocational responsibility of U.S. financial markets can be categorized into international and domestic efficiency. Also, since the overall concept of allocational efficiency is too general to test, operational efficiency must be focused upon as a testable concept.

The concept of capital-market efficiency is much less restrictive than the notion of perfect capital markets. In an efficient capital market prices fully and instantaneously reflect all available information; thus, when assets are traded, prices are accurate signals for capital allocation.

The question that follows immediately is what is meant by the words *fully* and *instantaneously*. The issue reduces to the definition of information considered relevant and the speed of adjustment of prices to new information. Fama (1970) defines three "types" of efficiency, each of which is based on a different notion of exactly what type of information is understood to be relevant. They are:

(1) **Weak form efficiency:** No investor can earn excess returns by developing trading rules based on historical price or return information.
(2) **Semi-strong form efficiency:** No investor can earn excess returns from trading rules based on publicly available information.
(3) **Strong form efficiency:** No investor can earn excess returns using any information, whether or not publicly available.

The concept of capital-market efficiency can now be stated precisely. Fama (1976a) defines efficient capital markets as those where the joint distribution of security prices (p_{jt}), given the set of information that the market uses (Φ_{t-1}^{m}) to determine security prices at time $t-1$, is identical to the joint distribution of prices that would exist if all relevant information (Φ_{t-1}) at $t-1$ were used. Formally:

$$f_m(p_{1t}, \ldots, p_{nt} \mid \Phi_{t-1}^{m}) = f(p_{1t}, \ldots, p_{nt} \mid \Phi_{t-1}).$$

However, empirical testing of the EMH needs still another input — namely, a theory about the time-series behavior of prices of capital assets. Three theories are considered.

(1) **The fair-game model.** Based on average returns across a large number of observations, the expected return on an asset equals its actual return — that is

$$z_{j,t+1} = r_{j,t+1} - E(r_{j,t+1} \mid \Phi_t),$$

and

$$E(z_{j,t+1}) = E(r_{j,t+1} - E(r_{j,t+1} \mid \Phi_t)) = 0,$$

in which $z_{j,t+1}$ is the error term between the jth stock's actual return $r_{j,t+1}$ at time $t+1$ and its expected return $E(r_{j,t+1} \mid \Phi_t)$. The fair-game model is an expected return efficient-market model. In search of a fair game, investors can invest in securities at their current prices and can be confident that these prices fully reflect all available information and are consistent with the risks involved.

(2) **The submartingale model.** A submartingale is a fair-game model where prices in the next period are expected to be greater than prices in the current period. Formally:

$$\frac{E(P_{j,t+1} \mid \Phi_t) - P_{j,t}}{P_{j,t}} = E(r_{r,t+1} \mid \Phi_t) \geq 0.$$

When the equality holds, it is a *martingale* model. A submartingale model is appropriate for an expanding economy, one with real economic growth, or an inflationary economy, one with nominal price increases.

(3) **The random walk model.** In this case, there is no difference between the distribution of returns conditional on a given information structure and the unconditional distribution of returns. The definition of capital-market efficiency is a random walk in prices. In returns form:

$$f(r_{1,t+1}, \ldots, r_{m,t+1}) = f(r_{1,t+1}, \ldots, r_{m,t+1} \mid \Phi_t).$$

It is immediately apparent that random walks are much stronger conditions than fair games or submartingales because they require that the joint distribution of returns remain stationary over time (all the parameters of the distribution should be the same with or without an information structure).

Some major empirical implications are outlined in Fama (1970). First, fair-game models rule out the possibility of profitable trading systems based only on historical information on Φ_t. Second, the submartingale model implies that trading rules based only on historical information on Φ_t, cannot have greater expected profits than a policy of buying and holding the security. Finally, Fama thinks it best to consider the random walk model as an extension of the general expected-return or fair-game efficient-market model.

With this as background, the discussion now turns to the empirical testing of the EMH. It is constructive, however, first to discuss the model used when this theory is tested. The determination of efficient security-market pricing can be usefully placed in the pricing framework of the market model and the CAPM as developed by Sharpe (1964), Lintner (1965), and Mossin (1966). These models express the required rate of return on any individual security as an additive function of the return required on a risk-free security and the return premium required to compensate investors for the assumption of risk.

12.2.1. *Market Model*

Following Chapters 3 and 9, the market model can be defined as

$$R_{j,t+1} = \alpha_j + \beta_j R_{m,t+1} + \mu_{j,t+1}, \tag{12.4}$$

where

$R_{j,t+1}$ = the rate of return on security j for the period for t to $t + 1$:
$R_{m,t+1}$ = the corresponding return on a market index m;
α_j and β_j = parameters that vary from security to security; and
$\mu_{j,t+1}$ = error term.

Using the context of an efficient-market pricing model in which Φ_t is the set of relevant information available for determining security prices at time t, Equation (12.4) may be rewritten:

$$E(R_{j,t+1} \mid \Phi_t) = \alpha_j(\Phi_t) + \beta_j(\Phi_t)E(R_{m,t+1} \mid \Phi_t). \tag{12.5}$$

The application of this model for the EMH test is explored later in this chapter. Since the riskless rate of return, $R_{f,t+1}$, is part of the information set Φ_t:

$$\alpha_j(\Phi_t) = R_{f,t+1}[1 - \beta_j(\Phi_t)], \tag{12.6}$$

and

$$\beta_j(\Phi_t) = \frac{\text{Cov}(R_{j,t+1}, R_{m,t+1}/\Phi_t)}{\sigma^2(R_{m,t+1}/\Phi_t)}. \tag{12.7}$$

12.2.2. *Sharpe–Lintner CAPM Model*

Following Chapter 9, the CAPM can be defined as

$$E(R_{j,t+1} \mid \Phi_t) = R_{f,t+1} + \left[\frac{E(R_{m,t+1} \mid \Phi_{it}) - R_{f,t+1}}{\sigma(R_{m,t+1} \mid \Phi_t)}\right] \times \left[\frac{\text{Cov}(R_{j,t+1}, R_{m,t+1} \mid \Phi_t)}{\sigma(R_{m,t+1} \mid \Phi_t)}\right], \tag{12.8}$$

where

$R_{m,t+1}$ = the return on the market portfolio, a market value weighted portfolio of all available investment assets;

$\sigma(R_{m,t+1} \mid \Phi_t) =$ the standard deviation about $R_{m,t+1}$ given Φ_t; and

$\text{Cov}(R_{j,t+1}, R_{m,t+1} \mid \Phi_t =$ the covariance between R_{jt} and R_{mt}, given Φ_t.

In the CAPM model the second bracketed term in Equation (12.8) is referred to as the risk of an individual asset, and the bracketed term by which it is multiplied is called the **market price of risk.**

12.3. Tests for Market Efficiency

As discussed above, there are three general categories that have been used to define market efficiency — (1) the weak form, (2) the semi-strong form, and (3) the strong form. Moreover, market efficiency is analyzed in both its static and dynamic forms. In a static analysis, efficiency is considered in terms of reflection boundaries, as discussed by Cootner (1962) and Shiller (1981b), and in a dynamic analysis by Hillmer and Yu (1979). The speed of adjustment of information impounded into security prices is their focus.

12.3.1. *Weak Form Efficiency*

The nature of the information set determines the distinctions of the three forms of efficiency. For the weak form, this set of information includes historical prices, price changes, and any related volume information. Current prices reflect all of this stock-market information, so that the use of such data cannot be of any assistance in the prediction of future price changes.

Two basic types of tests have been used to evaluate the weak form: (1) those that test for statistical independence in sequences of process and price changes, and (2) those that use technical trading rules to devise a profit beyond random selection. Many authors, including Samuelson (1973) and Fama (1965), have demonstrated that the evidence is against any significant dependence in successive price changes. The only contrary evidence seems to be from studies of individual transaction-price data as they become immediately available on the stock exchanges — for example, Niederhoffer and Osborne (1966) and Summers (1986). Nevertheless, it is not likely that the significant serial correlation found in the sequence of individual transaction prices could be used to generate excess profits after transaction costs.

The weak-form test of technical trading rules is characterized by the filter tests of Alexander (1961) and Fama and Blume (1966). A typical filter rule works as follows: buy a stock if its daily closing price increase by at least z percent from a previous low and hold it until its price decreases by at least z percent from a previous high. Then simultaneously sell and go short. When the stock price again increases by at least z percent above a previous low, close the short position and go long. Ignore price changes of less than z percent. This process is repeated continually over a fixed time period, at which time the results are compared with those from a buy-and-hold strategy over the same period. The conclusions reached from such studies have shown that only by using small filters and not taking into account trading costs can one achieve above-average profits.

Still another type of weak-form testing involves examining the correlation of excess returns (actual return minus expected return) to see if any correlation exists. Fama and MacBeth (1973) examined return series using the CAPM to estimate expected return on a security. They then examined the correlation of excess returns and found virtually no correlation.

Both Galai (1977) and Roll (1970) used different models of expected returns and then examined the correlation of excess returns. In both cases, the market is shown to be weak form efficient. Bernard and Thomas (1989) found that post-earnings announcement drift is essentially due to delayed price response.

12.3.2. *Semi-Strong Form Efficiency*

The information for semi-strong form efficiency includes not only stock market data but *all publicly available* information. Current prices under this form already include any piece of information that might otherwise be expected to be useful in achieving above-average rates of return. Tests of this form include examinations of the speed of adjustment of stock prices to new information and studies that consider whether investors can achieve above-average profits by trading on the basis of any publicly available information.

There are several problems with the filter tests discussed in the previous section. They test only the weak form of the EMH. The filter-rule test also fails to take into account the differential risk of assets; nevertheless, through a joint test of the EMH and CAPM, the various levels of risk across different securities can be taken into account. If capital markets are not efficient, the CAPM is invalid. The assumptions upon which the CAPM is based do not hold under conditions of market inefficiency; however, if capital markets are efficient and the CAPM is the right tool, the CAPM can be used simultaneously to test the efficiency of the capital market and the validity of the CAPM, as shown by Roll (1977).

The CAPM indicates that the only relevant risk is systematic risk. Based upon the CAPM the return of a security can be viewed as a fair-game model conditional on the security's systematic risk as measured by beta. A fair-game model says that the expected abnormal return for the security is zero.

Mathematically, the expected return on security j for time t can be written conditional upon the estimate of the firm's beta:

$$E(R_{jt} \mid \beta_{jt}) = R_{ft} + [E(R_{mt}) - R_{ft}]\beta_{jt}, \tag{12.9}$$

where

$$\beta_{jt} = \left[\frac{\mathrm{Cov}(R_{j,t+1}, R_{m,t+1})}{\sigma^2(R_{m,t+1})}\right].$$

The difference between the expected return and the actual return is defined as the residual:

$$\in_{jt} = R_{jt} - E(R_{jt} \mid \beta_{jt}). \tag{12.10}$$

The residual reflects the abnormal return of the security. If the CAPM is true and if markets are efficient:

$$E(\in_{jt}) = 0. \tag{12.11}$$

The joint tests of the EMH and the CAPM are made by evaluating this residual term.

Several studies have used a similar method, the **cumulative average residual (CAR),** to perform the tests. As before, the residual is defined for the jth firm, in time period t:

$$\in_{jt} = R_{jt} - E(R_{jt} \mid \beta_{jt}). \tag{12.12}$$

For a sample of N companies, a cross-sectional average residual for each time period can be defined:

$$AR_t = \frac{1}{N}\sum_{j=1}^{N} \in_{jt}. \tag{12.13}$$

By summing all the average residuals over time a CAR results:

$$CAR = \sum_{t=1}^{T} AR_t, \tag{12.14}$$

where

T = the number of months being summed ($T = 1, 2, \ldots, M$); and
M = the total number of months in the sample.

Finding that the CAR is not significantly different from zero would mean that the CAPM and EMH do hold.

The CAR method has been found appropriate for testing the semi-strong form by focusing on some information event — for example, a dividend or earnings announcement taken to occur at time $t = 0$. The residuals are studied for a number of periods prior to and after the announcement. Perhaps the best known of these studies is the Fama, Fisher, Jensen, and Roll (FFJR, 1969) analysis of the information impact of stock splits. It was hypothesized that any abnormal information to be derived from the split would show up in the residuals from a regression of individual stock returns on the returns in the market and would result in a permanently higher level of cash flows than would be expected by using only the CAPM. Their results indicate that those firms that also increased their cash dividend had slightly positive returns after the split, while those firms that did not increase their dividends had a negative return after the split. (The anomalies analysis related to these results is discussed later in this chapter.) It should be noted that in the FFJR study, the actual day of the stock split, rather than the announcement day, was used as the base period for their empirical study. This may have biased their results, but not to any significant degree.

Ball and Brown (1968), using methodology similar to FFJR, studied the effects of annual earnings announcements. From their study, they conclude that no more than about 10%–15% of the information in the annual earnings announcement had not been anticipated by the month of the announcement. This is viewed as further evidence consistent with the semi-strong theory of market efficiency.

The FFJR method has also been used by many scholars — including Gibbons and Hess (1981), Keim and Stambaugh (1984), and others — to investigate the phenomena known as the **weekend effect** in stock returns. The weekend effect refers to the fact that stock prices tend to rise all week long to a peak price level on Friday. The stock prices then tend to trade on Mondays at reduced prices. Recently, Cornell (1985) used a similar approach to show that a weekend effect exists in stock-index real return. However, he found that a weekend effect does not exist in real returns on stock-index futures.

Waud (1970) used the FFJR methodology to examine the effects of discount-rate changes by the Federal Reserve Bank. He finds evidence of a statistically significant **announcement effect** on stock returns for the first trading day following an announcement; the magnitude of the adjustment is small, however, never exceeding 0.5%.

The issue of an announcement effect for Federal Reserve policy changes was investigated by Lynge (1981), Urich and Wachtel (1981), and Cornell (1979, 1983a, 1983b). All of these studies find that only unanticipated money-supply changes affected the market rates. The anticipated component of the money-supply change was shown to have no significant impact on the market rate. This seems to indicate, on one hand, that the market is efficient while, on the other, it implies that the macro variables need to be analyzed by portfolio managers and security analysts.

In other studies, Sunder (1973, 1975) evaluates the effect of inventory methods, and Kaplan and Roll (1972) investigate the impact of accounting revisions that involve no changes in cash flow. These studies confirm that excess returns could be made with inside information, thus violating strong form efficiency but not semi-strong form efficiency.

Before leaving this discussion of the EMH with the conclusion that the semi-strong form holds all the time, it is necessary to consider several factors. All of these studies were made on widely held and heavily traded stocks. Research has shown that efficiency is at its best when the stock is heavily trade. Where there is thin or sporadic trading, efficiency may be impaired. Because the market mechanism does not function as well in thinly traded stocks, the new information cannot be impounded as easily in the stock's price. This implies that for thinly traded stocks the market may not be efficient and, therefore, the possibility for abnormal returns does exist.

Another problem related to the volume of trading is that of investors of differing ability. The theory assumes all investors have homogeneous expectations and abilities. However, as a result of greater skill or better resources, some investors are in a position to extract more valuable information from the historical data available. The information they can extract may be more valuable because they can figure it out sooner than the rest of the market and thus establish a position before the stocks; many talented investors compete against one another, ensuring the market's efficiency. However, in the thinly traded stocks, the investor with a greater ability may be able to secure an advantage. Thus, while semi-strong efficiency holds for a large part of the market, caution must be emphasized.

This section has examined the issue of market efficiency. The use of joint tests of the EMH and CAPM has shown that the validity of both is supported by research. Moreover, the value of using the CAPM in tests of market efficiency has been demonstrated. Because the CAPM allows adjustment for the risk involved, it allows the testing of a higher form of market efficiency, the semi-strong form, relative to using the filter tests to test the EMH. The filter tests generally only support the weak-form efficient market.

12.3.3. *Strong-Form Efficiency*

The mention of insider information leads naturally into a discussion of strong-form efficiency. The information set for the strong form includes not only all publicly available information but also insider information. It may seem that this form goes too far in its implication or impounding of "unavailable" information into stock prices. However, it really just shows that monopoly type information such as that possessed by company insiders and stock exchange specialists is also reflected in stock prices as it becomes available. The distinction between this information set and that assumed for the weak and semi-strong forms is that the strong-form information set is not available to all participants in the market but only to those relatively small groups that monopolize its source. As a result, there is only a partial reflection of the information in the market price of the stock. If the size of the monopoly group represents only 0.10% of the overall set of market participants, only a negligible impact should be expected as compared to what it would otherwise have been.

Niederhoffer and Osborne (1966) have pointed out that specialists on the NYSE apparently use their monopolistic access to information concerning unfilled limit orders to generate monopoly profits. Jaffe's (1974) and Finnerty's (1976a) studies, using insider-trading information, found that excess returns could be obtained. Their results indicate that even after eight months excess returns still occurred. Unless these insiders just happened to possess superior analytical ability, their excess returns must have resulted from the illegal exploitation of insider information. The Levine and Boesky scandal of 1987, the Wong and Lee scandal of 1988, and the SEC crackdown on insiders trading indicate that insiders can and do exploit their access to information in order to outperform the market.

The strong form has been shown to hold in test such as those that found that mutual-fund managers have been unable to outperform the market average consistently. In general, mutual funds performed worse than a naïve strategy of random selection or mixing the market with the riskless asset. It should be noted that in examining the question of strong form efficiency, it is relevant to look at performance after transaction costs involved with the purchase and sale of securities have been exceeded. Jensen (1968) found that mutual funds seem not to earn enough extra returns to cover the portion of the management fee that represents analysis costs. Thus, Jensen's evidence supports strong-form efficiency. Recent works by Merton (1981), Hendriksson and Merton (1981), and Hendriksson (1984) suggest that the poor performance of mutual funds may result from the methodology used to estimate the performance of the fund. (Mutual-fund performance is discussed in more detail in Chapter 17.)

12.4. Other Methods of Testing the EMH

This section discusses other methods and issues relating to testing the EMH. These include: (1) the random walk with reflecting barriers, (2) the variance-bound approach, (3) Hillmer and Yu's relative EMH test, and (4) market anomalies.

12.4.1. *Random Walk with Reflecting Barriers*

Cootner's (1962) analysis of stock-market behavior suggests that a random walk with reflecting barriers describes changes in stock prices over time. Cootner's model is a compromise model that allows both random and systematic changes in stock price to be taken into account.

Cootner's model has two types of investor, (1) the uninformed investor and (2) the informed investor. Uninformed investors engage in occupations in which they have comparative advantage and are compensated highly relative to other occupations. It is very costly, at least in terms of opportunity cost per unit of relevant information uncovered, for them to devote time to stock-market research. As a result they tend to accept present prices as roughly representing true differences in value, and they choose between stocks largely on the grounds of their attitudes toward risk. Therefore, for uninformed investors there exists a random walk of stock-market prices.

Informed investors, on the other hand, specialize in the stock market. As professionals their opportunity cost of research is much less than that of the uninformed. They do have an idea of what is going to happen in the future, but they cannot profit from it unless the current price deviates enough from the expected price to cover their opportunity costs. Their profits will come when prices have deviated enough from the expected price. Informed investors can expect future surprises to force prices toward their mean more often than not.

Another random walk environment operates within the informed-investor class. There is no reason that changes in the price expectations of professionals should occur in other than a random manner. Therefore, the path of stock prices over any substantial period of time would be composed of a random number of trends, each of which is a random walk with reflecting barriers.

Some believe that common-stock prices tend to move in a deterministic, cyclical manner, where the term **cyclical** is taken in the mechanical sense of a movement perfectly predictable in timing and extent. These cycles may be quite complex, but diligent effort will eventually unravel the patterns: excess returns can be captured through trading based on these patterns. Those who adhere to this point of view are known as **chartists** and their work as **technical analysis.**

Except for a small fringe of opinion largely confined to stock-market professionals, this point of view has largely been refuted by efficient-market-hypothesis scholar. These academics believe that securities markets are efficient enough to make technical analysts unable to obtain unusual profit using only past security prices. However, Cootner (1962) revived this theory by producing a model of stock-market behavior that he felt was perfectly compatible with much of what he interpreted Wall Street chart reading to be all about. More recently, Treynor and Ferguson (1985) have come to the defense of technical analysis. They have shown that past prices, when combined with other valuable information, can indeed be helpful in achieving unusual profit. However, they also argue that nonprice information creates this opportunity and that past prices serve only to permit its efficient exploitation. (Such technical analysis is discussed in Chapter 17.)

In understanding Cootner's work, it is first necessary to understand what **kurtosis** and **skewness** mean. In considering the effects of non-normality, it is convenient to use the measure γ_1 of skewness and γ_2 of kurtosis of the distribution of a random variable x. If the mean and variance of the distribution are denoted by μ and σ^2, respectively, its skewness γ_1 is defined as

$$\gamma_1 = \frac{E[(x-\mu)^3]}{\sigma^3}, \tag{12.15}$$

and its kurtosis γ_2 as

$$\gamma_2 = \frac{E[(x-\sigma^4]}{\sigma^4} - 3. \tag{12.16}$$

These measures do not depend on the location or scale of the distribution. For a symmetrical distribution, γ_1 is zero. Positive values for γ_1 indicate that the distribution is skewed to the right, so that the right tail is in a certain sense heavier than the left compared to a symmetric distribution. Imagine deforming a normal probability-density curve, keeping it symmetric and unimodal: a deformation in which the tails are heavier and the central part is more sharply peaked would have $\gamma_2 > 0$, and one in which the tails are lighter and the central part is flatter, giving an effect of shoulders (a pattern identified in technical analysis), would have $\gamma_2 < 0$.

According to Cootner, if the random walk hypothesis is correct, kurtosis of a price series should be near three at weekly intervals and get closer to three as time goes on. If the reflecting barrier or trend hypothesis is correct, kurtosis should be greater than three to begin with and should approach the kurtosis of the rectangular distribution in the limit if a single trend is involved. Cootner's result found the average kurtosis of the 45-price series was used to be 4.90. If successive changes were independent, price changes over longer intervals would be expected to more closely approach the average kurtosis of a normal distribution. In fact, in Cootner's results the kurtosis decreases so rapidly that it very soon falls below that of a normal distribution. This tends to refute the efficient-market theory that stock prices are independent.

Monthly data from the Dow Jones 30 during January 1, 1980–December 31, 1984, have been tested for any indication of skewness or kurtosis. Table 12.3 indicates evidence of both skewness and kurtosis in the price series. The average skewness and kurtosis are 0.5137 and 0.6137, respectively. As can be seen, the question of skewness and kurtosis for

Table 12.3. Statistical Estimates of Monthly Returns for the Dow Jones Average (January 2006–December 2010).

	TICKER	Company	Mean	Standard	Skewness	Kurtosis	Coefficient of Variation
1	MMM	3M	0.0019	0.0665	−0.4896	0.5488	35.7616
2	AA	Alcoa	−0.0211	0.1765	−3.0010	13.5221	−8.3725
3	AXP	American Express	−0.0094	0.1230	0.1616	4.2107	−13.0321
4	T	AT&T	0.0055	0.0616	−1.0458	0.8336	11.1907
5	BAC	Bank of America	−0.0370	0.2225	−2.5486	10.6076	−6.0210
6	BA	Boeing	−0.0036	0.0965	−1.0373	1.5956	−26.5438
7	CAT	Caterpillar	0.0029	0.1279	−1.9207	6.7557	43.4958
8	CVX	Chevron	0.0087	0.0624	−0.7818	0.6193	7.1677
9	CSCO	Cisco Systems	−0.0010	0.0892	−0.6297	0.6117	−86.4948
10	KO	Coca-Cola	0.0093	0.0510	−0.9161	3.8694	5.4828
11	DD	E.I. DuPont de Nemours	0.0024	0.0872	−0.7714	1.9378	36.0049
12	XOM	Exxon Mobil Corp	0.0048	0.0520	−0.4104	−0.0670	10.8100
13	GE	General Electric	−0.0135	0.1126	−1.0687	2.1340	−8.3216
14	HPQ	Hewlett-Packard	0.0044	0.0752	−1.0903	1.2700	17.1494
15	HD	Home Depot	−0.0028	0.0768	−0.3816	0.0906	−27.7587
16	INTC	Intel	−0.0041	0.0855	−0.9769	0.8779	−20.8216
17	IBM	International Business Machines	0.0093	0.0603	−1.6744	5.7418	6.4939
18	JNJ	Johnson & Johnson	0.0019	0.0443	−0.9569	1.8476	22.7633
19	JPM	JPMorgan Chase	−0.0016	0.0991	−0.6226	0.9468	−61.5612
20	KFT	Kraft Foods	0.0030	0.0623	−1.2024	2.4125	20.4741
21	MCD	McDonald's	0.0150	0.0454	−0.5133	0.0846	3.0338
22	MRK	Merck	0.0025	0.0801	−0.8158	1.3874	32.0949
23	MSFT	Microsoft	−0.0006	0.0811	−0.4540	0.1834	−135.0236
24	PFE	Pfizer	−0.0028	0.0653	−0.5603	0.7952	−23.0459
25	PG	Procter & Gamble	0.0027	0.0496	−0.6313	0.6330	18.6080
26	TRV	Travelers	0.0043	0.0542	−0.6674	2.0474	12.5164
27	UTX	United Technologies	0.0055	0.0629	−0.7546	0.3983	11.3590
28	VZ	Verizon Communications	0.0063	0.0569	−0.3339	−0.4991	9.0426
29	WMT	Wal-Mart Stores	0.0028	0.0482	−0.8825	3.1772	17.1172
30	DIS	Walt Disney	0.0059	0.0718	−0.9015	1.7228	12.1450
Mean			0.0001	0.0816	−0.9293	2.3432	−2.8095

security analysis and portfolio management is a nontrivial issue — one that will be taken up in later chapter.

12.4.2. *Variance-Bound Approach Test*

Shiller (1981a, 1981b), LeRoy and Porter (1981), and others have proposed a **variance-bound approach** to test the EMH. This kind of model, as defined in Equation (12.17), is based on the dividend-valuation model discussed in Chapter 4.

$$P_t = \sum_{k}^{\infty} \gamma^{k+1} E_t d_{t+k} = E_t P_t^*, \tag{12.17}$$

where

P_t = a price or yield;
$P_t^* = \sum_{k=0}^{\infty} \gamma^{k+1} d_{t+k}$ is an estimate based on perfect foresight of the *ex post* rational price or yield not known at time t;
E_t = a mathematical expectation conditional on information at time t;
$\gamma = \frac{1}{1+r}$ = a discount factor; and
r = a discount rate.

By using S&P 500 index data and yield-to-maturity data on long-term bonds, Shiller (1981a) showed that the movements in P_t appear to be too large to be justified by subsequent changes in dividends. Overall, Shiller concluded that the use of a random walk model for dividends to test the EMH does not appear to be promising. Other possibilities are that *ex ante* real interest rates show very large movements or, alternatively, that markets are irrational or subject to fads. This issue will be discussed in detail in the next chapter.

The use of volatility measures to assess market efficiency is conceptually similar to Cootner's random walk with reflecting barriers approach. Although the method used to perform the precise statistical testing is relatively complicated, it is conceptually easy to understand and useful for security analysis. Chapter 17 explores this topic in more detail.

12.4.3. *Hillmer and Yu's Relative EMH Test*

Hillmer and Yu (1979) propose a relative method for testing the EMH. Instead of dichotomizing the market into an efficient or nonefficient class, they emphasize that there are various degrees of efficiency based on the particular market variable and particular type of information. Consequently, Hillmer and Yu argue that the security analyst's efforts can be directed to discovering how various types of information affect different types of stocks. Hillmer and Yu's model for testing EMH is called a **relative** (instead of absolute) **EMH test**. Patell and Wolfson (1984) use this definition of EMH to study the intraday speed of adjustment of stock price to earnings and dividend announcements. They find that the speed of adjustment is generally less than an hour. The findings of Bernard and Thomas (1989) differ, however.

This section has discussed three alternative viewpoints to Fama's EMH test. These different hypotheses on EMH give some justification for active instead of passive approaches for security analysis and portfolio management. Despite the general applicability of EMH, there exist anomalies in the finance literature in which the efficient-market theory does not hold. These anomalies, dealing with the P/E ratio, size, effect, and January effect, are discussed in the next section.

12.5. Random Walk Hypothesis Versus EMH Test

Brown's (2010) paper entitled "The Efficient Markets Hypothesis: The Demise of the Demon of Chance?" have clearly defined the difference between the model of random walk hypothesis and the model of EMH.

Let Φ_t represent the common information all investors have after observing the current price p_t. Then according to the EMH, no investors can use this specific information z_{it} to have any kind of price advantage in the markets. If the trader's specific information z_{it} is already incorporated into the market price, then we can obtain Equation (12.18).

$$E_{\Phi_t}\{[r_{t+\tau} - E(r_{t+\tau} \mid z_{it})z_{it}]\} = 0. \qquad (12.18)$$

Equation (12.18) describes the condition of EMH.

However, most tests of the random walk hypothesis amount to a statement about serial covariance.

$$\gamma_\tau = E\{[r_{t+\tau} - E(r)][r_t - E(r)]\} = E\{[r_{t+\tau} - E(r)]r_t\} = 0. \qquad (12.19)$$

This expression corresponds to Eq. (12.A1) on the strong presumption that the market information Φ_t is time invariant.

Both Fama (1970) and Taylor (1982) have performed random walk hypothesis instead of EMH test. Fama (1970) used linear correlation model to test random walk, whereas Taylor used q-statistics to test the random walk hypothesis. Therefore, both Fama (1970) and Taylor (1982) did not directly test the EMH. Jarrow and Larsson (2011) have theoretically discussed how the EMH can be tested. Brown (2010) has argued that the filter test is a correct method for testing EMH. Lo *et al.* (2000) have used the filter rule to test the EMH and rejected the EMH. Lee *et al.* (2009 and 2011) have used alternative methods to test the EMH and also rejected the EMH hypothesis.

12.6. Market Anomalies

The idea of an efficient market is very important to the study of security analysis and portfolio management. If information is fully reflected in security prices, the market is efficient and it is not worthwhile to pay for information that is already impounded in security prices. The evidence seems to indicate that markets are efficient with respect to most types of information. However, there appear to be certain types of information associated with irregularities in the financial markets. Such irregularities are called **market anomalies**. Three of the most heavily researched anomalies are the P/E effect, the size effect, and the January effect.

12.6.1. *The P/E Effect*

The **price-earnings (P/E) effect** has been used to study whether the market is efficient.

Some security analysts have followed the strategy of buying stocks with below-average P/E ratios in order to earn above-average risk-adjusted returns. Basu (1977) found that high P/E or low P/E stocks produced excess returns for a sample of 750 NYSE stocks for the period September 1956 to August 1971. Ranking the stocks by their year and P/Es, he compared the yearly risk-adjusted returns for portfolios composed of 150 stocks with the highest P/E, 150 stocks with the next highest P/E, down to the final portfolio of 150 stocks with the lowest P/E. The results of this study show that the annual rate of return on a risk-adjusted basis was 9% for the high-P/E stocks and 16% for the low P/E stocks. Additionally, the low-P/E stock portfolio had lower risk than the high P/E portfolio.

12.6.2. *The Size Effect*

In a follow-up on the earlier study, Basu (1983) found that these results were continuing over time. The results indicate that with respect to certain types of publicly available information — that is, P/E ratios — the market may not be semi-strong form efficient. Reinganum (1981a) presents the argument that in actuality, the P/E-ratio effect found by Basu is a proxy for the small-firm or **size-effect**. Basu (1983) claims that the size effect is in reality more related to the P/E effect. In either case, evidence is available that the market may not be semi-strong form efficient.

Banz (1981) ranks all NYSE firms by the total market value of the firm. Reinganum (1981a) ranks all stocks on both the NYSE and the American Stock Exchange (ASE) in a similar fashion. They both divide their samples into five equal portfolios based on the market-value ranking. Their results indicate that the portfolios of the firm with the smallest market value experienced returns that were, both economically and statistically, significantly greater than the portfolios of the firms with large market value.

Much effort has been expended in trying to explain the size anomaly. Roll (1981, 1983) identifies statistical problems with measuring the riskiness of small, less frequently traded firms as being a probable explanation of the size-effect results. However, even after adjusting the methodology to account for Roll's criticism, the return pattern of the size effect still persists. Arbel *et al.* (1983) suggest that the size effect may be related to the disproportionate amount of institutional interest in the larger firms. Stoll and Whaley (1983) provide information on the trading costs of high-priced versus low-priced stocks and show that after the appropriate adjustment for size-related transaction costs, the small-firm effect is reduced. The size anomaly has not been adequately explained to date and still exists as evidence that refutes the semi-strong form of the EMH.

12.6.3. *The January Effect*

The final anomaly of interest is called the **January effect** (or the **year-end effect**). Branch (1977) provides evidence that investors tend to sell stocks in which they have experienced capital losses at the end of the year in order to take advantage of the U.S. tax laws. This selling pressure depresses stock prices during the month of December. During January, the selling is reversed as investors return to the market and buying pressure is evident. The returns calculated for the month of January are above average because the ending prices in December are lower than they should be and the ending prices in January are higher than they should be.

Keim (1983) presents evidence that supports the tax-loss explanation. However, Roll (1982) plays down the tax-loss selling argument and presents evidence that the January effect is size related. Reinganum (1983) dismisses the tax-selling effect because of evidence indicating that firms with both gains and losses during the previous year experience abnormal returns in January.

Haugen and Lakonishok (1988) offer a thorough review of the January effect with an explanation for its existence based on the trading behavior and patterns of institutional investors. As with the other anomalies, the January effect has not yet been completely explained in the context of an efficient market.

12.7. Summary

This chapter has examined the basic tenets and empirical support for the EMH and has outlined some of its implications for security valuation and portfolio management.

The relationship between market value and book value and its development into the concept of a q ratio was found to be very useful to security analysts in their estimates of the future value of a firm's financial securities. The EMH was categorized into three forms: weak, semi-strong, and strong. The main distinguishing feature among these forms was pointed out to be the information set assumed to be impounded into the market price of a firm's securities. For the weak form, the information set was shown to include historical prices, price changes, and related volume data; for the semi-strong form it was shown to include all publicly available information; and for the strong form it was shown to include all information, whether or not publicly available.

While empirical testing has provided good support for the weak and semi-strong forms of the EMH, the strong form has been upheld only in cases where, for example, mutual-fund managers have been unable to consistently outperform market averages. Tests involving corporate insiders and stock-exchange specialists have in general indicated that these groups do possess monopoly information and are able to use it to generate above-average returns.

Besides Fama's (1970) EMH, the discussion briefly included the random walk with reflecting barriers, the variance-bound test of EMH, and the market anomalies that refute EMH. This implies that the security-analysis and portfolio-management theory and methods discussed are worthwhile tools for security analysts and portfolio managers. The next chapter discusses timing and selectivity of stocks and mutual funds.

Questions and Problems

1. Define or explain the following:
   (a) weak form (b) semi-strong form
   (c) strong form (d) P/E ratio
   (e) Tobin's q (f) fair game
   (g) random walk (h) market anomalies.
2. What is the difference between a firm's market value and its book value? Which is a more meaningful measure?
3. What does the existence of market anomalies — that is, size, weekend, January effects, and so on — do to acceptance or rejection of the EMH?
4. ABC Bank's balance sheet is presented in the table. Calculate the market-to-book ratio for ABC and indicate what it implies about ABC. ABC stock trades at $8 per share.

ABC Bank's Balance Sheet ($ billions)

Cash	$10	Short-term deposits	$80
Investment	$50	Long-term deposits	$30
Loans	$50	Equity (1 billion	
Fixed assets	$10	shares outstanding)	$10
	$120		$120

5. ABC Bank has a P/E ratio of 4. Given the income statement for ABC, what does that ratio say about the bank? The current average P/E ratio for similar banks is 10.

ABC Bunk's Income Statement ($ billions)

Revenues	$10.20
Interest per year	$6.00
Operating earnings	$4.20
Provision for loan losses	$2.00
Taxed income	$2.20
Tax (10%)	$0.20
Earnings	$2.00

6. What is Tobin's q ratio for MNO Corp. given the following information? What does this value of q say about MNO?

Replacement cost of total assets	\$100
Market value of debt	\$50
Market value of equity	\$40

7. What is meant by a perfect market? Compare a perfect market to an efficient market.
8. How can the market model and the CAPM be used to test whether the market is efficient?
9. If the market is not efficient, what does this indicate about the validity of the CAPM?
10. How is volume of trading related to market efficiency?
11. Does the SEC crackdown on insider trading (in such cases as Levine and Boesky, Lee and Wong, and so on) imply that the market is becoming more strong-form efficient?
12. What do the results of Cootner's research imply about technical analysis?
13. What are the alternative viewpoints to Fama's EMH?
14. Explain an investment strategy or strategies that may be useful in taking advantage of the known market anomalies. If these strategies work, what will happen to the market anomalies?

Bibliography

Alexander, S. "Price Movements in Speculative Markets: Trends or Random Walks." *Industrial Management Review*, v. 2 (May 1961), pp. 7–26.

Arbel, A., S. Carvell and P. Strebel. "Giraffes, Institutions and Neglected Firms." *Financial Analysts Journal*, v. 39 (May/June 1983), pp. 2–8.

Ball, R. and P. Brown. "An Empirical Evaluation of Accounting Income Numbers." *Journal of Accounting Research*, v. 16 (Autumn 1968), pp. 159–178.

Banz, R. W. "The Relationship between Return and Market Value of Common Stocks." *Journal of Financial Economics*, v. 9 (March 1981), pp. 3–18.

Barry, C. and S. Brown. "Anomalies in Security Returns and the Specification of the Market Model." *Journal of Finance*, v. 39 (July 1984), pp. 807–818.

Basu, S. "Investment performance of Common Stocks in Relation to Their Price-Earnings Ratios: A Test of the Efficient Market Hypothesis." *Journal of Finance*, v. 32 (June 1977), pp. 663–682.

Basu, S. "The Relationship between Earnings Yield, Market Value, and the Return for NYSE Stocks; Further Evidence." *Journal of Financial Economics*, v. 12 (March 1983), pp. 129–156.

Bernard, V. L. and J. K. Thomas. "Post-Earnings Announcement Drift: Delayed Price Response or Risk Premium." *Journal of Accounting Research*, v. 27 (1989), pp. 1–36.

Bjerring, J., J. Lakonishok and T. Vermaelen. "Stock Prices and Financial Analysts' Recommendations." *Journal of Finance*, v. 38 (March 1983), pp. 187–204.

Branch, B. "A Tax Loss Trading Rule." *Journal of Business*, v. 50 (April 1977), pp. 198–207.

Brealey, R. *An Introduction to Risk and Return from Common Stocks.* Cambridge, MA: MIT Press, 1983.

Brown, L. and M. Rozeff. "The Superiority of Analysts' Forecasts as Measures of Expectations: Evidence from Earnings." *Journal of Finance*, v. 33 (March 1978), pp. 1–16.

Brown, S. J. "The Efficient Markets Hypothesis: The Demise of the Demon of Chance?" *Accounting & Finance*, v. 51, (March 2011), pp. 79–95.

Brown, S. and J. Warner. "Using Daily Stock Returns: The Case of Event Studies." *Journal of Financial Economics*, v. 14 (March 1985), pp. 3–32.

Brown, S. and W. Nichols. "Assimilating Earnings and Split Information: Is the Capital Market Becoming More Efficient?" *Journal of Financial Economics*, v. 10 (September 1981), pp. 309–314.

Constantinades, G. "Optimal Stock Trading with Personal Taxes: Implications for Prices and the Abnormal January Returns." *Journal of Financial Economics*, v. 13 (March 1984), pp. 65–90.

Cootner, P. "Stock Prices: Random vs. Systematic Changes." *Industrial Management Review*, v. 3 (Spring 1962), pp. 24–25.

Cornell, B. "Do Money Supply Announcements Affect Short-Term Interest Rates?" *Journal of Money Credit and Banking*, v. 11 (February 1979), 80–86.

Cornell, B. "Money Supply Announcements and Interest Rates: Another View." *Journal of Business*, v. 56 (January 1983a), pp. 1–24.

Cornell, B. "The Money Supply Announcements Puzzle: Review and Interpretation." *American Economic Review*, v. 73 (September 1983b), pp. 644–657.

Cornell, B. "The Weekly Pattern in Stock Returns: Cash versus Futures: A Note" *Journal of Finance*, v. 40 (June 1985), pp. 583–588.

Dimson, E. and P. Marsh. "An Analysis of Brokers' and Analysts' Unpublished Forecasts of UK Stock Returns." *Journal of Finance*, v. 39 (December 1984), pp. 1257–1292.

Elton, E. J., M. J. Gruber, S. J. Brown and W. N. Goetzmann. *Modern Portfolio Theory and Investment Analysis*, 7th ed. New York: John Wiley & Sons, 2006.

Emery, J. "The information Content of Daily Market Indicators." *Journal of Financial and Quantitative Analysis*, v. 8 (March 1973), pp. 183–190.

Epps, T. "Security Price Change and Transaction Volumes: Theory and Evidence." *American Economic Review*, v. 65 (September 1975), pp. 586–597.

Fama, E. F. "The Behavior of Stock Market Prices." *Journal of Business*, v. 38 (January 1965), pp. 34–105.

Fama, E. F. "Efficient Capital Markets: A Review of Theory and Empirical Work." *Journal of Finance*, v. 25 (May 1970), pp. 383–417.

Fama, E. F. *Foundation of Finance*. New York: Basic Books, Inc., 1976a.

Fama, E. F. "Market Efficiency, Long-Term Returns, and Behavioral Finance." *Journal of Financial Economics*, v. 49 (Issue 3 1998), pp. 283–306.

Fama, E. F. "A Note on the Market Model and the Two-Parameter Model." *Journal of Finance*, v. 28 (December 1973), pp. 1181–1185.

Fama, E. F. "Reply." *Journal of Finance*, v. 31 (March 1976b), pp. 143–147.

Fama, E. F. and M. Blume. "Filter Rules and Stock Market Trading Profits." *Journal of Business*, v. 39 (Special Supplement, January 1966), pp. 226–241.

Fama, E. F. and J. MacBeth. "Risk, Return and Equilibrium: Empirical Tests." *Journal of Political Economy*, v. 31 (May/June 1973), pp. 607–636.

Fama, E. F., L. Fisher, M. Jensen and R. Roll. "The Adjustment of Stock Prices to New Information." *International Economic Review*, v. 10 (February 1969), pp. 1–21.

Finnerty, J. "The CBOE and Market Efficiency." *Journal of Financial and Quantitative Analysis*, v. 13 (March 1978), pp. 29–38.

Finnerty, J. "Insiders' Activity and Inside Information: A Multivariate Analysis." *Journal of Financial and Quantitative Analysis*, v. 11 (June 1976a), pp. 205–215.

Finnerty, J. "Insiders and Market Efficiency." *Journal of Finance*, v. 31 (September 1976b), pp. 1141–1148.

Francis, J. "Intertemporal Differences in Systematic Stock Price Movements." *Journal of Financial and Quantitative Analysis*, v. 10 (June 1975), pp. 205–219.

French, K. "Stock Returns and the Weekend Effect." *Journal of Financial Economics*, v. 9 (March 1980), pp. 55–70.

Galai, D. "Tests of Market Efficiency of the Chicago Board Options Exchange." *Journal of Business*, v. 50 (April 1977), pp. 421–442.

Gibbons, M. and P. Hess. "Day of the Week Effects and Asset Returns." *Journal of Business*, v. 54 (October 1981), pp. 579–596.

Gonedes, N. "Evidence of the Information Content of Accounting Numbers: Accounting Based and Market Based Estimates of Systematic Risk." *Journal of Financial and Quantitative Analysis*, v. 8 (June 1973), pp. 407–443.

Haugen, R. and J. Lakonishok. *The Incredible January Effect: The Stock Market's Unsolved Mystery*. Homewood, IL: Dow Jones-Irwin, 1988.

Hawawini, G. *European Equity Markets: Price Behavior and Efficiency*. Monograph, Salomon Brothers Center, New York University, 1984.

Henriksson, R. D. "Mutual Fund Timing and Mutual Fund Performance: An Empirical Investigation." *Journal of Business*, v. 57 (January 1984), pp. 73–96.

Henriksson, R. D. and R. C. Merton. "On Market Timing and Investment Performance, II. Statistical Procedures for Evaluating Forecasting Skills." *Journal of Business*, v. 54 (October 1981), pp. 513–533.

Henriksson, R. D. and R. Westerfield. "The Weekend Effect in Common Stock Returns: The International Evidence." *Journal of Finance*, v. 40 (June 1985), pp. 433–454.

Hillmer, S. C. and P. L. Yu. "The Market Speed of Adjustment to New Information." *Journal of Financial Economics*, v. 7 (September 1979), pp. 321–345.

Ibbotson, R. and J. Jaffe. "Hot Issues Market." *Journal of Finance*, v. 30 (September 1975), pp. 1027–1042.

Jaffe, J. "The Effect of Regulation Changes on Insider Trading." *The Bell Journal of Economics and Management Science*, v. 5 (Spring 1974), pp. 93–121.

Jarrow, R. and M. Larsson. "The Meaning of Market Efficiency." Working Paper, 2011, Cornell University.

Jensen, M. C. "The Performance of Mutual Funds in the Period 1945–1964." *Journal of Finance*, v. 23 (May 1968), pp. 389–461.

Joy, M., R. Litzenberger and R. McEnally. "The Adjustment of Stock Prices to Announcements of Unanticipated Changes in Quarterly Earnings." *Journal of Accounting Research*, v. 25 (Autumn 1977), pp. 207–225.

Kaplan, R. S. and R. Roll. "Investor Evaluation of Accounting Information: Some Empirical Evidence." *Journal of Business*, v. 45 (April 1972), pp. 225–257.

Keim, D. B. "Size-Related Anomalies and Stock Return Seasonality: Further Empirical Evidence." *Journal of Financial Economics*, v. 11 (June 1983), pp. 13–32.

Keim, D. B. and R. F. Stambaugh. "A Further Investigation of the Weekend Effect in Stock Returns." *Journal of Finance*, v. 39 (July 1984), pp. 819–835.

Lee C. F., C. M. Tsai and A. C. Lee. "A Dynamic CAPM with Supply Effect: Theory and Empirical Results." *Quarterly Review of Economics and Finance*, v. 49, (August 2009), pp. 811–828.

Lee C. F., C. M. Tsai, and A. C. Lee. "Asset Pricing with Disequilibrium Price Adjustment: Theory and Empirical Evidence." *Quantitative Finance* (2011 forthcoming).

Lee, C. F., A. C. Lee and J. C. Lee . *Handbook of Quantitative Finance and Risk Management*. New York: Springer, 2010.

Lee C. F. and G. Yen. "Efficient Market Hypothesis.", *Review of Pacific Basin Financial Markets and Policies*, v. 11, No. 2 (2008), pp. 305-329.

Lee C. F., G. Yen, and C. F. Chang. "Informational Efficiency of Capital Market Revisited: Anomalous Evidence from a Refined Test.", *Advances in Quantitative Analysis of Finance and Accounting*, v. 2 (Part A 1993), pp. 39–65.

LeRoy, S. F. and R. Potter. "The Present Value Relation: Tests Based on Implied Variance Bounds." *Econometrica*, v. 49 (May 1981), pp. 555–574.

Lindenberg, E. B. and S. A. Ross. "Tobin's q Ratio and Industrial Organization." *Journal of Business*, v. 54 (January 1981), pp. 1–32.

Lintner, J. "The Valuation of Risk Assets and the Selection of Risky Investments in Stock Portfolios and Capital Budgets." *The Review of Economics and Statistics*, v. 47 (February 1965), pp. 13–37.

Lo, A. W., H. Mamaysky, and J. Wang. "Foundations of Technical Analysis: Computational Algorithms, Statistical Inference, and Empirical Implementation." *Journal of Finance*, v. 55 (August 2000), pp. 1705–1765.

Lynge, Jr, M. J. "Money Supply Announcements and Stock Prices." Journal of Portfolio Management, v. 8 (Fall 1981), pp. 40–43.

Merton, R. C. "On Market Timing and Investment Performance I. An Equilibrium Theory of Valuation for Market Forecasts." *Journal of Business*, v. 54 (July 1981), pp. 363–406.

Morgan, I. "Stock Prices and Heteroscedasticity." *Journal of Business*, v. 49 (October 1966), pp. 496–508.

Mossin, J. "Equilibrium in a Capital Asset Market." *Econometrica*, v. 34 (October 1966), pp. 768–783.

Niederhoffer, V. and M. F. M. Osborne. "Market Making and Reversal on the Stock Exchange." *Journal of the American Statistical Association*, v. 61 (December 1966), pp. 897–917.

Ohlson, J. and S. Penman. "Volatility Increases Subsequent to Stock Splits: An Empirical Observation." *Journal of Financial Economics*, v. 14 (June 1985), pp. 251–266.

Oppenheimer, H. and G. Schlarbaum . "Investing with Ben Graham: An Ex Ante Test of the EMH." *Journal of Financial and Quantitative Analysis*, v. 16 (September 1981), pp. 341–508.

Patell, J. M. and M. A. Wolfson. "The Intraday Speed of Adjustment of Stock Prices to Earnings and Dividend Announcements." *Journal of Financial Economics*, v. 13 (June 1984), pp. 223–252.

Penman, S. "Insider Trading and the Dissemination of Firm's Forecast Information." *Journal of Business*, v. 55 (October 1982), pp. 92–116.

Reinganum, M. R. "Abnormal Returns in Small Firms' Portfolios." *Financial Analysts Journal*, v. 37 (March/April 1981a), pp. 52–57.

Reinganum, M. R. "The Anomalies Stock Market Behavior of Small Firms in January: Empirical Tests for Tax-Loss Selling Effect." *Journal of Financial Economics*, v. 12 (March 1983), pp. 89–104.

Reinganum, M. R. "Misspecification of Capital Asset Pricing: Empirical Anomalies Based on Earnings Yields and Market Values." *Journal of Financial Economics*, v. 8 (March 1981b), pp. 13–32.

Roll, R. *The Behavior of Interest Rates: An Application of the Efficient Market Model to U. S. Treasury Bills.* New York: Basic Books, 1970.

Roll, R. "A Critique of the Asset Pricing Theory's Tests." *Journal of Financial Economics*, v. 4 (March 1977), pp. 129–176.

Roll, R. "On Computing Mean Returns and the Small Firm Premium." *Journal of Financial Economics*, v. 12 (November 1983), pp. 371–386.
Roll, R. "A Possible Explanation of the Small Firm Effect." *Journal of Finance*, v. 36 (September 1981), pp. 879–888.
Roll, R. "The Turn of the Year Effect and the Return Premium on Small Firms." *Journal of Portfolio Management*, v. 7 (1982), pp. 18–28.
Samuelson, P. "Proof that Properly Discounted Present Values of Assets Vibrate Randomly." *Bell Journal of Economics and Management Science*, v. 4 (Autumn 1973), pp. 369–374.
Schwartz, R. and D. Whitcomb. "Evidence on the Presence and Causes of Serial Correlation in the Market Model Residuals." *Journal of Financial and Quantitative Analysis*, v. 12 (June 1977), pp. 291–315.
Sharpe, W. F. "Capital Asset Prices: A Theory of Market Equilibrium under Conditions of Risk." *Journal of Finance*, v. 19 (September 1964), pp. 425–442.
Shiller, R. J. "Do Stock Prices Move Too Much to be Justified by Subsequent Changes in Dividends?" *American Economics Review*, v. 71 (June 1981a), pp. 421–436.
Shiller, R. J. "The Use of Volatility Measures in Assuming Market Efficiency." *Journal of Finance*, v. 36 (May 1981b), pp. 291–304.
Stevenson, R. and R. Bear. "Commodity Fixtures: Trends or Random Walks?" *Journal of Finance*, v. 25 (March 1970), pp. 65–81.
Stoll, H. and W. Whaley. "Transaction Costs and the Small Firm Effect." *Journal of Financial Economics*, v. 12 (June 1983), pp. 57–80.
Summers, L. H. "Do We Really Know that Financial Markets Are Efficient?" Harvard University Discussion Paper No. 1237, May 1986.
Sunder, S. "Relationship between Accounting Changes and Stock Prices: Problems of Measurement and Some Empirical Evidence." *Empirical Research in Accounting: Selected Studies*, 1973, 1–45.
Sunder, S. "Stock Price and Risk Related to Accounting Changes in Inventory Valuation." *Accounting Review*, v. 50 (April 1975), pp. 305–315.
Taylor, S. "Tests of the Random Walk Hypothesis against a Price Trend Hypothesis." *Journal of Financial and Quantitative Analysis*, v. 17 (March 1982), pp. 37–62.
Tobin, J. "A General Equilibrium Approach to Monetary Theory." *Journal of Money, Credit and Banking*, v. 1 (February 1969), pp. 15–29.
Treynor, J. L. and R. Ferguson. "In Defense of Technical Analysis." *Journal of finance*, v. 40 (July 1985), pp. 757–775.
Urich, T., and P. Wachtel. "Market Response to the Weekly Money Supply Announcements in the 1970s." *Journal of Finance*, v. 36 (December 1981), pp. 1063–1072.
Waud, R. N. "Public Interpretation of Federal Reserve Discount Rate Change: Evidence on the 'Announcement Effect."' *Econometrica*, v. 38 (March 1970), pp. 231–250.

West, R. "On the Difference between Internal and External Market Efficiency." *Financial Analysts Journal*, v. 31 (November/December 1975), pp. 30–34.

Westerfield, R. "The Distribution of Common Stock Price Changes: An Application of Transaction Time and Subordinate Stochastic Models." *Journal of Financial and Quantitative Analysis*, v. 12 (December 1977), pp. 743–766.

Chapter 13

Arbitrage Pricing Theory and Intertemporal Capital Asset Pricing Model

From the viewpoint of a security analyst, knowledge of an equilibrium-market pricing model is important because it allows the analyst to determine the theoretical value of a firm and estimate its cost of capital. The importance of these valuation concepts is demonstrated by the abundance of efforts from theoretician and practitioner alike to formula pricing models.

In finance, a great deal of the theoretical and empirical work is based on the modern portfolio theory (MPT) of Harry Markowitz (1952), out of which has evolved the **capital asset pricing model (CAPM)**. Although the CAPM has contributed greatly to our knowledge of how asset prices are determined, there are some deficiencies in the CAPM approach. These deficiencies, contained in the CAPM's stringent assumptions, have been demonstrated by the results of empirical studies. As an alternative approach to explaining the pricing of assets, Ross (1976, 1977) has developed **arbitrage pricing theory (APT)**.

APT offers many advantages over and above the traditional CAPM in terms of less stringent assumptions while retaining a higher degree of generality. Nevertheless, while theoretically APT seems to have opened up a whole new area in finance, its empirical testing still faces some problems that need to be resolved.

This chapter approaches APT by first extending the traditional CAPM to a multi-index model, thereby establishing a more congruent base from which to lead into APT. A discussion of multi-index models is followed by an examination of the specification of the arbitrage pricing model: its underlying arguments are developed and alternative model specifications are examined. The investigation then turns to the criteria of realism, and methodologies, results, and problems are examined with empirical tests. The APT and CAPM are then compared and contrasted, and the original CAPM is shown to be a special case of the APT. In addition, the intertemporal CAPM derived by Merton (1973) and others will be discussed in some detailed. The current and potential applications of APT are discussed along with future directions for model improvement. The appendices present an alternative specification of the APT as well as a method of identifying the APT model's common factors.

13.1. Multi-Index Models

Chapter 9 developed and examined the tenets of the CAPM. The CAPM implies that an asset's return is determined strictly by its inherent degree of systematic or nondiversifiable risk. This type of risk, which can also be referred to as *market risk*, is essentially a normalized measure of the covariability of returns between the individual asset and the market portfolio. Remember that beta, the measure of systematic risk, is defined as $\mathrm{Cov}(R_i, R_m)/\mathrm{Var}(R_m)$. Thus, the traditional CAPM suggests that only one independent variable, the market portfolio, is necessary for explaining asset expected returns. Nevertheless, both researchers and practitioners believe that there are influences beyond the market that cause stock prices to move. King (1966) presents evidence for the existence of industry influences. To handle additional influential factors for the explanation of asset returns and their movement over time, **multi-index models** have been proposed. Investment houses have organized their security analysis efforts along industry lines or sectors — for example, interest-sensitive stocks. Both practitioners and academics have begun to add additional factors to their models that are used to explain asset returns.

Simply adding these influences to the general return equation will, it is hoped, allow significant additional sources of covariance between securities to be taken into account. Hence, consider the following return-generating model:

$$R_i = a_i + b_{i1}I_1 + b_{i2}I_2 + \cdots + b_{iL}I_L + e_i, \tag{13.1}$$

where

I_h = the actual level of some index h ($h = 1, \ldots, \mathrm{L}$); and

b_{ih} = a measure of the responsiveness of the return on stock i to changes in index h or its sensitivity, to index h.

Essentially, then b_{ih} may be interpreted in much the same light as βi for the single-index model. Finally, the portion of security i's return that is not accounted for by the indexes is apportioned into variables, a_i and e_i. The a_i term represents the unique portion of the securities return that could be expected if it were to be unrelated to all of the explanatory indexes (i.e., all $b_{ih} = 0$). The e_i term corresponds to the random component of the return, with a mean of zero and variance of $\sigma_{e_i}^2$. Equation (13.1) is a multi-index model which has been carefully discussed in Appendix B of Chapter 10.

To simplify both the computation of risk and the selection of optimal portfolios in using the multi-index model, it is advantageous for the indexes to be uncorrelated (orthogonal). This poses no significant mathematical problem, as was shown in Chapter 10; thus, for the remainder of this section it can be assumed that the indexes do exhibit the mathematical properties associated with being uncorrelated with one another (i.e., they are independent, $\rho(I_h, I_k) = 0$).

Now, what do or should these explanatory indexes represent? While no precise answer exists for this question, theory, intuition, and empirical test can jointly suggest a number of possibilities. As was previously mentioned, King found that in addition to an overall market factor, various factors related to industry-type indexes are significant in explaining the returns-generating process for a particular security. Other potential additional indexes could be related to interest-rate movements and firm capitalization size. Sharpe (1984) finds quite a wide array of these additional factors, which he classifies as either a *systematic influence* or a *sector influence.* Among those defined as systematic influences on security returns, Sharpe finds five:

(1) Beta (the slope of the regression of excess return for the security against excess return on the S&P index);
(2) Dividend yield;
(3) Size;
(4) Bond beta; and
(5) Alpha.

The significant sector influences includes eight factors:

(1) Basic industries;
(2) Capital goods;
(3) Construction;
(4) Consumer goods;

(5) Energy;
(6) Finance;
(7) Transportation; and
(8) Utilities.

Another study by Fogler *et al.* (1981) find that the first three sources of variation in a study sample of 100 stocks are related to the market, the interest rate on U.S. government securities, and the interest rate on AA utility bonds.

Some of the other factors that have been considered include: (1) price/earnings ratio, (2) stock-issue size, (3) marketability and liquidity, (4) taxes, and (5) the time of year that the purchase or sale took place (the so-called January effect). There is no reason to believe that the number of important factors will stay constant over time or that the composition of the group of important factors will remain unchanged. Think of the OPEC oil crisis of the 1970s and its influence on pricing assets in financial markets during that period. Although during the 1980s OPEC's influence seems to have waned with respect to its influence on security pricing, perhaps in the future some other energy-related factor will emerge as an important influence in security prices.

Although empirical research supports the significance of additional explanatory indexes in addition to some market influence, the real question to put forward is how well multi-index models perform in explaining the pricing of securities. Nevertheless, to effectively carry on any discussion concerning performance, it is necessary to first reconsider the multi-index model's construction, the underlying assumptions, and the resultant implications.

By construction the equation

$$R_i = a_i + b_{i1}I_i + b_{i2}I_2 + \cdots + b_{iL}I_L + e_i, \tag{13.2}$$

has the following characteristics:

(1) The mean of e_i and $E(e_i) = 0$ for all stocks, where $i = 1, \ldots, n$.
(2) The covariance between indexes h and l equals $E[(I_h - \overline{I_h})(I_l - \overline{I_l})] = 0$ for all indexes, where $h = 1, \ldots, L$ and $l = 1, \ldots, L(h \neq l)$.
(3) The covariance between the residual for stock i and index h equals $\text{Cov}(e_i, I_h) = 0$ for all stocks and indexes, where $i = 1, \ldots, n$ and $h = 1, \ldots, L$.

(4) The covariance between e_i and e_j is zero. $[E(e_i, e_j) = 0]$ for all stocks, where $i = 1, \ldots, n$ and $j = 1, \ldots, n$ $(j \neq i)$.

If the multi-index model does sufficiently describe the return-generating process for common stocks, the expected return, variance, and covariance can then be computed between securities as follows (see Appendix 10B). The expected return for security i can be expressed:

$$\overline{R}_i = a_1 + b_{i1}\overline{I}_1 + b_{i2}\overline{I}_2 + \cdots + b_{iL}\overline{I}_L. \tag{13.3}$$

Its variance of return can be expressed:

$$\sigma_i^2 = b_{i1}^2\sigma_{I1}^2 + b_{i2}^2\sigma_{I2}^2 + \cdots + b_{iL}^2\sigma_{IL}^2 + \sigma_{ei}^2. \tag{13.4}$$

The covariance between securities i and j can be expressed:

$$\sigma_{ij}^2 = b_{i1}^2 b_{j1}\sigma_{I1}^2 + b_{i2}^2 b_{j2}\sigma_{I2}^2 + \cdots + b_{iL}^2 b_{jL}\sigma_{IL}^2. \tag{13.5}$$

It is necessary to examine the implication of the fourth model assumption, that $[E(e_i, e_j) = 0]$. This statistical requirement implies that the only reason stocks vary together is because of common co-movement with the set of indexes that have been specified in the model. No other factors beyond these indexes should account for any of the co-movement between two securities. However, there is nothing in the estimation of the model that requires this condition to be true. Rather, the model is more likely to be an approximation of reality. The model's performance is therefore dependent on how well the model approximates the true return-generating process for securities. Moreover, the accuracy of approximation will depend heavily upon how well the chosen indexes capture the actual pattern of co-movement between securities and to what extent historical patterns of co-movement persist into the future.

To judge the performance of multi-index models, it is first essential to point out that all index models lead to the same estimates of expected returns and a stock's own variance (but not covariance), when estimated from historical returns and variances. Moreover, if the stock analyst uses a personal estimate for the stock's expected return and variance, then all that is left for the model to estimate are the covariances. Yet since the covariance is the product of standard deviations and security coefficients, any disparities in performance that exist must arise from differences in estimating the correlation structure of security returns. Consequently, then, the most direct test of alternative models is to evaluate how well they estimate the future correlation matrix of security returns.

Upon measuring the difference between actual results and forecasts, it can be determined whether such forecasting deficiencies are statistically significant. Another mode of analysis for evaluation model performance is to test the economic significance of the difference in return or profit that result from basing forecasts on various models (for a prespecified level of risk).

The empirical results for testing the multi-index model on statistical and economic grounds do not offer a great deal of support. For instance, Elton and Gruber (1973) note that, in general, adding additional indexes to the single-index model leads to a decrease in performance on both statistical and economic grounds. These authors conclude that the addition of more indexes lead to a better explanation of the historical correlation matrix, yet it resulted in both a poorer prediction of the future correlation matrix and a selection of portfolios that at each risk level tended to have lower returns. Thus, the use of multiple indexes in the forecasting process results in the introduction of more random noise than real information.

In another test of the multi-index model, Cohen and Pogue (1967) formulate the additional explanatory indexes on the basis of standard industrial classifications. Comparing the forecasts of a single-index model to one including both a market and industry index, these authors conclude that the single-index model leads to lower expected risks and is much simpler to use.

As was previously mentioned, the performance of the multi-index model largely depends on which indexes are chosen and how they are formed. The study by Cohen and Pogue utilizes standard industrial classifications to devise their additional indexes. Nevertheless, this method has its problems. The increase in the number of multiproduct firms and the prevalence of company diversification has made the classification by product difficult and sometimes arbitrary. Moreover, classification by product or service may be useful for some purposes, but falls far short of being universal classification in all cases. For instance, although General Motors and Chrysler are in the same industry, there is substantial divergence between their performance and the degree of risk to which they are subject.

To combat this problem, Farrell (1974) formulates homogeneous groups of firms ("pseudo-industries") to form indexes as input to a multi-index model. Utilizing a procedure known as **principal-components analysis**, Farrell finds that his large sample of stocks can be classified into four pseudo-industries. Due to the nature of stocks in each group the author is able to associate characteristics with each of them and correspondingly labels the four groups:

(1) Growth stocks;
(2) Cyclical stocks;
(3) Stable stocks; and
(4) Oil stocks.

While it is not surprising that his model does a superior job of accounting for the historical correlation matrix of return, it is significant that this model performs somewhat better based on economic criteria than the models of Cohen and Pogue. Using *Economic criteria*, Farrell (1974) tested whether there is a better predictor of the correlation structure of returns. He found that when the explanation indexes are correctly formed the multi-index model can potentially outperform the single-index model, perhaps yielding greater insight into the inherent return-generating processes among securities. This chapter can now focus on the APT, which devises a more generalized equilibrium framework than the multi-index model for describing and forecasting security returns. Indeed, one of the central issues in APT concerns the formation, interpretation, and correct number of "pseudo-indexes" to use.

13.2. Model Specification of APT

Suppose there are two riskless assets offering rates of return r and r', respectively. Assuming no transaction costs, one of the strongest statements that can be made in positive economics is that

$$r = r'. \tag{13.6}$$

This is based on the law of one price, which says that the same good cannot sell at different prices. In terms of securities, the law of one price says that securities with identical risks must have the same expected return. Essentially, Equation (13.6) is an **arbitrage condition** that must be expected to hold in all but the most extreme circumstances. This is because if $r > r'$, the first riskless asset could be purchased with funds obtained from selling the second riskless asset. This arbitrage transaction would yield a return of $r - r'$ with no risk and no net wealth invested. If investors were to come across such a disequilibrium relationship, they would surely seize the opportunity to make a return of $r - r'$ without having to make any new investment of funds or taken on any additional risk. In the process of

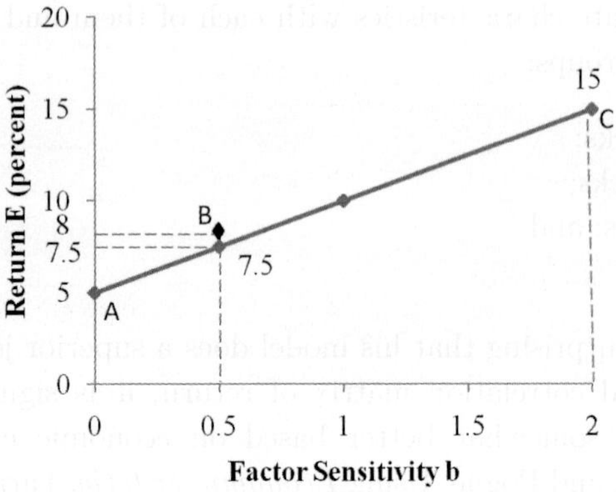

Security	Expected Return (percent)	Factor Sensitivity
A	5	0.0
B	8	0.5
C	15	2.0

Fig. 13.1. Expected Returns and Factor Sensitivity.

buying the first asset and selling the second, investors would bid up the former's price and bid down the latter's price. This repricing mechanism would continue up to the point where these two assets' respective prices equaled each other, and thus $r = r'$.

Put in the context of securities that are traded in markets and held in portfolios, consider the following simple example. There exist three assets A, B, and C, all of which are related to the same basic underlying factor. The characteristics of these three assets are shown in Fig. 13.1. Securities A and C are both correctly priced given the sensitivity they have to the factor.[1] However, security B appears to be mispriced; it offers a return of 8%, which exceeds the expected return of 7.5% for securities with a sensitivity of 0.5. To take advantage of this mispricing, an investor can perform an arbitrage among the three securities. By buying $1 worth of security B and short selling $0.75 of security A and $0.25 of security C, the investor can generate a risk-free return of 0.5%. This arbitrage is shown in Table 13.1. The arbitrage allows the investor to earn a return of 0.5% with no risk and no investment. There is only one factor in this example, but

[1]Strictly speaking, A, B, or C or some combination may be mispriced. However, the validity of the argument still holds.

Table 13.1. Arbitrage Results.

	Expected Return	Factor Sensitivity
Buy \$1 of B.	$(1 \times 8\% = 8\%)$	$(1 \times 0.5) = 0.5$
Sell \$0.75 of A short.	$-(0.75 \times 5\%) = -3.75\%$	$-(0.75 \times 0) = 0$
Sell \$0.25 of C short.	$-(0.25 \times 15\%) = -3.75\%$	$-(0.25 \times 2) = -0.5$
Total investment = 0	Total return = 0.5%	Total sensitivity = 0

the arbitrage argument can be extended to include many factors. As long as there exists a mispricing of one of the securities on one of the factors, an arbitrage opportunity will exist until investors drive the market into equilibrium.

APT utilizes this robust type of argument and extends its application to the pricing of risky assets. The net result of APT's development is a more generalized and less restrictive framework than the CAPM for the pricing of risky assets. More explicitly, to make its equilibrium statement for asset returns, APT does not require quadratic utility functions for investors or joint normality or returns between individual assets and the market portfolio. (APT does not require that market portfolio be mean-variance efficient or even that it exists at all.) Finally, APT is not limited to a single period, as is the original form of the CAPM.

13.2.1. *Ross's Arbitrage Model Specification*

This section focuses on two related forms of the arbitrage pricing model. The first of these is the model as originally proposed by Ross (1976).

The initial and probably the most prominent assumption made by APT concerns the return-generating process for assets. Specifically, individuals are assumed to believe (homogeneously) that the random returns on the set of assets being considered are governed by a k-factor generating model of the form:

$$\tilde{r}_i = E_i + b_{i1}\tilde{\delta}_1 + \cdots + b_{ik}\tilde{\delta}_k + \tilde{\epsilon}_i \quad (i = 1, \ldots, n), \tag{13.7}$$

where

$\tilde{r}_i$ = random return on the ith asset;
E_i = expected return on the ith asset;
$\tilde{\delta}_j$ = jth factor common to the returns of all assets under consideration with a mean of zero, common factors that in essence capture the systematic component of risk in the model;

b_{ij} = a coefficient called a *factor loading* that quantifies the sensitivity of asset i's returns to the movements in the common factor $\tilde{\delta}_j$ (and is analogous to the beta in the CAPM); and

$\tilde{\in}_i$ = an error term, or unsystematic risk component, idiosyncratic to the ith asset, with mean zero and variance equal to $\tilde{\sigma}^2_{\in}$.

Moreover, it is assumed that the $\tilde{\in}_i$ reflects the random influence of information that is unrelated to other assets. Thus, the following condition is assumed to hold:

$$E\{\tilde{\in}_i|\tilde{\in}_j\} = 0, \tag{13.8}$$

as well as $\bar{\in}_i$ and $\bar{\in}_j$ independence for all $i \neq j$. Also, for any two securities i and j:

$$E\{\tilde{\in}_i, \tilde{\in}_j\} = 0, \tag{13.9}$$

for all i and j, where $i \neq j$. If this last condition did not hold — that is, if there was too strong a dependence between $\tilde{\in}_i$ and $\tilde{\in}_j$ — it would be equivalent to saying that more than simply the k-hypothesized common factors existed. Finally, it is assumed that the set of n is much greater than the number of factors k.

Before developing Ross's riskless arbitrage argument, it is essential to examine Equation (13.7) more closely and draw some implications from its structure. First, consider the effect of omitting the unsystematic risk terms $\tilde{e}_i$. Equation (13.7) would then imply that each asset i has returns $\tilde{r}$ that are an exact linear combination of the returns on a riskless asset (with constant return) and the returns on k other factors or assets (or column vectors) $\delta_i, \ldots, \delta_k$. Moreover, the riskless return and each of the k factors can be expressed as a linear combination of $k + 1$ other returns — for example, r, through r_{k+1} — in this type of setting. Taking this logic one step further, since any other asset return is a linear combination of the factors, it must also be that a linear combination of the returns of the first $k + 1$ assets must be perfect substitutes for all other assets in the market. Consequently, there must be restrictions on the individual returns generated by the model, since perfect substitutes must be priced equivalently. This sequence of mathematical logic is the core of APT. That is, only a few systematic components of risk exist in the economy; and consequently many portfolios will be close substitutes, thereby demanding the same value.

To initiate Ross's arbitrage argument about APT, it is best to start with the assumption of Equation (13.7). Next, presume an investor who is contemplating an alteration of the currently held portfolio, The difference between any new portfolio and the old portfolio will be quantified by changes in the investment proportions x_i $(i = 1, \ldots, n)$. The x_i, represents the dollar amount purchased or sold of asset i as a fraction of total invested wealth. The investor's portfolio investment is constrained to hold to the following condition:

$$\sum_{i=1}^{n} x_i = 0. \tag{13.10}$$

In words, Equation (13.10) says that additional purchases of assets must be financed by sales of others. Portfolios that require no net investment such as $x \equiv (x_j, \ldots, x_n)$ are called *arbitrage portfolios.* Table 13.1 shows exactly this situation: the proceeds from the short sale of A and C were used to purchase B.

Now, consider an arbitrage portfolio chosen in the following manner. First the portfolio must be chosen to be well diversified by keeping each element, x, of order $1/n$ in size. Second, the x of the portfolio must be selected in such a way as to eliminate all systematic risk (for each h):

$$xb_h \sum_{i=1} x_i b_{ih} = 0 \quad (h = 1, \ldots, k). \tag{13.11}$$

The returns on any such arbitrage portfolios can be described:

$$\begin{aligned} x\tilde{r} &= (xE) + (xb)\tilde{\delta}_1 + \cdots + (xb_k)\tilde{\delta}_k + (x\tilde{\in}) \\ &\approx xE + (xb_1)\tilde{\delta}_1 + \cdots + (xb_k)\tilde{\delta}_k \\ &= xE, \end{aligned}$$

where $x\tilde{r} = \sum_{i=1}^{n} x_i \tilde{r}_i$ and $xE = \sum_{i=1}^{n} x_i E_i$. Note that the term $(x\tilde{\in})$ is (approximately) eliminated by the effect of holding a well-diversified portfolio of n assets, where n is large. Using the law of large numbers, if σ^2 denotes the average variance of the $\tilde{e}_i$ terms, and assuming for simplicity that each x, approximately equals $1/n$ and that the $\in_i$ are mutually independent:

$$\begin{aligned} \mathrm{Var}(x\tilde{\in}) &= \mathrm{Var}\left(\frac{1}{n}\sum_i \in_i\right) \\ &= \frac{\mathrm{Var}(\tilde{\in}_i)}{n^2} \\ &= \frac{\sigma^2}{n^2}. \end{aligned} \tag{13.12}$$

Thus if n is large the variance of $x\tilde{\in}$ will be negligible.

Reconsidering the steps up to this point, note that a portfolio has been created that has no systematic or unsystematic risk and using no wealth. Under **conditions of equilibrium** it can be stated unequivocally that *all portfolios of these n assets that satisfy the conditions of using no wealth and having no risk must also earn no return on average.* In other words, there are no free lunches in an efficient market, at least not for any extended period of time. Therefore the expected return on the arbitrage portfolio can be expressed as

$$x\tilde{r} = xE = \sum_{i=1}^{n} x_i E_i = 0. \tag{13.13}$$

Another way to state the preceding statements and results is through linear algebra. In general, any vector x with elements on the order of $1/n$ that is orthogonal to the constant vector and to each of the coefficient vectors b_h $(h = 1, \ldots, k)$ must also be orthogonal to the vector of expected returns. A further algebraic consequence of this statement is that the expected return vector E must be a linear combination of the constant vector and the b vectors. Using algebraic terminology, there exist $k + 1$ weights $(\lambda_0, \lambda_1, \ldots, \lambda_k)$ such that

$$E_i = \lambda_0 + \lambda_1 b_{il} + \cdots + \lambda_k b_{ik} \quad \text{for all } I. \tag{13.14}$$

In addition, if there exists a riskless asset with return E_0 which can be said to be the common return on all zero-beta assets — that is, $b_{ih} = 0$ (for all h) — then:

$$E_0 = \lambda_0.$$

Utilizing this definition and rearranging:

$$E_i - E_0 = \lambda_1 b_{il} + \cdots + \lambda_k b_{ik}. \tag{13.15}$$

The pricing relationship depicted in Equation (13.15) is the central conclusion of the APT. Before exploring the consequences of this pricing model through a simple numerical example, it is best to first give some interpretation to the λ_h, the factor risk premium. If portfolios are formed with a systematic risk of 1 relative to factor h and no risk on other factors, then each λ_h can be interpreted as

$$\lambda_h = E^h - E_0. \tag{13.16}$$

In words, each λ_h can be thought of as the excess return or market risk premium on portfolios with only systematic factor h risk. Hence, Equation (13.15) can be rewritten as

$$E_i - E_0 = (E^1 - E_0)b_{i1} + \cdots + (E^k - E_0)b_{ik}. \tag{13.17}$$

The implications that arise from the arguments concerning APT that have been constructed thus far can be summarized in the following statement: *APT yields a statement of relative pricing on subsets of the universe of assets.* Moreover, note that the arbitrage pricing model of Equations (13.15) or (13.17) can be tested by examining only subsets of the set of all return. Consequently, the market portfolio plays no special role in APT, since any well-diversified portfolio could serve the same purpose. Hence, it can be empirically tested on any set of data, and the results should be generalizable to the entire market. The following three sample problems give further illustration.

Sample Problem 13.1

To reinforce the concepts and workings of the arbitrage mechanism, consider a simple example. Suppose that the returns on two well-diversified portfolios can be described by a linear function in the following arbitrage pricing model (APM) form:

$$(E_i - E_0) = (\lambda_1 b_{i1} + \lambda_2 b_{i2}),$$

or,

$$= (E^1 - E_0)b_{i1} + (E^2 - E_0)b_{i2} + (E^3 - E_0)b_{i3},$$

in which E_0 is the constant return on the riskless asset.

Next, assume these portfolios have the following sensitivity coefficients (factor loadings) with the three identified factors (Table 13.2).

Assuming the riskless rate is 7% (E_0), the expected returns and their relative returns per unit of risk as defined by the Treynor performance

Table 13.2. Sensitivity Coefficients.

Portfolio	b_{i1}	b_{i2}	b_{i3}
1	0.6	1.0	0.8
2	0.3	0.7	0.5

Table 13.3. Expected Return Per Unit of Risk.

Portfolio	E_i (%)	$\frac{(E_i - E_0)}{(\sum_{i=1}^{3} b_{ih}/3)}$
1	12	6.25
2	8	2.00

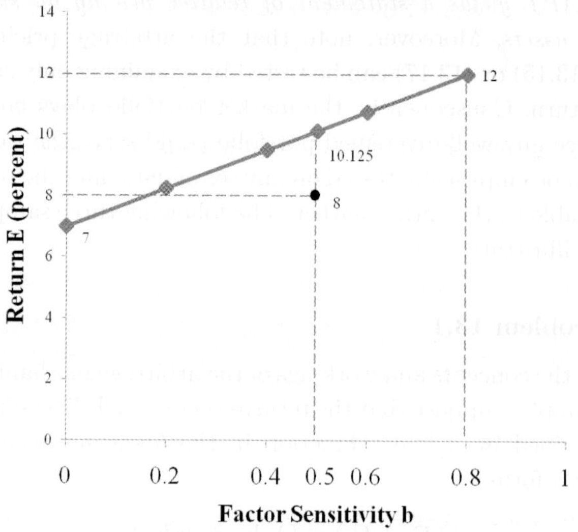

Fig. 13.2. Expected Return and Factor Sensitivity.

measure can be expressed in Table 13.3. In addition, a graph can be drawn of each portfolio's expected return versus the averaged value of its sensitivity coefficients, as indicated in the Fig. 13.2. This is somewhat analogous to the analysis in CAPM. Please note that 10.125% in fig. 13.2 is calculated as follows:

$$\frac{x - 7}{0.5} = \frac{12 - 7}{0.8}$$

$$x = 10.125,$$

where x is the theoretical expected return related to the factor sensitivity of the second portfolio.

As was demonstrated through the determination of each portfolio's expected return-per-risk measure, the graph again points out that the

Table 13.4. Excess Return of the Investment.

	Investment	Systematic Risk (b_{ih})	Expected Return (%)
For portfolio 2, sell short	\$1,000,000	−0.5	−0.8
For portfolio 1, buy	(\$625,000)	$(0.625 \times 0.8) = 0.5$	$(0.625 \times 12.0) = 7.5$
Invest remainder in bills	(\$375,000)	$(0.375 \times 0) = 0$	$(0.375 \times 7.0) = 2.625$
Net investment:	\$0		
Net risk:		0.0	
Total excess return earned:			2.125%

second portfolio is overpriced.[2] That is, its expected return per unit of risk is lower than that of the first portfolio relative to the riskless rate of 7%.

The proper "arbitrage strategy" to follow in order to profit from this apparent mispricing is shown in Table 13.4. However appealing the logic of the previous arbitrage argument, some specific assumptions are required for the APT.

(1) Investors are return maximizers.
(2) Borrowing and lending is done at the riskless rate.
(3) There are no market restrictions such as transaction costs, taxes, or restrictions on short selling.
(4) Investors agree on the number and identity of the factors that are priced.
(5) Riskless profitable opportunities above the risk-free rate are immediately arbitraged away.

Hence, since any market equilibrium must be consistent with no arbitrage profits, every equilibrium will be characterized by a linear relationship between each asset's expected return and its sensitivity to the common priced factors.

Sample Problem 13.2

Given the three portfolios in Table 13.5 with expected return R_i and sensitivity factors b_{i1} and b_{i2}, what is the equation of the plane in R_i, b_{i1}, and b_{i2} space defined by these portfolios?

[2]Suppose the second portfolio will pay \$10 per year. The price of this portfolio with the expected return 8% is \$10/0.08 = \$125, while the price with the theoretical return 10.125% is \$10/10.125% = \$98.77. The market price (\$125) is higher than its theoretical price (\$98.77), so the second portfolio is overpriced.

Table 13.5. Expected Return R_i and Sensitivity Factors b_{i1} and b_{i2}.

Portfolio	R_i	b_{i1}	b_{i2}
A	14.0	0.8	0.8
B	10.8	0.6	0.4
C	11.2	0.4	0.6

Solution

The information can be used to derive the equation for the risk-return plan of Equation (13.14) as follows. Substituting returns and sensitivity-factor information into Equation (13.14):

$$14 = \lambda_0 + 0.8\lambda_1 + 0.8\lambda \quad \text{(i)}$$

$$10.8 = \lambda_0 + 0.6\lambda_1 + 0.4\lambda_2 \quad \text{(ii)}$$

$$11.2 = \lambda_0 + 0.4\lambda_1 + 0.6\lambda_2. \quad \text{(iii)}$$

Subtract (ii) from (i):

$$3.2 = 0.2\lambda_1 + 0.4\lambda_2. \quad \text{(iv)}$$

Subtract (ii) from (iii):

$$0.4 = -0.2\lambda_1 + 0.2\lambda_2. \quad \text{(v)}$$

From Equation (iv) and (v) $\lambda_2 = 6$. From Equation (v) $\lambda_1 = 4$. Finally, from Equation (i), solving for λ_0:

$$\begin{aligned}\lambda_0 &= 14 + 0.8\lambda_1 - 0.8\lambda_2 \\ &= 14 + 3.2 - 4.8 \\ &= 6.\end{aligned}$$

Hence the equation of the plane describing equilibrium risk-return space can be expressed:

$$E_i = 6 + 4b_{i1} + 6b_{i2}.$$

Sample Problem 13.3

Using the portfolios in Sample Problem 13.2, determine how much arbitrage profit, if any, can be made by buying or selling (short) the following portfolios (individually) (Table 13.6).

Table 13.6. Expected Return R_i and Sensitivity Factors b_{i1} and b_{i2}.

Portfolio	$R_i(\%)$	b_{i1}	b_{i2}
D	14.0	0.5	0.7
E	15.2	0.8	1.0
F	9.0	0.6	0.5

Solution

From portfolios A, B, and C, the risk/return relationship is $E_i = 6 + 4b_{i1} + 6b_{i2}$.

For portfolio D, an equivalent portfolio can be composed from a linear combination of A, B, and C. Given sensitivity factors $b_{i1} = 0.5$ and $b_{i2} = 0.7$, the expected return would be

$$\begin{aligned} r_0 &= 6 + 4(0.5) + 6(0.7) \\ &= 12.2\%. \end{aligned}$$

Since $12.2\% < 14\%$, portfolio D is underpriced. A riskless, costless arbitrage profit can be made by buying portfolio D and selling an equivalent amount of a portfolio composed of A, B, and C.

For portfolio E, and equivalent portfolio can be constructed with yield:

$$r_{\text{equiv}} = 6 + 4(0.8) + 6(1.0) = 15.2\%.$$

This is exactly the yield of portfolio E; therefore, no arbitrage opportunities remain:

For portfolio F:

$$r_{\text{equiv}} = 6 + 4(0.8) + 6(0.5) = 11.4\%.$$

Since $11.4\% > 9\%$, the F portfolio is overpriced. Therefore, portfolio F should be sold and the equivalent portfolio should be bought.

A riskless, costless arbitrage profit of \$18,000 as indicated in Table 13.7 can be made by buying \$10 million worth of portfolio D and by selling \$10 million of an equivalent portfolio made up of A, B, and C.

A riskless, costless arbitrage profit of \$24,000 as indicated in Table 13.8 can be made by selling \$10 million worth of portfolio F and by buying \$10 million of an equivalent portfolio made up of A, B, and C.

Table 13.7. Arbitrage Profits of Portfolio D and the Equivalent Portfolio.

	Initial *CF*	Ending *CF*	Risk Factor b_{i1}	b_{i2}
Portfolio D	−\$10,000,000	+\$1,140,000	0.5	0.7
Equivalent portfolio	+\$10,000,000	−\$1,122,000	−0.5	−0.7
	0	+ 18,000	0	0

Table 13.8. Arbitrage Profits of Portfolio E and the Equivalent Portfolio.

	Initial *CF*	Ending *CF*	Sens. Factors b_{i1}	b_{i2}
Portfolio F	+\$10,000,000	−\$1,090,000	−0.8	−1.0
Equivalent portfolio	−\$10,000,000	+\$1,114,000	+0.8	+1.0
	0	+ 24,000	0	0

Even though the APT is very general and based on few assumptions, it provides little guidance concerning the identification of the priced factors. Hence empirical research must achieve two goals.

(1) Identify the number of factors.
(2) Identify the various economics underlying each factor.

13.2.2. *Empirical Test Methodology*

Empirical tests of the APT are evolving at an increasing rate as academicians attempt to verify its conclusions. In particular, recent empirical work in this area has sought to determine whether there exist multiple underlying factors for asset returns — and, if they exist, whether they are associated with risk premiums. It is hypothesized that there exist nonzero $\lambda_1, \ldots, \lambda_k$ such that

$$E_i - E_0 = \lambda_1 b_{i1} + \cdots + \lambda_k b_{ik}, \quad (13.18)$$

for all i. To empirically test this hypothesis, a two-step procedure is typically utilized. In the first step, the statistical technique of factor analysis is used to estimate the expected returns and the factor loading $(b_{i1}, \ldots, b_{ik})$ from time-series data of asset returns. In the second step, these estimates are used in the basic cross-sectional pricing equation of the APT to estimate the risk premium (λ_h), thereby performing the hypothesis test.

While this two-step procedure is analogous to familiar CAPM empirical work, it is free of some major conceptual difficulties in CAPM tests. Most important of these is that the APT can be applied to subsets of the universe of assets, eliminating any need to specify as well as justify any particular choice of a proxy for the market portfolio.

It would be ideal to perform the factor analysis in the first step on all asset returns as a whole; nevertheless, the resulting huge covariance matrix would be beyond the normal processing capacity of computers. To compromise with this technical constraint, several approaches have been taken in the empirical studies of APT. However, to date no one approach has yet been proposed that is free of shortcomings. To better clarify the testing procedures required for APT along with the inherent problems, some of the major empirical studies are now offered, followed by an example of an empirical test of the APT.

The most comprehensive and widely recognized study of the APT is that of Roll and Ross (RR, 1980). These authors use daily returns for a sample of 1,269 selected securities from both the NYSE and AMEX over the period July 3, 1962 to December 31, 1972. RR arranged the sample into 42 groups with 30 securities in each, on the basis of alphabetical order. Next, RR performs maximum-likelihood factor analysis on each of the 42 group to estimate the respective factor loadings. The estimated factor loadings are then used as the explanatory variables in the **second-stage cross-sectional regression test**.

The dominant problem associated with this approach is that the return-generating process cannot be compared across groups. This result from the complexity that factors in different groups might not lie in the same dimensionality. More explicitly, the first factor in one group may not correspond to the first factor in the other group. Quite conceivably then, the first factor in one group might be equivalent to the third factor in the other group. Hence, after the cross-sectional distributions of the loading coefficients are tabulated, there could be a mixing of estimates which apply to different "true" factors. Moreover, there is no way to ascertain that the same three (or four) factors (the number RR found) generate the returns in every group.

A second approach in testing the APT, called the **small-ample approach**, is employed by Chen (1983), and Oldfield and Rogalski (1981). Using the small-sample approach, assets are divided into several groups as before. However, now for only a single group (as opposed to every group) is factor analysis applied and corresponding factor loadings estimated. The estimates of factor loadings for in the remaining groups are inferred from the covariance of their returns with the loading coefficients of the factor analyzed group.

The small-sample approach assures the comparability of factors across groups, a definite strength over the RR approach. However, because only a relatively small number of asset returns are used in the factor-estimation procedure, the statistical problem of inefficient estimation is encountered. Moreover, as other researchers have demonstrated, the estimation bias in the original estimation of factor loadings can be magnified further when the remaining loadings are derived. The central consequence of this estimation bias is that "spurious" explanatory factors may be extracted.

To surpass the hindrance of inefficient estimation, Reinganum (1981) applies a third approach, the **portfolio approach**. Here assets are grouped into portfolios, and factor analysis is performed on the covariance matrix among these portfolio returns instead of the individual asset returns (as in the previous two approaches). The problem with this methodology is that as the number of assets in a portfolio increases, the portfolio returns tend to reflect a single-factor model even when a multifactor model is true. Thus, it is not surprising that the studies using the portfolio approach find but one significant factor.

Thus it has been shown that any efficient estimation procedure for testing the APT requires the utilization of all assets in the sample. Moreover, the portfolio approach stresses the importance of using the covariance matrix among individual assets in order to avoid the tendency toward a single-factor model. Yet the constraint of computer capacity makes the comparative analysis of the covariance matrix of the entire population of assets virtually impossible. Consequently, as Roll and Ross's study (1980) points out, dividing the population into a manageable number of smaller groups creates a problem in identifying what the explanatory factors are and determining whether their relative significance across groups is consistent.

13.3. APT: Empirical Results and Implications

Following the empirical tests of the APT, it is important to examine some of the findings in relation to the following questions:

(1) How many factors have been identified? How many should there be?
(2) Has empirical research been able to verify APT?
(3) If the theory is correct and significant factors have been identified, what do these factors represent?

In what has quickly become the classic article for testing the APT, Roll and Ross (1980) found that there are at least three, but probably no more than four, significant explanatory factors in the model structure. While the remaining empirical literature in this area is still somewhat scarce compared with that of the CAPM, most of the other studies settle on five as being the significant number of relevant factors (e.g., see Hughes (1981) and Chen (1983)). In a recent paper challenging the robustness of the APT, Cho *et al.* (1984) found at least five and as many as six explanatory factors while using the RR methodology.

Now consider whether four to six factors can constitute a correctly and significantly specified pricing model. While most of the previously mentioned researchers would say yes to the above, there remains a considerable amount of dissent in the finance corps. For instance, in their critical reexamination of the APT, Dhrymes *et al.* (1984) develop evidence indicating that the number of significant factors found tends to increase as the size of the sample groups is increased. This type of phenomenon is related to the factor-analysis methodology so widely used in tests of the APT.

Lee and Wei (2012) apply the Ramsey and Schmidt (1976) specification-error test to see whether a five-factor APT model may not be enough to explain the return-generating process of all securities. Using this type of F-test, these authors find specification error present in the five-factor model at the 5% level of significance. (However, this degree of specification error at the same significance level was not apparent when the same hypothesis was tested for a 10-factor model.) Their results are shown in Appendix 13B at the end of this chapter.

Thus, discrepancies in results among empirical tests may result from differing time periods of study, methodologies, and sample-group sizes. Moreover, the findings up to this point indicate that although relatively substantial evidence is accumulating that lends support to the APT's validity, its actual affirmation remains unsubstantiated. Part of this inability to develop conclusive proof of the APT relates to the potential inadequacy of factor analysis as a methodology for identifying common factors. Shanken (1982) exposes a previously unnoticed property of the factor-model representation of returns. By "repackaging" a given set of securities, the factor model can be manipulated rather arbitrarily. More specifically, Shanken shows that a new set of returns and a corresponding factor model can be produced, with virtually any prespecified random variables as the factors. Hence, formulating the APT model in terms of factor analytic methods can be taken to imply the proposition that all securities have the same expected return.

To combat some of this criticism, RR (1980) emphasize that if a more powerful test with factor analysis could be devised, as many factors as there are sets of assets would probably be found. Nevertheless, almost all of these additional factors would be diversifiable and thus irrelevant in terms of pricing.

Dybvig and Ross (1985) argue that the APT is a good approximation in theory. They counter Shanken's (1982) claim that the APT is untestable. They explain that empirical tests are performed using actual assets, not on arbitrage recombination as shown in Shanken's paper. Therefore Shanken's empirical version of the APT is unrelated to existing empirical work. They also show that the APT is testable.

Furthermore, Dybvig and Ross (1985) argue that Shanken's (1982) critique of the APT tests on two fallacies. First, the version of APT Shanken uses assumes that it can be applied to arbitrary portfolios, which is inconsistent with the theoretical and empirical work on the APT. Second, a good approximation that can be treated empirically as an equality can be manipulated arbitrarily as an equality. When Shanken creates the portfolios from the original assets, he finds all randomness, systematic factors, and idiosyncratic noise alike. That is, he treats all these factors as idiosyncratic noise. This is the opposite of diversification, and it is therefore not surprising that applying the APT to the transformed assets proves a paradox.

13.4. Identifying the Model Factors

Although APT still lacks a wide base of empirical support, its intuitive content and formulation remain quite appealing. Still, more testing is needed before the APT pricing relationship can be seriously applied by security analysis and other practitioners concerned with the correct allocation of resources in our economy. Some of the testing that is going on now takes a more universal scope in testing and interpreting the APT. These studies have focused on identifying the specific macroeconomic forces which influence security returns.

Chen *et al.* (CRR, 1986) developed a theoretical guide to help identify the economic-state variables that are likely to be important for asset pricing. The relevant affecting economic factors identified by these authors include:

(1) Unanticipated inflation;
(2) Expected inflation;
(3) Unanticipated change in the term structure of interest rates;
(4) Monthly and yearly growth rates in industrial production;

(5) Unexpected changes in the yearly growth in industrial production;
(6) Change in the expected rate of yearly growth in industrial production;
(7) Unanticipated changes in the risk premiums embedded in interest rates;
(8) Percentage changes in real consumption;
(9) Growth rate in oil prices;
(10) Return on the equal-weighted NYSE index;
(11) Return on the value-weighted NYSE index; and
(12) Treasury-bill (T-bill) rates.

CRR (1986) then devise data series to represent these economic-state variables and proceed to test their influence on stock-market returns. The results show a good number of these economic variables to be important explanators of expected stock returns. These results gain additional credibility due to the insignificance of the NYSE index variables when used in conjunction with the other state variables. Hence, the CRR study adds support to the dimension of APT, which argues that expected returns can be explained by the sensitivities of sock returns to innovations in macroeconomics-state variables.

In a related but more recent study, Lee and Wei (1984) attempted to uncover the pricing influences of a similar set of macroeconomic-state variables on the returns of securities. They classified these state variables into five categories.

(1) Money supply (MS);
(2) Real production;
(3) Inflation;
(4) Interest rate; and
(5) Market return.

In addition to the types of state variables used by CRR, this study also includes variables for transaction volume, the absolute level and velocity of MS, the risk premium decomposed into maturity and default components, and real auto and home production. A complete list of the explanatory state variables and results appears in Appendix 13B.

Summarizing these results, Lee and Wei find that in addition to the market index, only the risk-free rate, expected inflation, and industrial production significantly influence stock-market returns. In terms of relating some of their explanatory state variables to the common factors of the APT model, nothing conclusive was obtained. However, evidence does arise that associates the first factor with some market index, the second factor with expected inflation and industrial production, and the fourth factor with the risk-free rate and industrial production. No other state variables show significant correlation with the other two factors usually identified in APT tests.

Up to this point, intuitive arguments about APT have been provided as well as empirical support for its use. As APT can be viewed as a potentially preferable competitor of the CAPM, it seems appropriate at this time to relate, compare, and contrast these pricing theories.

13.5. APT Versus MPT and the CAPM

For more than two decades **MPT** has been the most widely accepted investment theory among academicians and practitioners alike. The best-known outcome of MPT has been the CAPM. Hence APT faces stiff competition in becoming a widely accepted and applied theory in the finance profession. A comparison and contrast of these two theories therefore seems appropriate at this point in order to understand the implications of the new versus the old.

First, recall the discussion of multi-index models at the beginning of this chapter. The focus was the return-generating process that utilized explanatory indexes of factors in addition to (or instead of) some market index. This model was of the type:

$$R_i = a_i + b_{i1}I_1 + b_{i2}I_2 + e_i, \tag{13.19}$$

in which I_1 and I_2 were indexes representing industry influences or broader economic effects such as interest rates or inflation. Once again look at the simple CAPM as discussed in Chapter 9:

$$\bar{R}_i = R_f + \beta_i(\bar{R}_m - R_f). \tag{13.20}$$

If the return-generating function is more complex than this, then can the simple CAPM still hold? The answer is yes. Recall from earlier discussions that the simple CAPM does not assume the market is the only source of covariance between returns. Therefore, Equation (13.20) could be extended to Equation (13.21) within the context of CAPM, as long as it is assumed that the set of indexes used capture all the sources of covariance between securities (e.g., $E(e_i, e_j) = 0$).

Within the framework of APT, the equilibrium model can be formulated for this same multifactor return-generating process, assuming some riskless asset, as follows:

$$\bar{R}_i = R_f + b_{i1}\lambda_1 + b_{i2}\lambda_2, \tag{13.21}$$

in which λ_1 and λ_2 represent the excess returns that occur for bearing the risk associated with that factor (or relatedly, the particular index of securities), and b_{i1} again is the sensitivity of security i to the explanatory factor λ_1.

If the CAPM is the equilibrium model for describing security returns, it must also hold for portfolios of securities. Suppose that the indexes in Equation (13.20) represent portfolios of securities. As is already been stated (and will be expanded upon later), the λ can be interpreted as the excess return for a portfolio with b_{ih} equal to 1 for one index and b_{ih} equal to zero for all other indexes:

$$\lambda_1 = \bar{R}_1 - R_f,$$
$$\lambda_2 = \bar{R}_2 - R_f.$$

Presuming that the CAPM holds, the R_h can be rewritten in terms of their equilibrium return as defined by the CAPM:

$$\begin{aligned}\lambda_1 &= c_1(\bar{R}_m - R_f),\\ \lambda_2 &= c_2(\bar{R}_m - R_f),\end{aligned} \tag{13.22}$$

in which c_1 and c_2 are adjustment factors. Then by substituting the equalities of (13.22) into the APT equation of (13.21):

$$\bar{R}_i = R_f + b_{i1}c_1(\bar{R}_m - R_f) + b_{i2}c_2(\bar{R}_m - R_f),$$
$$\bar{R}_i = R_f + (b_{i1}c_1 + b_{i2}c_2)(\bar{R}_m - R_f).$$

Now β_i needs to be defined to be equal to $(b_{i1}c_1 + b_{i2}c_2)$ in order to have the pricing relationship for R_i expressed within the CAPM framework:

$$\bar{R}_i = R_f + \beta_i(\bar{R}_m - R_f).$$

From this exercise it has been shown that the APT with multiple factors appropriately priced is fully consistent with the Sharpe–Lintner–Mossin form of the CAPM.

The proponents of APT contend that their theory is superior to that of MPT with the CAPM. The primary reason for viewing APT in this light is a result of its greater degree of generality, which is achieved utilizing fewer simplifying assumptions. In fact, the CAPM can be considered a special case of the APT. That case arises when only one explanatory factor exists for individual security returns, the market portfolio.

Among the ways that APT and MPT are similar is that both theories assume that investors prefer more wealth to less and that they are risk averse. These two assumptions together imply that investors have positive but diminishing marginal utility of wealth, and thus make investment decisions which will maximize their expected utility of wealth. This assumption on either theory's part is quite realistic.

Another assumption used by both theories is that capital markets are perfect. This condition is debatable in some financial arenas. Yet the resulting additional model complexity that generally arises if this assumption is not made is not worth the extra bit of market reality that the model is able to portray. However, the homogeneous-expectations assumption utilized in both APT and MPT is a weakness in each. Essentially, homogeneous expectations imply that all investors share the same risk and return perceptions for all assets in the market. By utilizing this assumption both models obviate the need to explain differences among investors' expectations.

The following assumptions are required for the CAPM but not the APT:

(1) The CAPM is restricted to a single-period planning horizon.
(2) The CAPM is restricted to rates of price change that conform to a normal (or log normal) empirical probability distribution of returns.
(3) The CAPM depends on rather strong assumptions about investors' utility functions in order to generate a two-parameter model.
(4) The CAPM requires the existence of a market portfolio that is a uniquely desirable investment medium.

From this rather extensive list of additional assumptions for the CAPM which the APT does not require, the greater generality of the APT is readily apparent. Thus, the APT provides a theoretically more robust and more testable alternative to the CAPM. Wei (1988) and Burmeister and McElroy (1988) have derived an asset pricing model unifying the CAPM and APT.

13.6. Intertemporal CAPM

Following Chen *et al.* (2011), both CAPM, developed by Sharpe (1964), Lintner (1965), and Mossin (1966), and APT developed by Ross (1976) are static asset pricing models. Dynamic asset pricing models can include Merton's (1973) intertemporal CAPM, and supply-side effect model developed by Black (1976) and Lee *et al.* (2009 and 2012). In this section, we will discuss the intertemporal CAPM by Merton (1973) in some detail.

The intertemporal CAPM developed by Merton (1973) can be defined as

$$\bar{R}_i = R_f + \lambda_1(\bar{R}_m - R_f) + \lambda_2(\bar{R}_n - R_f), \tag{13.23}$$

where

$\bar{R}_i$ = the expected return of security i,
R_f = the risk free rate,
$\bar{R}_m$ = the expected market rate of return,
$\bar{R}_n$ = the expected return on the asset which is negatively correlated with changes in the riskless interest rate,
$\rho_{m,n}$ = the correlation coefficient between R_m and R_n,

$$\beta_{im} = \frac{\text{cov}(R_i, R_m)}{\sigma_m^2}, \quad \beta_{in} = \frac{\text{cov}(R_i, R_m)}{\sigma_n^2}, \quad \beta_{mn} = \frac{\text{cov}(R_n, R_m)}{\sigma_m^2},$$

$$\lambda_1 = \frac{\beta_{im} - \beta_{in}\beta_{nm}}{1 - \sigma_{nm}^2}, \quad \text{and} \quad \lambda_2 = \frac{\beta_{in} - \beta_{im}\beta_{nm}}{1 - \sigma_{nm}^2}.$$

This model is derived in the context of the continuous time intertemporal asset pricing model, and it allows the shifting of the investment opportunity set. Merton assumed that the shift of the investment opportunity set can be characterized by changes of the riskless rate of interest.

Campbell (1993) has developed a simplified version of Merton model which is easier to be used for empirical study. Chang *et al.* (2003) have developed an intertemporal type of mutual fund performance model in accordance with Campbell's intertemporal CAPM model. In this new mutual fund performance model, they classified the performance into selectivity, timing and hedging components.

13.7. Applications of APT

Potential applications of the APT are similar to those of the CAPM. These include:

(1) Security analysis;
(2) Portfolio management;
(3) Performance measurement;
(4) Capital budgeting; and
(5) Cost of equity capital for public utilities and other types of companies.

The CAPM is probably the most widely accepted method in all of these corporate applications. Recently, the Federal Energy Regulation

Commission proposed that the CAPM be used as the principal measure of risk for the electric utilities it regulates. The CAPM beta (β) can be found to be the predominant measure of risk from a glance through the financial literature or a survey of the corporate world. However, the CAPM has been the target of a growing body of skeptics who have been finding significantly noticeable drawbacks in its empirical pricing framework.

Alternatively, the APT offers a more global framework for measuring a company's or a portfolio's sensitivity to various economic factors. However, at the current stage of the APT's development, it has seen little application in the domain of the practitioner. Nevertheless, empirical research has been emerging that not only points out differences in their estimates of company (portfolio) returns but, more importantly, suggests that the APT might be a preferable alternative to the CAPM in such uses.

The central application of APT is in estimating required rates of return, or equivalently the cost of equity capital. Recent work by Bower *et al.* (BBL, 1984) and Bubnys and Lee (1990) includes the use of the APT and the CAPM in a comparison of their respective abilities to effectively describe the return-generating process for stocks in terms of historical and forecasted results.

Utilizing a large sample of stocks from the NYSE and AMEX exchanges over the 1971–1979 period, these authors grouped their data into industry portfolios. Based on RR's previous results, the BBL factor analyzed the portfolio returns' covariance matrix to produce monthly scores for four factors. For comparison, the CAPM was run on the data as well to devise estimates of the portfolio betas and required return. Using the average betas and sensitivity coefficients from the cross-sectional tests, BBL summarizes the market model formulation results as shown in Table 13.9.

The results from these two models indicate conflicting information for regulators. The CAPM suggests that regulator should provide electric utilities the opportunity for a return of more than 1% above natural-gas distribution companies. Conversely, APT indicates that it is the gas distribution companies that require the higher rate of return and that the difference is close to 2%.

To discern which pricing model provides a better policy guide, BBL compared the CAPM and APT on the basis of two types of evidence. The first of these concerns what APT and CAPM can explain the returns used in their estimation.

$$E(R_i) = R_f + \beta_i(\bar{R}_m - R_f) \tag{13.24}$$

$$E(R_i) = R_0 + \lambda_1 b_{i1} + \lambda_2 b_{i2} + \lambda_3 b_{i3} + \lambda_4 b_{i4}. \tag{13.25}$$

Table 13.9. Market-Model Formulation Results Using CAPM and APT.

	CAPM	APT
Return-risk relationship	$E(R_j) = 0.0555 + 0.1085\beta$	$E(R_j) = 0.0621 - 1.8550b_{i1}$ $+1.4448b_{i2} + 0.1244b_{i3}$ $-2.7240b_{i4}$
Systematic risk Electrics	$\beta_t = 0.71$	$b_{i1} = -0.0318$
		$b_{i2} = -0.0114$
		$b_{i3} = -0.0022$
		$b_{i4} = -0.0017$
Gas distribution	$\beta_t = 0.58$	$b_{i1} = -0.0329$
		$b_{i2} = -0.0065$
		$b_{i3} = -0.0138$
		$b_{i4} = -0.0093$
Required return $E(R_t)$		
Electrics	13.2%	10.9%
Gas distribution	11.8%	13.7%

Source: Bower *et al.*, *Journal of Finance* (1984), p. 1044.

Table 13.10. Risk Premiums, *t*-Values, and Average R^2 for CAPM and APT.

	b_0	b_1	b_2	b_3	b_4	$\bar{R}$
CAPM						
Equation (11.25)	0.00463	0.00904	—	—	—	0.274
	(4.53)	(1.72)				
APT						
Equation (11.26)	0.00517	−0.15458	0.12040	0.01037	−0.2270	0.425
		(−0.159)	(0.81)	(0.11)	(−2.52)	

Source: Bower *et al.* (1984), p. 1046.

To test the CAPM defined in Equation (13.24) and APT defined in Equation (13.25), BBL use the CAPM β's and APT b_{ih}'s estimation for each portfolio in the time-series work just described. Cross-sectional regressions were run for each month with return as the dependent variable and the risk coefficients as independent variables. The mean values of the risk premiums for the 108 monthly CAPM and APT return/risk equations, the *t*-values (in parentheses), and the average R^2 for the 108 monthly cross-sectional regressions are listed in Table 13.10. Using the average $\bar{R}^2$ these findings favor the APT in terms of explanatory ability. However, a second, more convincing test is carried out since conclusions from the preceding test are limited due to the origin of the APT factor scores in the return date.

By forming a holdout group of 127 utilities not included in the original coefficient estimation for CAPM and APT, these authors forecast expected monthly returns for each utility over the 108 months from 1971–1979. The results are summarized in Table 13.11. To assess the quality of each model's forecast BBL used U^2, the sum of squared differences of each stock's average return $\bar{R}_i$ for the 1971–1979 period from its CAPM or APT forecast of return $\hat{R}_i$ and the sum of the squared differences of average return for each stock from the average return of all stocks $\bar{R}$.

The ratio of these squared differences, U^2, for all stocks is used to evaluate the contribution of the model as a forecasting device. It follows then that the smaller the ratio, the better is the model forecast relative to the naïve forecast. The results:

$$\begin{aligned} U^2 &= \frac{\sum_{i=1}^{127} (\bar{R}_i - \hat{R}_i)^2}{\sum_{i=1}^{127} (\bar{R}_i - \bar{R})^2} \\ &= 0.822 \text{ (APT)} \\ &= 1.115 \text{ (CAPM)}. \end{aligned}$$

Thus, as a forecasting model of required or expected return, APT does better than CAPM. Moreover, when the hold out sample is included in the original estimation of the APT (it is essentially included in both cases for the CAPM), the results are even more in favor of the APT. The figure from APT falls to 0.505 whereas that for the CAPM improves only a little, falling to 1.018.

While no single study can be taken to be the final word on which pricing theory is superior, these empirical findings do provide strong evidence in favor of the APT. More important, they show that the APT should be considered usable by practitioners for determining required rates of return of individual firms.

Lee and Cummins (1998) estimate the cost of equity capital for property/casualty insurers by applying three alternative asset pricing models: the capital asset pricing model (CAPM), the arbitrage pricing theory (APT), and a unified CAPM/APT model by Wei (1988). The in-sample forecast ability of the models is evaluated by applying the mean squared error method, the Theil U^2 statistic, and the Granger and Newbold (1977) conditional efficiency evaluation. Based on forecast evaluation procedures, the APT and Wei's unified CAPM/APT models perform better than the CAPM in estimating the cost of equity capital for the PC insurers and a combined forecast may outperform the individual forecasts.

Table 13.11. Required Return for Industries Represented in the Holdout Sample Using APT and CAPM Return/Risk Relationships Estimated from Monthly Data without Utility Portfolios for 1971–1979.

APT: $\bar{R}_i = 0.005173 - 0.154584b_{i1} + 0.120404b_{i2} + 0.010366b_{i3} - 0.227002b_{i4}$

CAPM: $\bar{R}_i = 0.004629 - 0.009038\beta_1$

	APT Sensitivity Coefficients				CAPM	Forecast Return		Actual Return
Industry	b_{i1}	b_{i2}	b_{i3}	b_{i4}	β_1	R_{APT}	R_{CAPM}	R
4911	−0.03181	−0.01141	−0.00219	−0.00168	0.70873	0.00870	0.01103	0.00457
4931	−0.03121	−0.01051	−0.00737	−0.00260	0.64692	0.00925	0.01048	0.00492
4922	−0.04212	−0.00601	+0.01387	−0.01214	0.95347	0.01386	0.01325	0.01140
4923	−0.03271	−0.01008	+0.00944	−0.01465	0.73650	0.01244	0.01129	0.01270
4924	−0.03290	−0.00649	−0.01382	−0.00932	0.57709	0.01150	0.00984	0.00807
4811	−0.02573	−0.00830	+0.00506	−0.00409	0.54211	0.00825	0.00953	0.00402
9999	−0.06471	−0.00814	+0.00372	+0.00433	1.32504	0.01413	0.01660	0.01595

Source: Bower *et al.* (1984), p. 1047.

13.8. Summary

This chapter has discussed extended versions of CAPM derived by Sharpe (1964), Lintner (1965), and Mossin (1966), APT and intertemporal CAPM. APT embodies a good deal of the more robust efforts of academicians to formulate less restrictive and more applicable models for asset pricing. Much research on APT and associated testing methodologies lies ahead; nevertheless, its alluring intuitive arguments and generalized construction make APT a formidable competitor to the CAPM. But perhaps APT should be considered an evolutionary step from the realm of CAPM theory rather than a revolutionary one. (In fact, it has been shown that the original CAPM is actually a special case of the APT model.)

Flaws and deficiencies within the methodologies used to empirically test APT have drawn the attention of a good part of the APT literature. Nevertheless, empirical results do lend some concrete support to APT pricing tenets. Much of the direction of the current research is focused on identifying the correct factor structure — that is, the appropriate number — along with identifying what economic-state variables might be associated with these explanatory factors.

The APT has not been developed to the stage of being usable by security analysts in predicting security returns. Studies at this point indicate that the APT describes the long-term expected return on a security and therefore would not be as beneficial to those concerned with short-term deviations in equilibrium conditions. Nevertheless, APT's potential ability to efficiently describe the long-run expected return for a firm's equity has valuable application in the area of capital budgeting.

Finally, this chapter has also briefly discussed the intertemperal CAPM developed by Merton (1973), Black (1976), and Campbell (1993).

Questions and Problems

1. What is an arbitrage opportunity? Carefully explain why arbitrage opportunities must not exist in an efficient market.
2. You are given the following information about two stocks, A and B, and the market.

$$E(R_m) = 10\%$$
$$R_f = 6\%$$

$$\beta_A = 1.5$$
$$\beta_B = 2.0$$

(a) Plot the SML.
(b) Calculate the expected returns for stocks A and B that are consistent with the CAPM.
(c) Now assume that stock A has an expected return of 14% while stock B has an expected return of 13%. Does an arbitrage opportunity exist? Carefully explain how you could exploit this opportunity.

3. Compare a one-factor APT model, where the factor is the expected return on the market with the CAPM.
4. What are the advantages of the APT over the CAPM? What are the disadvantages of the APT over the CAPM?
5. Assume that returns for XYZ company's stock are related to three factors in the following way.

$$E(R_{XYZ}) = \lambda_0 + b_{1,XYZ}\lambda_1 + b_{2,XYZ}\lambda_2 + b_{3,XYZ}\lambda_3$$

(a) Carefully explain what the b's measure.
(b) Assume $b_{1,XYZ} = 0.4$, $b_{2,XYZ} = 1.4$, $b_{3,XYZ} = 0.9$, and that the risk-free rate is 4%, the λ_1 risk premium is 5%, λ_2 is 6%, and λ_3 is 2%. What is the expected return for XYZ Company's stock?

6. Describe some of the problems associated with empirically testing the APT.
7. Assume that the following single-index model describes returns:

$$R_i = a_i + b_i I + e_i$$

Also use the information given in the table.

Portfolio	$E(R)$ (%)	b_{i1}
A	9	0.2
B	12	1.2

(a) Find the equation of the line that describes equilibrium returns.
(b) Explain the arbitrage opportunity that would exist if a new portfolio C existed with the following properties:

$$E(R_C) = 5\%, \quad b_C = 1.5$$

8. Suppose equilibrium returns are generated by the following two-index models.

$$R_j = a_j + b_{j1}I_1 + b_{j2}I_2 + e_j$$

And assume that we observe the portfolios in the table.

Portfolio	$E(R)$ (%)	b_{i1}	b_{i2}
G	8	1.0	0.3
H	12	1.5	0.4
K	17	1.7	−0.1

(a) Find the equation of the plane that describes equilibrium returns.
(b) Explain the arbitrage opportunity that would exist if a portfolio Z were observed with the following properties:

$$E(R_Z) = 20\%, \quad b_{Z1} = 0.5, \quad b_{Z2} = -0.4$$

9. Describe Lloyd and Lee's block recursive system asset pricing model (see Appendix 13A).
10. Describe how APT can be used to estimate cost of capital for an electric utility company.

Appendix 13A: Alternative Specifications of APT

By using the relationship between premium (excess) return and the factor scores, Jobson (1982) has derived a multivariate linear-regression model for testing the APT. Jobson concludes that individual company excess returns can be linearly related to all other returns in the market or some subset of returns. In relation to all other returns in the market, we can define Jobson's regression model as

$$r_{it} = \alpha_i + \sum_{j=1}^{n} \beta_j r_{jt} + \in_{jt} \quad i \neq j, \tag{13A.1}$$

where

r_{it} = excess return for company i at time t;
α_i = intercept term;
β_j = respective betas for excess return on company i and the excess returns on all other (N) companies;

$r_{jt} =$ excess returns on all other (N) companies in the market at time t; and

$\in_{jt}=$ error term at time t.

Even more significantly, Jobson has shown that his model can hold when the independent observations of r_{jt} are some subset k of the total set of returns, n. This testable form of the Jobson derivation can be defined:

$$r_{it} = \alpha_i + \sum_{j=1}^{k} \beta_j r_{jt} + \in_{jt} \quad (i \neq j), \tag{13A.2}$$

where $i \neq j$ and $k < n$.

If all excess returns are assumed to be multivariate normally distributed, and if all the r_{jt} (either individual or portfolio excess returns) are linearly independent, then testing the APT with Equation (13A.2) becomes equivalent to a test of the intercept term. For the APT to hold, the intercept term α_i in (13A.2) should not be significantly different from zero. By construction, Equation (13A.2) is equivalent to Equation (13A.1), which includes all excess returns in the market; therefore, if β_j is significantly different from zero, it implies that there are additional determinants that affect a company's excess return besides all other excess returns in the market. APT rests on the concept of relative pricing in that each company is priced relative to all others with regard to each respective risk-return characteristic. A significant intercept term in (13A.2) would substantially weaken this argument.

Jobson's model is similar to that proposed by Lloyd and Lee (1976) and Lee and Lloyd (1978), who utilized an econometric model called a "block recursive system" to explain the covariability among company returns. Applying this equation system to the 30 stocks that constitute the Dow-Jones Industrial Average, these authors empirically determined that other companies' rates of return can be utilized in addition to some market index to explain the return-generating process for individual companies.

The block recursive system can be represented by the following series of equations:

$$R_1 = \beta_{11} X_{11} + \beta_{12} X_{12} + \cdots + \beta_{1k} X_{1k} + \in_1$$

$$r_{21} + R_1 = \beta_{21} X_{21} + \beta_{22} X_{22} + \cdots + \beta_{2k} X_{2k} + \in_2$$

$$\vdots$$

$$r_{L1}R_1 + r_{L2}R_2 + \cdots + \gamma_{LL}R_{L-1} + R_L$$
$$= \beta_{L2}X_{L1} + \beta_{L2}X_{L2} + \cdots + \beta_{Lk}X_{Lk} + \in_L,$$

where

$L =$ number of jointly determined (dependent) variables;
$K =$ number of exogenous explanatory variables;
$\gamma_{LL-1} =$ coefficients on the jointly determined variables;
$\beta_{Lk} =$ coefficients on the exogenous variables;
$X_{Lk} =$ general economic or firm-related variables;
$R_L =$ returns on the Lth security in the model; and
$\in_L =$ error term.

Lloyd and Lee's application of this system uses only one exogenous variable (X) on the right-hand side of the equations, which is a proxy for the market index (the S&P 500). After breaking up the Dow 30 into eight homogeneous clusters using factor analysis, the stocks within each cluster (sub or system) are ordered according to their independence. That is, the stock most independent of the system is placed first, whereas the most dependent one is placed last. This type of ordering is a requirement of the equation system and is carried out by regressing each stock upon the other securities in the subsystem. The resulting $\bar{R}^2$ is then used as the measure of dependence.

The block recursive system is run as follows. For each subsystem the most independent security return is regressed on the market-index return. Consequently, the first run in each subsystem is equivalent to the traditional market-model formulation. Next, the second most independent variable is added to the left-hand side of the equation. This dependent variable is determined by the endogenous variables R_1 and $\in_2$. Since the random component of R_1 is $\in_1$, which is assumed to be independent of $\in_2$, R_1 may be regarded as predetermined with respect to R_2. This exact line of reasoning is continued for the rest of the equations in the subsystems.

As evidenced for the high explanatory potential of the bock recursive system, Table 13A.1 shows the eight stock clusters or subsystems, the ordering of securities within the subsystem, and a comparison of the percentage of variation in the individual security's return explained by the Sharpe market model and the percentage explained by the block recursive model. Notice, as mentioned earlier, that the first equation in each subsystem is equivalent to the Sharpe market model; thus $\bar{R}^2$ is the same. However, for many of

Table 13A.1. Grouping of Companies Based on Correlation with Common Factor.

	$\bar{R}^2$ Sharpe	$\bar{R}^2$ Recursive		$\bar{R}^2$ Sharpe	$\bar{R}^2$ Recursive
Subsystem 1			Subsystem 6		
Owens Illinois	0.275	0.275	Eastman Kodak	0.311	0.311
General Foods	0.234	0.237	United Aircraft	0.221	0.213
Subsystem 2			Subsystem 7		
Anaconda	0.309	0.309	Texaco	0.373	0.373
Woolworth	0.278	0.282	Standard Oil of California	0.347	0.612
American Brands	0.243	0.293			
American Can	0.210	0.224	Exxon	0.250	0.540
Subsystem 3			Subsystem 8		
Proctor & Gamble	0.235	0.235	ATT	0.380	0.380
Swift & Company	0.109	0.112	Dupont	0.251	0.243
			Chryster	0.449	0.469
Subsystem 4			Johns-Manville	0.292	0.279
International Nickel	0.316	0.316	Alcoa	0.350	0.340
			International Harvester	0.195	0.220
Subsystem 5			Goodyear	0.321	0.345
Sears	0.311	0.311	Intenational Paper	0.526	0.643
General Electric	0.416	0.411	Union Carbide	0.323	0.434
Westinghouse	0.243	0.302	General Motors	0.573	0.699
			Alied Chemical	0.357	0.493
			U.S. Steel	0.387	0.619
			Bethlehem Steel	0.390	0.793

Source: Lloyd and Lee (1976), p. 1107.

the other equations there are large increases in the explanatory power, as evidenced by the $\bar{R}^2$. For example, the $\bar{R}^2$ for Bethlehem Steel increased from 0.390 in the Sharpe model to 0.793 in the block recursive model. These improvements in explanatory power are a result of the significant relationships among individual securities, which emerge in addition to each individual security's relationship with the stock-market index. All of these interrelationships violate a basic assumption of the Sharpe market model — that is, $E(\in_1, \in_2) = 0$.

Appendix 13B: Lee and Wei's Empirical Results

Lee and Wei (2012) have proposed a multi-factor, multi-indicator approach to test the CAMP and the APT. This approach is able to solve the measuring problem in the market portfolio in testing the CAPM; and it

Table 13B.1. Lee and Wei's 11 Economic-State Variables Used to Identify the APT Model's Common Factors.

Variable	Definition
1. RM	*Return on the market portfolio*: the return on NYSE common stock composite index; equal weighted (RME), valued weighted (RMV).
2. VL	*Transaction volume*: the change rate in the transaction volume (shares) for all of the NYSE common stocks.
3. RF	*Real riskless rate*: the real interest rate on three-month Treasury bills.
4. MP	*Maturity risk premium*: the difference between the real interest rates on long-term Treasury bonds (ten or more years) and on three-month Treasury bills.
5. DP	*Default risk premium*: the difference between the real interest rates on new AA corporate bonds and three-month Treasury bills.
6. CPI	*Consumer price index inflation rate*: the change rate in urban consumer price index for all items.
7. M2	*Money supply*: the real change rate in money stock as measured by M2 (M1 + time deposits).
8. PI/M2	*Velocity of money supply*: the ratio of personal income to money supply M2. This is an alternative measure of money supply.
9. IP	*Read industrial production*: the change rate in real total industrial production.
10. IPA	*Real auto production*: the change in real automotive products.
11. IPH	*Real home production*: the change rate in real home goods.

Source: Lee and Wei (2012).

is also able to directly test the APT by linking the common factors to the macroeconomic indicators. Their results from testing the CAPM support Stambough's (1982) argument that the inference about the tests of the CAMP is insensitive to alternative market indexes. The results from testing the APT indicate that it is a one-factor model during 1963–1972, while it is a two-factor model during 1973–1982. Furthermore, the market variables (including the market portfolio and the transaction volume) play a major role in the pricing relation.

Table 13B.1 describes 11 economic-state variables which are used by Lee and Wei (2013) to identify common factors of the APT model. Table 13B.2 describes the regression relationship between the factors and economic variables. Other detailed empirical results can be found in Lee and Wei (2013).

Table 13B.2. Time-Series Regression Factors from Ross's APT on Indicators.

Indicator	Factor 1	Factor 2	Factor 3	Factor 4	Factor 5
Part A: RMV and VL Included					
RMV	0.206**	0.075**	−0.025	0.016	−0.037**
	(32.646)	(4.712)	(−1.527)	(0.973)	(−2.185)
VL	0.291**	−0.831**	0.057	−0.530	0.668*
	(2.119)	(−2.398)	(0.161)	(−1.465)	(1.832)
RF	−0.153	−0.808**	0.960**	−0.631	−0.356
	(−0.964)	(−2.017)	(2.352)	(−1.509)	(−0.843)
MP	−0.418	−2.316	0.509	0.422	0.269
	(−0.601)	(−1.318)	(0.284)	(0.230)	(0.145)
DP	0.096	2.472**	2.242*	−0.820	−0.107
	(0.196)	(1.990)	(1.770)	(−0.632)	(−0.082)
CPI	−0.257	−0.737*	0.480	0.160	0.064
	(−1.637)	(−1.865)	(1.191)	(0.387)	(0.155)
M2	0.005	−0.290	−0.634**	0.251	0.004
	(0.050)	(−1.202)	(−2.582)	(0.998)	(0.017)
IP	0.0324	−0.194**	−0.044	−0.058	−0.053
	(1.138)	(−2.708)	(−0.600)	(−0.778)	(−0.706)
Constant	−0.054	0.292	−0.189	−0.079	0.019
	(−0.593)	(1.282)	(−0.813)	(−0.334)	(0.080)
$\bar{R}^2$	0.860	0.1103	0.076	0.030	0.012
Part B: RME and VL Included					
RME	0.174**	0.001	0.011	0.021*	−0.000
	(89.236)	(0.047)	(0.869)	(1.662)	(−0.025)
VL	0.038	−0.166	−0.298	−0.643*	0.344
	(0.699)	(−0.453)	(−0.834)	(−1.770)	(0.926)
RF	−0.325**	−0.630	0.858	−0.674	−0.443
	(−5.130)	(−1.499)	(2.090)	(−1.614)	(−1.036)
MP	−0.862**	−1.348	−0.117	0.248	−0.203
	(−3.105)	(−0.732)	(−0.007)	(0.136)	(−0.109)
DP	0.652**	2.084	2.476*	−0.704	0.082
	(3.319)	(1.598)	(1.944)	(−0.544)	(0.062)
CPI	−0.364**	−0.682	0.445	0.140	0.038
	(−5.831)	(−1.647)	(1.099)	(0.339)	(0.089)
M2	−0.068*	−0.254	−0.657**	0.238	−0.013
	(−1.799)	(−1.008)	(−2.664)	(0.948)	(−0.051)
IP	0.013	−0.194**	−0.045	−0.061	−0.053
	(1.138)	(−2.584)	(−0.617)	(−0.813)	(−0.700)
Constant	−0.051	0.305	−0.195	−0.081	0.013
	(−1.417)	(1.279)	(−0.838)	(−0.341)	(0.053)
$\bar{R}^2$	0.978	0.025	0.070	0.038	−0.008

(*Continued*)

Table 13B.2. (*Continued*)

Indicator	Factor 1	Factor 2	Factor 3	Factor 4	Factor 5
Part C: Market Variables Excluded					
RF	0.405	−0.632	0.896	−0.603	−0.434
	(0.982)	(−1.521)	(2.202)	(−1.449)	(−1.035)
MP	2.855	−1.381	0.141	0.527	−0.116
	(1.582)	(−0.759)	(0.079)	(0.289)	(0.063)
DP	−1.143	2.090	2.384*	−0.877	0.061
	(−0.891)	(1.616)	(1.885)	(−0.677)	(0.046)
CPI	−0.024	−0.687*	0.455	0.157	0.050
	(−0.058)	(−1.668)	(1.129)	(0.382)	(0.118)
M2	0.069	−0.251	−0.643**	0.265	−0.019
	(0.275)	(−1.000)	(−2.618)	(1.054)	(−0.074)
IP	0.038	−0.194**	−0.044	−0.059	−0.053
	(0.515)	(−2.599)	(−0.606)	(−0.789)	(−0.691)
Constant	0.037	0.301	−0.197	−0.086	0.021
	(0.159)	(1.269)	(−0.850)	(−0.363)	(0.088)
$\bar{R}^2$	0.047	0.0322	0.074	0.029	−0.004

** and * indicate 10 percent and 5 percent significant level, respectively.
Source: Lee and Wei (2013).

Bibliography

Anderson, T. W. "An Introduction to Multivariate Statistical Analysis." 3rd ed (July 2003), Wiely.

Arnott, R. "Cluster Analysis and Stock Price Co-movement." *Financial Analysis Journal*, v. 36 (November/December 1980), pp. 56–62.

Black, F. "Capital Market Equilibrium with Restricted Borrowing." *Journal of Business*, v. 45 (July 1972), pp. 444–454.

Black, S. W. "Rational Response to Shocks in a Dynamic Model of Capital Asset Pricing." *American Economic Review*, v. 66, (December 1976), pp. 767–779.

Bower, D. "Arbitrage Pricing and Utility Stock Returns." *Journal of Finance*, v. 39 (September 1984), pp. 1041–1054.

Bower, D., R. Bower and D. Logue. "A Primer on APT." *Midland Corporate Finance Journal*, v. 2 (Fall 1984), pp. 31–40.

Breeden, D. "An Intertemporal Asset Pricing Model with Stochastic Consumption and Investment Opportunities." *Journal of Financial Economics*, v. 7 (September 1979), pp. 265–296.

Bubnys, E. L. and C. F. Lee. "Simulating and Forecasting Utility Stock Returns." *Financial Review*, v. 25 (1990), pp. 1–23.

Burmeister, E. and M. B. McElroy. "Joint Estimation of Factor Sensitivities and Risk Premia for the Arbitrage Pricing Theory." *Journal of Finance*, v. 43 (July 1988), pp. 721–735.

Campbell, John Y., "Intertemporal Asset Pricing Without Consumption Data." *American Economic Review*, v. 83 (June 1993), pp. 487–512.

Chamberlain, G. and M. Rothschild. "Arbitrage, Factor Structure, and Mean-Variance Analysis on Large Asset Markets." *Econometrica*, v. 51 (September 1983), pp. 1281–1304.

Chang, J. R., M. W. Hung and C. F. Lee, "An Intertemporal CAPM Approach to Evaluate Mutual Fund Performance." *Review of Quantitative Finance and Accounting*, v. 20 (June 2003), pp. 415–433.

Chen, N. F. "Some Empirical Tests of the Theory of Arbitrage Pricing." *Journal of Finance*, v. 38 (December 1983), pp. 1393–1414.

Chen, N., R. Roll and S. Ross. "Economic Forces and the Stock Market." *Journal of Business*, v. 59 (July 1986), pp. 383–403.

Chen, P. J., S. S. Chen, C. F. Lee and Y. C. Shih. "The Evolution of Capital Asset Pricing Models." Working Paper, Rutgers University, 2011.

Cheng, P. L. "An Alternative Test of the Capital Asset Pricing Model: Reply." *The American Economic Review*, v. 72 (December 1982), pp. 1201–1207.

Cheng, P. L. and R. Grauer. "An Alternative Test of the Capital Asset Pricing Model." *The American Economic Review*, v. 70 (September 1980), pp. 660–671.

Cho, D., E. Elton and M. Gruber. "On the Robustness of the Roll and Ross Arbitrage Pricing Theory." *Journal of Financial and Quantitative Analysis*, v. 19 (March 1984), pp. 1–10.

Cohen, K. and G. Pogue. "An Empirical Evaluation of Alternative Portfolio Models." *Journal of Business*, v. 40 (1967), pp. 166–193.

Connor, K. and G. Pogue. "An Empirical Evaluation of Alternative Portfolio Models." *Journal of Economic Theory*, v. 21 (October 1984), pp. 13–31.

Dhrymes, P. "Arbitrage Pricing Theory." *Journal of Portfolio Management*, v. 11 (Summer 1984), pp. 35–44.

Dhrymes, P., I. Friend and N. Gultekin. "A Critical Reexamination of the Empirical Evidence on the APT." *Journal of Finance*, v. 39 (June 1984), pp. 323–346.

Dybvig, P. and S. Ross. "Yes, the APT is Testable." *Journal of Finance*, v. 40 (September 1985), pp. 1173–1188.

Elton, E. J. and M. J. Gruber. "Estimating the Dependence Structure of Share Prices — Implications for Portfolio Selection." *Journal of Finance*, v. 27 (December 1973), pp. 1203–1233.

Elton, E. J. and J. Rentzler. "The Arbitrage Pricing Model and Returns on Assets Under Uncertain Inflation." *Journal of Finance*, v. 38 (May 1983), pp. 525–538.

Farrell, J. L. "Analyzing Covariation of Returns to Determine Homogeneous Stock Grouping." *Journal of Business*, v. 47 (April 1974), pp. 186–207.

Fogler, H. "Common Sense on CAPM, APT and Correlated Residuals." *Journal of Portfolio Management*, v. 9 (Summer 1982), pp. 20–28.

Fogler, H., K. John and J. Tipton. "Three Factors, Interest Rate Differentials and Stock Groups." *Journal of Finance*, v. 36 (May 1981), pp. 323–336.

Gibbons, M. "Multivariate Tests of Financial Models: A New Approach." *Journal of Financial Economics*, v. 10 (March 1982), pp. 3–27.

Granger, C. W. J. and P. Newbold. "Forecasting Economic Time Series." Academic, New York.

Huberman, G. "A Simple Approach to Arbitrage Pricing Theory." *Journal of Economic Theory*, v. 19 (October 1982), pp. 183–191.

Hughes, P. "A Test of the Arbitrage Pricing Theory." Working Paper, University of British Columbia, 1981.

Ingersoll, J., Jr. "Some Results in the Theory of Arbitrage Pricing." *Journal of Finance*, v. 39 (September 1984), pp. 1021–1054.

Jarrow, R. and A. Rudd. "A Comparison of the APT and CAPM." *Journal of Banking and Finance*, v. 17 (June 1983), pp. 295–303.

Jobson, J. "A Multivariate Linear Regression Test for the Arbitrage Pricing Theory." *Journal of Finance*, v. 37 (September 1982), pp. 1037–1042.

King, B. J. "Market and Industry Factors in Stock Price Behavior." *Journal of Business*, v. 39 (January 1966), pp. 139–190.

Kryzanowski, L. and M. To. "General Factor Models and the Structure of Security Returns." *Journal of Financial and Quantitative Analysis*, v. 18 (March 1983), pp. 48–49.

Lee, A. C. and J. D. Cummins. "Alternative Models for Estimating the Cost of Equity Capital for Property/Casualty Insurers." *Review of Quantitative Finance and Accounting*, v. 10 (May 1998), pp. 235–267.

Lee, C. F. and W. P. Lloyd. "Block Recursive Systems in Asset Pricing Models: An Extension." *Journal of Finance*, v. 32 (May 1978), pp. 640–644.

Lee, C. F., C. M. Tsai and A. C. Lee. "A Dynamic CAPM with Supply Effect: Theory and Empirical Results." *Quarterly Review of Economics and Finance*, v. 49 (August 2009), pp. 811–828.

Lee, C. F., A. C. Lee and J. C. Lee. *Handbook of Quantitative Finance and Risk Management.* New York: Springer, 2010.

Lee, C. F., C. M. Tsai and A. C. Lee. "Asset Pricing with Disequilibrium Price Adjustment: Theory and Empirical Evidence." *Quantitative Finance*, (2011 forthcoming).

Lee, C. F. and J. K. C. Wei. "Multi-Factor Multi-Indicator Approach to Asset Pricing Model: Theory and Empirical Evidence." *Handbook of Financial Econometrics and Statistics, eded. by* Lee, C. F., A. C. Lee and J. C. Lee, Springer, forthcoming 2012.

Lintner, J. "The Valuation of Risk Assets and the Selection of Risky Investments in Stock Portfolios and Capital Budgets." *Review of Economics and Statistics*, v. 47 (February 1965), pp. 13–37.

Lloyd, W. P. and C. F. Lee. "Block Recursive Systems in Asset Pricing Models." *Journal of Finance*, v. 30 (December 1976), pp. 1101–1114.

Long, J., Jr. "Stock Prices, Inflation and the Term Structure of Interest Rates." *Journal of Financial Economics*, v. 2 (July 1974), pp. 131–170.

Markowitz, H. "Portfolio Selection." *Journal of Finance*, v. 6 (March 1952), pp. 77–91.

Merton, R. "An Inter-Temporal Capital Asset Pricing Model." *Econometrica*, v. 41 (September 1973), pp. 867–887.

Mossin, J. "Equilibrium in a Capital Asset Market." *Econometrica*, v. 34 (October 1966), pp. 768–873.

Oldfield, G. S. and R. J. Rogalski. "Treasury Bill Factors and Common Stock Returns." *Journal of Finance*, v. 35 (May 1981), pp. 337–349.

Ramsey, J. B. and P. Schmidt. "Some Further Results on the Use of OLS and BLUS Residuals in Specification Error Tests." *Journal of American Statistical Association*, v. 66 (1976), pp. 471–474.

Reinganum, M. "The Arbitrage Pricing Theory: Some Empirical Results." *Journal of Finance*, v. 36 (May 1981), pp. 313–321.

Roll, R. "A Critique of the Asset Pricing Theory's Tests." *Journal of Financial Economics*, v. 5 (May 1977), pp. 129–176.

Roll, R. "The APT Approach to Strategic Portfolio Planning." *Financial Analysis Journal*, v. 40 (May/June 1984), pp. 14–26.

Roll, R. and R. Ross. "An Empirical Investigation of the Arbitrage Pricing Theory." *Journal of Finance*, v. 5 (December 1980), pp. 1073–1103.

Ross, S. "The Arbitrage Theory of Capital Asset Pricing." *Journal of Economic Theory*, v. 13 (December 1976), pp. 341–360.

Ross, S. "Mutual Fund Separation in Financial Theory — the Separating Distributions." *Journal of Economic Theory*, v. 15 (April 1978), pp. 254–286.

Ross, S. "Return, Risk and Arbitrage," in I. Friend and J. L. Bicksler (eds.), *Risk and Return in Finance*, Vol. 1. Cambridge, MA: Ballinger, 1977, pp. 187–208.

Schipper, K. and R. Thompson. "Common Stocks as Hedges against Shifts in the Consumption on Investment Opportunity Set." *Journal of Business*, v. 54 (April 1981), pp. 305–328.

Shanken, J. "The Arbitrage Pricing Theory: Is It Testable?" *Journal of Finance*, v. 37 (December 1982), pp. 1129–1140.

Shanken, J. "Multi-Beta CAPM or Equilibrium-APT?: A Reply." *Journal of Finance*, v. 40 (September 1985), pp. 1189–1190.

Sharpe W. "Capital Asset Prices: A Theory of Market Equilibrium under Conditions of Risk." *Journal of Finance*, v. 19 (September 1964), pp. 425–442.

Sharpe W. "Factor Models, CAPMs and the APT." *Journal of Portfolio Management*, v. 11 (Fall 1984), pp. 21–25.

Sharpe W. "Factors in NYSE Security Returns." *Journal of Portfolio Management*, v. 18 (Summer 1982), pp. 5–19.

Solnik, B. "International Arbitrage Pricing Theory." *Journal of Finance*, v. 38 (May 1983), pp. 449–458.

Stambaugh, R. "On the Exclusion of Assets from Tests of the Two-Parameter Model: A Sensitivity Analysis." *Journal of Financial Economics*, v. 10 (November 1982), pp. 237–268.

Theil, H. *Principles of Econometrics*. New York: John Wiley and Sons, Inc., 1971.

Varian, H. R. "The Arbitrage Principle in Financial Economics." *Journal of Economic Perspectives*, v. 1 (Fall 1987), pp. 55–72.

Wei, J. K. C. "An Asset-Pricing Theory Unifying the CAPM and APT." *Journal of Finance*, v. 43 (September 1988), pp. 881–892.

Part III

Futures and Option

Chapter 14

Futures Valuation and Hedging

A basic assumption of finance theory is that investors are risk averse. If we equate risk with uncertainty, can we question the validity of this assumption? What is the evidence?

As living, functional proof of the appropriateness of the risk aversion assumption, there exist entire markets whose sole underlying purpose is to allow investors to display their uncertainties about the future. These particular markets, which primarily focus on the future, are called just that, **futures markets**. These markets allow for the transfer of risk from hedgers (risk-averse individuals) to speculators (risk-seeking individuals); a key element necessary for the existence of futures markets is the balance between the number of hedgers and speculators who are willing to transfer and accept risk.

A **future contract** is a standardized legal agreement between a buyer and a seller, who promise to exchange a specified amount of money for goods or services at a future time. Of course, there is nothing really unusual about a contract made in advance of delivery. For instance, whenever something is ordered rather than purchased on the spot, a futures (or forward) contract is involved. Although the price is determined at the time of the order, the actual exchange of cash for the merchandise takes place later. For some items the lag is a few days, whereas for others (such as a car) it may be months. Moreover, a futures contract imparts a legal obligation to both parties of the contract to fulfill the specifications. To guarantee fulfillment of this obligation, a "good-faith" deposit, also called **margin**, may be required from the buyer (and the seller, if he or she does not already own the product).

To ensure consistency in the contracts and to help develop liquidity, futures exchanges have been established. These exchanges provide a central location and a standardized set of rules in order to enhance the credibility of these markets and thus generate an orderly, liquid arena for the price determination of individual commodities at distinct point in the future.

A substantial increase in the number of types of futures contracts offered by the exchanges has been occurring over the last decade. At the same time, the growth in futures trading volume has been phenomenal. Two explanations can be offered for this increase in futures activity. These increases can be intuitively correlated with the growing levels of uncertainty in many facets of the economic environment — for example, inflation and interest rates. A second view is based on the argument that even though the world has not become any more uncertain, the increased integration of financial and real markets has increased the risk exposure of any given individual. The tremendous growth in the home-mortgage and consumer-debt financial markets has allowed the purchase of more and more expensive and real assets. This increase in the rise of individual financial leverage has increased individual exposure to interest-rate fluctuations, thereby increasing the requirements for risk-sharing across markets or between individuals with varied portfolios. Futures markets have the potential to help people manage or transfer the uncertainties that plague the world today.

This chapter examines the basic types of futures contracts offered and the functioning of futures markets. In addition, the uses of financial and index futures are illustrated, and the theoretical pricing concepts related to these financial instruments are discussed. The important terms associated with futures contracts and futures markets are defined and the futures market is compared to the forward market. An analysis of futures market follows. A theory of valuation is introduced, and the chapter closes with a discussion of various hedging strategies and concepts.

The following section analyzes the differences between **forward contracts** and futures contracts.

14.1. Futures Versus Forward Markets

While futures and forward contracts are similar in many respects, their differences are more important to fully understanding the nature and uses of these financial instruments. Both futures and forward contracts specify a transaction to take place at a future date and include precise requirements for the commodity to be delivered, its price, its quantity, the delivery date, and the delivery point. Nevertheless, these two types of contracts for future delivery of a commodity and the markets in which they are traded differ in a number of significant ways, some of which are included in Table 14.1.

Although most people are unlikely ever to become involved in the forward market, it is important to understand some of its attributes, particularly as a good deal of the literature on pricing futures contracts typically refers to these two contracts interchangeably. Specifically, it might be inferred from Table 14.1 that differences resulting from liquidity, credit risk, search, margin, taxes, and commissions could cause futures and forward contracts not to be priced identically. Some of the major users of forward contracts include:

(1) *Public utilities*: Public utilities sometimes engage in fairly long-term perpetual forward contracts for the delivery of coal or natural gas.
(2) *Savings-and-loan associations*: A typical thrift institution might contract to deliver a pool of mortgages to another thrift in 90 days.
(3) *Apparel or toy manufacturers*: Stores often contract for the delivery of the "new fall line" in early spring.
(4) *Import–export businesses*: A U.S. exporter may contract for the delivery of a foreign currency in 60 days after it receives payment in the foreign currency for goods sold overseas.

In addition to the terminologies discussed in this section, some others related useful terminologies can be found in Appendix 14A. Some of the terminologies in this appendix have been used in this chapter. Furthermore, these terminologies will be used in chapter 15 and other chapters in this book.

14.2. Futures Markets: Overview

In the most general sense, the term **commodity futures** is taken to embrace all existing futures contracts. Nevertheless, for purposes of clarity and classification its meaning here is restricted to a limited segment of the total futures markets. Accordingly, futures contracts can be classified into three main types.

(1) Commodity futures;
(2) Financial futures; and
(3) Index futures.

Table 14.1. A Comparison of Futures and Forward Markets.

Futures Market	Forward Market
1. Trading is conducted in a competitive arena by "open outcry" of bids, offers, and amounts.	1. Trading is done by telex or telephone, with participants generally dealing directly with broker-dealers.
2. Contract terms are standardized with all buyers and sellers negotiating only with respect to price.	2. All contract terms are negotiated privately by the parties.
3. Nonmember participants deal through brokers (exchange members) who represent them on the exchange floor.	3. Participants deal typically on a principal-to-principal basis.
4. Participants include banks, corporations, financial institutions, individual investors, and speculators.	4. Participants are primarily institutions dealing with one other and other interested parties dealing through one or more dealers.
5. The clearinghouse of the exchange becomes the opposite side to each cleared transaction; therefore, the credit risk for a futures-market participant is always the same and there is no need to analyze the credit of other market participants.	5. A participant must examine the credit risk and establish credit limits for each opposite party.
6. Margin deposits are to be required of all participants.	6. Typically, no money changes hands until delivery, although a small margin deposit might be required of nondealer customers on certain occasions.
7. Settlements are made daily through the exchange clearinghouse. Gains on open positions may be withdrawn, and losses are collected daily.	7. Settlement occurs on date agreed upon between the parties to each transaction.
8. Long and short positions are usually liquidated easily.	8. Forward positions are not as easily offset or transferred to other participants.
9. Settlements are normally made in cash, with only a small percentage of all contracts resulting in actual delivery.	9. Most transactions result in delivery.
10. A single, round-trip (in and out of the market) commission is charged. It is negotiated between broker and customer and is relatively small in relation to the value of the contract. Commissions range from $18 to over $100 per round-turn.	10. No commission is typically charged if the transaction is made directly with another dealer. A commission is charged to both buyer and seller, however, if transacted through a broker.
11. Trading is regulated by the exchange and by a federal agency, the Commodity Futures Trading Commission (CFTC).	11. Trading is mostly unregulated.
12. The delivery price is the spot price.	12. The delivery price is the forward price.

Within this classification commodity futures include all agriculturally related futures contracts with underlying assets, such as corn, wheat, rye, barley, rice, oats, sugar, coffee, soybeans, frozen orange juice, pork bellies, live cattle, hogs, and lumber. Also within the commodity-futures framework are futures contracts written on precious metals, such as gold, silver, copper, platinum, and palladium, and contracts written on petroleum products, including gasoline, crude oil, and heating oil. Many of the futures contracts on metals and petroleum products have been introduced as recently as the early 1980s.

Producers, refineries, and distributors, to name only a few potential users, employ futures contracts to assure a particular price or supply — or both — for the underlying commodity at a future date.

Futures-market participants are divided into two broad classes: hedgers and speculators. **Hedging** refers to a futures-market transaction made as a temporary substitute for a cash-market transaction to be made at a later date. The purpose of hedging is to take advantage of current prices by using futures transactions. For example, banks and corporations can be hedgers when they use futures to fix future borrowing and lending rates.

Futures market **speculation** involves taking a short or long futures position solely to profit from price changes. If you think that interest rates will rise because of an increase in inflation, you can sell Treasury bills (T-bill) futures and make a profit if interest rates do rise and the value of T-bills falls. Sample Problem 14.1 provides further illustration.

Sample Problem 14.1

An investor has a portfolio of T-bills with a face value of \$1 million, currently worth \$950,000 in the cash market. A futures contract with a face value of \$1 million worth of T-bills is currently selling for $95\frac{16}{32}$ per \$100. Interest rates rise and the value of the T-bills falls to \$946.875, whereas the value of the T-bill futures contract falls to $95\frac{6}{32}$ per \$100. If the investor were to hedge the T-bill position with T-bill futures, what would be the net result of this interest-rate change on the value of the hedged position? If the investor were to speculate that interest rates would fall, what is the next effect of the portfolio value?

Solution

See Tables 14.2 and 14.3 that show the results of hedged and speculative positions, respectively.

Table 14.2. Hedged Position for Sample Problem 14.1.

Time	T-Bill Value in Cash Market	Time	Futures Value	
t	\$950,000	t	Sell ten T-bill contracts at $95\frac{16}{32}$ (1,000,000 × 0.955).	\$955.000
$t+1$	\$946,875	$t+1$	Buy ten T-bill contracts at $95\frac{6}{32}$ (1,000,000 × 0.951875).	\$951,875
Loss in cash market	−\$3,125		Gain on short position in futures	+\$3,125
	Net change in value of hedged portfolio = \$0			

Table 14.3. Speculative Position for Sample Problem 14.1.

Time	T-Bill Value in Cash Market	Time	Futures Value	
t	\$950,000	t	Buy ten T-bill contracts at $95\frac{16}{32}$ (1,000,000 × 0.955).	\$955.000
$t+1$	\$946,875	$t+1$	Sell ten T-bill contracts at $95\frac{6}{32}$ (1,000,000 × 0.951875).	\$951,875
Loss in cash market	−\$3,125		Loss on sale	−\$3,125
	Net change in value of unhedged portfolio plus speculation loss = \$6,250			

Financial futures are a trading medium initiated with the introduction of contracts on foreign currencies at the International Monetary Market (IMM) in 1972. In addition to future on foreign currencies, financial futures include contracts based on Treasury bonds (T-bonds), T-bills, Treasury notes (T-notes), bank certificates of deposit, Eurodollars, and GNMA mortgage securities. These latter types of financial futures contracts are also referred to as *interest-rate futures* since their underlying asset is an interest-bearing security. While foreign-currency futures arose with the abolition of the Bretton Woods fixed exchange-rate system during the early 1970s, interest-rate futures surged in popularity and number following the change in U.S. monetary policy in October 1979. The effect of the Federal Open Market Committee's decision to de-emphasize the traditional practice of "pegging" interest rates was to greatly increase the volatility of market

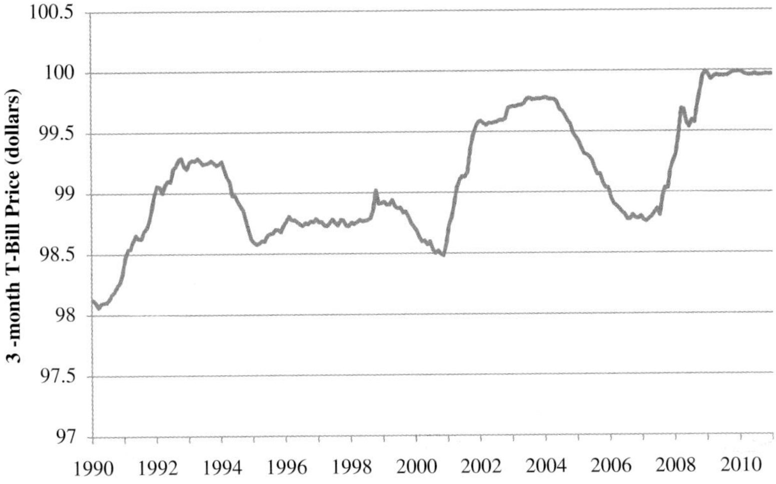

Fig. 14.1(a). Monthly Prices of Three-month T-Bill (1990–2010).

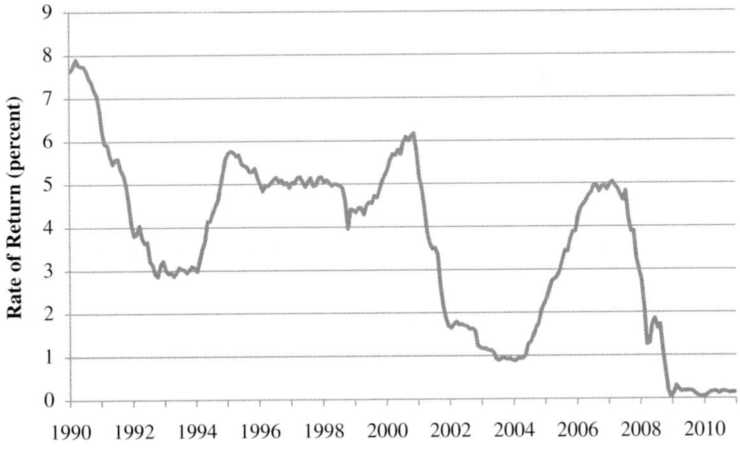

Fig. 14.1(b). Monthly Three-month T-Bill Returns (1990–2010).

interest rates. Thus, interest-rate changes have become a highly prominent risk to corporations, investors, and financial institutions. (Figures 14.1(a) and 14.1(b) exhibit the changing volatility of T-bill prices and rates of return from 1970 to 1988.)

Index futures represent the newest and boldest innovation in the futures market to date. An index-futures contract is one for which the underlying asset is actually a portfolio of assets — for example, the Major Market Index (MMI) includes 20 stocks traded on the NYSE and the S&P index includes the 500 stocks of the S&P index. Contracts on more diverse types of indexes include a high-quality bond index, an interest-rate index composed of interest-bearing market securities, and the consumer price index.

The S&P 500 index, requiring delivery of the 500 stocks constituting the S&P 500 stock index, would certainly have dampened enthusiasm for this and similar index contracts. Because of this, an index-futures contract is settled on the basis of its cash value when the contract matures. The cash value of the contract is equal to the closing index value on its last trading day, times a dollar amount of $500.

Many portfolio managers are taking advantage of index futures to alter their portfolios risk-return distributions. Some applications that have arisen are discussed later in this chapter.

14.3. Components and Mechanics of Futures Markets

This section discusses components and mechanics of futures markets: the exchanges, the clearinghouse, margin, order execution, and T-bill futures transactions.

14.3.1. *The Exchanges*

A **futures exchange**, just like a stock exchange, is the arena for the actual daily trading of futures contracts. The exchange is a nonprofit organization whose members include those allowed to trade on its floor. Members include individual traders, brokerage firms, and other types of institutions. The exchange's governing rules and procedures are determined by its members, who serve on various policy committees and elect the officers of the exchange.

The fees paid by an exchange's members support not only the daily operation of its trading venue but also other functions and services performed by staff members for the exchange, such as research, public relations, presentations and seminars for users, lobbying of government, and planning for the exchange's future.

Another term for an exchange membership is a seat. A prospective member may buy a full seat, allowing him or her to trade any of the offered futures contracts. To encourage volume on newer or less liquid contracts, most exchanges usually also offer a partial seat, permitting its owner to trade only a designated number of contracts. Usually, to get onto an exchange to trade, an investor needs to buy or lease a seat from a current owner. The value of an exchange seat can vary substantially; for example, the high and low prices for a full seat on the IMM exchange range from \$300,000 to \$100,000, respectively. Such exchanges are entrusted with clearinghouse responsibilities that are vital to the efficient operation of the futures market.

14.3.2. *The Clearinghouse*

Central to the operation of organized futures markets is the **clearinghouse** or clearing corporation for the exchange. Whenever someone enters a position in a futures contract on the long or short side, the clearinghouse always takes the opposite side of the contract. That is, it becomes a buyer to every seller and a seller to every buyer. The advantages of having a central organization providing this role are threefold.

(1) The clearinghouse eliminates concern over the creditworthiness of the party on the other side of the transaction.
(2) It frees the original trading partners from the obligation of delivery or offset with each other.
(3) It provides greater flexibility in opening or closing a position.

For example, if an investor originally bought a T-bill futures contract in January that matures in March, but in February desired to liquidate his position by selling the same contract at the current market price, he or she would not have to find the original seller of the contract. Instead, he or she needs only call up his or her broker with instructions to place an order to sell at the market price in the trading pit, allowing any other trader to buy the contract. On the other hand, if the investor decides to hold his or her T-bill futures contract to its March expiration and take delivery of the \$1 million of 13-week T-bills that the contract calls for, the investor need not locate the original seller of the contract. Rather, he or she would need only to notify the exchange's clearinghouse of his intentions; upon the contract's expiration, the clearinghouse would randomly select someone with an open short position in the same contract to make delivery.

The clearinghouse guarantees the integrity of such transactions by its guarantee fund, increased from \$33 million to \$36 million in July 1989 for the Chicago Mercantile Exchange. The fund is made up of contributions from clearing member firms and is available to be drawn upon in the event of a clearing member's failure to discharge financial obligations to the exchange's clearinghouse. The clearinghouse also oversees the daily marking to market of required margin deposits for all open accounts.

14.3.3. *Margin*

Whenever someone enters into a contract position in the futures market, a security deposit, commonly called a **margin requirement**, must be paid. While the futures margin seems to be a partial payment for the security on which the futures contract is based, it only represents security to cover any losses that could result from adverse price movements.

The minimum margin requirements set by the exchange must be collected by the clearing member firms (members of the exchange involved in the clearinghouse operations) when their customers take positions in the market. In turn, the clearing member firms must deposit a fixed portion of these margins with the clearinghouse. At the end of each trading day, every futures-trading account is incremented or reduced by the corresponding increase or decrease in the value of all open futures positions. This daily adjustment procedure is applied to the margin deposit and is called **marking to market**. For example, if an investor is long on a T-bill futures contract, and by the end of a day its market value has fallen \$1,000, he or she would be asked to add an additional \$1,000 to the margin account. The reason being that the investor is responsible for its initial value. For example, if a futures contract is executed at \$10,000 with initial margin of \$1,000 and the value of the position goes down from \$1,000 to \$9,000, the buyer would be required to put in additional margin of \$1,000 because if the investor who is responsible for paying refuses to do so, the clearing member firm that he or she trades through would automatically close out the position. On the other hand, if the contract's value was up \$1,000 for the day, the investor might immediately withdraw the profit if he or she so desires. The procedure of marking to market implies that all potential profits and losses are immediately realized.

Due to the difficulty of calling all customers whose margin accounts have fallen in value for the day, a clearing member firm will usually require that a sum of money be deposited at the initiation of any futures position. This additional sum is called **maintenance margin.** In most situations the original margin requirement may be established with a risk-free, interest-bearing security, such as a T-bill. However, the maintenance margin, which must be in cash, is adjusted for daily changes in the contract value.

Margin requirements may vary among brokerage houses and may certainly differ for the type of futures trading engaged in. The largest margin deposit is required of a speculator — that is, someone who has an outright long or short position in the futures, with no corresponding position in a related security or the actual underlying asset. This results from the fact that the speculator takes on the most risk and stands to lose the most. However, for someone who owns the asset underlying the futures contract and enters the market in order to hedge the spot position, margin requirements are significantly lower. That is, the hedger's spot position stands as collateral, and the overall position is subject to a much smaller degree of price risk. Lower margins are also required from *spreaders* — traders taking an opposite futures position in a distant contract month or a related contract, or who are taking a position in an option on the futures contract. For instance, if a spreader is long the September 1988 T-bill futures, and short the same but more distant March 1989 contract, the margin requirement would be lower than that required for an outright speculative position.

Although *margin calls* can be an inconvenience, they are disruptive to cash flow, and involve an interest opportunity cost, the actual size of the required margin deposit is very small compared to the value of the contract it controls. For a T-bill futures contract worth \$1 million the required margin might be as little as \$2,700. This is a leverage factor of 37×. For the much more volatile stock-index futures, such as the contract on the S&P 500 index, a speculative position requiring \$8,500 in total margin would typically control a position worth \$75,000 to \$85,000. This is still a leverage factor of roughly 10×, one reason that futures contracts are growing in popularity.

14.3.4. *Order Execution*

Each order to buy and sell futures contracts comes to the exchange floor either by telephone or by a computerized order-entry system. It is received by a member firm at its communications desk and is time-stamped. The person receiving the order is called a *phone clerk*.

The phone clerk then hands the order to a *runner*, who relays it to the appropriate trading area or *pit*. Futures contracts are traded in separate pits, which are divided into a number of sections designated for trading in specific contract months.

The runner gives the order to the firm's *floor broker*, who handles the firm's trades in a specific contract or delivery month and takes responsibility for executing the order. If the order is to buy, the floor broker sounds out a bid for the appropriate type and number of futures contracts at the requested price to the other brokers and traders in the pit. If the order is to sell, the floor broker sounds out an offer. Once someone calls back an acknowledgment to the broker's bid or offer, the order is executed.

When the order is executed, the floor broker endorses its time, price, and size while a specially trained employee of the exchange, the *pit observer*, records the price for immediate entry into the exchange's computerized price-reporting system. The system then instantaneously transmits information to market participants around the world.

Finally, the executed order is returned from the trading pit to the phone clerk again via the runner. Once more, at the firm's communications desk the phone clerk time-stamps the executed order and immediately confirms its execution to the customer who entered it. In all, the entire order-handling process on the exchange floor takes as little as two to three minutes.

As an aside, the time-stamping serves to indicate how long the firm took to execute or *fill* the order. Some orders — such as a market order, where the firm is instructed to buy or sell at the going market price — are typically allowed only three minutes for complete execution, and the firm can be penalized by the customer through the exchange if the order is not completed in the time allowed.

14.3.5. *A Sample T-bill Futures Transaction*

Suppose that on October 2, 1990, a trader buys one December 1990 T-bill futures contract at the opening index price of $94.83. Once the transaction is complete, the trader is contractually obligated to buy a $1 million face-value 13-week T-bill yielding 100 − 94.83 = 5.17% on a discount basis on the contract delivery date, which is December 18, 1990. At the time of the initial transaction, however, the trader pays only a commission and deposits the required margin with the broker.

Suppose the futures price falls two basis points during the next day's trading session, this means that the discount rate on T-bills for future delivery has been increased. Each basis-point change in the T-bill index is worth \$25. The trader in this case will lose \$50 if he or she sells the contract at the closing price. The procedure of handling this loss is now the focus for discussion.

The practice of marking futures contracts to market at the end of each trading session means that the trader is forced to realize this loss even if the trader does not sell the contract, because \$50 is subtracted from the trader's margin account. This money is then transferred to the seller's margin account. After the contract is marked to market, the trader is still obligated to buy a T-bill on December 18, 1990, but now at a discount yield of 5.19%. In effect, the trader pays \$50 less for the T-bill at delivery because he has paid \$50 to the potential seller by marking to market. Every day the old futures contract is essentially canceled and replaced by a new contract with a delivery price equal to the new futures price — that is, the settlement price at the end of the day.

If the trader chooses to hold the contract to maturity, the contract is marked to market one last time at the close of trading on December 18. All longs with open positions at that time must be prepared to buy the deliverable T-bill at a price determined by the closing futures price.

The final settlement price or purchase price for an IMM T-bill contract is determined as follows. First, the total discount is calculated from the face value of the T-bill:

$$\text{Discount} = \frac{\text{Days to maturity} \times [(100 - \text{Index}) \times 0.01] \times \$1{,}000{,}000}{360},$$

where (100 − Index) × 0.01 is the futures discount yield expressed as a fraction. Second, the purchase price is computed by subtracting the old discount from the face value of the deliverable bill. For example, if the final index price is \$94.81, the settlement price for the delivery is

$$\$986{,}880.83 = \$1{,}000{,}000 - \frac{91 \text{ days} \times 0.0519 \times \$1{,}000{,}000}{360},$$

where $0.0519 = [100 - \text{Index}] \times 0.01$

Because buying a futures contract during the last trading session is essentially equivalent to buying a T-bill in the spot market, futures prices tend to converge to the spot price of the deliverable security on the final day of futures trading for a given contract. Otherwise, risk-free arbitrage results. Thus the settlement futures discount yield should equal the spot market discount yield at the end of the trading day. Sample Problem 14.2 provides further illustration.

Sample Problem 14.2

What is the settlement value for delivery for a IMM T-bill contract when the final index is 93?

Solution

$$\begin{aligned}\text{Discount} &= \frac{\text{Days to maturity} \times [(100 - \text{Index}) \times 0.01] \times \$1{,}000{,}000}{360}\\ &= \frac{91[(100-93) - 0.01] - \$1{,}000{,}000}{360}\\ &= \$17{,}194.44\end{aligned}$$

$$\begin{aligned}\text{Settlement value} &= \$1{,}000{,}000 - \text{Discount}\\ &= \$1{,}000{,}000 - \$17{,}194.44\\ &= \$982{,}305.56.\end{aligned}$$

The minimum yield change for T-bill futures contracts is one basis point (0.001), or a hundredth of 1%. To calculate the change in dollar value for a change of one basis point, the discount relationship can be modified. For example, for a 90-day IMM T-bill contract each change of one basis point is equivalent to a change of $25.

$$\begin{aligned}\Delta(\$) &= \frac{\text{Days to maturity} \times \Delta(\text{basis points}) \times \$1{,}000{,}000}{360}\\ &= \frac{90 \times 0.001 \times \$1{,}000{,}000}{360}\\ &= \$25.\end{aligned}$$

The two important variables in the above relationship are the days to maturity and the face value of the contract.

14.4. The Valuation of Futures Contracts

The discussions of each of the three classifications of futures contracts have pointed out pricing idiosyncrasies and have examined specific pricing models for particular types of contracts. Nevertheless, the underlying tenets of any particular pricing model have their roots in a more general theoretical framework of valuation. Consequently, the focus is now on the traditional concepts of futures contracts valuation as a prelude to more specific discussions in Chapter 15.

14.4.1. *The Arbitrage Argument*

An instant before the futures contract matures, its price must be equal to the spot (cash) price of the underlying commodity, or:

$$F_{t,T} = S_t, \tag{14.1}$$

where

$F_{t,T}$ = the price of the futures contract at time t, which matures at time T, where $T > t$ and $T - t$ is a very small interval of time; and
S_t = the spot price of the underlying commodity at time t.

If Equation (14.1) did not hold, and arbitrage condition would prevail. More specifically, when $t = T$ at the maturity of the contract, all trading on the contract ceases and the futures price equals the spot price. If an instant before maturity $F_{t,T} < S_t$, one could realize a sure profit (an arbitrage profit) by simultaneously buying the futures contract (which is undervalued) and selling the spot commodity (which is overvalued). The arbitrage profit would equal:

$$S_t - F_{t,T}. \tag{14.2}$$

However, if $F_{t,T} > S_t$ is the market condition an instant before maturity, smart traders would recognize this arbitrage condition and sell futures contracts and buy the spot commodity until $t = T$ and $F_{t,T} = S_t$. In fact, the effect of selling the futures and buying the spot would bid their prices down and up, respectively. Thus, the arbitrage process would alleviate any such pricing disequilibrium between the futures contract and its underlying spot commodity.

14.4.2. *Interest Costs*

The previous simplified argument demonstrated that the futures and spot prices must be equal an instant before the contract's maturity. This development assumes no costs in holding the spot commodity or carrying it (storing it) across time. If such a market condition held, Equation (14.1) could be extended to apply to any point of time where $t < T$. However, by having to buy or sell the spot commodity to carry out the arbitrage process, the trader would incur certain costs. For instance, if the spot commodity were purchased because it is undervalued relative to the futures, the trader or *arbitrageur* would incur an opportunity or interest cost. Any funds he or she tied up in the purchase of the commodity could alternatively be earning some risk-free interest rate R_f through investment in an interest-bearing risk-free security. Therefore, the futures price should account for the interest cost of holding the spot commodity over time, and consequently Equation (14.1) can be modified to

$$F_{t,T} = S_t(1 + R_{f,T-t}), \tag{14.3}$$

where $R_{f,T-t}$ is the risk-free opportunity cost or interest income that is lost by tying up funds in the spot commodity over the interval $T - t$. Sample Problem 14.3 provides further illustration.

Sample Problem 14.3

On September 1, the spot price of a commodity is \$100. The current risk-free rate is 12%. What is the value on September 1 of a futures contract that matures on October 1 with a price of \$100?

Solution

$$F_{t,T} = S_t(1 + R_{f,T-t})$$

$$F_{t,T} = \$100\left(1 + \frac{0.12}{12}\right)$$

$$F_{\text{Sept. 1. Oct. 1}} = \$101.$$

Since the investment is for one month only, the annualized rate of 12% must be converted to a monthly rate of 1%; this is done for $R_{f,T-t}$ by dividing the annual rate by 12.

14.4.3. *Carrying Costs*

Since theories on the pricing of futures contracts were developed long before the introduction of financial or index futures, the costs of storing and insuring the spot commodity were considered relevant factors in the price of a futures contract. That is, someone who purchased the spot commodity to hold from time t to a later period T, incurs the costs of actually housing the commodity and insuring it in case of fire or theft. In the case of livestock such as cattle or hogs, the majority of this cost would be in feeding. The holder of a futures contract avoids these costs borne by the spot holder, making the value of the contract relative to the spot commodity increase by the amount of these carrying costs. Therefore, Equation (14.3) can be extended:

$$F_{t,T} = S_t(1 + R_{f,T-t}) + C_{T-t}, \tag{14.4}$$

where C_{T-t} is the carrying costs associated with the spot commodity for the interval $T - t$. Sample Problem 14.4 provides further illustration.

Sample Problem 14.4

Extending the problem in Sample Problem 14.3, if the carrying cost is \$0.04 per dollar of value per month, what is the value of the futures contract on September 1?

Solution

$$F_{t,T} = S_t(1 + R_{f,T-t}) + C_{T-t}$$

$$F_{t,T} = \$100\left(1 + \frac{0.12}{12}\right) + \$100(\$0.04/\text{month})(1\ \text{month})$$

$$F_{\text{Sept. 1. Oct. 1}} = \$105.$$

14.4.4. *Supply and Demand Effects*

As for other financial instruments or commodities, the price of a futures contract is affected by expectations of future supply and demand conditions. The effects of supply and demand for the current spot commodity (as well as for the future spot commodity) have not yet been considered in this analysis.

If the probability exists that future supplies of the spot commodity might significantly differ from current supplies, then this will affect the futures price. The discussion up to this point has assumed that the aggregate supply of the commodity was fixed over time and that demand remained constant; however, for agricultural, financial, and index futures, this is a very unrealistic assumption. For instance, if it is expected that the future available supply of wheat for time T will decline because of poor weather, and demand is expected to remain unchanged, one would then expect the future spot price of wheat to be higher than the current spot price. Furthermore, a futures contract on wheat that matures at time T can also be considered to represent the expected spot price at time T and consequently should reflect the expected change in supply conditions. In a more extreme fashion, if it is assumed that there is no current supply of wheat, then the futures price would reflect only future supply conditions and the expected future spot price at time T. This can be expressed as

$$F_{t,T} = E_t(\widetilde{S}_T), \tag{14.5}$$

where $E_t(\widetilde{S}_T)$ is the spot price at a future point T expected at time t, where $t < T$. The tilde above S_T indicates that the future spot price is a random variable because future factors such as supply cannot presently be known with certainty.

Equation (14.5) is called the **unbiased-expectations hypothesis** because it postulates that the current price of a futures contract maturing at time T represents the market's expectation of the future spot price at time T. Which of these expression for the price of a futures contract at time t will hold in the market — the arbitrage pricing relationship in Equation (14.4) or the unbiased-expectations hypothesis in Equation (14.5)? The answer is that, because the markets are assumed to be efficient, the market price of the futures contract will take on the minimum value of either of these two pricing relationship, or

$$F_{t,T} = \text{Min}[E_t(\widetilde{S}_T), S_t(1 + R_{f,T-t}) + C_{T-t}]. \tag{14.6}$$

Sample Problem 14.5 provides further illustration.

Sample Problem 14.5

Continuing Sample Problems 14.3 and 14.4, suppose that the consensus expectation is that the price of the commodity at time T will be \$103. What is the price that anyone would pay for a futures contract on September 1?

Solution

$$\begin{aligned} F_{t,T} &= \text{Min}[E_t(\widetilde{S}_T), S_t(1 + R_{f,T-t}) + C_{T-t}] \\ F_{t,T} &= \text{Min}(\$103, \$105) \\ F_{\text{Sept. 1. Oct. 1}} &= \$103. \end{aligned}$$

For any storable commodity on a given day t, the futures price $F_{t,T}$ will be higher than the spot price S_t on day t; $F_{t,T} > S_t$. The amount by which the futures price exceeds the spot price $(F_{t,T} - S_t)$ is called the **premium.** In most cases this premium is equal to the sum of financial costs $S_t R_{f,T-t}$ and carrying costs C_{T-t}. The condition of $F_{t,T} > S_t$ is associated with a commodity market called a **normal carrying-change market**.

In general, the difference between the futures price $F_{t,T}$ and spot price S_t is called the **basis**.

$$\textbf{Basis} = F_{t,T} - S_t. \tag{14.7}$$

14.4.5. *The Effect of Hedging Demand*

John Maynard Keynes (1930), who studied the futures markets as a hobby, proposed that for some commodities there was a strong tendency for hedgers to be concentrated on the short side of the futures market. That is, to protect themselves against the risk of a price decline in the spot commodity, the spot holder or producer (such as a farmer) would hedge the risk by selling futures contracts on his or her particular commodity. This demand for hedging, producing an abundant supply of futures contracts, would force the market price below that of the expected spot price at maturity (time T). Moreover, the hedgers would be transferring their price risk to speculators. This difference between $E_t(\widetilde{S}_T)$ and $F_{t,T}$ when $F_{t,T} < E_t(\widetilde{S}_T)$ can be thought of as a risk premium paid to the speculators for holding the long futures position and bearing the price risk of the hedger. This risk premium can be formulated as

$$E_t(R_P) = E_t(\widetilde{S}_T) - F_{t,T}, \tag{14.8}$$

where $E_t(R_P)$ is the expected risk premium paid to the speculator for bearing the hedger's price risk.

Keynes described this pricing phenomenon as **normal backwardation**. When the opposite conditions exist — hedgers are concentrated on the long side of the market and bid up the futures spot pricing $F_{t,T}$ over the expected future spot $E_t(\widetilde{S}_T)$ — the pricing relationship is called **contango** (i.e., $E_t(R_P) = F_{t,T} - E_t(\widetilde{S}_T)$). To reflect the effect of normal backwardation or contango on the current futures price, the $E_t(\widetilde{S}_T)$ term in Equation (14.8) must be adjusted for the effects of hedging demand:

$$F_{t,T} = \text{Min}[E_t(\widetilde{S}_T) + E(R_P), S_t(1 + R_{f,T-t}) + C_{T-t}]. \tag{14.9}$$

Equation (14.9) expresses a broad pricing framework for the value of a futures contract. Over the life of the futures contract the futures price must move toward the cash price, because at the maturity of the futures contract the futures price will be equal to the current cash price. If hedgers are in a net short position, then futures prices must lie below the expected future spot price, and futures prices would be expected to rise over the life of the contract. However, if hedgers are net long, then the futures price must lie above the expected futures spot price and the price of the futures would be expected to fall. Either a falling futures price (normal backwardation) or a rising futures price (contango) determines the boundaries within which the actual futures price will be located. This region is shown in Fig. 14.2.

However, numerous other factors can alter and distort the relationship shown by Equation (14.9). For instance, the analysis implicitly assumes that interest rates remain constant from time t to the contract's maturity date at time T. However, since market interest rates fluctuate, an increasing or decreasing term structure of interest rates would bias the price of the futures contract higher or lower. In fact, the more accurate one's forecast of future interest rates is, the more accurate the current valuation of the futures contract would be.

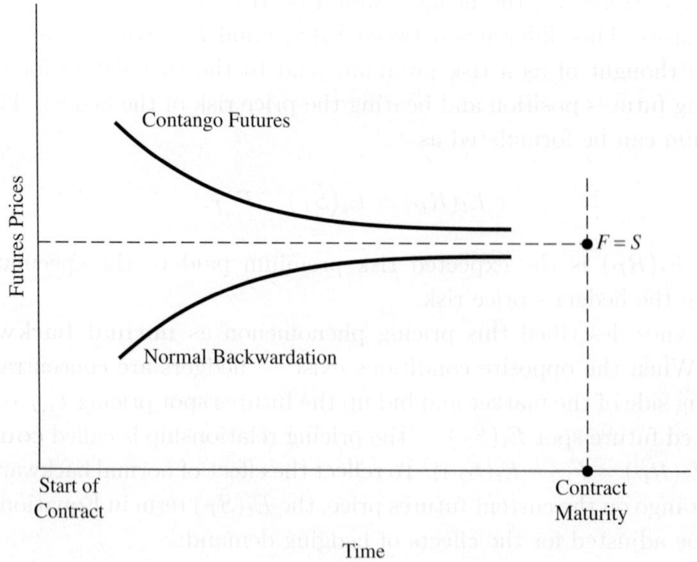

Fig. 14.2. Bounds for Futures Prices.

Empirical research casts rather strong doubt on the size of the expected risk-premium component of futures prices, particularly for financial and index futures. In fact, the expectation of speculators, along with actual futures contract supply and demand conditions in the pit, can combine to reverse the effect expected by Keynes. This results in part from the makeup of futures' users, a clear majority of whom are not hedgers as suggested by Keynes. Additionally, a futures contract for which an illiquid level of trading volume exists would put the bid and offer prices for the contract further apart. A seller of such a futures contract would require more than the theoretical fair price as compensation for the risk undertaken. The risk is of prices starting to rise in an illiquid market in which the position cannot be immediately closed out. It costs money to maintain the position; therefore, a premium is required to cover this cost.

14.5. Hedging Concepts and Strategies

The underlying motivation for the development of futures markets is to aid the holders of the spot commodity in hedging their price risk; consequently, the discussion now focuses on such an application of futures market. Four methodologies based on various risk-return criteria are examined; moreover, to fully clarify the hedger's situation some of the common problems and risks that arise in the hedging process are analyzed.

14.5.1. *Hedging Risks and Costs*

As mentioned previously, hedging refers to a process designed to alleviate the uncertainty of future price changes for the spot commodity. Typically this is accomplished by taking an opposite position in a futures contract on the same commodity that is held. If an investor owns the spot commodity, as is usually the case (a long position), the appropriate action in the futures market would be to sell a contract (a short position). However, disregarding for the moment the correct number of futures contracts to enter into, a problem arises if the prices of the spot commodity and the futures contract on this commodity do not move in a perfectly correlated manner. This nonsynchronicity of spot and futures prices is related to the basis and is called the **basis risk**.

The basis has been defined as the difference between the futures and spot prices. Basis risk is the chance that this difference will not remain constant over time. Four types of risk contribute to basis risk; these are

Table 14.4. The Components of Basis Risk.

Type of Risk	Components
Expiration-date risk	Futures contracts are not usually available for every month. If a hedger needed a futures contract for July and the only contracts that were available were for March, June, September, and December, the hedger would have to select either the June or September contract. Either of these contracts would have a different price series than a July contract (if one existed). Hence, the hedger cannot form a perfect hedge and is faced with the chance that the basis may change.
Location risk	The hedger requires delivery of the futures contract in location Y, but the only futures contracts available are for delivery in location X. Hence, the hedger cannot form a perfect hedge because of the transportation costs from X to Y; this may cause the basis to change.
Quality risk	The exact standard or grade of the commodity required by the hedger is not covered by the futures contract. Therefore, the price movement of commodity grade A may be different from the price movement of commodity grade B, which will cause the basis to change and prevent the hedger from forming a perfect hedge.
Quantity risk	The exact amount of the commodity needed by the hedger is not available by a single futures contract or any integer multiple thereof. Hence, the amount of the commodity is not hedged exactly; this prevents the hedger from forming a perfect hedge, and the underhedged or overhedged amount is subject to risk.

defined in Table 14.4. These four types of risks prevent the hedger from forming a perfect hedge (which would have zero risk). Even though the hedger is reducing the amount of risk, it has not been reduced to zero. It is often said that hedging replaces price risk with basis risk.

The potential causes of basis risk are not necessarily limited to those identified in Table 14.4. Hence, basis risk is the prominent source of uncertainty in the hedging process. Among other probable causes are: (1) supply-demand conditions, and (2) cross-hedging consequences.

Even if the futures contract is written on the exact commodity that the hedger holds, differing supply and demand conditions in the spot market and futures market could cause the basis to vary over time. Occasionally, speculators in the futures market will bid the futures price above or below its equilibrium position, due perhaps to the excitement induced by an unexpected news release. Of course, the market forces of arbitrage will eventually bring the spot and futures prices back in line. The limiting case is at the expiration of the futures contract, when its price must converge to the spot price.

Consequently, the disequilibrating influence on the basis stemming from supply-demand forces can be alleviated by entering a futures contract that matures on the exact day that the hedger intends to sell the spot commodity. But although most futures contracts are quite flexible, it is unlikely that any contract would correlate so precisely with the hedger's needs. In some cases (such as for agricultural commodities, where futures contracts are offered that mature each month), the basis risk due to nonsimultaneous maturities is not so great. However, for other commodities, particularly financial instruments, futures contracts maturing three months apart are more typically offered. Thus, at the time the hedger needs to sell the spot commodity in the market, any protection in price risk over the hedging period could conceivably be wiped out by a temporary adverse change in the basis.

Cross-hedging refers to hedging with a futures contract written on a nonidentical commodity (relative to the spot commodity). While not often necessary with agricultural futures, cross-hedging is frequently the best that can be done with financial and index futures. Changes in the basis risk induced by the cross-hedge are caused by less than perfect correlation of price movements between the spot and futures prices — even at maturity. That is, because the spot commodity and futures contract commodity are different, their respective prices will tend to be affected (even though minutely at times) by differing market forces. While the futures price must equal the price of its underlying spot commodity at the contract's maturity date, this condition does not necessarily hold when the hedger's commodity is not the "true" underlying asset. Therefore, even when the liquidation of the spot commodity coincides with the maturity of the futures contract, there is no guarantee of obtaining the original price of the commodity that was held at the initiation of the hedge.

Sample Problem 14.6

Basis risk is illustrated in Table 14.5. The spot price is \$100 and the futures price is \$105 on day t. The top half of the exhibit shows what can happen if the spot price falls at day $t+1$, and the bottom half shows what happens if the spot price rises. It is assumed that the hedger is trying to create a fully hedged position in each of the cases presented.

Table 14.5. Examples of Basis Risk.

	Spot Market		Futures Market		Basis ($F - S$)
Drop in Cash Price					
t	buy	100	sell	105	5
$t+1$	sell	95	buy	100	5
		−5		+5	change = 0
	Net hedge = 0			No change in basis	
t	buy	100	sell	105	5
$t+1$	sell	95	buy	101	6
		−5		+4	change = +1
	Net hedge = −1			Basis increases	
t	buy	100	sell	105	5
$t+1$	sell	95	buy	99	4
		−5		+6	change = −1
	Net hedge = +1			Basis decreases	
Increase in Cash Price					
t	buy	100	sell	105	5
$t+1$	sell	105	buy	110	5
		−5		−5	change = 0
	Net hedge = 0			No change in basis	
t	buy	100	sell	105	5
$t+1$	sell	105	buy	111	6
		+5		−6	change = +1
	Net hedge = −1			Basis increases	
t	buy	100	sell	105	5
$t+1$	sell	105	buy	109	4
		+5		−4	change = −1
	Net hedge = +1			Basis decreases	

If the basis is unchanged, the hedged position will neither gain nor lose. As can be seen in Table 14.5, the gain or loss on the hedged position is related to the change in the basis. Hence, the asset position's exposure to price risk is zero and the only risk the hedger faces is a change in the basis.

14.5.2. *The Classic Hedge Strategy*

The implicit assumption of the classic hedge ratio equal to one is that the prices of the spot commodity (in this case, the stock portfolio) and the futures contract will remain perfectly correlated over the entire hedge period. Then if the stock market does turn down as expected, any losses in the portfolio due to price declines in its composite stocks will be exactly offset by the gain on the futures position. Conversely, if stock prices rise, the portfolio's gains will be offset by equal losses on the futures position. Therefore, the portfolio manager attempts to lock in current profits by taking on a hedge position. Such a strategy implies that the objective of the classic hedge is risk minimization or elimination.

To apply the **classic hedge strategy** to the hedging problem, an opposite and equal position is taken in the futures market for the underlying commodity. More specifically, if a cautious portfolio manager believed that the stock market was going to turn downward for the next month and he or she wanted to lock in previously unrealized capital gains on his or her \$7.5 million stock portfolio, he or she would sell \$7.5 million worth of stock-index futures contracts. Furthermore, that portfolio manager would keep his or her initial futures position constant over the entire hedge period.

Sample Problem 14.7

In the example of the implementation of the classic hedge strategy shown in Table 14.6 the current scenario is extended and it is assumed that (1) there are no associated costs for entering or liquidating a futures position (e.g., commission costs or margin costs) and (2) a perfect correlation exists between the spot and futures price movements (e.g., there is not basis risk). The S&P 500 Index futures contract is used as the hedging instrument.

It is difficult to imagine the consequences of this strategy if the spot and futures prices are not perfectly correlated. In fact, if the spot- and futures-contract commodities are not identical, or if the hedging horizon does not coincide with the maturity of the futures contract, perfectly correlated spot and futures prices will always be the exception and not the rule.

Hence, there are identifiable risks associated with hedging. Two such types are (1) the risk of margin calls and (2) liquidity. Hedgers, like all participants in futures markets, must mark to market each day. In the simplified example, the decline (increase) in the value of the futures position is offset by gains (decreases) from the cash position. Nevertheless, gains from the cash position are typically not realized immediately, while futures contracts are marked to market at the end of each trading session. Thus practice of marking to market causes an imbalance in the cash flow of the hedger, who must balance paper gains in the cash market against realized (cash) outflows in the futures market. And although futures contracts are

Table 14.6. The Classic Hedge Strategy.

	Cash-Market Position	Future-Market Position (index = 150)
July 1, 1989	\$7,500,000 in well-diversified stock portfolio	Short (sell) 100 contracts, equal to 100 × (\$500 × 150) = \$7,500,000.
August 1, 1989	Scenario I: Stock prices fall (index = 145).	
	\$7,250,000 value of portfolio	Buy 100 contracts, equal to 100 × (\$500 × 145) = \$7,250,000
	Net Results from Hedging	
	Gain or (loss)	Gain or (loss)
	(\$250,000)	\$250,000
	Net Gain = \$0	
	Scenario II: Stock prices rise (index = 155)	
	\$7,750,000 value of portfolio	Buy 100 contracts, equal to 100 × (\$500 × 55) = \$7,750,000.
	Net Results from Hedging	
	Gain or (loss)	Gain or (loss)
	\$250,000	(\$250,000)
	Net Gain = \$0	

usually more liquid than the underlying cash instrument, liquidity may be a problem for some contracts. Hence hedgers who find it impossible to execute orders for the purchase or sale of a futures contract may need to be able to satisfy the delivery requirements of their hedge.

Liquidity is most likely a problem for futures contracts with delivery dates more than a year away. Trading activity in futures contracts is heaviest in contracts for the nearby delivery months. Trading in the most distant contract is typically very thin, hence less liquid.

Because of these problems with hedging, researchers have tried to incorporate the risk of hedging into the way the relative futures position is determined.

14.5.3. *The Working Hedge Strategy*

The **Working hedge strategy,** formulated by Holbrook Working (1953), makes explicit the speculative aspect of hedging. That is, in any hedged position the basis will not be constant over time. Therefore, the hedger in a certain sense is speculating on the future course of the basis. Yet it is expected that the changes in the basis will involve a smaller degree of risk than the corresponding price risk of the unhedged position.

This speculative aspect to hedging is exploited in Working's model by simultaneously determining positions in the spot and futures markets in order to capture increased return arising from relative movements in spot and futures prices. By studying the year-to-year constancy of the relation between spot and futures prices in various markets, Working discerned that a large *positive basis* (spot price less than futures price) was likely to be followed by a large negative change in the basis (basis narrows), and, conversely, a large negative basis by a large positive change in the basis. Figure 14.3 graphs a hypothetical basis relationship over time and designates the points considered indicative of large positive or negative basis.

The implications of Working's 1953 model for the hedger are as follows. A short position in futures (of equal magnitude to the commodity held) is entered into only if the basis is sufficiently wide and positive. Thus, on the expectation that this large positive basis will narrow over time, the hedger will (it is hoped) profit from the combined spot and futures position.

Sample Problem 14.8

As an example of the implementation of this hedging rule, assume that the manager of the well-diversified portfolio of stocks worth $7.5 million sees a difference between the stock-index futures price for the S&P 500

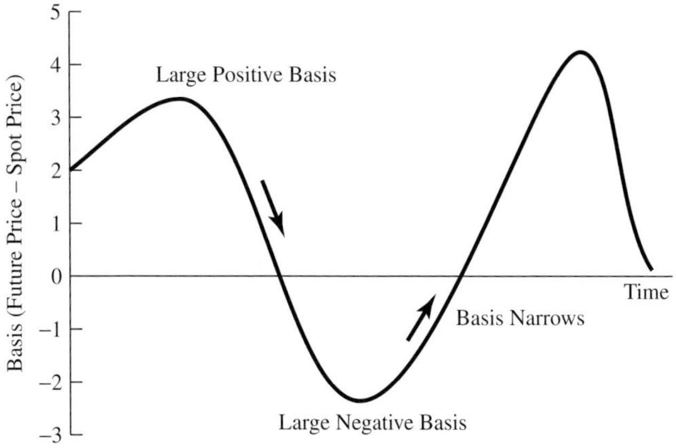

Fig. 14.3. A Hypothetical Basis Relationship Over Time.

Table 14.7. The Working Hedge Strategy.

	Spot-Market Position (Spot price = $150)	Futures-Market Position (futures price = $152.88)
July 1, 1989	$7,500,000 in well-diversified stock portfolio	Sell 98 contracts, equal to 98 × ($500 × 152.85) = $7,489,650. Basis = 2.85
August 1, 1989	$7,525,000 value of portfolio	Buy 98 contracts, equal to 98 × ($500 × 152.00) = $7,448,000. Basis = 1.50
Results from Hedging	Gain or (less) $25,000	Gain or (loss) $41,650
	Gross Profit = $66,650	

near-term contract and the spot price of 2.85 (152.85 – 150.00) on July 1. Her portfolio is highly correlated with the S&P 500 index, and she sells 98 contracts to achieve an approximately equally valued position in the futures. Table 14.7 summarizes the results of this hedge strategy one month later. As Table 14.7 shows for this simplified example, the hedger, by entering a short futures position when the basis was sufficiently positive, nearly triples the return on her portfolio. However, if the basis had widened over the hedging horizon, the net gain on the hedged position would have been reduced correspondingly.

For the most part, the Working strategy provides a relatively simple decision rule to facilitate speculation on the basis. Moreover, the hedger should create a hedged position with the futures only if the basis is sufficiently wide and positive at the beginning of the hedge period. Both the decision to hedge and the size of the hedging commitment are essentially predetermined and therefore relatively easy to implement. Finally, in order to evaluate the Working strategy versus the classic one-to-one hedge, the following *ex-post* measure of hedging effectiveness (HE) has been suggested:

$$\text{GP} = (S_2 - S_1) - H(F_2 - F_1), \tag{14.10}$$

where

GP = gross profit;
H = hedge ratio;
S_1, S_2 = beginning and end-of-period spot prices; and
F_1, F_2 = beginning and end-of-period futures prices.

In the example, gross profit is \$66,650. This sum could then be compared to either the gross profit (or loss) from an unhedged position or to the gross profit generated from an alternative hedging strategy.

14.5.4. *The Johnson Minimum-Variance Hedge Strategy*

Developed within the framework of modern portfolio theory, the **Johnson hedge model** (1960) retains the traditional objective of risk minimization but defines risk as the variance of return on a two-asset hedge portfolio. As in the two-parameter world of Markowitz (1959), the hedger is assumed to be infinitely risk averse (i.e., the investor desires zero variance). Moreover, with the risk-minimization objective defined as the variance of return of the combined spot and futures position, the Johnson hedge ratio is expressed in terms of expectations of variances and covariances for price changes in the spot and futures markets.

The Johnson hedge model can be expressed in regression form as

$$\Delta S_t = a + H\Delta F_t + e_t, \tag{14.11}$$

where

ΔS_t = change in the spot price at time t;
ΔF_t = change in the futures price at time t;
a = constant;
H = hedged ratio; and
e_t = residual term at time t.

Furthermore, the hedge ratio measure can be better understood by defining it in terms of its components:

$$\frac{X_f^*}{X_s} = -\frac{\sigma_{\Delta S,\Delta F}}{\sigma^2_{\Delta F}} = H, \tag{14.12}$$

where

X_f^* and X_s = the dollar amount invested in futures and spot;
$\sigma_{\Delta S,\Delta F}$ = the covariance of spot and futures price changes; and
$\sigma^2_{\Delta F}$ = the variance of futures price changes.

Thus H, the minimum-variance hedge ratio computed in variability, is also a measure of the relative dollar amount to be invested in futures per dollar of spot holdings. In a sense it is a localized beta coefficient similar in concept to the beta of a stock *a la* capital asset pricing theory.

As a measure of HE, Johnson utilizes the squared simple-correlation coefficient between spot and futures price changes, ρ^2. More formally, Johnson's hedging-effectiveness measure can be ascertained by first establishing the following expression:

$$HE = 1 - \frac{V_H}{V_u}, \tag{14.13}$$

where

V_u = variance of the unhedged spot position = $X_s^2\sigma_{\Delta S}^2$
$\sigma_{\Delta S}^2$ = variance of spot price changes; and
V_H = the variance of return for the hedged portfolio = $X_s^2\sigma_{\Delta S}^2(1-\rho^2)$.

By substituting the minimum-variance hedge position in the futures, X_f^*:

$$HE = \left[1 - \frac{X_S^2\sigma_{\Delta S}^2(1-\rho^2)}{X_S^2\sigma_{\Delta S}^2}\right] = \rho^2. \tag{14.14}$$

In simpler terms then, the Johnson measure of HE is the R^2 of a regression of spot-price changes on futures-price changes. To utilize this hedging method, it is necessary to regress historical data of spot-price changes on futures-price changes. The resulting beta coefficient from the regression would be the localized Johnson hedge ratio, and the regression R^2 would represent the expected degree of variance minimization using this hedge ratio over the hedging horizon. "Localized" and "expected" must be emphasized because, first of all, although the Johnson hedge ratio can be re-estimated, it nonetheless is a static measure based on historical data. What held for the past may not hold precisely for the future. Moreover, large price moves may distort this hedge ratio considerably. Hence, R^2 is what can be expected based on the past in terms of variance reduction for the total hedge position. It should not be expected to hold exactly. (A sample computation of a hedge ratio using the Johnson model is presented in a later section.)

14.5.5. *The Howard–D'Antonio Optimal Risk–Return Hedge Strategy*

The classic one-to-one hedge is a naïve strategy based upon a broadly defined objective of risk minimization. The strategy is naïve in the sense that a hedging coefficient of one is used regardless of past or expected correlations of spot- and futures-price changes. Working's strategy brings out the speculative aspects of hedging by analyzing changes in the basis and, accordingly exercising discrete judgment about when to hedge and when not to hedge. The underlying objective of Working's decision rule for hedgers is one of profit maximization. Finally, Johnson (1960), in applying the mean-variance criteria of modern portfolio theory, emphasizes the risk-minimization objective but defines risk in terms of the variance of the hedged position. Although Johnson's method improves on the naïve strategy of a one-to-one hedge, however, it essentially disregards the return component associated with a particular level of risk. Rutledge (1972) uses both mean and variance information to derive hedge ratio.

In a recent paper by Howard and D'Antonio (1984), a hedge ratio and measure of HE are derived in which the hedger's risk and return are both explicitly taken into account. Moreover, some of the variable relationships derived from their analysis help explain some of the idiosyncrasies of hedging that occur in practice.

Using a mean-variance framework, the **Howard–D'Antonio strategy** begins by assuming that the "agent" is out to maximize the expected return for a given level of portfolio risk. With a choice of putting money into three assets — a spot position, a futures contract, and a risk-free asset — the agent's optimal portfolio will depend on the relative risk-return characteristics of each asset. For a hedger, the optimal portfolio may contain a short futures position, a long futures position, or no futures position at all. In general, the precise futures position to be entered into will be determined by (1) the risk-free rate, (2) the expected returns and the standard deviations for the spot and futures positions, and (3) the correlation between the return on the spot position and the return on the futures.

Howard and D'Antonio arrive at the following expressions for the hedge ratio and the measure of HE:

$$\text{Hedge ratio } H = \frac{(\lambda - \rho)}{\gamma\pi(1 - \lambda\rho)}, \tag{14.15}$$

and

$$\text{Hedging effectiveness } HE = \sqrt{\frac{1 - 2\lambda\rho + \lambda^2}{1 - \rho^2}}, \tag{14.16}$$

where

$\pi = \sigma_f/\sigma_s$ = relative variability of futures and spot returns;
$\alpha = \bar{r}_f/(\bar{r}_s - i)$ = relative excess return on futures to that of spot;
$\gamma = P_f/P_s$ = current price ratio of futures to spot;
$\lambda = \alpha/\pi = (\bar{r}_f/\sigma_f)/[(\bar{r}_s - i)/\sigma_s]$ = risk-to-excess-return relative of futures versus the spot position;
P_s, P_f = the current price per unit for the spot and futures respectively;
ρ = simple correlation coefficient between the spot and futures returns;
σ_s = standard deviation of spot returns;
σ_f = standard deviation of futures returns;
$\bar{r}_s$ = mean return on the spot over some recent past interval;
$\bar{r}_f$ = mean return on the futures over some recent past interval; and
i = risk-free rate.

By analyzing the properties of λ, these authors discern some important insights for the coordinated use of futures in a hedge portfolio. Numerically, λ expresses the relative attractiveness of investing in futures versus the spot position. When $\lambda < 1$, $\lambda = 1$, and $\lambda > 1$, the futures contract offers less, the same, and more excess return per unit of risk than the spot position, respectively. Since this analysis is being undertaken from a hedger's point of view, it is assumed $\lambda < 1$. An assumption that $\lambda > 1$ would inappropriately imply that theoretically it is possible to hedge the futures position with the spot asset.

First, consider the effect of the relationship of λ to ρ on the optional hedge ratio, H. Table 14.8 summarizes the hedging implications for different magnitudes of the ratio of the risk-return relative λ to the simple correlation coefficient of spot and futures returns ρ. Of particular note is the case when $\lambda = \rho$. Such a condition implies that no benefit exists for going short or long in futures. Furthermore, this result rather clearly demonstrates that the holding of futures as a hedge against price risk is not simply related to ρ but is also dependent on the relative return-risk relationship between

Table 14.8. The Hedging Implications of Different Relative Magnitudes of λ and ρ.

Relative Magnitude	Hedge Ratio	Implied Futures Position
$\lambda < \rho$	$H < 0$	short
$\lambda = \rho$	$H = 0$	none
$\lambda > \rho$	$H > 0$	long

the futures and the spot asset. Chen *et al.* (2003) have shown that Howard D'Antonio hedge ratio will reduce to Johnson hedge ratio as indicated in (14.12) if $\bar{r}_f$ approaches to zero.

Next, a careful examination of Howard and D'Antonio's HE measure in Equation (14.6) is warranted. It is important to note that this hedging effectiveness measure *HE* is different from the measures studied so far because it takes into account the risk–return relationship between futures and spot as well as the correlation of returns. The Howard–D'Antonio *HE* measure indicates the degree (in terms of return) to which the hedger (investor) could enhance the portfolio by entering into the appropriate futures position, as indicated by Equation (14.14). For instance, if $\lambda = 0.60$ and $\rho = 0.80$, then $HE = 1.054$, meaning that a hedger could expect to enhance the excess return of the portfolio of the risk-free and spot assets by 5.4% by going short ($\lambda < \rho$) the number of futures contracts indicated by Equation (14.15).

The relationship among ρ, λ, and *HE* is seen more clearly in Fig. 14.4 and is summarized in Table 14.9. As can be seen from Fig. 14.6, *HE* is symmetrical about $\lambda = \rho$. Moreover, it is shown that as ρ approaches 1, *HE* increases. That is, the hedging properties of futures improve as ρ approaches 1. However, this effect is entirely contingent on $\lambda \neq \rho$. Even if $\rho \neq 1$ there will be no benefit to holding a futures contract if $\lambda = \rho$.

The last result is at odds with past studies on hedging, especially Johnson's (1960) work. Yet the implications from this result can help provide insight into the cross-hedging process. While past studies have indicated that the correlation of futures- and spot-price movements is the determinant of a hedge's effectiveness and would almost necessarily attribute superior hedging qualities to a futures contract on the true underlying asset (a straight hedge), these results indicate that the effectiveness of one's hedge — be it a cross-hedge or a straight hedge — depends on the relationship between λ and ρ.

From a practitioner's perspective it is also important to note that even when $\lambda \neq \rho$, a hedged position using the futures may not provide a real net improvement in the risk–return performance of a portfolio. Unless *HE* is significantly greater than 1, other factors such as transaction costs, taxes, the potential for margin calls, and liquidity may negate the overall benefit of hedging with futures. This point, along with the previous results about hedging, helps explain why certain futures contracts highly correlated with their underlying assets are not used extensively as hedging vehicles as might be expected.

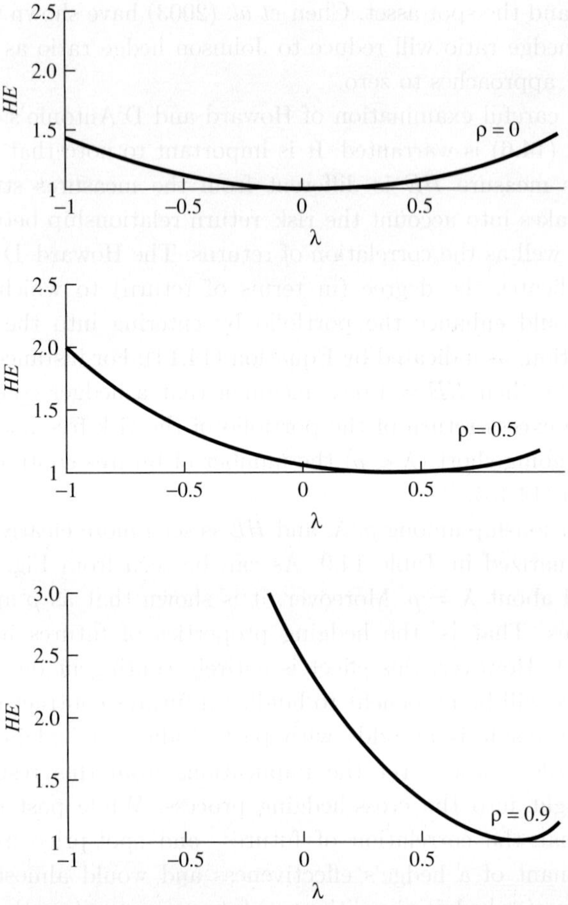

Fig. 14.4. Hedging Effectiveness (HE) versus the Risk–Return Relative for Various Correlations (ρ).
Source: C. T. Howard and L. J. D'Antonio, "A Risk-Return Measure of Hedging Effectiveness." *Journal of Financial and Quantitative Analysis*, v. 19 (March 1984), p. 109. Reprinted with permission.

Table 14.9. The Relationship of λ, ρ, and HE.

	Effect on the HE measure	Benefit of hedging with futures
$\lambda < \rho$	$HE > 1.0$	positive
$\lambda = \rho$	$HE = 1.0$	none
$\lambda > \rho$	$HE > 1.0$	positive

14.5.5.1. *Other Hedge Ratios*

Hsin *et al.* (1994) use quadratic utility function to derive a hedge ratio.

$$\text{Hedge Ratio } H = -\left[\frac{\bar{r}_f}{A\sigma_f^2} - \rho\frac{\sigma_s}{\sigma_f}\right], \tag{14.17}$$

where

ρ = simple correlation coefficient between the spot and futures returns;
σ_s = standard deviation of spot returns;
σ_f = standard deviation of futures returns;
$\bar{r}_f$ = mean return on the futures over some recent past interval; and
A = risk aversion parameter.

When A approaches to infinity, this hedge ratio will reduce to Johnson Hedge ratio as indicated in (14.12).

Chen *et al.* (2003) have reviewed alternative hedge ratios which have been developed until 2003. In addition, Chen *et al.* (2001) use Mean-Generalized Semivariance Approach to derive a new hedge ratio which is a generalized case of Johnson hedge ratio. Chen *et al.* (2008) have discussed implications of pure Martingale and joint normal distribution for deriving the Optimal Hedge Ratios.

14.6. Summary

This chapter has focused on the basic concepts of futures markets. Important terms were defined and basic models to evaluate futures contracts were discussed. The differences between futures and forward markets also received treatment. Finally hedging concepts and strategies were analyzed and alternative hedging ratios were investigated in detail. These concepts and valuation models can be used in security analysis and portfolio management related to futures and forward contracts. The next chapter investigates in depth commodity futures, financial futures, and index futures.

Questions and Problems

1. Define the following terms:
   (a) basis (b) backwardation
   (c) contango (d) hedger
   (e) speculator (f) arbitrager.

2. Carefully explain the difference between a futures contract and a forward contract.
3. Explain the importance of futures markets.
4. Carefully discuss the importance of the clearinghouse in futures markets.
5. What is marking to market? How does marking to market affect the cash flows of a futures contract?
6. What is the relationship between the price of the futures contract and the spot price of the underlying commodity as the expiration of the futures contract is approached?
7. Carefully explain how the interest rate determines the relationship between future and spot prices.
8. Carefully explain how carrying costs determine the relationship between future and spot prices.
9. On February 1, the spot price of a commodity is \$250 and the current risk-free rate is 9%. What is the value on February 1 of a futures contract that matures on March 1 and on April 1?
10. Carefully explain the difference between hedging and speculation.
11. Suppose an investor has a portfolio of T-bills with a face value of \$1 million, currently worth \$960,000. Assume the T-bills in this portfolio mature in three months. A three-month T-bill futures contract is currently selling for $96\frac{24}{32}$. Assume that interest rates rise and the value of the T-bills falls to \$950,125, while the value of the T-bills futures contract falls to $96\frac{8}{32}$.

    (a) Use the T-bill futures to hedge your T-bill position.
    (b) Is it possible to create a riskless hedge for this example?
    (c) If it is not possible to create a riskless hedge, what does this say about the market for T-bills and T-bill futures?
    (d) Calculate the net change in the value of the hedged portfolio.

12. Calculate the change in settlement for a T-bill contract for a six-basis-point change in the yield. Assume the contract matures in 180 days.
13. What is the settlement value for an IMM T-bill contract when the final index is 94?
14. Suppose the spot price for hog bellies is 44 cents per pound on July 1. What is the value on July 1 of a futures contract that matures on September 1 with a price of 44 cents per pound? Assume that the risk-free rate is 8%.

15. Recalculate the value of the futures contract presented in Sample Problem 14.4 if the carrying cost changes to $0.02 per pound per month.
16. Explain the logic behind the following formula.

$$F_{t,T} = \text{Min}[E_t(\widetilde{S}_T), S_t(1 + R_{f,T-t}) + C_{T-t}].$$

17. Explain the role of each of the following in the futures market.
    (a) hedger
    (b) speculator
    (c) arbitrager

    If any one of these groups is not participating in the futures market, what happens to the market? Answer this question for each group.
18. What are the various risk components of basis risk? What can be done about reducing or eliminating them?
19. What is the economic rationale for the existence of futures markets?
20. What is the difference between a forward market and a futures market?
21. An investor with $10 million in T-bills wishes to hedge his position. Given the following information, what is the gain or loss on the cash and futures position?

at $t = 0$	T-bills sell at 98% of par.
	Futures contract ($1 million face) is $98\frac{1}{4}$.
at $t \leq t + 1$	Interest rates have fallen.
	T-bills sell at $98\frac{1}{2}$% of par.
	Futures contract ($1 million face) is $98\frac{3}{4}$.

22. Compare and contrast the uses of the word *margin* in the stock market and in the futures market.
23. What is the current futures price of commodity X is the spot prices of X is $10 and the futures contract has two months to delivery? The current interest rate is 12%.
24. Given the information in question 23 and a carrying cost of $0.10 per dollar value per month, what is the current futures price?
25. Given the information in questions 23 and 24, if the spot price for X is expected to be $10, what is the futures price at $t = 0$? If the spot price of X is expected never to change, perhaps it is guaranteed by some sort of government program. Would you trade in futures contracts for X?
26. Given the following information, what is the basis at $t = 0$? What is the basis at $t \leq 1$? Why has basis changed?

$t = 0$ Spot price = \$10 $t \leq 1$ Spot price = 9.75
Futures price = \$11.50 Futures price = \$10.75

$$\text{Basis} = \text{Future} - \text{Spot}$$

$$f = \text{S}(1 + r) + \text{Carrying costs.}$$

27. Using the Howard–D'Antonio model, what is the hedge ratio if

$$\lambda = 0.5$$

$$\rho = 0.9$$

$$\gamma = 1.01$$

$$\pi = 1.2$$

What is the HE?

Appendix 14A: Basic Futures Terminology

Although related to other securities markets, such as those for stocks or bonds, the futures market is unique not only in nature but also with regard to some of its terminology. In this appendix, we define some commonly used terms for these markets as follows.

Term	Definition
Arbitrage	The simultaneous purchase and sale of similar financial instruments or commodity futures in order to benefit from an anticipated change (correction) in their price relationship.
Basis	The differece between futures price and the spot price. Basis is one kind of risk in investment: it is explored later in this chapter.
Bid	An offer to purchase at a specified price.
Car	A loose term sometimes used to describe the quantity of a contract — for example. "I am long *a car of bellies.*" (Derived from the fact that quantities of the product specified in a contract used to correspond closely to the capacity of a railroad car.)
Cash commodity	The actual physical commodity, as distinguished from a futures commodity. A commodity delivered at the time of sale is a cash commodity while a commodity to be delivered at a specific future date is a future commodity.
Clearinghouse	The third party of every futures contract, which guarantees that every futures contract will be carried out even if one of the parties defaults. The clearinghouse also facilitates trading of futures contracts before they are due for delivery.
Contract amount	The number of units of the good or service to be delivered.

(Continued)

(*Continued*)

Term	Definition
Contract month	The month in which a futures contract is scheduled to mature by making or accepting a delivery.
Contract specification	The precise definition of the good or service to be delivered in the futures contract.
Delivery	The tender and receipt of an actual commodity or financial instrument, or cash in settlement of a futures contract.
Delivery point	A point designated by a futures exchange at which the financial instrument or commodity covered by futures contract may be delivered in fulfillment of such contract.
Equity	The residual dollar value of a futures trading account (over and above margin requirements), assuming its liquidation at the going market price.
Floor broker	A licensed member of the exchange who is paid a fee for executing orders for clearing members or their customers.
Floor trader	An exchange member who generally trades only for his or her own account, or for an account controlled by him or her, (Also called "local.")
Forward contract	A prespecified contract similar to a futures contract except that it is tailored to suit the particular needs of the individual parties. Forward contracts are not generally traded on exchanges because they lack standardization, they do not have the daily mark-to-market requirement, and they typically require no transfers of money until delivery.
Futures contract	A legally binding, standardized agreement made within the confines of an exchange trading area, specifying the good or service involved, the quantity, and the future date and price at which the contract is to be fulfilled.
Hedger	A market participant who has or will have a position in the cash commodity and who attempts to eliminate or reduce risk exposure by taking an offsetting position in the futures or forward market.
Liquidation	Any transaction that offsets or closes out a long or short position. (Also called "evening up" or "offset.")
Long position	The purchase of a futures contract in anticipation of taking eventual delivery of the commodity (or financial instrument) or an expected increase in the underlying asset's price.
Margin	A cash amount of funds that must be deposited with the broker for each futures contract as a guarantee of its fulfillment.
Margin call	A demand for additional cash funds for each futures position held because of an adverse price movement.
Mark to market	The daily adjustment of a futures trading account to reflect profits or losses due to daily changes in the value of the futures contract.

(*Continued*)

(*Continued*)

Term	Definition
Open contracts	Contracts that have been bought or sold without the transactions having been completed by subsequent sale or purchase, or by making or taking actual delivery of the financial instrument or physical commodity. Measured by "Open interest," as reported in the press.
Settlement price	A figure determined by the closing-price range that is used to calculate daily gains and losses in futures-market accounts (and thus margin calls) and invoice prices for deliveries.
Short position	The sale of a futures contract in anticipation of a fall in the price of the underlying asset. Also obligates delivery of the commodity or financial instrument (and payment) if the position is left open to maturity.
Speculator	A market participant who is willing (for a price) to take on the risk the hedger wishes to eliminate. This trader goes long or short on a contract without having, or intending to take, an opposite position in the cash market.
Spot price	The current price of the commodity if purchased in the cash or "spot" market.
Spread	Refers to the simultaneous purchase and sale of futures contracts for (1) the name commodity or instrument with different maturity months or (2) commodities in different but related markets.
Tick	Refers to a change in price, either up or down. The amount varies with each contract.
Volume	The number of transactions in a futures contract made during a specified period of time.

Bibliography

Black, F. "The Pricing of Commodity Contracts." *Journal of Financial Economics*, v. 3 (September 1976), pp. 167–179.

Castelino, M. "Basis Volatility: Implications for Hedging." *Journal of Financial Research* v. 12 (Summer 1989), pp. 157–172.

Castelino, M. and J. Francis. "Basis Speculation in Commodity Futures: The Maturity Effect." *Journal of Futures Markets*, v. 2(2) (1982), pp. 195–207.

Chen, S. S., C. F. Lee and K. Shreshta. "Do the Pure Martingale and Joint Normality Hypotheses Hold for Futures Contracts? Implications for the Optimal Hedge Ratios." *Quarterly Review of Economics and Finance*, v. 48(1) (January 2008), pp 153–174.

Chen, S. S., C. F. Lee and K. Shreshta. "An Empirical Analysis of the Relationship between the Hedge Ratio and Hedging Horizon: A Simultaneous Estimation of the Short- and Long-Run Hedge Ratio." *Journal of Futures Markets*, v. 24 (2004), pp. 359–386.

Chen, S. S., C. F. Lee, and K. Shreshta. "Future Hedge Ratios: A Review." *Quarterly Review of Economics and Finance*, v. 43 (2003), pp.433–465.

Chen, S. S., C. F. Lee and K. Shreshta. "On a Mean-Generalized Semivariance Approach to Determining the Hedge Ratio." *Journal of Futures Markets*, v. 21(6) (2001), pp. 581–598.

Cheng, E. "Returns of Speculators and the Theory of Normal Backwardation." *Journal of Finance*, v. 40 (March 1985), pp. 193–208.

Chicago Board of Trade. *GNMA Futures.* Chicago: Chicago Board of Trade, 1987.

Chicago Board of Trade. *Ten-Year Treasury Futures.* Chicago: Chicago Board of Trade, 1987.

Chicago Board of Trade. *U.S. Treasury Bond Futures.* Chicago: Chicago Board of Trade, 1987.

Cornell, B. and K. French. "Taxes and the Pricing of Stock Index Futures." *Journal of Finance*, v. 38 (June 1983), pp. 675–694.

Cox, J., J. Ingersoll and S. Ross. "The Relation between Forward and Futures Prices." *Journal of Financial Economics*, v. 9 (December 1981), pp. 321–346.

Daigler, T. "Futures Bibliography." *Journal of Futures Markets*, v. 8 (Spring 1988), pp. 131–143.

Dusak, K. "Futures Trading and Investor Returns: An Investigation of Commodity Market Risk Premiums." *Journal of Political Economy*, v. 81 (November/December 1973), pp. 1306–1313.

Ederington, L. H. "The Hedging Performance of the New Futures Markets." *Journal of Finance*, v. 34 (March 1979), pp. 157–170.

Elton, E., M. Gruber and J. Rentzler. "Intraday Tests of the Efficiency of the T-Bill Futures Market." *Review of Economics and Statistics*, v. 66 (February 1984), pp. 129–137.

Fama, E. "Forward Rates as Predictors of Future Spot Rates." *Journal of Financial Economics*, v. 3 (October 1976), pp. 361–377.

Figlewski, S. *Hedging with Financial Futures for Institutional Investors.* Cambridge, MA: Ballinger Publishing Co., 1986.

Howard, C. T. and L. J. D'Antonio. "A Risk-Return Measure of Hedging Effectiveness." *Journal of Financial and Quantitative Analysis*, v. 19 (March 1984), pp. 101–112.

Hsin, C. W., J. Kuo and C. F. Lee. "A New Measure to Compare the Hedging Effectiveness of Foreign Currency Futures vs. Options." *Journal of Future Markets* v. 14 (September 1994), pp. 685–707.

International Monetary Market. *Inside CD Futures.* Chicago: IMM, 1988.

International Monetary Market. *Inside Eurodollar Futures.* Chicago: IMM, 1988.

International Monetary Market. *Inside SP500 Stock Index Futures.* Chicago: IMM, 1988.

International Monetary Market. "International Monetary Market." Chicago: IMM, 1988.

International Monetary Market. *Opportunities in Interest Rates: T-Bill Futures.* Chicago: IMM, 1988.

International Monetary Market. *The S & P 100 Stock Index Futures Contract: Flexibility for Today's Investor.* Chicago: IMM, 1988.

International Monetary Market. "Understanding Futures in Foreign Exchange." Chicago: IMM, 1988.
Jacob, N. L. and R. R. Pettit. *Investments.* Homewood, IL: Richard D. Irwin, Inc., 1984.
Jarrow, R. and G. Oldfield. "Forward Contracts and Futures Contracts." *Journal of Financial Economics*, v. 8 (December 1981), pp. 373–382.
Johnson, L. L. "The Theory of Hedging and Speculation in Commodity Futures." *Review of Economic Studies*, v. 27 (March 1960), pp. 139–151.
Junkus, J. C. and C. F. Lee. "Use of Three Stock Index Futures in Hedging Decisions." *Journal of Futures Markets*, v. 5 (Summer 1985), pp. 201–222.
Kamara, A. "Issues in Futures Markets: A Survey." *Journal of Futures Markets*, v. 2 (Fall 1982), pp. 261–294.
Keynes, J. M. A *Treatise on Money*, Vol. 2. London: Macmillan & Co., 1930.
Khoury, S. J. *Investing Management: Theory and Application.* New York: Macmillan Publishing Co., Inc., 1983.
Kolb, R. *Understanding Futures Markets.* Glenview, IL: Scott, Foresman and Co., 1984.
Loosigian, A. M. *Interest Rate Futures.* Princeton, NJ: Dow Jones-Irwin Inc., 1980.
Markowitz, H. *Portfolio Selection.* New York: John Wiley and Sons, Inc., 1959.
Modest, D.M. and M. Sundaresan. "The Relationship between Spot and Futures Prices in Stock Index Futures Markets: Some Preliminary Evidence." *The Journal of Futures Markets*, v. 3 (Spring 1983), pp. 15–42.
Poole, W. "Using T-Bill Futures to Gauge Interest Rate Expectations." *Federal Reserve Bank of San Francisco Economic Review* (Spring 1978), pp. 7–19.
Powers, M. and D. Vogel. *Inside the Financial Futures Markets.* New York: John Wiley and Sons, Inc., 1981.
Rutledge, D. J. S. "Hedgers' Demand for Futures Contracts: A Theoretical Framework with Applications to the United States Soybean Complex." *Food Research Institute Studies*, v. 11 (March 1972), pp. 237–256.
Schwarz, E., J. Hill and T. Schneeweis. *Financial Futures: Fundamentals Strategies, and Applications.* Homewood, IL: Richard D. Irwin, 1986.
Sharpe, W. F. *Investments*, 3rd ed. Englewood Cliffs, NJ: Prentice-Hall, Inc., 1987.
Telser, L. "Futures and Actual Markets: How They are Related." *Journal of Business*, v. 59 (April 1986), pp. 5–20.
Telser, L. "Why There are Organized Futures Markets." *Journal of Law and Economics*, v. 24 (April 1981), pp. 1–22.
Toevs, A. and D. Jacob. "Futures and Alternative Hedge Ratio Methodologies." *Journal of Portfolio Management*, v. 12 (Spring 1986), pp. 60–70.
Weiner, N. S. "The Hedging Rationale for a Stock Index Futures Contract." *Journal of Futures Market*, v. 1 (Spring 1981), pp. 59–76.
Weiner, N. S. *Stock Index Futures.* New York: John Wiley and Sons, Inc., 1984.
Working, H. "Hedging Reconsidered." *Journal of Farm Economics*, v. 35 (June 1953), pp. 544–561.

Chapter 15

Commodity Futures, Financial Futures, and Stock-Index Futures

From the viewpoint of a security analyst and portfolio manager, knowledge of alternative future instruments is important because these instruments allow the analyst and manager to invest for profit and/or to hedge for risk. (How to use futures as portfolio insurance is discussed in Chapter 24.)

Following the basic concepts, valuation, and hedging strategies of futures instruments and markets discussed in Chapter 14, Chapter 15 investigates commodity futures, financial futures, and index futures. The first topic for discussion is commodity futures, which is followed by a discussion of financial futures and a study of stock-index futures.

15.1. Commodity Futures

Futures trading in the U.S. originated in the early 1800s for agricultural commodities. With no organized trading exchanges at that time, these original **commodity futures** contracts were actually forward agreements. The use of forward contracts evolved from necessity as spot markets increasingly proved their inability to handle excess supply or demand for commodities. However, these forward contracts also proved to have their limitations in that they were not sufficiently liquid for hedgers.

Today, there are 17 commodity exchanges offering futures contracts on more than 30 different commodities. Why are futures contracts traded on some commodities and not others? Remember that price risk is the underlying reason for the existence of futures markets. Any good (or service) that has a volatile price, either due to macroeconomic or environmental factors that can affect future supply and demand conditions, is a prime candidate to be traded in a futures market. Think of agricultural crops for a moment. The annual supply of a particular crop can be devastatingly affected by adverse weather conditions. So, if heavy rains and unexpectedly cold weather damaged a large portion of the wheat crop, supply would be reduced and prices that processors have to pay would rise. Conversely, if weather conditions turned out better than expected and the wheat harvest was very large, an overabundant supply of the crop would push prices down, hurting the farmer. Thus for good reason the agricultural industry was the first to utilize forward-pricing arrangements to aid in transferring the inherent price risks to those more willing to bear it.

Consider the alternatives open to the farmer for dealing with price uncertainty. Assume it is spring and crop planting is taking place. The farmer observes that although market prices are comfortably high, the wheat harvest may be large enough to force prices to become significantly lower. If prices drop, the farmer will lose money on the invested efforts and expenses. If the farmer does nothing and waits to see what happens to prices, the risk is substantial, especially if the odds increase that weather conditions will be better than expected. The farmer's other alternative would be to hedge the price risk in the futures market. To do this, the farmer would go into the futures market (through a commodities broker) and sell (go short) wheat futures contracts that expire at the same time that the crop would be brought to market. By taking such an action the farmer is indicating satisfaction with the current contracted price, as taking a position in the futures market essentially "locks in" the contracted futures price. Sample Problem 15.1 provides further illustration.

Sample Problem 15.1

Suppose that Farmer Smith is planting enough wheat to yield 50,000 bushels to bring to market in July. Furthermore, Farmer Smith observes that while current market prices are quite attractive at \$5.00 per bushel, a record wheat crop is expected.

So, Farmer Smith decides to hedge his price risk by going into the futures market and effectively selling his crop ahead of time through the sale of 10 wheat futures contracts (a contract represents 5,000 bushels) at \$5.00 per bushel, expiring in July. Assuming there is no basis risk, the outcomes of this transaction for falling and rising prices over the interim period are shown in Table 15.1.

Table 15.1. Hedging the Price Risk by Futures Market.

	Cash Market	Futures Market
Prices fall	March 1: Plants 50,000 bu (spot price = \$5.00/bu).	Sells ten contracts at \$5.00.
	July 15: Sells 50,000 bu at \$4.50/bu.	Buys ten contracts at \$4.50.
	Profit (loss) = \$0.50/bu × 50,000 bu = (\$25,000)	Profit (loss) = \$0.50/bu × 10 × 5,000 bu = \$25,000
	Net gain = 0	
Prices rise	March 1: Plants 50,000 bu (spot price = \$5.00/bu).	Sells ten contracts at \$5.00.
	July 15: Sells 50,000 bu at \$5.50/bu.	Buys ten contracts at \$5.50.
	Profit (loss) = \$0.50/bu × 50,000 bu = \$25,000	Profit (loss) = (\$0.50/bu) × 10 × 5,000 bu = (\$25,000)
	Net gain = 0	

While Sample Problem 15.1 is simple, its purpose is to demonstrate how the futures market is used and how the locking in of a price is achieved through hedging. That is, the farmer received \$5.00 per bushel at market time whether prices went lower or higher over the interim. Of course, it would be logical to wonder who would buy the futures contracts from the farmer if prices were expected to fall. As a matter of fact, it is the market participants known as the **speculators** who would do so, contrary to the farmer, who as a hedger took a position in the futures market opposite to the actual commodity. Instead, the speculator would buy the futures contracts from the farmer on the chance that prices would actually rise and not fall as expected. If prices rose, the speculator, who is long the contract, would profit handsomely because of the leverage involved. However, the large potential return is balanced by a large potential loss should prices fall.

The speculator's role in the futures market has been questioned throughout the history of futures markets. Essentially, what the speculator appears to be doing is gambling. Yet without the speculator the futures markets would cease to function efficiently, if at all. That is, the farmer (hedger) who goes into the market to hedge the price risk is actually transferring it to someone else, the speculator. When the hedger needs to liquidate a futures position by buying 10 contracts (as in the Sample Problem), the speculator is there to sell them. So the speculator contributes to the functioning of futures markets in two invaluable ways: (1) risk transference and (2) liquidity. Finally, remember that the speculator does not intend to provide such invaluable economic services for no return; the speculator takes on price risk and provides liquidity in return for potential profits.

15.2. Futures Quotations

As indicated in Fig. 15.1, *The Wall Street Journal* reports daily information on various types of futures contracts. The classifications include agriculture, energy, index, interest rate, metals and others such as currency, lumber, and weather. To find a certain future contract, for example, corn future, click the item "Corn, Oats, Rice" under the agriculture category in Fig. 15.1 and then we can obtain the corn future price in Fig. 15.2. There are a number of important terms and quotations related to futures contracts (and used in *The Wall Street Journal*) that are useful to know; these are shown in Table 15.2.

Also of concern are *commodity, exchanges, contract size*, and *prices.* For example, the commodity trade is corn. The exchange refers to the place where the futures contracts are traded: CBT signifies the Chicago Board of Trade. The contract size refers to the amount of spot commodity that the contract represents — for example, 5,000 bushels of corn. The price is the manner in which the prices are quoted; for instance, corn at 162 means corn sells for $1.62 per bushel.

15.3. Financial Futures

Financial futures take many forms. The following discussion focuses on currency futures (foreign-exchange futures or FX futures) and interest rate futures.

Financial futures are standardized futures contracts whose market prices are established through open outcry and hand signals in regulated commodity exchange. They represent a legally enforceable commitment to buy and sell a prespecified quantity and quality of a specific financial instrument during a predetermined future delivery month.

15.3.1. *Currency Futures*

Currency futures and their valuation theory are discussed in this section. A currency futures contract is similar to other commodity-futures contracts.

COMPLETE COMMODITIES & FUTURES DATA

Intraday Futures Prices

All Contracts in These Categories; Plus, Options and More Charting

Agriculture
- Food, fiber
- Livestock, Meat
- Corn, Oats, Rice
- Oilseeds
- Wheat
- Ethanol

Energy
- Electricity
- Petroleum

Index
- U.S.
- International

Interest Rate
- Americas
- Europe
- Euro
- EuroDollar, Yen
- Asian, Pacific

Metals
- Copper
- Gold
- Platinum
- Palladium
- Silver

Other
- Currency
- Lumber
- Weather

Spot Prices
- Cash Commodity Prices
- Spot Lumber & Panel Prices

Settlement Prices, Indexes & Other Statistics
- API Energy Data: Weekly Snapshot
- Commodities Indexes
- Electricity Price Indexes
- Electricity Production
- Futures Settlements
- London Metals Exchange Prices
- Performance by Asset Class

Futures Options - Closing Snapshot
- Agricultural
- Currency
- Energy
- Index
- Interest Rate
- Livestock
- Metals

See Update Times, when and how often each data feature is updated

Fig. 15.1. Futures Prices Data.
Source: *The Wall Street Journal.* http://online.wsj.com/mdc/public/page/mdc_commodities.html?mod=mdc_topnav_2_3000.

Select commodity type: Agriculture - Corn, Oats, Rice **Then select contract:** Corn Day - cbot Help

Corn Day - cbot

Data retrieved at Aug 24 00:57:22 GMT • All quotes are in Greenwich Mean Time • Data provided by eSignal

Contract	Month	Last	Chg	Open	High	Low	Volume	OpenInt	Exchange	Date	Time
CORN (DAY)	Sep '10	**417'2**s	-4'0	421'4	422'0	415'4	9679	157994	CBT	08/23/10	18:41:17
CORN (DAY)	Dec '10	**432'6**s	-3'4	436'6	437'2	430'4	13253	783794	CBT	08/23/10	18:41:17
CORN (DAY)	Mar '11	**446'2**s	-2'4	449'0	450'0	444'0	1240	155147	CBT	08/23/10	18:41:17
CORN (DAY)	May '11	**453'0**s	-2'2	455'2	455'6	452'4	11	32937	CBT	08/23/10	18:41:17
CORN (DAY)	Jul '11	**459'0**s	-2'0	461'4	461'4	458'4	2166	87466	CBT	08/23/10	18:41:17
CORN (DAY)	Sep '11	**448'6**s	-2'2	451'6	451'6	451'6	5	12321	CBT	08/23/10	18:41:17
CORN (DAY)	Dec '11	**440'2**s	-2'0	443'4	443'4	439'2	42	115121	CBT	08/23/10	18:41:17
CORN (DAY)	Mar '12	**451'0**s	-2'2	451'0	451'0	451'0	0	7610	CBT	08/23/10	18:41:17
CORN (DAY)	May '12	**457'0**s	-2'2	457'0	457'0	457'0	0	1256	CBT	08/23/10	18:41:17
CORN (DAY)	Jul '12	**462'0**s	-2'2	463'4	463'4	463'4	1	3780	CBT	08/23/10	18:41:17
CORN (DAY)	Sep '12	**447'4**s	-0'6	447'4	447'4	447'4	0	662	CBT	08/23/10	18:41:17
CORN (DAY)	Dec '12	**433'2**s	1'0	433'2	433'2	433'2	0	10973	CBT	08/23/10	18:41:17
CORN (DAY)	Jul '13	**452'2**s	1'0	452'2	452'2	452'2	0	286	CBT	08/23/10	18:41:17
CORN (DAY)	Dec '13	**433'2**s	1'0	433'2	433'2	433'2	0	561	CBT	08/23/10	18:41:17
CORN (DAY)	Jul '14	**448'2**s	1'0	448'2	448'2	448'2	0	0	CBT	08/23/10	18:41:17

- Chart - Options - Quotes Save Quote Board

Fig. 15.2. Corn Future Prices.

Source: *The Wall Street Journal*, August 24, 2010.

Table 15.2. Future Terms.

Term	Definition
Open	The price for the day's first trade, registered during the period designated as the opening of the market.
High	Highest price at which the commodity is sold during the day.
Low	Lowest price at which the commodity is sold during the day.
Settle	Since each contract is marked to market each day, the settlement price or the marking-to-market price is very important to investors. The settlement price is a figure determined by formula from within the closing range or it may be the closing price.
Change	The amount by which the settlement price changed from the previous day.
Lifetime high or low	The highest and lowest prices recorded for each contract maturity from the first day it was traded to the present.
Open interest	The number represents the quantity of open long positions at the exchange's clearinghouse for each contract.
Volume	The number of contracts actually traded on the exchange for a given trading session.

It promises future delivery of a standard amount of a foreign currency at a specified time, place, and price. This instrument can be used to hedge foreign-exchange risk for investors and firms involved in the import and export business.

15.3.1.1. *Evolution*

The concept of financial futures on currencies emerged as an anticipatory reaction to the end of the Bretton Woods Agreement, which called for the elimination of fixed parities between major currencies. So on May 16, 1972, the International Monetary Market (IMM) division of the Chicago Mercantile Exchange (CME) opened and offered the first organized trading of standardized futures contracts on foreign currencies. The application of the futures market and its trading mechanics to financial products was supported by a number of economists at the time, including Milton Friedman.

The need for these exchange-rate hedging tools has intensified in the last decade. The change in U.S. monetary policy in October 1979, which went from essentially "pegging" interest rates to letting them float in accordance with market forces, resulted in a significant increase in the volatility of market interest rates. The effects of highly volatile U.S. interest rates were felt heavily in other countries as well. Consequently, the already volatile foreign-exchange-rate market became even more turbulent, as investors and governments moved their funds from one currency to another in search of higher returns.

As interest rates change in one country, so does the value of its currency relative to those of other countries. So a U.S. corporation that contracts to purchase materials from some foreign firm with payment to be made three months from now is exposing itself to foreign-exchange risk. If at the end of the three-month period the U.S. dollar's value falls against the home currency of the foreign firm, the U.S. company will actually end up paying more for the materials than originally intended.

15.3.1.2. *Advantages*

Although forward markets have existed for some time to help alleviate exchange-rate or currency risk, they generally do not offer the liquidity or flexibility of the futures market. The establishment of currency futures has provided a means by which Interbank dealers can hedge their positions in spot or forward markets. Moreover, because each trade is guaranteed by the exchange's clearinghouse, participants need not analyze the credit risk of a large number of market counterparts, as might be necessary in establishing a forward contract. The funds of participants are protected by daily settlement of the change in position values; they are also safeguarded by the exchange's clearing house, whose members together guarantee all trades. Finally, futures markets allow dealers to trade anonymously and provide price insurance and arbitrage opportunities in the spot and forward markets.

The **IMM** is today one of three divisions of the CME, the largest futures exchange in the U.S. Presently, the foreign currencies for which futures contracts are traded include U.K. pound (ticker code GBP); Canadian dollars (CAD); Euro (EUR); Swiss franc (CHF); Japanese yen (JPY); Russian Ruble (RUB); and Australian dollar (AUD). Trading volume is concentrated in the futures on pounds, euro, Swiss franc, yen, Australian dollar and Canadian dollar. The currency futures prices can be found in Market Data of *The Wall Street Journal* (Fig. 15.3). When dealing with foreign exchange, it is important to realize that the price of a currency is in terms of a second currency. Both the numerator and denominator of the price ratio are in terms of money. For example, in Fig. 15.4 the euro is worth \$1.2663 (0.7897 dollar per euro) and the yen is worth \$0.0117 (85.22 Yen per dollar). All foreign-exchange rates are related as reciprocals. For other currencies (usually the currencies of the major trading nations), not

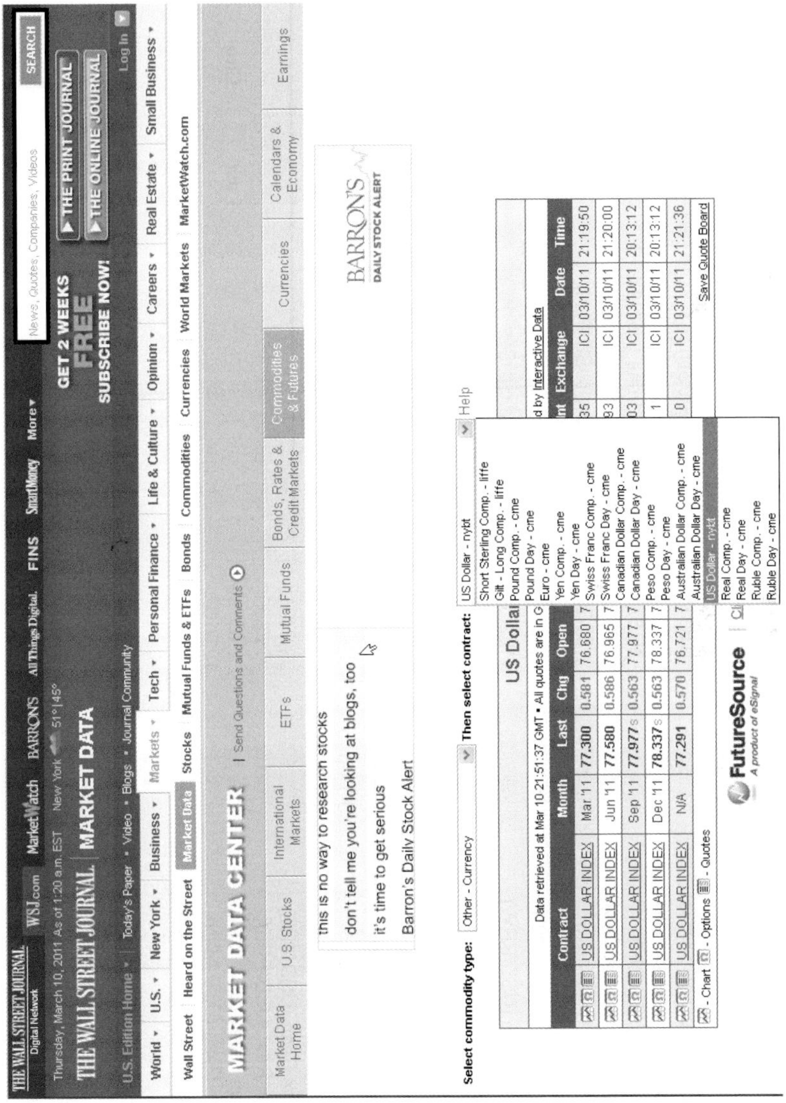

Fig. 15.3. Currency Futures Data.

Source: The Wall Street Journal, March 10, 2011.

CURRENCIES OVERVIEW

Asia — 3:14 p.m. EDT 08/24/10

	Last (bid)	Prior Day †
Australian Dollar (AUD/USD)	0.8850	0.8916
Hong Kong Dollar (USD/HKD)	7.7759	7.7742
Indian Rupee (USD/INR)	46.855	46.577
Indonesian Rupiah (USD/IDR)	8975	8969
Japanese Yen (USD/JPY)	84.19	85.22
Malaysian Ringitt (USD/MYR)	3.1418	3.1319
Singapore Dollar (USD/SGD)	1.3616	1.3570
S. Korean Won (USD/KRW)	1191.00	1182.31
Taiwanese Dollar (USD/TWD)	31.980	31.939
Thai Baht (USD/THB)	31.510	31.476

† Late Monday in New York.

Americas — 3:14 p.m. EDT 08/24/10

	Last (bid)	Prior Day †
Argentine Peso (USD/ARS)	3.9390	3.9401
Brazilian Real (USD/BRL)	1.7628	1.7690
Canadian Dollar (USD/CAD)	1.0594	1.0522
Mexican Peso (USD/MXN)	12.9299	12.9182

† Late Monday in New York.

Europe & Others — 3:14 p.m. EDT 08/24/10

	Last (bid)	Prior Day †
Euro (EUR/USD)	1.2679	1.2663
Czech Koruna (USD/CZK)	19.6110	19.5930
Denmark Krone (USD/DKK)	5.8726	5.8824
Norwegian Krone (USD/NOK)	6.2818	6.2344
Polish Zloty (USD/PLN)	3.1598	3.1716
Russian Ruble (USD/RUB)	30.8120	30.6940
Swedish Krona (USD/SEK)	7.4440	7.4074
Swiss Franc (USD/CHF)	1.0302	1.0412
U.K. Pound (GBP/USD)	1.5447	1.5516
Egyptian Pound (USD/EGP)	5.7028	5.6980
Israeli Shekel (USD/ILS)	3.8160	3.8124
S. African Rand (USD/ZAR)	7.3557	7.3638

† Late Monday in New York. Get this by E-mail

See Hourly Snapshots | See Full Daily Closing Prices

Currency Index — 3:13 p.m. EDT 08/24/10

	Last	Chg	% Chg
US Dollar Index	83.10	-0.03	-0.03

Fig. 15.4. Currency Rates.

Source: *The Wall Street Journal*, August 24, 2010.

only are the spot rates quoted but also the forward rates. For example, the Swiss franc, in addition to the spot rate, has quotes for the forward rates of 30, 60, and 90 days. The 30-day forward rate of 0.1576 means that a trader could buy French francs for delivery in 30 days at this price. The actual forward transaction takes place in 30 days. As is typical of forward markets, there is no specific location where trading takes place. Instead bankers around the world are linked together electronically. It is over this communication linkage that currencies are bought and sold in the spot and forward markets.

The futures market is different from the forward market. In the futures market, the maturity date of a given contract is fixed by the rules of the exchange. As each day passes, the futures contract gets closer to maturity. In the forward market, 30-, 60-, and 90-day contracts (or any other number of days) are available. However, contracts in the futures market mature four times a year (June, September, December, and March). In the forward market they mature every day.

In the forward market, the contract size is determined between the buyer and seller. In the futures market, only contracts of standardized amounts are traded — for example, 12.5 million yen for the Japanese-yen futures contract traded on the IMM.

15.3.1.3. *Pricing Currency Futures*

The arbitrage argument used to establish the price of a currency futures contract relative to the spot price is called **interest-rate parity** (which will be addressed again shortly). In the case of the U.S. dollar/British pound:

$$F_{t,T} = S_t \frac{(1 + R^{\$}_{t,T})}{(1 + R^{£}_{t,T})}, \tag{15.1}$$

where

$F_{t,T}$ = equilibrium price at time t for a currency futures contract maturing at time T;

S_t = spot price at time t for the foreign currency (to which the futures contract applies);

$R^{\$}_{t,T}$ = U.S. interest rate on risk-free securities maturing at time T; and

$R^{£}_{t,T}$ = British interest rate on risk-free securities maturing at time T.

Sample Problem 15.2 provides further illustration.

Sample Problem 15.2

As an example, suppose the U.S. dollar is currently quoted in the spot currency market for the British pound at $1.80/£. Interest rates in the U.S. and Britain for three months are 3% and 4%, respectively. What is the price of a three-month deposit futures contract for pounds?

Solution

Substituting all information into Equation (15.1):

$$F_{t,3\,\mathrm{mo}} = (\$1.80/£)\left(\frac{1+0.03}{1+0.04}\right)$$
$$= \$1.70/£.$$

Empirical tests have shown that the pricing relationship described by interest-rate parity holds very closely in the currency markets. The following is offered for clarification.

In the previous section on pricing theory for futures prices, spot prices of foreign currency were described as following a random walk. Thus, money as a liquid financial instrument incorporates anticipations of its future value into its current value. This is analogous to the manner in which future stock prices and dividend estimates are reflected in today's stock price. Using this rational-expectations hypothesis and momentarily assuming no inventory costs:

$$S_t = E_t(S_T), \tag{15.2}$$

or, today's price reflects the expected price for the foreign currency at time T.

Equation (15.2) can be reversed:

$$E_t(S_T) = S_t. \tag{15.3}$$

Hence, the best estimate for the spot price at some future point in time T is the current spot price of the currency. Since the currency-futures price at time t for a contract maturing at time T reflects the expected spot price for the foreign currency at time T (assuming no carrying costs):

$$F_{t,T} = E_t(S_T). \tag{15.4}$$

Consequently:

$$F_{t,T} = S_t. \tag{15.5}$$

So without carrying costs the current futures price equals the current spot price for any foreign currency. Sample Problem 15.3 provides further illustration.

Sample Problem 15.3

To see how the carrying cost (or relative opportunity cost) associated with interest has an effect on the valuation of foreign currency futures, assume that the spot and one-year futures prices for the British pound are \$1.30 and \$1.33, respectively. Suppose an American investor who bought \$1.3 million worth of pounds (£1 million) then invests £1 million at the 10% riskless rate yielded by one-year British-government securities. Furthermore, in order to hedge himself or herself against fluctuations in the dollar–pound exchange rate the investor sells £1 million worth of one-year futures contracts on pounds at 1.33 (equal to the value of 40 contracts). Assuming the investor holds his futures position to its maturity and then delivers the initial £1 million investment to close the position, here is a summary of the transactions and closing position value.

January 1, 1989	
Buy \$1.3 million worth of pounds.	
Invest proceeds at 10% British rate.	
Sell £1 million worth of futures at \$1.33.	
January 1, 1990	
Proceeds from earned interest	\$150,000
Deliver £1 million against short futures Position at \$1.33/£1.00	\$1,330,000
Gross revenue	\$1,460,000
Less initial investment	\$1,300,000
Net profit	\$160,000
Annual return	12.3%

From all these transactions the investor earns an annualized return of 12.3% on the original investment of \$1.3 million. This return is composed of the interest earned on the riskless British-government security and the 0.03 difference in spot and one-year futures prices for the pound (i.e., the investor sold the pound at \$1.33 but only paid \$1.30).

If the investor can borrow U.S. dollars at a rate less than 12.3%, then a riskless arbitrage opportunity is available. For instance, if the U.S. lending rate is 11.0%, the investor could borrow the initial capital of \$1.3 million and after one year repay the interest of 11% and clear a 1.3% risk-free return. However, this opportunity will not pass unnoticed. Arbitragers will buy pounds (bidding their price up), invest the pounds in one-year British-government securities yielding 10% (bidding their price up and yield down), and sell an equivalent number of futures contracts (forcing their price down). Finally, these arbitrage portfolios will be financed by borrowing U.S. dollars at the going 11.0% rate (forcing the rate to increase). All pressures discussed in this problem will continue until the arbitrage opportunity has dissipated. That point will be attained when:

$$S_t(1 + R^{\$}_{t,T}) = F_{t,T}(1 + R^{£}_{t,T}), \tag{15.6}$$

where $R^{\$}_{t,T}$ and $R^{£}_{t,T}$ interest rates on securities with the same maturity as the futures contract (one year, in this case).

Rearranging Equation (15.6) to solve for $F_{t,T}$, the futures price for a one-year contract on British pounds, we have

$$F_{t,T} = S_t \frac{(1 + R^{\$}_{t,T})}{(1 + R^{£}_{t,T})}. \tag{15.7}$$

This is the interest-rate parity relationship from Equation (15.1). Thus, the equilibrium one-year futures price for British pounds that would eliminate the arbitrage opportunity in the example can be computed as

$$\begin{aligned} F_{t,T} &= (\$1.30/£)\left(\frac{1 + 0.11}{1 + 0.10}\right) \\ &= \$1.3118/£. \end{aligned}$$

15.3.2. *The Traditional Theory of International Parity*

The writings of Keynes, Cassel, and Irving Fisher implicitly require four conditions for international currency parity.

(1) Financial markets are perfect. There are no controls, transaction costs, taxes, and so on.
(2) Goods markets are perfect. Shipment of goods anywhere in the world is costless.
(3) There is a single consumption good common to everyone.
(4) The future is known with certainty.

15.3.2.1. *Interest-Rate Parity*

For any two countries, the difference in their domestic interest rates must be equal to the forward exchange-rate differential:

$$\frac{1+R_i^t}{1+R_j^t} = \frac{F_{ij}^t}{S_{ij}^t},$$

where

R_i^t and R_j^t = the interest rate for countries i and j, respectively, in time t;
F_{ij}^t = the forward exchange rate of currency i in units of currency j quoted at time t for delivery at $t+1$; and
S_{ij}^t = the spot exchange rate of currency i in units of currency j at time t.

Keynes (1930) developed this relationship by using only the first assumption.

15.3.2.2. *Purchasing-Power Parity*

Cassel (1916a and 1916b) derived a **purchasing-power parity** theorem based on the first and third assumptions. According to the laws of one price in perfect markets, identical goods must have the same real price everywhere. Since it is assumed that every country consumes the same good (or basket of goods), a given currency has the same purchasing power in every country:

$$\frac{P_i^t}{P_j^t} = S_{ij}^t,$$

where

S_{ij}^t = the spot rate between countries i and j at time t; and
P_i^t and P_j^t = price level in countries i and j at time t, respectively.

15.3.2.3. *Fisherian Relation*

Using the first, third, and fourth assumption Irving Fisher (1930) showed that the nominal interest rate in every country will be equal to the real rate of interest plus the expected future inflation rate (this is called the **Fisherian relation**):

$$(1+R_j^t) = (1+r_j^t)(1+I_j^t),$$

where

r_j^t = the real rate of interest in country j at time t;
R_j^t = the nominal rate of interest at time t; and
I_j^t = the inflation rate at time t.

The implication of this relationship is that if the real rate of interest is equal everywhere, then the inflation differential between countries is fully reflected in their nominal interest rates.

15.3.2.4. *Forward Parity*

The forward exchange rate (F_{ij}^t) must be equal to the spot exchange rate at some future point in time (S_{ij}^{t+1}):

$$S_{ij}^{t+1} = F_{ij}^t.$$

This relationship **(forward parity)** must be true given the first three relationships derived above; otherwise, arbitrage opportunities would exist. Sample Problem 15.4 provides further illustration.

Sample Problem 15.4

Note that $\mathrm{I} + I_j^t = P_i^{t+1}/P_j^t$. Then, assuming that $1 + r_j^t = 1 + r_i^t$, it follows that

$$\frac{(1 + R_j^t)}{(1 + R_i^t)} = \frac{P_i^t}{P_j^t}\frac{P_j^{t+1}}{P_i^{t+1}} = \frac{S_{ij}^t}{S_{ij}^{t+1}},$$

which is equal to 1 plus the rate of currency appreciation (or depreciation).

In order to understand the pricing of futures contracts, the four relationships above must be used as building blocks. The linkages among interest rates, price levels, expected inflation, and exchange rates are all relevant in pricing a currency contract.

15.3.3. *Interest-Rate Futures*

Financial futures-related, interest-rate-sensitive instruments such as U.S. Treasury debt futures are the focus of this section. Sample daily price quotations for interest-rate futures are shown in Fig. 15.5.

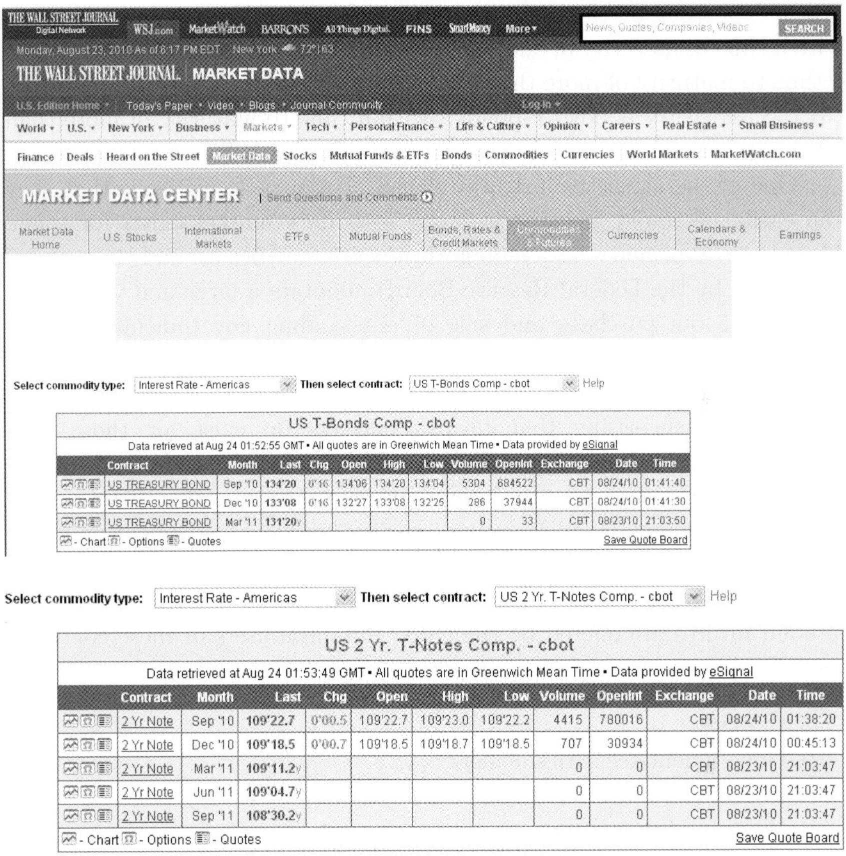

THE WALL STREET JOURNAL. Digital Network | WSJ.com | MarketWatch | BARRON'S | All Things Digital | FINS | SmartMoney | More

Monday, August 23, 2010 As of 8:17 PM EDT New York 72°|63

THE WALL STREET JOURNAL. MARKET DATA

U.S. Edition Home · Today's Paper · Video · Blogs · Journal Community · Log In

World · U.S. · New York · Business · Markets · Tech · Personal Finance · Life & Culture · Opinion · Careers · Real Estate · Small Business

Finance | Deals | Heard on the Street | Market Data | Stocks | Mutual Funds & ETFs | Bonds | Commodities | Currencies | World Markets | MarketWatch.com

MARKET DATA CENTER | Send Questions and Comments

Market Data Home | U.S. Stocks | International Markets | ETFs | Mutual Funds | Bonds, Rates & Credit Markets | Commodities & Futures | Currencies | Calendars & Economy | Earnings

Select commodity type: Interest Rate - Americas Then select contract: US T-Bonds Comp - cbot Help

US T-Bonds Comp - cbot

Data retrieved at Aug 24 01:52:55 GMT • All quotes are in Greenwich Mean Time • Data provided by eSignal

Contract	Month	Last	Chg	Open	High	Low	Volume	OpenInt	Exchange	Date	Time
US TREASURY BOND	Sep '10	**134'20**	0'16	134'06	134'20	134'04	5304	684522	CBT	08/24/10	01:41:40
US TREASURY BOND	Dec '10	**133'08**	0'16	132'27	133'08	132'25	286	37944	CBT	08/24/10	01:41:30
US TREASURY BOND	Mar '11	**131'20**y					0	33	CBT	08/23/10	21:03:50

- Chart - Options - Quotes Save Quote Board

Select commodity type: Interest Rate - Americas Then select contract: US 2 Yr. T-Notes Comp. - cbot Help

US 2 Yr. T-Notes Comp. - cbot

Data retrieved at Aug 24 01:53:49 GMT • All quotes are in Greenwich Mean Time • Data provided by eSignal

Contract	Month	Last	Chg	Open	High	Low	Volume	OpenInt	Exchange	Date	Time
2 Yr Note	Sep '10	**109'22.7**	0'00.5	109'22.7	109'23.0	109'22.2	4415	780016	CBT	08/24/10	01:38:20
2 Yr Note	Dec '10	**109'18.5**	0'00.7	109'18.5	109'18.7	109'18.5	707	30934	CBT	08/24/10	00:45:13
2 Yr Note	Mar '11	**109'11.2**y					0	0	CBT	08/23/10	21:03:47
2 Yr Note	Jun '11	**109'04.7**y					0	0	CBT	08/23/10	21:03:47
2 Yr Note	Sep '11	**108'30.2**y					0	0	CBT	08/23/10	21:03:47

- Chart - Options - Quotes Save Quote Board

Fig. 15.5. Interest Rate Futures Data.
Source: *The Wall Street Journal*, August 24, 2010.

15.3.4. *U.S. Treasury Debt Futures*

The U.S. Treasury issues debt securities to finance government operations and the federal deficit. These securities are backed by the government and are considered to be free of default risk. All Treasury debt is virtually identical except for differing maturities and yields. Corporations, financial institutions, investment funds, and state and local governments all utilize short-term U.S. Treasury securities as a repository for temporary surpluses of cash. Individual, institutional, and foreign investors use longer-term U.S. Treasury securities to secure their capital and insure its return for more extended periods of time. The U.S. Treasury debt can be classified into three types, depending on the time to maturity: (1) U.S. Treasury bills (T-bills), with a time to maturity of one year, (2) U.S. Treasury notes (T-notes), with a time to maturity of more than one year up to and including 10 years, and (3) U.S. Treasury bonds (T-bonds), with a time to maturity of more than 10 years.

One of the attractive features of U.S. Treasury securities is that they can easily be resold, because a strong secondary market exists for them. More then 30 primary dealers in government securities around the country (approved by the Federal Reserve Board) maintain a large and very liquid market for the purchase and sale of outstanding government securities (mostly those of the Treasury).

Considering the existence of such a well-developed secondary market, it might be surprising that futures markets do exist for those cash securities. The reason is interest-rate risk. Moreover, the homogeneity, relative risklessness, and correlation with the rates on other risky-market debt securities make U.S. Treasury securities an ideal instrument on which to trade futures for hedging purposes.

T-bill futures are traded at the IMM, while T-note futures and T-bond futures are offered by the CBT. Potential users of these contracts include:

(1) Banks;
(2) Government-securities dealers;
(3) Investment bankers;
(4) Bond-fund managers;
(5) Pension-fund managers;
(6) Trust-fund managers;
(7) Corporate treasurers;
(8) Insurance-company portfolio managers;
(9) Speculators; and
(10) Arbitragers.

The potential applications of T-bill, T-note, and T-bond futures include:

(1) Locking in yields on futures purchases of T-bills, T-notes, or T-bonds.
(2) Protecting the value of a portfolio comprised of government securities.
(3) Hedging participation in auctions for T-bills, T-notes, and T-bonds.
(4) Hedging corporate debt issuance.
(5) Cross-hedging other domestic and Eurodollar financial instruments.
(6) Pursuing speculative opportunity with risk capital.

(7) Profiting from price differentials (arbitrage).
(8) Discovering current and forward price information.

15.3.4.1. *Characteristics of T-Bill Futures*

A futures contract on 90-day T-bills was initiated by the IMM on January 6, 1976. This futures contract calls for the delivery of a 90-day T-bill with a face value of $1 million. T-bills (as well as T-notes and T-bonds) are traditionally quoted in terms of their yield to maturity. Since interest rates (or yields) and prices of debt securities move inversely, the common perception that a long position makes money as the quoted values increase does not apply to such instruments. That is, if someone bought a 90-day T-bill with a 10% yield and yields then rose, the investor would lose money on a long position.

The IMM quote system for its interest-rate securities is essentially an index based on the difference between the actual T-bill price and 100.00. Hence a T-bill yield of 10% would be quoted on the IMM at 90.00. This method fits the traditional quotation procedures in futures trading where the bid price is lower than the offer (to sell) price. Furthermore, each 0.01% move in the price of a T-bill futures contract is equal to one basis point, which is equal to $25.

When the IMM T-bill futures contract reaches the maturity date, the seller of the contract may have to make delivery of the underlying T-bill. Figure 15.6 illustrates the delivery process. The major function of the clearinghouse is to see that the transfer and payment (4B and 4S in Fig. 15.6) take place in a timely fashion. Should either party default in any way, the clearinghouse will complete the transaction and then seek to recover from the defaulting party.

15.3.4.2. *Pricing T-Bill Futures Contracts*

Studies by Poole (1978) and Rendleman and Carabini (1979) determined upper and lower bounds for the theoretical price of a T-bill futures contract. In following their derivation, which is based upon an arbitrage relationship between the spot and futures markets, first consider the situation of an investor faced with the following choice. (1) Invest in a 182-day T-bill, or (2) Invest in a 91-day T-bill and buy a futures contract maturing 91 days hence. In a perfectly efficient market, the investor should be indifferent between these equivalent investments, since both offer the same return.

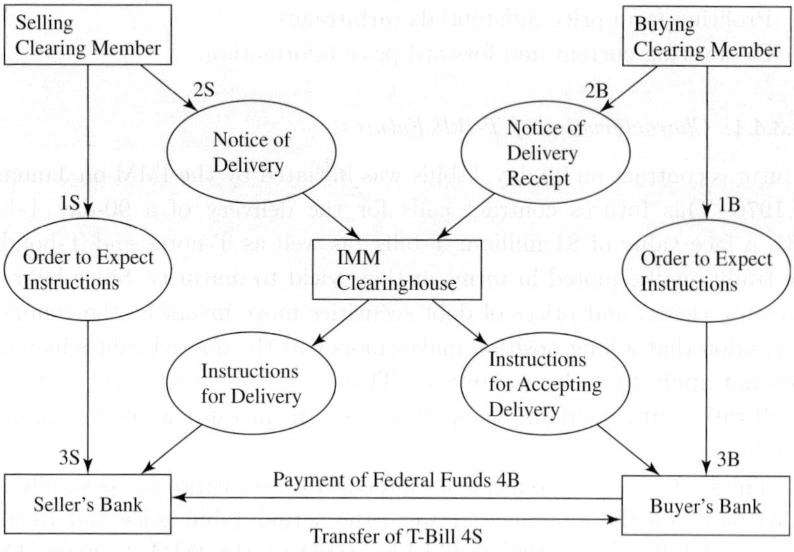

Fig. 15.6. Delivery of an IMM T-Bill Futures Contract.

Now let

$$\begin{aligned} Y_m &= \text{yield on a 91-day T-bill, } m = 1; \\ Y_n &= \text{yield on a 182-day T-bill, } m = 2; \\ Y_{Fu,m} &= \text{yield on a futures contract maturing } m \text{ days from now; and} \\ Y_{Fw,n-m} &= \text{implied forward rate on a T-bill with a life equal to } n - m. \end{aligned}$$

If the market is to be in equilibrium, then:

$$[(1+Y_m)(1+Y_{Fu,m})]^{1/n} = [(1+Y_m)(1+Y_{Fw,n-m})]^{1/n} = (1+Y_n). \quad (15.8)$$

In other words, investing in a 91-day T-bill and then buying a futures contract maturing in 91 more days is equivalent to initially investing in a 182-day T-bill.

Arbitrage conditions will arise if

$$\begin{aligned} Y_{Fu,m} &< Y_{Fw,n-m}, \\ Y_{Fu,m} &> Y_{Fw,n-m}. \end{aligned} \quad (15.9)$$

To compute $Y_{Fw,n-m}$, the implied forward rate of a T-bill with a life of $n - m$, the following example is utilized. Assume that the 182-day T-bill rate is 11% and the three-month T-bill rate is 10%. The implied three-month forward rate is then:

$$Y_{Fw,3} = \frac{(1+Y_n)^{n/m}}{(1+Y_m)} - 1 = \frac{(1+0.11)^2}{(1+0.10)} - 1. \tag{15.10}$$

If an arbitrager observed that the futures rate was above 12% (or had a price less than 88.00), he or she could profit from the following strategy.

(1) Borrow money at 11% (assuming lending and borrowing rates are equal) by selling short a six-month T-bill.
(2) Buy a three-month T-bill.
(3) Simultaneously, buy one T-bill futures contract with a time to maturity of three months.

Combining the spot and futures T-bill positions results in a synthetic six-month T-bill with a yield exceeding that realized on the actual six-month T-bill. For instance, if the futures contract has a rate of 15%, the six-month annualized return on the synthetic position is

$$\sqrt{(1+0.10)(1+0.13) - 1} = 11.48\%.$$

The **arbitrage profit** is equal to the realized yield on the synthetic position less the cost of establishing that position or 11.48% −11.00% = 0.48%. On a $1 million position, the arbitrager would have made $4,800 essentially risk-free.

Of course, this scenario could be reversed for the situation where the observed futures rate was less than 12% (or had a price greater than 88.00). Based on these examples, the theoretical price for a T-bill future can be derived from Equation (15.8). First, by taking its inverse:

$$\frac{1}{(1+Y_m)} \times \frac{1}{(1+Y_{Fu,m})} = \frac{1}{(1+Y_n)^n}, \tag{15.11}$$

or, equivalently:

$$P_m \times P_{Fu} = P_n, \tag{15.12}$$

where P_n is the price of an n-day T-bill paying $1 at maturity. And, therefore:

$$P_{Fu} = \frac{P_n}{P_m}, \tag{15.13}$$

where

P_{Fu} = price of a T-bill futures contract, quoted as the difference between \$100 and the annualized discount from par assuming 360 days in a year;
P_n = spot price of an n-day T-bill; and
P_m = spot price of an m-day T-bill ($n > m$).

Equation (15.13) can be altered to account for transaction costs such as commissions and a greater than zero bid-ask dealer spread (or bid-offer). In doing so the boundary conditions for the price of a T-bill futures contract are obtained:

$$100\frac{P_n^A}{P_m^B} - CC \le P_{Fu} \le 100\frac{P_n^A}{P_m^B} + CC,$$

where

CC = round-trip commission costs per \$100 of face value;
P_n^A = the price at which a dealer will sell an n-day T-bill; and
P_m^B = the price at which a dealer will buy an m-day T-bill.

Sample Problem 15.5 provides further illustration.

Sample Problem 15.5

Using Equation (15.13), compute the theoretical futures price for the IMM December 1989 contract as of June 7, 1988. Assume that the deliverable bill (in period) against the futures contract is the T-bill maturing March 21, 1989, with a bid price of 10.67 and ask price of 10.59. Also assume \$0.004 per \$100 of face value as the round-trip commission cost.

Solution

(1) Determine the T-bill rate corresponding to the m period — the interval between June 7, 1989, and the third Thursday of December 1989, the delivery date of the contract (i.e., $m = 188$ days).
(2) Find the price of this T-bill maturing in (approximately) 188 days (December 27) from the U.S. T-bill data listed earlier. Its bid price is 10.47 and its ask price is 10.41.
(3) Now calculate P_{Fu} without commission costs using Equation (15.13) and an average of the bid and ask prices for the m period and n period

and n-period T-bills.

$$P_{Fu} = \frac{100 - [10.63 \times (279/360)]}{100 - [10.44 \times (188/360)]}$$
$$= \frac{100 - 8.238}{100 - 5.452} = \frac{91.762}{84.548} = 0.97053.$$

Now, to get the quarterly yield (price) for the futures:

$$100 - 97.053 = 2.947.$$

And the annualized yield:

$$2.947 \times \frac{360}{91} = 11.658.$$

Finally, compute the theoretical futures price P_{Fu}:

$$P_{Fu} = 100 - 11.658 = 88.342.$$

In comparing this price with the market price of 88.32 for the December 1989 T-bill futures contract, it becomes clear that the calculated price is upwardly biased. This disparity could be due to neglect of transaction costs such as commissions. So the commission costs will be calculated on an annualized basis (like the futures price) and subtracted from the computed price.

$$0.004 \times \frac{360}{91} = 0.016,$$

and

$$P_{Fu} = 88.342 - 0.016 = 88.326.$$

15.3.4.3. *Characteristics of T-Note and T-Bond Futures*

T-bond futures as on the CBT require the delivery of a U.S. T-bond with a face value of $100,000 and maturing at least 15 years from maturity. Prices are quoted as a percentage of par in the same way as GNMA futures prices are quoted. With daily trading volume in excess of 100,000 contracts on average, the T-bond futures contract is currently the most successful futures contract ever. The depth of trading in this contract is revealed by the existence of outstanding T-bond contracts with maturities nearly three years into the future.

Growing in popularity is the **T-note futures** contract, also offered by the CBT. One of the underlying stimuli for its success is the growing proportion of total Treasury debt, which is represented by T-note securities. The T-note futures contract specifies the delivery of a U.S. Treasury note with a face value of $100,000 and a maturity of no less than 6.5 years and no more than 10 years form the date of delivery. Additional contract specification for T-note and T-bond futures are listed in Fig. 15.7.

15.3.5. *The Eurodollar Futures Market*

A **Eurodollar** is any dollar on deposit outside the U.S. Typically this refers to dollar balances on the books of the London branches of the U.S. and other major would-class banks. On occasion Eurodollars are also deposited in other locations, such as Nassau or the Grand Cayman Islands. An important aspect of these deposits is that, because of their location outside of the U.S. they do not fall under U.S. jurisdiction. Therefore, Eurodollars are not governed by the same regulations that apply to domestic deposits, set by the Federal Reserve.

15.3.5.1. *Evolution*

The Eurodollar market evolved in the 1950s in response to Federal Reserve restrictions on the maximum allowable interest rate to be paid on a deposit. Foreign merchant banks were able to pay a larger rate on dollar deposits than was allowed by Regulation Q and still make an arbitrage profit by selling dollars in their own country on a forward basis for a return even higher than that offered by the dollar depositors. To defend themselves against a loss of deposits, U.S. banks eventually reacted to this unconventional banking practice by allowing their London branches to enter this market and also take in dollar deposits.

By the mid 1960s the Eurodollar market had grown significantly and funds became available for dollar-denominated loans to be made by European banks to commercial lenders. Moreover, in 1966, Eurodollar CDs were issued by banks in the United Kingdom to increase the attractiveness of the Euro market to depositors and to meet the increased demand for funds from the U.S. These securities were negotiable instruments among the investor and the (foreign) banking institution. As the Eurodollar markets developed and matured, formal lines of credit and sovereign risk limitations were formalized by participants.

2-Year U.S. Treasury Note Futures

Underlying Unit	One U.S. Treasury note having a face value at maturity of $200,000.	
Deliverable Grades	U.S. Treasury notes with an original term to maturity of not more than five years and three months and a remaining term to maturity of not less than one year and nine months from the first day of the delivery month and a remaining term to maturity of not more than two years from the last day of the delivery month. The invoice price equals the futures settlement price times a conversion factor, plus accrued interest. The conversion factor is the price of the delivered note ($1 par value) to yield 6 percent.	
Price Quote	Points ($2,000) and quarters of 1/32 of a point. For example, 109-16 represents 109 16/32, 109-162 represents 109 16.25/32, 109-165 represents 109 16.5/32, and 109-167 represents 109 16.75/32. Par is on the basis of 100 points.	
Tick Size (minimum fluctuation)	One-quarter of one thirty-second (1/32) of one point ($15.625, rounded up to the nearest cent per contract), including intermonth spreads.	
Contract Months	The first five consecutive contracts in the March, June, September, and December quarterly cycle.	
Last Trading Day	Last business day of the calendar month. Trading in expiring contracts closes at 12:01 p.m. on the last trading day.	
Last Delivery Day	Third business day following the last trading day.	
Delivery Method	Federal Reserve book-entry wire-transfer system.	
Settlement	U.S. Treasury Futures Settlement Procedures	
Position Limits	Current Position Limits	
Block Minimum	Block Trade Minimums	
All or None Minimum	All or None Minimums	
Rulebook Chapter	CBOT Chapter 21	
Trading Hours (All times listed are Central Time)	OPEN OUTCRY	MON - FRI: 7:20 a.m. - 2:00 p.m.
	CME GLOBEX	SUN - FRI: 5:30 p.m. - 4:00 p.m.
Ticker Symbol	OPEN OUTCRY	TU
	CME GLOBEX	ZT
Exchange Rule	These contracts are listed with, and subject to, the rules and regulations of CBOT.	

U.S. Treasury Bond Futures

Underlying Unit	One U.S. Treasury bond having a face value at maturity of $100,000.	
Deliverable Grades	U.S. Treasury bonds that, if callable, are not callable for at least 15 years from the first day of the delivery month or, if not callable, have a remaining term to maturity of at least 15 years from the first day of the delivery month. **Note: Beginning with the March 2011 expiry, the deliverable grade for T-Bond futures will be bonds with remaining maturity of at least 15 years, but less than 25 years, from the first day of the delivery month.** The invoice price equals the futures settlement price times a conversion factor, plus accrued interest. The conversion factor is the price of the delivered bond ($1 par value) to yield 6 percent.	
Price Quote	Points ($1,000) and 1/32 of a point. For example, 134-16 represents 134 16/32. Par is on the basis of 100 points.	
Tick Size (minimum fluctuation)	One thirty-second (1/32) of one point ($31.25), except for intermonth spreads, where the minimum price fluctuation shall be one-quarter of one thirty-second of one point ($7.8125 per contract).	
Contract Months	The first three consecutive contracts in the March, June, September, and December quarterly cycle.	
Last Trading Day	Seventh business day preceding the last business day of the delivery month. Trading in expiring contracts closes at 12:01 p.m. on the last trading day.	
Last Delivery Day	Last business day of the delivery month.	
Delivery Method	Federal Reserve book-entry wire-transfer system.	
Settlement	U.S. Treasury Futures Settlement Procedures	
Position Limits	Current Position Limits	
Block Minimum	Block Trade Minimums	
All or None Minimum	All or None Minimums	
Rulebook Chapter	CBOT Chapter 18	
Trading Hours (All times listed are Central Time)	OPEN OUTCRY	MON - FRI: 7:20 a.m. - 2:00 p.m.
	CME GLOBEX	SUN - FRI: 5:30 p.m. - 4:00 p.m.
Ticker Symbol	OPEN OUTCRY	US
	CME GLOBEX	ZB
Exchange Rule	These contracts are listed with, and subject to, the rules and regulations of CBOT.	

Fig. 15.7. Contract Specification of T-Bonds and T-Note Futures.
Source: CME Group, U.S. Treasury Bond Futures and 2-Year U.S. Treasury Note Futures.

A bank lending funds in the Eurodollar market is exposed to essentially three risks:

(1) Interest-rate risk;
(2) Credit risk; and
(3) Sovereign risk.

The interest-rate risk involved with a Eurodollar loan is virtually identical to that in previous explanations and examples. Credit risk, while present to some extent in the U.S. cash CD market, is a larger concern in the Eurodollar market because of the difficulties that can arise when trying to analyze a foreign borrower's financial position. Finally, sovereign risk is unique to the arena of international lending. **Sovereign risk** refers to the unfavorable consequences that can have impact on a bank's investment if a foreign government is overthrown, becomes economically unstable, or passes detrimental regulations affecting the movement of funds. Most banks will have sovereign-risk limitations restricting the total amount placed on deposit with (or loaned to) institutions in any one country.

The relationship between three-month rates offered on Eurodollar deposits (as measured by the London Interbank Offered Rate (LIBOR) rate), U.S. CDs, and U.S. T-bills can be visualized for a two-year period in Fig. 15.8. A number of aspects of the relationship between these three securities can be noted from this chart. Most prominent among the rate

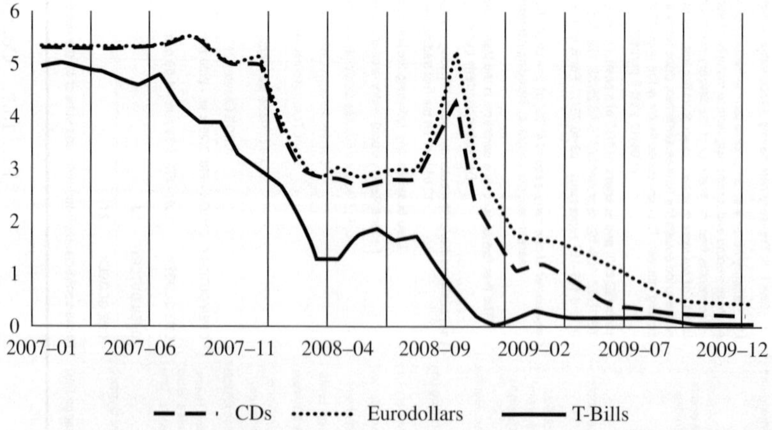

Fig. 15.8. Three-Month Rates on U.S. CDs, U.S. T-Bills, and Eurodollar deposits, Jan 2007–Jan 2010 (monthly data).
Source: Board of Governors of the Federal Reserve System, https://www.federalreserve.gov/default.htm.

relationships is that Eurodollar rates are higher than CD rates, which are higher than T-bill rates — a ranking consistent with the level of risk inherent in these securities. Not so obvious is the variation in the spread (difference) between Eurodollar rates and CD rates, which do not simply rise together when rates rise and fall together when rates fall. Rather, changes in the interest-rate spread are affected by a variety of unpredictable market forces and decisions of U.S. and foreign governments. For example, increasing U.S. interest rates tend to strengthen the dollar, narrowing the spread between Eurodollars and domestic CD rates. Unlike the behavior of the spread between Eurodollar and CD rates, the Eurodollar rates and Treasury rates have a less predictable tendency to rise together as rates rise.

The rationale for briefly discussing the Eurodollar market and the relationship of its rates to domestic rates is to provide a basis for understanding exactly what Eurodollar futures are, as well as to make it easier to understand why Eurodollar futures exist and how they can be used. Hence, the focus now turns to the Eurodollar futures contract and market.

15.3.5.2. *Eurodollar Futures*

Eurodollar futures are traded on the Chicago Mercantile Exchange (CME) (Fig. 15.9) and the London International Financial Exchange (LIFFE). The Eurodollar futures contract has as its underlying instrument a three-month Eurodollar time deposit in the amount of $1 million as shown in Fig. 15.10. The primary use of Eurodollar futures as a hedging vehicle is similar to that of other hedging vehicles; they are capable of protecting against detrimental changes in interest rates. Sample Problem 15.7 is offered to help clarify their application.

Sample Problem 15.7

A *Long Hedge with Eurodollar Futures.* Suppose that the London branch of a U.S. bank anticipates a decline in rates from September 16 to December 16. Furthermore, on June 12, the bank makes a three-month loan in the Eurodollar market and finances the loan with the funds from a six-month Eurodollar CD. When the three-month loan matures, the bank will relend the principal and interest received for another three months. Such a reverse liability-asset gap is partially the result of a downward-sloping yield curve where short-term rates are higher than longer-term rates.

Since the bank's profit is the spread between the higher rate at which they loan money and the lower rate at which they borrow money, a decline in the former without a corresponding decline in the latter will adversely affect

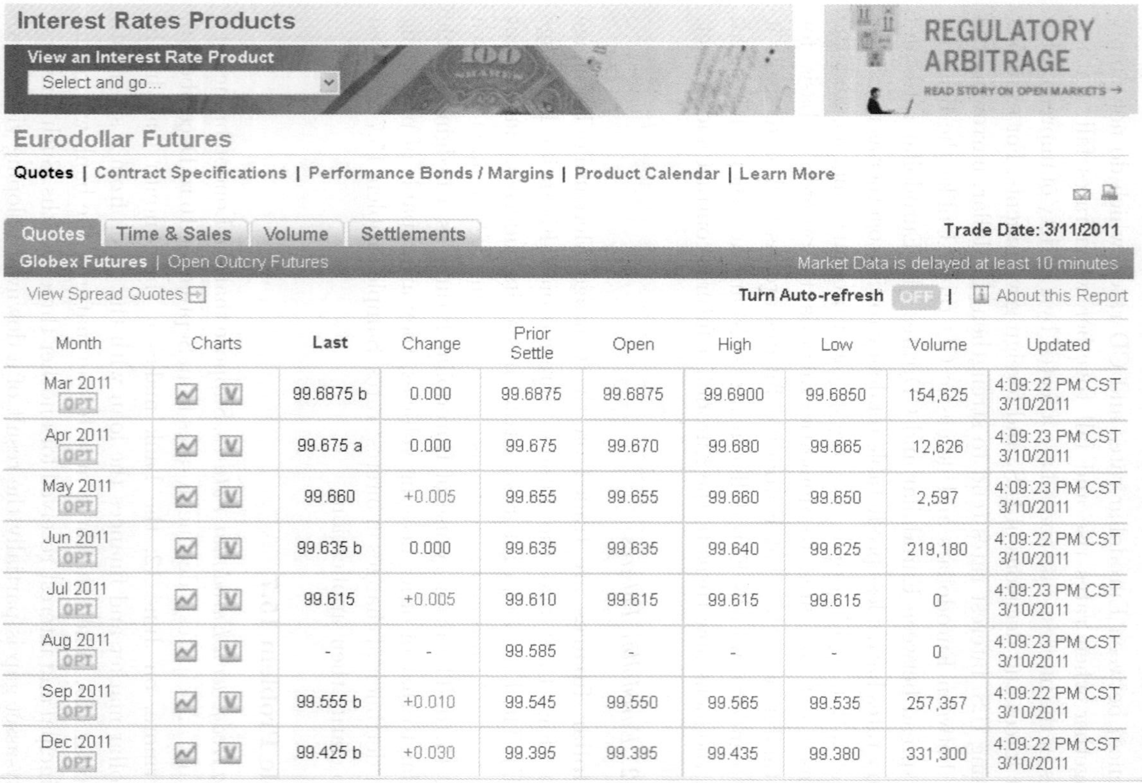

Month	Charts	Last	Change	Prior Settle	Open	High	Low	Volume	Updated
Mar 2011 OPT		99.6875 b	0.000	99.6875	99.6875	99.6900	99.6850	154,625	4:09:22 PM CST 3/10/2011
Apr 2011 OPT		99.675 a	0.000	99.675	99.670	99.680	99.665	12,626	4:09:23 PM CST 3/10/2011
May 2011 OPT		99.660	+0.005	99.655	99.655	99.660	99.650	2,597	4:09:23 PM CST 3/10/2011
Jun 2011 OPT		99.635 b	0.000	99.635	99.635	99.640	99.625	219,180	4:09:22 PM CST 3/10/2011
Jul 2011 OPT		99.615	+0.005	99.610	99.615	99.615	99.615	0	4:09:23 PM CST 3/10/2011
Aug 2011 OPT		-	-	99.585	-	-	-	0	4:09:23 PM CST 3/10/2011
Sep 2011 OPT		99.555 b	+0.010	99.545	99.550	99.565	99.535	257,357	4:09:22 PM CST 3/10/2011
Dec 2011 OPT		99.425 b	+0.030	99.395	99.395	99.435	99.380	331,300	4:09:22 PM CST 3/10/2011

Fig. 15.9. Eurodollar Futures Quotes.
Source: CME Group, March 10, 2011, http:// www.cmegroup.com/.

Eurodollar Futures

Underlying Instrument	Eurodollar Time Deposit having a principal value of USD $1,000,000 with a three-month maturity.	
Price Quote	Quoted in IMM Three-Month LIBOR index points or 100 minus the rate on an annual basis over a 360 day year (e.g., a rate of 2.5% shall be quoted as 97.50). 1 basis point = .01 = $25.	
Tick Size (minimum fluctuation)	One-quarter of one basis point (0.0025 = $6.25 per contract) in the nearest expiring contract month; One-half of one basis point (0.005 = $12.50 per contract) in all other contract months. The "new" front-month contract begins trading in 0.0025 increments on the same Trade Date as the Last Trading Day of the expiring "old" front-month contract.	
Contract Months	Mar, Jun, Sep, Dec, extending out 10 years (total of 40 contracts) plus the four nearest serial expirations (months that are not in the March quarterly cycle). The new contract month terminating 10 years in the future is listed on the Tuesday following expiration of the front quarterly contract month.	
Last Trading Day	The second London bank business day prior to the third Wednesday of the contract expiry month. Trading in the expiring contract closes at 11:00 a.m. London Time on the last trading day.	
Final Settlement	Expiring contracts are cash settled to 100 minus the British Bankers' Association survey of 3-month U.S. Dollar LIBOR on the last trading day. Final settlement price will be rounded to four decimal places, equal to 1/10,000 of a percent, or $0.25 per contract.	
Position Limits	None	
Block Minimum	Block Trading Minimums	
All or None Minimum	All or None Minimums	
Rulebook Chapter	CME Chapter 452	
Trading Hours (All times listed are Central Time)	OPEN OUTCRY	MON-FRI: 7:20 a.m. - 2:00 p.m.
	CME GLOBEX	SUN - FRI: 5:00 p.m. - 4:00 p.m. CT
Ticker Symbol	OPEN OUTCRY	ED
	CME GLOBEX	GE
Exchange Rule	These contracts are listed with, and subject to, the rules and regulations of CME.	

Fig. 15.10. Eurodollar Futures Contract.
Source: CME Group, http://www.cmegroup.com/.

profitability. In this scenario where declining rates are expected by the end of the first three-month loan, the bank is prone to reinvestment-rate risk.

To alleviate the problem, the bank chooses to fix the reinvestment rate for the latter three-month investment horizon through a long position in Eurodollar Futures. On June 12, the Eurodollar contract for September delivery was priced at an index of 86.53(100% − 13.47%), the six-month

Table 15.3. Hedging Interest Rate Risk by Future Market.

	Spot-Market Transaction	Futures-Market Transaction
June 12	Issue a $1,000,000 six-month Euro CD at 13.00 percent.	Buy one Eurodollar futures contract for September delivery at 86.53 (13.47 percent).
	Loan the $1,000,000 in the Euro market for three months at 14,00 percent.	
September 14: interest rates fall as expected.	Return the $1,000,000 principal plus interest of $33,299 at the current LIBOR rate of 12.00 percent (a net reinvestment rate decline of 2.0 percent).	Sell one Eurodollar futures contract at 88.00 (12.00 percent).
Results	Bought futures contract at	86.53 (13.47 percent)
	Sold futures contract at	88.00
	Profit on the contract (+147 basis points)	1.47 (1.47 percent)
	Dollar value of profit from futures transaction (each basis point is worth $25): 147 × $25 × 1 contract	$3,675
	Loss caused by decline in LIBOR lending rate: $[(1.02)^{0.25} - 1] \times \$1{,}033{,}299$	($5,128)
	Total net loss	($1,453)

Eurodollar CD rate was 13%, and the initial three-month loan was made at the LIBOR rate of 14%. Table 15.3 summarizes the transactions results. Note that a dollar-per-dollar hedge ratio for this example is assumed.

As Table 15.3 indicates, the use of the futures position to hedge the interest-rate risk allows the bank to reduce its reinvestment rate loss by 71%. Use of a more sophisticated hedge ratio such as Howard and D'Antonio's might have resulted in an even stronger position in futures, further cutting the bank's losses.

15.4. Stock-Index Futures

Stock-index futures offer the investor a medium for expressing an opinion on the general course of the market. In addition, these contracts can be used by portfolio managers in a variety of ways to alter the risk-return distribution of their stock portfolios. For instance, much of a sudden upward surge in the market could be missed by the institutional investor due to the time it takes to get money into the stock market. By purchasing stock-index futures contracts, the institutional investor can enter the market immediately and then gradually unwind the long futures position as he or she is able to get more funds invested in stocks. Conversely, after a run up in the value of the stock portfolio (assuming it is well diversified and correlates well with one of the major indexes), a portfolio manager might desire to lock in the profits until after being required to report the quarterly return on the portfolio. By selling an appropriate number of stock-index futures contracts, the institutional investor could offset any losses on the stock portfolio with corresponding gains on the futures position. Before presenting examples using stock-index futures, the origination of these contracts, the different types offered, and their theoretical pricing models are reviewed.

The first stock-index futures contract was offered by the Kansas City Board of Trade (KCBT) on the Value Line Composite Stock Index (VLCI) on February 24, 1982. Contracts on the S&P 500 stock index and NYSE composite stock index were soon offered by the IMM (a division of the Chicago Mercantile Exchange) and the NYSE, respectively. Most recently, there are multiple stock-index futures offered by CME Group, such as S&P 500 Futures, NASDAQ 100 Futures, and Dow Jones Futures.

The calculation of the market value for a stock-index futures contract on any given day is simply a matter of multiplying the current index price for the contract by the appropriate dollar amount. Each of the U.S. stock-index futures is listed in order of market popularity. Each contract bought and sold on a particular day is included in the calculation of daily trading volume. Fig. 15.11 shows prices, volume, and open interest for S&P 500 indexes future and Fig. 15.12 shows the contract specifications of S&P 500 Futures. Open interest represent the number of open contract positions on a given day with only one side counted — that is, when the buyer and seller make their transaction, only one position is counted as being open, not two.

The importance of trading-volume data is that is represents the relative liquidity of the various index-futures contracts. This is important information for users (particularly hedgers) trying to decide which would best suit their purposes. The higher a contract's liquidity, the easier to enter and exit positions and to trade in larger lots of contracts without overly impacting price. Of course, the extent to which an institutional investor's stock portfolio correlates with each of the underlying stock indexes will also influence the decision of which futures contract to hedge with.

All index-futures contracts call for cash settlement or delivery. This means that on the expiration date of the contract, no security or portfolio

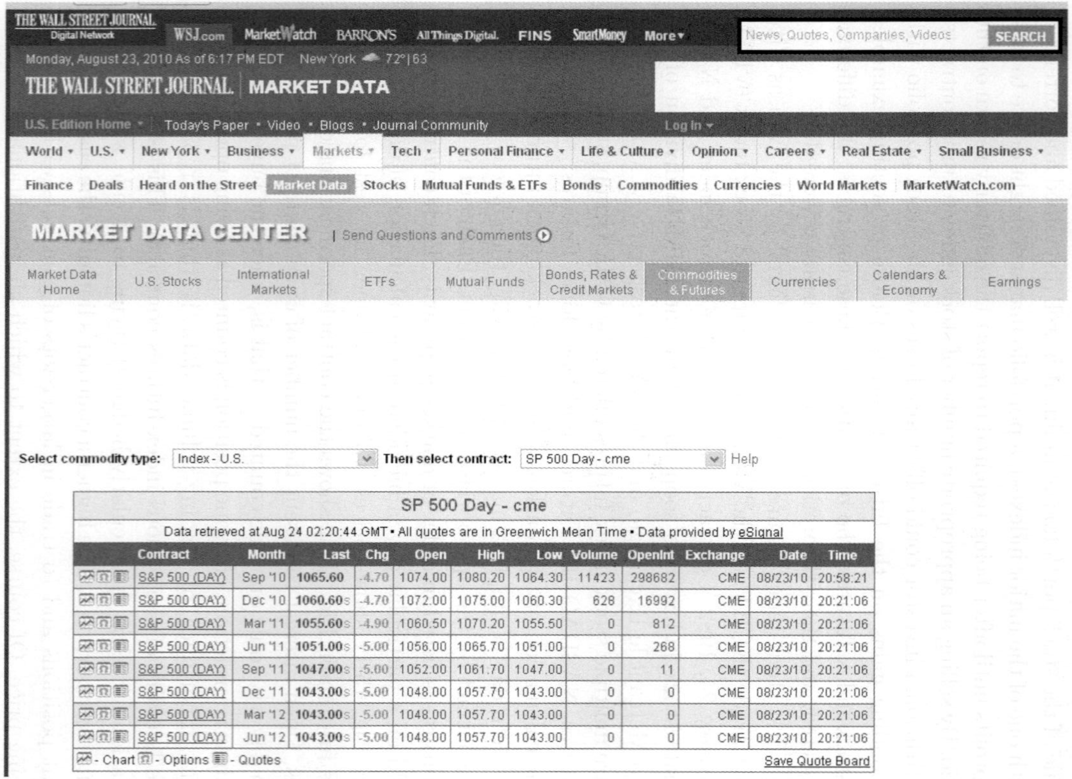

SP 500 Day - cme

Data retrieved at Aug 24 02:20:44 GMT • All quotes are in Greenwich Mean Time • Data provided by eSignal

Contract	Month	Last	Chg	Open	High	Low	Volume	OpenInt	Exchange	Date	Time
S&P 500 (DAY)	Sep '10	**1065.60**	-4.70	1074.00	1080.20	1064.30	11423	298682	CME	08/23/10	20:58:21
S&P 500 (DAY)	Dec '10	**1060.60**s	-4.70	1072.00	1075.00	1060.30	628	16992	CME	08/23/10	20:21:06
S&P 500 (DAY)	Mar '11	**1055.60**s	-4.90	1060.50	1070.20	1055.50	0	812	CME	08/23/10	20:21:06
S&P 500 (DAY)	Jun '11	**1051.00**s	-5.00	1056.00	1065.70	1051.00	0	268	CME	08/23/10	20:21:06
S&P 500 (DAY)	Sep '11	**1047.00**s	-5.00	1052.00	1061.70	1047.00	0	11	CME	08/23/10	20:21:06
S&P 500 (DAY)	Dec '11	**1043.00**s	-5.00	1048.00	1057.70	1043.00	0	0	CME	08/23/10	20:21:06
S&P 500 (DAY)	Mar '12	**1043.00**s	-5.00	1048.00	1057.70	1043.00	0	0	CME	08/23/10	20:21:06
S&P 500 (DAY)	Jun '12	**1043.00**s	-5.00	1048.00	1057.70	1043.00	0	0	CME	08/23/10	20:21:06

- Chart - Options - Quotes   Save Quote Board

Fig. 15.11. S&P 500 Future Quotes.

Source: *The Wall Street Journal*, August 23, 2010.

S&P 500 Futures

Quotes | **Contract Specifications** | Performance Bonds / Margins | Product Calendar | Learn Mc

Futures | Options

S&P 500 Futures

Opening Date	4/21/1982	
Ticker Symbol	SP SP= Clearing View product and vendor codes	
Contract Size	$250 x S&P 500 futures price	
Tick Size (minimum fluctuation)	OUTRIGHT	0.10 index points=$25
	CALENDAR SPREAD	0.05 index points=$12.50
Trading Hours All time listed are Central Time	Open Outcry	MON-FRI: 8:30 a.m.-3:15 p.m.
	CME Globex (Electronic Platform)	MON-THURS: 3:30 p.m.-8:15 a.m. (daily maintenance shutdown from 4:30 p.m.-5:00 p.m.) SUN: 5:00 p.m.-8:15 a.m
Contract Months	Open Outcry	Eight months in the March Quarterly Cycle (Mar, Jun, Sep, Dec)
	CME Globex	One month in the March Quarterly Cycle (Mar, Jun, Sep, Dec)
Last Trade Date/Time View Calendar	Open Outcry	3:15 p.m. on Thursday prior to 3rd Friday of the contract month
	CME Globex	On the rollover date (typcially eight days prior to last trade date for open outcry) when the lead month goes off the screen and the deferred month becomes the new lead month. View Rollover Dates
Final Settlement Procedure	Cash Settlement. All open positions at close of last day of trading are settled in cash to the Special Opening Quotation (SOQ) on Friday a.m. of the S&P 500 Index. See SOQ FAQ.	
Daily Price Limits	RTH: Successive 10%, 20%, 30% limits (downside only) ETH (overnight): 5% up or down View price limits details	
Position Limits	20,000 net long or short in all contract months combined.	
Block Trade Eligibility	No. View more on block-trade eligibile contracts.	
Block Minimum	N/A	
Rulebook Chapter	351	
Exchange Rule	These contracts are listed with, and subject to, the rules and regulations of CME.	

Fig. 15.12. S&P 500 Future Contract.
Source: CME Group, http://www.cmegroup.com/.

of securities is delivered. Rather, the difference in the value of the contract between buying and selling is delivered in cash. For example, if the S&P 500 contract was purchased when the index was 600 and delivered when the index was 620, the purchaser would receive \$5,000 from the seller (620 × \$250 = \$155,000 settlement value minus 600 × \$250 = \$150,000 purchase value).

15.4.1. *Pricing Stock-Index Futures Contracts*

Although the theoretical pricing of these contracts has not yet reached a conclusive level, an examination of the components of the models offered to date will further an understanding of the general pricing factors involved.

A paper by Modest and Sundaresan (1983) proposes theoretical pricing boundaries for a stock-index futures contract based on arbitrage conditions. First, for the case where no dividends are paid by the stocks in the underlying index, interest rates are nonstochastic, and there are no transaction costs, the price of a futures contract can be stated as

$$F_{t,T} = S_t(1 + R_{f,T-t}). \tag{15.14}$$

The argument for this relationship was presented earlier. Next, Modest and Sundaresan extend Equation (15.14) to a set of boundary conditions by taking into account transaction costs. To simplify, let the price of a discount bound $[1/(1 + R_{f,T-t})]$ be stated as $[1/(1 + R_{f,T-t})]$. So now:

$$\frac{S_t + C_{LS} + C_{SF}}{B_{t,T}} \geq F_{t,T} \geq \frac{S_t - C_{SS} - C_{LF}}{B_{t,T}}, \tag{15.15}$$

where

S_t = market value of the underlying stock index at time t;
$F_{t,T}$ = theoretically bounded price for a stock-index futures contract at time t, that matures at time T, where $T > t$;
$B_{t,T}$ = price of a discount bound $= 1/(1 + R_{f,T-t})$.

There are two steps to be taken to establish the validity of the arbitrage argument behind Equation (15.15). The first step is to show that $B_{t,T}F_{t,T} < (S_t + C_{LS} + C_{SF})$ (equivalent to $F_{t,T} \leq (S_t + C_{LS} + C_{SF})/B_{t,T}$). To do so, suppose that the reverse is true. Then at time t the following transactions can be undertaken to guarantee riskless profits.

(1) Buy the spot index by investing $\$(S_t + C_{LS})$;
(2) Sell futures short by incurring $\$C_{SF}$.

At time T, cover the short position in the futures by delivering the stock index (assuming this was allowed) and receive $F_{t,T}$ for certain. The present value at time t for the futures price received at time T is $B_{t,T}F_{t,T}$. Thus, if $B_{t,T}F_{t,T} > S_t + C_{L,S} + C_{SF}$ then arbitrage profits would be available. Hence:

$$B_{t,T}F_{t,T} < S_t + C_{L,S} + C_{SF}.$$

The second step is to show that $B_{t,T}F_{t,T} \geq (S_t - C_{SS} - C_{LF})$, or equivalently that $F_{t,T} \geq (S_t - C_{SS} - C_{LF})/B_{t,T}$. Once again, assume that the reverse pricing condition is true and pursue the following transactions at time t to obtain riskless profits.

(1) Sell the spot index short. This produces an inflow of $\$(S_t - C_{SS})$.
(2) Buy futures (long position) incurring $-\$C_{LF}$.

At time T, collect the stock in the futures market by paying $F_{t,T}$ and covering the short position. The inflow at time t is $(S_t - C_{SS} - C_{LF})$, and its value at time T is simply the same amount compounded from t to T by $B_{t,T}$ (i.e., divide the dollar sum by $B_{t,T}$, the price of a discount bound, which in the case of nonstochastic rates is the future-value interest factor). The outflow at time T is $F_{t,T}$, so, if $(S_t - C_{SS} - C_{LF})/B_{t,T} > F_{t,T}$, then arbitrage profits can be made. Therefore, efficient markets infer that the opposite condition is true.

To adjust the bounds for dividends paid out by the stocks in the spot index, simply subtract their discounted value from each side of the boundaries. The reason being that since the holder of a stock-index futures contract does not receive the dividends paid out by the underlying stock index, its value must be diminished by their present value. Assuming that dividends d are nonstochastic and paid out at known futures periods, such that $t < \tau < T$, their value can be discounted back to the present by a discount factor of $B_{t,t+T}$. Summing the present value of all future dividends paid by the spot index between t and T, the pricing boundary conditions can be adjusted downward in Equation (15.15):

$$\frac{S_t + C_{LS} + C_{SF} - \left(\sum_{\tau=1}^{T-t} B_{t,T} + \tau d\tau\right)}{B_{t,T}}$$

$$\geq F_{t,T} \geq \frac{S_t - C_{SS} - C_{LF} - \left(\sum_{\tau=1}^{T-t} B_{t,T} + \tau d\tau\right)}{B_{t,T}}. \quad (15.16)$$

Figures 15.13 and 15.14 show how well the price for S&P 500 futures contract maturing in June 1982 followed the boundary conditions in

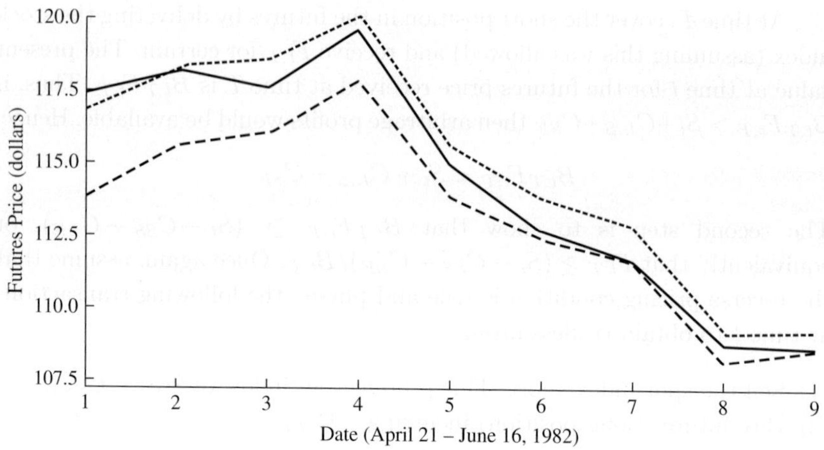

Fig. 15.13. Futures Prices and Bounds for S&P 500 Contracts Maturing June 1982: Zero Use of Proceeds, Adjustments for Dividends.
Source: D. M. Modest and M. Sundaresan. "The Relationship Between Spot and Futures Prices in Stock-Index Futures Markets: Some Preliminary Evidence." *Journal of Futures Markets*, v. 3 (Spring 1983), page 27. Copyright © 1983 by John Wiley and Sons, Inc. Reprinted by permission of John Wiley and Sons, Inc.

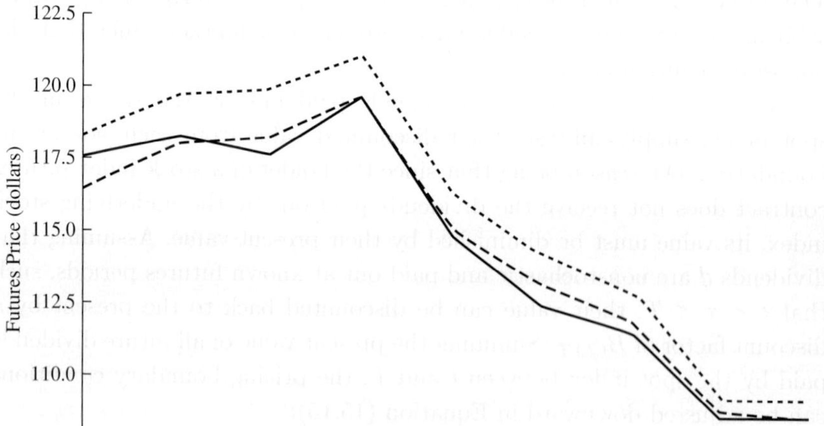

Fig. 15.14. Futures Prices and Bounds for S&P 500 Contracts Maturing June 1982: Half Use of Proceeds, No Adjustments for Dividends.
Source: D. M. Modest and M. Sundaresan. "The Relationship Between Spot and Futures Prices in Stock-Index Futures Markets: Some Preliminary Evidence." *Journal of Futures Markets*, v. 3 (Spring 1983), page 31. Copyright © 1983 by John Wiley and Sons, Inc. Reprinted by permission of John Wiley and Sons, Inc.

Equation (15.16). Figure 15.13 assumes that zero percent of any proceeds from a short sale of the spot index was available for use. Figure 15.14 assumes that 50% of such proceeds should be used by the investor for reinvestment. As can be seen, allowance for the use of 50% of short-sale proceeds increases the bounds and indicates that either they are upwardly biased or that the June 1982 futures contract was slightly undervalued during this period.

An analysis of the components in Equation (15.16) can help discern how the futures price should be affected by a change in any one of the variables.

$\frac{\partial F_{t,T}}{\partial B_{t,T}} > 0$ As the price of a discount bond increases or equivalently, interest rate falls, the futures price will increase. (15.17a)

$\frac{\partial F_{t,T}}{\partial S_t} > 0$ As the underlying spot price increases so will the futures price. (15.17b)

$\frac{\partial F_{t,T}}{\partial d} < 0$ As future dividend payments are expected to increase the futures price declines. (15.17c)

$\frac{\partial F_{t,T}}{\partial C} < 0$ As relevant transaction costs rise, the futures price will fall. (15.17d)

If more than one of the denominator variables changes at the same time, the expression cannot be generalized for the resulting effect on the futures price. The precise change in the futures price will depend on the relative size of the two or more changing parameters. Nevertheless, it can be concluded that a correct valuation for a stock-index futures contract requires accurate forecasts of future interest rates and dividends. Sample Problem 15.8 provides further illustration.

Sample Problem 15.8

Hedging with Stock-Index Futures. In this example an institutional investor is going to use S&P 500 stock-index futures contracts to hedge an expected market decline over the coming month. Assume the following: (1) the S&P 500 stock index is an exact proxy of the composition of the investor's stock portfolio, (2) no transaction costs are involved in entering or exiting either market, and (3) that the investor uses the Howard–D'Antonio hedge ratio equation [Chapter 14, Equation (14.15)] to determine how many futures contracts to sell. The figures used to compute the hedge ratio are from daily data over a two-month period.

The first step is to calculate the hedge ratio and corresponding hedging effectiveness measure. So, using the following figures:

$i = 0.10$ (the risk-free rate on 13-week T-bills);
$\overline{r}_f = 0.2241$ (average daily return, annualized, for the nearby futures);
$\overline{r}_s = 0.2025$ (average daily return, annualized, for the S&P 500 index);
$\sigma_f = 0.1851$ (standard deviation of daily returns on the nearby futures);
$\sigma_s = 0.0792$ (standard deviation of daily returns on the S&P 500 index);
$\rho = 0.9815$ (correlation coefficient among the returns on the S&P 500 index and nearby S&P 500 futures contract);
$\pi = \sigma_f/\sigma_s = 2.3371$;
$r = r_f/(r_s - i) = 2.1863$;
$\lambda = \alpha/\pi = 0.9355$ (risk–return relative);
$P_f = 167.60$ (current futures price for September contract);
$P_s = 165.54$ (current value of S&P 500 index); and
$\gamma = P_f/P_s = 1.0124$.

The hedge ratio is

$$\text{HHD} = \frac{(\lambda - \rho)}{\gamma\pi(1 - \lambda\rho)} = \frac{0.9355 - 0.9815}{1.0124(2.3371)[1 - (0.9355)(0.9815)]}$$
$$= -0.238.$$

The hedging effectiveness measure [Chapter 12, Equation (12.16)] is

$$\text{HE} = \sqrt{\frac{1 - 2\lambda\rho + \lambda^2}{1 - \rho^2}} = \sqrt{\frac{1 - 2(0.9355)(0.9815) + (0.92355)}{1 - (0.9815)^2}}$$
$$= 1.0284.$$

Assuming the investor's stock portfolio is 100× the value of the S&P 500 index, the investor should sell 24 futures contracts to hedge the portfolio. Based on the past risk–return relationship between the futures and the spot markets, the institutional investor can expect to enhance the excess return to risk on his or her portfolio by 2.8% over the hedging period [(1.0284 – 1) × 100%]. Table 15.4 summarizes the transactions and results from the hedge.

Utilizing the Howard and D'Antonio hedging strategy, the loss on the spot position was reduced by 38%.

Table 15.4. Transactions and Results.

	Spot-Market Transaction	Futures-Market Transaction
August 1	Holding a stock portfolio duplicating the S&P 500 index but 100 × its spot value or 100 × \$500 × 165.54 = \$8,277,000.	Sell 24 September-delivery S&P 500 futures contracts at a price of 167.60 (market value of 24 × \$500 × 167.60 = \$2,011,200).
September 1: stock-market prices fall as expected.	S&P 500 index falls to 163.04; value of portfolio is now 100 × \$500 × 163.04 = \$8,152,000.	Buy 24 September S&P 500 futures contracts at a price of 163.60 (market value = 24 × \$500 × 163.60 = \$1,963,200).
Results	Sell 24 contracts at	167.60
	Buy 24 contracts at	163.60
	Net profit on futures (+400 basis points)	4.00
	Dollar value of profit (each basis point worth \$5): 400 × \$5 × 24 contracts or \$2,011,200 − \$1,963,200	\$48,000
	Net loss on stock portfolio (\$8,152,000 − \$8,277,000)	(\$125,000)
	Net loss on hedge	(\$77,000)
	Portfolio loss reduced by hedge (percent)	38

15.4.2. *Stock-Index Futures: Does the Tail Wag the Dog?*

The rise in program trading based on a comparatively narrow blue-chip stock-market barometer, the **Major Market Index (MMI)**, is said to be fueling the volatile price swings in the stock market, a case of the tail wagging the dog. The MMI is a price-weighted index of 20 very actively traded stocks, 16 of which are included in the Dow Jones 30 Industrials. Because of its relatively small size, the MMI is expected to be more easily arbitragible than other stock-index futures contracts. Basically, program trading is taking a position (long or short) in a portfolio of stocks comprising the index and simultaneously taking an opposite position in the index-futures contracts. The objective of the program trade is to create a risk-free position that earns a return in excess of the currently available risk-free return.

These so-called program trades may move both the futures and the spot market. The chain of causality may work as follows.

(1) Investors believe the stock market will rise and they purchase futures contracts in expectation of higher equity values. The purchase of futures contracts is preferable because they entail no initial investment and lower transaction costs than a position in the stock market.
(2) The rise in futures prices causes an imbalance between the prices of the futures and the underlying index; as this premium between the futures and the index increases, it may become more profitable to execute a program trade.
(3) The simultaneous sale of the futures and purchase of the underlying index will cause the premium between the futures and the index to shrink.

Changes in other factors, such as interest rates, can also have an effect on the equilibrium relationship between the index price and the futures price, thereby changing the premium or discount between the two markets. Program traders can take advantage of any change in the spread between the markets. It does not matter what causes the change in spread, either internal factors like changes in investor expectations or external factors such as interest-rate changes. All program trading does is to bring cash and futures prices together. The program trade may be an essential mechanism insuring that futures prices and the underlying equity prices are efficiently determined. Chapter 24 discusses the relationship between portfolio insurance and program trading.

To date most of the literature on the impact of futures trading on the cash market has focused on the changes in the spot-price volatility because of the initiation or cessation of futures trading. A common conclusion of these studies is that the futures market has a smoothing effect on the cash market by stabilizing the spot price. The recent uproar about the "triple witching hour" and the so-called crisis at expiration caused by the expiration of stock-index futures and options at the close on the third Friday of March, June, September, and December brings to question the smoothing influence that futures contracts have on the underlying index.

If the market is efficient, prices adjust instantaneously to reflect all relevant information, and knowledge of such information cannot lead to excess risk-adjusted returns. The central concept in the efficient-market hypothesis is the fair-game model. A sequence of past returns over time is a fair game if today's price reflects the then-available information,

Table 15.5. Linkage between Futures-Price Changes and Subsequent Spot-Price Changes.

Maxi Major Market Index		Major Market Index	
Number of contracts studied	11		24
Number showing significance at the 10 percent level	7		16
Number showing significance if results were random	1		2
Number significant before December 1985/number of contracts	0/4	Number significant before April 1985/number of contracts	3/9
Number significant after December 1985/number of contracts	7/7	Number significant after April 1985/number of contracts	13/15

making it impossible to earn excess risk-adjusted returns by trading on that information. If the information set today contains all of the information known and used by the market participants in the spot market in determining the spot price, one of the components of the information set is the previous change in the price of futures contracts.

Using intraday spot and futures prices of the CBT's MMI over the period August 1984 to August 1986, Finnerty and Park (19871 provide the following and subsequent spot-price changes (Table 15.5). A majority of the contracts studied showed a significant relationship between the change in the futures price and the subsequent change in the index. This supports the notion that the tail is wagging the dog. This result was present for both the Maxi and the regular MMI contracts. Of interest is the fact that when each of the contracts was first traded, there existed a period of time when there was no relationship between the change in the futures price and subsequent change in the index. For the Maxi contract this was the first four months of trading, from September to December 1985. And for the MMI during the first nine months of trading, six out nine contracts showed no relationship between futures and subsequent spot-price changes. This could indicate either that arbitrage opportunities were not available during the initial trading of the contracts, or that program traders were unable immediately to take advantage of the opportunities if they were available.

However, after the initial start-up periods the results indicate that there exists a strong relationship between futures- and subsequent index-price changes in seven out of the last seven months for the Maxi and thirteen out of the last fifteen months for the MMI contracts. These results indicate that it is reasonable to answer in the affirmative: the tail is wagging the dog, at least in the case of the MMI and Maxi MMI.

15.5. Summary

In one sense, uncertainty and risk are equivalent; thus the more uncertain something is, the more risky it is. The futures markets evolved to alleviate one particular kind of risk that associated with unexpected price changes. The purpose of this chapter has been to help explain what futures contracts are, how markets for them operate, and most important, how they can be applied to the hedging of price risk for securities.

Although futures contracts originated on agricultural commodities, the 1970s saw the introduction of futures for financial instruments. Deregulation of the domestic financial sector, the 1979 change in monetary policy, elimination of fixed foreign-exchange rates, the growing interrelatedness of the world economy, and bouts with high levels of inflation are some of the major reasons for the growing need for and popularity of financial futures.

The general methodology for using futures to reduce price risk (or equivalently, interest-rate risk) should seem quite straightforward. We can long the spot commodity or instrument, and sell or short the related futures contract to lock in a price (or rate). Nevertheless, exactly how to determine the appropriate hedge ratio and evaluate the effectiveness of the hedge has no all-conclusive answer.

Questions and Problems

1. Carefully explain why a market for currency futures emerged.
2. What is interest-rate parity? What is the relationship between the concept of interest-rate parity and the futures and spot prices for foreign currency?
3. Assume that the six-month interest rate in the U.S. is 5%, while the rate is 7% in Japan. If the spot price of dollars in terms of yen is 124 yen/dollar, what is the price of a six-month futures contract for dollars?
4. Suppose IBM is planning to issue 30-year bonds to finance a new plant. Assume that it plans to issue these bonds in three months. Is there any way IBM can protect itself from unexpected increases in interest rates?
5. Carefully explain the function speculators serve in the futures markets.
6. Assume that 60-day spot T-bills sell for $97.75, while 90-day spot T-bills sell for $96.50. If the price of a 30-day T-bill future that matures

in 30 days is \$98.50, are there any arbitrage opportunities? If so, create a strategy to exploit this opportunity.

7. I. M. Ritch has a stock portfolio worth \$50,000. He plans to use it for a down payment on a house he will be purchasing in six months. Is there any way Mr. Ritch can protect himself from an adverse change in stock prices? Are there any conditions that must be met for this strategy to work?
8. Calculate the implied forward rate of a T-bill with a life of 182 days if the 91-day T-bill rate is 9% and the nine-month T-bill rate is 10.5%.
9. What are Eurodollars? Why do they exist?
10. Carefully explain why a bank might choose to have a long position in Eurodollar futures.
11. Carefully explain the difference between a long hedge and a short hedge. When would an investor wish to use a long hedge? A short hedge?
12. Juan Valdez is a coffee grower who is planning to harvest 112.500 pounds of coffee on June 1. The current price for coffee is \$1.34 per pound. A futures contract on coffee that matures on June 1 also costs \$1.34.

    (a) To hedge his position in coffee, should Mr. Valdez buy or sell futures contracts?
    (b) If a contract consists of 37,500 pounds of coffee, how many contracts does Mr. Valdez need to buy or sell to hedge his position perfectly?
    (c) Show the net gain or loss if the price of coffee rises to \$1.50 per pound on July 1.
    (d) Show the net gain or loss if the price of coffee falls to \$1.20 per pound.

13. The spot price for a T-bill that matures in 91 days is 98.875 while the spot price for a T-bill that matures in 273 days is 95.125.

    (a) Calculate the theoretical price of a futures contract for a 182-day T-bill with delivery in 91 days.
    (b) Recompute your answer in (a) assuming that there is a round-trip commission cost of \$0.006 per \$100 of face value.

Bibliography

Anderson, T. W. and J. P. Danthine. "Cross-hedging." *Journal of Political Economy*, v. 89 (November/December 1981), pp. 1182–1196.

Bacon, P. W. and R. Williams. "Interest Rate Futures: New Tools for the Financial Manager." *Financial Management*, v. 5 (Spring 1976), pp. 32–38.

Benninga, S. and M. Smirlock. "An Empirical Analysis of the Delivery Option, Marking to Market and the Pricing of T-Bond Futures." *Journal of Futures Markets*, v. 5 (Fall 1985), pp. 361–374.

Black, F. L. "The Pricing of Commodity Contracts." *Journal of Financial Economics*, v. 3 (June 1976), pp. 167–179.

Capozza, D. and B. Cornell. "Treasury Bill Pricing in the Spot and Futures Markets." *Review of Economics and Statistics*, v. 61 (November 1979), pp. 515–520.

Cassel, G. "The Present Situation of Foreign Exchange I." *Economic Journal*, v. 26 (March 1916a), pp. 62–65.

Cassel, G. "The Present Situation of Foreign Exchange II." *Economic Journal*, v. 26 (September 1916b), pp. 319–323.

Cornell, B. and K. French. "The Pricing of Stock Index Futures." *Journal of Futures Markets*, v. 3 (March 1983), pp. 1–14.

Cornell, B. and K. French. "Taxes and the Pricing of Stock Index Futures." *Journal of Finance*, v. 38 (June 1983), pp. 675–694.

Cornell, B. and M. Reinganum. "Forward and Futures Prices: Evidence from the Foreign Exchange Markets." *Journal of Finance*, v. 36 (September 1981), pp. 1035–1045.

Cox, J., J. Ingersoll, Jr. and S. Ross. "The Relation Between Forward and Futures Prices." *Journal of Financial Economics*, v. 9 (September 1981), pp. 321–346.

Duncan, W. H. "Treasury Bill Futures: Opportunities and Pitfalls." *Review*, Federal Reserve Bank of Dallas (July 1977), pp. 1–5.

Ederington, L. "The Hedging Performance of the New Futures Markets." *Journal of Finance*, v. 34 (March 1979), pp. 157–170.

Fabozzi, F. and G. Kipnis. *Stock Index Futures*. Homewood, IL: Dow Jones-Irwin, 1984.

Figlewski, S. "Hedging with Stock Index Futures: Theory and Application in a New Market." *Journal of Futures Markets*, v. 5 (Summer 1985), pp. 183–200.

Figlewski, S. and S. J. Kon. "Portfolio Management with Stock Index Futures." *Financial Analysts Journal*, v. 20 (January/Febuary1982), pp. 52–60.

Finnerty, J. and H. Park. "Does the Tail Wag the Dog?" *Financial Analysts Journal*, v. 43 (March/April 1987), pp. 57–60.

Fisher, I. *The Rate of Interest*. New York: Macmillan, 1907.

Fisher, I. *The Theory of Interest*. New York: Macmillan, 1930.

Francis, J. and M. Castelino, "Basis Speculation in Commodity Futures: The Maturity Effect." *Journal of Futures Markets*, v. 2 (Summer 1982), pp. 195–206.

Gay, R. and D. J. S. Rutledge. "The Economics of Commodity Futures Markets: A Survey." *Review of Marketing and Agricultural Economics*, v. 34 (March 1971), pp. 57–108.

Gay, R., R. Kolb and R. Chiang. "Interest Rate Hedging: An Empirical Test of Alternate Strategies." *Journal of Financial Research*, v. 6 (March 1983), pp. 187–197.

Hansen, L. P. and R. J. Hordrick. "Forward Exchange Rate as Optimal Predictors of Future Spot Rates: An Econometric Analysis." *Journal of Political Economy*, v. 88 (October 1980), pp. 829–853.

Hill, J. and T. Schneeweis. "Reducing Volatility with Financial Futures." *Financial Analysts Journal*, v. 40 (November/December 1984), pp. 34–40.

Hilliard, J. "Hedging Interest Rate Risk with Futures Portfolios under Term Structure Effects." *Journal of Finance*, v. 39 (December 1984), pp. 1547–1570.

Junkus, J. C. and C. F. Lee. "Use of Three Stock Index Futures in Hedging Decisions." *J. Futures Markets*, v. 5 (Summer 1985), pp. 201–222.

Kamara, A. "Issues in Futures Markets: A Survey." *Journal of Futures Markets*, v. 2 (Fall 1982), pp. 261–294.

Keynes, J. M. A *Treatise on Money*. London: Macmillan, 1930.

Khoury, S. *Speculative Markets*. New York; London: Macmillan, 1984.

Kolb, R. *Understanding Futures Markets*. Glenview, IL: Scott, Foresman and Co., 1985.

Kolb, R. and R. Chiang. "Duration, Immunization, and Hedging with Interest Rate Futures," in G. D. Gay and R. W. Kolb (eds.), *Interest Rate Futures: Concepts and Issues*, Investor Pubns (1982), pp. 353–364.

Kolb, R. and R. Chiang. "Improving Performance Using Interest Rate Futures." *Financial Management*, v. 10 (Autumn 1981), pp. 77–85.

Laufman, P. *Handbook of Futures Markets: Commodity, Financial Stock Indices and Options*. New York: John Wiley and Sons, 1986.

Loosigian, A. M. *Interest Rate Futures*. Homewood, IL: Dow Jones-Irwin, 1980.

Modest, D. M. and M. Sundaresan. "The Relationship between Spot and Futures Prices in Stock-Index Futures Markets: Some Preliminary Evidence." *Journal of Futures Markets*, v. 3 (Spring 1983), pp. 15–42.

Nelson, R. and R. Collins. "A Measure of Hedging Performance." *Journal of Futures Markets*, v. 5 (Spring 1985), pp. 45–55.

Poole, W. "Using T-Bill Futures to Gauge Interest Rate Expectations." *Economic Review*, Federal Reserve Bank of San Francisco (Spring 1978), pp. 7–19.

Powers, M. *Inside the Financial Futures Markets*. New York: John Wiley and Sons, 1984.

Rendleman, R. and C. Carabini. "The Efficiency of the T-Bill Futures." *Journal of Finance*, v. 34 (September 1979), pp. 895–914.

Rishard, S. and M. Sundaresan. "A Continuous Time Equilibrium Model of Forward Prices and Futures Prices in a Multigood Economy." *Journal of Financial Economics*, v. 9 (September 1981), pp. 347–372.

Rothstein, N. (ed.). *Handbook of Financial Futures*. New York: McGraw-Hill, 1986.

Rutledge, D. J. S. "Hedgers' Demand for Futures Contracts: A Theoretical Framework with Applications to the United States Soybean Complex." *Food Research Institute Studies*, v. 11 (March 1972), pp. 237–256.

Schwarz, E., J. Hill and T. Schneeweis. *Financial Futures: Fundamental Strategies and Applications*. Homewood, IL: Irwin, 1986.

Senchack, A. J., Jr. and J. C. Easterwood. "Cross Hedging CDs with Treasury Bill Futures." *Journal of Futures Markets*, v. 3 (Winter 1983), pp. 429–438.
Weiner, N. S. "The Hedging Rationale for a Stock Index Futures Contract." *Journal of Futures Market*, v. 1 (Spring 1981), pp. 59–76.

Chapter 16

Options and Option Strategies

The use of stock options for risk reduction and return enhancement has expanded at an astounding pace over the last two decades. Among the causes of this growth, two are most significant. First, the establishment of the Chicago Board Option Exchange (CBOE) in 1973 brought about the liquidity necessary for successful option trading, through public listing and standardization of option contracts. The second stimulus emanated from academia. In the same year that the CBOE was established, Professors Fischer Black and Myron Scholes published a paper in which they derived a revolutionary option-pricing model. The power of their model to predict an option's fair price has since made it the industry standard.

The development of option-valuation theory shed new light on the valuation process. Previous pricing models such as CAPM were based on very stringent assumptions, such as there being an identifiable and measurable market portfolio, as well as various imputed investor attributes, such as quadratic utility functions. Furthermore, previous theory priced only market risk since investors were assumed to hold well-diversified portfolios. The strength of the Black–Scholes and subsequent option-pricing models is that they rely on far fewer assumptions. In addition, the option-valuation models price total risk and do not require any assumptions concerning the direction of the underlying securities price. The growing popularity of the option concept is evidenced by its application to the valuation of a wide array of other financial instruments (such as common stock and bonds) as well as more abstract assets including leases and real estate agreements.

This chapter aims to establish a basic knowledge of options and the markets in which they are traded. It begins with the most common types of options, calls, and puts, explaining their general characteristics and discussing the institutions where they are traded. In addition, the concepts relevant to the new types of options on indexes and futures are introduced. The next focus is the basic pricing relationship between puts and calls, known as put–call parity. The final study concerns how options can be used as investment tools. The chapter on option valuation that follows utilizes all these essential concepts to afford a deeper conceptual understanding of valuation theory.

16.1. The Option Market and Related Definitions

This section discusses option-market and related definitions of options, which are needed to understand option valuations and option strategies.

16.1.1. *What is an Option?*

An **option** is a contract conveying the right to buy or sell a designated security at a stipulated price. The contract normally expires at a predetermined time. The most important element of an option contract is that there is no obligation placed upon the purchaser: it is an "option." This attribute of an option contract distinguishes it from other financial contracts. For instance, while the holder of an option has the opportunity to let his or her claim expire unused if so desired, futures and forward contracts obligate their parties to fulfill certain conditions.

16.1.2. *Types of Options and Their Characteristics*

A **call option** gives its owner the right to buy the underlying asset, while a **put option** conveys to its holder the right to sell the underlying asset.

An option is specified by five essential parts:

(1) The type (call or put);
(2) The underlying asset;
(3) The exercise price;
(4) The expiration date; and
(5) The option price.

While the most common type of underlying asset for an option is an individual stock, other underlying assets for options exist as well.

These include futures contracts, foreign currencies, stock indexes, and U.S. debt instruments. In the case of common stock options (on which this discussion is exclusively centered), the specified quantity to which the option buyer is entitled to buy or sell is 100 shares of the stock per option.

The **exercise price** (also called the **striking price**) is the price stated in the option contract at which the call (put) owner can buy (sell) the underlying asset up to the expiration date, the final calendar date on which the option can be traded. Options on common stocks have expiration dates three months apart in one of three fixed cycles.

(1) January/April/July/October;
(2) February/May/August/November; and
(3) March/June/September/December.

The normal expiration date is the third Saturday of the month. (The third Friday is the last trading date for the option.)

As an example, an option referred to as an "ABC June 25 call" is an option to buy 100 shares of the underlying ABC stock at $25 per share, up to its expiration date in June. Option prices are quoted on a per-share basis. Thus, a stock option that is quoted at $5 would cost $500 ($5 × 100 shares), plus commission and a nominal SEC fee.

A common distinction among options pertains to when they can be exercised. Exercising an option is the process of carrying out the right to buy or sell the underlying asset at the stated price. American options allow the exercise of this right at any time from when the option is purchased up to the expiration date. On the other hand, European options allow their holder the right of exercise only on the expiration date itself. The distinction between an American and European option has nothing to do with the location at which they are traded. Both types are currently bought and sold in the U.S. There are distinctions in their pricing and in the possibility of exercising them prior to expiration.

Finally, when discussing options, the two parties to the contract are characterized by whether they have bought or sold the contract. The party buying the option contract (call or put) is the option buyer (or holder), while the party selling the option is the option seller (or writer). If the writer of an option does not own the underlying asset, he or she is said to write a naked option.

Table 16.1 shows a listing of publicly traded options for Johnson & Johnson (JNJ) at March 29, 2011.

Table 16.1. Options Quotes for JNJ at March 29, 2011.

Strike	Symbol	Last	Bid	Ask	Vol	Open Int
Stock Price at March 29, 2011 = $59.38						
Call Options Expiring Fri. April 15, 2011						
35	JNJ110416C00035000	24.7	23.95	24.45	0	122
40	JNJ110416C00040000	17.85	18.95	19.35	33	360
45	JNJ110416C00045000	13.85	14.15	14.25	45	54
50	JNJ110416C00050000	8.75	9.2	9.35	2	213
52.5	JNJ110416C00052500	6.62	6.7	6.85	1	518
55	JNJ110416C00055000	4.25	4.2	4.3	5	1787
57.5	JNJ110416C00057500	1.84	1.89	1.94	40	4491
60	JNJ110416C00060000	0.3	0.3	0.31	399	23603
62.5	JNJ110416C00062500	0.04	0.03	0.04	232	24478
65	JNJ110416C00065000	0.02	N/A	0.02	407	12559
67.5	JNJ110416C00067500	0.02	N/A	0.02	24	8731
Put Options Expiring Fri. April 15, 2011						
47.5	JNJ110416P00047500	0.02	0.01	0.04	2	1983
50	JNJ110416P00050000	0.04	0.02	0.04	2	3518
52.5	JNJ110416P00052500	0.05	0.05	0.07	4	3355
55	JNJ110416P00055000	0.09	0.09	0.1	2	7993
57.5	JNJ110416P00057500	0.23	0.2	0.22	53	24464
60	JNJ110416P00060000	1.21	1.09	1.13	15	16678
62.5	JNJ110416P00062500	3.28	3.25	3.4	1	10861
65	JNJ110416P00065000	5.85	5.75	5.85	3	1038
67.5	JNJ110416P00067500	8.45	8.2	8.5	2	713

16.1.3. *Relationships between the Option Price and the Underlying Asset Price*

A call (put) option is said to be **in the money** if the underlying asset is selling above (below) the exercise price of the option. An **at-the-money** call (put) is one whose exercise price is equal to the current price of the underlying asset. A call (put) option is out of the money if the underlying asset is selling below (above) the exercise price of the option.

Suppose ABC stock is selling at $30 per share. An ABC June 25 call option is in the money ($\$30 - 25 > 0$), while an ABC June 35 call option is out of the money ($\$30 - 35 < 0$). Of course, the expiration dates could be any month without changing the option's standing as in, at, or out of the money.

The relationship between the price of an option and the price of the underlying asset indicates both the amount of intrinsic value and time value inherent in the option's price, as shown in Equation (16.1):

$$\text{Intrinsic value} = \text{Underlying asset price} - \text{Option exercise price}. \quad (16.1)$$

For a call (put) option that is in the money (underlying asset price > exercise price), its intrinsic value is positive. And for at-the-money and out-of-the-money options the intrinsic value is zero. An option's time value is the amount by which the option's premium (or market price) exceeds its intrinsic value. For a call or put option:

$$\text{Time value} = \text{Option premium} - \text{Intrinsic value}, \quad (16.2)$$

where intrinsic value is the maximum of zero or stock price minus exercise price. Thus an option premium or market price is composed of two components: intrinsic value, and time value. In-the-money options are usually most expensive because of their large intrinsic-value component. An option with an at-the-money exercise price will have only time value inherent in its market price. Deep out-of-the-money options have zero intrinsic value and little time value and consequently are the least expensive. Deep in-the-money cases also have little time value, and time value is the greatest for at-the-money options. In addition, time value (as its name implies) is positively related to the amount of time the option has to expiration. The theoretical valuation of options focuses on determining the relevant variables that affect the time-value portion of an option premium and the derivation of their relationship in option pricing.

In general, the call price should be equal to or exceed the intrinsic value:

$$\mathrm{C} \geq \mathrm{Max}(S - E, 0),$$

where

C = the value of the call option;
S = the current stock price; and
E = the exercise price.

Figure 16.1 illustrates the relationship between an option's time value and its exercise price. When the exercise price is zero, the time value of an option is zero. Although this relationship is described quite well in general by Fig. 16.1, the exact relationship is somewhat ambiguous. Moreover, the identification of options with a mispriced time-value portion in their total premium motivates interest in a theoretical pricing model.

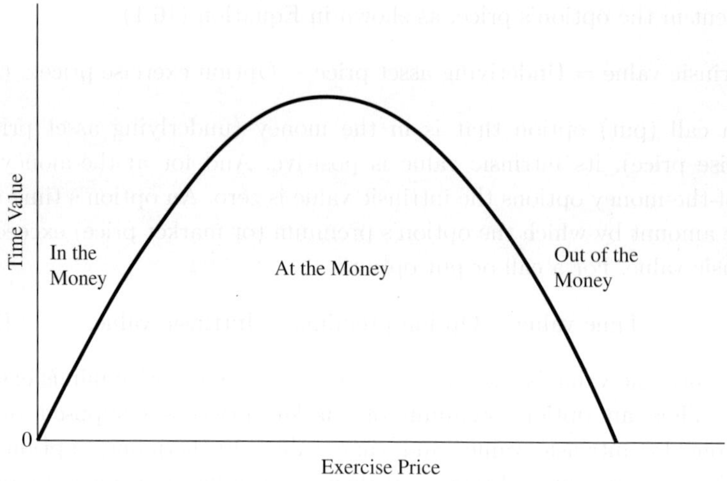

Fig. 16.1. The Relationship between an Option's Exercise Price and its Time Value.

One more aspect of time value that is very important to discuss is the change in the amount of time value an option has as its duration shortens. As previously mentioned, options with a longer time to maturity and those near to the money have the largest time-value components. Assuming that a particular option remains near to the money as its time to maturity diminishes, the rate of decrease in its time value, or what is termed the effect of time decay, is of interest. How time decay affects an option's premium is an important question for the valuation of options and the application of option strategies. To best see an answer to this question refer to Fig. 16.2.

In general, the value of call options with the same exercise price increases as time to expiration increases: $C(S_1, E_1, T_1) \leq C(S_1, E_1, T_2)$, where $T_1 \leq T_2$ and T_1 and T_2 are the time to expiration.

Notice that for the simple care in Fig. 16.2 the effect of time decay is smooth up until the last month before expiration, when the time value of an option begins to decay very rapidly. Why this effect occurs is made clearer in the next chapter, when the components of the option-pricing model are examined. Sample Problem 16.1 shows the effect of time decay.

Sample Problem 16.1

It is January 1, the price of the underlying ABC stock is $20 per share, and the time premiums are shown in the following Table 16.2. What is the value for the various call options?

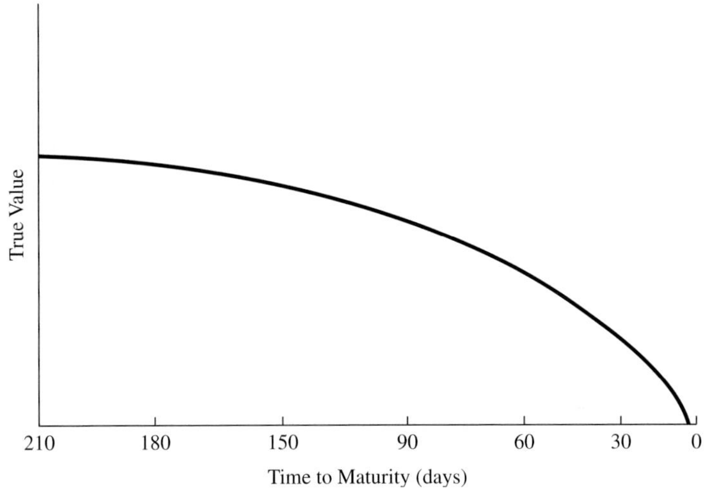

Fig. 16.2. The Relationship between Time Value and Time to Maturity for a Near-to-the-Money Option (Assuming a Constant Price for the Underlying Asset).

Table 16.2. Time Premiums.

Exercise Price X	January	April	July
15	\$0.50	\$1.25	\$3.50
20	1.00	2.00	5.00
25	0.50	1.25	3.50

Solution

$$\begin{aligned} \text{Call premium} &= \text{Intrinsic value} + \text{Time premium} \\ C_{15,Jan} &= \text{Max}(20-15,0)+0.50 \\ &= \$5.50 \text{ per share or } \$550 \text{ for 1 contract} \end{aligned}$$

Other values are shown in Table 16.3.

16.1.4. *Additional Definitions and Distinguishing Features*

Options may be specified in terms of their classes and series. A **class of options** refers to all call and put options on the same underlying asset. For example, all AT&T call and put options at various exercise prices and expiration months form one class. A **series** is a subset of a class and consists

Table 16.3. Call Premiums.

Exercise Price X	January	April	July
15	\$5.50	Max(20 − 15, 0) + 1.25 = \$6.25	Max(20 − 15, 0) + 3.50 = \$8.50
20	Max(20 − 20, 0) + 1.00 = \$1.00	Max(20 − 20, 0) + 2.00 = \$2.00	Max(20 − 20, 0) + 5.00 = \$5.00
25	Max(20 − 25, 0) + 5.0 = \$0.50	Max(20 − 25, 0) + 1.25 = \$1.25	Max(20 − 25, 0) + 3.50 = \$3.50

of all contracts of the same class (such as AT&T) having the same expiration date and exercise price.

When an investor either buys or sells an option (i.e., long or short) as the initial transaction, the option exchange adds this opening transaction to what is termed the **open interest** for an option series. Essentially, open interest represents the number of contracts outstanding at a particular point in time. If the investor reverses the initial position with a closing transaction (i.e., sells the option if he or she originally bought it or vice versa), then the open interest for the particular option series is reduced by one.

While open interest is more of a static variable, indicating the number of outstanding contracts at one point in time, **volume** represents a dynamic characteristic. More specifically, volume indicates the number of times a particular option is bought and sold during a particular trading day. Volume and open interest are measures of an option's liquidity, the ease with which the option can be bought and sold in large quantities. The larger the volume and/or open interest, the more liquid the option.

Again, an option holder who invokes the right to buy or sell is exercising the option. Whenever a holder exercises an option, a writer is assigned the obligation to fulfill the terms of the option contract by the exchange on which the option is traded. If a call holder exercises the right to buy, a **call writer** is assigned the obligation to sell. Similarly, when a put holder exercises the right to sell, a **put writer** is assigned the obligation to buy.

The seller or writer of a call option must deliver 100 shares of the underlying stock at the specified exercise price when the option is exercised. The writer of a put option must purchase 100 shares of the underlying stock when the put option is exercised. The writer of either option receives the premium or price of the option for this legal obligation. The maximum loss an option buyer can experience is limited to the price of the option. However, the maximum loss from writing a naked call is unlimited; the maximum loss possible from writing a naked put is the exercise price less the original price of that put. To guarantee that the option writer can meet these obligations, the exchange clearinghouse requires margin deposits.

The payment of cash dividends affects both the price of the underlying stock and the value of an option on the stock. Normally, no adjustment is made in the terms of the option when a cash dividend is paid. However, strike price or number of shares may be adjusted if the underlying stock realizes a stock dividend or stock split. For example, an option on XYZ Corporation with an exercise price of \$100 would be adjusted if XYZ Corporation stock split two for one. The adjustment in this case would be a change in the exercise price from \$100 to \$50, and the number of contracts would be doubled. In the case of a noninteger split (such as three for two), the adjustment is made to the exercise price and the number of shares covered by the option contracts. For example, if XYZ Corporation had an exercise price of \$100 per share and had a three-for-two split, the option would have the exercise price adjusted to \$66.66, and the number of shares would be increased to 150. Notice that the old exercise value of the option, \$10,000 (\$100 × 100 shares), is maintained by the adjustment (\$66⅔ × 150 shares).

16.1.5. *Types of Underlying Asset*

Although most people would identify common stocks as the underlying asset for an option, a variety of other assets and financial instruments can assume the same function. In fact, options on agricultural commodities were introduced by traders in the U.S. as early as the mid-1800s. After a number of scandals, agricultural commodity options were banned by the government. They were later reintroduced under tighter regulations and in a more standardized tradable form. Today, futures options on such agricultural commodities as corn, soybeans, wheat, cotton, sugar, live cattle, and live hogs are actively traded on a number of exchanges.

The biggest success for options has been realized for options on financial futures. Options on the S&P 500 index futures contracts, NYSE index futures, foreign-currency futures, 30-year U.S. Treasury bond futures, and gold futures have all realized extraordinary growth since their initial offerings back in 1982. Options on futures are very similar to options on the actual asset, except that the futures options give their holders the right (not the obligation) to buy or sell predetermined quantities of specified futures contracts at a fixed price within a predetermined period.

Options on the actual asset have arisen in another form as well. While a number of options have existed for various stock-index futures contracts, options now also exist on the stock index itself. Because of the complexity of having to provide all the stocks in an index at the spot price should a call holder exercise his or her buy right, options on stock indexes are always settled in cash. That is, should a call holder exercise his or her right to buy because of a large increase in the underlying index, that holder would be accommodated by a cash amount equal to the profit on his contract, or the current value of the option's premium. Although the options on the S&P 100 stock index at the CBOE are the most popular among traders, numerous index options are now traded as well. These include options on the S&P 500 index, the S&P OTC 250 index, the NYSE composite and AMEX indexes (computer technology, oil and gas, and airline), the Philadelphia Exchange indexes (gold/silver), the Value Line index, and the NASDAQ 100 index.

16.1.6. *Institutional Characteristics*

Probably two of the most important underlying factors leading to the success of options have been the standardization of contracts through the establishment of option exchanges and the trading anonymity brought about by the Option Clearing Corporations and clearinghouses of the major futures exchanges.

An important element for option trading is the interchangeability of contracts. Exchange contracts are not matched between individuals. Instead, when an investor or trader enters into an option contract, the Option Clearing Corporation (or clearinghouse for the particular futures exchange) takes the opposite side of the transaction. So rather than having to contact a particular option writer to terminate an option position, a buyer can simply sell it back to the exchange at the current market clearing price. This type of anonymity among option-market participants is what permits an active secondary market to operate.

The sources of futures options traded on the various futures exchanges mentioned earlier are determined by the **open-auction bidding**, probably the purest form of laissez-faire price determination that can be seen today. With the open-auction-bidding price mechanism there are no market makers, only a large octagonal pit filled with traders bidding among themselves to buy and sell contracts. While some traders buy and sell only for themselves, many of the participants are brokers representing large investment firms. Different sides of the pit usually represent traders who are dealing in particular expiration months. As brokers and other pit participants conduct trade, they mark down what they bought or sold, how much, at what price, and from whom. These cards are then collected by members of the exchange who record the trades and post the new prices. The prices are displayed on "scoreboards" surrounding the pit.

While stock options and options on commodities and indexes are traded in a similar fashion, one major difference prevails — the presence of **market makers**. Market makers are individuals who typically trade one type of option for their own account and are responsible for ensuring that a market always exists for their particular contract. In addition, some option exchanges utilize **board brokers** as well. These individuals are charged with the maintenance of the book of limit orders (orders from outside investors that are to be executed at particular prices or when the market goes up or down by a prespecified amount). Essentially, market makers and board brokers on the options exchanges share the duties performed by the specialists on the major stock exchanges.

Although stocks can be bought with as little as 50 percent margin, no margin is allowed for buying options-the cost of the contract must be fully paid. Because options offer a high degree of leverage on the underlying asset, additional leveraging through margins is considered by regulators to be excessive. However, if more than one option contract is entered into at the same time — for instance, selling and buying two different calls — then, of course, a lower cost is incurred, since the cost of one is partially (or wholly) offset by the sale of the other.

16.2. Put–Call Parity

This section addresses a most important concept, called **put–call parity** (for option valuation). The discussion includes European options, American options, and future options.

16.2.1. *European Options*

As an initial step to examining the pricing formulas for options, it is essential to discuss the relationships between the prices of put and call options on the same underlying asset. Such relationships among put and call prices are referred to as the *put–call parity theorems.* Stoll (1969) was the first to introduce the concept of put–call parity. Dealing strictly with European options, he showed that the value of a call option would equal the value of a portfolio composed of a long put option, its underlying stock, and a short discounted exercise price. Before stating the basic put–call parity theorem as originally devised by Stoll, it must be assumed that the markets for options, bonds, and stocks (or any other underlying asset we choose) are frictionless.

Theorem 1. *Put–Call Parity for European Options with No Dividends*

$$C_{t,T} = P_{t,T} + S_t - EB_{t,T}, \tag{16.3}$$

where

$C_{t,T}$ = value of a European call option at time t that matures at time $T(T > f)$;

$P_{t,T}$ = value of a European put option at time t, that matures at time T;

S_t = value of the underlying stock (asset) to both the call and put options at time t;

E = exercise price for both the call and put options;

$B_{t,T}$ = price at time t of a default-free bond that pays \$1 with certainty at time T (if it is assumed that this risk-free rate of interest is the same for all maturities and equal to r — in essence a flat-term structure — then $B_{t,T} = e^{-r(T-t)}$, under continuous compounding), or $B_{t,T} = 1/(1+r)^{T-t}$ for discrete compounding.

Equation (16.3) uses the following principle. If the options are neither dominant nor dominated securities, and if the borrowing and lending rates are equal, then the return patterns of a European call and a portfolio composed of a European put, a pure discount bond with a face value equal to the options exercise price E, and the underlying stock (or asset) are the same.[1]

In understanding why the put–call parity theorem holds, and to support the theorem, two additional properties of option pricing must be provided:

Property 1: At maturity (time T) the call option is worth the greater of $S_T - E$ dollars or zero dollars:

$$C_T = \text{Max}(0, S_T - E). \tag{16.4}$$

[1] Any security x is dominant over any security y if the rate of return on x is equal to or greater than that of y for all states of nature and is strictly greater for at least one state. For an expanded discussion of this subject, see Merton (1973) and Smith (1976).

As an example, suppose that the call option has an exercise price of \$30. At maturity, if the stock's (asset's) price is \$25, then the value of the call is the maximum of $(0, 25-30)$ or $(0, -5)$, which of course is zero. If an option sells for less than $(S, -E)$, its intrinsic value, an arbitrage opportunity will exist. Investors would buy the option and short sell the stock, forcing the mispricing to correct itself. Consequently, this first property implies that a call option's value is always greater than zero. An equivalent property and argument exist for the value of a put option as well.

Property 2: At maturity, the value of a put option is the greater of $E - S_T$ dollars or zero dollars:

$$P_T = \text{Max}(0, E - S_T). \tag{16.5}$$

Using the same line of reasoning and argument as for the call option, the second property also implies that the value of a put option is never less than zero. Table 16.4 provides proof of this first put–call parity theorem. Suppose at time t, two portfolios are formed: portfolio B is just a long call option on a stock with price S_t an exercise price of E, and a maturity date at T. Portfolio A consists of purchasing 100 shares of the underlying stock (since stock options represent one hundred shares), purchasing (going long) one put option on the same stock with exercise price E and maturity date T, and borrowing at the risk-free rate an amount equal to the present value of the exercise price or $EB_{t,T}$ with face value of E. (This portion of the portfolio finances the put, call, and stock position.)

At maturity date T, the call option (portfolio B) has value only if $S_T > E$, which is in accordance with Property 1. For portfolio A, under all these conditions the stock price and maturing loan values are the same,

Table 16.4. Call Parity for a European Option with No Dividends.

	Time T (Maturity)		
Time t Strategy	$S_T > E$	$S_T = E$	$S_T < E$
Portfolio A			
1. Buy 100 shares of the stock (S_t).	S_T	S_T	S_T
2. Buy a put (P_t, maturity at T with exercise price E).	0	0	$E - S_T$
3. Borrow $EB_{t,T}$ dollars.	$-E$	$-E$	$-E$
Portfolio A value at time T	$(S_T - E)$	0	0
Portfolio B			
1. Buy a call (C, maturing at T with exercise price E).	$(S_T - E)$	0	0

whereas the put option has value only if $E > S_T$. Under all three possible outcomes for the stock price S_T, it can be seen that the values of portfolios A and B are equal. Proof has been established for the first put–call parity theorem. Sample Problem 16.2 provides further illustration.

Sample Problem 16.2

A call option with one year to maturity and exercise price of $110 is selling for $5. Assuming discrete compounding, a risk-free rate of 10%, and a current stock price of $100, what is the value of a European put option with a strike price of $110 and one-year maturity?

Solution

$$P_{t,T} = C_{t,T} + EB_{t,T} - S_t$$

$$P_{0,1yr} = \$5 + \$110\left(\frac{1}{(1.1)^1}\right) - \$100$$

$$P_{0,1yr} = \$5.$$

16.2.2. *American Options*

Indeed, this first put–call parity theorem holds only under the most basic conditions (i.e., no early exercise and no dividends). Jarrow and Rudd (1983) give an extensive coverage of the effects of more complicated conditions on put–call parity. These authors demonstrate that the effect of known dividends is simply to reduce, by the discounted value (to time t) of the dividends, the amount of the underlying stock purchased. In considering stochastic dividends, the exactness of this pricing relationship breaks down and depends on the degree of certainty that can be maintained about the range of future dividends. Put–call parity for American options is also derived under various dividend conditions. Jarrow and Rudd demonstrate that as a result of the American option's early exercise feature, strict pricing relationships give way to boundary conditions dependent on the size and certainty of future dividends, as well as the level of interest rates and the size of the exercise price. To summarize, they state that for sufficiently high interest rates and/or exercise prices it may be optimal to exercise the put prior to maturity (with or without dividends). So the basic put–call parity for an American option with no dividends and constant interest rates is described by the following theorem.

Theorem 2. *Put–Call Parity for an American Option with No Dividends*

$$P_{t,T} + S - EB_{t,T} > C_{t,T} > P_{t,T} + S_t - E. \tag{16.6}$$

Increasing the generality of conditions results in increasing boundaries for the equilibrium relationship between put and call options. The beauty of these arguments stems from the fact that they require only that investors prefer more wealth to less. If more stringent assumptions are made, then the bounds can be made tighter. For an extensive derivation and explanation of these theorems, see Jarrow and Rudd (1983). Sample problem 16.3 provides further illustration.

Sample Problem 16.3

A put option with one year to maturity and an exercise price of \$90 is selling for \$15; the stock price is \$100. Assuming discrete compounding and a risk-free rate of 10%, what are the boundaries for the price of an American call option?

Solution

$$P_{t,T} + S - EB_{t,T} > C_{t,T} > P_{t,T} + S_t - E$$

$$\$15 + \$100 - \$90\left(\frac{1}{(1.1)^1}\right) > C_{t,T} > \$15 + \$100 - \$90$$

$$\$33.18 > C_{t,1yr} > \$25.$$

16.2.3. *Futures Options*

As a final demonstration of put–call parity, the analysis is extended to the case where the underlying asset is a futures contract. The topic of futures contracts and their valuation will be more fully examined in the next chapter. Nevertheless, this chapter takes time to apply put–call parity when the options are on a futures contract because of the growing popularity and importance of such futures options. A futures contract as described in Chapter 12 is a contract in which the party entering into the contract is obligated to buy or sell the underlying asset at the maturity date for some stipulated price. While the difference between European and American options still remains, the complexity of dividends can be ignored since futures contracts do not pay dividends. Put–call parity for a European futures option (when interest rates are constant) is as follows:

Theorem 3. *Put–Call Parity for a European Futures Option*

$$C_{t,T} = P_{t,T} + B_{t,T}(F_{t,T} - E), \tag{16.7}$$

where $F_{t,T}$ is the price at time t for a futures contract maturing at time T (which is the underlying asset to both the call and put options).

Option pricing Properties 1 and 2 for call and put options apply in an equivalent sense to futures options as well. However, to understand this relationship as stated in Equation (16.7), it must be assumed that the cost of a futures contract is zero. While a certain margin requirement is required, the majority of this assurance deposit can be in the form of interest-bearing securities. Hence as an approximation a zero cost for the futures contract is not unrealistic.

Again, the easiest way to prove this relationship is to follow the same path of analysis used in proving Theorem 1. Table 16.5 indicates that the argument for this theorem's proof is similar, with only a few notable exceptions. The value of the futures contract at time T (maturity) is equal to the difference between the price of the contract at time T and the price at which it was bought, or $F_{TT} - F_{t,T}$. This is an outcome of the fixed duration of a futures contract as opposed to the perpetual duration of common stock. Second, because no money is required to enter into the futures contract, the exercise price is reduced by the current futures price and the total is lent at the risk-free rate. (Actually this amount is either lent or borrowed depending on the relationship between $F_{t,T}$ and E at time t. If $F_{t,T} - E < 0$, then this amount will actually be borrowed at the risk-free rate.)

Table 16.5. Put–Call Parity for a European Futures Option.

	Time T (Maturity)		
Time t Strategy	$F_{TT} > E$	$F_{TT} = E$	$F_{TT} < E$
Portfolio A			
1. Buy a futures contract ($F_{t,T}$).	$F_{TT} - F_{t,T}$	$F_{TT} - F_{t,T}$	$F_{TT} - F_{t,T}$
2. Buy a put ($P_{t,T}$ on $F_{t,T}$ with exercise price E and maturity T).	0	0	$E - F_{TT}$
3. Lend $B_{t,T}(F_{t-T} - E)$ dollars.	$F_{t,T} - E$	$F_{t,T} - E$	$F_{t,T} - E$
Portfolio A's value at time T	$F_{TT} - E$	0	0
Portfolio B			
1. Buy a call ($C_{t,T}$ on $F_{t,T}$ with exercise price E and maturity T).	$F_{TT} - E$	0	0

Why are there options on spot assets as well as options on futures contracts for the spot assets? After all, at expiration the basis of a futures contract goes to zero and futures prices equal spot prices; thus, options in the spot and options on the future are related to the same futures value, and their current values must be identical. Yet a look at the markets shows that options on spot assets and options on futures for the same assets sell at different prices. One explanation for this is that investors who purchase options on spot must pay a large sum of money when they exercise their options, whereas investors who exercise an option on a future need only pay enough to meet the initial margin for the futures contract. Therefore, if the exercise of the option is important to an investor, that investor would prefer options on futures rather than options on spot and would be willing to pay a premium for the option on the future, whereas the investor who has no desire to exercise the option (remember, the investor can always sell it to somebody else to realize a profit) is not willing to pay for this advantage and so finds the option on spot more attractive.

16.2.4. *Market Application*

Put options were not listed on the CBOE until June 1977. Before that time, brokers satisfied their clients' demands for put option risk–return characteristics by a direct application of put–call parity. By combining call options and the underlying security, brokers could construct a **synthetic put**.

To illustrate, the put–call parity theorem is used when a futures contract is the underlying asset. Furthermore, to simulate the option broker's circumstances on July 1, 1984, the equation is merely rearranged to yield the put's "synthetic" value:

$$P_{t,T} = C_{t,T} - B_{t,T}F_{t,T} + B_{t,T}E. \tag{16.8}$$

So instead of a futures contract being purchased, it is sold. Assume the following values and use the S&P 500 index futures as the underlying asset.

$C_{t,T} = \$3.35$;
$F_{t,T} = 154.85$ (September contract);
$E = 155.00$; and
$B_{t,T} = 0.9770$ (current price of a risk-free bond that pays \$1 when the option and futures contract expire, average of bid and ask prices for T-bills from *The Wall Street Journal*).

According to Equation (16.8), the put's price should equal the theorem price: $P_{t,T} = \$3.497$. The actual put price on this day (July 1, 1984) with the same exercise price and expiration month was $P_{t,T} = \$3.50$. With repeated comparisons of the theorem using actual prices, it becomes clear that put–call parity is a powerful equilibrium mechanism in the market.

16.3. Risk–Return Characteristics of Options

One of the most attractive features of options is the myriad of ways in which they can be employed to achieve a particular combination of risk and return. Whether through a straight option position in combination with the underlying asset or some portfolio of securities, options offer an innovative and relatively low-cost mechanism for altering and enhancing the risk–return tradeoff. In order to better grasp these potential applications, this section analyzes call and put options individually and in combination, relative to their potential profit and loss and the effects of time and market sentiment.

16.3.1. *Long Call*

The purchase of a call option is the simplest and most familiar type of option position. The allure of calls is that they provide the investor a great deal of leverage. Potentially, large percentage profits can be realized from only a modest price rise in the underlying asset. In fact, the potential profit from buying a call is unlimited. Moreover, the option purchaser has the right but no obligation to exercise the contract. Therefore, should the price of the underlying asset decline over the life of the call, the purchaser need only let the contract expire worthless. Consequently, the risk of a long call position is limited. Figure 16.3 illustrates the profit profile of a **long call** position. The following summarizes the basic risk–return features for a long-call position.

Profit potential: unlimited.
Loss potential: limited (to cost of option).
Effect of time decay: negative (decrease option's value).
Market expectation: bullish.

As the profit profile indicates, the time value of a long call declines over time. Consequently, an option is a wasting asset. If the underlying asset's price does not move above the exercise price of the option E by its expiration

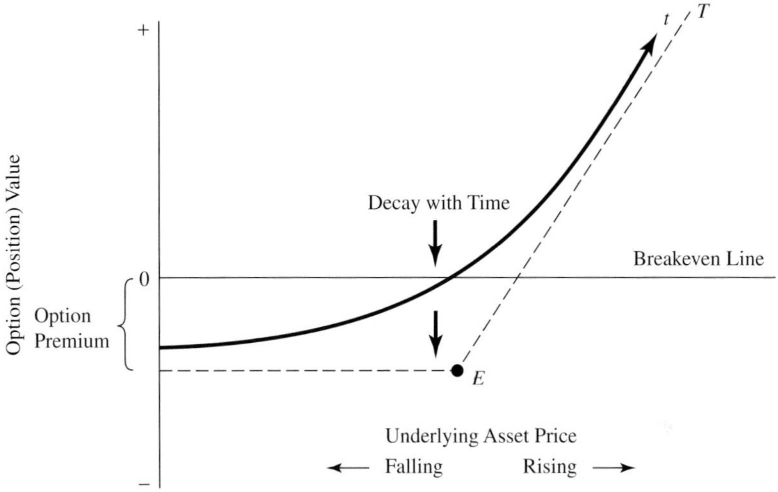

Fig. 16.3. Profit Profile for a Long Call.

date T, the buyer of the call will lose the value of his initial investment (the option premium). Consequently, the longer an investor holds a call, the more time value the option loses, thereby, reducing the price of the option. This leads to another important point — taking on an option position. As with any other investment vehicle, the purchaser of a call expresses an opinion about the market for the underlying asset. Whereas an investor can essentially express one of three different sentiments (bullish, neutral, or bearish) about future market conditions, the long call is strictly a bullish position. That is, the call buyer only wins if the underlying asset rises in price. However, depending on the exercise price of the call, the buyer can express differing degrees of bullishness. For instance, since out-of-the-money calls are the cheapest, a large price increase in the underlying asset will make these calls the biggest percentage gainers in value. So an investor who is extremely bullish would probably go with an out-of-the-money call, since its intrinsic value is small and its value will increase along with a large increase in the market.

16.3.2. *Short Call*

Selling a call (writing it) has risk–reward characteristics, which are the inverse of the long call. However, one major distinction arises when writing calls (or puts) rather than buying them. That is, the writer can either own

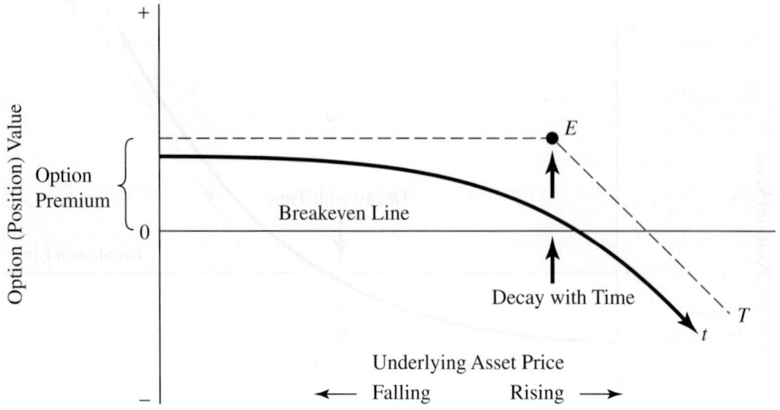

Fig. 16.4. Profit Profile for a Short Call.

the underlying asset upon which he or she is selling the option (a **covered write**), or simply sell the option without owning the asset (a **naked write**). The difference between the two is of considerable consequence to the amount of risk and return taken on by the seller. Let us first examine the profit profile and related attributes of the naked **short call**, displayed in Fig. 16.4.

When the writer of a call does not own the underlying asset, his or her potential loss is unlimited. Why? Because if the price of the underlying asset increases, the value of the call also increases for the buyer. The seller of a call is *obliged* to provide a designated quantity of the underlying asset at some prespecified price (the exercise price) at any time up to the maturity date of the option. So if the asset starts rising dramatically in price and the call buyer exercises his or her *right*, the naked-call writer must go into the market to buy the underlying asset at whatever the market price. The naked-call writer suffers the loss of buying the asset at a price S and selling it at a price E when $S > E$ (less the original premium collected). When common stock is the underlying asset, there is no limit to how high its price could go. Thus, the naked-call writer's risk is unlimited as well. Indeed, the naked-call writer could have reversed position by buying back the original option he sold — that is, zeroing out the position — however, this is also done at a loss. The following summarizes the basic risk–return features for a naked short-call position.

Profit potential: limited (to option premium).
Loss potential: unlimited.

Effect of time decay: positive (makes buyer's position less valuable).
Market expectation: bearish to neutral.

The naked short-call position is obviously a bearish position. If the underlying asset's price moves down, the call writer keeps the entire premium received for selling this call, since the call buyer's position becomes worthless. Once again, the naked-call writer can express the degree of bearishness by the exercise price at which he or she sells the call. By selling an in-the-money call, the writer stands to collect a higher option premium. Conversely, selling an out-of-the-money call conveys only a mildly bearish to neutral expectation. If the underlying asset's price stays where it is, the value of the buyer's position, which is solely time value, will decay to zero; and the call writer will collect the entire premium (though a substantially smaller premium than for an in-the-money call).

While the passing of time has a negative effect on the value of a call option for the buyer, it has a positive effect for the seller. One aspect of an option's time value is that in the last month before the option expires, its time value decays most rapidly. The reason being that time value is related to the probability that the underlying asset's price will move up or down enough to make an option position increase in value. This probability declines at an accelerating (exponential) rate as the option approaches its maturity date. The consideration of time value, then, is a major element when investing in or hedging with options. Unless an investor is extremely bullish, it would probably be unwise to take a long position in a call in its last month before maturity. Conversely, the last month of an option's life is a preferred time to sell since its time value can more easily and quickly be collected.

Now consider the other type of short-call position, covered-call writing. Because the seller of the call owns the underlying asset in this case, the risk is truncated. The purpose of writing a call on the underlying asset when it is owned is twofold. First, by writing a call option, one always decreases the risk of owning the asset. Second, writing a call can increase the overall realized return on the asset. The profit profile for a covered short call (or a covered write) in Fig. 16.5 provides further illustration. The following summarizes the basic risk–return features for the covered short-call position.

Profit potential: limited (exercise price − asset price + call premium).
Loss potential: limited (asset price − call premium).

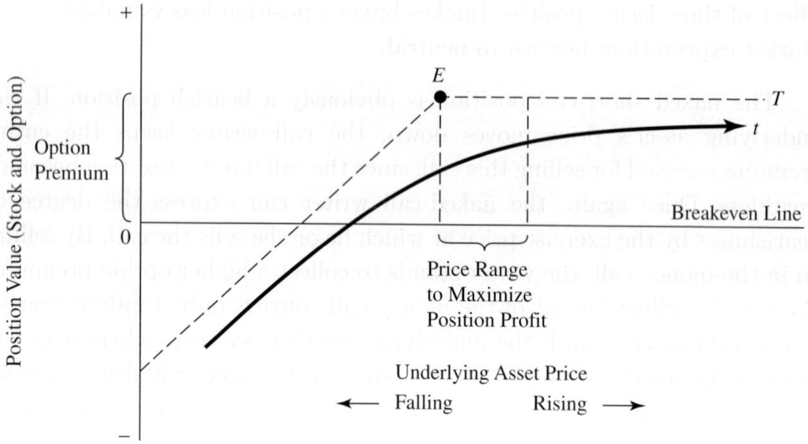

Fig. 16.5. Profit Profile for a Covered Short Call.

Effect of time decay: positive.
Market expectation: neutral to mildly bullish.

By owning the underlying asset, the covered-call writer's loss on the asset for a price decline is decreased by the original amount of the premium collected for selling the option. The total loss on the position is limited to the extent that the asset is one of limited liability, such as a stock, and cannot fall below zero. The maximum profit on the combined asset and option position is higher than if the option was written alone, but lower than simply owning the asset with no short call written on it. Once the asset increases in price by a significant amount the call buyer will very likely exercise the right to purchase the asset at the prespecified exercise price. Thus, covered-call writing is a tool or strategy for enhancing an asset's realized return while lowering its risk in a sideways market.

16.3.3. *Long Put*

Again, the put option conveys to its purchasers the right to sell a given quantity of some asset at a prespecified price on or before its expiration date. Similar to a long call, a **long put** is also a highly leveraged position, but the purchaser of the put makes money on the investment only when the price of the underlying asset declines. While a call buyer has unlimited profit potential, a put buyer has limited profit potential since the price of the underlying asset can never drop below zero. Yet like the long-call

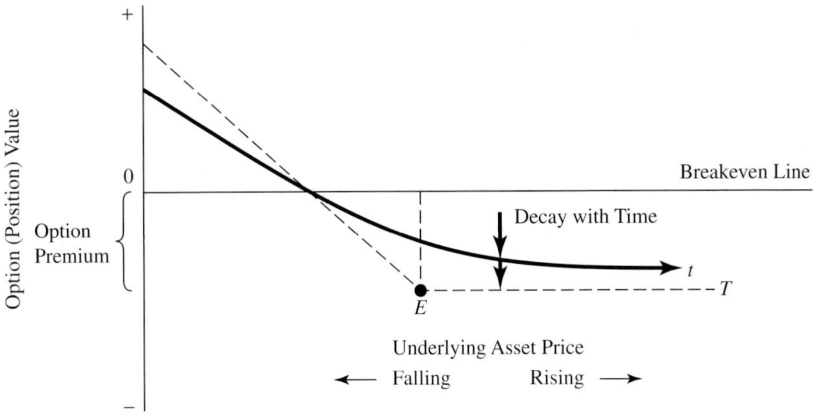

Fig. 16.6. Profit Profile for a Long Put.

position, the put buyer can never lose more than the initial investment (the option's premium). The profit profile for a long put is seen in Fig. 16.6. The following summarizes the basic risk–return features for the profit profile of a long-put position.

Profit potential: limited (asset price must be greater than zero).
Loss potential: limited (to cost of put).
Effect of time decay: negative or positive.
Market expectation: bearish.

An interesting pricing ambiguity for this bearish investment is how the put's price is affected by the time decay. With the long call there is a clear-cut relation — that is, the effect of the time decay is to diminish the value of the call. The relationship is not so clear with the long put. Although at certain prices for the underlying asset the value of the long-put position decreases with time, there exist lower asset prices for which its value will increase with time. It is the put's ambiguous relationship with time that makes its correct price difficult to ascertain. (This topic will be further explored in Chapter 17.)

One uniquely attractive attribute of the long put is its negative relationship with the underlying asset. In terms of the capital asset pricing model, it has a negative beta (though usually numerically larger than that of the underlying asset, due to the leverage affect). Therefore, the long put is an ideal hedging instrument for the holder of the underlying asset who wants to protect against a price decline. If the investor is wrong and the price of the asset moves up instead, the profit from the asset's price increase is only moderately diminished by the cost of the put. More on hedging and related concepts is discussed in Chapter 17.

16.3.4. *Short Put*

As was true for the short-call position, put writing can be covered or uncovered (naked). The risk–return features of the uncovered (naked) **short put** are discussed first.

For taking on the obligation to buy the underlying asset at the exercise price, the put writer receives a premium. The maximum profit for the uncovered-put-writer is this premium, which is initially received. Figure 16.7 provides further illustration.

While the loss potential is limited for the uncovered put-writer, it is nonetheless still very large. Thus, someone neutral on the direction of the market would sell out-of-the-money (lower exercise price) puts. A more bullish sentiment would suggest that at-the-money options be sold. The investor who is convinced that the market will go up should maximize return by selling a put with a larger premium. As with the long put, the time-decay effect is ambiguous and depends on the price of the underlying asset. The following summarizes the basic risk–return features for the profit profile of an uncovered short-put position.

Profit potential: limited (to put premium).
Loss potential: limited (asset price must be greater than zero).

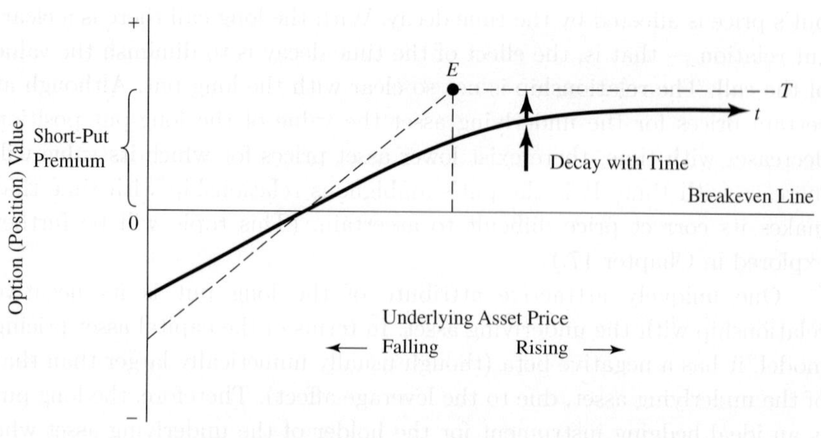

Fig. 16.7. Profit Profile for an Uncovered Short Call.

Effect of time decay: positive or negative.
Market expectation: neutral to bullish.

Referring again to Fig. 16.5 for the combined short-call and long-asset position, notice the striking resemblance of its profit profile at expiration to that for the uncovered short put. This relationship can be seen mathematically by using put–call parity. That is, the synthetic put price $P_T = E_c + C_T - S_T$, or at expiration the value of the put should equal the exercise price of the call option plus the call option's value minus the value at time T of the underlying asset. Buying (writing) a call and selling (buying) the underlying asset (or vice versa) allows an investor to achieve essentially the same risk–return combination as would be received from a long put (short put). This combination of two assets to equal the risk and return of a third is referred to as a synthetic asset (or synthetic option in this case). Synthesizing two financial instruments to resemble a third is an arbitrage process and is a central concept of finance theory.

Now a look at covered short puts is in order to round out the basics of option strategies. For margin purposes and in a theoretical sense, selling a put against a short-asset position would be the sale of a covered put. However, this sort of position has a limited profit potential that is obtained if the underlying asset is anywhere below the exercise price of the put at expiration. This position also has unlimited upside risk, since the short position in the asset will accrue losses while the profit from the put sale is limited. Essentially, this position is equivalent to the uncovered or naked short call, except that the latter has less expensive transaction costs. Moreover, because the time value for put options is generally less than that of calls, it will be advantageous to short the call.

Strictly speaking, a short put is covered only if the investor also owns a corresponding put with exercise price equal to or greater than that of the written put. Such a position, called a spread, is discussed later in this chapter.

16.3.5. *Long Straddle*

A straddle is a simultaneous position in both a call and a put on the same underlying asset. A **long straddle** involves purchasing both the call and the put. By combining these two seemingly opposing options, an investor can get the best risk–return combination that each offers. The profit profile

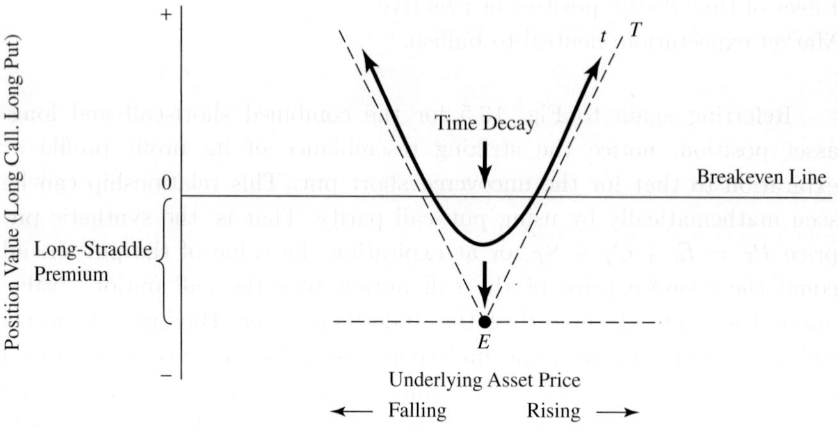

Fig. 16.8. Profit Profile for a Long Straddle.

for a long straddle in Fig. 16.8 illustrates the nature of this synthetic asset. The following summarizes the basic risk–return features for the profit profile of a long-straddle position.

Profit potential: unlimited on upside, limited on downside.
Loss potential: limited (to cost of call and put premiums).
Effect of time decay: negative.
Market sentiment: bullish or bearish.

The long straddle's profit profile makes clear that its risk–reward picture is simply that of the long call overlapped by the long put, with each horizontal segment truncated (represented by the horizontal dashed lines on the bottom). An investor will profit on this type of position as long as the price of the underlying asset moves sufficiently up or down to more than cover the original cost of the option premiums. Thus, a long straddle is an effective strategy for someone expecting the volatility of the underlying asset to increase in the future. In the same light, the investor who buys a straddle expects the underlying asset's volatility of price to be greater than that imputed in the option price.

Since time decay is working against the value of this position, it might be unwise to purchase a straddle composed of a call and put in their last month to maturity when their time decay is greatest. It would be possible to reduce the cost of the straddle by purchasing a high-exercise-price call and a low-exercise put (out-of-the-money options); however, the necessary up or down movement in the asset's price in order to profit is larger. Sample problem 16.4 provides further illustration.

Sample Problem 16.4

Situation: An investor feels the stock market is going to break sharply up or down but is not sure which way. However, the investor is confident that market volatility will increase in the near future. To express his position, the investor puts on a long straddle using options on the S&P 500 index, buying both at-the-money call and put options on the September contract. The current September S&P 500 futures contract price is 155.00. Assume the position is held to expiration.

Transaction:

1. Buy 1 September 155 call at $2.00	($1,000)
2. Buy 1 September 155 put at $2.00	($1,000)
Net initial investment (position value)	($2,000)

Results:

1. If futures price = 150.00:	
(a) 1 September call expires at $0	($1,000)
(b) 1 September put expires at $5.00	$2,500
(c) Less initial cost of put	($1,000)
Ending position value (net profit)	$500
2. If futures price = 155.00:	
(a) 1 September call expires at $0	($1,000)
(b) 1 September put expires at $0	($1,000)
Ending position value (net loss)	$2,000
3. If futures price = 160.00:	
(a) 1 September call expires at $5.00	$2,500
(b) 1 September call expires at $0	($1,000)
(c) Less initial cost of put	($1,000)
Ending position value (net profit)	$500

Summary:

Maximum profit potential: unlimited. If the market had contributed to move below 150.00 or above 160.00, the position would have continued to increase in value.

Maximum loss potential: \$2,000, the initial investment.
Breakeven points: 151.00 and 159.00, for the September S&P 500 futures contract.[2]
Effect of time decay: negative, as evidenced by the loss incurred, with no change in futures price (result 2).

16.3.6. *Short Straddle*

For the most part, the short straddle implies the opposite risk–return characteristics of the long straddle. A short straddle is a simultaneous position in both a short call and a short put on the same underlying asset. Contrary to the long-straddle position, selling a straddle can be an effective strategy when an investor expects little or no movement in the price of the underlying asset. A similar interpretation of its use would be that the investor expects the future volatility of the underlying asset's price that is currently impounded in the option premiums to decline. Moreover, since the time decay is a positive effect for the value of this position, one appropriate time to set a short straddle might be in the last month to expiration for the combined call and put. Figure 16.9 shows the short straddle's profit profile, and Sample problem 16.5 provides further illustration. The following summarizes the basic risk–return features for the profit profile of a short-straddle position.

Profit potential: limited (to call and put premiums).
Loss potential: unlimited on upside, limited on downside.
Effect of time decay: positive.
Market expectation: neutral.

Sample Problem 16.5

Situation: An investor feels the market is overestimating price volatility at the moment and that prices are going to remain stable for some time.

---

[2]Breakeven points for the straddle are calculated as follows:

$$\begin{aligned} \textit{Upside BEP} &= \text{Exercise price} + \text{Initial net investment (in points)} \\ 159.00 &= 155.00 + 4.00 \\ \textit{Downside BEP} &= \text{Exercise price} - \text{Initial net investment (in points)} \\ 159.00 &= 155.00 + 4.00 \\ 151.00 &= 155.00 - 4.00 \end{aligned}$$

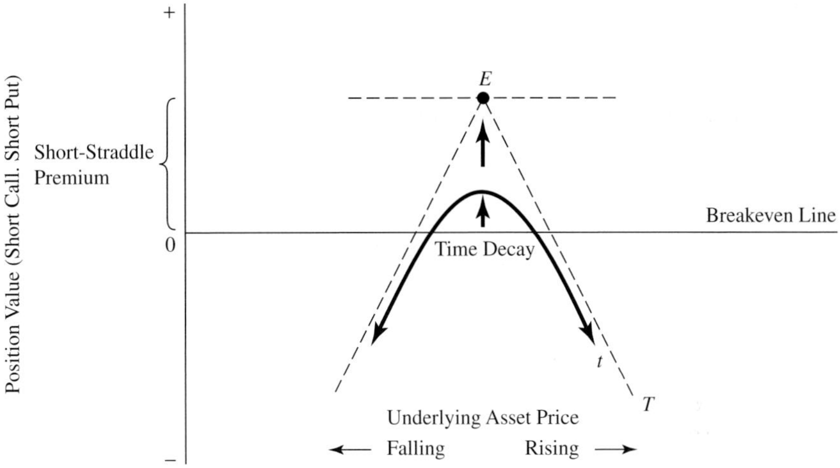

Fig. 16.9. Profit Profile for a Short Straddle.

To express his opinion, the investor sells a straddle consisting of at-the-money call and put options on the September S&P 500 futures contract, for which the current price is 155.00. Assume the position is held to expiration.

Transaction:

1. Sell 1 September 155 call at \$2.00 (× \$500 per point)	\$1,000
2. Sell 1 September 155 put at \$2.00	\$1,000
Net initial inflow (position value)	\$2,000

Results:

1. If futures price = 150.00:	
(a) 1 September 155 call expires at 0	\$1,000
(b) 1 September 155 put expires at \$5.00	(\$2,500)
(c) Plus initial inflow from sale of put	\$1,000
Ending position value (net loss)	(\$500)
2. If futures price = 155.00:	
(a) 1 September 155 call expires at 0	\$1,000
(b) 1 September 155 put expires at 0	\$1,000
Ending position value (net profit)	\$2,000

3. If futures price = 160.00:

(a) 1 September 155 call expires at \$5.00	(\$2,500)
(b) 1 September put expires at 0	\$1,000
(c) Plus initial inflow from sale of call	\$1,000
Ending position value (net loss)	(\$ 500)

Summary:

Maximum profit potential: \$2,000, result 2. where futures price does not move.
Maximum loss potential: unlimited. If futures price had continued up over 160.00 or down below 145.00, this position would have kept losing money.
Breakeven points: 151.00 and 159.00, an eight-point range for profitability of the position.[3]
Effect of time decay: positive, as evidenced by result 2.

16.3.7. *Long Vertical (Bull) Spread*

When dealing strictly in options, a spread is a combination of any two or more of the same type of options (two calls or two puts, for instance) on the same underlying asset. A vertical spread specifies that the options have the same maturity month. Finally, a long vertical spread designates a position for which one has bought a low-exercise-price call (or a low-exercise-price put) and sold a high-exercise-price call (or a high-exercise-price put) that both mature in the same month. A long vertical spread is also known as a **bull** spread because of the bullish market expectation of the investor who enters into it. Actually, the long vertical spread (or bull spread) is not a strongly bullish position, because the investor limits the profit potential in selling the high-exercise-price call (or high-exercise-price put). Rather, this is a popular position when it is expected that the market will more likely go up than down. Therefore, the bull spread conveys a bit of uncertainty about future market conditions. Of course, the higher the exercise price at which the call is sold, the more bullish the position. An examination of the profit profile for the long vertical spread (see Fig. 16.10) can tell more about its risk–return attributes. The following summarizes the basic risk–return features for the profit profile of a long-vertical-spread position.

[3]Breakeven points for the short straddle are calculated in the same manner as for the long straddle: exercise price plus initial prices of options.

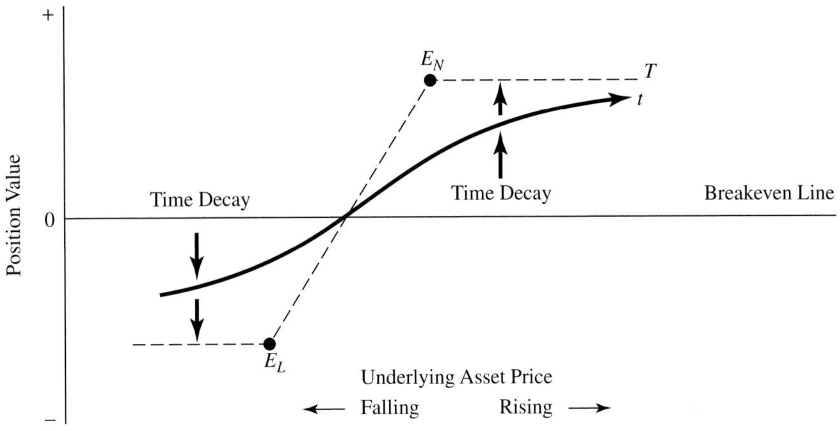

Fig. 16.10. Profit Profile for a Long Vertical Spread.

Profit potential: limited (up to the higher exercise price).
Loss potential: limited (down to the lower exercise price) Effect of time decay: mixed.
Market expectation: cautiously bullish.

Although profit is limited by the shorted call on the upside, the loss potential is also truncated at the lower exercise price by the same short call. There are other reasons for this being a mildly bullish strategy. The effect of time decay is ambiguous up to the expiration or liquidation of the position. That is, if the asset price, S_t, is near the exercise price of the higher-price option E_H, then the position acts more like a long call and time-decay effect is negative. Conversely, if S_t is near the exercise price of the lower-price option E_L, then the bull spread acts more like a short call and the time-decay effect is neutral.

Consequently, unless an investor is more than mildly bullish, it would probably be unwise to put on a bull spread with the low exercise price call near the current price of the asset while both options are in their last month to expiration. Sample problem 16.6 provides further illustration.

Sample Problem 16.6

Situation: An investor is moderately bullish on the West German mark. He would like to be long but wants to reduce the cost and risk of this position in case he is wrong. To express his opinion, the investor puts on a long vertical spread by buying a lower-exercise-price call and selling a higher-exercise-price call with the same month to expiration. Assume the position is held to expiration.

Transaction:

1. Buy 1 September 0.37 call at 0.0047 (×125.000 per point)	($587.50)
2. Sell 1 September 0.38 call at 0.0013	$162.50
Net initial investment (position value)	($425.00)

Results:

1. If futures price = 0.3700:	
(a) 1 September 0.37 call expires at 0	($587.50)
(b) 1 September 0.38 call expires at 0	$162.50
Ending position value (net loss)	($425.00)
2. If futures price = 0.3800:	
(a) 1 September 0.37 call expires at 0.0100	$1,250.00
(b) I September 0.38 call expires at 0	$162.50
Less initial cost of 0.37 call	($587.50)
Ending position value (net profit)	$825.00
3. If futures price = 0.3900:	
(a) 1 September 0.38 call expires at 0.0200	$2,500.00
(b) 1 September put expires at 0	($1,250.00)
Less initial premium of 0.37 call	($587.50)
Plus initial premium of 0.38 call	$162.50
Ending position value (net profit)	$825.00

Summary:

Maximum profit potential: $825.00, result 2.
Maximum loss potential: $425.00, result 1.
Breakeven point: 0.3734.[4]
Effect of time decay: mixed; positive if price is at high end of range and negative if at low end.

[4]Breakeven point for the long vertical spread is computed as lower exercise price plus price of long call minus price of short call (0.3734 = 0.3700 + 0.0047 − 0.0013).

16.3.8. *Short Vertical (Bear) Spread*

The **short vertical spread** is simply the reverse of the corresponding long position. That is, an investor buys a high-exercise-price call (or put) and sells a low-exercise-price call (or put), both having the same time to expiration left. As the more common name for this type of option position is bear spread, it is easy to infer the type of market sentiment consistent with this position. The profit profile for the short vertical spread is seen in Fig. 16.11.

As the profit profile indicates, this strategy is profitable as long as the underlying asset moves down in price. Profit is limited to a price decline in the asset down to the lower exercise price, while risk is limited on the upside by the long-call position. From the time-decay effects shown, a mildly bearish investor might consider using options in the last month to expiration with the E_L option near the money. The following summarizes the basic risk–return features for the profit profile of a short-vertical-spread position.

Profit potential: limited (down to E_L).
Loss potential: limited (up to E_H).
Effect of time decay: mixed (opposite to that of long vertical spread).
Market sentiment: mildly bearish.

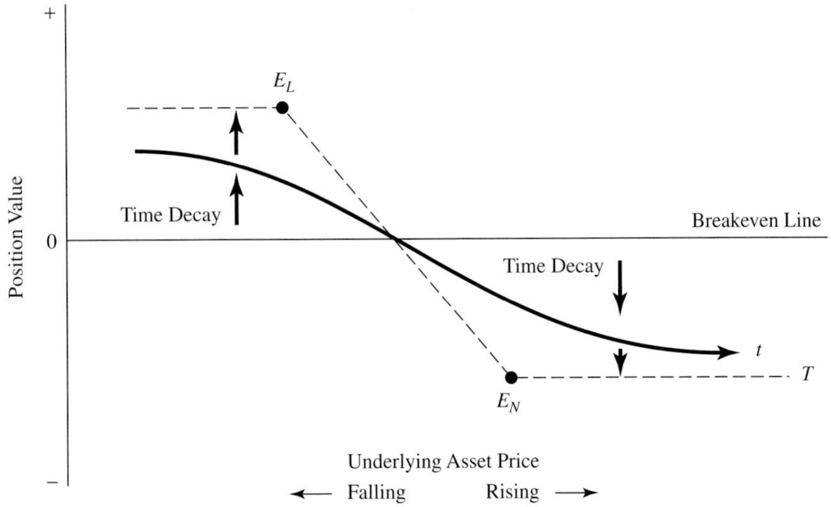

Fig. 16.11. Profit Profile for a Short Vertical Spread.

16.3.9. *Calendar (Time) Spreads*

A **calendar spread** (also called a **time** or **horizontal spread**) consists of the sale of one option and the simultaneous purchase of another option with the same exercise price but a longer term to maturity. The objective of the calendar spread is to capture the faster erosion in the time-premium portion of the shorted nearer-term-to-maturity option. By taking a position in two of the same type options (two calls or two puts), both with the same exercise price, the investor utilizing this strategy expresses a neutral opinion on the market. In other words, the investor is interested in selling time rather than predicting the price direction of the underlying asset. Thus, a calendar spread might be considered appropriate for a sideways-moving or quiet market. However, if the underlying asset's price moves significantly up or down, the calendar spread will lose part of its original value. Figure 16.12 displays the calendar spread's profit profile and related risk–return attributes.

The profit profile shows that this strategy will make money for a rather narrow range of price movement in the underlying asset. While similar in nature to the short straddle (both are neutral strategies), the calendar spread is more conservative. The reason being it has both a lower profit potential and lower (limited) risk than the short straddle. The lower potential profit is the result of only benefiting from the time decay in one option premium instead of two (the call and the put) for the short straddle. Moreover, taking opposite positions in the same type of option at the same

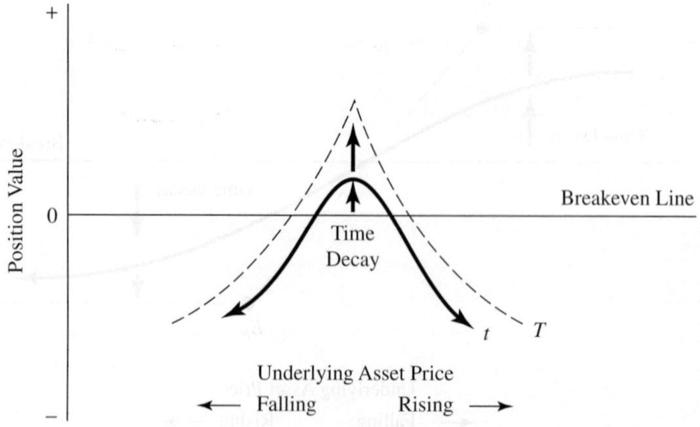

Fig. 16.12. Profit Profile for a Neutral Calendar Spread.

exercise price adds a loss limit on each side against adverse price moves. The following summarizes the basic risk–return features for the profit profile of a neutral calendar-spread position.

Profit potential: limited.
Loss potential: limited (to original cost of position).
Effect of time decay: positive. (Option sold loses value faster than option bought.)
Market sentiment: neutral.

The calendar spread does not have to be neutral in sentiment. By diagonalizing this spread it is possible to express an opinion on the market. For instance, by selling a near-term higher-exercise-price option and purchasing a longer-term lower-exercise-price option, the investor is being bullish in position. Such a position is thus referred to as a bullish calendar spread. Why is it bullish? Remember that with the neutral calendar spread we are concerned solely with benefiting from the faster time decay in the premium of the shorted near-term option. Any significant movement in price upwards, for instance, would have not been profitable because it would have slowed the time decay and increased the intrinsic value of the shorted near-term option. In fact we would eventually lose money because the difference in premiums between the near-term and the longer-term options (the spread) would narrow as the underlying asset's price increased. However, the bullish calendar spread is much like a long vertical (or bull) spread in that a modest increase in price for the asset up to the higher exercise price will be profitable. At the same time, though, the bullish calendar spread also reaps some of the benefits from the greater time decay in the nearer-term option's premium. While this strategy might sound superior to the straight bull spread, it really depends on market conditions. With a bullish calendar spread, its gain from time decay will probably not be as great as that from a neutral calendar spread, nor will its bullish nature be as profitable as a straight bull spread in the event of a modest price increase for the underlying asset. The real world application will be discussed in the next section.

16.4. Excel Approach to Analyze the Option Strategies

In this section we will show how excel program can be used to analyze the option strategies. We use the data of JNJ on March 29, 2011 as presented in Table 16.6 to analyze seven option strategies. Below is the information

Table 16.6. Call and Put Option Quotes for JNJ at March 29, 2011.

Strike	Symbol	Bid	Ask
Call Option Expiring close April 15, 2011			
35	JNJ110416C00035000	23.95	24.45
40	JNJ110416C00040000	18.95	19.35
45	JNJ110416C00045000	14.15	14.25
50	JNJ110416C00050000	9.2	9.35
52.5	JNJ110416C00052500	6.7	6.85
55	JNJ110416C00055000	4.2	4.3
57.5	JNJ110416C00057500	1.89	1.94
60	JNJ110416C00060000	0.3	0.31
62.5	JNJ110416C00062500	0.03	0.04
Put Option Expiring close April 15, 2011			
47.5	JNJ110416P00047500	0.01	0.04
50	JNJ110416P00050000	0.02	0.04
52.5	JNJ110416P00052500	0.05	0.07
55	JNJ110416P00055000	0.09	0.1
57.5	JNJ110416P00057500	0.2	0.22
60	JNJ110416P00060000	1.09	1.13
62.5	JNJ110416P00062500	3.25	3.4
65	JNJ110416P00065000	5.75	5.85
67.5	JNJ110416P00067500	8.2	8.5

published on March 29, 2011 for all options that expired in April 2011. JNJ stock closed at \$59.38 on March 29, 2011.

16.4.1. *Long Straddle*

Assume that an investor expects the volatility of JNJ stock to increase in the future, and then can use a long straddle to profit. The investor can purchase a call option and a put option with the same exercise price \$60. The investor will profit on this type of position as long as the price of the underlying asset moves sufficiently up or down to more than cover the original cost of the option premiums. Let S_0, S_T, and X denote the stock purchase price, future stock price at the expiration time T, and the strike price, respectively. Given $X = \$60$, and the premiums for the call option \$0.31 and put option \$1.13, Table 16.7 shows the values for long straddle at different stock prices at time T. The profit profile of the long straddle position is constructed in Fig. 16.13.

Table 16.7. Value of Long Straddle Position at Option Expiration.

Long a call at strike price	$60.00	Premium	$0.31
Long a put at strike price	$60.00	Premium	$1.13

Stock	Long Call (X = $60)		Long Put (X = $60)		Long Straddle	
Price	Payoff	Profit	Payoff	Profit	Payoff	Profit
$45.00	$0.00	−$0.31	$15.00	$13.87	$15.00	$13.56
$47.50	$0.00	−$0.31	$12.50	$11.37	$12.50	$11.06
$50.00	$0.00	−$0.31	$10.00	$8.87	$10.00	$8.56
$52.50	$0.00	−$0.31	$7.50	$6.37	$7.50	$6.06
$55.00	$0.00	−$0.31	$5.00	$3.87	$5.00	$3.56
$57.50	$0.00	−$0.31	$2.50	$1.37	$2.50	$1.06
$60.00	$0.00	−$0.31	$0.00	−$1.13	$0.00	−$1.44
$62.50	$2.50	$2.19	$0.00	−$1.13	$2.50	$1.06
$65.00	$5.00	$4.69	$0.00	−$1.13	$5.00	$3.56
$67.50	$7.50	$7.19	$0.00	−$1.13	$7.50	$6.06
$70.00	$10.00	$9.69	$0.00	−$1.13	$10.00	$8.56

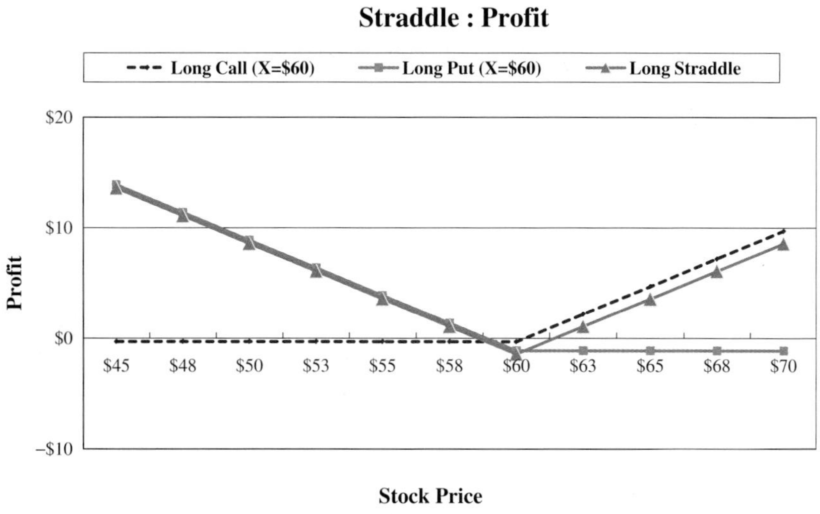

Fig. 16.13. Profit Profile for Long Straddle.

16.4.2. *Short Straddle*

Contrary to the long straddle strategy, an investor will use a short straddle via a short call and a short put on JNJ stock with the same exercise price $60 when he or she expects little or no movement in the price of JNJ stock.

Table 16.8. Value of Short Straddle Position at Option Expiration.

Short a call at strike price	$60.00	Premium	$0.30
Short a put at strike price	$60.00	Premium	$1.09

Stock	Short Call (X = $60)		Short Put (X = $60)		Short Straddle	
Price	Payoff	Profit	Payoff	Profit	Payoff	Profit
$45.00	$0.00	$0.30	−$15.00	−$13.91	−$15.00	−$13.61
$47.50	$0.00	$0.30	−$12.50	−$11.41	−$12.50	−$11.11
$50.00	$0.00	$0.30	−$10.00	−$8.91	−$10.00	−$8.61
$52.50	$0.00	$0.30	−$7.50	−$6.41	−$7.50	−$6.11
$55.00	$0.00	$0.30	−$5.00	−$3.91	−$5.00	−$3.61
$57.50	$0.00	$0.30	−$2.50	−$1.41	−$2.50	−$1.11
$60.00	$0.00	$0.30	$0.00	$1.09	$0.00	$1.39
$62.50	−$2.50	−$2.20	$0.00	$1.09	−$2.50	−$1.11
$65.00	−$5.00	−$4.70	$0.00	$1.09	−$5.00	−$3.61
$67.50	−$7.50	−$7.20	$0.00	$1.09	−$7.50	−$6.11
$70.00	−$10.00	−$9.70	$0.00	$1.09	−$10.00	−$8.61

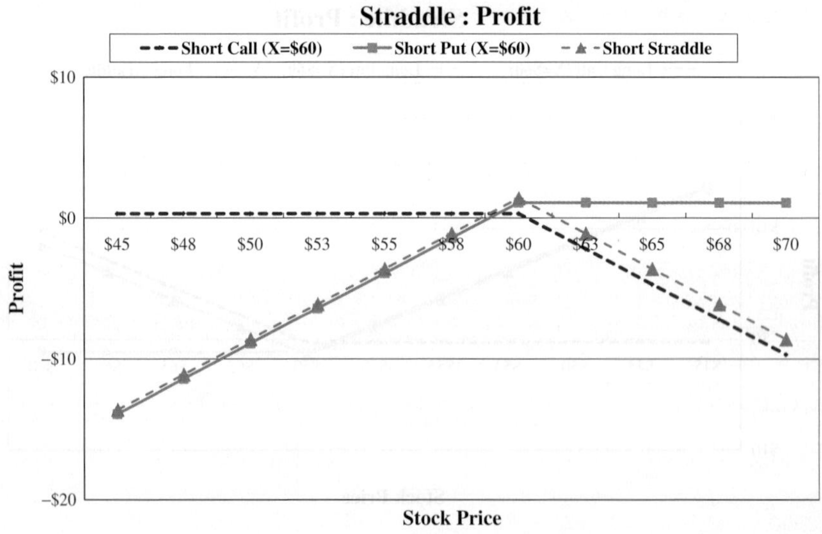

Fig. 16.14. Profit Profile for Short Straddle.

Given $X = \$60$, and the premiums for the call option $0.3 and put option $1.09, Table 16.8 shows the values for short straddle at different stock prices at time T. The profit profile of the short straddle position is constructed in Fig. 16.14.

16.4.3. *Long Vertical (Bull) Spread*

This strategy combines a long call (or put) with a low strike price and a short call (or put) with a high strike price. For example, an investor purchases a call with the exercise price \$57.50 and sells a call with the exercise price \$62.50. Given $X_1 = \$57.50$, $X_2 = \$62.50$ and the premiums for the long call option is \$1.94 and the short call option is \$0.03, Table 16.9 shows the values for Long Vertical Spread at different stock prices at time T. The profit profile of the Long Vertical Spread is constructed in Fig. 16.15.

16.4.4. *Short Vertical (Bear) Spread*

Contrary to a long vertical spread, this strategy combines a long call (or put) with a high strike price and a short call (or put) with a low strike price. For example, an investor purchases a call with the exercise price \$60 and sells a call with the exercise price \$57.50. Given $X_1 = \$60$, $X_2 = \$57.50$ and the premiums for the long call option is \$0.31 and the short call option is \$1.89, Table 16.10 shows the values for short vertical spread at different stock prices at time T. The profit profile of the short vertical spread is constructed in Fig. 16.16.

Table 16.9. Value of Long Vertical Spread Position at Option Expiration.

Long a call at strike price	\$57.50	Premium	\$1.94
Short a call at strike price	\$62.50	Premium	\$0.03

Stock	Short Call (X = \$62.50)		Long Call (X = \$57.50)		Long Vertical Spread	
Price	Payoff	Profit	Payoff	Profit	Payoff	Profit
\$45.00	\$0.00	\$0.03	\$0.00	−\$1.94	\$0.00	−\$1.91
\$47.50	\$0.00	\$0.03	\$0.00	−\$1.94	\$0.00	−\$1.91
\$50.00	\$0.00	\$0.03	\$0.00	−\$1.94	\$0.00	−\$1.91
\$52.50	\$0.00	\$0.03	\$0.00	−\$1.94	\$0.00	−\$1.91
\$55.00	\$0.00	\$0.03	\$0.00	−\$1.94	\$0.00	−\$1.91
\$57.50	\$0.00	\$0.03	\$0.00	−\$1.94	\$0.00	−\$1.91
\$60.00	\$0.00	\$0.03	\$2.50	\$0.56	\$2.50	\$0.59
\$62.50	\$0.00	\$0.03	\$5.00	\$3.06	\$5.00	\$3.09
\$65.00	−\$2.50	−\$2.47	\$7.50	\$5.56	\$5.00	\$3.09
\$67.50	−\$5.00	−\$4.97	\$10.00	\$8.06	\$5.00	\$3.09
\$70.00	−\$7.50	−\$7.47	\$12.50	\$10.56	\$5.00	\$3.09

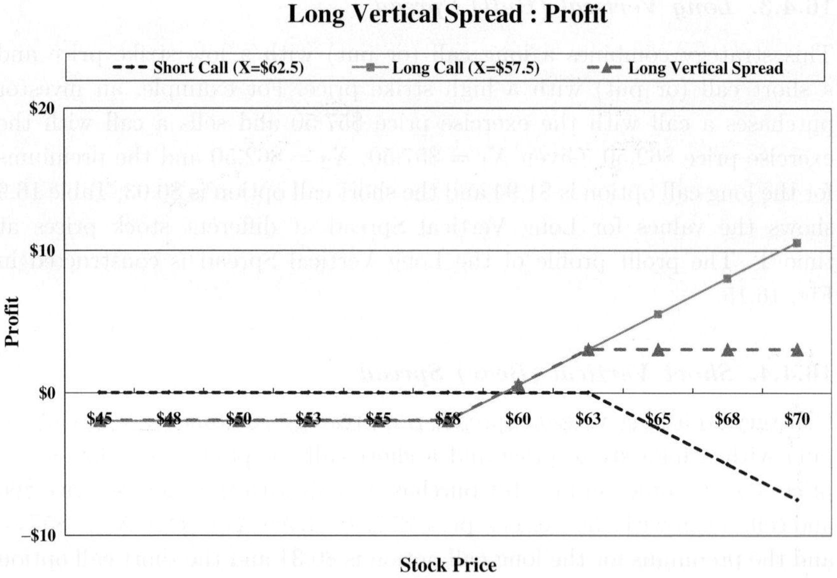

Fig. 16.15. Profit Profile for Long Vertical Spread.

Table 16.10. Value of Short Vertical Spread Position at Option Expiration.

Long a call at strike price	\$60.00	Premium	\$0.31
Short a call at strike price	\$57.50	Premium	\$1.89

Stock	Short Call (X = \$57.50)		Long Call (X = \$60)		Short Vertical Spread	
Price	Payoff	Profit	Payoff	Profit	Payoff	Profit
\$45.00	\$0.00	\$1.89	\$0.00	−\$0.31	\$0.00	\$1.58
\$47.50	\$0.00	\$1.89	\$0.00	−\$0.31	\$0.00	\$1.58
\$50.00	\$0.00	\$1.89	\$0.00	−\$0.31	\$0.00	\$1.58
\$52.50	\$0.00	\$1.89	\$0.00	−\$0.31	\$0.00	\$1.58
\$55.00	\$0.00	\$1.89	\$0.00	−\$0.31	\$0.00	\$1.58
\$57.50	\$0.00	\$1.89	\$0.00	−\$0.31	\$0.00	\$1.58
\$60.00	−\$2.50	−\$0.61	\$0.00	−\$0.31	−\$2.50	−\$0.92
\$62.50	−\$5.00	−\$3.11	\$2.50	\$2.19	−\$2.50	−\$0.92
\$65.00	−\$7.50	−\$5.61	\$5.00	\$4.69	−\$2.50	−\$0.92
\$67.50	−\$10.00	−\$8.11	\$7.50	\$7.19	−\$2.50	−\$0.92
\$70.00	−\$12.50	−\$10.61	\$10.00	\$9.69	−\$2.50	−\$0.92

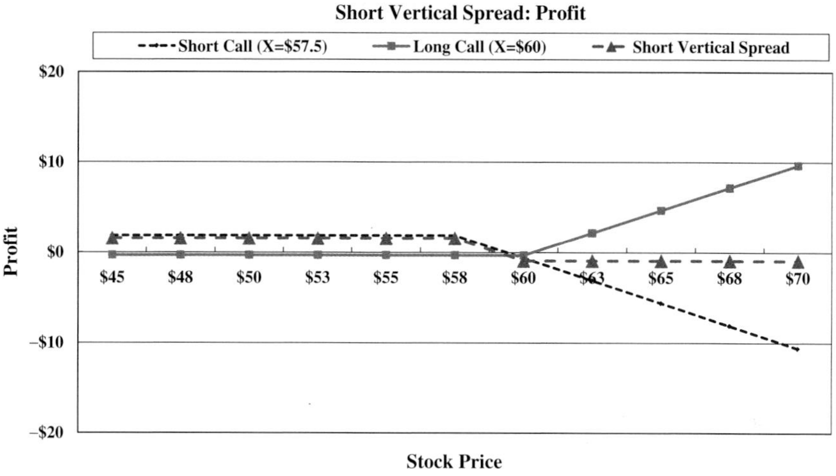

Fig. 16.16. Profit Profile for Short Vertical Spread.

16.4.5. *Protective Put*

Assume that an investor wants to invest in the JNJ stock on March 29, 2011, but does not desire to bear any potential loss for prices below $57.50. The investor can purchase JNJ stock and at the same time buy the put option with a strike price of $57.50. Given $S_0 = \$59.38$, $X = \$57.50$, and the premium for the put option $0.22 (the ask price), Table 16.11 shows the values for Protective Put at different stock prices at time T. The profit profile of the Protective Put position is constructed in Fig. 16.17.

16.4.6. *Covered Call*

This strategy involves investing in a stock and selling a call option on the stock at the same time. The value at the expiration of the call will be the stock value minus the value of the call. The call is "covered" because the potential obligation of delivering the stock is covered by the stock held in the portfolio. In essence, the sale of the call sold the claim to any stock value above the strike price in return for the initial premium. Suppose a manager of a stock fund holds a share of JNJ stock on March 29, 2011 and she plans to sell the JNJ stock if its price hits $62.50. Then she can write a share of a call option with a strike price of $62.50 to establish the position. She shorts the call and collects premiums. Given that $S_0 = \$59.38$, $X = \$62.50$, and the premium for the call option $0.03 (the bid price), Table 16.12 shows the values for covered call at different stock prices at

Table 16.11. Value of Protective Put Position at Option Expiration.

Long a put at strike price	$57.50	Premium	$0.22
Buy one share of stock		Price	$59.38

Stock	One Share of Stock		Long Put (X = $57.50)		Protective Put Value	
Price	Payoff	Profit	Payoff	Profit	Payoff	Profit
$45.00	$45.00	−$14.38	$12.50	$12.28	$57.50	−$2.10
$47.50	$47.50	−$11.88	$10.00	$9.78	$57.50	−$2.10
$50.00	$50.00	−$9.38	$7.50	$7.28	$57.50	−$2.10
$52.50	$52.50	−$6.88	$5.00	$4.78	$57.50	−$2.10
$55.00	$55.00	−$4.38	$2.50	$2.28	$57.50	−$2.10
$57.50	$57.50	−$1.88	$0.00	−$0.22	$57.50	−$2.10
$60.00	$60.00	$0.62	$0.00	−$0.22	$60.00	$0.40
$62.50	$62.50	$3.12	$0.00	−$0.22	$62.50	$2.90
$65.00	$65.00	$5.62	$0.00	−$0.22	$65.00	$5.40
$67.50	$67.50	$8.12	$0.00	−$0.22	$67.50	$7.90
$70.00	$70.00	$10.62	$0.00	−$0.22	$70.00	$10.40

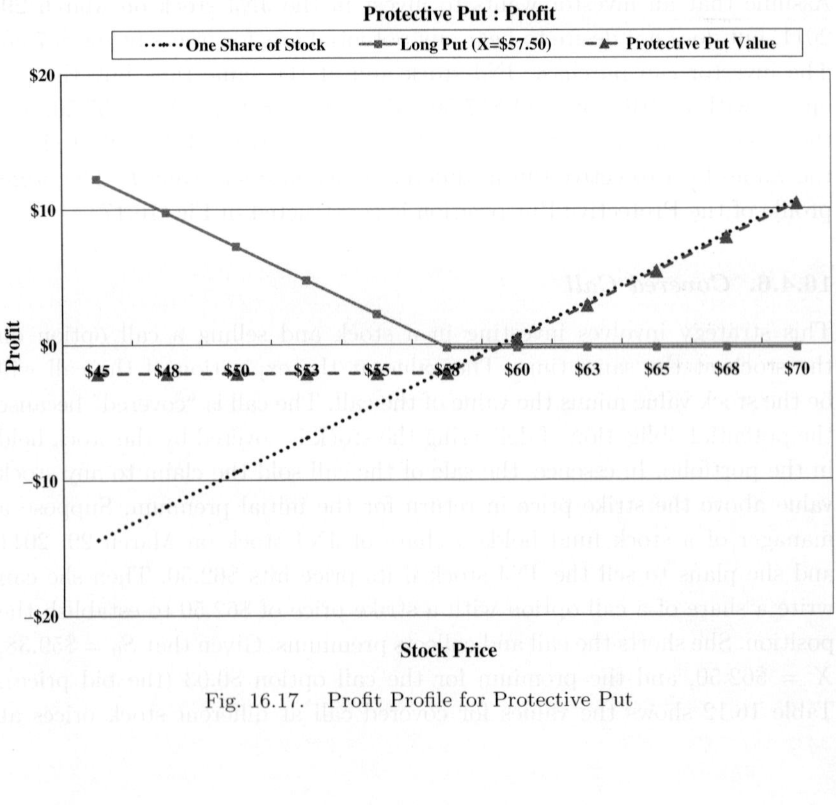

Fig. 16.17. Profit Profile for Protective Put

Table 16.12. Value of Covered Call Position at Option Expiration.

Write a call at strike price	$62.5 = 0	Premium	$0.03
Buy one share of stock		Price	$59.38

Stock	One Share of Stock		Written Call (X = $62.50)		Covered Call	
Price	Payoff	Profit	Payoff	Profit	Payoff	Profit
$45.00	$45.00	−$14.38	$0.00	$0.03	$45.00	−$14.35
$47.50	$47.50	−$11.88	$0.00	$0.03	$47.50	−$11.85
$50.00	$50.00	−$9.38	$0.00	$0.03	$50.00	−$9.35
$52.50	$52.50	−$6.88	$0.00	$0.03	$52.50	−$6.85
$55.00	$55.00	−$4.38	$0.00	$0.03	$55.00	−$4.35
$57.50	$57.50	−$1.88	$0.00	$0.03	$57.50	−$1.85
$60.00	$60.00	$0.62	$0.00	$0.03	$60.00	$0.65
$62.50	$62.50	$3.12	$0.00	$0.03	$62.50	$3.15
$65.00	$65.00	$5.62	−$2.50	−$2.47	$62.50	$3.15
$67.50	$67.50	$8.12	−$5.00	−$4.97	$62.50	$3.15
$70.00	$70.00	$10.62	−$7.50	−$7.47	$62.50	$3.15

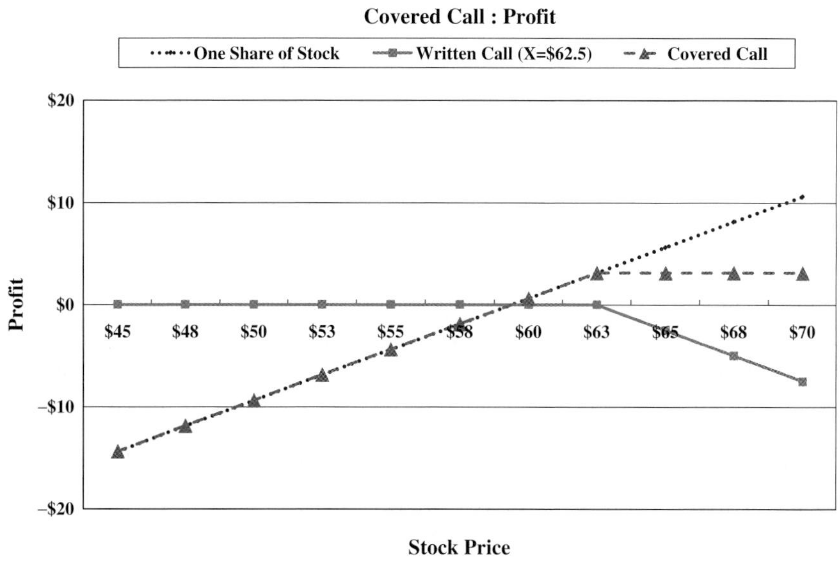

Fig. 16.18. Profit Profile for Covered Call.

time T. The profit profile of the covered call position is constructed in Fig. 16.18. It can be shown that the payoff pattern of covered call is exactly equal to shorting a put. Therefore, the covered call has frequently been used to replace shorting a put in dynamic hedging practice.

16.4.7. *Collar*

A collar combines a protective put and a short call option to bracket the value of a portfolio between two bounds. For example, an investor holds the JNJ stock selling at $59.38. Buying a protective put using the put option with an exercise price of $55 places a lower bound of $55 on the value of the portfolio. At the same time, the investor can write a call option with an exercise price of $62.50. The call and the put sell at $0.03 (the bid price) and $0.10 (the ask price), respectively, making the net outlay for the two options to be only $0.07. Table 16.13 shows the values of the collar position at different stock prices at time T. The profit profile of the collar position is shown in Fig. 16.19.

16.5. Summary

This chapter has introduced some of the essential differences between the two most basic kinds of option, calls and puts. Delineation was made of the relationship between the option's price or premium and that of the underlying asset. The option's value was shown to be composed of intrinsic value, or the underlying asset price less the exercise price, and

Table 16.13. Value of Collar Position at Option Expiration.

Write a call at strike price	$62.50	Premium	$0.03
Long a put at strike price	$55.00	Premium	$0.10
Buy one share of stock		Price	$59.38

Stock	One Share of Stock		Long Put (X = $55)		Write Call (X = $62.50)		Collar Value	
Price	Payoff	Profit	Payoff	Profit	Payoff	Profit	Payoff	Profit
$45.00	$45.00	−$14.38	$10.00	$9.90	$0.00	$0.03	$55.00	−$4.45
$47.50	$47.50	−$11.88	$7.50	$7.40	$0.00	$0.03	$55.00	−$4.45
$50.00	$50.00	−$9.38	$5.00	$4.90	$0.00	$0.03	$55.00	−$4.45
$52.50	$52.50	−$6.88	$2.50	$2.40	$0.00	$0.03	$55.00	−$4.45
$55.00	$55.00	−$4.38	$0.00	−$0.10	$0.00	$0.03	$55.00	−$4.45
$57.50	$57.50	−$1.88	$0.00	−$0.10	$0.00	$0.03	$57.50	−$1.95
$60.00	$60.00	$0.62	$0.00	−$0.10	$0.00	$0.03	$60.00	$0.55
$62.50	$62.50	$3.12	$0.00	−$0.10	$0.00	$0.03	$62.50	$3.05
$65.00	$65.00	$5.62	$0.00	−$0.10	−$2.50	−$2.47	$62.50	$3.05
$67.50	$67.50	$8.12	$0.00	−$0.10	−$5.00	−$4.97	$62.50	$3.05
$70.00	$70.00	$10.62	$0.00	−$0.10	−$7.50	−$7.47	$62.50	$3.05

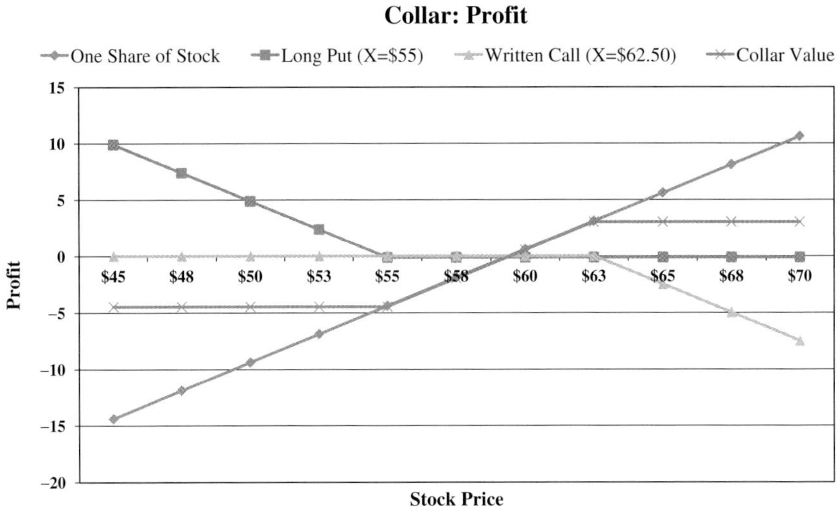

Fig. 16.19. Profit Profile for Collar.

time value. Moreover, it was demonstrated that the time value decays over time, particularly in the last month to maturity for an option.

Index and futures options were studied to introduce these important financial instruments. Put–call parity theorems were developed for European, American, and futures options in order to show the basic valuation relationship between the underlying asset and its call and put options. Finally, investment application of options and related combinations were discussed, along with relevant risk–return characteristics. A thorough understanding of this chapter is essential as a basic tool to successful study of option-valuation models in the next chapter.

Questions and Problems

1. Define the following terms.

(a) call option	(g) exercise price
(b) put option	(h) put–call parity
(c) striking price	(i) intrinsic value
(d) straddle	(j) European option
(e) option	(k) American option
(f) spread	(l) time value.

2. Compare the following pairs of investment strategies

   (a) Which is riskier, buying or selling a call option?

(b) Which is riskier, writing a naked call option or writing a covered call option?
(c) Other things being equal, which option has greater value, an American call option or a European call option?
(d) Other things being equal, which option should have greater value, the option written on a low-beta stock or the option written on a high-beta stock?

3. Plot profit versus the stock price for a call option with an exercise price of \$100 and a premium of \$3.
4. HHH, Inc. is a company doing medical research. It has decided to place all of its resources into finding a cure for AIDS. If HHH is successful, the value of its stock will increase tenfold. If the company is unsuccessful, it will be bankrupt in 10 years. (a) If you believe that there is a SO-percent chance of success, is there an investment strategy you can devise using put and call options to exploit this situation? (b) How might your answer in (a) change if you believe that there is only a 33% chance of success?
5. Carefully explain the difference between a vertical bull spread and a vertical bear spread. When would you use the vertical bull spread? When would you use the vertical bear spread?
6. You would like to purchase a put option on XYZ Company's stock. If only call options exist on XYZ's stock, explain how you could create your own put option.
7. What is the benefit of purchasing a call option over purchasing the underlying stock? What are the disadvantages?
8. Carefully explain why the value of an option can never be negative.
9. Compare an option to a futures contract. How are they similar? How are they different?
10. What is a butterfly spread? When would an investor purchase a calendar spread?
11. Plot the profit opportunities for an investor who purchases a long straddle. Assume that the exercise price on the put and call options is \$100.
12. Use the information given in the previous question to plot the profit opportunities for a short straddle. Compare these two positions.
13. Explain what is meant by an option that is

    (a) in the money.
    (b) at the money.
    (c) out of the money.

14. Explain how the time value of an option behaves as the option moves closer to expiration.
15. Given a stock valued at $25 on February 1, 1989, and the following information about call-option premiums, what is the time value for each of the options?

Exercise Price	March	June	September
20	$5.75	$6.75	$7.50
25	1.00	2.00	3.00
30	0.25	0.50	0.75

16. What impact does the payment of cash dividends by XYZ Company have on the put options of XYZ? How does it affect the call options of XYZ?
17. Discuss the uses of an option on foreign currencies.
18. Why would you never exercise an index option before the exercise date?
19. Explain the logic behind the put–call parity relationship shown in Table 16.4.
20. A call option with six months to maturity and an exercise price of 20 is selling for $3. Assuming discrete compounding, a risk-free rate of interest of 8%, and a current stock price of $19, what is the value of a European put option with a strike price of 20 and one year to maturity?
21. For a stock with a price of $10, a put option with three months to maturity and an exercise price of $12 is selling for $3. Assuming discrete compounding and a risk-free rate of 8%, what are the boundaries of the price for an American call option?
22. What are the major advantages of an option on futures over an option on an underlying asset?
23. What is a synthetic put? Why would a synthetic put be useful if you have listed put options?
24. Compare the risk–return features of a long call with a short naked call. If these two types of call positions were to be continued indefinitely, what would be the result?
25. Compare the risk–return features for a short covered call with an uncovered short put. Be sure to discuss the time decay.
26. An investor wants to use a long straddle, the current market index being 150. He buys the three-month 150 call for $5.00 and the three-month 150 put at $4.50. If the market rises to 180 at the end of three months,

what is the investor's profit or loss? If the market falls to 125 at the end of three months, what is the investor's profit or loss? If the market stays at 150 at the end of three months, what is the profit or loss?

27. Calculate the breakeven points (upside and downside) for the straddle described in the previous problem.
28. An investor wants to use a short straddle; the current market index is 100. He sells a one-month 100 call for \$1.50 and a one-month 100 put for \$1.75. At the end of one month the market index is: (a) 100, (b) 90, or (c) 80. What is the profit or loss for (a), (b), and (c)?
29. If an investor sells a high-exercise-price call and buys a low-exercise-price call of the same month to expiration, what does he or she hope for the price of the underlying asset?
30. How do you profit from a neutral calendar spread?
31. Firm A's common stock has been trading in a narrow price range for the past month. An investor is convinced that the price is going to break far out of that range in the next three months. However, this investor does not know whether the price will go up or down. The current price of the stock is \$90 per share and the price of a three-month call option at an exercise price of \$90 is \$8.

    (a) Assume the risk free rate is 6% per year, what is the price of a three-month put option on firm A's stock at an exercise price of \$90? (Assume the stock pays no dividend.)
    (b) What would be a simple option strategy to exploit your conviction about the stock price movement in the next three months? How far would it have to move in either direction for you to make a profit on your initial investment?

32. Firm B's common stock has been trading in a narrow price range around \$60 per share for a while. You believe the price is going to stay in the range for the next three months. The price of a three-month put option with an exercise price of \$60 is \$5.

    (a) Assume the risk-free rate is 6% per year, what is the price of a three-month call option on firm B stock at an exercise price of \$60 if it is in the money? (Assume the stock pays no dividend.)
    (b) What would be a simple option strategy to exploit your conviction about the stock price movement in the next three months? What is the most money you can make on this position? How far would it have to move in either direction before you lose money?

33. A manager in firm C receives 10,000 shares of company stock as part of his compensation package. The current market price of the stock is $50 per share. At this current price, this manager would receive $500,000 for the stock. This manager is considering buying a second house in April but is worried about the value of his stock holding. If the value of the stock holding falls below $450,000, he will not be able to come up with the down payment for the house. However, if the value of the stock rises above $550,000, he would be able to have a small cash reserve even after he makes his down payment. Please evaluate the following two strategies with respect to this manager's investment goal. What are the advantage and disadvantage of each strategy.

    (a) Strategy A: Write April call options on firm C's share with strike price $55. These calls are currently selling at $4 each.
    (b) Strategy B: Long April put options on firm C's share with strike price $45. These calls are currently selling at $4 each.

34. Please discuss why is owning a corporate bond similar to shorting a put option? A call option?
35. An investor is holding the following option portfolio. She is writing an April expiration call option on Dell with exercise price 80. She is also writing an April Dell put option with exercise price 75. The cost of the above options are $1 and $0.5, respectively.

    (a) Graph the payoff of this portfolio at option expiration as a function of Dell's stock price at that time.
    (b) What is the profit/loss on this position if Dell is selling at $78 on the option maturity data? What if Dell is selling at 88?
    (c) At what two stock prices will you just break even on your investment?

36. Consider the following portfolio. An investor writes a put option with exercise price 70 and buys a put option on the same stock with the same maturity date with exercise price 86.

    (a) Graph the *value* of the portfolio at the option maturity date.
    (b) Graph the *profit* of the portfolio. Determine which option costs more.

37. A GM put option with strike price $50 trading on the Acme options exchange sells for $3. However, a GM put with the same maturity selling on the Apex options exchange but with strike price $52 also sells for $3. If an investor plans to hold the option position to maturity, devise a

zero-net-investment arbitrage strategy to exploit the pricing anomaly. Please graph the diagram at maturity for your position.

38. John purchased a stock index fund currently selling at \$500 per share. He also purchases an at-the-money European put option on the fund for \$15 with exercise price \$500 and three-month time to expiration because he is worried about the losses. Investor A's financial adviser, Alice, points out that he is spending too much money on the put option. The adviser notes that three-month puts with the strike prices of \$480 cost only \$10 and suggest investor A to use the cheaper put.
    (a) For both John and Alice, draw the profit diagram for the stock-plus-put position for various stock prices in three months.
    (b) When does Alice's strategy do better? When does it do worse?
    (c) Which strategy has larger systematic risk?

39. An investment manager writes a call option with strike price \$30 and buys a call option with strike price \$40. The options are on the same stock and have the same maturity date. One of the call sells for \$2 and the other one sells for \$6.
    (a) Draw both payoff and profit graph for this strategy at the option maturity date.
    (b) What is the break even point for this strategy? Is this manager bullish or bearish on the stock?

Bibliography

Amram, M. and N. Kulatilaka. *Real Options*. New York: Oxford University Press, 2001.

Ball, C. and W. Torous. "Bond Prices Dynamics and Options." *Journal of Financial and Quantitative Analysis*, v. 18 (December 1983), pp. 517–532.

Bhattacharya, M. "Empirical Properties of the Black–Scholes Formula under Ideal Conditions." *Journal of Financial and Quantitative Analysis*, v. 15 (December 1980), pp. 1081–1106.

Black, F. "Capital Market Equilibrium with Restricted Borrowing." *Journal of Business*, v. 45 (July 1972), pp. 444–445.

Black, F. "Fact and Fantasy in the Use of Options." *Financial Analysts Journal*, v. 31 (July/August 1985), pp. 36–72.

Black, F. and M. Scholes. "The Pricing of Options and Corporate Liabilities." *Journal of Political Economy*, v. 31 (May/June 1973), pp. 637–654.

Bodhurta, J. and G. Courtadon. "Efficiency Tests of the Foreign Currency Options Market." *Journal of Finance*, v. 41 (March 1986), pp. 151–162.

Bookstaber, R. M. *Option Pricing and Strategies in Investing*. Reading, MA: Addison-Wesley Publishing Company, 1981.

Bookstaber, R. M. and R. Clarke. *Option Strategies for Institutional Investment Management.* Reading, MA: Addison-Wesley Publishing Company, 1983.

Brennan, M. and E. Schwartz. "The Valuation of American Put Options." *Journal of Finance*, v. 32 (May 1977), pp. 449–462.

Cox, J. C. "Option Pricing: A Simplified Approach." *Journal of Financial Economics*, v. 8 (September 1979), pp. 229–263.

Cox, J. C. and M. Rubinstein. *Option Markets.* Englewood Cliffs, NJ: Prentice-Hall, 1985.

Eckardt, W. and S. Williams. "The Complete Options Indexes." *Financial Analysts Journal*, v. 40 (July/August 1984), pp. 48–57.

Ervine, J. and A. Rudd. "Index Options: The Early Evidence." *Journal of Finance*, v. 40 (June 1985), pp. 743–756.

Finnerty, J. "The Chicago Board Options Exchange and Market Efficiency." *Journal of Financial and Quantitative Analysis*, v. 13 (March 1978), pp. 28–38.

Galai, D. and R. W. Masulis. "The Option Pricing Model and the Risk Factor of Stock." *Journal of Financial Economics*, v. 3 (March 1976), pp. 53–81.

Galai, D., R. Geske and S. Givots. *Option Markets.* Reading, MA: Addison-Wesley Publishing Company, 1988.

Gastineau, G. *The Stock Options Manual.* New York: McGraw-Hill, 1979.

Geske, R. and K. Shastri. "Valuation by Approximation: A Comparison of Alternative Option Valuation Techniques." *Journal of Financial and Quantitative Analysis*, v. 20 (March 1985), pp. 45–72.

Hull, J. *Options, Futures, and Other Derivatives*, 6th ed. Upper Saddle. River, New Jersey: Prentice Hall, 2005.

Jarrow, R. A. and A. Rudd. *Option Pricing.* Homewood, IL: Richard D. Irwin, 1983.

Jarrow R. and S. Turnbull. *Derivatives Securities*, 2nd ed. Cincinnati, OH: South-Western College Pub, 1999.

Liaw, K. T. and R. L. Moy, *The Irwin Guide to Stocks, Bonds, Futures, and Options*, New York: McGraw-Hill Co., 2000.

Lee, C. F. *Handbook of Quantitative Finance and Risk Management.* New York, NY: Springer, 2009.

Lee, C. F. and Alice C. Lee, *Encyclopedia of Finance.* New York, NY: Springer, 2006.

Macbeth, J. and L. Merville. "An Empirical Examination of the Black–Scholes Call Option Pricing Model." *Journal of Finance*, v. 34 (December 1979), pp. J173–J186.

McDonald, R. L. *Derivatives Markets*, 2nd ed. Boston, MA: Addison Wesley, 2005.

Merton, R. "Theory of Rational Option Pricing." *Bell Journal of Economics and Management Science*, v. 4 (Spring 1973), pp. 141–183.

Rendleman, R. J. Jr. and B. J. Barter. "Two-State Option Pricing." *Journal of Finance*, v. 34 (September 1979), pp. 1093–1110.

Ritchken, P. *Options: Theory, Strategy and Applications.* Glenview, IL: Scott, Foresman, 1987.

Rubinstein, M. and H. Leland. "Replicating Options with Positions in Stock and Cash." *Financial Analysts Journal*, v. 37 (July/August 1981), pp. 63–72.

Rubinstein, M. and J. Cox. *Option Markets.* Englewood Cliffs, NJ: Prentice-Hall, 1985.

Sears, S. and G. Trennepohl. "Measuring Portfolio Risk in Options." *Journal of Financial and Quantitative Analysis*, v. 17 (September 1982), pp. 391–410.

Smith, C. "Option Pricing: A Review." *Journal of Financial Economics*, v. 3 (January 1976), pp. 3–51.

Stoll, H. "The Relationships between Put and Call Option Prices." *Journal of Finance*, v. 24 (December 1969), pp. 801–824.

Summa, J. F. and J. W. Lubow, *Options on Futures.* New York: John Wiley & Sons, 2001.

Trennepohl, G. "A Comparison of Listed Option Premium and Black–Scholes Model Prices: 1973–1979." *Journal of Financial Research*, v. 4 (Spring 1981), pp. 11–20.

Weinstein, M. "Bond Systematic Risk and the Options Pricing Model." *Journal of Finance*, v. 38 (December 1983), pp. 1415–1430.

Welch, W. *Strategies for Put and Call Option Trading.* Cambridge, MA: Winthrop, 1982.

Whaley, R. "Valuation of American Call Options on Dividend Paying Stocks: Empirical Tests." *Journal of Financial Economics*, v. 10 (March 1982), pp. 29–58.

Zhang, P. G., *Exotic Options: A Guide to Second Generation Options*, 2nd ed. Singapore: World Scientific, 1998.

Chapter 17

Option Pricing Theory and Firm Valuation

The emergence of options and option pricing discusses several types of options and how their value is determined. We begin by looking at the basic concepts of options in Section 17.1, then go on to discuss factors that affect the value of options in Section 17.2. Hedging, hedge ratio, and option valuation are discussed in Section 17.3. Section 17.4 discusses how option pricing theory is used to investigate the capital structure question. We close the chapter with a look as the type of option called the warrant in Section 17.5. Summary of this chapter is discussed in Section 17.6. Appendix 17A discusses **the applications of the binomial distribution to evaluate call options**.

17.1. Basic Concepts of Options

In general, there are three types of equity options: (1) warrants, (2) executive stock options, and (3) publicly traded options. A *warrant* is a financial instrument issued by a corporation that gives the purchaser the right to buy a fixed number of shares at a set price for a specific period. There are two major differences between a warrant and a publicly traded option. The first is that the maturity of the warrant is normally less than nine months. The second difference is that the warrant is an agreement between the corporation and the warrant's buyer. This means that if the warrant's owner decides to exercise his right and purchase stock, the corporation issues new shares and receives the cash from the sale of those shares. The *publicly traded option* is an agreement between two individuals who have no relationship with the corporation whose shares are being optioned. When the publicly traded option is exercised, money is exchanged for shares between individuals and the corporation receives no funds, only a new owner.

Executive stock options are a means of compensation for corporate employees. For services rendered, the manager or the employee has the right to buy a specific number of shares for a set price during a given period. Unlike warrants and publicly traded options, executive stock options cannot be traded. The option's owner has only two choices: exercise the option or let it expire. Like a warrant, should the owner decide to exercise the option, the corporation receives money and issues new shares.

The use of executive stock options for management compensation raises an interesting agency question. The firm's managers may make investment and financing decisions that increase the firm's risk in order to increase the value of their stock options. Such action could have a detrimental effect on the bondholders and other creditors of the firm. Thus, we will see that the value of an option is directly related to the variability or riskiness of the underlying asset, which in this case in the firm.

Publicly traded options are probably the most widely known of the three types of equity option instruments. An important date in the history of these options is 1973, when the Chicago Board Options Exchange was founded. Although it was possible to trade options over the counter before that time, trading volume was relatively low. This date marks the beginning of a phenomenal growth in the popularity of options as a financial instrument. Indeed, in terms of the value of securities traded, the Chicago Board Options Exchange is running neck and neck with the New York and Tokyo stock exchanges as the world's largest securities market. There are now five options-trading centers in the U.S. — the Chicago Board Option Exchange, the American Stock Exchange, the Philadelphia Stock Exchange, the Pacific Stock Exchange, and the New York Stock Exchange — and there is a steady stream of proposals for new listings on these exchanges.

The share volume of trading and the general acceptance of these financial instruments renders options valuation an important subject for study. However, even more significant for our purposes, the theory of options valuation has important applications in financial management and in the valuation of other financial instruments. Black and Scholes (1973) point out that those corporate securities can be viewed as options or contingent claims on firm value. In viewing a firm's securities as options, we need to evaluate the interdependencies of bonds and stocks. As we have seen, a bond's price is the present value of future interest and principal payments, and a stock's price is determined by future dividends. The contingent-claims approach to security valuation differs in that it considers the valuation of all of the firm's classes of securities simultaneously. Bonds and stocks are valued in terms on the value placed on the firm's assets; that is, their value is contingent on the firm's assets or investments.

Banz and Miller (1978) developed an approach to making capital budgeting decisions based on a contingent claims framework. They created a method for calculating the net present value (NPV) of an investment based on estimates derived from using an option valuation model. In this chapter, we consider the question of option valuation and how options are used to make financial management decisions. However, before doing so, we must become acquainted with some of the terminology of options trading.

There are two basic types of options: puts and calls. A *call* gives the holder the right to buy a particular number of shares of a designated common stock at a specified price, called the *exercise price* (or strike price), on or before a given date, known as the *expiration date.* Hence, the owner of shares of common stock can create an option and sell it in the options market, thereby increasing the return or income on his or her stock investment. Such an option specifies both an exercise price and an expiration date. On the Chicago Board of Options Exchange, options are typically created for three, six, or nine months. The actual expiration date is the third Saturday of the month of expiration. A more venturesome investor may create an option in this fashion without owning any of underlying stock. This is called *naked option writing* and can be very risky, especially if the value of the underlying asset has a high degree of variability.

A *put* gives the holder the right to sell a certain number of shares of common stock at a set price on or before the expiration date of the option. In purchasing a put, the owner of shares has bought the right to sell these shares by the expiration date at the exercise price. As with calls, the creator can own the underlying shares (covered writing) or not (naked writing).

The owner of a put or call is not obligated to carry out the specified transaction, but has the *option* of doing so. If the transaction is carried out, it is said to have been *exercised.* For example, if you hold a call option on a stock that is currently trading at a price higher than the exercise price, because the stock could be immediately resold at a profit. (Or you could sell the option or hold it in the hope of further gains.) This call option is said to be "in the money." On the other hand, if the call option is "out of the money" — that is, the stock is trading at a price — you certainly would not want to exercise the option, as it would be cheaper to purchase the stock directly.

An American option can be exercised at any time up to the expiration date. A simpler instrument to analyze is the European option, which can only be exercised on the expiration date. In this case, the term to maturity of the option is known. Because of this simplifying factor, we will concentrate on the valuation of the European option. The factors determining the values of the two types of options are the same, although, all other things equal, an American option is worth more than a European option because of the extra flexibility permitted to the option holder.

Although our discussion is limited to equity options, many kinds of publicly traded options are available. Those include options in stick indexes, options on treasury bonds, options on future contracts, options on foreign currencies, and options on agricultural commodities.

The proceeding discussion presented quite a lot of new terminology. For convenience, we list and define those terms below.

Call An option to purchase a fixed number of shares of common stock.
Put An option to sell a fixed number of shares of common stock.
Exercise price contract Trading price set for the transaction as specified in an option.
Expiration date Time by which the option transaction must be carried out.
Exercise option Carrying out the transaction specified in an option.
American option An option in which the transaction can only be carried out at any time up to the expiration date.
European option An option in which the transaction can only be carried out in the expiration date.
Call option "in the money" If the stock price is above the exercise price.
Put option "in the money" If the stock price is below the exercise price.
Call option "out of the money" If the stock price is below the exercise price.
Put option "out of the money" If the stock price is above the exercise price.

17.1.1. *Option Price Information*

Each day the previous day's options trading are reported in the press. Table 17.1 is a partial listing of equity options traded on the Chicago Board of Options Exchange. In this table, we have highlighted the option

Table 17.1. Listed Options Quotations.

Close Price	Strike Price	Calls Sep	Calls Oct	Calls Jan	Puts Sep	Puts Oct	Puts Jan
JNJ							
65.12	45.00	20.40	N/A	N/A	N/A	N/A	N/A
65.12	50.00	N/A	N/A	N/A	N/A	N/A	N/A
65.12	55.00	10.30	10.40	11.10	N/A	0.02	0.30
65.12	60.00	5.30	N/A	6.40	N/A	N/A	0.70
65.12	65.00	0.10	1.15	2.60	0.05	0.85	1.95
65.12	70.00	N/A	0.05	0.55	4.80	4.50	5.00
MRK							
51.82	45.00	6.70	7.08	N/A	N/A	0.15	0.85
51.82	47.50	4.34	4.90	6.04	N/A	N/A	1.30
51.82	50.00	1.85	2.70	4.40	0.03	0.65	2.10
51.82	52.50	0.03	1.10	2.85	0.55	1.50	3.10
51.82	55.00	0.01	0.35	1.70	3.20	3.30	4.60
51.82	57.50	N/A	N/A	0.95	5.70	N/A	N/A
51.82	60.00	N/A	N/A	0.50	8.20	N/A	8.40
PG							
69.39	40.00	29.70	29.70	30.10	N/A	N/A	N/A
69.39	45.00	24.60	24.70	N/A	N/A	N/A	N/A
69.39	55.00	14.50	N/A	15.20	N/A	N/A	0.15
69.39	60.00	9.70	9.80	10.70	N/A	0.08	0.42
69.39	65.00	4.50	4.90	6.19	N/A	0.21	1.00
69.39	70.00	0.05	0.90	2.75	0.60	1.50	2.65
69.39	75.00	N/A	0.05	0.70	5.50	5.70	5.70
69.39	80.00	N/A	N/A	0.15	10.40	10.50	N/A

for Johnson & Johnson (JNJ). The first three months (September, October, and January) are for a call option contract on JNJ for 100 shares of stock at an exercise price of 65.12 represents the closing price of JNJ shares on the New York Stock Exchange. The numbers in the September column represents the price of one call option with a September expiration date. Since each option is the right to buy 100 shares, the cost of the call option with the strike price \$55 is \$1,030 or \$10.30 × 100. The values of the call options for September is somewhat higher, reflecting the fact that if you owned those options you would have a longer time to exercise them. In general, this time premium is reflected in higher prices for options with longer lives. The last three columns (September, October, and January) represent the value of put options on JNJ stock. Again, each put option contract is for 100 shares and worth 100 times the price, or \$2 for the October 55 JNJ. The specific factors that determine option value are discussed next.

How much should you pay for a put or call option? The answer is not easy to determine. However, it is possible to list the various factors that determine option value.

We begin with a simple question. How much is a call option worth on its expiration date? The question is simple because we are in a deterministic world. The uncertain future movement of the price of the stock in question is irrelevant. The call must be exercised immediately or not at all. If a call option is out of the money on its expiration date, it will not be exercised and the call becomes a worthless piece of paper. On the other hand, if the call option is in the money on its expiration date, it will be exercised. Stock can be purchased at the exercise price, and immediately resold at the market price, if so desired. The option value is the difference between these two prices. On the call option's expiration date, its value will be either 0 or some positive amount equal to the difference between the market price of the stock and the exercise price of the option. Symbolically, let $P=$ price of stock, $V_c=$ value of call option, and $E=$ exercise price. Then $V_c = P - E$ if $E \geq P$, and $V_c = 0$ if $P < E$. This relationship can be written as

$$V_c = \text{MAX}(0, P - E),$$

where MAX denoted the larger of the two bracketed terms. For a put option (V_p), $V_p = E - P$ if $E > P$, and $V_p = 0$ if $E \leq P$. This can be written as

$$V_p = \text{MAX}(0, E - P).$$

The call position is illustrated in Fig. 17.1(a), where we consider a call option with an exercise price of \$50. The figure shows the option value as a function of stock price to the option holder. For any price of the stock up to \$50, the call option is worthless. The option's value increases as the stock price rises above \$50. Hence, if on the expiration date the stock is trading at \$60, the call option is worth \$10.

Figure 17.1(b), which is the mirror image of (a), shows the option position from the view point of the writer of the call option. If the stock is trading below the exercise price on the expiration date, the call option will not be exercised and the exercise price on the expiration date, the call option will not be exercised and it seller incurs no loss. However, if the stock is trading at \$60, the seller of the call option will be required to sell

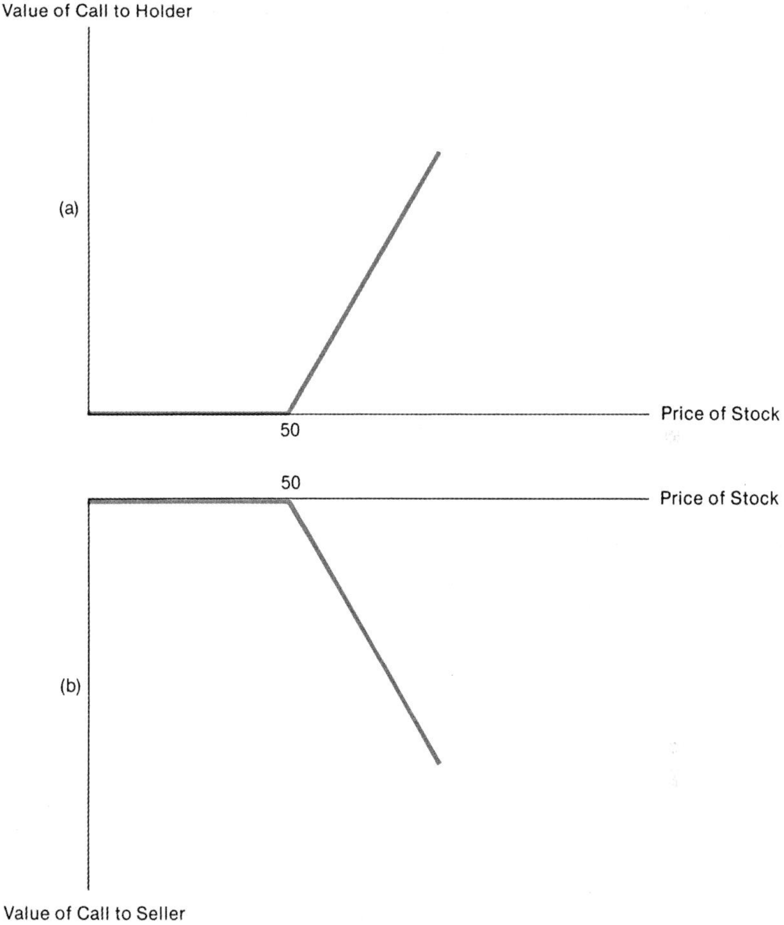

Fig. 17.1. Value of $50 Exercise Price Call Option (a) to Holder, (b) to Seller.

this stock for $50, which is $10 below the price that could be obtained on the market.

We have seen that once a call option have been purchased; the holder of the option has the possibility of obtaining gains but cannot incur losses. Correspondingly, the writer of the option may incur losses but cannot achieve any gains after receiving the premium. Further, there is no net gain in the sense that the profit incurred by one will balance the loss of the other. Thus, options are zero sum securities — they merely transfer wealth rather than create it. To acquire this instrument, a price must be paid to the writer, and it is this price that corresponds to the call value. This value is the price paid to acquire the chance of future profit and will therefore reflect uncertainty about the future market prices on the common stock. We will now discuss how to determine the value of an option before its expiration date.

17.2. Factors Affecting Option Value[1]

17.2.1. *Determining the Value of a Call Option Before the Expiration Date*

Suppose that you are considering the purchase of a call option, with an exercise price of $50, on a share of common stock. Let us try to determine what factors should be taken into account in trying to assess the value of such an option prior to the expiration date. As we have seen, the problem is trivial at the expiration date. However, determining the value of an option prior to expiration is more complex.

An important factor in this determination is the current price per share of the stock. Indeed, it is most straightforward to think of option value as a function of the market price. Given this framework, we can see fairly quickly how to set bounds on the value of a call option.

Lower bound: The value of a call cannot be less than the payoff that would accrue if it were exercised immediately. We can think of Fig. 17.1 as showing the payoff from immediate exercise of a call as a function on the current price of the stock. In our example, this payoff is zero for any market price below $50 and equal to the market price less for the $50 exercise price when market price is above $50. Suppose that the current stock price is $60 per share, and you are offered a call option for $8. This is certain to be profitable because you could immediately exercise the call and then resell the stock at a $10 gain. Subtracting the cost of the call option would yield a profit of $2. Of course, market participants are well aware of this, so that the excess of demand over supply for such immediate profits are unattainable.

Upper bound: The value of a call cannot be more than the market price of the stock.

[1]The mathematical derivations of the sensitivity between the factors and the option value are discussed in Chapter 20.

Suppose that, at the same cost, you are offered two alternatives:

(a) purchase a share of stock; or
(b) purchase an option on the same share of stock.

Looking into the future, option (b) will either be exercised or discarded as worthless. If the option is exercised, its value will be the difference between the future stock prices less the exercise price. This will be less than the future stock price, which is the value derived from option (a). Similarly, if the option turns out to have no value, this cannot be preferable to holding the stock, which, while it may have fallen in price, will have retained some value. Therefore, option (b) cannot be preferable to (a), so that the option value cannot exceed the market price of the stock.

These conclusions are illustrated in Fig. 17.2, which relates the call-option value to the market price of the stock. The ACD line shows the payoff that would be obtained if the option were exercised immediately. The AB line is the set of points at which the call value equals the market price of the stock. The call value must lie between these boundaries; that is, in the shaded area depicted in Fig. 17.2.

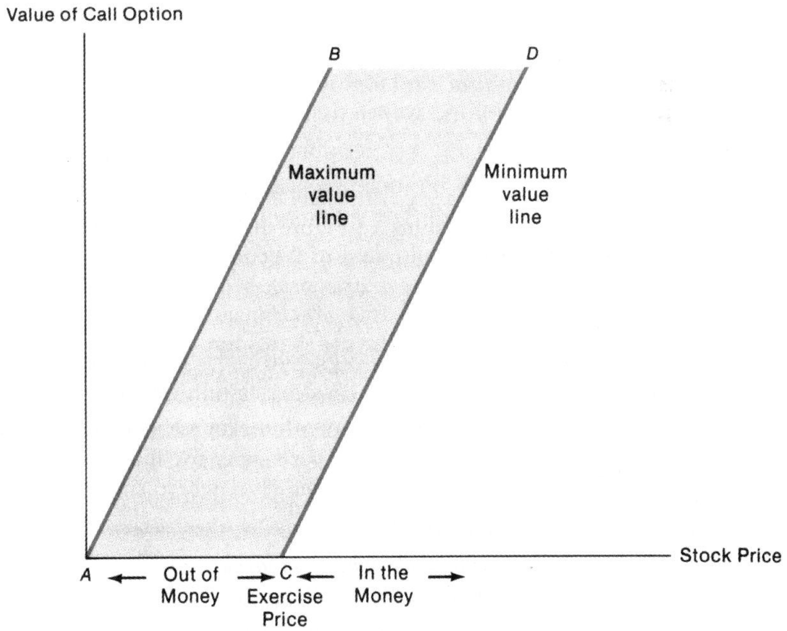

Fig. 17.2. Value of Call Option.

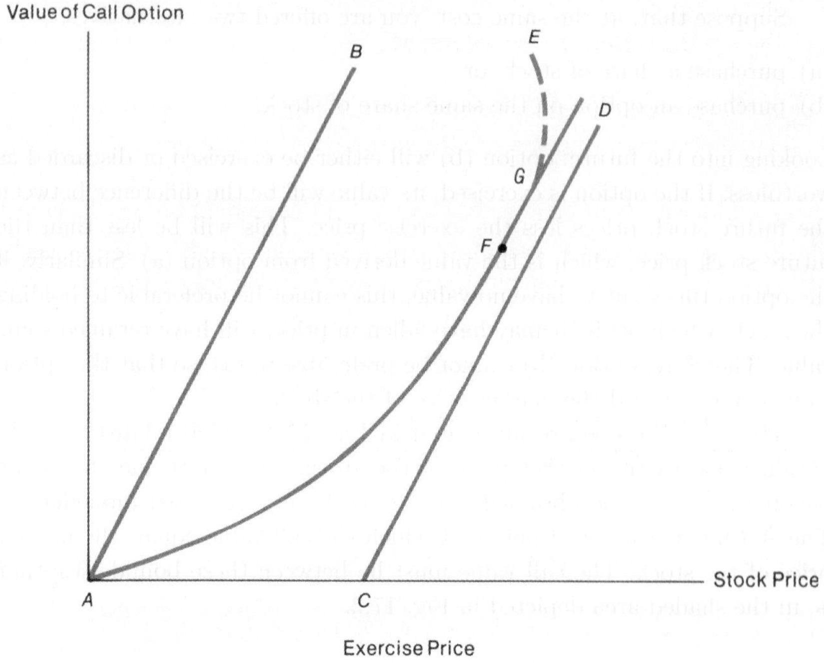

Fig. 17.3. Call Option Value as a Function of Stock Price.

So far, we have been able to determine a fairly wide range in which the option value must lie for any given value of the market price of the stock. Let us now see if we can be more precise in formulating the shape of the relationship between call-option value and market price stock. The following considerations should help in forming the appropriate picture of Fig. 17.3.

(1) *If the market price of the stock 0, the call value will also be 0, as indicated by point A.* This extreme case arises only when there is no hope that the stock will ever have any value, for otherwise investors would be prepared to pay some price, however small, for the stock. It follows, in such a dire circumstance, that the call option will never be exercised, and so it too has no value.
(2) *All other things equal, as the stock price increases, so does the call value (see lines AB and CD).* A call with an exercise price of $50 would be worth more if the current market price was $40 than if it was $35, all else equal. The probability that the market price will eventually exceed

the exercise price by any given amount is higher in the former case than in the latter, and so, consequently, is the payoff expected from the holding call.

(3) *If the price of the stock is high in relation to the exercise price, each dollar increase in price induces an increase of very nearly the same amount in the call value (shown by the slope of the line at point* F). Suppose that the market price of the stock exceeds the exercise price of a call by such a large amount that it is virtually impossible for the stock price to fall below the exercise price before the expiration date. Then, any change in stock price will induce a change of the same amount in the payoff expected from the call, since it is certain that the option will be exercised. The point is that if it is known that an option will eventually be exchanged for stock, this is tantamount to already owning stock. The call holder has effectively purchased the stock without paying the full amount for it right away. The balance owned is the exercise price to be paid at the expiration date. It follows that the value of the call option is the market value of the stock less the present value of the exercise price. Notice that in our previous notation, this will exceed $P-E$ if the exercise price does not have to be paid until some time in the future, because of the time value of money.

(4) *The call value rises at an increasing rate as the value of the stock price rises, as shown by curvature AFG.* The segment AF shows that as the stock price increases, the call value increases by a lesser amount. The segment FE shows the call price increasing by a larger amount than the increase in the stock price. Theoretically, this is impossible, because if it occurs, eventually the call price would exceed the price of the underlying stock.

Putting these four considerations together, we show in Fig. 17.3 a typical curve relating call-option value to the market price of a stock. Beginning at the origin, when both quantities are 0, the curve shows call value increasing as market price increases. Eventually, the curve becomes virtually parallel to the two 45-degree lines, forming the boundaries if the possible-values region. This is a result of the fourth consideration listed above.

The curve graphed in Fig. 17.3 shows the relationship between the call-option value and the market price of the stock, when all other relevant factors influencing call-option value are constant. Next, we must try to see what these other factors might be and assess their impact on call value.

We consider, in turn, five factors that influence the value of a call option:

(1) *Market price of the stock*: In Fig. 17.3, we have seen the curvilinear relationship between call-option value and market price of the stock. All other things equal, the higher the market price, the higher the call-option value on the stock. As already noted, the slope of this relationship increases as market price becomes higher, to the point where, eventually, each dollar increase in the stock price translates into an increase of about the same amount in the call option value on that stock.
(2) *The exercise price*: It offered two otherwise identical call options on the same stock; you would prefer the call with the lower exercise price. This would involve larger gains from any favorable movement in the price of the stock than would an option with a higher exercise price. Therefore, we conclude that the lower the exercise price, the higher the call-option value, all other things are equal.
(3) *The risk-free interest rate*: If a call option is eventually exercised, the holder of the option will reap some of the benefits of an increase in the market value of the stock. However, the holder will do so without having to immediately pay the exercise price. This payment will only be made at some future time when the call option is actually exercised. In the meantime, this money can be invested in government securities to earn a no-risk return. This opportunity confers an increment of value on the call option; the higher the risk-free rate of interest, the greater this incremental value or lower the present value of the exercise price. Therefore, we would expect to find, all else equal, that the higher the risk-free rate of interest, the greater the call-option value. Moreover, the longer the exercise of the option is postponed, the greater the risk-free interest earnings. Accordingly, we would expect the risk-free interest rate to determine call-option value in conjunction with the time remaining before the expiration date.
(4) *The volatility of the stock price*: Suppose that you are offered opportunity to purchase one of two call options, each with an exercise price of \$50. Table 17.2 lists probabilities for different market prices on the expiration date for each of the two stocks. In each case, the mean (expected) future price is the same. However, for the second stock, prices that differ substantially from the mean are far more likely than for the first stock. The price of such a stock is said to be relatively volatile. We now show that the expected price of such a stock is said to be relatively

Table 17.2. Probabilities for Future Prices of Two Stocks.

Less Volatile Stock		More Volatile Stock	
Future Price($)	Probability	Future Price ($)	Probability
42	0.10	32	0.15
47	0.20	42	0.20
52	0.40	52	0.30
57	0.20	62	0.20
62	0.10	72	0.15

volatile. We now show that the expected payoff on the expiration date is higher for a call option on the more volatile stock than for a call option on the less volatile stock. For less volatile stock, the option will not be exercised for prices below \$50, but for the three higher prices its exercise will result in payoffs of \$2, \$7, and \$12. Therefore, we find

$$\begin{aligned}&\text{expected payoff from call option on les volatile stock}\\&\quad= (0)(0.10) + (0)(0.20) + (2)(0.40) + (7)(0.20) + (12)(0.10)\\&\quad= \$3.40.\end{aligned}$$

Similarly, for a call option on more volatile stock,

$$\begin{aligned}&\text{expected payoff from call option on more volatile stock}\\&\quad= (0)(0.15) + (0)(0.20) + (2)(0.30) + (12)(0.20) + (22)(0.15)\\&\quad= \$6.30.\end{aligned}$$

We find, then, that although the expected future price is the same for the two stocks, the expected payoff is higher from a call option on the more volatile stock. This conclusion is quite general. For example, it does not depend on our having set the exercise price below the expected future stock price. The reader is invited to verify that the same qualitative finding would emerge if the exercise price were \$55. We can conclude that, all other things remaining the same, the greater the volatility in the price of the stock, the higher the call-option value on that stock.

One useful way to measure volatility is through the *variance* in day-to-day changes in the stock price. Figure 17.4 illustrates our assertion about the influence of stock-price volatility on call-option value. The figure shows the relationship between call value and current market price for three stocks. The three curves have the same general form depicted in Fig. 17.3. However,

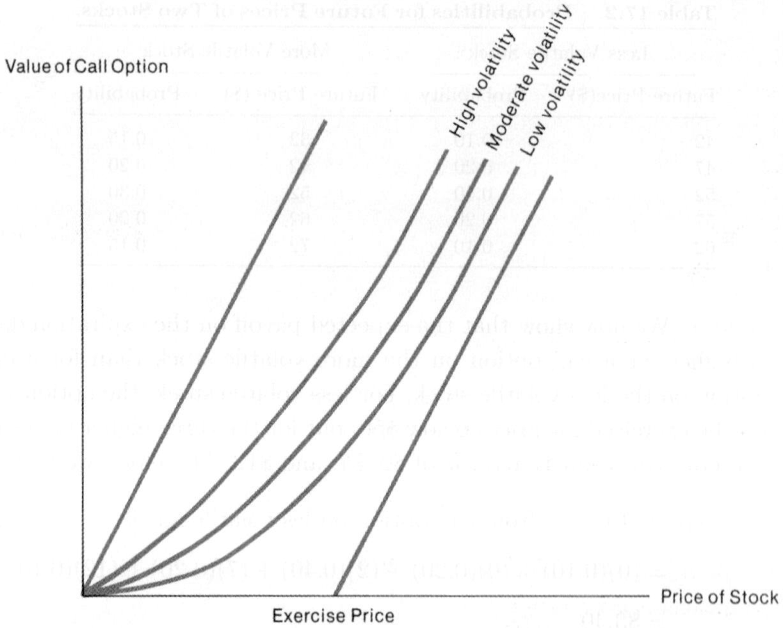

Fig. 17.4. Call-Option Value as Function of Stock Price for High-, Moderate-, and Low-Volatility Stocks.

notice that for any given current market price of the stock, the higher the variance of day-to-day price changes, the greater the call-option value.

The notion of volatility in future stock market prices is related to the length of the time horizon being considered. Specifically, if the variance of day-to-day changes is σ^2, the variance in the change from the present to t days is $\sigma^2 t$ if the price changes are serially independent. Therefore, the further ahead is the expiration date, the greater the volatility in price movements. This suggests that for a European option, which can only be exercised on the expiration date, the relevant measure of volatility is $\sigma^2 t$ where t is the number of days remaining to the expiration date. The larger this quantity is, the greater the call-option value.

(5) *Time remaining to expiration date*: We have seen in factor (3) and (4) above two reasons to expect that the longer the time remaining before the expiration date, the higher the call-option value, all else equal. The reason is that the extra time allows larger gains to be derived from postponing payment of the exercise price and permits greater volatility in price movements of the stock. These two considerations both operate in the same direction — toward increasing the call-option value.

We have seen that five factors influence the value of a call option. The interaction of these various factors in determining option value is rather complex.[2] We present a formula that, under certain assumptions, can be shown to determine a call-option value as a function of these five parameters. However, before proceeding to this somewhat complicated relationship, we discuss a simple situation in which option valuation is more straightforward. This is useful in explaining further the dependence of option value on the risk-free rate of interest.

Our aim here is to show, for a special set of assumptions, that an investor can guarantee a particular return from a combined strategy of holding shares in a stock and writing call options on that stock, even though there is some uncertainty about the future price of the stock. The essential simplifying assumption required to generate this result is that there are only two possible values for the future price per share of the stock. In addition, for convenience we will use European options, with an expiration date in one year. Further, we assume that the stock pays no dividend and that there are no transactions costs.

Within this framework, consider the factors in Table 17.3. An investor can purchase shares for \$100 each and write European call options with an exercise price of \$100. There are two possible prices of the stock on the expiration date, with uncertainty as to which will materialize.

In Table 17.4, we list the consequences to the investor for the two expiration-date stock prices. If the higher price prevails, each share of

Table 17.3. Data for a Hedging Example.

Current price per share:	\$100
Future price per share:	\$125 with probability 0.6
	\$85 with probability 0.4
Exercise price of call option:	\$100

Table 17.4. Possible Expiration-Date Outcomes for a Hedging Example.

Expiration-Date Stock Price	Value per Share of Stock Holdings	Value per Share of Options Written
\$125	\$125	−\$25
\$85	\$85	\$0

[2]Compared to the capital asset pricing model (CAPM), the OPM is a relative pricing approach In the CAPM, the major determinants are risk and return. In the OPM, the return of the asset or the market does not affect the option value.

stock will be worth \$125. However, the call options will be exercised, at a cost per share to the writer of the difference between the stock price and the exercise price. In Table 17.4, this is a negative value of \$25 from having written the call option. If the lower of the two possible stock prices materializes on the expiration date, each share owned will be worth \$85, and it will have cost nothing to write the option because it will not be exercised.

Suppose that the investor wants to form a *hedged portfolio* by both purchasing stock and writing call options, so as to guarantee as large a total value of holdings per dollar invested as possible, whatever the stock price on the expiration date. The hedge is constructed to be riskless, since any profit (or loss) from the stock is exactly offset with a loss (or profit) from the call option. This is called a *perfect* or *riskless hedge* and can be accomplished by purchasing H number of shares for each option written. We now determine H. If H shares are purchased and one option written, the total value on the expiration date will be \$125H–\$25 at the higher market price and \$85H–\$0 at the lower price. Suppose we choose H so that these two amounts are equal; that is

$$125H - 25 = 85H,$$

or

$$H = \frac{25}{40} = \frac{5}{8}.$$

Then, the same total value results whatever the stock's expiration-date market price. This ratio is known as the *hedge ratio* of stocks to options, the implication being that a hedged portfolio is achieved by writing eight options for each five shares purchased. More generally, it follows from the above argument that the hedge ratio is given by

$$H = \frac{P_U - E}{P_U - P_L},$$

where P_U = upper share price; P_L = lower share price; E = exercise price of option; and E is assumed to be between P_U and P_L.

Returning to our example, suppose that five shares are purchased and an option on eight shares is written. If the expiration-date price is \$125, then the total value of the investor's portfolio is

$$(5)(125) - (8)(25) = \$425.$$

If the expiration-date stock price is, \$85, total value is

$$(5)(85) + (8)(0) = \$425.$$

As predicted, the two are identical, so that this value is assured.

Next, we must consider the investor's income from the writing of call options. Let V_c denote the price per share of a call option. Then, the purchase of five shares costs \$500, but \$8 V_c is received from writing call options on eight shares, so that the net outlay will be \$500–\$8 V_c. For this outlay, a value one year hence of \$425 is assured. However, there is another simple mechanism for guaranteeing such a return. An investment could be made in government securities at the risk-free interest rate. Suppose that this rate is 8% per annum. On the expiration date, an initial investment of \$500–\$8 $V_c$will be worth \$1.08(500–8 V_c). If this is to be equal to the value of the hedged portfolio, then

$$1.08(500 - 8V_c) = 425,$$

so that

$$H = \frac{Max(0, P_U - E) - Max(0, P_L - E)}{P_U - P_L} = \frac{25 - 0}{125 - 85}.$$

Therefore, we conclude that if the price per share for the call option is \$13.31, the hedging strategy will yield an assured rate of return equal to the risk-free interest rate.

In a competitive market, this is the price that will prevail, and therefore is the value of the call option. Suppose that the price of the call option was above \$13.31. By forming a hedged portfolio in the manner just described, investors could ensure a return in excess of the risk-free rate. Such an opportunity would attract many to sell options, thus driving down the price. Conversely, if the price of the option was below \$13.31, it would be possible to achieve a return guaranteed to be in excess of the risk-free rate by both purchasing call options and selling short the stock. The volume of demand thus created for the call option would drive up its price. Hence, in a competitive market, \$13.31 is the only sustainable price for this option.

Our example shows that a hedged portfolio can achieve an assured rate of return of 8%. Notice that our analysis depends on the level of the risk-free rate. If that rate is 10% per annum, the call-option value is \$14.20. This illustrates the dependence of call-option value on the risk-free interest rate.

17.3. Determining The Value of Options

17.3.1. *Expected Value Estimation*

A higher *expected rate of return*, as compared with the hedged portfolio, can be achieved by the exclusive purchase either of shares or of call options. Suppose that a single share is purchased for \$100. One year hence, the expected value of that share is

$$\text{expected value of share} = (0.6)(125) + (0.4)(85) = \$109.$$

Hence, the expected rate of return from a portfolio consisting entirely of holdings of this stock is 9%. Similarly, suppose that a call option is purchased for \$13.31. The expected value of this option on the expiration date is

$$\text{expected value of call} = (0.6)(25) + (0.4)(0) = \$15.$$

Hence, the expected rate of return is

$$\text{expected rate of return on call} = \frac{15 - 13.31}{13.31} \times 100 = 12.7\%.$$

The increased expected rates of return from holding exclusively these two types of securities should not be surprising. They simply represent increases required by investors for assuming additional risk.

We have shown how call-option valuation can be determined within a simple framework in which only two values for the future market price of a stock are possible. We must move on to more realistic situations that involve a range of future market prices.

The value of a put option is determined by the same factors that determine the value of a call option, except that the factors have different relationships to the value of a put than they have to the value of a call. Figure 17.5 shows the relationship between put-option value and stock price.

The value of a put option is

$$V_P = MAX(E - P, 0),$$

where V_P = value of the put; E = exercise price; and P = value of the underlying stock. The maximum value of a put is equal to the exercise price of the option when the stock price is 0. This is shown by the line

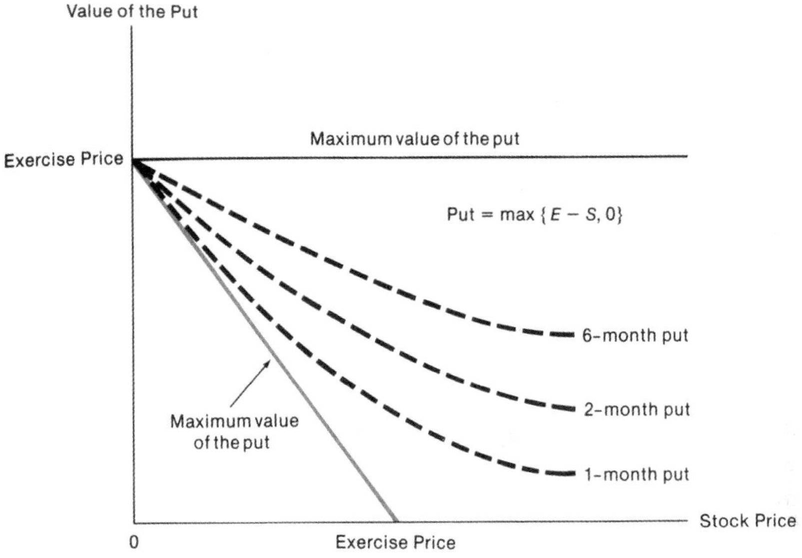

Fig. 17.5. Put-Option Value.

"Maximum value of the put" in Fig. 17.5. The minimum value of the put is 0, which occurs when the stock price exceeds the exercise price.

17.3.2. *The Black–Scholes Option Pricing Model*

The notion that the price of a call option should be such that the rate of return on a fully hedged portfolio is equal to the risk-free rate of interest has been used by Black and Scholes (1973) to derive a more generally applicable procedure for valuing an option. The assumption that only two future prices are possible is dropped for a more realistic view of future price movements. The complete set of assumptions on which the Black–Scholes formula is based is given below.

- Only European options are considered.
- Options and stocks can be traded in any quantities in a perfectly competitive market; there are no transactions costs and all relevant information is freely available to market participants.
- Short-selling of stocks and options in a perfectly competitive market is possible.
- The risk-free interest rate is known and is constant up to the expiration date. Market participants are able to borrow or lend at this rate.

- No dividends are paid on the stock.
- The stock price follows a random path in continuous time such that the variance of the rate of return is constant over time and known to market participants. The logarithm of future stock prices follows a normal distribution.

Under these assumptions, Black and Scholes show that the call-option value on a share of stock is given by

$$V_c = P[N(d_1)] - e^{-rt}E[N(d_2)], \tag{17.1}$$

where V = value of option; P = current price of stock; r = continuously compounded annual risk-free interest rate; t = time in years to expiration date; E = exercise price; $e = 2.71828$ is a constant; and $N(d_1)$ = probability that a standard normal random variable is less than or equal to $d_i (i = 1, 2)$, with

$$d_1 = \frac{ln\left(\frac{P}{E}\right) + \left(r + \frac{\sigma^2}{2}\right)t}{\sigma\sqrt{t}}, \tag{17.2a}$$

and

$$d_2 = \frac{ln\left(\frac{P}{E}\right) + \left(r - \frac{\sigma^2}{2}\right)t}{\sigma\sqrt{t}} = d_1 - \sigma\sqrt{t}, \tag{17.2b}$$

where σ^2 = variance of annual rate of return on the stock, continuously compounded; and logarithms are to base e. A binomial distribution approach to derive the option pricing model (OPM) can be found in Appendix 17A.

Although the specific form of the Black–Scholes option pricing formula is complicated, its interpretation is straightforward. The first term of Equation (17.1) is the value of an investor's right to that portion of the probability distribution of the stock's price that lies above the exercise price. This term equals the expected value of this portion of the stock's price distribution. N(d1) can be graphically described by Fig. 17.6.

The second term in Equation (17.1) is the present value of the exercise price times the probability that the exercise price will be paid (the option will be exercised at maturity). Overall, the Black–Scholes model involves the present value of a future cash flow, a common concern in finance. The Black–Scholes model equates option value to the present expected value of the stock price minus the present value of the cost of exercising the option.

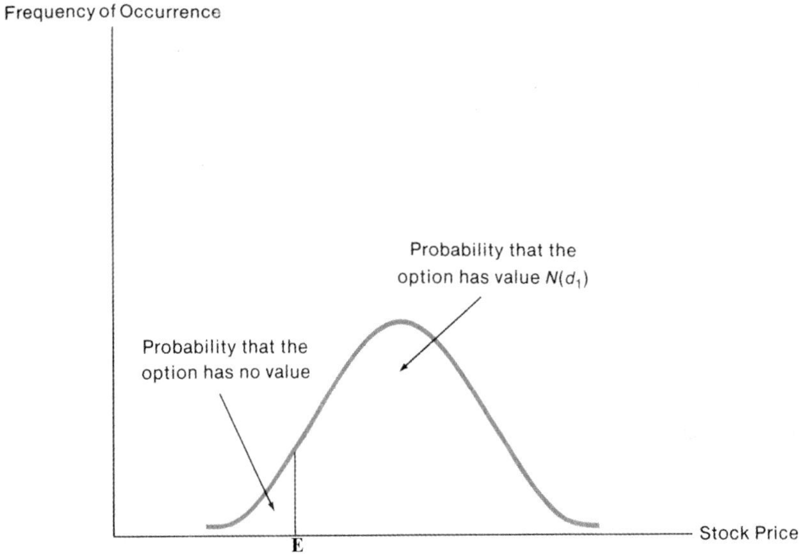

Fig. 17.6. Probability Distribution of Stock Prices.

More important for our purposes than the particular formula is the manner in which the model relates option value to the five factors discussed in the previous section. These relationships are as follows:

(1) All other things equal, the higher the current market price of the stock, the higher the call-option value.
(2) All other things equal, the higher the exercise price, the lower the option value.
(3) All other things equal, the higher the risk-free interest rate, the higher the option value.
(4) All other things equal, the greater the time to the expiration date, the higher the option value.
(5) All other things equal, the greater the volatility of the stock price (as measured by σ^2), the higher the option value

According to the Black–Scholes model, although the call-option value depends on the variance of rate of return, it does not depend on the stock's expected rate of return. This is because a change in expected rate of return affects stock price but not the relative value of the option and the stock. Recall from our earlier discussion that formation of the hedged portfolio was independent of expected return. For example, changing the two probabilities in Table 17.3 has no effect on call-option value.

The following example illustrates the computation of option value using the Black–Scholes formula.

Example 17.1

Suppose that the current market price of a share of stock is \$90 and an option is written to purchase the stock for \$100 in six months. The current risk-free rate of interest is 8% per annum. Since the time to the expiration date is half a year, we have, in the notation of the Black–Scholes model, $P = 90$; $E = 100$; $r = .08$; and $t = .50$.

All of this information is readily available to market participants. More problematic is an assessment of the likely volatility of returns on the stock over the next six months. One possible approach is to estimate this volatility using data on past price changes. For instance, we could compute the variance of daily changes in the logarithm of price (daily rate of return) over the last 100 trading days. Multiplying the result by the number of trading days in the year would then yield an estimate of the required variance on an annual basis.[3] For this stock, suppose that such a procedure yields the standard deviation

$$\sigma = 0.6.$$

This value or some alternative (perhaps developed subjectively) can then be substituted, together with the values of the other four factors, in Equation (17.1) to obtain an estimate of the market value of the call option. We now illustrate these calculations. First, we need the natural logarithm of P/E. This is

$$ln\left(\frac{P}{E}\right) = ln(.9) = -0.1054.$$

It follows that

$$\begin{aligned} d_1 &= \frac{ln\left(\frac{P}{E}\right) + rt + \sigma^2 \frac{t}{2}}{\sigma\sqrt{t}} \\ &= \frac{-0.1054 + (0.08)(0.50) + \frac{1}{2}(0.36)(0.50)}{0.6\sqrt{0.50}} = 0.06 \end{aligned}$$

[3]If we use monthly rate of return to calculate the variance, then the annualized variance will be 12 times the monthly variance.

$$\begin{aligned} d_2 &= \frac{ln\left(\frac{P}{E}\right) + rt - \sigma^2 \frac{t}{2}}{\sigma\sqrt{t}} \\ &= \frac{-0.1054 + (0.08)(0.50) - \frac{1}{2}(0.36)(0.50)}{0.6\sqrt{0.50}} \\ &= -0.37 \end{aligned}$$

Using the table of the cumulative distribution function of the standard normal distribution in the appendix at the back of this book, we find the probability that a standard normal random variable less than 0.06 is

$$N(d_1) = N(0.06) = 0.5239,$$

and the probability that a standard normal random variable is less than −0.37 is

$$N(d_2) = N(-0.37) = 1 - N(0.37) = 0.3557.$$

The detailed discussion of how to obtain $N(d_1)$ and $N(d_2)$ can be found in Chapter 19.

These numbers represent the probability that the stock price will be at least equal to the exercise price — 52% of the time over the life of the option — and the probability of exercise −35%. We also require

$$e^{-rt} = e^{-(0.08)(0.5)} = 0.9608.$$

Finally, on substitution into Equation (17.1), we find

$$\begin{aligned} V_c &= PN(d_1) - e^{rt}EN(d_2) \\ &= (90)(0.5239) - (0.9608)(100)(0.3557) = \$12.98 \end{aligned}$$

Therefore, according to the Black–Scholes model, the call option should be priced at $12.98 per share.

A further implication of the Black–Scholes model is that the quantity $N(d_1)$ provides the hedge ratio for a hedged portfolio of stocks and written options. We see, then, that to achieve such a portfolio, 0.5239 shares of stock should be purchased for each option written.

17.3.3. *Taxation of Options*

The taxation of option gains, losses, and income are a fairly complex and constantly changing part of the tax law. However, tax treatment can have a large impact on the usefulness of options for the individual investor. Income (premiums) received by the option writer is taxed as normal income, just as if the option writer were providing a service.

Options can be used to defer gains into the future, which reduces the investor's current tax liability. For example, an investor with a short-term gain on a stock can purchase a put to protect against a drop in the stock price. This allows the investor to hold the stock and not realize the gain until sometime in the future, perhaps the next year, thereby deferring the payment of tax from the present until some future period. Hence, the tax position of the investor is also a factor in determining the value or usefulness of options. However, because we do not have a homogeneous tax structure, it is difficult to incorporate the tax effect into a formulation such as the Black–Scholes model.

17.3.4. *American Options*

In our analysis of options, we have assumed the options are European and thus may only be exercised on the expiration date, and that no dividends are paid on the stock before the expiration date. Merton (1973) has shown that if the stock does not pay dividends, it is suboptimal to exercise an American call option before the expiration date. Therefore, if American and European call options on a nondividend-paying stock are otherwise identical, they should have the same value.

The effect of dividends on a call option depends on whether the firm is expected to pay dividends before the option's expiration date. Such action should reduce the option's value — the greater the expected dividend, the larger the reduction in option value. The reason is that a dividend payment amounts to the transfer to stockholders of part of the firm's value, a distribution in which option holders do not share. The larger this reduction in firm value, all other things equal, the lower the expected future price of the stock, because that price reflects firm value at any point in time. Therefore, the higher the dividend, the smaller the probability of any gains from exercising a call option on common stock and, hence, the lower the value of the option. The extreme case occurs if the firm is liquidated and the entire amount of funds realized from the liquidation is distributed as dividends to common stockholders. Once such a distribution is made, the stock and the call option have zero value.

If the firm pays dividends, the value of an American call option on its stock will exceed that of an otherwise identical European option. The reason is that the holder of the American call can exercise the option just before the ex-dividend date and thus receive the dividend payment. If the benefits from such an exercise outweigh the interest income that would have been earned on the exercise price had the option been held to the expiration date, it benefits the holder of an American call to exercise the option. Since this opportunity is not available to the holder of a European option, the American option should have a higher value.

The solution to valuing an option on a stock that pays dividends can be approximated by replacing P, the stock price in the Black–Scholes formula, with the stock price minus the present value of the known future dividend. This is justified because if the option is not exercised before maturity, the option holder will not receive the dividends, in which case the holder should subtract the present value of the dividend from the stock price.

17.4. Option Pricing Theory and Capital Structure

In this section we show how option pricing theory can be used to analyze the value of the components of a firm's capital structure. Suppose that management of an unlevered corporation decides to issue bonds. For simplicity, we assume these to be zero coupon bonds with face value $B$to be paid at the maturity date.[4] When the bonds mature, bondholders must be paid an amount B, if possible. If this money cannot be raised, bondholders have a first claim on the firm's assets and will be paid the firm's entire value, V_f which in this case will be less than B. Let us look at this arrangement from the point of view of the firm's stockholders. By using debt, stockholders can be regarded as having sold the firm to bondholders, with an option to purchase it back by paying an amount B at the maturity date of the bonds. Thus, the stockholders hold a call option on the firm, with expiration date at the date of maturity of the bonds. If the firm's value exceeds the value of the debt on the expiration date, the debt will be retired, so that stockholders will have exercised their call option. On the other hand, if the firm's value is less than the face value of the debt, stockholders' limited liability allows them to leave the firm in the hands of the bondholders. The call option will not be exercised, so that the stock will be worth nothing. However, stockholders will have no further obligations to bondholders. Therefore, on the date of expiration, the value of this call option, or, equivalently, the value of stockholders' equity, will be $V = V_f - B$

---

[4]These bonds will sell for less than the face value, the difference reflecting interest to be paid on the loan.

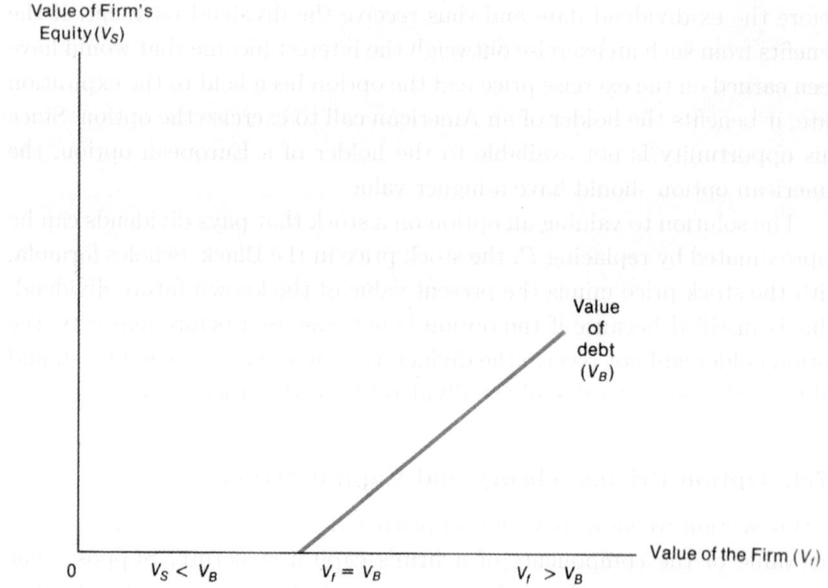

Fig. 17.7. Option Approach to Capital Structure.

if $V_f > B$ and 0 if $V_f < B$. Thus, we can write

$$V = \text{MAX}(0, V_f - B), \tag{17.3}$$

where V = value of stockholders' call option on the firm; V_f = value of the firm; and B = face value of debt. This relationship is shown in Fig. 17.7. As we can see, this is exactly the relationship shown in Fig. 17.1(a) for the value of a call option.

We see, then, that the theory of options can provide us with insights into the valuation of debt and stockholders' equity. This analysis indicates that the stockholders own a call option on the firm's assets. At any time, they could exercise this option by delivering the face value of the bonds to payoff the bondholders and realize the value of their option. This point is illustrated in the following example, where we employ the Black–Scholes model.

Example 17.2

An unlevered corporation is valued at $14 million. The corporation issues debt, payable in six years, with a face value of $10 million. The standard deviation of the continuously compounded rate of return on the total value of this corporation is 0.2. Assume that the risk-free rate of interest is 8% per annum.

In our previous notation, the current market price of the asset (in this case, the firm) is \$14 million, and the exercise price of the option is the face value of the debt. Therefore, we have $P = 14$, $E = 10$, $r = 0.08$, $t = 6$, and $\sigma = 0.2$, where we are measuring value in units of a million dollars.

We will use the Black–Scholes formula, Equation (17.1), to compute the value of stockholders' equity; that is, the value of the stockholders' call option on the firm. First, we require the natural logarithm of P/E, so that

$$ln\left(\frac{P}{E}\right) = ln(1.4) = 0.3365.$$

Next, we find

$$\begin{aligned} d_1 &= \frac{ln(\frac{P}{E}) + rt + \sigma^2 \frac{t}{2}}{\sigma\sqrt{t}} \\ &= \frac{0.3365 + (0.08)(6) + \frac{1}{2}(0.2)(6)}{0.2\sqrt{6}} = 1.91, \end{aligned}$$

and

$$\begin{aligned} d_2 &= \frac{ln\left(\frac{P}{E}\right) + rt - \sigma^2 \frac{t}{2}}{\sigma\sqrt{t}} \\ &= \frac{0.3365 + (0.08)(6) - \frac{1}{2}(0.2)(6)}{0.2\sqrt{6}} = 1.42. \end{aligned}$$

From tabulated values of the cumulative distribution function of the standard normal random variable, we find

$$N(d_1) = N(1.91) = 0.9719,$$

and

$$N(d_2) = N(1.42) = 0.9222.$$

We also require

$$e^{-rt} = e^{-(0.08)(6)} = 0.6188.$$

On substitution in Equation (17.1), we find the value of stockholders' equity

$$V = PN(d_1) - e^{-rt}EN(d_2)$$
$$= (14)(0.9719) - (0.6188)(10)(0.9222) = \$7.90 \text{ million.}$$

Since the total value of the firm is $14 million, the value of the debt is

$$\text{value of debt} = \$14 - \$7.9 = \$6.10 \text{ million}$$

Assuming the market is efficient, this firm could sell debt with a face value of $10 million for $6.1 million. These receipts could be distributed to stockholders, leaving them with an equity worth $7.9 million.

We now turn to examine the effects of two factors on our calculations.

17.4.1. *Proportion of Debt in Capital Structure*

Let us compare our results of Example 17.2 with an otherwise identical situation, but where now only $5 million face value of debt is to be issued. With $E = 5$ so that $P/E = 2.8$, we find $In(P/E)$ to be 1.0296. Using the same procedure as in Example 17.2, $d_1 = 3.33$ and $d_2 = 2.84$, so that $N(d_1) = .9996$ and $N(d_2) = .9977$. Using Equation (17.1), the value of stockholders' equity is

$$V = PN(d_1) - e^{-rt}EN(d_2)$$
$$= (14)(0.9996) - (0.6188)(5)(0.9977).$$
$$= \$10.91 \text{ million}$$

Therefore, the value of the debt is

$$\text{value of debt} = 14 - 10.91 = \$3.09 \text{ million.}$$

In Table 17.5, we compare, from the point of view of bondholders, the cases where the face values of issued debt are $5 million and $10 million. We see from the table that increasing the proportion of debt in the capital structure decreases the value of each dollar of face value of debt. If all

Table 17.5. Effect of Different Levels of Debt on Debt Value.

Face Value of Debt ($ millions)	Actual Value of Debt ($ millions)	Actual Value per Dollar Debt Face Value of Debt
5	3.09	$0.618
10	6.10	$0.610

the debt is issued at one time, this phenomenon, which simply reflects the increase in bondholders' risk as debt increases, will result in the demand for correspondingly higher interest rates. As our example illustrates, if the corporation sells only \$5 million of face-value bonds, a price of \$618,000 per million dollars in face value will be paid for these bonds. However, if bonds with face value of \$10 million are to be issued, this price will fall to \$610,000. In such a case, the market for bonds operates such that the risk to bondholders of future default is considered in establishing the price of the zero coupon bonds, or, more generally the interest rate attached to any bonds.

Suppose, however, that our company issues bonds with face value of \$5 million, at a cost to bond purchasers of \$3.09 million. One year later, this corporation decides to issue more debt. In valuing this new debt, potential purchasers of bonds will assess the risk of default. One factor taken into consideration will be the *total* level of debt of the corporation; that is, the amount of existing debt as well as the size of the new issue. Hence, the market price for the new bonds will reflect riskiness. Consider, however, the position of existing bondholders. The interest rates to be paid to these holders of old debt have already been established. The issue of new debt is going to increase the chance of default on all loans. Consequently, the value of existing bonds must fall when new bonds are issued. Therefore, the issue of new bonds entails a decrease in the wealth of existing bondholders. The beneficiaries are the stockholders of the company whose wealth increases by a corresponding amount. We see, then, that there is a conflict of interest between existing bondholders and holders of common stock. All other things equal, existing bondholders will prefer that no further debt be issued, while stockholders will prefer to see more debt issued. This provides an illustration of the agency problem. Purchasers of bonds will require covenants restricting the freedom of action of corporate management in order to protect the value of their investment.

17.4.2. *Riskiness of Business Operations*

Let us return to the corporation of Example 17.2, which is about to issue debt with face value of \$10 million. Leaving the other variables unchanged, suppose that the standard deviation of the continuously compounded rate of return on the corporation's total value is 0.4, rather than 0.2. This implies that the corporation is operating in an environment of greater business risk. Setting $\sigma^2 = 0.4$, with all other relevant variables as specified in

Example 17.2, we find $d_1 = 1.32$ and $d_2 = 0.34$, so that $N(d_1) = 0.9066$ and $N(d_2) = 0.6331$. From Equation (17.1), we find the value of stockholders' equity to be

$$\begin{aligned} V &= PN(d_1) - e^{-rt}EN(d_2) \\ &= (14)(0.9066) - (0.6188)(10)(0.6331) \\ &= \$8.77 \text{ million.} \end{aligned}$$

Thus, the value of the debt is

$$\text{value of debt} = 14 - 8.77 = \$5.23 \text{ million.}$$

Table 17.6 summarizes the comparison between these results and those of Example 17.2. We see that this increase in business risk, with its associated increase in the probability of default on the bonds, leads to a reduction from \$6.10 million to \$5.23 million in the market value of the \$10 million face value of debt. To the extent that potential purchasers of bonds are able to anticipate the degree of business risk, the higher interest rate on the bonds reflects the risk involved. The greater the degree of risk, the higher the interest rate that must be offered to sell a particular amount of debt.

However, suppose that having issued debt, corporate management embarks on new projects with a higher level of risk than could have been foreseen by the purchasers of the bonds. As we have just seen, this will lower the value of existing bonds. This decrease in bondholders' wealth accrues as a gain in wealth to holders of common stock. Once again, we find a conflict of interest between stockholders and bondholders. Once debt has been sold, it will be in the interests of stockholders for the firm to operate with a high degree of business risk, while bondholders will prefer lower levels of risk. Thus, the degree of business risk represents another example of an agency problem. Bondholders will want protection against the possibility that management will take on riskier than anticipated projects, and will demand protective covenants against such actions.

Table 17.6. Effect of Different Levels of Business Risk on the Value of \$10 Million Face Value of Debt.

Variance of Rate of Return	Value of Equity (\$ millions)	Value of Debt (\$ millions)
0.2	7.90	6.10
0.4	8.77	5.23

Because of this factor, the issue of a large volume of debt is likely to be accompanied by constraints on the freedom of management action in the firm's operation.

17.4.3. *Option Pricing Approach to Determine the Optimal Capital Structure*

Chapter 6 of Lee *et al.* (2009) discussed the traditional approach to determine the optimal capital structure. Leland (1994) has proposed an option approach to determine the optimal capital structure. Chen *et al.* (2010) have discussed traditional and option approaches to determine optimal capital structure. The option approach extended the M&M proposition 1 with tax from certainty to uncertainty case which includes the possibility of bankruptcy.

17.5. Warrants

A *warrant* is an option issued by a corporation to individual investors to purchase, at a stated price, a specified number of the shares of common stock of that corporation. Warrants are issued in two principal sets of circumstances:

(1) In raising venture capital, either to start a new company or to substantially increase the scope of operations of an existing company, warrants are often issued to lenders as an additional inducement to the promised interest payments or to purchasers of new stock issues.
(2) Often, when issuing bonds, a company will increase the bonds' attractiveness by attaching warrants. Thus, as well as receiving interest payments on the bonds, their purchasers obtain an option to buy stock in the corporation at a specified price. As we have seen, such options will have some value, and so their attachment to bonds should lead to a lowering of the interest rate paid on a fixed quantity of bonds or an increase in the number of bonds that can be sold at a given interest rate.

Since a warrant is essentially a call option on a specified number of shares of common stock, the principles underlying the valuation of call options are also applicable to the valuation of warrants. Suppose that a warrant entitles its holder to purchase N shares of common stock at a total cost E. If, at the expiration date, the price per share of common stock is

P, then shares of total value NP can be purchased at cost E.If NP exceeds E, the option to purchase will be exercised, and the difference between these quantities is the value of the warrant. On the other hand, if NP is less than E, it will not pay to exercise the option, so that the warrant will be worthless. The warrant's value on the expiration date can then be expressed as

$$V_w = \text{MAX}(0, NP - E),$$

where V = value of warrant; N = number of shares that can be purchased; P = market price per share of stock; and E = exercise price for the purchase of N shares of stock

Prior to the expiration date, for reasons discussed earlier in this chapter, the warrant's value will exceed this theoretical value. The same factors affecting the value of an ordinary call option are also relevant here. Thus, all other things equal, warrant value will increase with increases in the volatility of the stock price, in the risk-free interest rate, and in the time to the expiration date. However, the basic version of the Black–Scholes model generally will not be directly applicable, as it pertains to the valuation of warrants. The reason is that, generally, warrants differ in important respects from ordinary call options. These factors are as follows:

(1) The life of a call option typically is just a few months. However, the life of a warrant is several years. While it may not be unreasonable to expect volatility of rate of return to remain constant for a few months, it is less likely that it will do so for several years.
(2) Over a period of several years, it is likely that dividends will be paid. As we have seen, dividend payments, which do not accrue to warrantholders, reduce the value of options to purchase stock.
(3) For many warrants, the exercise price is not fixed to the expiration date, but changes at designated points in time. It may well pay to exercise the option to purchase shares immediately before such a change.
(4) It may be that the number of shares that all warrantholders are entitled to purchase represents a considerable fraction of the total number of shares of the corporation. Thus, if these options are all exercised, and total earnings are unaffected, then earnings per share will be diluted.

Let us look at this last point in more detail. Since by using warrants, a corporation can extract more favorable terms from bondholders, it follows that, in return, the company must have transferred something of value to these bondholders. This transfer can be visualized as giving the bondholders a stake in the corporation's equity. Thus, we should regard equity comprising both stockholdings and warrant value. We will refer to this total equity, prior to the exercise of the options, as *old equity* so that

$$\text{old equity} = \text{stockholders' equity} + \text{warrants.}$$

Suppose that the warrants are exercised. The corporation then receives additional money from the purchase of new shares, so that total equity is

$$\text{new equity} = \text{old equity} + \text{exercise money.}$$

We denote by N the number of shares outstanding and by N_w the number of shares that warrant holders can purchase. If the options are exercised, there will be a total of $N + N_w$ shares, a fraction $N_w/(N_w + N)$ of which is owned by former warrantholders. These holders then own this fraction of the new equity; that is

$$H\ (\text{new equity}) = H\ (\text{old equity}) + H(\text{exercise money}),$$

where $H = \frac{N_w}{N_w+N}$.

Thus, a fraction, $N_w/(N_w + N)$, of the exercise money is effectively returned to the former warrantholders. In fact, they have really spent $[1 - N_w/(N_w + N)] = N/(N_w + N)$ of the exercise money to acquire a fraction, $N_w/(N_w + N)$, of the old equity. Therefore, in valuing the warrants, the Black–Scholes formula must be modified. We need to make the appropriate substitutions in Equation (17.1) for the current stock price, P, and the exercise price of the option, E.

$$P = \left(\frac{N_w}{N_w + N}\right) (\text{value of old equity})$$

$$E = \left(\frac{N}{N_w + N}\right) (\text{exercise money})$$

It also follows that the appropriate measure of volatility, σ^2, is the variance of rate of return on the total old equity (including the value of warrants), not simply on stockholders' equity.

Suppose that a firm has one million shares outstanding, currently selling at \$100 per share. There are also 500,000 warrants with an exercise price of \$80 per share. The warrants are worth \$20, or the current stock price, \$100, less the exercise price of \$80. The value of the old equity is

$$\text{old equity} = 100(\text{lm}) + 20(0.5\text{m}) = \$110 \text{ million.}$$

If the warrants are exercised, the firm will receive \$40 million (\$80 $\times 0.5$ m) of new equity, so that the new equity is

$$\text{new equity} = \$110\text{m} + \$40\text{m} = \$150 \text{ million.}$$

When they exercise their warrants, the warrantholders will own one-third of the shares outstanding; that is,

$$H = \frac{N_w}{N_w + N} \quad \text{or} \quad \frac{500,000}{500,000 + 1,000,000},$$

and the old shareholders will own the remaining two-third of the shares outstanding.

The warrantholders now have an investment worth \$50 million, or

$$\frac{1}{3}(150\text{m}) = \frac{1}{3}(110\text{m}) + \frac{1}{3}(40\text{m}) = 50 \text{ million.}$$

It makes sense for the warrantholders to exercise their warrant; they spend \$40 million for shares that are worth \$50 million. In terms of the warrant value, the market should be willing to pay \$20 per warrant for 500,000 warrants, or \$10 million.

In Chapter 5, we discuss convertible bonds. A *convertible bond* is a security that gives its owner the right to exchange it for a given number of shares of common stock any time before the maturity date of the bond. Hence, a convertible bond is actually a portfolio of two securities: a bond and a warrant. The value of a convertible bond is the value of the bond portion of the portfolio plus the value of the warrant.

17.6. Summary

In Chapter 17, we have discussed the basic concepts of call and put options and have examined the factors that determine the value of an option. One procedure used in option valuation is the Black–Scholes model, which allows us to estimate option value as a function of stock price, option-exercise price, time-to-expiration date, and risk-free interest rate. The option pricing approach to investigating capital structure is also discussed, as is the value of warrants.

Questions and Problems

1. Find the expected value of an option with an exercise price of \$100 at the end of the period, given the following information. (Current stock price is \$100.)
2. A riskless hedge position can be constructed by buying a stock and writing options on the stock. Using the information in problem 1: (Assume the risk-free interest rate is 10%.)

   (a) Find the optimal hedge ratio.
   (b) Find the equilibrium option price.

3. The price of Goodsell Company stock on January 1 is \$100 per share. A call option maturing on April 1 has a \$100 exercise price. The standard deviation of Goodsell stock is 20% per year. What is the call option value if the risk-free rate is 10%?
4. Suppose an unleveraged firm is valued at \$10 million. The firm issues debt, payable in nine years, with a face value of \$7 million. The standard deviation of the rate of return on the total value of this firm is 0.4, and the risk-free interest rate is 8% per annum. Using the option valuation model, calculate the value of stockholders' equity.
5. How does the price of a call option respond to the following changes, other things equal?

   (a) Stock price increase
   (b) Exercise price increase
   (c) Risk-free interest rate increase
   (d) Extension of the expiration date
   (e) Volatility of the stock price increase.

6. If a call option has an exercise price of \$50, then over what stock price range would it be:

   (a) Out of the money?
   (b) In the money?

7. If a put option has an exercise price of \$50, then over what stock price range would it be:

   (a) Out of the money?
   (b) In the money?

8. Would an American option generally sell at a price higher or lower than a European option? Explain.
9. If a call option has an exercise price of $50, how much will it be worth on its exercise date (assuming no transaction costs) if the price of the underlying stock is
   (a) $30
   (b) $50
   (c) $80
10. If a call option has an exercise price of $60 and the price of the stock is $40, what is the value of the call option to the
    (a) Holder of the option
    (b) The seller of the option
11. Allison Merrick is considering two call options, each having exercise prices of $20 and being identical in all other respects except for the distribution of underlying stock values. The distributions of the values of the underlying stocks of Companies J and K are given below:
    Find the expected payoff for each and explain which one you would prefer.
12. The current price per share is $80 which can either go up to $100 or down to $60. The probabilities of upward and downward movement of the stock price is 0.6 and 0.4, respectively. Given an exercise price of $80 on a call option and an optimal hedge ratio of 0.4:
    (a) Find the lower bound of the stock price.
    (b) Find the expected value of the call option.
    (c) Demonstrate that the hedged portfolio is riskless.
13. The standard deviation of the return on the stock of Company A is .5 per year. A call option written on this stock is maturing six months from now and has an exercise price of $80. If the current stock price is

Table 17.7. Distributions of the Values of Companies J and K.

Probability	Stock J	Probability	Stock K
0.2	$15	0.1	$12
0.3	$18	0.3	$17
0.3	$22	0.4	$25
0.2	$25	0.2	$35

\$80 and the risk free rate of interest is 8%, find the optimal hedge ratio for a portfolio of stocks and options using the Black–Scholes model. (*Note*: This is equivalent to finding $N(d_1)$ in the Black–Scholes model.)

14. A firm has outstanding debt of \$12 million which matures in 5 years from now. The standard deviation of the rate of return of the firm's value is .3. The value of another otherwise identical firm with zero debt is \$20 million. Find the value of the firm's outstanding debt, given that the risk free interest rate is 8%.
15. $S_0 = 100$, $X = 120$, $R_f = 10\%$. There are two possibilities for S_T\$140 and \$70. Derive a two-state put option value in this problem.

    (a) Show that the range of S is 70 whereas that of P is 40 across state.
    (b) Form a portfolio of four shares of stocks and seven puts. What is the (nonrandom) payoff to this portfolio? What is the present value of the portfolio?
    (c) Given the stock is currently selling at 100, solve for the value of the put.

16. Use the Black–Scholes formula to find the value of a call option on the following stock and then use the put–call parity to calculate the put option value on the stock in the previous problem with the same exercise price and maturity as the call option.

Time of maturity	6 months
Standard deviation	20% per year
Exercise price	\$50
Stock price	\$50
Interest rate	5%

17. A call option with strike price \$50 on a stock currently priced at $S = \$65$ is selling for \$10. Using a volatility estimate of $\sigma = 0.30$, you find that $N(d1) = 0.6$ and $N(d2) = 0.4$. The risk free interest rate is 0. Is the implied volatility based on the option price more or less than 0.3? Explain.
18. The hedge ratio of an at-the-money call option on Dell is 0.3. The hedge ratio of an at-the-money put option is -0.6. What is the hedge ratio of an at-the-money straddle position on Dell?
19. A collar is established by buying a share of stock for \$50, buying a six-month put option with exercise price \$45, and writing a six-month

call option with exercise price \$55. Based on the volatility of the stock, you calculate that for a strike price of \$45 and maturity of six months, $N(d1) = 0.7$, whereas for the exercise price of \$55, $N(d1) = 0.3$.

(a) What will be the gain or loss on the collar if the stock price increases by \$1?

(b) What happens to the delta of the portfolio if the stock price becomes (i) very large or (ii) very small?

20. John is very bullish on Microsoft, much more so than the rest of the market. In each question, choose the portfolio strategy that will give you the largest dollar profit if John's bullish forecast turns out to be correct. Please briefly discuss your answer.

(a) Choice A: \$20,000 invested in calls with $X = 50$.
Choice B: \$20,000 invested in Microsoft.

(b) Choice A: 20 call options contracts (for 100 shares each) with $X = 50$
Choice B: 2000 shares of Microsoft stock.

21. Suppose you are a provider of portfolio insurance and are establishing a three-year program. The portfolio you manage is currently worth \$100 million and you hope to provide a minimum return of 0%. The equity portfolio has a standard deviation of 35% per year and T-bills pay 7% per year. Assume the portfolio pays no dividend. How much of the portfolio should be placed in equity? How much of the portfolio should be placed in bills?

22. Dennis wants to hold a protective put position on stock A to lock in a guaranteed minimum value of \$100 at year-end. Stock A currently sells for \$100. Over the next year the stock price will increase by 30% or decrease by 10%. The T-bill rate is 7%. Unfortunately, no put options are traded on stock A.

(a) If the desired put option were traded, how much would it cost to purchase?

(b) What would have been the cost of the protective put portfolio?

(c) What portfolio position in stock and T-bills will ensure a payoff that would be provided by a protective put with $X = 100$? Please show that the payoff to this portfolio and the cost of establishing the portfolio matches that of the desired protective put.

23. Richard is attempting to value a call option with an exercise price of \$100 and one year to expiration. The underlying stock pays no dividends, its current price is \$100 and Richard believes it has a 50% chance of increasing to \$110 and a 50% chance of decreasing to \$90. The risk free rate of interest is 6%. Calculate the call option's value using the two-state stock price model.
24. Consider an increase in the volatility of the stock in the previous problem. Suppose that if the stock increases in price, it will increase to \$120, and that if it falls, it will fall to \$80. Show that the value of the call option is now higher than the value derived previously.
25. Tim believes that market volatility will be 20% annually for the next three years. Three year at-the-money call and put options on the market index sell at an implied volatility of 22%. What options portfolio can Tim establish to speculate on its volatility belief without taking a bullish o bearish position on the market? Using Tim's estimate of volatility, three years at-the-money options have $N(d1) = 0.2$.
26. Suppose that call options on IBM stock with time to maturity six months and strike price \$60 are selling at an implied volatility of 30%. IBM stock currently is \$60 per share, and the risk free rate is 6%. If you believe the true volatility of the stock is 38%, how can you trade on your belief without taking on exposure to the performance of IBM? How many shares of stock will you hold for each option contract purchased or sold?
27. Suppose a firm sells call options on \$1.6 million worth of a stock portfolio with beta = 1.8. The option delta is 0.6. It wishes to hedge out its resultant exposure to a market advance by buying a market index portfolio.

    (a) How many dollars worth of the market index portfolio should the firm purchase to hedge its position?
    (b) What if the firm instead uses market index puts to hedge its exposure? Should it buy or sell puts? Each put option is on 100 units of the index, and the index at current prices represents \$1000 worth of stock.

28. John is holding call options on a stock. The stock's beta is 0.6, and John is concerned that the stock market is about to fall. The stock is currently selling for \$5 and John holds 1 million options on the stock (i.e., John holds 10,000 contracts for 100 shares each). The option delta

is 0.9. How much of the market index portfolio must you buy or sell to hedge your market exposure?

Appendix 17A: Applications of the Binomial Distribution To Evaluate Call Options

In this appendix, we show how the binomial distribution is combined with some basic finance concepts to generate a model for determining the price of stock options.

The simple binomial OPM

Before discussing the binomial option model, we must recognize its two major underlying assumptions. First, the binomial approach assumes that trading takes place in discrete time — that is, on a period-by-period basis. Second, it is assumed that the stock price (the price of the underlying asset) can take on only two possible values each period; it can go up or go down.

Say we have a stock whose current price per share S can advance or decline during the next period by a factor of either u(up) or d (down). This price either will increase by the proportion $u-1 \geq 0$ or will decrease by the proportion $1-d$, $0 < d < 1$. Therefore, the value Sin the next period will be either uS or dS. Next, suppose that a call option exists on this stock with a current price per share of C and an exercise price per share of X and that the option has one period left to maturity. This option's value at expiration is determined by the price of its underlying stock and the exercise price X. the value is either

$$C_u = \text{Max}(0, uS - X), \tag{17A.1}$$

or

$$C_d = \text{Max}(0, dS - X). \tag{17A.2}$$

Why is the call worth $\text{Max}(0, uS - X)$ if the stock price is uS? The option holder is not obliged to purchase the stock at the exercise price of X, so he or she will exercise the option only when it is beneficial to do so. This means the option can never have a negative value. When is it beneficial for the option holder to exercise the option? When the price per share of the stock is greater than the price per share at which he or she can purchase the stock by using the option, which is the exercise price, X. Thus if the stock price uS exceeds the exercise price X, the investor can exercise the option and buy the stock. Then he or she can immediately sell it for uS, making a profit of $uS - X$ (ignoring commission). Likewise, if the stock price declines to dS, the call is worth $\text{Max}(0, dS - X)$.

Also for the moment, we will assume that the risk-free interest rate for both borrowing and lending is equal to $r\%$ over the one time period and that the exercise price of the option is equal to X.

To intuitively grasp the underlying concept of option pricing, we must set up a *risk-free portfolio* — a combination of assets that produces the same return in every state of the world over our chosen investment horizon. The investment horizon is assumed to be one period (the duration of this period can be any length of time, such as an hour, a day, a week, etc.). To do this, we buy h share of the stock and sell the call option at its current price of C. Moreover, we choose the value of h such that our portfolio will yield the same payoff whether the stock goes up or down.

$$h(uS) - C_u = h(dS) - C_d. \tag{17A.3}$$

By solving for h, we can obtain the number of shares of stock we should buy for each call option we sell.

$$h = \frac{C_u - C_d}{(u - d)S}. \tag{17A.4}$$

Here h is called the *hedge ratio*. Because our portfolio yields the same return under either of the two possible states for the stock, it is without risk and therefore should yield the risk-free rate of return, $r\%$, which is equal to the risk-free borrowing and lending rate, the condition must be true; otherwise, it would be possible to earn a risk-free profit without using any money. Therefore, the ending portfolio value must be equal to $(1 + r)$ times the beginning portfolio value, $hS - C$.

$$(1 + r)(hS - C) = h(uS) - C_u = h(dS) - C_d. \tag{17A.5}$$

Note that S and C represent the beginning values of the stock price and the option price, respectively.

Setting $R = 1 + r$, rearranging to solve for C, and using the value of h from Equation (17A.4), we get

$$C = \left[\left(\frac{R - d}{u - d}\right) C_u + \left(\frac{u - R}{u - d}\right) C_d\right] \Big/ R, \tag{17A.6}$$

where $d < r < u$. To simplify this equation, we set

$$p = \frac{R - d}{u - d} \quad \text{so} \quad 1 - p = \left\{\frac{u - R}{u - d}\right\}. \tag{17A.7}$$

Table 17A.1. Possible Option Value at Maturity.

Today			
Stock (S)	Option (C)		Next Period (Maturity)
		$uS = \$110$	$C_u = \text{Max}(0, uS - X)$ $= \text{Max}(0, 110-100)$ $= \text{Max}(0, 10)$ $= \$10$
\$100	C		
		$dS = \$90$	$C_d = \text{Max}(0, dS - X)$ $= \text{Max}(0, 90-100)$ $= \text{Max}(0, -10)$ $= \$0$

Thus we get the option's value with one period to expiration:

$$C = [pC_u + (1 - p)C_d]/R. \tag{17A.8}$$

This is the binomial call option valuation formula in its most basic form. In other words, this is the binomial valuation formula with one period to expiration of the option.

To illustrate the model's qualities, let us plug in the following values, while assuming the option has one period to expiration. Let

$$X = \$100$$

$$S = \$100$$

$$u = (1.10). \text{ so } uS = \$110$$

$$d = (0.90), \text{ so } dS = \$90$$

$$R = 1 + r = 1 + 0.07 = 1.07.$$

First we need to determine the two possible option values at maturity, as indicated in Table 17A.1.

Next we calculate the value of p as indicated in Equation (17A.7).

$$p = \frac{1.07 - 0.90}{1.10 - 0.90} = 0.85 \quad \text{so} \quad 1 - p = \frac{1.10 - 1.07}{1.10 - 0.90} = 0.15.$$

Solving the binomial valuation equation as indicated in Equation (17A.8), we get

$$\begin{aligned} C &= [0.85(10) + 0.15(0)]/1.07 \\ &= \$7.94. \end{aligned}$$

The correct value for this particular call option today, under the specified conditions, is \$7.94. If the call option does not sell for \$7.94, it will be possible to earn arbitrage profits. That is, it will be possible for the investor to earn a risk-free profit while using none of his or her own money. Clearly, this type of opportunity cannot continue to exist indefinitely.

The Generalized Binomial OPM

Suppose we are interested in the case where there is more than one period until the option expires. We can extend the one-period binomial model to consideration of two or more periods. Because we are assuming that the stock follows a binomial process, from one period to the next it can only go up by a factor of u or go down by a factor of d. After one period the stock's price is either uS or dS. Between the first and second periods, the stock's price can once again go up by u or down by d, so the possible prices for the stock two periods from now are uuS, udS, and ddS. This process is demonstrated in the tree diagram (Fig. 17A.1) in Example 17A.1 later in this appendix.

Note that the option's price at expiration, two periods from now, is a function of the same relationship that determined its expiration price in the one-period model, more specifically, the call option's maturity value is always

$$C_T = \text{Max}[0, S_T - X], \tag{17A.9}$$

where T designated the maturity date of the option.

To derive the option's price with two periods to go ($T = 2$), it is helpful as an intermediate step to derive the value of C_u and C_d with one period to expiration when the stock price is either uS or dS, respectively.

$$C_u = [pC_{uu} + (1 - p)C_{ud}]/R \tag{17A.10}$$

$$C_d = [pC_{du} + (1 - p)C_{dd}]/R. \tag{17A.11}$$

Equation (17A.10) tells us that if the value of the option after one period is C_u, the option will be worth either C_{uu}(if the stock price goes up) or C_{ud} (if stock price goes down) after one more period (at its expiration date). Similarly, Equation (17A.11) shows that the value of the option is C_d after one period, the option will be worth either C_{du}or C_{dd} at the end of the second period. Replacing C_u and C_d in Equation (17A.8) with their expressions in Equations (17A.10) and (17A.11), respectively, we can simplify the resulting equation to yield the two-period equivalent of the one-period binomial pricing formula, which is

$$C = [p^2 C_{uu} + 2p(1-p)C_{ud} + (1-p)^2 C_{dd}]/R^2. \tag{17A.12}$$

In Equation (17A.12), we used the fact that $C_{ud} = C_{du}$ because the price will be the same in either case.

We know the values of the parameters S and X. If we assume that $R, u,$ and d will remain constant over time, the possible maturity values for the option can be determined exactly. Thus deriving the option's fair value with two periods to maturity is a relatively simple process of working backwards from the possible maturity values.

Using same procedure, we can extend two-period model to three-period model as

$$C = [p^3 C_{uuu} + 3p^2(1-p)C_{uud} + 3p(1-p)^2 C_{udd} + (1-p)^3 C_{ddd}]/R^3. \tag{17A.13}$$

We use a numerical example here to show how Equation (17A.13) can be applied to evaluation call option in a three-period case.

Example 17A.1

A Decision Tree Approach to Analyzing Future Stock Price and Determining Value of Call Option

By making some simplifying assumptions about how a stock's price can change from one period to the next, it is possible to forecast the future price of the stock by means of a decision tree. To illustrate this point, let us consider the following example.

Suppose the price of Company A's stock is currently \$100. Now let us assume that from one period to the next, the stock can go up by 17.5% or go down by 15%. In addition, let us assume that there is a 50% chance that the stock will go up and a 50% chance that the stock will go down. It is also assumed that the price movement of a stock (or of the stock market) today is completely independent of its movement in the past; in other words, the price will rise or fall today by a random amount. A sequence of these random increases and decreases is known as a **random walk**.

In addition, suppose a call option has three periods to expiration. The underlying asset is stock A, the exercise price is \$110, and the risk-free rate is 16%.

Given this information, we can lay out the paths that the stock's price may take. Figure 17A.1 shows the possible stock prices for company A for three periods.

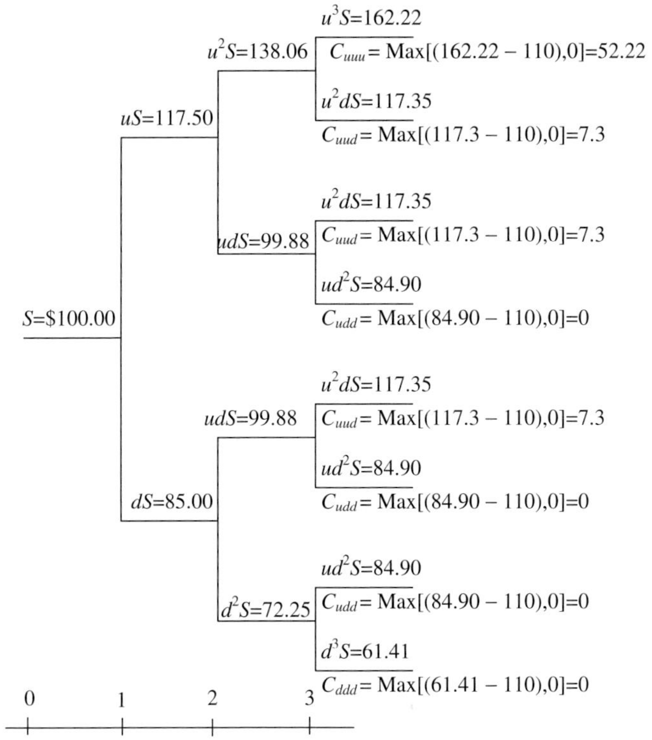

Fig. 17A.1. Price Path of Underlying Stock and Value of Call Option.

Note that in period 1, there are two possible outcomes: the stock can go up in value by 17.5% to \$117.50 or down by 15% to \$85.00. In period 2, there are four possible outcomes. If the stock went up in the first period, it can go up again to \$138.06 or down in the second period to \$99.88. Likewise, if the stock went down in the first period, it can go down again to \$72.25 or up in the second period to \$99.88. Using the same argument, we can trace the path of the stock's price for all three periods.

In addition, we can use Equation (17A.13) to determine the value of the call option.

$$p = \frac{R-d}{u-d} = \frac{(1.16) - 1.15}{1.175 - 1.15} = 0.4, \quad \text{and}$$

$$1-p = \frac{u-R}{u-d} = \frac{1.175 - 1.16}{1.175 - 1.15} = 0.6$$

$$\begin{aligned}C &= [p^3C_{uuu} + 3p^2(1-p)C_{uud} + 3p(1-p)^2C_{udd} + (1-p)^3C_{ddd}]/R^3\\&= [(0.4)^3 52.22 + 3(0.4)^2(0.6)(7.3) + 3(0.4)(0.6)^2(0)\\&\quad + (0.6)^3(0)]/(1.16)^3\\&= [(0.4)^3 52.22 + 3(0.4)^2(0.6)(7.3)]/(1.16)^3\\&= 3.4880.\end{aligned}$$

The cumulative binomial density function can be defined as

$$B(n,p) = \sum_{k=0}^{n} \frac{n!}{k!(n-k)!} p^{n-k}(1-p)^k, \qquad (17A.14)$$

where

n is the number of periods,
k is the number of successful trials,
$n! = n(n-1)(n-2)\cdots(1)$,
$k! = k(k-1)(k-2)\cdots(1)$, and
$(n-k)! = (n-k)(n-k-1)(n-k-2)\cdots(1)$.

We can use the cumulative binomial distribution as defined in Equation (17A.14) to generalize Equation (17A.13).

Then we can extend the binomial approach to its more generalized form, with n periods maturity:

$$C = \frac{1}{R^n} \sum_{k=0}^{n} \frac{n!}{k!(n-k)!} p^k (1-p)^{n-k} Max[0, u^k d^{n-k} S - X]. \qquad (17A.15)$$

To actually get this form of the binomial model, we could extend the two-period model to three periods, then from three periods to four periods, and so on. Equation (17A.15) would be the result of these efforts. To show how Equation (17A.14) can be used to assess a call option's value, we modify the example as follows: $S = \$100$, $X = \$100$, $R = 1.07$, $n = 3$, $u = 1.1$ and $d = 0.90$.

First we calculate the value of p from Equation (17A.7) as 0.85, so $1-p$ is 0.15. Next we calculate the four possible ending values for the call option after three periods in terms of $\text{Max}[0, u^k d^{n-k} S - X]$.

$$C_{uuu} = \text{Max}\,[0, (1.1)^3(0.90)^0(100) - 100] = 33.10$$

$$C_{uud} = \text{Max}\,[0, (1.1)^2(0.90)(100) - 100] = 8.90$$

$$C_{udd} = \text{Max } [0, (1.1)(0.90)^2(100) - 100] = 0$$

$$C_{ddd} = \text{Max } [0, (1.1)^0(0.90)^3(100) - 100] = 0.$$

Now we insert these numbers ($C_{uuu}, C_{uud}, C_{udd}$, and C_{ddd}) into the model and sum the terms.

$$\begin{aligned}
C &= \frac{1}{(1.07)^3}\left[\frac{3!}{0!3!}(0.85)^0(0.15)^3 X 0 + \frac{3!}{1!2!}(0.85)^1(0.15)^2 X 0\right.\\
&\quad \left. + \frac{3!}{2!1!}(0.85)^2(0.15)^1 X 8.90 + \frac{3!}{3!0!}(0.85)^3(0.15)^0 X 33.10\right]\\
&= \frac{1}{1.225}\left[0 + 0 + \frac{3X2X1}{2X1X1}(0.7225)(0.15)(8.90)\right.\\
&\quad \left. + \frac{3X2X1}{3X2X1X1} X(0.61413)(1)(33.10)\right]\\
&= \frac{1}{1.225}[(0.32513 X 8.90) + (0.61413 X 33.10)]\\
&= \$18.96.
\end{aligned}$$

As this example suggests, working out a multiple-period problem by hand with this formula can become laborious as the number of periods increases. Fortunately, programming this model into a computer is not too difficult.

Now let us derive a binomial option pricing model in terms of the cumulative binomial density function. As a first step, we can rewrite Equation (17A.14) as

$$\begin{aligned}
C &= S\left[\sum_{k=m}^{n} \frac{n!}{k!(n-K)!} p^K (1-p)^{n-k} \frac{u^k d^{n-k}}{R^n}\right]\\
&\quad - \frac{X}{R^n}\left[\sum_{k=m}^{n} \frac{n!}{k!(n-k)!} p^k (1-p)^{n-k}\right]. \qquad (17A.16)
\end{aligned}$$

This formula is identical to Equation (17A.9) except that we have removed the Max operator. In order to remove the Max operator, we need to make $u^k d^{n-k} S - X$ positive, which we can do by changing the counter in the summation from $k = 0$ to $k = m$. What is m? It is the minimum number of upward stock movements necessary for the option to terminate "in the money" (i.e., $u^k d^{n-k} S - X > 0$). How can we interpret Equation (17A.15)? Consider the second term in brackets; it is just a cumulative binomial distribution with parameters of n and p. Likewise, via a small algebraic manipulation we can show that the first term in the brackets is also a cumulative binomial distribution. this can be done by defining $P' \equiv (u/R)p$ and $1 - P' \equiv (d/R)(1 - p)$. Thus

$$p^k(1-p)^{n-k}\frac{u^k d^{n-k}}{R^n} = P'^k(1-P')^{n-k}.$$

Therefore the first term in brackets is also a cumulative binomial distribution with parameters of n and p'. We can write the binomial call option model as

$$C = SB_1(n, P', m) - \frac{X}{R^n}B_2(n, p, m), \tag{17A.17}$$

where

$$B_1(n, P', m) = \sum_{k=m}^{n} C_k^n P'^k(1-P')^{n-k}$$

$$B_2(n, p, m) = \sum_{k=m}^{n} C_k^n p^k(1-p)^{n-k},$$

and m is the minimum amount of time the stock has to go up for the investor to finish *in the money* (i.e., for the stock price to become larger than the exercise price).

In this appendix, we showed that by employing the definition of a call option and by making some simplifying assumptions, we could use the binomial distribution to find the value of a call option. Lee and Lin (2010) have shown how to binomial option pricing model approach to derive the Black–Scholes option pricing model. In the next chapter, we will show how the binomial distribution is related to the normal distribution and how this relationship can be used to derive one of the most famous valuation equations in finance, the Black–Scholes OPM. In Chapter 27, we show how we can use Itô's calculus and normal–lognormal approach to derive the OPM.

Bibliography

Amram, M. and N. Kulatilaka. *Real Options*. New York: Oxford University Press, 2001.

Banz, R. and M. Miller. "Prices for State Contingent Claims: Some Estimates and Applications." *Journal of Business*, v. 51 (1978), pp. 653–672.

Bhattachayra, M. "Empirical Properties of the Black–Scholes Formula under Ideal Conditions." *Journal of Financial and Quantitative Analysis*, v. 15 (December 1980), pp. 1081–1105.

Black, F. "Capital Market Equilibrium with Restricted Borrowing." *Journal of Business*, v. 45 (July 1972), pp. 444–445.

Black, F. and M. Scholes. "The Pricing of Options and Corporate Liabilities." *Journal of Political Economy*, v. 31 (May–June 1973), pp. 637–659.

Bookstaber, R. M. *Option Pricing and Strategies in Investing*. Reading, MA: Addison-Wesley, 1981.

Chen, S. S., C. F. Lee and H. H. Lee. "Alternative Methods to Determine Optimal Capital Structure: Theory and Application," in C. F. Lee, A. C. Lee and J. Lee (ed.), *Handbook of Quantitative Finance and Risk Management*, pp. 933–951. New York, NY: Springer, 2010.

Cox, J. C. and M. Rubinstein. *Option Markets*. Englewood Cliffs, NJ: Prentice-Hall, 1985.

Finnerty, J. "The Chicago Board Options Exchange and Market Efficiency." *Journal of Financial and Quantitative Analysis*, v. 13 (March 1978), pp. 29–38.

Galai, D. and R. W. Masulis. "The Option Pricing Model and the Risk Factor of Stock." *Journal of Financial Economics*, v. 3 (1976), pp. 53–81.

Hull, J. *Options, Futures, and Other Derivatives*, 6th ed. Upper Saddle. River, New Jersey: Prentice Hall, 2005.

Jarrow R. and S. Turnbull. *Derivatives Securities*, 2nd ed. Cincinnati, OH: South-Western College Pub, 1999.

Liaw, K. T. and R. L. Moy. *The Irwin Guide to Stocks, Bonds, Futures, and Options*. New York: McGraw-Hill Companies, 2000.

Leland, H. E. "Corporate Debt Value, Bond Covenants and Optimal Capital Structure." *Journal of Finance*, v. 49 (1994), pp. 1213–1252.

Lee, A. C., J. C. Lee and C. F. Lee. *Financial Analysis, Planning and Forecasting: Theory and Application*, 2nd ed. Singapore: World Scientific Publishing Company, 2009.

Lee, C. F. and A. C. Lee. *Encyclopedia of Finance*. New York, NY: Springer, 2006.

Lee, C. F., A. C. Lee and J. Lee. *Handbook of Quantitative Finance and Risk Management*. New York, NY: Springer, 2010.

Lee, C. F. and C. S-M. Lin. "Two Alternative Binomial Option Pricing Model Approaches to Derive Black–Scholes Option Pricing Model," in C. F. Lee, A. C. Lee and J. Lee (ed.), *Handbook of Quantitative Finance and Risk Management*, New York, NY: Springer, 2010, pp. 409–420.

MacBeth, J. and L. Merville. "An Empirical Examination of the Black–Scholes Call Option Pricing Model." *The Journal of Finance*, v. 34 (December 1979), pp. 1173–1186.

McDonald, R. L. *Derivatives Markets*, 2nd ed. Boston, MA: Addison Wesley, Boston, Massachusetts, 2005.

Merton, R. "An Inter-Temporal Capital Asset Pricing Model." *Econometrica*, v. 41 (September 1973), pp. 867–887.

Rendleman, R. J., Jr. and B. J. Barter. "Two-State Option Pricing," *Journal of Finance*, v. 24 (1979), pp. 1093–1110.

Ritchken, P. *Option: Theory, Strategy, and Applications.* Glenview, IL: Scott, Foresman 1987.

Summa, J. F. and J. W. Lubow. *Options on Futures.* New York: John Wiley & Sons, 2001.

Trennepohl, G. "A Comparison of Listed Option Premia and Black–Scholes Model Prices: 1973–1979." *Journal of Financial Research*, v. 4 (Spring 1981), pp. 11–20.

Zhang, P. G. *Exotic Options: A Guide to Second Generation Options*, 2nd ed. Singapore: World Scientific, 1998.

Chapter 18

Decision Tree and Microsoft Excel Approach for Option Pricing Model

The Binomial Option pricing model (OPM) derived by Rendleman and Barter (RB, 1979), and Cox *et al.* (CRR, 1979) is one the most famous models used to price options. Only the Black–Scholes model (1973) is more famous. One problem with learning the binomial OPM is that it is computationally intensive. This results in a very complicated formula to price an option.

The complexity of the binomial OPM makes it a challenge to learn the model. Most books teach the binomial option model by describing the formula. This is a not very effective because it usually requires the learner to mentally keep track of many details, many times to the point of information overload. There is a well-known principle in psychology that the average number of things that a person can remember at one time is seven.

In the Appendix A of Chapter 17, we have graphically and mathematically calculated call option value by a n-period decision tree. This chapter will first demonstrate that it is possible to create large Decision Trees for the binomial pricing model using Microsoft Excel. A 10-period Decision Tree would require 2,047 call calculations and 2,047 put calculations. This chapter will also show the Decision Tree for the price of a stock and the price of a bond, each requiring 2,047 calculations. Therefore, there would be 8,188 $(2,047 \times 4)$ calculations for a complete set of 10-period Decision Trees.

Second, this chapter will present the binomial option model in a less mathematical matter. By using Decision Trees, we can price call and put options without keeping track of many things at one time. Finally, this chapter will show the relationship between the binomial OPM and the Black–Scholes OPM.

Section 18.1 discusses the basic concepts of call and put options. Sections 18.2 demonstrate the one-period call and put OPMs. Section 18.3 presents the two-period OPM. Section 18.4 demonstrates how to use the Microsoft Excel workbook *binomialBS_OPM.xls* to create the Decision Trees for a n-period Binomical OPM. Section 18.5 demonstrate the use of the Black–Scholes model. Section 18.6 shows the relationship between the binomial OPM and the Black–Scholes OPM. Section 18.7 demonstrates how to use the the Microsoft Excel workboook *binomialBS_OPM.xls* to demonstrate the relationship between the binomial OPM and the Black–Scholes OPM.

This chapter uses a Microsoft Excel workbook called *binomialBS_OPM.xls* that contains the Visual Basic for Applications (VBA) code to create the Decision Trees for the binomial OPM. The VBA code is provided in Appendix 18A. The password for the workbook is *bigsky* for those who want to study the VBA code.[1]

18.1. Call and Put Options

A *call option* gives the owner the right but not the obligation to buy the underlying security at a specified price. The price in which the owner can buy the underlying price is called the *exercise price*. A call option becomes valuable when the exercise price is less than the current price of the underlying stock price.

For example, a call option on a GE stock with an exercise price of $20 when the stock price of an GE stock is $25 is worth $5. The reason it is worth $5 is because a holder of the call option can buy the GE stock at $20 and then sell the GE stock at the prevailing price of $25 for a profit of $5. Also, a call option on an GE stock with an exercise price of $30 when the stock price of an GE stock is $15 is worth $0.

A *put option* gives the owner the right but not the obligation to sell the underlying security at a specified price. A put option becomes valuable when the exercise price is more than the current price of the underlying stock price.

For example, a put option on an GE stock with an exercise price of $20 when the stock price of a GE stock is $15 is worth $5. The reason it is

[1]The Microsoft Excel workbook will be available upon request (JohnLeeExcelVBA@gmail.com).

worth $5 is because a holder of the put option can buy the GE stock at the prevailing price of $15 and then sell the GE stock at the put price of $20 for a profit of $5. Also, a put option on a GE stock with an exercise price of $20 when the stock price of the GE stock is $25 is worth $0.

Figures 18.1 and 18.2 are charts showing the value of call and put options of the above GE stock at varying prices.

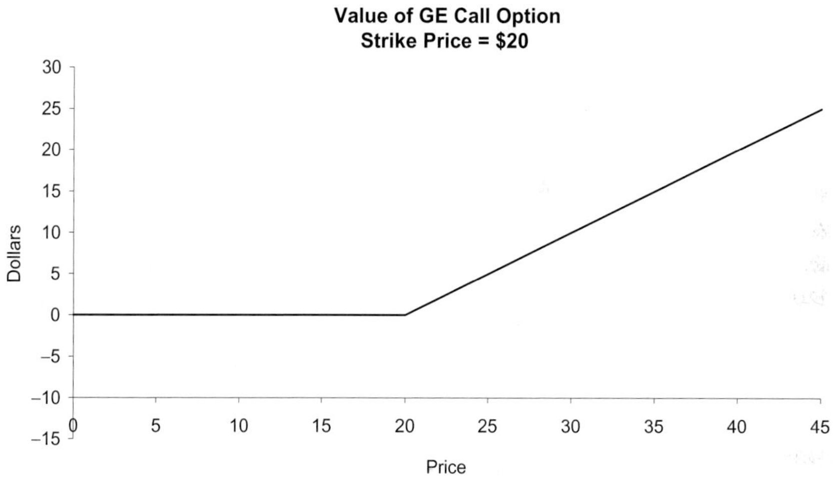

Fig. 18.1. Value of GE Call Option.

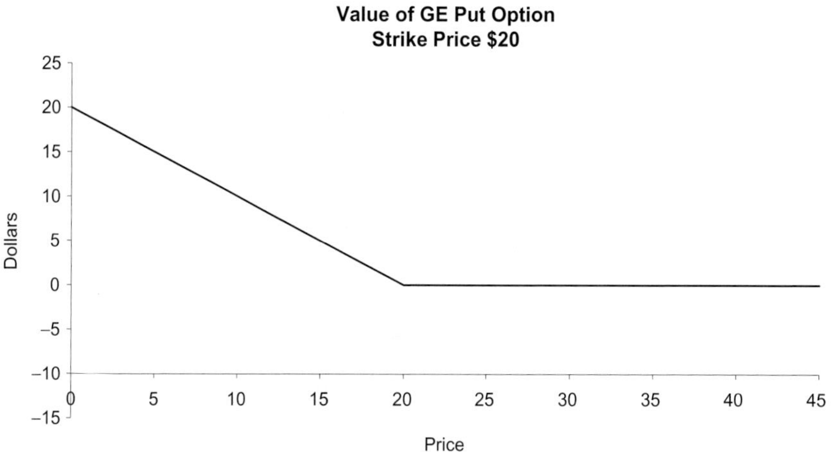

Fig. 18.2. Value of GE Put Option.

18.2. One-Period Option Pricing Model

What should be the value of these options? Let us look at a case where we are only concerned with the value of options for one period. In the next period a stock price can either go up or go down. Let us look at a case where we know for certain that a GE stock with a price of \$20 will either go up 5% or go down 5% in the next period and the exercise after one period is \$20. Figures 18.3, 18.4 and 18.5 show the Decision Tree for the GE stock price, the GE call option price, and the GE put option price, respectively.

Let us first consider the issue of pricing a GE call option. Using a one-period Decision Tree, we can illustrate the price of a GE stock if it goes up 5% and the price of a stock GE if it goes down 5%. Since we know the possible endings values of the GE stock, we can derive the possible ending values of a call option. If the stock price increases to \$21, the price of the GE call option will then be \$1 (\$21.5–\$20). If the GE stock price decreases to \$19, the value of the call option will worth \$0 because it would be below the exercise price of \$20. We have just discussed the possible ending value of a GE call option in period 1. But, what we are really interested in is what the value is now of the GE call option knowing the two resulting value of the GE call option.

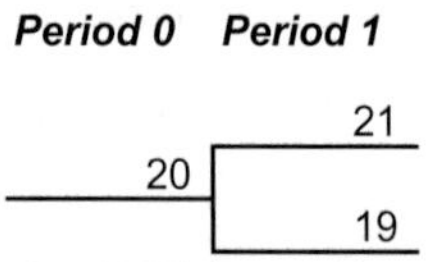

Fig. 18.3. GE Stock Price.

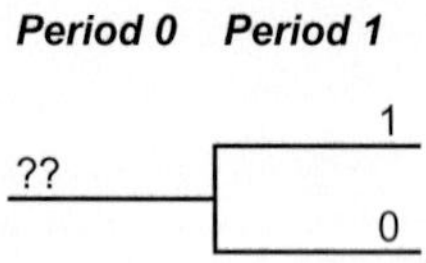

Fig. 18.4. GE Call Option Price.

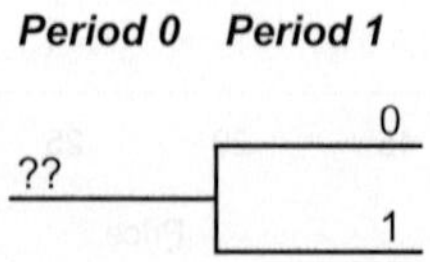

Fig. 18.5. GE Put Option Price.

To help determine the value of a one-period GE call option, it is useful to know that it is possible to replicate the resulting two states of the value of the GE call option by buying a combination of stocks and bonds. Below is the formula to replicate the situation where the price increases to \$21. We will assume that the interest rate for the bond is 3%.

$$21\text{S} + 1.03\text{B} = 1$$

$$19\text{S} + 1.03\text{B} = 0.$$

We can use simple algebra to solve for both S and B. The first thing that we need to do is to rearrange the second equation as follows:

$$1.03\text{B} = -19\text{S}.$$

With the above equation, we can rewrite the first equation as

$$21\text{S} + (-19S) = 1$$

$$2\text{S} = 1$$

$$\text{S} = 0.5.$$

We can solve for B by substituting the value 0.5 for S in the first equation.

$$21(0.5) + 1.03\text{B} = 1$$

$$10.5 + 1.03\text{B} = 1$$

$$1.03\text{B} = -9.5$$

$$\text{B} = -9.223.$$

Therefore, from the above simple algebraic exercise, we should at period 0 buy 0.5 shares of GE stock and borrow 9.223 at 3% to replicate the payoff of the GE call option. This means the value of a GE call option should be $0.5 \times 20 - 9.223 = 0.777$.

If this was not the case, there would then be arbitrage profits. For example, if the call option were sold for \$3, there would be a profit of 2.223. This would result in the increase in the selling of the GE call option. The increase in the supply of GE call options would push the price down for the call options. If the call option were sold for \$0.50, there would be a saving of 0.277. This saving would result in the increase demand for the GE call option. This increase demand would result in the price of the call option to increase. The equilibrium point would be \$0.777.

Using the above-mentioned concept and procedure, Benninga (2000) has derived a one-period call option model as

$$C = q_u \text{Max}[uSX, 0] + q_d \text{Max}[dS - X, 0], \tag{18.1}$$

where

$$q_u = \frac{(1+i) - d}{(1+i)(u-d)}$$

$$q_d = \frac{u - (1+i)}{(1+i)(u-d)},$$

$$u = \text{increase factor}$$

$$d = \text{down factor}$$

$$i = \text{interest rate.}$$

If we let $i = r$, $R = (1 + r)$, $p = (R - d)/(u - d)$, $1 - p = (u - R)/(u - d)$, $C_u = \text{Max}[uS - X, 0]$ and $C_d = \text{Max}[dS - X, 0]$, then we have

$$C = [pC_u + (1 - p)C_d]/R, \tag{18.2}$$

where,

C_u = call option price after increase
C_d = call option price after decrease.

Equation (18.2) is identical to Equation (17A.8) in Chapter 17.

Below calculates the value of the above one-period call option where the strike price, X, is \$20 and the risk-free interest rate is 3%. We will assume that that the price of a stock for any given period will either increase or decrease by 5%.

$$X = \$20$$

$$S = \$20$$

$$u = 1.05$$

$$d = 0.95$$

$$R = 1 + r = 1 + 0.03$$

$$p = (1.03 - 0.95)/(1.05 - 0.95)$$

$$C = [0.8(1) + 0.2(0)]/1.03 = \$0.777.$$

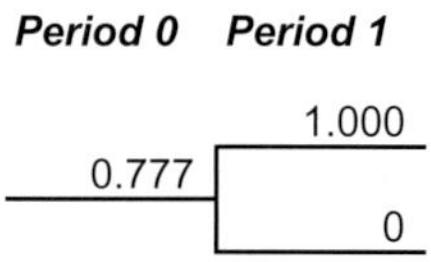

Fig. 18.6. Call Option Price.

Therefore from the above calculations, the value of the call option is \$7.94. Figure 18.6 shows the resulting Decision Tree for the above call option.

Like the call option, it is possible to replicate the resulting two state of the value of the put option by buying a combination of stocks and bonds. Below is the formula to replicate the situation where the price decreases to \$19.

$$21\text{S} + 1.03\text{B} = 0$$
$$19\text{S} + 1.03\text{B} = 1.$$

We will use simple algebra to solve for both S and B. The first thing we will do is to rewrite the second equation as follows:

$$1.03\text{B} = 1.5 - 19\text{S}.$$

The next thing to do is to substitute the above equation to the first put option equation. Doing this would result in the following:

$$21\text{S} + 1.5 - 19\text{S} = 0.$$

The following solves for S,

$$2\text{S} = -1.5$$
$$\text{S} = -0.5.$$

Now let us solve for B by putting the value of S into the first equation. This is shown below.

$$21(-0.5) + 1.03\text{B} = 0$$
$$1.03\text{B} = 10.5$$
$$\text{B} = 10.194.$$

From the above simple algebra exercise, we have S $= -0.5$ and B $= 10.194$. This tell us that we should in period 0 lend \$10.194 at 3% and sell 0.5 shares of stock to replicate the put option payoff for period 1. And, the value of the GE put option should be $20(-0.5) + 10.194 = 0.194$.

Using the same arbitrage argument that we used in the discussion of the call option, 0.194 has to be the equilibrium price of the put option.

As with the call option, Benninga (2000) has derived a one-period put option model as

$$P = q_u \text{Max}[X - uS, 0] + q_d \text{Max}[X - dS, 0], \tag{18.3}$$

where

$$q_u = \frac{(1+i) - d}{(1+i)(u-d)}$$

$$q_d = \frac{u - (1+i)}{(1+i)(u-d)}$$

$$u = \text{increase factor}$$

$$d = \text{down factor}$$

$$i = \text{interest rate.}$$

If we let $i = r$, $R = (1+r)$, $p = (R-d)/(u-d)$, $1-p = (u-R)/(u-d)$, $P_u = \text{Max}[X - uS, 0]$ and $P_d = \text{Max}[X - dS, 0]$, then we have

$$P = [pP_u + (1-p)P_d]/R, \tag{18.4}$$

where,

P_u = put option price after increase
P_d = put option price after decrease.

The calculation below shows the value of the above one-period put option where the strike price, X, is \$30 and the risk-free interest rate is 3%.

$$P = [0.8(0) + 0.2(1)]/1.03 = \$0.194.$$

From the above calculation, the put option pricing Decision Tree would look like the following.

Figure 18.7 shows the resulting Decision Tree for the above put option.

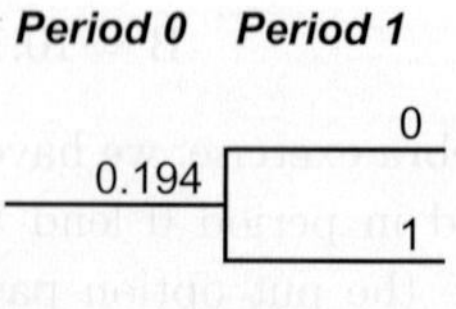

Fig. 18.7. GE Put Option Price.

There is a relationship between the price of a put option and the price of a call option. This relationship is called the put-call parity. Equation 18.5 shows the relationship between the price of a put option and the price of a call option.

$$P = C + X/R - S, \tag{18.5}$$

where

C = call price
X = strike price
R = 1+ interest rate
S = stock price.

The following uses the put-call parity to calculate the price of the GE put option.

$$\begin{aligned} P &= \$0.777 + \$20/(1.03) - \$20 \\ &= \$0.777 + \$19.417 - \$20 \\ &= \$0.194. \end{aligned}$$

18.3. Two-Period Option Pricing Model

We now will look at pricing options for two periods. Figure 18.8 shows the stock price Decision Tree based on the parameters indicated in the last section. This Decision Tree was created based on the assumption that a stock price will either increase by 5% or decrease by 5%.

How do we price the value of a call and put option for two periods?

The highest possible value for our stock based on our assumption is \$22.05. We get this value first by multiplying the stock price at period 0 by 105% to get the resulting value of \$21 of period 1. We then again multiply the stock price in period 1 by 105% to get the resulting value of \$22.05.

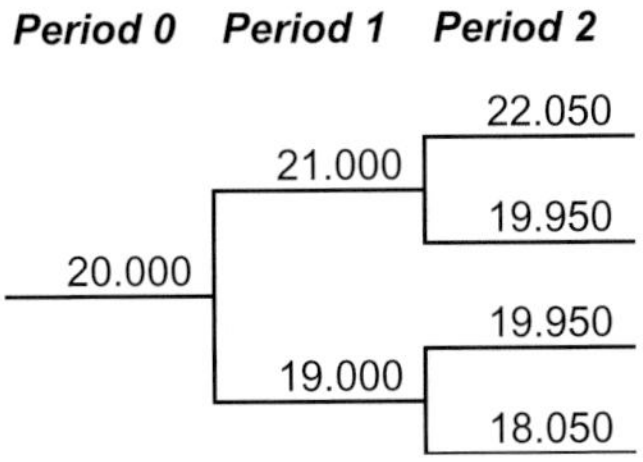

Fig. 18.8. GE Stock Price.

In period 2, the value of a call option when a stock price is \$22.05 is the stock price minus the exercise price, \$22.05 – \$20, or \$2.05. In period 2, the value of a put option when a stock price \$22.05 is the exercise price minus the stock price, \$20 – \$22.05, or –\$2.05. A negative value has no value to an investor so the value of the put option would be \$0.

The lowest possible value for our stock based on our assumptions is \$18.05. We get this value first by multiplying the stock price at period 0 by 95% (decreasing the value of the stock by 5%) to get the resulting value of \$19.0 of period 1. We then again multiply the stock price in period 1 by 95% to get the resulting value of \$18.05. In period 2, the value of a call option when a stock price is \$18.05 is the stock price minus the exercise price, \$18.05 – \$20, or –\$1.95. A negative value has no value to an investor so the value of a call option would be \$0. In period 2, the value of a put option when a stock price is \$18.05 is the exercise price minus the stock price, \$20 – \$18.05, or \$1.95. We can derive the call and put option value for the other possible value of the stock in period 2 in the same fashion.

Figures 18.9 and 18.10 show the possible call and put option values for period 2.

We cannot calculate the value of the call and put option in period 1 the same way we did in period 2 because it is not the ending value of the

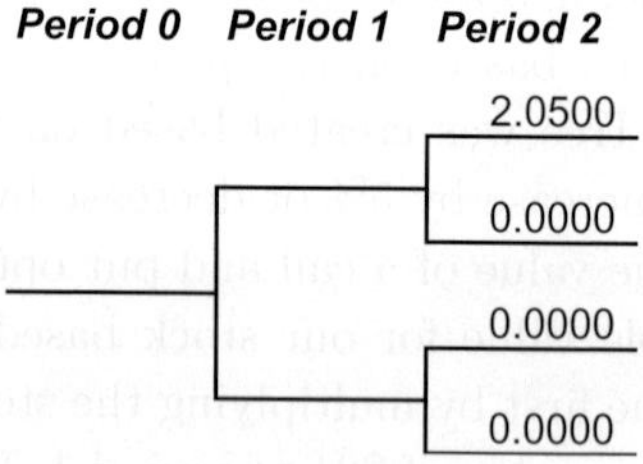

Fig. 18.9. GE Call Option.

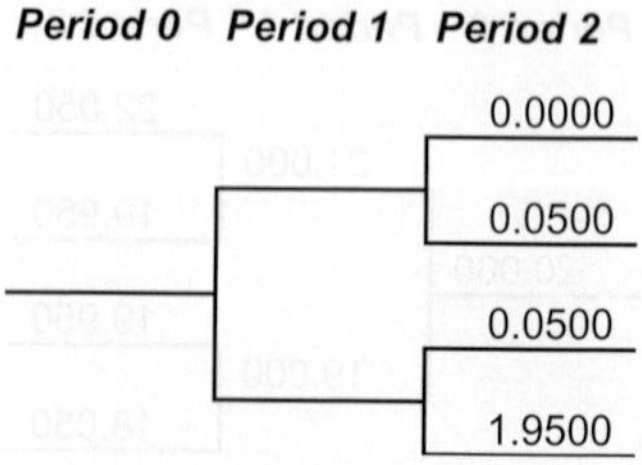

Fig. 18.10. GE Put Option.

stock. In period 1, there are two possible call values. One value is when the stock price increased, and one value is when the stock price decreased. The call option Decision Tree shown in Fig. 18.9 shows two possible values for a call option in period 1. If we just focus on the value of a call option when the stock price increases from period 1, we will notice that it is like the Decision Tree for a call option for one period. This is shown in Fig. 18.11.

Using the same method for pricing a call option for one period, the price of a call option when stock price increase from period 0 will be $1.5922. The resulting Decision Tree is shown in Fig. 18.12.

In the same fashion we can price the value of a call option when a stock price decreases. The price of a call option when a stock price decreases from period 0 is $0. The resulting Decision Tree is shown in Fig. 18.13.

In the same fashion we can price the value of a call option in period 0. The resulting Decision Tree is shown in Fig. 18.14.

We can calculate the value of a put option in the same manner as we did in calculating the value of a call option. The Decision Tree for a put option is shown in Fig. 18.15.

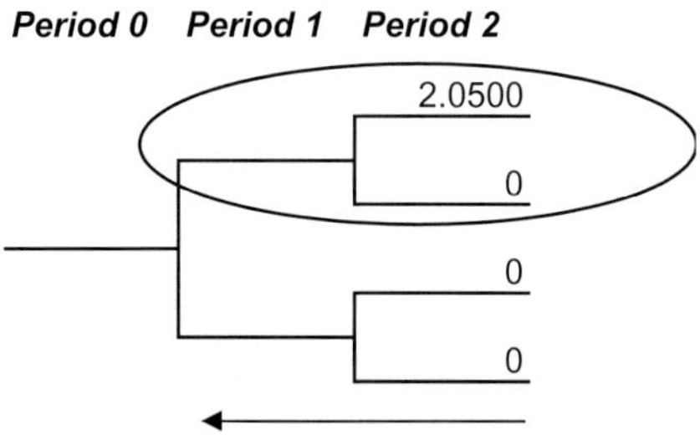

Fig. 18.11. GE Call Option.

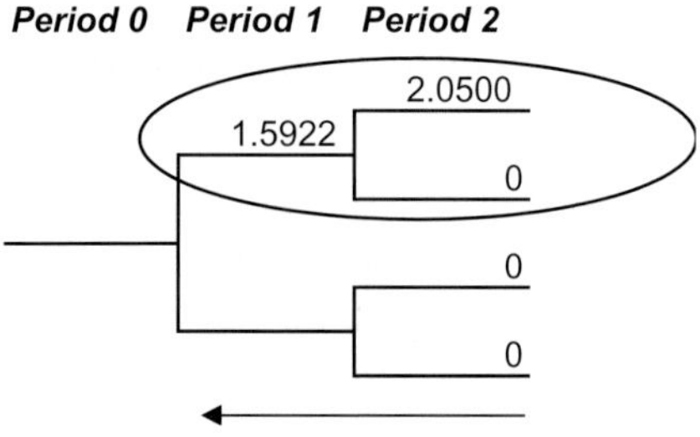

Fig. 18.12. GE Call Option.

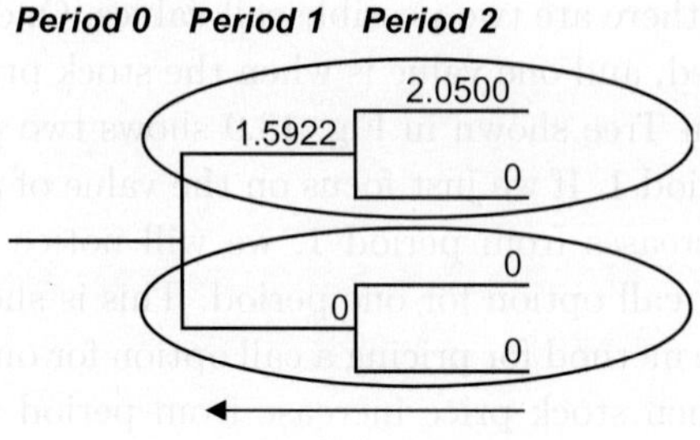

Fig. 18.13. GE Call Option.

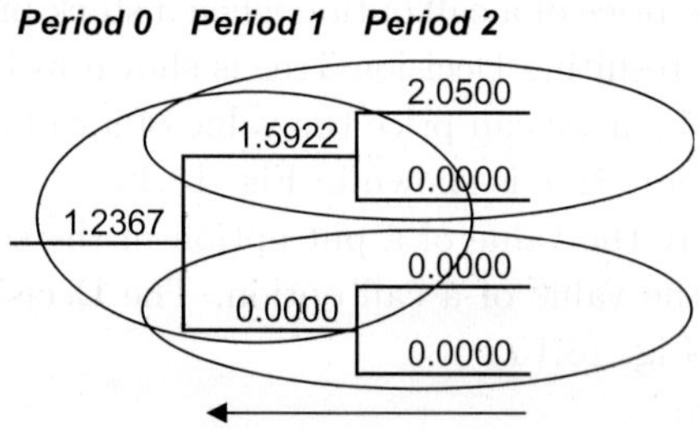

Fig. 18.14. GE Call Option.

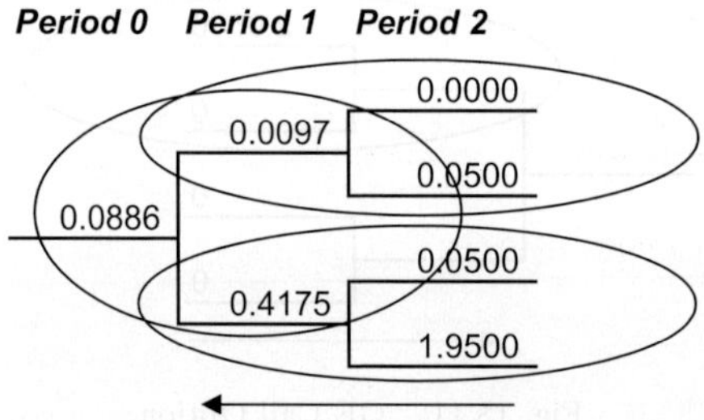

Fig. 18.15. GE Put Option.

18.4. Using Microsoft Excel to Create the Binomial Option Trees

In the previous section, we priced the value of a call and put option by pricing backward, from the last period to the first period. This method of pricing call and put options will work for any n-period. To price the value of a call options for two periods required seven sets of calculations. The number of calculations increases dramatically as n increases. Table 18.1 lists the number of calculations for specific number of periods.

Table 18.1. Number of Calculations for Specific Number of Periods.

Periods	Calculations
1	3
2	7
3	17
4	31
5	63
6	127
7	255
8	511
9	1023
10	2047
11	4065
12	8191

After two periods it becomes very cumbersome to calculate and create the Decision Trees for a call and put option. In the previous section, we saw that calculations were very repetitive and mechanical. To solve this problem, this chapter will use Microsoft Excel to do the calculations and create the Decision Trees for the call and put options. We will also use Microsoft Excel to calculate and draw the related Decision Trees for the underlying stock and bond.

To solve this repetitive and mechanical calculation of the Binomial OPM, we will look at a Microsoft Excel file called *binomialBS_OPM.xls*. We will use this Microsoft Excel workbook to produce four Decision Trees for the GE stock that was discussed in the previous sections. The four Decision Trees are

(1) Stock Price;
(2) Call Option Price;
(3) Put Option Price; and
(4) Bond Price.

This section will demonstrate how to use the *binomialBS_OPM.xls* Excel file to create the four Decision Trees. Figure 18.16 shows the Excel file *binomialBS_OPM.xls* after the file is opened. Pushing the button shown in Fig. 18.16 will get the dialog box shown in Fig. 18.17.

The dialog box shown in Fig. 18.17 shows the parameters for the *Binomial OPM*. These parameters are changeable. The dialog box in Fig. 18.17 shows the default values.

Pushing the *calculate* button shown in Fig. 18.17 will produce the four Decision Trees shown in Figs. 18.18, 18.19, 18.20, and 18.21.

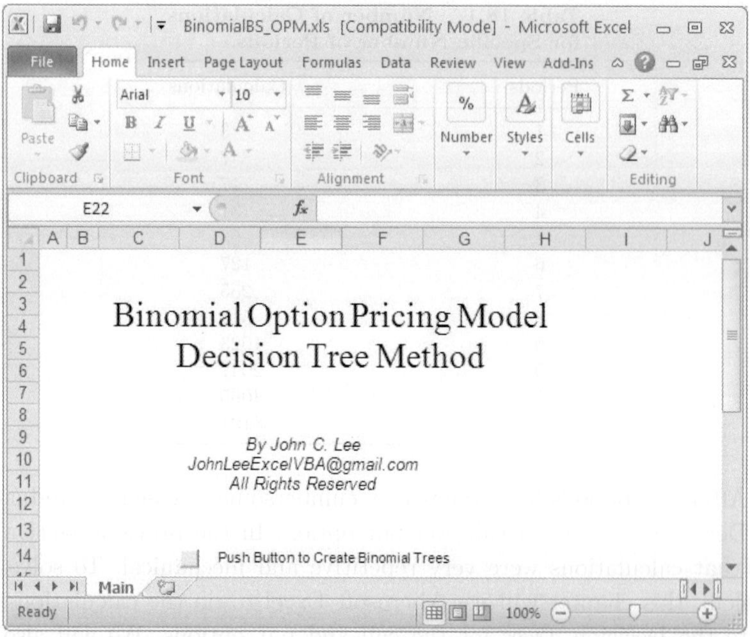

Fig. 18.16. Excel File BinomialBS_OPM.xls.

Table 18.1 indicated that 31 calculations were required to create a Decision Tree that has four periods. This section showed four Decision Trees. Therefore, the Excel file did $31 \times 4 = 121$ calculations to create the four Decision Trees.

Benninga (2000, p. 260) has defined the price of a call option in a Binomial OPM with n periods as

$$C = \sum_{i=0}^{n} \binom{n}{i} q_u^i q_d^{n-i} \max[S(u)^i (d)^{n-i}, 0], \tag{18.6}$$

and the price of a put option in a Binomial OPM with n-periods as

$$P = \sum_{i=0}^{n} \binom{n}{i} q_u^i q_d^{n-i} \max[X - S(u)^i (d)^{n-i}, 0]. \tag{18.7}$$

Lee *et al.* (2000, p. 237) has defined the pricing of a call option in a Binomial OPM with n period as

$$C = \frac{1}{R^n} \sum_{k=0}^{n} \frac{n!}{k!(n-k!)} p^k (1-p)^{n-k} \max[0, (u)^k (d)^{n-k}, S - X]. \tag{18.8}$$

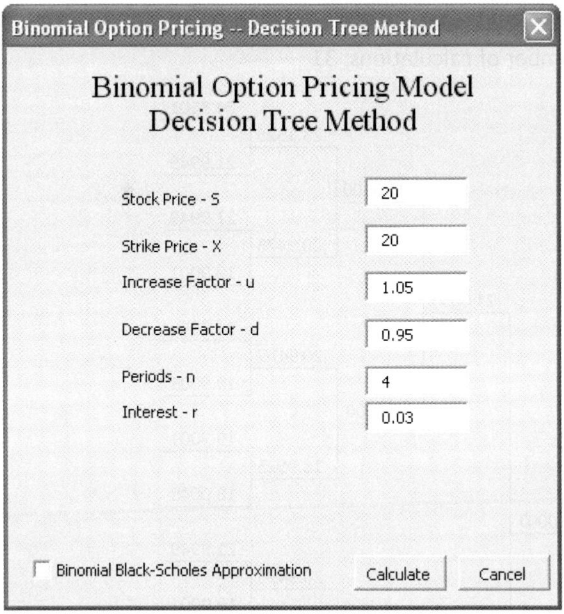

Fig. 18.17. Dialog Box Showing Parameters for the Binomial OPM.

The definition of the pricing of a put option in a Binomial OPM with n period would then be defined as

$$P = \frac{1}{R^n}\sum_{k=0}^{n}\frac{n!}{k!(n-k)!}p^k(1-p)^{n-k}\max[0, X-(u)^k(d)^{n-k}, S]. \quad (18.9)$$

18.5. Black–Scholes Option Pricing Model

The most famous OPM is the Black–Scholes OPM. In this section, we will demonstrate the usage of the Black–Scholes OPM. In latter sections, we will demonstrate the relationship between the Binomial OPM and the Black–Scholes pricing model. The Black–Scholes model prices European call and put options. The Black–Scholes model for a European call option is

$$\mathrm{C} = \mathrm{SN(d1)} - \mathrm{X}e^{-rT}\mathrm{N(d2)}, \quad (18.10)$$

where

C = Call price;
S = Stock price;
r = risk free interest rate;
T = time to maturity of option in years;

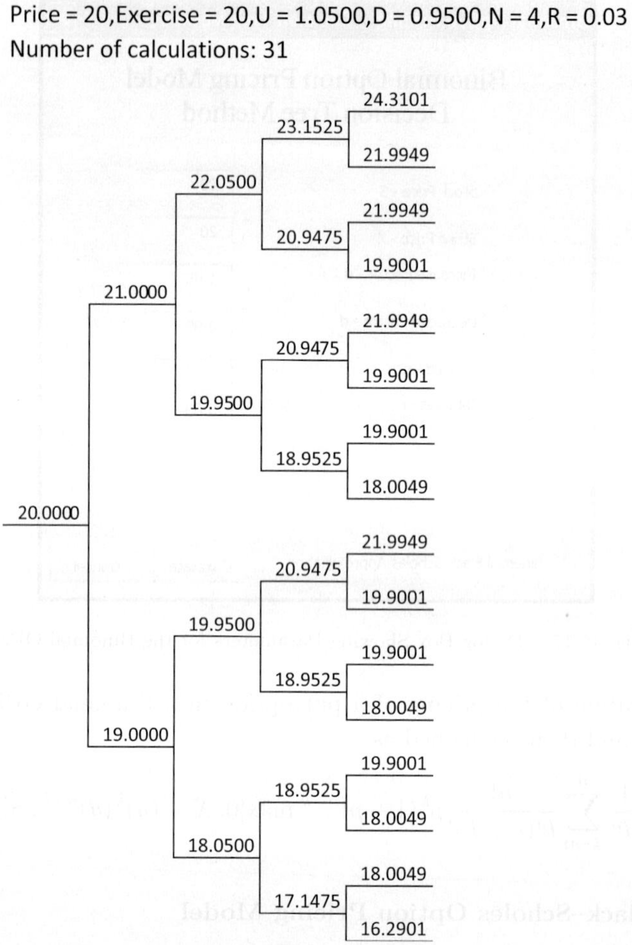

Fig. 18.18. Stock Price Decision Tree.

N(·) = standard normal distribution; and
σ = stock volatility.

$$d1 = \frac{\ln(S/X) + \left(r + \frac{\sigma^2}{2}\right)T}{\sigma\sqrt{T}}$$

$$d2 = d1 - \sigma\sqrt{T}.$$

Let us manually calculate the price of an European call option in terms of Equation (18.10) with the following parameter values, $S = 20$, $X = 2$, $r = 3\%$, $T = 4$, $\sigma = 20\%$

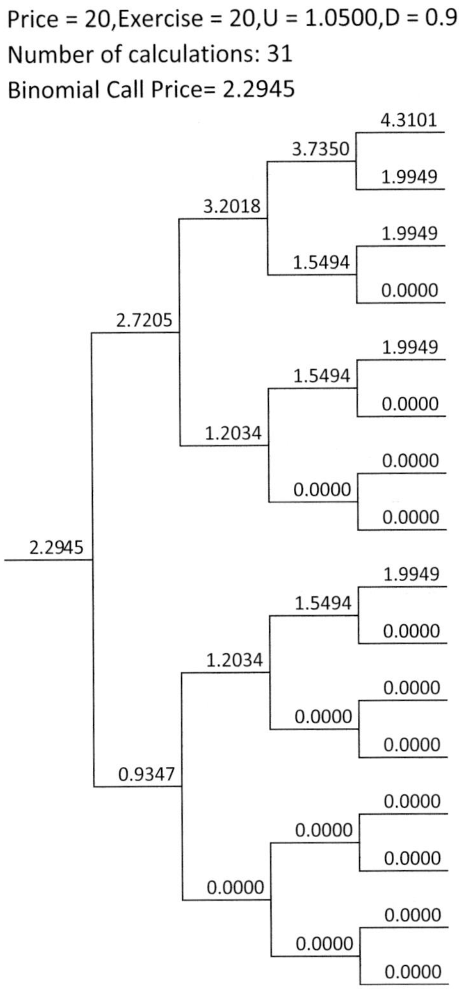

Fig. 18.19. Call Option Pricing Decision Tree.

Solution

$$d1 = \frac{\ln(S/X) + \left(r + \frac{\sigma^2}{2}\right)T}{\sigma\sqrt{T}} = \frac{\ln(30/30) + \left(0.03 + \cdot\frac{0.2^2}{2}\right)(4)}{0.2\sqrt{4}}$$

$$= \frac{(0.03 + 0.02)^{*}4}{0.4} = \frac{0.2}{0.4} = 0.5,$$

$$d2 = 0.5 - 0.2\sqrt{4} = 0.1$$

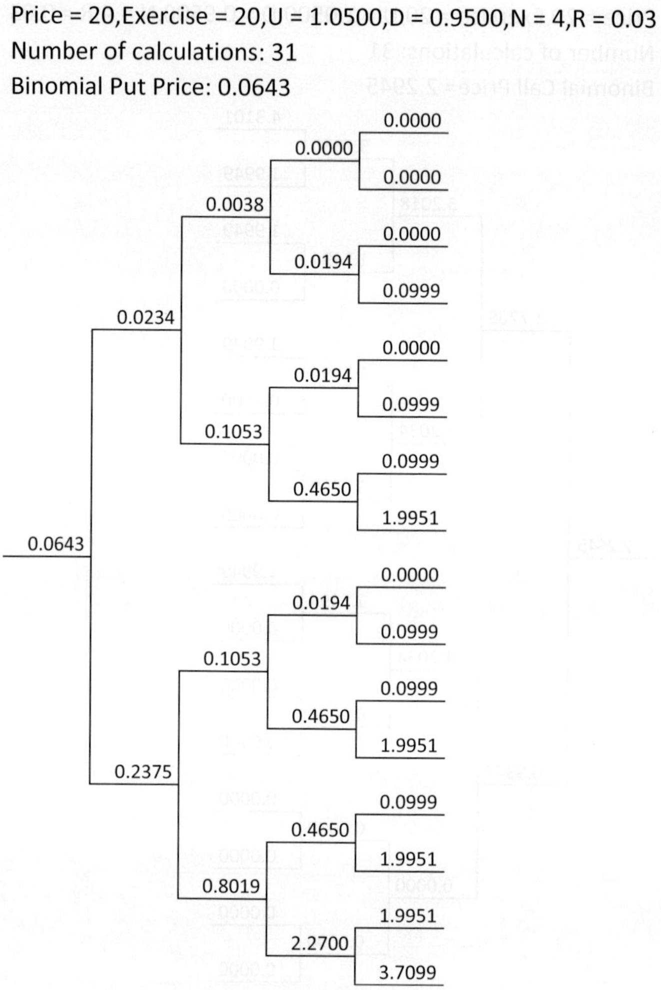

Fig. 18.20. Put Option Pricing Decision Tree.

$$\mathrm{N(d1)} = 0.69146, \quad \mathrm{N(d2)} = 0.5398, \quad e^{-rT} = 0.8869$$

$$\mathrm{C} = (20)^*(0.69146) - (20)^*(0.8869)^*0.5398$$

$$= 13.8292 - 9.5749724 = 4.2542276$$

The Black–Scholes put–call parity equation is

$$P = C - S + Xe^{-rT}.$$

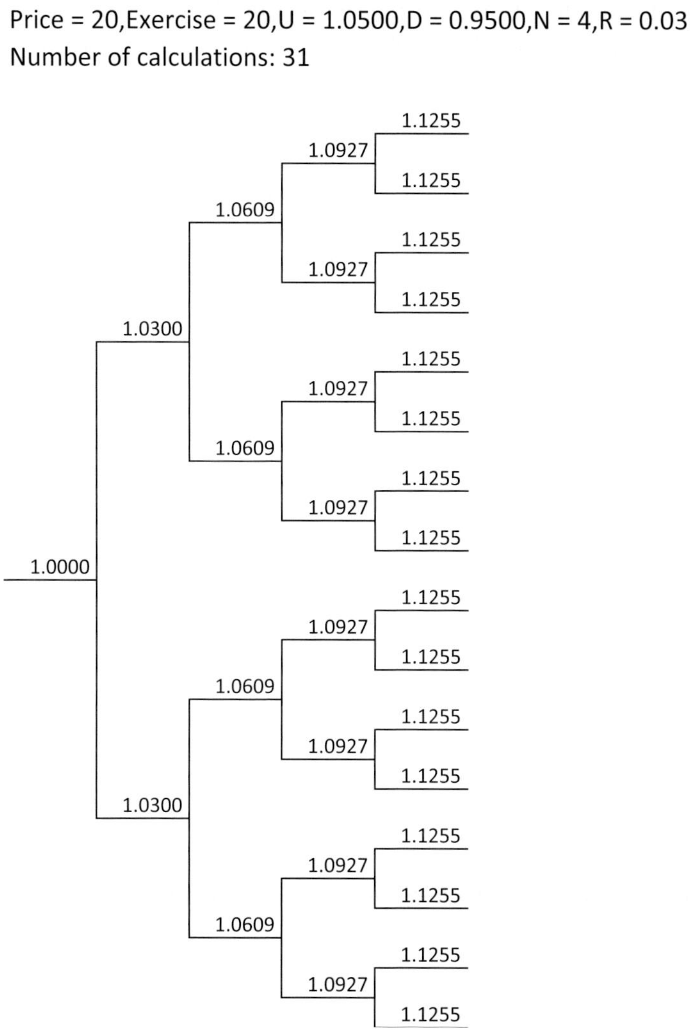

Fig. 18.21. Bond Pricing Decision Tree.

The put option value for the stock would be

$$
\begin{aligned}
P &= 4.25 - 20 + 20(0.8869) \\
&= 4.25 - 20 + 17.738 \\
&= 1.988.
\end{aligned}
$$

18.6. Relationship between the Binomial Option Pricing Model and the Black–Scholes Option Pricing Model

We can use either the Binomial model or Black–Scholes to price an option. They both should result in similar numbers. If we look at the parameters in both models, we will notice that the Binomial model has an *Increase Factor (U)*, a *Decrease Factor (D)*, and n-period parameters that the Black–Scholes model does not have. We also notice that the Black–Scholes model has the σ and T parameters that the Binomial model does not have. Benninga (2008) suggest the following translation between the Binomial and Black–Scholes parameters.

$$\Delta t = T/n \quad R = e^{r\Delta t} \quad U = e^{\sigma\sqrt{\Delta t}} \quad D = e^{-\sigma\sqrt{\Delta t}}.$$

In the Excel program, shown in Appendix 18A, we use Benninga's (2008) *Increase Factor* and *Decrease Factor* definitions. They are defined as follows:

$$q_u = \frac{R-d}{R(u-d)}, \quad q_d = \frac{u-R}{R(u-d)},$$

where

$u = 1+$ percentage of price increase;
$d = 1-$ percentage of price increase; and
$R = 1+$ interest rate.

18.7. Decision Tree Black–Scholes Calculation

We will now use the *BinomialBS_OPM.xls* Excel file to calculate the Binomial and Black–Scholes call and put values illustrated in Section 18.5. Notice that in Fig. 18.22 the *Binomial Black-Scholes Approximation* check-box is checked. Checking this box will cause T and σ parameters to appear and will adjust the *Increase Factor — u and Decrease Factor — d* parameters. The adjustment was done as indicated in Section 18.7.

Notice in Figs. 18.23 and 18.24 the Binomial OPM value does not agree with the Black–Scholes OPM. The Binomial OPM value will get very close to the Black–Scholes OPM value once the Binomial parameter n gets very large. Benninga (2008) demonstrated that the Binomial value will be close to the Black–Scholes when the Binomial n-parameter gets larger than 500.

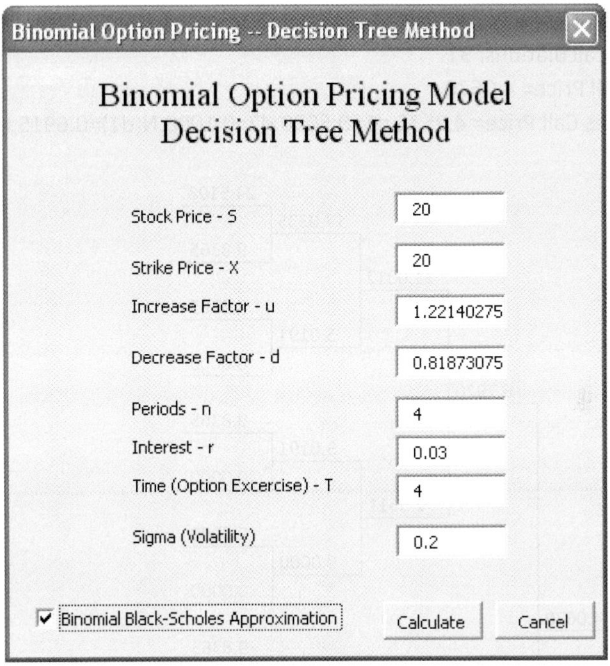

Fig. 18.22. Dialog Box Showing Parameters for the Binomial OPM.

18.8. Summary

This chapter demonstrated, with the aid of Microsoft Excel and Decision Trees, the Binomial Option model in a less mathematical fashion. This chapter allowed the reader to focus more on the concepts by studying the associated Decision Trees, which were created by Microsoft Excel. This chapter also demonstrated that using Microsoft Excel releases the reader from the computation burden of the Binomial Option Model.

This chapter also published the Microsoft Excel VBA code that created the Binomial Option Decision Trees. This allows for those who are interested in studying the many advanced Microsoft Excel VBA programming concepts that were used to create the Decision Trees. One major computer science programming concept used by the Excel VBA program in this chapter is recursive programming. Recursive programming is the ideal of a procedure calling itself many times. Inside the procedure there are statements to decide when not to call itself.

This chapter also used Decision Trees to demonstrate the relationship between the Binomial OPM and the Black–Scholes OPM.

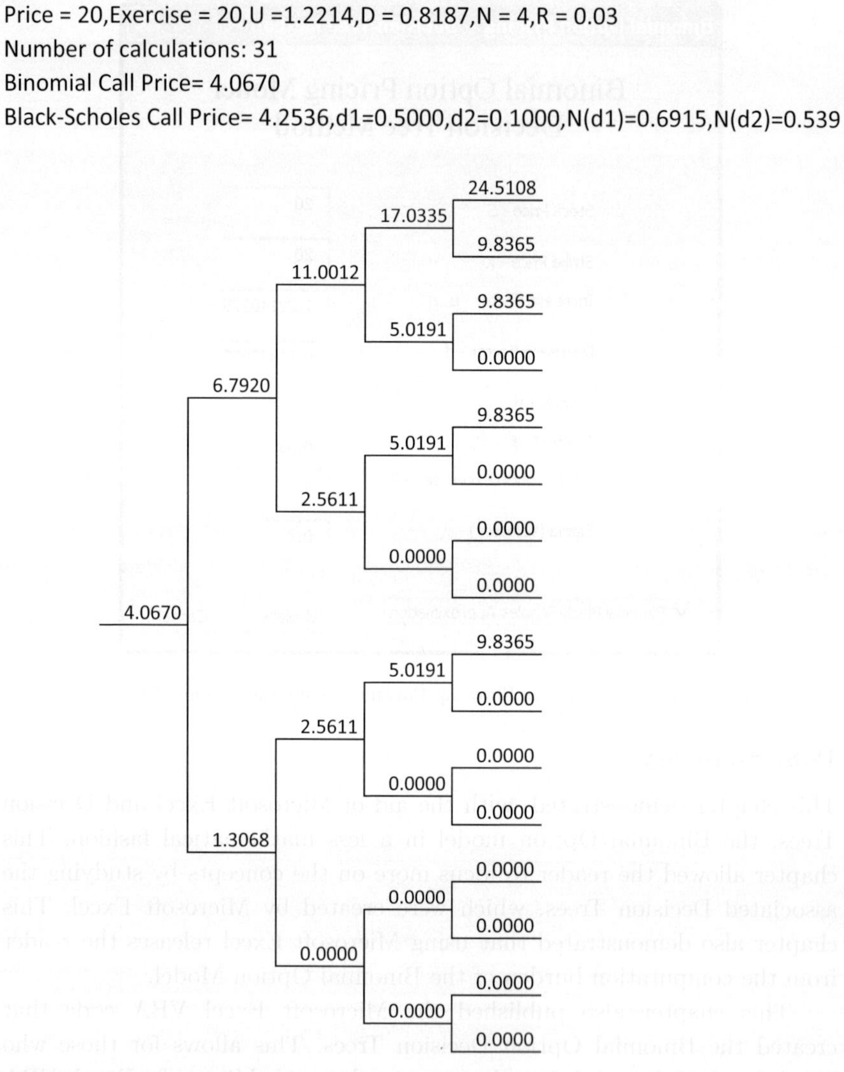

Fig. 18.23. Decision Tree Approximation of Black–Scholes Call Pricing.

Questions and Problems

1. What is the binomial distribution? What is cumulative density function of binomial distribution?
2. Please graphically and mathematically derive binomial call option model when time period (n) is 3.

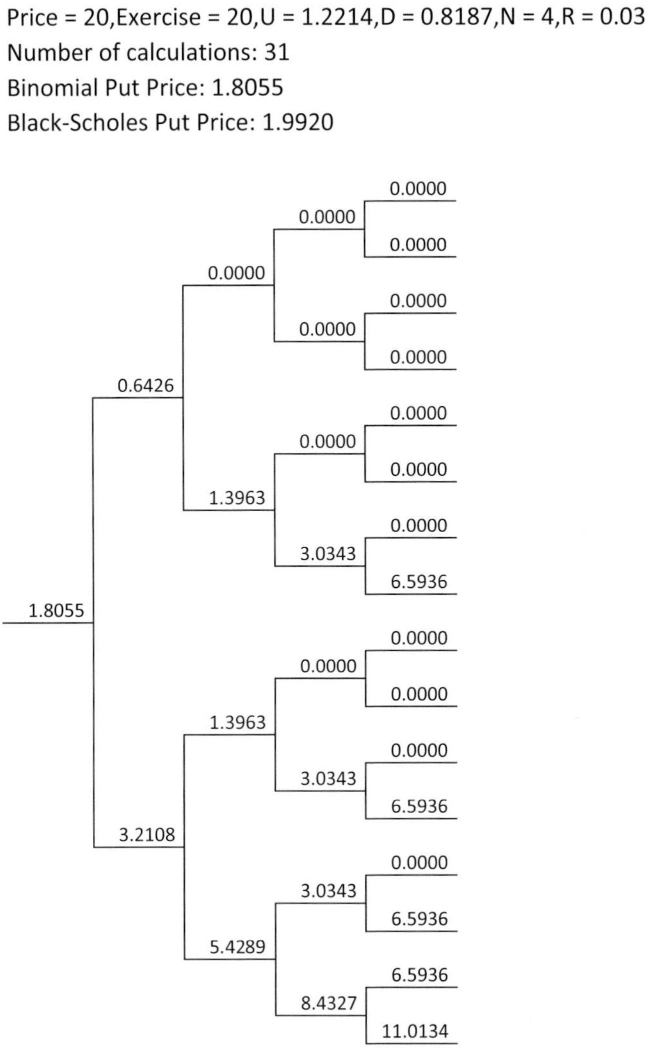

Fig. 18.24. Decision Tree Approximation of Black–Scholes Put Pricing.

3. What are the parameters used in the Binomial model? What are the parameters used in the Black–Scholes model? How are the parameters of two models related?
4. Explain how to form a risk-free portfolio by purchasing H shares of the stock for each call option written. How can the hedge ratio be obtained from this risk-free portfolio?

5. In Table 18.1, please graphically explain why there are seven calculations when the number of periods equals three.
6. You are given the following information about a stock:
   Stock Price $S = \$100$
   Strike Price $X = \$102$
   Increase Factor $u = 1.15$
   Decrease Factor $d = 0.90$
   Period (the number of months) $n = 5$
   Interest Rate (per month) $r = 0.005$
   Calculate the value of the call option if the stock goes up in three out of the five months.
7. If the parameters of question 6 change as follow, please calculate the call option value again
   (a) when $u = 1.20$
   (b) when $d = 0.85$
   (c) when $X = \$95$
   (d) when $S = \$110$
8. Answer question 6 again, finding the value of the option if the stock goes up in two out of the five months.
9. Given the parameters in question 6, calculate the value of the put option if the stock goes down in four out of the five months.

Appendix 18A: Excel VBA Code — Binomial Option Pricing Model

It is important to note that the thing that makes Microsoft Excel powerful is that it offers a powerful professional programming language called VBA. This section shows the VBA code that generated the Decision Trees for the Binomial Option pricing model. This code is in the form *frmBinomiaOption*. The procedure *cmdCalculate_Click* is the first procedure to run.

```
'/***************************************************************************
'/        Relationship Between the Binomial OPM
'/            and Black-Scholes OPM:
'/            Decision Tree and Microsoft Excel Approach
'/
'/                       by John Lee
'/                       JohnLeeExcelVBA@gmail.com
'/                       All Rights Reserved
'/***************************************************************************
Option Explicit
Dim mwbTreeWorkbook As Workbook
Dim mwsTreeWorksheet As Worksheet
```

```
Dim mwsCallTree As Worksheet
Dim mwsPutTree As Worksheet
Dim mwsBondTree As Worksheet
Dim mdblPFactor As Double
Dim mBinomialCalc As Long
Dim mCallPrice As Double   'jcl 12/8/2008
Dim mPutPrice As Double   'jcl 12/8/2008

'/***********************************************
'/Purpose:  Keep track the numbers of binomial calc
'/***********************************************
Property Let BinomialCalc(l As Long)
    mBinomialCalc = l
End Property
Property Get BinomialCalc() As Long
    BinomialCalc = mBinomialCalc
End Property
Property Set TreeWorkbook(wb As Workbook)
    Set mwbTreeWorkbook = wb
End Property
Property Get TreeWorkbook() As Workbook
    Set TreeWorkbook = mwbTreeWorkbook
End Property
Property Set TreeWorksheet(ws As Worksheet)
    Set mwsTreeWorksheet = ws
End Property
Property Get TreeWorksheet() As Worksheet
    Set TreeWorksheet = mwsTreeWorksheet
End Property
Property Set CallTree(ws As Worksheet)
    Set mwsCallTree = ws
End Property
Property Get CallTree() As Worksheet
    Set CallTree = mwsCallTree
End Property
Property Set PutTree(ws As Worksheet)
    Set mwsPutTree = ws
End Property
Property Get PutTree() As Worksheet
    Set PutTree = mwsPutTree
End Property
Property Set BondTree(ws As Worksheet)
    Set mwsBondTree = ws
End Property
Property Get BondTree() As Worksheet
    Set BondTree = mwsBondTree
End Property
Property Let CallPrice(dCallPrice As Double)
    '12/8/2008
    mCallPrice = dCallPrice
End Property
Property Get CallPrice() As Double
    Let CallPrice = mCallPrice
End Property
Property Let PutPrice(dPutPrice As Double)
    '12/10/2008
    mPutPrice = dPutPrice
End Property
Property Get PutPrice() As Double
```

```
    '12/10/2008
    Let PutPrice = mPutPrice
End Property

Property Let PFactor(r As Double)
    Dim dRate As Double

    dRate = ((1 + r) - Me.txtBinomialD) / (Me.txtBinomialU - Me.txtBinomialD)

    Let mdblPFactor = dRate
End Property
Property Get PFactor() As Double
    Let PFactor = mdblPFactor
End Property

Property Get qU() As Double
    Dim dblDeltaT As Double
    Dim dblDown As Double
    Dim dblUp As Double
    Dim dblR As Double

    dblDeltaT = Me.txtTimeT / Me.txtBinomialN
    dblR = Exp(Me.txtBinomialr * dblDeltaT)
    dblUp = Exp(Me.txtSigma * VBA.Sqr(dblDeltaT))
    dblDown = Exp(-Me.txtSigma * VBA.Sqr(dblDeltaT))


    qU = (dblR - dblDown) / (dblR * (dblUp - dblDown))
End Property

Property Get qD() As Double

    Dim dblDeltaT As Double
    Dim dblDown As Double
    Dim dblUp As Double
    Dim dblR As Double

    dblDeltaT = Me.txtTimeT / Me.txtBinomialN
    dblR = Exp(Me.txtBinomialr * dblDeltaT)
    dblUp = Exp(Me.txtSigma * VBA.Sqr(dblDeltaT))
    dblDown = Exp(-Me.txtSigma * VBA.Sqr(dblDeltaT))

    qD = (dblUp - dblR) / (dblR * (dblUp - dblDown))
End Property


Private Sub chkBinomialBSApproximation_Click()
    On Error Resume Next
        'Time and Sigma only BlackScholes parameter
        Me.txtTimeT.Visible = Me.chkBinomialBSApproximation
        Me.lblTimeT.Visible = Me.chkBinomialBSApproximation
        Me.txtSigma.Visible = Me.chkBinomialBSApproximation
        Me.lblSigma.Visible = Me.chkBinomialBSApproximation
        txtTimeT_Change

End Sub

Private Sub cmdCalculate_Click()
    Me.Hide
```

```
    BinomialOption
    Unload Me
End Sub

Private Sub cmdCancel_Click()
    Unload Me
End Sub


Private Sub txtBinomialN_Change()
    'jcl 12/8/2008
    On Error Resume Next
    If Me.chkBinomialBSApproximation Then
        Me.txtBinomialU = Exp(Me.txtSigma * Sqr(Me.txtTimeT / Me.txtBinomialN))
        Me.txtBinomialD = Exp(-Me.txtSigma * Sqr(Me.txtTimeT / Me.txtBinomialN))
    End If
End Sub



Private Sub txtTimeT_Change()

    'jcl 12/8/2008
    On Error Resume Next
    If Me.chkBinomialBSApproximation Then
        Me.txtBinomialU = Exp(Me.txtSigma * Sqr(Me.txtTimeT / Me.txtBinomialN))
        Me.txtBinomialD = Exp(-Me.txtSigma * Sqr(Me.txtTimeT / Me.txtBinomialN))
    End If
End Sub

Private Sub UserForm_Initialize()


   With Me

        .txtBinomialS = 20
        .txtBinomialX = 20
        .txtBinomialD = 0.95
        .txtBinomialU = 1.05
        .txtBinomialN = 4
        .txtBinomialr = 0.03
        .txtSigma = 0.2
        .txtTimeT = 4


        Me.chkBinomialBSApproximation = False
    End With

    chkBinomialBSApproximation_Click
    Me.Hide
End Sub

Sub BinomialOption()
    Dim wbTree As Workbook
    Dim wsTree As Worksheet
    Dim rColumn As Range
    Dim ws As Worksheet
```

```
    Set Me.TreeWorkbook = Workbooks.Add
    Set Me.BondTree = Me.TreeWorkbook.Worksheets.Add
    Set Me.PutTree = Me.TreeWorkbook.Worksheets.Add
    Set Me.CallTree = Me.TreeWorkbook.Worksheets.Add
    Set Me.TreeWorksheet = Me.TreeWorkbook.Worksheets.Add

    Set rColumn = Me.TreeWorksheet.Range("a1")

    With Me
        .BinomialCalc = 0
        .PFactor = Me.txtBinomialr
        .CallTree.Name = "Call Option Price"
        .PutTree.Name = "Put Option Price"
        .TreeWorksheet.Name = "Stock Price"
        .BondTree.Name = "Bond"
    End With

    DecisionTree rCell:=rColumn, nPeriod:=Me.txtBinomialN + 1, _
            dblPrice:=Me.txtBinomialS, sngU:=Me.txtBinomialU, _
            sngD:=Me.txtBinomialD

    DecitionTreeFormat
    TreeTitle wsTree:=Me.TreeWorksheet, sTitle:="Stock Price "
    TreeTitle wsTree:=Me.CallTree, sTitle:="Call Option Pricing"
    TreeTitle wsTree:=Me.PutTree, sTitle:="Put Option Pricing"
    TreeTitle wsTree:=Me.BondTree, sTitle:="Bond Pricing"

    Application.DisplayAlerts = False
    For Each ws In Me.TreeWorkbook.Worksheets
        If Left(ws.Name, 5) = "Sheet" Then
            ws.Delete
        Else
            ws.Activate
            ActiveWindow.DisplayGridlines = False
            ws.UsedRange.NumberFormat = "#,##0.0000_);(#,##0.0000)"
        End If
    Next
    Application.DisplayAlerts = True
    Me.TreeWorksheet.Activate
End Sub
Sub TreeTitle(wsTree As Worksheet, sTitle As String)
    wsTree.Range("A1:A5").EntireRow.Insert (xlShiftDown)
    With wsTree
        With .Cells(1)
              .Value = sTitle
              .Font.Size = 20
              .Font.Italic = True
        End With
        With .Cells(2, 1)
             .Value = "Decision Tree"
             .Font.Size = 16
             .Font.Italic = True
        End With
        With .Cells(3, 1)
             .Value = "Price = " & Me.txtBinomialS & _
                   ",Exercise = " & Me.txtBinomialX & _
                   ",U = " & Format(Me.txtBinomialU, "#,##0.0000") & _
                   ",D = " & Format(Me.txtBinomialD, "#,##0.0000") & _
                   ",N = " & Me.txtBinomialN & _
```

```
                ",R = " & Me.txtBinomialr
            .Font.Size = 14
        End With
        With .Cells(4, 1)
            .Value = "Number of calculations: " & Me.BinomialCalc
            .Font.Size = 14
        End With


        If wsTree Is Me.CallTree Then
            With .Cells(5, 1)
                .Value = "Binomial Call Price= " & Format(Me.CallPrice, "#,##0.0000")
                .Font.Size = 14
            End With

          If Me.chkBinomialBSApproximation Then
            wsTree.Range("A6:A7").EntireRow.Insert (xlShiftDown)

            With .Cells(6, 1)
                .Value = "Black-Scholes Call Price= " & Format(Me.BS_Call, "#,##0.0000") _
                          & ",d1=" & Format(Me.BS_D1, "#,##0.0000") _
                          & ",d2=" & Format(Me.BS_D2, "#,##0.0000") _
                          & ",N(d1)=" & Format(WorksheetFunction.NormSDist(BS_D1), "#,##0.0000") _
                          & ",N(d2)=" & Format(WorksheetFunction.NormSDist(BS_D2), "#,##0.0000")
                .Font.Size = 14
            End With
           End If
        ElseIf wsTree Is Me.PutTree Then
            With .Cells(5, 1)
                .Value = "Binomial Put Price: " & Format(Me.PutPrice, "#,##0.0000")
                .Font.Size = 14
            End With
           If Me.chkBinomialBSApproximation Then
            wsTree.Range("A6:A7").EntireRow.Insert (xlShiftDown)

            With .Cells(6, 1)
                .Value = "Black-Scholes Put Price: " & Format(Me.BS_PUT, "#,##0.0000")
                .Font.Size = 14
            End With
           End If
        End If

    End With
End Sub
Sub BondDecisionTree(rPrice As Range, arCell As Variant, iCount As Long)
    Dim rBond As Range
    Dim rPup As Range
    Dim rPDown As Range

    Set rBond = Me.BondTree.Cells(rPrice.Row, rPrice.Column)
    Set rPup = Me.BondTree.Cells(arCell(iCount - 1).Row, arCell(iCount - 1).Column)
    Set rPDown = Me.BondTree.Cells(arCell(iCount).Row, arCell(iCount).Column)

    If rPup.Column = Me.TreeWorksheet.UsedRange.Columns.Count Then
        rPup.Value = (1 + Me.txtBinomialr) ^ (rPup.Column - 1)
        rPDown.Value = rPup.Value
    End If
```

```
    With rBond
        .Value = (1 + Me.txtBinomialr) ^ (rBond.Column - 1)
        .Borders(xlBottom).LineStyle = xlContinuous
    End With
            rPDown.Borders(xlBottom).LineStyle = xlContinuous
            With rPup
                .Borders(xlBottom).LineStyle = xlContinuous
                .Offset(1, 0).Resize((rPDown.Row - rPup.Row), 1). _
                    Borders(xlEdgeLeft).LineStyle = xlContinuous
            End With

End Sub


Sub PutDecisionTree(rPrice As Range, arCell As Variant, iCount As Long)
    Dim rCall As Range
    Dim rPup As Range
    Dim rPDown As Range

    Set rCall = Me.PutTree.Cells(rPrice.Row, rPrice.Column)
    Set rPup = Me.PutTree.Cells(arCell(iCount - 1).Row, arCell(iCount - 1).Column)
    Set rPDown = Me.PutTree.Cells(arCell(iCount).Row, arCell(iCount).Column)

    If rPup.Column = Me.TreeWorksheet.UsedRange.Columns.Count Then
        rPup.Value = WorksheetFunction.Max(Me.txtBinomialX - arCell(iCount - 1), 0)
        rPDown.Value = WorksheetFunction.Max(Me.txtBinomialX - arCell(iCount), 0)
    End If

    With rCall

            '12/10/2008
            If Not Me.chkBinomialBSApproximation Then
                .Value = (Me.PFactor * rPup + (1 - Me.PFactor) * rPDown) / (1 + Me.txtBinomialr)
            Else
                .Value = (Me.qU * rPup) + (Me.qD * rPDown)
            End If

             Me.PutPrice = .Value   '12/8/2008

            .Borders(xlBottom).LineStyle = xlContinuous
    End With

    rPDown.Borders(xlBottom).LineStyle = xlContinuous
    With rPup
        .Borders(xlBottom).LineStyle = xlContinuous
        .Offset(1, 0).Resize((rPDown.Row - rPup.Row), 1). _
        Borders(xlEdgeLeft).LineStyle = xlContinuous
    End With

End Sub
Sub CallDecisionTree(rPrice As Range, arCell As Variant, iCount As Long)
    Dim rCall As Range
    Dim rCup As Range
    Dim rCDown As Range

    Set rCall = Me.CallTree.Cells(rPrice.Row, rPrice.Column)
    Set rCup = Me.CallTree.Cells(arCell(iCount - 1).Row, arCell(iCount - 1).Column)
    Set rCDown = Me.CallTree.Cells(arCell(iCount).Row, arCell(iCount).Column)
```

```
    If rCup.Column = Me.TreeWorksheet.UsedRange.Columns.Count Then
        With rCup
            .Value = WorksheetFunction.Max(arCell(iCount - 1) - Me.txtBinomialX, 0)
            .Borders(xlBottom).LineStyle = xlContinuous
        End With
        With rCDown
                .Value = WorksheetFunction.Max(arCell(iCount) - Me.txtBinomialX, 0)
                .Borders(xlBottom).LineStyle = xlContinuous
        End With
    End If

    With rCall

        If Not Me.chkBinomialBSApproximation Then
            .Value = (Me.PFactor * rCup + (1 - Me.PFactor) * rCDown) / (1 + Me.txtBinomialr)
        Else
            .Value = (Me.qU * rCup) + (Me.qD * rCDown)
        End If

        Me.CallPrice = .Value  '12/8/2008

        .Borders(xlBottom).LineStyle = xlContinuous
    End With

    rCup.Offset(1, 0).Resize((rCDown.Row - rCup.Row), 1). _
                Borders(xlEdgeLeft).LineStyle = xlContinuous

End Sub

Sub DecitionTreeFormat()
    Dim rTree As Range
    Dim nColumns As Integer
    Dim rLast As Range
    Dim rCell As Range
    Dim lCount As Long
    Dim lCellSize As Long
    Dim vntColumn As Variant
    Dim iCount As Long
    Dim lTimes As Long
    Dim arCell() As Range
    Dim sFormatColumn As String
    Dim rPrice As Range


    Application.StatusBar = "Formatting Tree.. "
    Set rTree = Me.TreeWorksheet.UsedRange
    nColumns = rTree.Columns.Count


    Set rLast = rTree.Columns(nColumns).EntireColumn.SpecialCells(xlCellTypeConstants, 23)
    lCellSize = rLast.Cells.Count
    For lCount = nColumns To 2 Step -1
        sFormatColumn = rLast.Parent.Columns(lCount).EntireColumn.Address
        Application.StatusBar = "Formatting column " & sFormatColumn
        ReDim vntColumn(1 To (rLast.Cells.Count / 2), 1)

        Application.StatusBar = "Assigning values to array for column " & _
            rLast.Parent.Columns(lCount).EntireColumn.Address
        vntColumn = rLast.Offset(0, -1).EntireColumn.Cells(1).Resize(rLast.Cells.Count / 2, 1)
```

```
        rLast.Offset(0, -1).EntireColumn.ClearContents

        ReDim arCell(1 To rLast.Cells.Count)
        lTimes = 1
        Application.StatusBar = "Assigning cells to arrays. Total number of cells: " & lCellSize
        For Each rCell In rLast.Cells
            Application.StatusBar = "Array to column " & sFormatColumn & " Cells " & rCell.Row
            Set arCell(lTimes) = rCell
            lTimes = lTimes + 1
        Next

        lTimes = 1

        Application.StatusBar = "Formatting leaves for column " & sFormatColumn
        For iCount = 2 To lCellSize Step 2

            Application.StatusBar = "Formatting leaves for cell " & arCell(iCount).Address
            If rLast.Cells.Count <> 2 Then
                Set rPrice = arCell(iCount).Offset(-1 * ((arCell(iCount).Row - arCell(iCount -
                 1).Row) / 2), -1)
                rPrice.Value = vntColumn(lTimes, 1)
            Else
                Set rPrice = arCell(iCount).Offset(-1 * ((arCell(iCount).Row - arCell(iCount -
                 1).Row) / 2), -1)
                rPrice.Value = vntColumn
            End If


            arCell(iCount).Borders(xlBottom).LineStyle = xlContinuous
            With arCell(iCount - 1)
                .Borders(xlBottom).LineStyle = xlContinuous
                .Offset(1, 0).Resize((arCell(iCount).Row - arCell(iCount - 1).Row), 1). _
                    Borders(xlEdgeLeft).LineStyle = xlContinuous
            End With
            lTimes = 1 + lTimes

            CallDecisionTree rPrice:=rPrice, arCell:=arCell, iCount:=iCount
            PutDecisionTree rPrice:=rPrice, arCell:=arCell, iCount:=iCount
            BondDecisionTree rPrice:=rPrice, arCell:=arCell, iCount:=iCount
        Next

        Set rLast = rTree.Columns(lCount - 1).EntireColumn.SpecialCells(xlCellTypeConstants, 23)
        lCellSize = rLast.Cells.Count
    Next ' / outer next

    rLast.Borders(xlBottom).LineStyle = xlContinuous
    Application.StatusBar = False
End Sub

'/*******************************************************************
'/Purpse: To calculate the price value of every state of the binomial
'/        decision tree
'/*******************************************************************
Sub DecisionTree(rCell As Range, nPeriod As Integer, _
            dblPrice As Double, sngU As Single, sngD As Single)
    Dim lIteminColumn As Long

    If Not nPeriod = 1 Then
        'Do Up
```

```
        DecisionTree rCell:=rCell.Offset(0, 1), nPeriod:=nPeriod - 1, _
                dblPrice:=dblPrice * sngU, sngU:=sngU, _
                sngD:=sngD
        'Do Down
        DecisionTree rCell:=rCell.Offset(0, 1), nPeriod:=nPeriod - 1, _
                dblPrice:=dblPrice * sngD, sngU:=sngU, _
                sngD:=sngD
    End If


    lIteminColumn = WorksheetFunction.CountA(rCell.EntireColumn)


    If lIteminColumn = 0 Then
        rCell = dblPrice

    Else
        If nPeriod <> 1 Then
            rCell.EntireColumn.Cells(lIteminColumn + 1) = dblPrice
        Else
            rCell.EntireColumn.Cells(((lIteminColumn + 1) * 2) - 1) = dblPrice
            Application.StatusBar = "The number of binomial calcs are : " & Me.BinomialCalc _
            & " at cell " & rCell.EntireColumn.Cells(((lIteminColumn + 1) * 2) - 1).Address
        End If

    End If
    Me.BinomialCalc = Me.BinomialCalc + 1

End Sub
Function BS_D1() As Double
    Dim dblNumerator As Double
    Dim dblDenominator As Double

    On Error Resume Next
    dblNumerator = VBA.Log(Me.txtBinomialS / Me.txtBinomialX) + _
                ((Me.txtBinomialr + Me.txtSigma ^ 2 / 2) * Me.txtTimeT)
    dblDenominator = Me.txtSigma * Sqr(Me.txtTimeT)


    BS_D1 = dblNumerator / dblDenominator

End Function
Function BS_D2() As Double

    On Error Resume Next
    BS_D2 = BS_D1 - (Me.txtSigma * VBA.Sqr(Me.txtTimeT))

End Function
Function BS_Call() As Double

    BS_Call = (Me.txtBinomialS * WorksheetFunction.NormSDist(BS_D1)) _
            - Me.txtBinomialX * Exp(-Me.txtBinomialr * Me.txtTimeT) * _
            WorksheetFunction.NormSDist(BS_D2)

End Function
'Used put-call parity theorem to price put option
Function BS_PUT() As Double

    BS_PUT = BS_Call - Me.txtBinomialS + _
            (Me.txtBinomialX * Exp(-Me.txtBinomialr * Me.txtTimeT))
End Function
```

Bibliography

Benninga, S. *Financial Modeling.* Cambridge, MA: MIT Press, 2000.

Benninga, S. *Financial Modeling.* Cambridge, MA: MIT Press, 2008.

Black, F. and M. Scholes. "The Pricing of Options and Corporate Liabilities." *Journal of Political Economy*, v. 31 (May–June 1973), pp. 637–659.

Cox, J., S. A. Ross and M. Rubinstein. "Option Pricing: A Simplified Approach." *Journal of Financial Economics*, v. 7 (1979), pp. 229–263.

Daigler, R. T. *Financial Futures and Options Markets Concepts and Strategies.* New York: Harper Collins, 1994.

Jarrow, R. and S. TurnBull. *Derivative Securities.* Cincinnati: South-Western College Publishing, 1996.

Lee, C. F. *Handbook of Quantitative Finance.* New York, NY: Springer, 2009.

Lee, C. F. and A. C. Lee. *Encyclopedia of Finance.* New York, NY: Springer, 2006.

Lee, C. F., J. C. Lee and A. C. Lee (2000). *Statistics for Business and Financial Economics.* Singapore: World Scientific.

Lee, J. C., C. F. Lee, R. S. Wang and T. I. Lin. "On the Limit Properties of Binomial and Multinomial Option Pricing Models: Review and Integration," in *Advances in Quantitative Analysis of Finance and Accounting New Series*, Vol. 1. Singapore: World Scientific, 2004.

Lee, C. F., C. M. Tsai and A. C. Lee, "Asset Pricing with Disequilibrium Price Adjustment: Theory and Empirical Evidence." *Quantitative Finance* (2012, forthcoming).

Lee, J. C., "Using Microsoft Excel and Decision trees to Demonstrate the Binomial Option Pricing Model." *Advances in Investment Analysis and Portfolio Management*, v. 8 (2001), pp. 303–329.

Lo, A. W. and J. Wang. "Trading Volume: Definition, Data Analysis, and Implications of Portfolio Theory." *Review of Financial Studies*, v. 13 (2000), pp. 257–300.

Rendleman, R. J., Jr. and B. J. Barter. "Two-State Option Pricing." *Journal of Finance*, v. 34(5) (December 1979), pp. 1093–1110.

Wells, E. and S. Harshbarger. *Microsoft Excel 97 Developer's Handbook.* Redmond, WA: Microsoft Press, 1997.

Walkenbach, J. *Excel 2003 Power Programming with VBA.* Indianapolis, In: Wiley Publishing, Inc., 2003.

Chapter 19

Normal, Log-Normal Distribution, and Option Pricing Model

The normal (or Gaussian) distribution is the most important distribution in probability and statistics. One of the justifications for using the normal distribution is the central limit theorem. Also, most of the statistical theory is based on the normality assumption. However, in finance research, the log-normal distribution is playing a most important role. Part of the reason is the fact that in finance, we are dealing with random quantities which are positive in nature. Hence, taking the natural logarithm is quite reasonable. Also, empirical data quite often support the assumption of the lognormality for random quantity such as the stock price movements.

In Sections 19.1 and 19.2, we discuss the normal distribution and the log-normal distribution, respectively. Section 19.3 explains the relationship between the log-normal distribution and the normal distribution. In Section 19.4, the multivariate normal and log-normal distributions are introduced. Section 19.5 applies the normal distribution to the binomial distribution. Section 19.6 covers the applications of the log-normal distribution in option pricing. Section 19.7 introduces the bivariate normal distribution. In Sections 19.8, we price the American call options by the bivariate normal distribution and illustrate the calculation process by given an example. In Section 19.9, we derive the price bounds of options written on the stocks with or without dividends. In Section 19.10, we summarize and conclude our findings in the previous sections.

19.1. The Normal Distribution

A random variable X is said to be normally distributed with mean μ and variance σ^2 if it has the probability density function (PDF)

$$f(x) = \frac{1}{\sqrt{2\pi}\sigma} e^{-\frac{1}{2}\left(\frac{x-\mu}{\sigma}\right)^2}, \quad \sigma > 0. \tag{19.1}$$

The normal distribution is symmetric around μ, which is the mean and the mode of the distribution. It is easy to see that the PDF of $Z = \frac{X-\mu}{\sigma}$ is

$$g(z) = \frac{1}{\sqrt{2\pi}} e^{-\frac{z^2}{2}}, \tag{19.2}$$

which is the PDF of the standard normal and is independent of the parameters μ and σ^2.

The cumulative distribution function (CDF) of Z is

$$P(Z \leq z) = N(z), \tag{19.3}$$

which has been well tabulated. Also, software package or system such S-plus will provide the value $N(z)$ instantly. For a discussion of some approximations for $N(z)$, the reader is referred to Johnson and Kotz (1970). For the CDF of X we have

$$P(X \leq x) = P\left(\frac{X-\mu}{\sigma} \leq \frac{x-\mu}{\sigma}\right) = N\left(\frac{x-\mu}{\sigma}\right). \tag{19.4}$$

The normal distribution as given in Equation (19.1) is very important in practice. It is very useful in describing the phenomena such as the scores of tests, heights of students in a certain school. It is useful in serving as an approximation for binomial distribution. It is also quite useful in studying the option pricing.

We next discuss some properties of the normal distribution. If X is normally distributed with mean μ and variance σ^2, then the Moment generating function (MGF) of X is

$$M_x(t) = e^{\mu t + t^2\sigma^2/2}, \tag{19.5}$$

which is useful in deriving the moment of X. Equation (19.5) is also useful in deriving the moments of the log-normal distribution. From Equation (19.5), it is easy to verify that

$$E(X) = \mu \quad \text{and} \quad \mathrm{Var}(X) = \sigma^2.$$

If $X_1, \cdots, X_n$ are independent, normally distributed random variable, then any linear function of these variables is also normally distributed. In fact, if X_i is normally distributed with mean μ_i and variance σ_i^2, then $\sum_{i=1}^n a_i X_i$ is normally distributed with mean $\sum_{i=1}^n a_i \mu_i$ and variance $\sum_{i=1}^n a_i^2 \sigma_i^2$, when $a_i' s$ are constants. If X_1 and X_2 are independent, and each is normally distributed with mean 0 and variance σ^2, then $(X_1^2 - X_2^2)/(X_1^2 + X_2^2)$ is also normally distributed.

19.2. The Log-Normal Distribution

A random variable X is said to be log-normality distributed with parameters μ and σ^2 if

$$Y = \log X \tag{19.6}$$

is normally distributed with mean μ and variance σ^2. It is clear that X has to be a positive random variable. This distribution is quite useful in studying the behavior of stock prices.

For the log-normal distribution as described above, the PDF is

$$g(x) = \frac{1}{\sqrt{2\pi}\sigma x} e^{-\frac{1}{2\sigma^2}(\log x - \mu)^2}, \quad x > 0. \tag{19.7}$$

The log-normal distribution is sometimes called the antilog-normal distribution, because it is the distribution of the random variable X which is the antilog of the normal random variable Y. However, "log-normal" is most commonly used in the literature. When applied to economic data, especially production function, it is often called the Cobb–Douglas distribution.

We next discuss some properties of the log-normal distribution, as defined in Equation (19.6). The rth moment of X is

$$\mu_r' = E(X^r) = E(e^{rY}) = e^{\mu r + \frac{r^2\sigma^2}{2}}. \tag{19.8}$$

It is noted that we have utilized the fact the MGF of the normal random variable Y with mean μ and variance σ^2 is $M_Y(t) = e^{\mu t + \frac{t^2\sigma^2}{2}}$. Thus, $E(e^{rY})$ is simply $M_Y(r)$, which is the right-hand side of Equation (19.8). From Equation (19.8) we have

$$E(X) = e^{\mu + \frac{\sigma^2}{2}}, \tag{19.9}$$

$$Var(X) = e^{2\mu} e^{\sigma^2}[e^{\sigma^2} - 1]. \tag{19.10}$$

It is noted that the moment sequence $\{\mu'_r\}$ does not belong only to log-normal distribution. Thus, the log-normal distribution cannot be defined by its moments.

The CDF of X is

$$P(X \leq x) = P(\log X \leq \log x) = N\left(\frac{\log x - \mu}{\sigma}\right), \tag{19.11}$$

because $\log X$ is normally distributed with mean μ and variance σ^2.

The distribution of X is unimodal with the mode at

$$\text{mode}(X) = e^{(\mu-\sigma^2)}. \tag{19.12}$$

Let x_α be the $(100)\alpha$ percentile for the log-normal distribution and z_α be the corresponding percentile for the standard normal, then

$$P(X \leq x_\alpha) = P\left(\frac{\log X - \mu}{\sigma} \leq \frac{\log x_\alpha - \mu}{\sigma}\right) = N\left(\frac{\log x_\alpha - \mu}{\sigma}\right). \tag{19.13}$$

Thus $z_\alpha = \frac{\log x_\alpha - \mu}{\sigma}$, implying that

$$x_\alpha = e^{\mu+\sigma z_\alpha}. \tag{19.14}$$

Thus, the percentile of the log-normal distribution can be obtained from the percentile of the standard normal.

From Equation (19.13), we also see that

$$median(X) = e^{\mu}, \tag{19.15}$$

as $z_{0.5} = 0$. Thus $median(X) > \text{mode}(X)$. Hence the log-normal distribution is not symmetric.

19.3. The Log-Normal Distribution and Its Relationship to the Normal Distribution

By comparing the PDF of normal distribution given in Equation (19.1) and the PDF of log-normal distribution given in Equation (19.7), we know that

$$f(x) = \frac{f(y)}{x}. \tag{19.16}$$

In addition, from Equation (19.6), it is easy to see that

$$dx = xdy. \tag{19.17}$$

The CDF for the log-normal distribution can be expressed as

$$\begin{aligned} F(a) &= \Pr(X \leq a) = \Pr(\log X \leq \log a) \\ &= \Pr\left(\frac{\log X - \mu}{\sigma} \leq \frac{\log a - \mu}{\sigma}\right) \\ &= N(d) \end{aligned} \tag{19.18}$$

where

$$d = \frac{\log a - \mu}{\sigma}, \tag{19.19}$$

and $N(d)$ is the CDF of the standard normal distribution which can be obtained from Normal Table; $N(d)$ can also be obtained from S-plus or other software package. Alternatively, the value of $N(d)$ can be approximated by the following formula:

$$N(d) = a_0 e^{-\frac{d^2}{2}}(a_1 t + a_2 t^2 + a_3 t^3), \tag{19.20}$$

where

$$t = \frac{1}{1 + 0.33267d}$$

$$a_0 = 0.3989423, \quad a_1 = 0.4361936, \quad a_2 = -0.1201676, \quad a_3 = 0.9372980$$

In case we need $\Pr(X > a)$, then we have

$$\Pr(X > a) = 1 - \Pr(X \leq a) = 1 - N(d) = N(-d). \tag{19.21}$$

Since for any h, $E(X^h) = E(e^{hY})$, the hth moment of X, the following moment generating function of Y, which is normally distributed with mean μ and variance σ^2,

$$M_Y(t) = e^{\mu t + \frac{1}{2}t^2\sigma^2}. \tag{19.22}$$

For example,

$$\begin{aligned} \mu_X &= E(X) = E(e^Y) = M_Y(1) = e^{\mu + \frac{1}{2}t^2\sigma^2}. \\ E(X^h) &= E(e^{hY}) = M_Y(h) = e^{\mu h + \frac{1}{2}t^2\sigma^2}. \end{aligned} \tag{19.23}$$

Hence

$$\begin{aligned} \sigma_X^2 &= E(X^2) - (EX)^2 = e^{2\mu + 2\sigma^2} - e^{2\mu + \sigma^2} \\ &= e^{2\mu + \sigma^2}(e^{\sigma^2} - 1) \end{aligned} \tag{19.24}$$

Thus, fractional and negative moment of a log-normal distribution can be obtained from Equation (19.23)

The mean of a log-normal random variable can be defined as

$$\int_0^{\infty} xf(x)dx = e^{\mu+\frac{\sigma^2}{2}}. \tag{19.25}$$

If the lower bound a is larger than 0; then the partial mean of x can be shown as

$$\int_0^{\infty} xf(x)dx = \int_{\log(a)}^{\infty} f(y)e^y dy = e^{\mu+\frac{\sigma^2}{2}} N(d), \tag{19.26}$$

where

$$d = \frac{\mu - \log(a)}{\sigma} + \sigma.$$

This implies that partial mean of a log-normal variable is the mean of x times an adjustment term, $N(d)$.

19.4. Multivariate Normal and Log-Normal Distributions

The normal distribution with the PDF given in Equation (19.1) can be extended to the p-dimensional case. Let $X = (X_1, \ldots, X_p)'$ be a $p \times 1$ random vector. Then we say that $X \sim N_p(\mu, \Sigma)$, if it has the PDF

$$f(x) = (2\pi)^{-p/2} |\Sigma|^{-1/2} \exp\left[-\frac{1}{2}(x-\mu)'\Sigma^{-1}(x-\mu)\right]. \tag{19.27}$$

In Equation (19.27), μ is the mean vector and Σ is the covariance matrix which is symmetric and positive definite. The moment generating function of $\boldsymbol{X}$ is

$$M_x(t) = E(e^{t'x}) = e^{t'\mu+\frac{1}{2}t'\Sigma t}, \tag{19.28}$$

where $t = (t_1, \ldots, t_p)'$ is a $p \times 1$ vector of real values.

From Equation (19.28), it can be shown that

$$E(X) = \mu \quad \text{and} \quad Cov(X) = \Sigma.$$

If $\mathbf{C}$ is a $q \times p$ matrix of rank $q \le p$. Then $\mathbf{CX} \sim N_q(\mathbf{C}\mu, \mathbf{C}\Sigma\mathbf{C}')$. Thus, linear transformation of a normal random vector is also a multivariate normal random vector.

Let $\mathbf{X} = \begin{pmatrix} \mathbf{X}^{(1)} \\ \mathbf{X}^{(2)} \end{pmatrix}$, $\mu = \begin{pmatrix} \mu^{(1)} \\ \mu^{(2)} \end{pmatrix}$, and $\Sigma = \begin{pmatrix} \Sigma_{11} & \Sigma_{12} \\ \Sigma_{21} & \Sigma_{22} \end{pmatrix}$, where $\mathbf{X}^{(i)}$ and $\mu^{(i)}$ are $p_i \times 1$, $p_1 + p_2 = p$, and Σ_{ij} is $p_i \times p_j$.

Then the marginal distribution of $X^{(i)}$ is also a multivariate normal with mean vector $\mu^{(i)}$ and covariance matrix Σ_{ii}, that is, $\mathbf{X}^{(i)} \sim N_{p_i}(\mu^{(i)}, \Sigma_{ii})$. Furthermore, the conditional distribution of $\mathbf{X}^{(1)}$ given $\mathbf{X}^{(2)} = x^{(2)}$, where $x^{(2)}$ is a known vector, is normal with mean vector $\mu_{1\cdot 2}$ and covariance matrix $\Sigma_{11\cdot 2}$

where

$$\mu_{1\cdot 2} = \mu^{(1)} + \Sigma_{12}\Sigma_{22}^{-1}(x^{(2)} - \mu^{(2)}), \tag{19.29}$$

and

$$\Sigma_{11\cdot 2} = \Sigma_{11} - \Sigma_{12}\Sigma_{22}^{-1}\Sigma_{21}, \tag{19.30}$$

that is, $\mathbf{X}^{(1)}|\mathbf{X}^{(2)} = x^{(2)} \sim N_{p_1}(\mu_{1\cdot 2}, \Sigma_{11\cdot 2})$.

We next consider a bivariate version of correlated log-normal distribution.

Let $\begin{pmatrix} Y_1 \\ Y_2 \end{pmatrix} = \begin{pmatrix} \log(X_1) \\ \log(X_2) \end{pmatrix} \sim N\left(\begin{pmatrix} \mu_1 \\ \mu_2 \end{pmatrix}, \begin{pmatrix} \sigma_{11} & \sigma_{12} \\ \sigma_{21} & \sigma_{22} \end{pmatrix}\right)$.

The joint PDF of X_1 and X_2 can be obtained from the joint PDF of Y_1 and Y_2 by observing that

$$dx_1 dx_2 = x_1 x_2 dy_1 dy_2, \tag{19.31}$$

which is an extension of Equation (19.17) to the bivariate case.

Hence, the joint PDF of X_1 and X_2 is

$$g(x_1, x_2) = \frac{1}{2\pi|\Sigma|x_1 x_2} \exp\left\{-\frac{1}{2}[(\log x_1, \log x_2) - \mu]'\Sigma^{-1}[(\log x_1, \log x_2) - \mu]\right\}. \tag{19.32}$$

From the property of the multivariate normal distribution, we have $Y_i \sim N(\mu_i, \sigma_{ii})$. Hence, X_i is log-normal with

$$E(X_i) = e^{\mu_i + \frac{\sigma_{ii}}{2}}, \tag{19.33}$$

$$Var(X_i) = e^{2\mu_i} e^{\sigma_{ii}}[e^{\sigma_{ii}} - 1]. \tag{19.34}$$

Furthermore, by the property of the moment generating for the bivariate normal distribution, we have

$$\begin{aligned} E(X_1X_2) &= E(e^{Y_1+Y_2}) \\ &= e^{\mu_1+\mu_2+\frac{1}{2}(\sigma_{11}+\sigma_{22}+2\sigma_{12})} \\ &= E(X_1)E(X_2)\cdot\exp(\rho\sqrt{\sigma_{11}\sigma_{22}}). \end{aligned} \tag{19.35}$$

Thus, the covariance between X_1 and X_2 is

$$\begin{aligned} Cov(X_1, X_2) &= E(X_1X_2) - E(X_1)E(X_2) \\ &= E(X_1)E(X_2)\cdot(\exp(\rho\sqrt{\sigma_{11}\sigma_{22}}) - 1) \\ &= \exp\left(\mu_1+\mu_2+\frac{1}{2}(\sigma_{11}+\sigma_{22})\right)\cdot(\exp(\rho\sqrt{\sigma_{11}\sigma_{22}}) - 1). \end{aligned} \tag{19.36}$$

From the property of conditional normality of Y_1 given $Y_2 = y_2$, we also see that the conditional distribution of Y_1 given $Y_2 = y_2$ is log-normal.

The extension to the p-variate log-normal distribution is trivial. Let $\boldsymbol{Y} = (Y_1, \ldots, Y_p)'$, where $Y_i = \log X_i$. If $\boldsymbol{Y} \sim N_p(\boldsymbol{\mu}, \boldsymbol{\Sigma})$, where $\boldsymbol{\mu} = (\mu_1 \cdots \mu_p)'$ and $\boldsymbol{\Sigma} = (\sigma_{ij})$.

The joint PDF of $X_1, \ldots, X_p$, can be obtained from the following theorem.

Theorem 1. (Anderson, 2003)

Let the PDF of $Y_1, \ldots, Y_p$ be $f(y_1, \ldots, y_p)$, consider the p-valued functions

$$x_i = x_i(y_1, \ldots, y_p), \quad i = 1, \ldots, p. \tag{19.37}$$

We assume that the transformation from the y-space to the x-space is one-to-one with the inverse transformation

$$y_i = y_i(x_1, \ldots, x_p), \quad i = 1, \ldots, p. \tag{19.38}$$

Let the random variables $X_1, \ldots, X_p$, be defined by

$$X_i = x_i(Y_1, \ldots, Y_p), \quad i = 1, \ldots, p. \tag{19.39}$$

Then the PDF of $X_1, \ldots, X_p$ is

$$g(x_1, \ldots, x_p) = f(y_1(x_1, \ldots, x_p), \ldots, y_p(x_1, \ldots, x_p))J(x_1, \ldots, x_p), \tag{19.40}$$

where $J(x_1, \ldots, x_p)$ is the Jacobian of transformations

$$J(x_1, \ldots, x_p) = \text{mod} \begin{vmatrix} \dfrac{\partial y_1}{\partial x_1} & \cdots & \dfrac{\partial y_1}{\partial x_p} \\ \vdots & \ddots & \vdots \\ \dfrac{\partial y_p}{\partial x_1} & \cdots & \dfrac{\partial y_p}{\partial x_p} \end{vmatrix}, \tag{19.41}$$

where "mod" means a modulus or absolute value.

Applying the above theorem with $f(y_1, \ldots, y_p)$ being a p-variate normal, and

$$J(x_1, \ldots, x_p) = \text{mod} \begin{vmatrix} \dfrac{1}{x_1} & 0 & \cdots & 0 \\ 0 & \dfrac{1}{x_2} & \cdots & 0 \\ \vdots & & \ddots & \vdots \\ 0 & \cdots & & \dfrac{1}{x_p} \end{vmatrix} = \prod_{i=1}^{p} \frac{1}{x_i}, \tag{19.42}$$

we have the following joint PDF of $X_1, \ldots, X_p$

$$\begin{aligned} g(x_1, \ldots, x_p) & \\ = (2\pi)^{-p/2} |\Sigma|^{-\frac{p}{2}} & \left(\prod_{i=1}^{p} \frac{1}{x_i} \right) \\ \times \exp & \left\{ -\frac{1}{2} [(\log x_1, \ldots, \log x_p) - \mu]' \Sigma^{-1} [(\log x_1, \ldots, \log x_p) - \mu] \right\}. \end{aligned} \tag{19.43}$$

It is noted that when $p = 2$, Equation (19.43) reduces to the bivariate case given in Equation (19.32).

Then the first two moments are

$$E(X_i) = e^{\mu_i + \frac{\sigma_{ii}}{2}}, \tag{19.44}$$

$$Var(X_i) = e^{2\mu_i} e^{\sigma_{ii}} [e^{\sigma_{ii}} - 1]. \tag{19.45}$$

$$Cor(X_i, X_j) = \exp\left(\mu_i + \mu_j + \frac{1}{2}(\sigma_{ii} + \sigma_{jj}) \right) \cdot (\exp(\rho_{ij} \sqrt{\sigma_{ii}\sigma_{jj}}) - 1), \tag{19.46}$$

where ρ_{ij} is the correlation between Y_i and Y_j.

For more details concerning properties of the multivariate log-normal distribution, the reader is referred to Johnson and Kotz (1972).

19.5. The Normal Distribution as an Application to the Binomial and Poisson Distribution

The cumulative normal density function tells us the probability that a random variable Z will be less than some value x. Note in Fig. 19.1 that $P(Z < x)$ is simply the area under the normal curve from $-\infty$ up to point x.

One of the many applications of the cumulative normal distribution function is in valuing stock options. A call option gives the option holder the right to purchase, at a specified price known as the exercise price, a specified number of shares of stock during a given time period. A call option is a function of the following five variables:

(1) Current price of the firm's common stock (S);
(2) Exercise price (or strike price) of the option (X);
(3) Term to maturity in years (T);
(4) Variance of the stock's price (σ^2); and
(5) Risk-free rate of interest (r).

The binomial option pricing model defined in Equation (19.22) can be written as

$$C = S\left[\sum_{k=m}^{T} \frac{T!}{k!(T-k)!} p'^k (1-p')^{T-k}\right] - \frac{X}{(1+r)^T}\left[\sum_{k=m}^{T} \frac{T!}{k!(T-k)!} p^k (1-p)^{T-k}\right] \tag{19.47}$$

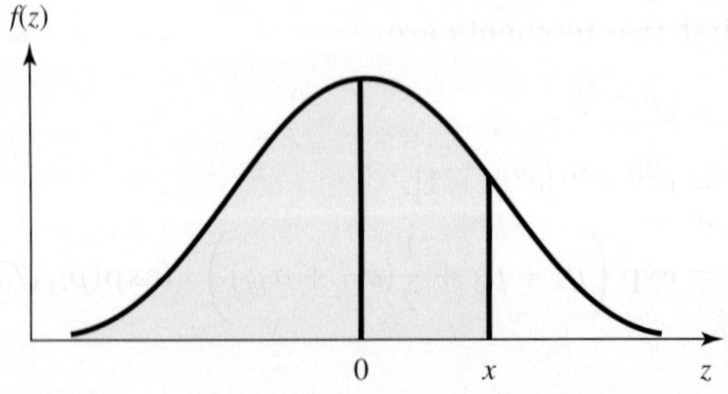

Fig. 19.1. The Cumulative Normal Density Function.

$$= SB(T, p', m) - \frac{X}{(1+r)^T} B(T, p, m),$$

and $C = 0$ if $m > T$,
where

$S =$ Current price of the stock,
$T =$ term to maturity in years,
$m =$ minimum number of upward movements in stock price that is necessary for the option to terminate "in the money,"
$p = \frac{R-d}{u-d}$ and $1 - p = \frac{u-R}{u-d}$,
$X =$ option exercise price (or strike price),
$R = 1 + r = 1+$ risk-free rate of return,
$u = 1+$ percentage of price increase,
$d = 1+$ percentage of price decrease,
$p' = (\frac{u}{R})p$,

$$B(n, p, m) = \sum_{k=m}^{n} {}_nC_k p^k (1-p)^{n-k}.$$

By a form of the central limit theorem, we showed in Section 19.7 as $T \to \infty$, the option price C converges to C below[1]

$$C = SN(d_1) - XR^{-T} N(d_2), \tag{19.48}$$

where

$C =$ Price of the call option,

$$d_1 = \frac{\log\left(\frac{S}{Xr^{-t}}\right)}{\sigma\sqrt{t}} + \frac{1}{2}\sqrt{t},$$

$$d_2 = d_1 - \sigma\sqrt{t}$$

$N(d)$ is the value of the cumulative standard normal distribution,

t is the fixed length of calendar time to expiration and h is the elapsed time between successive stock price changes and $T = ht$.

If future stock price is constant over time, then $\sigma^2 = 0$. It can be shown that both $N(d_1)$ and $N(d_2)$ are equal to 1 and that Equation (19.48)

[1]See Cox, J., S. Ross and M. Rubinstein. "Option Pricing: A Simplified Approach." *Journal of Financial Economics*, v. 7 (1979), pp. 229–263.

becomes

$$C = S - Xe^{-rT}. \tag{19.49}$$

Alternatively, Equations (19.48) and (19.49) can be understood in terms of the following steps:

Step 1: The future price of the stock is constant over time.

Because a call option gives the option holder the right to purchase the stock at the exercise price X, the value of the option, C, is just the current price of the stock less the present value of the stock's purchase price. Mathematically, the value of the call option is

$$C = S - \frac{X}{(1+r)^T}. \tag{19.50}$$

Note that Equation (19.50) assumes discrete compounding of interest, whereas Equation (19.49) assumes continuous compounding of interest. To adjust Equation (19.50) for continuous compounding, we substitute e^{-rT} for $\frac{1}{(1+r)^T}$ to get

$$C = S - Xe^{-rT}. \tag{19.51}$$

Step 2: Assume the price of the stock fluctuates over time (S_t).

In this case, we need to adjust Equation (19.49) for the uncertainty associated with that fluctuation. We do this by using the cumulative normal distribution function. In deriving Equation (19.48), we assume that S_t follows a log-normal distribution, as discussed in Section 19.3.

The adjustment factors $N(d_1)$ and $N(d_2)$ in the Black–Scholes option valuation model are simply adjustments made to Equation (19.49) to account for the uncertainty associated with the fluctuation of the price of the stock.

Equation (19.48) is a continuous option pricing model. Compare this with the binomial option price model given in Equation (19.47), which is a discrete option pricing model. The adjustment factors $N(d_1)$ and $N(d_2)$ are cumulative normal density functions. The adjustment factors $B(T, p', m)$ and $B(T, p, m)$ are complementary binomial distribution functions.

We can use Equation (19.48) to determine the theoretical value, as of November 29, 1991, of one of IBM's options with maturity on April 1992. In this case we have $X = \$90$, $S = \$92.50$, $\sigma = 0.2194$, $r = 0.0435$, and

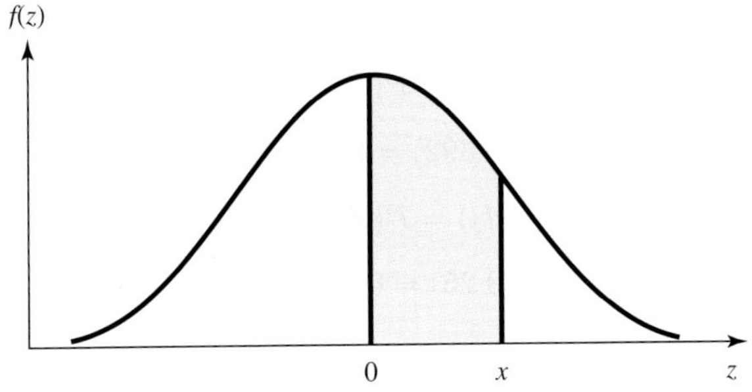

Fig. 19.2. Probability of a Variable Z between 0 and x.

$T = \frac{5}{12} = 0.42$ (in years).[2] Armed with this information we can calculate the estimated d_1 and d_2.

$$x = \frac{\left\{\ln\left(\frac{92.5}{90}\right) + [(0.0435) + \frac{1}{2}(0.2194)^2](0.42)\right\}}{(0.2194)(0.42)^{\frac{1}{2}}} = 0.392,$$

$$x - \sigma\sqrt{t} = x - (0.2194)(0.42)^{\frac{1}{2}} = 0.25.$$

In Equation (19.45), $N(d_1)$ and $N(d_2)$ are the probabilities that a random variable with a standard normal distribution takes on a value less than d_1 and a value less than d_2, respectively. The values for $N(d_1)$ and $N(d_2)$ can be found by using the tables in the back of the book for the standard normal distribution, which provide the probability that a variable Z is between 0 and x (see Fig. 19.2).

To find the cumulative normal density function, we need to add the probability that Z is less than zero to the value given in the standard normal distribution table. Because the standard normal distribution is symmetric around zero, we know that the probability that Z is less than zero is 0.5, so

$$P(Z < x) = P(Z < 0) + P(0 < Z < x) = 0.5 + \text{value from table.}$$

[2]Values of $X = \$90$, $S = \$92.50$, $r = 0.0435$ were obtained from Section C of the *Wall Street Journal* on December 2, 1991. And $\sigma = 0.2194$ is estimated in terms of monthly rate of return during the period January 1989 to November 1991.

We can now compute the values of $N(d_1)$ and $N(d_2)$.

$$N(d_1) = P(Z < d_1) = P(Z < 0) + P(0 < Z < d_1)$$
$$= P(Z < 0.392) = 0.5 + 0.1517 = 0.6517$$
$$N(d_2) = P(Z < d_2) = P(Z < 0) + P(0 < Z < d_2)$$
$$= P(Z < 0.25) = 0.5 + 0.0987 = 0.5987$$

Then the theoretical value of the option is

$$C = (92.5)(0.6517) - [(90)(0.5987)]/e^{(0.0435)(0.42)}$$
$$= 60.282 - 53.883/1.0184 = \$7.373.$$

and the actual price of the option on November 29, 1991, was \$7.75.

19.6. Applications of the Log-Normal Distribution in Option Pricing

To derive the Black–Scholes formula it is assumed that there are no transaction costs, no margin requirements, and no taxes; that all shares are infinitely divisible; and that continuous trading can be accomplished. It is also assumed that the economy is risk neutral and the stock price follows a log-normal distribution. Denote the current stock price by S and the stock price at the end of jth period by S_j.

Then $\frac{S_j}{S_{j-1}} = \exp[K_j]$ is a random variable with a log-normal distribution, where K_j is the rate of return in jth period and is a random variable with normal distribution. Let K_t have the expected value μ_k and variance σ_k^2 for each j. Then $K_1 + K_2 + \cdots + K_t$ is a normal random variable with expected value $t\mu_k$ and variance $t\sigma_k^2$. Thus, we can define the expected value (mean) of $\frac{S_t}{S} = \exp[K_1 + K_2 + \cdots + K_t]$ as

$$E\left(\frac{S_t}{S}\right) = \exp\left[t\mu_k + \frac{t\sigma_k^2}{2}\right]. \tag{19.52}$$

Under the assumption of a risk-neutral investor, the expected return $E(\frac{S_t}{S})$ is assumed to be $\exp(rt)$ (where r is the riskless rate of interest). In other words,

$$\mu_k = r - \frac{\sigma_k^2}{2}. \tag{19.53}$$

In the risk-neutral assumptions of Cox and Ross (1976) and Rubinstein (1976), the call option price C can be determined by discounting the expected value of the terminal option price by the riskless rate of interest:

$$C = \exp[-rt]E[Max(S_T - X, 0)], \tag{19.54}$$

where T is the time of expiration and X is the striking price.

Note that

$$\begin{aligned} Max(S_T - X, 0) &= \left(S\left(\frac{S_T}{S} - \frac{X}{S}\right)\right), \quad \text{for} \quad \frac{S_T}{S} > \frac{X}{S} \\ &= 0 \qquad\qquad\qquad\qquad\quad \text{for} \quad \frac{S_T}{S} < \frac{X}{S}. \end{aligned} \tag{19.55}$$

Equations (19.54) and (19.55) say that the value of the call option today will be either $S_t - X$ or 0, whichever is greater. If the price of stock at time t is greater than the exercise price, the call option will expire in the money. This simply means that an investor who owns the call option will exercise it. The option will be exercised regardless of whether the option holder would like to take physical possession of the stock. If the investor would like to own the stock, the cheapest way to obtain the stock is by exercising the option. If the investor would not like to own the stock, he or she will still exercise the option and immediately sell the stock in the market. Since the price the investor paid (X) is lower that the price he or she can sell the stock for (S_t), the investor realizes an immediate the profit of $S_t - X$. If the price of the stock (S_t) is less than the exercise price (X), the option expires out of the money. This occurs because in purchasing shares of the stock the investor will find it cheaper to purchase the stock in the market than to exercise the option.

Let $X = \frac{S_T}{S}$ be log-normally distributed with parameters $\mu = tr - \frac{t\sigma_k^2}{2}$ and $\sigma^2 = t\sigma_k^2$. Then

$$\begin{aligned} C &= \exp[-rt]E[Max(S_t - X)] \\ &= \exp[-rt]\int_{\frac{X}{S}}^{\infty} S\left[x - \frac{X}{S}\right] g(x)dx \\ &= \exp[-rt]S\int_{\frac{X}{S}}^{\infty} xg(x)dx - \exp[-rt]S\frac{X}{S}\int_{\frac{X}{S}}^{\infty} g(x)dx, \end{aligned} \tag{19.56}$$

where $g(x)$ is the probability density function of $X_t = \frac{S_t}{S}$.

Substituting $\mu = tr - t\sigma_k^2/2, \sigma^2 = t\sigma_k^2$ and $a = \frac{X}{S}$ into Equations (19.18) and (19.26) in Section 19.4, we obtain

$$\int_{\frac{X}{S}}^{\infty} xg(x)dx = e^{rt}N(d_1) \quad (19.57)$$

$$\int_{\frac{X}{S}}^{\infty} g(x)dx = N(d_2), \quad (19.58)$$

where

$$d_1 = \frac{tr - \frac{t}{2}\sigma_k^2 - \log\left(\frac{X}{S}\right)}{\sqrt{t}\sigma_k} + \sqrt{t}\sigma_k = \frac{\log\left(\frac{S}{X}\right) + \left(r + \frac{1}{2}\sigma_k^2\right)t}{\sqrt{t}\sigma_k}, \quad (19.59)$$

and

$$d_2 = \frac{\log\left(\frac{S}{X}\right) + \left(r - \frac{1}{2}\sigma_k^2\right)t}{\sqrt{t}\sigma_k} = d_1 - \sqrt{t}\sigma_k. \quad (19.60)$$

Substituting Equation (19.58) into Equation (19.56), we obtain

$$C = SN(d_1) - X\exp[-rt]N(d_2). \quad (19.61)$$

This is Equation (19.48) defined in Section 19.6.

We have defined a put option as a contract conveying the right to sell a designated security at a stipulated price. It can be shown that the relationship between a call option (C) and a put option (P) can be defined as

$$C + Xe^{-rt} = P + S. \quad (19.62)$$

Substituting Equation (19.33) into Equation (19.34), we obtain the put option formula as

$$P = Xe^{-rt}N(-d_2) - SN(-d_1), \quad (19.63)$$

where S, C, r, t, d_1, and d_2 are identical to those defined in the call option model.

19.7. The Bivariate Normal Density Function

In correlation analysis, we assume a population where both X and Y vary jointly. It is called a joint distribution of two variables. If both X and Y are normally distributed, then we call this known distribution a bivariate normal distribution.

We can define the PDF of the normally distributed random variables X and Y as

$$f(X) = \frac{1}{\sigma_X\sqrt{2\pi}} \exp\left[\frac{-(X-\mu_X)}{2\sigma_X^2}\right], \quad -\infty < X < \infty, \tag{19.64}$$

$$f(Y) = \frac{1}{\sigma_Y\sqrt{2\pi}} \exp\left[\frac{-(Y-\mu_Y)}{2\sigma_Y^2}\right], \quad -\infty < Y < \infty, \tag{19.65}$$

Where μ_X and μ_Y are population means for X and Y, respectively; σ_X and σ_Y are population standard deviations of X and Y, respectively; $\pi = 3.1416$; and exp represents the exponential function.

If ρ represents the population correlation between X and Y, then the PDF of the bivariate normal distribution can be defined as

$$f(X,Y) = \frac{1}{2\pi\sigma_X\sigma_Y\sqrt{1-\rho^2}} \exp(-q/2), \quad -\infty < X < \infty, -\infty < Y < \infty, \tag{19.66}$$

where $\sigma_X > 0$, $\sigma_Y > 0$, and $-1 < \rho < 1$,

$$q = \frac{1}{1-\rho^2}\left[\left(\left(\frac{X-\mu_X}{\sigma_X}\right)^2 - 2\rho\left(\frac{X-\mu_X}{\sigma_X}\right)\left(\frac{Y-\mu_Y}{\sigma_Y}\right) + \left(\frac{X-\mu_Y}{\sigma_Y}\right)^2\right)\right].$$

It can be shown that the conditional mean of Y, given X, is linear in X and given by

$$E(Y|X) = \mu_Y + \rho\left\{\frac{\sigma_Y}{\sigma_X}\right\}(X-\mu_X). \tag{19.67}$$

It is also clear that given X, we can define the conditional variance of Y as

$$\sigma(Y|X) = \sigma_Y^2(1-\rho^2). \tag{19.68}$$

Equation (19.67) can be regarded as describing the population linear regression line. For example, if we have a bivariate normal distribution of heights of brothers and sisters, we can see that they vary together and there is no cause-and-effect relationship. Accordingly, a linear regression in terms of the bivariate normal distribution variable is treated as though there were a two-way relationship instead of an existing causal relationship. It should be noted that regression implies a causal relationship only under a "prediction" case.

Equation (19.66) represents a joint PDF for X and Y. If $\rho = 0$, then Equation (19.66) becomes

$$f(X, Y) = f(X)f(Y). \tag{19.69}$$

This implies that the joint PDF of X and Y is equal to the PDF of X times the PDF of Y. We also know that both X and Y are normally distributed. Therefore, X is independent of Y.

Example 19.1

Using a Mathematics Aptitude Test to Predict Grade in Statistics

Let X and Y represent scores in a mathematics aptitude test and numerical grade in elementary statistics, respectively. In addition, we assume that the parameters in Equation (19.66) are

$$\mu_X = 550 \quad \sigma_X = 40 \quad \mu_Y = 80 \quad \sigma_Y = 4 \quad \rho = 0.7.$$

Substituting this information into Equations (19.67) and (19.68), respectively, we obtain

$$E(Y|X) = 80 + 0.7(4/40)(X - 550) = 41.5 + 0.07X, \tag{19.70}$$

$$\sigma^2(Y|X) = (16)(1 - 0.49) = 8.16. \tag{19.71}$$

If we know nothing about the aptitude test score of a particular student (say, John), we have to use the distribution of Y to predict his elementary statistics grade.

$$95\% \text{ interval} = 80 \pm (1.96)(4) = 80 \pm 7.84.$$

That is, we predict with 95% probability that John's grade will fall between 87.84 and 72.16.

Alternatively, suppose we know that John's mathematics aptitude score is 650. In this case, we can use Equations (19.70) and (19.71) to predict John's grade in elementary statistics.

$$E(Y|X = 650) = 41.5 + (0.07)(650) = 87,$$

and

$$\sigma^2(Y|X) = (16)(1 - 0.49) = 8.16.$$

We can now base our interval on a normal probability distribution with a mean of 87 and a standard deviation of 2.86.

$$95\% \text{ interval} = 87 \pm (1.96)(2.86) = 87 \pm 5.61.$$

That is, we predict with 95% probability that John's grade will fall between 92.61 and 81.39.

Two things have happened to this interval. First, the center has shifted upward to take into account the fact that John's mathematics aptitude score is above average. Second, the width of the interval has been narrowed from $87.84 - 72.16 = 15.68$ grade points to $92.61 - 81.39 = 11.22$ grade points. In this sense, the information about John's mathematics aptitude score has made us less uncertain about his grade in statistics.

19.8. American Call Options

19.8.1. *Price American Call Options by the Bivariate Normal Distribution*

An option contract which can be exercised only on the expiration date is called European call. If the contract of a call option can be exercised at any time of the option's contract period, then this kind of call option is called American call.

When a stock pays a dividend, the American call is more complex. Following Whaley (1981), the valuation equation for American call option with one known dividend payment can be defined as

$$\begin{aligned} C(S,T,X) &= S^x[N_1(b_1) + N_2(a_1, -b_1; -\sqrt{t/T})] \\ &\quad - Xe^{-rt}[N1(b_2)e^{r(T-t)} + N_2(a_2, -b_2; -\sqrt{t/T})] \qquad (19.72\text{a}) \\ &\quad + De^{-rt}N_1(b_2), \end{aligned}$$

where

$$a_1 = \frac{\ln\left(\frac{S^x}{X}\right) + \left(r + \frac{1}{2}\sigma^2\right)T}{\sigma\sqrt{T}}, \quad a_2 = a_1 - \sigma\sqrt{T}, \qquad (19.72\text{b})$$

$$b_1 = \frac{\ln\left(\frac{S^x}{S_t^*}\right) + \left(r + \frac{1}{2}\sigma^2\right)t}{\sigma\sqrt{t}}, \quad b_2 = b_1 - \sigma\sqrt{t}, \qquad (19.72\text{c})$$

$$S^x = S - De^{-rt}, \qquad (19.73)$$

S^x represents the correct stock net price of the present value of the promised dividend per share (D); t represents the time dividend to be paid.

S_t^* is the exdividend stock price for which

$$C(S_t^*, T-t) = S_t^* + D - X. \tag{19.74}$$

S, X, r, σ^2, T have been defined previously in this chapter.

Both $N_1(b_1)$ and $N_2(b_2)$ are cumulative univariate normal density function; $N_2(a, b; \rho)$ is the cumulative bivariate normal density function with upper integral limits, a and b, and correlation coefficient, $\rho = -\sqrt{t/T}$.

American call option on a nondividend-paying stock will never optimally be exercised prior to expiration. Therefore, if no dividend payments exist, Equation (19.72) will reduce to European Option pricing model with no dividend payment.

We have shown how the cumulative univariate normal density function can be used to evaluate the European call option in previous sections of this chapter. If a common stock pays a discrete dividend during the option's life, the American call option valuation equation requires the evaluation of a cumulative bivariate normal density function. While there are many available approximations for the cumulative bivariate normal distribution, the approximation provided here relies on Gaussian quadratures. The approach is straightforward and efficient, and its maximum absolute error is 0.00000055.

Following Equation (19.66), the probability that $x^{'}$ is less than a and that $y^{'}$ is less than b for the standardized cumulative bivariate normal distribution

$$P(X^{'} < a, Y^{'} < b)$$

$$= \frac{1}{2\pi\sqrt{1-\rho^2}} \int_{-\infty}^{a} \int_{-\infty}^{b} \exp\left[\frac{2x^{'2} - 2\rho x^{'} y^{'} + y^{'2}}{2(1-\rho^2)}\right] dx^{'} dy^{'},$$

where $x^{'} = \frac{x-\mu_x}{\sigma_x}$, $y^{'} = \frac{y-\mu_y}{\sigma_y}$ and p is the correlation between the random variables $x^{'}$ and $y^{'}$.

The first step in the approximation of the bivariate normal probability $N_2(a, b; \rho)$ is as follows:

$$\varphi(a, b; \rho) \approx 0.31830989\sqrt{1-\rho^2} \sum_{i=1}^{5} \sum_{j=1}^{5} w_i w_j f(x_i^{'}, x_j^{'}), \tag{19.75}$$

where

$$f(x_i^{'}, x_j^{'}) = \exp[a_1(2x_i^{'} - a_1) + b_1(2x_j^{'} - b_1) + 2\rho(x_i^{'} - a_1)(x_j^{'} - b_1)].$$

The pairs of weights, (w) and corresponding abscissa values $(x^{'})$ are

i, j	w	$x^{'}$
1	0.24840615	0.10024215
2	0.39233107	0.48281397
3	0.21141819	1.0609498
4	0.033246660	1.7797294
5	0.00082485334	2.6697604

(This portion is based upon Appendix 13.1 of Stoll H. R. and R. E Whaley. *Futures and Options*. Cincinnati, OH: South Western Publishing, 1993.)

and the coefficients a_1 and b_1 are computed using

$$a_1 = \frac{a}{\sqrt{2(1-\rho^2)}} \quad \text{and} \quad b_1 = \frac{b}{\sqrt{2(1-\rho^2)}}.$$

The second step in the approximation involves computing the product $ab\rho$; if $ab\rho \leq 0$, compute the bivariate normal probability,$N_2(a, b; \rho)$, using the following rules:

(1) If a ≤ 0, b ≤ 0, and $\rho \leq 0$, then $N_2(a, b; \rho) = \varphi(a, b; \rho)$;
(2) If a ≤ 0, b ≥ 0, and $\rho > 0$, then $N_2(a, b; \rho) = N_1(a) - \varphi(a, -b; -\rho)$;
(3) If a ≥ 0, b ≤ 0, and $\rho > 0$, then $N_2(a, b; \rho) = N_1(b) - \varphi(-a, b; -\rho)$;
(4) If a ≥ 0, b ≥ 0, and $\rho \leq 0$, then $N_2(a, b; \rho) = N_1(a) + N_1(b) - 1 + \varphi(-a, -b; \rho)$. (19.76)

If $ab\rho > 0$, compute the bivariate normal probability, $N_2(a, b; \rho)$, as

$$N_2(a, b; \rho) = N_2(a, 0; \rho_{ab}) + N_2(b, 0; \rho_{ab}) - \delta, \tag{19.77}$$

where the values of $N_2(\bullet)$ on the right-hand side are computed from the rules, for $ab\rho \leq 0$

$$\rho_{ab} = \frac{(\rho a - b)Sgn(a)}{\sqrt{a^2 - 2\rho ab + b^2}}, \quad \rho_{ba} = \frac{(\rho b - a)Sgn(b)}{\sqrt{a^2 - 2\rho ab + b^2}},$$

$$\delta = \frac{1 - Sgn(a) \times Sgn(b)}{4},$$

and

$$Sgn(x) = \begin{cases} 1 & x \geq 0 \\ -1 & x < 0 \end{cases},$$

$N_1(d)$ is the cumulative univariate normal probability.

19.8.2. *Pricing an American Call Option: An Example*

An American call option whose exercise price is \$48 has an expiration time of 90 days. Assume the risk-free rate of interest is 8% annually, the underlying price is \$50, the standard deviation of the rate of return of the stock is 20%, and the stock pays a dividend of \$2 exactly for 50 days. (a) What is the European call value? (b) Can the early exercise price predicted? (c) What is the value of the American call?

(a) The current stock net price of the present value of the promised dividend is

$$S^x = 50 - 2e^{-0.08(50/365)} = 48.0218.$$

The European call value can be calculated as

$$C = (48.0218)N(d_1) - 48e^{-0.08(90/365)}N(d_2),$$

where

$$d_1 = \frac{[\ln(48.208/48) + (0.08 + 0.5(0.20)^2)(90/365)]}{0.20\sqrt{90/365}} = 0.25285$$

$$d_2 = 0.292 - 0.0993 = 0.15354.$$

From standard normal table, we obtain

$$N(0.25285) = 0.5 + 0.3438 = 0.599809$$

$$N(0.15354) = 0.5 + 0.3186 = 0.561014.$$

So the European call value is

$$C = (48.516)(0.599809) - 48(0.980)(0.561014) = 2.40123.$$

(b) The present value of the interest income that would be earned by deferring exercise until expiration is

$$X(1 - e^{-r(T-t)}) = 48(1 - e^{-0.08(90-50)/365}) = 48(1 - 0.991) = 0.432.$$

Since $d = 2 > 0.432$, therefore, the early exercise is not precluded.

(c) The value of the American call is now calculated as

$$C = 48.208[N_1(b_1) + N_2(a_1, -b_1; \sqrt{50/90})]$$
$$- 48e^{-0.08(90/365)}[N_1(b_2)e^{-0.08(40/365)} + N_2(a_2, -b_2; -\sqrt{50/90})]$$
$$+ 2e^{-0.08(50/365)}N_1(b_2) \quad (19.78)$$

since both b_1 and b_2 depend on the critical exdividend stock price S_t^*, which can be determined by

$$C(S_t^*, 40/365; 48) = S_t^* + 2 - 48.$$

By using trial and error, we find that $S_t^* = 46.9641$. An Excel program used to calculate this value is presented in Table 19.1.

Table 19.1. Calculation of S_t^* (Critical Exdividend Stock Price).

S^*(critical exdividend stock price)	46	46.962	46.963	46.9641	46.9	47
X(exercise price of option)	48	48	48	48	48	48
r(risk-free interest rate)	0.08	0.08	0.08	0.08	0.08	0.08
volalitity of stock	0.2	0.2	0.2	0.2	0.2	0.2
$T-t$(expiration date-exercise date)	0.10959	0.10959	0.10959	0.10959	0.10959	0.10959
d_1	−0.4773	−0.1647	−0.1644	−0.164	−0.1846	−0.1525
d_2	−0.5435	−0.2309	−0.2306	−0.2302	−0.2508	−0.2187
D(divent)	2	2	2	2	2	2
c(value of European call option to buy one share)	0.60263	0.96319	0.96362	0.9641	0.93649	0.9798
p(value of European put option to sell one share)	2.18365	1.58221	1.58164	1.58102	1.61751	1.56081
$C(S_t^*, T-t; X) - St^* - D + X$	0.60263	0.00119	0.00062	$2.3E{-06}$	0.03649	−0.0202

(Continued)

Table 19.1. (*Continued*)

	Calculation of S_t^* (critical exdividend stock price)	
1*		Column C*
2		
3	S^*(critical exdividend stock price)	46
4	X(exercise price of option)	48
5	r(risk-free interest rate)	0.08
6	volatility of stock	0.2
7	$T-t$(expiration date-exercise date)	= (90 – 50)/365
8	d_1	=(LN(C3/C4) + (C5 + C6^2/2)*(C7))/(C6*SQRT(C7))
9	d_2	=(LN(C3/C4) + (C5 – C6^2/2)*(C7))/(C6*SQRT(C7))
10	D(divent)	2
11		
12	c(value of European call option to buy one share)	= C3*NORMSDIST(C8)–C4*EXP(–C5*C7)*NORMSDIST(C9)
13	p(value of European put option to sell one share)	= C4*EXP(–C5*C7)*NORMSDIST(–C9)–C3*NORMSDIST(–C8)
14		
15	$C(S_t^*, T-t; X) - S_t^* - D + X$	$= C12 - C3 - C10 + C4$

* The table above shows the number of the row and the column in the excel sheet.

Substituting $S^x = 48.208$, $X = \$48$ and S_t^* into Equations (19.72b) and (19.72c), we can calculate a_1, a_2, b_1, and b_2:

$$a_1 = d_1 = 0.25285.$$

$$a_2 = d_2 = 0.15354.$$

$$b_1 = \frac{\ln\left(\frac{48.208}{46.9641}\right) + \left(0.08 + \frac{0.2^2}{2}\right)\left(\frac{50}{365}\right)}{(0.20)\sqrt{50/365}} = 0.4859.$$

$$b_2 = 0.485931 - 0.074023 = 0.4119.$$

In addition, we also know $\rho = -\sqrt{50/90} = -0.7454$.

From the above information, we now calculate related normal probability as follows:

$$N_1(b_1) = N_1(0.4859) = 0.6865$$

$$N_1(b_2) = N_1(0.7454) = 0.6598$$

Following Equation (19.77), we now calculate the value of $N_2(0.25285, -0.4859; -0.7454)$ and $N_2(0.15354, -0.4119; -0.7454$ as follows:

Since $ab\rho > 0$ for both cumulative bivariate normal density function, therefore, we can use Equation $N_2(a, b; \rho) = N_2(a, 0; \rho_{ab}) + N_2(b, 0; \rho_{ba}) - \delta$ to calculate the value of both $N_2(a, b; \rho)$ as follows:

$$\begin{aligned}\rho_{ab} &= \frac{[(-0.7454)(0.25285) + 0.4859](1)}{\sqrt{(0.25285)^2 - 2(0.7454)(0.25285)(-0.4859) + (0.4859)^2}} \\ &= 0.87002 \\ \rho_{ba} &= \frac{[(-0.7454)(-0.4859) - 0.25285](1)}{\sqrt{(0.25285)^2 - 2(0.7454)(0.25285)(-0.4859) + (0.4859)^2}} \\ &= -0.31979 \\ \delta &= (1 - (1)(-1))/4 = 1/2\end{aligned}$$

$$\begin{aligned}&\mathrm{N}_2(0.292, -0.4859; -0.7454) \\ &\quad = \mathrm{N}_2(0.292, 0.0844) + \mathrm{N}_2(-0.5377, 0.0656) - 0.5 \\ &\quad = \mathrm{N}_1(0) + \mathrm{N}_1(-0.5377) - \Phi(-0.292, 0; -0.0844) \\ &\qquad - \Phi(-0.5377, 0; -0.0656) - 0.5 = 0.07525\end{aligned}$$

Using a Microsoft Excel program presented in Appendix 19A, we obtain

$$\mathrm{N}_2(0.1927, -0.4119; -0.7454) = 0.06862.$$

Then substituting the related information into the Equation (19.78), we obtain $C = \$3.08238$ and all related results are presented in Appendix 19B.

19.9. Price Bounds for Options

19.9.1. *Options Written on Nondividend-Paying Stocks*

To derive the lower price bounds and the put–call parity relations for options on nondividend-paying stocks, simply set the cost-of-carry rate, b, equal to the risk-less rate of interest, r. Note that the only cost of carrying the stock is interest.

The lower price bounds for the European call and put options are

$$c(S,T;X) \geq \max[0, S - Xe^{-rT}], \quad (19.79a)$$

and

$$p(S,T;X) \geq \max[0, Xe^{-rT} - S], \quad (19.79b)$$

respectively, and the lower price bounds for the American call and put options are

$$C(S,T;X) \geq \max[0, S - Xe^{-rT}], \quad (19.80a)$$

and

$$P(S,T;X) \geq \max[0, Xe^{-rT} - S], \quad (19.80b)$$

respectively. The put–call parity relation for nondividend-paying European stock options is

$$c(S,T;X) - p(S,T;X) = S - Xe^{-rT}, \quad (19.81a)$$

and the put–call parity relation for American options on nondividend-paying stocks is

$$S - X \leq C(S,T;X) - P(S,T;X) \leq S - Xe^{-rT}. \quad (19.81b)$$

For nondividend-paying stock options, the American call option will not rationally be exercised early, while the American put option may be done so.

19.9.2. *Options Written on Dividend-Paying Stocks*

If dividends are paid during the option's life, the above relations must reflect the stock's drop in value when the dividends are paid. To manage this modification, we assume that the underlying stock pays a single dividend during the option's life at a time that is known with certainty. The dividend amount is D and the time to exdividend is t.

If the amount and the timing of the dividend payment are known, the lower price bound for the European call option on a stock is

$$c(S,T;X) \geq \max[0, S - De^{-rt} - Xe^{-rT}]. \quad (19.82a)$$

In this relation, the current stock price is reduced by the present value of the promised dividend. Because a European-style option cannot be exercised before maturity, the call option holder has no opportunity to exercise the option while the stock is selling cum dividend. In other words, to the call option holder, the current value of the underlying stock is its observed market price less the amount that the promised dividend contributes to the current stock value, that is, $S - De^{-rt}$. To prove this pricing relation, we use the same arbitrage transactions, except we use the reduced stock price $S - De^{-rt}$ in place of S. The lower price bound for the European put option on a stock is

$$p(S, T; X) \geq \max[0, Xe^{-rT} - S - De^{-rt}]. \tag{19.82b}$$

Again, the stock price is reduced by the present value of the promised dividend. Unlike the call option case, however, this serves to increase the lower price bound of the European put option. Because the put option is the right to sell the underlying stock at a fixed price, a discrete drop in the stock price, such as that induced by the payment of a dividend, serves to increase the value of the option. An arbitrage proof of this relation is straightforward when the stock price, net of the present value of the dividend is used in place of the commodity price.

The lower price bounds for American stock options are slightly more complex. In the case of the American call option, for example, it may be optimal to exercise just prior to the dividend payment because the stock price falls by an amount D when the dividend is paid. The lower price bound of an American call option expiring at the exdividend instant would be 0 or$S - Xe^{-rt}$, whichever is greater. On the other hand, it may be optimal to wait until the call option's expiration to exercise. The lower price bound for a call option expiring normally is (19.82a). Combining the two results, we get

$$C(S, T; X) \geq \max[0, S - Xe^{-rt}, S - De^{-rt} - Xe^{-rT}]. \tag{19.83a}$$

The last two terms on the right-hand side of (19.83a) provide important guidance in deciding whether to exercise the American call option early, just prior to the exdividend instant. The second term in the squared brackets is the present value of the early exercise proceeds of the call. If the amount is less than the lower price bound of the call that expires normally, that is, if

$$S - Xe^{-rt} \leq S - De^{-rT} - Xe^{-rt}, \tag{19.84}$$

the American call option will not be exercised just prior to the exdividend instant.

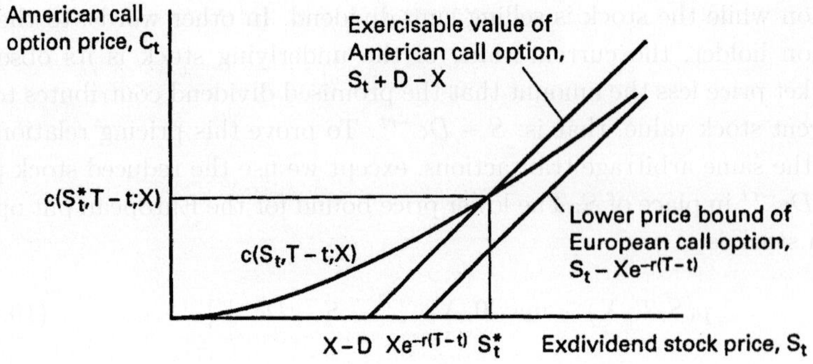

Fig. 19.3. American Call Option Price as a Function of the Exdividend Stock Price Immediately Prior to the Exdividend Instant. Early Exercise may be Optimal.

To see why, simply rewrite (19.84) so it reads

$$D < X[1 - e^{-r(T-t)}]. \tag{19.85}$$

In other words, the American call will not be exercised early if the dividend captured by exercising prior to the exdividend date is less than the interest implicitly earned by deferring exercise until expiration.

Figure 19.3 depicts a case in which early exercise could occur at the exdividend instant, t. Just prior to exdividend, the call option may be exercised, yielding proceeds $S_t + D - X$, where S_t, is the exdividend stock price. An instant later, the option is left unexercised with value $c(S_t, T - t; X)$, where $c(\cdot)$ is the European call option formula. Thus, if the exdividend stock price, S_t is above the critical exdividend stock price where the two functions intersect, S_t^*, the option holder will choose to exercise his or her option early just prior to the exdividend instant. On the other hand, if $S_t \leq S_t^*$, the option holder will choose to leave her position open until the option's expiration.

Figure 19.4 depicts a case in which early exercise will not occur at the exdividend instant, t. Early exercise will not occur if the functions, $S_t + D - X$ and $c(S_t, T-t; X)$ do not intersect, as is depicted in Fig. 19.4. In this case, the lower boundary condition of the European call, $S_t - Xe^{-r(T-t)}$, lies above the early exercise proceeds, $S_t + D - X$, and hence the call option will not be exercised early. Stated explicitly, early exercise is not rational if

$$S_t + D - X < S_t - Xe^{-r(T-t)}.$$

This condition for no early exercise is the same as (19.84), where S_t is the exdividend stock price and where the investor is standing at the exdividend

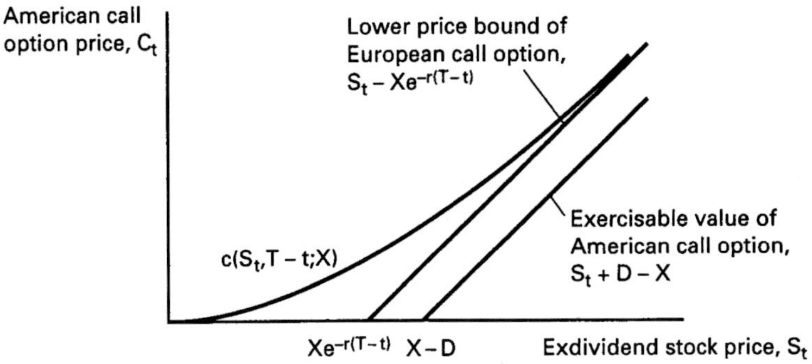

Fig. 19.4. American Call Option Price as a Function of the Exdividend Stock Price Immediately Prior to the Exdividend Instant. Early Exercise will not be Optimal.

instant, t. The condition can also be written as

$$D < X[1 - e^{-r(T-t)}]. \tag{19.85}$$

In other words, if the exdividend stock price decline — the dividend — is less than the present value of the interest income that would be earned by deferring exercise until expiration, early exercise will not occur. When condition (19.85) is met, the value of the American call is simply the value of the corresponding European call.

The lower price bound of an American put option is somewhat different. In the absence of a dividend, an American put may be exercised early. In the presence of a dividend payment, however, there is a period just prior to the exdividend date when early exercise is suboptimal. In that period, the interest earned on the exercise proceeds of the option is less than the drop in the stock price from the payment of the dividend. If t_n represents a time prior to the dividend payment at time t, early exercise is suboptimal, where $(X - S)e^{-r(t-t_n)}$ is less than $(X - S + D)$. Rearranging, early exercise will not occur between $t_n$and t if[3]

$$t_n > t - \frac{\ln\left(1 + \frac{D}{X-S}\right)}{r}. \tag{19.86}$$

[3]It is possible that the dividend payment is so large that early exercise prior to the dividend payment is completely precluded. For example, consider the case where $X = 50$, $S = 40$, $D = 1$, $t = 0.25$, and $r = 0.10$. Early exercise is precluded if $r, = 0.25 - \ln[1 - 1/(50-40)]/0.10 = -0.7031$. Because the value is negative, the implication is that there is no time during the current dividend period (i.e., from 0 to t) where it will not pay the American put option holder to wait until the dividend is paid to exercise his option.

Early exercise will become a possibility again immediately after the dividend is paid. Overall, the lower price bound of the American put option is

$$P(S,T;X) \geq \max[o, X - (S - De^{-rt})]. \tag{19.83b}$$

Put–call parity for European options on dividend-paying stocks also reflects the fact that the current stock price is deflated by the present value of the promised dividend, that is

$$c(S,T;X) - p(S,T;X) = S - De^{-rt} - Xe^{-rT}. \tag{19.87}$$

That the presence of the dividend reduces the value of the call and increases the value of the put is again reflected here by the fact that the term on the right-hand side of (19.87) is smaller than it would be if the stock paid no dividend.

Put–call parity for American options on dividend-paying stocks is represented by a pair of inequalities, that is

$$S - De^{-rt} - X \leq C(S,T;X) - P(S,T;X) \leq S - De^{-rt} - Xe^{-rT}. \tag{19.88}$$

To prove the put–call parity relation (19.88), we consider each inequality in turn. The left-hand side condition of (19.88) can be derived by considering the values of a portfolio that consists of buying a call, selling a put, selling the stock, and lending $X + De^{-rt}$ risklessly. Table 19.2 contains these portfolio values.

In Table 19.2, it can be seen that, if all of the security positions stay open until expiration, the terminal value of the portfolio will be positive, independent of whether the terminal stock price is above or below the exercise price of the options. If the terminal stock price is above the exercise price, the call option is exercised, and the stock acquired at exercise price X is used to deliver, in part, against the short stock position. If the terminal stock price is below the exercise price, the put is exercised. The stock received in the exercise of the put is used to cover the short stock position established at the outset. In the event the put is exercised early at time T, the investment in the riskless bonds is more than sufficient to cover the payment of the exercise price to the put option holder, and the stock received from the exercise of the put is used to cover the stock sold when the portfolio was formed. In addition, an open call option position that may still have value remains.

In other words, by forming the portfolio of securities in the proportions noted above, we have formed a portfolio that will never have a negative

Table 19.2. Arbitrage Transactions for Establishing Put–Call Parity for American Stock Options.

$$S - De^{-rt} - X \leq C(S,T;X) - P(S,T;X)$$

		Exdividend Day (t)	Put Exercised Early (γ)	Put Exercised Normally (T)	
Position	Initial Value		Intermediate Value	Terminal Value $\tilde{S}_T \leq X$	$\tilde{S}_T > X$
Buy American Call	$-C$		$\tilde{C}_\gamma$	0	$\tilde{S}_T - X$
Sell American Put	P		$-(X - \tilde{S}_\gamma)$	$-(\tilde{X} - \tilde{S}_T)$	0
Sell Stock	S	$-D$	$-\tilde{S}_\gamma$	$-\tilde{S}_T$	$-\tilde{S}_T$
Lend De^{-rt}	$-De^{-rt}$	D		Xe^{rT}	Xe^{rT}
Lend X	$-X$		$Xe^{r\gamma}$		
Net Portfolio Value	$-C + P + S$ $-De^{-rt} - X$	0	$\tilde{C}_\gamma + X(e^{r\gamma} - 1)$	$X(e^{rT} - 1)$	$X(e^{rT} - 1)$

future value. If the future value is certain to be non-negative, the initial value must be nonpositive, or the left-hand inequality of (19.88) holds.

The right-hand side of (19.88) may be derived by considering the portfolio used to prove European put–call parity. Table 19.2 contains the arbitrage portfolio transactions. In this case, the terminal value of the portfolio is certain to equal zero, should the option positions stay open until that time. In the event the American call option holder decides to exercise the call option early, the portfolio holder uses his long stock position to cover his stock obligation on the exercised call and uses the exercise proceeds to retire his outstanding debt. After these actions are taken, the portfolio holder still has an open long put position and cash in the amount of $X[1 - e^{-r(T-t)}]$. Since the portfolio is certain to have non-negative outcomes, the initial value must be nonpositive or the right-hand inequality of (19.88) must hold.

19.10. Summary

In this chapter, we first introduced univariate and multivariate normal distribution and log-normal distribution. Then we showed how normal distribution can be used to approximate binomial distribution. Finally, we used the concepts normal and log-normal distributions to derive

Black–Scholes formula under the assumption that investors are risk neutral.

In this chapter, we first reviewed the basic concept of the Bivariate normal density function and presented the Bivariate normal CDF. The theory of American call stock option pricing model for one dividend payment was also presented. The evaluations of stock option models without dividend payment and with dividend payment were discussed, respectively. Finally, we provided an excel program for evaluating American option pricing model with one dividend payment.

Questions and Problems

1. Briefly explain the relationship between the normal distribution and the binomial distribution in valuing stock call options.
2. Briefly describe the relationship between the expected stock return and risk-free rate under the risk neutral assumption.
3. What does the Black–Scholes stock option model assume about the probability distribution of the stock price?
4. Let X follow the normal distribution with mean $\mu = 0$ and variance $\sigma^2 = 1$, find the following probabilities.

   (a) $P(X > 1.65)$
   (b) $P(X < -2.38)$
   (c) $P(X > -1.37)$
   (d) $P(-2.43 < X < 1.72)$.

5. As the assumption in question1, find the following values of z.

   (a) $P(X < z) = 0.99$
   (b) $P(X > z) = 0.05$
   (c) $P(z < X < 0) = 0.0130$
   (d) $P(-z < X < z) = 0.5408$.

6. Let Y follow the normal distribution with a mean of 5 and a standard deviation of 2. Find the probabilities as follows:

   (d) Y is between 5 and 9.
   (b) Y is between -1 and 3.
   (c) Y is greater than 6.
   (d) Y is less than 10.

7. The manager in the local bank discovers that people come in to cash their pay checks on Friday. The amount of money withdrawn on Friday

follows a normal distribution with 6 million as the mean and 1 million as the standard deviation. The bank manager wants to make sure that the amount money in the bank can cover 99.9% of the Friday withdrawals. What is the minimum amount of money he or she should plan to have on hand?

8. A consumer rights organization wants to find out whether a local dairy farm actually puts 20 ounces of milk into a container that is labeled 20 ounces. Assume the milk put into the container by the local dairy farm follows a normal distribution with a mean of 20.05 and a standard deviation of 0.05.
   (a) What is the probability that a certain container contains more than 20 ounces of milk?
   (b) The consumer rights organization bought 400 bottles of milk. What is the probability that among them, it found fewer than 12 bottles that do not contain enough milk?
9. Use the Black–Scholes option formula to price the value of call option under the assumption as follows:

$$S = \$105$$
$$X = \$110$$
$$r = 0.05$$
$$t = 0.8$$
$$\sigma = 0.45.$$

10. In question 9, what is the value of call option when $X = \$90$? Briefly describe the relationship between the strike price and call option in terms of the probability following the log-normal distribution.

Appendix 19A: Microsoft Excel Program for Calculating Cumulative Bivariate Normal Density Function

```
Option Explicit

Public Function Bivarncdf(a As Double, b As Double, rho As Double) As Double

    Dim rho_ab As Double, rho_ba As Double
    Dim delta As Double

    If (a * b * rho) <= 0 Then

        If (a <= 0 And b <= 0 And rho <= 0) Then
            Bivarncdf = Phi(a, b, rho)
        End If
```

```
        If (a <= 0 And b >= 0 And rho > 0) Then
            Bivarncdf = Application.WorksheetFunction.NormSDist(a) - Phi(a, -b, -rho)
        End If

        If (a >= 0 And b <= 0 And rho > 0) Then
            Bivarncdf = Application.WorksheetFunction.NormSDist(b) - Phi(-a, b, -rho)
        End If

        If (a >= 0 And b >= 0 And rho <= 0) Then
            Bivarncdf = Application.WorksheetFunction.NormSDist(a) +
Application.WorksheetFunction.NormSDist(b) - 1 + Phi(-a, -b, rho)
        End If
    Else

        rho_ab = ((rho * a - b) * IIf(a >= 0, 1, -1)) / Sqr(a ^ 2 - 2 * rho * a * b + b ^ 2)
        rho_ba = ((rho * b - a) * IIf(b >= 0, 1, -1)) / Sqr(a ^ 2 - 2 * rho * a * b + b ^ 2)
        delta = (1 - IIf(a >= 0, 1, -1) * IIf(b >= 0, 1, -1)) / 4
        Bivarncdf = Bivarncdf(a, 0, rho_ab) + Bivarncdf(b, 0, rho_ba) - delta

    End If
End Function

Public Function Phi(a As Double, b As Double, rho As Double) As Double

    Dim a1 As Double, b1 As Double
    Dim w(5) As Double, x(5) As Double
    Dim i As Integer, j As Integer
    Dim doublesum As Double

    a1 = a / Sqr(2 * (1 - rho^2))
    b1=b/Sqr(2*(1-rho^2))

    w(1) = 0.24840615
    w(2) = 0.39233107
    w(3) = 0.21141819
    w(4) = 0.03324666
    w(5) = 0.00082485334

    x(1) = 0.10024215
    x(2) = 0.48281397
    x(3) = 1.0609498
    x(4) = 1.7797294
    x(5) = 2.6697604

    doublesum = 0

    For i = 1 To 5
        For j = 1 To 5
        doublesum = doublesum + w(i)*w(j)*Exp(a1*(2*x(i) - a1) + b1*(2*x(j) - b1)
+ 2 * rho * (x(i) - a1) * (x(j) - b1))
        Next j
    Next i

    Phi = 0.31830989 * Sqr(1 - rho ^ 2) * doublesum

End Function
```

Appendix 19B: Microsoft Excel Program for Calculating the American Call Options

Number*	A	B	C*
1	Option Pricing Calculation		
2			
3	S(current stock price) =	50	
4	S_t^* (critical exdividend stock price) =	46.9641	
5	S(current stock price NPV of promised dividend) =	48.0218	=B3 – B11*EXP(–B7*B10)
6	X(exercise price of option) =	48	
7	r(risk-free interest rate) =	0.08	
8	σ(volatility of stock) =	0.2	
9	T(expiration date) =	0.24658	
10	t (Exercise date) =	0.13699	
11	D(Dividend) =	2	
12	d_1(nondividend-paying) =	0.65933	= (LN(B3/B6) + (B7 + 0.5* B8ˆ2)*B9)/(B8*SQRT(B9))
13	d_2(nondividend-paying) =	0.56001	= B12 – B8*SQRT(B9)
14	d_1*(critical exdividend stock price) =	–0.16401	= (LN(B4/B6) + (B7 + 0.5* B8ˆ2)*(B9 – B10))/ (B8*SQRT (B9 – B10))
15	d_2*(critical exdividend stock price) =	–0.23022	= B14 – B8*SQRT (B9 – B10)

(*Continued*)

Number*	A	B	C*
16	d_1(dividend-paying) =	0.25285	=(LN(B5/B6) +(B7+0.5* B8^2)*(B9))/(B8*SQRT(B9))
17	d_2(dividend-paying) =	0.15354	=B16 − B8*SQRT(B9)
18	$a_1 =$	0.25285	=(LN((B3 − B11*EXP(−B7*B10))/B6) + (B7 +0.5*B8^2)*(B9))/(B8*SQRT(B9))
19	$a_2 =$	0.15354	=B18 − B8*SQRT(B9)
20	$b_1 =$	0.48593	=(LN((B3 − B11*EXP(−B7*B10))/B4) +(B7+0.5*B8^2)*(B10))/(B8*SQRT(B10))
21	$b_2 =$	0.41191	=B20 − B8*SQRT(B10)
22			
23	$C(S_t^*, T-t; X) =$	0.9641	=B4*NORMSDIST(B14) − B6*EXP(−B7*(B9 − B10)) *NORMSDIST(B15)
24	$C(S_t^*, T-t; X) - S_t^* - D + X =$	$2.3E-06$	=B23 − B4 − B11 + B6
25			
26	$N_1(a_1) =$	0.59981	=NORMSDIST(B18)
27	$N_1(a_2) =$	0.56101	=NORMSDIST(B19)
28	$N_1(b_1) =$	0.68649	=NORMSDIST(B20)
29	$N_1(b_2) =$	0.6598	=NORMSDIST(B21)
30	$N_1(-b_1) =$	0.31351	=NORMSDIST(−B20)
31	$N_1(-b_2) =$	0.3402	=NORMSDIST(−B21)
32	$\rho =$	−0.74536	= −SQRT(B10/B9)
33	$a = a_1; b = -b_1$		
34	$\Phi(a, -b; -\rho) =$	0.20259	=phi(−B20, 0, −B37)
35	$\Phi(-a, b; -\rho) =$	0.04084	=phi(−B18, 0, −B36)

(*Continued*)

Number*	A	B	C*
36	$\rho ab =$	0.87002	=((B32*B18−(−B20))*IF(B18 >= 0, 1, −1))/SQRT(B 18^2 − 2*B32 *B18*− B20 + (−B20)^2)
37	$\rho ba =$	−0.31979	=((B32*−B20 − (B18))*IF (−B20 >= 0,1,−1))/SQRT (B18^2 − 2*B32*B18*−B20 + (−B20)^2)
38	$N_2(a, 0; \rho ab) =$	0.45916	= bivarncdf(B18, 0, B36)
39	$N_2(b, 0; \rho ba) =$	0.11092	= bivarncdf(−B20, 0, B37)
40	$\delta =$	0.5	=(1−IF(B18 >= 0, 1, −1)* IF(−B20 >= 0, 1, −1))/4
41	$a = a_2; b = b_2$		
42	$\Phi(a, -b; -\rho) =$	0.24401	= phi(−B21, 0, −B45)
43	$\Phi(-a, b; -\rho) =$	0.02757	= phi(−B19, 0, −B44)
44	$\rho ab =$	0.94558	=((B32* B19−(−B21))* IF(B19 >= 0, 1, −1))/SQRT (B19^2 − 2*B32* B19*−B21 + (−B21)^2)
45	$\rho ba =$	−0.48787	= ((B32*−B21 − (B19))* IF(−B21 >= 0, 1, −1))/SQRT (B19^2 − 2* B32* B19*−B21 + (−B21)^2)
46	$N_2(a, 0; \rho ab) =$	0.47243	= bivarncdf(B19,0,B44)
47	$N_2(b, 0; \rho ba) =$	0.09619	= bivarncdf(−B21,0,B45)
48	$\delta =$	0.5	= (1−IF(B19 >= 0,1,−1)* IF(−B21 >= 0,1,−1))/4
49			
50	$N_2(a_1, -b_1; \rho) =$	0.07007	= bivarncdf(B18,−B20,B32)
51	$N_2(a_2, -b_2; \rho) =$	0.06862	= bivarncdf(B19,−B21,B32)
52			
53	***c* (value of European call option to buy one share)**	2.40123	=B5*NORMSDIST(B16) − B6*EXP(−B7*B9)*NO RMSDIST(B17)

(*Continued*)

Number*	A	B	C*
54	***p* (value of European put option to sell one share)**	1.44186	= –B5*NORMSDIST(–B16) + B6*EXP(–B7*B9)*NO RMSDIST(–B17)
55	***c* (value of American call option to buy one share)**	3.08238	=(B3 – B11*EXP (–B7*B10))* (NORMSDIST(B20) + bivarncdf(B18, –B20, –SQRT(B10/B9)))–B6*EXP (–B7*B9)*(NORMSDIST (B21)*EXP(B7*(B9 – B10)) + bivarncdf(B19, –B21, –SQRT(B10/B9))) + B11*EXP (–B7*B10)*NORMSDIST (B21)

* The table shows the number of the row and the column in the excel sheet.

Bibliography

Anderson, T. W. *An Introduction to Multivariate Statistical Analysis*, 3rd ed. New York: Wiley-Interscience, 2003.

Cox, J. C. and S. A. Ross. "The Valuation of Options for Alternative Stochastic Processes." *Journal of Financial Economics*, v. 3 (January–March 1976), pp. 145–166.

Cox, J., S. Ross and M. Rubinstein. "Option Pricing: A Simplified Approach." *Journal of Financial Economics*, v. 7 (1979), pp. 229–263.

Johnson, N. L. and S. Kotz. *Distributions in Statistics: Continuous Multivariate Distributions.* New York: Wiley, 1972.

Johnson, N. L. and S. Kotz. *Distributions in Statistics: Continuous Univariate Distributions 2.* New York: Wiley, 1970.

Rubinstein, M. "The Valuation of Uncertain Income Streams and the Pricing of Options." *Bell Journal of Economics and Management Science*, v. 7 (1976), 407–425.

Whaley, R. E. "On the Valuation of American Call Options on Stocks with Known Dividends." *Journal of Financial Economics*, v. 9 (1981), pp. 207–211.

Stoll, H. R. "The Relationship Between Put and Call Option Prices." *Journal of Finance*, v. 24 (December 1969), pp. 801–824.

Chapter 20

Comparative Static Analysis of the Option Pricing Models

In Chapter 17, we have discussed how the call option value can be affected by stock price per share, exercise price per share, the contract period of the option, the risk-free rate, and the volatility of the stock return. In this chapter, we will mathematically analyze these kinds of relationships. Parts of these mathematical relationships are called "Greek letters" by finance professionals. Here we specifically derive Greek letters for call (put) options on nondividend stock and dividends-paying stock. Some examples will be provided to explain applications of these Greek letters. Sections 20.1 to 20.5 discuss the derivations and applications of Delta, Theta, Gamma, Vega, and Rho, respectively. Section 20.6 derives the partial derivative of stock options with respect to their exercise prices. Section 20.7 describes the relationship between Delta, Theta, and Gamma, and their implication in delta neutral portfolio. Finally in Section 20.8, we summarize and conclude this chapter.

20.1. Delta (Δ)

The delta of an option, Δ, is defined as the rate of change of the option price respected to the rate of change of underlying asset price:

$$\Delta = \frac{\partial \Pi}{\partial S},$$

where Π is the option price and S is underlying asset price. We next show the derivation of delta for various kinds of stock option.

20.1.1. *Derivation of Delta for Different Kinds of Stock Options*

From Black–Scholes option pricing model, we know the price of call option on a nondividend stock can be written as

$$C_t = S_t N(d_1) - Xe^{-r\tau} N(d_2), \tag{20.1}$$

and the price of put option on a nondividend stock can be written as

$$P_t = Xe^{-r\tau} N(-d_2) - S_t N(-d_1), \tag{20.2}$$

where

$$d_1 = \frac{\ln\left(\frac{S_t}{X}\right) + \left(r + \frac{\sigma_s^2}{2}\right)\tau}{\sigma_s\sqrt{\tau}},$$

$$d_2 = \frac{\ln\left(\frac{S_t}{X}\right) + \left(r - \frac{\sigma_s^2}{2}\right)\tau}{\sigma_s\sqrt{\tau}} = d_1 - \sigma_s\sqrt{\tau},$$

$$\tau = T - t,$$

$N(\cdot)$ is the cumulative density function of normal distribution.

$$N(d_1) = \int_{-\infty}^{d_1} f(u)du = \int_{-\infty}^{d_1} \frac{1}{\sqrt{2\pi}} e^{-\frac{u^2}{2}} du$$

First, we calculate

$$N'(d_1) = \frac{\partial N(d_1)}{\partial d_1} = \frac{1}{\sqrt{2\pi}} e^{-\frac{d_1^2}{2}} \tag{20.3}$$

$$\begin{aligned} N'(d_2) &= \frac{\partial N(d_2)}{\partial d_2} \\ &= \frac{1}{\sqrt{2\pi}} e^{-\frac{d_2^2}{2}} \\ &= \frac{1}{\sqrt{2\pi}} e^{-\frac{(d_1 - \sigma_s\sqrt{\tau})^2}{2}} \\ &= \frac{1}{\sqrt{2\pi}} e^{-\frac{d_1^2}{2}} \cdot e^{d_1\sigma_s\sqrt{\tau}} \cdot e^{-\frac{\sigma_s^2\tau}{2}} \\ &= \frac{1}{\sqrt{2\pi}} e^{-\frac{d_1^2}{2}} \cdot e^{\ln\left(\frac{S_t}{X}\right) + \left(r + \frac{\sigma_s^2}{2}\right)\tau} \cdot e^{-\frac{\sigma_s^2\tau}{2}} \\ &= \frac{1}{\sqrt{2\pi}} e^{-\frac{d_1^2}{2}} \cdot \frac{S_t}{X} \cdot e^{r\tau} \end{aligned} \tag{20.4}$$

Equations (20.2) and (20.3) will be used repetitively in determining following Greek letters when the underlying asset is a nondividend paying stock.

For a European call option on a nondividend stock, delta can be shown as

$$\Delta = N(d_1). \tag{20.5}$$

The derivation of Equation (20.5) is in the following:

$$\begin{aligned}
\Delta &= \frac{\partial C_t}{\partial S_t} \\
&= N(d_1) + S_t \frac{\partial N(d_1)}{\partial S_t} - Xe^{-r\tau} \frac{\partial N(d_2)}{\partial S_t} \\
&= N(d_1) + S_t \frac{\partial N(d_1)}{\partial d_1} \frac{\partial d_1}{\partial S_t} - Xe^{-r\tau} \frac{\partial N(d_2)}{\partial d_2} \frac{\partial d_2}{\partial S_t} \\
&= N(d_1) + S_t \frac{1}{\sqrt{2\pi}} e^{-\frac{d_1^2}{2}} \cdot \frac{1}{S_t \sigma_s \sqrt{\tau}} - Xe^{-r\tau} \frac{1}{\sqrt{2\pi}} e^{-\frac{d_1^2}{2}} \cdot \frac{S_t}{X} \cdot e^{r\tau} \cdot \frac{1}{S_t \sigma_s \sqrt{\tau}} \\
&= N(d_1) + S_t \frac{1}{S_t \sigma_s \sqrt{2\pi\tau}} e^{-\frac{d_1^2}{2}} - S_t \frac{1}{S_t \sigma_s \sqrt{2\pi\tau}} e^{-\frac{d_1^2}{2}} \\
&= N(d_1).
\end{aligned}$$

For a European put option on a non-dividend stock, delta can be shown as

$$\Delta = N(d_1) - 1. \tag{20.6}$$

The derivation of Equation (20.6) is

$$\begin{aligned}
\Delta &= \frac{\partial P_t}{\partial S_t} \\
&= Xe^{-r\tau} \frac{\partial N(-d_2)}{\partial S_t} - N(-d_1) - S_t \frac{\partial N(-d_1)}{\partial S_t} \\
&= Xe^{-r\tau} \frac{\partial (1 - N(d_2))}{\partial d_2} \frac{\partial d_2}{\partial S_t} - (1 - N(d_1)) - S_t \frac{\partial (1 - N(d_1))}{\partial d_1} \frac{\partial d_1}{\partial S_t} \\
&= -Xe^{-r\tau} \frac{1}{\sqrt{2\pi}} e^{-\frac{d_1^2}{2}} \cdot \frac{S_t}{X} \cdot e^{r\tau} \cdot \frac{1}{S_t \sigma_s \sqrt{\tau}} - (1 - N(d_1)) \\
&\quad + S_t \frac{1}{\sqrt{2\pi}} e^{-\frac{d_1^2}{2}} \cdot \frac{1}{S_t \sigma_s \sqrt{\tau}}
\end{aligned}$$

$$= -S_t \frac{1}{S_t \sigma_s \sqrt{2\pi\tau}} e^{-\frac{d_1^2}{2}} - N(d_1) - 1 + S_t \frac{1}{S_t \sigma_s \sqrt{2\pi\tau}} e^{-\frac{d_1^2}{2}}$$

$$= N(d_1) - 1.$$

If the underlying asset is a dividend-paying stock providing a dividend yield at rate q, Black–Scholes formulas for the prices of a European call option on a dividend-paying stock and a European put option on a dividend-paying stock are

$$C_t = S_t e^{-q\tau} N(d_1) - X e^{-r\tau} N(d_2), \tag{20.7}$$

and

$$P_t = X e^{-r\tau} N(-d_2) - S_t e^{-q\tau} N(-d_1), \tag{20.8}$$

where

$$d_1 = \frac{\ln\left(\frac{S_t}{X}\right) + \left(r - q + \frac{\sigma_s^2}{2}\right)\tau}{\sigma_s \sqrt{\tau}},$$

$$d_2 = \frac{\ln\left(\frac{S_t}{X}\right) + \left(r - q - \frac{\sigma_s^2}{2}\right)\tau}{\sigma_s \sqrt{\tau}} = d_1 - \sigma_s \sqrt{\tau},$$

To make the following derivations more easily, we calculate Equations (20.9) and (20.10) in advance.

$$\mathrm{N}'(\mathrm{d}_1) = \frac{\partial N(d_1)}{\partial d_1} = \frac{1}{\sqrt{2\pi}} e^{-\frac{d_1^2}{2}}, \tag{20.9}$$

$$\begin{aligned} N'(d_2) &= \frac{\partial N(d_2)}{\partial d_2} \\ &= \frac{1}{\sqrt{2\pi}} e^{-\frac{d_2^2}{2}} \\ &= \frac{1}{\sqrt{2\pi}} e^{-\frac{(d_1 - \sigma_s\sqrt{\tau})^2}{2}} \\ &= \frac{1}{\sqrt{2\pi}} e^{-\frac{d_1^2}{2}} \cdot e^{d_1 \sigma_s \sqrt{\tau}} \cdot e^{-\frac{\sigma_s^2 \tau}{2}} \\ &= \frac{1}{\sqrt{2\pi}} e^{-\frac{d_1^2}{2}} \cdot e^{\ln\left(\frac{S_t}{X}\right) + \left(r - q + \frac{\sigma_s^2}{2}\right)\tau} \cdot e^{-\frac{\sigma_s^2 \tau}{2}} \\ &= \frac{1}{\sqrt{2\pi}} e^{-\frac{d_1^2}{2}} \cdot \frac{S_t}{X} \cdot e^{(r-q)\tau}. \end{aligned} \tag{20.10}$$

For a European call option on a dividend-paying stock, delta can be shown as

$$\Delta = e^{-q\tau} N(d_1). \tag{20.11}$$

The derivation of (20.11) is

$$\begin{aligned}
\Delta &= \frac{\partial C_t}{\partial S_t} \\
&= e^{-q\tau} N(d_1) + S_t e^{-q\tau} \frac{\partial N(d_1)}{\partial S_t} - X e^{-r\tau} \frac{\partial N(d_2)}{\partial S_t} \\
&= e^{-q\tau} N(d_1) + S_t e^{-q\tau} \frac{\partial N(d_1)}{\partial d_1} \frac{\partial d_1}{\partial S_t} - X e^{-r\tau} \frac{\partial N(d_2)}{\partial d_2} \frac{\partial d_2}{\partial S_t} \\
&= e^{-q\tau} N(d_1) \\
&\quad + S_t e^{-q\tau} \frac{1}{\sqrt{2\pi}} e^{-\frac{d_1^2}{2}} \cdot \frac{1}{S_t \sigma_s \sqrt{\tau}} - X e^{-r\tau} \frac{1}{\sqrt{2\pi}} e^{-\frac{d_1^2}{2}} \cdot \frac{S_t}{X} \cdot e^{(r-q)\tau} \cdot \frac{1}{S_t \sigma_s \sqrt{\tau}} \\
&= e^{-q\tau} N(d_1) + S_t e^{-q\tau} \frac{1}{S_t \sigma_s \sqrt{2\pi\tau}} e^{-\frac{d_1^2}{2}} - S_t e^{-q\tau} \frac{1}{S_t \sigma_s \sqrt{2\pi\tau}} e^{-\frac{d_1^2}{2}} \\
&= e^{-q\tau} N(d_1).
\end{aligned}$$

For a European call option on a dividend-paying stock, delta can be shown as

$$\Delta = e^{-q\tau} [N(d_1) - 1]. \tag{20.12}$$

The derivation of (20.12) is

$$\begin{aligned}
\Delta &= \frac{\partial P_t}{\partial S_t} \\
&= X e^{-r\tau} \frac{\partial N(-d_2)}{\partial S_t} - e^{-q\tau} N(-d_1) - S_t e^{-q\tau} \frac{\partial N(-d_1)}{\partial S_t} \\
&= X e^{-r\tau} \frac{\partial (1 - N(d_2))}{\partial d_2} \frac{\partial d_2}{\partial S_t} - e^{-q\tau} (1 - N(d_1)) - S_t e^{-q\tau} \frac{\partial (1 - N(d_1))}{\partial d_1} \frac{\partial d_1}{\partial S_t} \\
&= -X e^{-r\tau} \frac{1}{\sqrt{2\pi}} e^{-\frac{d_1^2}{2}} \cdot \frac{S_t}{X} \cdot e^{(r-q)\tau} \cdot \frac{1}{S_t \sigma_s \sqrt{\tau}} - e^{-q\tau} (1 - N(d_1)) \\
&\quad + S_t e^{-q\tau} \frac{1}{\sqrt{2\pi}} e^{-\frac{d_1^2}{2}} \cdot \frac{1}{S_t \sigma_s \sqrt{\tau}}
\end{aligned}$$

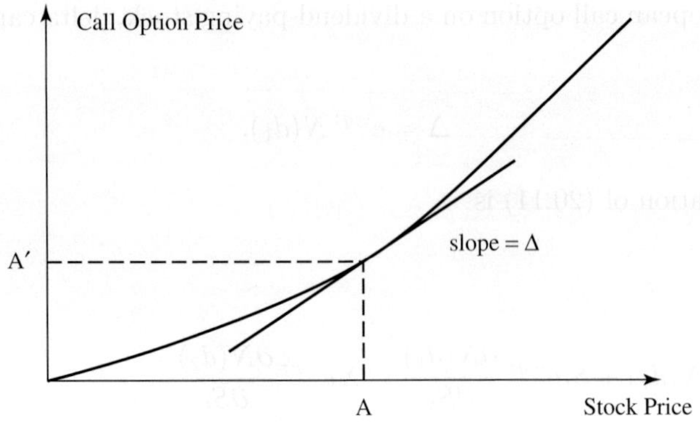

Fig. 20.1. The Relationship between Call Option Price and Stock Price.

$$= -S_t e^{-q\tau}\frac{1}{S_t\sigma_s\sqrt{2\pi\tau}}e^{-\frac{d_1^2}{2}} + e^{-q\tau}(N(d_1)-1) + S_t e^{-q\tau}\frac{1}{S_t\sigma_s\sqrt{2\pi\tau}}e^{-\frac{d_1^2}{2}}$$

$$= e^{-q\tau}(N(d_1)-1).$$

20.1.2. *Application of Delta* (Δ)

Figure 20.1 shows the relationship between the price of a call option and the price of its underlying asset. The delta of this call option is the slope of the line at the point of A corresponding to current price of the underlying asset.

By calculating delta ratio, a financial institution that sells option to a client can make a delta neutral position to hedge the risk of changes of the underlying asset price. Suppose that the current stock price is \$100, the call option price on stock is \$10, and the current delta of the call option is 0.4. A financial institution sold 10 call option to its client, so that the client has right to buy 1,000 shares at time to maturity. To construct a delta hedge position, the financial institution should buy $0.4 \times 1{,}000 = 400$ shares of stock. If the stock price goes up to \$1, the option price will go up by \$0.40. In this situation, the financial institution has a \$400 (\$1 × 400 shares) gain in its stock position and a \$400 (\$0.40 × 1,000 shares) loss in its option position. The total payoff of the financial institution is zero. On the other hand, if the stock price goes down by \$1, the option price will go down by \$0.40. The total payoff of the financial institution is also zero.

However, the relationship between option price and stock price is not linear, so delta changes over different stock price. If an investor wants to remain his portfolio in delta neutral, he should adjust his hedged

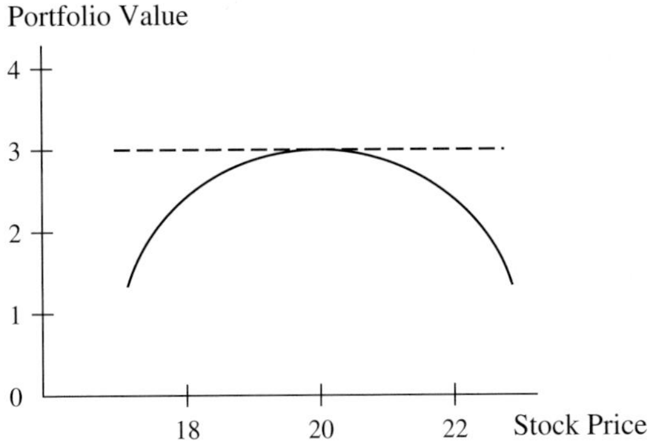

Fig. 20.2. The Relationship between Portfolio Value and Stock Price.

ratio periodically. The more frequent adjustments he does, the better delta-hedging he gets.

Figure 20.2 exhibits the change in delta affecting the delta-hedges. If the underlying stock has a price equal to \$20, then the investor who uses only delta as risk measure will consider that his or her portfolio has no risk. However, as the underlying stock prices changes, either up or down, the delta changes as well and thus he or she will have to use different delta hedging. Delta measure can be combined with other risk measures to yield better risk measurement. We will discuss it further in the following sections.

20.2. Theta (Θ)

The theta of an option, Θ, is defined as the rate of change of the option price with respect to the passage of time:

$$\Theta = \frac{\partial \Pi}{\partial t},$$

where Π is the option price and t is the passage of time.

If $\tau = T - t$, theta (Θ) can also be defined as minus one timing the rate of change of the option price respected to time to maturity. The derivation of such transformation is easy and straight forward:

$$\Theta = \frac{\partial \Pi}{\partial t} = \frac{\partial \Pi}{\partial \tau}\frac{\partial \tau}{\partial t} = (-1)\frac{\partial \Pi}{\partial \tau},$$

where $\tau = T - t$ is time to maturity. For the derivation of theta for various kinds of stock option, we use the definition of negative differential on time to maturity.

20.2.1. *Derivation of Theta for Different Kinds of Stock Options*

For a European call option on a nondividend stock, theta can be written as

$$\Theta = -\frac{S_t\sigma_s}{2\sqrt{\tau}}\cdot N'(d_1) - rX\cdot e^{-r\tau}N(d_2). \tag{20.13}$$

The derivation of (20.13) is

$$\begin{aligned}
\Theta &= -\frac{\partial C_t}{\partial \tau} \\
&= -S_t\frac{\partial N(d_1)}{\partial \tau} + (-r)\cdot X\cdot e^{-r\tau}N(d_2) + Xe^{-r\tau}\frac{\partial N(d_2)}{\partial \tau} \\
&= -S_t\frac{\partial N(d_1)}{\partial d_1}\frac{\partial d_1}{\partial \tau} - rX\cdot e^{-r\tau}N(d_2) + Xe^{-r\tau}\frac{\partial N(d_2)}{\partial d_2}\frac{\partial d_2}{\partial \tau} \\
&= -S_t\frac{1}{\sqrt{2\pi}}e^{-\frac{d_1^2}{2}}\cdot\left(\frac{r+\frac{\sigma_s^2}{2}}{\sigma_s\sqrt{\tau}} - \frac{\ln\left(\frac{s_t}{X}\right)}{2\sigma_s\tau^{3/2}} - \frac{r+\frac{\sigma_s^2}{2}}{2\sigma_s\sqrt{\tau}}\right) - rX\cdot e^{-r\tau}N(d_2) \\
&\quad + Xe^{-r\tau}\cdot\left(\frac{1}{\sqrt{2\pi}}e^{-\frac{d_1^2}{2}}\cdot\frac{S_t}{X}\cdot e^{r\tau}\right)\cdot\left(\frac{r}{\sigma_s\sqrt{\tau}} - \frac{\ln\left(\frac{s_t}{X}\right)}{2\sigma_s\tau^{3/2}} - \frac{r+\frac{\sigma_s^2}{2}}{2\sigma_s\sqrt{\tau}}\right) \\
&= -S_t\frac{1}{\sqrt{2\pi}}e^{-\frac{d_1^2}{2}}\cdot\left(\frac{r+\frac{\sigma_s^2}{2}}{\sigma_s\sqrt{\tau}} - \frac{\ln\left(\frac{s_t}{X}\right)}{2\sigma_s\tau^{3/2}} - \frac{r+\frac{\sigma_s^2}{2}}{2\sigma_s\sqrt{\tau}}\right) - rX\cdot e^{-r\tau}N(d_2) \\
&\quad + S_t\frac{1}{\sqrt{2\pi}}e^{-\frac{d_1^2}{2}}\cdot\left(\frac{r}{\sigma_s\sqrt{\tau}} - \frac{\ln\left(\frac{s_t}{X}\right)}{2\sigma_s\tau^{3/2}} - \frac{r+\frac{\sigma_s^2}{2}}{2\sigma_s\sqrt{\tau}}\right) \\
&= -S_t\frac{1}{\sqrt{2\pi}}e^{-\frac{d_1^2}{2}}\cdot\left(\frac{\frac{\sigma_s^2}{2}}{\sigma_s\sqrt{\tau}}\right) - rX\cdot e^{-r\tau}N(d_2) \\
&= -\frac{S_t\sigma_s}{2\sqrt{\tau}}\cdot N'(d_1) - rX\cdot e^{-r\tau}N(d_2).
\end{aligned}$$

For a European put option on a nondividend stock, theta can be shown as

$$\Theta = -\frac{S_t\sigma_s}{2\sqrt{\tau}}\cdot N'(d_1) + rX\cdot e^{-r\tau}N(-d_2). \tag{20.14}$$

The derivation of (20.14) is

$$\begin{aligned}
\Theta &= -\frac{\partial P_t}{\partial \tau} \\
&= -(-r)\cdot X\cdot e^{-r\tau}N(-d_2) - Xe^{-r\tau}\frac{\partial N(-d_2)}{\partial \tau} + S_t\frac{\partial N(-d_1)}{\partial \tau}
\end{aligned}$$

$$= -(-r)X \cdot e^{-r\tau}(1 - N(d_2)) - Xe^{-r\tau}\frac{\partial(1 - N(d_2))}{\partial d_2}\frac{\partial d_2}{\partial \tau}$$

$$+ S_t\frac{\partial(1 - N(d_1))}{\partial d_1}\frac{\partial d_1}{\partial \tau}$$

$$= -(-r)X \cdot e^{-r\tau}(1 - N(d_2))$$

$$+ Xe^{-r\tau} \cdot \left(\frac{1}{\sqrt{2\pi}}e^{-\frac{d_1^2}{2}} \cdot \frac{S_t}{X} \cdot e^{r\tau}\right) \cdot \left(\frac{r}{\sigma_s\sqrt{\tau}} - \frac{\ln\left(\frac{S_t}{X}\right)}{2\sigma_s\tau^{3/2}} - \frac{r + \frac{\sigma_s^2}{2}}{2\sigma_s\sqrt{\tau}}\right)$$

$$- S_t\frac{1}{\sqrt{2\pi}}e^{-\frac{d_1^2}{2}} \cdot \left(\frac{r + \frac{\sigma_s^2}{2}}{\sigma_s\sqrt{\tau}} - \frac{\ln\left(\frac{S_t}{X}\right)}{2\sigma_s\tau^{3/2}} - \frac{r + \frac{\sigma_s^2}{2}}{2\sigma_s\sqrt{\tau}}\right)$$

$$= rX \cdot e^{-r\tau}(1 - N(d_2)) + S_t\frac{1}{\sqrt{2\pi}}e^{-\frac{d_1^2}{2}} \cdot \left(\frac{r}{\sigma_s\sqrt{\tau}} - \frac{\ln\left(\frac{S_t}{X}\right)}{2\sigma_s\tau^{3/2}} - \frac{r + \frac{\sigma_s^2}{2}}{2\sigma_s\sqrt{\tau}}\right)$$

$$- S_t\frac{1}{\sqrt{2\pi}}e^{-\frac{d_1^2}{2}} \cdot \left(\frac{r + \frac{\sigma_s^2}{2}}{\sigma_s\sqrt{\tau}} - \frac{\ln\left(\frac{S_t}{X}\right)}{2\sigma_s\tau^{3/2}} - \frac{r + \frac{\sigma_s^2}{2}}{2\sigma_s\sqrt{\tau}}\right)$$

$$= rX \cdot e^{-r\tau}(1 - N(d_2)) - S_t\frac{1}{\sqrt{2\pi}}e^{-\frac{d_1^2}{2}} \cdot \left(\frac{\frac{\sigma_s^2}{2}}{\sigma_s\sqrt{\tau}}\right)$$

$$= rX \cdot e^{-r\tau}(1 - N(d_2)) - \frac{S_t\sigma_s}{2\sqrt{\tau}} \cdot N'(d_1)$$

$$= rX \cdot e^{-r\tau}N(-d_2) - \frac{S_t\sigma_s}{2\sqrt{\tau}} \cdot N'(d_1).$$

For a European call option on a dividend-paying stock, theta can be shown as

$$\Theta = q \cdot S_te^{-q\tau}N(d_1) - \frac{S_te^{-q\tau}\sigma_s}{2\sqrt{\tau}} \cdot N'(d_1) - rX \cdot e^{-r\tau}N(d_2). \qquad (20.15)$$

The derivation of (20.15) is

$$\Theta = -\frac{\partial C_t}{\partial \tau}$$

$$= q \cdot S_te^{-q\tau}N(d_1) - S_te^{-q\tau}\frac{\partial N(d_1)}{\partial \tau} + (-r) \cdot X \cdot e^{-r\tau}N(d_2)$$

$$+ Xe^{-r\tau}\frac{\partial N(d_2)}{\partial \tau}$$

$$
\begin{aligned}
&= q \cdot S_t e^{-q\tau} N(d_1) - S_t e^{-q\tau} \frac{\partial N(d_1)}{\partial d_1} \frac{\partial d_1}{\partial \tau} - rX \cdot e^{-r\tau} N(d_2) \\
&\quad + X e^{-r\tau} \frac{\partial N(d_2)}{\partial d_2} \frac{\partial d_2}{\partial \tau} \\
&= q \cdot S_t e^{-q\tau} N(d_1) \\
&\quad - S_t e^{-q\tau} \frac{1}{\sqrt{2\pi}} e^{-\frac{d_1^2}{2}} \cdot \left(\frac{r - q + \frac{\sigma_s^2}{2}}{\sigma_s \sqrt{\tau}} - \frac{\ln\left(\frac{S_t}{X}\right)}{2\sigma_s \tau^{3/2}} - \frac{r - q + \frac{\sigma_s^2}{2}}{2\sigma_s \sqrt{\tau}} \right) \\
&\quad - rX \cdot e^{-r\tau} N(d_2) + X e^{-r\tau} \cdot \left(\frac{1}{\sqrt{2\pi}} e^{-\frac{d_1^2}{2}} \cdot \frac{S_t}{X} \cdot e^{(r-q)\tau} \right) \\
&\quad \cdot \left(\frac{r - q}{\sigma_s \sqrt{\tau}} - \frac{\ln\left(\frac{S_t}{X}\right)}{2\sigma_s \tau^{3/2}} - \frac{r - q + \frac{\sigma_s^2}{2}}{2\sigma_s \sqrt{\tau}} \right) \\
&= q \cdot S_t e^{-q\tau} N(d_1) - S_t e^{-q\tau} \frac{1}{\sqrt{2\pi}} e^{-\frac{d_1^2}{2}} \cdot \left(\frac{r + \frac{\sigma_s^2}{2}}{\sigma_s \sqrt{\tau}} - \frac{\ln\left(\frac{S_t}{X}\right)}{2\sigma_s \tau^{3/2}} - \frac{r + \frac{\sigma_s^2}{2}}{2\sigma_s \sqrt{\tau}} \right) \\
&\quad - rX \cdot e^{-r\tau} N(d_2) + S_t e^{-q\tau} \frac{1}{\sqrt{2\pi}} e^{-\frac{d_1^2}{2}} \cdot \left(\frac{r}{\sigma_s \sqrt{\tau}} - \frac{\ln\left(\frac{S_t}{X}\right)}{2\sigma_s \tau^{3/2}} - \frac{r + \frac{\sigma_s^2}{2}}{2\sigma_s \sqrt{\tau}} \right) \\
&= q \cdot S_t e^{-q\tau} N(d_1) - S_t e^{-q\tau} \frac{1}{\sqrt{2\pi}} e^{-\frac{d_1^2}{2}} \cdot \left(\frac{\frac{\sigma_s^2}{2}}{\sigma_s \sqrt{\tau}} \right) - rX \cdot e^{-r\tau} N(d_2) \\
&= q \cdot S_t e^{-q\tau} N(d_1) - \frac{S_t e^{-q\tau} \sigma_s}{2\sqrt{\tau}} \cdot N'(d_1) - rX \cdot e^{-r\tau} N(d_2).
\end{aligned}
$$

For a European call option on a dividend-paying stock, theta can be shown as

$$
\Theta = rX \cdot e^{-r\tau} N(-d_2) - q S_t e^{-q\tau} N(-d_1) - \frac{S_t e^{-q\tau} \sigma_s}{2\sqrt{\tau}} \cdot N'(d_1). \quad (20.16)
$$

The derivation of (20.16) is

$$
\begin{aligned}
\Theta &= -\frac{\partial P_t}{\partial \tau} \\
&= -(-r) \cdot X \cdot e^{-r\tau} N(-d_2) - X e^{-r\tau} \frac{\partial N(-d_2)}{\partial \tau} \\
&\quad + (-q) S_t e^{-q\tau} N(-d_1) + S_t e^{-q\tau} \frac{\partial N(-d_1)}{\partial \tau}
\end{aligned}
$$

$$= rX \cdot e^{-r\tau}(1 - N(d_2)) - Xe^{-r\tau} \frac{\partial(1 - N(d_2))}{\partial d_2} \frac{\partial d_2}{\partial \tau} - qS_t e^{-q\tau} N(-d_1)$$

$$+ S_t e^{-q\tau} \frac{\partial(1 - N(d_1))}{\partial d_1} \frac{\partial d_1}{\partial \tau}$$

$$= rX \cdot e^{-r\tau}(1 - N(d_2)) + Xe^{-r\tau} \cdot \left(\frac{1}{\sqrt{2\pi}} e^{-\frac{d_1^2}{2}} \cdot \frac{S_t}{X} \cdot e^{(r-q)\tau} \right)$$

$$\cdot \left(\frac{r-q}{\sigma_s \sqrt{\tau}} - \frac{\ln\left(\frac{S_t}{X}\right)}{2\sigma_s \tau^{3/2}} - \frac{r - q + \frac{\sigma_s^2}{2}}{2\sigma_s \sqrt{\tau}} \right) - qS_t e^{-q\tau} N(-d_1)$$

$$- S_t e^{-q\tau} \frac{1}{\sqrt{2\pi}} e^{-\frac{d_1^2}{2}} \cdot \left(\frac{r - q + \frac{\sigma_s^2}{2}}{\sigma_s \sqrt{\tau}} - \frac{\ln\left(\frac{S_t}{X}\right)}{2\sigma_s \tau^{3/2}} - \frac{r - q + \frac{\sigma_s^2}{2}}{2\sigma_s \sqrt{\tau}} \right)$$

$$= rX \cdot e^{-r\tau}(1 - N(d_2)) + S_t e^{-q\tau} \frac{1}{\sqrt{2\pi}} e^{-\frac{d_1^2}{2}}$$

$$\cdot \left(\frac{r-q}{\sigma_s \sqrt{\tau}} - \frac{\ln\left(\frac{S_t}{X}\right)}{2\sigma_s \tau^{3/2}} - \frac{r - q + \frac{\sigma_s^2}{2}}{2\sigma_s \sqrt{\tau}} \right) - qS_t e^{-q\tau} N(-d_1)$$

$$- S_t e^{-q\tau} \frac{1}{\sqrt{2\pi}} e^{-\frac{d_1^2}{2}} \cdot \left(\frac{r - q + \frac{\sigma_s^2}{2}}{\sigma_s \sqrt{\tau}} - \frac{\ln\left(\frac{S_t}{X}\right)}{2\sigma_s \tau^{3/2}} - \frac{r - q + \frac{\sigma_s^2}{2}}{2\sigma_s \sqrt{\tau}} \right)$$

$$= rX \cdot e^{-r\tau}(1 - N(d_2)) - qS_t e^{-q\tau} N(-d_1) - S_t e^{-q\tau} \frac{1}{\sqrt{2\pi}} e^{-\frac{d_1^2}{2}} \cdot \left(\frac{\frac{\sigma_s^2}{2}}{\sigma_s \sqrt{\tau}} \right)$$

$$= rX \cdot e^{-r\tau}(1 - N(d_2)) - qS_t e^{-q\tau} N(-d_1) - \frac{S_t e^{-q\tau} \sigma_s}{2\sqrt{\tau}} \cdot N'(d_1)$$

$$= rX \cdot e^{-r\tau} N(-d_2) - qS_t e^{-q\tau} N(-d_1) - \frac{S_t e^{-q\tau} \sigma_s}{2\sqrt{\tau}} \cdot N'(d_1).$$

20.2.2. *Application of Theta* (Θ)

The value of option is the combination of time value and stock value. When time passes, the time value of the option decreases. Thus, the rate of change of the option price withrespect to the passage of time, theta, is usually negative.

Because the passage of time on an option is not uncertain, we do not need to make a theta hedge portfolio against the effect of the passage of time. However, we still regard theta as a useful parameter, because it is a proxy of gamma in the delta neutral portfolio. For the specific detail, we will discuss in the following sections.

20.3. Gamma (Γ)

The gamma of an option, Γ, is defined as the rate of change of delta respective to the rate of change of underlying asset price:

$$\Gamma = \frac{\partial \Delta}{\partial S} = \frac{\partial^2 \Pi}{\partial S^2},$$

where Π is the option price and S is the underlying asset price.

Because the option is not linearly dependent on its underlying asset, delta-neutral hedge strategy is useful only when the movement of underlying asset price is small. Once the underlying asset price moves wider, gamma-neutral hedge is necessary. We next show the derivation of gamma for various kinds of stock option.

20.3.1. *Derivation of Gamma for Different Kinds of Stock Options*

For a European call option on a nondividend stock, gamma can be shown as

$$\Gamma = \frac{1}{S_t \sigma_s \sqrt{\tau}} N'(d_1). \tag{20.17}$$

The derivation of (20.17) is

$$\begin{aligned}
\Gamma &= \frac{\partial^2 C_t}{\partial S_t^2} \\
&= \frac{\partial \left(\frac{\partial C_t}{\partial S_t}\right)}{\partial S_t} \\
&= \frac{\partial N(d_1)}{\partial d_1} \cdot \frac{\partial d_1}{\partial S_t} \\
&= N'(d_1) \cdot \frac{\frac{1}{S_t}}{\sigma_s \sqrt{\tau}} \\
&= \frac{1}{S_t \sigma_s \sqrt{\tau}} N'(d_1).
\end{aligned}$$

For a European put option on a nondividend stock, gamma can be shown as

$$\Gamma = \frac{1}{S_t \sigma_s \sqrt{\tau}} N'(d_1). \tag{20.18}$$

The derivation of (20.18) is

$$\begin{aligned}\Gamma &= \frac{\partial^2 P_t}{\partial S_t^2}\\ &= \frac{\partial\left(\frac{\partial P_t}{\partial S_t}\right)}{\partial S_t}\\ &= \frac{\partial(N(d_1)-1)}{\partial d_1}\cdot\frac{\partial d_1}{\partial S_t}\\ &= N'(d_1)\cdot\frac{\frac{1}{S_t}}{\sigma_s\sqrt{\tau}}\\ &= \frac{1}{S_t\sigma_s\sqrt{\tau}}N'(d_1).\end{aligned}$$

For a European call option on a dividend-paying stock, gamma can be shown as

$$\Gamma = \frac{e^{-q\tau}}{S_t\sigma_s\sqrt{\tau}}N'(d_1). \tag{20.19}$$

The derivation of (20.19) is

$$\begin{aligned}\Gamma &= \frac{\partial^2 C_t}{\partial S_t^2}\\ &= \frac{\partial\left(\frac{\partial C_t}{\partial S_t}\right)}{\partial S_t}\\ &= \frac{\partial\left(e^{-q\tau}N(d_1)\right)}{\partial S_t}\\ &= e^{-q\tau}\cdot\frac{\partial N(d_1)}{\partial d_1}\cdot\frac{\partial d_1}{\partial S_t}\\ &= e^{-q\tau}\cdot N'(d_1)\cdot\frac{\frac{1}{S_t}}{\sigma_s\sqrt{\tau}}\\ &= \frac{e^{-q\tau}}{S_t\sigma_s\sqrt{\tau}}N'(d_1).\end{aligned}$$

For a European call option on a dividend-paying stock, gamma can be shown as

$$\Gamma = \frac{e^{-q\tau}}{S_t\sigma_s\sqrt{\tau}}N'(d_1). \tag{20.20}$$

The derivation of (20.20) is

$$\begin{aligned}\Gamma &= \frac{\partial^2 P_t}{\partial S_t^2}\\ &= \frac{\partial\left(\frac{\partial P_t}{\partial S_t}\right)}{\partial S_t}\\ &= \frac{\partial\left(e^{-q\tau}(N(d_1)-1)\right)}{\partial S_t}\\ &= e^{-q\tau}\cdot\frac{\partial[(N(d_1)-1)]}{\partial d_1}\cdot\frac{\partial d_1}{\partial S_t}\\ &= e^{-q\tau}\cdot N'(d_1)\cdot\frac{\frac{1}{S_t}}{\sigma_s\sqrt{\tau}}\\ &= \frac{e^{-q\tau}\cdot}{S_t\sigma_s\sqrt{\tau}}N'(d_1).\end{aligned}$$

20.3.2. *Application of Gamma* (Γ)

One can use delta and gamma together to calculate the changes of the option due to changes in the underlying stock price. This change can be approximated by the following relations.

$$\begin{aligned}&\text{change in option value}\\ &\quad\approx \Delta\times\text{change in stock price}+\frac{1}{2}\times\Gamma\times(\text{change in stock price})^2.\end{aligned}$$

From the above relation, one can observe that the gamma makes the correction for the fact that the option value is not a linear function of underlying stock price. This approximation comes from the Taylor series expansion near the initial stock price. If we let V be option value, S be stock price, and S_0 be initial stock price, then the Taylor series expansion around S_0 yields the following.

$$\begin{aligned}V(S) &\approx V(S_0)+\frac{\partial V(S_0)}{\partial S}(S-S_0)+\frac{1}{2!}\frac{\partial^2 V(S_0)}{\partial S^2}(S-S_0)^2\\ &\quad+\cdots+\frac{1}{2!}\frac{\partial^n V(S_0)}{\partial S^n}(S-S_0)^n\\ &\approx V(S_0)+\frac{\partial V(S_0)}{\partial S}(S-S_0)+\frac{1}{2!}\frac{\partial^2 V(S_0)}{\partial S^2}(S-S_0)^2+o(S)\end{aligned}$$

If we only consider the first three terms, the approximation is then

$$V(S) - V(S_0) \approx \frac{\partial V(S_0)}{\partial S}(S - S_0) + \frac{1}{2!}\frac{\partial^2 V(S_0)}{\partial S^2}(S - S_0)^2$$
$$\approx \Delta(S - S_0) + \frac{1}{2}\Gamma(S - S_0)^2.$$

For example, if a portfolio of options has a delta equal to \$10,000 and a gamma equal to \$5,000, the change in the portfolio value if the stock price drop to \$34 from \$35 is approximately

$$\text{change in portfolio value}$$
$$\approx (\$10{,}000) \times (\$34 - \$35) + \frac{1}{2} \times (\$5{,}000) \times (\$34 - \$35)^2$$
$$\approx -\$7{,}500.$$

The above analysis can also be applied to measure the price sensitivity of interest rate related assets or portfolio to interest rate changes. Here we introduce *Modified Duration* and *Convexity* as risk measure corresponding to the above delta and gamma. Modified duration measures the percentage change in asset or portfolio value resulting from a percentage change in interest rate.

$$\text{Modified Duration} = \left(\frac{\text{Change in price}}{\text{Change in interest rate}}\right)\Big/\text{Price}$$
$$= -\Delta/P$$

Using the modified duration,

$$\text{Change in Portfolio Value} = \Delta \times \text{Change in interest rate}$$
$$= (-\mathit{Duration} \times \mathrm{P}) \times \text{Change in interest rate},$$

we can calculate the value changes of the portfolio. The above relation corresponds to the previous discussion of delta measure. We want to know how the price of the portfolio changes given a change in interest rate. Similar to delta, modified duration only shows the first-order approximation of the changes in value. In order to account for the nonlinear relation between the interest rate and portfolio value, we need a second-order approximation similar to the gamma measure before, this is then the convexity measure. Convexity is the interest rate gamma divided by price,

$$\mathit{Convexity} = \Gamma/\mathrm{P},$$

and this measure captures the nonlinear part of the price changes due to interest rate changes. Using the modified duration and convexity together allows us to develop first as well as second-order approximation of the price changes similar to previous discussion.

$$\text{Change in Portfolio Value} \approx -\textit{Duration} \times \text{P} \times (\text{change in rate}) + \frac{1}{2} \times \textit{Convexity} \times \text{P} \times (\text{change in rate})^2$$

As a result, (−Duration × P) and (Convexity × P) act like the delta and gamma measure, respectively, in the previous discussion. This shows that these Greeks can also be applied in measuring risk in interest-rate related assets or portfolio.

Next we discuss how to make a portfolio gamma neutral. Suppose the gamma of a delta-neutral portfolio is Γ, the gamma of the option in this portfolio is Γ_o, and ω_o is the number of options added to the delta-neutral portfolio. Then, the gamma of this new portfolio is

$$\omega_o \Gamma_o + \Gamma.$$

To make a gamma-neutral portfolio, we should trade $\omega_o^* = -\Gamma/\Gamma_o$ options. Because the position of option changes, the new portfolio is not in the delta-neutral. We should change the position of the underlying asset to maintain delta-neutral.

For example, the delta and gamma of a particular call option are 0.7 and 1.2. A delta-neutral portfolio has a gamma of −2,400. To make a delta-neutral and gamma-neutral portfolio, we should add a long position of 2,400/1.2 = 2,000 shares and a short position of 2,000 × 0.7 = 1,400 shares in the original portfolio.

20.4. Vega (ν)

The vega of an option, ν, is defined as the rate of change of the option price respective to the volatility of the underlying asset:

$$\nu = \frac{\partial \Pi}{\partial \sigma},$$

where Π is the option price and σ is volatility of the stock price. We next show the derivation of vega for various kinds of stock option.

20.4.1. *Derivation of Vega for Different Kinds of Stock Options*

For a European call option on a nondividend stock, vega can be shown as

$$\nu = S_t\sqrt{\tau} \cdot N'(d_1). \tag{20.21}$$

The derivation of (20.21) is

$$\begin{aligned}
\nu &= \frac{\partial C_t}{\partial \sigma_s} \\
&= S_t \frac{\partial N(d_1)}{\partial \sigma_s} - Xe^{-r\tau}\frac{\partial N(d_2)}{\partial \sigma_s} \\
&= S_t \frac{\partial N(d_1)}{\partial d_1}\frac{\partial d_1}{\partial \sigma_s} - Xe^{-r\tau}\frac{\partial N(d_2)}{\partial d_2}\frac{\partial d_2}{\partial \sigma_s} \\
&= S_t \frac{1}{\sqrt{2\pi}}e^{-\frac{d_1^2}{2}} \cdot \left(\frac{\sigma_s^2\tau^{3/2} - \left[\ln\frac{S_t}{X} + \left(r + \frac{\sigma_s^2}{2}\right)\tau\right]\cdot \tau^{\frac{1}{2}}}{\sigma_s^2\tau}\right) \\
&\quad - Xe^{-r\tau}\left(\frac{1}{\sqrt{2\pi}}e^{-\frac{d_1^2}{2}} \cdot \frac{S_t}{X} \cdot e^{r\tau}\right) \cdot \left(\frac{-\left[\ln\frac{S_t}{X} + \left(r + \frac{\sigma_s^2}{2}\right)\tau\right]\cdot \tau^{\frac{1}{2}}}{\sigma_s^2\tau}\right) \\
&= S_t \frac{1}{\sqrt{2\pi}}e^{-\frac{d_1^2}{2}} \cdot \left(\frac{\sigma_s^2\tau^{3/2} - \left[\ln\frac{S_t}{X} + \left(r + \frac{\sigma_s^2}{2}\right)\tau\right]\cdot \tau^{\frac{1}{2}}}{\sigma_s^2\tau}\right) \\
&\quad - S_t \frac{1}{\sqrt{2\pi}}e^{-\frac{d_1^2}{2}} \cdot \left(\frac{-\left[\ln\frac{S_t}{X} + \left(r + \frac{\sigma_s^2}{2}\right)\tau\right]\cdot \tau^{\frac{1}{2}}}{\sigma_s^2\tau}\right) \\
&= S_t \frac{1}{\sqrt{2\pi}}e^{-\frac{d_1^2}{2}} \cdot \left(\frac{\sigma_s^2\tau^{3/2}}{\sigma_s^2\tau}\right) \\
&= S_t\sqrt{\tau} \cdot N'(d_1).
\end{aligned}$$

For a European put option on a nondividend stock, vega can be shown as

$$\nu = S_t\sqrt{\tau} \cdot N'(d_1). \tag{20.22}$$

The derivation of (20.22) is

$$\begin{aligned}
\nu &= \frac{\partial P_t}{\partial \sigma_s} \\
&= Xe^{-r\tau}\frac{\partial N(-d_2)}{\partial \sigma_s} - S_t\frac{\partial N(-d_1)}{\partial \sigma_s} \\
&= Xe^{-r\tau}\frac{\partial (1-N(d_2))}{\partial d_2}\frac{\partial d_2}{\partial \sigma_s} - S_t\frac{\partial (1-N(d_1))}{\partial d_1}\frac{\partial d_1}{\partial \sigma_s} \\
&= -Xe^{-r\tau}\left(\frac{1}{\sqrt{2\pi}}e^{-\frac{d_1^2}{2}}\cdot\frac{S_t}{X}\cdot e^{r\tau}\right)\cdot\left(\frac{-\left[\ln\frac{S_t}{X}+\left(r+\frac{\sigma_s^2}{2}\right)\tau\right]\cdot\tau^{\frac{1}{2}}}{\sigma_s^2\tau}\right) \\
&\quad + S_t\frac{1}{\sqrt{2\pi}}e^{-\frac{d_1^2}{2}}\cdot\left(\frac{\sigma_s^2\tau^{3/2}-\left[\ln\frac{S_t}{X}+\left(r+\frac{\sigma_s^2}{2}\right)\tau\right]\cdot\tau^{\frac{1}{2}}}{\sigma_s^2\tau}\right) \\
&= -S_t\frac{1}{\sqrt{2\pi}}e^{-\frac{d_1^2}{2}}\cdot\left(\frac{-\left[\ln\frac{S_t}{X}+\left(r+\frac{\sigma_s^2}{2}\right)\tau\right]\cdot\tau^{\frac{1}{2}}}{\sigma_s^2\tau}\right) \\
&\quad + S_t\frac{1}{\sqrt{2\pi}}e^{-\frac{d_1^2}{2}}\cdot\left(\frac{\sigma_s^2\tau^{3/2}-\left[\ln\frac{S_t}{X}+\left(r+\frac{\sigma_s^2}{2}\right)\tau\right]\cdot\tau^{\frac{1}{2}}}{\sigma_s^2\tau}\right) \\
&= S_t\frac{1}{\sqrt{2\pi}}e^{-\frac{d_1^2}{2}}\cdot\left(\frac{\sigma_s^2\tau^{3/2}}{\sigma_s^2\tau}\right) \\
&= S_t\sqrt{\tau}\cdot N'(d_1).
\end{aligned}$$

For a European call option on a dividend-paying stock, vega can be shown as

$$\nu = S_t e^{-q\tau}\sqrt{\tau}\cdot N'(d_1). \tag{20.23}$$

The derivation of (20.23) is

$$\begin{aligned}
\nu &= \frac{\partial C_t}{\partial \sigma_s} \\
&= S_t e^{-q\tau}\frac{\partial N(d_1)}{\partial \sigma_s} - Xe^{-r\tau}\frac{\partial N(d_2)}{\partial \sigma_s} \\
&= S_t e^{-q\tau}\frac{\partial N(d_1)}{\partial d_1}\frac{\partial d_1}{\partial \sigma_s} - Xe^{-r\tau}\frac{\partial N(d_2)}{\partial d_2}\frac{\partial d_2}{\partial \sigma_s}
\end{aligned}$$

$$= S_t e^{-q\tau} \frac{1}{\sqrt{2\pi}} e^{-\frac{d_1^2}{2}} \cdot \left(\frac{\sigma_s^2 \tau^{3/2} - \left[\ln \frac{S_t}{X} + \left(r - q + \frac{\sigma_s^2}{2}\right)\tau\right] \cdot \tau^{\frac{1}{2}}}{\sigma_s^2 \tau} \right)$$

$$- X e^{-r\tau} \left(\frac{1}{\sqrt{2\pi}} e^{-\frac{d_1^2}{2}} \cdot \frac{S_t}{X} \cdot e^{(r-q)\tau} \right) \cdot \left(\frac{-\left[\ln \frac{S_t}{X} + \left(r - q + \frac{\sigma_s^2}{2}\right)\tau\right] \cdot \tau^{\frac{1}{2}}}{\sigma_s^2 \tau} \right)$$

$$= S_t e^{-q\tau} \frac{1}{\sqrt{2\pi}} e^{-\frac{d_1^2}{2}} \cdot \left(\frac{\sigma_s^2 \tau^{3/2} - \left[\ln \frac{S_t}{X} + \left(r - q + \frac{\sigma_s^2}{2}\right)\tau\right] \cdot \tau^{\frac{1}{2}}}{\sigma_s^2 \tau} \right)$$

$$- S_t e^{-q\tau} \frac{1}{\sqrt{2\pi}} e^{-\frac{d_1^2}{2}} \cdot \left(\frac{-\left[\ln \frac{S_t}{X} + \left(r - q + \frac{\sigma_s^2}{2}\right)\tau\right] \cdot \tau^{\frac{1}{2}}}{\sigma_s^2 \tau} \right)$$

$$= S_t \frac{1}{\sqrt{2\pi}} e^{-\frac{d_1^2}{2}} \cdot \left(\frac{\sigma_s^2 \tau^{3/2}}{\sigma_s^2 \tau} \right)$$

$$= S_t e^{-q\tau} \sqrt{\tau} \cdot N'(d_1).$$

For a European call option on a dividend-paying stock, vega can be shown as

$$\nu = S_t e^{-q\tau} \sqrt{\tau} \cdot N'(d_1). \tag{20.24}$$

The derivation of (20.24) is

$$\nu = \frac{\partial P_t}{\partial \sigma_s}$$

$$= X e^{-r\tau} \frac{\partial N(-d_2)}{\partial \sigma_s} - S_t e^{-q\tau} \frac{\partial N(-d_1)}{\partial \sigma_s}$$

$$= X e^{-r\tau} \frac{\partial(1 - N(d_2))}{\partial d_2} \frac{\partial d_2}{\partial \sigma_s} - S_t e^{-q\tau} \frac{\partial(1 - N(d_1))}{\partial d_1} \frac{\partial d_1}{\partial \sigma_s}$$

$$= -X e^{-r\tau} \left(\frac{1}{\sqrt{2\pi}} e^{-\frac{d_1^2}{2}} \cdot \frac{S_t}{X} \cdot e^{(r-q)\tau} \right) \cdot \left(\frac{-\left[\ln \frac{S_t}{X} + \left(r - q + \frac{\sigma_s^2}{2}\right)\tau\right] \cdot \tau^{\frac{1}{2}}}{\sigma_s^2 \tau} \right)$$

$$+ S_t e^{-q\tau} \frac{1}{\sqrt{2\pi}} e^{-\frac{d_1^2}{2}} \cdot \left(\frac{\sigma_s^2 \tau^{3/2} - \left[\ln \frac{S_t}{X} + \left(r - q + \frac{\sigma_s^2}{2}\right)\tau\right] \cdot \tau^{\frac{1}{2}}}{\sigma_s^2 \tau} \right)$$

$$= -S_t e^{-q\tau} \frac{1}{\sqrt{2\pi}} e^{-\frac{d_1^2}{2}} \cdot \left(\frac{-\left[\ln \frac{S_t}{X} + \left(r - q + \frac{\sigma_s^2}{2}\right)\tau\right] \cdot \tau^{\frac{1}{2}}}{\sigma_s^2 \tau} \right)$$

$$+ S_t e^{-q\tau} \frac{1}{\sqrt{2\pi}} e^{-\frac{d_1^2}{2}} \cdot \left(\frac{\sigma_s^2 \tau^{3/2} - \left[\ln \frac{S_t}{X} + \left(r - q + \frac{\sigma_s^2}{2}\right)\tau\right] \cdot \tau^{\frac{1}{2}}}{\sigma_s^2 \tau} \right)$$

$$= S_t e^{-q\tau} \frac{1}{\sqrt{2\pi}} e^{-\frac{d_1^2}{2}} \cdot \left(\frac{\sigma_s^2 \tau^{3/2}}{\sigma_s^2 \tau} \right)$$

$$= S_t e^{-q\tau} \sqrt{\tau} \cdot N'(d_1).$$

20.4.2. *Application of Vega (ν)*

Suppose a delta-neutral and gamma-neutral portfolio has a vega equal to ν and the vega of a particular option is ν_o. Similar to gamma, we can add a position of $-\nu/\nu_o$ in option to make a vega-neutral portfolio. To maintain delta-neutral, we should change the underlying asset position. However, when we change the option position, the new portfolio is not gamma-neutral. Generally, a portfolio with one option cannot maintain its gamma-neutral and vega-neutral at the same time. If we want a portfolio to be both gamma-neutral and vega-neutral, we should include at least two kinds of option on the same underlying asset in our portfolio.

For example, a delta-neutral and gamma-neutral portfolio contains option A, option B, and underlying asset. The gamma and vega of this portfolio are −3,200 and −2,500, respectively. Option A has a delta of 0.3, gamma of 1.2, and vega of 1.5. Option B has a delta of 0.4, gamma of 1.6, and vega of 0.8. The new portfolio will be both gamma-neutral and vega-neutral when adding ω_A of option A and ω_B of option B into the original portfolio.

$$\text{Gamma Neutral: } -3200 + 1.2\omega_A + 1.6\omega_B = 0.$$

$$\text{Vega Neutral: } -2500 + 1.5\omega_A + 0.8\omega_B = 0.$$

From two equations shown above, we can get the solution that $\omega_A = 1000$ and $\omega_B = 1250$. The delta of new portfolio is $1000 \times 0.3 + 1250 \times 0.4 = 800$. To maintain delta-neutral, we need to short 800 shares of the underlying asset.

20.5. RHO (ρ)

The rho of an option is defined as the rate of change of the option price respected to the interest rate:

$$\text{rho} = \frac{\partial \Pi}{\partial r},$$

where Π is the option price and r is interest rate. The rho for an ordinary stock call option should be positive because higher interest rate reduces the present value of the strike price which in turn increases the value of the call option. Similarly, the rho of an ordinary put option should be negative by the same reasoning. We next show the derivation of rho for various kinds of stock option.

20.5.1. *Derivation of Rho for Different Kinds of Stock Options*

For a European call option on a nondividend stock, rho can be shown as

$$\text{rho} = X\tau \cdot e^{-r\tau} N(d_2). \tag{20.25}$$

The derivation of (20.25) is

$$\begin{aligned}
\text{rho} &= \frac{\partial C_t}{\partial r} = S_t \frac{\partial N(d_1)}{\partial r} - (-\tau) \cdot X \cdot e^{-r\tau} N(d_2) - X e^{-r\tau} \frac{\partial N(d_2)}{\partial r} \\
&= S_t \frac{\partial N(d_1)}{\partial d_1} \frac{\partial d_1}{\partial r} + X\tau \cdot e^{-r\tau} N(d_2) - X e^{-r\tau} \frac{\partial N(d_2)}{\partial d_2} \frac{\partial d_2}{\partial r} \\
&= S_t \frac{1}{\sqrt{2\pi}} e^{-\frac{d_1^2}{2}} \cdot \left(\frac{\sqrt{\tau}}{\sigma_s}\right) + X\tau \cdot e^{-r\tau} N(d_2) \\
&\quad - X e^{-r\tau} \cdot \left(\frac{1}{\sqrt{2\pi}} e^{-\frac{d_1^2}{2}} \cdot \frac{S_t}{X} \cdot e^{r\tau}\right) \cdot \left(\frac{\sqrt{\tau}}{\sigma_s}\right) \\
&= S_t \frac{1}{\sqrt{2\pi}} e^{-\frac{d_1^2}{2}} \cdot \left(\frac{\sqrt{\tau}}{\sigma_s}\right) + X\tau \cdot e^{-r\tau} N(d_2) - S_t \frac{1}{\sqrt{2\pi}} e^{-\frac{d_1^2}{2}} \cdot \left(\frac{\sqrt{\tau}}{\sigma_s}\right) \\
&= X\tau \cdot e^{-r\tau} N(d_2).
\end{aligned}$$

For a European put option on a nondividend stock, rho can be shown as

$$\text{rho} = -X\tau \cdot e^{-r\tau} N(-d_2). \tag{20.26}$$

The derivation of (20.26) is

$$\text{rho} = \frac{\partial P_t}{\partial r} = (-\tau)\cdot X \cdot e^{-r\tau} N(-d_2) + Xe^{-r\tau}\frac{\partial N(-d_2)}{\partial r} \quad S_t\frac{\partial N(-d_1)}{\partial r}$$

$$= -X\tau \cdot e^{-r\tau}(1 - N(d_2)) + Xe^{-r\tau}\frac{\partial(1-N(d_2))}{\partial d_2}\frac{\partial d_2}{\partial r}$$

$$- S_t\frac{\partial(1-N(d_1))}{\partial d_1}\frac{\partial d_1}{\partial r}$$

$$= X\tau \cdot e^{-r\tau}(1-N(d_2)) - Xe^{-r\tau}\cdot\left(\frac{1}{\sqrt{2\pi}}e^{-\frac{d_1^2}{2}}\cdot\frac{S_t}{X}\cdot e^{r\tau}\right)\cdot\left(\frac{\sqrt{\tau}}{\sigma_s}\right)$$

$$+ S_t\frac{1}{\sqrt{2\pi}}e^{-\frac{d_1^2}{2}}\cdot\left(\frac{\sqrt{\tau}}{\sigma_s}\right)$$

$$= X\tau\cdot e^{-r\tau}(1-N(d_2)) - S_t\frac{1}{\sqrt{2\pi}}e^{-\frac{d_1^2}{2}}\cdot\left(\frac{\sqrt{\tau}}{\sigma_s}\right) + S_t\frac{1}{\sqrt{2\pi}}e^{-\frac{d_1^2}{2}}\cdot\left(\frac{\sqrt{\tau}}{\sigma_s}\right)$$

$$= -X\tau\cdot e^{-r\tau}N(-d_2).$$

For a European call option on a dividend-paying stock, rho can be shown as

$$\text{rho} = X\tau \cdot e^{-r\tau}N(d_2). \tag{20.27}$$

The derivation of (20.27) is

$$\text{rho} = \frac{\partial C_t}{\partial r} = S_t e^{-q\tau}\frac{\partial N(d_1)}{\partial r} - (-\tau)\cdot X\cdot e^{-r\tau}N(d_2) - Xe^{-r\tau}\frac{\partial N(d_2)}{\partial r}$$

$$= S_t e^{-q\tau}\frac{\partial N(d_1)}{\partial d_1}\frac{\partial d_1}{\partial r} + X\tau\cdot e^{-r\tau}N(d_2) - Xe^{-r\tau}\frac{\partial N(d_2)}{\partial d_2}\frac{\partial d_2}{\partial r}$$

$$= S_t e^{-q\tau}\frac{1}{\sqrt{2\pi}}e^{-\frac{d_1^2}{2}}\cdot\left(\frac{\sqrt{\tau}}{\sigma_s}\right) + X\tau\cdot e^{-r\tau}N(d_2)$$

$$- Xe^{-r\tau}\cdot\left(\frac{1}{\sqrt{2\pi}}e^{-\frac{d_1^2}{2}}\cdot\frac{S_t}{X}\cdot e^{(r-q)\tau}\right)\cdot\left(\frac{\sqrt{\tau}}{\sigma_s}\right)$$

$$= S_t e^{-q\tau}\frac{1}{\sqrt{2\pi}}e^{-\frac{d_1^2}{2}}\cdot\left(\frac{\sqrt{\tau}}{\sigma_s}\right) + X\tau\cdot e^{-r\tau}N(d_2)$$

$$- S_t e^{-q\tau}\frac{1}{\sqrt{2\pi}}e^{-\frac{d_1^2}{2}}\cdot\left(\frac{\sqrt{\tau}}{\sigma_s}\right)$$

$$= X\tau\cdot e^{-r\tau}N(d_2).$$

For a European put option on a dividend-paying stock, rho can be shown as

$$\text{rho} = -X\tau \cdot e^{-r\tau} N(-d_2). \tag{20.28}$$

The derivation of (20.28) is

$$\begin{aligned}
\text{rho} &= \frac{\partial P_t}{\partial r} \\
&= (-\tau) \cdot X \cdot e^{-r\tau} N(-d_2) + X e^{-r\tau} \frac{\partial N(-d_2)}{\partial r} - S_t e^{-q\tau} \frac{\partial N(-d_1)}{\partial r} \\
&= -X\tau \cdot e^{-r\tau}(1 - N(d_2)) + X e^{-r\tau} \frac{\partial(1 - N(d_2))}{\partial d_2} \frac{\partial d_2}{\partial r} \\
&\quad - S_t e^{-q\tau} \frac{\partial(1 - N(d_1))}{\partial d_1} \frac{\partial d_1}{\partial r} \\
&= X\tau \cdot e^{-r\tau}(1 - N(d_2)) - X e^{-r\tau} \cdot \left(\frac{1}{\sqrt{2\pi}} e^{-\frac{d_1^2}{2}} \cdot \frac{S_t}{X} \cdot e^{(r-q)\tau} \right) \cdot \left(\frac{\sqrt{\tau}}{\sigma_s} \right) \\
&\quad + S_t e^{-q\tau} \frac{1}{\sqrt{2\pi}} e^{-\frac{d_1^2}{2}} \cdot \left(\frac{\sqrt{\tau}}{\sigma_s} \right) \\
&= X\tau \cdot e^{-r\tau}(1 - N(d_2)) - S_t e^{-q\tau} \frac{1}{\sqrt{2\pi}} e^{-\frac{d_1^2}{2}} \cdot \left(\frac{\sqrt{\tau}}{\sigma_s} \right) \\
&\quad + S_t e^{-q\tau} \frac{1}{\sqrt{2\pi}} e^{-\frac{d_1^2}{2}} \cdot \left(\frac{\sqrt{\tau}}{\sigma_s} \right) \\
&= -X\tau \cdot e^{-r\tau} N(-d_2).
\end{aligned}$$

20.5.2. *Application of Rho* (ρ)

Assume that an investor would like to see how interest rate changes affect the value of a three-month European put option she holds with the following information. The current stock price is \$65 and the strike price is \$58. The interest rate and the volatility of the stock is 5% and 30% per annum, respectively. The rho of this European put can be calculated as follows.

$$\begin{aligned}
\text{Rho}_{\text{put}} &= X\tau e^{-r\tau} N(d_2) \\
&= (\$58)(0.25) e^{-(0.05)(0.25)} N\left(\frac{\ln(65/58) + \left[0.05 - \frac{1}{2}(0.3)^2\right](0.25)}{(0.3)\sqrt{0.25}} \right) \\
&\cong -3.168.
\end{aligned}$$

This calculation indicates that given 1% change increase in interest rate, say from 5% to 6%, the value of this European call option will decrease 0.03168 (0.01×3.168). This simple example can be further applied to stocks that pay dividends using the derivation results shown previously.

20.6. Derivation of Stock Options with Respect to Exercise Price

For a European call option on a nondividend stock, the sensitivity can be shown as

$$\frac{\partial C_t}{\partial X} = -e^{-r\tau}N(d_2). \tag{20.29}$$

The derivation of (20.29) is

$$\begin{aligned}
\frac{\partial C_t}{\partial X} &= S_t\frac{\partial N(d_1)}{\partial X} - e^{-r\tau}N(d_2) - Xe^{-r\tau}\frac{\partial N(d_2)}{\partial X}\\
&= S_t\frac{\partial N(d_1)}{\partial d_1}\frac{\partial d_1}{\partial X} - e^{-r\tau}N(d_2) - Xe^{-r\tau}\frac{\partial N(d_2)}{\partial d_2}\frac{\partial d_2}{\partial X}\\
&= S_t\frac{1}{\sqrt{2\pi}}e^{-\frac{d_1^2}{2}}\cdot\frac{1}{\sigma_s\sqrt{\tau}}\cdot\left(-\frac{1}{X}\right) - e^{-r\tau}N(d_2)\\
&\quad - Xe^{-r\tau}\left(\frac{1}{\sqrt{2\pi}}e^{-\frac{d_1^2}{2}}\cdot\frac{S_t}{X}\cdot e^{r\tau}\right)\frac{1}{\sigma_s\sqrt{\tau}}\cdot\left(-\frac{1}{X}\right)\\
&= \frac{1}{\sigma_s\sqrt{2\pi\tau}}e^{-\frac{d_1^2}{2}}\left(-\frac{S_t}{X}\right) - e^{-r\tau}N(d_2) - \frac{1}{\sigma_s\sqrt{2\pi\tau}}e^{-\frac{d_1^2}{2}}\left(-\frac{S_t}{X}\right)\\
&= -e^{-r\tau}N(d_2).
\end{aligned}$$

For a European put option on a nondividend stock, the sensitivity can be shown as

$$\frac{\partial P_t}{\partial X} = e^{-r\tau}N(-d_2). \tag{20.30}$$

The derivation of (20.30) is

$$\begin{aligned}
\frac{\partial P_t}{\partial X} &= e^{-r\tau}N(-d_2) + Xe^{-r\tau}\frac{\partial N(-d_2)}{\partial X} - S_t\frac{\partial N(-d_1)}{\partial X}\\
&= e^{-r\tau}(1 - N(d_2)) + Xe^{-r\tau}\frac{\partial(1 - N(d_2))}{\partial d_2}\frac{\partial d_2}{\partial X} - S_t\frac{\partial(1 - N(d_1))}{\partial d_1}\frac{\partial d_1}{\partial X}
\end{aligned}$$

$$= e^{-r\tau}(1 - N(d_2)) - Xe^{-r\tau}\left(\frac{1}{\sqrt{2\pi}}e^{-\frac{d_1^2}{2}} \cdot \frac{S_t}{X} \cdot e^{r\tau}\right)\frac{1}{\sigma_s\sqrt{\tau}} \cdot \left(-\frac{1}{X}\right)$$

$$+ S_t\frac{1}{\sqrt{2\pi}}e^{-\frac{d_1^2}{2}} \cdot \frac{1}{\sigma_s\sqrt{\tau}} \cdot \left(-\frac{1}{X}\right)$$

$$= e^{-r\tau}(1 - N(d_2)) + \frac{1}{\sigma_s\sqrt{2\pi\tau}}e^{-\frac{d_1^2}{2}}\left(\frac{S_t}{X}\right) - \frac{1}{\sigma_s\sqrt{2\pi\tau}}e^{-\frac{d_1^2}{2}}\left(\frac{S_t}{X}\right)$$

$$= e^{-r\tau}N(-d_2).$$

For a European call option on a dividend-paying stock, the sensitivity can be shown as

$$\frac{\partial C_t}{\partial X} = -e^{-r\tau}N(d_2). \tag{20.31}$$

The derivation of (20.31) is

$$\frac{\partial C_t}{\partial X} = S_te^{-q\tau}\frac{\partial N(d_1)}{\partial X} - e^{-r\tau}N(d_2) - Xe^{-r\tau}\frac{\partial N(d_2)}{\partial X}$$

$$= S_te^{-q\tau}\frac{\partial N(d_1)}{\partial d_1}\frac{\partial d_1}{\partial X} - e^{-r\tau}N(d_2) - Xe^{-r\tau}\frac{\partial N(d_2)}{\partial d_2}\frac{\partial d_2}{\partial X}$$

$$= S_te^{-q\tau}\frac{1}{\sqrt{2\pi}}e^{-\frac{d_1^2}{2}} \cdot \frac{1}{\sigma_s\sqrt{\tau}} \cdot \left(-\frac{1}{X}\right) - e^{-r\tau}N(d_2)$$

$$- Xe^{-r\tau}\left(\frac{1}{\sqrt{2\pi}}e^{-\frac{d_1^2}{2}} \cdot \frac{S_t}{X} \cdot e^{(r-q)\tau}\right)\frac{1}{\sigma_s\sqrt{\tau}} \cdot \left(-\frac{1}{X}\right)$$

$$= \frac{1}{\sigma_s\sqrt{2\pi\tau}}e^{-\frac{d_1^2}{2}}\left(-\frac{S_te^{-q\tau}}{X}\right) - e^{-r\tau}N(d_2) - \frac{1}{\sigma_s\sqrt{2\pi\tau}}e^{-\frac{d_1^2}{2}}\left(-\frac{S_te^{-q\tau}}{X}\right)$$

$$= -e^{-r\tau}N(d_2).$$

For a European put option on a dividend-paying stock, the sensitivity can be shown as

$$\frac{\partial P_t}{\partial X} = e^{-r\tau}N(-d_2). \tag{20.32}$$

The derivation of (20.32) is

$$\frac{\partial P_t}{\partial X} = e^{-r\tau}N(-d_2) + Xe^{-r\tau}\frac{\partial N(-d_2)}{\partial X} - S_te^{-q\tau}\frac{\partial N(-d_1)}{\partial X}$$

$$= e^{-r\tau}(1 - N(d_2)) + Xe^{-r\tau}\frac{\partial(1 - N(d_2))}{\partial d_2}\frac{\partial d_2}{\partial X}$$

$$
\begin{aligned}
&- S_t e^{-q\tau} \frac{\partial(1 - N(d_1))}{\partial d_1} \frac{\partial d_1}{\partial X} \\
&= e^{-r\tau}(1 - N(d_2)) - X e^{-r\tau} \left(\frac{1}{\sqrt{2\pi}} e^{-\frac{d_1^2}{2}} \cdot \frac{S_t}{X} \cdot e^{(r-q)\tau} \right) \frac{1}{\sigma_s \sqrt{\tau}} \cdot \left(-\frac{1}{X} \right) \\
&+ S_t e^{-q\tau} \frac{1}{\sqrt{2\pi}} e^{-\frac{d_1^2}{2}} \cdot \frac{1}{\sigma_s \sqrt{\tau}} \cdot \left(-\frac{1}{X} \right) \\
&= e^{-r\tau}(1 - N(d_2)) + \frac{1}{\sigma_s \sqrt{2\pi\tau}} e^{-\frac{d_1^2}{2}} \left(\frac{S_t e^{-q\tau}}{X} \right) \\
&- \frac{1}{\sigma_s \sqrt{2\pi\tau}} e^{-\frac{d_1^2}{2}} \left(\frac{S_t e^{-q\tau}}{X} \right) \\
&= e^{-r\tau} N(-d_2).
\end{aligned}
$$

20.7. Relationship between Delta, Theta, and Gamma

So far, the discussion has introduced the derivation and application of each individual Greeks and how they can be applied in portfolio management. In practice, the interaction or trade-off between these parameters is of concern as well. For example, recall the Black–Scholes–Merton differential equation with nondividend paying stock can be written as

$$\frac{\partial \Pi}{\partial t} + rS \frac{\partial \Pi}{\partial S} + \frac{1}{2} \sigma^2 S^2 \frac{\partial^2 \Pi}{\partial S^2} = r\Pi,$$

where Π is the value of the derivative security contingent on stock price, S is the price of stock, r is the risk-free rate, and σ is the volatility of the stock price, and t is the time to expiration of the derivative. Given the earlier derivation, we can rewrite the Black–Scholes partial differential equation (PDE) as

$$\Theta + rS\Delta + \frac{1}{2}\sigma^2 S^2 \Gamma = r\Pi.$$

This relation gives us the trade-off between delta, gamma, and theta. For example, suppose there are two delta neutral ($\Delta = 0$) portfolios, one with positive gamma ($\Gamma > 0$) and the other one with negative gamma ($\Gamma < 0$) and they both have value of \$1 ($\Pi = 1$). The trade-off can be written as

$$\Theta + \frac{1}{2}\sigma^2 S^2 \Gamma = r.$$

For the first portfolio, if gamma is positive and large, then theta is negative and large. When gamma is positive, change in stock prices result in higher value of the option. This means that when there is no change in stock prices, the value of the option declines as we approach the expiration date. As a result, the theta is negative. On the other hand, when gamma is negative and large, change in stock prices result in lower option value. This means that when there is no stock price changes, the value of the option increases as we approach the expiration and theta is positive. This gives us a trade-off between gamma and theta and they can be used as proxy for each other in a delta neutral portfolio.

20.8. Summary

In this chapter, we have shown the partial derivatives of stock option with respect to five variables. Delta (Δ), the rate of change of option price to change in price of underlying asset, is first derived. After Delta is obtained, Gamma (Γ) can be derived as the rate of change of delta with respect to underlying asset price. Another two risk measures are Theta (Θ) and Rho (ρ); they measure the change in option value with respect to passing time and interest rate, respectively. Finally, one can also measure the change in option value with respect to the volatility of the underlying asset and this gives us the Vega (v). The applications of these Greeks letter in the portfolio management have also been discussed. In addition, we use the Black–Scholes PDE to show the relationship between these risk measures. In sum, risk management is one of the important topics in finance for both academics and practitioners. Given the recent credit crisis, one can observe that it is crucial to properly measure the risk related to the even more complicated financial assets. The comparative static analysis of option pricing models gives an introduction to the portfolio risk management. Further discussion of the comparative statics analysis can be found in Hull (2011) and McDonald (2005).

Questions and Problems

1. What does the $\Delta = 0.7$ of a call option mean?
2. Briefly describe the meanings of Theta Θ and Gamma Γ, respectively.
3. Describe the relationship between volatility of stock price and option price via Vega.
4. How to calculate the changes of option price by using Delta and Gamma together?

5. What is the value of the Delta of an at-the-money call option when $r = 5\%$ per year, $\sigma_s = 15\%$, and the maturity $\tau = 2$?
6. Calculate Delta, Gamma, Vega, Theta, and Rho of a call option on a nondividend paying stock under the following information.

$$S = \$110, \quad X = \$100, \quad r = 0.05, \quad \sigma_s = 15\%, \quad \text{and} \quad \tau = 7 \text{ months.}$$

7. Based on information provide in question 6, if the stock pays dividend with 1% dividend yield, please calculate Delta, Gamma, Vega, Theta, and Rho.
8. Derive the relationship between the Deltas of a call option and of a put option by put–call parity.
9. Describe the relationship between the Gamma of a call option and the Gamma of a put option.
10. Given the table of option portfolio as below

Type	**Position**	**Delta**	**Gamma**	**Vega**
Call	−1,500	0.3	0.4	1.6
Call	−100	0.9	1.3	0.2
Put	−1,000	−0.5	0.9	0.3
Call	−300	0.7	2.5	1.5

Let a traded option is available with Delta = 0.8, Gamma = 2.0, Vega = 0.8.

(a) What position in the traded option and the options in the table can make the portfolio with Delta neutral?
(b) What position in the traded option and the options in the table can make the portfolio with Gamma neutral?
(c) What position in the traded option and the options in the table can make the portfolio with both Delta and Gamma neutral?

Bibliography

Bjork, T. *Arbitrage Theory in Continuous Time.* New York: Oxford University Press, 1998.

Boyle, P. P. and D. Emanuel. "Discretely Adjusted Option Hedges." *Journal of Financial Economics*, v. 8(3) (1980), pp. 259–282.

Duffie, D. *Dynamic Asset Pricing Theory.* Princeton, NJ: Princeton University Press, 2001.

Fabozzi, F. J. *Fixed Income Analysis*, 2nd Edn. New York: Wiley, 2007.

Figlewski, S. "Options Arbitrage in Imperfect Markets." *Journal of Finance*, v. 44(5) (1989), pp. 1289–1311.

Galai, D. "The Components of the Return from Hedging Options against Stocks." *Journal of Business*, v. 56(1) (1983), pp. 45–54.

Hull, J. *Options, Futures, and Other Derivatives*, 8th Edn. Upper Saddle River, NJ: Pearson, 2011.

Hull, J. and A. White. "Hedging the Risks from Writing Foreign Currency Options." *Journal of International Money and Finance*, v. 6(2) (1987), pp. 131–152.

Karatzas, I. and S. E. Shreve. *Brownian Motion and Stochastic Calculus*. Berlin: Springer, 2000.

Klebaner, F. C. *Introduction to Stochastic Calculus with Applications*. London: Imperial College Press, 2005.

McDonald, R. L. *Derivatives Markets*, 2nd Edn. Boston, MA: Addison-Wesley, 2005.

Shreve, S. E. *Stochastic Calculus for Finance II: Continuous Time Model*. New York: Springer, 2004.

Tuckman, B. *Fixed Income Securities: Tools for Today's Markets*, 2nd Edn. New York: Wiley, 2002.

Part IV

Applied Portfolio Management

Chapter 21

Security Analysis and Mutual Fund Performance

The role of security analysts and portfolio managers is to select the right stocks at the right time. They can generally use theory and methods (as discussed in most of the previous chapters) to determine which stock (or stocks) they should buy or sell at the appropriate point. Security-analysis and portfolio-management methodologies can be classified into fundamental analysis and technical analysis.

This chapter discusses methods and applications of fundamental analysis and technical analysis. In addition, it investigates the ranking performance of the Value Line and the timing and selectivity of mutual funds. A detailed investigation of technical versus fundamental analysis is first presented. This is followed by an analysis of regression time-series and composite methods for forecasting security rates of return. Value Line ranking methods and their performance then are discussed, leading finally into a study of the classification of mutual funds and the mutual-fund managers' timing and selectivity ability. In addition, the hedging ability is also briefly discussed. All of these topics can help improve performance in security analysis and portfolio management.

21.1. Fundamental Versus Technical Analysis

This section explores the relationship between two components of security analysis and portfolio management: fundamental analysis and technical analysis.

21.1.1. *Fundamental Analysis*

The job of a security analyst is to estimate the value of securities. If a security's estimated value is above its market price, the security analyst will recommend buying the stock; if the value is below the market price, the security should be sold before its price drops. Underpriced stocks are purchased until their price is bid up to equal their value; overpriced stocks are sold, driving their price down until it equals their value.

There are two schools of thought as to how one determines an overpriced or underpriced security. **Fundamental analysis** (the fundamentalist school) studies the fundamental facts affecting a stock's value. Fundamental analysts delve into companies' earnings, their management, earnings forecasts, the firm's competition, market conditions, and many other business and economic factors. The second school of thought determines an overpriced or underpriced security by studying the way security prices behave over time. **Technical analysis** concentrates almost totally on charts of security-market prices and related summary statistics of security trading.

The macro approach to fundamental analysis first emphasizes the analysis of the aggregate economy and market, then industry analysis, and finally the examination of specific companies within the industry. Changes in the national economy and credit conditions are associated with changes in interest rates, capitalization rates, and multipliers. Therefore, and aggregate economic and market analysis must be done in conjunction with determining the security's appropriate multiplier. A multiplier of 10 may be appropriate for normal economic conditions, whereas a multiple of 15 may be more realistic in an environment of rapid economic growth and prosperity.

All of the fundamentalist's research is based upon some valuation model. The analyst prepares his or her estimate of the intrinsic value per share at time 0, P_{i0}, by multiplying the ith stock's normalized earnings per share at time 0, E_{i0} times the share's earnings multiplier, m_{it}:

$$P_{i0} = E_{i0} m_{it}, \quad t = 0, \tag{21.1}$$

where

$$m_{it} = \frac{P_{i0}}{E_{i0}} = \frac{\frac{d_{i1}}{E_{i0}}}{k_i - g_i}.$$

The earnings multiplier P_{i0}/E_{i0} is called the **price-earnings (P/E) ratio**. The ratio d_{i1}/E_{i0} is called the **dividend-payout ratio**; k_i and g_i

are the **required rate of return** and **growth rate**, respectively. This model was explored in detail in Chapter 4.

Much of the fundamental analyst's work centers on determining the appropriate capitalization rate, or equivalently the appropriate multiplier to use in valuing a particular security's income. This encompasses the micro approach to estimating future values for the stock market. It involves using a two-step approach: (1) estimating the expected earnings for some market-indicator series (Dow-Jones Industrial Average or Standard & Poor's Industrial Index) or some stock, and (2) estimating the expected earnings multiplier for the market series or stock. The main factors that must be considered in determining the correct multiplier are (1) the risk of the security, (2) the growth rate of the dividend stream, (3) the duration of any expected growth, and (4) the dividend-payout ratio.

In determining the P/E ratio to use in valuing a firm's securities, three factors must be estimated: (1) the capitalization rate, (2) the dividend growth rate, and (3) the dividend-payout ratio. Algebraically:

$$\frac{P_0}{E} = \frac{d_1}{k-g} \quad \text{or} \quad \frac{P_0}{E} = \frac{d_1}{k-g} = \frac{d_0(1+g)}{k-g}, \tag{21.2}$$

where

$d_1/E =$ the dividend-payout ratio;
$K =$ the capitalization rate; and
$g =$ the expected growth of dividends.

Given this equation, a positive relationship is expected between the earnings multiplier and the dividend payout, and with the growth rate of dividends, all things being equal. Alternatively, there should be a negative relationship between the earnings multiplier and the capitalization rate. Sample Problems 21.1 and 21.2 provide further illustration.

Sample Problem 21.1

The stock of XYZ Corporation is currently paying a dividend of \$1.00 per share. The firm's dividend growth rate is expected to be 10%. For firms in the same risk class as XYZ, market analysts agree that the capitalization rate is approximately 15%. Current earnings for XYZ are \$2.00 per share and they are expected to grow at 10%. What are the P/E ratio and the price of XYZ shares given this information?

Solution

$$P/E = \frac{d_1/E}{k-g} = \frac{\$1.00(1+0.1)/2.00(1+0.1)}{15-10} = 10$$

$$P = \frac{d_0(1+g)}{k-g} = \frac{1.00(1+0.1)}{0.15-0.10} = \$22/\text{share}.$$

Sample Problem 21.2

XYZ in Sample Problem 21.1 is expected to experience an increase in growth rate from 10% to 12%. What is the impact on XYZ's P/E ratio and price?

Solution

$$P/E = \frac{d_1/E}{k-g} = \frac{\$1.00(1.12)/2.00(1+1.12)}{0.15-0.12} = 16.67$$

$$P = \frac{d_0(1+g)}{k-g} = \frac{1.00(1.12)}{0.15-0.12} = \$37.33.$$

As can be seen from comparing Sample Problems 21.1 and 21.2, a 20% increase in growth has led to a 67% increase in P/E ratio and a 69% increase in price. It is clear, therefore, that the accuracy of the analyst's growth estimate is very important.

The capitalization rate varies with a firm's risk class and the prevailing market conditions (therefore, the necessity of the macro approach). Since future expectations are influenced by past experience, one way to estimate a firm's risk class is to examine historical data. The capitalization rate is determined by (1) the economy's risk-free rate, (2) the expected rate of price increases (annual rate of inflation), and (3) a risk premium for common stocks that reflects investor uncertainty regarding future returns.

The capital asset pricing model (CAPM) discussed in Chapter 9 suggests using the systematic risk for common stocks to determine the size of the risk premium. In theory, this measure of risk should be the beta for common stocks relative to the market portfolio for all risky assets. Since a portfolio of all risky assets does not exist, an alternative is to examine fundamental factors. These factors examine the relationship between the systematic risk (beta) for a security and various proxies for business risk and financial risk. A generally accepted measure of a firm's business risk is the coefficient of variation of the firm's operating income.

Financial risk is determined by the financing decisions of the firm, or, more specifically, by the extent of financial leverage employed. The most common measures of financial risk are the debt/equity ratio and the fixed-charge coverage ratio.

Studies of securities listed on the New York Stock Exchange (NYSE) have shown that their historical average-earnings capitalization rate varied directly with the security's volatility coefficient. The fundamental analyst can measure the risk of the company in recent periods, adjust these historical risk statistics for any expected changes, and then use these forecasted risk statistics to obtain capitalization rates. (Chapters 8 and 9 explain how to measure a stocks' risk in more detail.)

The growth of dividends is a function of the growth of earnings and changes in the dividend-payout ratio. It is usually fairly simple to estimate the growth rate in cash dividends or earnings per share. (Measuring these growth rates is discussed in Chapter 3.) The growth rate is as important as the capitalization rate in estimating multipliers. The effects of the dividend-payout ratio are more direct than the effect of the growth rate. If other things remain constant, reducing a corporation's dividend payout cuts its multiplier and thus its intrinsic value proportionately. For companies whose payout ratio fluctuates widely, it is necessary to estimate the corporation's normalized earnings per share averaged over a complete business cycle. After a share's normal earnings are estimated, all that needs be done is to divide normalized earnings per share into the corporation's regular cash dividend per share to find the payout ratio for use in the determination of an earnings multiplier.

Reilly *et al.* (1983) found that the fundamental factors such as the payout ratio, growth, risk-free rate, earnings variability, the debt/equity ratio, and the failure rate of firms going bankrupt combine to form the determinants of the aggregate stock-market earnings multiple. Using these fundamental factors as independent variables in an ordinary least-squares (OLS) regression and multiple discriminate analysis, predictions are made for the multiplier.

They then use the OLS model to simulate investment strategies. If the model predicted a decline in the multiple, investment in T-bills was indicated; if the model predicted an increase in the multiple, and investment in common stock was indicated. Their results strongly support the multiple-prediction model compared to buying and holding common stocks. Not only is the rate of return substantially higher, but risk as measured by the standard deviation is lower for the model stock portfolio than for the buy-and-hold portfolio. Their results indicate that on the basis of analyzing macro variables, it is possible to estimate the likely future direction of the market-earnings multiple, which in turn is a major indicator of total stock-market movements over time. For those portfolio managers who invest in stocks, using this model is superior to a buy-and-hold strategy.

Technical analysts study charts of aggregate stock movements in an attempt to determine trends in the stock market that influence movements in individual stocks. It is the fundamental analysts, however, who have delved into the driving forces behind these movements. Shiller (1984) presented a demand-side theory explaining the market movement. He considered the supply of corporate stock to be fixed, at least in the short run, while investment demand for stocks fluctuates according to economic states. The decline in the demand for shares may not be accompanied by a decline in supply. Therefore, when many investors wish to sell their shares, for whatever reason, the price of those shares must fall. Shiller proposed that the demand-side accounts for the majority of stock-market movements.

A competing story that is equally attractive is the supply-side story. By this explanation, the main reason for the decline in stock prices is the decline in the expected future supply of dividends. However, in its extreme form, the theory implies that stock prices move only because of new information about future dividends. The theory is generally expressed today in conjunction with the assumption of efficient markets. Therefore, stock prices equal the present value of optimally forecasted future dividends.

The third theory of stock market fluctuations rests on a "market fads" theory. According to this theory, stock prices move because people tend to be vulnerable to waves of optimism or pessimism, not because of any economically identifiable shocks either to demand or supply. Highly publicized events or statements by influential figures have an impact on the market far beyond their true importance. The great crash of October 19, 1987, might well be thought of in this light.

Shiller (1984) used the following model to test the supply-side theory:

$$P_t = \sum_{k=1}^{\infty} \frac{E_t/(D_{t+k})}{(1+r)^k}, \tag{21.3}$$

where $P_t =$ the real ex-dividend price of a share at time t; $E_t/(D_{t+k}) =$ the mathematical expectation conditional on information at time t of the real dividend accruing to a share at time $t+k$; and $r =$ the real discount rate.

Since dividends are not known to infinity, and there is roughly a century of dividends on Standard and Poor's stock, Shiller evaluated the model over historical data using:

$$P_t = E_t(P_t^*), \tag{21.4a}$$

$$P_t^* = \sum_{k=1}^{1981-t} \frac{D_{t+k}}{(1+r)^k} + \frac{P_{1981}^*}{(1+r)^{1981-t}}, \quad t \le 1981. \tag{21.4b}$$

The variable P_t^* is the "perfect foresight" or "*ex-post* rational" stock price.

By replacing P_t^* with P_{1981} Shiller was able to obtain an approximation P_{st}^* (the subscript s refers to the supply-side theory) to the *ex-post* rational price:

$$P_{st}^* = \sum_{k=1}^{1981-t} \frac{D_{t+k}}{(1+r)^k} + \frac{P_{1981}^*}{(1+r)^{1981-t}}, \quad t \le 1981. \tag{21.5}$$

By plotting P_{st}^* along with the real Standard & Poor's price index P_t (Fig. 21.1), Shiller found that the two series are quite divergent. It appears that P_{st}^* behaves much like a simple growth trend, while P_t oscillates wildly around it; P_{st}^* is smooth increasing because it is a weighted moving average of dividends, and moving averages serve to smooth the series averaged. Moreover, real dividends are a fairly stable and upward trending series.

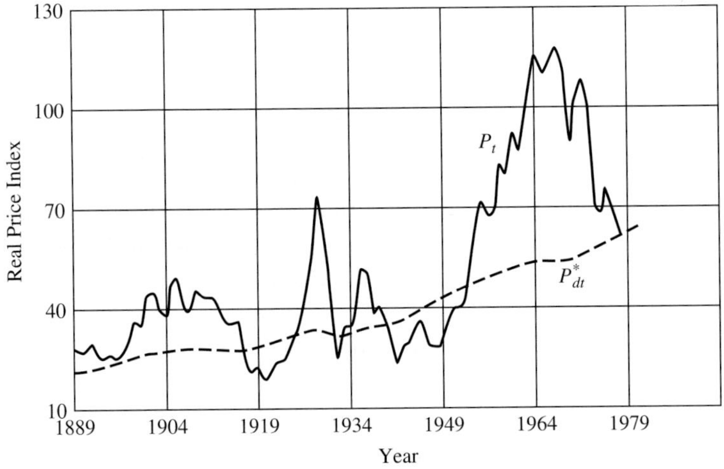

Fig. 21.1. Real Stock-Price Index P_t^* and *Ex-Post* Rational Counterpart P_{st}^* Based on Real Dividends, 1889–1981.
Source: Shiller (1984).

Using a basic economic theory of the two-period consumption with marginal rate of substitution s_t to derive a consumption beta similar to Breeden (1979), Shiller constructed a demand-side model to explain aggregate stock-price movements. Shiller showed that if i_t is the return on stock (found by dividing the sum of capital gain and dividend by price) between t and $t+1$ and if $E_t(1+i_t)s_t = 1$ at all times, then the price is the expected value of P^*_{st}, where P^*_{st} is the present value of dividends discounted by marginal rates of substitution:

$$P_t = E_t(P^*_t), \tag{21.4a}$$

$$P^*_{st} = \sum_{k=1}^{\infty} s_t^{(k)} D_{t+k}, \tag{21.6}$$

and $s_t^{(k)}$ is the marginal rate of substitution between C_t and C_{t+k}. The function for the marginal rate of substitution is $s_t^{(k)} = \delta^k (C_t/C_{t+k})^4$; that is, $s_t^{(k)}$ is proportional to the consumption ratio to the fourth power. This functional form embodies the concavity we expect in indifference curves — that is, the marginal rate of substitution declines as C_{t+k} rises relative to C_t. The fourth power was chosen because it makes P^* roughly fit the data. The δ^k represents impatience, so that (if $\delta < 1$) at a zero interest rate the person would consume more this period than in future periods.

Substituting Equation (21.6) for the marginal rate of substitution and assuming that dividends are expected to follow the trend $D_t = D_0(1+g)^t$ with certainty:

$$P^*_{dt} = C_t^4 \left[D_0(1+g)^t \sum_{k=1}^{\infty} \delta(1+g)^k C_{t+k}^{-4} \right]. \tag{21.7}$$

This expression and the assumption that $P_t = E_t(P^*_{dt})$ means essentially that stock prices should be high when aggregate consumption is high and low when consumption is low. The subscript d for P^*_{dt} means "according to the demand-side theory."

By plotting P^*_{dt} along with real price per share P_t (Fig. 21.2), Shiller finds that P^*_{dt} moves a great deal more than P^*_{st}; P^*_{dt} and P_t resemble each other much more than P^*_{st} and P_t. Unfortunately, Shiller finds that the theory seems to break down after 1950. Shiller concludes that movements over the last century in aggregate real dividends just fail to explain the movements in aggregate stock prices. Therefore, the supply-side efficient-market theory does not look promising. On the other hand,

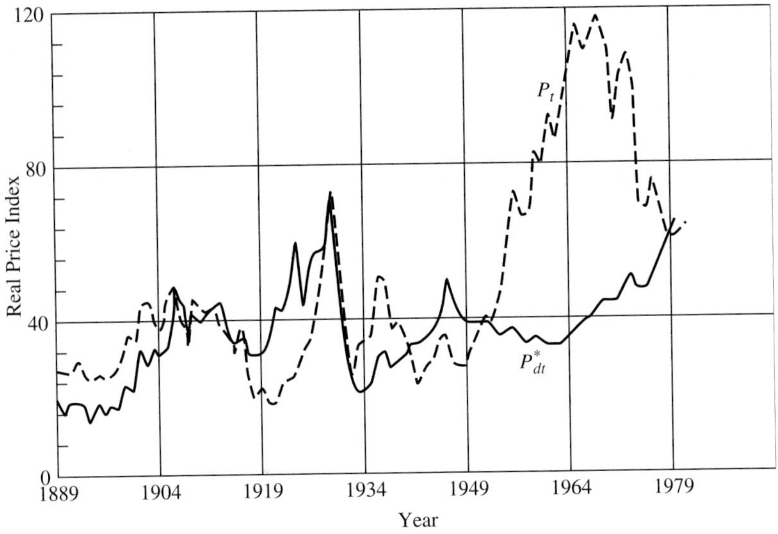

Fig. 21.2. Real Stock-Price Index P_t and *Ex-Post* Rational Counterpart P^*_{dt} Based on Real Consumption, 1889–1981.
Source: Shiller (1984).

the demand-side theory looks more promising then the supply-side theory. It predicts a business-cycle correlation for stock prices that was, until 1950, actually observed. However, since 1950 the demand-side theory has failed to explain the dramatic increase of real stock prices.

Regardless of the reasons fundamentalists will find for aggregate stock movements, technicians will continue to ignore the driving forces, whatever they may be, and will make their stock predictions based upon shapes seen in the plotting aggregate stock movements.

21.1.2. *Technical Analysis*

Technical analysts, rather than working through the large amount of fundamental information about an investment such as company earnings, competitive products, and forthcoming legislation, searched for a summary of all facts by studying the way security prices behave historically. Over the past decades, technical analysts have focused their attention almost totally on charts of security market prices and related summary statistics.

Technical analysis is based on the widely accepted premise that security prices are determined by the supply of and the demand for securities. Typically technical analysts record historical financial data on charts, study these charts in an effort to find meaningful patterns, and use these patterns to predict future prices. Technical analysts believe that past patterns of market action will recur in the future and that past patterns can be used for predictive purposes.

Rather than try to evaluate the intrinsic value of a security, the technical analysts seek to estimate security prices; that is, they try to forecast short-run shifts in supply and demand that will affect the market price of one or more securities. Some of the tools used by chartists to measure supply and demand and to forecast security prices are the Dow theory chart, odd-lot theory, confidence index, breadth-of-market indicators, relative-strength analysis, and trading-volume data.

21.1.3. *Dow Theory*

One of the tools used by technical analysts to measure supply and demand and forecast security prices is the **Dow theory**. The Dow theory is used to indicate reversals and trends in the market as a whole or in individual securities. According to the theory, there are three movements going on in the markets at all times. These movements are (1) daily fluctuations (the narrow movement from day-to-day), (2) secondary movements (short-run movements over two weeks to a month or more), and (3) primary trends, major movements covering at least four years in duration. The theory asserts that daily fluctuations are meaningless. However, daily asset prices or the market average must be plotted in order to outline the primary and secondary trends. In plotting the asset prices, the Dow theorists search for price patterns indicating market tops and bottoms.

Technical analysts use three basic types of charts: (1) line charts, (2) bar charts, and (3) point-and-figure charts. Bar charts have vertical bars representing each day's price movement. Each bar spans the distance from the day's highest price to the day's lowest price with a small cross on the bar marking the closing price. Lines are used to connect successive day's prices. Patterns indicating market tops or bottoms are then searched for in these line charts by technical analysis. *The Wall Street Journal* uses the bar charts to show daily fluctuations in the Dow Jones Average.

Point-and-figure charts are more complex than line or bar charts. These charts draw the percentage change directly. They are not only used to detect reversals in a trend but are also employed to set actual price forecasts.

The construction of a point-and-figure chart varies with the price level of the stock being charted. Only significant changes are posted to a point-and-figure chart. As a result there are one-point, two-point, three-point, and five-point, point-and-figure charts.

To set the price target (forecasted stock price), which a stock is expected to attain, point-and-figure chartists begin by finding a congestion area. A congestion area is a horizontal band created by a series of reversals around a given price level. Congestion areas are supposed to result when supply and demand are equal. A breakout is said to have occurred when a column of price increase rises above the top of a congestion area. Breakout refers to a price rise or fall in which the price rises above or falls below the horizontal band which contained the congestion area. A penetration of the top of a congestion area is a signal for continued price rise. Penetration of the bottom of a congestion area by a column of price declines is a bearish signal.

To establish estimates of the new prices that a security should attain, point-and-figure chartists measure the horizontal width of a congestion area as they watch for a breakout. When a breakout occurs, the chartist projects the horizontal count upward or downward in the same direction as the breakout to establish the new price target.

21.1.4. *The Odd-Lot Theory*

The **odd-lot theory** is one of several theories of contrary opinion. In essence, the theory assumes that the common man is usually wrong, and it is therefore advantageous to pursue strategies opposite to his thinking. In order to find out what the common man is doing, statistics on odd-lot trading are gathered. Most odd-lot purchases are made by amateur investors with limited resources — that is, by the common man, who is a small, unsophisticated investor.

Odd-lot trading volume is reported daily. The odd-lot statistics are broken down into the number of shares purchased, sold, and sold short. The index of odd-lot purchases less odd-lot sales is typically plotted concurrently with some market index. The odd-lotter's net purchases are used by chartists as a leading indicator of market prices. That is, positive net purchases are presumed to forecast falls in market prices, and net selling by odd-lotters is presumed to occur at the end of a bear market.

21.1.5. *The Confidence Index*

The **confidence index** is designed to measure how willing investors are to take a chance in the market. It is the ratio of high-grade bond yields to low-grade bond yields. This ratio is started below one. When bond investors grow more confident about the economy, they shift their holdings from high-grade to lower-grade bonds, lowering their yield relative to high-grade bonds and increasing the confidence index. In other words, the confidence ratio moves close to one.

Confidence-index technicians believe that the confidence index leads the stock market by two to eleven months. An upturn in the confidence index is supposed to foretell the rising optimism and rising prices in the stock market. A fall in the confidence index represents the fact that low-grade bond yields are rising faster or falling more slowly than high-grade yields. This is supposed to reflect increasing risk aversion by institutional money managers who foresee an economic downturn and rising bankruptcies and defaults. Analysts who have examined the confidence index conclude that it conveys some information for security analysis.

21.1.6. *Trading Volume*

Many technical analysts believe that it is possible to detect whether the market in general and/or certain security issues are bullish or bearish by studying the volume of trading. Volume is supposed to be a measure of the intensity of investors' emotions. If high volume occurs on days when prices move up, the overall nature of the market is considered to be bullish. If the high volume occurs on days when prices are falling, this is a bearish sign.

21.1.7. *Moving Average*

Moving-average (or rate-of-change) technicians focus on prices and/or moving averages of prices. The moving average is used to provide a smoothed stable reference point against which the daily fluctuations can be gauged. When the daily prices penetrate above the moving-average line, technicians interpret this penetration as a bearish signal. When the daily prices move downward through the moving average, they frequently fail to rise again for many months.

Moving-average analysts recommend buying a stock when: (1) the 200-day moving average flattens out and the stock's price rises through the moving average, (2) the price of a stock falls below a moving-average line that is rising, and (3) the price of a stock that is above the moving-average line falls but turns around and begins to rise again before it ever reaches the moving-average line.

Moving-average chartists recommend selling a stock when: (1) the moving-average line flattens out and the stock's price drops downward through the moving-average line, (2) a stock's price rises above a moving-average line that is declining, and (3) a stock's price falls downward through the moving-average line and turns around to rise but then falls again before getting above the moving-average line.

There are many tools for technical analysts. All the technical-analysis tools have one thing in common — they attempt to measure the supply and demand for some group of investors. Shifts in supply and demand are presumed to be gradual, not instantaneous. When changes in prices are detected, they are presumed to be the result of gradual shifts in supply and demand rather than a series of instantaneous shifts. Since these shifts are expected to continue as the price gradually reacts to news or other factors, they are used to predict further price changes.

There has been a lack of published research on technical analysis. Most of the work that has been done is held privately and forms the basis of trading recommendations. Academic studies in this area have concentrated on the random-walk model, which implies that daily price changes are uncorrelated. A paper by Irwin and Uhrig (1984) combined trading-system optimization and efficient-market tests to investigate the validity of technical analysis for the future market. Irwin and Uhrig's specific objectives were (1) to test whether the random-walk model is a reasonable description of daily future-price behavior, (2) to simulate the trading of four technical systems, and (3) to deduce the market-efficiency implications of both sets of results.

If the futures market is either weak-form efficient or the random-walk model describes price generation, the implication is that the expected profit of a technical trading system will be no greater than zero. Two approaches have been adopted to test futures-market efficiency. The first, statistical analysis of the random-walk model, by Taylor (1982), has been rejected as a description of price behavior for futures markets in the U.S., United Kingdom, and Australia. The second approach is to simulate the trading of a technical system and examine the resulting profits or losses. These two applications have been confined almost exclusively to examining **Alexander's** (1961) **filter rule**, which results in the existence of trading profits. However, the significance and importance of filter-rule research are difficult to assess objectively (see Sweeny, 1988). Lee *et al.* (2011) use price per share, dividend per share, and shares outstanding to test the existence of a price disequilibrium adjustment process with international index data and U.S. equity data. They found that a disequilibrium price adjustment process does, in fact, exist in our empirical data. These results support Lo and Wang's (2000) findings that trading volume is an important factor in capital asset pricing.

Irwin and Uhrig (1984) tried to improve upon earlier efforts by: (1) testing both the random-walk model and the trading-system tests over the same data, (2) optimizing the trading systems and then simulating the optimized system over out-of-sample data, (3) deducting for both commission and transaction costs, and (4) examining trading systems actively used by trading advisors. Their data consist of eight series of daily future-price closes.

The authors examined four technical trading systems selected as representative of the three main types of trading systems: price channels, moving averages, and momentum oscillators. The four systems examined are the Donchian system (DONCH), and the moving-average with a percentage price band system (MAPB), the dual moving-average crossover system (DMAC), and the directional indicator system (DI).

The **DONCH system** is part of a family of technical systems known as price channels. The system generates a buy signal any time the daily high price is outside (greater than) the highest price in the specified time interval. A sell signal is generated any time the daily high breaks outside (lower than) the lowest price in the same interval. The system always generates a signal for the trader to take a position, long or short, in the futures market.

The **MAPB system** belongs to a technical family derived from moving averages. Moving averages come in many forms — that is, simple moving averages, exponentially weighted, linearly weighted, and so on. The MAPB system employs a simple moving average with a band based on a percentage of price centered around it. A signal to exit a position occurs when the price recrosses the moving average. The band creates a neutral zone in which the trader is neither long nor short.

The **DMAC system** employs logic similar to the MAPB system by seeking to find when the short-run trend rises above or below the long-term trend. The MAPB represents the short-term trend by the daily price and the long-term trend by the moving average. The DMAC uses a short-term moving average and long-term moving average to represent the short- and long-term trend. A change in the price trend is signaled when these two moving averages cross. Specifically, a buy signal is generated when the shorter moving average is greater than (above) the longer moving average, and a sell signal when the shorter moving average is less than (below) the longer moving average. The trader always maintains a long or short position in the futures market.

The **DI system** is from a technical family known as momentum oscillators. Whereas the previous systems outlined deal with the futures-price level, oscillators deal with price changes. The logic employed by the directional-indicator system is that any trending period can be characterized as having a significant excess of either positive or negative price movements. Periods when prices are quickly moving upward will have more upward price change than downward price change, and *vice versa*. It is this relative price change that the DI estimates.

Irwin and Uhrig (1984), using the Lyung-Box test on the autocorrelation analysis for nonrandomness, found that their results indicated that the random-walk model could be rejected for futures on corn, soybeans, sugar, wheat, cocoa, and live cattle. However, the random-walk model could not be rejected for futures on copper and live hogs.

The data are divided into three sample periods (1960–1981, 1960–1972, and 1973–1981) to account for the structural and policy changes that occurred in the early 1970s. Each trading system is optimized; that is, the highest profit parameter is found. The optimum parameters are used as the basis for trading in a time period after their development. Substantial trading-system profits are evident over the 1960–1981 period for all commodities. However, these are almost exclusively concentrated in the years from 1973 to 1981. As a result futures-market efficiency cannot be rejected for the 1960–1972 period and was rejected for the 1973–1981 period. It is felt that structural and policy changes during 1973–1981 prevented futures prices from adjusting instantaneously to new information, resulting in significant profits from technical trading systems utilizing significant price trends.

Technical analysis seems to have some merit when the market involved is not efficient. By studying price trends, the analyst is able to realize excess profits.

21.2. Anomalies and Their Implications

Chapter 16 briefly introduced the anomalies in the efficient-market literature. Four authors — Basu, Banz, Reinganum, and Keim — deal with the anomalies centered around the P/E ratio, size effect, and January effect. This section looks at these anomalies in the context of technical and fundamental analysis.

21.2.1. *Basu's Findings*

Basu (1977) tries to determine empirically whether the investment performance of common stocks is related to their P/E ratios. The primary data for this study come from a data base that includes the Compustat file of NYSE industrial firms, the investment–return file from the Center for Research in Security Prices (CRSP) tape, and a delisted file containing selected accounting data and investment returns for securities delisted from the NYSE. The database represents 1,400 industrial firms, all of which actually traded on the NYSE between September 1956 and August 1971.

For any given year under consideration, three criteria are used in selecting sample firms: (1) the fiscal year ends on December 31, (2) the firm actually traded on the NYSE as of the beginning of the portfolio-holding period and is included in the merged tape, and (3) the relevant investment–return and financial-statement data are not missing.

Beginning with 1956, the P/E ratio of every sample security is computed. The numerator of the ratio is defined as the market value of common stock as of December 31, and the denominator as reported annual earnings available for common stockholders. These ratios are ranked and five portfolios are formed.

This procedure, repeated annually on each April 1, gives 14 years (April 1967–March 1971) of return data for each of the P/E portfolios.

Basu uses the performance-evaluation measures of Jensen, Sharpe, and Treynor. His results indicate that during the period April 1957–March 1971 low-P/E portfolios seem to have (on average) earned higher absolute and risk-adjusted rates of return than the high-P/E portfolios. Even after accounting for a bias in the performance measure resulting from the effect of risk, above-normal returns are found.

The results are consistent with the view that P/E-ratio information is not fully reflected in security prices in as rapid a manner as postulated by the semi-strong form of the efficient-market hypothesis (EMH). To the extent that low-P/E portfolios did earn superior returns on a risk-adjusted basis, the proposition of the price-ratio hypothesis (on the relationship between investment performance of equity securities and their P/E ratios) seems to be valid. There appear to be lags and frictions in the process of adjusting security prices to publicly available information. Therefore, publicly available P/E ratios may possess information content and may warrant an investor's attention at the time of portfolio formation or revision.

21.2.2. *Reinganum's Findings*

Reinganum's (1981) study documents an empirical anomaly that suggests that either the simple one-period CAPM is misspecified or that capital markets are inefficient. He forms portfolios based upon firm size or E/P ratios. The data, collected primarily from *The Wall Street Journal*, consists of corporate quarterly earnings and announcement dates from the fourth quarter of 1975 and the subsequent eight quarters. The sample consists of 566 NYSE and American Stock Exchange (AMEX) stocks with fiscal-year ends in December.

The sample is divided into portfolios based upon standardized unexpected earnings (SUE). The high-SUE portfolio contains the 20 securities with the highest SUE, while the low-SUE portfolio consists of 20 firms with the lowest SUE. Each 20-security portfolio is subdivided into two equal-weighted portfolios of 10 securities. One portfolio contains the 10 securities with the highest estimated betas, and the other consists of the 10 firms with the lowest estimated betas. Weights are selected for the two 10-security portfolios so that the overall 20-security portfolio has an estimated beta equal to one.

Reinganum's results indicate that abnormal returns cannot be earned over the period studied by constructing portfolios on the basis of a firm's SUE. These results offer support for the assumption of market efficiency.

Reinganum uses the same data source computed earnings/price (E/P) ratios for the firms in his sample. The E/P ratios are computed as the quarterly net income divided by the value of the common stock. The value of the common stock is calculated with both pre-earnings and post-earnings announcement prices. If capital markets rapidly incorporate information into prices, then rankings based upon post-announcement prices should reflect only the equilibrium effect between E/P ratios and asset pricing.

Results indicate that during 1976 and 1977, an abnormal return of about 0.1% per day on the average can be earned by forming portfolios based on E/P ratios. That is, the mean return of a high-E/P portfolio exceeds the mean return of a low-E/P portfolio by about 0.1% per day, even after adjusting for beta risk. Ignoring transaction costs, this mean spread is greater than 6% per quarter, and it persists for at least two quarters. Reinganum suggests that the evidence indicates a misspecification in CAPM rather than any informational inefficiencies.

The evidence in this study suggests that the simple one-period CAPM is misspecified. The set of factors omitted from the equilibrium pricing mechanism seems to be more closely related to firm size than E/P ratios. According to Reinganum, the misspecification does not appear to be a market inefficiency in the sense that abnormal returns arise because of transaction costs or informational lags. Rather, the source of the misspecification seems to be risk factors that are omitted from the CAPM as is evidenced by the persistence of abnormal returns for at least two years.

21.2.3. *Banz's Findings*

Banz (1981) examines the empirical relationship between the return and the total market value of NYSE common stocks. His sample includes all common stocks quoted on the NYSE for at least five years between 1926 and 1975. The securities are assigned to one of 25 portfolios containing similar numbers of securities, first from one to five on the basis of the market value of the stock, then the securities in each of those five are in turn assigned to one of five portfolios on the basis of their beta. Five years of data are used for the estimation of the security beta; the next five year's data are used for the re-estimation of the portfolio betas. Stock price and number of shares outstanding at the end of the five-year periods are used for the calculation of the market proportions. The portfolios are updated every year.

The results indicate that shares of firms with large market values have had smaller risk-adjusted returns, on average, than similar small firms over a 40-year period. This size effect is not linear in proportion to market value, but is most pronounced for the smallest firms in the sample. In addition, the effect is not very stable through time. Banz argues that the P/E ratio serves as a proxy for the size of a firm and not *vice versa*. He cites a study by Reinganum (1981), where the results show that the P/E effect disappears for both NYSE and AMEX stocks when Reinganum controls for size, but that there is a significant size effect even when he controls for the P/E ratio.

To summarize, the size effect exists, but it is not clear why it exists. Although it has been conjectured that the effect may be due to restricted distribution of information about small firms, it has not been established that size is not just a proxy for yet another effect.

21.2.4. *Keim's Findings*

Keim (1983) examines, month by month, the empirical relation between abnormal returns and the market value of NYSE and AMEX common stocks. Evidence is provided that daily abnormal return distributions in January have large means relative to the remaining 11 months, and that the relation between abnormal returns and size is always negative and more pronounced in January than in any other months. In particular, nearly 50% of the average magnitude of the size effect over the period 1963–1979 is due to January abnormal returns. Further, more than 50% of the January premium is attributable to large abnormal returns during the first week of trading in the year, particularly on the first trading day. In addition, Lee *et al.* (1998) have used mutual fund to study small firm January effect.

The data for this study are drawn from the CRSP daily stock files for a 17-year period, 1963–1979. The sample consists of firms listed on the NYSE and AMEX that had returns on the CRSP files during the entire calendar year under consideration.

21.2.5. *Additional Findings*

Although several hypotheses regarding the January effect have been suggested, the more prominent are a tax-loss selling hypothesis by Branch (1977) and an information hypothesis. However, neither has been theoretically or empirically linked to the seasonal return.

Since February 1984 (and prior to February 1980), each Thursday, following the close of financial markets, the Federal Reserve has released an estimate of the seasonally adjusted average M-1 money supplies prevailing over the week ending Wednesday eight days earlier. (Between February 1980 and February 1984, the weekly money-supply announcement was moved from Thursday to Friday afternoon.) Therefore the announcement effect cannot occur until the markets open on Monday. Other events over the weekend may have camouflaged the money-supply announcement effect during this period.

Cornell (1983) examined the money-supply announcement effect upon various assets, including three-month Treasury bills, 30-year Treasury bonds, German marks, and the Standard & Poor's 500 stock index. Notationally his model can be described as follows:

$$DA_t = A_0 + a_1 UM_t + a_2 EM_t + U_t, \tag{21.8}$$

where $DA_t =$ the change in asset return; $UM_t =$ the unexpected monetary announcement; $EM_t =$ the expected monetary announcement; and $U_t =$ the random disturbance.

Cornell summarized four major hypotheses that explain why money-supply announcements affect asset prices. First, the expected-inflation hypothesis states that the announcements alter analysts' inflation forecasts. Second, the Keynesian hypothesis predicts that in response to an announced innovation in the money stock, analysts expect the Fed to take offsetting action. Third, the real-activity hypothesis alleges that money-supply announcements provide the market with information about future output, and thereby future money demand. Finally, the risk-premium hypothesis states that money-supply announcements alter the required real return on financial assets by providing the market with information about aggregate risk preferences and beliefs. None of the hypotheses explained the reaction of all four assets. Therefore, at best, the market is responding to money-supply announcements in an eclectic manner.

Using data from January 5, 1978 to December 18, 1981, divided into two intervals to take account of the Federal Reserve's stated change in operating procedure on October 6, 1979, Cornell finds that the market was only responsive to monetary announcements after October 6, 1979. Others, notably Urich and Wachtel (1981) have found some evidence that the announcement effect did exist prior to the change in Fed policy. In addition, Cornell finds that only the unanticipated portion of the announcement is significant, and that a definite relationship exists between the asset-price change and the unanticipated money-supply change. In summary, the existence of anomalies tends to indicate that the market is not perfectly efficient. Due to this inefficiency, technical analysts have hope for some success in capturing excess profits.

Treynor and Ferguson (1985) further defended the use of technical analysis by using a Bayesian probability estimate to assess whether, in using past price data, the market has already incorporated some firm-specific information available to the investor. If the market has not discovered this information and past price data confirms this, the informed investor may be able to realize excess returns. Their results showed that past prices, combined with other valuable information, can be used to achieve excess returns. However, they noted that it is the firm-specific information that creates the opportunity while past prices serve to permit its exploitation.

21.3. Security Rate-of-Return Forecasting

This section discusses alternative methods to forecast security rate of return in security analysis. In order to do security-return forecasting, regression analysis, time-series analysis, and a composite approach are often utilized.

In forecasting security rates of return, both the fundamental and the technical analyst may use the regression approach. The time-series approach is more often associated with the technical school.

21.3.1. *Regression Approach*

A **regression approach** captures the relationship between independent variables(s) X_{it} and a dependent variable R_{jt} in a linear format. One can choose either a linear or log-linear model as defined below:

$$R_{jt} = a + bX_t + \in_t, \tag{21.9a}$$

$$\log R_{jt} = a' + b' \log X_t + \in'_t, \tag{21.9b}$$

in which $\in_t$ and $\in'_t$ are error terms. The choice between Equations (21.9a) and (21.9b) depends on whether the related variables, X_t and R_{jt} are normally or log-normally distributed.

In order to obtain the best linear model to predict R_{jt} given X_t, it is necessary to find the equation that minimizes the squared error term. The error term ($\in_t$) represents the difference between the actual value of R_{jt} and the predicted value of R_{jt}. The estimated value of R_{jt}, $\hat{R}_{jt}$ can be defined as

$$\hat{R}_{jt} = \hat{a} + \hat{b}X_t.$$

In general, if X_t is the series to be forecasted and y_{it} is the possible explanatory series, then a further example of an explanatory model is

$$X_t = a + b_1 y_{1t} + b_2 y_{2t} + \cdots + b_n y_{nt} + e_t.$$

To forecast one step ahead, write this as

$$X_{t+1} = a + b_1 y_{1t+1} + b_2 y_{2t+1} + \cdots + b_n y_{nt+1} + e_{t+1}.$$

Another model is therefore required to provide a forecast for y_{it+1} so that a forecast for X_{t+1} can be constructed. The regression model can be classified into fixed-coefficient and time-varying-coefficient versions. These two versions are now discussed using the market model of Chapters 9 and 10.

21.3.1.1. *Fixed-Coefficient Market Model*

A common model found in finance literature that is used to estimate the return on security j is the **fixed-coefficient market model**.

$$R_{jt} = \alpha_j + \beta_j R_{mt} + \in_{jt}, \tag{21.10}$$

where R_{jt} = return on security in period t; α_j = regression intercept term in period t; R_{mt} = return on the market portfolio in period t; β_j = estimated parametric coefficient in period t; and $\in_{jt}$ = error term in period t.

Using the estimated coefficient α_j and β_j from period t and forecasting the return on the market for time period $t+1$, $R_{m,t+1}$, the return on security j can be forecasted for period $t+1$:

$$R_{j,t+1} = \alpha_j + \beta_j R_{m,t+1} + \in_{j,t+1}. \tag{21.11}$$

21.3.1.2. *Time-Varying-Coefficient Market Model*

A variation of the fixed-coefficient market model, the **time-varying-coefficient market model** allows the coefficient to vary with time. Algebraically:

$$R_{jt} = \alpha_j + \beta_{jt} R_{mt} + \in_{jt}, \tag{21.12a}$$

$$\beta_{jt} = \beta_j + \gamma_1 X_1 + \gamma_2 X_2 + \cdots + \gamma_n X_n + \tau_{jt}. \tag{21.12b}$$

Rosenberg and McKibben (1973) used this format to predict stock returns. In their analysis, they used historical accounting variables (X) to predict the time-varying data.

Substituting Equation (21.12b) into Equation (21.12a) leads to a multiple-regression format where

$$R_{jt} = \alpha_j + \beta R_{mt} + \gamma_1(X_1 R_{mt}) + \gamma_2(X_2 R_{mt}) + \cdots + \gamma_n(X_n R_{mt}) + (\in_{jt} + \tau_{jt} R_{mt}). \tag{21.13}$$

In order to use this format to forecast $R_{j,t+1}$, not only must R_{mt+1} be forecasted but also $\beta_{j,t+1}$, which indicates that a forecast of variable X_j must be available. As one can see this is a much more complex situation than forecasting using a constant beta.

21.3.2. *Time-Series Approach*

A **time series** is a set of observations generated sequentially in time. If the set is continuous, the time series is said to be *continuous*. If the set is discrete, the time series is said to be *discrete*.

The use at time t of available observations from a time series to forecast its value at some future time $t+1$ can provide a base for economic and business planning, production planning, inventory and production control, and optimization of industrial processes. To calculate the best forecasts, it is also necessary to specify their accuracy, so that the risks associated with decisions based upon the forecasts may be calculated.

Two major approaches to time-series analysis are component analysis and sample-function analysis. **Component analysis** regards the time series as being composed of several influences or components that are generally taken to be trend-cycle, seasonal, and random movements. In component analysis the seasonal and trend movements are modeled in a deterministic manner. The trend might be fitted by a polynomial of a given degree and the seasonal component by a Fourier series (a trigonometric function with a given period and amplitude).

Sample-function analysis regards a time series as an observed sample function representing a realization of an underlying stochastic process. Complicated parametric statistical-estimation procedures are used to determine the properties of time-series data. Since empirical results obtained from component analysis are easier to understand and interpret, henceforth this chapter concerns only component analysis.

21.3.2.1. *Component Analysis*

Component analysis is based on the premise that seasonal fluctuations can be measured in an original series of economic data and separated from trend, cyclical, trading-day, and random fluctuation. The seasonal component reflects a long-term pattern of variation which is repeated constantly or in an evolving fashion from year to year. The trend-cycle component includes the long-term trend and the business cycle. The trading-day component consists of variations which are attributed to the composition of the calendar. The random component is composed of residual variations that reflect the effect of random or unexplained events in the time series.

Decomposing past time series and discovering the relative percentage contribution of the trend, seasonal, and random components to changes in the series provide insight to financial analysts. The trend-cycle component reflects permanent information in both a short- and long-run economic time series. The seasonal component is considered to represent a permanent pattern underlying the short-run time series. The random component contains the randomness that exists in the time series for both short- and long-run analysis. The higher the relative percentage contribution of the random component in a time series, the greater the uncertainty and thus the greater the probability of forecasting errors.

Gentry and Lee (1987) used the decomposition method known as the X-II to measure the relative percentage contribution of trend-cycle, seasonal, and random components to changes in the original series of income-statement variables. Their results indicated that the relative percentage contribution of the trend-cycle, seasonal, and random components were directly affected by the length of the time period of data. The shorter the time period of data, the greater is the relative percentage contribution of the irregular component. The longer the time period, the greater is the relative contribution of the trend-cycle component and the smaller the seasonal component. In addition, the relative percentage contribution of the components varied widely among companies for all of the income-statement variables tested. These results have serious implications both for internal management and external analysis. An industry index of the percentage contribution of the random components for each income statement variable would provide a useful benchmark to measure the reliability of an analyst's forecast.

21.3.2.2. *ARIMA Models*

This section examines a class of models used in forecasting time-series data. It is best to begin by examining the simplest of all possible time series, a purely random series. A series that is purely random is sometimes referred to as a white-noise or **random-walk** model. Mathematically such a series can be described by the following equation:

$$y_t = a_t, \tag{21.14}$$

in which the series a_t is assumed to have a mean of zero, to be unrelated to its past values, and to have a constant variance over time. Mathematically, these assumptions can be summarized as (i) $E(a_t) = 0$, (ii) $E(a_t, a_{t-i}) = 0$ for all t and $i \neq 0$ (iii) $\text{Var}(a_t) = \sigma_a^2$ for all t.

Modifying Equation (21.14) to allow the series to be concentrated around a nonzero mean δ, the series could now be described:

$$y_t = \delta + a_t. \tag{21.15}$$

Equation (21.15) is a model that can be used to represent many different time series in economics and finance. For example, in an efficient market a series of stock prices might be expected to randomly fluctuate around a constant mean. So the actual stock price observed in time period t would be equal to its average price plus some random shock in time period t.

The question now is how to model a purely random series. Fortunately, a theorem known as **Wold's decomposition** provides the answer. Wold's decomposition proves that any stationary time series (a series is stationary if it is centered around a constant mean) can be considered as a sum of self-deterministic components. This theorem states that a time series can be generated from a weighted average of past random shocks of infinite order. A model such as this is known as a **moving average of infinite order** and can be expressed by the following equation:

$$y_t = \delta + \Theta_1 a_{t-1} + \Theta_2 a_{t-2} + \cdots + \Theta_\infty a_{t-\infty} + a_t, \tag{21.16}$$

where δ = mean of the process; $a_{t-\infty}$ = random shock that occurred ∞ periods earlier; and Θ_∞ = parameter that relates the random shock ∞ periods earlier to the current value of y.

The moving-average model just discussed should not be confused with the moving-average concept previously discussed in this chapter. Previously, the term *moving average* was used to refer to an arithmetic average of stock prices over a specified number of days. The term *moving average* was used because the average was continually updated to include the most recent series of data. In time-series analysis, a moving-average process refers to a series generated by a weighted average of past random shocks.

Because it would be impossible to estimate a model of infinite order, in practice it is best to specify a model of finite order. A moving-average process of order q with zero mean would be expressed:

$$y_t = \Theta_1 a_{t-1} + \cdots + \Theta_q a_{t-q} + a_t. \tag{21.17}$$

A moving-average process is not the only way to model a stationary time series. Again, consider a moving-average process of infinite order:

$$y_t = \Theta_1 a_{t-1} + \Theta_2 a_{t-2} + \cdots + a_t. \tag{21.18}$$

Equation (21.18) can be rewritten in terms of the error term a_t:

$$a_t = y_t - \Theta_1 a_{t-1} - \Theta_2 a_{t-2} - \cdots. \tag{21.19}$$

Because Equation (21.19) is recursive in nature, it is easy to generate an expression for a_{t-1}:

$$a_{t-1} = y_{t-1} - \Theta_1 a_{t-2} - \Theta_2 a_{t-3} - \cdots. \tag{21.20}$$

By substituting the expression for a_{t-1} into Equation (21.19):

$$\begin{aligned} a_t &= y_t - \Theta_1(y_{t-1} - \Theta_1 a_{t-2} - \Theta_2 a_{t-3} - \cdots) - \Theta_2 a_{t-2} - \Theta_3 a_{t-3} - \cdots \\ &= y_t - \Theta_1 y_{t-1} + (\Theta_1^2 - \Theta_2) a_{t-2} + (\Theta_1\Theta_2 - \Theta_3) a_{t-3} + \cdots. \end{aligned} \quad (21.21)$$

By generating expressions for $a_{t-2}\, a_{t-3}, \ldots$ and substituting them into Equation (21.21) a_t can be expressed in terms of past values of y_t:

$$a_t = y_t + \phi_1 y_{t-1} + \phi_2 y_{t-2} + \cdots. \quad (21.22)$$

Rearranging Equation (21.22) in terms of y_t:

$$y_t = -\phi_1 y_{t-1} - \phi_2 y_{t-2} - \cdots + a_t, \quad (21.23)$$

where $\phi_1 = \phi_1$ and $\phi_2 = \Theta_1^2 - \Theta_2$.

Equation (21.23) is known as an **autoregressive process of infinite order**. The term *autoregressive* refers to the fact that y_t is expressed in terms of its own past values $y_{t-1}, y_{t-2}, \ldots, y_{t-p}$.

Again, because it is impossible to estimate a model of infinite order, an approximate model of finite order is specified. An autoregressive process of order p can be expressed:

$$y_t = -\phi_1 y_{t-1} - \cdots - \phi_p y_{t-p} - \cdots + a_t. \quad (21.24)$$

Thus a stationary time series can be expressed in two ways: (1) as a moving-average process in which the series can be represented as a weighted average of past random shocks, or (2) as an autoregressive process in which the series can be represented as a weighted average of its past values. A third possibility is that a series may involve some combination of the two processes. This process is referred to as a mixed **autoregressive moving-average (ARMA) process**.

An ARMA process of infinite order can be expressed:

$$y_t = \Theta_1 a_{t-1} + \Theta_2 a_{t-2} + \cdots - \phi_1 y_{t-1} - \phi_2 y_{t-2} - \cdots + a_t. \quad (21.25)$$

Again, an ARMA process of finite order must be specified in order to make estimation possible. An ARMA (p, q) process can be expressed:

$$y_t = \Theta_1 a_{t-1} + \cdots + \Theta_q a_{t-q} - \phi_1 y_{t-1} - \cdots - \phi_p y_{t-p} + a_t. \quad (21.26)$$

So far the discussion has focused on the estimation of stationary time series. Suppose the process of interest is not stationary. Fortunately, a nonstationary series can usually be made stationary by transforming the data in an appropriate manner. The most popular method of transforming a nonstationary series to a stationary one is by differencing the series. For example, suppose the series $y_1, y_2, \ldots, y_t$ is nonstationary. By differencing the series a new series, $Z_1, Z_2, \ldots, Z_{t-1}$, is created. The new series can be defined as (i) $Z_1 = y_2 - y_1$ (ii) $Z_2 = y_3 - y_2 \ldots$ (iii) $Z_{t-1} = y_t - y_{t-1}$.

If the series Z_t is nonstationary, it may be necessary to differentiate the series Z_t.

The modeling of a series that has been differenced is referred to as an **autoregressive integrated moving-average (ARIMA) process**. A detailed discussion of ARIMA modeling is beyond the scope of this book; nevertheless, a brief outline of the ARIMA modeling procedure is in order. (See Nelson (1973) or Nazem (1988), for details of the ARIMA procedure.)

The ARIMA process uses the following three steps as (1) Identification, (2) Estimation and (3) Forecasting.

The first step is to identify the appropriate model. Identification involves determining the degree of differencing necessary to make the series stationary and to determine the form (ARMA or ARIMA) and order of the process.

After a suitable model is identified, the parameters $\phi_1, \ldots, \phi_p$, $\Theta_1, \ldots, \Theta_q$, need to be estimated. The final step in the ARIMA process is to use the model for forecasting. Oftentimes the adequacy of the model is checked by using the model to forecast within the sample. This allows a comparison of the forecasted values to the actual values. If the model is determined to be adequate, the model can be used to forecast future values of the series.

21.3.3. *Composite Forecasting*

Numerous approaches running from sophisticated multiple-equation regression techniques to rather naïve extrapolations or intuitive estimates are being utilized to produce forecasts. Bessler and Brandt (1979) examined three alternative procedures for forecasting time-dependent quarterly observations on hog, cattle, and broiler prices along with composite forecasts based on various linear combinations of these three procedures. The alternative methods for forecasting these prices are econometric models, time series (ARIMA), and expert opinion.

The results obtained by Bessler and Brandt for selected performance measures (mean-squared error and turning points) applied to the forecasts of each method over the period 1976 quarter I through 1979 quarter II suggest that no method consistently outperformed or was outperformed by the other two methods. In terms of mean-squared error performance forecasts based on the ARIMA processes are lowest for hog and cattle prices, while the econometric model gives lowest mean-squared error forecasts for broiler prices.

The mean forecast error is determined by taking the average of the difference between the summation of the overpredictions and the summation of the underpredictions. A negative sign would indicate that the average forecast series is above the mean of the actual series; a positive sign suggests an average forecast which is low. The mean absolute forecast error is simply the average of the absolute values of the forecast errors.

Composite forecasts based on the forecasts of the individual methods are formed using three procedures; minimum variance, adaptive weighting, and simple average composites. The empirical results from all three composite forecasting schemes generate performance levels that are at least as good as any of the individual forecasts and usually much better. In particular, the mean-squared error of the best individual forecasting method is compared with that of the best composite for each of the three commodities. The composite forecast errors of the three commodities average 14% lower than the errors of the best individual forecasts.

The **econometric model** is essentially based on representations of the underlying economic behavioral system for a particular commodity. These representations attempt to identify and model the relevant supply-and-demand factors that together determine market price and quantity.

As an alternative to statistical models for forecasting, forecasts based upon expert opinions are available. These forecasts represent an accumulation of knowledge about the particular industry, commodity, or stock in question. In many respects, the forecasts of experts are like those of econometric- or ARIMA-model forecasting in that they incorporate much of the same information from the same data sources. Expert opinions, however, are less restrictive or structures, in that the expert can change the weights assigned to different bits of information, or can select with relative ease the sources from which to draw the data. In addition, these expert forecasts are able to incorporate information that cannot, perhaps, be included in a more quantitative model in the form of data.

Recognizing that most forecasts contain some information that is not used in other forecasts, it seems possible that a combination of forecasts will quite often outperform any of the individual forecasts. Bessler and Brandt (1979) construct composite forecasts based upon composite weighting schemes. Bessler and Brandt use various tests or measures of performance to evaluate the price forecasts of econometric, ARIMA, expert-opinion, and composite methods. Of the single-variable measures, they use the mean-squared error, the mean forecast error, and the mean absolute forecast error. The mean-squared error is a nonparametric statistic that provides a measure of the size of individual forecast errors from the actual values. Because the error is squared, large errors detract significantly from the performance of the method.

Performance indicators that track the movements of actual and forecast price series are called tracking measures. Examples of tracking measures are the number of turning points missed or falsely predicted compared with those correctly forecasted. Although these measures will not indicate which forecasting method most closely approximates the actual series, they are particularly useful when the forecaster is interested in knowing when a series is likely to turn upward or downward from its current pattern.

Bessler and Brandt's study does not find any specific forecasting method to be universally superior in terms of the performance measures. Although the ARIMA model performs best for two of three commodities, its performance is poorest for the third commodity in terms of the mean-squared error criterion. The composite forecasting method's mean-squared errors are lower than or nearly as low as the best of the individual methods. More important, in no case does a composite method of forecast generate errors that are as large as the worst of the individual methods.

The results of the performance evaluation suggest that forecasters should seriously consider using composite forecasting techniques. The idea that alternative forecasting methods use a variety of different information sources and means for assimilating the information and generating forecasts, a variety that can be captured by a composite forecast, is not only theoretically appealing but, in Bessler's and Brandt's study, somewhat empirically substantiated. Appendix 21A presents the composite forecasting method.

21.4. Value Line Ranking

The **Value Line Investment Survey** is an independent weekly investment-advisory service registered with the U.S. Securities and Exchange Commission. The weekly Value Line survey comes in three sections:

(1) *Rating and Reports* contains full-page reports on each of 1,700 stocks. The stocks are classified into 92 industry groups. A report on the industry precedes reports on the stocks in it. Every week, about 130

stocks in seven or eight industries are covered on a preset sequential schedule.

(2) The *Summary and Indexes* is a weekly alphabetical catalog of all 1,700 stocks at their most recent prices, with their current ranking for timeliness and safety.

(3) *Selection and Opinion* gives Value Line's opinion of business prospects, the stock-market outlook, and the advisable investment strategy.

21.4.1. *Criteria of Ranking*

By means of the two rankings, timeliness and safety, Value Line relays its expectations about the performance of individual stocks and industries. The timeliness rank runs on a scale from 1 (highest) down to 5 (lowest). The safety rank is a measure of risk avoidance. It is based mainly on the company's relative financial strength and the stock's price stability. The safety rank changes infrequently and may be taken as a forecast of risk avoidance. Safety ranks run on a scale of 1 (safest) to 5 (riskiest).

The rankings are drawn almost completely from published information about the earnings and price history of the companies that are followed, and are based on 10 years of history of the companies that are followed, and are based on 10 years of history on earnings and prices. The rankings are produced primarily by a computer using as input the earnings and price history. The system tends to assign high ranks to stocks with low P/E ratios relative to historic norms and to the current P/E ratio of the market. The system also tends to assign high ranks to stocks whose quarterly earnings reports show an upward momentum, relative to the quarterly earnings on the market as a whole, and to stocks that have upward price momentum. These factors are chosen by doing a cross-sectional regression on past data. The set of weights that seems to give the best predictive ability is then chosen. In sum, the one-year rankings are based on growth in earnings, price momentum, and the P/E ratio of each stock relative to the market and to historical standards for the stock.

The evaluation of a single stock involves:

(1) Choosing stocks that are acceptable in terms of timeliness rankings;
(2) Among the stocks chosen for timeliness, picking those that are in industries also shown to be timely;
(3) Among the most timely stocks in the most timely industries, picking those that conform to the investor's safety constraints;

(4) Among those stocks that meet the investor's timeliness and safety constraints, choosing those that meet the investor's current yield requirement.

21.4.2. *Performance Evaluation*

In studies to determine the profitability of the investment advice given by various brokerages and investment advisors, Value Line recommendations yield a portfolio that earns a few percentage points more return per year than could be earned by picking a large portfolio randomly. Fischer Black (1972), advocate of the buy-and-hold strategy, using monthly data over a given year commencing with April 1965, tested for the investment performance of the Value Line rankings. He used Jensen's time-series test of consistency of performance, calculating the return on the market at frequent intervals. A time-series regression of the excess return on the portfolio against the excess on the market was run; the intercept of that regression shows the extra returns the portfolio is able to achieve adjusted for risk. The intercept is then tested for significance.

Black constructed portfolios of all the stocks in each ranking and weighted each stock equally each month. Purchases were assumed to occur at the close of the markets on Friday, which is when most subscribers receive their reports. The results of Black's tests show that the success of the rankings are very consistent over time, and thus very significant in a statistical sense. The extra return of rank 1 stocks is about 10% per year; it is about −10% per year for the rank 5 stocks. Black notes that if weekly returns and associated portfolio revisions had been used, rank 1 would have earned an extra 20% per year rather than an extra 10% per year.

In sum, the use of Jensen's CAPM time-series test tends to indicate that rankings clearly provide a profitable portfolio strategy for investors who can execute orders at low transaction costs. Even in reducing the turnover activity involved, significant excess returns were achieved.

Similar studies were performed by Holloway (1981) and Copeland and Mayer (1982). Holloway (1981) found significant performance for rank 1 firms over the 1974–1977 period. Copeland and Mayers (1982) noted that rank 1 firms outperformed rank 5 firms by 6.8% per year on a risk-adjusted basis over the 1965–1978 period for portfolios updated semi-annually. A later work by Chen *et al.* (1987) using an APT framework has results that are similar to the Copeland and Mayers (1982) results.

Stickel (1985), using an event-study methodology, examined evidence on (1) the differential impact of the various types of rank change and (2) the speed of adjustment of individual security prices to new information. His results indicated that although Value Line rank changes have information content, the effect varies by the type of rank change. Changes from rank 2 to rank 1 have the most dramatic effect on prices. A cross-sectional analysis finds that smaller firms have a greater reaction to a rank change than larger firms. Finally, a speed-of-adjustment test suggests that individual securities with significant abnormal performance on event day 0 or +1 adjust to the information in rank change over a multiple-day period.

Lee and Park (1987), using a specification-analysis approach, investigated the effect of Value Line ranking changes for the beta coefficients. Following Equation (21.12), they generalized the additional market model:

$$R_{jt} = \alpha + \beta_{jt} R_{mt} + \in_{jt}, \tag{21.27a}$$

$$\beta_{jt} = \beta_j + CV_{jt}, \tag{21.27b}$$

where R_{jt} = rate of return for the jth firm in period t; R_{mt} = market rate of return in period t; β_{jt} = beta coefficient for the jth firm in period t; and V_{jt} = Value Line ranking for the firm in period t.

Substituting Equation (21.27b) into (21.27a):

$$R_{jt} = \alpha_j + \beta R_{mt} + C(V_{jt} R_{mt}) + E_{jt}. \tag{21.28}$$

In Equation (21.28), the interaction variable $V_{jt}R_{mt}$ can be used to test whether the Value Line ranking exhibits some market-timing ability on the jth firm's rate-of-return determination. Their empirical results using monthly stock-return data and Value Line weekly rankings over the period July 1978 to February 1983 suggest that firm's betas are affected by the change of a Value Line ranking more than 40% of the time. Most of the estimated Cs are negative; hence it can be concluded that an increase in rank will reduce the beta coefficient and rate of return of the firm.

These studies suggest that Value Line's recommendations are better than picking stocks randomly. Such favorable studies have never been published for other investment-advisory services by unbiased outside researchers.

21.5. Mutual Funds

Mutual funds are one of the most important investments for individual investors. In this section, mutual-fund classification and mutual-fund managers' timing and selectivity abilities are discussed.

21.5.1. *Mutual-Fund Classification*

According to the Investment Company Act of 1940, mutual funds must publish a written statement of their investment objectives and make it available to their shareholders. This objective can be changed only if the majority of the shareholders consent in advance to the new objective. The investment objectives of mutual funds can be classified into four categories as (1) Growth, (2) Income and growth, (3) Income and (4) Income, growth, and stability (balanced fund).[1]

These objectives are listed in descending order of the aggressiveness with which the fund's management implies it will seek a high average rate of return and assume the corresponding risks.

The **balanced funds** offer a complete investment program to their clients, so far as marketable securities are concerned. Their portfolios are presumably structured to include bonds and stocks in a ratio considered appropriate for an average individual investor given the return outlook for each sector and possibly a risk and volatility constraint.

Generally, however, these funds have been much less popular with investors than growth founds. **Growth funds** are structured to include a well-diversified combination of common stocks. Basically, three reasons may be cited. First, empirical studies of common stocks have almost invariably shown their long-term total returns to exceed those on bonds. Second, stock is generally conceded to be a better hedge against inflation risk than bonds. Third, many small investors may prefer to hold obligations of financial institutions as their major fixed-income securities because of their convenience and safety resulting from government insurance programs.

Income funds are composed of well-diversified selection of bonds. Empirical studies of long-term bond returns have indicated a widely diversified list of medium-quality bonds that have been superior to high-quality bonds. In order to obtain appropriate representation in this sector of the bond universe, which includes both corporate and municipals, a large pool of funds is required to obtain the desired degree of diversification. One should be alert to the possibility that in order to show highly attractive yields on a competitive basis, and income fund may acquire a heavy proportion of speculative bonds on which the default risk is high.

---

[1]Bodie *et al.* (2010) have classified mutual funds by investment policy into money market funds, equity funds, sector funds, bond funds, international funds, balance funds, asset allocation and flexible funds, and index funds.

Income-and-growth funds are composed of a combination of common stock and bonds. Whether the emphasis is on income or growth determines what percentage of bonds or common stock is in the portfolio.

21.5.2. *Mutual-Fund Manager's Timing and Selectivity*

When faced with the problem of deriving a performance measure, there are two considerations: (1) the collective performance of the security portfolio and (2) the relative performance of the security portfolio. Evidence about the collective performance is relevant to the EMH, and thereby to an understanding of the process of security-price determination. Evidence about the relative performance of individual mutual funds or portfolios is of obvious interest to entities with investment funds to allocate. In examining relative performance, market-timing activities as well as careful selection of individual securities are of concern.

Performance evaluations originally employed a one-parameter risk–return benchmark like that developed by Jensen (1968, 1969) and refined by Black *et al.* (1972), and Blume and Friend (1973). Such investigations have effectively focused on the fund manager's security-selection skills, since the examined portfolios' risk levels have been assumed to be stationary through time. Fama (1972) and Jensen (1972) pointed out the empirical measurement problems involved in evaluating properly the constituents of investment performance when portfolio risk levels are nonstationary as indicated by Chang and Lewellen (1984).

Fama (1972), rather than following previous research on performance measurement by Sharpe (1966), Treynor (1965), and Jensen (1968) (where performance was evaluated in a two-dimensional framework of risk and return), looked for a finer breakdown of performance. Up to that time the notion underlying performance measurement was a comparison of the returns on a managed portfolio relative to an annually selected portfolio with similar risk. The Sharpe–Lintner–Mossin version of the CAPM was used to obtain the benchmark portfolio return of the naively selected portfolio.

To obtain the benchmark portfolio, Fama (1972) used Sharpe's (1964) method to derive the efficient portfolio and *ex-ante* security-market line (SML). The efficient portfolios are formed according to

$$R_x = xR_f + (1 - x)R_m, \quad x \leq 1, \tag{21.29}$$

so that

$$E(R_x) = xR_f + (1-x)E(R_m), \tag{21.30}$$

$$\sigma(R_x) = (1-x)\sigma(R_m), \tag{21.31}$$

in which R_m, $E(R_m)$ and $\sigma(R_m)$ are one-period return, expected return, and standard deviation of return for the market portfolio m, respectively, and x is the weight associated with the risk-free asset.

Following Appendix 9A, the *ex-ante* SML can be defined:

$$E(R_j) = R_f + \left[\frac{E(R_m) - R_f}{\sigma(R_m)}\right]\frac{\text{Cov}(R_j, R_m)}{\sigma(R_m)}, \tag{21.32}$$

in which $\text{Cov}(R_j, R_m)$ is the covariance between the return on asset j and the return on the market portfolio.

The benchmark or naively selected portfolios are just the combination of the riskless asset R_f and the market portfolio R_m obtained with different values of x (where x is a weight). Given the *ex-post* or realized return R_m for the market portfolio for the naively selected portfolio *ex-post* return is

$$R_x = xR_f + (1-x)R_m. \tag{21.33}$$

Moreover:

$$\begin{aligned}\beta_x &= \frac{\text{Cov}(R_x, R_m)}{\sigma(R_m)} = \frac{\text{Cov}[(1-x)R_m, R_m]}{\sigma(R_m)},\\ &= (1-x)\sigma(R_m) = \sigma(R_x).\end{aligned} \tag{21.34}$$

That is, for the benchmark portfolio risk and standard deviation of return are equal.

For the naively selected portfolios, Equations (21.33) and (21.34) imply the following relationship between risk of an asset β_x and *ex-post* return R_x:

$$R_x = R_f + \left(\frac{R_m - R_f}{\sigma(R_m)}\right)\beta_x. \tag{21.35}$$

That is, for the naively selected portfolios, there is a linear relationship between risk and return. In performance-evaluation models using this methodology as a benchmark is provided against which the returns on managed portfolios are judged.

To use Equation (21.35) as a benchmark for evaluating *ex-post* portfolio returns requires estimates of risk β_p and dispersion $\sigma(R_p)$ of the managed portfolios, as well as an estimate of $\sigma(R_m)$, the dispersion of the return on the market portfolio. In order for the performance evaluation to be objective, it must be possible to obtain reliable estimates of these parameters from historical data. Evidence suggests that, at least for portfolios of 10 or more securities, β_p and $\sigma(R_p)$ seem to be fairly stationary over long periods of time and likewise for $\sigma(R_m)$. However, if market timing is to be a consideration, the problem of nonstationary β_p, $\sigma(R_p)$, and $\sigma(R_m)$ must be considered.

In addition, an assumption of normal return distributions is held, even though evidence suggests that actual return distributions conform more closely to non-normal, two-parameter stable distributions. Finally, the available empirical evidence indicates that the average returns over time on securities portfolios deviate systematically from the predictions of the standard CAPM model. In short, the evidence suggests that CAPM does not provide the best benchmark for the average return–risk tradeoffs available in the market from naively selected portfolios.

Fama (1972) first introduced the concept of **selectivity**, defined as how well a chosen portfolio does relative to a naïve portfolio with the same level of risk. Algebraically, this measure of performance of the chosen portfolio a is

$$\text{Selectivity} = R_a - R_x(\beta_a), \tag{21.36}$$

where

$$R_a = \frac{V_{a,t+1} - V_{a,t}}{V_{a,t}};$$

$V_{a,t}, V_{a,t+1} =$ the total market values at t and $t+1$ of the actual portfolio chosen at time t; and

$R_x(\beta_a) =$ the return on the combination of the riskless asset f and the market portfolio m that makes risk β_x equal to β_a, the risk of the chosen portfolio a.

Selectivity is the sole measure of performance in the work of Sharpe, Treynor, and Jensen, as discussed in Chapters 7 and 9. Fama introduced the concept of overall performance. Overall performance is the difference between the return on the chosen portfolio and the return on the riskless asset. Overall performance is in turn split into two parts, (1) selectivity and (2) risk. Algebraically:

$$\overset{\text{Overall performance}}{[R_a - R_f]} = \overset{\text{Selectivity}}{[R_a - R_x(\beta_a)]} + \overset{\text{Risk}}{[R_x(\beta_a) - R_f]}. \tag{21.37}$$

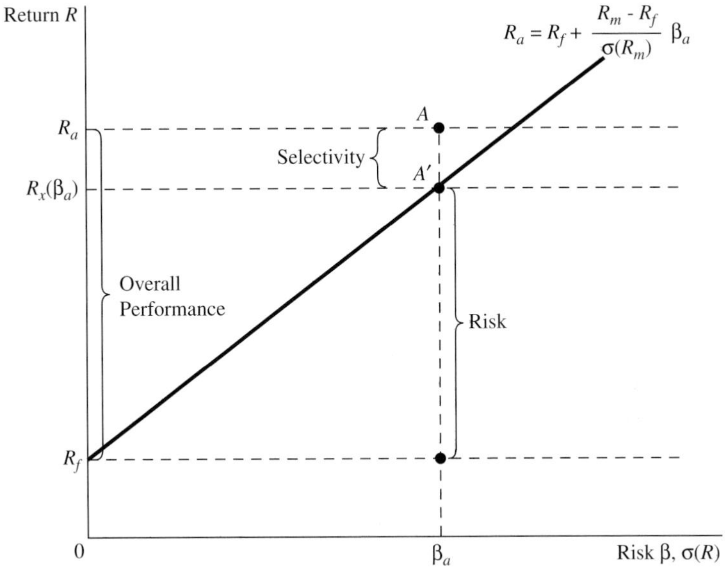

Fig. 21.3. Overall Components of Mutual-Fund Performance.

Figure 21.3 graphically presents the components related to mutual-fund performance of Equation (21.37). Jensen's measure of performance, is, of course, the height of the line $A'A$. Fama referred to this distance as the return due to selectivity. In addition, Fig. 21.3 indicates overall performance $R_a - R_f$ and risk $R_x(\beta_a) - R_f$. The risk measures the return for the decision to take one positive amount of risk. It will be determined by the level of risk chosen (the value of β_a) and the SML defined in Equation (21.35).

It does not matter whether this portfolio is a small part of the holdings of an investor, because diversifiable risk will be diversified away when looking at the investor's total holdings. If, on the other hand, the portfolio represents their entire holdings, it does matter. The question that now arises is whether beta or the standard deviation is the appropriate measure of risk for evaluating portfolio management. If total risk is the appropriate measure, then a Sharpe measure is the appropriate measurement tool.

Fama (1972) further decomposed Equation (21.37) by breaking up risk into two parts, (1) total portfolio risk $\sigma(R_a)$ and (2) market risk β_a. Fama then showed that the portfolio risk $\sigma(R_a)$ will be greater than the market risk β_a as long as the portfolio's returns are not perfectly correlated with the returns on the market. This can be seen by looking at the correlation coefficient $\rho_{a.m}$ between R_a and R_m:

$$\rho_{a,m} = \frac{\text{Cov}(R_a, R_m)}{\sigma(R_a)\sigma(R_m)}.$$

Multiplying both sides by $\sigma(R_a)$ yields:

$$\rho_{a,m}\sigma(R_a) = \frac{\text{Cov}(R_a, R_m)}{\sigma(R_m)}.$$

Notice that the right-hand side of the equation is just the measure of market risk β_a. So β_a can be written as

$$\rho_{a,m}\sigma(R_a) = \beta_a.$$

So

$$\beta_a \leq \sigma(R_a) \quad \text{when} \quad \rho_{a.m} \leq 1.$$

Because total risk $\sigma(R_a)$ is greater than market risk β_a, Fama was able to decompose selectivity into two parts, net selectivity and diversification. In Fig. 21.4, the quantity $R_x[\sigma(R_a)] - R_a$ is a measure of the extra return earned on portfolio as compared to a naïve portfolio with the same total risk.

Fama called $R_x[\sigma(R_a)] - R_a$ net selectivity. He called the distance $R_x[\sigma(R_a)] - R_x(\beta_a)$ diversification, decomposing $R_x[\sigma(R_a)] - R_x(\beta_a)$ into $R_a - R_x(\beta_a)$, selectivity, and $R_x[\sigma(R_a)] - R_a$, net selectivity.

The decomposition of selectivity can be seen algebraically:

$$\overbrace{[R_a - R_x(\beta_a)]}^{\text{Selectivity}} = \text{Net Selectivity} + \overbrace{[R_x(\sigma(R_a)) - R_x(\beta_a)]}^{\text{Diversification}}, \tag{21.38a}$$

$$\begin{aligned}\text{Net Selectivity} &= \overbrace{[R_a - R_x(\beta_a)]}^{\text{Selectivity}} + \overbrace{\{R_x(\sigma(R_a)) - R_x(\beta_a)]}^{\text{Diversification}} \\ &= R_a - R_x[\sigma(R_a)].\end{aligned} \tag{21.38b}$$

Diversification measures the extra portfolio return that a less-than optimally diversified portfolio must earn to justify itself. When the return on the market is greater than the return on the risk-free asset, diversification measures the additional return that would just compensate the investor for the diversifiable dispersion $[\sigma(R_a) - (\beta_a)]$. However, when the return on the market is less than the return on the risk-free asset, diversification measures the return lost form taking on diversifiable dispersion rather than choosing the naively selected portfolio with market risk and standard deviation both equal to β_a, the market risk of the portfolio actually chosen.

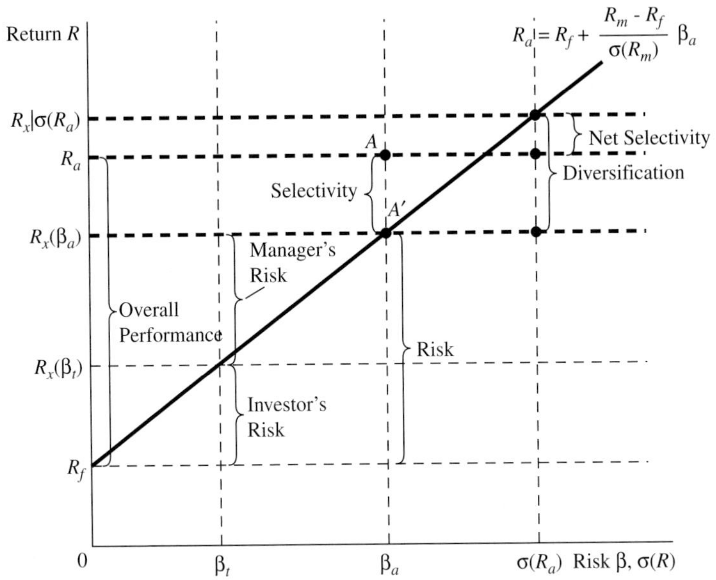

Fig. 21.4. Detailed Components of Mutual-Fund Performance.

Net selectivity may be negative, if a manger's selectivity was not sufficient to make up for the avoidable risk taken. In Fama's example shown in Fig. 21.4 related to $\sigma(R_a)$, you can see that the area measured by the diversification is larger than the area measured by selectivity. Therefore, net selectivity must be negative, according to Equation (21.38b).

If the investor has a target risk level β_T, the part of the overall performance due to risk can be allocated to the investor and to the portfolio manager as follows:

$$\overset{\text{Risk}}{[R_x(\beta_a) - R_f]} = \overset{\text{Manager's risk}}{[R_x(\beta_a) - R_x(\beta_T)]} + \overset{\text{Investor's risk}}{[R_x(\beta_T) - R_f]}, \tag{21.39}$$

in which $R_x(\beta_T)$ is the return on the investor's newly selected portfolio with the target level of market risk the investor has chosen. The manager's risk is composed of the risk assumed by the manager by taking on a level of risk β_a different from the investor's target level β_T. This decomposition is indicated in Fig. 21.4 related to β_T.

Manager's risk might in part result from a timing decision. That is, the manager might have chosen a portfolio with a higher or lower level of risk than desired by the investor due to his evaluation of economic or industry trends. Using *an ex-ante* CAPM market line, risk can be subdivided as follows:

$$\overbrace{\{R_x(\beta_a) - R_f\}}^{\text{Risk}} = \overbrace{\underbrace{\{R_x(\beta_a) - E[R_x(\beta_T)]\}}_{\text{Total timing}} - \underbrace{\{R_x(\beta_T) - E[R_x(\beta_T)]\}}_{\text{Market conditions}}}^{\text{Manager's timing}}$$
$$+ \overbrace{\{E[R_x(\beta_T)] - E[R_x(\beta_T)]\}}^{\text{Manager's expected risk}} + \overbrace{\{R_x(\beta_T) - R_f\}}^{\text{Investor's risk}}. \tag{21.40}$$

The manager's risk of Equation (21.39) is the sum of the first three terms. The manager's expected risk is the incremental expected return from the manager's decision to take on a nontarget level of risk. The expression for market conditions measures how much the market deviated from expectations at the target level of risk. Total timing is the difference between the *ex-post* return on the naively selected portfolio with risk β_a and the *ex-ante* expected return. When the return on the market is greater than the expected return on the market, total timing is positive (and more positive the larger the value of β_a). When the return on the market is less than expected return, total timing is negative (and more negative the larger the value of β_a). Manager's timing is the difference between total timing and market conditions. The manager's timing is only positive (negative) when the chosen level of market risk is above (below) the target level and return on the market is above (below) the expected return on the market. It is, therefore, a more sensitive indicator of the manager's timing ability than total timing.

At times, a target level of risk may not be relevant; if this is the case, the market portfolio may be treated as the target portfolio. That is

$$\overbrace{\{R_x(\beta_a) - R_f\}}^{\text{Risk}} = \overbrace{\underbrace{\{R_x - E[R_x(\beta_a)]\}}_{\text{Total timing}} - \underbrace{\{R_m - E(R_m)\}}_{\text{Market conditions}}}^{\text{Manager's timing}}$$
$$+ \overbrace{\{E[R_x(\beta_a)] - E(R_m)\}}^{\substack{\text{Expected deviation} \\ \text{From the market}}} + \overbrace{\{R_m - R_f\}}^{\substack{\text{Market} \\ \text{risk}}}. \tag{21.41}$$

Fama was, therefore, one of the first to suggest that the return on a portfolio could be subdivided into two parts: the return from security selection and the return from the bearing of risk in attempting to predict general market-price movements. Therefore, a manger's performance can be attributed either to skill in selecting an underpriced security or in market-timing ability. However, Fama noted his concerns about current benchmark portfolios. They included the fact that β_p, $\sigma(R_p)$, and $\sigma(R_m)$ are stable for long periods of time (e.g., 10 years); but in order to capture market timing, the relevant period for evaluation must be considerably shorter. Although the observed return–risk relationships seem to be linear, the trade-off of risk for return is in general less than predicted by the standard CAPM. In short, evidence suggests that standard CAPM framework may not provide the best benchmarks for the average return–risk tradeoffs available in the market from naively selected portfolios.

One of the principal applications of modern capital-market theory has been to propose a structural specification within which to measure investment performance and thereby to identify superior performers if they exist. In this structure, it is usually assumed that forecasting skills can be partitioned into two distinct components: (1) forecasts of price movements of selected individual stocks (**microforecasting**), and (2) forecasts of price movements of the general stock market as a whole (**macroforecasting**). Usually microforecasting involves the identification of individual stocks that are undervalued or overvalued relative to an index for equities. Using the CAPM as a framework, a microforecaster attempts to identify individual stocks whose expected returns lie significantly above or below the SML. The microforecaster, in essence, forecasts the nonsystematic or nonmarket-explained component of the return on individual stocks. Using the CAPM framework, the random variable return per dollar $Z_j(t)$ on security j at time t can be algebraically shown as

$$Z_j(t) = R(t) + \beta_j[Z_m(t) - R(t)] + \in_j (t). \tag{21.42}$$

In Equation (21.42), $Z_m(t)$ is the return on the market, $R(t)$ is the return on the riskless asset, and $\in_j (t)$ is the error term with the property that its expectation is conditional on knowing that the outcome of $Z_m(t)$ is equal to its unconditional expectation ($\in_j (t)$ follows a martingale process). Given such a model, a microforecaster would be interested in forecasting based on the properties of $\in_j (t)$.

A macroforecaster, on the other hand, attempts to identify when equities in general are undervalued or overvalued relative to other types of security, such as fixed-income securities. Macroforecasters try to forecast when stocks will outperform bonds using bonds as a proxy for other types of securities, that is, $Z_m(t) > R(t)$ and when bonds will outperform stocks, that is, $Z_m(t) < R(t)$. Therefore, a microforecaster tries to forecast $Z_m(t) - R(t)$. As a result, macroforecasters' forecasts can only be used to predict differential performance among individual stocks arising from the systematic or market-explained components of their returns, $\{\beta_j[Z_m(t) - R(t)] + R(t)\}$.

Jensen (1972) developed a theoretical structure for the evaluation of the micro- and macro-forecasting performance of investment managers where the basis for the evaluation is a comparison of *ex-post* performance of the manager's fund with the returns on the market. In the Jensen analysis, the market timer is assumed to forecast the actual return on the market portfolio, and the forecasted return and the actual return on the market are assumed to have a joint normal distribution. Under these assumptions, a market timer's forecasting ability can be measured by the correlation between the market timer's forecast and the realized return on the market. Jensen points out that the separate contributions of micro- and macro-forecasting cannot be identified using the structure of the CAPM framework unless for each period the market-timing forecast, the portfolio adjustment corresponding to that forecast, and the expected return on the market are known.

Grant (1977) showed that market-timing actions will affect the results of empirical tests that focus only on microforecasting skills. That is, using the following CAPM framework:

$$Z_j(t) - R(t) = \alpha_j + \beta_j[Z_m(t) - R(t)] + \in_j(t), \qquad (21.43)$$

where $Z_j(t)$ is the return on security j, $R(t)$ is the return on the risk-free asset, and α_j is the expected excess return from microforecasting. Market-timing ability will cause the regression estimate α_j to be downward-biased due to microforecasting ability.

Treynor and Mazuy (1966) added a quadratic term to the previous CAPM framework to test for market-timing ability. They argued that the performance measure should not be a linear function. They contend that the investment manager who can forecast market returns will hold a greater proportion of the market portfolio when the return on the market is high and a lower proportion when the market return is low. Therefore, the portfolio return will be a nonlinear function of the market return.

Kon and Jen (1979) used the Quandt (1972) switching regression technique in a CAPM framework to examine the possibility of changing levels of market-related risk over time for mutual-fund portfolios. Using a maximum likelihood test, they find evidence that many mutual funds do have discrete changes in the level of market-related risk they choose.

Merton (1981) developed a model that is not based on the CAPM framework; from it he was able to analyze market timing through the theoretical structure of the pattern of future returns based upon a posterior distribution of returns. Merton was able to show that up to an additive noise term, the pattern of returns from an investment strategy based upon market timing will be the same as the pattern of returns from a partial protective put-option investment strategy. If this noise (which is caused by forecast error) is diversifiable then, independent of investor's preference, endowments, or probability beliefs, the equilibrium management fee is proportional to the price of a put option on the market portfolio. These results are obtained with no specific assumptions about the distribution of returns on the market or the way in which the option prices are determined.

Henriksson and Merton's (1981) forecast model, which assumes that a manager's forecasts are observable, is as follows. Let $\gamma(t)$ be the market timer's forecast variable where $\gamma(t) = 1$ if the forecast, made at time $t - 1$ for the time period t, is that $Z_m(t) > R(t)$ and $\gamma(t) = 0$ if the forecast is that $Z_m(t) \leq R(t)$. The probabilities for $\gamma(t)$ conditional upon the realized return on the market are defined by (i) $P_1(t) = \Pr\text{ob}[\gamma(t) = 0|Z_m(t) \leq R(t)]$, (ii) $1 - P_1(t) = \Pr\text{ob}[\gamma(t) = 1|Z_m(t) \geq R(t)]$, (iii) $P_2(t) = \Pr\text{ob}[\gamma(t) = 1|Z_m(t) > R(t)]$, (iv) $1 - P_2(t) = \Pr\text{ob}[\gamma(t) = 0| Z_m(t) < R(t)]$.

Therefore, $P_1(t)$ is the conditional probability of a correct forecast given that $Z_m(t) \leq R(t)$, and $P_2(t)$ is the conditional probability of a correct forecast given that $Z_m(t) > R(t)$. Assuming that $P_1(t)$ and $P_2(t)$ do not depend upon the magnitude of $|Z_m(t) \leq R(t)|$, the sum of the conditional probabilities of a correct forecast, $P_1(t) + P_2(t)$ is a sufficient statistic for the evaluation of forecasting ability.

However, if a manger's forecasts are not observable, Henriksson and Merton consider a parametric test for the joint hypothesis of no market-timing ability and an assumed generating process for the returns or securities. They assume a pattern of equilibrium security returns that is consistent with the SML of the CAPM. They further assume that as a function of a manger's forecast there are discretely different systematic-risk levels that depend on whether or not the return on the market portfolio is forecasted to exceed the return on riskless securities for those portfolios chosen by the portfolio manager. That is, the manager is assumed to have one target beta when predicting that $Z_m(t) > R(t)$ and another target beta when predicting that $Z_m(t) \leq R(t)$: their parametric tests are open to the same criticisms that any performance measure is when based upon a CAPM structure.

Using the parametric and nonparametric techniques presented in Henriksson and Merton (1981), Henriksson (1984) evaluated the market-timing performance of 116 open-end mutual funds using monthly data from February 1968 to June 1980. Using a weighted least-squares regression analysis with a correction for heteroscedasticity, the separate contribution from forecasting and market timing were obtained. Results show little evidence of market-timing ability. In fact, 62% of the funds had negative estimates of market-timing. Further examination of the estimates for the individual funds shows the existence of a strong negative correlation between microforecasting (selectivity) and macroforecasting (market timing). This negative correlation seems to imply that funds that earn superior returns from stock selection also seem to have negative market-timing ability and performance.

These results tend to be somewhat disturbing, and the possibility of misspecification of the return-generating process must be considered. One potential source of error is the misspecification of the market portfolio. This results from the fact that the proxy used for the market portfolio does not include all risk assets. Another potential source of error is omission of relevant factors in addition to the return on the market portfolio from the return-generating process. If the omitted factor can be identified, then the return-generating process can be modified to take into account the omitted factor.

Chang and Lewellen (1984) compared the performance estimates derived from Henriksson and Merton's (1981) model and the single-factor market model. In order to test Henriksson and Merton's model, first they divided data into two subsets based on the sign of $X(t) = Z_m(t) - R(t)$, the market risk premium. Second, they estimated the least-squares lines in each of the two market conditions for every mutual fund, pursuant to the requirement that the line share a common intercept for each fund. And finally they tested whether the coefficient estimates for the two lines β_1^* and β_2^* differ significantly.

Chang and Lewellen's results indicate that the fit of the single-factor market model is little different from Henriksson and Merton's model for the mutual-fund return data examined. Out of the 67 mutual funds studied, only four funds indicate any statistical evidence of market timing. Approximately this number might be expected to emerge by chance alone. A similar conclusion applies to the evaluation of the fund manager's security-selection abilities. Only five funds indicate any statistical evidence of selectivity ability. Again, chance alone could produce virtually the same findings.

Their findings show that not much, if any, systematic market-timing activity was undertaken by portfolio managers in the 1970s — and to the extent that it was undertaken, it was often in the wrong direction. This may explain why the fit of the single-factor market model is not very different from the Henriksson and Merton model. Lee and Rahman (1990, 1991) updated and improved Chang and Lewellen's results by using better econometric techniques. In addition, they estimated the risk-aversion parameter empirically. They found that mutual-fund managers indeed have some timing and selectivity abilities. Chang and Hung (2003) have used Campbell's intertemporal version of CAPM model to test the performance of hedge factor for mutual fund. Chen *et al.* (1992) have performed a cross-sectional analysis of mutual funds' market timing and security selection skill.

Nevertheless, if the individual fund level is considered, it can be seen that Henriksson and Merton's approach has the clear potential to provide a much richer insight into the nature and sources of managed-portfolio performance differentials. For example, of the seven funds that indicate excess-return intercepts from the single-factor market model, only one of the cases coincides with those for which the Henriksson–Merton regression specification gives rise to a significant intercept. Of the other six funds, four have negative and two have positive estimate intercepts according to the single-factor market model; but the Henriksson–Merton model suggests that these differentials can be imputed to market-timing behavior rather than to security-selection activities. In addition, the Henriksson–Merton-model estimates indicate for several additional funds that a combination of significant timing and selectivity phenomena is present — but in opposite directions, resulting in statistically insignificant intercepts.

In short, Chang and Lewellen's results show that although Henriksson and Merton's model is an enhancement of the CAPM that provides a more complete appraisal of the constituents of that model and can eliminate certain biases in the estimates provided by it, neither skillful market timing nor clever security selections are evident in observed mutual-fund return data — nor does their model address the general critique of the CAPM as a benchmark.

Kon and Jen (1979) point out that Jensen's assumption of stationarity of risk through time may be in direct conflict with a managed portfolio. If in a managed portfolio the level systematic risk is adjusted substantially in either direction, a violation of the specifications of the OLS model occurs. The effect is that the loss of the known distributional properties of the OLS parameter is made conditional on these estimates. One possible problem could be heteroscedastic disturbances, which increase sampling variances of the OLS estimates and reduce their t-values.

Kon and Jen's model assumes a sequence of discrete risk-level decisions; thereby each observation of excess return (total returns on a portfolio minus the risk-free rate) over the measurement interval of n observation was generated by one of N distinct regression equations. In the Jensen model's estimating equation:

$$R'_{jt} = \alpha_j + \beta_j R'_{mt} + \in_{jt},$$

where $R'_{jt} = R_j - R_{ft}$; $R'_{mt} = R_{mt} - R_{ft}$; $\in_{jt}$ =normally distributed with a mean of zero and a constant variance; α_j = the performance measure; and β_j = assumed stationary.

The stationary assumption is only valid if the fund manager never engages in market timing and if the expected excess return on the market, the variance of the market given information at time $t - 1$, and the percentage change of the variance of the excess return of the portfolio remain constant. However, if the observations can be indexed according to risk, the Jensen performance measure conditional on the risk level chosen by fund manager in period t can be applied.

Kon and Jen's model is the performance of the portfolio over the measurement interval relative to a naively selected portfolio with risk level β_i. Total overall selectivity investment performance is the summation of the weighted αs of each subset. Their model is a Jensen model over N distinct risk levels. The actual number (N) of distinct risk levels chosen during the measurement interval is an empirical issue; the actual number of regression regimes must be determined for each mutual fund by statistical inference.

The change in β_t may be merely a change in the target level rather than an active timing decision. Therefore, even if the target risk-level evidence indicates $N > 1$, the timing performance measure may not be meaningful without additional procedure to estimate $R_{ft} - E_t(R_{ft})$ and $R_{mt} - E_t(R_{mt})$. Nevertheless, the empirical methodology used implies that selectivity performance can still be estimated if changes in risk level are the result of a changing investment-opportunity set.

Kon and Jen's methodology utilizes the N regime-switching regression model proposed by Quandt (1972), with a new identifiability condition. In order to ensure that the parameters are identified, the identifiability condition $\beta_N > \beta_{N-1} > \cdots > \beta_1$ is imposed. The strict ordering of risk levels is a result of the ordering of fund managers' forecasts of the unanticipated returns on the market portfolio, $E_t(R_{mt}) - E_t(R_{mt}|\phi_{t-1})$. It is this additional prior information that identifies the model.

Because Kon and Jen's maximum-likelihood estimation procedure presented here assumes an unknown probability that the fund manager will choose regime i for generating observations, the estimation procedure is only applicable to analyzing selectivity performance given the timing decision. In addition, it faces the problem of nonstationarity of market-level parameters. The third problem is a proxy for the fund's target risk level.

The Kon–Jen data consist of mutual funds with complete monthly return data from January 1960 to December 1971. The market proxy is the equal-weighted market-index-form CRSP with a 30-day Treasury bill rate as a proxy for the risk-free rate. Their simulated results provide confidence in their methodology. Tests of the model specification on a sample of 49 mutual funds indicate that for many individual funds it is more likely that the data were generated by a mixture of two or three regression equations rather than by that of a standard linear model. The null hypothesis of risk-level stationarity was rejected by many individual funds, giving specification for each fund determined by the likelihood-ratio test. This could explain Jensen's (1968) finding of so few significant t-values in his evidence on selectivity performance. By neglecting this phenomenon and utilizing OLS, the resulting heteroscedastic disturbances increase the sampling variance and reduce the t-statistics.

In addition, Jensen's (1968) frequency distribution of $\hat{\alpha}$ was negatively skewed, whereas Kon and Jen found their frequency distribution of $\hat{\alpha}s$ to be approximately symmetric about zero. Moreover, if management expenses were added to the mutual fund's rate of return as in the Jensen study, there would certainly be many more significantly positive performance measures. This evidence is clearly inconsistent with the EMH.

It can be argued that one could expect managers to be successful in forecasting from time to time, whether by uncovering special information or by keener insight into the implications of publicly available information. However, in an efficient market they cannot do this consistently over time. There is very little evidence that any individual fund was able to consistently generate significantly superior performance. In addition, the evidence for the EMH is based on the bias in favor of low-risk securities using the SML benchmark. Therefore, Kon and Jen's evidence is not inconsistent with the hypothesis that mutual-fund managers individually and on average are unable to forecast the future prices on individual securities consistently enough to recover their research expenses, management fees, and commission expenses.

Much of the empirical evidence (Chang and Lewellen (1984), Henriksson (1984), and Kon (1983)) indicates that timing ability is rare. In addition, if timing ability is present, it is often negative, and those funds that do exhibit significant timing performance show negative performance more often than positive performance. Henriksson (1984) found a negative correlation between the measure of security selection and market timing. A number of potential explanations for these results has been suggested, including errors-in-variables bias, misspecification of the market portfolio, and use of a single-factor rather than a multifactor asset-pricing model. Jagannathan and Korajczk (1986) suggest another explanation for the empirical results, which relies on the nonlinear payoff structure of options and option-like securities as well as the specification of the proxy for the market portfolio. They show that the portfolio strategy of buying call options exhibits positive timing performance and negative security selection even though no market forecasting or security-specific forecast is done. If market-timing occurs but the return is reduced by the premium paid for the option, thereby leading to negative security-selection evidence.

The **market proxy** is a portfolio of stocks that are, to a greater or lesser extent, options. The sign of market-timing performance of a given mutual fund may depend on whether the average stock held by the mutual fund has more or less of an option effect than the average stock in the index. The average negative timing performance found in Kon (1983), Chang and Lewellen (1984), and Henriksson (1984) may be due to the fact that the mutual funds in the sample tend to invest in firms that are larger, better established, and less leveraged than the average firm on the NYSE.

Jagannathan and Korajczyk (1986), using the option-pricing model, found that when the proxy for the market portfolio contains option-like securities, portfolios with greater (lower) concentration in option-like securities will show positive (negative) timing performance and negative (positive) selectivity. This provides a possible explanation of previous empirical findings indicating that mutual funds have negative timing ability on average, and that selectivity and timing performance are negatively correlated. If mutual funds tend to invest in higher-quality securities, then average timing performance would be expected to be negative. Also, negative correlation would be expected between selectivity and timing performance if investments were in securities that are less like options. However, Lehman and Modest (1987) and Lee and Rahman (1990) have found that mutual-fund managers have positive timing ability. In addition, Chang *et al.* (2003) have extended Lee and Rahman's (1990) model to allow selective ability, market timing ability, and hedging timing ability. They also performed some empirical test for 65 U.S. mutual funds during the period from January 1980 to September 1996.[2]

A possible explanation for the lack of evidence of timing ability on the aggregate is the possible use of an immunization strategy by the funds. Although timing may be an important aspect within the fund, where assets are bought and sold to maintain a fund's duration, the fund in the aggregate may not display any timing influences. If, indeed, mutual funds do follow an immunization strategy, this could aid in explaining the empirical results, revealing timing activity within funds but not at the aggregate level.

21.6. Summary

This chapter has employed the concepts and theory of technical and fundamental analysis to show that security analysts and portfolio managers might utilize theory, methodology, and data information to outperform the market. Both Value Line ranking performance and mutual-fund managers' performance are used to support this conclusion. Overall, this chapter has culled information discussed in previous chapters to explore how security analysis and portfolio management can more effectively be executed.

Questions and Problems

1. Define or explain the following terms.

(a) technical analysis	(b) fundamental analysis
(c) P/E ratio	(d) Dow theory
(e) market anomalies	(f) selectivity
(g) time series	(h) ARIMA.

[2]Chang *et al.* (2003) have used Campbell's (1993) Intertemporal CAPM to generalize Lee and Rahman's (1990) model to allow for testing the existence of selectivity, timing, and hedging performance for a mutual fund.

2. ABC Corporation is currently paying $2.00 per share in dividends with a payout ratio of 50%. Its growth rate is expected to be 10% for both earnings and dividends. The firm's cost of capital is 16%. What is the current price per share and the P/E ratio for ABC?
3. For ABC Corporation in Question 2, the growth rate is expected to fall to 5% for both dividends and earnings. What will happen to the price and P/E ratio if this occurs?
4. If you were interested in testing the relationship between dividends and share value, how would you design a research project to investigate the relationship?
5. Compare technical analysis and fundamental analysis. Which approach makes more sense from an economic viewpoint?
6. Discuss Basu's findings on the relationship between P/E ratios and investment performance. What does this mean in the context of the EMH?
7. Discuss the two major approaches to time-series analysis.
8. Discuss the procedure Value Line uses in its ranking. What does the success of Value Line's ranking mean in the context of the EMH?
9. Given the various investment objectives for mutual funds — growth; income and growth; income; and income, growth, and stability — what sort of strategies or investment policies do mutual-fund managers follow in order to achieve these objectives?
10. Compare and contrast Fama's overall performance measure with the performance measures of Sharpe, Treynor, and Jensen.
11. Compare the approaches of a macroforecaster and a microforecaster.
12. Suppose a portfolio manager's performance has been evaluated as superior when compared to the Dow Jones, the S&P, and the NYSE composite index. Does this evaluation make you feel comfortable about this manager's true ability?
13. What is the January effect? Offer some explanations for this anomaly.
14. Discuss how the timing and selectivity of a mutual fund's performance can be tested empirically.

Appendix 21A: Composite Forecasting Method

Most forecasts contain some information that is independent of that contained in other forecasts; thus a combination of the forecasts will, quite often, outperform any of the individual forecasts.

Nelson (1973) has shown that a composite forecast of unbiased forecasts is unbiased. For n individual unbiased forecasts $X_i (i = 1, 2, \ldots, n)$ with n weights a_i, each greater than or equal to zero and all weights summing to one, and a composite forecast X, the value of X is then given as

$$X = \sum_{i=1}^{n} a_i X_i, \quad \sum_{i=1}^{n} a_i = 1, \quad a_i \geq 0.$$

The expected value of X is

$$E(X) = E\left(\sum_{i=1}^{n} a_i X_i\right) = \sum_{i=1}^{n} a_i E(X_i) = \sum_{i=1}^{n} a_i(\mu_x) = \mu_x,$$

in which μ_x is the expected value of X_i. Therefore, the expected value of combination of n unbiased forecasts is itself unbiased.

If, however, a combination of n forecasts is formed, m of which are biased, the result is generally a biased composite forecast. By letting the expected value of the ith biased forecast be represented as $E(X_i) = \mu_x + \in_i$ the composite bias can be represented as follows:

$$\begin{aligned} E(X) &= \sum_{i=1}^{n} a_i E(X_i) \\ &= \sum_{i=1}^{m} a_i(\mu + \in_i) + \sum_{i=m+1}^{n} a_i(\mu_x) \\ &= \mu_x + \sum_{i=1}^{m} a_i \in_i. \end{aligned}$$

The composite of m-biased forecasts has a bias given by a combination of the individual forecast biases. This suggests that the composite of a biased forecast can be unbiased only if $\sum_{i=1}^{m} a_i \in_i = 0$. In particular, combining two forecasts, one with a positive bias and one with a negative bias, can, for proper choices of weights, result in an unbiased composite, However, for biased forecasts that do not balance each other, and assuming the assignment of zero weights to biased forecasts is not desired, numerous combinations of weights can be selected, each of which gives a composite that is unbiased.

The choice of weights can follow numerous approaches. These range from the somewhat naïve rule of thumb to more involved additive rules. One rule of thumb is that when several alternative forecasts are available but a history of performance on each is not, the user can combine all forecasts by finding their simple average.

Some additive rules may combine the econometric and ARIMA forecasts into a linear composite prediction of the form:

$$A_t = B_1(\text{Econometric})_t + B_2(\text{ARIMA})_t + \in_t, \tag{21A.1}$$

where

$A_t =$ actual value for period t;
B_1 and $B_2 =$ fixed coefficients; and
$\in_t =$ composite prediction error.

Least-squares fitting of (21A.1) requires minimization of the sum of errors over values of B_1 and B_2 and, therefore, provides the minimum mean-square-error linear composite prediction for the sample period. In the case that both the econometric model and ARIMA predictions are individually unbiased, then (21A.1) can be rewritten as

$$A_t = B(\text{Econometric}) + (1 - B)(\text{ARIMA})_t + \in_t\,. \tag{21A.2}$$

The least-squares estimate of B in (21A.2) is then given by

$$\hat{B} = \frac{\sum_{t=1}^{N} [(\text{ECM})_t - (\text{ARIMA})_t][A_t - (\text{ARIMA})_t]}{\sum_{t=1}^{N} [(\text{ECM})_t - (\text{ARIMA})_t]^2}, \tag{21A.3}$$

in which $(\text{ECM})_t$ and $(\text{ARIMA})_t$ represent forecasted values from econometric model and ARIMA model, respectively. Equation (21A.3) is seen to be the coefficient of the regression of ARIMA prediction errors $[A_t - (\text{ARIMA})_t]$ on the difference between the two predictions. As would seem quite reasonable, the greater the ability of the difference between the two predictions to account for error committed by $(\text{ARIMA})_t$, the larger will be the weight given to $(\text{Econometric})_t$.

Composite predictions may be viewed as portfolios of predictions. If the econometric model's and ARIMA's errors are denoted by u_{1t}, and u_{2t}, respectively, then from (21A.2) the composite prediction error is seen to be

$$\in_t = B(u_{1t}) + (1 - B)(u_{2t}). \tag{21A.4}$$

The composite error is the weighted average of individual errors. The objective is to minimize the variance of the weighted average, given its expected value. In the case of prediction portfolios the weighted average always has expectation zero if individual predictions are unbiased; or it may be given expectation zero by addition of an appropriate constant.

Minimizing composite error variance over a finite sample of observations leads to the estimate of B given by

$$\hat{B} = \frac{s_2^2 - s_{12}}{s_1^2 + s_2^2 - 2s_{12}}, \tag{12A.5}$$

where s_1^2, s_2^2, and s_{12} are the sample variance of u_{1t}, the sample variance of u_{2t}, and the sample covariance of u_{1t} and u_{2t}, respectively. For large samples, or in the case that the variances $\mathrm{Var}(u_{1t})$ and $\mathrm{Var}(u_{2t})$ and the covariance $\mathrm{Cov}(u_{1t}\, u_{2t})$ are known, Equation (12A.5) becomes

$$B = \frac{\mathrm{Var}(u_{2t}) - \mathrm{Cov}(u_{1t}, u_{2t})}{\mathrm{Var}(u_{1t}) + \mathrm{Var}(u_{2t}) - 2\mathrm{Cov}(u_{1t}, u_{2t})}. \tag{21A.6}$$

The minimum variance weight is seen to depend on the covariance between individual errors as well as on their respective variance. Holding the covariance constant, the larger the variance of the ARIMA error relative to that of the econometric error, the larger the weight given to the econometric prediction.

Bibliography

Alexander, S. "Price Movements in Speculative Markets: Trends or Random Walks." *Industrial Management Review*, v. 2 (May 1961), pp. 7–26.

Banz, R. W. "The Relationship between Return and Market Value of Common Stocks." *Journal of Financial Economics*, v. 9 (March 1981), pp. 3–18.

Basu, S. "Investment Performance of Common Stocks in Relation to Their Price-Earnings Ratios: A Test of the Efficient Markets Hypothesis." *Journal of Finance*, v. 32 (June 1977), pp. 663–682.

Bessler, D. A. and J. A. Brandt. "Composite Forecasting of Live-stock Prices: An Analysis of Combining Alternative Forecasting Methods." Department of Agricultural Economics Agricultural Experiment Station, Station Bulletin No. 265 (December 1979). Purdue University, West LaFayette, Indiana.

Black, F. "Active and Passive Monetary Policy in a Neoclassical Model." *Journal of Finance*, v. 27 (September 1972), pp. 801–814.

Black, F., M. C. Jensen and M. Scholes. "'The Capital Asset.' Pricing Model: Some Empirical Test," in M. C. Jensen (ed.), *Studies in the Theory of Capital Markets*. New York: Prager, 1972, pp. 79–121.

Blume, M. E. and I. Friend. "A New Look at the Capital Asset Pricing Model." *Journal of Finance*, v. 28 (March 1973), pp. 19–34.

Bodie, Z., A. Kane and A. Marcus. *Investments*. New York: McGraw-Hill/Irwin, 2010.

Bower, D. H., R. S. Bower and D. F. Logue. "Arbitrage Pricing Theory and Utility Stock Returns." *Journal of Finance*, v. 39 (September 1984), pp. 1041–1054.

Box, G. P. and G. M. Jenkins. *Time Series Analysis: Forecasting and Control.* New York: Holden-Day, 1976.

Branch, B. "A Tax Loss Trading Rule." *Journal of Business*, v. 50 (April 1977), pp. 198–207.

Breeden, D. T. "An Intertemperal Asset Pricing Model with Stochastic Consumption and Investment Opportunities." Journal of Financial Economics, v. 7 (September 1979), pp. 265–296.

Campbell, John Y. "Intertemporal Asset Pricing Without Consumption Data." *American Economic Review*, v. 83 (June 1993), pp. 487–512.

Chang, E. C. and W. G. Lewellen. "Market Timing and Mutual Fund Investment Performance." *Journal of Business*, v. 57 (January 1984), pp. 57–72.

Chang J. R., M. W. Hung and C. F. Lee. "An Intertemporal CAPM Approach to Evaluate Mutual Fund Performance." *Review of Quantitative Finance and Accounting*, v. 20 (June 2003), pp. 415–433.

Chen, C. R., C. F. Lee, S. Rahman and A. Chen. "A Cross-sectional Analysis of Mutual Funds' Market Timing and Security Selection Skill." *Journal of Business Finance and Accounting*, v. 19 (September 1992), pp. 659–675.

Chen, N-F., R. Roll and S. A. Ross. "Economic Forces and the Stock Market: Testing the APT and Alternative Asset Pricing Theories." *Journal of Business*, v. 59 (July 1986). pp. 383–404.

Chen, N., T. E. Copeland and D. Mayers. "A Comparison of Single and Multifactor Portfolio Performance Methodologies." *Journal of Financial and Quantitative Analysis*, v. 22 (December 1987), pp. 401–417.

Chen S. and C. F. Lee. "Bayesian and Mixed Estimators of Time Varying Betas." *Journal of Economics and Business*, v. 34 (November 1982), pp. 291–301.

Cho, C., E. J. Elton and M. J. Gruber. "On the Robustness of the Roll and Ross Arbitrage Theory." *Journal of Financial and Quantitative Analysis*, v. 19 (March 1984), pp. 1–10.

Copeland, T. E. and D. Mayers. "The Value Line Enigma (1965–1978): A Case Study of Performance Evaluation Issues." *Journal of Financial Economics*, v. 10 (November 1982), pp. 289–322.

Cornell, B. "Asymmetric Information and Portfolio Performance Measurement." *Journal of Financial Economics*, v. 7 (December 1979), pp. 381–390.

Cornell, B. "The Money Supply Announcements Puzzle: Review and Interpretation." *American Economic Review*, v. 73 (June 1983), pp. 644–657.

Dhrymes, P. J., I. Friend and N. B. Gultekin. "A Critical Re-examination of the Empirical Evidence on the Arbitrage Pricing Theory." *Journal of Finance*, v. 39 (June 1984), pp. 323–346.

Dybvig, P. H. "The Analytics of Performance Measurement Using a Security Market Line." *Journal of Finance*, v. 40 (June 1985a), pp. 401–416.

Dybvig, P. H. "Yes, the APT is Testbale." *Journal of Finance*, v. 40 (September 1985b), pp. 1173–1188.

Dybvig, P. H. and S. A. Ross. "Differential Information and Performance Measurement Using a Security Market Line." *Journal of Finance*, v. 40 (June 1985), pp. 383–399.

Fabozzi, F. J., C. F. Lee and S. Rahman. "Errors-in-Variables, Functional Form and Mutual Fund Returns." Chicago: Mimeo, 1989.

Fabozzi, F. J., J. C. Francis and C. F. Lee. "Generalized Functional Form for Mutual Fund Returns." *Journal of Financial and Quantitative Analysis*, v. 15 (December 1980), pp. 1107–1120.

Fama, E. F. "Components of Investment Performance." *Journal of Finance*, v. 27 (June 1972), pp. 551–567.

Gehr, A., Jr. "Some Tests of the Arbitrage Pricing Theory." *Journal of the Midwest Finance Association*, v. 7 (March 1976), pp. 91–105.

Gentry, J. A. and C. F. Lee. "Financial Forecasting and the X-11 Model: Preliminary Evidence," in C. F. Lee (ed.), *Advances in Planning and forecasting*. Greenwich, CT: JAI Press, 1987.

Grant, D. "Portfolio Performance and the 'Cost' of Timing Decisions." *Journal of Finance*, v. 32 (June 1977), pp. 837–846.

Guerard, J. B. Handbook of Portfolio and Construction: Contemporary Applications of Markowitz Techniques. New York: Springer, 2010.

Henriksson, R. D. "Market Timing and Mutual Fund Performance: An Empirical Investigation." *Journal of Business*, v. 57 (January 1984), pp. 73–96.

Henriksson, R. D. and R. C. Merton. "On Market Timing and Investment Performance II, Statistical Procedures for Evaluating Forecasting Skills." *Journal of Business*, v. 54 (October 1981), pp. 513–533.

Holloway, C. "A Note on Testing and Aggressive Investment Strategy Using Value Line Ranks." *Journal of Finance*, v. 36 (June 1981), pp. 711–719.

Irwin, S. H. and J. W. Uhrig. "Do Technical Analysts Have Holes in Their Shoes?" *Review of Research and Future Markets*, v. IV (Winter 1984), pp. 264–277.

Jagannathan, R. and R. A. Korajczyk. "Assessing the Market Timing Performance of Managed Portfolios." *Journal of Business*, v. 59 (April 1986), pp. 217–235.

Jensen, M. C. "Optimal Utilization of Market Forecasts and the Evaluation of Investment Performance," in G. P. Szego and K. Shell (eds.), *Mathematical Methods in Investment and Finance*. Amsterdam: North-Holland, 1972.

Jensen, M. C. "The Performance of Mutual Funds in the Period 1945–1964." *Journal of Finance*, v. 39 (May 1968), pp. 389–416.

Jensen, M. C. "Risk, the Pricing of Capital Assets and the Evaluation of Investment Portfolios." *Journal of Business*, v. 42 (April 1969), pp. 167–247.

Keim, D. B. "Size-Related Anomalies and Stock Return Seasonality: Further Empirical Evidence." *Journal of Financial Economics*, v. 11 (June 1983), pp. 13–32.

Kon, S. J. "The Market-Timing Performance of Mutual Fund Managers." *Journal of Business*, v. 56 (July 1983), pp. 323–347.

Kon, S. J. and F. C. Jen. "The Investment Performance of Mutual Funds: An Empirical Investigation of Timing, Selectivity, and Market Efficiency." *Journal of Business*, v. 52 (July 1979), pp. 363–389.

Lee, C. F. and E. Bubnys. "The Stability of Return, Risk and the Cost of Capital for the Electric Utility Industry," in R. E. Burns (ed.), *Proceedings of the Fifth MARUC Biennial Regulating Information Conference*, 1986.

Lee, C. F. and H. Park. "Value Line Investment Survey Rank Changes and Beta Coefficients." *Financial Analysts Journal*, v. 43 (November/December 1987), pp. 70–72.

Lee, C. F. and J. K. C. Wei. "Multi-Factor Multi0Indicator Approach to Asset Pricing Model: Theory and Empirical Evidence." *Handbook of Financial Econometrics and Statistics, eded. by* Lee, C. F., A. C. Lee and J. C. Lee, Springer, forthcoming 2013.

Lee, C. F. and S. Rahman. "Market Timing, Selectivity and Mutual Fund Performance: An Empirical Investigation." *Journal of Business*, v. 63 (1990), pp. 261–278.

Lee, C. F. and S. Rahman. "New Evidence on Timing and Security Selection Skill of Mutual Fund Managers." *Journal of Portfolio Management*, v. 17 (Winter 1991), pp. 80–83.

Lee, C. F., D. C. Porter and D. G. Weaver. "Indirect Test of the Haugen–Lakonishok Small Firm/January Effect Hypothesis: Window Dressing versus Performance Hedging." *Financial Review*, v. 33 (May 1998), pp. 177–194.

Lee, C. F., C. M. Tsai, and A. C. Lee. "Asset Pricing with Disequilibrium Price Adjustment: Theory and Empirical Evidence." *Quantitative Finance*, (2012 forthcoming).

Lehman, B. N. and D. Modest. "Mutual Fund Performance Evaluation: A Comparison of Benchmarks and Benchmark Comparisons." *Journal of Finance*, v. 42 (June 1987), pp. 233–265.

Lintner, J. "The Valuation of Risk Assets and the Selection of Risky Investments in Stock 'Portfolios and Capital Budgets." *Review of Economics and Statistics*, v. 47 (February 1965), pp. 13–37.

Litzenberger, R. H. and K. Ramaswamy. "The Effect of the Personal Taxes and Dividends on Capital Asset Prices." *Journal of Financial Economics*, v. 76 (June 1979), pp. 163–195.

Lo, Andrew W. and Jiang Wang, "Trading Volume: Definition, Data Analysis, and Implications of Portfolio Theory." *Review of Financial Studies* v. 13 (March 2000), pp. 257–300.

Mayers, D. and E. M. Rice. "Measuring Portfolio Performance and the Empirical Content of Asset Pricing Models." *Journal of Financial Economics*, v. 7 (March 1979), pp. 3–28.

Merton, R. C. "On Market Timing and Investment Performance. I, An Equilibrium Theory of Value for Market Forecasts." *Journal of Business*, v. 54 (July 1981), pp. 363–406.

Mossin, J. "Equilibrium in a Capital Asset Market." *Econometrica*, v. 34 (October 1966), pp. 768–783.

Nazer, S. M. *Applied Time Series Analysis for Business and Economic Forecasting*. New York: Marcel Dekker, 1988.

Nelson, C. R. *Applied Time Series Analysis for Managerial Forecasting*. New York: Holden-Day, 1973.

Quandt, R. E. "A New Approach to Estimating Switching Regressions." *Journal of the American Statistical Association*, v. 67 (June 1972), pp. 306–310.

Reilly, F. K., F. T. Griggs and W. Wong. "Determinants of the Aggregate Stock Market Earnings Multiple." *Journal of Portfolio Management*, v. 10 (Fall 1983), pp. 36–45.

Reinganum, M. R. "Misspecification of Capital Asset Pricing: Empirical Anomalies Based on Earnings Yields and Market Values." *Journal of Financial Economics*, v. 8 (March 1981), pp. 19–46.

Roll, R. "A Critique of the Asset Pricing Theory's Test Part I: On Past and Potential Testability of the Theory." *Journal of Financial Economics*, v. 4 (March 1977), pp. 129–176.

Roll, R. "Ambiguity When Performance is Measured by the Securities Market Line." *Journal of Finance*, v. 33 (September 1978), pp. 1051–1069.

Roll, R. "A Reply to Mayers and Rice (1979)." *Journal of Financial Economics*, v. 7 (September 1979), pp. 391–400.

Roll, R. and S. A. Ross. "An Empirical Investigation of the Arbitrage Pricing Theory." *Journal of Finance*, v. 35 (December 1980), pp. 1073–1103.

Rosenberg, B. and W. McKibben. "The Prediction of Systematic and Specific Risk in Common Stocks." *Journal of Financial and Quantitative Analysis*, v. 8 (March 1973), pp. 317–333.

Ross, S. A. "The Arbitrage Theory of Capital Asset Pricing." *Journal of Economic Theory*, v. 13 (December 1976), pp. 341–360.

Shanken, J. "The Arbitrage Pricing Theory: Is It Testable?" *Journal of Finance*, v. 37 (December 1982), pp. 1129–1140.

Sharpe, W. F. "Capital Asset Prices: A Theory of Market Equilibrium under Condition of Risk." *Journal of Finance*, v. 19 (September 1964), pp. 425–442.

Sharpe, W. F. "Mutual Fund Performance." *Journal of Finance*, v. 39 (January 1966), pp. 119–138.

Shiller, R. J. "Theories of Aggregate Stock Price Movements." *Journal of Portfolio Management*, v. 10 (Winter 1984), pp. 28–37.

Stickel, S. E. "The Effect of Value Line Investment Survey Rank Changes on Common Stock Prices." *Journal of Financial Economics*, v. 14 (March 1985), pp. 121–143.

Sweeny, R. J. "Some New Filter Rule Tests: Methods and Results." *Journal of Financial and Quantitative Analysis*, v. 23 (September 1988), pp. 285–300.

Taylor, S. J. "Tests of the Random Walk Hypothesis against a Price-Trend Hypothesis." *Journal of Financial and Quantitative Analysis*, v. 17 (March 1982), pp. 37–61.

Treynor, J. L. "How to Rate Management of Investment Funds." *Harvard Business Review*, v. 43 (January/February 1965), pp. 63–75.

Treynor, J. L. and F. Mazuy. "Can Mutual Funds Outguess the Market?" *Harvard Business Review*, v. 44 (July/August 1966), pp. 131–136.

Treynor, J. L. and R. Ferguson. "In Defense of Technical Analysis." *Journal of Finance*, v. 40 (July 1985), pp. 757–775.

Ulrich, T. and P. Wachtel. "Market Response of the Weekly Money Supply Announcements in the 1970s." *Journal of Finance*, v. 36 (December 1981), pp. 1063–1071.

Chapter 22

International Diversification and Asset Pricing

A large number of investors, both sophisticated money managers and individual portfolio holders, routinely restrict their investment activities to only a few of the available world investment opportunities. This chapter explores the broad topic of international diversification, with emphasis on providing an understandable overview of the theoretical issues involved as well as a review of the mechanics and risks of international investing.

Section 22.1 discusses foreign-currency markets and exchange-rate risk. The foreign-exchange market adds a significant additional variable to investing that is not a factor in domestic investment. The theoretical effects of international diversification and the international investment markets are discussed in Section 22.2. This chapter examines whether the world markets are integrated or segmented; also examined are the implications of extending the capital asset pricing and arbitrage pricing theory (APT) security-valuation models to the international markets, developed using data collected on U.S. securities. Other issues, notably the impact of differential inflation rates and empirical evidence on international diversification, are examined as well. An analysis of applied international diversification is then presented that summarizes the various investment vehicles available and discusses their relative advantages and disadvantages.

Section 22.3 discusses applied international diversification. Investing in the world market and buying foreign securities have become very popular. Hence, the impact of international investments on the diversification of a portfolio is important for both security analysts and portfolio managers.

Using empirical results of Eun and Resnick (1987) and Chiou *et al.* (2010), we show how international diversification can be used in real world investment decision. Section 22.4 introduces currency option which underlying asset is a spot of exchange rate instead of either individual stock or stock index. Using the Black–Scholes Model, we show how to calculate the value of the currency option. In addition, we are also going to discuss index option in this section. Final section will summarize this chapter.

22.1. Exchange-Rate Risk

Securities denominated in a currency other than the currency used by the purchaser have an additional element of risk, **exchange-rate** (or **currency**) risk. That is, the total return an investor receives will equal the stock return times the change in the currency the security is denominated in relative to the investor's domestic currency, or:

$$\text{Total return} = \begin{matrix}\text{Security}\\ \text{return}\end{matrix} \times \begin{matrix}\text{Change in relative}\\ \text{exchange rate}\end{matrix}. \tag{22.1}$$

In this chapter the primary investment vehicle is assumed to be the foreign security; the use of the foreign-exchange markets as an investment tool in their own right is a separate subject.

Equation (22.1) can be rewritten in a modified security-return format:

$$R_1^f = \left(\frac{D_1^f + P_1^f}{P_0^f}\right)\left(\frac{S_1^{d/f}}{S_0^{d/f}}\right) - 1, \tag{22.2}$$

where

R_1^f = total return on the foreign investment;

P_0^f and P_1^f = prices of the foreign security at the time of purchase and the time of sale;

D_1^f = total dividends paid during the folding period; and

$S_0^{d/f}$ and $S_1^{d/f}$ = the prices of the foreign currency in units of domestic currency in time periods 0 and 1, respectively.

It can be seen from Equation (22.2) that the foreign-security yield R_1^f can be modified by the change in the exchange rate $S_1^{d/f}/S_0^{d/f}$.

Table 22.1 illustrates this principle, from the U.S. perspective, for the period from November 1986 through November 1987 for 19 stock markets. As is clear, the currency return can affect the total both negatively and positively. Investing in the French stock market, for example, would

Table 22.1. Global Stock Markets.

	In Local Currencies			In U.S. Dollars[a]		
Index	Change (%)	11/5/87	52-week Range	Change (%)	11/5/87	52-week Range
The World	+2.0	318.5	410.2–295.9	+3.6	399.6	495.9–334.1
E.A.F.E.[b]	+1.2	447.3	574.5–412.5	+3.7	720.5	876.1–550.0
		240.1	433.2–235.2		144.6	285.3–115.0
	−2.4	211.8	270.2–208.8		465.9	532.2–421.6
Belgium	+0.0	267.1	395.0–267.1	+2.6	377.8	514.1–339.6
Canada	+3.2	333.6	460.4–316.3	+2.3	271.4	374.5–252.2
Denmark	+1.4	342.9	417.5–338.3	+3.9	3%.1	463.5–345.2
France	−0.7	309.5	467.6–295.6		301.5	427.4–279.2
Germany	−2.8	169.7	264.0–169.7	−0.3	369.3	505.4–369.2
Hong Kong	−9.0	1415.0	2803.4–1415.0		1006.6	1994.1–1006.6
Italy	−2.8	392.9	598.9–392.9	−0.8	198.0	290.0–198.0
	+3.4	1097.4	1360.1–835.0	+6.1	2921.4	3439.2–1831.5
Mexico	−21.0	34114.7	78086.7–7592.2	−21.9	257.7	618.2–115.2
Netherlands	−3.4	219.2	332.5–216.5		418.4	567.3–194.3
Norway	−4.2					784.3–420.2
Singapore/ Malaya	+2.8	462.9	848.3–450.2	+3.8	694.7	1236.4–669.2
Spain	+12.1	205.3	284.6–163.0	+15.3	127.4	163.7–84.2
Sweden	−2.9	724.5	1058.3–698.4		619.0	857.3–563.0
Switzerland	−4.3	151.1	220.7–151.1	−1.0	469.7	619.6–464.9
U.K.	−2.8	491.9	736.2–475.5		363.6	500.7–280.8
U.S.	+3.8	238.0	313.9–210.5	+3.8	238.0	313.9–210.5

Base: Jan 1, 1970 = 100
[a]Adjusted for foreign exchange fluctuation relative to the U.S. dollar.
[b]Europe, Australia, Far East Index.
Source: Morgan Stanley Capital International Perspective, Geneva, 1988.

have yielded a return of about −0.7% in the local currency. Because of the weakness of the U.S. dollar, however, from the perspective of a U.S. investor the return would have been 1.6% during this period. On the other hand, investing in the Canadian stock market would have yielded a 3.2% return offset by a 0.9% foreign-exchange loss, for a net return of 2.3%. The impression that the effect of the currency return, on average over time and country, is largely positive is erroneous. It depends on the movement of the dollar vis à vis the other currencies. Sometimes the dollar strengthens (foreign returns are lowered) and sometimes the dollar weakens (foreign returns are enhanced). Most of the time period covered by Table 22.1 is one in which the dollar was declining relative to most foreign currencies, resulting, on average, in improved yields for nondollar-denominated investments.

The above discussion leads to the following pertinent questions.

(1) Is currency risk related in any systematic way to security risk, or is it random?
(2) If there is a correlation between security risk and currency risk, is it positive, tending to exaggerate swings, or is it negative, tending to dampen swings?
(3) Are currency-return changes systematic across' a portfolio of foreign securities, or are they random and thus diversifiable?
(4) Do the added risks and transaction costs of going from dollars to foreign currency to foreign security to foreign currency and back to dollars make foreign investing unattractive?
(5) If the investment goal is primarily foreign-security diversification, is there any way that currency effects can be eliminated?

The first two questions have been the subject of several studies but have not been conclusively answered. Grubel (1968) and Levy and Sarnat (1970) showed that the optimum portfolios were entirely different with and without incorporating foreign-exchange-rate risk. Grubel found that accounting for foreign-exchange risk did not have a significant impact on the variance of returns. Other studies have attempted to show that since investors evaluate their investment opportunities in real terms only, and since changes in currency rates are caused only by inflationary expectations, the exchange rate risk is irrelevant to investors.

Solnik (1974a) explored the implications of financial markets in a world where individuals in different countries consume different baskets of goods. His conclusion is that "exchange risk," less the effects of differential inflation is really just "business" risk. The following example, from Solnik's (1974a) paper, illustrates this point.

> We consider an idealized situation in which there is no inflation and only two countries are considered, Japan and France. Additionally, at time zero (super-script 0) the conversion rate is one yen to one franc and the price of one unit of wine is the same as one unit of sake. There are only two goods in each country's baskets, sake (s), produced in Japan, and wine (w), produced in France. The French consumption basket is $9w_F^0 + 1s_F^0 = 10$, and the Japanese consumption basket is $9s_J^0 + 1w_J^0 = 10$. Suppose a "shock" occurs (say, significant damage to the French wine crop). The new relative price (at time 1) is $w_F^1 = 1.5s_J^1$ and $w_J^1 = 1.5s_J^1$. The new

consumption baskets are $8w_F^1 + 1.5s_F^1 = 12s_F^1 + 1.5s_F^1 = 13.5s_F^1$ for France, and $9.5s_J^1 + 0.33w_J^1 = 9.5s_J^1 + 0.5s_J^1 + 0.5s_J^1 = 10s_J^1$ for Japan.

Because there is no inflation and because of the law of one price, the price of sake must be the same in both countries. Therefore, after the shock the new exchange rate is $10/13.5 = 0.741$. Thus, those in France who have invested in Japan when the exchange rate was $1\,\text{F} = 1$ yen get only 0.741 of what they expected to get in francs without exchange-rate effect. Because the "risk was caused by a change in the relative price of goods," it is an exchange-rate risk; however, it is essentially no different than a business risk.

The bad harvest caused the exchange rate to change. An event like a bad harvest is the type of risk faced by any agricultural business. The answer to the first question is that, since currency risk is a business-type risk, it is not systematically related to stock-price movements in general and therefore can be diversified away. The correlation between security risk and currency risk is probably very close to zero.

The third question concerns the correlation, or lack of correlation, of different foreign currencies with the domestic currency and with each other. Table 22.2 shows the correlation of returns for seven local bond markets and currency (1971–1985). Generalizing on these and other results:

(1) Some reduction in currency risk can be obtained through diversification into several countries' securities.
(2) Nevertheless, a substantial portion of the risk will remain for U.S. investors because of the tendency of the foreign currencies' movements to be correlated positively with each other.

Table 22.2. Correlations of Returns from Local Bond Markets and Currency (1971–1985).

U.S.	1						
Japan	0.20	1					
Germany	0.37	0.37	1				
U.K.	0.23	0.19	0.21	1			
Yen	0.13	0.34	0.15	0.14	1		
DM	0.11	0.23	0.25	0.01	0.54	1	
Sterling	0.16	0.14	0.20	0.25	0.46	0.54	1

Source: From Beidleman, C. (ed.) *Handbook of International Investing*. Chicago: Probus Publishing Company, 1987, p. 622. Reprinted by permission of Probus Publishing Company. Data from J.P. Morgan Investment, 1986.

(3) If the domestic currency were not the U.S. dollar, diversification benefits could be greater due to the negative correlation with the dollar.

These results are consistent, to a great extent, with the dollar's position as the world currency variations consist of two components: the random fluctuations of all currencies with each other due to specific local conditions and general changes in tastes, and the general fluctuation of all nondollar currencies with the world (dollar) standard. For the U.S. investor, the first risk can be diversified completely, and the second risk can be modified only by adjusting the total portion of the portfolio in nondollar investments in relation to the total in dollar investments.

The fourth of the questions posed earlier is that, since domestic investors in each country do not face currency risks and currency-exchange transaction costs, and since each of the domestic markets should be priced efficiently, would not investors be worse off by adding the risks and transaction costs of foreign diversification? The answer is that the diversification benefits (i.e., the reduction in the market-portfolio risk premium due to the expanded market portfolio) have to outweigh the increased risk and transaction costs. (This diversification benefit is the subject of much of the rest of this chapter.) Some of the increased currency risk can be diversified, as discussed above. The additional transaction costs are comparatively small, at least for all major world currencies, as a result of the immense volume, easy divisibility, and consequent liquidity of the currency markets. Additionally, there are ways to hedge this risk and ways to diversify internationally in dollar-denominated investments.

Foreign-exchange risk can be minimized by covering all transactions in the foreign-exchange forward or futures markets. Two markets are available: the Interbank Foreign Exchange Market and the International Monetary Market. The first is made up of both a spot and a forward market, while the second, a subsidiary of the Chicago Mercantile Exchange, is a futures market only. By purchasing futures contracts for an amount equal to the expected net proceeds of the future dividends and sales price, Equation (22.2) becomes

$$R_1 = \left(\frac{D_1^f + P_1^f}{P_0^f}\right)\left(\frac{F_{0,1}^{d/f}}{S_0^{d/f}}\right) - 1. \tag{22.3}$$

Note that the second term does not reduce to one because $F_{0,1}^{d/f}$, the future exchange rate (period 1) at time zero of the foreign currency, does not equal the current exchange rate. Thus, the currency effect has not been eliminated, but the unknown price, or the price risk, has. Nevertheless, the total risk still has not been eliminated, because it has been necessary to use an estimate of the future net receipts in the foreign currency. The risk will still remain in proportion to the difference in actual receipts from forecast receipts. Also, this procedure adds two more transaction costs, on the purchase and on the sale of the futures contract.

The question of interest to most investors is what happens when the securities of several countries are included in a portfolio. According to the information discussed so far, the potential exists for higher return, lower risk, or both. Portfolio theory indicates that as we diversify internationally, as long as all of the economies of the world are not perfectly positively correlated with each other we should expect gains from diversification. It is a fact that, given any particular group of assets, various optimal weightings of those assets exist that create portfolios with the maximum possible return for a given level of risk. These are the so-called **efficient-frontier portfolios**.

The efficient frontier for an internationally diversified portfolio lies above the efficient frontier for portfolios limited to their own domestic market, because the range of potential returns is wider internationally and because the correlations of return are typically lower. As a result, the internationally diversified investor has the potential to achieve a higher level of return than the domestic investor for any given level of risk, or, viewed from a different perspective, to expect a lower variability of return than a domestic investor for any given level of return. These relationships are shown in Fig. 22.1.

22.2. Theoretical Effects of International Diversification

This section analyzes theoretical issues related to international diversification. Empirical evidence of international diversification is discussed in the next section.

22.2.1. *Segmented Versus Integrated World Markets*

This section presents the results of research for the past decade with the objective of discovering whether international markets are segmented or integrated, and how this will affect the risk–return tradeoff available to the investor.

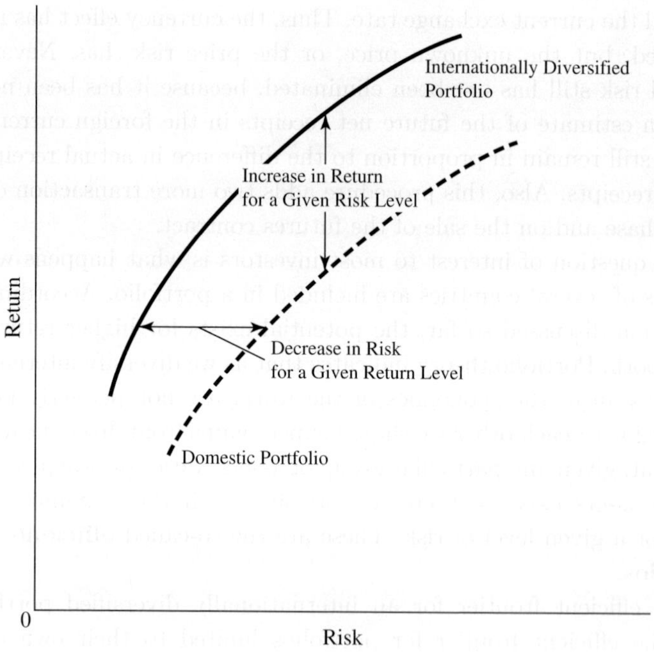

Fig. 22.1. International versus Domestic Efficient Frontiers.

The question of whether the international market is integrated or segmented appears particularly elusive. The difficulty surrounding this important issue was made clear by Solnik (1974d). The segmented market theory states that capital assets are priced in terms of their "domestic systematic risk." The capital asset pricing model (CAPM) can be extended to account for the correlation between national securities markets in determination of securities on a given international market:

$$E(R_i^j) = R_f + \beta_{di}^j [E(R_m) - R_f], \tag{22.4}$$

where

$E(R_i^j)$ = expected rate of return on ith security (or portfolio) in jth country;
$E(R_m)$ = expected market rates of return in jth country;
β_{di}^j = the beta coefficient for jth country in terms of domestic countrys market rate of return; and
R_f = the risk-free rate in the domestic country.

Equation (22.4) is a nationalistic model that postulates that security rates of return on each marketplace have in common a national factor, R_m. This national factor R_m is in turn dependent on a single common world factor, R_w (return for the world market portfolio), defined:

$$E(R_m) = R_f + \beta_w^j[E(R_w) - R_f], \tag{22.5}$$

where β_w^j is the **international systematic risk** of country j.

From Equation (22.5), it can be concluded that the lower the correlation between the two markets the lower the β_w^j, the lower the expected return, and the higher the value of international diversification. So it can be inferred that an investor who holds a portfolio of domestic securities would hold an underdiversified portfolio with respect to world diversification. Therefore, by holding an international portfolio (or security), the investor can reduce the systematic risk of his portfolio. Solnik, using his **international asset pricing model (IAPM)** to test whether assets are best regarded as being traded in segmented (national) or integrated (international) markets, found some evidence that markets are integrated. Furthermore, in his international mean-variance (MV) analysis, Solnik (1977) showed that as long as expected excess returns are positive and covariances low, MV analysis will produce optimal internationally diversified portfolios to reduce risk. Solnik's work was recently tested by Cho *et al.* (1986). The result of the test "lend tentative support" that only "mild segmentation" exists and that this segmentation does not affect required returns on "eligible securities."

Suppose for a moment that the world is one big economy and that markets are fully integrated. Then the risk- (world beat-) adjusted average return across national markets should be similar to those of U.S. markets. The integrated-market theory stipulates that all securities in the world are priced in terms of their global systematic risk. This can be stated as

$$E(R_i^j) = R_f + \beta_{wi}^j[E(R_w) - R_f], \tag{22.6}$$

where

$E(R_i^j)$ = expected rate of return on ith security (or portfolio) in country j;
R_f = the risk-free rate of interest;
$E(R_w)$ = expected rate of return on the world market portfolio;
β_{wi}^j = $(\rho_{i,w}\sigma_i\sigma_w)/\sigma_w^2$ or the correlation coefficient between the rate of return on security i in country j and the world market, times the standard deviation of security i, times the standard deviation of

the world market, divided by the variance of the world market portfolio.

Solnik (1974c) shows that the relationship between β^j_d, β^j_w, and β^j_{wi} can be defined:

$$\beta^j_{wi} = \beta^j_w \beta^j_{di}. \tag{22.7}$$

Equation (22.7) indicates that the international systematic risk of a security i in country $j(\beta^j_{wi})$ is equal to the product of the national systematic risk of that security (β^j_{di}) and the international systematic risk (β^j_w). In Table 22.6 we present international systematic risk for 34 countries.

From the formula it can be inferred that the riskiness of a portfolio results from the covariance of a portfolio rate of return with a national stock-market index. Nevertheless, that index is not the only way to determine the price of a portfolio since the national market now has a relationship with the world market and has a certain influence on the world portfolio. That influence depends on the weight that the nation's financial market index has on the world market index. Grubel and Fadner (1971) measured the strength of relationship between the U.S. portfolio and foreign portfolios. Specifically, they were measuring the correlation among pairs of identical industries. Their results are summarized in Table 22.3. From this table, it can be concluded that the correlation is greater the larger the ratio of an industry's exports plus imports over output, which means that international diversification pays off.

The following conclusions can be drawn from the available knowledge on the subject of world market integration:

(1) The world market lies in an area of being "mildly segmented" — that is, the economy of each country is its own world, to a significant degree of integration (the economy of each country has a substantial impact on the world economy, depending on the role that the particular country plays in the world markets as a whole).
(2) International diversification can substantially reduce the risk and increase the wealth of the portfolio holders of any country, provided that the portfolio is properly constructed to accommodate the utility function of the portfolio holder.

The argument for segmented markets relies on the existence of barriers that prevent the free flow of capital around the world. These barriers include: (1) legal restrictions, (2) transaction costs, (3) lack of information,

Table 22.3. Industries' Foreign Trade and Levels of Correlation Quarterly Holding Periods.

	U.S. 1958 (Import and Export)		Correlation of U.S. Industry with			
			West Germany		United Kingdom	
Industry	Output	Rank	R	Rank	R	Rank
Shipping	0.107	1	0.43	7	0.39	12
Machinery	0.107	2	0.44	5	0.68	2
Paper	0.106	3	0.49	2	0.45	11
Chemicals	0.082	4	0.52	1	0.77	1
Tobacco	0.075	5	0.37	11	0.12	18
Rubber	0.069	6	−0.06	18	0.28	15
Electrical equipment	0.065	7	0.38	10	0.68	3
Automobile	0.062	8	0.45	4	0.55	9
Food	0.061	9	0.39	8	0.65	5
Aircraft	0.048	10	0.31	13	0.24	17
Household goods	0.046	11	0.46	3	0.63	6
Steel	0.039	12	0.44	6	0.37	13
Electronics	0.037	13	0.29	14	0.57	8
Textiles	0.034	14	0.38	9	0.67	4
Retail Store	0.015	15	0.36	12	0.51	10
Oil	0.013	16	0.27	16	0.28	16
Publishing	0.010	17	0.29	15	0.36	14
Finance Company	0.005	18	0.25	17	0.63	7

Note: In some cases rank was determined by digits computed but not reproduced here.
Source: Trade data, U.S. 1958 Input-Output Table, Survey of Current Business, September 1965, pp. 33–39; Grubel and Fadner, "The Interdependence of International Equity Markets." Journal of Finance, v. 26 (March 1971), p. 93.

and (4) discrimination against foreign investors either by taxation or outright exclusion. Whether the world markets are segmented or integrated seems to ebb and flow as world conditions change. Presently, the trend appears to be toward a greater degree of integration as the barriers mentioned are reduced or eliminated.

22.2.2. *The CAPM and the APT Applied Internationally*

The CAPM assumes that each investor faces the same efficient frontier of potential portfolios. In general, the efficient frontier will differ among investors because of differences in expectations. In a portfolio context, the concern of the investor with the characteristics of individual securities is justified in terms of the effect that each security has on the distribution of the rate of return of the portfolio. Specifically, the CAPM states that the relevant risk of a single security is the nondiversifiable risk, beta, the covariance of the security with the market divided by the variance of the market. The issue in an international context, therefore, is how international diversification affects the riskiness of the portfolio and its rate of return. Asset-pricing models similar in form to the CAPM have been derived for international financial assets in a manner parallel to the CAPM. Solnik (1974c) developed an IAPM and tested it. In his empirical tests, Solnik used daily data on stocks of eight European countries and the U.S. The results were weakly consistent with his IAPM. However, Solnik generated some empirical estimates for the risk of an internationally diversified portfolio compared to a purely domestic portfolio. Using weekly data on stocks in eight major European countries and the U.S., Solnik found that an internationally diversified portfolio would be one-tenth as risky as a typical security and one-half as risky as a well-diversified U.S. portfolio.

A new development in the field of IAPM parallels an advance in the **domestic asset pricing theory**. Breeden (1979) developed an asset-pricing model which explicitly noted that individuals derive their utility from consumption. Maximizing lifetime utility from consumption, Breeden developed a more complete model for asset pricing, wherein pricing of an asset depended on covariances with aggregate consumption rather than any market index or portfolio. Application of the Breeden model to various economies of the world may give some insight into how financial assets are priced.

The APT, formulated by Ross in 1976, offers a feasible alternative to the CAPM. It is worthwhile in the context of this chapter to examine the implications of extending the APT to include the world market. The APT assumes that the rate of return on any security is a linear function of k factors, or:

$$\tilde{R}_i = E(\tilde{R}_i) + b_{i1}\tilde{F}_1 + \cdots + b_{ik}\tilde{F}_k + \tilde{e}_i, \tag{22.8}$$

where

$\tilde{R}_i$ = the random rate of return on the ith asset;
$E(\tilde{R}_i)$ = the expected rate of return on the ith asset;
b_{ik} = the sensitivity of the ith assets returns to the kth factor;
$\tilde{F}_k$ = the kth factor common to all assets; and
$\tilde{e}_i$ = a random mean noise term for the ith asset.

The most important feature of the APT is that in equilibrium all portfolios that can be selected from among the set of assets under consideration and that satisfy the two conditions of (1) using no wealth and (2) having no risk must earn no return on average.

Solnik (1974c) extended the APT to the international capital markets, leading to the **international arbitrage pricing theory (IAPT)**. In this article, Solnik shows that IAPT overcomes the problem of aggregation when asset demands are summed in the universe of investors who use different numeration to measure returns. This is because the portfolios in the IAPT context represent weighted averages of individual assets. Further, Solnik shows that even in foreign terms the domestic arbitrage portfolio bears no risk and hence should earn zero return in equilibrium.

Cho *et al.* (1987) empirically tested the IAPT and rejected the first hypothesis that the international capital market is integrated and that the APT is valid internationally. However, their study used international common factors. Abeysekera and Mahajan (1985) utilized domestic common factors and directly tested Solnik's (1983) claim on the IAPT. The results of their study "strongly support the hypothesis that the IAPT accurately predicts the risk-free rate."

22.2.3. *Inflation and Exchange-Rate Risks*

It is appropriate to question how, from a theoretical point of view, two significant potential differences between one-country investing and world investing affect the risk and return potential for an investor. These two variables are (1) exchange-rate difference and (2) differences in the rates of inflation. Domestic investors do not face exchange-rate risk, so it is a substantive theoretical difference with models developed purely for domestic purposes. This issue was discussed in the previous section; it is enough to restate here that much of the risk can be either diversified away or hedged against. Additionally, as pointed out by Solnik (1974c), exchange-rate risk is essentially just another form of business risk.

Inflation differential risk is the second added dimension of international diversification. Suppose an investor in the U.S. has a security in England whose return is fixed in terms of the pound. Assuming that there is no inflation in the U.S. but that the inflation rate in England is uncertain. The dollar value of the investment at the end of the period is uncertain and hence risky. The position has an **exchange risk**, which in this case is an inflation risk. This connection between exchange risk and inflation risk is not coincidental. There is an explicit set of connections between any country's exchange rate and its inflation rate. The Fisher effect, used to take into account inflation, can be expanded internationally:

$$(1 + R_m^d) = (1 + R_{\text{real}}^d)(1 + I^d), \tag{22.9}$$

$$(1+ R_m^f) = (1+ R_{\text{real}}^f)(1+ I^f), \tag{22.10}$$

where R_{real} is the real rate of interest, R_m is the nominal interest rate, and I is the inflation rate. The superscript d and f indicate domestic and foreign rates, respectively. Equations (22.9) and (22.10) can be combined to solve for the relative nominal rates:

$$\frac{1 + R_m^f}{1 + R_m^d} = \left(\frac{1 + R_{\text{real}}^f}{1 + R_{\text{real}}^d}\right)\left(\frac{1 + I^f}{1 + I^d}\right). \tag{22.11a}$$

This equation can be interpreted to state that, for every country, the nominal interest rate is connected to its own real rate and inflation and the real rate and the inflation of the other country.

As a first-order approximation, the nominal interest-rate differential between two countries can be shown to be

$$R_m^f - R_m^d = R_{\text{real}}^f - R_{\text{real}}^d + I^f - I^d. \tag{22.11b}$$

That is, the difference in the nominal rates is approximately equal to the difference in the real rates and the rates of inflation between the two countries. Sample Problem 22.1 provides further illustration.

Sample Problem 22.1

The real rate of interest in the U.S. and Germany is 4%, the inflation rate in the U.S. is expected to be 5%, and the inflation rate in Germany is expected to be 1%. What is the difference in the nominal rates between the two countries?

Solution

Using Equation (22.11b) as an approximation:

$$\begin{aligned} R_m^{\text{US}} - R_m^{\text{Ger}} &= R_{\text{real}}^{\text{US}} - R_{\text{real}}^{\text{Ger}} + I^{\text{US}} - I^{\text{Ger}} \\ &= 0.05 - 0.05 + 0.05 - 0.01 \\ &= 0.04. \end{aligned}$$

The nominal rate in the U.S. should be 4% higher than the nominal rate in Germany. If Equation (22.11a) were used to solve this problem, the exact difference in the nominal interest rates would be 3.9604%. This is approximately equal to the 4% found using Equation (22.11b).

Recall for a moment the example with the U.S. and England. Suppose that the inflation in England is known precisely and that inflation in the U.S. is somewhat less than in England. The inflation rate in each country will have an impact on the value of the currency in that particular country. The amount of the impact can be determined relatively precisely since the parity between currencies must be observed by the law of price equilibrium. This relationship can be expressed in the following formula:

$$\frac{E(S_1^{d/f}) - S_0^{d/f}}{S_0^{d/f}} = \frac{E(I^d) - E(I^f)}{1 + E(I^d)}, \tag{22.12}$$

where $E(S_1^{d/F})$ is the expected future exchange rate between the foreign and the domestic currency and $S_0^{d/F}$ is the current spot exchange rate.

Equation (22.12) states that the difference between current and future exchange rates is equal to the differences in inflation rates. Thus, it appears inflation is fixed into exchange rates in the marketplace. The exposure of a business firm to exchange risk is defined by its cash-flow and asset-stock position. These in turn depend on expected future receipts and payments on the firm's net monetary position — that is, on the relationship between current assets and current liabilities. So unless payment and receipts in relation to the future net monetary position of the firm exactly balance, the firm is exposed to declines or increases in the value of foreign currencies. This exposure to risk can be eliminated in the world of inflation by appropriate indexation of contracts in real terms. Sample Problem 22.2 provides further illustration.

Sample Problem 22.2

The current spot exchange rate between the U.S. dollar and the British pound is \$2.00/£ , the expected inflation in the U.S. is 5%, and the expected inflation in England is 10%. What is the expected future spot rate (\$/£)?

Solution

Using Equation (22.12):

$$\frac{E(S^d/_{\pounds}^1) - \$2.00/_{\pounds}}{\$2.00/_{\pounds}} = \frac{0.05 - 0.10}{1.05}$$

$$E(S_1^{d/\pounds}) = \$2.00/_{\pounds} + \$2.00/_{\pounds} - \left(\frac{0.05}{1.05}\right)$$

$$= \$1.9048/_{\pounds}.$$

The higher inflation rate in England will cause the pound to devalue relative to the dollar, so that instead of \$2.00/£ , it will only cost \$1.9048 to buy £ 1.00 in the future.

This discussion on inflation and exchange-rate risk can be concluded by stating that there are two types of exchange-rate risk to consider: the risk of inflation and **relative price risk.** Since the risk of inflation is nominal, this risk can be eliminated by appropriate indexing of contracts in real terms. The relative price risk is due to changes in supply-and-demand conditions in various countries. Eliminating inflation risk results in an exchange risk that is a form of business risk resulting from changes in relative prices, which reflect changes in supply-and-demand conditions. This aspect of exchange risk is much more difficult to hedge or eliminate.

22.2.4. *Are World Markets Efficient?*

A final issue of importance in the theoretical discussion of international diversification is whether the world market is efficient. Domestic theoretical models such as the CAPM and the APT are dependent to a considerable extent on the assumption of market efficiency. The validity of extending these models to world markets will be seriously threatened if the international market is not as efficient as the U.S. market.

An efficient market, again, is a market where any new information would be immediately and fully reflected in prices, and the adjustment in price would be very rapid. Therefore, investors using publicly available information will not be able to earn above-average returns.

The issue of **world market efficiency** has been tested by Roll (1979). He set the expected return on international speculation conditional on information at the beginning of the period equal to zero, using **purchasing-power parity (PPP)**, which means that people will value currencies for what they will buy. He concludes that the deviations from PPP attributable to relative price fluctuations are dominated by the effects of inflation on the exchange rate. Hence relative inflation is an important determinant of exchange rates.

One requirement of market efficiency is that arbitrage profits are zero. Frankel and Levich (1975) tested whether deviations of interest-rate parity outside of the countries of transactions can exist. They concluded that if arbitrage assets are comparable, arbitrage opportunities do not exist.

Simple tests of market efficiency have implied that the forward exchange rate should be an unbiased predictor of the spot rate. However, Stockman's (1980) theoretical development states that a bias should exist, since a premium is associated with the risk investors face in forward exchange markets. Nevertheless, Stockman (1977) and Cornell (1977) have found evidence of a bias for only a few countries and then only when the risk premium changes erratically.

There have been many studies on the efficiency of national stock markets around the world. Hawawini (1984), Kato and Schallheim (1985), Jaffe and Westerfield (1985), and Ang and Pohlman (1978), to name a few, all conclude that the national stock markets they studied are at least semi-strong-form efficient. Given the increasing interest in financial analysis and portfolio management in these markets, these findings are not too suprising.

One issue remains unresolved at present: the efficiency of the world market. In other words, is it possible for portfolio managers to allocate funds to certain national markets and thereby generate performance that is better than a world market index? To date there is little empirical evidence to resolve this issue. What is required is a simultaneous evaluation of financial markets, currency markets, and real markets to ascertain whether they are efficient from a world perspective.

22.2.5. *Empirical Evidence Supporting International Diversification*

As early as 1968, evidence was being accumulated in empirical studies regarding the potential advantages of international diversification. Grubel (1968) found that international diversification can pay off, if portfolios are properly selected. More recently, Stehle (1977) showed that low-beta securities of internationally diversified portfolios outperformed high-beta securities of domestically diversified portfolios, on a beat-adjusted basis.

Adler and Dumas (1983) stated in their study that "the potential of international diversification to reduce the risk seems unquestionable."

The growth of international financial markets coincided with the increasing integration of national financial institutions through international firms. Integration of financial institutions as well as portfolio investment was a major phenomenon of the 1970s and 1980s. The effect of market integration has important implications in many sectors of the economy. It is important, therefore, when studying effects of international financial integration, to realize the benefits that could be used as a reference for policy making.

Studies by Senchack and Beedles (1980) and Jacquillat and Solnik (1978) suggest that U.S. investors who hold portfolios of U.S. multinational firms do not receive the same risk reduction as investors who hold portfolios of U.S. and foreign securities. This probably results from the restrictions imposed on the multinational management by the various governments of the countries in which they operate.

22.3. Applied International Diversification

Once the investor or portfolio manager has decided to diversify internationally, how does he or she go about doing so? There are several different vehicles: (1) direct purchase of foreign securities, (2) purchase of securities of American-listed firms with large foreign operations, (3) American depository receipts, (4) Eurobonds, and (5) international mutual funds. Along with deciding which vehicle to use, the investor must consider how to obtain information, what will be the impact of market imperfections such as local taxes and restrictions on capital flow, and whether to hedge against currency risk.

22.3.1. *Direct Foreign Investment*

The manager of a large portfolio would probably consider the direct foreign investment option first. The costs of gathering information and the additional currency-transaction cost would be a much smaller proportion of the total portfolio return and therefore a worthwhile tradeoff to achieve a higher degree of choice in the selection of securities and countries, as well as greater flexibility in the timing of transactions. The following are brief discussions of some of the most easily available foreign investment opportunities.

22.3.1.1. *Canada*

The Canadian stock market has had a correlation with the U.S. market (S&P 500) ranging from 0.83 to 0.91 over the last two decades. Thus, diversification benefits (beyond those due only to the increased number of available securities) are minimal. This makes sense in light of the economic and geographic proximity of the two countries. Additionally, Canada imposes a 15% withholding tax on returns earned by U.S. investors. Canada has three major stock exchanges, in Toronto, Montreal, and Vancouver. The Toronto Stock Exchange is the most important.

22.3.1.2. *Germany*

Germany is the third-largest Western industrial nation. The correlation of the German stock market with the U.S. stock market has ranged from −0.58 to +0.56 over the two decades. Diversification benefits should therefore be substantial.

Germany has eight stock exchanges; the two most important are the Frankfurt and Düsseldorf exchanges. Trading is thin by U.S. standards. The debt market has always been of interest to U.S. investors due to the stability of the mark. There is a 15% withholding tax on dividends but none on interest.

22.3.1.3. *Japan*

The Japanese stock market correlation with the U.S. market has ranged from 0.07 to 0.84. Japan has had one of the healthiest economies in the world and has been increasing its market share in many high-growth industries. Japan imposes a 10% withholding tax on interest and dividends. There are eight stock exchanges, of which the Tokyo Exchange is the most important.

22.3.1.4. *Other Pacific-Basin Countries*

The Pacific basin is considered the best growth area in the world for the next decade or longer. Hong Kong has been a leader as a result of its inexpensive labor, its location on key Asian trade routes, and its position as a financial center for Asia. The uncertainty of Hong Kong's outlook after the UK lease expires in 1997 has been somewhat resolved and remains less of a risk than in prior years.

Taiwan, South Korea, and Singapore are also growth economies as a result of inexpensive labor and the general attitude of both the governments and the labor forces. All three areas are benefiting from the trend to manufacture electronics and other goods outside the higher-cost, more developed countries. Additionally, Singapore is geographically well situated and is a major regional center for finance, commerce, and oil refining. Australia and Malaysia are both resource-rich countries. They are favorably located for growth with the expanding Pacific-basin manufacturing economies.

22.3.1.5. *United Kingdom*

The United Kingdom's stock market has an historical correlation coefficient range of 0.17 to 0.79 with the U.S. market. The British economy has been plagued with negative growth, high inflation, and heavy government interference. The large North Sea oil discoveries and the reform programs of the Thatcher government have given some hope of a remedy for these economic ills. However, large transaction costs and taxes are incurred when trading on the London exchange.

On the positive side, the current weakness may provide more potential for growth. The United Kingdom is still the world's most important financial center. The London Stock Exchange is organized in a fashion similar to the U.S. exchanges, and trading volume is heavier than on other European exchanges.

22.3.2. *Indirect Foreign Investment*

The purchase of U.S. securities with large foreign operations can be a lower-cost, lower-risk way to diversify internationally. Foreign-exchange risks are not incurred directly, information is more easily available, and the markets and regulations are the ones that are familiar to the investor.

Unfortunately, as discussed earlier, statistical studies have found that U.S. multinational firms seem to track the U.S. stock market very closely. One study (Jacquillat and Solnik, 1978) found that when the returns of 23 U.S.-based multinationals were regressed on various countries' market indexes, the only significant explanatory variable was the U.S. market. It seems that this low-cost, low-risk alternative does not result in significant international diversification benefits.

22.3.2.1. *American Depository Receipts*

American depository receipts (ADRs) were introduced in 1927 by the Morgan Guaranty Trust Company. They are financial instruments issued by

U.S. banks (called depositories) against shares deposited with the bank's overseas branch or a custodian. The ADRs allow U.S. investors to buy, sell, and own foreign securities without ever taking physical possession of them. They are ordinarily issued on a one-to-one basis, one ADR for every share, and they can be traded in exactly the same way as shares of U.S. corporations. The issuing bank acts as the intermediary in all transactions; it notifies the ADR holder of dividends and distributes these dividends in dollars; it deducts foreign taxes; and it furnishes information on stock rights, stockholders' meetings, new issues, and tender offers. For these services, the band charges a fee.

Although ADRs are dollar-denominated, they include the full effect of changes in both the underlying security and the exchange rate. Investors who do not want to incur exchange-rate risk must still hedge in the foreign-exchange markets exactly as if they were purchasing securities on a foreign market. On the other hand, investors who feel that changes in foreign-exchange rates may work in their favor can use ADRs without having to incur the added transaction costs and complications of investing directly in foreign markets.

Other advantages of utilizing ADRs rather than direct foreign investment include (1) avoidance of some foreign taxes; (2) improved and more easily obtained information, which is also from one source (the bank) and in English; (3) avoidance of foreign regulations; (4) improved security (an ADR is registered with a major U.S. bank, whereas many foreign securities are bearer securities and their value will be gone if the security is lost or stolen); and (5) improved liquidity. There is an active domestic ADR market, and transactions can be performed by a broker over the phone. Foreign securities, on the other hand, must often be mailed overseas; and it is sometimes necessary to wait long periods for the proceeds of the sale.

22.3.2.2. *Foreign Bonds and Eurobonds*

Following Eun and Resnick (2012), foreign bond market and Eurobond market are two important international bond markets. A **foreign bond** issue is one offered by a foreign borrower to the investors in a national capital market and denominated in that nation's currency. An example is a German MNC issuing dollar-denominated bonds to U.S. investors. A **Eurobond** issue is one denominated in a particular currency but sold to investors in national capital markets other than the country that issued the denominating currency. An example is a Dutch borrower issuing dollar-denominated bonds to investors in the U.K., Switzerland, and the Netherlands. The markets for foreign bonds and Eurobonds operate in parallel with the domestic national bond markets, and all three market groups compete with one another.

Eun and Resnick (2012) have classified the international bond in according with four different major instruments such as: (i) straight fixed-rate, (ii) floating-rate notes, (iii) convertible issues, and (iv) with equity warrants. The international bond amounts outstanding for these major instruments can be found from international banking and financial market developments, bank for international settlements.

Eurobonds are extremely flexible financial instruments. In addition to issues in the major currencies — dollar, yen, mark, pound, and Swiss franc — **currency cocktails** (combinations of currencies) are also used. It is very common for Eurobonds to be convertible or to have warranties attached so that bondholders can participate in the profits and growth of the firm's equity. Both fixed- and floating-rate bonds are issued.

Despite the broad variety, some features are common to almost all Eurobonds. Generally Eurobonds (1) have low default risk, as they are high-quality issues; (2) have intermediate maturities, usually about seven years; (3) are thinly traded issues with very small secondary markets; (4) have extremely complex trading; (5) give higher yields than comparable U.S. bonds; (6) are bearer bonds, with all of the accompanying risk; (7) pay interest not subject to foreign taxes; and (8) provide (mostly) for a sinking fund or a repurchase fund. Given these characteristics, it seems obvious that while Eurobonds can be very attractive for the skilled professional with adequate resources, they should be avoided by individual investors. However, individuals can participate through mutual funds.

22.3.2.3. *International Mutual Funds*

Investors, both small and large, may want the advantages of international diversification without having to be experts on the subject themselves. In this case, they may delegate the management of the international portion of their investments to a mutual fund. Many funds are available to choose from. The Dean Witter Worldwide Investment Trust Fund is a typical one. Appendix 22A gives excerpts from the 1984 prospectus for this fund, which has typical objectives and policies. The last few decades has witnessed a dramatic growth of U.S.-based mutual funds that invest in non-U.S. stock markets. By 2003, the size of the U.S. international mutual fund market is now almost $300 billion. Furthermore, there are almost 1,500 such mutual funds. Clearly, this is an important and growing sector of the U.S. economy.

Proffitt and Seitz (1983) evaluated the performance of U.S. international funds over the period 1974–1982. Using both the Sharpe and Treynor performance measures discussed in Chapter 17, they find that 10 international mutual funds outperformed the S&P 500 index for both measures. They conclude, at least for the time period of their study, that U.S. investors were better off investing internationally than investing in the U.S. market.

The Morgan Guaranty Trust Company (1979) presents the empirical evidence which is necessary for evaluating international portfolio investment. The return, variance of return, and correlation coefficients between the U.S. and foreign markets are presented. Figure 22.2 shows the rates of return for the U.S. and five major foreign stock markets. The average annual compounded rate of return is calculated in two ways, with the assets valued in the local currency and with the assets valued in U.S. dollars. The U.S. returns fall in the middle of the six markets studied over the period.

As has been noted, the variability of return on any portfolio depends both on the standard deviation of return of the individual assets and on the correlation of returns among them. If the standard deviations of

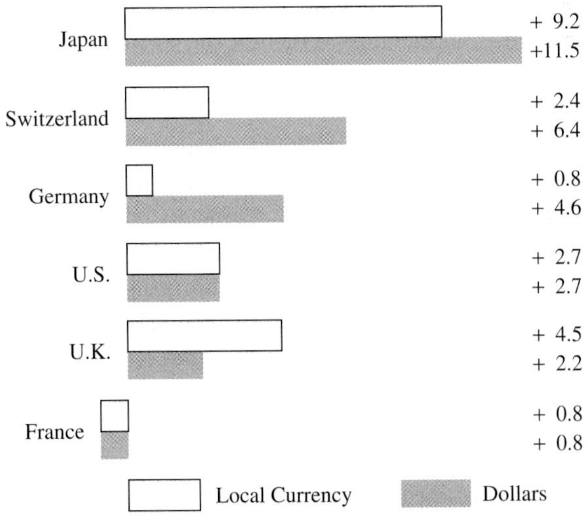

Fig. 22.2. Historical Compound Annual Rates of Return (Price Only — 20-Year, 1959–1978, percentage).
Source: Morgan Guaranty Trust Company. *Investing Internationally*, 1978.

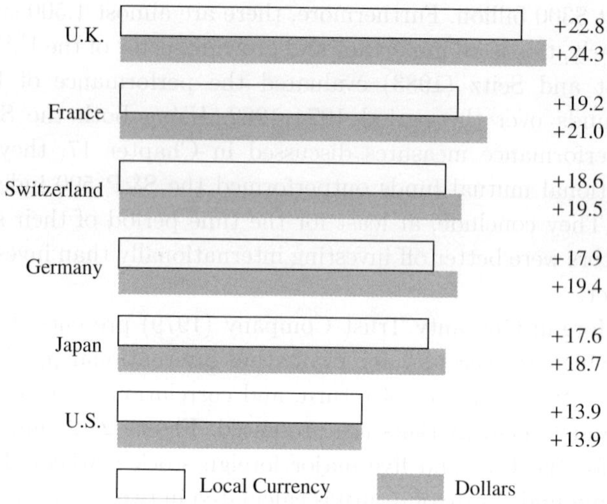

Fig. 22.3. Historical Standard Deviations of Return (Price Only — 20-Year, 1959–1978, percentage).
Source: Morgan Guaranty Trust Company. *Investing Internationally*, 1978.

foreign markets are very high, this will tend to make international portfolios more variable than domestic portfolios. However, if the correlations among returns are very low, this will tend to make international portfolios less volatile than domestic portfolios. Which of these two effects is stronger, the high standard deviations or the low correlations?

Unlike rates of return, which can be substantially different when measured in dollars rather than in local currency units, the variability of return is not significantly different whether measured in local currencies or in dollars. This is evident in Fig. 22.3. Typically, the variability in dollars is slightly more than the variability measured in local currency units; thus, the focus of concentration can be the variability measured in dollars. The U.S. market has been one of the least variable markets over the time period studied. Table 22.4 shows correlation coefficients of foreign equity markets.

The basic conclusions to be drawn from the correlation coefficients shown in Table 22.4 are as follows.

(1) The correlations of returns have not been constant but have tended to increase somewhat as world markets have become more integrated.
(2) Very substantial variations exist in the degree to which other equity markets tend to move with the U.S. market.

Table 22.4. Correlaltion Coefficient of Foreign Equity Markets with the United States (Monthly Data).

	1959–1978	1959–1963	1964–1968	1969–1973	1974–1978
Local currencies					
Australia	0.40	−0.01	0.29	0.34	0.61
Austria	0.13	0.33	0.09	−0.06	0.29
Belgium	0.49	0.50	0.51	0.37	0.58
Canada	0.75	0.79	0.83	0.77	0.70
Denmark	0.15	−0.02	0.03	0.15	0.30
France	0.34	0.45	0.01	0.25	0.46
Germany	0.31	0.48	0.12	0.37	0.24
Italy	0.22	0.34	0.05	0.04	0.33
Japan	0.20	0.02	0.06	0.42	0.27
Netherlands	0.56	0.67	0.60	0.50	0.53
Norway	0.32	0.38	0.05	0.06	0.62
Spain	0.11	0.05	0.01	0.12	0.17
Sweden	0.34	0.34	0.34	0.33	0.35
Switzerland	0.49	0.52	0.34	0.53	0.54
United Kingdom	0.41	0.29	0.20	0.39	0.52
Average of 15	0.35	0.34	0.22	0.30	0.43
U.S. dollars					
Australia	0.41	−0.01	0.29	0.35	0.60
Austria	0.16	0.33	−0.09	0.01	0.24
Belgium	0.46	0.50	0.52	0.33	0.55
Canada	0.75	0.81	0.84	0.76	0.69
Denmark	0.19	−0.03	0.05	0.19	0.34
France	0.33	0.46	0.01	0.20	0.47
Germany	0.33	0.48	0.12	0.38	0.29
Italy	0.21	0.34	0.04	0.09	0.26
Japan	0.21	0.02	0.06	0.44	0.27
Netherlands	0.57	0.67	0.61	0.53	0.54
Norway	0.34	0.38	0.04	0.06	0.68
Spain	0.12	0.11	0.02	0.10	0.16
Sweden	0.36	0.33	0.34	0.34	0.38
Switzerland	0.48	0.52	0.34	0.49	0.51
United Kingdom	0.39	0.29	0.19	0.38	0.48
Average of 15	0.35	0.35	0.23	0.31	0.43

Source: Morgan Guaranty Trust Company. *Investing Internationally*, 1978.

(3) The size of the correlations tends to be low, which indicates that there can be substantial risk reductions through international diversification.

By using international mutual funds data during 1970-2003, Patro (2010) provided a comprehensive analysis of the growth of U.S.-based international mutual funds to understand what drives investors to buy these funds. His analysis uncovers several new and unique features of flows into international mutual funds. His empirical findings show a strong relationship between flows into U.S.-based international mutual funds and the correlation of the fund's assets and the U.S. market and standard deviation of the fund's returns, consistent with the international diversification argument. Second, the flows are related to contemporaneous and past fund returns supporting an "information asymmetry" as well as "return chasing" or "trend following" hypothesis for international capital flows.

22.3.3. *Return, Risk, and Sharpe Performance Measure for International Indexes*

In this section, we follow two different studies to explore issues in international diversification and performance. First, following Eun and Resnick (1987), summary statistics of monthly returns for 15 major stock markets (1973–1982) are presented in Table 22.5. In Table 22.5, correlation coefficients, mean and standard deviation (SD) of monthly returns, beat coefficient, and Sharpe performance measure (SHP) are presented. The beat coefficient is the β_w^j defined in Equation (22.5); the Sharpe measure is as defined in Chapters 7 and 11.

Based on the available evidence, it would appear that investors can improve returns and lower risk by investing internationally.

As the caveats in the Dean Witter prospectus point out (see Appendix 22A), foreign investing involves many risks and problems not normally encountered by U.S. investors. Nevertheless, the research, while not conclusive, appears substantial enough to indicate that the benefits outweigh the risks. Care must be taken to choose the countries and the investment vehicles that are appropriate to the investor's individual utility function, portfolio size, and the time the investor can afford to personally spend on the foreign portion of the portfolio.

The correlation coefficients of foreign markets with the U.S. market indicate that the world markets lie somewhere between the theoretical extremes of totally segmented individual-country markets and the integrated one-world market. This lack of complete integration is one of the attractions of international diversification.

Second, we updated the data used by Chiou *et al.* (2010) calculate return, standard deviation, beta coefficient, and SHP for 34 countries during the period from January 1988 to January 2011. The correlation coefficient

Table 22.5. Summary Statistics of the Monthly Return for 15 Major Stock Markets, 1973–1982 (all returns converted to U.S. dollars).

	Correlation Coefficient														Mean	SD		
Stock Market	AU	BE	CA	FR	GE	HK	IT	JA	NE	SG	SP	SD	SW	UK	(percent)	(percent)	β	SHP
Australia (AU)															0.63	7.97	1.25	0.027
Belgium (BE)	0.36														0.80	5.92	0.84	0.065
Canada (CA)	0.62	0.36													0.78	6.52	1.16	0.056
France (FR)	0.46	0.61	0.46												0.67	8.04	1.16	0.032
Germany (GE)	0.33	0.65	0.31	0.52											0.83	5.44	0.73	0.076
Hong Kong (HK)	0.34	0.36	0.27	0.30	0.33										1.10	14.54	1.52	0.047
Italy (IT)	0.29	0.36	0.28	0.39	0.28	0.21									0.27	8.47	0.74	0.017
Japan (JA)	0.34	0.43	0.29	0.40	0.49	0.45	0.37								0.85	5.77	0.78	0.075
Netherlands (NE)	0.43	0.69	0.53	0.59	0.70	0.45	0.30	0.44							1.01	5.80	1.06	0.102
Singapore (SG)	0.46	0.40	0.41	0.38	0.38	0.48	0.23	0.43	0.54						1.08	10.20	1.54	0.065
Spain (SP)	0.28	0.28	0.24	0.26	0.28	0.20	0.25	0.32	0.31	0.15					−0.46	6.12	0.45	−0.143
Sweden (SD)	0.30	0.44	0.28	0.29	0.42	0.24	0.16	0.35	0.46	0.34	0.23				1.18	5.89	0.66	0.130
Switzerland (SW)	0.48	0.72	0.46	0.60	0.75	0.38	0.38	0.46	0.78	0.53	0.25	0.52			0.77	6.01	1.00	0.059
United Kingdom (UK)	0.46	0.50	0.48	0.53	0.40	0.36	0.38	0.32	0.63	0.58	0.22	0.32	0.54		1.02	9.27	1.47	0.065
United States (U.S.)	0.53	0.37	0.68	0.41	0.32	0.24	0.16	0.27	0.58	0.48	0.15	0.36	0.49	0.46	0.57	4.84	1.03	0.032

Source: C. Eun and B. Resnick, "International Diversification under Estimation Risk: Actual vs Potential Gains." Reprinted by permission of the publisher from *Recent Developments in International Banking and Finance*, Vol. I. ed. Sarkis J. Khoury and Alo Ghosh. Lexington. MA: Lexington Books, D.C Heath & Co. Copyright 1987. D.C. Heath.

Table 22.6. Return, Standard Deviation, Beta Coefficient, and SHP for 34 Countries (January 1988–January 2011).

	Mean	STD	Skewness	Kurtosis	CV	Beta	Sharp Ratio
Argentina	0.0151	0.1459	0.3273	4.1369	9.6658	1.1669	0.0366
Brazil	0.0161	0.1561	−1.4184	10.1559	9.7206	1.6820	0.1033
Chile	0.0152	0.0711	−0.6659	2.9861	4.6883	0.8035	0.0839
Greece	0.0060	0.1032	0.2377	3.3966	17.3246	0.9723	0.0081
Indonesia	0.0096	0.1391	0.1584	4.5995	14.4776	1.2055	0.0783
Korea, S.	0.0065	0.1083	0.1719	2.7586	16.5915	1.2870	0.0480
Malaysia	0.0074	0.0842	−0.2862	4.2311	11.3453	0.9243	0.0611
Mexico	0.0166	0.0942	−1.0255	3.3591	5.6935	1.2437	0.0407
Philippines	0.0057	0.0924	−0.1694	1.8251	16.2543	0.9355	0.1205
Portugal	0.0035	0.0674	−0.3659	1.8614	19.0031	0.9082	−0.0283
Thailand	0.0066	0.1129	−0.5554	2.2973	17.1143	1.3491	0.0814
Turkey	0.0096	0.1642	−0.0646	0.9757	17.1590	1.5413	0.0092
Taiwan	0.0057	0.1063	−0.0892	1.3749	18.7579	1.0157	0.0549
Australia	0.0093	0.0608	−0.6971	2.3590	6.5580	0.9495	−0.0083
Austria	0.0057	0.0793	−1.1969	6.1916	13.9107	0.8565	0.1317
Belgium	0.0068	0.0639	−1.9759	11.7819	9.3457	0.9039	0.1015
Canada	0.0087	0.0573	−1.1023	4.5658	6.6077	0.9999	0.1008
Switzerland	0.0092	0.0505	−0.4242	0.9746	5.4808	0.8228	0.1405
Germany	0.0076	0.0677	−0.8028	2.3144	8.8894	1.1774	0.1207
Denmark	0.0107	0.0587	−0.8923	3.0645	5.4711	0.8830	0.0821
Spain	0.0082	0.0693	−0.6651	2.0310	8.4730	1.1997	0.1619
Finland	0.0079	0.0941	−0.3418	1.3981	11.8856	1.4447	0.1458
France	0.0080	0.0608	−0.5704	1.4090	7.6351	1.0696	0.1089
UK	0.0066	0.0490	−0.3360	1.4346	7.4116	0.8892	0.1023
Hong Kong	0.0103	0.0758	−0.2862	2.3506	7.3769	1.1193	0.0992
Ireland	0.0021	0.0675	−1.0533	2.8264	31.5529	1.0153	0.0522
Italy	0.0046	0.0703	−0.3014	0.7596	15.3637	0.9806	0.0509
Japan	0.0001	0.0630	0.0060	0.7152	539.3905	1.0901	0.0829
Netherlands	0.0085	0.0573	−1.2320	3.7439	6.7735	1.0575	−0.0422
Norway	0.0090	0.0796	−1.2088	4.3929	8.8803	1.2166	0.0901
New Zealand	0.0044	0.0681	−0.3600	1.3037	15.5247	0.9331	0.0980
Singapore	0.0082	0.0733	−0.7323	3.3036	8.9700	1.1241	0.0530
Sweden	0.0108	0.0764	−0.6249	1.7951	7.0891	1.4012	0.0508
U.S.	0.0079	0.0435	−0.8011	1.6418	5.4871	0.8629	0.1160

matrix for both 13 developing markets and 21 developed countries are also calculated. Table 22.6 indicates that the rates of return for developed countries are generally higher than those of developing countries for the period from January 1988 to January 2011. In addition, the standard deviation of developed countries is generally lower than those of developing countries. Therefore, the SHPs for developed countries are generally higher than those of developing countries. It should be noted that the beta coefficient presented in Table 22.6 is made by regressing individual countries' market rates of return against the rate of return for the world index. Therefore, this beta coefficient expressed international systematic risk.

Table 22.7 shows the correlation coefficient matrix for developing countries. For example, the correlation coefficient between Argentina and Indonesia is 0.0045, and the correlation coefficient between Argentina and Taiwan is 0.0043. These figures indicate that the stock rates of return between these countries are not highly correlated. In addition, Table 22.7 also indicates that the correlation coefficients among different countries are relatively low. Therefore, if we formulate a portfolio to invest in these countries, the uncorrelated nature allows for diversification in the portfolio.

Table 22.8 shows the correlation coefficient matrix for developed countries. Overall, the correlation coefficients among the 21 countries are relatively low. For example, the correlation coefficient between Canada and the United Kingdom is 0.0018, and the correlation between Canada and Japan is 0.0017. It also implies that if we formulate a portfolio by investing in these 21 countries, we will enjoy a large diversification effect.

Chiou *et al.* (2009) have used both Markowitz model and SHP approaches which have been discussed in Chapters 8 and 11, respectively, to obtian the optimal investment allocation among 44 international market indexes. They found that diversifying portfolios internationally is beneficial in terms of Markowitz model and SHP. Therefore, although financial market are becoming more integrated, the international diversification effect exists and can be used in portfolio investment decision.

22.4. Currency Option and Index Option

22.4.1. *Currency Option*

Currency option is option on spot exchange rate instead of either individual stock or stock index. An exchange rate is the price of one currency in terms of another currency. For example, the exchange rate between the Japanese yen and U.S. dollar is 130.77 on December 15, 1997.

The valuation model for the European type of currency call option can be defined as

$$C = Se^{-r_f t}N(d_1) - Xe^{-rt}N(d_2), \tag{22.13}$$

Table 22.7. Correlation Coefficient Matrix for Developing Countries.

	AR	BZ	CH	GR	IN	KO	ML	MX	PH	PG	TH	TK	TW
Argentina (AR)	0.0212												
Brazil (BZ)	0.0065	0.0243											
Chile (CH)	0.0035	0.0047	0.0050										
Greece (GR)	0.0043	0.0051	0.0023	0.0106									
Indonesia (IN)	0.0045	0.0051	0.0035	0.0040	0.0193								
Korea, S. (KO)	0.0028	0.0036	0.0025	0.0029	0.0062	0.0117							
Malaysia (ML)	0.0024	0.0031	0.0024	0.0021	0.0060	0.0033	0.0071						
Mexico (MX)	0.0064	0.0057	0.0031	0.0027	0.0045	0.0037	0.0028	0.0089					
Philippines (PH)	0.0035	0.0038	0.0028	0.0026	0.0068	0.0032	0.0044	0.0032	0.0085				
Portugal (PG)	0.0025	0.0039	0.0014	0.0041	0.0027	0.0021	0.0016	0.0017	0.0019	0.0045			
Thailand (TH)	0.0045	0.0048	0.0036	0.0029	0.0080	0.0065	0.0055	0.0045	0.0065	0.0023	0.0127		
Turkey (TK)	0.0064	0.0079	0.0038	0.0068	0.0050	0.0041	0.0035	0.0048	0.0034	0.0041	0.0049	0.0269	
Taiwan (TW)	0.0043	0.0048	0.0029	0.0021	0.0037	0.0044	0.0038	0.0040	0.0041	0.0015	0.0054	0.0044	0.0113

Table 22.8. Correlation Coefficient Matrix for Developed Countries.

	AU	AS	BE	CA	SW	GE	DE	SP	FN	FR	UK	HK	IR	IT	JP	NL	NW	NZ	SG	SD	US
AU	0.0037																				
AS	0.0027	0.0063																			
BE	0.0021	0.0034	0.0041																		
CA	0.0024	0.0025	0.0021	0.0033																	
SW	0.0016	0.0024	0.0021	0.0015	0.0025																
GE	0.0024	0.0037	0.0032	0.0024	0.0024	0.0046															
DE	0.0019	0.0029	0.0027	0.0021	0.0019	0.0029	0.0034														
SP	0.0026	0.0032	0.0029	0.0023	0.0022	0.0034	0.0027	0.0048													
FN	0.0030	0.0030	0.0025	0.0030	0.0021	0.0036	0.0028	0.0035	0.0088												
FR	0.0023	0.0031	0.0030	0.0022	0.0022	0.0036	0.0025	0.0032	0.0032	0.0037											
UK	0.0020	0.0025	0.0022	0.0018	0.0018	0.0024	0.0020	0.0024	0.0026	0.0023	0.0024										
HK	0.0025	0.0026	0.0021	0.0027	0.0016	0.0025	0.0020	0.0026	0.0029	0.0023	0.0021	0.0057									
IR	0.0024	0.0033	0.0029	0.0021	0.0019	0.0029	0.0025	0.0029	0.0031	0.0025	0.0024	0.0021	0.0045								
IT	0.0021	0.0033	0.0028	0.0022	0.0020	0.0033	0.0026	0.0035	0.0036	0.0030	0.0021	0.0021	0.0026	0.0049							
JP	0.0018	0.0019	0.0016	0.0017	0.0016	0.0017	0.0017	0.0021	0.0024	0.0018	0.0016	0.0019	0.0020	0.0019	0.0040						
NL	0.0023	0.0031	0.0030	0.0022	0.0022	0.0033	0.0025	0.0029	0.0030	0.0029	0.0023	0.0023	0.0028	0.0028	0.0018	0.0033					
NW	0.0032	0.0042	0.0035	0.0032	0.0023	0.0035	0.0033	0.0035	0.0040	0.0033	0.0028	0.0030	0.0034	0.0033	0.0022	0.0033	0.0063				
NZ	0.0030	0.0028	0.0019	0.0021	0.0017	0.0022	0.0017	0.0026	0.0028	0.0019	0.0018	0.0024	0.0022	0.0021	0.0018	0.0022	0.0030	0.0046			
SG	0.0027	0.0030	0.0024	0.0027	0.0018	0.0027	0.0022	0.0028	0.0029	0.0023	0.0022	0.0041	0.0024	0.0024	0.0021	0.0025	0.0035	0.0029	0.0054		
SD	0.0030	0.0031	0.0029	0.0028	0.0024	0.0039	0.0031	0.0039	0.0047	0.0034	0.0026	0.0030	0.0031	0.0034	0.0024	0.0033	0.0041	0.0030	0.0033	0.0058	
US	0.0017	0.0017	0.0018	0.0019	0.0013	0.0020	0.0015	0.0020	0.0024	0.0019	0.0015	0.0018	0.0019	0.0017	0.0012	0.0018	0.0021	0.0015	0.0020	0.0023	0.0019

where

$$\begin{aligned}
S &= \text{spot exchange rate,}\\
r &= \text{domestic risk-free rate,}\\
r_f &= \text{foreign risk free rate,}\\
X &= \text{exercise price,}\\
\sigma &= \text{standard deviation of spot exchange rate,}\\
t &= \text{time to expiration,}\\
d_1 &= \frac{\ln\left(\frac{P}{E}\right)+(r-r_f)t+\sigma^2\frac{t}{2}}{\sigma\sqrt{t}}, \text{ and}\\
d_2 &= \frac{\ln\left(\frac{P}{E}\right)+(r-r_f)t-\sigma^2\frac{t}{2}}{\sigma\sqrt{t}} = d_1 - \sigma\sqrt{t}.
\end{aligned}$$

By comparing standard Black and Scholes option pricing model, it is found that Equation 22.13 can be obtained by replacing q by r_f.

Example

Valuation of Currency Option

Consider a four-month European call option on the Japanese yen. Suppose that the current exchange rate is 130, the exercise price is 125, the risk-free rate in the U.S. is 6% per annum, the risk-free rate in Japan is 2% per annum. The volatility of foreign exchange rate is 15%.

Substituting $S = 130$, $X = 125$, $r = 0.06$, $r_f = 0.02$, $\sigma = .15$, $T = 4/12$ into Equation (22.13), we obtain

$$d_1 = \frac{\ln\left(\frac{130}{125}\right) + (0.06 - 0.02) + \left(\frac{(0.15)^2}{2}\right)\left(\frac{4}{12}\right)}{(0.15)\sqrt{\frac{4}{12}}} = \frac{0.0392 + .0171}{0.0866} = 0.6501$$

$$d_2 = 0.6501 - (0.15)\sqrt{\frac{4}{12}} = 0.5635$$

From standard normal distribution table, we obtain

$$N(0.65) = 0.7422 \quad N(0.56) = 0.7123.$$

Substituting all related information into Equation (22.13), we obtain

$$\begin{aligned}
C &= 130e^{-\frac{0.02}{3}}(0.7422) - (125)e^{-\frac{0.06}{3}}(0.7123)\\
&= 95.8395 - 87.2746\\
&= 8.5649
\end{aligned}$$

22.4.2. *Index Option*

Index option is the option on stock index instead of individual stocks. Many different index options currently trade in the U.S. The most popular contracts are those on the S&P 500 Index and the S&P 100 Index (CBOE). Index options may be European or American. The contract on the S&P 500 is European, whereas that on the S&P 100 is American. For example, one CBOE contract is to buy or sell 100 times the index at the specified strike price of 280. If it is exercised when the value of the index is 292, the writer of the contract pays the holder (292 − 280) × 100 = $1,200. This cash payment is based on the index value at the end of the day in which the exercise instructions are issued. Not surprisingly, investors usually wait until the end of a day before issuing these instructions.

In valuing index, assume that it could be treated as a security paying a known dividend yield. Therefore, the European style of index call options can be evaluated in terms of the European style of stock call option formula defined as

$$C = S'N(d_1) - Xe^{-rt}N(d_2), \tag{22.14}$$

where

$S' = Se^{-qt}$,
S = spot exchange rate,
q = dividend yield,
r = risk-free rate,
X = exercise price,
σ = standard deviation of spot exchange rate,
t = time to expiration,
$d_1 = [\ln(S/X) + (r - q + \frac{1}{2}\sigma^2)t]/\sigma\sqrt{t}$, and
$d_2 = d_1 - \sigma\sqrt{t}$.

Example

Index Option Valuation

Consider a European call option on the S&P 500 that is two months from maturity. The current value of the index is 950, the exercise price is 900, the risk-free interest rate is 6% per annum, and the volatility of the index is 15 per annum. Dividend yields of 0.2% and 0.3% are expected in the first and the second month, respectively. In this case, $S = 950$, $X = 900$,

$r = 0.06$, $\sigma = 0$ and $T = 2/12$. The total dividend yield during the option's life is $0.2 + 0.3 = 0.5\%$. This is 3% per annum. Hence, $q = 0.03$ and

$$d_1 = \frac{\left[\ln(950/900) + (0.06 - 0.03 + (0.15)^2(0.5))\left(\frac{2}{12}\right)\right]}{(0.15)\sqrt{2/12}}$$
$$= \frac{0.054 + 0.007}{0.061} = 1$$
$$d_2 = 1 - (0.15)\sqrt{2/12} = 0.93$$

From Appendix Table V, we obtained that

$$N(d_1) = 0.8413 \quad N(d_2) = 0.8238,$$

so that the call price, C, is given by Equation (22.14)

$$C = 950(0.8413)e^{-0.03\times 2/12} - 900(0.8238)e^{-0.006\times 212}$$
$$= 795.24 - 734.01 = 61.23.$$

One contract would cost $61.23 × 100 = $6,123.

If the absolute amount of the dividend that will be paid on the stocks underlying the index (rather than the dividend yield) is assumed to be known, the basic Black–Scholes formula can be used with the initial stock price reduced by the present value of the dividends.

22.5. Summary

This chapter has explored international diversification from both theoretical and empirical viewpoints. It was demonstrated that the exchange risk and inflation risk will affect the return of international investment and, therefore, should be a major factor for analyzing international diversification.

Theoretically, the question of whether the world market is segmented or integrated has been shown to be important in investigating the effectiveness of international diversification. Both international CAPM and APT were used to discuss these related issues.

Both direct and indirect investments in foreign securities were used to show the benefit of international diversification. International mutual funds were employed to illustrate the usefulness of international diversification. Finally, the currency option, the index option, and their corresponding valuation models were discussed. In Chapter 25 of this book, we will discuss alternative ways of crafting long/short investment strategies to capture sources of equity risk premia by using international equity data.

Questions and Problems

1. Define the following terms.

   (a) exchange-rate risk
   (b) segmented market
   (c) integrated market
   (d) the Fisher effect
   (e) spot rate
   (f) forward rate
   (g) direct foreign investment
   (h) international portfolio investment
   (i) ADR.

2. What are the returns to a U.S. investor for the investments shown in the table?

	Foreign Return (%)	Currency Change (%)
A	12	2
B	10	−5
C	7	0
D	10	−20

3. Can currency risk be diversified away for the U.S. investor?
4. Show the efficient frontiers for domestic portfolios and international diversified portfolios. Give some reasons why this relationship should exist.
5. Why would world capital markets be segmented?
6. The nominal interest rate in the U.S. is 10%; the nominal rate in Germany is 5%. What impact will this difference have on the exchange rate? On what factors does it depend?
7. The spot rate for the French franc is \$1 = 6FF. The inflation rate is 5% in the U.S. and 10% in France. What is the expected future spot rate for the franc in dollars?
8. Are world capital markets efficient? What factors need to be considered in answering this question?
9. What are the advantages of an ADR for the U.S. investor?
10. What is a Eurobond? Why would a U.S. investor want to own such a security?
11. Consider a European call option on the Japanese yen is maturing one year from now on. Suppose that the current exchange rate is 80, the exercise price is 85, the risk-free rate in the U.S. is 3% per annum, the risk-free rate in Japan is 2% per annum. The volatility of foreign exchange rate is 15%. What is the value of the currency call option?

12. Consider a European call option on the S&P 500 that is three months from maturity. The current value of the index is 1000, the exercise price is 950, the risk-free interest rate is 6% per annum, and the volatility of the index is 15 per annum. Total dividend yields during the option's life will be 1%. What is the value of the index call option?
13. Suppose you have $1,200 and invest in a Japanese company, ABC. The stock price of ABC is ¥200 per share. The exchange rate at that time is ¥100. That is, ¥100 can exchange to $1. One year later, the ABC stock price is ¥250 per share and pays ¥20 dividends per share, and the exchange rate is ¥90. What is the rate of return on your investment in terms of Japanese Yen? What is the rate of return on your investment in terms of U.S. dollar?

Appendix 22A: Objectives and Policies of an International Mutual Fund

The investment objective of the Fund is to seek total return on its assets primarily through long-term capital growth and to a lesser extent from income. The Fund will seek to achieve such objective through investment in all types of common stocks and equivalents, preferred stocks and bonds, and other debt obligations of domestic and foreign companies and governments and international organizations. There is no limitation on the percentage or amount of the Fund's assets which may be invested for growth or income.[1]

> ... The percentage of the Fund's assets invested in particular geographic sectors will shift from time to time in accordance with the judgment of the Investment Advisers ....
>
> Notwithstanding the Fund's investment objective of seeking total return, the fund may, for defensive purposes, with limitation, invest in: obligations of the U.S. Government, its agencies or instrumentalities, cash and cash equivalents in major currencies, repurchase agreements, money market instruments, and high quality commercial paper.
>
> The Fund may also invest in securities of foreign issuers in the form of American Depository Receipts, European Depository Receipts or similar securities convertible into securities of foreign issuers ....

[1] Reproduced by courtesy of Dean Witter Worldwide Investment Trust Fund.

The Fund may enter into forward foreign currency exchange contracts as a hedge against fluctuations in future foreign exchange rates.

Since investments in foreign companies will usually involve currencies of foreign countries, and since the Fund may temporarily hold funds in bank deposits in foreign currencies during the course of investment programs, the value of the assets of the Fund as measured in U.S. dollars may be affected by changes in foreign currency exchange rates, exchange control regulations, and the Fund may incur costs in connection with conversion between various currencies.

...when management of the Fund believes that the currency of a particular foreign country may suffer a substantial decline against the U.S. dollar, it may enter into a forward contract to sell, for a fixed amount of dollars, the amount of foreign currency approximating the value of some or all of the Fund's portfolio securities denominated in such foreign currency. The precise matching of the forward contract amounts and the value of the securities involved will not generally be possible since the future value of such securities in foreign currencies will change as a consequence of market movements in the value of those securities between the date the forward contract is entered into and the date it matures.

...In making the allocation of assets among the various markets, the Investment Advisers will consider such factors as recent developments in the various countries, the condition and growth potential of various economies and securities markets, currency and tax considerations and other pertinent financial social, national and political factors...

...there may be the possibility of expropriations or confiscatory taxation, political, economic or social instability or diplomatic developments which could affect assets of the Fund held in foreign countries.

There may be less publicly available information about foreign companies comparable to reports and ratings published about U.S. companies. Foreign stock markets have substantially less volume that the New York Stock Exchange and securities of some foreign companies are less liquid and more volatile than securities of comparable U.S. companies. Brokerage commissions and other transactions costs on foreign securities exchanges are generally higher than in the U.S.

Bibliography

Abeysekera, S. P. and A. Mahajan. "The International Arbitrage Pricing theory: An Empirical Investigation." Working paper, presented June 1985, Western Finance association Annual Meeting.

Adler, M. and B. Dumas. "International Portfolio Choice and Corporate Finance: A Synthesis." *Journal of Finance*, v. 38 (June 1983), pp. 925–984.

Adler, M. and D. Simon. "Exchange Risk Surprises in International Portfolios." *Journal of Portfolio Management*, v. 12 (Winter 1986), pp. 44–53.

Ang, J. and R. Pohlman. "A Note on the Price Behavior of Far Eastern Stocks." *Journal of International Business Studies*, v. 9 (Spring 1978), pp. 103–107.

Bae, K., W. Bailey and C. X. Mao. "Stock Market Liberalization and the Information Environment." *Journal of International Money and Finance*, v. 25 (2006), pp. 404–428.

Beck, T., A. Demirg¨uc-Kunt and R. Levine. "Law, Endowments, and Finance." *Journal of Financial Economics*, v. 70 (2003), pp. 137–181.

Bekaert, G. and C. R. Harvey. "Emerging Equity Market Volatility." *Journal of Financial Economics*, v. 43 (1997), pp. 29–77.

Bekaert, G. and C. R. Harvey. "Emerging Markets Finance." *Journal of Empirical Finance*, v. 10 (2003), pp. 3–56.

Bekaert, G. and C. R. Harvey. "Foreign Speculators and Emerging Equity Markets." *Journal of Finance*, v. 55 (2000), pp. 565–614.

Bekaert, G. and C. R. Harvey. "Time-Varying World Market Integration." *Journal of Finance*, v. 50 (1995), pp. 403–444.

Bekaert, G., C. R. Harvey and A. Ng. "Market Integration and Contagion." *Journal of Business*, v. 78 (2005), pp. 39–70.

Bekaert, G., C. R. Harvey, C. T. Lundblad and S. Siegel. "What Segments Equity Markets?" Working paper, 2008, Columbia University.

Bekaert, G., R. Hodrick and X. Zhang. "International Stock Return Comovements." *Journal of Finance*, v. 64 (December 2009), pp. 2591–2626.

Bekaert, G. and G. Wu. "Asymmetric Volatility and Risk in Equity Markets." *Review of Financial Studies*, v. 13 (2000), pp. 1–42.

Black, F. "The Ins and Outs of Foreign Investment." *Financial Analysts Journal*, v. 34 (May/June 1978), pp. 25–32.

Black, F. "International Capital Market Equilibrium with Investment Barriers." *Journal of Financial Economics*, v. 1 (December 1974), pp. 337–352.

Bodie, Z., A. Kane and A. J. Marcus. *Investments.* McGraw-Hill, 9th ed., 2011.

Bollerslev, T. "Generalized Autoregressive Conditional Heteroscedasticity." *Journal of Econometrics*, v. 31 (1986), pp. 307–327.

Bomberger, W. A. and W. J. Frazer. "Interest Rates, Uncertainty, and the Livingston Data." *Journal of Finance*, v. 36 (June 1981), pp. 661–679.

Box, G. E. P., G. M. Jenkins and G. C. Reinsel. *Time Series Analysis: Forecasting and Control*, 3rd edn. Upper Saddle River, NJ: Prentice Hall, 1994.

Breeden, D. T. "An Intertemporal Asset Pricing Model with Stochastic Consumption and Investment Opportunities." *Journal of Financial Economics*, v. 7 (September 1979), pp. 265–296.

Carrieri, F., V. Errunza and S. Sarkissian. "Industry Risk and Market Integration." *Management Science*, v. 50 (2004), pp. 207–221.

Chen, S. and C. F. Lee. "The Effects of the Sample Size, the Investment Horizon and Market Conditions on the Validity of Composite Performance Measures: A Generalization." *Management Science*, v. 32 (1986), pp. 1410–1421.

Chen, S. and C. F. Lee. "The Sampling Relationship between Sharpe's Performance Measure and Its Risk Proxy: Sample Size, Investment Horizon and Market Conditions." *Management Science*, v. 27 (1981), pp. 607–618.

Chiou, W. P., A. C. Lee and C. C. A. Chang. "Do Investors still Benefit from International Diversification with Investment Constraints?" *Quarterly Review of Economics and Finance*, v. 49 (2009), pp. 448–483.

Chiou, W. P., A. C. Lee and C. F. Lee. "Stock Return, Risk and Legal Environment around the World." *International Review of Economics and Finance*, v. 19 (2010), pp. 95–105.

Chiou, W. P., A. C. Lee and C. F. Lee. "Variation in Stock Return Risks: An International Comparison." *Review of Pacific Basin Financial Markets and Policies*, v. 12 (2009), pp. 245–266.

Cho, D. C., C. S. Eun and L. W. Senbet. "International Arbitrage Pricing Theory: An Empirical Investigation." *Journal of Finance*, v. 41 (June 1986), pp. 313–329.

Cohn, R. A. and J. J. Pringle. "Imperfection in International Financial Markets: Implications for Risk Premium and the Cost of Capital to Firms." *Journal of Finance*, v. 28 (March 1973), pp. 59–66.

Cornell, B. "Inflation, Relative Price Changes, and Exchange Risk." *Financial Management*, v. 9 (Autumn 1980), pp. 30–34.

Cornell, B. "Spot Rates, Forward Rates, and Exchange Market Efficiency." *Journal of Financial Economics*, v. 5 (August 1977), pp. 55–65.

Demirg¨uc-Kunt, A. and V. Maksimovic. "Bank-based and Market-based Financial Systems: Evidence from Firm-level Data." *Journal of Financial Economics*, v. 65 (2002), pp. 337–363.

Demirg¨uc-Kunt, A. and V. Maksimovic. "Law, Finance, and Firm Growth." *Journal of Finance*, v. 53 (1998), pp. 2107–2137.

De Santis, G. and S. ˙Imrohoro˘glu. "Stock Returns and Volatility in Emerging Financial Markets." *Journal of International Money and Finance*, v. 16 (1997), pp. 561–579.

Dumas, B., J. Fleming and R. E. Whaley. "Implied Volatility Functions: Empirical Tests." *Journal of Finance*, v. 53 (1998), pp. 2059–2106.

Errunza, V. R. and L. Senbet. "The Effects of International Operations on the Market Value of the Firm: Theory and Evidence." *Journal of Finance*, v. 36 (May 1981), pp. 401–417.

Eun, C. S. "International Portfolio Diversification," in D. K. Eiteman and A. I. Stonehill, *Multinational Business Finance*. New York: Addison-Wesley, 1989.

Eun, C. S. and B. Resnick. "Estimating the Correlation Structure of International Share Prices." *Journal of Finance*, v. 39 (December 1984), pp. 1311–1324.

Eun, C. S. and B. Resnick. "Estimating the Dependence Structure of Share Prices: A Comparative Study of the U.S. and Japan." *The Financial Review*, v. 23 (November 1988), pp. 387–401.

Eun, C. S. and B. Resnick. "International Diversification under Estimation Risk: Actual vs. Potential Gains," in S. Khoury and A. Gosh (eds.), *Recent Developments in International Banking and Finance*, pp. 135–147. Lexington, MA: Lexington Books, 1987.

Eun, C. S. and B. Resnick. International Financial Management, sixth ed. McGraw-Hill, 2012.

Fama, E. F. and A. Farber. "Money Bonds and Foreign Exchange." *American Economic Review*, v. 69 (September 1979), pp. 639–650.

Frankel, J. and R. Levich. "Covered Interest Arbitrage: Unexploited Profits?" *Journal of Political Economy*, v. 83 (April 1975), pp. 325–338.

Grauer, F., R. Litzenberger and R. Stehle. "Sharing Rules and Equilibrium in an International Capital Market under Uncertainty." *Journal of Financial Economics*, v. 3 (June 1976), pp. 233–256.

Grinold, R. C. and R. N. Kahn. Active Portfolio Management: A Quantitative Approach for Providing Superior Returns and Controlling Risk, 2nd ed. McGraw-Hill, 1999.

Grubel, H. G. "International Diversified Portfolios: Welfare Gains and Capital Flows." *American Economic Review*, v. 58 (December 1968), pp. 1299–1314.

Grubel, H. G. and K. Fadner, "The Interdependence of International Equity Markets." *Journal of Finance*, v. 26 (March 1971), pp. 89–94.

Guerard, J. B. Handbook of Portfolio and Construction: Contemporary Applications of Markowitz Techniques. New York: Springer, 2010.

Hamilton, J. D. and G. Lin. "Stock Market Volatility and the Business Cycle." *Journal of Applied Econometrics*, v. 11 (1996), pp. 573–593.

Harvey, C. "The World Price of Covariance Risk." *Journal of Finance*, v. 46 (1991), pp. 111–157.

Haugen, R. A., E. Talmor and W. N. Torous. "The Effect of Volatility Changes on the Level of Stock Prices and Subsequent Expected Returns." *Journal of Finance*, v. 46 (1991), pp. 985–1007.

Hawawini, G. *European Equity Markets: Price Behavior and Efficiency.* Salomon Brothers Center, New York University, Monograph 1984–1989.

Ibbotson, R., L. Siegel and K. Love. "World Wealth: Market Values and Returns." *Journal of Portfolio Management*, v. 11 (Fall 1985), pp. 4–23.

Jacob, N. L. and R. R. Pettit. *Investments.* Homewood, ILL: Richard D. Irwin, Inc., 1984.

Jacquillat, B. and B. Solnik. "Multinationals are Poor Tools for Diversification." *Journal of Portfolio Management*, v. 4 (Winter 1978), pp. 8–12.

Jaffe, J. and R. Westerfield. "Patterns in Japanese Common Stock Returns: Day of the Week and Turn of the Year Effects." *Journal of Finance and Quantitative Analysis*, v. 20 (June 1985), pp. 259–278.

John, L. M., L. M. Donald, E. P. Jerald and W. M. Dennis. *Managing Investment Portfolios: A Dynamic Process*. CFA Institute, 3rd ed., 2007.

Jorion, R. "International Portfolio Diversification with Estimation Risk." *Journal of Business*, v. 58 (July 1985), pp. 259–278.

Kato, K. and J. S. Schallheim. "Seasonal and Size Anomalies in the Japanese Stock Market." *Journal of Financial and Quantitative Analysis*, v. 20 (June 1985), pp. 243–260.

Kim, E. H. and V. Singal. "Stock Markets Openings: Experience of Emerging Economies." *Journal of Business*, v. 73 (2000), pp. 25–66.

Karolyi, G. A. and R. M. Stulz. "Are Financial Assets Priced Locally or Globally?" *Handbook of the Economics of Finance*, v. 1B (2003), pp. 975–1020.

La Porta, R., F. Lopez-de-Silanes, A. Shleifer and R. Vishny. "Investor Protection and Corporate Governance." *Journal of Financial Economics*, v. 58 (2000), pp. 141–186.

La Porta, R., F. Lopez-de-Silanes, A. Shleifer and R. Vishny. "Law and Finance." *Journal of Political Economy*, v. 106 (1998), pp. 1113–1155.

La Porta, R., F. Lopez-de-Silanes, A. Shleifer and R. Vishny. "The Quality Government." *Journal of Law, Economics, and Organization*, v. 15 (1999), pp. 222–279.

Lee, W. Y. and K. Sachdeva. "The Role of Multinational Firm in the Integration of Segmented Capital Markets." *Journal of Finance*, v. 32 (May 1977), pp. 479–492.

Lessard, D. R. "International Portfolio Diversification: A Multivariate Analysis for a Group of Latin American Countries." *Journal of Finance*, v. 28 (June 1973), pp. 619–633.

Lessard, D. R. "World, Country, and Industry Relationships in Equity Returns: Implications for Risk Reduction through International Diversification." *Financial Analysis Journal*, v. 32 (January/February 1976), pp. 32–38.

Levy, H. and M. Sarnat. "International Diversification of Investment Portfolios." *American Economic Review*, v. 60 (September 1970), pp. 668–675.

Madhavan, A., M. Richardson and M. Roomans. "Why Do Security Prices Change? A Transaction-level Analysis of NYSE Stocks." *Review of Financial Studies*, v. 10 (1997), pp. 1035–1064.

Maldonado, R. and A. Saunders. "International Portfolio Diversification and International stability of International Stock Market Relationships." *Financial Management*, v. 10 (Autumn 1981), pp. 54–63.

Morgan Guaranty Trust Company. *Investing Internationally*. New York: 1978.

Patro, D. K. "Determinants of Flows into U.S.-Based International Mutual Funds" in Lee *et al.*, Handbook of Quantitative Finance and Risk Management, pp. 1235–1255, Springer, 2010.

Pindyck, R. S. "Risk, Inflation, and the Stock Market." *American Economic Review*, v. 74 (1984), pp. 335–351.

Proffitt, D. and N. Seitz. "The Performance of Internationally Diversified Mutual Funds." *Journal of the Midwest Finance Association*, v. 12 (March 1983), pp. 39–53.

Robichek, A. A. and M. R. Eaker. "Foreign Exchange Hedging and Capital Asset Pricing Model." *Journal of Financial*, v. 33 (June 1978), pp. 1011–1018.
Roll, R. "A Critique of Asset Pricing Theories Tests. Part I: On Past and Potential Testability of the Theory." *Journal of Economics*, v. 4 (March 1977), pp. 129–176.
Roll, R. "Violations of Purchasing Power Parity and Their Implications for Efficient International Commodity Markets," in M. Sarnat and G. Szego (eds.), *International Finance and Trade*. Cambridge, MA: Ballinger, 1979.
Roll, R. and B. Solnik. "A Pure Foreign Exchange Asset Pricing Model." *Journal of International Economics*, v. 13 (May 1977), pp. 161–179.
Senchack, A. and W. Beedles. "Is Indirect International Diversification Desirable?" *Journal of Portfolio Management*, v. 6 (Winter 1980), pp. 49–57.
Solnik, B. "An Equilibrium Model of the International Capital Market." *Journal of Economic Theory*, v. 8 (August 1974a), pp. 500–525.
Solnik, B. *International Investments*. Reading, MA: Addison-Wesley, 1988.
Solnik, B. "An International Model of Security Price Behavior." *Journal of Financial and Quantitative Analysis*, v. 9 (September 1974b), pp. 537–554.
Solnik, B. "The International Pricing of Risk: An Empirical Investigation of the World Capital Market Structure." *Journal of Finance*, v. 29 (May 1974c), pp. 365–378.
Solnik, B. "Testing International Asset Pricing: Some Pessimistic Views." *Journal of Finance*, v. 32 (May 1977), pp. 503–512.
Solnik, B. "Why Not Diversity Internationally Rather than Domestically?" *Financial Analysis Journal*, v. 29 (July/August 1974d), pp. 48–54.
Stehle, R. "An Empirical Test of the Alternate Hypothesis of National and International Pricing of Risky Assets." *Journal of Finance*, v. 32 (May 1977), pp. 493–507.
Stockman, A. "A Theory of Exchange Rate Determination." *Journal of Political Economy*, v. 88 (August 1980), pp. 673–699.
Stulz, R. "A Model of International Asset Pricing." *Journal of Financial Economics*, v. 9 (December 1981), pp. 383–406.
Stulz, R. "On the Effects of Barriers to International Investment." *Journal of Finance*, v. 36 (September 1981), pp. 923–934.
Stulz, R. M. and R. Williamson. "Culture, Openness, and Finance." *Journal Financial Economics*, v. 70 (2003), pp. 313–349.
Subrahmanyam, M. "On the Optimality of International Capital Market Integration." *Journal of Financial Economics*, v. 2 (August 1975), pp. 3–28.
Veronesi, P. "Stock Market Overreaction to Bad News in Good Times: A Rational Expectations Equilibrium Model." *Review of Financial Studies*, v. 12 (1999), pp. 975–1007.
Witter, D. "Dean Witter World Wide Investment Trust." Prospectus, June 1984.

Chapter 23

Bond Portfolios: Management and Strategy

Portfolio theory has had a limited impact on the management of fixed-income portfolios. For the most part, the techniques and strategies used in managing a bond portfolio are unique. This chapter presents techniques that are commonly used in bond-portfolio management and discusses the impact that portfolio theory has had on bond-portfolio management.

This chapter first focuses on the bond strategies of riding the yield curve and structuring the maturity of the bond portfolio in order to generate additional return. This is followed by a discussion of swapping. Next is an analysis of duration or the measure of the portfolio sensitivity to changes in interest rates with and without convexity, after which immunization is the focus. Finally, a case study is presented of bond-portfolio management in the context of portfolio theory.

23.1. Bond Strategies

How are yield curves useful for investors and analysts? The primary ways in which they are used in the market include: (1) to improve the forecasting of interest rates, (2) as a measure to help identify mispriced debt securities, (3) to "ride the yield curve," and (4) to help investors manage their portfolio-maturity structures. This section concerns the third and fourth uses of yield curves.

23.1.1. *Riding the Yield Curve*

Riding the yield curve is an investment strategy designed to take advantage of yield-curve shapes that are expected to be maintained for a period of time. Given the yield-curve shape, an investor then decides whether to purchase a debt security that matures at the end of his or her time horizon or to purchase a longer-term debt security which can be sold at time T. (The investor may also purchase securities that mature before T and reinvest out to T.) If the yield curve is upward sloping and is expected to remain stable over the investor's horizon period, purchasing a longer-term security and holding on to it as the end of the horizon period approaches would lead to an increasing selling price (bond value) as the yield declines. Even though reinvestment rates (RRs) for coupons would also be declining, the total realized yield (RY) would be higher than the direct investment in a shorter-term security that matures at the end of the holding period. Similar strategies could be illustrated for other yield-curve shapes. The problem with successfully using such strategies is that yield curves do not remain unchanged for long periods of time; they can and do change abruptly and seemingly without warning. The best advice to those with a specific horizon period but little forecasting skill would likely be to invest in short-maturity bonds to maintain reinvestment flexibility.

23.1.2. *Maturity-Structure Strategies*

A common practice among bond-portfolio managers is to evenly space the maturity of their securities. Under the **staggered-maturity plan** bonds are held to maturity, at which time the principal is reinvested in another long-term maturity instrument. Little managerial expertise is required to maintain the portfolio, and the maturing bonds and regular interest payments provide some liquidity.

An alternative to a staggered portfolio is the dumbbell strategy. Dumbbell portfolios are characterized by the inclusion of some proportion of short and intermediate term bonds that provide a liquidity buffer to protect a substantial investment in long-term securities. In Fig. 23.1, it is apparent why this is called the dumbbell strategy — the resulting graph looks like a weightlifter's dumbbell.

The dumbbell portfolio divides its funds between two components. The shortest maturity is usually less than three years, and the longest maturities are more than 10 years. The portfolio is weight at both ends of the maturity spectrum (again like a dumbbell). The logic and mechanics of the dumbbell strategy are straightforward: the short-term Treasury notes (T-notes) provide the least risk and highest liquidity, while long-term bonds

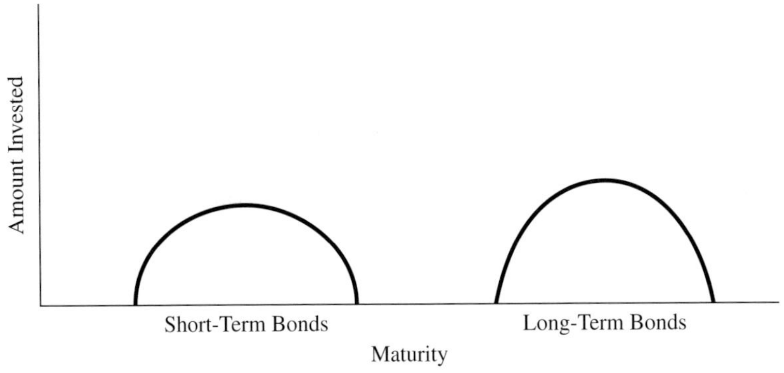

Fig. 23.1. Dumbbell Maturity Strategy.

provide the highest return. The best risk/return portfolio combination may very well be a combination of these extremes. Assuming an upward-sloping yield curve, no intermediate bonds will be held since they have (1) less return than the longest-maturity bonds, and (2) less liquidity and safety than the shortest T-note.

The performance of staggered and dumbbell strategies differs with respect to price fluctuations and return. During periods when interest rates are expected to increase, the return will most likely be over for a dumbbell portfolio than for a staggered portfolio. When rates are constant or cyclical and the yield curve is upward sloping, the dumbbell is superior to the staggered portfolio in yield; nevertheless, the price fluctuation will be greater for a dumbbell than for a staggered-maturity structure.

23.1.3. *Swapping*

When a market is in turmoil, great distortions take place. Some bonds drop further than they should, others less. A bond swapper can improve yield and pick up a substantial capital gain. In swapping, timing is very important.

Swapping strategies generally concentrate on highly specialized trading relationships. A commonly accepted method for classifying such swaps is Homer and Leibowitz's four types: (1) pure yield-pickup swap, (2) interest-rate anticipations, (3) intermarket swap, and (4) substitution swap. The expected return from any swap is usually based upon several motives, not just one — thus, these "types" of swaps are really just sources of return.

23.1.3.1. *Substitution Swap*

The substitution swap is the simplest of all. The swap attempts to profit from a change in yield spread between two nearly identical bonds. The trade is based upon a forecasted change in the yield spread between the two nearly bonds. The forecast is generally based upon the past history of the yield-spread relationship between the two bonds, with the assumption that any aberration from the past relationship is temporary, thereby allowing profit by buying the bond with the lower (higher) yield if the spread will become wider (or narrower). This trade is later reversed, leaving the investor in the original position, but with a trading profit from the relative changes in prices.

The substitution swap is simple in concept. Both the H-bond (the bond now held) and the P-bond (the proposed purchase) are equality, coupon, and maturity. The swap is executed at a time when the bonds are mispriced relative to each other. This mispricing is expected to be corrected by the end of the workout period. Sample Problem 23.1 provides further illustration.

Sample Problem 23.1

Substitution Swap. Suppose the investor holds a 30-year Aa utility 7% coupon bond (the H-bond), currently priced at par. He is offered to swap another 30-year Aa utility 7% coupon bond (the P-bond) at a yield to maturity (YTM) of 7.10%. Assume the workout period is one year. During this period, the prevailing RR for coupon remains unchanged at 7%. At the end of the workout period, both the H-bond and the P-bond are priced at par to yield 7%. See the evaluation worksheet (Table 23.1) that follows.

The worksheet gain of 129 basis points in realized compound yield is achieved only during the single year of the workout period. To obtain such a realized compound yield over the extended 30-year period, the investor must continue to swap an average of once a year, picking up 10 basis points with each swap, or at least averaging such a pickup on balance.

At the very worst, the workout period may take the entire 30 years, at which time the realized compound-yield gain would be 4.3 basis points. This is less than the initial 10-basis-point gain in YTM because the same RR will prevail for reinvesting the coupons of both the H-bond and the P-bond. This RR benefits the bond with the lower starting yield relative to the bond with the higher starting yield. Thus, it pulls the total returns together. The relative benefit of the RR to the lower-yield issue will be greater at low future RRs and less at high future rates.

Table 23.1. Evaluation Worksheet for a Sample Substitution Swap.

	H-Bond 30-year 7s @ 7.00%	P-Bond 30-year 7s @ 7.10%
	Workout time: 1 year RR: 7%	
Original investment per bond	$1,000.00	$987.70
Two coupons during year	70.00	70.00
Interest on one coupon @ 7% for one-half year	1.23	1.23
Principal value at end of year @ 7.00 YTM	1,000.00	1,000.00
Total accrued	1,071.23	1,071.23
Total gain	71.23	83.53
Gain per invested dollar	0.07123	0.08458
Realized compound yield (%)	7.00	8.29
Value of swap	129 basis points in one year	

Source: Homer, S. and M. L. Leibowitz. *Inside the Yield Book.* New York: Prentice-Hall and New York Institute of Finance (1972), p. 84.

Table 23.2. Effect of Workout Time on Substitution Swap: 30-Year 7s Swapped from 7% YTM to 7.10% YTM.

Workout Time	Realized Compound Yield Gain
30 years	4.3 basis points/year
20	6.4
10	12.9
5	25.7
2	64.4
1	129.0
6 months	258.8
3 months	527.2

Source: Homer and Leibowitz (1972), p. 85.

As the workout time is reduced, the relative gain in realized compound yield over the workout period rises dramatically, as seen in Table 23.2, above. The substitution swap may not work out exactly as anticipated due to: (1) a slower workout time than anticipated, (2) adverse interim spreads, (3) adverse changes in overall rates and (4) the P-bond's not being a true substitute. In the substitution swap, major changes in overall market yields affect the price and reinvestment components of both the H- and P-bond. However, as these effects tend to run parallel for both the H- and P-bond,

Table 23.3. Effect of Major Rate Changes on the Substitution Swap: 30-Year 7s Swapped from 7% to 7.1%, Realized Compound Yields — Principal Plus Interest.

	1-Year Workout			30-Year Workout		
RR and YTM (%)	*H*-Bond	*P*-Bond	Gain (Basis Points)	*H*-Bond	*P*-Bond	Gain (Basis Points)
5	34.551	36.013	146.2	5.922	5.965	4.3
6	19.791	21.161	137.0	6.445	6.448	4.3
7	7.00	8.29	129.0	7.000	7.043	4.3
8	(4.117)	(2.896)	122.1	7.584	7.627	4.3
9	(13.811)	(12.651)	116.0	8.196	8.239	4.3

Source: Homer and Leibowitz (1972), p. 87.

the relative gain from the swap is insensitive even to major rate changes, as seen in Table 23.3.

23.1.3.2. *Intermarket-Spread Swap*

The intermarket spread swap works on trading between sector-quality-coupon categories, based upon a forecasted change in yield spread between two different categories. The most common forecasting method is to observe historical yield spreads at various points in the interest-rate cycle, and then to adjust for current supply-and-demand effects. However, this is most difficult, as shown by the 1977–1978 period of extremely narrow spreads between AA's and U.S. government issues. Many managers bought government issues early in 1977, expecting the spread to widen, only to have to sit on their position through the next 18 months as both inflation and government spending continued unabated.

In the intermarket-spread swap the offered *P*-bond is essentially a different bond from the investor's *H*-bond, and the yield spread between the two bonds is largely determined by the yield spread between two segments of the bond market itself. The investor believes the "intermarket" yield spread is temporarily out of line, and the swap is executed in the hope of profiting when the discrepancy in this spread is resolved.

The intermarket-spread swap can be executed in two directions. The swap can be made into a *P*-bond having a greater YTM than the *H*-bond. This is done either for the extra yield (in belief that the spread will not widen), or in the belief that the intermarket spread will narrow, resulting in a lower relative YTM for the *P*-bond, thus a higher relative price for the P-bond. The investor is always assured of a gain of the initial basis-point spread, less any adjustment to the YTM of the swapped bond due to reinvestments at a higher coupon rate by maturity. Sample Problem 23.2 provides further illustration.

Sample Problem 23.2

Intermarket-Spread Swap. Suppose an investor holds the 30-year 4s priced at 67.18 to yield 6.50% and views the 30-year 7s at par as appropriate for an intermarket-spread swap. This investor feels that the 50-basis-point spread is excessive and anticipates a shrinkage of 10 basis points over the coming year. The price of the H-bond (4s) is kept constant for ease in computation. Table 23.4 illustrates this situation.

The 24.5-basis-point gain over 30 years (see Table 23.5) is less than the initial 50-basis-point gain due to the fact that the same RR benefits the bond with lower starting yield relative to the bond with the higher starting yield. Thus, it pulls the total returns together.

Table 23.4. Evaluation Worksheet for a Sample Intermarket-Spread Swap in a Yield-Pickup Direction.

	H-Bond 30-year 4s @ 6.50%	P-Bond 30-year 7s @ 7.00%
Initial YTM (%)	6.50	7.00
YTM at workout	6.50	6.90
Spread narrows 10 basis points from 50 basis points to 40 basis points.		
	Workout time: 1 year RR: 7%	
Original investment per bond	$671.82	$1,000.00
Two coupons during year	40.00	70.00
Interest on one coupon @ 7% for 6 months	0.70	1.23
Principal value at end of year	675.55	1,012.46
Total accrued	716.25	1,083.69
Total gained	44.43	83.69
Gain per invested dollar	0.0661	0.0837
Realized compound yield (%)	6.508	8.200
Value of swap	169.2 basis points in one year	

Source: Homer and Leibowitz (1972), p. 90.

Table 23.5. Effect of Various Spread Realignments and Workout Times on the Sample Yield-Pickup Intermarket Swap: Basis-Point Gain (Loss) in Realized Compound Yields (Annual Rate).

Spread	Workout Time				
Shrinkage	6 Months	1 Year	2 Years	5 Years	30 Years
40	1,083.4	539.9	273.0	114.3	24.5
30	817.0	414.6	215.8	96.4	24.5
20	556.2	291.1	159.1	78.8	24.5
10	300.4	169.2	103.1	61.3	24.5
0	49.8	49.3	47.8	44.0	24.5
(10)	(196.0)	(69.3)	(6.9)	26.8	24.5
(20)	(437.0)	(186.0)	(61.0)	9.9	24.5
(30)	(673.0)	(301.2)	(114.5)	(6.9)	24.5
(40)	(904.6)	(414.8)	(167.4)	(23.4)	24.5

Source: Homer and Leibowitz (1972), p. 91.

The **yield-giveup** version of the intermarket-spread swap works against the investor over time. Therefore, when a swap involves a loss in yield, there is a high premium to be placed on achieving a favorable spread change within a relatively short workout period. Here the investor trades the higher YTM H-bond for a lower YTM bond (P-bond). The investor will profit only if the yield spread widens, leading to relatively lower P-bond prices, which would more than offset the yield loss.

As an example, assume the H-bond is the 30-year 7s priced at par, and the P-bond is the 30-year 4s period at 67.18 to yield 6.50%. The investor believes that the present 50-basis-point spread is too narrow and will widen, as shown in Table 23.6.

General market moves over the short term would have little effect on the swap's value provided the spread changes as originally anticipated. The potential risk of this swap must be viewed in the context of changes in overall rate levels and the realignment of spread relationships among the many market components. As can be seen in Table 23.7, there is a high premium to be placed on achieving a favorable spread change within a relatively short workout period.

23.1.3.3. *Interest-Rate Anticipation Swap*

The investor who feels that the overall level of interest rates is going to change will want to affect a swap that will net a relative gain if this happens. Most commonly these swaps consist of shortening maturities if

Table 23.6. Evaluation Worksheet for a Sample Intermarket-Spread Swap with Yield Giveup.

	H-Bond 30-year 7s @ 7%	*P*-Bond 30-year 4s @ 6.50%
Initial YTM (%)	7	6.5
YTM at workout	7	6.4
	Spread growth: 10 basis points	
	Workout time: 1 year RR: 7%	
Original investment per bond	$1,000.00	$671.82
Two coupons during year	70.00	40.00
Interest on one coupon @ 7% for 6 months	1.23	0.70
Principal value at end of year	1,000.00	685.34
Total accrued	1,071.23	726.04
Total gained	71.23	54.22
Gain per invested dollar	0.0712	0.0807
Realized compound yield (%)	7	7.914
Value of swap	91.4 basis points in one year	

Source: Homer and Leibowitz (1972), p. 88.

Table 23.7. Effect on Various Spread Realignments and Workout Times on the Sample Yield-Giveup Intermarket Swap: Basis-Point Gain (Loss) in Realized Compound Yields (Annual Rate).

Spread Shrinkage	Workout Time: 6 Months	1 Year	2 Years	5 Years	30 Years
40	1,157.6	525.9	218.8	41.9	(24.5)
30	845.7	378.9	150.9	20.1	(24.5)
20	540.5	234.0	83.9	(1.5)	(24.5)
10	241.9	91.4	17.6	(22.9)	(24.5)
0	(49.8)	(49.3)	(47.8)	(44.0)	(24.5)
(10)	(335.3)	(187.7)	(112.6)	(64.9)	(24.5)
(20)	(614.9)	(324.1)	(176.4)	(85.6)	(24.5)
(30)	(888.2)	(458.4)	(239.1)	(106.0)	(24.5)
(40)	(1,155.5)	(590.8)	(302.1)	(126.3)	(24.5)

Source: Homer and Leibowitz (1972), p. 89.

higher long-term yields are expected, and lengthening maturities if lower long-term yields are expected.

The decisive factor is the expected long rate: the change in the long rate will almost always be the chief determinant of the value of the swap. Maturity swaps are highly speculative. If yields do not rise or fall as expected in a short period of time, often a large penalty due to the immediate loss in yield will occur. If the yield curve is positive, as one moves from long to short a large yield loss occurs. Conversely, if the curve is negative, moving from short to long involves little or no yield pickup and sometimes a yield loss. Time works heavily against the swapper. Nevertheless, these periods of maximum yield loss are usually the best times to make maturity swaps in both directions.

In evaluating maturity swaps, capital gains or losses will be critical over the first year or so. As time goes on, coupon income and compounded interest become more important. The concept of duration easily explains this fact, for as time increases the present-value factor declines. Therefore, capital gains or losses are valued at the lower present-value factor. Sample Problem 23.3 provides further illustration.

Sample Problem 23.3

Interest-Rate-Anticipation Swap. Suppose an investor holds a 7% 30-year bond selling at par. He expects rate to rise from 7% to 9% within the year. Therefore, a trade is made into a 5% T-note maturing in one year and selling at par, as in Table 23.8.

The portfolio manager who shortens maturities drastically at a large loss in yield within the long range must expect a substantial increase in

Table 23.8. Evaluation Worksheet for a Sample Interest-Rate-Anticipation Swap.

	H-Bond 30-year 7s @ 100	*P*-Bond 30-year 5s @ 100
	Anticipated rate change: 9%	
	Workout time: 1 year	
Original investment per bond	$1,000.00	$1,000
Two coupons during year	70.00	50
Interest on one coupon @ 7% for 6 months	1.23	
Principal value at end of year	748.37	
Total accrued	819.60	—
Total gained	(180.4)	1,000
Gain per invested dollar	(0.1804)	1,050
Realized compound yield (%)	(13.82)	50
		0.05
		5.00
Value of swap	1,885 basis points in one year	

Source: Homer and Leibowitz (1972), p. 94.

yields within the short range — otherwise his long-range yield loss will exceed his short-term gain. The swapper into longs at a big yield increase has time in his favor, but over the near term he can fare badly if long yields rise further. Finally, the swapper from short to long at a yield loss also has time against him.

23.1.3.4. *Pure Yield-Pickup Swap*

In a pure yield-pickup swap there is no expectation of market changes, but a simple attempt to increase yield. Basically, two bonds are examined to establish their difference in YTM, with a further adjustment to consider the impact of interim reinvestment of coupons at an assumed rate or return between now and the maturity date. Sample Problem 23.4 provides further illustration.

Sample Problem 23.4

Pure Yield-Pickup Swap. Suppose an investor swaps from the 30-year 4s at 671.82 to yield 6.50% into 30-year 7s at 100 to yield 7% for the sole purpose of picking up the additional 105 basis points in current income or the 50 basis points in the YTM. The investor is not motivated by a judgment that the intermarket spread will shrink or that yields will rise or fall. He has no explicit concept of a workout period — he intends to hold the 7s to maturity.

To evaluate a swap of this sort, which is based on holding the P-bond to maturity, three factors must be taken into account: (1) the coupon income, (2) the interest on interest, and (3) the amortization to par. Interim market-price changes may be ignored. A simple addition of the three money flows just listed, divided by the dollars invested, will give a total return in dollars which, with the aid of a compound-interest table, will give the total realized compound yield as a percentage of each dollar invested, as shown in Table 23.9.

Although the principal invested in both issues is only $671.82 per bond, over a period of 30 years, the switch results in a gain of $210.82 per bond in coupon income, a gain of $479.68 per bond in interest on interest, and a loss of $328.18 per bond in capital gain. These three factors add up to a net gain of $362.32 per bond, or a net gain of 24 basis points per year.

23.2. Duration

The traditional role of bonds as an asset category has changed over the past 15 years due to surging interest rates and the resultant price volatility.

Table 23.9. Evaluation Worksheet for a Sample Pure Yield-Pickup Swap.

	H-Bond 30-year 4s @ 6.50%	*P*-Bond 30-year 7s @ 7.00%
	(one bond)	(0.67182 of one bond)
Coupon income over 30 years	$1,200.00	$1,410.82
Interest on interest at 7%	2,730.34	3,210.02
Amortization	328.18	0
Total return	$4,258.52	$4,620.84
Realized compound yield (%)	6.76	7.00
Value of swap	24 basis points per annum at 7% RR	

Source: Homer and Leibowitz (1972), p. 99.

The use of bond maturity to reduce interest-rate risk in bond portfolios through maturity matching has become increasingly inadequate. By the 1970s, several researchers had recognized that maturity is an incomplete measure of the life and risk of a coupon bond.

In 1971, Fisher and Weil recommended a practical measurement tool that could help immunize bond portfolios against interest-rate risk, and in 1973 Hopewell and Kaufman demonstrated that it could also be used as a measure of price risk for bonds. This concept is **duration**, which has emerged as an important tool for the measurement and management of interest-rate risk. Bierwag, Kaufman, and Toevs (BKT) noted in 1983 that only the introduction of beta in the 1960s has generated as much interest in the investment community as has duration.

The purpose of this section is to review briefly the historical development of duration and to examine its potential use by investors in alternative bond-portfolio immunization strategies, as well as to look at certain reservations that should be considered when using duration to immunize bond portfolios.

In 1938, Frederick Macaulay developed the concept of duration as part of an overall analysis of interest rates and bond prices. He was attempting to develop a more meaningful summary measure of the life of a bond that would correlate well with changes in bond price; he arrived at a weighted average of the time to each bond payment, with the weights being the present values of each payment relative to the total present value of all the flows:

$$D = \frac{\sum_{t=0}^{n} t\left[\frac{C_t}{(1+k_d)^t}\right]}{\sum_{t=0}^{n} \frac{C_t}{(1+k_d)^t}}, \tag{23.1}$$

where

$C_t =$ the coupon-interest payment in periods 1 through $n - 1$;
$C_n =$ the sum of the coupon-interest payment and the face value of the bond in period n;
$k_d =$ the YTM or required rate of return of the bondholders in the market; and
$t =$ the time period in years.

Thus, for the first semi-annual payment in the series between 0 and n, t would equal 0.5. The denominator of this equation is equal to the current price of the bond as estimated by the present value of all future cash flows.

The duration of a bond with a fixed maturity date declines just as maturity with the passage of time. The duration of a coupon bond, however, is always shorter than its maturity. Only for pure discount (zero-coupon) bonds will duration equal maturity. Duration is also affected by the size of the coupon and its YTM, decreasing as either increases.

It is useful to place the concept of duration in the perspective of other summary measures of the timing of an asset's cash flow. Because the cash flows from bonds are specific, both as to timing and amount, analysts have derived a precise measure of the timing for bonds. The most commonly used timing measure is term to maturity (TM), the number of years prior to the final payment on the bond. The advantage of TM is that it is easily identified and measured. However, the disadvantage is that TM ignores interim cash flows. Moreover, TM ignores the substantial difference in coupon rates and the difference in sinking funds.

23.2.1. *Weighted-Average Term to Maturity*

In an attempt to rectify the deficiency of TM, a measure that considered the interest payments and the final principal payment was constructed. The **weighted-average term to maturity (WATM)** computes the proportion of each individual payment as a percentage of all payments and makes this proportion the weight for the year the payment is made:

$$\text{WATM} = \frac{\text{CF}_1}{\text{TCF}}(1) + \frac{\text{CF}_2}{\text{TCF}}(2) + \cdots + \frac{\text{CF}_n}{\text{TCF}}(n), \tag{23.2}$$

where

$\text{CF}_t =$ the cash flow in year t;
$t =$ the year when cash flow is received;

$n =$ maturity; and
TCF $=$ the total cash flow from the bond.

Sample Problem 23.5 provides further illustration.

Sample Problem 23.5

Suppose a 10-year, 4% bond will have total cash-flow payments of \$1,400. Thus, the \$40 payment in CF_1 will have a weight of 0.0287 (\$40/\$1,400), each subsequent interest payment will have the same weight, and the principal in year 10 will have a weight of 0.74286 (\$1,040/1,400). Therefore:

$$\text{WATM} = \frac{\$40}{\$1{,}400}(1) + \frac{\$40}{\$1{,}400}(2) + \frac{\$40}{\$1{,}400}(3) + \cdots + \frac{\$40}{\$1{,}400}(9) + \frac{\$1{,}040}{\$1{,}400}(10) = 8.71 \text{ years.}$$

The WATM is definitely less than the TM, because it takes account of all interim cash flows in addition to the final payment. In addition, a bond with a larger coupon has a shorter WATM because a larger proportion of its total cash flows is derived from the coupon payments prior to maturity — that is, the coupon-weighted average of the larger coupon is larger than the smaller coupon bond. The weighted-average term can be utilized to take into account sinking-fund payments, thus lowering the WATM.

23.2.2. *WATM Versus Duration Measure*

A major advantage of WATM is that it considers the timing of all cash flows from the bond, including interim and final payments. One disadvantage is that it does not consider the time value of the flows. The interest payment of the first period is valued the same as the last period.

The **duration measure** is simply a weighted-average maturity, where the weights are stated in present value terms. In the same format as the WATM, duration is

$$\text{D} = \frac{\text{PVCF}_1}{\text{PVTCF}}(1) + \frac{\text{PVCF}_2}{\text{PVTCF}}(2) + \cdots + \frac{\text{PVCF}_n}{\text{PVTCF}}(n), \tag{23.3}$$

where

$\text{PVCF}_t =$ the present value of the cash flow in year t discounted at current yield to maturity;
$t =$ the year when cash flow is received;

$n =$ maturity; and
PVTCF = the present value of total cash flow from the bond discounted at current YTM.

The time in the future when a cash flow is received is weighted by the proportion that the present value of that cash flow contributes to the total present value or price of the bond. Similar to the WATM, the duration of a bond is shorter than its TM because of the interim interest payment. Duration is inversely related to the coupon of the bond. The one variable that does not influence the average TM but can affect duration is the prevailing market yield. Market yield does not affect WATM because this measure does not consider the present value of flows. Nevertheless, market yield affects more on both the numerator of WATM and TM. As a result, there is an inverse relation between a change in the market yield and a bond's duration.

Tables 23.10 and 23.11, taken from Reilly and Sidhu's (1980) article, "The Many Uses of Bond Duration," illustrate the difference between the timing measures. These two tables show the WATM and the duration, respectively. Due to the consideration of the time value of money in the duration measurement, duration is the superior measuring technique.

Table 23.10. WATM (Assuming Annual Interest Payments).

Bond A $1,000, 10 years, 4%				Bond B $1,000, 10 years, 8%			
(1)	(2)	(3)	(4)	(5)	(6)	(7)	(8)
Year	Cash Flow ($)	Cash Flow/TCF	(1)×(3)	Year	Cash Flow ($)	Cash Flow/TCF	(5)×(7)
1	40	0.02857	0.02857	1	80	0.04444	0.04444
2	40	0.02857	0.05714	2	80	0.04444	0.08888
3	40	0.02857	0.08571	3	80	0.04444	0.13332
4	40	0.02857	0.11428	4	80	0.04444	0.17776
5	40	0.02857	0.14285	5	80	0.04444	0.22220
6	40	0.02857	0.17142	6	80	0.04444	0.26664
7	40	0.02857	0.19999	7	80	0.04444	0.31108
8	40	0.02857	0.22856	8	80	0.04444	0.35552
9	40	0.02857	0.28713	9	80	0.04444	0.39996
10	1,040	0.74286	7.42860	10	1,080	0.60000	6.00000
Sum	$1,400	1.00000	8.71425	Sum	$1,800	1.00000	7.99980
	WATM = 8.71 years				WATM = 8.00 years		

Source: Reilly and Sidhu, "The Many Uses of Bond Duration." *Financial Analysts Journal*, v. 36 (July/August 1980), p. 60.

Table 23.11. Duration (Assuming 8% Market Yield).

(1) Year	(2) Cash Flow	(3) PV at 8%	(4) PV of Flow	(5) PV as % of Price	(6) (1)×(5)
Bond A					
1	\$ 40	0.9259	\$ 37.04	0.0506	0.0506
2	40	0.8573	34.29	0.0469	0.0938
3	40	0.7938	31.75	0.0434	0.1302
4	40	0.7350	29.40	0.0402	0.1608
5	40	0.6806	27.22	0.0372	0.1860
6	40	0.6302	25.21	0.0345	0.2070
7	40	0.5835	23.34	0.0319	0.2233
8	40	0.5403	21.61	0.0295	0.2360
9	40	0.5002	20.01	0.0274	0.2466
10	1,040	0.4632	481.73	0.6585	6.5850
Sum			\$ 731.58	1.0000	8.1193
Duration = 8.12 years					
Bond B					
1	\$ 80	0.9259	\$ 74.07	0.0741	0.0741
2	80	0.8573	68.59	0.0686	0.1372
3	80	0.7938	63.50	0.0635	0.1906
4	80	0.7350	58.80	0.0588	0.1906
5	80	0.6806	54.44	0.0544	0.2720
6	80	0.6302	50.42	0.0504	0.3024
7	80	0.5835	46.68	0.0467	0.3269
8	80	0.5403	43.22	0.0432	0.3456
9	80	0.5002	40.02	0.0400	0.3600
10	1,080	0.4632	500.26	0.5003	5.0030
Sum			\$ 1,000.00	1.0000	7.2470
Duration = 7.25 years					

WATM is always longer than the duration of a bond, and the difference increases with the market rate used in the duration formula. This is consistent with the duration property of an inverse relation between duration and the market rate.

23.2.3. *Yield to Maturity*[1]

Based upon Chapter 5, **Yield to maturity** is an average maturity measurement in its own way because it is calculated using the same rate

[1]Malkiel (1962) and Bodie *et al.* (2011) have carefully discussed the sensitivity of bond prices to changes in market interest rate, i.e., interest rate sensitivity. They have carefully proposed several propositions to describe this kind of relationship. It is well-known

to discount all payments to the bondholder — thus, it is an average of spot rates over time. For example, if the spot rate for period two, r_2, is greater than that for period one, r_1, the YTM on a two-year coupon bond would be between r_1 and r_2 — an underestimate of the two-year spot rate. Likewise, the opposite condition would overestimate the two-year spot rate. With the high volatility of interest rates that has existed in recent years, the difference can be dramatic. For example, in Britain during 1977, the 20-year spot rate of interest was approximately 20%, while the YTM on 20-year coupon bonds was only 13%. The reason for the larger discrepancy was that YTM was calculated as an average of the relatively low short-term spot rates and the relatively high long-term spot rates.

Until the 1970s, when interest-rate and bond-price volatility increased dramatically, the significance of the superiority of duration over average-measurement of bond-portfolio risk was required for immunization against interest-rate risk. Studies comparing the success of portfolios immunized with a duration strategy and a maturity strategy have shown that duration outperforms maturity 75% of the time for a variety of planning periods. Duration also produces lower variances between realized and promised returns than either the maturity strategy or the naïve strategy of annually rolling over 20-year bonds.

The motivation for bond investment is to secure a fixed cash flow over a particular investment horizon. Asset and liability portfolios of financial institutions often generate future cash-flow patterns that must conform to certain solvency and profitability restrictions. For example, insurance companies and pension funds, with definite future commitments of funds, invest now so that their future cash-flow stream will match well with their future commitment stream. Bond-immunization strategies are designed to guarantee the investor in default-free and option-free bonds at rate of return that approximates the promised rate (or YTM) computed at the outset of the investment. Nevertheless, the YTM will be equal to the RY only if the interim coupon payments are reinvestable at the YTM. If interest rates change, the RY will be lower or higher than YTM, depending upon the relationship between the bond's measured duration D and the investor's expected holding period H. It has been shown that realized yield (RY) can be computed as a weighted average of the YTM and the average

---

that bond characteristics such as coupon rate or yield to maturity affect interest rate sensitivity. Therefore, the yield to maturity discussed in Chapter 5 and this section can be used to analysis the interest rate sensitivity of bond prices.

reinvestment rate (RR) available for coupon payments:

$$\text{RY} = \left(\frac{D}{H}\right)(\text{YTM}) + \left(1 - \frac{D}{H}\right)(\text{RR}). \tag{23.4}$$

Therefore, the RY would equal the YTM only if the duration on the bond were kept equal to the time horizon of the investor. An increase in the RR would increase the return from reinvested coupons, but would at the same time decrease the bond value. Only holding the bond to maturity would prevent this value reduction from affecting the RY. Therefore, the overall impact of RR increases depends upon the extent to which the income effect offsets the value reduction. On the other hand, a decrease in the RR will decrease the return from reinvested coupons, but it will increase the bond values in the market. As shown in Equation (23.4), these opposite impacts on RY will exactly offset each other only when D equals H.

If a more complete time spectrum of zero-coupon bonds of all types were readily available, bond-portfolio immunization would be a relatively simple process. Simply by choosing bonds with maturities equal to the length of an investor's investment horizon, the rate of return would always be as promised by the YTM, regardless of interest-rate changes. Beginning with Treasury-bond sales of February 15, 1985, the U.S. Treasury has been cooperating with Wall Street firms in the stripping of coupon payments from new Treasury issues through separate registration of coupon and maturity payments, thus manufacturing a series of zero-coupon issues. However, since this applies only to Treasury issues, it is still necessary for investors to use duration models to immunize portfolios of non-Treasury bonds.

To immunize a bond portfolio, investors must match the duration of the portfolio with the length of their investment horizons. This must be accomplished within their assumed stochastic process of interest-rate movements and changes in the yield curve. If the yield curve changes during the holding period, the immunization process will break down and the RY will not equal the YTM as promised.

Since the hoped-for results of the passive duration-immunization method can be upset by interest-rate shifts, some investors may prefer to try to predict interest-rate changes and undertake an active immunization strategy. This would involve the formation of bond portfolios with durations intentionally longer or shorter than the investment-planning period. Since it is usually assumed that the market consensus about future interest rates is the most likely possibility, investors should pursue active strategies only if their forecasts of rates differ from those of the market. The investor, who expects the interest rate to be higher than the market forecast, should form a bond portfolio with a duration shorter than the length of the investment horizon. If successful, the income gains from reinvestment of coupons and maturing bonds will exceed the value loss on unmatured bonds: RY will exceed the YTM promised. If unsuccessful, the reinvestment return will not be enough to offset the value loss and RY will be less than YTM.

If the investor expects interest rates to be lower than the market forecast, the procedure would be the reverse of that described above — that is, to purchase a bond portfolio with a duration longer than the investment horizon. If successful, the lower reinvestment returns will be more than offset by the bond-value gains. Thus the active immunization strategy relies solely upon the ability of the investor to predict the direction of future interest-rate changes and to take full advantage of market opportunities for realized returns greater than market rates. While this provides the investor with an opportunity for substantial returns, it can also result in substantial losses. Because of this, Leibowitz and Weinberger (LW, 1981) derived a "stop loss" active immunization strategy which they called contingent immunization. In this method, the portfolio manager pursues higher returns through active management unless the value of the portfolio declines to a level that threatens a minimum target return. At this point, the portfolio is switched into a pure immunization mode designed to provide the minimum target specified at the outset. Other researchers have developed similar strategies that rely on two portfolios — one actively and the other passively immunized. Interest changes could take place that would virtually wipe out the active portfolio, but they would not greatly affect the minimum target return of the two-portfolio combination.

23.2.4. *The Macaulay Model*

The duration model that is still most widely used because of its simplicity is the **Macaulay model**. However, basic limitations affect the use of this model. First, the current and forward spot rates are assumed to be equal over a specific planning horizon — that is, the yield curve is assumed to be flat. This is also one of the basic weakness of the YTM measurement. Second, this model provides an accurate measure of interest-rate risk only when there is a single parallel shift in the term of structure of interest rates — that is, there is only one shift within the holding period and it does not involve a change in yield-curve shape.

Most studies surveyed seem to indicate that the Macaulay model assumptions are unrealistic and too restrictive. Cox *et al.* (1979) noted that it does not take into account the dynamic nature of the term structure observed in the real world, in which yield curves can and do change in shape as well as location. As a result, a number of more complex duration models have been developed to measure risk when multiple term-structure shifts can affect the shape and location of the yield curve. Because the actual underlying stochastic process governing interest-rate changes is not known, only empirical analysis can determine whether the extra complexity of these models justifies their usage. Bierwag *et al.* (1982) extensively tested the Macaulay model along with four more complex duration models and found that duration-matching strategies generated realized returns consistently closer to promised yields than a maturity-matching strategy. Even more interesting, the Macaulay measure appeared to perform as well as the more complex models. Their findings suggest that single-factor duration matching is a feasible immunization strategy that works reasonably well, even with the less complex (and thus less costly) Macaulay model.

Duration appears a better measure of a bond's life than maturity because it provides a more meaningful relationship with interest-rate changes. This relationship has been expressed by Hopewell and Kaufman (1973) as:

$$\frac{\Delta P}{P} = \frac{D}{(1+i)}\Delta i = D{*}\Delta i, \tag{23.5}$$

Where $\Delta =$ "change in"; $P =$ bond price; $D =$ duration; and $i =$ market interest rate or bond yield.

For example, a bond with five years' duration will decline in price by approximately 10% when market yield increases by 2%. Note that $\Delta P/P$ on the left-hand side of Equation (23.5) is the percentage change in price, and Δi is the absolute change in yield level and not percentage change.

Other useful generalizations can be made concerning the relationships of duration to various bond characteristics, as follows.

1. The higher the coupon, the shorter the duration, because the face-value payment at maturity will represent a smaller proportional present-value contribution to the makeup of the current bond value. In other words, bonds with small coupon rates will experience larger capital gains or losses as interest rates change. Additionally, for all bonds except zero-coupon-rate bonds, as the maturity of the bond lengthens the duration at the limit will approach (1 + YTM)/YTM. Table 23.12 shows the relationship between

Table 23.12. Duration, Maturity, and Coupon Rate.

	Coupon Rate			
Maturity (years)	0.02	0.04	0.06	0.08
1	0.995	0.990	0.985	0.981
5	4.756	4.558	4.393	4.254
10	8.891	8.169	7.662	7.286
20	14.981	12.98	11.904	11.232
50	19.452	17.129	16.273	15.829
100	17.567	17.232	17.120	17.064
∞	17.667	17.667	17.667	17.667

duration, maturity, and coupon rates for a bond with a YTM of 6%. At the limit (maturity goes to infinity), the duration will approach 17.667 (i.e., $(1 + 0.06)/0.06$).

As can be seen in Table 23.12, the limit is independent of the coupon rate: it is always 17.667. However, when the coupon rate is the same as or greater than the yield rate (the bond is selling at a premium), duration approaches the limit directly. Conversely, for discount-priced bonds (coupon rate is less than YTM), duration can increase beyond the limit and then recede to the limit. In the case of the bond with the 2% coupon at a maturity of 50 years, the duration is 19.452 — and this approaches the limit as maturity keeps increasing. These relationships are shown in Fig. 23.2.

Regardless of coupon size, it is nearly impossible to find bonds with durations in excess of 20 years; most bonds have a limit of about 15 years.

2. The higher the YTM, the shorter the duration, because YTM is used as the discount rate for the bond's cash flows and higher discount rates diminish the proportional present-value contribution of more distant payments. As has been shown, at the limit duration is equal to (1 +

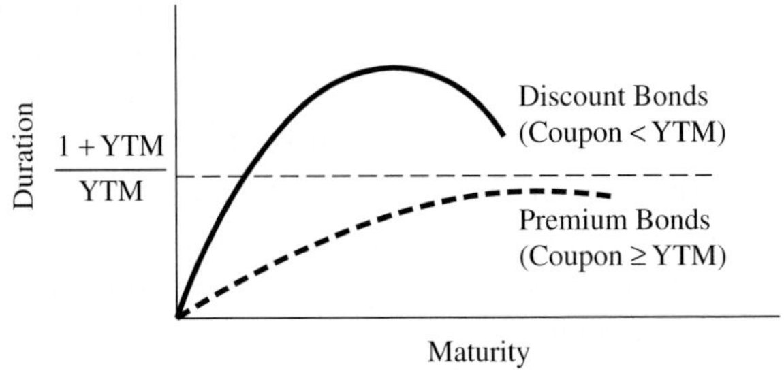

Fig. 23.2. Duration and Maturity for Premium and Discount Bonds.

Table 23.13. Duration and YTM.

YTM	Duration at Limit (maturity $\to \infty$)
0.02	51
0.04	26
0.08	13.5
0.10	11
0.20	6
0.30	4.33
0.50	3

YTM)/YTM; in Table 23.13 the relationship between duration and YTM is shown.

3. A typical sinking fund (one is which the bond principal is gradually retired over time) will reduce duration. Duration can be reduced by the sinking-fund or call provision. A large proportion of current bond issues do have sinking funds, and these can definitely affect a bond's duration. An example will illustrate this fact. A 10-year 4% bond with a sinking fund of 10% of face value per year starting at the end of the fifth year has a duration of 7.10 years as compared to the duration of 8.12 years of a similar bond without a sinking fund. Table 23.14 provides further illustration.

The effect of a sinking fund on the time structure of cash flows for a bond is certain to the issuer of the bond, since the firm must make the payments: they represent a legal cash-flow requirement that will affect the firm's cash flow. However, the sinking fund may not affect the investor since the money put into the sinking fund may not necessarily be used to retire outstanding bonds. Even if it is, it is not certain that a given investor's bonds will be called for retirement.

4. For bonds of less than five years to maturity, the magnitudes of duration changes are about the same as those for maturity changes. For bonds of 5 to 15 years' maturity, changes in the magnitude of duration are considerably less than those of maturity. For bonds with more than 20 years to maturity, changes in the magnitude of duration are very small relative to changes in maturity. As can be seen in Fig. 23.3, in the range of zero to five years the relationship between duration and maturity is shown approximately by a straight line with a slope of 45 degrees. In the range of five to ten years, the slope of the line is less, indicating a smaller change in duration for a given change in maturity. And for more than 20 years, the

Table 23.14. Duration with and without Sinking Funds (Assuming 8% Market Yield).

	Cash flow	Present-Value Factor	Present Value of Cash Flow	Weight	Duration
Bond A—No Sinking Fund					
1	$ 40	0.9259	$ 37.04	0.0506	0.0506
2	40	0.8573	34.29	0.0469	0.0938
3	40	0.7938	31.75	0.0434	0.1302
4	40	0.7350	29.40	0.0402	0.1608
5	40	0.6806	27.22	0.0372	0.1860
6	40	0.6302	25.21	0.0345	0.2070
7	40	0.5835	23.34	0.0319	0.2233
8	40	0.5403	21.61	0.0295	0.2360
9	40	0.5002	20.01	0.0274	0.2466
10	1,040	0.4632	481.73	0.6585	6.5850
Sum			$ 731.58	1.0000	8.1193
Duration = 8.12 years					
Bond A — Sinking Fund (10% per year from fifth year)					
1	$40	0.9259	$ 37.04	0.04668	0.04668
2	40	0.8573	34.29	0.04321	0.08642
3	40	0.7938	31.75	0.04001	0.12003
4	40	0.7350	29.40	0.03705	0.14820
5	140	0.6806	95.28	0.12010	0.60050
6	140	0.6302	88.23	0.11119	0.66714
7	140	0.5835	81.69	0.10295	0.72065
8	140	0.5403	75.64	0.09533	0.76264
9	140	0.5002	70.03	0.08826	0.79434
10	540	0.4632	250.13	0.31523	3.15230
Sum			$ 793.48	1.00000	7.09890
Duration = 7.10 years					

Source: Reilly and Sidhu (1980), pp. 61–62.

line is almost horizontal, showing a smaller change in duration for a given change in maturity.

5. In contrast to a sinking fund, all bondholders will be affected if a bond is called. The duration of a callable bond will be shorter than a noncallable bond.

When a bond is callable, the cash flow implicit in the YTM figure is subject to possible early alteration. Most corporate bonds issued today are callable, but with a period of call protection before the call option can be exercised. At the expiration of this period, the bond may be called at a specified call price, which usually involves some premium over par.

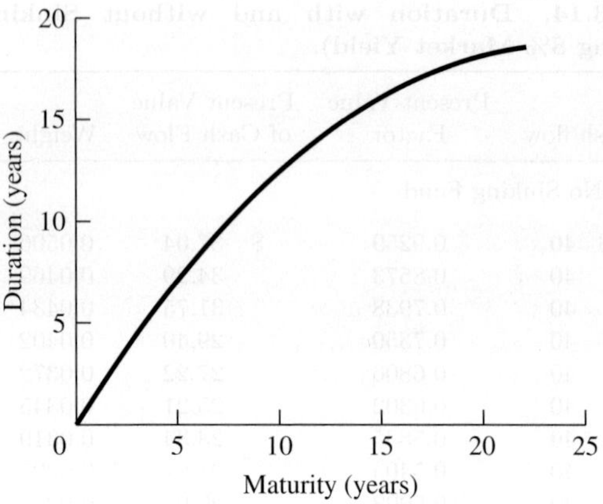

Fig. 23.3. Duration versus Maturity.

To provide some measure of the return in the event that the issuer exercises the call option at some future point, the yield to call is calculated instead of the YTM. This computation is based on the assumption that the bond's cash flow is terminated at the "first call date" with redemption of principal at the specified call price. The crossover yield is defined as that yield where the YTM is equal to the yield to call. When the price of the bond rises to some value above the call price, and the market yield declines to value below the crossover yield, the yield to call becomes the minimum yield. At this price and yield, the firm will probably exercise a call option when it is available. When prices go below the call price, the YTM is the minimum yield. Sample Problem 23.6 provides further illustration.

Sample Problem 23.6

To calculate the crossover yield for a 8%, 30-year bond selling at par with 10-year call protection, the annual return flow divided by the average investment can be used as an approximation for the yield. The implied crossover yield is 8.46%:

$$\text{Crossover yield: } \frac{80 + \frac{1080-1000}{10}}{\frac{1080+1000}{2}} = 8.46\%.$$

In one year's time the bond's maturity will be 29 years with nine years to call. If the market rate has decline to the point where the YTM of the bond is 7%, which is below the crossover yield of 8.46%, the bond's yield to call will be 6%.

$$\text{Yield to call} = \frac{80 + \frac{1000-1123.43}{9}}{\frac{1080+1123.43}{2}} = 6\%.$$

If a bond-portfolio manager ignored the call option and computed the duration of this bond to maturity at a market yield of 7%, the duration would be 12.49 years. If duration was computed recognizing the call option at a price of $1,080 and using the yield to call of 6%, it would be 6.83 years.

Since a majority of corporate bonds have a call option, the effect of the call option upon a bond's duration could have an effect on the bond manager's investment decision. Therefore, the bond's duration, both disregarding the call option and regarding the call option, must be considered in an investment decision. That is, if interest rates stabilize or continue to rise, the call-option duration is of less importance than the bond's duration disregarding the call option. If interest rates fall, the call-option duration is of more importance.

23.3. Convexity

The duration rule in Equation (23.5) is a good approximation for small changes in bond yield, but it is less accurate for large changes. Equation (23.5) implies that percentage change in bond price is linearly related to change in yield to maturity. If this linear relationship is not hold, then Equation (23.5) can be generalized as

$$\frac{\Delta P}{P} = -D * \Delta i + 0.5 \times Convexity \times (\Delta i)^2. \tag{23.6}$$

Where the *Convexity* is the rate of change of the slope of the price-yield curve as follows:

$$Convexity = \frac{1}{P} \times \frac{\partial^2 P}{\partial i^2} = \frac{1}{P \times (1+i)^2} \sum_{t=1}^{n} \left[\frac{CF_t}{(1+i)^t} (t^2 + t) \right]$$
$$\approx 10^8 \left[\frac{\Delta P-}{P} + \frac{\Delta P+}{P} \right]. \tag{23.7}$$

Where CF_t is the cash flow at time t as definition in Equation (23.2); n is the maturity; CF_t represents either a coupon payment before maturity or final coupon plus par value at the maturity date. $\Delta P-$ is the capital loss from a one-basis-point (0.0001) increase in interest rates and $\Delta P+$ is the capital gain from a one-basis-point (0.0001) decrease in interest rates[2].

In Equation (23.6), the first term of on the right-hand side is the same as the duration rule, Equation (23.5). The second term is the modification for convexity. Notice that for a bond with positive convexity, the second term is positive, regardless of whether the yield rises or falls.

The more accurate Equation (23.6), which accounts for convexity, always predicts a higher bond price than Equation (23.5). Of course, if the change in yield is small, the convexity term, which is multiplied by $(\Delta y)^2$ in Equation (23.6), will be extremely small and will add little to the approximation. In this case, the linear approximation given by the duration rule will be sufficiently accurate. Thus convexity is more important as a practical matter when potential inertest rate changes are large. Sample Problem 23.7 provides further illustration.

Sample Problem 23.7

Figure 23.4 is drawn by the assumptions that the bond with 20-year maturity and 7.5% coupon sells at an initial yield to maturity of 7.5%. Because the coupon rate equals yield to maturity, the bond sells at par

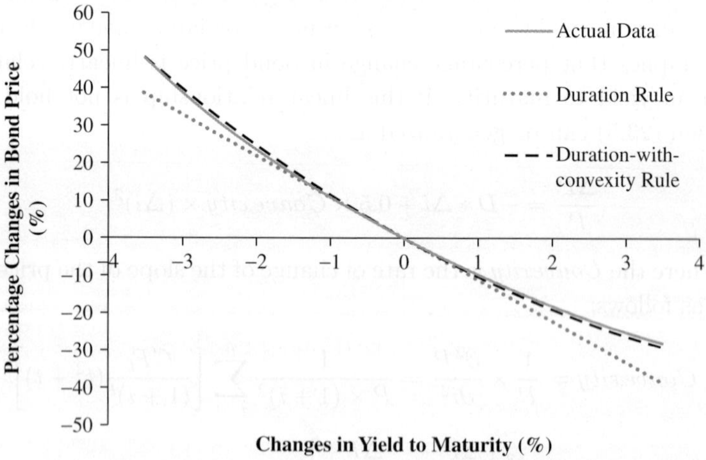

Fig. 23.4. The Relationship between Percentage Changes in Bond Price and Changes in YTM.

[2]The approximation of convexity is referred to *Financial Institutions Management: A Risk Management Approach* by Saunders and Cornett, 7th ed., 2010.

value, or \$1,000. The modified duration and convexity of the bond are 10.95908 and 155.059 calculated by Equation (23.1) and the approximation formula in Equation (23.7), respectively.

If the bond's yield increases from 7.5% to 8.0% ($\Delta i = 0.005$), the price of the bond actually falls to \$950.9093. Based on the duration rule, the bond price falls from \$1,000 to \$945.2046 with a decline of 5.47954% Equation (23.5) as follows

$$\frac{\Delta P}{P} = -D * \Delta i = -10.95908 * 0.005 = -0.0547954, \text{ or } -5.47954\%$$

If we use Equation (23.6) instead of Equation (23.5), we get the bond price falls from \$1,000 to \$947.1482 with a decline of 5.28572% by Equation (23.6):

$$\begin{aligned}\frac{\Delta P}{P} &= -D * \Delta i + 0.5 \times Convexity \times (\Delta i)^2 \\ &= -10.95908 \times 0.005 + 0.5 \times 155.059 \times (0.005)^2 \\ &= -0.0528572, \text{ or } -5.28572\%\end{aligned}$$

The duration rule used by Equation (23.5) is close to the case with accounting for convexity in terms of Equation (23.6).

However, if the change in yield are larger, 3% ($\Delta i = 0.03$), the price of the bond actually fall to \$753.0727 and convexity becomes an important matter of pricing the percentage change in bond price. Without accounting for convexity, the price of the bond on dash line actually falls from \$1,000 to \$671.2277 with a decline of 32.8772% based on the duration rule, Equation (23.5) as follows

$$\frac{\Delta P}{P} = -D * \Delta i = -10.95908 * 0.03 = -0.328772, \text{ or } -32.8772\%$$

According to the duration-with-convexity rule, Equation (23.6), the percentage change in bond price is calculated in following equation

$$\begin{aligned}\frac{\Delta P}{P} &= -D * \Delta i + 0.5 \times Convexity \times (\Delta i)^2 \\ &= -10.95908 \times 0.03 + 0.5 \times 155.059 \times (0.03)^2 \\ &= -0.258996, \text{ or } -25.8996\%\end{aligned}$$

The bond price \$741.0042 estimated by the duration-with-convexity rule is close to the actual bond price \$753.0727 rather than the price

\$671.2277 estimated by the duration rule. As the change in interest rate becomes larger, the percentage change in bond price calculated by Equation (23.5) is significantly different from it calculated by Equation (23.6). Saunders and Cornett (2011) have discussed why convexity is important in the risk management of financial institutions.

23.4. Contingent Immunization

Contingent immunization allows a bond-portfolio manager to pursue the highest yields available through active strategies while relying on the techniques of bond immunization to assure that the portfolio will achieve a given minimal return over the investment horizon. Using this strategy, the portfolio manager attempts to earn returns in excess of the immunized return, but at the same time attempts to constrain or control losses that may result from poor forecasts of interest-rate movements.

Risk control is the major objective of contingent immunization. At the inception of the strategy, the manager determines the degree of risk he or she is willing to accept. If a sequence of interest-rate movements causes the portfolio to approach the predetermined risk level, the manager alters the portfolio's duration to completely immunize it from any further risk. On the other hand, if the interest-rate movements provide additional returns, the portfolio manager does nothing.

The difference between the minimal, or floor, rate of return and the rate of return on the market is called the cushion spread. Equation (23.8) shows the relationship between the market rate of return R_m and the cushion C to be the floor rate of return, R_{FL}.

$$R_{FL} = R_m - C. \tag{23.8}$$

Interest-rate movement favorable to the bond-portfolio manager's position will enlarge the spread — that is, R_m goes up and the portfolio is long bonds, thereby increasing the realized return. Adverse interest-rate movements will reduce the cushion spread $R_m - C$ up to the point that $R_{FL} = R_m$. At this point, the portfolio manager will immunize the portfolio, which will ensure that the realized return will equal R_{FL}.

Figure 23.5 is a graphical presentation of contingent immunization. The realized change in the market rate of return is shown on the horizontal axis, and the potential rate of return for the portfolio is shown on the vertical axis. The potential return is a function of the market return, the floor return, and the cushion. If the interest-rate change is +2%, the portfolio

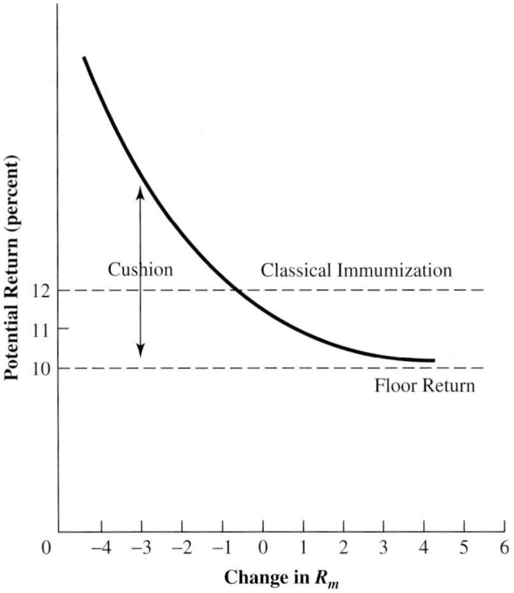

Fig. 23.5. Contingent Immunization.

manager shifts to an immunization strategy that locks in the R_{FL} at 10% for the planning horizon. Regardless of interest-rate movements thereafter, the portfolio will realize a return of 10%. If interest rates were to go down, the portfolio would earn a return in excess of the R_{FL} because of the manager's ability to have a portfolio with a duration larger than the investment horizon.

The contingent-immunization approach allows the portfolio manager the ability to follow the active investment strategies discussed earlier in this chapter. At the same time, the manager is able to protect a minimum return by using a duration-based immunization strategy. There is an old saying in the market: "Let your winners run and cut your losses." This is exactly the philosophy behind the contingent-immunization strategy.

23.5. Bond Portfolios: A Case Study

Ron Allen is the President of Merchant's Bank and Trust Co.[3] Mr. Allen has been the CEO of the $80-million community bank for less than a

[3]This case study is based on Altmix (1984). Raymond A. Altmix is currently vice-president, First of America Bank-Kankakee.

year. The bank has always been successful and, in years past, provided its stockholders with a slightly better return than its peers. However, the return on the bank's investment portfolio had suffered somewhat in the early 1980s because of its inability to cope with the dramatic rise and continued fluctuation of interest rates. Now Allen wants the bank to become more of an investment manager than simply a buyer and seller of bonds. It is Allen's belief that by using duration theory he can achieve a bond portfolio that is not as sensitive to changes in rates and yet will still produce a better-than-average return.

Duration is the weighted-average number of years until an initial cash investment is recovered, with the weight expressed as the relative present value of each payment of interest and principal. For example, suppose a bank bought a five-year, \$1,000 bond with a 10% coupon at par. If the going rate of interest remains at 10%, what would be the duration of the bond? The bond would produce a cash income in the amount of \$100.00 per year for five years before maturing. To calculate the weighted present value, it is necessary to find the present value of each payment and multiply it by the number of periods until the payment is received. In the first year, the bank will receive \$100.00 in coupon income. Discounted at 10%, the present value of the payment is \$90.01 (see Table 23.15). Column 3, the present-value interest factor (PVIF), is obtained by using the formula $1/(1+i)^n$, in which n is the number of compounding periods and i is the interest rate.

The present value of the second year's coupon income of \$100 will be \$82.64. The value is multiplied by two — that is, the number of years until receipt; the weighted present value of \$165.28 is obtained. The present value of the third-year cash flow is \$75.13; the weighted present value is \$225.39.

Table 23.15. Weighted Present Value.

(1) Year	(2) Coupons	(3) $\frac{1}{(1+i)^n}$	(4) (2)×(3) Unweighted PV	(5) (1)×(4) Weighted P
1	100.00	0.9091	90.91	90.91
2	100.00	0.8264	82.64	165.28
3	100.00	0.7513	75.13	225.39
4	100.00	0.6830	68.30	273.20
5	1,100.00	0.6211	683.01	3,415.05
	1,500.00		1,000.00	4,169.83

$4{,}169.83 \div 1{,}000.00 = 4.17$ years duration

For the fourth year, the present value is \$68.30 and the weighted present value is \$273.20. For the last year, it is necessary to calculate both the present value of the \$100 coupon and that of the maturing \$1,000 bond. This sum is equal to \$683.01, which when multiplied by five equals \$3,415.05. As presented in Table 23.6, the cumulative weighted present values total \$4,169.83. When this total is divided by the unweighted present value of the bond, \$1,000, we have the duration of the bond, 4.1698 years. Thus, the initial duration of a five-year, 10% bond selling at par is 4.17 years. (This example assumes that no costs are incurred in buying and selling of bonds and in reinvesting the funds received as bond coupon are paid.)

The basic problem that faces Mr. Allen, as with any bond portfolio manager, is obtaining a given rate of return to satisfy the yield requirements of a specific date — that is, the investment horizon. If the market rates never changed between the purchase and the maturity of a bond, it would be possible to acquire a bond that would guarantee return overall of a portfolio manager's investment horizon. However, the term structure of interest rates is dynamic and the market rates are constantly changing. Because of the changes in the term structure, bond-portfolio managers are faced with interest-rate risk. Interest-rate risk is the combination of two risks, price risk and coupon-reinvestment risk.

Price-risk occurs if interest rates change before the target date and the bond is sold prior to maturity. At that time the market price will differ from the value at the time of purchase. If rates increase after the purchase date, the price the bond would be sold at would be below what had been anticipated. If the rates decline, the realized price would be above what had been expected.

Increases in interest rates will reduce the market value of a bond below its par value. But it will increase the return from the reinvestment of the coupon interest payments. Conversely, decreases in interest will increase the market value of a bond above its par value but decrease the return on the reinvestment of the coupons. In order for a bond to be protected from the changes in interest rates after purchase, the price risk and coupon reinvestment must offset each other.

Of equal importance is **coupon-reinvestment risk**. It is the expected yield calculated by assuming that all coupon cash flows would be reinvested at the same yield that exists at the time of purchase. If rates begin to fall, it would be impossible to reinvest the coupon at a rate high enough to produce the anticipated yield. Obviously, if rates increase, the coupon cash flow will be reinvested at higher rates and produce a return above expectations.

Duration is the time period at which the price risk and coupon-reinvestment risk of a bond are of equal magnitude but opposite in direction. The result is that the expected yield is realized.

The duration strategy may protect the bank's bond portfolio from these unexpected changes in the yield. Merchant's Bank set its desired holding period at four years in order to protect the portfolio. This means that the duration of the bond portfolio should equal four years. In order to give the portfolio a four-year duration, the weighted-average duration is set at the desired length and the bank invests all future cash flows with duration equal to the remaining expected value.

An example of the effect of attempting to protect a portfolio by matching the investment horizon and the duration of a bond portfolio is contained in Table 23.16 using a single bond. Merchant's Bank has an investment horizon of four years. The current YTM for a four-year bond is 10.50%. Therefore, the ending wealth ratio should be 1.4909 ($1/(1.105)^4$). This assumes a completely protected portfolio. Two investment strategies are computed in Table 23.16. The first is the maturity strategy, where the TM is set at four years. The second is the duration strategy, where the duration is four years. In this case, the bank would acquire a five-year,

Table 23.16. Comparison of the Maturity Strategy and Duration Strategy for a Five-Year Bond.

Year	Cash Flow	RR(%)	Value
Maturity Strategy			
1	105.00	10.5	105.00
2	105.00	10.5	221.03
3	105.00	8.0	343.71
4	105.00	8.0	1,476.01
			2,145.75
Duration Strategy			
1	105.00	10.5	105.00
2	105.00	10.5	221.03
3	105.00	8.0	343.71
4	1,125.10*	8.0	1,496.31
			2,166.05

Expected wealth ratio is 1,491.00.

*The bond could be sold at its market value of $1,125.12, which is the value for a 10.5% bond with one year to maturity priced to yield 8%.

10.5% bond that has a duration of 4.13 years, assuming a 10.5% YTM. For this example, it is assumed that there is a single interest-rate change at the end of year two and the market yield goes from 10.5% to 8% through the fourth year.

As Table 23.16 shows, the wealth ratio for the maturity strategy fell short of the desired ending wealth ratio on this particular bond. This is due to the interest-rate change in year two, which results in a lower RR. In the maturity strategy, the price risk of the bond itself is eliminated because the bond matures in the fourth year. However, the duration strategy actually created a wealth ratio above what was expected. This is because the return that was lost in the reinvestment was offset by the increase in the value of the bond in its fourth year. In this case, a premium would be paid for a bond with a coupon $2\frac{1}{2}\%$ over the market rate by the purchaser in a secondary market.

The fact that a premium would be paid for this five-year bond at the end of four years is an important factor in the effectiveness of the duration concept. There is a direct relationship between the duration of a bond and the price volatility for the bond assuming given changes in the market rates of interest. This relationship can be expressed in the formula:

$$\text{BPC} = -D * (r),$$

where

$\text{BPC} =$ the percent of change in price for the bond;
$D* =$ the adjusted duration of the bond in years, equal to $D/(1+r)$; and
$r =$ the change in the market yield in basis points divided by 100 (e.g., a 50-basis-point decline would be -0.5).

Using the values from Tale 23.16, the percentage of change in the price of the five-year bond can be calculated. The duration is 4.13 years and interest-rate range from 8% to 10.5%.

$$D* = 3.738$$

$$\begin{aligned}\text{BPC} &= -3.738(100/100)\\ &= -3.738(1)\\ &= -3.738.\end{aligned}$$

In this example, the price of the bond should decline by about 3.7% for every 100-basis-point increase in market rates. The accuracy of the formulas may vary depending on the length of duration. However, the important point is in the relationship between duration and interest-rate risk. The longer the duration of a bond, the greater the price volatility of the bond for changes in interest rates.

Developing an interest-rate forecast is essential in any bond-portfolio manager's program. To aid them in the development of this forecast, Merchant's Bank has secured the services of two well-known investment firms. Both firms publish monthly forecasts that will be used along with forecasts provided by Mr. Allen's staff. Investment Firm A predicts that short-term interest rates, over 0–6 months, will average between $9\frac{1}{2}\%$ and 11%, and long-term rates will fluctuate between 11% and 12%. Firm B has a similar forecast for short-term rates, but Firm B predicts a downward-sloping yield curve with long-term interest rates in the 9%–10% range. Mr. Allen's problem here is that the firms' forecasts of long-term interest rates move in opposite directions. If interest rates increase, the bank's bond portfolio will not perform well unless it is protected using duration. However, if interest rates fall, the return provided by using duration will not be as great as the maturity strategy would provide. In this case, Mr. Allen may miss an opportunity to earn above-average returns.

Mr. Allen now must develop an interest-rate forecast for his Board of Directors. At the same time, he will attempt to show them that duration can be an effective management tool. Merchant's Bank and Trust Co. has $750,000 in bonds maturing from the existing portfolio. Table 23.17 is a list of bonds Mr. Allen is considering for purchase. His decisions, based on the future of interest rates, will be closely monitored by the Board of Directors. It is important that Mr. Allen consider the advantages and disadvantages of using duration as a bond-portfolio management tool.

23.6. Summary

The management of a fixed-income portfolio involves techniques and strategies that are unique to the specific area of bonds. This chapter has discussed riding the yield curve, swaps, and duration as three techniques that are familiar to all managers of fixed-income portfolios. A comparison of these techniques was presented in the previous section in the context of a case situation.

Overall, this chapter has related bond-valuation theory to bond-portfolio theory and has developed bond-portfolio management strategies.

Table 23.17. Bonds being Considered for Purchase by Merchant's Bank and Trust Co.

Amount*	Name	Rate (%)	Maturity
$150,000	Agency A	10.90	3
$200,000	Government 1	10.85	3
$100,000	Government 2	11.00	4
$100,000	Agency B	11.10	4
$150,000	Agency C	11.25	4
$100,000	Government 3	11.25	5
$200,000	Agency D	11.35	5
$250,000	Agency E	11.40	5
$100,000	Agency F	11.30	5
$200,000	Government 4	11.25	6
$150,000	Agency G	11.70	6
$200,000	Government 5	12.50	10

*All bonds are purchased at par and are assumed to have an annual coupon.

The next chapter discusses portfolio insurance, using not only valuation concepts and valuation theory for stocks and bonds, but also valuation concepts and theory for futures and options, discussed in Chapters 14–17.

Questions and Problems

1. Define the following terms.

   (a) riding the yield curve (b) swapping
   (c) workout period (d) duration
   (e) immunization (f) crossover yield.

2. What is the duration of bond A if it has the following characteristics?

   PV = $1,000 principal = $1,000
   coupon rate = 15% YTM = 15%
   $n = 3$ years

3. What kinds of risks does duration involve?
4. What is the value of a substitution swap for the following two bonds?

H-(Hold) Bond	*P*-(Purchaser) Bond
20-year 10% purchased at par	20-year 10% priced at $950
Workout time: 1 year	
RR: 10%	

5. What is the value of an intermarket swap for the following two bonds?

H-(Hold) Bond	*P*-(Purchaser) Bond
Price of bond: 5% @ beginning $680	Price of bond: 10% @ beginning $1,000
YTM: 10%	YTM: 11%
YTM at workout: 10%	YTM: 10%
Workout time: 1 year	
RR: 10%	
Price of bond in one year: $685	Price of bond in one year: $1,105

6. What impact does a longer workout period have on the value of swaps?
7. Explain an interest-rate-anticipation swap. What are the tradeoffs that the bond investor is relying on?
8. What is the relationship between maturity and duration for a zero-coupon bond? What is the relationship between maturity and duration for a coupon bond selling at par? What is the relationship between maturity and duration for a coupon bond selling at a discount? What is the relationship between maturity and duration for a coupon bond selling at a premium?
9. What is the relationship between WATM and duration?
10. Calculate the duration and WATM for the following bonds. What impact do changing market interest rates have on duration and WATM?

Bond A	Bond B	Bond C
Principal $1,000	Principal $1,000	Principal $1,000
Maturity 5 years	Maturity 5 years	Maturity 5 years
Coupon 5%	Coupon 5%	Coupon 5%
PV $957.60	PV $1,044.65	PV $1,000

11. If you expect interest rates to fall, how should you structure your bond portfolio with respect to duration and holding period?
12. For a given maturity, how does coupon rate affect the duration of a bond?
13. How is the duration of a callable bond related to the duration of a noncallable bond?
14. Explain the convexity of a bond. What is the relationship between convexity and bond price? What is the difference between the duration rule with and without convexity?

15. What is the crossover yield of a bond with a 10% coupon selling at \$1,100 with a call protection of 10 years?
16. What is the duration of a 20-year 10% bond selling at par that is callable in 5 years at \$1,050?
17. Assume a bond with 8-year maturity and 6% coupon sells at an initial yield to maturity of 6%, that is, the bond sells at par value, \$1,000. What is the duration and modified duration of the bond? What is the approximation value and exactly value of convexity?
18. For the given bond in Question 16, what are the bond prices estimated by the duration rule and duration-with-convexity rule when the yield to maturity increase from 6% to 8%? What is the actual bond price when the yield to maturity is 8%?
19. According to the assumption of bond in Question 16, what are the percentage changes in bond price based on the duration rule and duration-with-convexity rule when the yield to maturity decline from 6% to 5.5%?

Bibliography

Altmix, R. A. "Duration, Bond Portfolio Protection: Case study." Unpublished manuscript, 1984.

Bierwag, G. O. *Duration Analysis: Managing Interest Rate Risk.* Cambridge, MA: Ballinger Publishing Co., 1987.

Bierwag, G. O. "Immunization Strategies for Funding Multiple Liabilities." *Journal of Financial and Quantitative Analysis*, v. 18 (March 1983), pp. 113–123.

Bierwag, G. O., G. G. Kaufman and D. Khang. "Duration and Bond Portfolio Analysis: An Overview." *Journal of Financial and Quantitative Analysis*, v. 13 (November 1978), pp. 671–681.

Bierwag, G. O., G. G. Kaufman and A. Toevs. "Single-Factor Duration Models in a Discrete General Equilibrium Framework." *Journal of Finance*, v. 37 (May 1982), pp. 325–338.

Bodie, Z., A. Kane, and A. J. Marcus. *Investments.* McGraw-Hill, 9th ed., 2011.

Bookstaber, R. *The Complete Investment Book.* Glenview, IL: Scott, Foresman and Co., 1985.

Boquist, J. A., G. Racette and G. G. Schlarbaum. "Duration and Risk Assessment for Bonds and Common Stocks." *Journal of Finance*, v. 30 (December 1975), pp. 1360–1365.

Chua, J. "A Closed Form Formula for Calculating Bond Duration." *Financial analysts Journal*, v. 40 (May/June 1984), pp. 76–78.

Cox, J., J. E. Ingersoll and S. A. Ross. "Duration and Measurement of Basis Risk." *Journal of Business*, v. 52 (January 1979), pp. 51–61.

Fisher, L. and R. Weil. "Coping with the Risk of Interest Rate Fluctuations: Returns to Bondholders from Naïve and Optimal Strategies." *Journal of Business*, v. 44 (October 1971), pp. 408–431.

Fong, H. and F. Fabozzi. *Fixed Income Portfolio Management*. Homewood, IL: Dow Jones-Irwin, 1985.

Fabozzi F. *The Handbook of Fixed Income Securities*. McGraw-Hill, 7th ed., 2005.

Fabozzi F. *Bond Markets, Analysis, and Strategies*. Prentice Hall, 7th ed., 2009.

Hawawini, G (ed.). *Bond Duration and Immunization: Early Developments and Recent Contributions*. New York and London: Garland Publishing, 1982.

Hessel, C. and L. Huffman. "The Effect of Taxation on Immunization Rules and Duration Estimation." *Journal of Finance*, v. 36 (December 1981), pp. 1127–1142.

Homer, S. and M. L. Leibowitz. *Inside the Yield Book*. New York: Prentice-Hall, and New York Institute of Finance, 1972.

Hopewell, M. and G. G. Kaufman. "Bond Price Volatility and Terms to Maturity: A Generalized Respecification." *American Economic Review*, v. 63 (September 1973), pp. 749–753.

Ingersoll, J., J. Skelton and R. Weil. "Duration: Forty Years Later." *Journal of Financial and Quantitative Analysis*, v. 13 (November 1978), pp. 627–650.

John, L. M., L. M. Donald, E. P. Jerald, and W. M. Dennis. *Managing Investment Portfolios: A Dynamic Process*. CFA Institute, 3rd ed, 2007.

Lanstein, R. and W. Sharpe. "Duration and Security Risk." *Journal of Financial and Quantitative Analysis*, v. 13 (November 1978), pp. 653–668.

Leibowitz, M. L. "Contingent Immunization, Part I: Risk Control Procedures." *Financial Analysts Journal*, v. 38 (November/December 1982), pp. 17–32.

Leibowitz, M. L. "Contingent Immunization, Part II: Problem Cases." *Financial Analysts Journal*, v. 39 (January/February 1983), pp. 35–50.

Leibowitz, M. L. and A. Weinberger. "The Uses of Contingent Immunization." *Journal of Portfolio Management*, v. 8 (Fall 1981), pp. 51–55.

Malkiel, B. "Expectations, Bond Prices, and the Term Structure of Interest Rates." *Quarterly Journal of Economics*, v. 76 (May 1962), pp. 197–218.

Macaulay, F. *Some Theoretical Problems Suggested by the Movement of Interest Rates, Bond Yields, and Stock Prices in the U.S. Since 1865*. New York: National Bureau of Economic Research, 1938.

McEnally, R. "Duration as a Practical Tool in Bond Management." *Journal of Portfolio Management*, v. 3 (Summer 1977), pp. 53–57.

Reilly, F. K. and R. S. Sidhu. "Many Uses of Bond Duration." *Financial Analysts Journal*, v. 36 (July/August 1980), pp. 58–72.

Saunders, A., and M. M. Cornett. *Financial Markets and Institutions*. McGraw-Hill, 5th ed., 2011.

Saunders, A., and M. M. Cornett. *Financial Institutions Management.* McGraw-Hill, 7th ed., 2010.

Weil, R. "Macaulay's Duration: An Appreciation." *Journal of Business*, v. 46 (October 1973), pp. 589–592.

Yawitz, J. "The Relative Importance of Duration and Yield Volatility on Bond Price Volatility." *Journal of Money Credit and Banking*, v. 9 (February 1977), pp. 97–102.

Chapter 24

Portfolio Insurance and Synthetic Options

Previous chapters of this book have discussed concepts, valuation models, and theory to evaluate stocks, bonds, futures, options, and futures options. In addition, portfolio diversification concepts and the selection method have been developed for domestic equity portfolios, international equity portfolios, and bond portfolios. This chapter discusses how futures, options, and futures options can be used in portfolio insurance (dynamic hedging). In addition, the techniques of combining stocks and futures to derive synthetic options are explored.

Portfolio insurance is a strategy that may allow portfolio managers and investors to limit downside risk while maintaining upside potential. In this context, the word *insurance* is somewhat misleading: portfolio insurance is not a true form of insurance, where the insured pays a premium to someone who accepts the risk of some adverse event. Rather, portfolio insurance is an asset-allocation or hedging strategy that allows the investor to alter the amount of risk he or she is willing to accept by giving up some return. This chapter looks at the basic concept of portfolio insurance, the various alternative methods available to the portfolio manager to hedge the portfolio, the impact of portfolio insurance on the stock market, and the pricing of equity securities and market regulation, and finally, empirical studies of portfolio insurance.

24.1. Basic Concepts of Portfolio Insurance

Portfolio insurance refers to any strategy that protects the value of a portfolio of assets. It can be used for stock, bonds, or real assets. If the

Table 24.1. Mechanics of Portfolio Insurance: An Example.

Initial investment	\$100
Cost of portfolio insurance	−\$5
Amount of investment going toward securities	\$95
Amount invested = \$100	

Value of Portfolio at Year End (dollars)	Return on Uninsured Portfolio (percent)	Value of Insured Portfolio (dollars)	Net Return on Insured Portfolio (percent)
75	−25	95	−5
80	−20	95	−5
85	−15	95	−5
90	−10	95	−5
95	−5	95	−5
100	0	95	−5
105	5	100	0
110	10	105	5
115	15	110	11
120	20	115	15
125	25	120	20
130	30	125	25

value of the asset declines, the insurance or hedge will increase in value to help offset the decline in price of hedged assets. If the price of the asset increases, the increase of the insured portfolio will be less than the increase in the asset but will nevertheless still increase.

Table 24.1 illustrates how portfolio insurance works. In this example, the underlying asset is purchased for \$95 and \$5 is spent on portfolio insurance. The minimum amount that the insured investor can realize is \$95, but the uninsured portfolio can fall in value to a low of \$75 if the market falls. If the value of the asset increases, the value of the insured portfolio will increase, but at a smaller rate. Figure 24.1 illustrates the profit and loss of the insured and uninsured portfolio.

Rubinstein (1985) stated that the portfolio shown in Figure 24.1 has the three properties of an insured portfolio.

(1) The loss is limited to a prescribed level.
(2) The rate of return on the insured portfolio will be a predictable percentage of the rate of return on the uninsured portfolio.
(3) The investments of the portfolio are restricted to a market index and cash. The expected return on the market index is above the expected return from holding cash, and the insurance is fairly priced. This

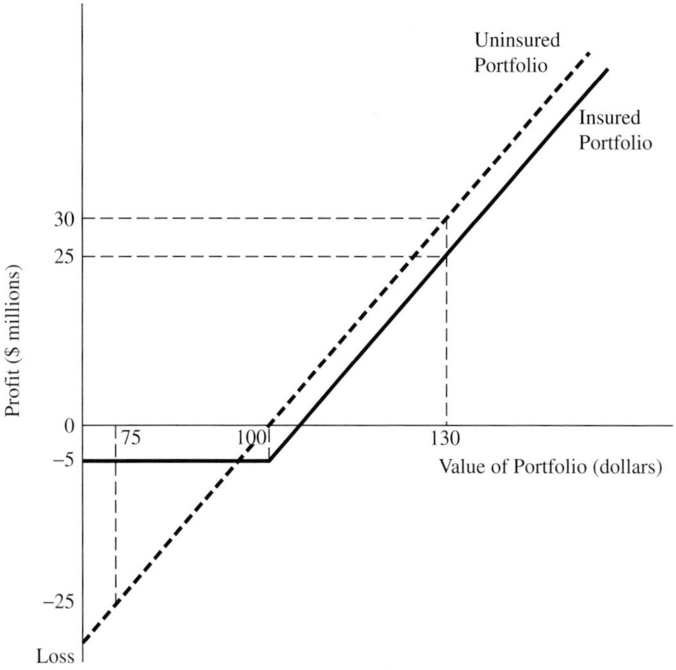

Fig. 24.1. Gains and Losses of Insured and Uninsured Portfolios: An Example.

guarantees that the insured portfolio has a higher expected return than the uninsured portfolio.

Portfolio insurance allows market participants to alter the return distribution to fit investors' needs and preferences for risk. Figure 24.2 shows the effect of insurance on the expected returns of a portfolio. Notice that the expected return of the uninsured portfolio is greater than the expected return of the uninsured portfolio, according to the third property listed above. It should be noted that in an efficient market at a fair price the insurance will be used until the expected return on insured and uninsured portfolios are the same.

The uninsured portfolio has greater upside potential as well as greater downside risk, whereas the insured portfolio limits the downside loss to the cost of the hedge. The upside potential of the insured portfolio is always below that of the uninsured portfolio. The cost of the insurance is the lower return for the insured portfolio should prices increase. While some investors would prefer the greater upside potential that the uninsured portfolio offers,

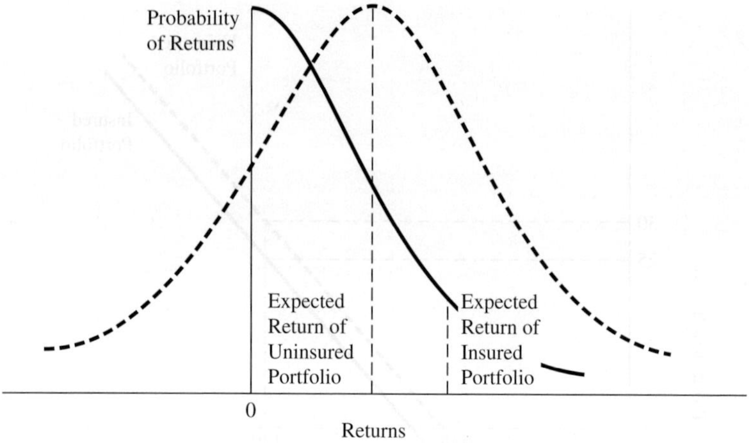

Fig. 24.2. Expected Returns on Insured and Uninsured Portfolios.

risk-averse investors would prefer the limited-risk characteristics that the hedged portfolio offers.

In general, portfolio insurance can be thought of as holding two portfolios. The first portfolio can be viewed as the safe or riskless portfolio with value equal to the level of protection desired. This level is called the **floor** and is the lowest value the portfolio can have. For certain strategies this can be held constant or allowed to change over time as market conditions or needs change. The second portfolio consists of the difference between the total value of the portfolio and the floor, commonly called the **portfolio cushion**. These assets consist of a leveraged position in risky assets. To insure the portfolio, the cushion should be managed so as to never fall below zero in value because of the limited-liability property of common stock. Figure 24.3 shows the relationship between the total value of the portfolio, the cushion, and the floor. The actual investment or allocation of the portfolio funds between risky and risk-free assets is determined by changing market conditions or the changing requirements of the portfolio manager.

A simple example of changing the mix between risky and risk-free assets in response to market changes offers the opportunity to demonstrate the dynamic nature of portfolio insurance. As shown in Figure 24.3, half the current portfolio is invested in risky assets and half in risk-free assets. The exposure at this point is \$500. The cushion is \$200. If this is a reasonable relationship that the portfolio manager wishes to maintain, the

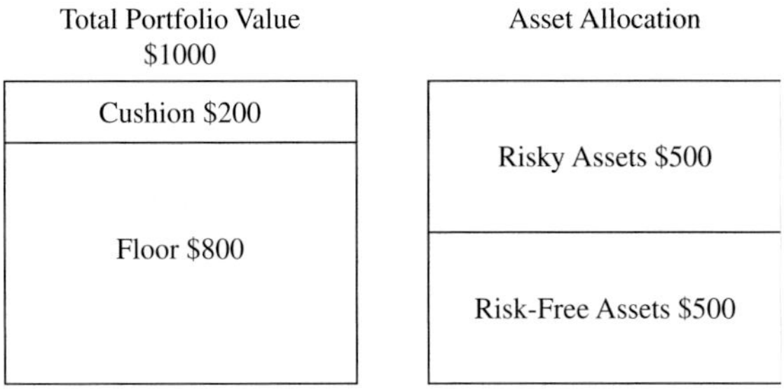

Fig. 24.3. Components of an Insured Portfolio Valued at $1,000.

relationship between these two, defined as the **multiple**, can be calculated:

$$\text{Multiple} = \frac{\text{Exposure}}{\text{Cushion}}, \tag{24.1}$$

$$m = \frac{e}{c}$$

$$= \frac{500}{200} = 2.5. \tag{24.2}$$

As the market for the risky assets changes, the exposure and the cushion value change, causing a change in the multiple. Given a predetermined trigger or change in multiple, the portfolio manager can trade to restore the balance between the cushion and the exposure. If, for example, the market value of the risky asset rises 20%, the value of the cushion increases to $300 and the value of the risky assets rises to $600. The total value of the portfolio is the value of the risky assets plus the value of the risk-free assets ($500 + $600, or $1,100). The value of the floor remains at $800 so that the cushion goes to $\$300(\$1,100 - \$800)$. The multiple has fallen to

$$m = \frac{e}{c} = \frac{600}{300} = 2. \tag{24.3}$$

If the target multiple is 2.5, an adjustment must be made by the portfolio manager, who must sell some of the risk-free assets and purchase risky assets until the multiple is 2.5. Hence, the manager needs to rebalance the portfolio so that $750 is invested in risky assets and $350 is invested in risk-free assets. This mix will restore the multiple to the desired level of 2.5:

$$m = \frac{e}{c} = \frac{750}{300} = 2.5. \tag{24.4}$$

Figure 24.4 shows the portfolio after rebalancing.

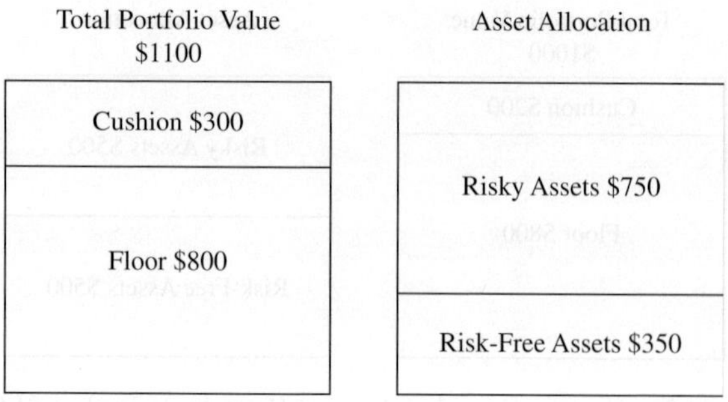

Fig. 24.4. Components of an Insured Portfolio Rebalanced after a Market Rise.

Increasing the portfolio's risky assets as the market rises allows the manager to participate in the bull market. As long as the market continues its rise, the manager continues to shift assets to the risky-asset portfolio to participate in the market gain. However, when the market turns bearish and begins to go down, the manager needs to sell off risky assets and invest in risk-free assets. For example, if the market declined by $16\frac{2}{3}\%$ back to its original level at the beginning of this example, the value of the risky assets would be \$625 (\$750 × 0.8333). At this new level, the multiple would be

$$m = \frac{e}{c} = \frac{625}{175} = 3.56. \tag{24.5}$$

The target multiple of 2.5 is below the actual multiple of 3.56, so the portfolio manager must sell some of the risky assets and place the proceeds into risk-free assets. The total value of the portfolio has fallen to \$975 (\$625 + \$350). The value of the cushion has fallen to \$175 (\$975 – \$800). In order to have a multiple of 2.5 the risky assets have to be reduced to

$$\begin{aligned} m &= \frac{e}{175} = 2.5 \\ e &= \$437.50. \end{aligned} \tag{24.6}$$

Hence \$187.50 of the risky assets must be sold and this amount must be invested in the risk-free assets. The position of the insured portfolio after this rebalancing is shown in Figure 24.5.

As the market falls, the portfolio manager sells off risky assets and invests the proceeds in risk-free assets, thereby reducing exposure to a falling market. In general, this strategy can best be described as "run

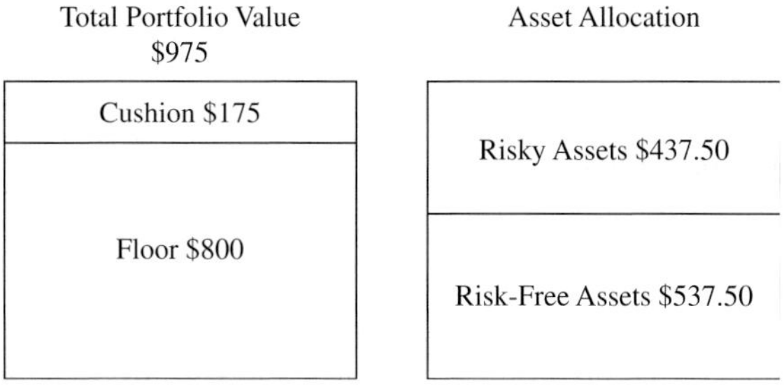

Fig. 24.5. Components of an Insured Portfolio Rebalanced after a Market Fall.

with your winners and cut your losses." *Underlying this discussion are the assumptions that the rise and fall of the market takes place over a time interval long enough for the portfolio manager* to *rebalance the position, and that the market has sufficient liquidity to absorb the value of the risky assets.* This may not always be the case, however. October 19, 1987, commonly called Black Monday, and October 26, 1987, commonly called Blue Monday, as well as October 13, 1989, are examples of a rapid fall in prices in a very illiquid market for risky assets.

This general discussion of portfolio insurance is based on an article by Perold (1986). The simplicity of this approach makes it an ideal way to explain the general way of accomplishing portfolio insurance or portfolio hedging. Perold has called this **constant-proportion portfolio** insurance **(CPPI)**. As has been seen, it involves holding the risk-free asset in an amount equal to the level of protection desired (floor), plus holding the remainder of the portfolio in a risky asset. The multiple of the risky asset to the cushion is then held in a constant proportion.

As will be seen, there are a number of ways of insuring or hedging a portfolio to keep the multiple constant. These are discussed in the next section.

24.2. Strategies and Implementation of Portfolio Insurance

Portfolio insurance allows the investor to participate in the appreciation of value of a risky portfolio while limiting the potential losses of the portfolio. This is very similar to the features available from an investment in options. There are four basic strategies to implementing a portfolio-insurance program: (1) the use of stop-loss orders, (2) the purchase of exchange-traded put options, (3) the creation of synthetic put options, and

(4) dynamic hedging using futures contracts. All of these strategies are detailed below.

24.2.1. *Stop-Loss Orders*

A **stop-loss order** is a conditional market order to sell portfolio stock if the value of the stock drops to a given level. For example, if you held an index portfolio when the market index is at \$100 and you expected the market to rise, you could limit your downside risk by placing a stop-loss order at \$95. If the market fell to \$95, your stop-loss order would become a market sell order, and the portfolio would be sold at the prevailing market price. The use of a stop-loss order does not guarantee that you would get exactly \$95; you could get more or less. Still, you would begin to liquidate your position at a predetermined level. As you can see, the placement of stop-loss orders is a kind of crude portfolio insurance in that it allows you to make money if the market goes up and cuts your losses (approximately) to a predetermined level should the market fall.

As pointed out by Rubinstein (1985), the major problem of using stop-loss orders to approximate portfolio insurance is the path dependence of this technique — that is, if the market falls, the stop-loss order is executed, and the portfolio is sold, the portfolio manager needs to make a decision about when to get back into the market. The worst thing that could happen would be for the market to rebound immediately after the execution of the stop-loss order and sale of the portfolio. In such a case, the portfolio would consist of 100% cash. Because of this cash position, the portfolio would not benefit from the increase in stock price as the market rises. On the other hand, if the market were to continue to fall after the execution of the stop-loss order, the portfolio manager with 100% cash would be in a position enhanced by the portfolio insurance — that is, 100% cash in a falling market. Hence, the success of the portfolio-insurance strategy is dependent on the subsequent market movement. Ideally, portfolio insurance should work regardless of the subsequent movement of the market; thus it should be **path independent**. Clearly, in the case of stop-loss orders it is path dependent, and this strategy is not a very useful form of portfolio insurance.

24.2.2. *Portfolio Insurance with Listed Put Options*

Put options can be purchased on a stock index on various exchanges and used for creating an insured portfolio. Table 24.2 lists the indexes and

Table 24.2. Listed Options on Market Indexes.

Chicago Mercantile Exchange	*Chicago Board Options Exchange*	*American Stock Exchange*
S & P 500 Index	S & P 100 Index S & P 500 Index	Major Market Index Computer Technology Index Oil Index Institutional Index
Philadelphia Stock Exchange	*New York Stock Exchange*	*Pacific Exchange*
Utilities Index	NYSE Composite Index	Financial News Composite Index
Value Line Index National OTC Index	NYSE Beta Index	

exchanges on which options are available. If the market falls, the drop in the value of the portfolio will be offset by the gain in value of the put option. On the other hand, if the market increases in value, the portfolio will increase in value but the premium paid for the put option will be lost. For example, a portfolio manager with a \$100-million portfolio purchases 4,000 Major Market Index (MMI) options with an exercise price of \$250 with the cost of each option at \$500. If the market value of the portfolio declines by \$10 million by the expiration date of the option and the MMI index drops to \$225, the portfolio manager can exercise the puts to offset the losses on the stock portfolio. The portfolio manager delivers the 4,000 put options and receives \$10 million. Since the puts cost \$2 million, the net gain on the puts is \$8 million. The \$8 million gain on the puts offsets some of the \$10 million loss on the portfolio, for a net loss of \$2 million. If the portfolio increases in value by \$20 million and the MMI index closes above \$250, the net gain on the portfolio will be \$20 million from the increase in equity value minus the \$2 million premium paid for the options — a net gain of \$18 million. The portfolio returns for this example are depicted in Figure 24.6.

A perfect hedge is usually not possible because the correlation between the market index and the portfolio may not be perfect. This is called the **tracking problem**. The greater the correlation between the portfolio and the index, the more effective the hedge. The lower the correlation, the less effective the hedge as a portfolio insurance strategy.

In the example it was assumed that the beta coefficient between the portfolio and the MMI was equal to one. If the beta in reality were not equal to one, more or less put contracts would be needed to insure the portfolio.

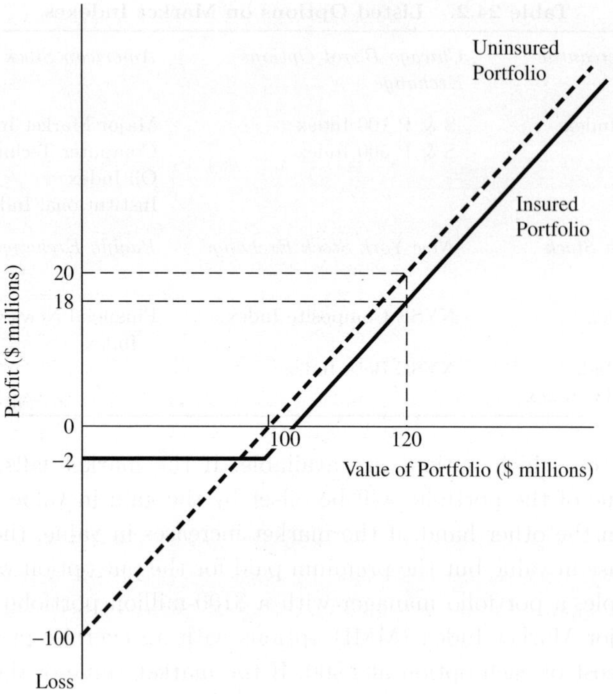

Fig. 24.6. Gains and Losses of Insured and Uninsured Portfolios.

For a beta less than one fewer puts would be needed, and for a beta greater than one more puts would be needed. For example, if the portfolio had a beta of 1.20, 20% more put options would be needed to hedge the portfolio.

The price change of the market index and the value of the portfolio, as well as the movement of the price of the option on the index, are all related. The success of a portfolio-insurance strategy depends on correct determination of the hedge ratio. The hedge ratio is the ratio of the value of the portfolio to the value of the options contracts used to hedge the portfolio:

$$\text{Hedge ratio} = \frac{\text{Number of contracts} \times \text{Face value of contracts}}{\text{Face value of portfolio}}.$$

In discussing the use of put options for portfolio insurance, two characteristics were assumed about the nature of the options used.

(1) They are available with long maturities or with maturities that match the portfolio manager's investment horizon.

(2) They are exercisable only at maturity — that is, they are European-type options.

Unfortunately, all the index options listed in Table 24.2 are American options. American options can be exercised at any time before expiration, hence have higher values to certain investors. This is so because American options have all the advantages of European options plus the privilege of early exercise. The portfolio manager who uses American options for portfolio insurance finds that he or she is paying for the early exercise privilege when in fact he or she does not really need it. Second, listed options are not protected against normal cash-dividend payments. When a firm's stock goes ex-dividend, the price of the stock is expected to fall by the amount of the dividend payment. This expected fall in the price of the stock is not offset by any changes in the option contract; hence the market price of the option will be affected by the exdividend behavior of the stock's price. As a result, options can be used to insure the capital-appreciation component of the stock return but not the dividend component. Third, all listed options have a maximum maturity of nine months, with most of the trading taking place in the near contracts with maturities of three months or less. Given these problems, the usefulness of index put options for portfolio insurance is somewhat questionable.

24.2.3. *Portfolio Insurance with Synthetic Options*

Rubinstein and Leland (1981) suggest a strategy that replicates the returns on a call option by continuously adjusting a portfolio consisting of stock and a risk-free asset (T-bill, cash). This is called a synthetic call-option strategy; it involves increasing the investment in stock by borrowing when the value of stocks is increasing, and selling stock and paying off borrowing or investing in the risk-free asset when market values are falling. The key variable in this strategy is the delta value, which measures the change in the price of a call option with respect to the change in the value of the portfolio of risky stocks (see also Chapter 20). For deep-in-the-money options, the delta value will be close to one because a \$1 change in the stock value will result in approximately a \$1 change in the option value. Thus to replicate the option with cash and stock, almost one share must be purchased and the amount borrowed will be approximately equal to the exercise price. For deep out-of-the-money options, the value of the delta will be close to zero, and the replicating portfolio will contain very few shares and little or no borrowing. Hence in its simplest form, the delta value largely depends on the relationship between the exercise price and the stock price. As the market moves to new levels, the value of the delta will change; hence the synthetic option portfolio must be rebalanced periodically to maintain the proper mix between equity and borrowing or cash.

In a similar manner, a portfolio manager can create replicated put options through a combination of selling short the asset and lending. The amount of stock sold short is equal to the delta value minus one. As the market decreases in value, more of the equity is sold (the short position increases), with the proceeds invested at the risk-free rate. If the market increases in value, money is borrowed to buy the stock and reduce the short position.

The logic behind a call-replicating strategy is shown in Figure 24.7, when the exercise price of the option and current share price are $100. The

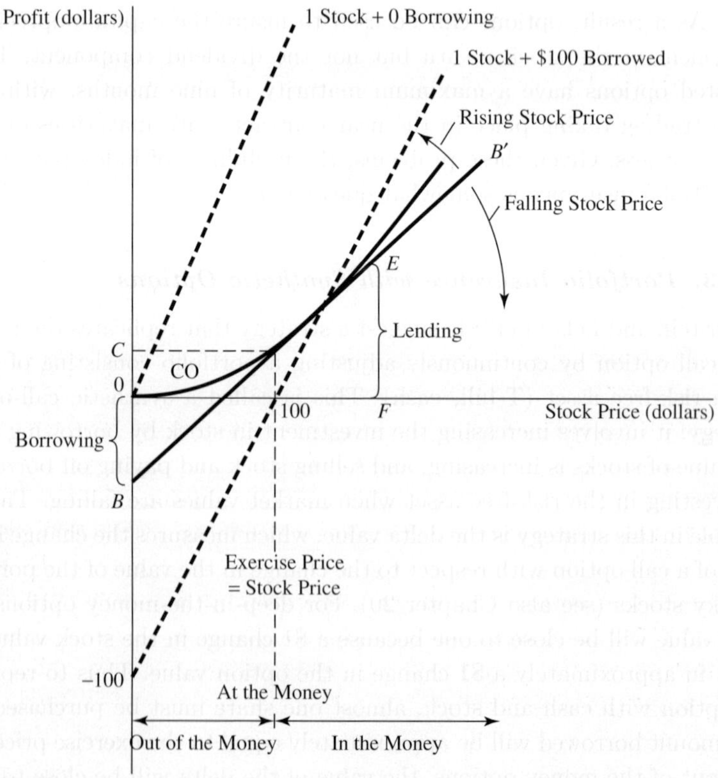

Fig. 24.7. Synthetic Call Option.

straight line starting from the origin and labeled "1 Stock + 0 Borrowing" is the value of an unleveraged long position in the stock. When the stock is worth zero, the option is worth zero; and for every \$1 increase in the value of the stock, the value of the position increases by \$1. The straight line that starts from −100 on the profit axis (labeled "1 Stock + \$100 Borrowed") is the leveraged position in which one share of stock is owned and the exercise price of the call (\$100) is borrowed. The curved line labeled CO is the value of the call option and is an increasing function of the stock price. When the option is deep out of the money, changes in the stock price do not have much effect on the value of the call option (delta is small); hence the line is almost horizontal. However, as the stock price increases, the rate of change in the call price (the slope of CO) increases until it approaches one for an in-the-money call. The slope of CO is the number of shares to be held in the replicating portfolio. At low stock prices, few shares are held; at higher share price more shares are held.

The amount of borrowing needed to replicate the portfolio is represented by the dotted line BB'. The intercept of BB' and the stock-price axis represents the amount of borrowing and the line segment EF represents the amount of paying off borrowing or holding a risk-free asset. As the stock price rises, the dashed line BB' pivots counterclockwise, taking on increasing slope and an intercept farther from zero along the vertical axis. As the stock price falls, the BB' line pivots clockwise, with decreasing slope and an intercept closer to zero. The value C of the call option is shown on the profit axis. Thus at any stock price, the value of the portfolio invested in stock is the value of the call C plus the amount of borrowing B minus the amount borrowed B or C. The line CO shows how the value of the insured portfolio reacts to changes in the stock price. As the stock price increases (decreases), the slope of the curved line becomes steeper (flatter) and the amount of borrowing increases (decreases).

If the call is in the money at the expiration date, the investor will own one share in the replicating portfolio and owe an amount equal to the exercise price. If the call finishes out of the money, no stock will be owned and the borrowing will be fully repaid. This is equivalent to the position of the call buyer at expiration. Hence a purchased call position can be replicated by a strategy of buying shares plus borrowing, where shares are bought (sold) and the borrowing is increased (decreased) as the stock price rises (falls). The accuracy of the replicating strategy depends on four considerations. First, since the strategy may involve frequent trading, it is necessary that transaction costs be low. Second, it must be possible

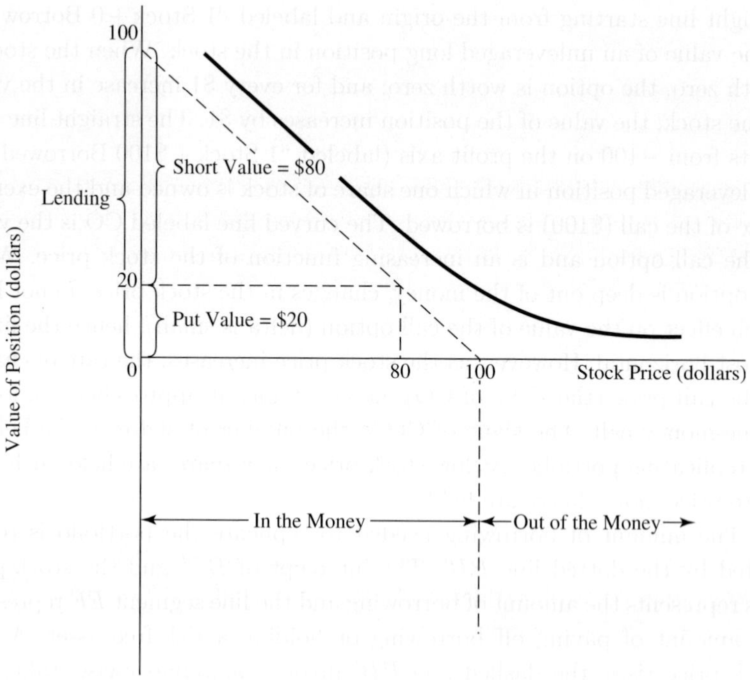

Fig. 24.8. Synthetic Put Option.

to borrow whatever amount is required. Third, trading in the stock may not provide continuous prices; there may be jumps or gaps. In this case, the strategy will not be able to exactly replicate the price movement of a traded call. Fourth, there may be uncertainty surrounding future interest rates, stock volatility, or dividends. This may affect the price of a traded call with an accompanying change in stock price. Hence, the value of the replicated option would not change, while the traded option price would change.

Figure 24.8 shows a synthetic put position in which the stock and exercise prices are \$100. As the stock value increases (decreases), the slope of a line tangent to the put-value curve becomes flatter (steeper) and the number of shares sold short in the synthetic put decreases (increases). The intersection of the value axis gives the lending amount. The lending position increases as the stock declines in value because more proceeds are available from the short sale of the stock. If the put is in the money at expiration, the investor will be short one share of the stock (e.g., \$80) and will simultaneously lend the amount equal to the exercise price, \$100. The total value of this position will equal the value of the listed put, \$20.

24.2.4. *Portfolio Insurance with Dynamic Hedging*

As a practical matter, rather than buying, selling, or short selling stocks, a portfolio manager may trade (buy or sell) stock-index futures to adjust the exposure of a portfolio. If the stock market is declining, futures contracts are sold to effectively reduce the position in the portfolio. The selling of stock-index futures has the same effect on the portfolio as the sale of stocks and the investment in a risk-free asset. As the market turns around and begins to go up in value, the portfolio manager purchases futures contracts to cover the short position by liquidating the investment in the risk-free asset. This procedure is called **dynamic hedging**. Whether it works depends upon a high degree of correlation between the value of index-futures contracts and the value of the underlying index. For most time periods there is a very high degree of comovement between the index and the futures contract. However, this may not always be the case.

Suppose that a portfolio manager wishes to insure a portfolio of well-diversified stocks with a value of \$1 million, and the portfolio beta is 1.1 when measured relative to the S&P 500. (This means that if the S&P 500 goes up or down by 1%, the change in the value of the portfolio will be 1.1%.) If the portfolio manager is worried about a market decline, he or she can insure his or her portfolio by selling S&P 500 index futures contracts. By selling futures contracts, the fall in value of the portfolio would be offset by gains in the futures market. If the strategy for portfolio insurance incorporates the beta, the following relationship is necessary to determine the number of contracts required to insure the portfolio:

$$\text{Number of contracts} = \frac{\text{Value of portfolio}}{\text{Value of futures contracts}} \times \beta. \tag{24.7}$$

Assume the S&P 500 index is selling at \$110, and the portfolio is worth \$1 million on day 1. If the market falls by 10%, the value of the portfolio falls 11% to \$890,000, the value of the S&P 500 futures contract falls to \$99, and the scenario is as follows.

(1) The portfolio has lost \$110,000.
(2) Each S&P 500 futures contract sold can be repurchased for $\$99 \times 500$ or \$49,500, for a gain of \$5500 ($\$55,000 - \$49,500$).

In order to have a perfect hedge, the portfolio manager would need $\$110,000/5500 = 20$ contracts. Using Equation (24.7), we see that adjusting the number of contracts for the volatility or beta of the portfolio yields:

$$\text{Number of contracts} = \frac{\$1,000,000}{\$110 \times 500} \times 1.1 = 20 \text{ contracts.}$$

This result of a perfect hedge is dependent upon two critical assumptions.

(1) The relationship of the volatility of the portfolio to the volatility of the index remains the same or the beta does not change; and
(2) The movement of the price of the futures contract is in lock step with the movement of the index; they are perfectly correlated.

In spite of the problems for portfolio insurance associated with the validity of these critical assumptions, the use of futures contracts for portfolio hedging is widespread. The main reason why futures have been accepted as a trading vehicle for portfolio insurance is the low trading costs. This and the reasons below have led to rapid growth in the use of futures contracts for insuring portfolios during the early part of the 1980s.

(1) Low trading costs allow for rapid and frequent adjustments in implementing the portfolio strategy.
(2) Futures markets are liquid enough for insurance programs for large institutional portfolios.
(3) The use of futures allows for independence between management of the risky assets in the portfolio and the portfolio insurance.

24.3. Comparison of Alternative Portfolio-Insurance Strategies

This section compares alternative portfolio-insurance strategies — that is, synthetic options, listed put options, and dynamic hedging.

24.3.1. *Synthetic Options*

As previously discussed, **synthetic options** are not options but a strategy for allocating assets that replicates the return on a call option. There are four advantages to using a dynamic-hedging strategy instead of synthetic-option approach. First, the futures contracts have lower transaction costs than stocks. Kidder, Peabody reports that index funds pay one-way transaction costs of \$125 for \$100,000 of stock, or 0.125% (they assume a commission of \$0.05 per share at an average price of \$40), and institutional clients pay approximately \$0.06 per share.[1] In contrast, one-way futures transaction costs for institutional investors are \$15 per \$100,000, or 0.015%. Thus the transaction costs for futures are one-eighth to one-tenth of the cost of trading stocks, thereby reducing the cost of dynamic hedging compared with synthetic options. Second, liquidity is much greater in the futures market than in options or stock markets. For example, during the large downside movement in the stock market on September 11–12, 1986, the consulting from of Leland O'Brien Rubinstein Associates sold more than \$500 million of stock-index futures.[2] Such large transactions could not be made in options markets.

The third advantage is that futures contracts are highly levered and less cash is necessary to carry out a dynamic-hedging strategy. As little as \$2,000 can control each futures contract. The fourth advantage is that because stocks are not sold, the management of the stock portfolio is independent of the portfolio insurance. In contrast, managers must be active when implementing a synthetic option because the underlying stock is bought or sold to replicate the returns on an option.

The main disadvantage of dynamic hedging with respect to synthetic options is the tracking error that might occur because the futures are not perfectly correlated with the stock. This is not a problem with synthetic options because the stock itself is purchased or sold.

Another disadvantage of implementing either a dynamic-hedging or synthetic-option strategy is that they require continuous monitoring to insure that the delta of the replicated put equals the delta of a theoretical option. The replicated put must be rebalanced at certain intervals to maintain a proper mix of stock and futures. Here a tradeoff results: the more frequent the rebalancing, the better the replication of the theoretical put; however, more frequent rebalancing also results in higher transaction costs. Thus determining when to rebalance the portfolio is a major decision when implementing a synthetic-option or dynamic-hedging strategy in the presence of transaction costs.

---

[1] Hill, J. M. *Portfolio Insurance: Volatility Risk and Futures Mispricing.* New York: Kidder Peabody Financial Futures Department, 1987.

[2] Anders, G. "Investors Rush for Portfolio Insurance." *The Wall Street Journal* (October 14, 1986), p. 6.

Table 24.3. Profit or Loss of Expensive Futures.

Value of Stock at Expiration of Futures	Value of Futures at Expiration	Profit or Loss on Stock	Profit or Loss on Futures	Profit or Loss
270	270	+20	−10	+10
230	230	−20	+30	+10

Table 24.4. Profit or Loss of Cheap Futures.

Value of Stock at Expiration of Futures	Value of Futures at Expiration	Profit or Loss on Stock	Profit or Loss on Futures	Profit or Loss
270	270	+20	−25	−5
230	230	−20	+15	−5

There might be a price advantage or disadvantage to a dynamic-hedging strategy due to futures mispricing. When shorting futures for hedging purposes, the manager hopes that the futures sell at a premium and the basis (the cash price minus the futures price) widens. By selling futures when they are expensive and buying them back at a lower price, a profit results on the hedge. On the other hand, losses on the hedge will probably result if "cheap" futures are sold for hedging purposes. The following example illustrates these concepts. Suppose that a manager holds a portfolio worth \$250 and shorts futures on the same portfolio that are worth \$260. The basis is \$250 − \$260 = −\$10. Because the basis is equal to zero at expiration, the negative basis will have to increase.

In this example the investor makes a profit of \$10 on the hedge, regardless of how the portfolio performs. The profit is a result of selling "expensive" futures and waiting for the basis to increase. In contrast, suppose that an investor with a portfolio worth \$250 shorts futures worth \$245. In this example, the investor will lose money if he waits until expiration, because the basis will decrease.

Here, the basis decreases and losses result for the hedger. Cheap futures will increase the costs of implementing a dynamic-hedging strategy and expensive futures will reduce the costs. The dynamic hedger hopes to sell futures selling at a premium and buy the futures at a discount.

The synthetic-call approach is usually used when implementing a portfolio-insurance strategy without futures. Thus, more of the risky asset is purchased when performance is favorable and the stock is sold when the asset declines. When implementing a dynamic-hedging strategy, the underlying stocks are not bought or sold, but rather stock-index futures are shorted to create a put option on the portfolio. In both cases, insurance is created for the portfolio, but the methods are different. In the synthetic-option case, the underlying portfolio behaves like a call option. For the dynamic-hedging case, the portfolio is not altered, only the futures position is changed to create a put option. A further discussion of the synthetic-call approach can be found in Becker (1988).

24.3.2. *Listed Put Options*

Portfolio insurance with **listed put options** does not require continuous monitoring because the delta of the listed option is automatically changed when the price of the underlying asset changes. Because of the automatic adjustment of the delta value, a listed-put strategy requires less monitoring and lower trading frequency than a synthetic-option or dynamic-hedging strategy.

There are a number of problems with using stock-index puts for portfolio insurance. First, because index options have at most a nine-month life, an investor may have to buy these short-term options even though the planning horizon might be much longer. These cumulative purchases of puts would result in a much greater cost than a longer-term option. This is due to the fact that for the long-term one-year put to be in the money, the market price must be below the exercise price after one year. In contrast, the value of the short-term options will have a positive value if the market price finished below the exercise price after nine months.

Second, the purchaser of portfolio insurance is not interested in exercising the option early, because this would leave the portfolio uninsured. The purchaser of insurance would prefer European options over American options because European options are cheaper. (However, the most popular index option, the OEX S&P 100, is American.) This early-exercise feature is of no value to the purchaser of portfolio insurance and adds to the cost of the insurance.

The third problem is that large-portfolio managers cannot purchase put options for insurance purposes because options markets do not provide the liquidity necessary to purchase large amounts of put options. Low liquidity might be even more of a problem for deep in- or out-of-the-money options or options that expire in the six- to nine-month range of maturities.

Like futures, there might be a lacking problem between the underlying stock or stocks and the instrument underlying the portfolio.

A replicated-option approach requires more management than a listed put-option strategy. The dynamic-hedging approach uses the highly liquid futures market to rebalance the portfolio. On the other hand, portfolio managers of large portfolios cannot purchase listed puts for portfolio insurance because of lack of liquidity in the options market. Futures mispricing will increase or decrease the cost of dynamic hedging; if the short hedger shorts expensive futures, profits will result from the hedges. If expensive futures are shorted, losses will be incurred.

24.3.3. *Dynamic Hedging and Listed Put Options*

The first difference between dynamic hedging and listed put options for portfolio insurance is that the delta value of a put option changes automatically while it must be adjusted continuously in a dynamic-hedging framework. Thus, dynamic hedging requires continuous monitoring and more frequent trading than listed puts.

Second, insurance costs (the premium paid for the option) for a listed-put strategy are known and paid up front. After the put is purchased, no more adjustments or monitoring are necessary. In contrast, insurance costs are unknown at the beginning of the period and are realized as the dynamic-hedging strategy is implemented. The cost of a dynamic-hedging strategy is the forgone profits that result from shorting futures. For example, suppose that a portfolio consists of $10,000 of stock and that $50,000 of futures contracts are shorted to replicate a put option (assume that this is one futures contract).

In the second period, the value of the portfolio increased to $120,000, whereas the value of the futures contract appreciated to $60,000. If no futures were held, profit on the portfolio would be $20,000; however, the dynamic hedger lost $10,000 on the futures. Thus the cost of the

Table 24.5. Dynamic Hedging.

	Portfolio Value	Futures Value	Profit on Portfolio	Loss on Futures	Profit on Insured Portfolio
Period 1	100,000	50,000			
Period 2	120,000	60,000	20,000	−10,000	10,000

dynamic-hedging strategy is the gain on the insured portfolio minus the gain on the uninsured portfolio ($\$10,000 - \$20,000 = -\$10,000$).

Another difference is that listed-option strategy is confined to fixed-interval exercise prices. In contrast, a dynamic-hedging strategy can be implemented around any exercise price.

Changing volatility can affect the cost of a portfolio-insurance strategy. For options, the cost of put protection is higher if the volatility declines. This is because the purchaser of the put locks in the volatility at the time of purchase. Thus, if the volatility declines, the put value declines. In contrast, an increase in volatility lowers the cost of put protection because the price of the put increases.

With a dynamic-hedging strategy, costs are lowered if volatility declines because the delta value will be reduced and not as many futures will be sold.

A replicated-option approach can be used for any asset-portfolios of stocks, various types of bonds, agricultural commodities, currencies, or metals. Since options markets are limited, replicated options must be created to simulate the returns of these investments.

24.4. Impact of Portfolio Insurance on the Stock Market and Pricing of Equities

Portfolio insurance is not formal insurance in the sense of a guarantee against loss. Rather, it is a method of hedging a portfolio either by selling a certain portion of the risky assets themselves, or futures contracts on stock indexes, when the market falls. Both techniques ultimately have the same effect, but index futures tend to be more popular because they entail smaller transaction costs.

When the stock market rises as it did almost uninterruptedly from December 1986 to August 1987, the hedge was hardly used as investors participated in the bull market. But when stocks began to fall in autumn 1987, investors started selling futures, usually contracts tied to the S&P 500 index, thereby making up any losses from falling prices by the gain on the futures contracts. The portfolio insurer sells futures contracts at index levels that, in a falling market, are higher than they will be later. The money from the sale of the futures is then invested in money-market instruments until it is needed to buy back the futures contracts at lower prices in the future when the market has bottomed out.

Consider the following sequence of events involving the linkages between the sale of futures contracts for portfolio insurance and the market index.

(1) Your portfolio, valued at \$100, is equally divided between the risk-free asset and risky assets. The market index is 1000, and there is no futures discount from the index level.
(2) The market declines to an index of 900, and futures give a discount from the index of 10. As the market declines, portfolio insurance requires reducing your investment in the risky asset. This can be done by selling stock directly or by selling futures on the index. You increase your investment in the risk-free asset to \$55, leaving your investment in the risky asset long stocks 45, short index 5.
(3) Market arbitrageurs can now take advantage of mispricing between the index level and the price of futures because the investor has sold futures contracts, thereby increasing the discount between the futures price and the market index level. The discount has gone from 0 to −10. These so-called program traders begin to sell stocks and buy index futures to lock in a risk-free return. This causes the market index to fall; and in a falling market the investor will want to reduce his exposure to the risky asset by selling futures and investing the funds in the risk-free asset. This action will increase the discount between the index and the futures value and again encourage program traders to execute arbitrage trades. Once the cycle starts, it may be difficult to stop.

Could the scenario described in the last few paragraphs ever really take place? Unfortunately, the answer is yes. On Monday, October 19, 1987 — ever after to be known as Black Monday — this is precisely what happened on the New York Stock Exchange. Figures 24.9–24.11 show the precipitous drop of 508 points on the Dow Jones index that took place on Black Monday. Figure 24.10 shows that for most of the day futures were selling at a discount to the index. What is more revealing is that every time the discount got wider, the index started to fall faster. The bottom panels in Figures 24.10 and 24.11 show the percentages of trading volume for futures and the NYSE. It is apparent that a substantial amount of the record trading was being done by institutions trying to implement their portfolio-insurance strategies. What is especially unfortunate about Black Monday is that no one foresaw what would happen if every institution implemented a similar portfolio strategy simultaneously. Even the generally

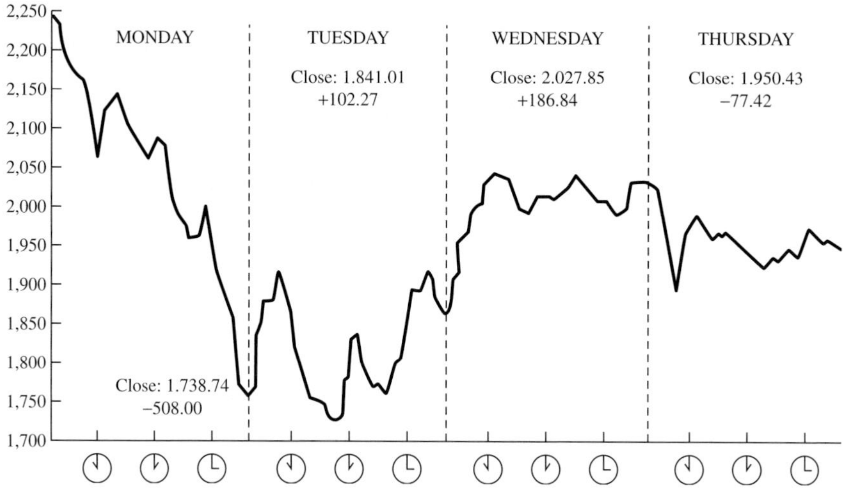

Fig. 24.9. Daily Movement of the Dow Jones Industrial Average, October 19–22, 1987. *Source*: Knight-Ridder Tradecenter, 1988. Courtesy of Knight-Ridder Financial Information.

liquid NYSE could not handle the crushing volume of orders to sell as a result of portfolio-insurance strategies. Most recently, Blume *et al.* (1989) have shown the breakdown in the linkage between futures prices and the spot index on October 19 and October 20, 1987. In addition they have found breakdowns in the linkage among NYSE stocks.

24.4.1. *Regulation and the Brady Report*

In the aftermath of the October 1987 crash, the role of regulation in both the futures and the stock markets was hotly debated. Figure 24.12 shows the relationships of the Congress, Federal agencies, and the Federal Reserve with the two leading futures and stock exchanges. Some have argued that the separate regulation of futures and stocks contributed to the severity of the October 1987 crash. The role of portfolio insurance and index arbitrage in linking the futures and stock markets has brought into question the separation of regulatory authority. At the present time, what form the future regulatory structure will take is a matter of conjecture. One reasoned answer has been presented by the Brady Commission report. This report is likely to provide the framework for the debate of how to regulate U.S. security markets.

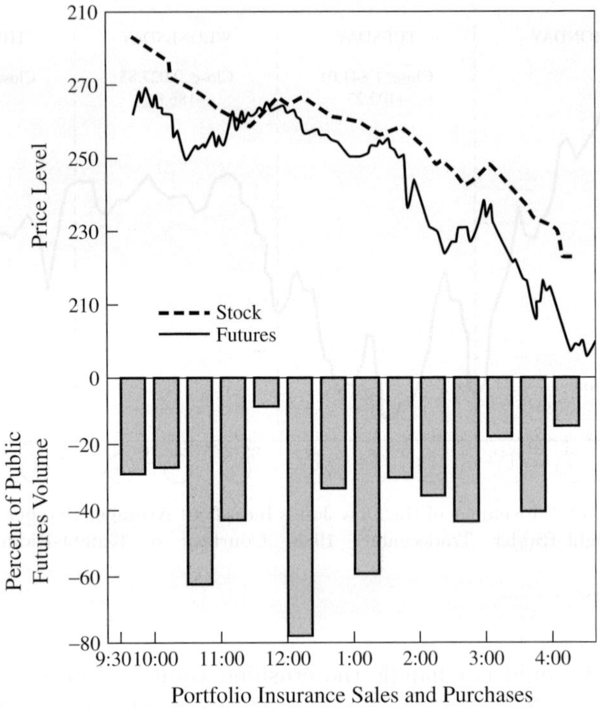

Fig. 24.10. S&P Index and Futures Contracts, Monday, October 19, 1987. *Source*: *The Washington Post*, October 9, 1988. Copyright @ 1988 by *The Washington Post*.

The Brady report makes five primary recommendations.

(1) Information systems should be established to monitor transactions and conditions in related markets.
(2) Clearing methods should be unified across marketplaces to reduce financial risk.
(3) Margins should be made consistent across marketplaces to control speculation and financial leverage.
(4) One agency should coordinate the few but critical regulatory issues that have an impact across the related market segments and throughout the financial system. The Federal Reserve is considered a reasonable candidate for this role.
(5) Circuit-breaker mechanisms such as price limits and coordinated trading halts should be formulated and implemented to protect the market system.

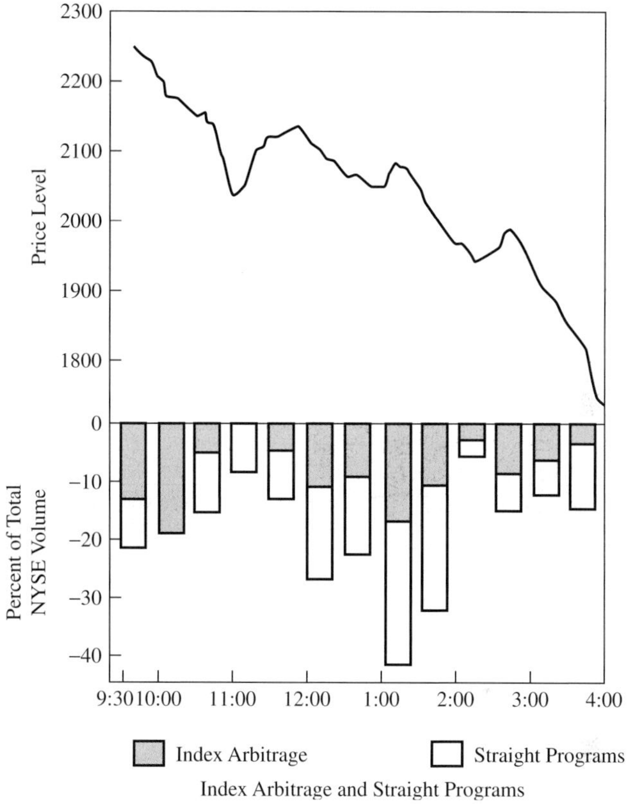

Fig. 24.11. Dow Jones Industrial One-Minute Chart, Monday, October 19, 1987. *Source*: *The Washington Post*, October 9, 1988. Copyright @ 1988 by *The Washington Post*.

How many of these recommendations are acted upon in restructuring the futures and stock markets remains to be seen. However, it is clear that practices such as portfolio insurance that link different markets together have forced study of the problems of a segmented regulatory system.

24.5. Empirical Studies of Portfolio Insurance[3]

Much of the early research on portfolio insurance focused on simulation models to see whether synthetic-option strategies could successfully limit

[3]Part of this section is from the "Portfolio Insurance Strategies" by L. C. Ho (2013, forthcoming).

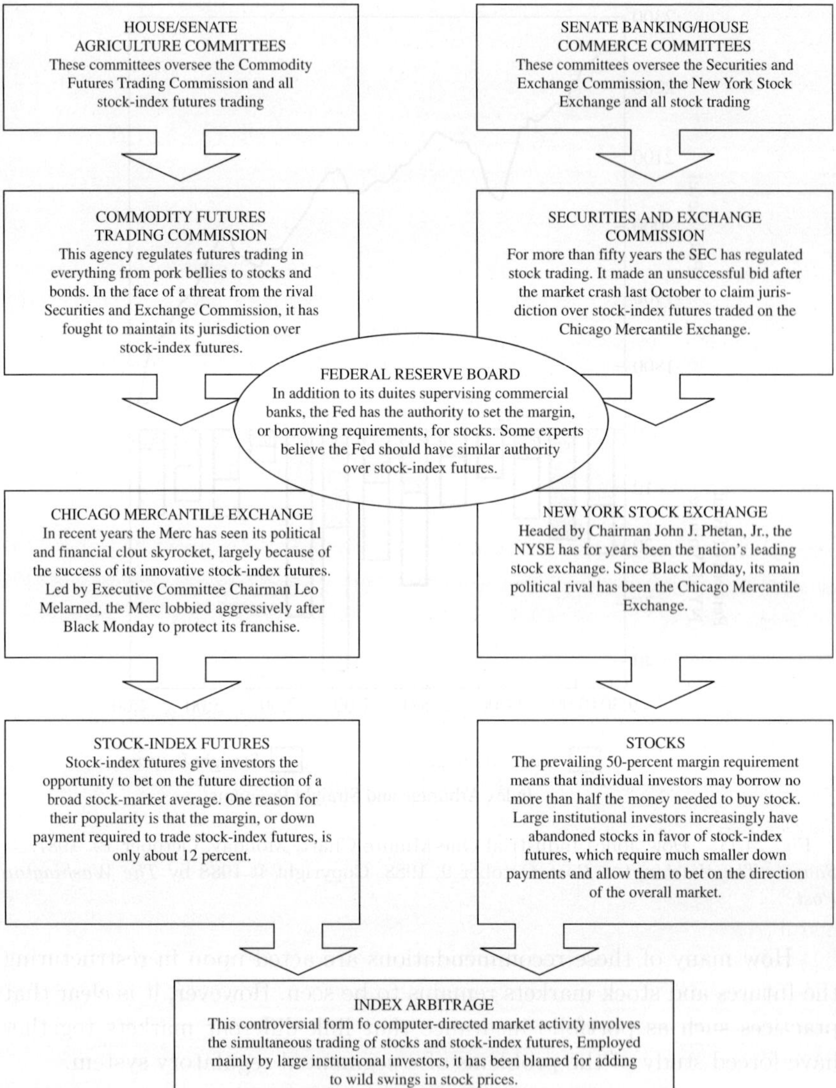

Fig. 24.12. Regulating the Markets.

Source: *The Washington Post*, October 9, 1988. Copyright @ 1988 by *The Washington Post*.

losses on portfolios of risky assets. In the early to mid-1980s, most of the empirical research on portfolio insurance was conducted by financial institutions such as Drexel, Burnham, Lambert and Salomon Brothers. However, more articles on the subject have appeared recently in journals such as *The Financial Analyst's Journal* and *Journal of Portfolio Management.*

24.5.1. *Leland (1985)*

Leland (1985) developed a replication strategy in the presence of transaction costs and tested this approach by using a simulation. As Leland pointed out, because transaction costs increase without limit as the revision period becomes shorter, it may be very costly to assure a given level of accuracy in the synthetic option. In addition, "transaction costs associated with replicating strategies are path-dependent: they depend not only on the initial and final stock prices, but also on the entire sequence of stock prices in between." Another problem with trying to create portfolio insurance in the presence of transaction costs is that transaction costs are correlated with the market. Leland poses the question, "In the presence of transaction costs, is there an alternative to the Black–Scholes replicating strategy which will overcome these problems?"

Leland proposed a procedure that adjusts upward the volatility estimate to the replicating procedure. The modification is a positive function of transaction costs and the replication period. This increase in the volatility estimate is due to the fact that each time a transaction occurs, the associated trading costs cause the purchase cost to be higher and the selling proceeds to be lower than without these costs. With transaction costs, the cost of purchasing stock is higher than without these costs; similarly, the price of selling the stock is lower, inclusive of these costs. "This accentuation of up or down movements of the stock price can be modeled as if the volatility of the actual stock price was higher." The adjustment to volatility is

$$\sigma_A^2 = \sigma^2\left(1 + \frac{\sqrt{2/\pi k}}{\sigma\sqrt{t}}\right), \tag{24.8}$$

where

σ_A^2 = the transaction-cost adjusted volatility;
σ = the annualized standard deviation of the natural logarithm of the price;

k = round-trip transaction costs as a proportion of the volume of transaction; and
t = the revision interval as a proportion of a year.

The modification to the volatility estimate has the following characteristics.

(1) Transaction costs remain bounded as the revision period becomes short.
(2) The strategy replicates the option return inclusive of transaction costs, with an error that is uncorrelated with the market and approaches zero as the revision period becomes short.
(3) Expected turnover and associated transaction costs of the modified replicating strategy can easily be calculated, given the revision interval. Since the error inclusive of transaction costs is uncorrelated with the market, these transaction costs put bounds on the option prices.

The delta value of this strategy takes into account transaction costs and will be higher than without transaction costs. As can be seen from Equation (24.8), the volatility estimate increases as the revision period and transaction costs increase. Leland believes that the modified replication strategy is superior to following the Black–Scholes strategy and paying transaction costs that result from the strategy because the expected error is negative, "reflecting the fact that transaction costs are not 'covered' by the initial option price." He assumes that the Black–Scholes strategy will result in higher turnover than the modified strategy because the latter "is based on a higher volatility which tends to 'smooth' the required trading."

Leland uses a simulation to determine the effectiveness of this strategy. The risk-free rate in the simulation is 10%; the expected return for the stock is 16%, with a standard deviation of 20%. Leland uses rebalancing periods of one week, four weeks, and eight weeks to replicate options expiring in three months, six months, and twelve months. Here H is the difference between the listed call and the synthetic option after the revision period, Δt.

$$\Delta H = \Delta C - [C_s S + r(C - C_s S)]\,, \tag{24.9}$$

where ΔC is the change in the listed call option over the revision period, C_s is the delta value and is the number of shares in the replicated portfolio, and r is the interest rate over the revision period. If the replicated option perfectly matches the changes in the listed option, ΔH will equal zero. For each of the revision periods, the mean and standard deviation of the errors is calculated.

Using simulated data with no transaction costs, the Black–Scholes strategy replicates the option with mean errors equal to zero for a revision period of one week. The standard deviation increases as the time until expiration decreases. As expected, the mean error increases as the revision period increases, with the greatest error occurring for the eight-week rebalancing period.

Leland uses his modification to the volatility estimate to calculate the accuracy of option replication with transaction costs. He compares the errors from the modified strategy with a Black–Scholes replicating scheme in which delta values and borrowing amounts are derived from the Black–Scholes model and then transaction costs are added on. In every case, the preciseness of the modified strategy exceeds the accuracy of the Black–Scholes design when round-trip transaction costs of 1% are used.

24.5.2. *Asay and Edelsburg (1986)*

Asay and Edelsburg used Monte Carlo simulations to determine how closely a synthetic-option strategy can match the returns on options on Treasury-bill futures. They state that there are three objections to a synthetic-option plan. First, changing delta values mean that positions must be continuously adjusted for the returns to be similar. However, rebalancing may not be possible if prices change overnight. If the position changes, too few or too many shares will be held in the underlying asset and the returns will not be the same as in the option position. The second problem with a synthetic strategy is that transaction costs may be significant, particularly if the rebalancing period is short.

The third problem is that the position could be whipsawed. **Whipsawing** occurs when the underlying asset increases enough to trigger rebalancing. After more shares are added, the underlying asset decreases in value and the additional shares are sold at a lower price than what was paid for them. A common remedy for this problem is to use a larger adjustment gap or filter rule; however, the wrong number of shares could be held if the filter rule was increased, particularly if the stock moved in a linear manner. Whipsawed positions commonly occur when the asset fluctuates around a constant level. Asay and Edelsburg used a Monte Carlo simulation of an option on a Treasury-bill future to determine if these and other problems would cause a divergence between the theoretical and synthetic positions. Profits and losses on the synthetic option are compared with those that would be earned through the purchase and sale of the option at the theoretical price if it were held to maturity. The profit on the replicated option is equal to the value of the option at maturity minus the price paid for option. They use adjustment gaps of 5–50 basis points in the simulated one-year interest-rate futures to trigger rebalancing.

Fifty simulations on six-month options were run. The option prices generated by the synthetic approach were very close to the options purchased at their theoretical values. Larger adjustment gaps proved more accurate when the futures traded in a narrow range, but the larger gaps were "disastrous" when the futures moved in one direction. Thus, they were unable to recommend a best adjustment gap. Asay and Edelsburg found the transaction cost of the replicating strategy to be insignificant.

To determine the amount of mispricing due to using an incorrect volatility estimate, they used a "correct" volatility measure for the listed option and an "incorrect" measure for the synthetic option. They found that input of a wrong estimate into the option-pricing model seems "to have only a minimal effect through the resulting incorrect hedge ratio." The authors concluded that problems such as transaction costs, whipsawing, and frequent rebalancing do not negate the effectiveness of the synthetic option on Treasury-bill futures.[4]

24.5.3. *Eizman (1986)*

The purpose of Eizman's paper is to determine which rebalancing strategy is the most effective in a dynamic-hedging portfolio-insurance framework. He considered three rebalancing disciplines: (1) to fully rebalance the required stock/cash mix at discrete time intervals, (2) to fully rebalance every time the market changes by a specified percentage, and (3) to rebalance only when the actual mix lags the required mix by more than a specified lag factor in either direction, "and then rebalance only to the extent of bringing the actual mix up to a lag factor away from the required mix. . . ."

Log normal returns to generate one-year puts are obtained using a multiyear Monte Carlo simulation. Eizman assumes a standard deviation of 13%, an interest rate of 8%, futures transaction costs of 0.15%, and a dividend yield of 4%. Put premiums and delta values for the synthetic put were generated by the Black–Scholes model. Then average annual

[4]Asay, M. and C. Edelsburg. "Can a Dynamic Strategy Replicate the Returns of an Option." "*Journal of Futures Markets*." v. 6 (Spring 1986), pp. 63–70. Copyright ©1986 by John Wiley and Sons, Inc. Reprinted by permission of John Wiley and Sons. Inc.

transaction costs and average annual replication errors are calculated. In all three strategies, there is a tradeoff between transaction costs and accuracy; the liberal adjustment strategies had lower transaction costs and higher replication errors.

For the discrete-time adjustment strategy, he rebalanced monthly, weekly, semiweekly, daily, and hourly. The transaction costs increased and replication errors decreased as the rebalance periods shortened. He used a utility function of Min $(X + Y)$, where X is average annual transaction costs and r is average annual replication error, to determine the most effective rebalance period. Using this criterion, the best method is the weekly method, with the semiweekly strategy coming in second.

For the second strategy, market moves from 5% to 0% were used to trigger rebalancing. Again, larger percentage rebalance periods lead to lower transaction costs and larger errors. The third discipline, in which the portfolio is rebalanced only if the actual futures/stock mix lags the required mix by more than a prescribed percentage, works the best, according to Eizman. Under this method, the adjustment is made so that the actual mix is brought up to the 3% boundary and not up to the required mix. The lag that provided the best cost/error tradeoff was 3%.

24.5.4. *Rendleman and McEnally (1987)*

This study addresses the issue of portfolio-insurance cost. It tries to answer the following questions.

(1) What is the probability that the portfolio will earn no more than its insured floor return?
(2) What are the expected returns and utilities of return of the insured portfolio versus those of a reasonable alternative strategy?
(3) What are the probabilities that the insured portfolio or the alternative will have the higher return?
(4) Over the long run, how will the accumulation of value from the insured portfolio stack up against the alternative?

They used a Monte Carlo simulation with a 16% expected return and a 10% interest rate. The Black–Scholes model is used to derive delta values for the put option. In addition, a logarithmic utility function is specified to measure the utility of a portfolio-insurance strategy. Rendleman and McEnally simulate one- and three-year put options using minimum returns of 5%, 0%, and −5%, stock volatility of 20% and 18%, and interest rates of

10% and 6%. Various simulations are run and the costs of the put positions are calculated along with expected utility for the insured portfolio and an uninsured portfolio.

Probability distributions are generated to determine the probability that the insured and uninsured portfolios have a return greater than the minimum floor. They concluded that the "insured portfolio is ... more likely than the optimal portfolio to achieve only the guaranteed minimum return." In addition, they found that portfolio insurance strategies "... suffer in comparison with an 'optimal' portfolio designed to maximize the rate of growth of portfolio value over time." Using the various inputs on the simulations, they determined that the insured portfolio can expect to have a lower return than a similar optimal portfolio. They concluded that portfolio-insurance strategies are optimal only when investors are highly risk averse.

24.5.5. *Garcia and Gould (1987)*

The main goal of this article is to compute the costs of a synthetic-call portfolio-insurance strategy. They do not deal with dynamic hedging because "... sufficient historical experience is not yet available to simulate meaningfully the results from long equities/short futures implementations." They use closing prices of the S&P 500 index from January 1, 1963, to December 31, 1983. They generate returns for 240 overlapping years by taking 20 January to January returns, then 20 February to February returns, and so on. This is the first published portfolio-insurance study to use real data as opposed to simulated data.

The returns for hedged and unhedged portfolios were calculated. Over the period of study, the arithmetic mean of the unhedged S&P 500 returns was 9.63% with a standard deviation of 16.22%; the mean return for a portfolio insurance strategy with a 0% floor and 0.5% transaction costs was 7.08 with a lower standard deviation of 9.33%. The mean return for the strategy with a −5% floor was 8.18% with a standard deviation of 11.80%.

Opportunity costs of the portfolio insurance were calculated. If the return on the unhedged portfolio was 10% and the return on the hedged portfolio was 0.10%, the opportunity cost is 5%. They conclude that with a zero floor insurance investors gain 10.27% in a down year. When the market is up, hedged portfolios forgo 7.21%.

They concluded that the cost of portfolio insurance is 170 basis points for zero-floor insurance and 83 basis points for a −5% strategy, and that a dynamically balanced portfolio will not outperform a buy-and-hold (BH) portfolio.

24.5.6. *Zhu and Kavee (1988)*

They evaluated and compared the performances of the two traditional portfolio strategies, the synthetic-put approach of Rubinstein and Leland (1981) and the constant-proportion approach of Black and Jones (1987). They employed a Monte Carlo simulation methodology, assuming log-normally distributed daily returns with an annual mean return of 15% and paired with different values for market volatility, in order to discover whether these strategies can really guarantee the floor return and how much investors have to pay for the protection.

Both strategies are able to reshape the return distribution so as to reduce downside risk and retain a certain part of the upside gains. However, they demonstrated that a certain degree of protection can be achieved at a considerable cost. There are two types of costs in implementing a portfolio insurance strategy. The first is the explicit cost, that is, the transactions costs. The other is the implicit cost, which is the average return forgone in exchange for protection against the downside risk. When the market becomes volatile, the protection error of the synthetic-put approach increases, and the transaction costs may be unbearable. On the contrary, while the constant proportion approach may have lower transactions costs, its implicit cost may still be substantial.

24.5.7. *Perold and Sharpe (1988)*

Using simulated stocks and bills prices, they examined and compared how the four dynamic asset allocation strategies, namely, the BH, constant mix (CM), CPPI, and option-based portfolio insurance (OBPI), perform in bull, bear, and flat markets and in volatile and not-so-volatile markets.

CPPI and OBPI strategies sell stocks as the market falls and buy stocks as the market rises. This dynamic allocation rule represents the purchase of portfolio insurance and has a convex payoff function, which results in a better downside protection and a better upside potential than a BH strategy. However, they do worse in relatively trendless, volatile markets.

On the contrary, a CM strategy — holding a constant fraction of wealth in stocks — buys stocks as the market falls and sells them as it rises. This rebalancing rule effectively represents the sale of portfolio insurance and has a concave payoff function, which leads to less downside protection than, and not as much upside as, a BH strategy. However, it does best in relatively trendless and volatile markets.

They suggested that no one particular type of dynamic strategy is best in all situations. Financial analysts can help investors understand the implications of various strategies, but they cannot, and should not, choose a strategy without a substantial understanding of an investor's circumstances and desires.

24.5.8. *Rendleman and O'Brien (1990)*

They addressed the issue that the misestimation of volatility input can have a significant impact on the final payoffs of a portfolio using a synthetic put strategy. In an OBPI strategy, the daily portfolio adjustments depend on the delta of the put option on the risky asset. In the original Black and Scholes (1973) valuation equation, the delta at each day is a function of the following variables:

$$D_t = f(S_t, \bar{k}_0, \bar{r}_0, \sigma_0, T), \tag{24.10}$$

where S_t is the price of the risky asset at date t, k_0 the strike price, r_0 the annual continuously compounded riskless rate of interest, σ_0 the *ex ante* volatility parameter at the beginning of the insurance period, and T the maturity of the option.

Assume that at the beginning of the insurance period, one manager predicts a high-volatile market and a 20% annualized volatility, while a second manager believes a low-volatile market and a 10% volatility. The delta for the first manager is higher which means he would buy more insurance and allocate less to a position in the risky asset. Assume that the *ex-post* volatility turns out to be 10%. The second manager will have made the proper allocation between risky and riskless assets. In contrast, the high-estimate manager will have invested too little in the risky asset. This misallocation would lose the opportunity of participating in the price appreciation in a strong market. Thus, a manager who underestimates volatility will typically end up buying less insurance than is necessary to ensure a given return, while a manager who overestimates volatility will buy more insurance than is necessary and forgo gains.

As for the issue of portfolio rebalancing, they examined adjustment frequencies by time intervals, namely, daily, weekly, monthly, and bimonthly. The effect (error) is measured as the difference of the horizon insurance values between noncontinuous and continuous trading. They suggested that weekly rebalancing produces an amount of error that appears to be tolerable by most portfolio managers.

More importantly, they addressed the biggest potential risk of implementing portfolio insurance strategies — the gap risk, by simulating the performance of the OBPI strategy over the period of the October 1987 market crash. They indicated that most insured portfolios would have fallen short of their promised values because the managers would not be able to adjust the portfolio in time before a big drop in the market. The gap risk will be discussed further in the financial stability section.

24.5.9. *Loria, Pham, and Sim (1991)*

They simulated the performance of a synthetic-put strategy using futures contracts based on the Australian All Ordinaries Index for the period from April 1984 to March 1989. Their study contains 20 consecutive nonoverlapping three-month insurance periods whose expiration dates coincide with the expiration dates of each SPI futures contract traded on the Sydney Futures Exchange. Four implementation scenarios are examined: a zero floor versus 5% floor which correspond to a portfolio return of 0% and −5% per annual, respectively; and a realized volatility versus Leland's (1985) modified volatility. They reported that there is no perfect guarantee of loss prevention under any scenario. Even in the scenario with a 5% floor and modified volatility, two out of 20 contracts do not meet the desired floor. In addition, the OBPI strategy is most effective under severe market conditions. In other periods characterized by insignificant market declines, the value of the insured portfolio is below that of the market portfolio. They suggested futures mispricing may be one potential culprit for this outcome.

24.5.10. *Do and Faff (2004)*

This empirical paper is an extension of Loria *et al.* (1991). They examined two approaches (the OBPI and CPPI) and conducted simulations across two implementation strategies (via Australia stock index and bills, and via SPI futures and stock index). Furthermore, they considered the use of implied volatility as an input into the model, and the use of a zero floor versus 5% floor. The dataset consists of 59 nonoverlapping three-month insurance periods, which span from October 1987 to December 2002. Thus, their key contributions relative to Loria *et al.* (1991) are the examination of a futures-based CPPI, a fine-tuned algorithm that allows for dividend payments, the consideration of *ex ante* volatility information, and more up-to-date data.

In terms of floor protection, the futures-based portfolio insurance implementation generally dominates its index-and-bill rival in both floor specifications, which reflects the low transaction costs in the futures market. Furthermore, the perfect floor protection is possible when implied volatility is used rather than using *ex post* volatilities. From the cost of insurance perspective, the futures-based strategy generally induces a lower cost of insurance than its index-and-bill rival in both floor specifications, which reflects the same reason as above. However, the cost of insurance is higher when implied volatility is used compared to *ex post* volatilities. The possible explanation is that the implied volatility is often higher than the same period *ex post* volatility, which results in over-hedging. As for the performances between the OBPI and CPPI approaches, there is no strong evidence to distinguish between them. Within the futures-based implementation, the synthetic put appears to dominate the CPPI with respect to floor protection, while the latter appears to slightly outperform in terms of upside participation.

They also examined whether portfolio insurance strategies work under stress conditions by assessing the strategies' effectiveness during tranquil and turbulent periods. Tranquil periods are defined as ones that return more than −4% and have a realized volatility of less than 15%; violation of either one or both of these conditions is regarded as indicating a turbulent period. All portfolio insurance strategies achieve 100% floor protection during tranquil periods, whereas the futures-based OBPI approach records the highest portfolio return. During turbulent times, futures-based portfolio insurance continues to perform quite well. The 1987 stock market crash makes the assessment difficult because of trading halts. However, assuming the futures continued to trade during that crisis, from the algorithm's perspective, the futures-based CPPI maintains a positive return, while the OBPI results in a negative return.

24.5.11. *Cesari and Cremonini (2003)*

This study is an extensive comparison of a wide variety of traditional portfolio insurance strategies. There are basically five dynamic asset allocation strategies: (1) BH, (2) CM, (3) constant proportion (without and with the lock-in of profits, CP and CPL), (4) the option-based approach (with three variations, BCDT, NL, and PS), and (5) technical strategy (with two kinds of stop-loss mechanism, MA and MA2); therefore, nine strategies in total are considered.

For each strategy, eight measures for risk, return, and risk-adjusted performance are calculated, namely, mean return, standard deviation, asymmetry, kurtosis, downside deviation, Sharpe ratio, Sortino ratio and return at risk. The strategies are then compared in different market situations (bear, no-trend, bull markets) and with different market volatility periods (low, medium, and high periods), taking into account transaction costs and discrete rebalancing of portfolios. The three market situations are defined accordingly if market average returns fall into the three ranges: (−30%, −5%), (−5%, +5%), (+5%, +30%), and the three ranges for the volatile periods are: (10%, 15%), (15%, 25%), (25%, 30%). Transaction costs are treated in two ways: a proportional cost to the value traded, and a correction to the Leland's (1985) option volatility. Two main rebalancing disciplines are used: a time discipline with weekly adjustment and a price discipline with adjustment only when prices are increased/decreased by 2.5% with respect to the previous rebalance time.

Monte Carlo simulations of MSCI World, North America, Europe, and Pacific stock market returns show that no strategy is dominant in all market situations. However, in bear and no-trend markets, CP and CPL strategies appear to be the best choice. In a bull market or in no-trend but with high volatility market, the CM strategy is preferable. If the market phase is unknown, CP, CPL, and BCDT strategies are recommended. In addition, these results are independent of the volatility level and the risk-adjusted performance measure adopted.

24.5.12. *Herold, Maurer, and Purschaker (2005)*

By constructing a fixed income portfolio, in which the risky asset is the JPMorgan government bond index and the riskless asset is cash (one-month yield), they compared the hedging performances between the traditional CPPI strategy and the risk-based (specifically, VaR-based) strategy with a one-year investment horizon that begins at each year from 1987 to 2003. CPPI avoids losses in the bear years of 1994 and 1999. The mean return is inferior to (about 40 bp below) that of the risk-based strategy. CPPI also produces a higher turnover.

24.5.13. *Hamidi, Jurczenko, and Maillet (2007)*

Although they proposed a conditional CPPI multiplier determined either by VaR or by ES, only a VaR-based measure is studied in this empirical work, and the ES measure is absent for future research.

The data set contains 29 years of daily returns of the Dow Jones Index, from January 2, 1987 to May 20, 2005, 4,641 observations in total. They used a rolling window of 3,033 returns to estimate the VaR, and there are 1,608 VaRs in the out-of-sample period. They resorted to eight methods of VaR calculation: one nonparametric method using the historical simulation approach; three parametric methods based on distributional assumptions, namely, the normal VaR, the RiskMetrics VaR based on the normal distribution, and the GARCH VaR based on the Student-t distribution; four semiparametric methods using quantile regression to estimate the conditional autoregressive VaR (CAViaR), namely, the symmetric Absolute Value CAViaR, the Asymmetric Slope CAViaR, the IGARCH(1,1) CAViaR, and the Adaptive CAViaR.

According to the 1,608 back-testing results, the Asymmetric Slope CAViaR is the best model to fit the data. After having calculated the VaR values, the conditional multipliers can be determined. The estimations spread between 1.5 and 6, which are compatible with multiple values used by practitioners in the market (between 3 and 8).

Using the time-varying CPPI multipliers estimated by different methods, and a "multi-start" analysis — the fixed one-year investment horizon beginning at every day of the out-of-sample period, they found that the final returns of these insured portfolios are not significantly different.

24.5.14. *Ho, Cadle, and Theobald (2008)*

This empirical study presents a complete structure of comparing traditional portfolio insurance strategies (OBPI, CPPI) with modern risk-based portfolio insurance strategies (VaR-, ES-based RBPI). By constructing a currency portfolio, in which the risky asset is the Australian dollar and the riskless asset is a US dollar overnight deposit, they compared the dynamic hedging performances between the traditional and the modern strategies with a one-year investment horizon that begins at each year from 2001 to 2007.

When implementing the OBPI strategy, the delta is calculated based on the modified Black–Scholes formula, $D_t = f(S_t, \bar{k}_0, r_t, \sigma_t, T)$. That is, daily annualized historical volatilities are used as inputs in the put-replication process instead of the constant *ex ante* or the implied volatility in the original model to mitigate the volatility misestimation problem. Besides, the latter two parameters would make the portfolio daily returns more volatile. The interest rates are also updated daily for the same reason. When CPPI is implemented, the possible upper bounds of the multiplier are examined via the extreme value theory, which ranges from 4 to 6 corresponding to different confidence levels. When risk-based approaches are employed, both a historical distribution and a normal distribution with exponentially weighted volatility of risky asset returns are assumed. A daily rebalancing principle is adopted in their research without any modification to show the original results of hedging.

The performances are evaluated from six differing perspectives. In terms of the Sharpe ratio and the volatility of portfolio returns, the CPPI is the best performer, while the VaR based upon the normal distribution is the worst. From the perspective that the return distribution of the hedged portfolio is shifted to the right and in terms of both the average and the cumulative portfolio returns across years, the ES-based strategy using the historical distribution ranks first. Moreover, the ES-based strategy results in a lower turnover within the investment horizon, thereby saving transaction costs.

24.6. Summary

This chapter has discussed basic concepts and methods of portfolio insurance for stocks. Strategies and implementation of portfolio insurance have also been explored in detail. Other issues related to portfolio insurance and dynamic hedging have also been studied.

Portfolio insurance was described not as an insurance technique but rather as an asset-allocation or hedging technique. The general methods of portfolio insurance — (1) stop-loss orders, (2) market-traded index options, (3) synthetic options, and (4) futures trading — were discussed. One of the major issues facing investors and regulators during the later 1980s was introduced — the effect of portfolio insurance on the stock market.

Overall, this chapter has integrated most of the material discussed in previous chapters. It can be regarded as a synthesis of the whole book although another chapter follows. Chapters 17 and 27 shows how high-power mathematical and statistical tools can be used to derive the Black–choles option-pricing model more precisely.

Questions and Problems

1. What is portfolio insurance? Identify and explain the various strategies that can be used to insure a portfolio.
2. What is the difference between hedging and portfolio insurance?
3. A manager is running a $10-million portfolio. She has decided to allocate $5 million to risky assets and $5 million to risk-free assets. She has set the floor of the portfolio at $7 million.
   (a) What is the cushion for this portfolio?
   (b) What is the exposure for this portfolio?
   (c) What is the multiple for this portfolio?
4. Given the information in question 3, if the market for risky assets increases by 30%:
   (a) What is the value of the total portfolio?
   (b) What is the new multiple?
   (c) What should the portfolio manager do to restore the portfolio to its target multiple?
5. Given the information in question 3, if the market for risky assets decreases by 10%:
   (a) What is the value of the total portfolio?
   (b) What is the new multiple?
   (c) What should the portfolio manager do to restore the portfolio to its target level?
6. What does the term *path dependence* mean? Why is it important for portfolio-insurance strategies to be path independent?
7. Define a synthetic option. Explain how the option position is adjusted in a rising or falling market.
8. What is a delta value? Why is it important?
9. A portfolio manager has $10 million invested in a well-diversified portfolio of common stock with a portfolio beta of 0.9 measured relative to the S&P 500. How many S&P 500 futures contracts are needed to insure the portfolio if the futures are currently selling for $105?
10. How could the strategy of hedging with futures contracts not provide a perfect hedge?
11. Compare and contrast portfolio insurance with options to portfolio insurance with futures.

12. Identify and discuss the linkage between trading futures contracts for portfolio insurance and market volatility. Does the tail wag the dog?
13. What is the difference between margin on equities and margin on futures?

Bibliography

Anders, G. "Investors Risk for Portfolio Insurance." *The Wall Street Journal* (October 14, 1986), p. 6.

Asay, M. and C. Edelsburg. "Can a Dynamic Strategy Replicate the Returns of an Option?" *The Journal of Futures Markets*, v. 6 (Spring 1986), pp. 63–70.

Becker, K. "Rebalancing Strategies for Synthetic Call Options." Doctoral dissertation, University of Illinois, 1988.

Benninga, S. and M. Blume. "On the Optimality of Portfolio Insurance." *The Journal of Finance*, v. 40 (December 1985), pp. 1341–1352.

Bertrand, P. and J. L. Prigent. "Portfolio Insurance Strategies: OBPI versus CPPI." *Finance*, v. 26(1) (2005), pp. 5–32.

Black, F. and R. Jones. *Simplifying Portfolio Insurance.* New York: Goldman Sachs, 1986.

Black, F. and R. Jones. "Simplifying Portfolio Insurance." *Journal of Portfolio Management*, v. 14 (1987), pp. 48–51.

Black, F. and M. Scholes. "The Pricing of Options and Corporate Liabilities." *Journal of Political Economy*, v. 81 (1973), pp. 637–659.

Blume, M. E., A. C. Mackinlay and B. Terker. "Order Imbalances and Stock Price Movements on October 19 and 20, 1987." *Journal of Finance*, v. 44 (September 1989), pp. 827–848.

Bodie, Z., A. Kane, and A. J. Marcus. *Investments.* McGraw-Hill, 9th ed., 2011.

Brennan, M. J. and R. Solanki. "Optimal Portfolio Insurance." *Journal of Financial and Quantitative Analysis*, v. 16 (September 1981), pp. 279–300.

Cesari, R. and D. Cremonini. "Benchmarking, Portfolio Insurance and Technical Analysis: A Monte Carlo Comparison of Dynamic Strategies of Asset Allocation." *Journal of Economic Dynamics & Control*, v. 27 (2003), pp. 987–1011.

Do, B. H. and R. W. Faff. "Do Futures-Based Strategies Enhance Dynamic Portfolio Insurance?" *Journal of Futures Markets*, v. 6 (June 2004), pp. 591–608.

Dreher, W. "Does Portfolio Insurance Ever Make Sense?" *Journal of Portfolio Management*, v. 14 (Summer 1988), pp. 25–32.

Eizman, E. S. "Rebalance Disciplines for Portfolio Insurance." *Journal of Portfolio Management*, v. 13 (Fall 1986), pp. 59–62.

Finnerty, J. and H. Park. "How to Profit from Program Trading." *Journal of Portfolio Management*, v. 14 (Winter 1988), pp. 40–46 .

Finnerty, J. and H. Park. "Stock Index Futures: Does the Tail Wag the Dog?" *Financial Analysts Journal*, v. 43 (March/April 1987), pp. 57–61.

Garcia, C. B. and F. J. Gould. "An Empirical Study of Portfolio Insurance." *Financial Analysts Journal*, v. 43 (July/August 1987), pp. 44–54.

Grossman, S. "An Analysis of the Implications for Stock and Futures Price Volatility of Program Trading and Dynamic Hedging Strategies." *Journal of Business*, v. 61 (July 1988), pp. 275–298.

Grossman, S. "Insurance Seen and Unseen: The Impact on Markets." *Journal of Portfolio Management*, v. 14 (Summer 1988), pp. 5–8.

Hamidi, B., E. Jurczenko and B. Maillet. "An extended expected CAViaR approach for CPPI." Working paper, Variances, University of Paris-1, 2007.

Herold, U., R. Maurer and N. Purschaker. "Total Return Fixed-Income Portfolio Management: A Risk-Based Dynamic Strategy." *Journal of Portfolio Management*, v. 31 (Spring 2005), pp. 32–43.

Hill, J. *Portfolio Insurance: Volatility Risk and Futures Mispricing.* New York: Kidder, Peabody, and Co., 1987.

Ho, L. C. "Portfolio Insurance Strategies," in C. F. Lee and A. C. Lee (eds.), *Encyclopedia Finance*, 2nd edn. New York:Springer, Forthcoming, 2013.

Ho, L. C., J. Cadle and M. Theobald. "Portfolio Insurance Strategies: Review of Theory and Empirical Studies," in C. F. Lee, A. C. Lee and J. Lee (eds.), *Handbook of Quantitative Finance and Risk Management.* New York: Springer, 2010, pp. 319–332.

Ho, L. C., J. Cadle and M. Theobald. "An Analysis of Risk-Based Asset Allocation and Portfolio Insurance Strategies." Working paper, Central Bank of the Republic of China (Taiwan), 2008.

John, L. M., L. M. Donald, E. P. Jerald, and W. M. Dennis. *Managing Investment Portfolios: A Dynamic Process.* CFA Institute, 3rd ed., 2007.

Kritzman, M. "What's Wrong with Portfolio Insurance?" *The Journal of Portfolio Management*, v. 13 (Fall 1986), pp. 13–16.

Leland, H. E. "Option Pricing and Replication with Transaction Costs." *Journal of Finance*, v. 40 (December 1985), pp. 1283–1307.

Leland, H. E. "Who Should Buy Portfolio Insurance." *Journal of Finance*, v. 35 (May 1980), pp. 581–594.

Loria, S., T. M. Pham and A. B. Sim. "The Performance of a Stock Index Futures-Based Portfolio Insurance Scheme: Australian Evidence." *Review of Futures Markets*, v. 10(3) (1991), pp. 438–457.

Luskin, D. *Portfolio Insurance: A Guide to Dynamic Hedging.* Wiley, 1988.

Malkiel, B. "The Brady Commission Report: A Critique." *Journal of Portfolio Management*, v. 14 (Summer 1988), pp. 9–13.

Nolan E., M. A. Sola, and S. Crouch. *The Insured Portfolio: Your Gateway to Stress-Free Global Investments.* Wiley, 2010.

O'Brien, T. "The Mechanics of Portfolio Insurance." *Journal of Portfolio Management*, v. 14 (Spring 1988), pp. 40–47.

Perold, A. F. "Constant Proportion Portfolio Insurance." Working Paper, Harvard Business School, 1986.

Perold, A. F. and W. F. Sharpe. "Dynamic Strategies for Asset Allocation." *Financial Analysts Journal*, v. 44 (1) (1988), pp. 16–27.

Presidential Task Force on Market Mechanisms. *Tire Brady Report.* Washington, DC: U.S. Government Printing Office, 1988.

Rendleman, R. J. and R. W. McEnally. "Assessing the Cost of Portfolio Insurance." *Financial Analysts Journal*, v. 43 (May/June 1987), pp. 27–37.

Rendleman, R. J. Jr. and T. J. O'Brien. "The Effects of Volatility Misestimation on Option-Replication Portfolio Insurance." *Financial Analysts Journal*, v. 46(3) (1990), pp. 61–70.

Rubinstein, M. "Alternative Paths to Portfolio Insurance." *Financial Analysts Journal*, v. 41 (July/August 1985), pp. 42–52.

Rubinstein, M. and H. Leland. "Replicating Options with Positions in Stock and Cash." *Financial Analysts Journal*, v. 37 (July/August 1981), pp. 63–72.

Singleton, C. and R. Grieves. "Synthetic Puts and Portfolio Insurance Strategies." *Journal of Portfolio Management*, v. 10 (Spring 1984), pp. 63–69.

Tilley, J. A. and G. O. Latainer. "A Synthetic Option Framework for Asset Allocation." *Financial Analysts Journal*, v. 41 (May/June 1985), pp. 32–41.

Zhu, Y. and R. C. Kavee. "Performance of Portfolio Insurance Strategies." *Journal of Portfolio Management*, v. 14(3) (1988), pp. 48–54.

Part V

Special Topics

Chapter 25

Capturing Equity Risk Premia*

The global equity markets can be treacherous. From 1900–2000, the standard deviation of U.S. equity returns exceeded 20% per annum, as reported by Dimson *et al.* (2002). In the five worst individual years during this period, the U.S. equity market dropped by more than 30%. Other markets were even riskier. For example, the Japanese market had an annualized volatility exceeding 30%, while UK equities lost 71% of their value during the 1973–1974 bear market.

Naturally, investors expect compensation for bearing this risk. Historically, they have received it. During 1900–2000, the annualized geometric mean return (net of inflation) was positive in all developed markets, with the median value near 5%.

The Capital Asset Pricing Model (CAPM) provides a formal framework for analyzing the risk/return tradeoff (Sharpe, 1964). According to this theory, in an efficient market no investor can expect to outperform the market on a risk-adjusted basis. In financial parlance, there is no "alpha." That is, under CAPM, the only risk premium comes from the market itself, or "beta."

Nonetheless, there is considerable evidence that other sources of equity risk premia (i.e., alpha factors), in fact, do exist. These premia include — but are not limited to — Value, Size, and Momentum. The Value premium, first analyzed by Basu (1977), is an effect whereby stocks that are priced low

*This chapter was written by Jose Menchero (MSCI), Andrei Morozov (MSCI), and John Guerard (McKinley Capital Management).

relative to fundamentals (e.g., earnings or book value) tend to outperform. The Size effect, investigated by Banz (1981), describes the observation that small firms tend to outperform large firms. In the Momentum effect, stocks that have performed well over the previous 6–12 months tend to continue their outperformance, as documented by Jegadeesh and Titman (1993).

There are many ways of crafting long/short investment strategies to capture sources of equity risk premia. In this chapter, the authors examine three such approaches. The first approach considered is to simply go long stocks with positive exposure to the factor, and to short those with negative exposure. The authors refer to this as the "simple" factor approach. While this strategy certainly achieves exposure to the desired factor, it may also introduce unintentional and unwanted exposure to other factors. For instance, a simple Value strategy tends to overweight the Financials sector and underweight Information Technology. These incidental exposures may increase portfolio risk while potentially reducing returns.

Another strategy is to maintain unit exposure to the desired factor, while eliminating exposures to all other factors. The authors refer to this as the "pure" factor strategy. A strength of this approach is that it allows the portfolio manager to surgically control the exposures. A limitation of this technique, however, is that it does not take risk into account.

The third approach considered for capturing equity risk premia is to construct a portfolio that retains unit exposure to the desired factor, while minimizing risk. It is referred as the "optimized" factor strategy.

In this chapter, the risk and return profiles of these three different investment strategies are investigated. The World factor as well as the eight style factors contained within the Barra Global Equity Model, GEM2 are considered. In Section 25.1, the relevant aspects of the GEM2 model are briefly described, such as estimation universe and factor structure. This model has been described in detail by Menchero *et al.* (2010). In Section 25.2, the construction methodology for the three types of factor portfolios are described. In Section 25.3, the results for the risk and return of these factors spanning a 13-year period from 1997 to 2010 are presented. In Section 25.4, lagged correlations between the Leading Economic Indicators (LEI) and GEM2 factor returns are examined. Also the results of a "factor timing" strategy based upon these relationships are analyzed. Finally, in Section 25.5, we summarize and conclude.

25.1. Global Equity Risk Model

25.1.1. *Estimation Universe*

The estimation universe is the set of stocks that is used to estimate the model. Judicious selection of the estimation universe is a critical component to building a sound risk model. The estimation universe must be sufficiently broad to accurately represent the investment opportunity set of global investors, without being so broad as to include illiquid stocks that may introduce spurious return relationships into the model. Furthermore, the estimation universe should be reasonably stable to ensure that factor exposures are well behaved across time. *Representation, liquidity,* and *stability*, therefore, represent the three primary goals that must be attained when selecting a risk model estimation universe.

A well-constructed equity index must address and overcome these very issues, and therefore serves as an excellent foundation for the estimation universe. The GEM2 estimation universe utilizes the MSCI *All Country World Investable Market Index* (ACWI IMI), part of the MSCI Global Investable Market Indices family, which represents the latest in MSCI index-construction methodology. MSCI ACWI IMI aims to reflect the full breadth of global investment opportunities by targeting 99% of the float-adjusted market capitalization in both developed and emerging markets. The index-construction methodology applies innovative rules designed to achieve index stability, while reflecting the evolving equity markets in a timely fashion. Moreover, liquidity screening rules are applied to ensure that only investable stocks with reliable pricing are included for index membership.

25.1.2. *GEM2 Factor Structure*

The equity factor set in GEM2 includes a World factor (w), countries (c), industries (i), and styles (s). Every stock is assigned an exposure of 1 to the World factor. Hence, the local excess returns (i.e., currency hedged) r_n can be written as

$$r_n = f_w + \sum_c X_{nc} f_c + \sum_i X_{ni} f_i + \sum_s X_{ns} f_s + u_n, \tag{25.1}$$

where X_{nk} is the exposure of stock n to factor k, f_k is the return of the factor, and u_n is the specific return of the stock. Mathematically, the World factor represents the intercept term in the cross-sectional regression. Economically, it describes the aggregate up-and-down movement of the global equity market. Typically, the World factor is the dominant source of risk for a diversified long-only portfolio.

For most institutional investors, however, the primary concern is the risk of *active* long/short portfolios. If both the portfolio and benchmark are fully invested — as is typically the case — then the active exposure to the World factor is zero. Thus, we must look beyond the World factor to other sources of risk.

Country factors play a critical role in global equity risk modeling. One reason is that they are powerful indicator variables for explaining the cross section of global equity returns. A second, related, reason is that the country allocation decision is central to many global investment strategies, and portfolio managers often must carefully monitor their exposures to these factors. It is therefore included that the explicit country factors for all markets are covered.

In Table 25.1, we present a list of the 48 countries in the GEM2 estimation universe. The country exposures X_{nc} in GEM2 are set equal to 1

Table 25.1. GEM2 Country Factors.

Country Name	Average Weight	Jan-08 Weight	Jan-08 # Stocks	Jan-08 Float-Cap	Jan-08 Total-Cap
Argentina	0.10	0.09	13	0.02	0.04
Australia	1.62	2.48	236	1.05	1.20
Austria	0.17	0.37	35	0.09	0.18
Belgium	0.64	0.69	47	0.20	0.33
Brazil	0.65	1.87	140	0.53	0.90
Canada	2.59	3.44	297	1.37	1.66
Chile	0.18	0.26	34	0.05	0.13
China International	0.67	2.96	215	0.64	1.43
Colombia	0.03	0.07	11	0.01	0.03
Czech Republic	0.06	0.15	8	0.03	0.07
Denmark	0.39	0.46	57	0.15	0.22
Egypt	0.05	0.17	31	0.03	0.08
Finland	0.59	0.69	52	0.28	0.33
France	4.18	5.24	184	1.61	2.53
Germany	3.31	3.71	184	1.43	1.79
Greece	0.28	0.48	62	0.14	0.23
Hong Kong	1.07	1.50	165	0.40	0.72
Hungary	0.06	0.09	8	0.03	0.04
India	0.54	2.41	251	0.38	1.16
Indonesia	0.13	0.34	54	0.07	0.16
Ireland	0.26	0.27	30	0.11	0.13
Israel	0.20	0.32	69	0.09	0.15

(*Continued*)

Table 25.1. (*Continued*)

Country Name	Average Weight	Jan-08 Weight	Jan-08 # Stocks	Jan-08 Float-Cap	Jan-08 Total-Cap
Italy	2.05	2.09	161	0.63	1.01
Japan	11.52	8.96	1160	3.20	4.32
Jordan	0.03	0.05	17	0.00	0.02
Korea	1.02	2.06	332	0.60	0.99
Malaysia	0.43	0.53	119	0.11	0.26
Mexico	0.43	0.59	40	0.17	0.29
Morocco	0.03	0.09	10	0.01	0.05
Netherland	1.47	1.34	70	0.45	0.65
New Zealand	0.09	0.07	22	0.02	0.03
Norway	0.34	0.71	68	0.19	0.34
Pakistan	0.03	0.06	24	0.01	0.03
Peru	0.04	0.11	16	0.03	0.05
Philippines	0.06	0.14	27	0.02	0.07
Poland	0.11	0.33	66	0.07	0.16
Portugal	0.20	0.24	21	0.06	0.12
Russia	0.49	2.83	71	0.31	1.36
Singapore	0.48	0.72	104	0.19	0.35
South Africa	0.63	0.86	116	0.29	0.42
Spain	1.41	2.11	88	0.66	1.02
Sweden	1.05	1.05	105	0.39	0.51
Switzerland	2.54	2.41	118	1.02	1.16
Taiwan	1.25	1.34	411	0.44	0.65
Thailand	0.19	0.36	66	0.06	0.17
Turkey	0.18	0.45	68	0.07	0.21
UK	8.65	7.65	463	3.46	3.69
US	47.53	34.80	2468	15.74	16.79
Total	100.00	100.00	8414	36.92	48.27

Average weights (based on total capitalization) are from January 1997 to January 2008. Market capitalizations are reported in trillions of U.S. dollars.

if stock n is in country c, and set equal to 0 otherwise. We assign country exposures based on country membership within the MSCI ACWI IMI.

In Table 25.1, the average and ending weights (based on total market capitalization) over the period from January 1997 to January 2008 is also shown. It is interesting to note the relative decline of the U.S. and Japanese markets, and the rise of markets such as Brazil, Russia, and India. The number of securities in the estimation universe for each country and the market capitalization (float-adjusted and total) in trillions of U.S. Dollars as of January 2008 are also reported.

Industries are also important variables in explaining the sources of global equity return co-movement. One of the major strengths of GEM2 is to employ the Global Industry Classification Standard (GICS®) for the industry factor structure. The GICS scheme is hierarchical, with 10 top-level sectors, which are then divided into 24 industry groups, 68 industries, and 154 sub-industries. GICS applies a consistent global methodology to classify stocks based on careful evaluation of the firm's business model and economic operating environment. The GICS structure is reviewed annually by MSCI and Standard & Poor's to ensure that it remains timely and accurate.

Identifying which industry factors to include in the model involves a combination of judgment and empirical analysis. At one extreme, the 10 GICS sectors could be used as industry factors. Such broad groupings, however, would certainly fail to capture much of the cross-sectional variation in stock returns. At the other extreme, all 154 sub-industries could be used as the factor structure. Besides the obvious difficulties associated with using so many factors (e.g., risk reporting, thin industries), such an approach would present a more serious problem for risk forecasting: although adding more factors always increases the in-sample R^2 of the cross-sectional regressions, many of the factor returns would not be statistically significant. Allowing noise-dominated "factors" into the model defeats the very purpose of a factor risk model.

In GEM2, selection of the industry factor structure begins at the second level of the GICS hierarchy, with each of the 24 industry groups automatically qualifying as a factor. This provides a reasonable level of granularity, without introducing an excessive number of factors. Each industry group is then analyzed, carefully examining the industries and sub-industries contained therein to determine if a more granular factor structure is warranted. The basic criteria used to guide industry factor selection are: (a) the groupings of industries into factors must be economically intuitive, (b) the industry factors should have a strong degree of statistical significance, (c) incorporating an additional industry factor should significantly increase the explanatory power of the model, and (d) thin industries (those with few assets) should be avoided.

The result of this process is the set of 34 GEM2 industry factors, presented in Table 25.2. Industries that qualify as factors tend to exhibit volatile returns and have significant weight. It is found that this relatively parsimonious set of factors captures most of the in-sample R^2 explained by the 154 sub-industries, but with a much higher degree of statistical significance. Also reported in Table 25.2 are the average and end-of-period industry weights from January 1997 to January 2008. Only five industries

Table 25.2. GEM2 Industry Factors.

GICS Sector	GEM2 Code	GEM2 Industry Factor Name	Average Weight	Jan-08 Weight
Energy	1	Energy Equipment & Services	0.75	1.29
	2	Oil, Gas & Consumable Fuels	4.88	9.32
	3	Oil & Gas Exploration & Production	1.00	1.72
Materials	4	Chemicals	2.36	2.84
	5	Construction, Containers, Paper	1.38	1.24
	6	Aluminum, Diversified Metals	1.05	2.41
	7	Gold, Precious Metals	0.37	0.58
	8	Steel	0.79	1.83
Industrials	9	Capital Goods	7.33	8.60
	10	Commercial & Professional Services	1.43	0.77
	11	Transportation Non-Airline	1.82	2.32
	12	Airlines	0.37	0.45
Consumer Discretionary	13	Automobiles & Components	2.52	2.29
	14	Consumer Durables & Apparel	2.33	1.93
	15	Consumer Services	1.35	1.39
	16	Media	3.24	2.11
	17	Retailing	3.42	2.08
Consumer Staples	18	Food & Staples Retailing	1.82	1.76
	19	Food, Beverage & Tobacco	4.56	4.37
	20	Household & Personal Products	1.43	1.20
Health Care	21	Health Care Equipment & Services	2.13	1.93
	22	Biotechnology	0.78	0.68
	23	Pharmaceuticals, Life Sciences	6.17	3.82
Financials	24	Banks	10.52	10.83
	25	Diversified Financials	5.63	5.06
	26	Insurance	4.61	4.14
	27	Real Estate	2.08	3.07
Information Technology	28	Internet Software & Services	0.62	0.74
	29	IT Services, Software	3.24	2.56
	30	Communications Equipment	2.46	1.41
	31	Computers, Electronics	3.69	2.81
	32	Semiconductors	2.47	1.52
Telecom	33	Telecommunication Services	7.11	5.84
Utilities	34	Utilities	4.31	5.08

Weights are computed within the GEM2 estimation universe using total market capitalization. Average weights are computed from January 1997 to January 2008.

have end-of-period weights less than 100 bps, and these tend to be highly volatile, thus making them useful risk factors.

Investment style represents another important source of systematic risk. Style factors are designed to capture these sources of risk. They are constructed from financially intuitive stock attributes called *descriptors*, which serve as effective predictors of equity return covariance. Since the descriptors within a particular style factor are meant to capture the same underlying driver of returns, these descriptors tend to be strongly collinear. For instance, price-to-book ratio, dividend yield, and earnings yield are all attributes used to identify value stocks, and they tend to exhibit significant cross-sectional correlation. Although these descriptors have high explanatory power on their own, naively including them as separate factors in the model may lead to serious multicollinearity problems. Combining these descriptors into a single style factor overcomes this difficulty, and also leads to a more parsimonious factor structure.

Unlike country and industry factors, which are assigned exposures of either 0 or 1, style factor exposures are continuously distributed. To facilitate comparison across style factors, they are standardized to have a mean of 0 and a standard deviation of 1. Each descriptor is also standardized similarly. That is, if d_{nl}^{Raw} is the raw value of stock n for descriptor l, then the standardized descriptor value is given by

$$d_{nl} = \frac{d_{nl}^{\text{Raw}} - \mu_l}{\sigma_l}, \tag{25.2}$$

where μ_l is the cap-weighted mean of the descriptor (within the estimation universe), and σ_l is the equal-weighted standard deviation. The convention of standardizing using the cap-weighted mean is adopted so that a well-diversified cap-weighted portfolio, such as MSCI ACWI IMI, has approximately zero exposure to all style factors. For the standard deviation, however, the equal-weighted mean is used to prevent large-cap stocks from having an undue influence on the overall scale of the exposures.

Formally, descriptors are combined into style factors as follows:

$$X_{nk} = \sum_{l \in k} w_l d_{nl}, \tag{25.3}$$

where w_l is the descriptor weight, and the sum takes place over all descriptors within a particular risk index. Descriptor weights are determined using an optimization algorithm to maximize the explanatory power of the model. Style factor exposures are rescaled to have a standard deviation of 1.

Some of the style factors are standardized on a *global-relative* basis, others on a *country-relative* basis. In the former case, the mean and standard deviation in Equation 25.2 are computed using the entire global cross section. In the latter case, the factors have mean 0 and standard deviation 1 within each country. When deciding which standardization convention to adopt, both the intuitive meaning of the factor and its explanatory power are considered.

GEM2 uses eight style factors. Specific details on the individual descriptors comprising each style factor can be found in Menchero *et al.* (2010). Below, a qualitative description of each of the style factors is provided:

(1) The *Volatility* factor is typically the most significant style factor. In essence, it captures market risk that cannot be explained by the World factor. The most important descriptor within the Volatility index is historical beta relative to the World portfolio (as proxied by the estimation universe). To better understand this factor, consider a fully invested long-only portfolio that is strongly tilted toward high-beta stocks. Intuitively, this portfolio has greater market risk than a portfolio with beta equal to one. This additional market risk is captured through positive exposure to the Volatility factor. Note that the time-series correlation between the World factor and the Volatility factor is typically very high, so that these two sources of risk add coherently in this example. If, by contrast, the portfolio is invested in low-beta stocks, then the risk from the Volatility and the World factors is partially canceled, as intuitively expected. The Volatility factor on a global-relative basis is standardized. As a result, the mean exposure to Volatility within a country can deviate significantly from zero. This standardization convention is a natural one for a global model, as most investors regard stocks in highly volatile markets as having more exposure to the factor than those in low-volatility markets. This view is reflected in the data, as it is found that the explanatory power of the factor is greater using the global-relative standardization.

(2) The *Momentum* factor often ranks second in significance after Volatility. Momentum differentiates stocks based on recent relative performance. Descriptors within Momentum include historical alpha from a 104-week regression and relative strength (over trailing 6 and 12 months) with a one-month lag. As with Volatility, Momentum is standardized on a global-relative basis. This is also an intuitive convention for a global model. From the perspective of a global investor, a stock that strongly outperforms the World portfolio is likely to be considered a positive momentum stock, even if it slightly underperforms its country peers. The empirical results support this view, as the

Momentum factor standardized globally has greater explanatory power than one standardized on a country-relative basis.

(3) The *Size* factor represents another well-known source of return covariance. It captures the effect of large-cap stocks moving differently from small-cap stocks. Size is measured by a single descriptor: log of market capitalization. The explanatory power of the model is quite similar whether Size is standardized globally or on a country-by-country basis. The country-relative standardization is adopted, however, since it is more intuitive and consistent with investors' perception of the markets. For instance, major global equity indices, such as the MSCI Global Investable Market Indices, segment each country according to size, with the largest stocks inside each country always being classified as large-cap stocks. Moreover, standardizing the Size factor on a global-relative basis would serve as an unintended proxy for developed markets versus emerging markets, and increases collinearity with the country factors.

(4) The *Value* factor describes a major investment style which seeks to identify stocks that are priced low relative to fundamentals. Value is standardized on a country-relative basis. This again is consistent with the way major indices segment each market, with each country divided roughly equally into value and growth subindices. This convention also circumvents the difficulty of comparing fundamental data across countries with different accounting standards. GEM2 utilizes official MSCI data items for Value factor descriptors, as described in the *MSCI Barra Fundamental Data Methodology* handbook (2008).

(5) *Growth* differentiates stocks based on their prospects for sales or earnings growth. It is standardized on a country-relative basis, consistent with the construction of the MSCI Value and Growth Indices. Therefore, each country has approximately half the weight in stocks with positive Growth exposure, and half with negative exposure. The GEM2 Growth descriptors also utilize official MSCI data items, as described in the *MSCI Barra Fundamental Data Methodology* handbook.

(6) The *Nonlinear Size* (NLS) factor captures nonlinearities in the payoff to size exposure across the market-cap spectrum. NLS is based on a single raw descriptor: the cube of the log of market capitalization. Since this raw descriptor is highly collinear with Size, it is orthogonalized to the Size factor. This procedure does not affect the fit of the model, but does mitigate the confounding effects of collinearity, and thus preserves an intuitive meaning for the Size factor. The NLS factor is represented

by a portfolio that goes long mid-cap stocks, and shorts large-cap and small-cap stocks.

(7) The *Liquidity* factor describes return patterns to stocks based on relative trading activity. Stocks with high turnover have positive exposure to Liquidity, whereas low-turnover stocks have negative exposure. Liquidity is standardized on a country-relative basis.

(8) *Leverage* captures the return difference between high-leverage and low-leverage stocks. The descriptors within Leverage include market leverage, book leverage, and debt-to-assets ratio. This factor is standardized on a country-relative basis.

It is also important to understand the sources of collinearity among factors. One way to measure collinearity is through the cross-sectional correlation of factor exposures. In Table 25.3, we present the average

Table 25.3. Regression-Weighted Cross-sectional Correlation of Style and Industry Factor Exposures.

Factor	Volatility	Momentum	Size	Value	Growth	NL Size	Liquidity	Leverage
Volatility	1.00	−0.05	−0.09	−0.25	0.27	−0.06	0.42	−0.07
Momentum	−0.05	1.00	0.12	−0.17	0.08	0.15	0.09	−0.08
Size	−0.09	0.12	1.00	−0.11	−0.05	0.11	0.10	−0.03
Value	−0.25	−0.17	−0.11	1.00	−0.24	−0.03	−0.15	0.22
Growth	0.27	0.08	−0.05	−0.24	1.00	−0.02	0.18	−0.17
Non-linear Size	−0.06	0.15	0.11	−0.03	−0.02	1.00	0.11	0.01
Liquidity	0.42	0.09	0.10	−0.15	0.18	0.11	1.00	−0.03
Leverage	−0.07	−0.08	−0.03	0.22	−0.17	0.01	−0.03	1.00
Energy Equipment & Services	0.06	0.02	−0.03	−0.02	0.06	0.02	0.07	−0.03
Oil, Gas & Consumable Fuels	−0.02	0.02	0.11	0.06	−0.03	−0.04	0.00	−0.01
Oil & Gas Exploration & Production	0.01	0.02	−0.01	0.01	0.00	0.00	0.02	0.01
Chemicals	−0.03	0.00	−0.01	0.04	−0.04	0.03	−0.01	0.00
Construction, Containers, Paper	−0.04	−0.01	−0.02	0.07	−0.06	0.04	−0.04	0.06
Aluminum, Diversified Metals	0.03	0.02	0.02	0.03	0.00	0.01	0.03	0.00

(Continued)

Table 25.3. (*Continued*)

Factor	Volatility	Momentum	Size	Value	Growth	NL Size	Liquidity	Leverage
Gold, Precious Metals	0.00	−0.01	0.00	−0.06	0.00	0.00	−0.01	−0.04
Steel	0.04	0.02	−0.01	0.09	−0.02	0.01	0.03	0.03
Capital Goods	0.01	0.01	−0.07	0.04	−0.02	0.01	0.00	−0.01
Commercial & Professional Services	0.01	0.00	−0.09	−0.05	0.06	−0.01	−0.02	−0.03
Transportation Non-Airline	−0.06	0.01	0.00	0.02	−0.02	0.02	−0.04	0.08
Airlines	0.02	−0.02	0.01	0.02	−0.01	0.02	0.02	0.08
Automobiles & Components	0.01	0.00	0.01	0.10	−0.02	0.00	−0.01	0.00
Consumer Durables & Apparel	0.01	−0.01	−0.07	0.05	0.00	0.00	0.03	−0.06
Consumer Services	−0.02	0.00	−0.06	−0.03	0.04	0.02	0.01	0.02
Media	−0.01	−0.03	0.01	−0.12	0.02	0.02	−0.03	0.00
Retailing	0.03	0.01	−0.05	−0.01	0.05	0.01	0.04	−0.06
Food & Staples Retailing	−0.07	−0.01	0.02	−0.02	0.00	0.01	−0.03	−0.01
Food, Beverage & Tobacco	−0.14	0.00	0.02	−0.01	−0.05	0.02	−0.07	−0.01
Household & Personal Products	−0.05	0.00	0.03	−0.04	−0.02	−0.01	−0.03	−0.03
Health Care Equipment & Services	−0.02	0.02	−0.06	−0.08	0.09	0.01	0.04	−0.05
Biotechnology	0.09	0.00	−0.05	−0.17	0.07	−0.03	0.07	−0.05
Pharmaceuticals, Life Sciences	−0.04	0.00	0.06	−0.10	0.02	−0.04	0.00	−0.10
Banks	−0.08	0.00	0.12	0.12	−0.09	−0.05	−0.10	0.10
Diversified Financials	0.05	0.00	0.02	0.04	0.01	0.01	−0.03	0.04
Insurance	−0.06	0.00	0.04	0.11	−0.05	0.03	−0.06	−0.10
Real Estate	−0.13	0.02	−0.09	0.07	−0.08	0.03	−0.07	0.17
Internet Software & Services	0.15	−0.02	−0.04	−0.12	0.12	−0.03	0.07	−0.06
IT Services, Software	0.15	−0.01	−0.06	−0.14	0.12	−0.02	0.09	−0.12
Communications Equipment	0.16	−0.02	−0.01	−0.09	0.06	−0.03	0.08	−0.07

(*Continued*)

Table 25.3. (*Continued*)

Factor	Volatility	Momentum	Size	Value	Growth	NL Size	Liquidity	Leverage
Computers, Electronics	0.11	−0.02	−0.02	−0.05	0.04	−0.03	0.09	−0.09
Semiconductors	0.21	−0.02	0.00	−0.10	0.09	−0.02	0.16	−0.08
Telecommunication Services	0.04	−0.02	0.15	−0.07	0.01	−0.07	0.01	0.05
Utilities	−0.17	0.01	0.06	0.11	−0.13	0.04	−0.07	0.20

Results are averages over the period from January 1997 to June 2008. Correlations above 0.10 in absolute value are shaded in gray.

pair-wise cross-sectional correlations among styles as well as between styles and industries. The highest collinearities are generally among style factors. For instance, stocks with positive exposure to Value tend to have negative exposure to Volatility, Momentum, and Growth. Similarly, stocks with positive exposure to Volatility (i.e., high beta) tend to have negative exposure to Value, and positive exposure to Growth and Liquidity.

While collinearities may be strongest among style factors, industries can also exhibit significant cross-sectional correlation. This is especially true of the Financials, Information Technology, and Utilities sectors. Over the period from January 1997 to June 2008, Information Technology stocks tended to have positive exposure to Volatility and Growth, and negative exposure to Value and Leverage; for Financials and Utilities, the opposite holds. It should be beared in mind that the results in Table 25.3 represent averages over multiple years, and that these relationships may change over time. For instance, during the financial crisis of 2008/2009, Financial stocks tended to have a large positive exposure to Volatility and a large negative exposure to Momentum.

25.2. Factor Portfolios

25.2.1. *Simple Factor Portfolios*

Simple factor portfolios are formed from a univariate regression of local excess returns,

$$r_n = f_w^s + X_{ns} f_s^s + u_n^s, \tag{25.4}$$

where the intercept term f_w^s is the return to the simple World factor, f_s^s is the return to the simple style factor, and u_n^s is the residual. The GEM2 model uses square root of market cap for the regression weights. This is appropriate for risk model construction since to a good approximation it minimizes sampling error. In this chapter, however, the objective is to study the performance of long/short investment strategies. For this purpose, it is more appropriate to focus on large-cap stocks which are more easily shorted than relatively illiquid small-cap stocks. Therefore, market-cap weights w_n are used in the regression.

As discussed by Menchero (2010), with style factor exposures standardized to be cap-weighted mean 0 and standard deviation 1, the World factor return is given by

$$f_w^s = \sum_n w_n r_n, \tag{25.5}$$

which is simply the cap-weighted return (currency hedged) of the World portfolio. The simple style factor returns are given by

$$f_s^s = \sum_n (w_n X_{ns}) r_n, \tag{25.6}$$

which represents the return of a factor-replicating portfolio that goes long stocks with positive exposure to the factor, and shorts stocks with negative exposure. The weights are also proportional to the market cap, so that the portfolio is dominated by large-cap stocks.

The simple factor portfolio described in Equation (25.6) has unit exposure to the desired style factor. As seen in Table 25.3, however, collinearity may cause these portfolios to have significant exposures to other factors as well.

25.2.2. *Pure Factor Portfolios*

Pure factor returns f_k^p are estimated by cross-sectional regression of local excess returns against *all* the factors,

$$r_n = \sum_k X_{nk} f_k^p + u_n^p. \tag{25.7}$$

The index k runs over the World factor, countries, industries, and styles. Again, although the GEM2 risk model uses square root of market cap for the regression weights, in this study market cap weights for the regression is employed.

Every stock has unit exposure to the World factor, and exposure of 0 or 1 to countries and industries. As a result, the sum of all country factor exposures X_{nc} equals the World factor exposure, and similarly for industries, i.e.,

$$\sum_c X_{nc} = 1, \quad \text{and} \quad \sum_i X_{ni} = 1, \tag{25.8}$$

for all stocks n. The GEM2 factor structure, therefore, exhibits exact two-fold collinearity. Constraints must be applied to obtain a unique solution.

We adopt constraints as in Heston and Rouwenhorst (1994) that require the cap-weighted country and industry factor returns to sum to zero,

$$\sum_c W_c f_c^p = 0, \quad \text{and} \quad \sum_i W_i f_i^p = 0, \tag{25.9}$$

where W_c is the cap weight of the estimation universe in country c, and W_i is the corresponding weight in industry i. These constraints remove the exact collinearities from the factor exposure matrix, without reducing the explanatory power of the model.

A more precise interpretation to the factors can be provided now. Consider the cap-weighted world portfolio, with asset weights w_n. The currency-hedged return of this portfolio R_w can be attributed using the GEM2 factors,

$$R_w = f_w^p + \sum_c W_c f_c^p + \sum_i W_i f_i^p + \sum_s X_s^w f_s^p + \sum_n w_n u_n^p. \tag{25.10}$$

The first two sums in Equation (25.10) are equal to zero by virtue of the constraints of Equation (25.9). The third sum is zero since the style factors are standardized to be cap-weighted mean zero for the world portfolio; i.e., $X_s^w = 0$, for all styles s. The final sum in Equation (25.10) is the cap-weighted specific return of the estimation universe, which is equal to zero by virtue of using cap-weights in the regression. Therefore,

$$R_w = f_w^p, \tag{25.11}$$

which means that the return of the pure World factor is exactly the cap-weighted return of the world portfolio. That is, for this regression setting, the simple and pure World factors are identical.

The pure style factor returns can be written as

$$f_s^p = \sum_n \Omega_{ns}^p r_n, \tag{25.12}$$

where Ω_{ns}^p is the weight of stock n in pure factor portfolio s. The pure factor portfolio has unit exposure to the particular style, but zero exposure to all other factors. This implies, for example, that the pure style factor portfolio has net zero weight in every industry and every country. For a more extensive discussion of pure factor portfolios, see Menchero (2010).

25.2.3. *Optimized Factor Portfolios*

Simple factor portfolios have unit exposure to the particular factor, and nonzero exposure to other factors. Pure factor portfolios have unit exposure to the particular factor, and zero exposure to all other factors. There is another important factor portfolio to consider. This is given by the minimum risk portfolio with unit exposure to the factor.

The solution, as shown by Grinold and Kahn (2000), is given by

$$\Omega_{ns}^{o} = \left(\sum_{m} V_{mn}^{-1} X_{ms}\right)\left(\sum_{mn} X_{ns} V_{mn}^{-1} X_{ms}\right)^{-1}, \tag{25.13}$$

where V_{mn}^{-1} is the element (between stocks m and n) of the inverse asset covariance matrix. The intuition behind optimized factor portfolios is straightforward: the portfolio maintains unit exposure to the particular factor but reduces the risk by acquiring exposures to other factors.

It is worth pointing out that, unlike the case for simple and pure factor portfolios, the weights in the optimal portfolio are not computed by regression. Instead, they depend only on the factor exposures and the asset covariance matrix through Equation (25.13). In this study, the asset covariance matrix is taken from the short-horizon version (GEM2S) of the GEM2 model, as described by Menchero *et al.* (2010).

25.3. Results

25.3.1. *Cumulative Factor Returns*

In Fig. 25.1, cumulative performance (represented by index levels) for the World factor is shown. As noted previously, the simple and pure World factor returns are identical, given by the cap-weighted return (currency hedged) of the world portfolio. Figure 25.1 clearly illustrates the main market features over the last 13 years. The strong bull market is observed from 1997 to 2000, followed by the sharp downturn with the collapse of the internet bubble. In 2003, a market recovery begins, lasting until the onset of the financial crisis in late 2007. From November 2007 to March 2009, however, the global equity market plunged by more than 50%. Since then,

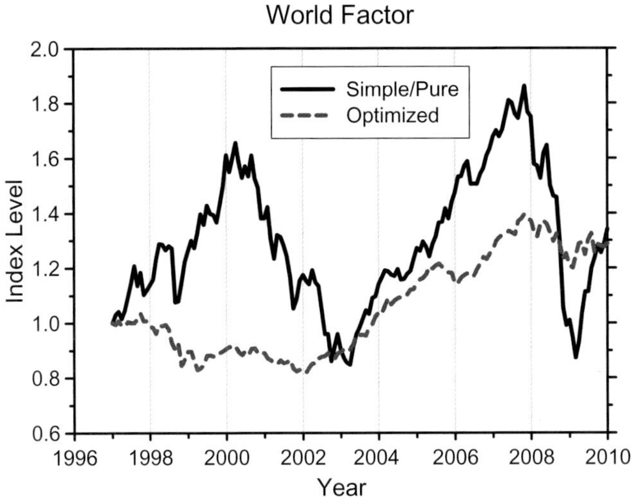

Fig. 25.1. Cumulative Performance of World Factor.

there has been a modest recovery, although the market remains well below its former peak.

The optimized World factor represents the minimum-risk fully invested portfolio. From 1997 to 2002, the factor portfolio declines slightly, but is largely insensitive to both the bull and the bear market. From 2003 to 2008, however, the factor strongly participates in the market rally. Later, when the performance of the Volatility factor is considered, additional insight is gained into the behavior of the optimized world portfolio.

In Fig. 25.2, cumulative performance for the Value factor is presented. Simple Value performed very poorly up to the collapse of the internet bubble. Pure Value, by contrast, was essentially flat during this same period. This shows that the poor performance of simple Value was explained mostly by incidental exposures to other factors (e.g., industries), and was not driven by the pure effect. Similarly, during the financial crisis of 2008, simple Value declined much more sharply than pure Value. Over the 13-year period, all three Value strategies performed well and trended strongly upward. However, the pure and optimized strategies exhibited considerably lower volatility.

In Fig. 25.3, performance results for the Momentum factor is presented. The simple and optimized Momentum strategies have similar cumulative returns over the 13-year period, although the optimized approach

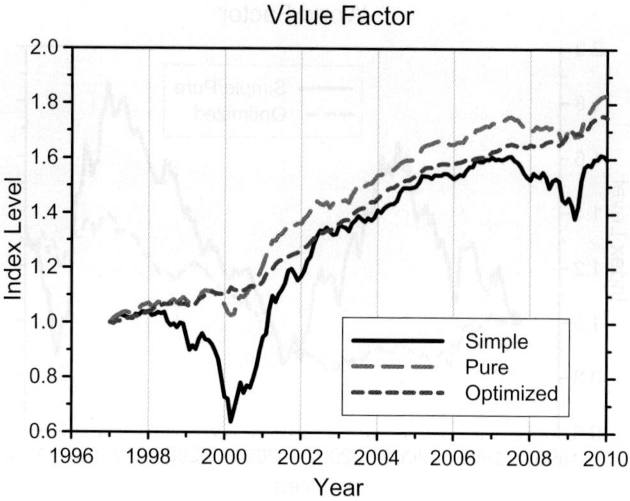

Fig. 25.2. Cumulative Performance of Value Factor.

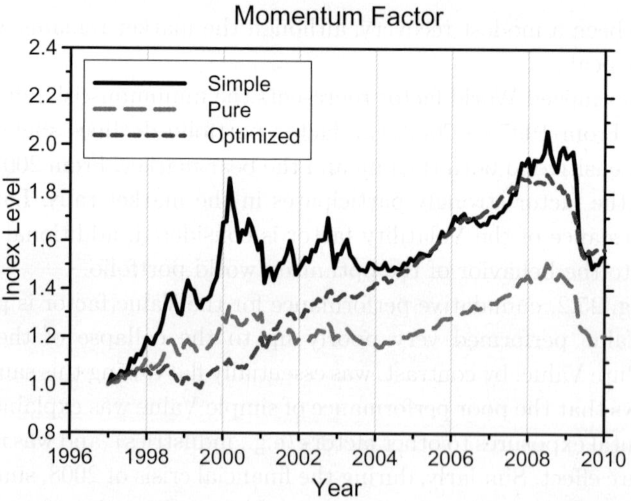

Fig. 25.3. Cumulative Performance of Momentum Factor.

achieves this with considerably lower volatility. All three strategies perform extremely poor during the financial crisis of 2008/2009.

In Fig. 25.4, the performance of the Size factor portfolios is plotted. From 1997 to 2000, the simple Size factor had strong positive returns,

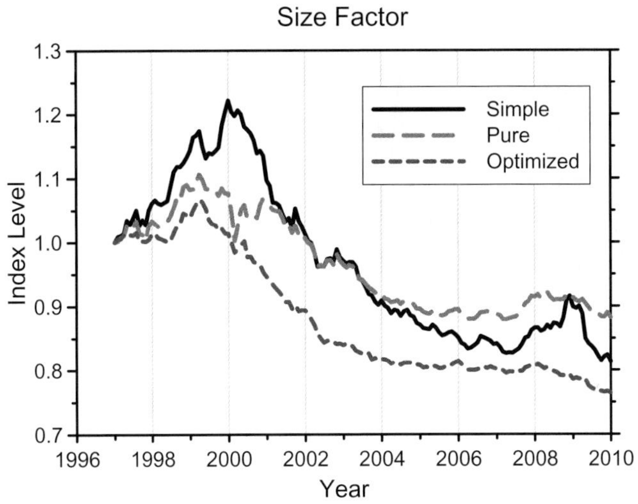

Fig. 25.4. Cumulative Performance of Size Factor.

indicating large-cap stocks outperformed small-caps during this period. The collapse of the internet bubble, however, ushered in a long era of large-cap underperformance. A notable exception to this occurred in late 2008, which may reflect a flight-to-quality effect during the financial crisis. Over the entire sample period, the optimized Size factor declined by the greatest amount, and did so with the least volatility. It is worth pointing out once again that the Size factor is defined so that large stocks have positive exposure. To describe a *small-firm* effect, therefore, the signs on the exposures must be reversed. This inverts the plots in Fig. 25.4, leading to an *upward* trend consistent with a small-cap premium.

In Fig. 25.5, cumulative performance for the Volatility factor portfolios is displayed. The simple factor spikes up in late 1999 and early 2000, but then plummets over the next several years. From 2004 to 2008, the simple factor remains largely flat, but then declines sharply during the financial crisis of 2008 before again recovering with the market rally in early 2009. The pure Volatility factor behaves qualitatively quite similar to the simple factor over the 13-year period considered in this paper. The optimized Volatility factor, on the other hand, is essentially flat over the entire 13-year sample period.

The behavior of the pure Volatility factor helps explain the performance of the optimized World factor portfolio in Fig. 25.1. To a good

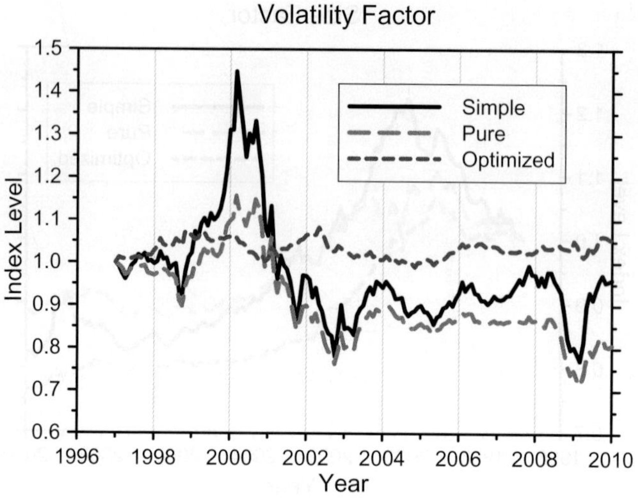

Fig. 25.5. Cumulative Performance of Volatility Factor.

approximation, the optimized World factor is long the pure World factor and short the pure Volatility factor (which acts as a risk-reducing hedge). During the internet bubble, the optimized World factor was helped on the long side by the pure World factor but this was offset by the strong performance of the pure Volatility factor on the short side. Following the collapse of the internet bubble (2000–2002), the poor performance of the long side was again offset by the poor performance of the pure Volatility factor on the short side. As a result, the optimized World factor remained essentially flat from 1997 to 2002. From 2004 to 2008, however, the pure Volatility factor moves sideways, while the pure World factor moves up sharply, which lead to a strong upward trend for the optimized World factor.

Another interesting observation from Fig. 25.5 is that, although the simple and pure Volatility factor portfolios are both down over the 13-year period, the World factor was *up* over the same period. Since the Volatility factor portfolios have high beta, the CAPM predicts that these portfolios would have performed well over the period, contrary to the finding. The results are consistent with Fama and French (1992), who observeed that high beta stocks do not outperform low beta stocks.

In Fig. 25.6, the performance of the Growth factors is presented. In 1999 and early 2000, the simple Growth factor performed extremely

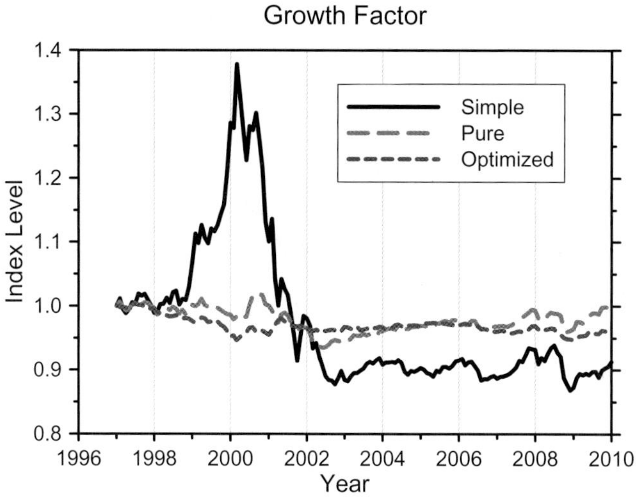

Fig. 25.6. Cumulative Performance of Growth Factor.

well. However, it plummeted following the collapse of the internet bubble. Interestingly, the pure and optimized Growth factors have remained largely flat over the entire period. This clearly shows that the dramatic rise and collapse of the simple Growth strategy was driven primarily by incidental exposures to other factors (e.g., industries), and not by pure Growth.

In Fig. 25.7 the performance of the NLS factor is plotted. Interestingly, the simple NLS factor is nearly the mirror image of the simple Size factor shown in Fig. 25.4. In the simple Size factor portfolio, large-caps have positive weight and mid-caps have negative weight. For the NLS factor, however, the opposite holds. The pure and optimized NLS portfolios are largely flat over the 13-year period.

The Liquidity factor is presented in Fig. 25.8. The simple Liquidity factor behaves qualitatively similar to the simple Volatility factor in Fig. 25.5. This is not too surprising, given that the two factors have high cross-sectional correlation (0.42), as indicated in Table 25.3. An important distinction between the two, however, is that the simple Liquidity factor has a positive return over the sample period, in contrast to the Volatility factor. Over the 13-year period, the pure Liquidity factor has earned roughly the same cumulative return as the simple Liquidity factor, although with considerably lower volatility.

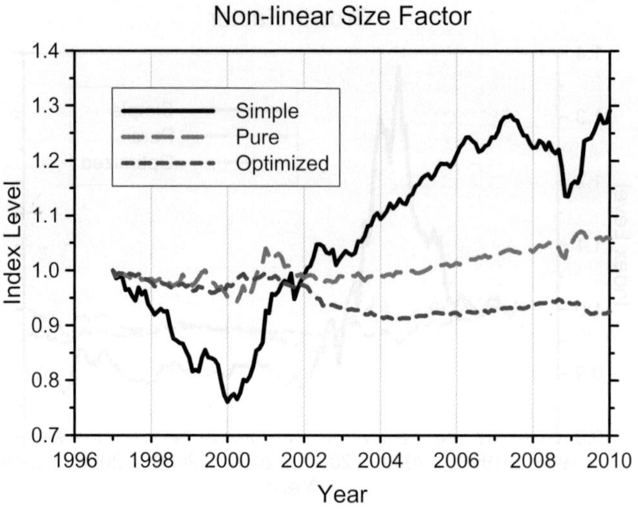

Fig. 25.7. Cumulative Performance of NLS Factor.

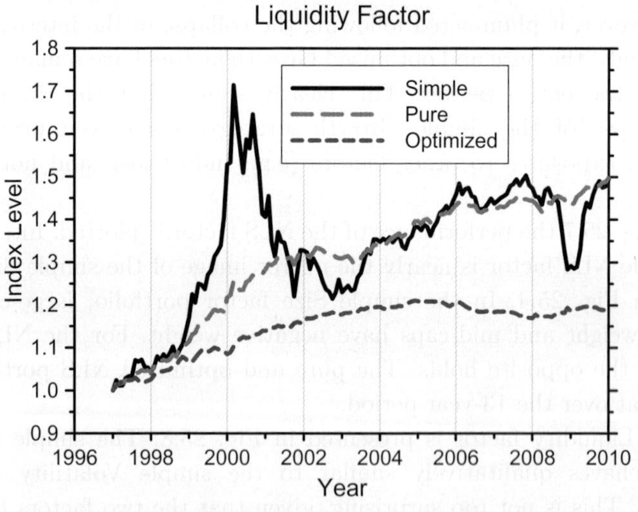

Fig. 25.8. Cumulative Performance of Liquidity Factor.

In Fig. 25.9, cumulative performance for the Leverage factor is presented. The simple factor performed very poorly during the internet bubble, but then recovered and performed strongly from 2000 to 2007. The simple factor again plummeted in 2007 and 2008, before staging a partial comeback

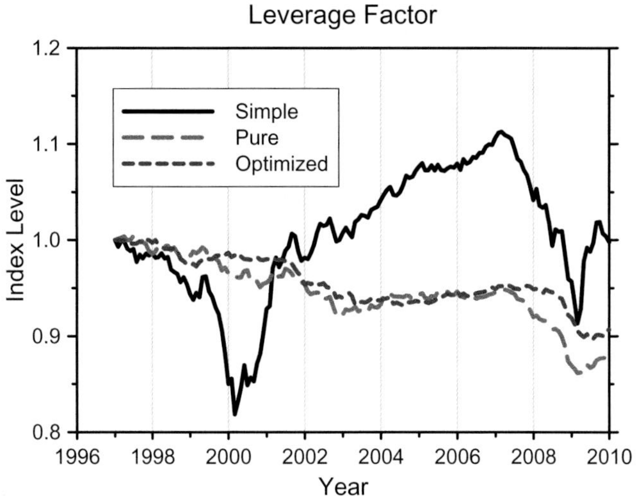

Fig. 25.9. Cumulative Performance of Leverage Factor.

in 2009. The pure and optimized Leverage factor portfolios generally had a downward drift, and both performed, especially, poorly during the financial crisis of 2008.

It is also interesting to compare the behavior of the simple factor portfolios across style factors. Every style factor showed a sharp turning point at the peak of the internet bubble. Value, NLS, and Leverage factors hit bottom at this point, and then strongly rebounded; the other five style factors peaked before subsequently collapsing. During the financial crisis of 2008/2009, many simple style factors also experienced strong signatures. For instance, Value, Volatility, Liquidity and Leverage seemed to move with the market, whereas simple Momentum and Size seemed to move against it.

25.3.2. *Summary Statistics*

In Table 25.4, the annualized return, risk, and information ratio (*IR*) for all factor portfolios considered in this study are presented. The annualized return is computed as the geometric mean over the 13-year period. The annualized risk is given by the standard deviation of realized monthly returns, multiplied by $\sqrt{12}$. The *IR* is obtained as the ratio of the annualized return to annualized risk.

To convert the *IR* to a t-statistic, it is multiplied by the square root of the number of years in the sample ($\sqrt{13}$). *IR*s above 0.55 in absolute terms

Table 25.4. Factor Returns, Volatilities, and *IR*s, January 1997 to December 2009.

Factor Portfolio	Annualized Return	Annualized Risk	Information Ratio
Simple World	2.27%	16.11%	0.14
Pure World	2.27%	16.11%	0.14
Optimized World	1.96%	6.85%	0.29
Simple Value	3.64%	8.98%	0.41
Pure Value	4.73%	3.37%	1.40
Optimized Value	4.37%	1.69%	2.59
Simple Momentum	3.35%	10.60%	0.32
Pure Momentum	1.46%	6.11%	0.24
Optimized Momentum	3.49%	4.70%	0.74
Simple Volatility	−0.31%	11.50%	−0.03
Pure Volatility	−1.62%	7.97%	−0.20
Optimized Volatility	0.40%	2.96%	0.14
Simple Size	−1.57%	3.87%	−0.41
Pure Size	−0.95%	3.07%	−0.31
Optimized Size	−2.03%	2.01%	−1.01
Simple Growth	−0.70%	6.90%	−0.10
Pure Growth	0.01%	1.91%	0.01
Optimized Growth	−0.31%	1.07%	−0.29
Simple Non-linear Size	1.97%	5.26%	0.38
Pure Non-linear Size	0.43%	2.38%	0.18
Optimized Non-linear Size	−0.59%	1.38%	−0.43
Simple Liquidity	3.13%	8.47%	0.37
Pure Liquidity	3.14%	2.23%	1.40
Optimized Liquidity	1.35%	1.33%	1.01
Simple Leverage	−0.02%	4.29%	0.00
Pure Leverage	−1.03%	1.45%	−0.71
Optimized Leverage	−0.75%	1.03%	−0.72

Note: Statistically significant *IR*s are highlighted in gray.

are considered significant at the 95% confidence level, and are highlighted in gray in Table 25.4.

The simple and pure World factor, both represented by the cap-weighted world portfolio, had an annualized return of 2.27% and a risk of 16.11%. This gives an *IR* of 0.14, which is not statistically significant. Clearly, the presence of two bear markets during the sample period adversely impacted performance. The optimized World factor returned slightly less (1.96%), but with much lower volatility (6.85%), leading to an *IR* of 0.29.

For the style factors, there are several interesting observations. In all cases, the simple factor portfolios were more volatile than the pure factor portfolios. This is not too surprising, since the simple factors are exposed to industries and other styles, which tends to increase risk. It is interesting, however, to compare the relative volatilities of the simple and pure factors. For factors such as Size and Volatility, the pure factors were nearly as volatile as the simple factors. For these factors, the simple factor is expected to be driven primarily by the pure factor, and the two factors should track each other quite well. This view is consistent with Figs. 25.4 and 25.5. For other factors, such as Growth, Liquidity, or Leverage, the volatility of the pure factor is small compared to the simple factor. In this case, the simple and pure factors is expected to track poorly, as observed in Figs. 25.6, 25.8, and 25.9.

It is also interesting to observe in Table 25.4 that the optimized factor portfolios in all cases have had lower volatility than the pure factor portfolios. Since these are out-of-sample realized volatilities, it indicates that the risk model was successful in identifying and exploiting risk-reducing hedges.

Another notable result is that none of the simple style factors had statistically significant *IR*s over the sample period. This was not necessarily due to low returns, but rather because of high risk. For instance, the simple, pure and optimized Value strategies all exhibited comparable returns, but the volatility of the simple factor strategy was far higher.

Three of the pure factor strategies (Value, Liquidity, and Leverage) had statistically significant *IR*s. For the optimized style factors, five were statistically significant. For Value, Momentum, and Size, the optimized *IR* was much higher than the pure *IR*. Value performed best on a risk-adjusted basis, with an *IR* of 2.59.

In Table 25.5, the time-series correlations between the simple, pure, and optimized factor portfolios, as well as with the cap-weighted world portfolio are reported. Correlation coefficients are measured over the 13-year period spanning from 1997 to 2010. Correlations between simple and pure factor portfolios were generally high, ranging from 0.47 for NLS to 0.94 for Volatility. Correlations between the optimized and pure factors were generally lower, ranging from 0.27 for Liquidity to 0.70 for Momentum.

It is also interesting to consider correlations between the style factors and the World factor. For the simple factor portfolios, the highest correlations were for Volatility (0.79) and Liquidity (0.68). The pure

Table 25.5. Time-Series Correlations, January 1997 to December 2009.

Factor Portfolio	Simple	Pure	Optimized	World
Simple World	1.00	1.00	0.25	1.00
Pure World	1.00	1.00	0.25	1.00
Optimized World	0.25	0.25	1.00	0.25
Simple Value	1.00	0.67	0.10	−0.15
Pure Value	0.67	1.00	0.38	0.11
Optimized Value	0.10	0.38	1.00	0.12
Simple Momentum	1.00	0.90	0.63	−0.15
Pure Momentum	0.90	1.00	0.70	−0.18
Optimized Momentum	0.63	0.70	1.00	−0.06
Simple Volatility	1.00	0.94	0.38	0.79
Pure Volatility	0.94	1.00	0.41	0.79
Optimized Volatility	0.38	0.41	1.00	0.31
Simple Size	1.00	0.61	0.47	−0.17
Pure Size	0.61	1.00	0.68	−0.06
Optimized Size	0.47	0.68	1.00	−0.02
Simple Growth	1.00	0.53	−0.15	0.54
Pure Growth	0.53	1.00	0.30	0.35
Optimized Growth	−0.15	0.30	1.00	−0.04
Simple Non-linear Size	1.00	0.47	0.15	0.12
Pure Non-linear Size	0.47	1.00	0.46	−0.06
Optimized Non-linear Size	0.15	0.46	1.00	−0.07
Simple Liquidity	1.00	0.69	−0.02	0.68
Pure Liquidity	0.69	1.00	0.27	0.40
Optimized Liquidity	−0.02	0.27	1.00	−0.08
Simple Leverage	1.00	0.51	0.16	0.00
Pure Leverage	0.51	1.00	0.39	0.28
Optimized Leverage	0.16	0.39	1.00	0.17

Volatility factor retained the high correlation (0.79), but the pure Liquidity factor was considerably less correlated (0.40). Pure Growth and pure Leverage were also strongly correlated with the World factor, whereas pure Momentum was negatively correlated.

25.4. Leading Economic Indicators and Barra Factor Returns

Economic indicators are descriptive and anticipatory time-series data used to analyze and forecast changing business conditions. Cyclical indicators are comprehensive series that are systemically related to the business cycle.

Business cycles are recurrent sequences of expansions and contractions in aggregate economic activity. Coincident indicators have cyclical movements that approximately correspond with the overall business cycle expansions and contractions. Lagging indicators reach their turning points after the corresponding turns in the business cycle. Leading indicators, by contrast, reach their turning points before the corresponding business cycle turns.

An important aspect of financial decision making may depend on the forecasting effectiveness of the composite index of leading economic indicators, or LEI. As described in The Conference Board Handbook (2001), the LEI is made up of a weighted average of several components, such as yield spread, stock index levels, and money supply (M2), among others.

An interesting question to investigate is whether there exist relationships between the LEI and the GEM2 factor returns. If such relationships were economically grounded and statistically significant, they could be potentially exploited as investment strategies. For instance, suppose that a rise in the LEI one month could be associated with a rise in a GEM2 factor return three months later. An investor might then profit by taking a long position in the factor whenever the three-month lagged LEI were positive.

For this study, the Euro LEI series published by The Conference Board (TCB) is used. The relationships between the Euro LEI and the GEM2 factor returns are observed. Ideally, LEI data from other economic regions would be included, but here the European data for illustrative purposes is only used.

Let $LEI(t)$ be the LEI level at the end of month t. Generally, these values are published with a one or two-month lag. The "return" to the LEI over month t is then given by

$$L_t = \frac{LEI(t) - LEI(t-1)}{LEI(t-1)}. \tag{25.14}$$

The lagged correlation between the GEM2 factor return and the LEI return is

$$\rho_k^m = \mathrm{corr}(f_{kt}^P, L_{t-m}), \tag{25.15}$$

where f_{kt}^P is the pure return to factor k over period t, and m is the number of lags in months. In Table 25.6, the lagged correlations between the pure GEM2 style factors and the lagged Euro LEI series are reported. The row corresponding to zero lags represents the contemporaneous case. Many of these correlations are quite large, and are generally intuitive. For instance, the contemporaneous correlations between LEI and the Volatility

Table 25.6. Lagged Correlations between Monthly GEM2 Pure Factor Returns and Monthly Percentage Changes in the European LEI Levels.

Lags	Momentum	Volatility	Value	Size	NL Size	Growth	Liquidity	Leverage
0	−0.08	0.40	0.12	−0.17	−0.12	0.06	0.17	0.36
1	0.14	0.03	0.00	−0.17	−0.18	−0.03	0.05	0.23
3	0.08	0.10	0.04	0.04	−0.08	0.03	0.03	0.22
6	0.30	−0.05	−0.13	0.12	0.06	0.03	0.04	−0.02
9	0.13	0.00	−0.05	0.16	0.09	0.08	0.10	−0.01
12	0.03	−0.04	0.01	0.09	0.16	−0.01	0.00	0.20

Analysis period: January 1997 to December 2009.

and Leverage factors are quite strong. This says that when the LEI moves upward, high beta stocks tend to outperform low beta stocks, and high-leverage stocks outperform low-leverage stocks. The Size factor, on the other hand, is negatively correlated, which says that small-cap stocks tend to outperform large-cap stocks when the LEI moves upward.

These contemporaneous relationships, of course, are impossible to exploit as an investment strategy since the LEI information is not available without a time lag. However, using LEI data lagged three months or more certainly does correspond to an implementable investment strategy. The strongest correlation in Table 25.6 for lags of three months or more is for the Momentum factor with a six-month lag. The strong positive correlation suggests a positive relationship between changes in the LEI and corresponding changes in Momentum six months later.

A factor-timing strategy can be devised whose returns are given by

$$R_t = f_{kt}^P \cdot L_{t-m}. \tag{25.16}$$

In other words, the strategy takes long or short positions in the pure factor portfolio depending on the changes in the LEI m months prior.

In Fig. 25.10, the returns to a Momentum timing strategy based on the six-month lagged LEI series are represented. The cumulative performance of the pure Momentum factor, as well as the Euro LEI series are also presented. The Momentum timing returns have been scaled to have the same realized volatility as the pure Momentum factor over the 13-year period. The Momentum timing strategy greatly outperforms the pure Momentum strategy over this sample period, with the former climbing more than 60%, compared to only 20% return for the pure factor.

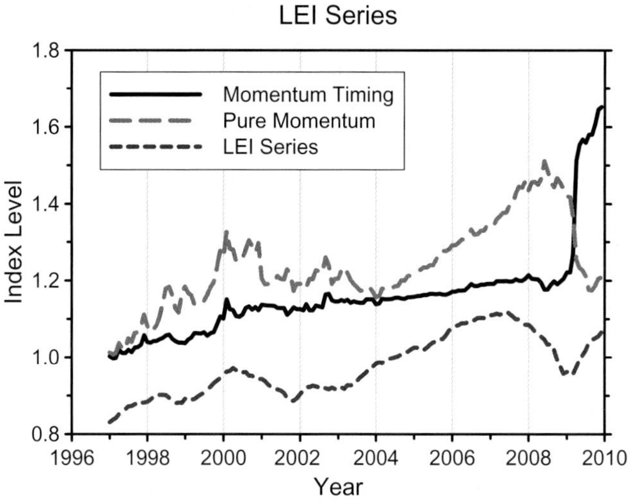

Fig. 25.10. Leading Economic Indicators Index Level, and Cumulative Performance of Pure Momentum Factor and Momentum Timing Strategy.
The LEI Series has been Divided by 100 to be Placed on the Same Scale as the Other Lines.

Two observations are in order when examining the results of the Momentum timing strategy shown in Fig. 25.10. First, the results seem to be dominated by a single observation, April 2009. During that month, the pure Momentum factor return plunged by about 8%. That event coincides exactly six months after the dramatic drop in LEI which occurred in October 2008. It is worth pointing, however, that the *IR* of the Momentum timing strategy actually *increases* if the observation is removed: Even though April 2009 dominated the return of the strategy, it had an even larger impact on the risk.

The second observation is that since the strategy was devised after the fact, one must naturally exercise great caution when interpreting these results. Ideally, there should be an economic or financial basis for explaining the positive correlation between Momentum returns and the six-month lagged LEI series. Of course, even with such an explanation, there is no guarantee that the relationship will continue to hold in the future.

25.5. Summary

The three long/short strategies for capturing equity risk premia were presented. The simple approach goes long stocks with positive exposure, and shorts those with negative exposure. Although this provides the desired exposure to the factor, it also leads to incidental exposures to other factors. This may increase the volatility of the portfolio and potentially be detrimental to the performance.

In the pure approach, the portfolio obtains an exposure of 1 to the desired factor, but has zero exposure to all other factors. This has the benefit of precisely controlling portfolio exposures, but does not explicitly take risk into consideration.

The optimized approach leads to portfolios with unit exposure to the desired factor, while achieving minimum risk. This is accomplished through volatility-reducing hedges to other factors.

The performance of eight style factors and the World factor over a 13-year period was examined. None of the simple strategies achieved a statistically significant *IR* over this period. For the pure style factors, three were statistically significant, versus five for the optimized factors. For Value, Size, and Momentum, the optimized strategies had far higher *IR*s than the pure counterparts.

Finally, an illustrative example of a Momentum "factor timing" strategy that uses lagged LEI values as the input signal was considered. It was found that, on a risk-adjusted basis, the factor timing strategy outperformed the pure Momentum factor over the sample period.

Questions and Problems

1. Discuss three long/short strategies to capture sources of equity premia.
2. Please discuss GEM2 Factor Structure as defined in Equation (25.1) in some detail.
3. Please discuss the relationship among (a) simple factor portfolios (b) pure factor portfolios and (c) optimized factor portfolios.
4. Please discuss leading economic indicators.
5. Please discuss the topics in this chapter related to prior chapters in this text.

Bibliography

Banz, R. "The Relationship between Return and Market Value of Common Stock." *Journal of Financial Economics*, v. 9 (1981), pp. 3–18.

Basu, S. "Investment Performance of Common Stocks in Relation to their Price-Earnings Ratio: A Test of the Efficient Market Hypothesis." *Journal of Finance*, v. 32 (June 1977), pp. 663–682.

The Conference Board LEI for the Euro Area. *Business Cycle Indicators Handbook*. New York: The Conference Board LEI for the Euro Area.

Dimson, E., P. Marsh and M. Staunton. *Triumph of the Optimists*. Princeton, NJ: Princeton University Press, 2002.

Fama, E. and R. French. "The Cross-Section of Expected Stock Returns." *Journal of Finance*, v. 47(2) (1992), pp. 427–465.

Grinold, R. and R. Kahn. *Active Portfolio Management*. New York, NY: McGraw Hill, 2000.

Heston, S. L. and K. G. Rouwenhorst. "Does Industrial Structure Explain the Benefits of International Diversification?" *Journal of Financial Economics*, v. 36 (1994), pp. 3–27.

Jegadeesh, N. and S. Titman. "Returns to Buying Winners and Selling Losers: Implications for Stock Market Efficiency." *Journal of Finance*, v. 48 (1993), pp. 65–92.

Menchero, J. "Characteristics of Factor Portfolios," *MSCI Barra Research* Insight, 2010.

Menchero, J., A. Morozov, and P. Shepard. "Global Equity Risk Modeling," in J. B. Guerard (ed.), *The Handbook of Portfolio Construction: Contemporary Applications of Markowitz Techniques*, pp. 439–480. New York, NY: Springer, 2010.

MSCI Barra Fundamental Data Methodology Handbook, 2008, http://www.msci.com/methodology/meth_docs/MSCI_Sep08_Fundamental_ Data.pdf.

Sharpe, W.F. "Capital Asset Prices: A Theory of Market Equilibrium under Conditions of Risk." *Journal of Finance*, v. 19(3) (September 1964), pp. 425–442.

Chapter 26

Simultaneous Equation Models for Security Valuation

Following Lee *et al.* (2009), either the linear-programming approach or the simultaneous-equation approach can be used to perform security variation. In this chapter, we will consider two models based upon a simultaneous-equation approach to financial planning. The first model we consider in this chapter is the Warren and Shelton (1971) (hereafter, *WS*) model. The other model, that of Francis and Rowell (1978) (hereafter, *FR*), is an expansion of the *WS* model. Both models allow the financial planner/manager to analyze important operating and financial variables. Both models are also computer-based and much less complicated for the user than the Carleton model.

To certify some of the uses of WS type of simultaneous equation models, we will use a case study of Johnson and Johnson. In addition, we have discussed Felthan–Ohlson model for determining equity value. Finally, we have explored the usefulness of integrating WS model and Felthan–Ohlson model to improve the determination of equity value.

26.1. Warren and Shelton Model[1]

A good financial-planning model will have the following characteristics:

(1) The model results and the assumptions should be plausible and/or credible.

[1]The case study of the *WS* model by employing the annual report data of Johnson and Johnson will be presented in Section 26.2 in detail.

(2) The model should be flexible so that it can be adapted and expanded to meet a variety of circumstances.
(3) It should improve on current practice in a technical or performance manner.
(4) The model inputs and outputs should be comprehensible to the user without extensive additional training.
(5) It should take into account the interrelated investments, financing, dividend, and production decisions and their effect on the market value of the firm.
(6) The model should be fairly simple for the user to operate without extensive intervention of nonfinancial personnel and tedious formulation of the input.

With the exception of point (6), Carleton's (1970) model fits this framework. In an effort to improve upon Carleton's model, *WS* devised a simultaneous-equation model. The *WS* model has some similarities to Carleton's model. *WS* do take greater account of the interrelation of the financing, dividend, and investment decisions. They rely upon a sales forecast as a critical input to the model. Unlike Carleton, *WS* explicitly used various operating ratios in their model. Carleton had those ratios in his model implicitly through the manner in which the forecasts were made up. The explicit positioning of the ratios means that the *WS* method is computationally less tedious, and thus its use is more time-efficient.

As can be seen from examining Table 26.1, the *WS* model has four distinct segments corresponding to the sales, investment, financing, and return-to-investment concepts in financial theory. The entire model is a system of 20 equations of a semi-simultaneous nature. The actual solution algorithm is recursive, between and within segments.

Now, we will consider in detail an Excel computer program called FINPLAN, which is used to solve the *WS* model.[2] First, we will consider the inputs to the *WS* model. Second, we will develop into the interaction of the equations in the model. Third, we will look at the inputs to the FINPLAN model.

[2]The original FINPLAN is a financial-forecasting model using FORTRAN computer program based upon Warren and Shelton (1971) simultaneous-equation approach to financial planning. The detailed description of the computer program can be found in Appendix 26B.

Table 26.1. The *WS* Model.

I. Generating of Sales and Earnings Before Interest and Taxes for Period t

(1) $Sales_t = Sales_{t-1} \times (1 + GSALS_t)$

(2) $EBIT_t = REBIT_t \times SALES_t$

II. Generating of Total Assets Required for Period t

(3) $CA_t = RCA_t \times SALES_t$

(4) $FA_t = RFA_t \times SALES_t$

(5) $A_t = CA_t + FA_t$

III. Financing the Desired Level of Assets

(6) $CL_t = RCL_t\, SALES_t$

(7) $NF_t = (A_t - CL_t - PFDSK_t) - (L_{t-1} - LR_t) - S_{t-1} - R_{t-1}$
$-b_t\{(1 - T_t)[EBIT_t - i_{t-1}(L_{t-1} - LR_t)] - PFDIV_t\}$

(8) $NF_t + b_t(1 - T_t)[i_t^e NL_t + U_t^1 NL_t] = NL_t + NS_t$

(9) $L_t = L_{t-1} - LR_t + NL_t$

(10) $S_t = S_{t-1} + NS_t$

(11) $R_i = R_{t-1} + b_t\{(1 - T_t)[EBIT_t - i_t L_t - U_t^1 NL_t] - PFDIV_t\}$

(12) $i_t = i_{t-1}(\frac{L_{t-1} - LR_t}{L_t}) + i_t^e \frac{NL_t}{L_t}$

(13) $\frac{L_t}{S_t + R_t} = K_t$

IV. Generation of Per Share Data for Period t

(14) $EAFCD_t = (1 - T_t)[EBIT_t - i_t L_t - U_t^1 NL_t] - PFDIV_t$

(15) $CMDIV_t = (1 - b_t)EAFCD_t$

(16) $NUMCS_t = NUMCS_{t-1} + NEWCS_t$

(17) $NEWCS_t = \frac{NS_t}{(1 - U_t^s)P_t}$

(18) $P_t = m_t EPS_t$

(19) $EPS_t = \frac{EAFCD_t}{NUMCS_t}$

(20) $DPS_t = \frac{CMDIV_t}{NUMCS_t}$

The above system is "complete" in 20 equations and 20 unknows. The unknows are listed and defined in Table 23.2, together with the parameters (inputs) that management is required to provide.
Source: Warren, J. M. and J. P. Shelton. "A Simultaneous-Equation Approach to Financial Planning." *Journal of Finance* (December 1971): Appendix I. Reprinted by permission.

The 20-equation model appears in Table 26.1, and the parameters used as inputs to the model are demonstrated in the second part of Table 26.2. As in the Carleton model, the driving force of the model is the sales-growth estimates ($GSALS_t$). Equation (1) shows that the sales for period t is simply the product of sales in the prior period multiplied by the growth rate in sales for the period t. We then derive earning before interest and taxes ($EBIT$) as a percentage of sales ratio, as in Equations (3) and (4) through the use of the $CA/SALES$ and $FA/SALES$ ratios. The sum of CA and FA is total assets for the period (Equation (5)).

The financing of the desired level of assets is undertaken in Section III. In Equation (6), current liabilities in period t is derived from the ratio of $CL/SALES$ multiplied by $SALES$. Equation (7) is the funds required (NF_t). Like Carleton's model, FINPLAN assumes that the amount of preferred stock is constant over the planning horizon. In determining needed funds, FINPLAN uses accounting identities. As Equation (7) shows, the assets for period t are the basis for financing needs. Current liabilities, as determined in Equation (6), are one source of funds and are therefore subtracted from asset levels. As mentioned above, preferred stock is constant and therefore must be subtracted. After the first parenthesis in Equation (7), we have the financing that must come from internal sources (retain earnings) and long-term external sources (debt and stock issues). The second parenthesis takes into account the remaining old debt outstanding, after retirements, in period t. Then the funds provided by existing stock and retained earnings aresubtracted. The last quantity is the funds provided by operations during period t.

Once the funds needed for operations are defined, Equation (8) specifies that new funds, after taking into account underwriting costs and additional interest costs from new debt, are to come from long-term debt and new stock issues. Equations (9) and (10) simply update the debt and equity accounts for the new issuances. Equation (11) updates the retained earnings account for the portion of earnings available to common shares as a result of operations during period t. The term b_t is the retention rate in period t (i.e., the complement of the payout ratio) and $(1 - T_t)$ is the after-tax percentage, which is multiplied by the earnings from the period after netting out interest costs on both new and old debt. Since preferred stockholders must be paid before common stockholders, preferred dividends must be subtracted from funds available for common. Equation (12) calculates the new weighted-average interest rate for the firm's debt. Equation (13) is the new debt-to-equity ratio, for period t.

Table 26.2. List of Unknowns and List of Parameters Provided by Management.

I. Unknowns	
1. $SALES_t$	Sales
2. CA_t	Current Assets
3. FA_t	Fixed Assets
4. A_t	Total Assets
5. CL_t	Current Payables
6. NF_t	Needed Funds
7. $EBIT_t$	Earnings before Interest and Taxes
8. NL_t	New Debt
9. NS_t	New Stock
10. L_t	Total Debt
11. S_t	Common Stock
12. R_t	Retained Earnings
13. i_t	Interest Rate on Debt
14. $EAFCD_I$	Earnings Available for Common Dividends
15. $CMDIV_t$	Common Dividends
16. $NUMCS_t$	Number of Common Shares Outstanding
17. $NEWCS_t$	New Common Shares Issued
18. P_t	Price per Share
19. EPS_t	Earnings per Share
20. DPS_t	Dividends per Share
II Provided by Management	
21. $SALES_{t-1}$	Sales in Previous Period
22. $GSALS_t$	Growth in Sales
23. RCA_t	Current Assets as a Percent of Sales
24. RFA_t	Fixed Assets as a Percent of Sales
25. RCL_t	Current Payables as a Percent of Sales
26. $PFDSK_t$	Preferred Stock
27. PFDIV_t	Preferred Dividends
28. L_{t-1}	Debt in Previous Period
29. LR_t	Debt Repayment
30. S_{t-1}	Common Stock in Previous Period
31. R_{t-1}	Retained Earnings in Previous Period
32. b_t	Retention Rate
33. T_t	Average Tax Rate
34. i_{t-1}	Average Interest Rate in Previous Period
35. i_t^e	Expected Interest Rate on New Debt
36. $REBIT_t$	Operating Income as a Percent of Sales
37. U_t^1	Underwriting Cost of Debt
38. U_t^s	Underwriting Cost of Equity
39. K_t	Ratio of Debt to Equity
40. $NUMCS_{t-1}$	Number of Common Shares Outstanding in Previous Period
41. m_t	Price-Earnings Ratio

Source: Warren, J. M. and J. P. Shelton. "A Simultaneous-Equation Approach to Financial Planning." *Journal of Finance* (December 1971): Table 1. Reprinted by permission.

Section IV of Table 26.1 is concerned with the common stockholder, dividends, and market value. Equation (14) is the earnings available for common dividends. It is the same as the portion Equations (11) through (15) by using the complement of the retention rate multiplied by the earnings available for common dividends. Equation (16) updates the number of common shares for new issues.

As Equation (17) shows, the number of new common shares is determined by the total amount of the new stock issue divided by the stock price after discounting for issuance costs. Equation (18) determines the price of the stock through the use of a price-earnings ratio (m_t) of the stock purchase. Equation (19) determines *EPS*, as usual, by dividing earnings available for common by the number of common shares outstanding. Equation (20) determines dividends per share in a similar manner. This completes the model of 20 equations in 20 unknowns. Table 26.3 shows the variable numbers and their input format. A sample FINPLAN input is demonstrated, together with a sensitivity analysis.

Sensitivity analysis is accomplished by changing one parameter and noting the effect the change has on the result. FINPLAN allows sensitivity analysis to be built into a single-input deck through the use of the run code. The procedure for performing the sensitivity analysis is indicated in Table 26.3. Sensitivity analysis is very helpful in answering questions about what the results might have been if a different decision had been made.

Since the future cannot be forecast with perfect certainty, the manager/planner must know how a deviation from the forecast will affect his or her plans. The financial manager/planner must also make contingency plans for probable deviations from his or her forecast.

While the *WS* model allows the user a greater control over more details than does the Carleton model, it does not explicitly consider the production segment of the firm. In an effort to deal with the production function and other issues, *FR* have formulated a simultaneous-equation model that expands on the *WS* model.

26.2. Johnson & Johnson as a Case Study

In this section, a case study is used to demonstrate how *WS*'s model set forth in Table 26.1 can be used to perform financial analysis, planning, and forecasting for an individual firm.

Table 26.3. FINPLAN Input Format.

Variable* Number	Data**	Variable	Description
21	61897.0	$SALE_{t-1}$	Net Sales at $t-1 = 2009$
22	−0.2900	$GCALS_t$	Growth in Sales
23	0.6388	RCA_{t-1}	Current Assets as a Percentage of Sales
24	0.8909	RFA_{t-1}	Fixed Assets as a Percentage of Sales
25	0.3109	RCL_{t-1}	Current Payables as a Percentage of Sales
26	0.0000	$PFDSK_{t-1}$	Preferred Stock
27	0.0000	$PFDIV_{t-1}$	Preferred Dividends
28	8223.0	L_{t-1}	Term Debt in Previous Period
29	219.0	LR_{t-1}	Long-Term Debt Repayment (Reduction)
30	3120.0	S_{t-1}	Common Stock in Previous Period
31	67248.0	R_{t-1}	Retained Earnings in Previous Period
32	0.5657	b_{t-1}	Retention Rate
33	0.2215	T_{t-1}	Average Tax Rate (Income Taxes/Pretax Income)
34	0.0671	i_{t-1}	Average Interest Rate in Previous Period
35	0.0671	i^e_{t-1}	Expected Interest Rate on New Debt
36	0.2710	$REBIT_{t-1}$	Operating Income as a Percentage of Sales
37	0.0671	U^L	Underwriting Cost of Debt
38	0.1053	U^E	Underwriting Cost of Equity
39	0.1625	K_t	Ratio of Debt to Equity
40	2754.3	$NUMCS_{t-1}$	Number of Common Shares Outstanding in Previous Period
41	14.5	m_{t-1}	Price–Earnings Ratio

*Variable number as defined in Table 26.2.

**Data obtained from JNJ Balance Sheets and Income Statements.

Table 26.3. (*Continued*)

Historical or Base-Period Input

Balance Sheet

JOHNSON & JOHNSON
TICKER SYMBOL: JNJ
SIC Code: 2834
ANNUAL BALANCE SHEET
($ MILLIONS)

	Dec-09	Dec-08	Dec-07	Dec-06	Dec-05	Dec-04	Dec-03	Dec-02	Dec-01
ASSETS									
Cash and Short-Term Investments	19,425.00	12,809.00	9, 315.00	4,084.00	16,138.00	12,884.00	9,523.00	7,475.00	7,972.00
Receivables	9,646.00	9,719.00	9,444.00	8,712.00	7,010.00	6,831.00	6,574.00	5,399.00	4,630.00
Inventories — Total	5,180.00	5,052.00	5,110.00	4,889.00	3,959.00	3,744.00	3,588.00	3,303.00	2,992.00
Prepaid Expense	.	.	.	.	.	.	.	.	.
Other Current Assets	5,290.00	6,797.00	6,076.00	5,290.00	4,287.00	3,861.00	3,310.00	3,089.00	2,879.00
	—	—	—	—	—	—	—	—	—
Total Current Assets	39,541.00	34,377.00	29,945.00	22,975.00	31,394.00	27,320.00	22,995.00	19,266.00	18,473.00
Property, Plant, and Equipment — Total (Gross)	29,251.00	27,392.00	26,466.00	24,028.00	19,716.00	18,664.00	17,052.00	14,314.00	12,458.00
Depreciation, Depletion, and Amortization (Accumulated)	14,492.00	13,027.00	12,281.00	10,984.00	8,886.00	8,228.00	7,206.00	5,604.00	4, 739.00
	—	—	—	—	—	—	—	—	—

Table 26.3. (*Continued*)

Property, Plant, and Equipment — Total (Net)	14,759.00	14,365.00	14,185.00	13,044.00	10,830.00	10,436.00	9,846.00	8,710.00	7,719.00
Investments and Advances — Equity Method	0	0	0	0	0	0	0	0	.
Investments and Advances — Other	.	4	2	16	20	46	84	121	969
Intangibles	31,185.00	27,695.00	28,763.00	28,688.00	12,175.00	11,842.00	11,539.00	9,246.00	9,077.00
Deferred Charges	266	136	481	259	1,218.00	1,001.00	1,021.00	959	0
Other Assets — Sundry	8,931.00	8,335.00	7,578.00	5,574.00	2,388.00	2,672.00	2,778.00	2,254.00	2,250.00
—	—	—	—	—	—	—	—	—	—
TOTAL ASSETS LIABILITIES	94,682.00	84,912.00	80,954.00	70,556.00	58,025.00	53,317.00	48,263.00	40,556.00	38,488.00
Debt — Due in One Year	34	221	9	9	12	18	224	77	228
Notes Payable	6,284.00	3,511.00	2,454.00	4,570.00	656	262	915	2,040.00	337
Accounts Payable	5,541.00	7,503.00	6,909.00	5,691.00	4,315.00	5,227.00	4,966.00	3,621.00	2,838.00
Income Taxes Payable	442	417	223	724	940	1,506.00	944	710	537
Accrued Expense	9,430.00	9,200.00	10,242.00	8,167.00	6,712.00	6,914.00	6,399.00	5,001.00	4,104.00
Other Current Liabilities	9,430.00	9,200.00	10,242.00	8,167.00	6,712.00	6,914.00	6,399.00	5,001.00	4,104.00
—	—	—	—	—	—	—	—	—	—

(*Continued*)

Table 26.3. (*Continued*)

	Dec-09	Dec-08	Dec-07	Dec-06	Dec-05	Dec-04	Dec-03	Dec-02	Dec-01
Total Current Liabilities	21,731.00	20,852.00	19,837.00	19,161.00	12,635.00	13,927.00	13,448.00	11,449.00	8,044.00
Long-Term Debt — Total	8,223.00	8,120.00	7,074.00	2,014.00	2,017.00	2,565.00	2,955.00	2,022.00	2,217.00
Deferred Taxes	1,424.00	1,432.00	1,493.00	1,319.00	211	403	780	643	493
Investment Tax Credit	0	0	0	0	0	0	0	0	0
Minority Interest	0	0	0	0	0	0	0	0	0
Other Liabilities	12,716.00	11,997.00	9,231.00	8,744.00	5,291.00	4,609.00	4,211.00	3,745.00	3,501.00
EQUITY									
Preferred Stock — Redeemable	0	0	0	0	0	0	0	0	0
Preferred Stock — Nonredeemable	0	0	0	0	0	0	0	0	0
	—	—	—	—	—	—	—	—	—
Total Preferred Stock	0	0	0	0	0	0	0	0	0
Common Stock	3,120.00	3,120.00	3,120.00	3,120.00	3,120.00	3,120.00	3,120.00	3,120.00	3,120.00
Capital Surplus	0	0	0	0	0	−11	−18	−25	−30
Retained Earnings	67,248.00	58,424.00	54,587.00	47,172.00	40,716.00	34,708.00	29,913.00	25,729.00	22,536.00
Less: Treasury Stock — Total Dollar Amount	19,780.00	19,033.00	14,388.00	10,974.00	5,965.00	6,004.00	6,146.00	6,127.00	1,393.00
	—	—	—	—	—	—	—	—	—

Table 26.3. (*Continued*)

Total Common Equity	50,588.00	42,511.00	43,319.00	39,318.00	37,871.00	31,813.00	26,869.00	22,697.00	24,233.00
	—	—	—	—	—	—	—	—	—
TOTAL STOCKHOLDERS' EQUITY	50,588.00	42,511.00	43,319.00	39,318.00	37,871.00	31,813.00	26,869.00	22,697.00	24,233.00
	—	—	—	—	—	—	—	—	—
TOTAL LIABILITIES AND STOCKHOLDERS' EQUITY	94,682.00	84,912.00	80,954.00	70,556.00	58,025.00	53,317.00	48,263.00	40,556.00	38,488.00
COMMON SHARES OUTSTANDING	2,754.32	2,769.18	2,840.22	2,893.23	2,974.48	2,971.02	2,967.97	2,968.30	3,047.22

(*Continued*)

Table 26.3. (*Continued*)

Income Statement

JOHNSON & JOHNSON
TICKER SYMBOL: JNJ
SIC: 2834
ANNUAL INCOME STATEMENT COMPARING HISTORICAL AND RESTATED INFORMATION
($ MILLIONS, EXCEPT PER SHARE)

	Dec-09	Dec-08	Dec-07	Dec-06	Dec-05	Dec-04	Dec-03	Dec-02	Dec-01
Sales	61,897.00	63,747.00	61,035.00	53,194.00	50,434.00	47,348.00	41,862.00	36,298.00	33,004.00
Cost of Goods Sold	15,560.00	15,679.00	14,974.00	12,880.00	11,861.00	11,298.00	10,307.00	8,785.00	7,931.00
Selling, General, and Administrative Expense	26,787.00	29,067.00	28,131.00	24,558.00	23,189.00	21,063.00	18,815.00	16,173.00	15,583.00
	—	—	—	—	—	—	—	—	—
Operating Income Before Depreciation	19,550.00	19,001.00	17,930.00	15,756.00	15,384.00	14,987.00	12,740.00	11,340.00	9,490.00
Depreciation and Amortization	2,774.00	2,832.00	2,777.00	2,177.00	2,093.00	2,124.00	1,869.00	1,662.00	1,605.00
Interest Expense	552	582	426	181	165	323	315	258	248
Nonoperating Income (Expense)	−54	515	551	996	812	316	440	295	513
	—	—	—	—	—	—	—	—	—
Pretax Income	15,755.00	16,929.00	13,283.00	14,587.00	13,656.00	12,838.00	10,308.00	9,291.00	7,898.00
Income Taxes — Total	3,489.00	3,980.00	2,707.00	3,534.00	3,245.00	4,329.00	3,111.00	2,694.00	2,230.00
Minority Interest	0	0	0	0	0	0	0	0	0
	—	—	—	—	—	—	—	—	—

Table 26.3. (*Continued*)

Income Before Extraordinary Items	12,266.00	12,949.00	10,576.00	11,053.00	10,411.00	8,509.00	7,197.00	6,597.00	5,668.00
Extraordinary Items and Discontinued Operations	0	0	0	0	0	0	0	0	0
Net Income (Loss)	12,266.00	12,949.00	10,576.00	11,053.00	10,411.00	8,509.00	7,197.00	6,597.00	5,668.00
Earnings Per Share (Primary) — Excluding Extraordinary Items	4.45	4.62	3.67	3.76	3.5	2.87	2.42	2.2	1.87
Earnings Per Share (Primary) — Including Extraordinary Items	4.45	4.62	3.67	3.76	3.5	2.87	2.42	2.2	1.87
Common Shares Used to Calculate Primary EPS	2,759.50	2,802.50	2,882.90	2,936.40	2,973.90	2,968.40	2,968.10	2,998.30	3,033.80
Earnings Per Share (Fully Diluted) — Excluding Extraordinary Items	4.4	4.57	3.63	3.73	3.46	2.84	2.4	2.16	1.84
Earnings Per Share (Fully Diluted) — Including Extraordinary Items	4.4	4.57	3.63	3.73	3.46	2.84	2.4	2.16	1.84

(*Continued*)

Table 26.3. (*Continued*)

Statement of Cash Flows

JOHNSON & JOHNSON
TICKER SYMBOL: JNJ
SIC: 2834
ANNUAL STATEMENT OF CASH FLOWS
($ MILLIONS)

	Dec-09	Dec-08	Dec-07	Dec-06	Dec-05	Dec-04	Dec-03	Dec-02	Dec-01
INDIRECT OPERATING ACTIVITIES									
Income Before Extraordinary Items	12,266.00	12,949.00	10,576.00	11,053.00	10,411.00	8,509.00	7,197.00	6,597.00	5,668.00
Depreciation and Amortization	2,774.00	2,832.00	2,777.00	2,177.00	2,093.00	2,124.00	1,869.00	1,662.00	1,605.00
Extraordinary Items and Disc. Operations	0	0	0	0	0	0	0	0	0
Deferred Taxes	−436	22	−1,762.00	−1,168.00	−46	−498	−720	−74	−106
Equity in Net Loss (Earnings)	0	0	0	0	.	.	.	.	.
Sale of Property, Plant, and Equipment and Sale of Investments — Loss (Gain)	0	0	0	0	0	0	0	0	0
Funds from Operations — Other	686	894	2,205.00	1,204.00	331	21	924	183	204

(*Continued*)

Table 26.3. *(Continued)*

Accounts Receivable — Decrease (Increase)	453	−736	−416	−699	−568	−111	−691	−510	−258
Inventory — Decrease (Increase)	95	−101	14	−210	−396	11	39	−109	−167
Accounts Payable and Incrued Liab. — Increase (Decrease)	−507	−272	2,642.00	1,750.00	−911	607	2,192.00	1,420.00	1,401.00
Income Taxes — Accrued — Increase (Decrease)	.	.	.	.	.	.	.	.	.
Other Assets and Liabilities — Net Change	1,240.00	−616	−787	141	963	468	−215	−993	517
Operating Activities — Net Cash Flow	16,571.00	14,972.00	15,249.00	14,248.00	11,877.00	11,131.00	10,595.00	8,176.00	8,864.00
INVESTING ACTIVITIES									
Investments — Increase	10,040.00	3,668.00	9,659.00	467	5,660.00	11,617.00	7,590.00	6,923.00	8,188.00
Sale of Investments	7,232.00	3,059.00	7,988.00	426	9,187.00	12,061.00	8,062.00	7,353.00	5,967.00
Short-Term Investments — Change	.	.	.	.	.	.	.	.	.
Capital Expenditures	2,365.00	3,066.00	2,942.00	2,666.00	2,632.00	2,175.00	2,262.00	2,099.00	1,731.00
Sale of Property, Plant, and Equipment	.	.	.	.	.	.	.	.	.
Acquisitions	2,470.00	1,214.00	1,388.00	18,023.00	987	580	2,812.00	478	225

(Continued)

Table 26.3. (*Continued*)

Investing Activities — Other	45	702	−138	439	−187	−36	76	−50	84
Investing Activities — Net Cash Flow	−7,598.00	−4,187.00	−6,139.00	−20,291.00	−279	−2,347.00	−4,526.00	−2,197.00	−4,093.00
FINANCING ACTIVITIES									
Sale of Common and Preferred Stock	882	1,486.00	1,562.00	1,135.00	696	642	311	390	514
Purchase of Common and Preferred Stock	2,130.00	6,651.00	5,607.00	6,722.00	1,717.00	1,384.00	1,183.00	6,538.00	2,570.00
Cash Dividends	5,327.00	5,024.00	4,670.00	4,267.00	3,793.00	3,251.00	2,746.00	2,381.00	2,047.00
Long-Term Debt — Issuance	9	1,638.00	5,100.00	6	6	17	1,023.00	22	14
Long-Term Debt — Reduction	219	24	18	13	196	395	196	245	391
Current Debt — Changes	2,693.00	1,111.00	−2,065.00	3,752.00	483	−777	−1,072.00	1,799.00	−771
Financing Activities — Other	0	0	0	0	0	0	0	0	0
Financing Activities — Net Cash Flow	−4,092.00	−7,464.00	−5,698.00	−6,109.00	−4,521.00	−5,148.00	−3,863.00	−6,953.00	−5,251.00
Exchange Rate Effect	161	−323	275	180	−225	190	277	110	−40
Cash and Cash Equivalents — Increase (Decrease)	5,042.00	2,998.00	3,687.00	−11,972.00	6,852.00	3,826.00	2,483.00	−864	−520
DIRECT OPERATING ACTIVITIES									
Interest Paid — Net	533	525	314	143	151	222	206	141	185
Income Taxes Paid	2,363.00	4,068.00	4,099.00	4,250.00	3,429.00	3,880.00	3,146.00	2,006.00	2,090.00

The above data of financial statements is downloaded from the COMPUSTAT dataset; @NA represents data is not available.

26.2.1. *Data Sources and Parameter Estimations*

In this case study, Johnson & Johnson (JNJ) company is chosen, to perform financial planning and analysis using the *WS* model. The base year of the planning is 2009 and the planning period is one year, that is, 2010. Accounting and market data are required to estimate the parameters of *WS* financial-planning model. The *COMPUSTAT* data file is the major sources of accounting and market information. The following paragraphs briefly discuss the parameter-estimation processes. All dollar terms are in millions, and the number of shares outstanding is also millions.

Using these parameter estimates given in Table 26.3, the 20 unknown variables related to income statement and balance sheet can be solved for algebraically. The calculations are set forth in the following subsection.

26.2.2. *Procedure for Calculating WS Model*

By using the data above, we are able to calculate the unknown variables below:

(1) $$\begin{aligned} Sales_t &= Sales_{t-1} \times (1 + GCALS_t) \\ &= 61897.0 \times 0.71 \\ &= 43,946.87 \end{aligned}$$

(2) $$\begin{aligned} EBIT_t &= REBIT_{t-1} \times Sales_t \\ &= 0.2710 \times 43{,}946.87 \\ &= 11{,}909.60 \end{aligned}$$

(3) $$\begin{aligned} CA_t &= RCA_{t-1} \times Sales_t \\ &= 0.6388 \times 43{,}946.87 \\ &= 28{,}073.26 \end{aligned}$$

(4) $$\begin{aligned} FA_t &= RFA_{t-1} \times Sales_t \\ &= 0.8909 \times 43{,}946.87 \\ &= 39{,}152.27 \end{aligned}$$

(5) $$\begin{aligned} A_t &= CA_t + FA_t \\ &= 28{,}073.26 + 39{,}152.27 \\ &= 67{,}225.53 \end{aligned}$$

(6) $$\begin{aligned} CL_t &= RCL_{t-1} \times Sales_t \\ &= 0.3109 \times 43{,}946.87 \\ &= 13{,}663.08 \end{aligned}$$

(7) $NF_t = (A_t - CL_t - PFDSK_t) - (L_{t-1} - LR_t) - S_{t-1} - R_{t-1} - b_t \times \{(1-T_t)[EBIT_t - i_{t-1}(L_{t-1} - LR_t)] - PFDIV_t\}$

$= (67{,}225.53 - 13{,}663.08 - 0) - (8{,}223.0 - 219.0) - 3{,}120.0 - 67{,}248.0 - 0.5657 \times \{(1-0.2215) \times [11{,}909.60 - 0.0671 \times (8{,}223.0 - 219.0)] - 0\}$

$= -29{,}817.99$

(12) $i_t L_t = i_{t-1}(L_{t-1} - LR_t) + i^e_{t-1} \times NL_t$

$= 0.0671 \times (8{,}223.0 - 219.0) + 0.0671 \times NL_t$

$= 537.0684 + 0.0671 \times NL_t$

(8) $NF_t + b_t(1-T)[i_{t-1} \times NL_t + U^L_t \times NL_t] = NL_t + NS_t$

$-29{,}817.99 + 0.5657 \times (1 - 0.2215) \times [0.0671NL_t + 0.0671NL_t) = NL_t + NS_t$

$-29{,}817.99 + 0.0591 \times NL_t = NL_t + NS_t$

(a) $NS_t + 0.9409NL_t = -29{,}817.99$

(9) $L_t = L_{t-1} - LR_t + NL_t$

(b) $L_t = 8{,}223.0 - 219.0 + NL_t$

$L_t - NL_t = 8{,}004$

(10) $S_t = S_{t-1} + NS_t$

(c) $-NS_t + S_t = 3{,}120.0$

(11) $R_t = R_{t-1} + b_t\{(1-T_t)[EBIT_t - i_t L_t - U^L_t NL_t] - PFDIV_t\}$

$= 67{,}248.0 + 0.5657 \times \{(1-0.2215) \times [11{,}909.60 - i_t L_t - 0.0671NL_t] - 0\}$

Substitute (12) into (11)

$R_t = 67{,}248.0 + 0.5657 \times \{0.7785 \times [11{,}909.60 - (537.0684 + 0.0671 \times NL_t) - 0.0671NL_t]\}$

$= 67{,}248.0 + 5{,}008.4347 - 0.0591NL_t$

(d) $72{,}256.435 = R_t + 0.0591NL_t$

(13) $L_t = (S_t + R_t)K_t$

$L_t = 0.1625S_t + 0.1625R_t$

(e) $L_t - 0.1625S_t - 0.1625R_t = 0$

(b)–(e) = (f)

$0 = (L_t - NL_t - 8{,}004) - (L_t - 0.1625S_t - 0.1625R_t)$

$8{,}004 = 0.1625S_t + 0.1625R_t - NL_t$

(f)−0.1625 (c) = (g)

$$8{,}004 - 507 = (0.1625S_t + 0.1625R_t - NL_t) - 0.1625(-NS_t + S_t)$$
$$7{,}497 = 0.1625NS_t - NL_t + 0.1625R_t$$

(g)−0.1625 (d) = (h)

$$7{,}497 - 0.1625 \times 72,256.435$$
$$= (0.1625NS_t - NL_t + 0.1625R_t) - 0.1625(R_t + 0.0591NL_t)$$
$$-4{,}244.67 = 0.1625NS_t - 1.0096NL_t$$

(h)−0.1625 (a) = (i)

$$0.1625NS_t - 1.0096NL_t - 0.1625(NS_t + 0.9409NL_t)$$
$$= -4{,}244.67 + 0.1625(29,817.99)$$
$$NL_t = -600.7533/1.1625 = -516.777$$

Substitute NL_t in (a)

$$NS_t + 0.9409 \times (-516.777) = -29{,}817.99$$
$$NS_t = -29{,}331.755$$

Substitute NL_t in (b)

$$L_t = 8{,}223.0 - 219.0 - 516.777$$
$$= 7{,}487.223$$

Substitute NL_t in (c)

$$29{,}331.755 + S_t = 3{,}120.0$$
$$S_t = -26{,}211.755$$

Substitute NL_t in (d)

$$72{,}256.43 = R_t + 0.0591NL_t$$
$$R_t = 72{,}256.43 - 0.0591(-516.777)$$
$$R_t = 72{,}286.98$$

Substitute NL_tL_t in (12)...

$$i_t(7{,}487.223) = 537.0684 + 0.0671 \times (-516.777)$$
$$i_t = 0.0671$$

(14) $EAFCD_t = (1 - T_t)(EBIT_t - i_tL_t - U_t^L NL_t) - PFDIV_t$
$= 0.7785 \times [11{,}909.60 - (0.0671)(7{,}487.223)$
$-0.0671(-516.777)]$
$= 8{,}907.51$

(15) $CMDIV_t = (1 - b_t)EAFCD_t$
$= 0.4343(8{,}907.51)$
$= 3{,}868.53$

(16) $NUMCS_t = X_1 = NUMCS_{t-1} + NEWCS_t$
$X_1 = 2{,}754.3 + NEWCS_t$
(17) $NEWCS_t = X_2 = NS_t/(1 - U_t^E)P_t$
$X_2 = -29{,}331.755/(1 - 0.1053)P_t$
(18) $P_t = X_3 = m_t EPS_t$
$X_3 = 14.5(EPS_t)$
(19) $EPS_t = X_4 = EAFCD_t/NUMCS_t$
$X_4 = 8{,}907.5075/NUMCS_t$
(20) $DPS_t = X_5 = CMDIV_t/NUMCS_t$
$X_5 = 3{,}868.53/NUMCS_t$

(A) = For (18) and (19), we obtain $X_3 = 14.5(8,907.51)/NUMCS_t = 129{,}158.9/X_1$

Substitute (A) into Equation (17) to calculate (B)

(B) $= X_2 = -29{,}331.755/[(1 - 0.1053) \times 129{,}158.9/X_1]$
(B) $= X_2 = -0.2538X_1$

Substitute (B) into Equation (16) to calculate (C)

(C) $= X_1 = 2{,}754.3 - 0.2538X_1$
(C) $= X_1 = 2{,}196.76$

Substitute (C) into (B)...

(B) $= X_2 = -0.2538 \times 2{,}196.76$
(B) $= X_2 = -557.54$

From Equation (19) and (20) we obtain X_4, X_5 and X_3

$X_4 = 8{,}907.5075/2{,}196.76 = 4.0548$
$X_5 = 3{,}868.53/2{,}196.76 = 1.7610$
$X_3 = 14.5(4.0548) = 58.79$

The results of the above calculations allow us to forecast the following information regarding JNJ in the 2010 fiscal year (dollars in thousands, except for per share data):

- Sales = \$43,946.87
- Current Assets = \$28,073.26
- Fixed Assets = \$39,152.27
- Total Assets = \$67,225.53
- Current Payables = \$13,663.08
- Needed Funds = (\$29,817.99)

- Earnings before Interest and Taxes = \$11,909.60
- New Debt = (\$516.777)
- New Stock = (\$−29,331.755)
- Total Debt = \$7,487.223
- Common Stock = (\$26,211.755)
- Retained Earnings = \$72,286.98
- Interest Rate on Debt = 6.71%
- Earnings Available for Common Dividends = \$8,907.51
- Common Dividends = \$3,868.53
- Number of Common Shares Outstanding = 2,196.76
- New Common Shares Issued = (557.54)
- Price per Share = \$58.79
- Earnings per Share = \$4.0548
- Dividends per Share = \$1.7610.

About 18 out of 20 unknowns are listed in Table 26.4, the actual data is also listed to allow calculation of the forecast errors. In the last column of Table 26.4, the relative absolute forecasting errors ($|(\mathrm{A} - \mathrm{F})/\mathrm{A}|$) are calculated to indicate the performance of the *WS* model in forecasting important financial variables. It was found that the quality of the sales-growth rate estimate is the key to successfully using the *WS* model in financial planning and forecasting.

By comparing the forecast and actual values in Table 26.4, we find that the forecasting numbers generated by FINPLAN are very close to the ones on actual financial statements. During the financial-planning period, the company's financial policy does not change and the economy is neither in a big recession nor booming. This provides us with an environment in which the historical data are useful for financial planning. From the solution, we know that, under the assumed parameter values, the company must issue both debt and equity. If the company wants to avoid equity financing, *WS* model also enables us to investigate alternative methods to achieve this goal by changing the parameter values. Therefore, the model can answer "*what if*" questions and, hopefully, the company can choose the best alternative. Finally, the model also can help us to understand the impacts of changes in parameters on key financial variables, such as earnings per share (*EPS*), price per share (*PPS*), dividend per share (*DPS*), and earning before interest and taxes (*EBIT*), through the complicated interactions among the investment, financial, and dividend policies.

Table 26.4. The Comparison of Financial Forecast of JNJ: Hand Calculation and FINPLAN Forecasting.

Category	Manual Calculation	Financial Plan Model	Variance (|(A − F)/A|)(%)
INCOME STATEMENT			
Sales	43,946.87	43,946.87	0.0
Operating Income	11,909.60	11,909.60	0.0
Interest Expense	502.39	502.39	0.0
Income before taxes	11,372.53	11,372.53	0.0
Taxes	2,519.02	2,519.02	0.0
Net Income	8,853.52	8,853.52	0.0
Common Dividends	3,868.53	3,845.08	0.6
Debt Repayments	219.00	219.00	0.0
BALANCE SHEET			
Assets			
Current Assets	28,073.26	28,073.26	0.0
Fixed Assets	39,152.27	39,152.27	0.0
Total Assets	67,225.53	67,225.53	0.0
LIABILITIES AND NET WORTH			
Current Payables	13,663.08	13,663.24	0.0
Total Debt	7,487.22	7,487.20	0.0
Common Stock	(26,211.7)	(26,211.89)	0.0
Retained Earnings	72,286.98	72,286.98	0.0
Total Liabilities and Net Worth	67,225.53	67,225.53	0.0
PER SHARE DATA			
Price per Share	58.79	58.51	0.5
Earnings per Share (EPS)	4.05	4.04	0.5
Dividends per Share (DPS)	1.76	1.75	0.5

To do multiperiod forecasting and sensitivity analysis, the program of FINPLAN of Microsoft Excel, as listed in Appendix 26A, can be used. Using these program provided, the *pro forma* financial statements listed in Tables 26.6 and 26.7 can be produced. The input parameters and the values used to produce the output in Tables 26.6 and 26.7 are listed in Table 26.5. The list of these parameters can be found in Table 26.3. To perform the sensitivity analysis, both high and low values are assigned to the growth rate of sales (g), retention rate (b), and target leverage ratio (k). The results of the sensitivity analysis related to *EPS*, *DPS* and *PPS* are demonstrated in Table 26.8. Table 26.8 indicates that the

Table 26.5. FINPLAN Input 2009.

Value of Data	Variable Number*	Beginning Period	Last Period	Description
4	1	0	0	The number of years to be simulated
61897.0000	21	0	0	Net Sales at $t-1=2009$
−0.2900	22	1	4	Growth in Sales
0.6388	23	1	4	Current Assets as a Percentage of Sales
0.8909	24	1	4	Fixed Assets as a Percentage of Sales
0.3109	25	1	4	Current Payables as a Percentage of Sales
0.0000	26	1	4	Preferred Stock
0.0000	27	1	4	Preferred Dividends
8223.0000	28	0	0	Long-Term Debt in Previous Period
219.0000	29	1	4	Long-Term Debt Repayment (Reduction)
3120.0000	30	0	0	Common Stock in Previous Period
67248.0000	31	0	0	Retained Earnings in Previous Period
0.5657	32	1	4	Retention Rate
0.2215	33	1	4	Average Tax Rate (Income Taxes/Pretax Income)
0.0671	34	0	0	Average Interest Rate in Previous Period
0.0671	35	1	4	Expected Interest Rate on New Debt
0.2710	36	1	4	Operating Income as a Percentage of Sales
0.0671	37	1	4	Underwriting Cost of Debt
0.1053	38	1	4	Underwriting Cost of Equity
0.1625	39	1	4	Ratio of Debt to Equity
2,754.321	40	0	0	Number of Common Shares Outstanding in Previous Period
14.4700	41	1	4	Price–Earnings Ratio

*Variable numbers except the number of years to be simulated are as defined in Table 26.2.

increases in g, b, and k will generally have positive impacts on EPS, DPS, and PPS.

26.3. Francis and Rowell Model[3]

The model presented below extends the simultaneous linear-equation model of the firm developed by *WS* in 1971. The object of this model is to

[3]A major portion of this section is reprinted from Francis, J. C. and D. R. Rowell. "A simultaneous equation model of the firm for financial analysis and planning." *Financial Management* (Spring 1978), pp. 29–44, by permission of the authors and *Financial Management*.

Table 26.6. ***Pro forma* Balance Sheet of JNJ: 2010–2013.**

Item/Year	2010	2011	2012	2013
Assets				
Current assets	28,073.26	19,932.01	14,151.73	10,047.73
Fixed assets	39,152.27	27,798.11	19,736.66	14,013.03
Total assets	67,225.53	47,730.12	33,888.39	24,060.76
Liabilities and Net Worth				
Current liabilities	13,663.24	9,700.90	6,887.64	4,890.22
Long-term debt	7,489.12	5,317.28	3,775.27	2,680.44
Preferred stock 0.00	0.00	0.00	0.00	
Common stock	−26,214.00	−43,199.96	−55,258.11	−63,817.52
Retained earnings	72,287.17	75,911.90	78,483.59	80,307.61
Total liabilities and net worth	67,225.53	47,730.12	33,888.39	24,060.76
Computed DBT/EQ	0.16	0.16	0.16	0.16
Int. rate on total debt	0.07	0.07	0.07	0.07
Per Share Data				
Earnings	4.04	3.43	2.95	2.54
Dividends	1.75	1.49	1.28	1.10
Price	58.42	49.59	42.68	36.74

Table 26.7. ***Pro forma* Income Statement of JNJ: 2010–2013.**

Item/Year	2010	2011	2012	2013
Sales	43,946.87	31,202.28	22,153.62	15,729.07
Operating income	11,909.60	8,455.82	6,003.63	4,262.58
Interest expense	502.74	356.94	253.43	179.93
Underwriting commission–debt	34.56	131.09	88.81	58.79
Income before taxes	11,372.30	7,967.78	5,661.39	4,023.85
Taxes	2,518.44	1,764.49	1,253.73	891.10
Net income	8,853.87	6,203.29	4,407.65	3,132.75
Preferred dividends	0.00	0.00	0.00	0.00
Available for common dividends	8,853.87	6,203.29	4,407.65	3,132.75
Common dividends	3,845.14	2,694.03	1,914.20	1,360.52
Debt repayments	219.00	219.00	219.00	219.00
Actual funds needed for investment	−29,848.88	−18,938.80	−13,381.16	−9,435.24

generate *pro forma* financial statements that describe the future financial condition of the firm for any assumed pattern of sales. Parameters of various equations in the system can be changed to answer "*what if*" question, perform sensitivity analysis, and explore various paths toward some goals

Table 26.8. Results of Sensitivity Analysis.

Year			2010	2011	2012	2013
$GSALS_t =$	$b_{t-1} =$	$K_t =$				
−0.2900	0.5657	0.1625				
$EPS =$			4.04	3.43	2.95	2.54
$DPS =$			1.75	1.49	1.28	1.10
$PPS =$			58.42	49.59	42.68	36.74
$GSALSt =$	$b_{t-1} =$	$K_t =$				
−0.4	0.5657	0.1625				
$EPS =$			3.69	2.88	2.29	1.82
$DPS =$			1.60	1.25	0.99	0.79
$PPS =$			53.47	41.71	33.10	26.27
$GSALS_t =$	$b_{t-1} =$	$K_t =$				
0.09	0.5657	0.1625				
$EPS =$			5.09	5.65	6.23	6.86
$DPS =$			2.21	2.46	2.70	2.98
$PPS =$			73.61	81.81	90.11	99.26
$GSALS_t =$	$b_{t-1} =$	$K_t =$				
−0.2900	0.3	0.1625				
$EPS =$			3.97	3.31	2.80	2.37
$DPS =$			2.78	2.32	1.96	1.66
$PPS =$			57.46	47.92	40.52	34.27
$GSALS_t =$	$b_{t-1} =$	$K_t =$				
−0.2900	0.7	0.1625				
$EPS =$			4.07	3.49	3.03	2.63
$DPS =$			1.22	1.05	0.91	0.79
$PPS =$			58.90	50.44	43.80	38.03
$GSALS_t =$	$b_{t-1} =$	$K_t =$				
−0.2900	0.5657	0.1				
$EPS =$			3.97	3.46	2.99	2.58
$DPS =$			1.72	1.50	1.30	1.12
$PPS =$			57.42	50.02	43.23	37.37
$GSALS_t =$	$b_{t-1} =$	$K_t =$				
−0.2900	0.5657	0.5				
$EPS =$			3.94	3.39	2.86	2.42
$DPS =$			1.71	1.47	1.24	1.05
$PPS =$			56.97	49.01	41.40	34.98

or goals that may or may not be optimal. The *FR* model is composed of 10 sectors with a total of 36 equations (see Tables 26.9 and 26.10).

The model incorporates an explicit treatment of risk by allowing for stochastic variability in industry sales forecasts. The exogenous input of

Table 26.9. List of Variables for FR Model.

Endogenous		Exogenous	
Sales_t^P	Potential industry sales (units)	GSALS_t	Growth rate in potential industry sales
S_t^{FC}	Full capacity unit output (company)	Sales_{t-1}^P	Previous period potential industry sales (units)
S_t^a	Actual company unit output	S_{t-1}^{FC}	Previous period company full capacity unit output
S_t^P	Potential company unit output	INV_{t-1}	Previous period company finished goods inventory
γ_{1t}	Measure of necessary new investment (based on units)	FA_{t-1}	Previous period company fixed asset base ($)
γ_{2t}	Measure of slack due to underutilization of existing resources	γ_t	Capacity utilization index
K_t	Units of capital stock	c_t	Desire market share
NK_t	Desired new capital (capital units)	θ	Proportionality coefficient of S_t^{RC} to K_t
FA_t	Fixed assets (current $)	P_{kt}	GNP component index for capital equipment
NF_t	Desired new investment (current $)	P	Percentage markup of output price over ratio of $\text{GOP}_t/\text{INV}_t$
P_{ts}	Output price	δ_2	Proportionality coefficient of OC_t to $\$S_t$
$\$S_t$	Sales dollars (current $)	Φ	Proportionality coefficient of D_t to FA_t
COG_t	Cost of goods (current $)	N	Proportionality coefficient of INV_t to $\$S_t$
OC_t	Overhead, selling, cost of goods (current $)	LR_t	Repayment of long-term debt
$OC2_t$	Nonoperating income (current $)	T_t	Corporate tax rate
D_t	Depreciation expense (current $)	b_t	Retention rate
INV_t	Inventory (current $)	U_t^L	Underwriting cost of new debt
L_t	Long-term debt	PFDIV_t	Preferred dividend
i_t^L	Cost of new debt (%)	i_{t-1}^A	Previous period weighted average cost of long-term debt
NL_t	New long-term debt needed ($)	L_{t-1}	Previous period long-term debt
NS_t	New common stock (equity) needed ($)	k	Optimal capital structure assumption
NIAT_t	Net income after tax (current $)	α_L, β_L	Coefficients in risk-teturn tradeoff for new debt

(*Continued*)

Table 26.9. (*Continued*)

Endogenous		Exogenous	
RE_t	Retained earnings	α_s, β_s	Coefficients in risk-return tradeoff for new stock
EBIT_t	Earnings before interest and taxes	GOP_{t-1}	Gross operating profit of previous period
i_t^A	Weighted average cost of long term debt	δ_1	Ratio of COG_t to actual net sales
v_{EBIT}	Coefficient of variation of EBIT	δ_3	Ratio of OC2 to net sales
i_t^s	Cost of new stock issue	$\alpha_1, \alpha_2, \alpha_3$	Production function coefficients
v_{NIAT}	Coefficient of variation of NIAT	$\sum_1$	Ratio of CA_t to net sales
TEV_t	Total equity value	$\sum_2$	Ratio of CL_t to net sales
g_t^a	Growth rate in $\$S_t$	$\sigma^{\rho}_{\mathrm{Sale}\delta^2_P}$	Standard deviation of potential industry sales
EAFCD_t	Earnings available for common dividend		
CMDIV_t	Common dividend		
$\Delta\mathrm{RE}_t$	Contributions to RE made in the tth period		
GPO_t	Gross operating profit (current \$)		

sales variance is transformed (through simplified linear relations in the model) to coefficients of variation for *EBIT* and net income after taxes (*NIAT*) (see Table 26.10). These are used in risk–return functions that determine the costs of new financing.

Lee and Rahman (1997) use dynamic optimal control model to discuss the interactions of investment, financing, and dividend decisions. Lee and Rahman's approach can integrate with *FR*'s model.

The model also incorporates some variables external to the firm that are important from a financial-planning viewpoint. These industry or economy-wide variables are introduced in every sector to enable the financial planner to explore their influence on plans. They include: market share, an industry capacity-utilization index, the tax rate, and a GNP component price index for explicit analysis of the effects of inflation.

The *FR* model explicitly allows for divergence between planned (or potential) and actual levels in both sales and production. That is, sales forecasts and production potential are compared to determine the existence of slack or idle capacity and company expansion possibilities. Any positive

Table 26.10. List of Equations for FR Model.

1. *Industry Sales*
   (1) $\text{Sales}_t^p = \text{Sales}_{t-1}^p(1 + \text{GSALS}_t)$
2. *Company Production Sector*
   (2) $S_t^{FC} = \alpha_1 S_{t-1}^{FC} + \alpha_2 \text{INV}_{t-1} + \alpha_3 \text{FA}_{t-1}$
   (3) $\frac{S_t^a}{S_t^{FC}} = \gamma_t \rightarrow S_t^a = \gamma_t S_t^{FC}$
   (4) $S_t^p = c_t \text{Sales}_t^p$
3. *Capital Stock Requirements Sector*
   (5) $S_t^p - S_t^a = (S_t^{FC} - S_t^a) + (S_t^p - S_t^{FC})$
   (6) $S_t^{FC} - S_t^a = \gamma_{2t}$
   (7) $S_t^p - S_t^{FC} = \gamma_{1t} \quad (0 \leq \gamma_{1t})$
   (8) $K_1 = \theta S_t^{FC}$
   (9) $NK_t = \theta\gamma_{1t}$
4. *Pricing Sector*
   (10) $P_{Kt} \cdot K_t = FA_t$ or $FA_t/K_t = P_{Kt}$
   (11) $P_{Kt} \cdot NK_t = NF_t$
   (12) $P_{st} \cdot S_t^a = \$S_t^a$
   (13) $P_{ts} = p(\text{GOP}_{t-1}/\text{INV}_{t-1})$
5. *Production Cost Sector*
   (14) $\text{OC}_t = \delta_2(\$S_t^a)$
   (15) $\text{COG}_t = \delta_1(\$S_t^a)$
   (16) $\text{GOP}_t = \$S_t^a - \text{COG}_t$
   (17) $\text{OC2}_t = \delta_3(\$S_t^a)$
6. *Income Sector*
   (18) $\text{INV}_t = N(\$S_t^a)$
   (19) $\text{EBIT}_t = \$S_t^a - \text{OC}_t + \text{OC2}_t - D_t$
   (20) $\text{NIAT}_t = (\text{EBIT}_2 - i_t^A L_t)(1 - T)$
   (20′) $\text{CL}_t = \sum_2(\$S_t^a)$
7. *New Financing Required Sector*
   (21) $\text{NF}_t + b_t\{(1-T)[i_t^L \text{NL}_t + U_t^L \text{NL}_t]\} = \text{NLS}_t + \Delta\text{RE}_t + (\text{CL}_t - \text{CL}_{t-1})$
   (22) $\text{NLS}_t = \text{NS}_t + \text{NL}_t$
   (23) $\Delta\text{RE}_t = b_t\{(1-T)[\text{EBIT}_t - i_t^A L_t - U_t^L \text{NL}_t] - \text{PFDIV}_t$
   (24) $i_t^A = i_{t-1}^A\left[\frac{L_{t-1} - \text{LR}_t}{L_t}\right] + i_t^L \frac{\text{NL}_t}{L_t}$
   (25) $\frac{\text{NL}_t}{\text{NS}_t + \Delta\text{RE}_t} = k$
   (26) $L_t = L_{t-1} - \text{LR}_t + \text{NL}_t$
8. *Risk Sector*
   (27) $\sigma_{\text{ebit}}^2 = \theta_1^2 \cdot \theta_2^2 \cdot \sigma_{\text{Sales}_t^p}^2$
   (28) $\sigma_{\text{niat}}^2 = \theta_5^2 \cdot \theta_6^2 \cdot \theta_2^2 \cdot \sigma_{\text{Sales}_t^p}^2$
9. *Costs of Financing Sector*
   (29) $i_t^L = \alpha_L + \beta_L v_{\text{EBIT}}$
   (30) $v_{\text{EBIT}} = \frac{\sigma_{\text{EBIT}}}{\bar{R}_{\text{EBIT}}}$
   (31) $i_t^a = \alpha_s + \beta_s v_{\text{NIAT}}$
   (32) $v_{\text{NIAT}} = \frac{\sigma_{\text{NIAT}}}{\bar{R}_{\text{NIAT}}}$
10. *Valuation of Equity Sector*
   (33) $\text{TEV}_t = \frac{\text{CMDIV}_t}{i_t^s - g_t^s}$
   (34) $\text{EAFCD}_t = (1 - T_t) \times [\text{EBIT}_t - i_t^A L_t - U_t^L \text{NL}_t] - \text{PFDIV}_t$
   (35) $\text{CMDIV}_t = (1 - b_t)\text{EAFCD}_t$[3pt]
   (36) $g_t^a = \frac{\$S_t - \$S_{t-1}}{\$S_{t-1}}$

difference between potential or forecasted company sales and actual company sales is decomposed into the portion facilities. As a result, a forecasted sales increase need not lead to investment in new capital. Likewise, a forecasted sales downturn would not lead to a divestiture of capital. An advantage of this disaggregation is that it allows for greater realism — that it, it permits both a lagged production response to sales upturns and downturns, as well as lags, overadjustment, and underadjustment in new investment decisions.

The *FR* model offers a disaggregation of the sales equation into separate market share, production, and pricing equations, which has several distinct advantages. It offers the opportunity to treat sales forecast in physical units that can be compared to technical production capabilities in physical units for both potential and actual levels of sales and production. Such disaggregation also allows distinction between physical units of sales and production and dollar units. Therefore, the pricing decision can be treated separately. This feature is helpful in analyzing the effect of changing prices.

Another aspect of the *FR* financial-forecasting model is the econometrical advantage. The *FR* model's risk–return function and its production function are estimated econometrically. Additionally, standard econometric techniques to evaluate goodness-of-fit and predictive power of a simultaneous equation system are reported. In the remaining subsections of this section, the *FR* model is explained in its general form. Then the coefficients of the equations are set to equal to the values that characterize the operations of an existing company, and then the active operations of a well-known firm are simulated, to test this financial model empirically.

26.3.1. *FR Model Specification*

The *FR* model is composed of 10 sectors: (1) industry sales, (2) production sector, (3) fixed capital-stock requirements, (4) pricing, (5) production costs, (6) income, (7) new financing required, (8) risk, (9) costs of financing, and (10) common stock valuation. These sectors are illustrated in the equation specifications as defined in Table 26.10.

The flow chart conveniently illustrates the simultaneity discussed above. All 10 sectors are portrayed, labeled, and outlined by dot-dash borders with arrows displaying their interaction. This is summarized for sectors one through ten in the interdependence table (Table 26.11). An "**X**" is placed in the table to represent the direction of an arrow (from explaining to explained) on the flow chart.

Looking more deeply reveals that the *FR* model is, to a large extent (but not entirely), recursive between sectors. All entries of the sector-interdependence table, with the exception of one (between sectors seven and nine), are below the diagonal. It has been structures in this manner for the specific purpose of ease of exposition and computation. The simultaneity of the FR model is primarily within each sector's equations. For example, this is illustrated for sector seven in the variable interdependence table shown in Table 26.12.

Table 26.11. Sector Interdependence.

		Earning Sector									
		1	2	3	4	5	6	7	8	9	10
Explained Sector	1										
	2	×									
	3		×								
	4			×							
	5				×						
	6					×					
	7				×		×			×	
	8	×	×	×	×	×	×	×			
	9								×		
	10							×		×	

Table 26.12. Variable Interdependence within Sector Seven.

		Explaining Variables					
		RE_t	L_t	NL_t	NS_t	i_t^A	NLS_t
Explained Variables	RE_t		X	X		X	
	L_t		X				
	NL_t		X		X		
	NS_t			X			X
	i_t^A		X	X			
	NLS_t	X		X			

SECTOR ONE: INDUSTRY SALES

Following Francis and Rowell (1978), the industry sales forecast sector influences directly the risk sector and production sector and, indirectly, every sector of the model.

The industry sales sector can be any size and is abbreviated here to merely a single equation; (see *FR* example (1) in Table 26.10). The industry-sales equation shows that an industry-sales forecast must be made by some means over a predefined forecast period and given as an exogenous input to the *FR* model.

Although sales remain the driving force for the *FR* model, it is industry instead of the company sales that drive the model, since forecasting experience indicates that industry sales can usually be more accurately forecasted than company sales. In addition, two parameters of the industry sales forecast are employed, the mean and the standard deviation. The mean enters the model in the conventional way, whereas the standard deviation is mathematically transformed to obtain the standard deviation of its derivative quantities, the company's *NIAT* and *EBIT*.[4]

SECTOR TWO: COMPANY SALES AND PRODUCTION

Company sales are obtained through a market-share assumption, which is typically a more stable parameter than a company's dollar sales level. Potential company sales is obtained from forecasted industry sales through this market-share assumption. Equation (4) in Table 26.10 shows the relationship explicitly.

The *FR* model distinguishes between potential and actual sales levels; this allows a realistic treatment of slack or idle capacity in the firm. Because of the possibility of directly underutilized assets, it is not necessary that every sales upturn be translated directly into an increase in the asset base. Some or all of the sales upturn can be absorbed by more complete utilization of available resources.

Company production potential is obtained from a production function that defines full-capacity company production. This is determined by previous-period full-capacity production sales, inventory, and fixed assets (see Equation (2) in Table 26.10 for the exact specification). Actual company production is derived from full-capacity production by a capacity-utilization index in Equation (3) of Table 26.10.

The production function allows explicit definition of the company's full-capacity production levels. It serves the useful purpose of relaxing the unrealistic assumption (used in many models) that whatever is produced is sold. Full-capacity production is typically adjusted gradually, or dynamically, over the long run, to upward changes in potential sales and is often not responsive to downturns. The nonproportionality and asymmetry discussed earlier with respect to the distinctions between actual

[4]The *FR* model could easily be linked to macroeconomic forecasting model to obtain the sales forecast for the industry and the firm. The expanded macroeconomics and microeconomics model could provide detailed forecasts of the economy, the firm's industry, the firm itself, and the firm's equity returns. A small simultaneous-equation model to explain a single firm's changes in earnings per share and stock price per share has been developed by Francis (1977). Francis' model is driven by macroeconomics factors, with some forces from within the firm treated as unexplained residuals (called unsystematic risk). If the Francis quarterly equity-returns model were provided with exogenous input data about aggregate profits and a stock-market index, it could be modified to operate with the FR model and provide detail analysis of period-by-period equity returns.

and potential sales also applies to the distinctions between potential full capacity and actual production. For instance, slack (that is, idle capacity) may be decreased to meet a sales upturn without increasing the firm's investment in manufacturing machinery.

SECTOR THREE: FIXED CAPITAL-STOCK REQUIREMENTS

Necessary new investments is not linked directly to company sales in the FR model, but instead results from comparison between potential and actual company sales. Equation (7) of Table 26.10 measures the company expansion possibility by the difference between potential company sales (influenced by management's industry-sales forecast and company market-share assumption) and full-capacity sales. The units of required new capital are derived from this difference in Equation (9), shown in Table 26.10.[5]

A capacity–utilization index for the simulated company and industry translates full-capacity output (from the production function) into actual company sales, just as a market-share assumption is used to translate potential industry sales into potential company sales. Any positive difference between potential company sales and actual company sales is decomposed into the contribution due to idle capacity and the contribution due to company expansion possibility, as shown mathematically in Equation (5) of Table 26.10.

SECTOR FOUR: PRICING

The pricing sector of the model plays a key role by relating real or units sector to the nominal or dollar sectors. The real sectors of industry sales, company sales and production, and fixed capital-stock requirements are all denominated in physical units of output. However, the nominal sectors of production costs, income, financing required, and valuation are all dollar-denominated. The real sectors and the nominal sectors are connected by the pricing sector.

[5]Through this specification the *FR* model recognizes the asymmetrical response of the asset base to changes in sales levels. A strict ratio between sales and asset levels, such as those used in other pro forma models derived by Pindyck and Rubinfeld (1976) and by Salzman (1967), presume a proportionate and symmetrical response of asset levels to both sales upturns and downturns. The *FR* distinction between actual and potential sales and the concept of slack allows a realistic nonproportionality and asymmetry in the simulation. (For instance, a sales downturn need not and usually does not lead to a reduction in asset levels; instead, it typically causes a decrease in capacity utilization.)

This sector separation allows explicit treatment of the product-pricing decision apart from the sales and production decisions. Also, it maintains the important distinction between real and nominal quantities and thus permits an analysis of inflation's impact on the firm (as suggested by the Securities and Exchange Commission (1976)).

FR Equation (13) is a simple formula that generates product price by relating it, through a markup, to the ratio of previous-period gross operating profit to inventory. Real units of company sales are priced out in *FR* Equation (12). Required new capital units are priced out using the average unit capital cost specified in *FR* Equation (11) of Table 26.10.

SECTOR FIVE: PRODUCTION COSTS

The production cost sector is similar to previous models; production cost and inventory are related directly to actual company sales dollars. Also, depreciation is linked directly to existing fixed investment.

SECTOR SIX: INCOME

As in the production cost sector, the income-sector ties inventory, earnings before interest and taxes, and net income after taxes directly to actual company sales dollars. This simplicity is preserved here to create a linear-determined income statement that produces $EBIT$ as a function of actual company sales (given a few simplifying assumptions). The $NIAT$ is derived from $EBIT$ after deduction of interest expense (also linearly related to actual sales levels and taxes).

SECTOR SEVEN: NEW FINANCING REQUIRED

The new-financing-required sector is composed primarily of accounting relationships that determine the dollar amount of external financing required from the new capital requirements (Sector Three) and internal financing capability (Sector Six). In *FR* model, Equation (21) obtains this external financing requirement. The retained-income portion of internal financing is derived from *FR* Equation (23) of Table 26.10.

Finally, the breakdown of new external financing into new equity and new debt occurs in *FR* Equation (25), where the notion of optimal capital structure is exploited. The weighted-average cost of debt, *FR* Equation (24), consists of a weighted sum of new debt costs and the cost of existing debt. The cost of the new debt is not exogenous in this model; it is estimated in a simplified risk–return tradeoff from Sector Nine.

SECTOR EIGHT: RISK

The linear derivation of both *EBIT* and *NIAT* in the income sector is used (with simplifying assumptions) in the risk sector to obtain the standard deviation of each income measure. The derivation (presented in Table 26.13) demonstrates how management's judgment as to the variability (i.e., standard deviation) of forecasting industry sales affects the risk character (of both the business and financial risk) of the company. This risk character influences the costs of financing new stock and debt in risk–return tradeoff equations of Sector Nine. In this way, risk is explicitly accounted for as the principal determinant of financing costs, and financing costs are made endogenous to the model. In addition, the risk relationship from the ratio of fixed to variable cost (an operating leverage measures) to the standard deviation of *EBIT*. The debt-to-equity ratio (a financial leverage ratio) also positively influences the *NIAT* standard deviation. Thus, the leverage structure of the firm endogenously influences the costs of financing in a realistic way.

SECTOR NINE: COST OF FINANCING

Market factors enter into the determination of financing costs through the slope (β_1 and β_2) and intercept (α_1 and α_2) coefficients of the risk–return tradeoff functions — namely Equations (29) and (31) of Table 26.10. At the present time, all four coefficients must be exogenously provided by management. However, this is not a difficult task. Historical coefficients can be estimated empirically using simple linear regression. The regression coefficients would establish a plausible range of values that might be used by management to determine the present or future coefficient values.

SECTOR TEN: COMMON STOCK VALUATION

The valuation model used finds the present value of dividends, which are presumed to grow perpetually at a constant rate. This venerable model can be traced from Williams (1938) through more recent analysts. Algebraically reduced to its simplest form, the single-share valuation model is shown below:

$$\text{Share price} = \frac{\text{Cash dividend per year}}{(\text{Equity capitalization rate}\,, i_t^{\mathrm{s}}) - (\text{Growth rate, } g_t^{\mathrm{a}})}.$$

Equation (33) of Table 26.10 differs slightly from the per-share valuation model above because it values the firm's total equity outstanding. This change was accomplished merely by multiplying both sides of the

Table 26.13. Transformation of Industry Sales Moments to Company *NIAT* and *EBIT* Moments.

EBIT

$$\begin{aligned}\text{EBIT}_t &= \$S_t^a - \text{OC}_t - D_t\\ &= \$S_t^a - \delta_2\$S_t^a - \Phi\text{FA}_t\\ &= \$S_t^a - \delta_2\$S_t^a - \Phi P_{kt}\theta \cdot \frac{1}{\gamma_t} \therefore \frac{\$S_t^a}{P_{st}}\\ &= \{1 - \delta_2 - \Phi[(\tfrac{P_{kt}}{P_{ts}}) \cdot \theta(\tfrac{1}{\gamma_t})]\}\$S_t^a\\ &= \theta_1\$S_t\end{aligned}$$

If $S_t^p = S_t^{FC}$ then $S_t^{FC} = c_t\text{Sales}_t^p$

$\therefore S_t^p = c_t\text{Sales}_t^p$

Since: $S_t^a = \gamma_t S_t^{FC} = \gamma_t[c_t\text{Sales}_t^a]$

so: $P_{ts}S_t^a = \$S_t = P_{ts}\gamma_t[c_t\text{Sales}_t^p]$

and: $\$S_t^a = \theta_2\text{Sales}_t^p$

Hence: $\text{EBIT}_t = \theta_1^2 \cdot \theta_2^2\sigma^2_{\text{Sales}_t^p}$

then: $\sigma^2_{\text{EBIT}} = \theta_1^2 \cdot \theta_2^2\sigma^2_{\text{Sales}_t^p}$

NIAT

$\text{NIAT}_t = [1 - T][\text{EBIT}_t - i^A L_t - U^L\text{NL}_t]$

if $U^I = 0$

also:

$$L_t = \frac{[\Sigma_1 + \frac{P_k\theta_t}{\gamma_t P_{ts}} - \Sigma_2]}{[1+\frac{1}{k}]}\$S_t^a$$

$= \theta_4\$S_t$

$$\begin{aligned}\text{NIAT} &= [1 - T][\theta_1 \cdot \$S_t^a - i_t^A\theta_4 \cdot \$S_t^a]\\ &= [1 - T][\theta_1 - i_t^A\theta_4]\$S_t^a\\ &= [1 - T][\theta_1 - i_t^A\theta_4]\theta_2\text{Sales}_t^p\\ &= \theta_5 \cdot \theta_6 \cdot \theta_2\text{Sales}_t^p\end{aligned}$$

$\text{NIAT}_t = \theta_5 \cdot \theta_6 \cdot \theta_2\text{Sales}_t^p$

then

$\sigma^2_{\text{NIAT}} = \theta_5^2 \cdot \theta_6^2 \cdot \theta_2^2 \cdot \theta^2_{\text{sales}_t^{\text{P}}}$

where

$\theta_1 = [1 - \delta_2 - \Phi(\frac{P_k}{P_{ts}}) \cdot \theta(\frac{1}{\gamma_t})]$

$\theta_2 = P_{ts}\gamma_t c_t$

$$\theta_4 = \left\{\frac{\left[\Sigma_1 + \frac{\theta_k P_k}{1+\frac{1}{k}} - \Sigma_2\right]}{[1+\frac{1}{k}]}\right\}$$

$\theta_5 = [1 - T_t]$

$\theta_6 = [\theta_1 - i_t^A\theta_4]$

and

$CA_t = \sum_1 \cdot\$S_t^a$

$D_t = \Phi\text{FA}_t$

also, parameters $\delta_2, \theta, \gamma_t, \sum_2$, are defined in the List of Equations (Table 26.10).

valuation equation shown above by the number of shares outstanding. The remaining equations of this sector are then accounting statements.

26.3.2. *A Brief Discussion of FR'S Empirical Results*

FR (1978) used Anheuser-Busch Company annual reports to perform full simulation experiments, and show one prediction comparison for the *FR* model and the *WS* model.

Overall, *FR* found that their model is very useful in performing financial planning and forecasting. In addition, *FR* also argued that their model has superior explanatory power over a wide range of applications (see footnote 4). Detailed discussion of *FR*'s empirical results is beyond the scope of this book. Hence it is omitted and left for students' further study. A case study of using both *FR* and Carleton's (1970) models to analyze a forecast General Motors' financial position can be found in Lee (1984).

26.4. Feltham–Ohlson Model for Determining Equity Value

Ohlson Model introduced the clean surplus relations (CSR) assumption requiring that income over a period equals net dividends and the change in book value of equity. CSR ensures that all changes in shareholder equity that do not result from transactions with shareholders (such as dividends, share repurchases or share offerings) are reflected in the income statement. In other words, CSR is an accounting system recognizing that the periodically value created is distinguished from the value distributed.

Let NIAT_t denote the earnings for period $(t-1, t)$, TEV_t denote the book value of equity at time t, R_f denote the risk-free rate plus one, CMDIV_t denote common dividends, and $\text{NIAT}_t^a = \text{NIAT}_t - (R_f - 1)\text{TEV}_t$ denote the abnormal earnings at time t. The change in book value of equity between two days equals earnings minus dividends, so the clean surplus relations $(\text{CSR})\text{TEV}_t = \text{TEV}_{t-1} + \text{NIAT}_t - \text{CMDIV}_t$ implies that

$$P_{ts} = \text{TEV}_t + \sum_{\tau=1}^{\infty} R_f^{-\tau} E_t[\text{NIAT}_{t+\tau}^a]. \tag{26.1}$$

The price of firm's equity (P_{ts}) is equal to its book value of equity adjusted for the present value of expected future abnormal earnings. The variables on the right-hand side of (26.1) are still forecasts, not past realizations. To deal with this problem, Ohlson Model introduced the information dynamics to link the value to the contemporaneous accounting data. Assume $\{\widetilde{\text{NIAT}}_t^a\}_{\tau \geq 1}$ follows the stochastic process

$$\begin{aligned}\widetilde{\text{NIAT}}_{t+1}^a &= \omega \text{NIAT}_t^a + v_t + \tilde{\varepsilon}_{1,t+1},\\ \tilde{v}_{t+1} &= \gamma v_t + \tilde{\varepsilon}_{2,t+1},\end{aligned} \tag{26.2}$$

where v_t is value relevant information other than abnormal earnings and $0 \leq \omega, \gamma \leq 1$. Based on Equations (26.1) and (26.2), Ohlson Model demonstrated that the value of the equity is a function of contemporaneous accounting variables as follows.

$$P_{ts} = \text{TEV}_t + \hat{\alpha}_1 \text{NIAT}_t^a + \hat{\alpha}_2 v_t, \tag{26.3}$$

where $\hat{\alpha}_1 = \hat{\omega}/(R_f - \hat{\omega})$ and $\hat{\alpha}_2 = R_f/(R_f - \hat{\omega})(R_f - \hat{\gamma})$. Or equivalently,

$$P_{ts} = \kappa(\varphi \text{NIAT}_t - d_t) + (1 - \kappa)\text{TEV}_t + \alpha_2 v_t, \tag{26.4}$$

where $\kappa = (R_f - 1)\hat{\omega}/(R_f - \hat{\omega})$ and $\varphi = R_f/(R_f - 1)$. Equations (26.3) and (26.4) imply that the market value of the equity is equal to the book value adjusted for (i) the current profitability as measured by abnormal earnings and (ii) other information that modifies the prediction of future profitability.

One major limitation of the Ohlson Model is that it assumed unbiased accounting. Feltham and Ohlson (1995) (hereafter *FO*) introduce additional dynamics to deal with the issue of biased (conservative) accounting data. The *FO* Model analyzes how firm value relates to the accounting information that discloses the results from both operating and financial activities. For the financial activities, there are relatively perfect markets and the accounting measures for book value and market value of these assets are reasonably close. However for the operating assets, accrual accounting usually results in difference between the book value and the market value of these assets since they are not traded in the market. Accrual accounting for the operating assets consequently results in discrepancy between their book value and market value and thus influences the goodwill of the firm. Similar to Ohlson Model, the information dynamics in the *FO* Model is

$$\begin{aligned}\widetilde{ox}_{t+1}^a &= \omega_{10} + \omega_{11} ox_t^a + \omega_{12} oa_t + \omega_{13} v_{1t} + \tilde{\varepsilon}_{1t+1},\\ \widetilde{oa}_{t+1} &= \omega_{20} + \omega_{22} ox_t^a + \omega_{24} v_{2t} + \tilde{\varepsilon}_{2t+1},\\ \tilde{v}_{1t+1} &= \omega_{30} + \omega_{33} v_{1t} + \tilde{\varepsilon}_{3t+1},\\ \tilde{v}_{2t+1} &= \omega_{40} + \omega_{44} v_{2t} + \tilde{\varepsilon}_{4t+1},\end{aligned} \tag{26.5}$$

where ox_t^a is the abnormal operating earnings, oa_t is the operating assets, v_{1t} and v_{2t} are the other value relevant information variables for firm at time t, respectively. The operating assets and the financial assets are calculated as follows.

$$\begin{aligned}
\text{Operating Assets} &= \text{Total assets} - \text{Financial Assets}\\
\text{Operating Liabilities} &= \text{Preferred Shares} + \text{Total Liabilities}\\
&\quad - \text{Financial Liabilities}\\
\text{Financial Assets} &= \text{Cash and Cash Equivalent}\\
&\quad + \text{Investments and Advancements}\\
&\quad + \text{Short term Investments}\\
\text{Financial Liabilities} &= \text{Long term debt} + \text{Debt in Current Liabilities}\\
&\quad + \text{Notes Payable}\\
\text{Net Operating Assets} &= \text{Operating Assets} - \text{Operating Liabilities}\\
\text{Net Financial Assets} &= \text{Financial Assets} - \text{Financial Liabilities}
\end{aligned}$$

The derived implied pricing function is

$$P_t = y_t + \hat{\lambda}_0 + \hat{\lambda}_1 ox_t^a + \hat{\lambda}_2 oa_t + \hat{\lambda}_3 v_{1t} + \hat{\lambda}_4 v_{2t}, \tag{26.6}$$

where

$$\begin{aligned}
\hat{\lambda}_0 &= \frac{(1+r)\begin{bmatrix}\hat{\omega}_{10}(1+r-\hat{\omega}_{22})(1+r-\hat{\omega}_{33})(1+r-\hat{\omega}_{44}),\\ +\hat{\omega}_{12}\hat{\omega}_{20}(1+r-\hat{\omega}_{33})+\hat{\omega}_{13}\hat{\omega}_{30}(1+r-\hat{\omega}_{22})\\ +\hat{\omega}_{14}\hat{\omega}_{40}(1+r-\hat{\omega}_{44})\end{bmatrix}}{r(1+r-\hat{\omega}_{11})(1+r-\hat{\omega}_{22})(1+r-\hat{\omega}_{33})(1+r-\hat{\omega}_{44})},\\
\hat{\lambda}_1 &= \frac{\hat{\omega}_{11}}{r(1+r-\hat{\omega}_{11})},\\
\hat{\lambda}_2 &= \frac{(1+r)\hat{\omega}_{12}}{(1+r-\hat{\omega}_{11})(1+r-\hat{\omega}_{22})},\\
\hat{\lambda}_3 &= \frac{(1+r)\hat{\omega}_{13}}{(1+r-\hat{\omega}_{11})(1+r-\hat{\omega}_{33})},\\
\hat{\lambda}_4 &= \frac{(1+r)\hat{\omega}_{14}}{(1+r-\hat{\omega}_{11})(1+r-\hat{\omega}_{44})},
\end{aligned} \tag{26.7}$$

Or equivalently,

$$P_t = k(\phi x_t - d_t) + (1-\kappa)y_t + \hat{\alpha}_2 oa_t + \hat{\lambda}_3 v_{1t} + \hat{\lambda}_4 v_{2t}, \tag{26.8}$$

where $\kappa = (R_f - 1)\hat{\omega}_{11}/(R_f - \hat{\omega}_{11})$ and $\phi = R_f/(R_f - 1)$. The implied valuation function in Equations (26.6) and (26.8) is a weighted average of firm's operating earnings, firm's book value, and the other value-relevant information with an adjustment for the understatement of the operating assets resulting from accrual accounting. The major contribution of the *FO* Model is that it considered the accounting conservatism in the equity valuation.

26.5. Combined Forecasting Method to Determine Equity Value

Lee *et al.* (2012) investigate the stock price forecast ability of Ohlson (1995) model, *FO* (1995) model, and *WS* (1971) Model. They use simultaneous equation estimation approach to estimate the information dynamics for Ohlson model and *FO* model and forecast future stock prices. Empirical results show that the simultaneous equation estimation of the information dynamics improves the ability of the Ohlson Model and *FO* model in capturing the dynaic of the abnormal earnings process.

Lee *et al.* (2012) also find that *WS* model can generate smaller future stock prices prediction errors than those predicted by the Ohlson model and *FO* model, indicating that *WS* model has better forecast ability to determing future stock prices. The superior accuracy comparing to the Ohlsen model and *FO* model are due to the incorporation of both operation and financing decisions of the firms.

Using various time-varying parameters models proposed by Granger and Newbold (1973) and Diebold and Pauly (1987), Lee *et al.* (2012) further examine whether forecast combination provides better prediction accuracy. They also employ the linear and quadratic deterministic time-varying parameters model to produce time-varying weights. The evidence shows that combined forecast method can reduce the prediction errors.

26.6. Summary

Two simultaneous-equation financial planning models were discussed in detail in this chapter. There are 20 equations and 20 unknowns in the *WS* model. Annual financial data from JNJ company were used to show how the *WS* model can be used to perform financial analysis and planning. A computer program of the *WS* model is presented in Appendix 26B.

The *FR* model is a generalized *WS* financial-planning model. There are 36 equation and 36 unknown in the *FR* model. The two simultaneous-equation financial-planning models discussed in this chapter are an alternative to Carleton's linear-programming model, to perform financial analysis, planning, and forecasting.

In this chapter, we have also briefly discussed Felthan-Ohlson model for determining equity value. In addition, we have explored the usefulness of integrating WS model and Felthan-Ohlson model to improve the determination of equity value.

Questions and Problems

1. According to Warren and Shelton (1971), what are the characteristics of a good financial-planning model?
2. Briefly discuss the *WS* model of using a simultaneous-equations approach to financial planning. How this model can be used to forecast price per share of the company?
3. How does the *FR* simultaneous model extend the *WS* model? Briefly discuss the *FR* model specification.
4. Please compare the Ohlson model with Feltham and Ohlson model. Which model is more suitable for determining stock price per share? Why?
5. Use a flow chart to interpret the computer program listed in Appendix 26B of this chapter. Then use these concepts to discuss how the *WS* model can be solved by this computer program.

Appendix 26A: Procedure of Using Microsoft Excel to Run Finplan Program

	A	B	C	D	E	F	G	H	I	J	K
1	FINPLAN input										
2	2009										
3	Value of Data	Variable	Beginning	Last							
4		Number	Period	Period	Value						
5	4	1	0	0	The number of years to be simulated						
6	61897.0000	21	0	0	Net Sales at t-1=2009						
7	-0.2900	22	1	4	Growth in Sales						
8	0.6388	23	1	4	Current Assets as a Percent of Sales						
9	0.8909	24	1	4	Fixed Assets as a Percent of Sales						
10	0.3109	25	1	4	Current Payables as a Percent of Sales						
11	0.0000	26	1	4	Preferred Stock						
12	0.0000	27	1	4	Preferred Dividends						
13	8223.0000	28	0	0	Long Term Debt in Previous Period						
14	219.0000	29	1	4	Long Term Debt Repayment (Reduction)						
15	3120.0000	30	0	0	Common Stock in Previous Period						
16	67248.0000	31	0	0	Retained Earnings in Previous Period						
17	0.5657	32	1	4	Retention Rate						
18	0.2215	33	1	4	Average Tax Rate (Income Taxes / Pretax Income)						
19	0.0671	34	0	0	Average Interest Rate in Previous Period						
20	0.0671	35	1	4	Expected Interest Rate on New Debt						
21	0.2710	36	1	4	Operating Income as a Percentage of Sales						
22	0.0671	37	1	4	Underwriting Cost of Debt						
23	0.1053	38	1	4	Underwriting Cost of Equity						
24	0.1625	39	1	4	Ratio of Debt to Equity						
25	2,754.321	40	0	0	Number of Common Shares Outstanding in Previous Period						
26	14.4700	41	1	4	Price-Earnings Ratio						
27											
28											
29											
30											
31											
32											

	A	B	C	D	E	F	G	H	I	J	K
33		**Pro forma Income Statement**									
34											
35		2009	2010	2011	2012	2013					
36											
37	Sales	61897.00	43946.87	31202.28	22153.62	15729.07					
38	Operating income	0.00	11909.60	8455.82	6003.63	4262.58					
39	Interest expense	0.00	502.61	356.85	253.36	179.89					
40	Underwriting commission -- debt	0.00	34.69	131.05	88.79	58.77					
41	Income before taxes	0.00	11372.30	7967.91	5661.48	4023.91					
42	Taxes	0.00	2518.44	1764.52	1253.75	891.11					
43	Net income	0.00	8853.87	6203.39	4407.73	3132.80					
44	Preferred dividends	0.00	0.00	0.00	0.00	0.00					
45	Available for common dividends	0.00	8853.87	6203.39	4407.73	3132.80					
46	Common dividends	0.00	3845.23	2694.13	1914.28	1360.58					
47	Debt repayments	0.00	219.00	219.00	219.00	219.00					
48	Actl funds needed for investment	0.00	-29848.90	-18938.76	-13381.13	-9435.22					
49											
50											
51											
52											
53		**Pro forma Balance Sheet**									
54											
55		2009	2010	2011	2012	2013					
56	**Assets**										
57	Current assets	0.00	28073.26	19932.01	14151.73	10047.73					
58	Fixed assets	0.00	39152.27	27798.11	19736.66	14013.03					
59	Total assets	0.00	67225.53	47730.12	33888.39	24060.76					
60	**Liabilities and net worth**										
61	Current liabilities	0.00	13663.24	9700.90	6887.64	4890.22					
62	Long term debt	8223.00	7487.20	5315.91	3774.30	2679.75					
63	Preferred stock	0.00	0.00	0.00	0.00	0.00					
64	Common stock	3120.00	-26212.11	-43198.58	-55257.09	-63816.76					
65	Retained earnings	67248.00	72287.19	75911.89	78483.54	80307.54					
66	Total liabilities and net worth	0.00	67225.53	47730.12	33888.39	24060.76					
67	Computed DBT/EQ	0.0000	0.1625	0.1625	0.1625	0.1625					
68	Int. rate on total debt	0.0671	0.0671	0.0671	0.0671	0.0671					
69	Per share data										
70	Earnings	0.0000	4.0371	3.4269	2.9494	2.5387					
71	Dividends	0.0000	1.7533	1.4883	1.2809	1.1026					
72	Price	0.0000	58.4172	49.5865	42.6783	36.7356					

The program of FINPLAN is available on the website: http://centerforpbbefr. rutgers.edu/

Appendix 26B: Program of Finplan with an Example

This program is composed under Visual Basic Application (VBA) environment.

```
Sub FinPlan()
  Dim i As Integer            'Looping control variable
  Dim bNYEARFound As Boolean 'Check if Year Being Simulated is found
  Dim NDATE As Integer        'Year immediately preceeding the first forecasted year
  Dim NUMVR As Integer        'Variable code number
  Dim NYEAR() As Integer      'Year being simulated

  Dim N As Integer            '1 The number of years to be simulated
  Dim SALES() As Double       '21 Sales in the simulation year
  Dim GSALS() As Double       '22 Growth rate of sales
  Dim CARAT() As Double       '23 Ratio of current assets to sales
  Dim FARAT() As Double       '24 Ratio of fixed assets to sales
  Dim CLRAT() As Double       '25 Ratio of current liabilities to sales
  Dim PFDSK() As Double       '26 Preferred stock
  Dim PFDIV() As Double       '27 Preferred dividends
  Dim ZL() As Double          '28 Long term debt
  Dim ZLR() As Double         '29 Debt repayments
  Dim S() As Double           '30 Common stock
  Dim R() As Double           '31 Retained earnings
  Dim B() As Double           '32 Retention rate
  Dim T() As Double           '33 Federal income tax rate
  Dim ZI() As Double          '34 Interest rate on total debt
  Dim ZIE() As Double         '35 Interest rate on new debt
  Dim ORATE() As Double       '36 Operating income rate (EBIT/SALES)
  Dim UL() As Double          '37 Underwriting commission of new debt
  Dim US() As Double          '38 Underwriting commission of new stock
  Dim ZK() As Double          '39 Desired debt to equity ratio
  Dim ZNUMC() As Double       '40 Cummulative number of common stock shares
                                 outstanding
  Dim PERAT() As Double       '41 Price / Earnings ratio

  Dim O() As Double           'Operating income
  Dim CA() As Double          'Current assets
  Dim FA() As Double          'Fixed assets
  Dim A() As Double           'Total assets
  Dim CL() As Double          'Current liabilities
  Dim ZNF() As Double         'Estimated needed funds
  Dim ZNL() As Double         'Value of new debt issued
  Dim EXINT() As Double       'Interest expense
  Dim DBTUC() As Double       'Debt underwriting commission
  Dim EAIBT() As Double       'Earnings after interest and before tax
  Dim TAX() As Double         'Federal income taxes
  Dim EAIAT() As Double       'Earnings after interest and after tax
```

```
Dim EAFCD() As Double            'Earnings available for common dividends
Dim COMDV() As Double            'Common stock dividends
Dim ZNS() As Double              'Value of new common stock issued
Dim TLANW() As Double            'Total liabilities and net worth
Dim COMPK() As Double            'Computed debt to equity
Dim ANF() As Double              'Actual needed funds
Dim P() As Double                'Per share market price of common stock
Dim ZNEW() As Double             'Value of new common stock shares issued
Dim EPS() As Double              'Common stock earnings per share
Dim DPS() As Double              'Common stock dividends per share

On Error GoTo ErrorHandler

Columns("a").ColumnWidth = 29    'Set default column A width

Range("a2").Select               'Get the year being simulated from cell A2
NDATE =ActiveCell.Value

Range("b5").Select               'Get the variable code number from cell
                                   B5
NUMVR = ActiveCell.Value

bNYEARFound = False
While NUMVR <> Empty And Not bNYEARFound
  If NUMVR = 1 Then              'If the number of years to be simulated
                                   is found
    N = ActiveCell.Previous.Value + 1
    bNYEARFound = True
  End If
  ActiveCell.Offset(1, 0).Activate
  NUMVR =ActiveCell.Value
Wend
If Not bNYEARFound Then N = 5    'If the number of years to be simulated
                                   is not found
                         'then set the default of N as 5
ReDim NYEAR(N)
ReDim SALES(N)
ReDim GSALS(N)
ReDim ORATE(N)
ReDim T(N)
ReDim CARAT(N)
ReDim FARAT(N)
ReDim CLRAT(N)
ReDim ZL(N)
ReDim ZI(N)
ReDim ZIE(N)
ReDim ZLR(N)
ReDim PFDSK(N)
ReDim PFDIV(N)
```

```
ReDim S(N)
ReDim ZNUMC(N)
ReDim R(N)
ReDim B(N)
ReDim ZK(N)
ReDim PERAT(N)
ReDim UL(N)
ReDim US(N)

NYEAR(1) = NDATE
For i = 2 To N
  NYEAR(i) = NYEAR(i - 1) + 1
Next

Range("b5").Select
NUMVR = ActiveCell.Value

While NUMVR <> Empty
  Select Case NUMVR

    Case 21
      SALES(1) = ActiveCell.Previous.Value

    Case 22
      For i = ActiveCell.Next.Value + 1 To ActiveCell.Next.Next.Value + 1
        GSALS(i) = ActiveCell.Previous.Value
      Next

    Case 23
      For i = ActiveCell.Next.Value + 1 To ActiveCell.Next.Next.Value + 1
        CARAT(i) = ActiveCell.Previous.Value
      Next

    Case 24
      For i = ActiveCell.Next.Value + 1 To ActiveCell.Next.Next.Value + 1
        FARAT(i) = ActiveCell.Previous.Value
    Next

    Case 25
      For i = ActiveCell.Next.Value + 1 To ActiveCell.Next.Next.Value + 1
        CLRAT(i) = ActiveCell.Previous.Value
    Next

    Case 26
      For i = ActiveCell.Next.Value + 1 To ActiveCell.Next.Next.Value + 1
        PFDSK(i) = ActiveCell.Previous.Value
    Next

    Case 27
      For i = ActiveCell.Next.Value + 1 To ActiveCell.Next.Next.Value + 1
        PFDIV(i) = ActiveCell.Previous.Value
    Next
```

```
Case 28
  ZL(1) = ActiveCell.Previous.Value
Case 29
  For i = ActiveCell.Next.Value + 1 To ActiveCell.Next.Next.Value + 1
    ZLR(i) = ActiveCell.Previous.Value        Next
Case 30
  S(1) = ActiveCell.Previous.Value
Case 31
  R(1) = ActiveCell.Previous.Value
Case 32
  For i = ActiveCell.Next.Value + 1 To ActiveCell.Next.Next.Value + 1
    B(i) = ActiveCell.Previous.Value
Next
Case 33
  For i = ActiveCell.Next.Value + 1 To ActiveCell.Next.Next.Value + 1
    T(i) = ActiveCell.Previous.Value
Next
Case 34
  ZI(1) = ActiveCell.Previous.Value
Case 35
  For i = ActiveCell.Next.Value + 1 To ActiveCell.Next.Next.Value + 1
    ZIE(i) = ActiveCell.Previous.Value
Next
Case 36
  For i = ActiveCell.Next.Value + 1 To ActiveCell.Next.Next.Value + 1
    ORATE(i) = ActiveCell.Previous.Value
Next
Case 37
  For i = ActiveCell.Next.Value + 1 To ActiveCell.Next.Next.Value + 1
    UL(i) = ActiveCell.Previous.Value
Next
Case 38
  For i = ActiveCell.Next.Value + 1 To ActiveCell.Next.Next.Value + 1
    US(i) = ActiveCell.Previous.Value
Next
Case 39
  For i = ActiveCell.Next.Value + 1 To ActiveCell.Next.Next.Value + 1
    ZK(i) = ActiveCell.Previous.Value
Next
Case 40
  ZNUMC(1) = ActiveCell.Previous.Value
```

```
        Case 41
            For i = ActiveCell.Next.Value + 1 To ActiveCell.Next.Next.Value + 1
                PERAT(i) = ActiveCell.Previous.Value
        Next
    End Select
    ActiveCell.Offset(1, 0).Activate
    NUMVR = ActiveCell.Value
Wend
ReDim O(N)
ReDim CA(N)
ReDim FA(N)
ReDim A(N)
ReDim CL(N)
ReDim ZNF(N)
ReDim ZNL(N)
ReDim EXINT(N)
ReDim DBTUC(N)
ReDim EAIBT(N)
ReDim TAX(N)
ReDim EAIAT(N)
ReDim EAFCD(N)
ReDim COMDV(N)
ReDim ZNS(N)
ReDim TLANW(N)
ReDim COMPK(N)
ReDim ANF(N)
ReDim P(N)
ReDim ZNEW(N)
ReDim EPS(N)
ReDim DPS(N)
For i = 2 To N              'Solve simultaneous equations for N periods
    SALES(i) = SALES(i - 1) * (1 + GSALS(i))
    O(i) = ORATE(i) * SALES(i)
    CA(i) = CARAT(i) * SALES(i)
    FA(i) = FARAT(i) * SALES(i)
    A(i) = CA(i) + FA(i)
    CL(i) = CLRAT(i) * SALES(i)
    ZNF(i) = (A(i) - CL(i) - PFDSK(i)) - (ZL(i - 1) - ZLR(i)) - S(i - 1) - R(i - 1)_
        - B(i) * ((1 - T(i)) * (O(i) - ZI(i - 1) * (ZL(i - 1) - ZLR(i))) - PFDIV(i))
    ZNL(i) = (ZK(i) / (1 + ZK(i))) * (A(i) - CL(i) - PFDSK(i))
        - (ZL(i - 1) - ZLR(i))
    ZL(i) = (ZL(i - 1) - ZLR(i)) + ZNL(i)
    ZI(i) = ZI(i - 1) * ((ZL(i - 1) - ZLR(i)) / ZL(i)) + ZIE(i) * (ZNL(i) / ZL(i))
    If ZNL(i) <= 0 Then ZI(i) = ZI(i - 1)
    EXINT(i) = ZI(i) * ZL(i)
```

```
    DBTUC(i) = Abs(UL(i) * ZNL(i))
    EAIBT(i) = O(i) - EXINT(i) - DBTUC(i)
    TAX(i) = T(i) * EAIBT(i)
    EAIAT(i) = EAIBT(i) - TAX(i)
    EAFCD(i) = EAIAT(i) - PFDIV(i)
    COMDV(i) = (1 - B(i)) * EAFCD(i)
    R(i) = R(i - 1) + B(i) * ((1 - T(i)) * (O(i) - ZI(i) * ZL(i) - UL(i) *_
        ZNL(i)) - PFDIV(i))
    S(i) = ZL(i) / ZK(i) - R(i)
    ZNS(i) = S(i) - S(i - 1)
    TLANW(i) = CL(i) + PFDSK(i) + ZL(i) + S(i) + R(i)
    COMPK(i) = ZL(i) / (S(i) + R(i))
    ANF(i) = ZNF(i) + B(i) * (1 - T(i)) * (ZI(i) * ZL(i) + UL(i) *_
        ZNL(i) - ZI(i - 1) * (ZL(i - 1) - ZLR(i)))
    P(i) = (PERAT(i) * EAFCD(i) - ZNS(i) / (1 - US(i))) / ZNUMC(i - 1)
    ZNEW(i) = ZNS(i) / ((1 - US(i)) * P(i))
    ZNUMC(i) = ZNUMC(i - 1) + ZNEW(i)
    EPS(i) = EAFCD(i) / ZNUMC(i)
    DPS(i) = COMDV(i) / ZNUMC(i)
Next

Range(ActiveCell.Offset(0, -1), ActiveCell.Offset(70, N)).Clear 'Clear the
  report area

ActiveCell.Offset(6, 0).Activate      'Select the Income Statemet Starting Cell

With ActiveCell.Font
  .Bold = True
  .Size = 11
End With

ActiveCell.Value = "Pro forma Income Statement"   'Generate Income Statement
ActiveCell.Offset(2, -1).Activate
For i = 1 To N
  ActiveCell.Offset(0, i).Value = NYEAR(i)
Next

ActiveCell.Offset(2, 0).Activate
Range(ActiveCell, ActiveCell.Offset(15, N)).NumberFormat = "###0.00"

ActiveCell.Value = "Sales"
For i = 1 To N
  ActiveCell.Offset(0, i).Value = SALES(i)
Next

ActiveCell.Offset(1, 0).Activate
ActiveCell.Value = "Operating income"
For i = 1 To N
  ActiveCell.Offset(0, i).Value = O(i)
Next
```

```
ActiveCell.Offset(1, 0).Activate
ActiveCell.Value = "Interest expense"
For i = 1 To N
  ActiveCell.Offset(0, i).Value = EXINT(i)
Next
ActiveCell.Offset(1, 0).Activate
ActiveCell.Value = "Underwriting commission – debt"
For i = 1 To N
  ActiveCell.Offset(0, i).Value = DBTUC(i)
Next
ActiveCell.Offset(1, 0).Activate
ActiveCell.Value = "Income before taxes"
For i = 1 To N
  ActiveCell.Offset(0, i).Value = EAIBT(i)
Next
ActiveCell.Offset(1, 0).Activate
ActiveCell.Value = "Taxes"
For i = 1 To N
  ActiveCell.Offset(0, i).Value = TAX(i)
Next
ActiveCell.Offset(1, 0).Activate
ActiveCell.Value = "Net income"
For i = 1 To N
  ActiveCell.Offset(0, i).Value = EAIAT(i)
Next
ActiveCell.Offset(1, 0).Activate
ActiveCell.Value = "Preferred dividends"
For i = 1 To N
  ActiveCell.Offset(0, i).Value = PFDIV(i)
Next
ActiveCell.Offset(1, 0).Activate
ActiveCell.Value = "Available for common dividends"
For i = 1 To N
  ActiveCell.Offset(0, i).Value = EAFCD(i)
Next
ActiveCell.Offset(1, 0).Activate
ActiveCell.Value = "Common dividends"
For i = 1 To N
  ActiveCell.Offset(0, i).Value = COMDV(i)
Next
ActiveCell.Offset(1, 0).Activate
ActiveCell.Value = "Debt repayments"
```

```
For i = 1 To N
   ActiveCell.Offset(0, i).Value = ZLR(i)
Next
ActiveCell.Offset(1, 0).Activate
ActiveCell.Value = "Actl funds needed for investment"
For i = 1 To N
   ActiveCell.Offset(0, i).Value = ANF(i)
Next
ActiveCell.Offset(5, 1).Activate      'Generate Balance Sheet
With ActiveCell.Font
   .Bold = True
   .Size = 11
End With
ActiveCell.Value = "Pro forma Balance Sheet"
ActiveCell.Offset(2, -1).Activate
For i = 1 To N
   ActiveCell.Offset(0, i).Value = NYEAR(i)
Next
ActiveCell.Offset(1, 0).Activate
ActiveCell.Font.Bold = True
ActiveCell.Value = "Assets"
ActiveCell.Offset(1, 0).Activate
Range(ActiveCell, ActiveCell.Offset(9, N)).NumberFormat = "###0.00"
Range(ActiveCell.Offset(10, 0), ActiveCell.Offset(15, N)).NumberFormat
   = "###0.0000"
ActiveCell.Value = "Current assets"
For i = 1 To N
   ActiveCell.Offset(0, i).Value = CA(i)
Next
ActiveCell.Offset(1, 0).Activate
ActiveCell.Value = "Fixed assets"
For i = 1 To N
   ActiveCell.Offset(0, i).Value = FA(i)
Next
ActiveCell.Offset(1, 0).Activate
ActiveCell.Value = "Total assets"
For i = 1 To N
   ActiveCell.Offset(0, i).Value = A(i)
Next
ActiveCell.Offset(1, 0).Activate
ActiveCell.Font.Bold = True
ActiveCell.Value = "Liabilities and net worth"
```

```
ActiveCell.Offset(1, 0).Activate
ActiveCell.Value = "Current liabilities"
For i = 1 To N
  ActiveCell.Offset(0, i).Value = CL(i)
Next

ActiveCell.Offset(1, 0).Activate
ActiveCell.Value = "Long term debt"
For i = 1 To N
  ActiveCell.Offset(0, i).Value = ZL(i)
Next

ActiveCell.Offset(1, 0).Activate
ActiveCell.Value = "Preferred stock"
For i = 1 To N
  ActiveCell.Offset(0, i).Value = PFDSK(i)
Next

ActiveCell.Offset(1, 0).Activate
ActiveCell.Value = "Common stock"
For i = 1 To N
  ActiveCell.Offset(0, i).Value = S(i)
Next

ActiveCell.Offset(1, 0).Activate
ActiveCell.Value = "Retained earnings"
For i = 1 To N
  ActiveCell.Offset(0, i).Value = R(i)
Next

ActiveCell.Offset(1, 0).Activate
ActiveCell.Value = "Total liabilities and net worth"
For i = 1 To N
  ActiveCell.Offset(0, i).Value = TLANW(i)
Next

ActiveCell.Offset(1, 0).Activate
ActiveCell.Value = "Computed DBT/EQ"
For i = 1 To N
  ActiveCell.Offset(0, i).Value = COMPK(i)
Next

ActiveCell.Offset(1, 0).Activate
ActiveCell.Value = "Int. rate on total debt"
For i = 1 To N
  ActiveCell.Offset(0, i).Value = ZI(i)
Next

ActiveCell.Offset(1, 0).Activate
ActiveCell.Value = "Per share data"
```

```
ActiveCell.Offset(1, 0).Activate
ActiveCell.Value = "Earnings"
For i = 1 To N
  ActiveCell.Offset(0, i).Value = EPS(i)
Next

ActiveCell.Offset(1, 0).Activate
ActiveCell.Value = "Dividends"
For i = 1 To N
  ActiveCell.Offset(0, i).Value = DPS(i)
Next

ActiveCell.Offset(1, 0).Activate
ActiveCell.Value = "Price"
For i = 1 To N
  ActiveCell.Offset(0, i).Value = P(i)
Next

Exit Sub 'Exit to avoid ErrorHandler.

ErrorHandler: 'Error-handling routine.
  Select Case Err.Number ' Evaluate error number.
    Case 9
      MsgBox "'The number of years to be simulated' does not match your "&_
      "'Last Period' input.", vbExclamation
    Case 11
      MsgBox Str$(Err.Number) & ", " & Err.Description & Chr$(10) & _
      "'The number of years to be simulated' does not match your " & _
      "'Last Period' input.", vbExclamation
    Case Else
      MsgBox Str$(Err.Number) & ", " & Err.Description
  End Select
End Sub
```

Bibliography

Brealey, R. A. and S. C. Myers. *Principles of Corporate Finance*, 6th edn. Burr Ridge, IL: McGraw-Hill, 2000.

Carleton, W. T. "An Analytical Model for Long-Range Financial Planning." *Journal of Finance*, v. 25 (May 1970), pp. 291–315.

Davis, B. E., G. J. Caccappolo and M. A. Chandry. "An Econometric Planning Model for American Telephone and Telegraph Company." *The Bell Journal of Economics and Management Science*, v. 4 (Spring 1973), pp. 29–56.

Diebold, F. X. and P. Pauly. "Structural Change and the Combination of Forecasts." *Journal of Forecasting*, v. 6 (January–March 1987), pp. 21–40.

Elliott, J. W. "Forecasting and Analysis of Corporate Financial Performance with an Econometric Model of the Firm." *Journal of Financial and Quantitative Analysis* (March 1972), pp. 1499–1526.

Feltham, G. A. and J. A. Ohlson. "Valuation and Clean Surplus Accounting for Operating and Financial Activities." *Contemporary Accounting Research*, v. 11 (1995), pp. 689–731.

Francis, J. C. "Analysis of Equity Returns: A Survey with Extensions." *Journal of Economics and Business* (Spring/Summer 1977), pp. 181–192.

Francis, J. C. and D. R. Rowell. "A Simultaneous-Equation Model of the Firm for Financial Analysis and Planning." *Financial Management*, v. 7 (Spring 1978), pp. 29–44.

Gershefski, G. W. "Building a Corporate Financial Model." *Harvard Business Review* (July/August 1969), pp. 61–72.

Granger, C. W. J. and P. Newbold. "Some Comments on the Evaluation of Economic Forecasts." *Applied Economics*, v. 5 (March 1973), pp. 35–47.

Lee, C. F. Alternative Financial Planning and Forecasting Models: An Integration and Extension. Mimeo: The University of Illinois at Urbana-Champaign, 1984.

Lee, C. F. and S. Rahman. "Interaction of Investment, Financing, and Dividend Decisions: A Control Theory Approach." *Advances in Financial Planning and Forecasting*, v. 7 (1997).

Lee, C. F. J. E. Finnerty and E. A. Norton. *Foundations of Financial Management*, 3rd edn. Minneapolis/St. Paul: West Publishing Co., 1997.

Lee, C. F., J. C. Lee and A. C. Lee. *Statistics for Business and Financial Economics*. Singapore: World Science Publishing Co., 2000.

Lee, A. C., J. C. Lee, and C. F. Lee. *Financial Analysis, Planning and Forecasting: Theory and Application*, 2nd ed. Singapore: World Scientific Publishing Company, 2009.

Lee, C. F., W. K. Shih, and H. Y. Chen. "Alternative Equity Valuation Models." 2012 Working Paper.

Lerner, E. and W. T. Carleton. "The Integration of Capital Budgeting and Stock Valuation." *American Economics Review*, v. 54 (September 1964), pp. 683–702.

Myers. S. C. and A. Pogue. "A Programming Approach to Corporate Financial Management." *Journal of Finance*, v. 29 (May 1974), pp. 579–599.

Ohlson, J. A. "Earnings, Book Values, and Dividends in Equity Valuation." *Contemporary Accounting Research*, v. 11 (1995), pp. 661–687.

Pindyck, R. S. and D. L. Rubinfeld. *Econometric Models and Economic Forecasts*. New York: McGraw-Hill Book Co., 1976.

Ross, S. A., R. W. Westerfield and J. F. Jaffe. *Corporate Finance*, 6th edn. Boston, MA: McGraw-Hill Irwin Publishing Co., 2002.

Salzman, S. "An Econometric Model of a Firm." *Review of Economics and Statistics*, v. 49 (August 1967), pp. 332–342.

Securities and Exchange Commission, Release No. 5695. "Notice of Adoption of Amendments to Regulations S-X Requiring Disclosure of Certain Replacement Cost Data," March 23, 1976.

Securities and Exchange Commission, Release No. 33-5699. April 23, 1976.

Warren, J. M. and J. P. Shelton. "A Simultaneous-Equation Approach to Financial Planning." *Journal of Finance*, v. 26 (December 1971), pp. 1123–1142.

Williams, J. B. *The Theory of Investment Value.* Cambridge, MA: Harvard University Press, 1938.

Websites

http://finance.yahoo.com.

Chapter 27

Itô's Calculus: Derivation of the Black–Scholes Option Pricing Model*

The purpose of this chapter is to develop certain relatively recent mathematical discoveries known generally as **stochastic calculus** (or more specifically as **Itô's Calculus**) and to illustrate their application in the pricing of options. The topic is motivated by a desire to provide an *intuitive* understanding of certain probabilistic methods that have found significant use in financial economics. A rigorous presentation of the same ideas is presented briefly in Malliaris and Brock (1982) and more recently, Chalamandaris and Malliaris (2011).

Itô's Calculus was prompted by purely mathematical questions originating in Wiener's work in 1923 on stochastic integrals and was developed by the Japanese probabilist Kiyosi Itô during 1944–1951. Two decades later economists such as Merton (1973) and Black and Scholes (1973) started using Itô's stochastic differential equation to describe the behavior of asset prices. Because stochastic calculus is now used regularly by financial economists, some attention must be given to its mathematical meaning, its appropriateness in economic modeling, and its applications in economic modeling, and to finance.

27.1. The Itô Process and Financial Modeling

Stochastic calculus is the mathematical of random change in continuous time, unlike ordinary calculus, which deals with deterministic change. A key

* This chapter was written by Professor A. G. Malliaris, Loyola University of Chicago.

notion in stochastic calculus is the equation

$$dS(t,w) = \mu[t, S(t,w)]dt + \sigma[t, S(t,w)]dZ(t,w), \qquad (27.1)$$

which is analogous to the ordinary differential equation $dS(t)/dt = \mu[t, S(t)]$. This section defines intuitively the Itô equation in Equation (27.1) and discusses its appropriateness to financial modeling.

A stochastic process is an Itô process if the random variable $dS(t,w)$ can be represented by Equation (27.1). The first term, $\mu[t, S(t,w)]dt$, is the expected change in $S(t,w)$ at time t. The second term, $\sigma[t, S(t,w)]dZ(t,w)$, reflects the uncertain term.

The Itô equation is a random equation. The domain of the equation is $[0,\infty) \times \Omega$, with the first argument t denoting time and taking values continuously in the interval $[0,\infty)$, and the second argument w denoting a random element taking values from a random set Ω. The range of the equation is the real numbers or real vectors. For simplicity, only the real numbers, denoted by R, are considered as the range of Equation (27.1). Because time takes values continuously in $[0,\infty)$, the Itô equation is a **continuous-time random equation**.

Although at first a real random variables $S(t,w): [0,\infty) \times \Omega \to R$ is used — that is, a function having as domain $[0,\infty) \times \Omega$ and as range real numbers — Equation (27.1) expresses not the values of $S(t,w)$, but its infinitesimal differences $dS(t,w)$ as a function of two terms. For example, in finance $S(t,w)$ denotes the price of a stock at time t affected by the state of the economy described by the random element w; and (27.1) expresses the small changes in the stock price, $dS(t,w)$, at time t affected by the random element w. The mathematical meaning of this small difference can be explained as follows: $dS(t,w)$ may be viewed as the limit of large finite differences $\Delta S(t,w)$ as Δt approaches zero. Note that $\Delta S(t,w) = S(t + \Delta t, w) - S(t,w)$, where Δt denotes the difference in the change in time. Thus, the Itô equation, expresses random changes in the values of a variable taking place continuously in time.

Moreover, these random changes are given as the sum of two terms. The first term, $\mu[t, S(t,w)]$, is called the **drift component** of the Itô equation, and in finance it is used to compute the instantaneous expected value of the change in the random variable $S(t,w)$. Observe that $\mu[t, S(t,w)]$, as a function used in the computation of a statistical mean, is affected by both time and randomness. If at a given time t the expected change in $dS(t,w)$, expressed as $E[dS(t,w)]$, is desired, this can be answered by computing $E\{\mu[t, S(t,w)]dt\}$.

The second term $\sigma[t, S(t, w)]dZ(t, w)$ is itself the product of two factors. Each factor is important and needs special attention. The first factor, $\sigma[t, S(t, w)]$, is used in the calculation of the instantaneous standard derivation of the change in the random variable $S(t, w)$; it is a function of both time t and the range of values taken by $S(t, w)$. When $\sigma[t, S(t, w)]$ is squared to compute the instantaneous variance, it is usually called the **diffusion coefficient**; it measures the variability of $dS(t, w)$ at a given instance in time.

The second factor, $dZ(t, w)$, is called **white noise**; it models financial uncertainty in continuous time. Actually, $dZ(t, w)$ denotes an infinitesimal change in the **Wiener process**, $Z(t, w) : [0, \infty) \times \Omega \to R$, a process with increments that are statistically independent and normally distributed with mean zero and variance equal to the increment in time. In other words, for every pair of disjoint time intervals $[t_1, t_2], [t_3, t_4]$ with, say, $t_1 < t_2 \leq t_3 < t_4$, the increments $Z(t_4, w) - Z(t_3, w)$ and $Z(t_2, w) - Z(t_1, w)$ are independent and normally distributed random variables with means

$$E[Z(t_3, w) - Z(t_4, w)] = E[Z(t_2, w) - Z(t_1, w)] = 0,$$

and respective variances

$$\begin{aligned}\text{Var}[Z(t_4, w) - Z(t_3, w)] &= t_4 - t_3,\\ \text{Var}[Z(t_2, w) - Z(t_1, w)] &= t_2 - t_1.\end{aligned}$$

By convention it is assumed that at time $t = 0$, the Wiener process is zero — that is, $Z(0, w) = 0$.

The two factors have been described separately; an intuitive explanation of the product of $\sigma[t, S(t, w)]$ and $dZ(t, w)$ is now presented. Because $\sigma[t, S(t, w)]$ measures the instantaneous standard derivation or volatility of $dS(t, w)$ and because $dZ(t, w)$ is an infinitesimal increment (which is, by definition, purely random with mean zero and variance dt), the expression of $\sigma[t, S(t, w)]dZ(t, w)$ is the product of two independent random variables, with

$$E\{\sigma[t, S(t, w)]dZ(t, w)\} = 0, \tag{27.2}$$

$$\begin{aligned}Var\{\sigma[t, S(t, w)]dZ(t, w)\} &= E\{\sigma[t, S(t, w)]dZ(t, w)\}^2\\ &= E\{\sigma^2[t, S(t, w)]dt\}.\end{aligned} \tag{27.3}$$

Therefore, the product $\sigma[t, S(t, w)]dZ(t, w)$ is a random variable with mean and variances given by Equations (27.2) and (27.3), which, for a given time t and state of nature w, yields a real number. This number may be either positive or negative depending on the value of $dZ(t, w)$ since $\sigma[t, S(t, w)]$ represents a measure of standard derivation and is always positive. Furthermore, the magnitude of the product $\sigma[t, S(t, w)]dZ(t, w)$ depends on the magnitude of each of the two terms. Indeed, the methodological foundation of the Itô model is that the uncertainty magnitude, $dZ(t, w)$ is multiplied by $\sigma[t, S(t, w)]$ to produce the **total contribution of uncertainty**. Therefore, $\sigma[t, S(t, w)]dZ(t, w)$ describes the total fluctuation produced by volatility as this volatility is aggrandized or reduced by pure randomness.

This analysis explains why uncertainty given by $dZ(t, w)$ is being modeled as a multiplicative factor in the product $\sigma[t, S(t, w)]dZ(t, w)$: to repeat once again, the multiplicative modeling of uncertainty allows the generation of values for $dS(t, w)$ that are above or below the instantaneous expected value, depending on whether uncertainty is positive or negative, respectively. In other words, the product $\sigma[t, S(t, w)]dZ(t, w)$ can be viewed as the total contribution of uncertainty to $dS(t, w)$, with such uncertainty being the product of two factors: the instantaneous standard derivation of changes and the purely random white noise.

The conceptual components of the Itô process can now be collected to offer a more general interpretation of its meaning in finance. If at a given time t the possible future change in the price of an asset during the next trading interval is being evaluated, this change can be decomposed into two nonoverlapping components: the *expected* change and the *unexpected* change. The expected change, $E[dS(t, w)]$, is described by $E\{\sigma[t, S(t, w)]dt\}$ and the unexpected change is given by $E\{\sigma[t, S(t, w)]dZ(t, w)\}$. As already noted, this unexpected change depends on the asset's volatility and pure randomness, and because uncertainty cannot be anticipated, the unexpected change is zero. This holds because $\sigma[t, S(t, w)]$ and $dZ(t, w)$ are independent random variables; and therefore, from Equation (27.2):

$$E\{\sigma[t, S(t, w)]dZ(t, w)\} = E\{\sigma[t, S(t, w)]\}E[dZ(t, w)] = 0.$$

Because by definition $E[dZ(t, w)] = 0$. Thus, Equation (27.1), which was developed by mathematicians, captures the spirit of financial modeling admirably because it is an equation that involves three important concepts in finance: *mean, standard derivation, and randomness.*

However, Equation (27.1) captures the spirit of finance not only because it involves means, standard derivations, and randomness but, more important, because it also expresses key methodological elements of modern financial theory. In an elegant paper, Merton (1982) identified several foundational notions of the appropriateness of the Itô equation in modern finance.

(1) Itô's equation allows uncertainty not to disappear even as trading intervals become extremely short. In the real world of financial markets, uncertainty evolves continuously, and $dZ(t, w)$ captures this uncertainty because the value of $dZ(\Delta t, w)$ is not zero even as Δt becomes small. On the other hand, as trading intervals increase uncertainty increases because by definition

$$\text{Var}[Z(t + \Delta t, w) - Z(t, w)] = \Delta t.$$

(2) Itô's equation incorporates uncertainty for all times. This means that uncertainty is present at all trading periods.
(3) The rate of change described by $\mu[t, S(t, w)]dt$ is finite, and uncertainty does not cause the term $\mu[t, S(t, w)]dZ(t, w)$ to become unbounded. These notions of the Itô equation are consistent with real-world observations of finite means, finite variances, and uncertainty (which evolves nicely by obtaining continuously finite values).
(4) Finally, all that counts in an Itô equation is the present time t. In other words, the past and future are independent. This notion expresses mathematically the concept of economic markets efficiency. That is, knowledge of past price behavior does not allow for above-average returns in the future.

Sample Problems 27.1 and 27.2 provide illustrations of the concepts discussed.

Sample Problem 27.1

Consider the following example of an Itô process describing the price of given stock.

$$dS(t, w) = 0.001\ S(t, w)dt + 0.025\ S(t, w)dZ(t, w).$$

If both sides are divided by $S(t, w)$ we get:

$$\frac{dS(t, w)}{S(t, w)} = 0.001\ dt + 0.025\ dZ(t, w), \tag{27.4}$$

which gives the proportional change in the price of the stock. Assume that dt equals one trading period, such as one day. Using appropriate coefficients in Equation (27.4), dt could be denoted as one second. In Equation (27.4), the expected daily proportional change is given by

$$E\left[\frac{dS(t,w)}{S(t,w)}\right] = E[0.001\ dt + 0.025\ dZ(t,w)] = 0.001, \tag{27.5}$$

which means that at any given trading day, the price of the stock is expected to change by 0.1%. The standard derivation of the proportional change is $\sigma = 0.025$ or 2.5%.

What actually occurs at a given trading period depends on the evolution of the uncertainty as modeled by the normally distributed random variable $dZ(t,w)$, with mean 0 and variance 1. From the properties of the normal distribution, it can be deduced that although Equation (27.5) says that the expected daily proportional change is 0.001 and there is a 68.26% probability that the daily proportional change will be between $0.001 \pm (1)(0.025)$, or a 95.46% probability that it will be between $0.001 \pm (2)(0.025)$, or a 99.74% probability that it will be between $0.001 \pm (3)(0.025)$.

Sample Problem 27.2

This second example shows how the Itô equation combines the notion of a trading interval dt, the expected change in the price of the stock μ, the volatility of the stock μ, and pure uncertainty $dZ(t,w)$ to describe changes in the price of an asset. The same example will be used later to show the behavior of the price of the stock $S(t,w)$. Equation (27.5) illustrates only approximately the infinitesimal proportional change in the price of the stock and in order to obtain the solution of the stochastic differential equation in (27.5), we need the following useful lemma.

27.2. Itô Lemma

The preceding two sections dealt with the Itô process, both its intuitive mathematical meaning and its financial interpretation. This section presents briefly Itô's lemma of stochastic differentiation. By formally integrating Equation (27.1):

$$S(t,w) = S(0,w) + \int_0^t \mu(u,w)du + \int_0^t \mu(u,w)dZ(u,w), \tag{27.6}$$

this last equation describes Itô's process in terms of the original random variable $S(t,w)$ rather than infinitesimal differences (differential form), as in Equation (27.1). Mathematically, Equations (27.1) and (27.6) are equivalent and (27.1) obtains clear meaning through integration, which is not developed here because of its complexity. Nevertheless, note that it is the second integral, $\int_0^t \mu(u,w)dZ(u,w)$, that presents the difficulties. The problem arises because uncertainty given by $dZ(u,w)$ in its limit does not have a precise meaning, and therefore the second integral cannot be treated like an ordinary Riemann integral. Itô's great accomplishment was to define the second integral as a random variable, that is, the limit in probability of a certain sequence of integrals of step functions multiplied by the uncertainty $dZ(u,w)$.

Suppose that a stochastic process is given by Equation (27.6) and that a new process $Y(t,w)$ is formed by letting $Y(t,w) = u[t, S(t,w)]$. Because stochastic calculus studies random changes in continuous time, the question arises: what is $dY(t,w)$? This question is important for both mathematical analysis and finance. The answer is given in Itô's lemma.

Itô's Lemma. *Consider the nonrandom continuous function* $u(t,S)$: $[0,\infty)\times R \to R$ *and suppose that it has continuous partial derivatives* u_t,u_S, and u_{SS}.

Let

$$Y(t,w) = u[t, S(t,w)], \tag{27.7}$$

with

$$dS(t,w) = \mu[t, S(t,w)]dt + \sigma[t, S(t,w)]dZ(t,w). \tag{27.8}$$

Then the process $Y(t,w)$ has a differential given by

$$\begin{aligned} dY(t,w) = \{&u_t[t,S(t,w)] + u_S[t,S(t,w)]\mu[t,S(t,w)] \\ &+ \frac{1}{2}u_{SS}[t,S(t,w)]\sigma^2[t,S(t,w)]\}dt \\ &+ u_S[t,S(t,w)]\sigma[t,S(t,w)]dZ(t,w). \end{aligned} \tag{27.9}$$

The proof is presented in Gikhman and Skorokhod (1969, pp. 387–389), and extensions of this lemma may be found in Arnold (1974, pp. 90–99). Here the analysis is limited to three remarks.

(1) Itô's lemma is a useful result because it allows the computation of stochastic differentials of arbitrary functions having as an argument a stochastic process that itself is assumed to possess a stochastic differential. In this respect, Itô's formula is as useful as the chain rule of ordinary calculus.
(2) Given an Itô stochastic process $S(t, w)$ with respect to a given Wiener process $Z(t, w)$, and letting $Y(t, w) = u[t, S(t, w)]$ be a new process, Itô's formula gives the stochastic differential of $Y(t, w)$, where $dY(t, w)$ is given with respect to the same Wiener process — that is, both processes have the same source of uncertainty.
(3) An inspection of the proof of Itô's lemma reveals that it consists of an application of Taylor's theorem of advanced calculus and several probabilistic arguments to establish the convergence of certain quantities to appropriate integrals. Therefore, Itô's formula may be obtained by applying Taylor's theorem instead of remembering the specific result in Equation (27.6). More specifically, the differential of $Y(t, w) = u[t, S(t, w)]$, where $S(t, w)$ is a stochastic process with differential given by Equation (27.1), may be computed by using Taylor's theorem and the following multiplication rules:

$$dt \times dt = 0, \quad dZ \times dZ = dt, \quad dt \times dZ = 0 \tag{27.10}$$

as

$$\begin{aligned} dY &= u_t dt + u_S dS + \frac{1}{2}(dS)^2 \\ &= u_t dt + u_S(\mu dt + \sigma dZ) + \frac{1}{2}u_{SS}(\mu dt + \sigma dZ)^2. \end{aligned}$$

By carrying out these multiplications and using the rules in Equation (27.10), Equation (27.9) is obtained.

27.3. Stochastic Differential-Equation Approach to Stock-Price Behavior

This section demonstrates how a stochastic equation can be used to describe the price behavior of an asset. We begin with Sample Problem 27.3

Sample Problem 27.3

As a special case of Equation (27.1) consider:

$$dS(t, w) = \mu S(t, w)dt + \sigma S(t, w)dZ(t, w) \tag{27.11}$$

in which μ and σ are constants as in Sample Problem 27.1. Assume that Equation (27.11) describes the price behavior of a certain stock with $S(0, w)$ given. The solution $S(t, w)$ of Equation (27.11) is given by

$$S(t,w) = S(0,w)\exp\left[\left(\mu - \frac{1}{2}\sigma^2\right)t + \sigma Z(t,w)\right]. \tag{27.12}$$

To show that the behavior of Equation (27.12) is the solution of Equation (27.11), use Itô's lemma as follows. First, start with Equation (27.12), which corresponds to the function $Y(t, w)$. In this case, Equation (27.12) is a function of t and $Z(t, w)$, and instead of Equation (27.8):

$$dZ(t,w) = 0 \cdot dt + 1 \cdot dZ(t,w).$$

Next, compute the first- and second-order partials denoted by S_t, S_Z, and S_{ZZ}:

$$\begin{aligned} S_t(t,w) &= \left(\mu - \frac{\sigma^2}{2}\right)S(t,w), \\ S_Z(t,w) &= \sigma S(t,w), \\ S_{ZZ}(t,w) &= \sigma^2 S(t,w). \end{aligned}$$

Collect these results and use Equation (27.9) to conclude that Equation (27.11) holds:

$$\begin{aligned} dS(t,w) &= \left[\left(\mu - \frac{\sigma^2}{2}\right)S(t,w) + \sigma S(t,w)\cdot 0 + \frac{\sigma^2}{2}S(t,w)\cdot 1\right]dt \\ &\quad + \sigma S(t,w)\cdot 1 \cdot dZ(t,w) \\ &= \mu S(t,w)dt + \sigma S(t,w)dZ(t,w). \end{aligned}$$

This result is not only mathematically interesting; in finance it means that, assuming stock price are given by an Itô process as in Equation (27.11), then Equation (27.12) holds as well. To see if Equation (27.12) accurately describes stock prices in the real world, rewrite it as

$$\ln\frac{S(t,w)}{S(0,w)} = \left(\mu - \frac{\sigma^2}{2}\right)t + \sigma Z(t,w), \tag{27.13}$$

which is a random variable normally distributed with mean $(\mu - \sigma^2/2)t$ and variance $\sigma^2 t$. This means that if the stock price follows an Itô process, it has a log-normal probability distribution. Such a distribution for stock price is reasonable because it is consistent with reality, where negative stock prices are not possible; the worst that can happen is that the stock price reaches zero. For a detailed analysis of the properties of a log-normal random distribution, see Cox and Rubinstein (1985, pp. 201–204); for a list of bibliographical references on the empirical distribution of stock-price changes, see Cox and Rubinstein (1985, pp. 485–488). Sample Problem 27.4 provides further illustration.

Sample Problem 27.4

The analysis of this problem applies the results of the last two sections to the example in Sample problem 27.1. Suppose that instead of Equation (27.11) Equation (27.14) is given. Then Equation (27.12) describes the solution of Equation (27.14):

$$S(t, w) = S(0, w) \exp\left[\left(0.001 - \frac{0.025^2}{2}\right) t + 0.025 Z(t, w)\right]. \qquad (27.14)$$

From Equation (27.14), the exact evolution of the price of the stock as influences by a mean, a variance, time, and uncertainty is obtained. Using Equation (27.14) for $t = 1$ to compute:

$$E\left[\ln \frac{S(t, w)}{S(0, w)}\right] = \left(\mu - \frac{\sigma^2}{2}\right) t = \left[0.001 - \frac{(0.025)^2}{2}\right] (0.1) = 0.0006875, \qquad (27.15)$$

$$\text{Var}\left[\frac{S(t, w)}{S(0, w)}\right] = \sigma^2 t = (0.025)^2 (0.1) = 0.000625, \qquad (27.16)$$

which means that for a given trading day, the price of the stock is expected to experience a continuous change of 0.068% with a standard derivation of 0.025%. Computing Equations (27.15) and (27.16) for any t can be done easily; the same computations cannot be performed readily in Equation (27.4).

Sample Problem 27.5

Here we give an intuitive description of Equation (27.1) with reference to Table 27.1 using Excel. In Table 27.1, we collect from Yahoo.com 40 recent daily closing Google Inc. prices. These prices are also illustrated graphically in Fig. 27.1.

For modeling purposes, the Black–Scholes equation requires a mathematical expression for prices, such as shown in Table 27.1 and Fig. 27.1.

Table 27.1. Daily Price Data for Google Inc.

Day	Price	r_i	dZ
1	610.21		
2	630.08	0.03256	2.91992
3	625.26	−0.00765	−0.66558
4	624.22	−0.00166	−0.13180
5	624.15	−0.00011	0.00651
6	628.15	0.00641	0.58794
7	624.5	−0.00581	−0.50160
8	616.44	−0.01291	−1.13427
9	616.5	0.00010	0.02519
10	618.38	0.00305	0.28841
11	614.29	−0.00661	−0.57323
12	610.98	−0.00539	−0.46394
13	610.15	−0.00136	−0.10462
14	612	0.00303	0.28686
15	611.04	−0.00157	−0.12336
16	600.36	−0.01748	−1.54193
17	600.99	0.00105	0.11008
18	616.79	0.02629	2.36063
19	616.5	−0.00047	−0.02541
20	619.91	0.00553	0.50970
21	611.08	−0.01424	−1.25354
22	611.83	0.00123	0.12594
23	626.77	0.02442	2.19377
24	631.75	0.00795	0.72496
25	639.63	0.01247	1.12868
26	624.18	−0.02415	−2.13721
27	616.69	−0.01200	−1.05344
28	616.87	0.00029	0.04253
29	616.01	−0.00139	−0.10780
30	614.21	−0.00292	−0.24403
31	616.44	0.00363	0.34024
32	613.5	−0.00477	−0.40874
33	609.07	−0.00722	−0.62733
34	602.12	−0.01141	−1.00093
35	604.35	0.00370	0.34674
36	593.97	−0.01718	−1.51493
37	598.86	0.00823	0.75057
38	601	0.00357	0.33513
39	598.92	−0.00346	−0.29208
40	602.38	0.00578	0.53162
41	604.23	0.00307	0.29035
$\mu_{\mathbf{ri}}$		−0.000185	
$\sigma_{\mathbf{ri}}$		0.011215	
$\mu_{\mathbf{dz}}$			0
$\sigma_{\mathbf{dz}}$			1

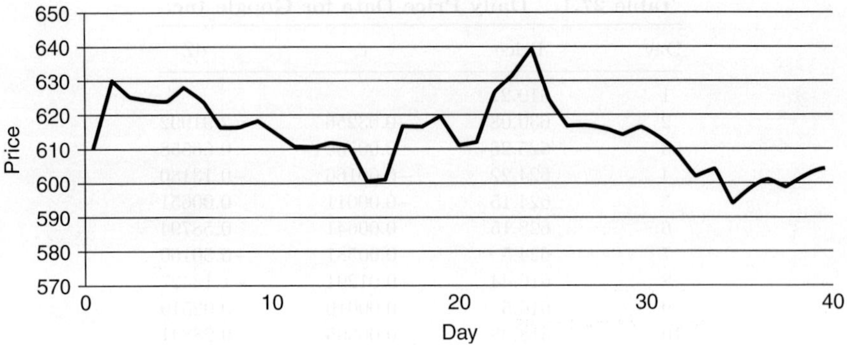

Fig. 27.1. Daily Google Inc. Closing Prices.

How can we check to see if the prices in these figures follow an Itô process? In column 3 of Table 27.1, we compute the daily Google returns and calculate the average historical return of the 40 daily returns. This daily average is 0.000185, which annualized becomes $0.000185 \times 250 = 0.04625$. The volatility of these 40 returns is computed as the annualized standard deviation of daily returns and is computed as $0.011215 \times \sqrt{250} = 0.177324$. Both these calculations assume 250 trading days per year. To complete checking the prices in Table 27.1 satisfy Equation (27.8), we solve for dZ. Since these prices are daily, we use the daily constant average return and constant daily volatility to obtain daily dZs in column 4 of Table 27.1 using

$$dZ_i = \frac{r_i - \mu_{ri}}{\sigma_{ri}}.$$

We also compute the mean and variance of the dZ in the last column. Recall that earlier we postulated that $E(dZ) = 0$ and $\text{Var}(dZ) = 1$ is assumed. Indeed, the mean and variance of the dZ values in Table 27.1 are as postulated.

Note that if we were to graph the distribution of Google stock prices, it would follow a log-normal distribution while its returns would follow a normal distribution. Furthermore, the daily dZs, as an approximation to the continuous random walk dZ of Equation (27.8), also are normally distributed with mean 0 and variance 1. Figures 27.2 and 27.3 are frequency approximations to a normal distribution and illustrate the distributions of returns and distributions of dZs of Table 27.1.

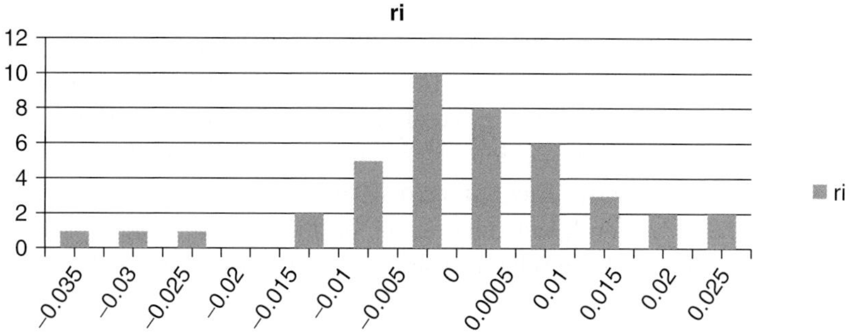

Fig. 27.2. Frequency Distribution of Returns.

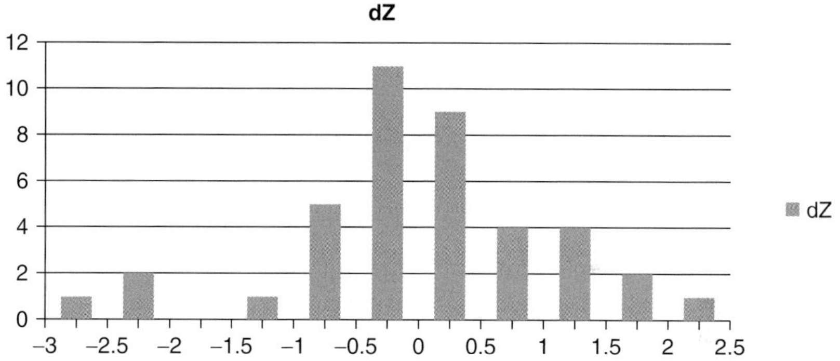

Fig. 27.3. Frequency Distribution of Errors.

27.4. The Pricing of an Option

An **option** is a contract giving the right to buy or sell an asset within a specified period of time subject to certain conditions. The simplest kind of option is the **European call option**, which is a contract to buy a share of a certain stock at a given date for a specified price. The date the option expires is called the **expiration date (maturity date)** and the price that is paid for the stock when the option is exercised is called the **exercise price (striking price)**.

In terms of economic analysis, several propositions about call-option pricing seem clear. The value of an option increases as the price of the stock increases. If the stock price is much greater than the exercise price, it is almost certain that the option will be exercised; and, analogously, if the price of the stock is much less than the exercise price, the value of the option will be near zero and the option will expire without being exercised. If the expiration date is very far in the future, the value of the option will be approximately equal to the price of the stock. If the expiration date is very near, the value of the option will be approximately equal to the stock price minus the exercise price, or zero if the stock price is less than the exercise price. In general, the value of the option is more volatile than the price of the stock, and the relative volatility of the option depends on both the stock price and maturity.

The first rigorous formulation and solution of the problem of option pricing was achieved by Black and Scholes (1973) and Merton (1973). Consider a stock option denoted by C whose price at time t can be written:

$$C(t, w) = C[t, S(t, w)], \tag{27.17}$$

in which C is a twice continuously differentiable function. Here $S(t, w)$ is the price of some stock upon which the option is written. The price of this stock is assumed to follow Itô's stochastic differential equation:

$$dS(t, w) = \mu[t, S(t, w)]dt + \sigma[t, S(t, w)]dZ(t, w). \tag{27.18}$$

Assume, as a simplifying case, that $\mu[t, S(t, w)] = \mu S(t, w)$ and $\sigma[t, S(t, w)] = \sigma S(t, w)$. For notational convenience, w is suppressed from the various expressions, and sometimes t as well. Therefore, Equation (27.18) becomes

$$dS(t) = \mu S(t)dt + \sigma S(t)dZ(t). \tag{27.19}$$

Consider an investor who builds up a portfolio of stocks, options on the stocks, and a riskless asset (for example, government bonds) yielding a riskless rate r. The nominal of the portfolio, denoted by $P(t)$, is

$$P(t) = N_1(t)S(t) + N_2C(t) + Q(t), \tag{27.20}$$

where

N_1 = the number of shares of the stock;
N_2 = the number of call options; and
Q = the value of dollars invested in riskless bonds.

Assume that the stock pays no dividends or other distributions. By Itô's lemma, the differential of the call price using Equations (27.17) and (27.19) is

$$\begin{aligned} dC &= C_t dt + C_S dS + \frac{1}{2} C_{SS} dS^2 \\ &= \left(C_t + C_S \mu S + \frac{1}{2} C_{SS} \sigma^2 S^2 \right) dt + C_S \sigma S dZ \\ &= \mu_C C dt + \sigma_C C dZ. \end{aligned} \tag{27.21}$$

Observe that in Equation (27.21):

$$\mu_C C = C_t + C_S \mu S + \frac{1}{2} C_{SS} \sigma^2 S^2, \tag{27.22}$$

$$\sigma_C C = C_S \sigma S. \tag{27.23}$$

In other words, $\mu_C C$ is the expected change in the call-option price and $\sigma_C^2 C^2$ is the variance of such a change per unit of time. Itô's lemma simply indicates that if the call-option price is a function of a spot stock price that follows an Itô process, then the call-option price also follows an Itô process with mean and standard derivation parameters that are more complex than those of the stock price. The Itô process for a call is given by Equations (27.22) and (27.23).

The change in the normal value of the portfolio dP results from the change in the prices of the assets because at a point in time the equations of option and stock are given — that is, $dN_1 = dN_2 = 0$. More precisely:

$$\begin{aligned} dP &= N_1(dS) + N_2(dS) + dQ \\ &= (\mu dt + \sigma dZ) N_1 S + (\mu_C dt + \sigma_C dZ) N_2 C + rQdt. \end{aligned} \tag{27.24}$$

Let w_1 be the fraction of the invested in stock, w_2 be the fraction invested in options, and w_3 be the fraction of the invested in the riskless asset. As before, $w_1 + w_2 + w_3 = 1$, that is, all of the funds available are invested in some type of asset. Set $w_1 = N_1 S/P$, $w_2 = N_2 C/P$, $w_3 = Q/P = 1 - w_1 - w_2$. Then Equation (27.24) becomes

$$\frac{dP}{P} = (\mu dt + \sigma dZ) w_1 + (\mu_C dt + \sigma_C dZ) w_2 + (r\, dt) w_3. \tag{27.25}$$

At this point, the notion of **economic equilibrium** (also called **risk-neutral** or **preference-free pricing**) is introduced in the analysis. This notion plays an important role in modeling financing behavior, and its appropriate formulation is considered to be a major breakthrough in financial analysis.

More specifically, design the proportions w_1, w_2 so that the position is *riskless* for all $t \geq 0$ — that is, let w_1 and w_2 be such that

$$\text{Var}\left(\frac{dP}{P}\right) = \text{Var}\,(w_1\sigma dZ + w_2\sigma_C dZ) = 0. \tag{27.26}$$

In the last equation, Var_t denotes variance conditioned on $S(t)$, $C(t)$, and $Q(t)$. In other words, choose $(w_1, w_2) = (\bar{w}_1, \bar{w}_2)$ so that

$$\bar{w}_1\sigma + \bar{w}_2\sigma_C = 0. \tag{27.27}$$

Then from Equation (27.25), because the portfolio is riskless it follows that the portfolio must be expected to earn the riskless rate of return, or:

$$E_t\left(\frac{dP}{P}\right) = [\mu\bar{w}_1 + \mu_C\bar{w}_2 + r(1 - \bar{w}_1 - \bar{w}_2)]dt = r(t)dt. \tag{27.28}$$

Equations (27.27) and (27.28) yield the Black–Scholes–Merton equations:

$$\frac{\bar{w}_1}{\bar{w}_2} = -\frac{\sigma_C}{\sigma}, \tag{27.29}$$

and

$$r = \mu\bar{w}_1 + \mu_C\bar{w}_2 - r\bar{w}_1 - r\bar{w}_2 + r, \tag{27.30}$$

which simplify to

$$\frac{\mu - r}{\sigma} = \frac{\mu_C - r}{\sigma_C}. \tag{27.31}$$

Because of the law of one price, Equation (27.31) says that the net rate of return per unit of risk must be the two assets and describes an appropriate concept of economic equilibrium in this problem. If this were not the case, there would exist an arbitrage opportunity until this equality held. Using Equation (27.31) and making the necessary substitutions from Equations (27.22) and (27.23), the partial differential equation of the pricing of an option is obtained:

$$\frac{1}{2}\sigma^2 S^2 C_{SS}(t, S) + rSC_S(t, S) - rC(t, S) + C_t(t, S) = 0. \tag{27.32}$$

The equation along with the boundary conditions for call options fully characterize the call price: $C(S, T) = \text{Max}(0, S - X), S \geq 0, 0 \geq E \geq T$. The solution to the differential Equation (27.32) given these boundary conditions is the Black–Scholes formula.

27.5. A Reexamination of Option Pricing

To illustrate the notion of economic equilibrium once again, consider the nominal value of a portfolio consisting of a stock and a call option on this stock and write:

$$P(t) = N_1(t)S(t) + N_2(t)C(t), \tag{27.33}$$

using the same notation as in the previous section. Equation (27.33) differs from Equation (27.20) because the term $Q(t)$ has been deleted. Now concentrating on the two assets of the portfolio — that is, the stock and the call option — and using Equations (27.33) and (27.21), the change in the value of the portfolio is given by

$$dP = N_1 dS + N_2 dC = N_1 dS + N_2[(C_t + \frac{1}{2}C_{SS}\sigma^2 S^2)dt + C_S dS]. \tag{27.34}$$

Note that $dN_1 = dN_2 = 0$, since at any given point in time the equations of stock and option are given. For arbitrary quantities of stock and option, Equation (27.34) shows that the change in the nominal value of the portfolio dP is stochastic because dS is a random variable. Suppose the quantities of stock and call option are chosen as that

$$\frac{N_1}{N_2} = -C_S. \tag{27.35}$$

Note that C_S in Equation (27.35) denotes a hedge ration and is called **delta**. Then,

$$N_1 dS + N_2 C_S dS = 0,$$

and inserting Equation (27.35) into Equation (27.34) yields:

$$\begin{aligned} dP &= -N_2 C_S dS + N_2 \left[\left(C_t + \frac{1}{2}C_{SS}\sigma^2 S^2\right) dt + C_S dS\right] \\ &= N_2 \left(C_t + \frac{1}{2}C_{SS}\sigma^2 S^2\right) dt. \end{aligned} \tag{27.36}$$

Let $N_2 = 1$ in Equation (27.36) and observe that in equilibrium the rate of return of the riskless portfolio must be the same as the riskless rate $r(t)$. Therefore:

$$\frac{dP}{p} = r\, dt. \tag{27.37}$$

Equation (27.37) can be used to derive the partial differential equation for the value of the option. Making the necessary substitutions in Equation (27.36):

$$\frac{(C_t + \frac{1}{2}C_{SS}\sigma^2 S^2)\,dt}{-C_S S + C} = r\,dt,$$

which upon rearrangement gives Equation (27.32). Note that the option-pricing equation is a second-order linear partial differential equation of the parabolic type. The boundary conditions of Equation (27.32) are determined by the specification of the asset. For the case of an option that can be exercised only at the expiration date t^* with an exercise price X, the boundary conditions are

$$C(t, S = 0) = 0, \tag{27.38}$$

$$C(t = t^*, S) = \text{Max}(0, S - X). \tag{27.39}$$

Observe that Equation (27.38) says that the call-option price is zero if the stock price is zero at any date t; Equation (27.39) says that the call-option price at the expiration date $t = t^*$ must equal the maximum of either zero or the difference between the stock price and the exercise price.

The solution of the option-pricing equation for a call and a put option subject to the boundary conditions are given in Equations (27.40a) and (27.40b) for $T = t^* - t$, as

$$C(T, S, \sigma^2, X, r) = SN(d_1) - Xe^{-rT}N(d2), \tag{27.40a}$$

$$P(T, S, \sigma^2, X, r) = Xe^{-rT}(-N(d_2) - S(-N(d_1)), \tag{27.40b}$$

where N denotes the cumulative normal distribution, namely:

$$N(y) = -\frac{1}{\sqrt{2\pi}}\int_{-\infty}^{y} \mathrm{e}^{-x^2/2}dx.$$

In Equation (27.40a), T is time to expiration (measured in years) and d_1 and d_2 are given by

$$d_1 = \frac{\ln(S/X) + (r + \frac{1}{2}\sigma^2)T}{\sigma\sqrt{T}}, \tag{27.41}$$

$$\begin{aligned} d_2 &= \frac{\ln(S/X) + (r - \frac{1}{2}\sigma^2)T}{\sigma\sqrt{T}} \\ &= d_1 - \sigma\sqrt{T}. \end{aligned} \tag{27.42}$$

It can be shown that

$$\frac{\partial C}{\partial T} > 0, \quad \frac{\partial C}{\partial S} > 0, \quad \frac{\partial C}{\partial \sigma^2} > 0, \quad \frac{\partial C}{\partial X} < 0, \quad \frac{\partial C}{\partial r} > 0. \tag{27.43}$$

These partial derivatives justify the intuitive behavior of the price of an option, as was indicated in the beginning of the previous section. More specifically, these partials show the following:

(1) As the stock price rises, so does the option price.
(2) As the variance rate of the underlying stock rises, so does the option price.
(3) With a higher exercise price, the expected payoff decreases.
(4) The value of the option increases as the interest rate rises.
(5) With a longer time to maturity, the price of the option is greater.

Before giving an example, it is appropriate to sketch the solution of Equation (27.32) subject to the boundary conditions of Equations (27.38) and (27.39). Let t denote the current trading period that is prior to the expiration date t^*. At time t, two outcomes can be expected to occur at t^*. (1) $S(t^*) > X$ — that is the price of the stock at the time of the expiration of the call option is greater than exercise price, or (2) $S(t^*) \leq X$. Note that the first outcome occurs with probability $P_0 \equiv P[S(t^*) > X]$ and the second occurs with probability $1 - p$. Obviously, the only interesting possibility is the first case when $S(t^*) > X$, because this is when the price of the call has positive value. If $S(t^*) \leq X$, then $C(t^*) = 0$ from Equation (27.39). Again from Equation (27.39), if $S(t^*) > X$, then the price of the call option at expiration $C(t^*)$ can be computed from the expiration of Equation (27.39):

$$C(t^*) = E\{Max[0, S(t^*) - X]\} = E[S(t^*) - X]. \tag{27.44}$$

What is the price of a call option if the first outcome materializes at t instead of t^*? This can be answered immediately by appropriate continuous discounting. Using Equation (27.44):

$$C(t) = \mathrm{e}^{-r(t^*-t)} E[S(t^*) - X]. \tag{27.45}$$

Recall, however, that $C(t)$ in Equation (27.45) holds only with probability p. Combine both possibilities to write:

$$\begin{aligned} C(t) &= p \cdot \mathrm{e}^{-r(t^*-t)} E[S(t^*) - X] + (1-p) \cdot 0 \\ &= p \cdot \mathrm{e}^{-r(t^*-t)} E[S(t^*)|S(t^*) > X] - p \cdot \mathrm{e}^{-r(t^*-t)} X. \end{aligned} \tag{27.46}$$

Detailed calculation in Jarrow and Rudd (1983, pp. 92–94) shows that because the price of the underlying stock is distributed log normally, it follows that

$$p = P[S(t^*) > X] = N\left[\frac{\ln\frac{S(t)}{X} + \left(r + \frac{1}{2}\sigma^2\right)(t^* - t)}{\sigma\sqrt{t^* - t}}\right], \tag{27.47}$$

$$p \cdot E[S(t^*)|S^* > X] = S(t)\mathrm{e}^{r(t^*-t)}N\left[\frac{\ln\frac{S(t)}{X} + \left(r + \frac{1}{2}\sigma^2\right)(t^* - t)}{\sigma\sqrt{t^* - t}}\right]. \tag{27.48}$$

Combining Equations (27.47) and (27.48) with $T = t^* - t$ into Equation (27.46) yields Equation (27.40a).

It is worth observing that two terms of Equations (27.40a) and (27.40b) have economic meaning. The first term, $SN(d_1)$, denotes the present value of receiving the stock provided that $S(t^*) > X$. The second term gives the present value of paying the striking price provided that $S(t^*) > X$. In the special case when there is no uncertainty and $\sigma = 0$, observe that

$$\begin{gathered} N(d_1) = N(d_2) = N(\infty) = 1; \quad \text{and} \\ C = S(t) - \mathrm{e}^{-r(t^*-t)}X, \end{gathered} \tag{27.49}$$

that is, a call is worth the difference between the current value of the stock and the discounted value of the striking price provided $S(t^*) > X$; otherwise the call price would be zero. When $\sigma \neq 0$ — that is, when uncertainty exists and the stock price is volatile — the two terms in Equation (27.49) are multiplied by $N(d_1)$ and $N(d_2)$, respectively, to adjust the call price for the prevailing uncertainties. These two probabilities can also be given an economic interpretation. As mentioned earlier, $N(d_1)$ is called delta; it is the partial derivative of the call price with respect to the stock price; $N(d_2)$ gives the probabilities that the call option will be in the money, as Equation (27.47) shows.

Assuming that investors in the economy have risk-neutral preferences, it will be possible to derive the Black–Scholes formula without using stochastic differential equations. Garven (1986) has shown that to derive Equation (27.40a) knowledge is required of normal and log-normal distributions and basic calculus, as presented in Appendix 27A.

Sample Problem 27.6

Equations (27.40a) and (27.40b) indicate that the Black–Scholes option-pricing model is a function of only five variables: T, the time to expiration,

S, the stock price, σ^2, the instantaneous variance rate on the stock price, X, the exercise price, and r, the riskless interest rate. Of these five variables, only the variance rate must be estimated; the other four variables are directly observable. A simple example is presented to illustrate the use of Equation (27.40). The values of the observable variables are taken from *Yahoo! Finance*.

On Wednesday, March 16, 2011, at 3:58 pm EDT, IBM Corp. had a stock price of \$152.93. The July 11 call-option with a strike price of 150.00 was priced at \$10.50. We estimate the riskless rate at 0.25% from the U.S. Treasury bill rate. The only missing piece of information is the instantaneous variance of the stock price.

Several different techniques have been suggested for estimating the instantaneous variance. In this regard, the work of Latané and Rendleman (1976) must be mentioned; they derived standard derivations of continuous price-relative returns that are implied in actual call-option prices on the assumption that investors behave as if they price options according to the Black–Scholes model. In the example the implicit variance is calculated by using a numerical search to approximate the standard derivation implied by the Black–Scholes formula with these parameters: stock price $S = 152.93$, exercise price $X = 150$, time to expiration $T = 121/365 = 0.3315$, riskless rate $r = 0.0025$, and call-option price $C = 10.50$. The approximated implied volatility is found to be $\sigma = 0.264$.

Sample Problem 27.7

Using the information about the implied volatility presented above and a stock price of $S = 155$, we present the following example. Given $S = 155$, $X = 150$, $T = 0.3315$, $r = 0.0025$, and $\sigma = 0.264$, use Equation (27.40) to compute C. Using Equation (27.41) and (27.42) calculate:

$$d_1 = \frac{\ln\left(\frac{155}{150}\right) + \left[0.0025 + \left(\frac{0.264^2}{2}\right)\right] 0.3315}{0.264\sqrt{0.3315}} = 0.29717,$$

$$d_2 = \frac{\ln\left(\frac{155}{150}\right) + \left[0.0025 - \left(\frac{0.264^2}{2}\right)\right] 0.3315}{0.264\sqrt{0.3315}} = 0.14517.$$

From a standard normal distribution table, giving the area of a standard normal distribution, $N(0.29717) = 0.616836$ and $N(0.14517) = 0.557923$. Finally,

$$C = 152.93 \times 0.616836 - 150e^{-0.0025*0.3315} \times 0.557923 = \$10.71.$$

These calculations show that as the price of the underlying stock increases from 152.93 to 155, the call price increases as indicated in (27.43) from \$10.50 to \$10.71, while all other variables are the same.

Sample Problem 27.8

Using the information from the above example, we will calculate a call with a strike price of \$160 using Equation (27.40a)

$$d_1 = \frac{\ln\left(\frac{155}{160}\right) + \left[0.0025 + \left(\frac{0.264^2}{2}\right)\right] 0.3315}{0.264\sqrt{0.3315}} = -0.127419,$$

$$d_2 = \frac{\ln\left(\frac{155}{160}\right) + \left[0.0025_{-}\left(\frac{0.264^2}{2}\right)\right] 0.3315}{0.264\sqrt{0.3315}} = -0.268425.$$

From a standard normal distribution table, giving the area of a standard normal distribution, $N(-0.127419) = 0.449314$ and $N(-0.268425) = 0.394208$. Finally,

$$C = 152.93 \times 0.449314 - 160e^{-0.0025 * 0.3315} \times 0.394208 = \$9.63.$$

As expected, the price of this call option, $C = \$9.63$, with $X = 160$ has a lower calculated price than the call option with $X = 150$, as indicated in (27.43).

This simple example shows how to use the Black–Scholes model to price a call option under the assumptions of the model. The example is presented for illustrative purposes only, and it relies heavily on the implicit estimate of the variance, its constancy over time, and all the remaining assumptions of the model. The appropriateness of estimating the implicit instantaneous variance is ultimately an empirical question, as is the entire Black–Scholes pricing formula. Boyle and Ananthanarayanan (1977) studied the implications of using an estimate of the variance in option-valuation models and showed that this procedure produces biased option values. However, the magnitude of this bias is not large.

One additional remark must be made. The closeness of a calculated call option price to the actual call price is not necessary evidence of the validity of the Black–Scholes model. Extensive empirical work has taken place to investigate how market prices of call options compare with price predicted by Black–Scholes; see MacBeth and Merville (1979) and Bhattacharya (1980).

27.6. Remarks on Option Pricing

For a review on the literature on option pricing, see the two papers by Smith (1976, 1979). It is appropriate here to make a few remarks on the Black–Scholes option-pricing model to clarify its significance and its limitation.

First, the Black–Scholes model for a European call as original derived, and as reported here, is based on several simplifying assumptions.

(1) The stock price follows an Itô equation;
(2) The market operates continuously;
(3) There are no transaction costs in buying or selling the option or the underlying stock;
(4) There are no taxes;
(5) The riskless rate is known and constant, and;
(6) There are no restrictions on short sales.

Several researchers have extended the original Black–Scholes model by modifying these assumptions. Merton (1973) generalized the model to include dividend payments, exercise-price changes, and the case of a stochastic interest rate. Roll (1977) had solved the problem of valuing a call option that can be exercised prior to its expiration date when the underlying stock is assumed to make known dividend payments before the option matures. Ingersoll (1976) studied the effect of differential taxes on capital gains and income, while Scholes (1976) determined the effects of the tax treatment of options on the pricing model. Furthermore, Merton (1976) and Cox and Ross (1976) showed that if the stock-price movements are discontinuous, under certain assumptions the valuation model still holds. These and other modifications of the original Black–Scholes analysis indicate that the model is quite robust about the relaxation of its fundamental assumptions.

Second, it is worth repeating that the use of Itô's calculus and the important insight concerning the appropriate concept of an equilibrium by creating a riskless hedge portfolio have let Black and Scholes obtain a closed-form solution for option pricing. In this closed-form solution, several variables do not appear, such as (1) the expected rate of return of the stock, (2) the expected rate of return of the option, (3) a measure of investor's risk preference, (4) investor expectations, and (5) equilibrium conditions for the entire capital market.

Third, the Black–Scholes pricing model has found numerous applications. Among these are: (1) pricing the debt and equity of a firm;

(2) the effects of corporate policy and, specially, the effects of mergers, acquisitions, and scale expansions on the relative values of the debt and equity of the firm; (3) the pricing of convertible bonds; (4) the pricing of underwriting contracts; (5) the pricing of leases; and (6) the pricing of insurance. Smith (1976, 1979) summarized most applications and indicates the original reference. See also Brealey and Myers (1988).

Fourth, Black (1976) showed that the original call-option formula for stocks can be easily modified to be used in pricing call options on futures. The formula is

$$C(T, F, \sigma^2, X, r) = \mathrm{e}^{-rT}[FN(d_1) - XN(d_2)], \tag{27.50}$$

$$d_1 = \frac{\ln(F/X) + \frac{1}{2}\sigma^2 T}{\sigma\sqrt{T}}, \tag{27.51}$$

$$d_2 = \frac{\ln(F/X) - \frac{1}{2}\sigma^2 T}{\sigma\sqrt{T}}. \tag{27.52}$$

In Equation (27.50), F now denotes the current futures price. The other four variables are as before — time to maturity, volatility of the underlying futures price, exercise price, and risk-free rate. Note that Equation (27.50) differs from Equation (27.40) only in one respect: by substituting $\mathrm{e}^{-rT}F$ for S in the original Equation (27.40), Equation (27.50) is obtained. This holds because the investment in a futures contract is zero, which causes the interest rate in Equations (27.51) and (27.52) to drop out.

Fifth, three important papers by Harrison and Kreps (1979) and Kreps (1981, 1982) consider some foundational issues that arise in conjunction with the arbitrage theory of option pricing. The important point to consider is this: the ability to trade securities frequently can enable a few multiperiod securities to span many states of nature. In the Black–Scholes theory, there are two securities and uncountable many state of nature, but because there are infinitely many trading opportunities and because uncertainty resolves nicely, markets are effectively complete. Thus, even though there are far fewer securities than states of nature, markets are complete and risk is allocated efficiently. An interesting result of Harrison and Kreps (1979) is that certain self-trading strategies can create something out of nothing when there are infinitely many trading opportunities. The doubling strategies are the well-known illustrations of this phenomenon. Harrison and Kreps introduce the concept of a simple strategy to eliminate free lunches and conjecture that a non-negative wealth constraint could rule out the doubling strategies. Duffie and Huang (1985) gave an interpretation of admissible strategy as a limit of a sequence of simple strategies and use an integrability condition on the trading strategies. Dybvig and Huang (1986) showed that under certain conditions the integrability condition and the non-negative wealth constraint are functionally equivalent.

Finally, for an intensive survey of numerous empirical tests, see Galai (1983).

27.7. Summary

This chapter has discussed the basic concepts and equations of stochastic calculus (Itô's calculus), which has become a very useful tool in understanding finance theory and practice. By using these concepts and equations, the manner by which Black and Scholes derived their famous option-pricing model was also illustrated. Although this chapter is not required to understand the basic ingredients of security analysis and portfolio management discussed in Chapters 1–26, it is useful for those with training in advanced mathematics to realize how advanced mathematics can be used in finance.

Questions and Problems

1. Briefly describe Itô's lemma and Itô's process.
2. Describe the meaning of the process of a stock price $S(t, w)$ that follows the stochastic process

$$dS(t, w) = \mu S(t, w)dt + \sigma S(t, w)dZ(t, w).$$

3. Derive the Black–Scholes call option model by using Itô's lemma and the stochastic process of a stock price $S(t, w)$ in question 2.
4. Suppose the stock price $S(t, w)$ in question 2, what is the process of the variable $S^n(t, w)$? (Hint: show that $S^n(t, w)$ also follows the same stochastic process.)
5. Assume the stock price $S(t, w)$ in question 2. Let $\mu = 0.15$ and $\sigma = 0.2$ in the first two years and $\mu = 0.28$ and $\sigma = 0.35$ in the last year. Today stock price is \$50.

   (a) What is the probability distribution of the stock price at the end of two years?
   (b) What is the probability distribution of the stock price at the end of three years?

6. Assume the stock price $S(t, w)$ follows the stochastic process

$$dS(t, w) = \mu dt + \sigma dZ(t, w).$$

   Is this process more appropriate than the process in question 2? Why or Why not?

7. Assume the stock price $S(t, w)$ in question 6. Let $\mu = 1.5$, $\sigma = 2$ and now stock price is \$110.

   (a) What is the probability distribution of the stock price in the next year?

   (b) What are 95% confidence limits for the stock price in the next year?

8. Assume the stock price $S(t, w)$ in question 2 again. Suppose the expected return of stock price equal 7% and volatility is 25% per year, now the stock price is \$100.

   (a) What is the expected stock price at the end of six months?

   (b) What is the standard deviation of the stock price at the end of six months?

   (c) What is the expected stock price next year?

9. Assume the stock price $S(t, w)$ in question 2 again. Derive the process of Y under the condition as follows:

   (a) $Y = 3S(t, w)$

   (b) $Y = S^n(t, w)$

   (c) $Y = e^{r(T-t)}S(t, w)$.

10. Assume the stock price $S(t, w)$ in question 5, what is the probability that the stock price will be greater than \$130 in two years?

Appendix 27A: An Alternative Method to Derive the Black–Scholes Option Pricing Model

Perhaps it is unclear why it is assumed that investors have risk-neutral preferences when the usual assumption in finance courses is that investors are risk averse. It is feasible to make this simplistic assumption because investors are able to create riskless portfolios by combining call options with their underlying securities. Since the creation of a riskless hedge places no restrictions on investor preferences other than nonsatiation, the valuation of the option and its underlying asset will be independent of investor risk preferences. Therefore, a call option will trade at the same price in risk-neutral economy as it will in a risk-averse or risk-preferent economy.

27A.1. *Assumptions and the Present Value of the Expected Terminal Option Price*

To derive the Black–Scholes formula, it is assumed that there are no transaction costs, no margin requirements, and no taxes; that all shares are infinitely divisible, and that continuous trading can be accomplished. It is also assumed that the economy is risk neutral.

In the risk-neutral assumptions of Cox and Ross (1976) and Rubinstein (1976), today's option price can be determined by discounting the expected value of the terminal option price by the riskless rate of interest. As was seen earlier, the terminal call-option price can take on only two values: $S_t - X$, if the call option expires in the money, or 0 if the call expires out of the money. So today's call option price is

$$C = \exp(-rt)\text{Max}(S_t - X, 0), \tag{27A.1}$$

where

C = the market value of the call option;
r = riskless rate of interest;
t = time to expiration;
S_t = the market value of the underlying stock at time t; and
X = exercise or striking price.

Equation (27A.1) says that the value of the call option today will be either $S_t - X$ or 0, whichever is greater. If the price of stock at time t is greater than the exercise price, the call option will expire in the money. This simply means that an investor who owns the call option will exercise it. The option will be exercised regardless of whether the option holder would like to take physical possession of the stock. If the investor would like to own the stock, the cheapest way to obtain the stock is by exercising the option. If the investor would not like to own the stock, he or she will still exercise the option and immediately sell the stock in the market. Since the price the investor paid (X) is lower that the price he or she can sell the stock for (S_t), the investor realizes an immediate the profit of $S_t - X$. If the price of the stock (S_t) is less than the exercise price (X), the option expires out of the money. This occurs because in purchasing shares of the stock the investor will find it cheaper to purchase the stock in the market than to exercise the option.

Assuming that the call option expires in the money, then the present value of the expected terminal option is equal to the present value of the difference between the expected terminal stock price and the exercise price, as indicated in Equation (27A.2):

$$\begin{aligned} C &= \exp(-rt)E[Max(S_t - X, 0)] \\ &= \exp(-rt)\int_x^{\infty}(S_t - X)h(S_t)dS_t, \end{aligned} \tag{27A.2}$$

where $h(S_t)$ is the log-normal density function of S_t. To evaluate the integral in (27A.2), rewrite it as the difference between two integrals:

$$\begin{aligned} C &= \exp(-rt)\left[\int_x^{\infty} S_t h(S_t)dS_t - X\int_x^{\infty} h(S_t)dS_t\right] \\ &= E_x(S_t)\cdot\exp(-rt) - X\cdot\exp(-rt)\cdot[1 - H(X)], \end{aligned} \tag{27A.3}$$

where

$E_x(S_t) =$ the partial expectation of S_t, truncated from below at x; and
$H(X) =$ the probability that $S_t \leq X$.

Equation (27A.3) says that the value of the call option is present value of the partial expected stock price (assuming the call expires in the money) minus the present value of the exercise price (adjusted by the probability that the stock's price will be less than the exercise price at the expiration of the option). The terminal stock price S_t, can be rewritten as the product of the current price (S) and the t-period log-normally distributed price ratio S_t/S, so $S_t = S(S_t/S)$. Equation (27A.3) can also be rewritten as

$$\begin{aligned} C &= \exp(-rt)\left[S\int_{x/s}^{\infty}\frac{S_t}{S}g\left(\frac{S_t}{S}\right)\left(\frac{dS_t}{S}\right) - X\int_{x/s}^{\infty}g\left(\frac{S_t}{S}\right)\left(\frac{dS_t}{S}\right)\right] \\ &= S\exp(-rt)E_{x/S}\left(\frac{S_t}{S}\right) - X\exp(-rt)\left[1 - G\left(\frac{X}{S}\right)\right], \end{aligned} \tag{27A.4}$$

where

$g\left(\frac{S_t}{S}\right) =$ log normal density function of S_t/S;
$E_{x/S}\left(\frac{S_t}{S}\right) =$ the partial expextation of S_t/S, truncated from below at x/S;
$G\left(\frac{X}{S}\right) =$ the probability that $S_t/S \leq X/S$.

27A.2. *Present Value of the Partial Expectation of the Terminal Stock Price*

The right-hand side of Equation (27A.4) is evaluated by considering the two integrals separately. The first integral, $S\exp(-rt)E_{x/S}(S_t/S)$, can be solved by assuming the return on the underlying stock follows a stationary random walk. That is

$$\frac{S_t}{S} = \exp(Kt), \tag{27A.5}$$

where K is the rate of return on the underlying stock per unit of time. Taking the natural logarithm of both sides of Equation (27A.5) yields:

$$\ln\left(\frac{S_t}{S}\right) = (Kt).$$

Since the ratio S_t/S is log normally distributed, it follows that Kt is log normally distributed with density $f(Kt)$, mean $\mu_K t$, and variance $\sigma_K^2 t$. Because $S_t/S = \exp(Kt)$, the differential can be rewritten as $dS_t/S = \exp(Kt)t\,dK$; $g(S_t/S)$ is a density function of a log-normally distributed variable S_t/S; so following Garven (1986), it can be transformed into a density function of a normally distributed variable Kt according to the relationship $S_t/S = \exp(Kt)$ as

$$g\left(\frac{S_t}{S}\right) = f(Kt)\left(\frac{S_t}{S}\right). \tag{27A.6}$$

These transformations allow the first integral in Equation (27A.4) to be rewritten as

$$S\exp(-rt)E_{x/S}\left(\frac{S_t}{S}\right) = S\exp(-rt)\int_{\ln(x/S)}^{\infty} f(Kt)\exp(Kt)\,t\,dK.$$

Because Kt is normally distributed, the density $f(Kt)$ with mean $\mu_K t$ and variance $\sigma_K^2 t$ is

$$f(Kt) = \left(2\pi\sigma_K^2 t\right)^{-1/2}\exp\left[-\frac{1}{2}\left(Kt-\mu_K t\right)^2/\sigma_K^2\right].$$

Substitution yields:

$$S\exp(-rt)E_{x/S}\left(\frac{S_t}{S}\right) = S\exp(-rt)(2\pi\sigma_K^2 t)^{-1/2} \times\int_{\ln(x/S)}^{\infty}\exp[Kt]\exp\left[-\frac{1}{2}(Kt-\mu_K t)^2/\sigma_K^2 t\right] t\,dK. \tag{27A.7}$$

Equation (27A.7)'s integrand can be simplified by adding the terms in the two exponents, multiplying and dividing the result by $\exp\left(-\frac{1}{2}\sigma_K^2 t\right)$. First, expand the term $(Kt - \mu_K t)^2$ and factor out t so that

$$\exp[Kt]\exp\left[-\frac{1}{2}(Kt - \mu_K t)^2/\sigma_K^2 t\right].$$

Next, factor out t so

$$\exp(Kt)\exp\left\{-\frac{1}{2}t\left[(K^2 - 2\mu_K K + \mu_K^2)/\sigma_K^2\right]\right\}.$$

Now combine the two exponents

$$\exp\left\{-\frac{1}{2}t\left[(K^2 - 2\mu_K K + \mu_K^2 - 2\sigma_K^2 K)/\sigma_K^2\right]\right\}.$$

Now, multiply and divide this result by $\exp\left(-\frac{1}{2}\sigma_K^2 t\right)$ to get:

$$\exp\left\{-\frac{1}{2}t\left[(K^2 - 2\mu_K K + \mu_K^2 - 2\sigma_K^2 K + \sigma_K^4 - \sigma_K^4)/\sigma_K^2\right]\right\}.$$

Next, rearrange and combine terms to get:

$$\exp\left\{\left(-\frac{1}{2}t\right)\left[(K - \mu_K - \sigma_K^2)^2 - \sigma_K^4 - 2\mu_K\sigma_K^2\right]/\sigma_K^2\right\}$$

$$= \exp\left[\left(\mu_K + \frac{1}{2}\sigma_K^2\right)t\right]\exp\left\{-\frac{1}{2}\left[Kt - (\mu_K + \sigma_K^2)t\right]^2/\sigma_K^2 t\right\}. \quad (27A.8)$$

In Equation (27A.8), $\exp[(\mu_K + \frac{1}{2}\sigma_K^2)t] = E(S_t/S)$, the mean of the t-period log-normally distributed price ratio S_t/S. So, Equation (27A.7) becomes:

$$S\exp(-rt)E_{x/S}\left(\frac{S_t}{S}\right)$$

$$= SE\left(\frac{S_t}{S}\right)\exp(-rt)\left(2\pi\sigma_K^2 t\right)^{-1/2}$$

$$\times \int_{\ln(x/S)}^{\infty} \exp(Kt)\exp\left\{-\frac{1}{2}\left[Kt - (\mu_K + \sigma_K^2)t\right]^2/\sigma_K^2 t\right\} \quad (27A.9)$$

Since the equilibrium rate of return in a risk-neutral economy is the riskless rate, $E(S_t/S)$ may be rewritten as $\exp(rt)$:

$$SE\left(\frac{S_t}{S}\right)\exp(-rt) = S\exp(rt)\exp(-rt)$$

$$= S.$$

So Equation (27A.9) becomes

$$\begin{aligned} &S\exp(-rt)E_{x/S}\left(\frac{S_t}{S}\right) \\ &\quad = S\left(2\pi\sigma_K^2 t\right)^{-1/2} \\ &\quad \times \int_{\ln(x/S)}^{\infty} \exp\left\{-\frac{1}{2}\left[Kt - \left(\mu_K + \sigma_K^2\right)t\right]^2/\sigma_K^2 t\right\} t\,dK \qquad (27A.10) \end{aligned}$$

To complete the simplification of this part of the Black–Scholes formula, define a standard normal random variable y:

$$y = \left[Kt - \left(\mu_K + \sigma_K^2\right)t\right]/\sigma_K^2 t^{1/2}.$$

Solving for Kt yields:

$$Kt = \left(\mu_K + \sigma_K^2\right)t + \sigma_K t^{1/2} y,$$

and therefore:

$$t\,dK = \sigma_K t^{1/2} dy.$$

By making the transformation from Kt to y, the lower limit of integration becomes

$$[\ln(x/S) - (\mu_K + \sigma_K^2)t]/\sigma_K t^{1/2}.$$

Further simplify the integrand by noting that the assumption of a risk-neural economy implies:

$$\exp\left[\left(\mu_K + \frac{1}{2}\sigma_K^2\right)t\right] = \exp(rt).$$

Taking the natural logarithm of both sides yields:

$$\left(\mu_K + \frac{1}{2}\sigma_K^2\right)t = (rt).$$

Hence, $\left(\mu_K + \frac{1}{2}\sigma_K^2\right)t = \left(r + \frac{1}{2}\sigma_K^2\right)t$.

The lower limit of integration is now:

$$-\left[\ln(S/x) + \left(r + \frac{1}{2}\sigma_K^2\right)t\right]/\sigma_K t^{1/2} = -d_1.$$

Substituting this into Equation (27A.10) and making the transformation to y yields:

$$S\exp(-rt)E_{x/S}\left(\frac{S_t}{S}\right) = S\int_{-d_1}^{\infty}\exp\left(-\frac{1}{2}y\right)^2/(2\pi)^{1/2}\,dy.$$

Since y is a standard normal random variable (distribution is symmetric around zero) the limits of integration can be exchanged:

$$\begin{aligned} S\exp(-rt)E_{x/S}\left(\frac{S_t}{S}\right) &= S\int_{\infty}^{-d_1}\exp\left(-\frac{1}{2}y^2\right)/(2\pi)^{1/2}\,dy \\ &= S\,N(d_1), \end{aligned} \tag{27A.11}$$

where $N(d_1)$ is the standard normal cumulative distribution function evaluated at $y = d_1$.

27A.3. *Present Value of the Exercise Price under Uncertainty*

To complete the derivation, the integrals that correspond to the term $X\exp(-rt)[1 - G(X/S)]$ must be evaluated. Start by making the logarithmic transformation:

$$\ln\left(\frac{S_t}{S}\right) = Kt.$$

This transformation allows the rewriting of $g(S_t/S)$ to $(S/S_t)f(Kt)$ as mentioned previously. The differential can be written as

$$d\frac{S_t}{S} = \exp(Kt)t\,dK.$$

Therefore,

$$\begin{aligned} X\exp(-rt)[1 - G(X/S)] &= X\exp(-rt)\int_{\ln(X/S)}^{\infty} f(Kt)t\,dK \\ &= X\exp(-rt)\left(2\pi\sigma_K^2 t\right)^{-1/2}\int_{\ln(X/S)}^{\infty}\exp\left[-\frac{1}{2}(Kt-\mu_K t)^2/\sigma_K^2 t\right]t\,dK. \end{aligned} \tag{27A.12}$$

The integrand is now simplified by following the same procedure used in simplifying the previous integral. Define a standard normal random variable Z:

$$Z = \left[\frac{Kt - \mu_K t}{\sigma_K t^{1/2}}\right].$$

Solving for Kt yields:

$$Kt = \mu_K t + \sigma_K t^{1/2} Z,$$

and $t\,dK = \sigma_K t^{1/2} dZ$. Making the transformation from Kt to Z means the lower limit of integration becomes

$$\frac{\ln(X/S) - \mu_K t}{\sigma_K t^{1/2}}.$$

Again, note that the assumption of a risk-neutral economy implies:

$$\exp\left(\mu_K + \frac{1}{2}\sigma_K^2 t\right) = \exp(rt).$$

Taking the natural logarithm of both sides yields:

$$\left(\mu_K + \frac{1}{2}\sigma_K^2\right) t = rt,$$

or:

$$\mu_K t = \left(r - \frac{1}{2}\sigma_K^2\right) t.$$

Therefore, the lower limit of integration becomes:

$$\begin{aligned}\frac{-\left[\ln(S/x) + \left(r - \frac{1}{2}\sigma_K^2\right) t\right]}{\sigma_K t^{1/2}} &= -\left(d_1 - \sigma_K t^{1/2}\right) \\ &= -d_2.\end{aligned}$$

Substitution yields:

$$\begin{aligned} x\exp(-rt)[1 - G(X/S)] &= x\exp(-rt)\int_{-d_2}^{\infty} \exp\left[-\frac{1}{2}Z^2/(2\pi)^{1/2}\right] dZ \\ &= x\exp(-rt)\int_{-\infty}^{d_2} \exp\left[-\frac{1}{2}Z^2/(2\pi)^{1/2}\right] dZ \\ &= x\exp(-rt)N(d_2), \qquad (27A.13)\end{aligned}$$

where $N(d_2)$ is the standard normal cumulative distribution function evaluated at $Z = d_2$.

Substituting, Equations (27A.11) and (27A.13) into Equation (27A.4) completes the derivation of the Black–Scholes formula:

$$C = S\,N(d_1) - X\exp(-rt)\,N(d_2). \tag{27A.14}$$

This appendix provides a simple derivation of the Black–Scholes call-option pricing formula. Under an assumption of risk neutrality the Black–Scholes formula was derived using only differential and integral calculus and a basic knowledge of normal and log-normal distributions.

Bibliography

Arnold, L. *Stochastic Differential Equation: Theory and Applications.* New York: John Wiley & Sons, 1974.

Bhattacharya, M. "Empirical Properties of the Black-Scholes Formula under Ideal Conditions." *Journal of Financial Quantitative Analysis*, v. 15 (December 1980), pp. 1081–1105.

Black, F. "The Pricing of Commodity Contracts." *Journal of Financial Economics*, v. 3 (January–March 1976), pp. 167–178.

Black, F. and M. Scholes. "The Pricing of Options and Corporate Liabilities." *Journal of Political Economy*, v. 81 (May/June 1973), pp. 637–654.

Boyle, P. P. and A. L. Ananthanarayanan. "The Impact of Variance Estimation in Option Valuation Models." *Journal of Financial Economics*, v. 5 (September 1977), pp. 375–387.

Brealey, R. and S. Myers. *Principles of Corporate Finance*, 3rd edn. New York: McGraw-Hill, 1988.

Brennan, M. and E. Schwartz. "A Continuous Time Approach to the Pricing of Bonds." *Journal of Banking and Finance*, v. 3 (July 1979), pp. 133–155.

Brennan, M. and E. Schwartz. "Finite Difference Method and Jump Processes Arising in the Pricing of Contingent Claims: A Synthesis." *Journal of Financial Quantitative Analysis*, v. 13 (September 1978), pp. 461–474.

Courtadon, G. "A More Accurate Finite Difference Approximation for the Valuation of Options." *Journal of Financial Quantitative Analysis*, v. 17 (December 1982), pp. 697–705.

Cox, J. C. and S. A. Ross. "The Valuation of Options for Alternative Stochastic Processes." *Journal of Financial Economics*, v. 3 (March 1976), pp. 145–226.

Cox, J. C. and M. Rubinstein. *Options Markets.* Englewood Cliffs, NJ: Prentice-Hall.

Duffie, D. and C. Huang. "Implementing Arrow-Debreu Equilibria by Continuous Trading of Few Long-Lived Securities." *Econometrica*, v. 53 (December 1985), pp. 1337–1356.

Dybvig, P. and C. Huang. "Optimal Portfolios and Positive Wealth Constraint." Yale University School of Management Working Paper, 1986.

Galai, D. "A Survey of Empirical Tests of Option-Pricing Models." in M. Brenner (ed.), *Option Pricing*, pp. 45–80. Lexington, MA: Lexington Books, 1983.

Garven, J. R. "A Pedagogic Note on the Derivation of the Black–Scholes Option Pricing Formula." *The Financial Review*, v. 21 (November 1986), pp. 337–344.

Geske, R. and K. Shostri. "Valuation by Approximation: A Comparison of Alternative Option Valuation Techniques." *Journal of Financial Quantitative Analysis*, v. 20 (March 1985), pp. 45–71.

Gikhman, I. and A. V. Skorokhod. *Investment to the Theory of Random Processes.* Philadelphia, PA : W. B. Saunders, 1969.

Harrison, J. M. and D. M. Kreps. "Martingales and Arbitrage in Multiperiod Securities Markets." *Journal of Economic Theory*, v. 20 (1979), pp. 381–408.

Harrison, J. and S. Pliska. "Martingales and Stochastic Integrals in the Theory of Continuous Trading." *Stochastic Processes and Their Application*, v. 2 (1981), pp. 261–271.

Ingersoll, J. E. "A Theoretical and Empirical Investigation of the Dual Purpose Funds: An Application of Contingent Claims and Analysis." *Journal of Financial Economics*, v. 3 (March 1976), pp. 83–123.

Itô, K. and H. McKean. *Diffusion Processes and Their Sample Paths.* New York: Academic Press, 1964.

Jarrow, R. and A. Rudd. *Option Pricing.* Homewood, IL: R. D. Irwin, 1983.

Jarrow, R. and A. Rudd. "Approximate Option Valuation for Arbitrary Stochastic Processes." *Journal of Financial Economics*, v. 10 (November 1982), pp. 347–370.

Kreps, D. M. "Arbitrage and Equilibrium in Economics with Infinitely Many Commodities." *Journal of Mathematical Economics*, v. 8 (March 1981), pp. 15–35.

Kreps, D. M. "Multiperiod Securities and the Efficient Allocation of Risk: A Comment on the Black–Scholes Option Pricing Model," in J. J. McCall (eds.), *The Economics of Information and Uncertainty*, pp. 203–232. Chicago: University of Chicago Press, 1982.

Latané, H. A. and R. J. Rendleman, Jr. "Standard Derivations of Stock Price Ratios Implied in Option Prices." *Journal of Finance*, v. 31 (May 1976), pp. 369–381.

MacBeth, J. D. and L. J. Merville. "An Empirical Examination of the Black–Scholes Call Option Pricing Model." *Journal of Finance*, v. 34 (December 1979), pp. 1173–1186.

Malliaris, A. G. and W. A. Brock. *Stochastic Methods in Economics and Finance.* Amsterdam: North-Holland, 1982.

Merton, R. C. "Option Pricing When Underlying Stock Returns are Discontinuous." *Journal of Financial Economics*, v. 3 (January–March 1976), pp. 125–144.

Merton, R. C. "On the Mathematics and Economics Assumption of Continuous-Time Model," in W. F. Sharpe and C. M. Cootner (eds.), *Financial*

Economics: Essay in Honor of Paul Cootner, pp. 19–51. Englewood Cliffs, NJ: Prentice-Hall, 1982.

Merton, R. C. "Theory of Finance from the Perspective of Continuous Time." *Journal of Financial Quantitative Analysis*, v. 10 (December 1975), pp. 659–674.

Merton, R. C. "The Theory of Rational Option Pricing." *Bell Journal of Economics and Management Science*, v. 4 (Spring 1973), pp. 141–183.

Roll, R. "An Analytic Valuation Formula for Unprotected American Call Options on Stocks with Known Dividends." *Journal of Financial Economics*, v. 5 (May 1977), pp. 251–281.

Rubinstein, M. "The Valuation of Uncertain Income Streams and the Pricing of Options." *Bell Journal of Economics*, v. 7 (Fall 1976), pp. 407–425.

Scholes, M. "Taxes and the Pricing of Options." *Journal of finance*, v. 31 (May 1976), pp. 319–332.

Smith, C. W., Jr. "Applications of Option Pricing Analysis," in J. L. Bicksler (ed.), *Handbook of Financial Economics.* Amsterdam: North-Holland, 1979.

Smith, C. W., Jr. "Option Pricing: A Review." *Journal of Financial Economics*, v. 3 (January–March 1976), pp. 3–51.

Appendix Tables

Table I	Compound Sum of $1 for n Years
Table II	Present Value of $1
Table III	Sum of an Annuity for $1 for n Years
Table IV	Present Value of $1 Received Annually
Table V	Areas Under the Standard Normal Distribution

Table I Compound Sum of \$1: $S_n = P(1+r)^n$

Year	1%	2%	3%	4%	5%	6%	7%	8%	9%	10%	11%	12%	13%	14%	15%	16%
1	1.010	1.020	1.030	1.040	1.050	1.060	1.070	1.080	1.090	1.100	1.110	1.120	1.130	1.140	1.150	1.160
2	1.020	1.040	1.061	1.082	1.102	1.124	1.145	1.166	1.188	1.210	1.232	1.254	1.277	1.300	1.322	1.346
3	1.030	1.061	1.093	1.125	1.158	1.191	1.225	1.260	1.295	1.331	1.368	1.405	1.443	1.482	1.521	1.561
4	1.041	1.082	1.126	1.170	1.216	1.262	1.311	1.360	1.412	1.464	1.518	1.574	1.631	1.689	1.749	1.811
5	1.051	1.104	1.159	1.217	1.276	1.338	1.403	1.469	1.539	1.611	1.685	1.762	1.842	1.925	2.011	2.100
6	1.062	1.126	1.194	1.265	1.340	1.419	1.501	1.587	1.677	1.772	1.870	1.974	2.082	2.195	2.313	2.436
7	1.072	1.149	1.230	1.316	1.407	1.504	1.606	1.714	1.828	1.949	2.076	2.211	2.353	2.502	2.660	2.826
7	1.083	1.172	1.267	1.369	1.477	1.594	1.718	1.851	1.993	2.144	2.305	2.476	2.658	2.853	3.059	3.278
9	1.094	1.195	1.305	1.423	1.551	1.689	1.838	1.999	2.172	2.358	2.558	2.773	3.004	3.252	3.518	3.803
10	1.105	1.219	1.344	1.480	1.629	1.791	1.967	2.159	2.367	2.594	2.839	3.106	3.395	3.707	4.046	4.411
11	1.116	1.243	1.384	1.539	1.710	1.898	2.105	2.332	2.580	2.853	3.152	3.479	3.836	4.226	4.652	5.117
12	1.127	1.268	1.426	1.601	1.796	2.012	2.252	2.518	2.813	3.138	3.499	3.896	4.335	4.818	5.350	5.936
13	1.138	1.294	1.469	1.665	1.886	2.133	2.410	2.720	3.066	3.452	3.883	4.363	4.898	5.492	6.153	6.886
14	1.149	1.319	1.513	1.732	1.980	2.261	2.579	2.937	3.342	3.797	4.310	4.887	5.535	6.261	7.076	7.988
15	1.161	1.346	1.558	1.801	2.079	2.397	2.759	3.172	3.642	4.177	4.785	5.474	6.254	7.138	8.137	9.266
16	1.173	1.373	1.605	1.873	2.183	2.540	2.952	3.426	3.970	4.595	5.311	6.130	7.067	8.137	9.358	10.748
17	1.184	1.400	1.653	1.948	2.292	2.693	3.159	3.700	4.328	5.054	5.895	6.866	7.986	9.276	10.761	12.468
18	1.196	1.428	1.702	2.026	2.407	2.854	3.380	3.996	4.717	5.560	6.544	7.690	9.024	10.575	12.375	14.463
19	1.208	1.457	1.754	2.107	2.527	3.026	3.617	4.316	5.142	6.116	7.263	8.613	10.197	12.056	14.232	16.777
20	1.220	1.486	1.806	2.191	2.653	3.207	3.870	4.661	5.604	6.728	8.062	9.646	11.523	13.743	16.367	19.461

Table II Present Value of \$1: $P = S_n(1+r)^{-n}$

Years Hence	1%	2%	4%	6%	8%	10%	12%	14%	15%	16%	18%	20%	22%	24%	25%	26%	28%	30%	35%	40%	45%	50%
1	0.990	0.980	0.962	0.943	0.926	0.909	0.893	0.877	0.870	0.862	0.847	0.833	0.820	0.806	0.800	0.794	0.781	0.769	0.741	0.714	0.690	0.667
2	0.980	0.961	0.925	0.890	0.857	0.826	0.797	0.769	0.756	0.743	0.718	0.694	0.672	0.650	0.640	0.630	0.610	0.592	0.549	0.510	0.476	0.444
3	0.971	0.942	0.889	0.840	0.794	0.751	0.712	0.675	0.658	0.641	0.609	0.579	0.551	0.524	0.512	0.500	0.477	0.455	0.406	0.364	0.328	0.296
4	0.961	0.924	0.855	0.792	0.735	0.683	0.636	0.592	0.572	0.552	0.516	0.482	0.451	0.423	0.410	0.397	0.373	0.350	0.301	0.260	0.226	0.198
5	0.951	0.906	0.822	0.747	0.681	0.621	0.567	0.519	0.497	0.476	0.437	0.402	0.370	0.341	0.328	0.315	0.291	0.269	0.223	0.186	0.156	0.132
6	0.942	0.888	0.790	0.705	0.630	0.564	0.507	0.456	0.432	0.410	0.370	0.335	0.303	0.275	0.262	0.250	0.227	0.207	0.165	0.133	0.108	0.088
7	0.933	0.871	0.760	0.665	0.583	0.513	0.452	0.400	0.376	0.354	0.314	0.279	0.249	0.222	0.210	0.198	0.178	0.159	0.122	0.095	0.074	0.059
8	0.923	0.853	0.731	0.627	0.540	0.467	0.404	0.351	0.327	0.305	0.266	0.233	0.204	0.179	0.168	0.157	0.139	0.123	0.091	0.068	0.051	0.039
9	0.914	0.837	0.703	0.592	0.500	0.424	0.361	0.308	0.284	0.263	0.225	0.194	0.167	0.144	0.134	0.125	0.108	0.094	0.067	0.048	0.035	0.026
10	0.905	0.820	0.676	0.558	0.463	0.386	0.322	0.270	0.247	0.227	0.191	0.162	0.137	0.116	0.107	0.099	0.085	0.073	0.050	0.035	0.024	0.017
11	0.896	0.804	0.650	0.527	0.429	0.350	0.287	0.237	0.215	0.195	0.162	0.135	0.112	0.094	0.086	0.079	0.066	0.056	0.037	0.025	0.017	0.012
12	0.887	0.788	0.625	0.497	0.397	0.319	0.257	0.208	0.187	0.168	0.137	0.112	0.092	0.076	0.069	0.062	0.052	0.043	0.027	0.018	0.012	0.008
13	0.879	0.773	0.601	0.469	0.368	0.290	0.229	0.182	0.163	0.145	0.116	0.093	0.075	0.061	0.055	0.050	0.040	0.033	0.020	0.013	0.008	0.005
14	0.870	0.758	0.577	0.442	0.340	0.263	0.205	0.160	0.141	0.125	0.099	0.078	0.062	0.049	0.044	0.039	0.032	0.025	0.015	0.009	0.006	0.003
15	0.861	0.743	0.555	0.417	0.315	0.239	0.183	0.140	0.123	0.108	0.084	0.065	0.051	0.040	0.035	0.031	0.025	0.020	0.011	0.006	0.004	0.002
16	0.853	0.728	0.534	0.394	0.292	0.218	0.163	0.123	0.107	0.093	0.071	0.054	0.042	0.032	0.028	0.025	0.019	0.015	0.008	0.005	0.003	0.002
17	0.844	0.714	0.513	0.371	0.270	0.198	0.146	0.108	0.093	0.080	0.060	0.045	0.034	0.026	0.023	0.020	0.015	0.012	0.006	0.003	0.002	0.001
18	0.836	0.700	0.494	0.350	0.250	0.180	0.130	0.095	0.081	0.069	0.051	0.038	0.028	0.021	0.018	0.016	0.012	0.009	0.005	0.002	0.001	0.001
19	0.828	0.686	0.475	0.331	0.232	0.164	0.116	0.083	0.070	0.060	0.043	0.031	0.023	0.017	0.014	0.012	0.009	0.007	0.003	0.002	0.001	
20	0.820	0.673	0.456	0.312	0.215	0.149	0.104	0.073	0.061	0.051	0.037	0.026	0.019	0.014	0.012	0.010	0.007	0.005	0.002	0.001	0.001	
21	0.811	0.660	0.439	0.294	0.199	0.135	0.093	0.064	0.053	0.044	0.031	0.022	0.015	0.011	0.009	0.008	0.006	0.004	0.002	0.001		
22	0.803	0.647	0.422	0.278	0.184	0.123	0.083	0.056	0.046	0.038	0.026	0.018	0.013	0.009	0.007	0.006	0.004	0.003	0.001	0.001		
23	0.795	0.634	0.406	0.262	0.170	0.112	0.074	0.049	0.040	0.033	0.022	0.015	0.010	0.007	0.006	0.005	0.003	0.002	0.001			
24	0.788	0.622	0.390	0.247	0.158	0.102	0.066	0.043	0.035	0.028	0.019	0.013	0.008	0.006	0.005	0.004	0.003	0.002	0.001			
25	0.780	0.610	0.375	0.233	0.146	0.092	0.059	0.038	0.030	0.024	0.016	0.010	0.007	0.005	0.004	0.003	0.002	0.001	0.001			
26	0.772	0.598	0.361	0.220	0.135	0.084	0.053	0.033	0.026	0.021	0.014	0.009	0.006	0.004	0.003	0.002	0.002	0.001				
27	0.764	0.586	0.347	0.207	0.125	0.076	0.047	0.029	0.023	0.018	0.011	0.007	0.005	0.003	0.002	0.002	0.001	0.001				
28	0.757	0.574	0.333	0.196	0.116	0.069	0.042	0.026	0.020	0.016	0.010	0.006	0.004	0.002	0.002	0.002	0.001	0.001				
29	0.749	0.563	0.321	0.185	0.107	0.063	0.037	0.022	0.017	0.014	0.008	0.005	0.003	0.002	0.002	0.001	0.001	0.001				
30	0.742	0.552	0.308	0.174	0.099	0.057	0.033	0.020	0.015	0.012	0.007	0.004	0.003	0.002	0.001	0.001	0.001					
40	0.672	0.453	0.208	0.097	0.046	0.022	0.011	0.005	0.004	0.003	0.001	0.001										
50	0.608	0.372	0.141	0.054	0.021	0.009	0.003	0.001	0.001	0.001												

Table III Sum of an Annuity for \$1 for n Years: $S_{n,r} = \$1\left[\frac{(1+r)^n-1}{r}\right] = \$1C_{n,r}$

Year	1%	2%	3%	4%	5%	6%	7%	8%	9%	10%	11%	12%	13%	14%	15%	16%
1	1.000	1.000	1.000	1.000	1.000	1.000	1.000	1.000	1.000	1.000	1.000	1.000	1.000	1.000	1.000	1.000
2	2.010	2.020	2.030	2.040	2.050	2.060	2.070	2.080	2.090	2.100	2.110	2.120	2.130	2.140	2.150	2.160
3	3.030	3.060	3.091	3.122	3.152	3.184	3.215	3.246	3.278	3.310	3.342	3.374	3.407	3.440	3.473	3.506
4	4.060	4.122	4.184	4.246	4.310	4.375	4.440	4.506	4.573	4.641	4.710	4.779	4.850	4.921	4.993	5.066
5	5.101	5.204	5.309	5.416	5.526	5.637	5.751	5.867	5.985	6.105	6.228	6.353	6.480	6.610	6.742	6.877
6	6.152	6.308	6.468	6.633	6.802	6.975	7.153	7.336	7.523	7.716	7.913	8.115	8.323	8.536	8.754	8.977
7	7.214	7.434	7.662	7.898	8.142	8.394	8.654	8.923	9.200	9.487	9.783	10.089	10.405	10.730	11.067	11.414
8	8.286	8.583	8.892	9.214	9.549	9.897	10.260	10.637	11.028	11.436	11.859	12.300	12.757	13.233	13.727	14.240
9	9.369	9.755	10.159	10.583	11.027	11.491	11.978	12.488	13.021	13.579	14.164	14.776	15.416	16.085	16.786	17.518
10	10.462	10.950	11.464	12.006	12.578	13.181	13.816	14.487	15.193	15.937	16.722	17.549	18.420	19.337	20.304	21.321
11	11.567	12.169	12.808	13.486	14.207	14.972	15.784	16.645	17.560	18.531	19.561	20.655	21.814	23.044	24.349	25.733
12	12.683	13.412	14.192	15.026	15.917	16.870	17.888	18.977	20.141	21.384	22.713	24.133	25.650	27.271	29.002	30.850
13	13.809	14.680	15.618	16.627	17.713	18.882	20.141	21.495	22.953	24.523	26.212	28.029	29.985	32.089	34.352	36.786
14	14.947	15.974	17.086	18.292	19.599	21.051	22.550	24.215	26.019	27.975	30.095	32.393	34.883	37.581	40.505	43.672
15	16.097	17.293	18.599	20.024	21.579	23.276	25.129	27.152	29.361	31.772	34.405	37.280	40.417	43.842	47.580	51.659

Table IV Present Value of $1 Received Annually: $A_{n,r} = \$1\left[\frac{1-(1+r)^{-n}}{r}\right] = \$1P_{n,r}$

Year (n)	1%	2%	4%	6%	8%	10%	12%	14%	15%	16%	18%	20%	22%	24%	25%	26%	28%	30%	35%	40%	45%	50%
1	0.990	0.980	0.962	0.943	0.926	0.909	0.893	0.877	0.870	0.862	0.847	0.833	0.820	0.806	0.800	0.794	0.781	0.769	0.741	0.714	0.690	0.667
2	1.970	1.942	1.886	1.833	1.783	1.736	1.690	1.647	1.626	1.605	1.566	1.528	1.492	1.457	1.440	1.424	1.392	1.361	1.289	1.224	1.165	1.111
3	2.941	2.884	2.775	2.673	2.577	2.487	2.402	2.322	2.283	2.246	2.174	2.106	2.042	1.981	1.952	1.923	1.868	1.816	1.696	1.589	1.493	1.407
4	3.902	3.808	3.630	3.465	3.312	3.170	3.037	2.914	2.855	2.798	2.690	2.589	2.494	2.404	2.362	2.320	2.241	2.166	1.997	1.849	1.720	1.605
5	4.853	4.713	4.452	4.212	3.993	3.791	3.605	3.433	3.352	3.274	3.127	2.991	2.864	2.745	2.689	2.635	2.532	2.436	2.220	2.035	1.876	1.737
6	5.795	5.601	5.242	4.917	4.623	4.355	4.111	3.889	3.784	3.685	3.498	3.326	3.167	3.020	2.951	2.885	2.759	2.643	2.385	2.168	1.983	1.824
7	6.728	6.472	6.002	5.582	5.206	4.868	4.564	4.288	4.160	4.039	3.812	3.605	3.416	3.242	3.161	3.083	2.937	2.802	2.508	2.263	2.057	1.883
8	7.652	7.325	6.733	6.210	5.747	5.335	4.968	4.639	4.487	4.344	4.078	3.837	3.619	3.421	3.329	3.241	3.076	2.925	2.598	2.331	2.108	1.922
9	8.566	8.162	7.435	6.802	6.247	5.759	5.328	4.946	4.772	4.607	4.303	4.031	3.786	3.566	3.463	3.366	3.184	3.019	2.665	2.379	2.144	1.948
10	9.471	8.983	8.111	7.360	6.710	6.145	5.650	5.216	5.019	4.833	4.494	4.192	3.923	3.682	3.571	3.465	3.269	3.092	2.715	2.414	2.168	1.965
11	10.368	9.787	8.760	7.887	7.139	6.495	5.937	5.453	5.234	5.029	4.656	4.327	4.035	3.776	3.656	3.544	3.335	3.147	2.752	2.438	2.185	1.977
12	11.255	10.575	9.385	8.384	7.536	6.814	6.194	5.660	5.421	5.197	4.793	4.439	4.127	3.851	3.725	3.606	3.387	3.190	2.779	2.456	2.196	1.985
13	12.134	11.343	9.986	8.853	7.904	7.103	6.424	5.842	5.583	5.342	4.910	4.533	4.203	3.912	3.780	3.656	3.427	3.223	2.799	2.468	2.204	1.990
14	13.004	12.106	10.563	9.295	8.244	7.367	6.628	6.002	5.724	5.468	5.008	4.611	4.265	3.962	3.824	3.695	3.459	3.249	2.814	2.477	2.210	1.993
15	13.865	12.849	11.118	9.712	8.559	7.606	6.811	6.142	5.847	5.575	5.092	4.675	4.315	4.001	3.859	3.726	3.483	3.268	2.825	2.484	2.214	1.995
16	14.718	13.578	11.652	10.106	8.851	7.824	6.974	6.265	5.954	5.669	5.162	4.730	4.357	4.033	3.887	3.751	3.503	3.283	2.834	2.489	2.216	1.997
17	15.562	14.292	12.166	10.477	9.122	8.022	7.120	6.375	6.047	5.749	5.222	4.775	4.391	4.059	3.910	3.771	3.518	3.295	2.840	2.492	2.218	1.998
18	16.398	14.992	12.659	10.828	9.372	8.201	7.250	6.467	6.128	5.818	5.273	4.812	4.419	4.080	3.928	3.786	3.529	3.304	2.844	2.494	2.219	1.999
19	17.226	15.678	13.134	11.158	9.604	8.365	7.366	6.550	6.198	5.877	5.316	4.844	4.442	4.097	3.942	3.799	3.539	3.311	2.848	2.496	2.220	1.999
20	18.046	16.351	13.590	11.470	9.818	8.514	7.469	6.623	6.259	5.929	5.353	4.870	4.460	4.110	3.954	3.808	3.546	3.316	2.850	2.497	2.221	1.999
21	18.857	17.011	14.029	11.764	10.017	8.649	7.562	6.687	6.312	5.973	5.384	4.891	4.476	4.121	3.963	3.816	3.551	3.320	2.852	2.498	2.221	2.000
22	19.660	17.658	14.451	12.042	10.201	8.772	7.645	6.743	6.359	6.011	5.410	4.909	4.488	4.130	3.970	3.822	3.556	3.323	2.853	2.498	2.222	2.000
23	20.456	18.292	14.857	12.303	10.371	8.883	7.718	6.792	6.399	6.044	5.432	4.925	4.499	4.137	3.976	3.827	3.559	3.325	2.854	2.499	2.222	2.000
24	21.243	18.914	15.247	12.550	10.529	8.985	7.784	6.835	6.434	6.073	5.451	4.937	4.507	4.143	3.981	3.831	3.562	3.327	2.855	2.499	2.222	2.000
25	22.023	19.523	15.622	12.783	10.675	9.077	7.843	6.873	6.464	6.097	5.467	4.948	4.514	4.147	3.985	3.834	3.564	3.329	2.856	2.499	2.222	2.000
26	22.795	20.121	15.983	13.003	10.810	9.161	7.896	6.906	6.491	6.118	5.480	4.956	4.520	4.151	3.988	3.837	3.566	3.330	2.856	2.500	2.222	2.000
27	23.560	20.707	16.330	13.221	10.935	9.237	7.943	6.935	6.514	6.136	5.492	4.964	4.524	4.154	3.990	3.839	3.567	3.331	2.856	2.500	2.222	2.000
28	24.316	21.281	16.663	13.406	11.051	9.307	7.984	6.961	6.534	6.152	5.502	4.970	4.528	4.157	3.992	3.840	3.568	3.331	2.857	2.500	2.222	2.000
29	25.066	21.844	16.984	13.591	11.158	9.370	8.022	6.983	6.551	6.166	5.510	4.975	4.531	4.159	3.994	3.841	3.569	3.332	2.857	2.500	2.222	2.000
30	25.808	22.396	17.292	13.765	11.258	9.427	8.055	7.003	6.566	6.177	5.517	4.979	4.534	4.160	3.995	3.842	3.569	3.332	2.857	2.500	2.222	2.000
40	32.835	27.355	19.793	15.046	11.925	9.779	8.244	7.105	6.642	6.234	5.548	4.997	4.544	4.166	3.999	3.846	3.571	3.333	2.857	2.500	2.222	2.000
50	39.196	31.424	21.482	15.762	12.234	9.915	8.304	7.133	6.661	6.246	5.554	4.999	4.545	4.167	4.000	3.846	3.571	3.333	2.857	2.500	2.222	2.000

Table V Areas Under the Standard Normal Distribution

z	0.00	0.01	0.02	0.03	0.04	0.05	0.06	0.07	0.08	0.09
0.0	0.0000	0.0040	0.0080	0.0120	0.0160	0.0199	0.0239	0.0279	0.0319	0.0359
0.1	0.0398	0.0438	0.0478	0.0517	0.0557	0.0596	0.0636	0.0675	0.0714	0.0753
0.2	0.0793	0.0832	0.0871	0.0910	0.0948	0.0987	0.1026	0.1064	0.1103	0.1141
0.3	0.1179	0.1217	0.1255	0.1293	0.1331	0.1368	0.1406	0.1443	0.1480	0.1517
0.4	0.1554	0.1591	0.1628	0.1664	0.1700	0.1736	0.1772	0.1808	0.1844	0.1879
0.5	0.1915	0.1950	0.1985	0.2019	0.2054	0.2088	0.2123	0.2157	0.2190	0.2224
0.6	0.2257	0.2291	0.2324	0.2357	0.2389	0.2422	0.2454	0.2486	0.2517	0.2549
0.7	0.2580	0.2611	0.2642	0.2673	0.2704	0.2734	0.2764	0.2794	0.2823	0.2852
0.8	0.2881	0.2910	0.2939	0.2967	0.2995	0.3023	0.3051	0.3078	0.3106	0.3133
0.9	0.3159	0.3186	0.3212	0.3238	0.3264	0.3289	0.3315	0.3340	0.3365	0.3389
1.0	0.3413	0.3438	0.3461	0.3485	0.3508	0.3531	0.3554	0.3577	0.3599	0.3621
1.1	0.3643	0.3665	0.3686	0.3708	0.3729	0.3749	0.3770	0.3790	0.3810	0.3830
1.2	0.3849	0.3869	0.3888	0.3907	0.3925	0.3944	0.3962	0.3980	0.3997	0.4015
1.3	0.4032	0.4049	0.4066	0.4082	0.4099	0.4115	0.4131	0.4147	0.4162	0.4177
1.4	0.4192	0.4207	0.4222	0.4236	0.4251	0.4265	0.4279	0.4292	0.4306	0.4319
1.5	0.4332	0.4345	0.4357	0.4370	0.4382	0.4394	0.4406	0.4418	0.4429	0.4441
1.6	0.4452	0.4463	0.4474	0.4484	0.4495	0.4505	0.4515	0.4525	0.4535	0.4545
1.7	0.4554	0.4564	0.4573	0.4582	0.4591	0.4599	0.4608	0.4616	0.4625	0.4633
1.8	0.4641	0.4649	0.4656	0.4664	0.4671	0.4678	0.4686	0.4693	0.4699	0.4706
1.9	0.4713	0.4719	0.4726	0.4732	0.4738	0.4744	0.4750	0.4756	0.4761	0.4767
2.0	0.4772	0.4778	0.4783	0.4788	0.4793	0.4798	0.4803	0.4808	0.4812	0.4817
2.1	0.4821	0.4826	0.4830	0.4834	0.4838	0.4842	0.4846	0.4850	0.4854	0.4857
2.2	0.4861	0.4864	0.4868	0.4871	0.4875	0.4878	0.4881	0.4884	0.4887	0.4890
2.3	0.4893	0.4896	0.4898	0.4901	0.4904	0.4906	0.4909	0.4911	0.4913	0.4916
2.4	0.4918	0.4920	0.4922	0.4925	0.4927	0.4929	0.4931	0.4932	0.4934	0.4936
2.5	0.4938	0.4940	0.4941	0.4943	0.4945	0.4946	0.4948	0.4949	0.4951	0.4952
2.6	0.4953	0.4955	0.4956	0.4957	0.4959	0.4960	0.4961	0.4962	0.4963	0.4964
2.7	0.4965	0.4966	0.4967	0.4968	0.4969	0.4970	0.4971	0.4972	0.4973	0.4974
2.8	0.4974	0.4975	0.4976	0.4977	0.4977	0.4978	0.4979	0.4979	0.4980	0.4981
2.9	0.4981	0.4982	0.4982	0.4983	0.4984	0.4984	0.4985	0.4985	0.4986	0.4986
3.0	0.4987	0.4987	0.4987	0.4988	0.4988	0.4989	0.4989	0.4989	0.4990	0.4990

Acknowledgments

The authors would like to acknowledge the usage of the following tables and figures in the book:

Page 3: Table 1.1 reprinted by permission of the Federal Reserve Bulletin. Pages 4–5: Table 1.2 and Figure 1.2 reprinted by permission of the NYSE Statistics Archive in NYSE Euronext website. Pages 6–7: Table 1.3 adapted from *Future's Magazine's 1989 Reference Guide to Futures-Options Markets*, pp. 112–127. Page 97: Table 3.3 reprinted by permission of Moody's Industrial Manual © 1987. Page 157: Table 5.1 reprinted by permission of *The Wall Street Journal* © February 16, 2011. Page 158: Figure 5.1 reprinted by permission of the U.S. Department of The Treasury © 2011. Page 173: Table 5.3 reprinted by permissions of Moody's Investors Service and Standard & Poor's Bond Guide, October 1989 edition. Page 201: Reprinted by permission of the author and publisher, Lawrence Fisher, "Some New Stock Market Indexes," *Journal of Business*, v. 39 (1966), pp. 191–225, © 1966, University of Chicago. Page 210: Table 6.3 reprinted by permission of the Department of Commerce, Handbook of Cyclical Indicators © May 1977. Page 213: Figure 6.2 reprinted by permission of *Wilshire Associates*. Pages 217–223: Table 6A.1 and Table 6A.2 reprinted by permission of *Wilshire Associates*.

Pages 248–249: Reprinted by permission of the author and publisher from William F. Sharpe, "Mutual-Fund Performance," *Journal of Business*, v. 39 (1966), pp. 119–138, © 1966 by the University of Chicago. Page 251: Reprinted by permission of the author and publisher from Michael C. Jensen, "Risk, The Pricing of Assets, and the Evaluation of Investment Portfolios," *Journal of Business*, v. 42 (1969), pp. 167–185, © 1969 by the University of Chicago. Pages 267–268: Excerpt from J. C. M. Mao, Quantitative Analysis of Financial Decisions, © 1968 by J. C. M. Mao,

Reprinted by permission of Macmillan Publishing Company. Page 280: Figure 8.7 reprinted by permission of the author and publisher from Haim Levy and Marshall Sarnat, "A Note on Portfolio Selection and Investors' Wealth," *Journal of Financial and Quantitative Analysis*, v. 6 (January 1971), pp. 639–642, © 1971 by School of Business Administration, University of Washington. Page 282: Figure 8.8 reprinted by permission of the author and publisher from Edward A. Dyl, "Negative Betas: The Attractions of Selling Short," *Journal of Portfolio Management*, v. 1 (Spring 1975), pp. 74–76, © 1975 by Institutional Investor Systems. Page 336: Reprinted by permission from J. Mincer and V. Zarnowitz, "The Evaluation of Economic Forecasts," in J. Mincer, ed., Economic Forecasts and Expectations, © 1969 by National Bureau of Economic Research, Inc., Cambridge, Massachusetts. Pages 337–338: Tables 9.2, 9.3 and 9.4 reprinted by permission of the author and publisher from Cheng F. Lee, Paul Newbold, Joseph E. Finnerty, and Chen-Chin Chu, "On Accounting-Based, Market-Based and Composite-Based Beta Predictions: Methods and Implications," *The Financial Review*, v. 21 (February 1986), pp. 51–68, © 1986 by Wiley Online Library. Page 345: Reprinted by permission of Harcourt Brace Jovanovich from Fischer Black, Michael C. Jensen, and Myron Scholes, "The Capital Asset Pricing Model: Some Empirical Tests," in Michael C. Jensen, ed., Studies in the Theory of Capital Markets, Praeger Publishers Inc., 1972, © 1972 by Harcourt Brace Jovanovich, Inc. Page 346: Reprinted by permission of the authors and publisher from Eugene F. Fama and J. MacBeth, "Risk, Return and equilibrium Empirical Tests," *Journal of Political Economy*, v. 31 (1973), pp. 607–636, © 1973 by the University of Chicago. Page 347: Reprinted by permission of the author and Elsevier Science Publishers B. V. from Robert C. Merton, "On Estimating the Expected Return on the Market, An Exploratory Investigation," *Journal of Financial economics*, v. 9 (1980), pp. 323–361. Page 347: Reprinted by permission of the author and Elsevier Science Publishers B. V. from Richard Roll, "A Critique of the Asset Pricing Theory's Tests — Part I: On Past and Potential Testability of the Theory," *Journal of Financial Economics*, v. 4 (1977), pp. 13–37. Pages 399–408: Adapted by permission of Elsevier Science Publishers B. V. from J. Lintner, "The Valuation of Risk Assets on the Selection of Risky Investments in Stock Portfolio and Capital Budgets," *Review of Economics and Statistics*, v. 57 (1965), pp. 13–37. Page 440: Reprinted by permission of Ohio State University Press from J. Tobin, "A General Equilibrium Approach to Monetary Theory," *Journal of Money, Credit, and Banking*, v. 1 (1969), pp. 15–29. Page 443: Adapted by permission from E. F. Fama, *Foundations of Finance*, Basic Books, 1976, pp. 134–137. Pages 452–453: Adapted from Paul Cootner, "Stock Prices: Random vs. Systematic Changes," *Industrial Management Review*, v. 3 (1962), pp. 24–25, © 1962 by the Sloan Management Review Association. All rights reserved. Page 477: Adapted by permission of Academic Press from S. Ross, "The Arbitrage Theory of Capital Asset Pricing," *Journal of Economic Theory*, v. 13 (1976), pp. 341–360. Page 490: Reprinted by permission of the authors and publisher from N. Chen, R. Roll, and S. Ross, "Economic Forces and the Stock Market," *Journal of Business*, v. 59 (1986), pp. 383–403, © 1986 by the University of Chicago. Pages 497–499: Tables 13.9, 13.10, and 13.11 reprinted by permission of the author and publisher from Dorothy H. Bower, Richard S. Bower and Dennis E. Logue, "Arbitrage Pricing and Utility Stock Returns," *Journal of Finance*, v. 39 (September 1984), pp. 1041–1054, © 1984 by Blackwell Publishing for the American Finance Association. Page 505: Table 13A.1 reprinted by permission of the author and publisher from William P. Lloyd and Cheng F. Lee, "Block Recursive Systems in Asset Pricing Models," *Journal of Finance*, v. 30 (December 1976), pp. 1101–1114, © 1976 by Blackwell Publishing for the American Finance Association. Pages 506 and 508: Tables 13B.1 and 13B.2 reprinted by permission of the author and publisher from Cheng F. Lee and K. C. John Wei, "Multi-Factor Multi-Indicator Approach to Asset Pricing Model: Theory and Empirical Evidence," *Handbook of Financial Econometrics and Statistics*, Cheng F. Lee, Alice C. Lee and John C. Lee, eds., Springer, forthcoming 2013, © 2013 by Springer.

Pages 543–544: Reprinted by permission of the publisher from L. L. Johnson, "The Theory of Hedging and Speculation in Commodity Futures," *Review of Economic Studies*, v. 27 (1960), pp. 139–151. Page 548: Figure 14.4 reprinted by permission of the author and publisher from Charles T. Howard and Louis J. D'Antonio, "A Risk-Return Measure of Hedging Effectiveness," *Journal of Financial and Quantitative Analysis*, v. 19 (March 1984), p. 109, © 1984 by School of Business Administration, University of Washington. Pages 561, 562, 565, 566, 573, and 588: Figures reprinted by permission of *The Wall Street Journal*. Pages 581, 584, 585, and 589: Figures reprinted by permission of CME Group. Page 582: Figure 15.8 reprinted by Board of Governors of the Federal Reserve System. Page 592: Figures 15.13 and 15.14 reprinted by permission of the author and publisher from David M. Modest and Mahadevan Sundaresan, "The Relationship Between Spot and Futures Prices in Stock-Index Futures Markets: Some Preliminary Evidence," *Journal of Futures Markets*, v. 3

(Spring 1983), pp. 15–41, © 1983 by John Wiley and Sons, Inc. Page 673: Adapted by permission of the authors and publisher from F. Black and M. Scholes, "The Pricing of Options and Corporate Liabilities," *Journal of Political Economy*, v. 31 (1973), pp. 637–659, © 1973 by the University of Chicago. Page 759: Adapted by permission of the author and publisher from Hans R. Stoll and Robert E. Whaley, *Futures and Options*, © 1993 by Cincinnati, OH: South Western Publishing.

Pages 815 and 817: Figures 21.1 and 21.2 reprinted by permission of the author and publisher from Robert J. Shiller, "Theories of Aggregate Stock Price Movements," *Journal of Portfolio Management*, v. 10 (Winter 1984), pp. 28–37, © 1984 by Institutional Investor Systems. Page 825: Reprinted by permission of the author and Elsevier Science Publishers B. V. from M. Reinganum, "Misspecification of Capital Asset Pricing: Empirical Anomalies Based on Earning Yields and Market Values," *Journal of Financial Economics*, v. 8 (1981), pp. 19–46. Page 826: Reprinted by permission of the author and Elsevier Science Publishers B. V. from R. W. Banz, "The Relationship Between Return and Market Value of Common Stocks," *Journal of Financial Economics*, v. 9 (1981), pp. 3–18. Pages 835–837: Adapted by permission of the School of Agriculture, Purdue University, from David A. Bessler and Jon A. Brandt, *Composite Forecasting of Livestock Prices, An Analysis of Combining Alternative Forecasting Methods*, Station Bulletin No. 265, Department of Agricultural Economics, Agricultural Experiment Station, Purdue University. Page 851: Reprinted by permission of the authors and publisher from Roy D. Henriksson and Robert C. Merton, "On Marketing Timing and Investment Performance II, Statistical Procedures for Evaluating Forecasting Skills," *Journal of Business*, v. 54 (1981), pp. 513–533, © 1981 by the University of Chicago. Pages 853–854: Reprinted by permission of the authors and publisher from Stanley J. Kon and Frank C. Jen, "The Investment Performance of Mutual Funds: An Empirical Investigation of Timing, Selectivity, and Market Efficiency," *Journal of Business*, v. 52 (1979), pp. 363–389, © 1979 by the University of Chicago. Page 869: Table 22.1 reprinted by permission of Morgan Stanley Capital International Perspective, Geneva © 1988. Page 871: Table 22.2 reprinted by permission of the author and publisher from Carl R. Beidleman, *Handbook of International Investing*, © 1987 by Chicago, Probus Publishing Company. Page 877: Table 22.3 reprinted by permission of Survey of Current Business, and permission of the author and publisher from Herbert G. Grubel and Kenneth Fadner, "The Interdependence of International Equity Markets," *Journal of Finance*,

v. 26 (March 1971), pp. 89–94, © 1971 by Blackwell Publishing for the American Finance Association. Pages 889–891: Tables and Figures reprinted by permission of Morgan Guaranty Trust Company, Investing Internationally, © 1978. Page 893: Table 22.5 reprinted by permission of the author and publisher from Cheol S. Eun and Bruce G. Resnick, "International Diversification under Estimation Risk: Actual vs Potential Gains", *Recent Developments in International Banking and Finance*, v. 1., © 1987 by Lexington Books, D.C Heath & Co. Pages 913–920: Tables reprinted by permission of the author and publisher from Sidney Homer and Martin L. Leibowitz, *Inside the Yield Book*, © 1972 by Prentice-Hall, Inc. Used by permission of the publisher, Prentice-Hall, Inc., Englewood Cliffs, New Jersey. Page 920: Reprinted by permission from F. Macaulay, *Some Theoretical Problems Suggested by the Movement of Investment Rates, Bonds Yields, and Stock Prices in the United States Since 1865*, © 1938 by National Bureau of Economic Research, Inc., and Cambridge, Massachusetts. Pages 923 and 931: Tables 23.10 and 23.14 reprinted by permission of the author and publisher from Frank K. Reilly and Rupinder S. Sidhu, "Many Uses of Bond Duration," *Financial Analysts Journal*, v. 36 (July/August 1980), pp. 58–72, © 1980 by CFA Institute. Page 971: Figure 24.9 reprinted by permission of Knight-Ridder Tradecenter, © 1988. Pages 972–974: Figures reprinted by permission of The Washington Post, © 1988.

Pages 1029 and 1031: Tables 26.1 and 26.2 reprinted by permission of the author and publisher from James M. Warren and John P. Shelton, "A Simultaneous-Equation Approach to Financial Planning," *Journal of Finance*, v. 26 (December 1971), pp. 1123–1142, © 1971 by Blackwell Publishing for the American Finance Association. Pages 1081–1089: Adapted by permission from K. Itô and H. P. McKean, Jr., *Diffusion Processes and Their Sample Paths,* Grundlehren der mathematischen Wissenschaften, Band 125, © 1974 by Springer-Verleg Berlin-Heidelberg. Page 1085: From Robert C. Merton, "On the Mathematical and Economic Assumptions of Continuous-Time Model," in W. F. Sharpe and Paul Cootner, eds., *Financial Economics: Essays in Honor of Paul Cootner*, pp. 37–39, © 1982 by Prentice-Hall, Inc. Adapted by permission of Prentice-Hall, Inc., Englewood Cliffs, New Jersey. Page 1094: Adapted by permission of the authors and publisher from F. Black and M. Scholes, "The Pricing of Options and Corporate Liabilities," *Journal of Political Economy*, v. 31 (1973), pp. 637–659, © 1973 by the University of Chicago.

Author Index

J

K

L

W

Y

Z

Subject Index

B

C

M

N

T

Y